PINSTRIPE

United States CITY TO CITY ATLAS

For the traveling professional

Cover Photo: Mark E. Gibson

PRINTED IN CANADA

Contents

4-5   Mileage Chart

6-7   U.S. Interstate Highway System

8-9   Canada

10-11   Mexico

12   State Map Legend

13-88   State Maps

89-170   Vicinity Maps (see listing)

171-238   City Center Maps (see listing)

239-272   Index to U.S. Cities (listed alphabetically by state)

State, City Center, Vicinity Maps & Driver's Information

(*denotes detailed city center map)

ALABAMA 13
Birmingham *174, 96
Huntsville 120
Mobile 138

ALASKA 14

ARIZONA 16-17
Phoenix *220, 151
Tucson 166

ARKANSAS 15
Little Rock 127

CALIFORNIA 18-21
Anaheim/Orange County 131
Fresno 118
Long Beach 129
Los Angeles *199, 128-131
Monterey 138
Oakland *214, 161
Sacramento 157
San Bernardino 130
San Diego *232, 160
San Francisco *234, 161
San Jose 162

COLORADO 22-23
Denver *187, 114

CONNECTICUT 24-25
Hartford *193, 120
New Haven/Stratford 141

DELAWARE 42-43

DISTRICT OF COLUMBIA
Washington *238, 168

FLORIDA 26-27
Daytona Beach 113
Fort Lauderdale *190, 118
Jacksonville 124
Miami *203, 135
Orlando *217, 149
St. Petersburg *228, 165
Tampa *236, 165

GEORGIA 28-29
Atlanta *171, 92
Augusta 93
Columbus 108

HAWAII 30

IDAHO 31

ILLINOIS 32-33
Chicago *180, 102-105
Moline/Rock Island 112
Peoria 154

INDIANA 34-35
Evansville 117
Fort Wayne 117
Gary 103
Indianapolis *196, 122

IOWA 36
Council Bluffs 148
Davenport/Bettendorf 112
Des Moines 113

KANSAS 37
Kansas City 125
Wichita 170

KENTUCKY 38-39
Lexington 127
Louisville *201, 132

LOUISANA 40
Baton Rouge 95
New Orleans *210, 140

MAINE 41

MARYLAND 42-43
Baltimore *173, 94

MASSACHUSETTS 24-25
Boston *175, 97

MICHIGAN 44-45
Detroit *189, 115
Grand Rapids 119

MINNESOTA 46-47
Minneapolis *206, 137
St. Paul *227, 137

MISSISSIPPI 50
Jackson 123

MISSOURI 48-49
Kansas City *197, 125
St. Louis *226, 158

MONTANA 51

NEBRASKA 52-53
Omaha 148

NEVADA 54
Las Vegas *198, 126

NEW HAMPSHIRE 57
Manchester 133

NEW JERSEY 56-57
Atlantic City 91
Newark *208, 143

NEW MEXICO 62
Albuquerque 90

NEW YORK 58-61
Albany 90
Buffalo *177, 98
New York *211, 142-145
Rochester *225, 156
Syracuse 164

NORTH CAROLINA 64-65
Asheville 91
Charlotte *178, 101
Durham 155
Fayetteville 118
Greensboro 169
High Point 169
Raleigh 155
Winston-Salem 169

NORTH DAKOTA 63

OHIO 66-67
Akron 89
Canton 99
Cincinnati *181, 106
Cleveland *182, 107
Columbus *183, 109
Dayton *186, 112
Toledo 166
Youngstown 170

OKLAHOMA 68-69
Oklahoma City *216, 147
Tulsa 167

OREGON 70-71
Eugene 116
Portland *223, 153

PENNSYLVANIA 72-73
Allentown 91
Bethlehem 91

Erie 116
Harrisburg 119
Philadelphia *219, 150
Pittsburgh *222, 152
Scranton 164
Wilkes-Barre 164

RHODE ISLAND 24-25
Providence 154

SOUTH CAROLINA 64-65
Charleston 100
Columbia 108

SOUTH DAKOTA 74

TENNESSEE 38-39
Chattanooga 99
Knoxville 126
Memphis *202, 134
Nashville *207, 139

TEXAS 75-79
Austin 93
Beaumont/Port Arthur 95
Dallas *184, 111
El Paso 116
Fort Worth *192, 110
Houston *194, 121
San Antonio *231, 159

UTAH 80-81
Salt Lake City *230, 157

VERMONT 55

VIRGINIA 82-83
Arlington 168
Norfolk *213, 146
Richmond *224, 156

WASHINGTON 84-85
Seattle *235, 163
Tacoma 164

WEST VIRGINIA 82-83
Charleston 100

WISCONSIN 86-87
Madison 133
Milwaukee *205, 136

WYOMING 88

Mileage Chart

	Albany, NY	Albuquerque, NM	Amarillo, TX	Atlanta, GA	Austin, TX	Baltimore, MD	Billings, MT	Birmingham, AL	Boise, ID	Boston, MA	Brownsville, TX	Buffalo, NY	Charleston, SC	Charleston, WV	Charlotte, NC	Chicago, IL	Cincinnati, OH	Cleveland, OH	Columbia, SC	Columbus, OH	Dallas, TX	Daytona Beach, FL	Denver, CO	Des Moines, IA	Detroit, MI	El Paso, TX	Fargo, ND	Fort Lauderdale, FL	Fort Wayne, IN	Fort Worth, TX	Grand Rapids, MI	Greensboro, NC	Hartford, CT	Houston, TX	Indianapolis, IN	Jackson, MS	Jacksonville, FL	Kansas City, MO	Knoxville, TN	Las Vegas, NV	Lincoln, NE	Little Rock, AK
Albany, NY	0	2125	1825	1007	1882	332	2073	1112	2601	170	2007	292	932	639	795	795	729	496	823	657	1679	1209	1853	1193	690	2327	1463	1403	705	1682	710	661	106	1825	836	1320	1111	1279	836	2609	1336	1370
Albuquerque, NM	2125	0	300	1387	716	1881	1022	1260	970	2214	988	1801	1695	1583	1628	1346	1394	1606	1598	1468	673	1716	446	1013	1537	267	1314	1953	1410	632	1491	1677	2084	870	1289	1087	1678	811	1407	576	837	883
Amarillo, TX	1825	300	0	1087	485	1581	1037	965	1235	1914	784	1501	1517	1304	1338	1046	1094	1306	1298	1168	363	1467	454	806	1289	508	999	1670	1109	344	1191	1377	1822	608	989	787	1378	552	1107	876	596	607
Atlanta, GA	1007	1387	1087	0	884	669	1804	160	2252	1068	1175	912	300	495	251	695	438	692	211	543	805	446	1401	924	726	1453	1364	681	612	837	749	348	969	816	543	397	329	810	204	1947	1013	540
Austin, TX	1882	716	485	884	0	1550	1449	793	1716	1930	331	1566	1247	1251	1237	1100	1127	1371	1095	1233	203	1158	1009	897	1333	583	1333	1326	1200	192	1288	1281	1867	162	1111	519	1057	680	1051	1297	851	520
Baltimore, MD	332	1881	1581	669	1550	0	1875	804	2416	409	1825	352	567	339	430	697	510	355	513	405	1347	876	1692	997	511	1997	1339	1036	550	1379	624	346	308	1409	584	1006	770	1078	503	2408	1192	1037
Billings, MT	2073	1022	1037	1804	1449	1875	0	1759	586	2232	1771	1857	2222	1762	2027	1214	1479	1662	2075	1654	1395	2173	579	959	1579	1284	625	2466	1405	1406	1396	1958	2169	1739	1400	1743	2227	1078	1723	1060	836	1439
Birmingham, AL	1112	1260	965	160	793	804	1759	0	2101	1267	1065	941	460	539	411	669	468	722	359	584	637	505	1370	838	721	1304	1311	764	610	702	739	493	1058	676	497	251	472	724	255	1822	953	394
Boise, ID	2601	970	1235	2252	1716	2416	586	2101	0	2794	1921	2271	2503	2246	2408	1777	1983	2058	2289	2069	1610	2576	870	1402	2020	1241	1245	2820	1871	1598	1917	2408	2652	1854	1890	2091	2579	1476	2022	662	1205	1781
Boston, MA	170	2214	1914	1068	1930	409	2232	1267	2794	0	2255	454	989	728	828	965	875	632	928	738	1727	1257	1953	1305	795	2376	1623	1492	847	1761	908	739	105	1878	933	1395	1167	1435	871	2765	1500	1472
Brownsville, TX	2007	988	784	1175	331	1825	1909	1065	1921	2255	0	1865	1500	1479	1426	1430	1426	1670	1360	1533	526	1353	1251	1184	1694	806	1601	1542	1455	518	1585	1480	2094	357	1427	791	1264	1008	1320	1573	1216	819
Buffalo, NY	292	1801	1501	912	1566	352	1857	941	2271	454	1865	0	947	430	666	543	438	195	822	333	1363	1069	1602	867	366	2011	1185	1400	381	1395	419	641	397	1492	512	1119	1068	1007	671	2254	1057	1046
Charleston, SC	932	1695	1517	300	1247	567	2222	460	2503	989	1500	947	0	479	203	912	628	750	113	670	1164	351	1743	1185	874	1729	1557	586	740	1116	959	271	867	1027	743	702	248	1135	368	2247	1287	814
Charleston, WV	639	1583	1304	495	1251	339	1762	539	2246	728	1479	430	479	0	276	469	178	284	376	156	1134	726	1377	761	371	1672	1126	1004	284	1056	457	227	662	1246	328	790	676	777	284	1788	960	707
Charlotte, NC	795	1628	1338	251	1237	430	2027	411	2408	828	1426	666	203	276	0	738	446	543	100	453	1054	469	1548	1029	607	1710	1414	721	602	1061	791	89	763	1053	551	640	413	940	219	2173	1151	743
Chicago, IL	795	1346	1046	695	1100	697	1214	669	1777	965	1430	543	912	469	738	0	291	348	794	340	932	1096	1037	357	284	1435	649	1348	159	945	178	729	875	1160	186	762	999	543	537	1749	527	675
Cincinnati, OH	729	1394	1094	438	1127	510	1479	468	1983	875	1426	438	628	178	446	291	0	249	502	105	924	861	1199	583	260	1472	940	1086	184	956	357	458	746	1053	109	680	786	591	246	1921	715	608
Cleveland, OH	496	1606	1306	692	1371	355	1662	722	2058	632	1670	195	750	284	543	348	249	0	627	138	1168	952	1407	672	171	1716	997	1232	211	1200	284	486	539	1297	317	924	908	803	489	2059	867	851
Columbia, SC	823	1598	1298	211	1095	513	2075	359	2289	928	1360	822	113	376	100	794	502	627	0	513	1032	381	1616	1126	745	1668	1446	622	671	1057	858	188	836	1066	625	610	290	1025	267	2162	1199	759
Columbus, OH	657	1469	1168	543	1233	405	1654	584	2069	738	1533	333	670	156	453	340	105	138	513	0	1030	901	1270	657	195	1540	989	1126	150	1062	311	381	641	1159	179	786	850	665	351	1995	776	713
Dallas, TX	1679	673	363	805	203	1347	1395	637	1610	1727	526	1363	1164	1134	1054	932	924	1168	1032	1030	0	1123	806	714	1203	648	1131	1097	1030	33	1110	1122	1664	243	908	422	1005	511	820	1249	648	317
Daytona Beach, FL	1209	1716	1467	446	1158	876	2173	505	2576	1257	1353	1069	351	726	469	1096	883	952	381	901	1123	0	1823	1329	1103	1728	1714	227	1006	1126	1143	551	1138	952	880	688	97	1209	603	2316	1401	904
Denver, CO	1853	446	454	1401	1009	1692	579	1370	870	1953	1251	1602	1743	1377	1548	1037	1199	1407	1616	1270	806	1823	0	695	1321	705	915	2067	1186	773	1201	1621	1988	1060	1091	1246	1779	608	1341	743	507	992
Des Moines, IA	1193	1013	806	924	897	997	959	838	1402	1305	1184	867	1185	761	1029	357	583	672	1126	657	714	1329	695	0	600	1114	475	1581	516	747	502	1028	1283	930	478	846	1270	203	821	1399	203	562
Detroit, MI	690	1537	1289	726	1330	511	1579	721	2020	795	1694	366	874	371	607	284	260	171	745	195	1203	1103	1321	600	0	1701	922	1346	170	1240	162	567	701	1304	293	923	1046	791	506	2011	819	850
El Paso, TX	2327	267	508	1453	583	1997	1274	1304	1241	2376	806	2011	1729	1672	1710	1435	1372	1716	1668	1540	648	1728	705	1114	1701	0	1460	1869	1573	609	1554	1783	2263	743	1460	1070	1626	915	1488	722	946	960
Fargo, ND	1463	1314	999	1364	1333	1339	625	1311	1245	1625	1601	1185	1557	1126	1414	649	940	997	1446	989	1131	1714	915	475	922	1460	0	2007	808	1072	827	1412	1531	1334	835	1335	1704	609	1195	1535	451	1091
Fort Lauderdale, FL	1435	1953	1670	681	1326	1036	2466	764	2820	1492	1542	1400	586	1004	721	1348	1086	1232	622	1126	1097	227	2067	1581	1346	1869	2007	0	1271	1129	1342	786	1403	1191	1232	883	332	1459	860	2530	1670	1184
Fort Wayne, IN	705	1410	1109	612	1200	550	1405	610	1871	847	1455	381	740	284	602	159	184	219	671	150	1030	1006	1186	516	170	1573	808	1271	0	1053	172	551	768	1176	122	784	929	648	430	1878	686	711
Fort Worth, TX	1682	632	344	837	192	1379	1406	702	1598	1761	518	1395	1116	1056	1061	945	956	1200	1057	1062	33	1126	773	747	1236	609	1072	1129	1053	0	1121	1154	1696	264	912	446	1037	513	853	1203	648	349
Grand Rapids, MI	710	1491	1191	749	1288	624	1396	739	1917	908	1585	419	959	457	791	178	357	284	858	311	1110	1143	1201	502	162	1554	827	1342	172	1121	0	707	794	1196	263	957	1071	638	573	1889	699	799
Greensboro, NC	661	1677	1377	348	1281	346	1958	493	2408	739	1480	641	271	227	89	729	458	486	188	381	1122	551	1621	1028	567	1783	1412	786	551	1154	707	0	650	1167	563	770	483	1013	283	2237	1202	778
Hartford	106	2084	1822	969	1867	308	2169	1058	2652	105	2044	397	867	662	763	875	746	539	836	641	1664	1138	1988	1283	701	2263	1531	1403	768	1696	794	650	0	1773	805	1306	1071	1297	841	2675	1378	1344
Houston, TX	1825	870	608	816	162	1409	1639	676	1854	1878	357	1492	1027	1246	1053	1160	1053	1297	1066	1159	243	952	1060	930	1304	743	1334	1191	1176	264	1196	1167	1773	0	1041	406	891	754	922	1468	892	446
Indianapolis, IN	836	1289	989	543	1111	584	1400	497	1890	933	1427	512	743	328	551	186	105	317	625	179	908	980	1091	478	293	1460	835	1232	122	912	263	563	805	1041	0	681	867	486	351	1816	673	608
Jackson, MS	1320	1087	787	397	519	1006	1743	251	2091	1395	991	1119	702	790	640	762	680	924	610	786	422	688	1246	846	923	1070	1335	883	784	446	957	770	1306	406	681	0	591	716	506	1650	874	251
Jacksonville, FL	1111	1678	1378	329	1057	770	2227	472	2579	1167	1264	1068	248	676	413	999	786	908	290	850	1005	97	1779	1270	1046	1626	1704	332	929	1037	1071	483	1071	891	867	591	0	1110	555	2238	1321	843
Kansas City, MO	1279	811	552	810	680	1078	1078	724	1476	1435	1008	1007	1135	777	940	543	591	803	1025	665	511	1209	608	203	791	916	609	1459	648	513	638	1013	1297	754	486	716	1110	0	752	1345	211	409
Knoxville, TN	836	1407	1107	204	1051	503	1723	255	2022	871	1320	671	368	284	219	537	246	489	267	351	820	603	1341	821	506	1488	1195	860	430	872	573	283	841	922	351	506	555	752	0	1983	944	523
Las Vegas, NV	2609	576	876	1947	1297	2408	1060	1822	662	2765	1573	2254	2247	2119	2173	1749	1921	2059	2162	1995	1249	2316	743	1399	2011	722	1535	2530	1878	1203	1889	2237	2675	1468	1816	1650	2238	1345	1983	0	1224	1483
Lincoln, NE	1336	837	596	1013	851	1192	836	953	1205	1500	1216	1057	1287	960	1151	527	802	867	1199	776	648	1401	507	203	819	946	451	1670	686	648	699	1202	1378	892	673	874	1321	211	944	1224	0	616
Little Rock, AK	1370	883	607	540	520	1037	1439	394	1781	1472	819	1046	814	707	743	675	608	851	759	713	317	904	992	562	850	960	1091	1184	711	349	799	778	1344	446	608	251	843	409	523	1483	616	0
Los Angeles, CA	2911	823	1095	2197	1410	2676	1254	2067	837	2993	1678	2587	2521	2394	2617	1989	2164	2392	2426	2254	1401	2407	1009	1654	2270	818	1844	2704	2137	1361	2148	2478	2829	1581	2075	1880	2402	1589	2201	275	1476	1678
Louisville, KY	868	1332	1041	421	1022	608	1550	373	1908	976	1321	543	608	253	468	300	105	349	494	211	819	801	1127	591	365	1467	949	1078	222	851	373	462	867	948	129	575	729	518	246	1861	730	502
Memphis, TN	1232	1021	721	397	658	900	1557	239	1833	1379	957	908	689	653	604	551	469	713	612	575	455	749	1151	599	712	1103	1224	989	592	487	690	640	1209	584	470	211	697	470	385	1581	647	138
Miami, FL	1439	1994	1694	665	1338	1095	2580	788	2860	1516	1580	1524	630	1046	745	1338	1086	1264	658	1210	1321	259	2131	1582	1386	1958	1986	24	1326	1353	1356	810	1427	1207	1208	907	356	1475	859	2570	1673	1208
Milwaukee, WI	933	1443	1143	784	1203	794	1143	766	1777	1078	1530	640	1032	566	835	92	388	445	891	448	1013	1180	1070	365	389	1528	576	1443	256	1059	275	826	948	1155	283	884	1067	568	643	1752	560	772
Minneapolis, MN	1215	1256	1062	1105	1120	1105	812	1088	1488	1362	1456	948	1316	874	1143	405	696	753	1276	753	1013	1458	956	251	698	1520	244	1723	564	1001	583	1135	1257	1266	591	1123	1376	459	932	1630	409	881
Mobile, AL	1322	1265	965	340	656	990	1854	269	2343	1379	851	1184	607	825	575	908	745	989	555	834	592	502	1372	954	988	1236	1413	705	839	624	1006	681	1290	478	749	178	413	819	449	1841	1039	430
Montgomery, AL	1178	1345	1042	164	804	833	1836	93	2346	1232	1041	1076	464	632	405	762	561	815	379	707	677	458	1412	1311	814	1325	1521	671	686	701	819	512	1133	709	590	255	379	867	348	2015	975	470
Nashville, TN	993	1232	932	243	869	688	1640	195	2059	1062	1168	722	576	458	399	474	283	527	458	389	666	639	1167	712	536	1314	1136	900	385	698	534	429	973	795	302	422	592	590	174	1792	770	349
New Orleans, LA	1453	1187	875	493	535	1136	1820	352	2191	1526	730	1273	727	891	721	925	820	1078	701	940	530	632	1323	978	1077	1127	1494	843	916	519	1071	810	1436	367	857	193	551	857	607	1800	1114	430
New York City, NY	146	1995	1695	855	1728	201	1926	1019	2571	203	2002	390	786	524	625	794	628	446	715	551	1525	1054	1775	1070	620	2173	1450	1289	691	1557	706	561	101	1679	730	1192	957	1192	771	2520	1274	1235
Norfolk, VA	505	1905	1632	551	1403	237	2098	711	2551	660	1735	569	454	369	341	851	681	493	412	559	1359	702	1800	1202	711	1998	1581	964	709	1382	802	227	471	1362	669	948	632	1179	412	2534	1354	1025
Oakland, CA	2982	1134	1430	2488	1786	2864	1218	2321	671	3124	2034	2745	2788	2600	2755	2098	2317	2498	2703	2391	1803	2831	1223	1742	2350	1194	1870	3041	2257	1723	2308	2809	2909	1957	2212	2270	2771	1799	2509	582	1604	1984
Oklahoma City, OK	1523	559	267	863	414	1322	1188	701	1451	1659	680	1242	1176	1031	1069	804	835	1047	1091	909	211	1257	660	576	1030	708	989	1481	852	210	932	1118	1546	454	730	575	1181	373	847	1119	433	324
Omaha, NE	1308	905	754	989	847	1143	904	904	1274	1443	1249	1005	1303	899	1135	464	721	824	1283	795	693	1402	559	146	726	1256	464	1604	634	634	640	1208	1321	949	616	914	1305	195	930	1249	57	690
Orlando, FL	1249	1751	1451	446	1142	917	2277	545	2695	1297	2034	1306	401	814	559	1127	892	1046	440	997	1078	81	1896	1363	1143	1735	1826	208	1059	1110	1188	648	1208	964	989	697	138	1266	665	2311	1452	965
Philadelphia, PA	251	1922	1622	766	1630	97	2051	880	2488	327	1954	397	688	517	522	757	559	430	627	460	1427	914	1762	998	585	2075	1370	1127	604	1459	672	438	220	1581	624	1094	859	1134	646	2449	1260	1110
Phoenix, AZ	2512	446	746	1810	1030	2311	1220	1700	1022	2644	1289	2269	2222	2045	2061	1776	1808	2045	2075	1907	1013	2101	802	1497	2019	438	1791	2244	1831	983	1906	2099	2523	1110	1719	1500	2100	1277	1845	284	1236	1379
Pittsburgh, PA	471	1654	1354	712	1412	245	1681	778	2203	584	1713	219	778	211	504	470	291	128	572	186	1209	859	1475	770	304	1833	1112	1216	336	1241	397	438	486	1345	349	965	882	851	515	2181	965	899
Portland, Or	2869	1378	1636	2763	2059	2765	867	2571	439	3149	2468	2677	2952	2615	2757	2140	2474	2416	2972	2478	2051	3018	1233	1816	2368	1661	1484	3204	2299	2003	2251	2823	2877	2369	2335	2518	3042	1809	2550	991	1641	2270
Providence, RI	178	2156	1856	1027	1898	356	2238	1189	2701	41	2222	454	956	699	785	924	790	600	888	713	1695	1201	1961	1256	746	2335	1566	1459	799	1727	859	706	73	1849	892	1362	1127	1378	935	2683	1451	1395
Raleigh, NC	656	1759	1459	397	1355	324	2273	557	2560	713	1506	721	300	297	162	802	540	559	215	453	1152	559	1694	1123	643	1800	1485	794	603	1184	754	73	624	1233	635	815	486	1086	356	2319	1263	851
Reno, NV	2763	1056	1345	2411	1775	2562	1021	2363	404	2871	2068	2433	2765	2407	2570	1897	2221	2238	2626	2295	1731	2758	1030	1606	2190	1183	1660	3008	2056	1608	2067	2591	2749	1932	2116	2143	2716	1606	2363	478	1411	1986
Richmond, VA	482	1833	1533	527	1463	155	1655	699	2594	544	1646	552	462	251	280	788	356	583	390	498	1313	713	1904	1293	609	2023	1481	946	635	1333	722	191	455	2291	907	946	693	1205	440	2406	1249	963
Rochester,NY	219	1857	1557	1015	1623	300	1922	965	2352	381	1891	81	871	495	689	608	502	268	789	397	1420	1176	1637	932	424	2036	1249	1410	464	1452	499	600	324	1555	551	1183	1102	1062	710	2371	1135	1111
Saint Louis, MO	1028	1054	754	588	806	827	1381	539	1727	1184	1216	747	884	544	689	292	340	552	737	414	641	956	859	377	585	1238	872	1206	369	698	437	762	1030	835	251	495	859	251	497	1581	462	422
Saint Paul, MN	1215	1362	1062	1105	1120	1095	812	1118	1398	892	1565	948	1316	870	1143	405	696	753	1320	745	1013	1458	956	251	698	1541	244	1753	564	987	583	1138	1257	1266	591	1160	1376	459	951	1630	408	881
Salt Lake City, UT	2290	621	1324	1900	1341	2051	579	1825	349	2417	1775	1922	2254	1896	2059	1386	1710	1727	2115	1711	1287	2283	519	1085	1679	892	1172	2578	1527	1184	1556	2059	2238	1460	1605	1742	2286	1095	1766	413	900	1462
San Antonio, TX	1986	684	530	965	81	1646	1600	895	1709	2052	300	1638	1371	1419	1272	1208	1208	1443	1180	1305	284	1175	975	1022	1500	576	1402	1378	1269	283	1353	1321	1965	203	1200	649	1086	795	1150	1273	916	592
San Diego, CA	2855	787	1078	2174	1313	2714	1309	2034	1010	2992	1574	2613	2505	2402	2423	2335	2193	2334	2389	2277	1369	2418	1054	1760	2419	721	1934	2621	2189	1332	2269	2457	2944	1484	2067	1783	2329	1627	2269	349	1573	1743
San Francisco, CA	2966	1135	1396	2511	1776	2765	1239	2371	595	3133	2044	2403	2923	2616	2756	2108	2329	2408	2738	2461	1865	2827	1233	1832	2360	1184	1886	3073	2304	1735	2318	2740	3019	1947	2224	2183	2781	1869	2549	592	1614	1994
Seattle, WA	2855	1500	1805	2656	2157	2685	815	2475	524	2961	2521	2531	2960	2748	2765	2043	2334	2336	2971	2408	2203	3070	1371	1889	2299	1775	1440	3882	2202	2071	2221	2773	2918	2498	2229	2585	3090	1884	2553	1209	1636	2320
Shreveport, LA	1599	868	568	624	340	1229	1691	474	1912	1618	644	1265	945	899	885	916	826	1070	833	902	189	903	1112	827	1069	844	1229	1144	909	228	1018	937	1519	271	827	223	814	624	729	1468	727	219
Spokane, WA	2652	1346	1563	2367	1981	2417	541	2469	369	2693	2359	2263	2700	2503	2505	1775	2066	2068	2572	2115	1978	2811	1095	1556	2020	1686	1166	3014	1921	1978	1941	2503	2650	2222	1961	2205	2822	1727	2298	1119	1460	2092
Tallahassee, FL	1249	1508	1208	268	899	932	2306	302	2512	1312	1094	1155	364	868	559	957	706	949	408	828	835	259	1727	1216	957	1492	1598	462	871	867	1022	608	1223	721	818	421	170	1045	584	2068	1227	679
Tampa, FL	1281	1759	1459	476	1150	949	2143	553	2763	1329	1345	1346	479	903	584	1143	908	1091	497	1013	1086	141	1858	1460	1200	1743	1849	268	1092	1118	1219	673	1240	972	1069	672	195	1296	730	2319	1477	958
Toledo, OH	633	1526	1220	641	1315	454	1557	673	2020	742	1622	309	973	284	533	243	203	114	683	138	1112	1063	1272	567	65	1699	885	1289	105	1144	170	516	624	1249	243	876	989	717	449	1954	762	803
Tuscon, AZ	2442	486	656	1785	908	2246	1342	1621	1144	2571	1176	2166	2100	2039	1913	1711	1750	1971	2080	1833	964	1999	835	1484	1938	316	1897	2271	1783	932	1856	2059	2433	1079	1668	1378	2010	1281	1755	389	1246	1257
Tulsa, OK	1409	674	336	803	462	1208	1293	636	2020	1532	835	1128	1103	941	989	673	721	933	1018	795	259	1156	714	471	916	788	972	1409	738	305	818	1037	1411	504	616	510	1167	283	782	1224	416	259
Washington, DC	378	1864	1564	630	1509	41	2006	781	2441	430	1787	429	559	299	334	697	478	341	498	418	1306	802	1654	1054	506	1954	1322	1062	531	1338	608	309	341	1220	551	965	730	1046	554	2376	1184	832
West Palm Beach, FL	1396	1938	1638	632	1329	1046	2736	702	2942	1426	1524	1443	568	982	673	1289	1063	1192	586	1146	1265	195	2157	1646	1305	1922	2028	41	1157	1297	1476	737	1339	1151	1176	851	284	1052	806	2498	1598	1101
Youngstown, OH	462	1632	1346	719	1368	298	1632	738	2090	568	1695	190	709	251	502	413	275	74	561	170	1193	986	1421	737	239	1804	1038	1219	275	1225	340	482	470	1322	341	949	958	843	521	2124	923	876

Mileage Chart 5

	Los Angeles, CA	Louisville, KY	Memphis, TN	Miami, FL	Milwaukee, WI	Minneapolis, MN	Mobile, AL	Montgomery, AL	Nashville, TN	New Orleans, LA	New York City NY	Norfolk, VA	Oakland,CA	Oklahoma City, OK	Omaha, NE	Orlando, FL	Philadelphia, PA	Phoenix, AZ	Pittsburgh, PA	Portland, OR	Providence, RI	Raleigh, NC	Reno, NV	Richmond, VA	Rochester, NY	Saint Louis, MO	Saint Paul, MN	Salt Lake City, UT	San Antonio, TX	San Diego, CA	San Francisco, CA	Seattle, WA	Shreveport, LA	Spokane, WA	Tallahassee, FL	Tampa, FL	Toledo, OH	Tucson, AZ	Tulsa, OK	Washington, DC	West Palm Beach, FL	Youngstown, OH
Albany, NY	2911	868	1232	1439	933	1215	1322	1178	993	1453	146	505	2982	1523	1308	1249	251	2512	471	2869	178	656	2763	482	219	1028	1215	2290	1986	2855	2966	2855	1599	2652	1249	1281	633	2442	1409	378	1396	462
Albuquerque, NM	823	1332	1021	1994	1443	1256	1265	1345	1232	1187	1995	1905	1134	559	905	1751	1922	446	1654	1378	2156	1759	1056	1833	1857	1054	1362	621	684	787	1135	1500	868	1346	1508	1759	1526	486	674	1864	1938	1646
Amarillo, TX	1095	1041	721	1694	1143	1062	965	1045	932	875	1695	1632	1430	267	754	1451	1622	746	1354	1636	1856	1458	1345	1533	1557	754	1062	917	530	1078	1396	1805	568	1563	1208	1459	1220	656	336	1564	1638	1346
Atlanta, GA	2197	421	397	665	784	1105	340	164	243	493	855	551	2488	863	989	446	766	1810	712	2763	1027	397	2411	527	1015	588	1105	1900	965	2174	2511	2656	624	2367	268	476	641	1785	803	630	632	719
Austin, TX	1410	1022	658	1338	1203	1120	656	804	869	535	1728	1403	1786	414	847	1142	1630	1030	1412	2059	1898	1355	1775	1463	1623	806	1120	1341	81	1313	1776	2157	340	1981	899	1150	1315	908	462	1509	1329	1368
Baltimore, MD	2676	608	900	1095	794	1105	990	833	688	1136	201	237	2864	1322	1143	917	97	2311	245	2765	356	324	2562	155	300	827	1095	2051	1646	2714	2765	2686	1229	2417	932	949	454	2246	1208	41	1046	298
Billings, MT	1254	1550	1557	2580	1143	812	1854	1836	1640	1820	1926	2098	1218	1168	904	2277	2051	1220	1681	867	2238	2273	1021	1655	1922	1381	812	579	1600	1309	1239	815	1691	541	2306	2143	1557	1342	1293	2006	2736	1632
Birmingham, AL	2067	373	239	788	766	1088	269	93	195	352	1019	711	2321	701	904	545	880	1700	778	2571	1189	557	2363	699	965	539	1118	1825	895	2034	2371	2475	474	2469	302	553	673	1621	636	781	702	738
Boise, ID	837	1908	1833	2860	1777	1488	2143	2346	2059	2191	2571	2551	671	1451	1274	2695	2498	1022	2203	439	2701	2560	404	2594	2352	1727	1398	349	1709	1010	595	524	1912	369	2512	2763	2020	1144	1582	2441	2492	2090
Boston, MA	2993	976	1379	1516	1078	1362	1379	1232	1062	1525	203	560	3124	1659	1443	1297	327	2644	584	3149	41	713	2871	544	381	1184	892	2417	2052	2992	3133	2961	1618	2693	1312	1329	742	2571	1532	430	1426	568
Brownsville, TX	1678	1321	957	1580	1530	1456	851	1041	1168	730	2002	1735	2034	680	1249	2034	1954	1289	1713	2468	2222	1506	2068	1646	1891	1216	1565	1609	300	1574	2044	2521	644	2359	1094	1345	1622	1176	835	1787	1524	1695
Buffalo, NY	2587	543	908	1424	640	948	1184	1076	722	1273	390	569	2745	1242	1005	1306	397	2269	219	2677	454	721	2433	552	81	747	948	1922	1638	2613	2667	2531	1265	2263	1155	1346	309	2166	1128	429	1443	190
Charleston, SC	2521	608	689	630	1032	1316	607	464	576	727	787	454	2788	1176	1303	401	688	2222	778	2952	956	300	2765	462	871	884	1316	2254	1371	2505	2923	2960	945	2700	364	479	973	2100	1103	559	568	709
Charleston, WV	2394	258	653	1046	566	874	825	632	458	891	524	369	2600	1031	899	814	517	2045	211	2615	699	297	2407	251	495	544	870	1896	1419	2402	2616	2748	899	2503	868	903	284	2039	941	299	982	251
Charlotte, NC	2417	438	592	604	835	1143	575	415	399	721	625	341	2755	1069	1135	559	522	2061	504	2757	785	162	2570	280	689	689	1143	2059	1272	2423	2756	2765	885	2505	559	584	583	1913	989	334	673	502
Chicago, IL	1989	300	551	1338	92	405	908	762	474	925	794	851	2098	804	454	1127	757	1776	470	2140	924	802	1897	788	608	292	405	1386	1208	2306	2108	2043	916	1775	957	1143	243	1711	673	697	1289	413
Cincinnati, OH	2164	105	469	1086	388	696	712	561	283	810	628	601	2317	835	721	892	559	1808	291	2369	790	540	2201	503	502	340	696	1671	1208	2193	2329	2334	813	2066	706	908	203	1756	721	478	1051	275
Cleveland, OH	2392	349	713	1264	445	753	989	815	527	1078	446	493	2498	1047	824	1046	430	2045	128	2416	600	559	2238	583	268	552	753	1727	1443	2384	2408	2336	1070	2068	949	1091	114	1971	933	341	1192	74
Columbia, SC	2426	494	612	658	891	1276	555	379	458	701	715	412	2703	1091	1283	440	627	2025	572	2972	888	215	2626	390	789	737	1320	2115	1180	2389	2738	2971	833	2572	408	497	683	2080	1018	498	586	561
Columbus, OH	2254	211	575	1210	448	753	834	707	389	940	551	559	2391	909	795	997	460	1907	186	2478	713	453	2295	498	397	414	745	1711	1305	2277	2461	2408	592	2115	828	1513	138	1833	795	418	1146	170
Dallas, TX	1401	819	455	1321	1013	1013	592	677	666	530	1525	1359	1803	211	693	1078	1427	1013	1209	2059	1695	1152	1731	1313	1420	641	1013	1287	284	1369	1865	2203	196	1978	835	1086	1112	964	259	1306	1265	1193
Daytona Beach, FL	2407	801	749	259	1180	1458	502	458	639	632	1054	702	2831	1257	1402	81	914	2102	859	3018	1201	559	2758	713	1176	956	1458	2283	1175	2418	2827	3070	903	2811	259	141	1063	1999	1156	802	195	986
Denver, CO	1009	1127	1151	2131	1070	956	1372	1412	1167	1323	1775	1800	1223	660	559	1896	1762	802	1475	1283	1961	1694	1030	1904	1637	859	956	519	975	1054	1233	1371	1112	1095	1727	1858	1272	835	714	1654	2157	1421
Des Moines, IA	1654	591	599	1582	365	251	954	1131	712	978	1070	1202	1742	576	146	1363	1037	1479	770	1816	1256	1123	1606	1293	932	377	251	1085	1022	1760	1832	1889	827	1556	1216	1460	567	1484	471	1054	1646	737
Detroit, MI	2270	365	712	1386	389	698	988	814	536	1077	620	711	2350	1030	726	1143	585	2019	304	2368	746	643	2190	609	424	535	698	1679	1500	2419	2360	2299	1069	2020	957	1200	65	1938	916	506	1305	239
El Paso, TX	818	1467	1103	1958	1528	1520	1236	1325	1314	1127	2173	1998	1194	708	1256	1735	2073	438	1833	1661	2335	1800	1185	2023	2036	1238	1541	894	576	721	1184	1775	844	1686	1492	1743	1699	316	788	1954	1922	1804
Fargo, ND	1844	949	1224	1987	576	244	1413	1525	1138	1521	1450	1581	1870	989	464	1826	1370	1791	1112	1484	1566	1485	1660	1481	1249	872	244	1172	1402	1934	1886	1440	1229	1166	1598	1849	885	1897	972	1322	2028	1038
Fort Lauderdale, FL	2704	1078	989	24	1443	1723	705	671	900	843	1289	964	3041	1481	1604	208	1127	2244	1216	3204	1459	794	3008	946	1410	1208	1753	2578	1378	2621	3073	3382	1144	3014	462	268	1289	2271	1409	1062	41	1219
Fort Wayne, IN	2137	222	592	1326	256	564	839	686	385	916	691	709	2257	852	634	1059	604	1831	336	2299	799	603	2056	635	464	369	564	1527	1269	2189	2304	2202	909	1921	871	1092	105	1783	738	531	1157	275
Fort Worth, TX	1361	851	487	1353	1059	1001	624	701	698	519	1557	1382	1723	210	634	1110	1459	983	1241	2003	1727	1184	1608	1333	1452	698	987	1184	283	1332	1735	2071	228	1978	867	1118	1144	932	305	1338	1297	1225
Grand Rapids, MI	2148	373	690	1356	275	583	1006	819	534	1071	706	802	2308	932	640	1188	672	1906	397	2251	859	754	2067	722	499	437	583	1556	1353	2269	2318	2221	1018	1941	1022	1219	170	1856	818	608	1476	340
Greensboro, NC	2478	462	640	810	826	1135	681	512	429	810	561	227	2809	1118	1208	648	438	2099	438	2823	706	73	2591	191	600	762	1138	2059	1321	2457	2740	2773	937	2503	608	673	516	2059	1037	309	737	482
Hartford, CT	2829	867	1209	1427	948	1257	1290	1133	973	1436	101	471	2909	1546	1321	1208	220	2523	486	2877	73	624	2749	455	324	1030	1257	2238	1965	2944	3019	2918	1529	2656	1223	1240	624	2433	1411	341	1339	470
Houston, TX	1581	948	584	1207	1155	1266	478	709	795	367	1679	1362	1957	454	949	964	1581	1110	1345	2369	1849	1233	1932	2291	1555	835	1266	1460	203	1484	1947	2498	271	2222	721	972	1249	1079	504	1420	1151	1322
Indianapolis, IN	2075	129	470	1208	283	591	749	590	302	857	730	669	2212	730	616	989	624	1719	349	2335	892	635	2116	907	551	251	591	1605	1200	2067	2224	2229	827	1961	818	1069	243	668	616	551	1176	341
Jackson, MS	1880	575	211	907	884	1123	178	255	422	193	1192	948	2270	575	914	697	1094	1500	965	2518	1362	815	2143	946	1183	495	1160	1742	649	1783	2183	2585	223	2205	421	672	876	1378	510	965	851	949
Jacksonville, FL	2402	729	697	356	1067	1374	413	379	592	551	957	632	2771	1181	1305	138	859	2100	882	3030	1127	584	2716	693	1102	867	1374	2286	1086	2329	2781	3042	814	2822	170	195	989	2010	1167	730	284	958
Kansas City, MO	1589	519	470	1475	568	459	819	867	590	857	1192	1179	1799	373	195	1266	1134	1277	851	1809	1378	1086	1606	1205	1062	251	459	1095	795	1627	1869	1834	624	1727	1045	1296	717	1281	283	1052	144	843
Knoxville, TN	2201	246	385	859	643	932	449	348	174	607	753	412	2509	847	930	665	646	1845	515	2550	951	356	2363	440	710	497	935	1766	1150	2269	2549	2553	729	2298	584	730	449	1755	782	554	806	521
Las Vegas, NV	275	1861	1581	2570	1752	1630	1841	2015	1792	1800	2520	2534	582	1119	1249	2311	2449	284	2181	991	2683	2319	478	2406	2371	1581	1630	413	1273	349	592	1209	1468	1119	2068	2319	1954	389	1224	2376	2498	2124
Lincoln, NE	1476	730	647	1673	560	409	1039	975	770	1014	1274	1354	1604	433	57	1452	1260	1236	965	1641	1451	1263	1411	1249	1135	462	408	900	916	1573	1614	1636	727	1460	1227	1477	762	1246	416	1184	1598	923
Little Rock	1678	502	138	1208	772	881	430	470	349	430	1235	1025	1984	324	690	965	1110	1379	899	2270	1395	851	1986	963	1111	422	881	1462	592	1743	1994	2368	219	2092	679	958	803	1257	259	832	1101	876
Los Angeles, CA	0	2136	1816	2828	2238	1905	2013	2035	2027	1883	2790	2809	372	1354	1508	2585	2717	389	2449	989	2902	2554	511	2641	2400	1849	1905	672	1378	121	382	1159	1687	1406	2342	2578	2213	502	1459	2659	2772	2424
Louisville, KY	2136	0	364	1102	397	705	626	466	178	729	707	607	2333	738	671	907	664	1782	381	2298	421	525	2132	686	608	290	705	1638	1103	2119	2388	2320	721	2075	664	915	300	1697	633	533	1094	373
Memphis, TN	1816	364	0	1013	673	949	389	332	211	397	1095	876	2122	462	705	770	989	1444	795	2408	1257	712	2124	825	973	300	949	1613	730	1881	2132	2506	357	2230	527	778	665	1370	397	875	957	738
Miami, FL	2828	1102	1013	0	1435	1743	729	695	908	867	1313	988	3087	1524	1670	227	1215	2448	1248	3366	1483	818	3032	988	1435	1231	1743	2602	1402	2645	3097	3406	1130	3138	486	292	1293	2326	1483	1086	65	1264
Milwaukee, WI	2238	397	673	1435	0	332	981	859	571	1045	851	948	2171	884	503	1224	834	1873	567	2002	1021	899	1930	832	697	389	332	1419	1305	2109	2175	1970	1013	1702	1053	1240	332	1808	770	770	1386	510
Minneapolis, MN	1905	705	949	1743	332	0	1227	1281	892	1346	1160	1337	2065	803	381	1673	1126	1679	868	1670	1322	1241	1776	1237	1005	628	1	1475	1265	1975	2075	1638	985	1370	1354	1589	641	1702	705	1078	1737	794
Mobile, AL	2013	626	389	729	981	1227	0	176	462	146	1176	884	2351	786	1011	486	1078	1593	1050	2611	1346	738	2278	867	1273	673	1158	1903	697	1971	2361	2710	401	2342	243	494	940	1542	713	949	673	1005
Montgomery, AL	2035	466	332	695	859	1281	176	0	288	322	1010	715	2295	794	1037	452	930	1655	843	2632	1191	561	2456	792	1179	632	1281	1918	904	2127	2464	2838	478	2562	209	460	766	1633	765	794	639	831
Nashville, TN	2027	178	211	908	571	892	462	288	0	551	859	665	2374	673	735	689	761	1671	575	2376	1029	502	2189	614	770	323	892	1678	941	2092	2375	2384	669	2124	486	737	478	1581	608	632	875	543
New Orleans, LA	1883	729	397	867	1045	1346	146	322	551	0	1322	1054	2317	681	1021	624	1224	1540	1078	2505	1492	876	2278	1114	1362	681	1346	1842	551	1824	2327	2574	309	2409	381	632	1005	1419	657	1095	811	1095
New York, NY	2790	707	1095	1313	851	1160	1176	1010	859	1322	0	389	2876	1436	1208	1094	101	2425	381	2880	162	510	2635	366	320	941	1160	2124	1832	2773	2886	2837	1415	2569	1109	1126	556	2360	1331	252	1223	403
Norfolk, VA	2809	607	876	988	948	1337	884	715	665	1054	389	0	2957	1349	1362	770	268	2393	365	2968	527	197	2789	98	535	927	1337	2262	1606	2669	2967	2975	1203	2700	802	827	592	2271	1234	190	916	438
Oakland, CA	372	2333	2122	3087	2171	2065	2351	2295	2374	2317	2876	2957	0	1660	1596	2844	2913	744	2528	614	2974	2865	201	2988	2681	2003	2065	545	1734	493	9	777	2052	979	2601	2836	2293	878	1766	2772	3055	2463
Oklahoma City, OK	1354	738	462	1524	884	803	786	794	673	681	1436	1349	1660	0	495	1281	1363	998	1095	1946	1597	1200	1662	1287	1298	495	803	1151	478	1345	1670	2044	389	1768	1038	1289	961	908	105	1305	1468	1087
Omaha, NE	1508	671	705	1670	503	381	1110	1037	735	1021	1208	1362	1596	495	0	1421	1200	1427	908	1605	1394	1281	1395	1400	1078	446	381	947	949	1641	1606	1679	729	1403	1241	1492	705	1400	401	1151	1671	875
Orlando, FL	2585	907	770	227	1224	1673	486	452	689	624	1094	770	2844	1281	1421	0	1005	2205	1025	3123	1273	608	2789	776	1200	1030	1551	2359	1159	2402	2854	3163	920	2895	243	89	1086	2083	1240	876	194	1052
Philadelphia, PA	2717	664	989	1215	834	1126	1078	930	761	1224	101	268	2913	1363	1200	1005	0	2374	292	2830	259	412	2627	252	324	868	1126	2209	1734	2911	2923	2780	1270	2512	1020	1037	502	2287	1249	133	1134	357
Phoenix, AZ	389	1782	1444	2448	1873	1679	1593	1655	1671	1540	2425	2393	744	998	1427	2205	2374	0	2084	1322	2586	2172	754	2285	2281	1484	1808	673	989	357	754	1492	1282	1386	1962	2213	1950	122	1103	2367	2392	2061
Pittsburgh, PA	2449	381	795	1248	567	868	1050	843	575	1078	381	365	2528	1095	908	1025	292	2084	0	2538	559	519	2335	333	284	600	868	1824	1468	2441	2538	2513	1087	2190	932	998	227	2021	981	219	1111	65
Portland, OR	985	2298	2408	3366	2002	1670	2611	2632	2376	2505	2880	2968	614	1946	1605	3123	2830	1322	2538	0	3000	2903	616	3012	2676	2068	1670	764	2168	1078	624	170	2255	365	2880	3131	2311	1483	1987	2846	3310	2481
Providence, RI	2902	421	1257	1483	1021	1322	1346	1191	1029	1492	162	527	2974	1597	1394	1273	259	2586	559	3000	0	673	2814	511	381	1102	1322	2303	2002	2978	2984	2967	1585	2644	1288	1322	689	252	1483	397	1402	538
Raleigh, NC	2554	525	713	818	899	1241	738	561	502	876	510	197	2865	1200	1281	608	412	2172	519	2903	673	0	2716	175	600	835	1241	2205	1427	2529	2797	2911	538	2651	624	657	584	2124	1103	283	754	535
Reno, NV	511	2132	2124	3032	1930	1776	2278	2456	2189	2278	2635	2789	201	1662	1395	2789	2627	754	2335	616	2814	2716	0	2803	2489	1881	1776	511	1768	535	211	810	1927	770	2546	2797	2133	867	1702	2579	2976	2303
Richmond, VA	2641	686	825	988	832	1237	867	792	614	1114	366	98	2988	1287	1400	776	252	2285	333	3012	511	175	2803	0	455	976	1237	2324	1555	2643	2989	3029	1173	2761	794	827	630	2425	1222	114	924	662
Rochester, NY	2400	608	973	1435	697	1005	1273	1179	770	1362	320	535	2681	1298	1078	1200	324	2281	284	2676	381	600	2489	455	0	803	1005	1978	1686	2674	2691	2660	1361	2384	1208	1257	381	2222	1398	341	1346	265
Saint Louis, MO	1849	290	300	1231	389	628	673	632	323	681	941	927	2003	495	446	1030	868	1484	600	2068	1102	835	1881	976	803	0	628	1370	916	1840	2075	2076	624	1881	795	1030	466	1419	381	795	1241	592
Saint Paul, MN	1905	705	949	1743	332	1	1158	1281	892	1346	1160	1337	2065	803	381	1551	1126	1808	868	1670	1322	1241	1776	1237	1005	628	0	1475	1265	1975	2075	1638	985	1370	1354	1589	641	1702	705	1078	1737	794
Salt Lake City, UT	672	1638	1613	2602	1419	1475	1903	1918	1678	1842	2124	2262	545	1151	947	2359	2209	673	1824	764	2303	2205	511	2324	1978	1370	1475	0	1447	762	714	851	1563	706	2116	2318	1715	795	1223	2141	2490	1805
San Antonio, TX	1378	1103	730	1402	1305	1265	697	904	941	551	1832	1606	1734	478	949	1159	1734	989	1468	2168	2002	1427	1768	1555	1686	916	1265	1447	0	1274	1774	2255	474	2110	916	1151	1387	876	535	1605	1370	1477
San Diego, CA	121	2119	1881	2645	2109	1975	1971	2127	2092	1824	2773	2669	493	1345	1641	2402	2911	357	2441	1078	2978	2529	535	2643	2674	1840	1975	762	1274	0	527	1276	1565	1403	2213	2464	2604	405	1403	2733	2072	2456
San Francisco, CA	382	2388	2132	3097	2175	2075	2361	2464	2375	2327	2886	2967	9	1670	1606	2854	2923	754	2538	624	2984	2797	211	2989	2691	2075	2075	714	1774	527	0	787	2061	852	2611	2846	2415	868	1776	2949	3065	2569
Seattle, WA	1159	2343	2506	3406	1970	1638	2710	2838	2384	2574	2837	2975	777	2044	1679	3163	2780	1492	2513	170	2967	2911	810	3029	2660	2076	1638	851	2255	1276	787	0	2335	274	2920	3155	2231	1573	2034	2684	3388	2456
Shreveport, LA	1687	721	357	1130	1013	985	401	478	669	309	1415	1203	2052	389	729	920	1270	1282	1087	2255	1585	538	1927	1173	1361	624	985	1563	474	1565	2061	2335	0	2038	644	895	1099	1160	356	953	507	1081
Spokane, WA	1406	2075	2230	3138	1702	1370	2342	2562	2124	2409	2569	2700	979	1768	1403	2895	2512	1386	2190	365	2644	2651	770	2761	2384	1816	1370	706	2110	1403	852	274	2038	0	2652	2887	2100	1496	1727	2417	3196	2125
Tallahassee, FL	2342	664	527	486	1053	1354	243	209	486	381	1109	802	2601	1038	1241	243	1020	1962	932	2880	1288	624	2546	794	1208	795	1354	2116	916	2213	2611	2920	644	2652	0	251	900	1840	955	891	430	1005
Tampa, FL	2578	915	778	292	1240	1589	494	460	737	632	1126	827	2836	1289	1492	89	1037	2213	998	3131	1322	657	2797	827	1251	1030	1589	2318	1151	2464	2846	3155	895	2887	251	0	1143	2076	1182	908	219	1088
Toledo, OH	2213	300	665	1293	332	641	940	766	478	1005	556	592	2293	961	705	1086	502	1950	227	2311	689	584	2133	630	381	466	641	1715	1387	2604	2415	2231	1099	2100	900	1143	0	2051	867	438	1248	170
Tuscon, AZ	502	1697	1370	2326	1808	1702	1542	1633	1581	1419	2360	2271	878	908	1400	2083	2287	122	2021	1483	252	2124	867	2425	2222	1419	1702	795	876	405	868	1573	1160	1496	1840	2076	2051	0	1038	2254	2270	2003
Tulsa, OK	1459	633	397	1483	770	705	713	765	608	657	1331	1234	1766	105	401	1240	1249	1103	981	1987	1483	1103	1702	1222	1398	381	705	1223	535	1403	1776	2034	356	1727	955	1182	867	1038	0	1284	1167	964
Washington, DC	2659	533	875	1086	770	1078	949	796	632	1095	252	190	2772	1305	1151	876	133	2367	219	2846	397	283	2579	114	341	795	1078	2141	1605	2733	2949	2684	953	2417	891	908	438	2254	1284	0	1005	283
West Palm Beach, FL	2772	1094	957	65	1386	1737	673	639	875	811	1223	916	3055	1468	1671	194	1134	2392	1111	3310	1402	754	2976	924	1346	1241	1737	2490	1370	2072	3065	3388	507	3196	430	219	1248	2270	1167	1005	0	1167
Youngstown, OH	2424	373	738	1238	510	794	1005	831	543	1095	403	438	2463	1087	875	1052	357	2076	65	2481	527	535	2303	662	265	592	794	1877	1477	2432	2569	2456	1181	2125	1005	1088	170	2003	964	283	1167	0

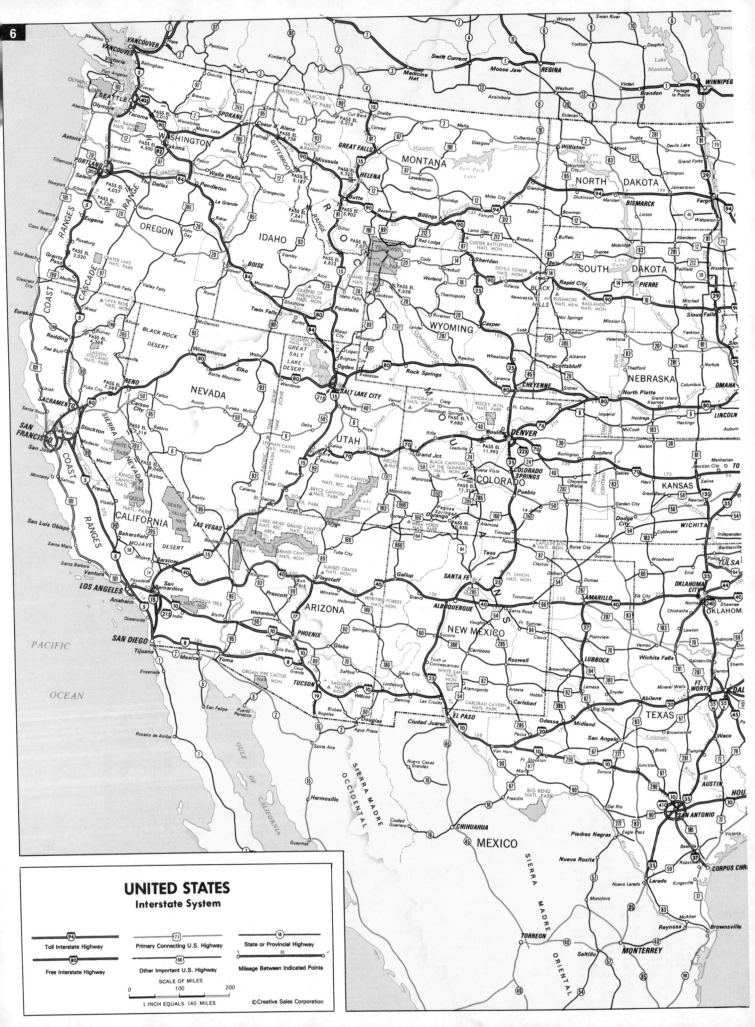

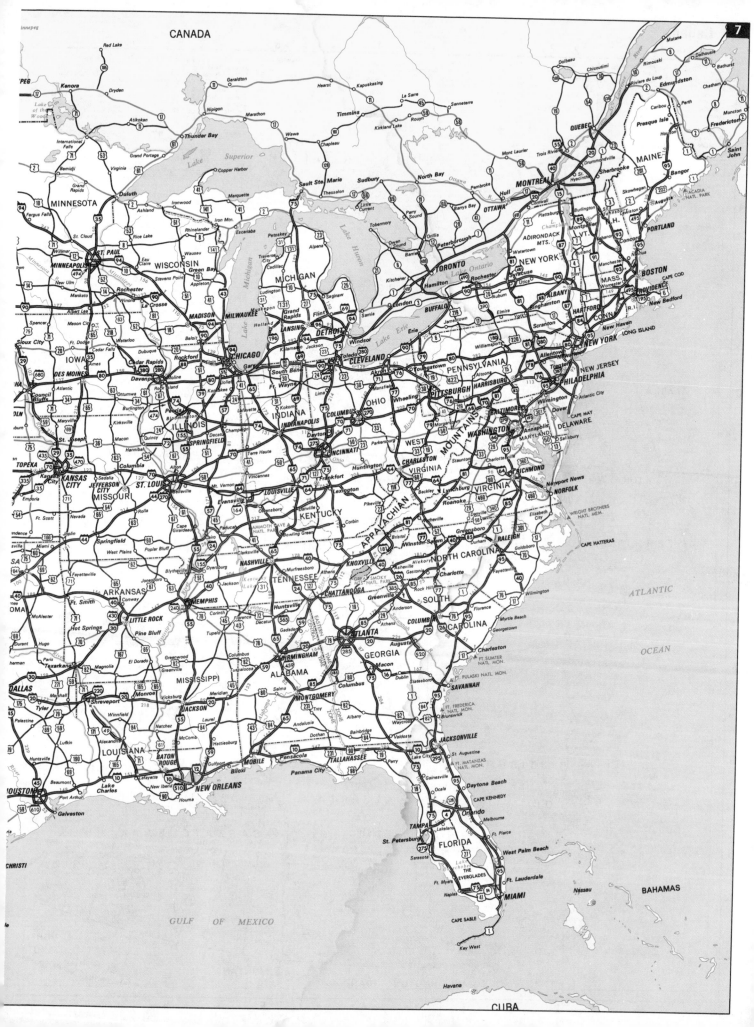

Goose Bay	C-12	
Grand Falls	C-14	
Hebron	C-11	
Hopedale	C-11	
Labrador City	D-11	
Makkovik	C-12	
Marystown	D-14	
Northwest River	C-12	
Nutak	C-11	
Placentia	C-14	
St. John's	C-14	

St. Pierre (France)	D-14	
Stephenville	D-13	
Wabana	C-14	

N.W. TERRITORY

Aklavik	C-2	
Artic Bay	A-6	
Artic Red River	D-2	
Baker Lake	D-6	
Bathurst Inlet	C-5	
Cambridge Bay	C-5	
Cape Dorset	C-8	
Cape Dyer	A-9	
Chesterfield Inlet	D-7	
Clyde	A-8	
Colville Lake	D-4	
Coppermine	D-4	
Echo Bay (Port Radium)	D-4	
Eskimo Point	E-7	
Ft. Franklin	D-3	
Ft. Good Hope	D-3	
Ft. Laird	F-3	
Ft. McPherson	C-2	
Ft. Norman	D-3	
Ft. Providence	E-4	
Ft. Resolution	E-4	
Ft. Simpson	E-3	
Ft. Smith	F-4	
Frobisher Bay	B-9	
Gjoa Haven	C-6	
Hall Beach	B-7	
Hay River	E-4	
Holman	C-4	
Igloolik	B-7	
Inuvik	C-2	
Lac la Martre	E-4	
Lake Harbour	B-9	
Mould Bay	A-4	
Norman Wells	D-3	
Panguirtung	B-8	
Paulatuk	C-3	
Pine Point	F-4	
Pond Inlet	A-7	
Rae	E-4	
Rankin Inlet	D-7	
Reliance	E-5	
Repulse Bay	C-7	
Resolute	A-5	
Resolution Island	B-10	
Sachs Harbour	B-3	
Snowdrift	E-5	
Spence Bay	B-6	
Trout Lake	F-3	
Tukloyaktuk	C-2	
Wrigley	E-3	
Yellowknife	E-4	

NOVA SCOTIA

Amherst	E-13	
Bridgewater	F-14	
Canso	E-14	
Glace Bay	E-14	
Halifax	F-14	
Kentville	F-13	
New Glasgow	E-14	
Shelburne	F-14	
Sydney	E-14	
Truro	E-13	
Yarmouth	F-13	

ONTARIO

Armstrong	G-9	
Atikokan	H-8	
Barrie	H-11	
Belleville	H-12	
Blind River	H-10	
Brantford	J-11	
Brockville	G-12	
Chatham	J-11	
Cochrane	G-10	
Cornwall	G-12	
Deep River	G-11	
Favourable Lake	G-8	
Ft. Albany	F-9	
Ft. Frances	H-8	
Ft. Severn	F-8	
Geraldton	H-9	
Goderich	J-11	
Guelph	H-11	
Hamilton	H-12	
Hearst	G-10	
Kapuskasing	G-10	
Kenora	H-8	
Kingston	H-12	
Kirkland Lake	G-11	
Kitchener	H-11	
Lec Seul	H-8	
London	J-11	
Marathon	H-9	
Moosonee	F-10	
Nakina	G-9	
Niagra Falls	H-12	
Nipigon	H-9	
North Bay	H-11	
Oshawa	H-11	
Ottawa	G-12	
Owen Sound	H-11	
Parry Sound	H-11	
Pembroke	G-11	
Peterborough	H-12	
Pickle Lake	G-9	
Red Lake	H-8	
Renfrew	G-12	
St. Catharines	H-12	
St. Thomas	J-11	
Sault Ste. Marie	H-10	
Sioux Lookout	H-8	
Smith's Falls	G-12	
Sudbury	H-10	
Thunder Bay	H-9	
Timmins	G-10	
Toronto	H-11	
Trenton	H-12	
Wawa	H-10	
Windsor	J-11	
Winisk	F-9	

PRINCE EDWARD ISLAND

Charlottetown	E-13	
Summerside	E-13	

QUEBEC

Alma	F-12	
Amos	G-11	
Arvida	F-12	
Baie Comeau	E-12	
Belin (Payne)	C-10	
Cape Smith	D-9	
Chandler	E-12	
Chicoutimi	F-12	
Deception	C-9	
Desmaraisville	F-11	
Drummondville	G-12	
Eastmain	F-10	
Ft. Chimo	C-10	
Ft. George	E-10	
Ft. Rupert	F-10	
Gagnon	E-11	
Gaspe	E-12	
Granby	G-12	
Harve St. Pierre	D-12	
Hull	G-12	
Inoucdjouac (Port Harrison)	D-9	
Ivujivik	C-9	
Koartac	C-9	
La Tugue	F-12	
Lac-Allard	D-12	
Levis	F-12	
Manicourgan	E-12	
Maniwaki	G-11	
Maricourt (Wakeham)	C-9	
Matagami	F-11	
Matane	E-12	
Mont-Laurier	G-12	
Montreal	G-12	
Nitchequon	E-11	
Noranda	G-10	
Nouveau-Quebec (George River)	C-10	
Port Alfred	F-12	
Port Cartier	E-12	
Poste-de-la-Baleine	E-10	
Povungnitak	D-9	
Quebec	F-12	
Rimouski	E-12	
Riviere-du-Loup	F-12	
Rouyn	G-10	
St. Hyacinthe	G-12	
St. Jean	G-12	
St. Jerome	G-12	
Ste. Anne-des-Monts	E-12	
Schefferville	D-11	
Senneterre	G-11	
Sept. Iles	E-12	
Shawinigan	G-12	
Sherbrooke	G-12	
Shibougamau	F-11	
Sorel	G-12	
Thetford Mines	G-12	
Trois-Rivieres	G-12	
Val-d'Or	G-11	

SASKATCHEWAN

Assiniboia	J-6	
Biggar	H-5	
Estevan	H-5	
La Loche	G-5	
La Rouge	G-6	
Lloydminster	H-5	
Meadow lake	H-5	
Melfort	H-6	
Missinipe	G-6	
Moose Jaw	J-6	
North Battleford	H-5	
Prince Albert	H-6	
Regina	H-6	
Saskatoon	H-6	
Stoney Rapids	F-5	
Swift Current	J-5	
Uranium City	F-5	
Weyburn	J-6	
Wollaston Lake	F-6	
Yorkton	H-6	

YUKON

Beaver Creek	E-1	
Carcross	E-1	
Carmacks	D-1	
Clinton Creek	D-1	
Dawson	D-1	
Elsa	D-2	
Faro	E-1	
Haines Jct.	E-1	
Mayo	E-1	
Old Crow	C-1	
Teslin	F-2	
Watson Lake	F-2	
Whitehorse	E-2	

CANADA

▬▬▬ EXPRESSWAYS	㉗ INTERSTATE HIGHWAYS
─── PRIMARY HIGHWAYS	⑵ U.S. HIGHWAYS
─── OTHER HIGHWAYS	③ CANADIAN HIGHWAYS

⬡ TRANS-CANADA HIGHWAY

MILES
0   100   200   300   400   500

KILOMETERS
0   160   320   480   640   800

© Creative Sales Corporation

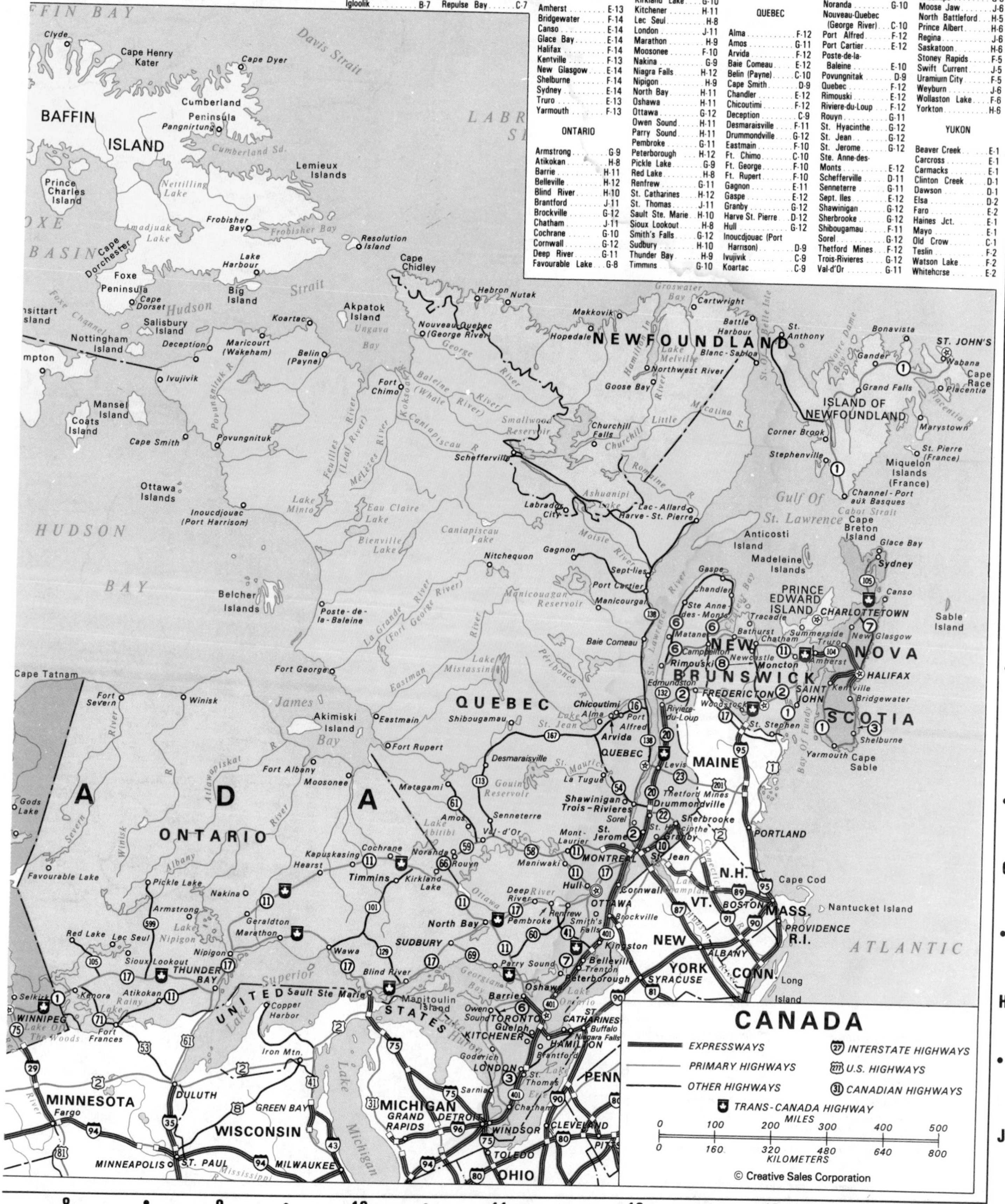

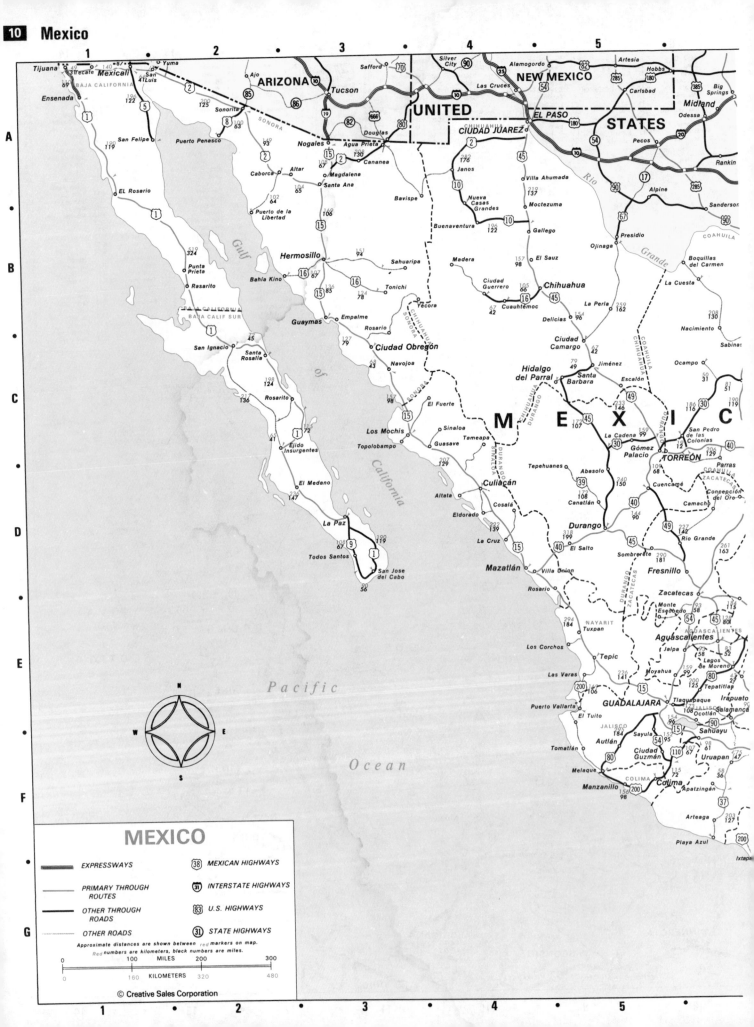

MEXICO

	EXPRESSWAYS	38	MEXICAN HIGHWAYS
	PRIMARY THROUGH ROUTES	31	INTERSTATE HIGHWAYS
	OTHER THROUGH ROADS	83	U.S. HIGHWAYS
	OTHER ROADS	31	STATE HIGHWAYS

Approximate distances are shown between *red* markers on map.
Red numbers are kilometers, black numbers are miles.

MILES 0   100   200   300

KILOMETERS 0   160   320   480

© Creative Sales Corporation

MEXICO

Cities and Towns

Abasolo	D-5	Ciudad del Maiz	E-7
Acambaro	F-6	Coatzacoalcos	F-9
Acapulco	G-6	Colima	F-5
Acatlan	F-7	Comitan	G-9
Acayucan	F-8	Conception de Oro	D-6
Agua Prieta	A-3	Cordoba	F-8
Aguascalientes	E-6	Cosala	D-4
Altar	A-3	Cuauhtemoc	B-4
Altata	D-4	Cuencame	D-5
Alvarado	F-8	Cuernavaca	F-7
Apatzingan	F-6	Culiacan	D-4
Arcelia	F-6	Delicias	B-5
Arriga	G-9	Durango	D-5
Arteaga	F-6	Dzilam de Bravo	E-10
Arlixco	F-7	Ejido Insurgentes	C-3
Autlan	F-5	El Fuerte	C-4
Bahia Kino	B-2	El Medana	D-3
Bavispe	A-4	El Rosario	A-1
Becal	E-10	El Sauz	B-4
Boquillas de		El Tuito	E-5
Carmen	B-6	Empalme	B-3
Buenaventura	B-4	Ensanada	A-1
Caborca	A-2	Escalon	C-5
Camacho	D-6	Escarcega	F-10
Campeche	E-10	Fresnillo	D-5
Cananea	A-3	Gallego	B-4
Canatlan	D-5	Gomez Palacio	C-5
Cardenas	F-9	Guadalajara	E-5
Celaya	E-6	Guasave	C-4
Celestun	E-10	Guaymas	B-3
Champoton	F-10	Hermosillo	B-3
Chetumal	F-11	Hidalgo del Parral	C-5
Chihuahua	B-5	Hopelchen	E-10
Chilpancingo	F-7	Huajuapan de Leon	F-7
China	C-7	Iguala	F-7
Ciudad Acuna	B-6	Irapuato	E-6
Ciudad Camargo	C-5	Iturbide	F-10
Ciudad Guerrero	B-4	Jalapa	F-8
Ciudad Guzman	F-5	Jalpa	E-5
Ciudad Juarez	A-4	Janos	A-4
Ciudad Madero	E-7	Jimenez	C-5
Ciudad Mante	E-7	Juchitan	G-8
Ciudad Victoria	D-7	La Cruz	D-4
Ciudad de Carmen	F-9	La Cadena	C-5
Ciudad de Valles	E-7	La Cuesta	B-6
		La Paz	D-3
		La Perla	B-5

La Pesca	D-7	Paraiso	F-9
La Piedad	E-6	Parras	C-6
Las Varas	E-5	Peto	E-10
Leon	E-6	Piedras Negras	B-6
Linares	D-7	Pijijiapan	G-9
Los Corchos	E-5	Pinotepa Nacional	G-7
Los Mochis	C-3	Piste	E-11
Madera	B-4	Playa Azul	F-6
Magdalena	A-3	Pochutla	G-8
Malpaso	F-8	Poza Pica	E-7
Manuel	E-7	Progreso	E-10
Manzanillo	F-5	Puebla	F-7
Matamoros	C-7	Puerto de la	
Matehuala	D-6	Libertad	B-2
Matias Romero	G-8	Puerto Escondido	G-8
Mazatlan	D-4	Puerto Juarez	E-11
Melaque	F-5	Puerto Madero	G-9
Merida	E-10	Puerto Penasco	A-2
Mexicali	A-1	Punta Prieta	B-2
Mexico City	F-7	Queretaro	E-6
Miahuatlan	G-8	Rasarito	B-2
Mier	C-7	Reynosa	C-7
Minatitlan	F-8	Rio Grande	D-6
Moctezuma	B-4	Rio Lagartos	E-11
Molango	E-7	Rosario	C-3
Moncloya	C-6	Rosario	D-4
Monte Escobedo	E-5	Sabinas	B-6
Montemorelos	D-7	Sabinas Hidagalo	C-6
Monterrey	C-6	Sahuaripa	B-3
Morelia	F-6	Salamanca	E-6
Morelos	B-6	Salinas	D-6
Moyahua	E-5	Salina Cruz	G-8
Nacimiento	C-6	Saltillo	C-6
Nautla	E-8	San Andres Tuxtla	F-8
Navojoa	C-3	San Cristobal	G-9
Nogales	A-3	San Felipe	A-2
Nueva Casas		San Fernando	D-7
Grandes	B-4	San Ignacio	C-2
Nueva Rosita	C-6	San Jose del Cabo	D-3
Nuevo Laredo	C-7	San Luis	A-2
Oaxaca	G-8	San Luis Potosi	E-6
Ocampo	C-6	San Pedro de las	
Ocotlan	E-6	Colonias	C-6
Ojinaga	B-5	Santa Ana	A-3
Ometepec	G-7	Santa Barbara	C-5
Orizaba	F-8	Santa Rosalia	C-2
Pachuca	E-7	Sayula	F-5
Palenque	F-9	Sinaloa	C-4
Papantla	E-7	Sombrerete	D-5

Sonorita	A-2	
Soto La Marina	D-7	
Tameapa	C-4	
Tampico	E-7	
Tapachula	G-9	
Tapanatepec	G-9	
Taxco	F-7	
Teapa	F-9	
Tecate	A-1	
Tehuacan	F-7	
Tehuantepec	G-8	
Temporal	E-7	
Tepatitlan	D-5	
Tepehuanes	D-5	
Tepic	E-5	
Ticul	E-10	
Tijuana	A-1	
Tiquicheo	F-6	
Tlaciaco	G-7	
Tlaxcala	F-7	
Tlaxiaco	G-7	
Todos Santos	D-3	
Toluca	F-7	
Tomatian	F-5	
Tonichi	B-3	
Topolobampo	C-3	
Torreon	C-5	
Totolapan	G-8	
Tulancingo	F-7	
Tulum	E-11	
Tuxpan	E-5	
Tuxpan	F-8	
Tuxtepec	F-8	
Tuxtla Gutierrez	G-9	
Uruapan	F-6	
Valladolid	E-11	
Veracruz	F-8	
Villa Ahumada	A-4	
Villagran	D-7	
Villahermosa	F-9	
Villa Union	D-4	
Xcan	E-11	
Yecora	B-4	
Zacatal	F-9	
Zacatecas	E-6	
Zamora	F-6	
Zihuatanejo	F-6	
Zimapan	E-7	
Zitacuaro	F-6	

STATE MAP LEGEND

ROAD CLASSIFICATIONS & RELATED SYMBOLS

Free Interstate Hwy.	90
Toll Interstate Hwy.	76
Divided Federal Hwy.	14
Federal Hwy.	20
Divided State Hwy.	31
State Hwy.	147
Other Connecting Road	258
Trans - Canada Hwy.	
Point to Point Milage	17
State Boundaries	

LAND MARKS & POINTS OF INTEREST

Indian Reservation		Desert	
National & State Forest or Wildlife Preserve		River, Lake, Ocean or other Drainage	
Military Installation		Urban Area	**Denver**
National & State Park or Recreation Area		Airport	✈
		State Capital	✳
		Park, Monument, University or other Point of Interest	■
Grassland		Roadside Table or Rest Areas	▲

ABBREVIATIONS

A.F.B. - Air Force Base	Mgmt. - Management	Prov. - Province	S. F. - State Forest
Hist. - Historical	Mon. - Monument	Rec. - Recreation	St. Pk. - State Park
Mem. - Memorial	Nat. - Natural	Ref. - Refuge	W.M.A. - Wildlife Management Area

CITIES & TOWNS - Type size indicates the relative population of cities and towns

Mapleton	Kenhorst	Somerset	Butler	Auburn	Harrisburg	Madison	Chicago
under 1000	1000-5,000	5,000-10,000	10,000-25,000	25,000-50,000	50,000-100,000	100,000-500,000	500,000 and over

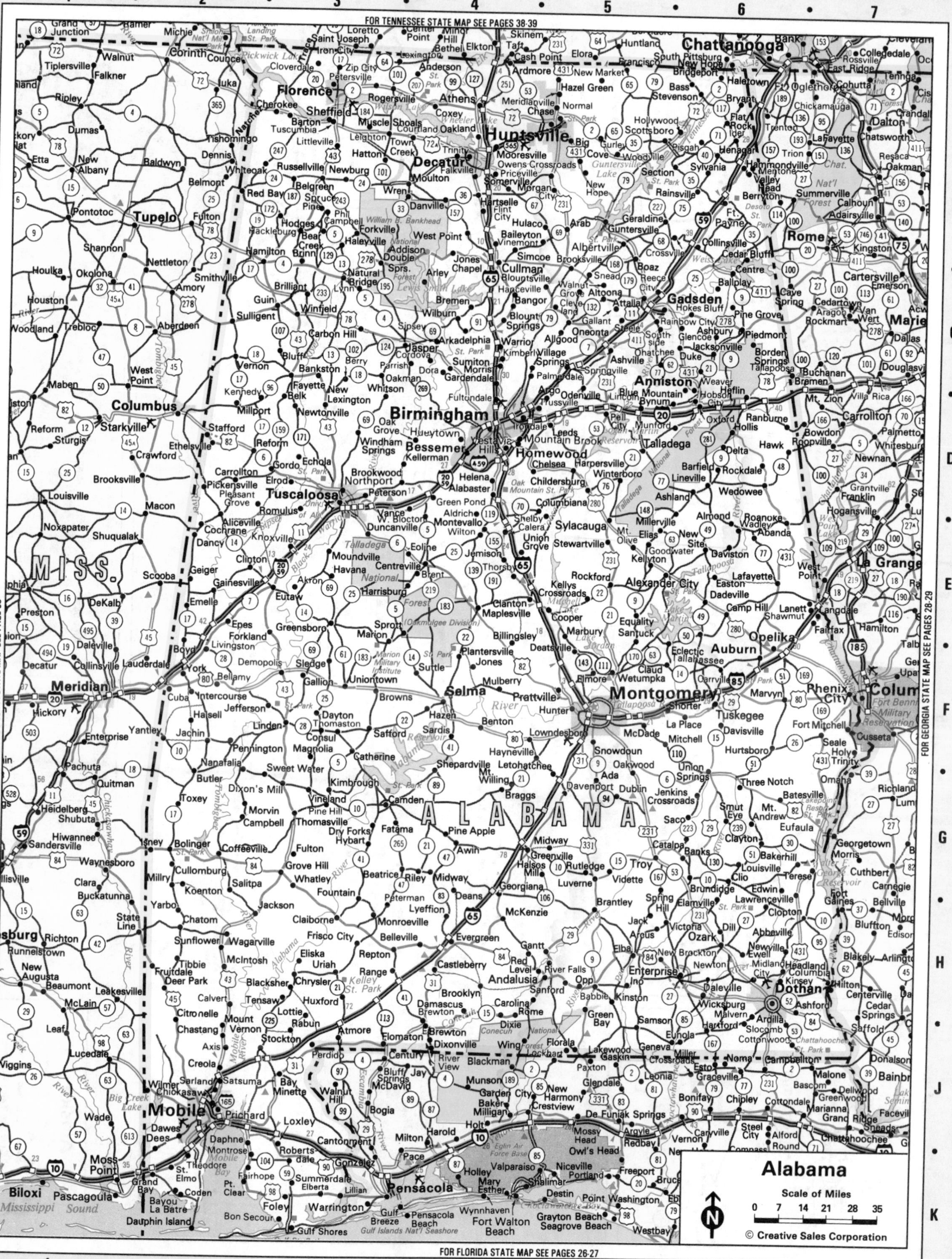
FOR TENNESSEE STATE MAP SEE PAGES 38-39
FOR MISSISSIPPI STATE MAP SEE PAGE 50
FOR GEORGIA STATE MAP SEE PAGES 28-29
FOR FLORIDA STATE MAP SEE PAGES 26-27
MISS.
ALABAMA
Birmingham
Montgomery
Huntsville
Mobile
Tuscaloosa
Chattanooga
Alabama
Scale of Miles
0 7 14 21 28 35
N
© Creative Sales Corporation

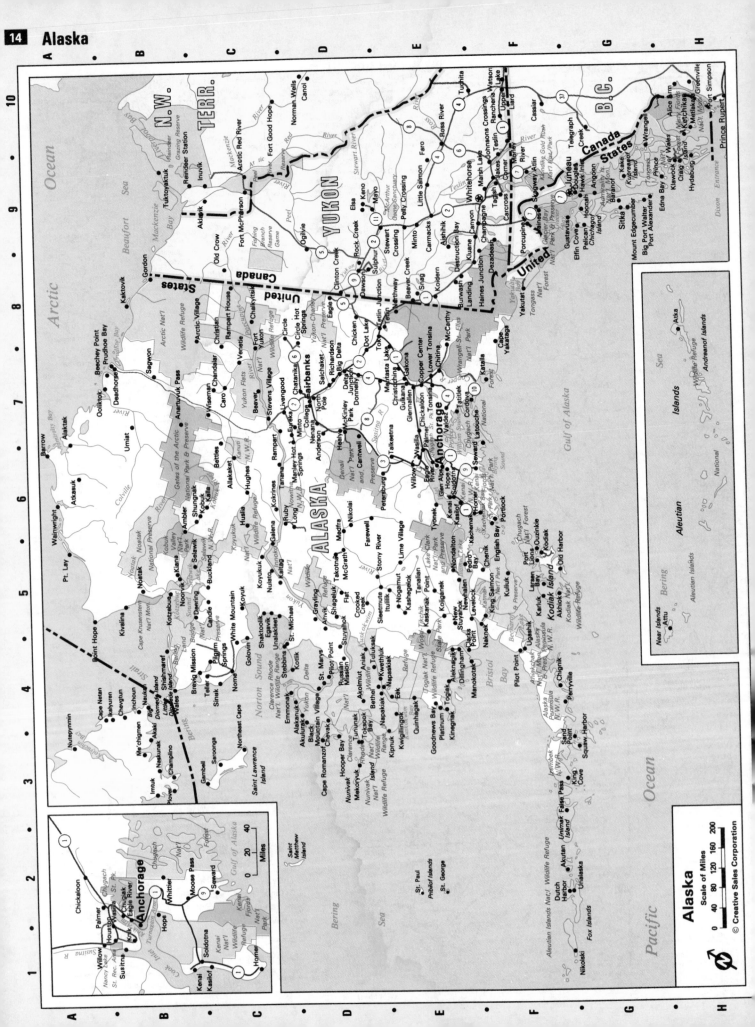

Alaska

Scale of Miles

0 40 80 120 160 200

© Creative Sales Corporation

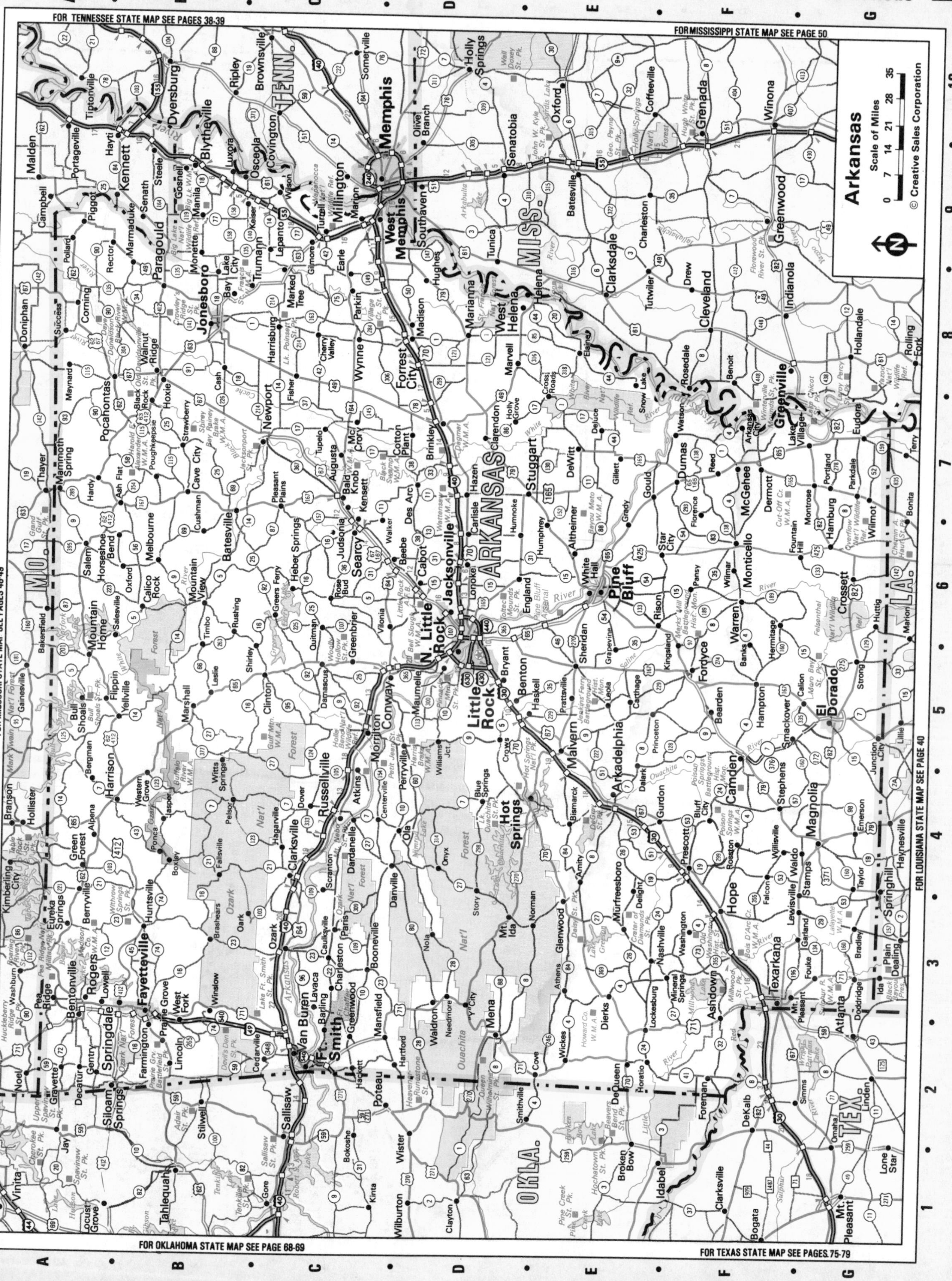
FOR TENNESSEE STATE MAP SEE PAGES 38-39
FOR MISSISSIPPI STATE MAP SEE PAGE 50
FOR MISSOURI STATE MAP SEE PAGES 48-49
FOR LOUISIANA STATE MAP SEE PAGE 40
FOR OKLAHOMA STATE MAP SEE PAGE 68-69
FOR TEXAS STATE MAP SEE PAGES 75-79
Arkansas
Scale of Miles
0 7 14 21 28 35
© Creative Sales Corporation
ARKANSAS
MO.
TENN.
MISS.
OKLA.
TEX.
LA.
Little Rock
N. Little Rock
Memphis
West Memphis
Jonesboro
Fort Smith
Fayetteville
Springdale
Hot Springs
Pine Bluff
Texarkana
El Dorado
Conway
Jacksonville
Searcy
Russellville
Harrison
Mountain Home
Batesville
Blytheville
Forrest City
Helena
Stuttgart
Camden
Hope
Arkadelphia
Malvern
Benton
Magnolia
Monticello
Greenville
Clarksdale
Cleveland
Grenada
Oxford
Dyersburg
Tahlequah
Mena
Paragould
Newport

FOR COLORADO STATE MAP SEE PAGES 22-23
FOR NEW MEXICO STATE MAP SEE PAGE 62
FOR UTAH STATE MAP SEE PAGES 80-81
FOR NEVADA STATE MAP SEE PAGE 54

UTAH

NEVADA

ARIZONA

La Sal, La Sal Jct., Summit Pt., Eastland, Monticello, Blanding, Manti-La Sal National Forest, Canyonlands National Park, Hanksville, Fry Canyon, Bluff, Montezuma Creek, Aneth, Teec Nos Pos, Rock Point, Round Rock, Tsaile, Cross Canyon, St. Michaels, Window Rock, Luptonn, Sanders, Navajo, Houck, Chambers, Greasewood (Lower), Ganado, Keams Canyon, Polacca, Cedar Springs, Indian Wells, Dilkon, Sun Valley, Holbrook, Joseph City, Winslow

Mexican Hat, Mexican Water, Tes Nez Iha, Dinnehotso, Kayenta, Tsegi, Chilchinbito, Rough Rock, Cow Springs, Red Lake, Old Oraibi, Oraibi, Second Mesa, Seba Dalkai, Sunrise, Leupp, Angell, Winona

Torrey, Grover, Boulder, Escalante, Widtsoe Jct., Henrieville, Cannonville, Tropic, Bryce Canyon, Ruby's Inn, Long Valley Jct., Alton, Glendale, Orderville, Mt. Carmel, Mt. Carmel Jct., Kanab, Fredonia, Colorado City, Jacob Lake, Marble Canyon, Page, Cedar Ridge, The Gap, Tonalea, Tuba City, Cameron, Gray Mountain, Desert View, North Rim, Grand Canyon, Moqui, Tusayan, Valle, Flagstaff, Mountainaire, Munds Park, Lake Montezuma, McGuireville

Panguitch, Hatch, Bryan Head, Brian Head, Cedar City, Hamilton Fort, Kanarraville, New Harmony, Pintura, La Verkin, Toquerville, Virgin, Springdale, Rockville, Hurricane, Washington, St. George, Littlefield, Beaver Dam, Mesquite, Bunkerville, Glendale, Logandale, Overton, Moapa, Sedona, Cottonwood, Clarkdale, Jerome, Cornville, Prescott Valley, Prescott, Pauldenn, Chino Valley, Ash Fork, Williams, Bellemont, Pine Springs, Parks, Seligman

Yampai, Peach Springs, Nelson, Truxton, Valentine, Hackberry, Kingman, Chloride, Dolan Springs, Meadview, Temple Bar, Cottonwood Cove, Katherine, Bullhead City, Riviera, Golden Shores, Topock, Lake Havasu City, Needles, Oatman, Yucca, Wikieup, Goldroad

N. Las Vegas, Henderson, Boulder City, Nelson, Cal Nev Ari, Searchlight, Laughlin

Alamo, Caliente, Panaca, Pioche, Ursine, Elgin, Modena, Newcastle, Uvada, Enterprise, Central, Pine Valley, Gunlock, Veyo, Ivins, Santa Clara, Shivwits

Dixie National Forest, Zion National Park, Kaibab National Forest, Grand Canyon National Park, Coconino National Forest, Prescott National Forest, Petrified Forest National Park, Navajo Indian Reservation, Hopi Indian Reservation, Hualapai Indian Reservation, Lake Mead National Recreational Area, Lake Mohave, Lake Powell, Colorado River, Little Colorado River, Paria River, Virgin River

Interstate 15, Interstate 40, U.S. 89, U.S. 93, U.S. 180, U.S. 191

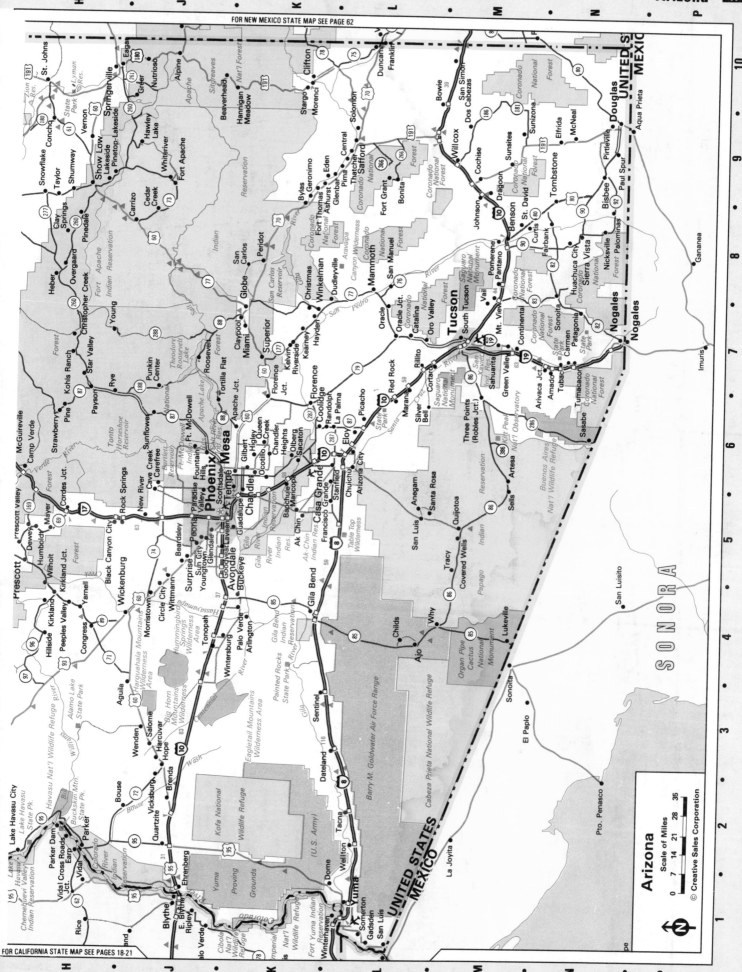

FOR NEW MEXICO STATE MAP SEE PAGE 62

FOR CALIFORNIA STATE MAP SEE PAGES 18-21

UNITED STATES
MEXICO

SONORA

Arizona

Scale of Miles

0 7 14 21 28 35

© Creative Sales Corporation

FOR NEVADA STATE MAP SEE PAGE 54

California

Scale of Miles

0 7 14 21 28 35

© Creative Sales Corporation

N

FOR OREGON STATE MAP SEE PAGES 70-71

OREGON

NEVADA

CALIFORNIA

Medford · Ashland · Talent · Cave Junction · Brookings · Crescent City · Klamath Falls · Lakeview · Alturas · Cedarville · Lake City · Ft. Bidwell · Davis Cr. · Willow Ranch · Newell · Tulelake · Merrill · Bonanza · Dorris · Macdoel · Montague · Yreka · Weed · Mt. Shasta · Dunsmuir · McCloud · Big Bend · Burney · Fall River Mills · McArthur · Adin · Canby · Lookout · Nubieber · Bieber · Madeline · Likely · Termo · Ravendale · Madeline

Susanville · Litchfield · Standish · Wendel · Herlong · Doyle · Milford · Johnstonville · Janesville · Westwood · Chester · Greenville · Crescent Mills · Taylorsville · Canyon Dam · Quincy · Twain · Keddie · Portola · Beckwourth · Loyalton · Sierraville · Vinton · Hallelujah Jct. · Hobart Mills · Truckee · Sierra City · Downieville · Washington · Nevada City · Grass Valley · Colfax · Foresthill

Redding · Anderson · Cottonwood · Red Bluff · Corning · Orland · Chico · Paradise · Oroville · Marysville · Yuba City · Linda · Willows · Colusa · Williams · Arbuckle · Clearlake · Lucerne · Ukiah · Willits · Ft. Bragg · Mendocino · Point Arena

Arcata · Eureka · Fortuna · Scotia · Ferndale · Rio Dell · Garberville · Redway · Laytonville · Covelo · Willow Cr. · Hoopa · Weaverville · Hayfork · Junction City · Big Bar · Forks Of Salmon · Somes Bar · Orleans · Happy Camp · Ft. Jones · Etna · Callahan · Gazelle · Hornbrook · Hilt

Reno · Sparks · Carson City · Virginia City · Dayton · Fernley · Fallon · Wabuska · Silver Springs · Nixon · Wadsworth · Gerlach · Sutcliffe

Pyramid Lake · Honey Lk. · Eagle Lake · Clear Lake Res. · Goose Lk. · Tule Lake · Shasta Lake · Lake Almanor · Lake Oroville · Lake Pillsbury · Lake Tahoe

Klamath Nat'l Forest · Modoc Nat'l Forest · Shasta Nat'l Forest · Trinity Nat'l Forest · Lassen Nat'l Forest · Plumas Nat'l Forest · Tahoe Nat'l Forest · Mendocino Nat'l Forest · Six Rivers Nat'l Forest · Redwood Nat'l Park · Lassen Volcanic Nat'l Park · Lava Beds Nat'l Mon.

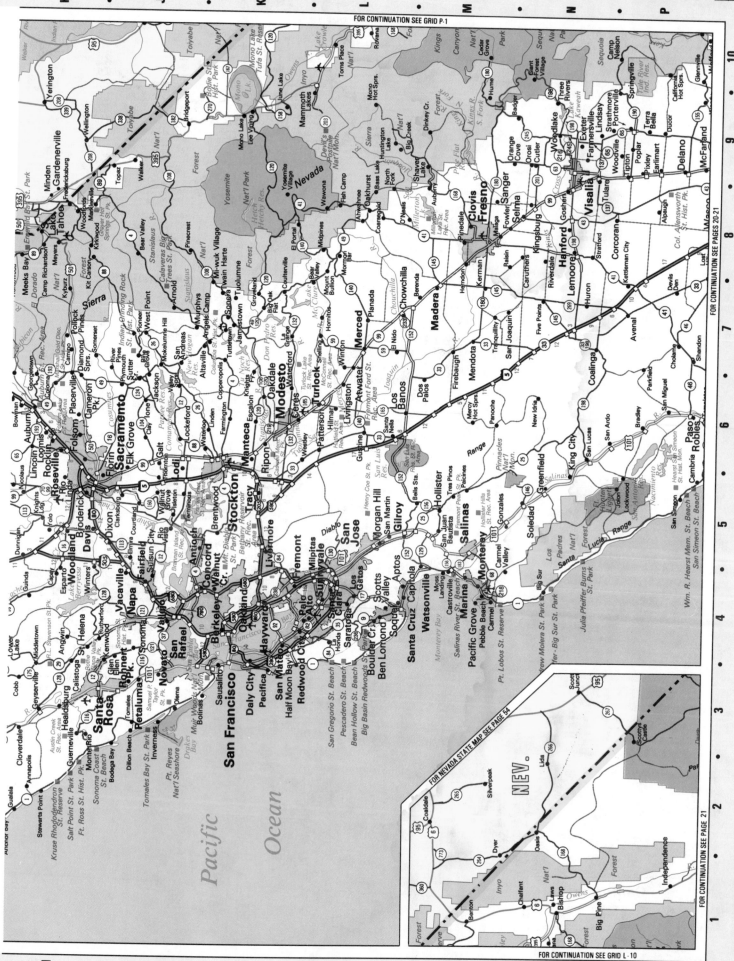

FOR CONTINUATION SEE GRID P-1

FOR CONTINUATION SEE PAGES 20-21

FOR CONTINUATION SEE PAGE 21

FOR CONTINUATION SEE GRID L-10

FOR NEVADA STATE MAP SEE PAGE 54

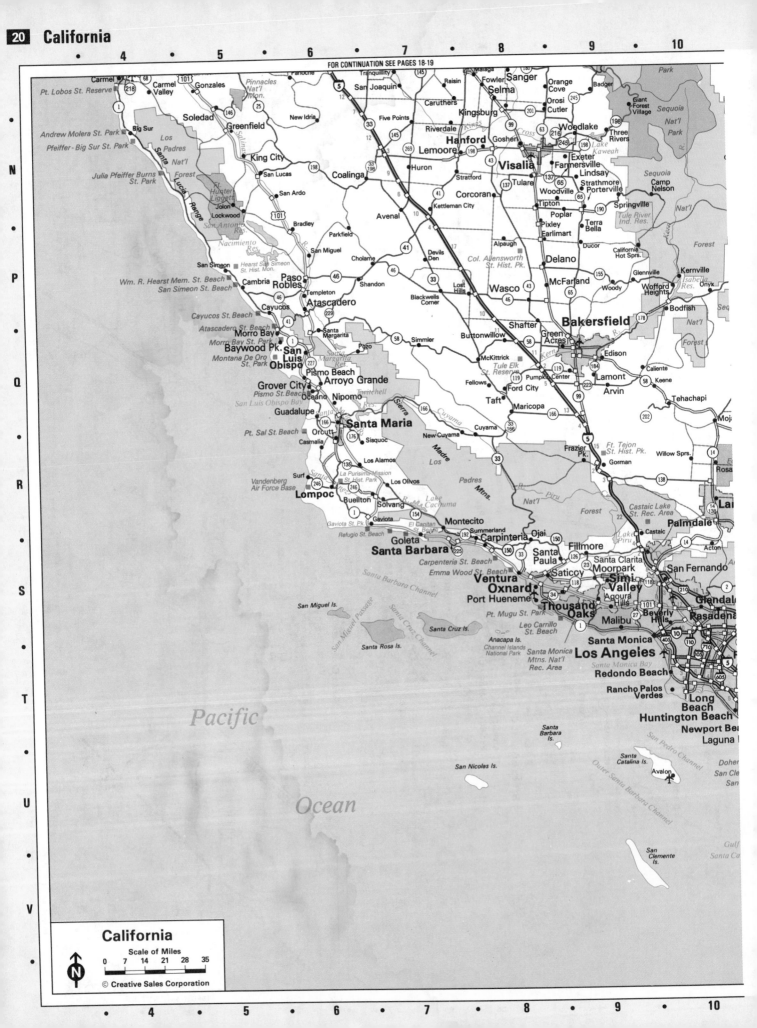

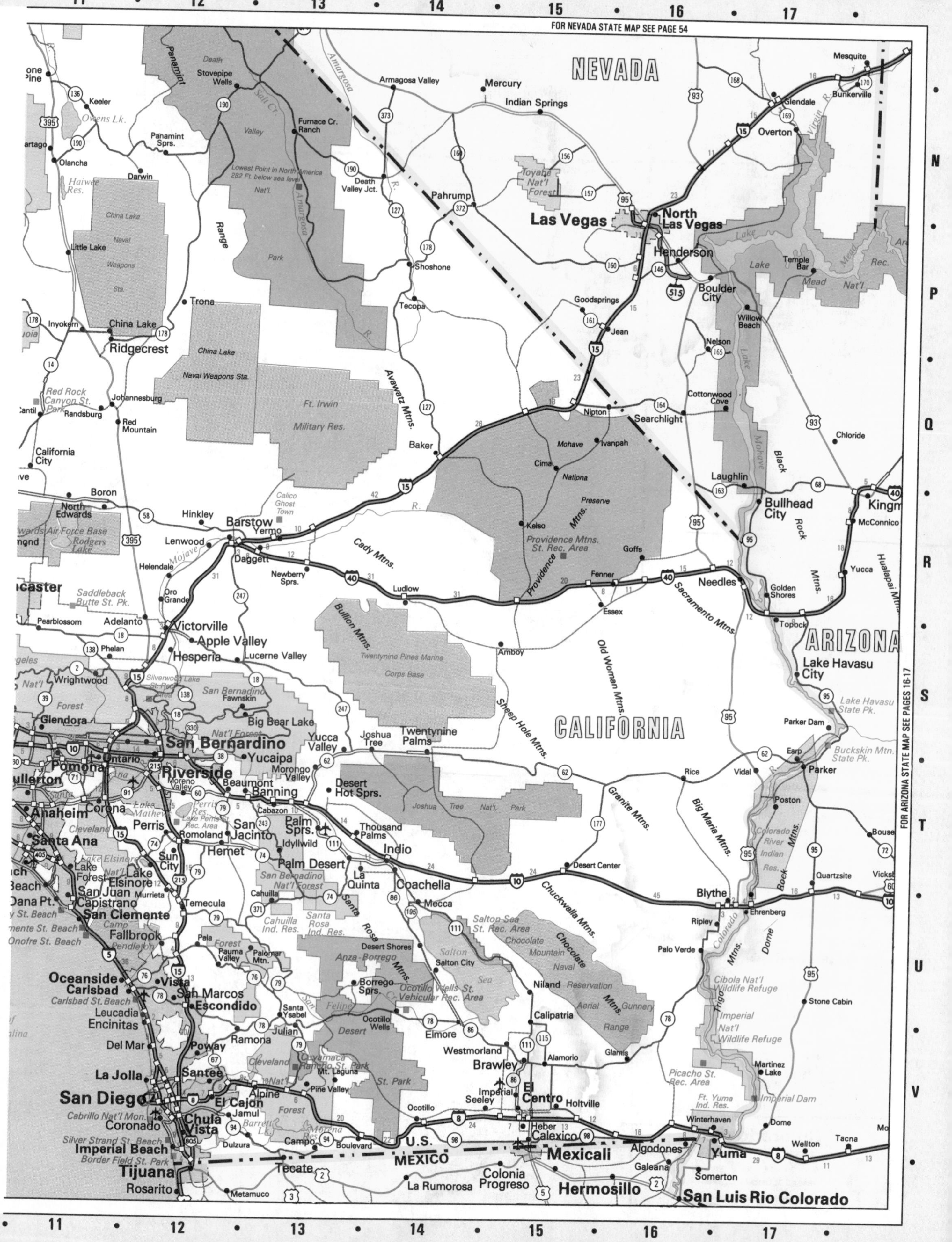
FOR NEVADA STATE MAP SEE PAGE 54
FOR ARIZONA STATE MAP SEE PAGES 16-17
NEVADA
CALIFORNIA
ARIZONA
MEXICO
U.S.
Las Vegas
North Las Vegas
Henderson
Boulder City
Mesquite
Bunkerville
Glendale
Overton
Mercury
Indian Springs
Armagosa Valley
Pahrump
Death Valley Jct.
Shoshone
Tecopa
Goodsprings
Jean
Nipton
Searchlight
Cottonwood Cove
Nelson
Willow Beach
Temple Bar
Laughlin
Bullhead City
Kingman
McConnico
Chloride
Yucca
Needles
Golden Shores
Topock
Lake Havasu City
Lake Havasu State Pk.
Parker Dam
Earp
Parker
Buckskin Mtn. State Pk.
Poston
Bouse
Quartzsite
Ehrenberg
Blythe
Ripley
Palo Verde
Stone Cabin
Martinez Lake
Imperial Dam
Dome
Wellton
Tacna
Yuma
Winterhaven
Somerton
San Luis Rio Colorado
Algodones
Galeana
Mexicali
Calexico
Heber
El Centro
Holtville
Imperial
Seeley
Brawley
Westmorland
Calipatria
Niland
Glamis
Alamorio
Ocotillo
Boulevard
Campo
Tecate
Colonia Progreso
La Rumorosa
Hermosillo
Metamuco
Tijuana
Rosarito
Imperial Beach
Coronado
Chula Vista
San Diego
El Cajon
Jamul
Dulzura
Alpine
Pine Valley
Mt. Laguna
Santee
La Jolla
Del Mar
Poway
Ramona
Julian
Santa Ysabel
Encinitas
Leucadia
Escondido
San Marcos
Vista
Carlsbad
Oceanside
Fallbrook
Pala
Pauma Valley
Palomar Mtn.
Temecula
Murrieta
San Clemente
San Juan Capistrano
Dana Pt.
Lake Elsinore
Lake Forest
Sun City
Perris
Romoland
Hemet
San Jacinto
Santa Ana
Anaheim
Corona
Fullerton
Pomona
Ontario
Riverside
San Bernardino
Yucaipa
Beaumont
Banning
Cabazon
Palm Sprs.
Palm Desert
Thousand Palms
Idyllwild
Indio
La Quinta
Coachella
Mecca
Desert Hot Sprs.
Morongo Valley
Yucca Valley
Joshua Tree
Twentynine Palms
Big Bear Lake
Fawnskin
Glendora
Wrightwood
Hesperia
Apple Valley
Victorville
Lucerne Valley
Phelan
Adelanto
Pearblossom
Oro Grande
Helendale
Barstow
Yermo
Daggett
Lenwood
Hinkley
Newberry Sprs.
Ludlow
Amboy
Essex
Fenner
Goffs
Kelso
Cima
Ivanpah
Baker
Boron
North Edwards
Edwards Air Force Base
California City
Randsburg
Johannesburg
Red Mountain
Ridgecrest
China Lake
Inyokern
Trona
Little Lake
Olancha
Keeler
Darwin
Panamint Sprs.
Stovepipe Wells
Furnace Cr. Ranch
Desert Center
Rice
Vidal
Desert Shores
Salton City
Borrego Sprs.
Ocotillo Wells
Elmore
Death Valley Nat'l Park
Mojave National Preserve
Joshua Tree Nat'l Park
Twentynine Pines Marine Corps Base
China Lake Naval Weapons Sta.
Ft. Irwin Military Res.
Chocolate Mountain Naval Reservation Aerial Gunnery Range
Anza-Borrego Desert St. Park
Salton Sea
Lake Mead Nat'l Rec. Area
Colorado River Indian Res.
Cibola Nat'l Wildlife Refuge
Imperial Nat'l Wildlife Refuge
Picacho St. Rec. Area
Ft. Yuma Ind. Res.
Providence Mtns. St. Rec. Area
Red Rock Canyon St. Park
Saddleback Butte St. Pk.
Calico Ghost Town
Lowest Point in North America 282 Ft. below sea level
Cady Mtns.
Bullion Mtns.
Old Woman Mtns.
Sheep Hole Mtns.
Granite Mtns.
Big Maria Mtns.
Chuckwalla Mtns.
Chocolate Mtns.
Sacramento Mtns.
Avawatz Mtns.
Black Mtns.
Hualapai Mtns.
Dome Rock Mtns.
Trigo Mtns.

FOR WYOMING STATE MAP SEE PAGES 88-89

FOR UTAH STATE MAP SEE PAGE 80-81

WYOMING

UTAH

Carter · Fort Bridger · Lyman · Urie · Mountain View · Robertson · Lonetree · Burntfork · McKinnon · Manila · Green Lake · Ashley · Oak Park Res. · Whiterocks · Monarch · Neola · Lapoint · Maeser · Vernal · Naples · Jensen · Boneta · Altamont · Bluebell · Cedarview · Gusher · Mt. Emmons · Arcadia · Ioka · Upalco · Fort Duchesne · Roosevelt · Duchesne · Myton · Ouray · Leota · Bridgeland · Blue Mountain · Dinosaur · Rangely

Qualey · Green River · Hiawatha · Browns Park Nat'l. Wildlife Refuge · Dinosaur National Monument · Sunbeam · Maybell · Lay · Craig · Elk Springs · Hamilton · Pagoda · Meeker · Buford

High Uintas Wilderness Area · Uinta National Forest · Hill Creek Extension Uintah and Ouray Indian Reservation

Sunnyside · East Carbon City · Woodside · Green River · Thompson · Cisco · Crescent Jct. · Mack · Loma · Fruita · Grand Junction · Clifton · Palisade · Cameo · Mesa · Collbran · Molina · Skyway · Whitewater · Cedaredge · Orchard City · Austin · Delta · Lazear · Hotchkiss · Paonia · Somerset · Bowie · Crawford · Maher · Olathe · Montrose · Cimarron · Sapinero

Moab · Gateway · Uravan · Paradox · Bedrock · Nucla · Naturita · Vancorum · Redvale · Norwood · Ridgway · Placerville · Saw Pit · Telluride · Ophir · Red Mountain · Gladstone · Silverton · Slick Rock · Egnar · Dunton · Rico · Stoner · Rockwood · Hermosa

Monticello · Eastland · Dove Creek · Cahone · Pleasant View · Yellow Jacket · Lewis · Arriola · Cortez · Lebanon · Dolores · Mancos · Hesperus · Durango · Breen · Kline · Marvel · Redmesa · Oxford · Ignacio · Bayfield

La Sal Jct. · La Sal · Summit Pt. · Fry Canyon · Blanding · Bluff · Montezuma Creek · Aneth · Mexican Hat · Towaoc · Fort Lewis

Baggs · Dixon · Savery · Saratoga · Riverside · Encampment · Medicine Bow Nat'l Forest · Larkspur · Centennial · Albany · Woods Landing · Mountain Home · Cowdrey · Walden · Gould · Rand · Rustic · Steamboat Sprs. · Milner · Hayden · Coalmont · Oak Creek · Phippsburg · Yampa · Toponas · McCoy · Bond · State Bridge · Wolcott · Kremmling · Parshall · Hot Sulphur Springs · Granby · Grand Lake · Nederland · Rollinsville · Fraser · Tabernash · Winter Park · Estes Park · Deer Ridge · Raymond

Rio Blanco · New Castle · Silt · Rifle · Parachute · DeBeque · Carbondale · Glenwood Sprs. · Dotsero · Gypsum · Eagle · Edwards · Avon · Dowd · Gilman · Vail · Frisco · Dillon · Echo Lake · Silverthorne · Breckenridge · Blue River · Alma · Fairplay · Como · Jefferson · Garo Park · Basalt · Snowmass · Woody Creek · Aspen · Redstone · Marble · Snowmass Village · Twin Lakes · Granite · Leadville · Malta · Climax · Red Cliff · Crested Butte · Buena Vista · Gunnison · Parlin · Doyleville · Sargents · Poncha Springs · Salida · Coaldale · Howard · Monarch Hot Springs · Mount Princeton Hot Springs · Nathrop · Johnson Village · Almont · Maher

Gunnison National Forest · Curecanti National Recreation Area · Blue Mesa Res. · Powderhorn · Lake City · Creede · Wagon Wheel Gap · Spar City · South Fork · Del Norte · Monte Vista · Summitville · Platoro · Saguache · Moffat · Villa Grove · Mineral Hot Springs · Center · Hooper · Homelake · Mosca · Alamosa · Capulin · La Jara · Sanford · Romeo · Manassa · Conejos · Antonito · Chama · Brazos

San Juan National Forest · Rio Grande National Forest · Great Sand Dunes National Monument · Pagosa Sprs. · Chimney Rock · Arboles · Chromo · Lumberton · Dulce · Monero · Los Ojos · Rutheron · La Puente · Ensenada · Tierra Amarilla · Tres Piedras

Ute Mountain Indian Reservation · Mesa Verde National Park · Navajo Lake · Aztec · Flora Vista · Kirtland · Shiprock · Beklabito · Farmington · Bloomfield · Turley · Archuleta · La Plata · Cedar Hill

FOR NEW MEXICO STATE MAP SEE PAGE 62

FOR WYOMING STATE MAP SEE PAGES 88-89
FOR NEBRASKA STATE MAP SEE PAGES 52-53
FOR KANSAS STATE MAP SEE PAGE 37
FOR OKLAHOMA STATE MAP SEE PAGES 68-69

NEBRASKA

KANSAS

OKLA.

NEW MEXICO

COLORADO

Laramie, Horse Creek, Cheyenne, Pine Bluffs, Burns, Hillsdale, Carpenter, Egbert, Bushnell, Kimball, Dix, Potter, Gurley, Sidney, Lodgepole, Big Springs, Brule, Ogallala, Keystone, Sutherland, Hershey, Paxton, North Platte, McConnaughy

Tie Siding, Federal, Virginia Dale, Rockport, Nunn, Pierce, Briggsdale, Chappell, Ovid, Julesburg, Sedgwick, Peetz, Crook, Proctor, Iliff, Grant, Venango, Brandon, Madrid, Elsie, Grainton, Wallace, Dickens, Maywood, Hayes Center

The Forks, Poudre Park, Bellvue, Fort Collins, Ault, Buckingham, Raymer, Stoneham, Merino, Sterling, Atwood, Fleming, Haxtun, Paoli, Holyoke, Amherst, Lamar, Imperial, Enders, Champion, Wauneta, Palisade, Trenton, Culbertson

Drake, Loveland, Windsor, Eaton, Greeley, Kersey, Orchard, Barnesville, Weldona, Hillrose, Snyder, Akron, Otis, Yuma, Wray, Eckley, Laird, Haigler, Parks, Benkelman, Stratton, Max, McCook

Estes Park, Pinewood Springs, Lyons, Berthoud, Milliken, Evans, La Salle, Gilcrest, Platteville, Masters, Goodrich, Wiggins, Fort Morgan, Brush, Woodrow, Clarkville

Longmont, Meeker Park, Frederick, Fort Lupton, Keenesburg, Roggen, Prospect Valley, Lindon, Anton, Abarr, Idalia, Wheeler, St. Francis, Bird City, McDonald, Atwood, Herndon

Boulder, Lafayette, Broomfield, Northglenn, Thornton, Hudson, Lochbuie, Brighton, Commerce City, Bennett, Strasburg, Deer Trail, Last Chance, Joes, Cope, Bonny Res., Rexford, Colby

Black Hawk, Empire, Golden, Wheat Ridge, Aurora, Denver, Watkins, Byers, Cope

Idaho Sprs., Lakewood, Englewood, Littleton, Greenwood Village, Parker, Agate, Flagler State Wildlife Area, Seibert, Vona, Stratton, Bethune, Burlington, Kanorado, Goodland, Brewster, Halford, Oakley

Conifer, Bailey, Shawnee, Sedalia, Franktown, Elizabeth, Kiowa, Simla, Matheson, Limon, Genoa, Arriba, Hugo, Winona, Russell Springs

Castle Rock, Larkspur, Ramah, Boyero, Firstview, Sharon Springs, Wallace

Palmer Lake, Monument, Peyton, Calhan, Boyero, Wild Horse, Arapahoe, Cheyenne Wells

Woodland Park, Divide, Chipita Park, Manitou Spgs., Colorado Springs, Security-Widefield, Fountain, Falcon, Ellicott, Yoder, Rush, Punkin Center, Aroya, Kit Carson

Florissant, Lake George, Cripple Creek, Victor, Canon City, Penrose, Fort Carson, Galatea, Eads, Brandon, Towner, Tribune, Leoti, Scott City, Sand Creek Massacre

Hartsel, Guffey, Parkdale, Royal Gorge, Florence, Pueblo West, Pueblo, Baxter, Boone, Olney Springs, Ordway, Sugar City, Haswell, Chivington, Sheridan Lake

Texas Creek, Cotopaxi, Hillside, Wetmore, Vineland, Avondale, Fowler, Manzanola, Rocky Ford, Crowley, Cheraw, Arlington, McClave, Wiley, Fort Lyon, Las Animas, Hasty, Kornman, Bristol, Holly, Granada, Coolidge, Syracuse, Lakin, Deerfield, Holcomb

Westcliffe, Silver Cliff, Beulah, Colorado City, Rye, Gardner, Farisita, Walsenburg, Hawley, La Junta, Toonerville, Cheney Center, Lamar, Carlton

Blanca, La Veta, Cuchara, Aguilar, Pryor, Hoehne, Thatcher, Tyrone, Model, Delhi, Springfield, Two Buttes, Vilas, Walsh, Lycan, Bartlett, Manter, Johnson City, Richfield, Moscow, Ulysses, Sublette

San Acacio, San Luis, Fort Garland, Monument Park, Stonewall, Weston, Segundo, Jansen, Trinidad, Starkville, Valdez, Branson, Tobe, Kim, Utleyville, Campo, Pritchett, Elkhart, Rolla, Hugoton

Chama, San Pablo, San Francisco, Garcia, Costilla, Amalia, Raton, Sugarite State Park, Kenton, Sturgis, Surrey Hills, Hooker, Guymon, Hardesty

Cerro, Red River, Questa, Cimarron Canyon, Capulin, Folsom, Des Moines, Boise City, Keyes, Eva, Four Corners, Goodwell, Texhoma

Comanche National Grassland
Pawnee National Grassland
Pike National Forest
Cheesman Lake
Rocky Mountain National Park
Great Sand Dunes National Monument
John Martin Lake
Adobe Creek Res.
Two Buttes Res.
North Sterling St. Park
Jackson Lake Res.
Summit Springs Battlefield
Beecher Island Battleground
Bonny Res.
Neeso Pah Res.
Nee Nashe Res.
Muddy Creek Res.
Kiowa National Grasslands
Curt Gowdy State Park

FOR VERMONT STATE MAP SEE PAGE 55

FOR NEW YORK STATE MAP SEE PAGES 58-61

N.H.

VT.

MASS.

CONN.

N.Y.

Long Island Sound

Albany
Rensselaer
Troy
Williamstown
North Adams
Adams
Pittsfield
Dalton
Hinsdale
Lenox
Stockbridge
Great Barrington
Sheffield
Hudson
Chatham
Nassau
Canaan
Sharon
Salisbury
Norfolk
Winsted
Torrington
Litchfield
Kent
New Milford
Danbury
Bethel
Ridgefield
New Fairfield
Brookfield
Southbury
Newtown
Monroe
Shelton
Derby
Ansonia
Naugatuck
Waterbury
Southington
Bristol
Plymouth
Thomaston
Watertown
Wolcott
Meriden
Wallingford
Cheshire
Hamden
Woodbridge
New Haven
West Haven
Milford
Stratford
Bridgeport
Fairfield
Westport
Norwalk
Darien
Stamford
Greenwich
New Canaan
Wilton
Trumbull
Orange
East Haven
North Haven
North Branford
Branford
Guilford
Madison
Clinton
Westbrook
Old Saybrook
Old Lyme
East Lyme
New London
Waterford
Groton
Mystic
Stonington
Pawcatuck

Northampton
Easthampton
Westhampton
Holyoke
Chicopee
West Springfield
Springfield
Agawam
Longmeadow
East Longmeadow
Amherst
Hadley
South Hadley
Belchertown
Ware
Palmer
Monson
Wilbraham
Enfield
Windsor Locks
Suffield
Granby
East Granby
Simsbury
Canton
Avon
Farmington
West Hartford
Hartford
East Hartford
Manchester
Vernon
Newington
Wethersfield
Glastonbury
New Britain
Berlin
Rocky Hill
Cromwell
Middletown
Durham
Haddam
Chester
Deep River
Essex

Greenfield
Deerfield
Montague
Sunderland
Hatfield
Orange
Athol
Gardner
Fitchburg
Leominster
Worcester
Barre
Spencer
Leicester
Sturbridge
Southbridge
Webster
Putnam
Woodstock
Pomfret
Storrs
Coventry
Mansfield Center
Willimantic
Windham
Plainfield
Jewett City
Norwich
Colchester
Hebron
Marlborough
Salem
Ledyard
North Stonington

Peterborough
Jaffrey
Rindge
Winchendon
Swanzey
Winchester

Long Island Sound

Greenport
Southold
Shelter Island
Montauk
Peconic
Gardiners Island
Fishers Island

FOR NEW HAMPSHIRE STATE MAP SEE PAGE 55

Merrimack Derry Hampstead Amesbury Salisbury
Wilton Litchfield Atkinson Merrimac Salisbury Beach St. Res.
Milford Windham West Newburyport
Silver Lake St. Pk. Nashua Hudson Salem Newbury Newbury
Townsend Hollis Haverhill Parker River Nat'l Wildlife Ref.
Methuen Groveland Rowley Plum Is.
Tyngsborough Lawrence Georgetown Plum Is. St. Pk.
Pepperell Dracut Ipswich Halibut Point State Park
Lunenburg Lowell Andover Topsfield Essex Rockport
Westford Tewksbury North Reading Wenham Hamilton
Ayer Chelmsford Wilmington Danvers Manchester-by-the-Sea Gloucester
Shirley Billerica Lynnfield Beverly
Harvard Littleton Acton Carlisle Reading Salem Marblehead
Sterling Bolton Bedford Wakefield Peabody Swampscott
Clinton Stow Concord Woburn Saugus Lynn Nahant
Boylston Hudson Maynard Lexington Revere
Northborough Marlborough Lincoln Cambridge Chelsea Winthrop
Shrewsbury Wayland Newton Boston Massachusetts Bay
Westborough Cochituate Wellesley Hull
Millbury Natick Milton Quincy
Grafton Framingham Hingham Scituate
Upton Hopkinton Westwood Weymouth
Northbridge Millis Medfield Norwood Braintree Norwell
Milford Walpole Canton Randolph
Whitinsville Hopedale Medway Holbrook Rockland Hanover Marshfield
Mendon Norfolk Sharon Avon Abington Hanson Pembroke
Uxbridge Bellingham Wrentham Stoughton Brockton Whitman Duxbury
Blackstone Foxborough Easton East Bridgewater
Slatersville N. Attleborough Mansfield Bridgewater Halifax Kingston
Woonsocket Norton Plympton Plymouth
Harrisville Ashton Berkley Raynham Attleboro Carver
Mapleville Chepachet Esmond Taunton Middleborough
North Foster Harmony Pawtucket Rehoboth Dighton Buzzards Bay Sandwich
N. Scituate Providence Seekonk Freetown Sagamore
Foster Center Clayville Cranston Somerset Wareham Bourne Barnstable
Vernon Hope East Providence Swansea Rochester Marion Hyannis
Barrington Warren Fall River Acushnet Centerville Yarmouth
West Greenwich Warwick Bristol Mattapoisett Osterville Dennis
Nooseneck East Greenwich Fairhaven Falmouth South Yarmouth Harwich Chatham
Millville Exeter Tiverton Westport New Bedford Otis A.F.B. Dennis Port
Wickford Portsmouth Dartmouth East Falmouth
Hope Valley Middletown Little Compton Falmouth
Kingston Jamestown Newport Naushon Tisbury Oak Bluffs Nantucket
Wakefield Vineyard Haven Edgartown Chappaquiddick Island
Narragansett Pier Conanicut Is. Cuttyhunk Is. Chilmark Gay Head West Tisbury
Charlestown Martha's Vineyard Island Nantucket Island
Westerly Block Island Sound Nantucket Mem. Airport

Atlantic Ocean

Cape Cod Bay Provincetown Truro Wellfleet Eastham Orleans Brewster

Buzzards Bay Nantucket Sound Vineyard Sound

Block Island Block Island State Beach Block Island Nat'l W.R.

Florida

Scale of Miles

0 7 14 21 28 35

© Creative Sales Corporation

N

FOR GEORGIA STATE MAP SEE PAGES 28-29

Atlantic

Ocean

Gulf

of

Mexico

GEORGIA

Tallahassee

Jacksonville

Atlantic Beach
Neptune Beach
Jacksonville Beach

Fernandina Beach

St. Augustine
St. Augustine Beach

Flagler Beach
Ormond By The Sea
Ormond Beach
Daytona Beach
Port Orange
New Smyrna Beach
Edgewater

Mims
Titusville
Cocoa
Cape Canaveral
Merritt Island
Cocoa Beach
Rockledge
Satellite Beach
Indian Harbour Beach
Melbourne
W. Melbourne
Palm Bay

Gifford
Vero Beach
Sebastian
Fellsmere

Winter Springs
Winte Pk.
Casselberry
Sanford
DeBary
Deltona
DeLand
Orange City

Orlando
Apopka
Winter Garden
Lake Buena Vista
Kissimmee
St. Cloud

Haines City
Lake Wales
Winter Haven
Lakeland
Bartow
Fort Meade
Avon Park
Frostproof

Plant City
Brandon
Temple Terrace
Tampa
Riverview
Sun City Center
Apollo Beach

St. Petersburg
Clearwater
Largo
Dunedin
Treasure Island
St. Petersburg Beach

New Port Richey
Tarpon Springs
Zephyrhills
Dade City
Brooksville

Hudson
Homosassa Springs
Crystal River
Inverness
Inglis

Ocala
Dunnellon
Belleview
Wildwood
Bushnell
Ridge Manor
Lacoochee
Clermont
Mt. Dora
Eustis
Umatilla
Mt. Plymouth

Williston
Reddick
Archer
Chiefland
Suwanee
Cedar Key

Gainesville
Hawthorne
Palatka
East Palatka
Crescent City
Bunnell
Hastings

Keystone Heights
Green Cove Springs
Orange Park
Starke
Lake Butler
Alachua
High Springs
Newberry
Trenton
Bell
Old Town
Cross City

Baldwin
Callahan
Hilliard
Kingsland
Folkston
St. George
Fargo

Lake City
Macclenny
Waterfown

Live Oak
Jasper
Mayo
Day
Perry
Madison
Greenville
Monticello
Lamont
Thomas City
Woodville
Crawfordville
Carrabelle
Sopchoppy

Quitman
Valdosta
Lakeland
Homerville

Bainbridge
Thomasville
Cairo
Quincy
Gretna
Havana
Chattahoochee
Donalsonville
Blountstown
Bristol

Okefenokee Nat'l Wildlife Refuge

Osceola Nat'l Forest

Ocala Nat'l Forest

St. Johns River

Apalachicola Nat'l Forest

Apalachee Bay

St. George Is. St. Pk.

John F. Kennedy Space Ctr.
Cape Canaveral Air Force Station
Patrick Air Force Base
Canaveral Nat'l Seashore
Merritt Is. Wildlife Ref.

Lake Okeechobee area roads

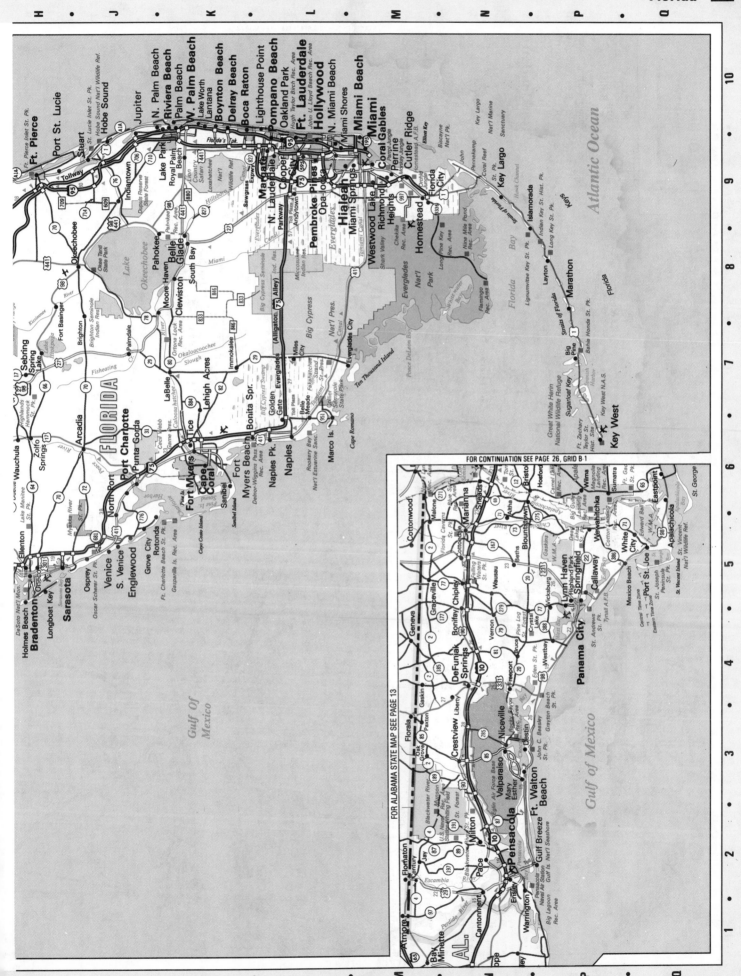

FOR CONTINUATION SEE PAGE 26, GRID B-1

FOR ALABAMA STATE MAP SEE PAGE 13

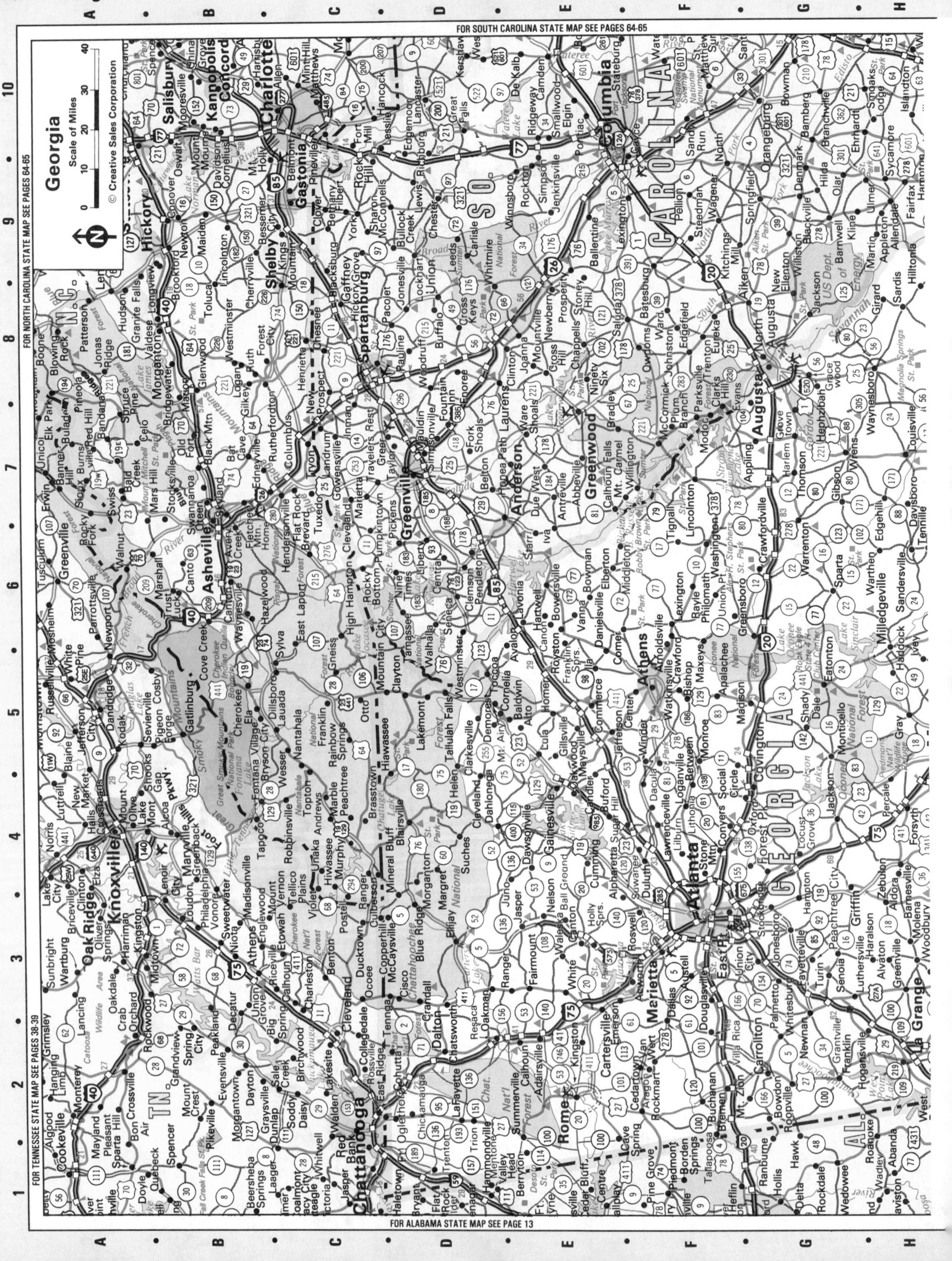

FOR SOUTH CAROLINA STATE MAP SEE PAGES 64-65
FOR NORTH CAROLINA STATE MAP SEE PAGES 38-39
FOR TENNESSEE STATE MAP SEE PAGES 38-39
FOR ALABAMA STATE MAP SEE PAGE 13

Georgia

Scale of Miles

© Creative Sales Corporation

N

FOR FLORIDA STATE MAP SEE PAGES 26-27

FOR ALABAMA STATE MAP SEE PAGE 13

A B C D E F G

Hawaii

Scale of Miles

0 4 8 12 16 20

© Creative Sales Corporation

N

Maui

Pukaulua Pt.
Kahului
Hana
Waipanapapa St. Pk.
Kipahulu
Mooea Pt.
Kalahu Pt.
360
Wailua
Makawao
Haleakala Nat'l Park
Haleakala Crater
Kaupo
Apole Pt.
378
377
Haiku
37
Paia
Pauwela
Spreckelsville
Puunene
Ulupalakua
Cape Hanamanioa
36
Kihei
Keokea
Kahului
311
Puunene
Waiea
31
Makena
Nukuleo Pt.
Wailuku
30
Maalaea
Kahului Bay
Maalaea Bay
Kamaole Beach Park
Hekili Pt.
Maui
Nakalele Pt.
340
Kahakuloa Pt.
Iao Valley
Olowalu
Mopua
Honokahua
30
Lahaina

Pacific Ocean

Molokai

Lamaloa Head
Halawa
Cape Halawa
Pauwalu
Waialua
Pukoo
Ualapue
Kikipua Pt.
Kamalo
Makanalua Pen.
450
Kalaupapa
Kalae
Kualapuu
Kaunakakai
Kamiloloa
Kahiu Pt.
Ilio Pt.
Mauna Loa
460
Kolo
Laau Pt.
Molokai

Kalohi Channel

Pacific Ocean

Kauai Co. / Honolulu Co.

Honolulu Co. / Maui Co.

HAWAII

Maui (inset)

Hana
360
Haleakala
Ulupalakua
Honokahua
Kahului
36
37
Lahaina
31
Keomuku
30
Kaanapali
Maui

Molokai (inset)

Halawa
Kualapuu
450
Kamalo
460
Mauna Loa
Molokai

Lanai

Koele
Lanai City
Lanai
Kaka Pt.

Kahoolawe

Kaho'olawe
Kaʻula Channel
Kealaikahiki Channel
Alalakeiki Channel

Hawaii

Waiakea
Pohoiki
Honohina
Pepeekeo Pt.
Papaaloa
Papaikou
Hilo
Oophikao
Kalapana
130
Pahoa
Kaimu
Papaaloa
Waiakea
19
Kurtistown
Punaluu Black Sand Beach
Ookala
Apua Pt.
Mountain View
Glenwood
Honuapo
Kukuihaele
Honokaa
200
Hawaii Volcanoes National Park
Waimea
Mauna Kea 13,796 ft.
Mauna Loa 13,680 ft.
11
Hawi
Niulii
Weleka
190
Pahala
Naalehu
Kaalualu
250
Kalaoa
Honokohau
Kainaliu
Keokea
Papa
Waiohinu
11
Waiahukini
Ka Lee
Mahukona
270
Puako
19
Captain Cook
Napoopoo
Honaunau
Hookena
Hanamaulu Pt.
Kawaihae
Kailua
Keauhou
Milolii
Kauna Pt.
Keahole Pt.
Upolu Pt.
Hawaii
Alenuihaha Channel

Maui Co. / Hawaii Co.

Oahu

Mokapu Pt.
Sea Life Park
Makapuu Pt.
Kailua
Waimanalo
72
Koko Head
Kaneohe Bay
Kualoa Pt.
Kahana Beach
H3
Kaneohe Marine Air Station
61
Hawaii Kai
Waikiki
92
Diamond Head
Kailua
Koko Head Park
Kahuku
Laie
63
Kaneohe
Pearl City
Aiea
Honolulu
H1
Kahaluu
Polynesian Cultural Center
83
Range
78
99
Hauula
Sacred Falls
Waiahole
Koolau
H2
Kahuku Pt.
Sunset Beach
Waialua
Wahiawa
Schofield Barracks
Mililani Town
750
Ewa
Pearl Harbor
Hickam Air Force Base
95
Haleiwa
99
83
Range
Barbers Pt. Air Sta.
Waianae
780
Makaha
Maili
Nanakuli
Waipahu
Dillingham Air Force Base
930
Kepuhi Pt.
93
Keaau Pt.
Waianae
Barbers Pt.
Oahu

Kaiwi Channel

Kauai Channel

Pacific Ocean

Kauai (inset)

Haena
Anahola
56
Lihue
Lawai
50
Kauai
Mana
Waimea

Kauai

Anahola
Moloaa
Keaalia
Kapaa
Wailua
Hanamaulu
Lihue Airport
Nawiliwili
Ninini Pt.
56
Lihue
580
583
50
Puhi
Kilauea
Koloa
Hanalei
Lawai
Eleele
Port Allen
Koloa
Kalaheo
Haena
Haena Pt.
Mt. Waialeale 5,148 ft.
Makahuena Pt.
Kalalau
Koheo Pt.
550
Waimea Canyon State Park
Kokee State Park
50
Waimea
550
Kaumakani
Hanapepe
Makaha Pt.
Mana
Kekaha
Kauai

Pacific Ocean

Niihau

Kaunakakai
Kaulakahi Channel
Puuwai
Niihau (Private)

Kauai Co. / Honolulu Co.

Pacific Ocean

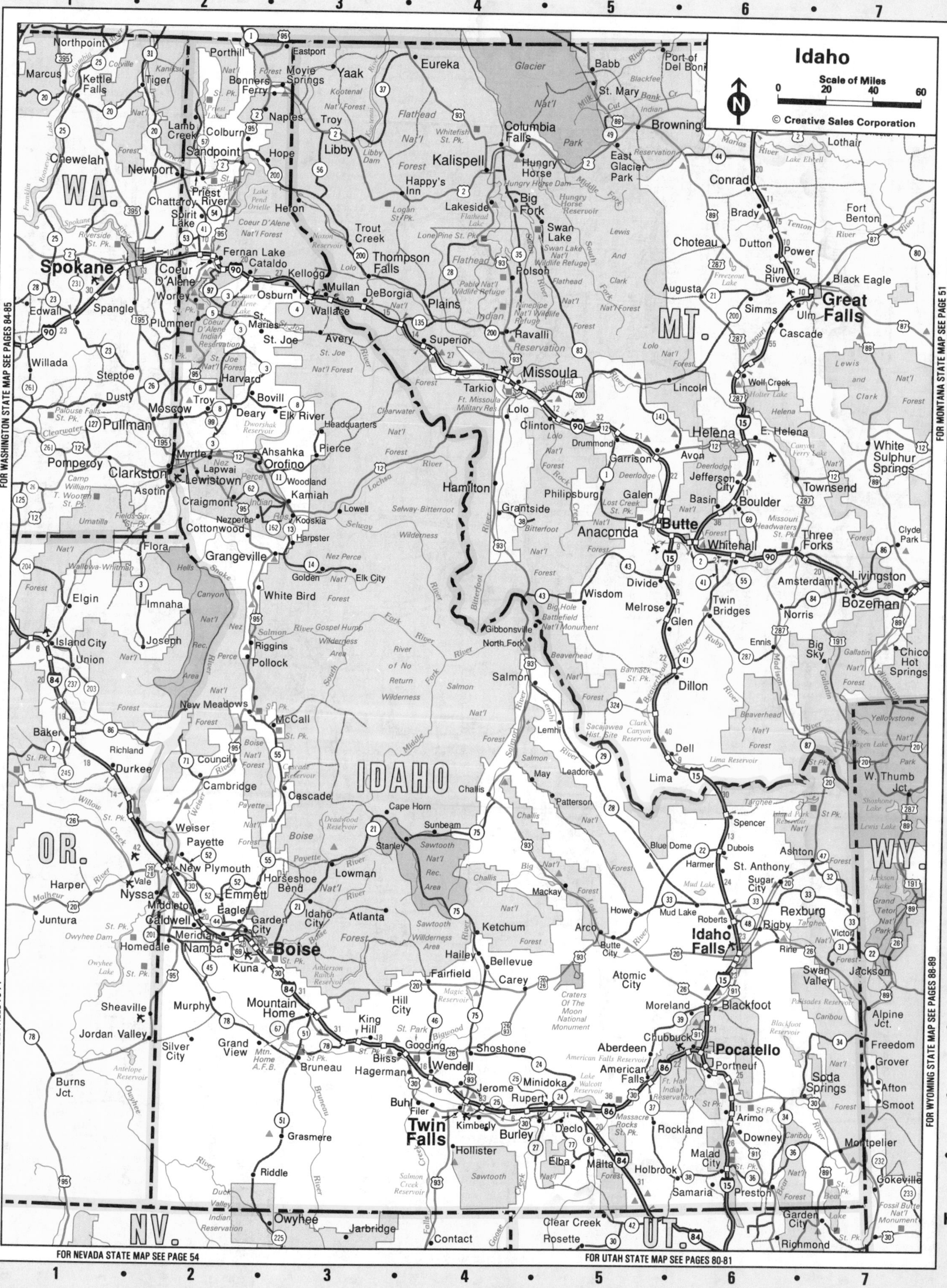

Idaho

Scale of Miles

© Creative Sales Corporation

FOR WASHINGTON STATE MAP SEE PAGES 84-85
FOR OREGON STATE MAP SEE PAGES 70-71
FOR MONTANA STATE MAP SEE PAGE 51
FOR WYOMING STATE MAP SEE PAGES 88-89
FOR UTAH STATE MAP SEE PAGES 80-81
FOR NEVADA STATE MAP SEE PAGE 54

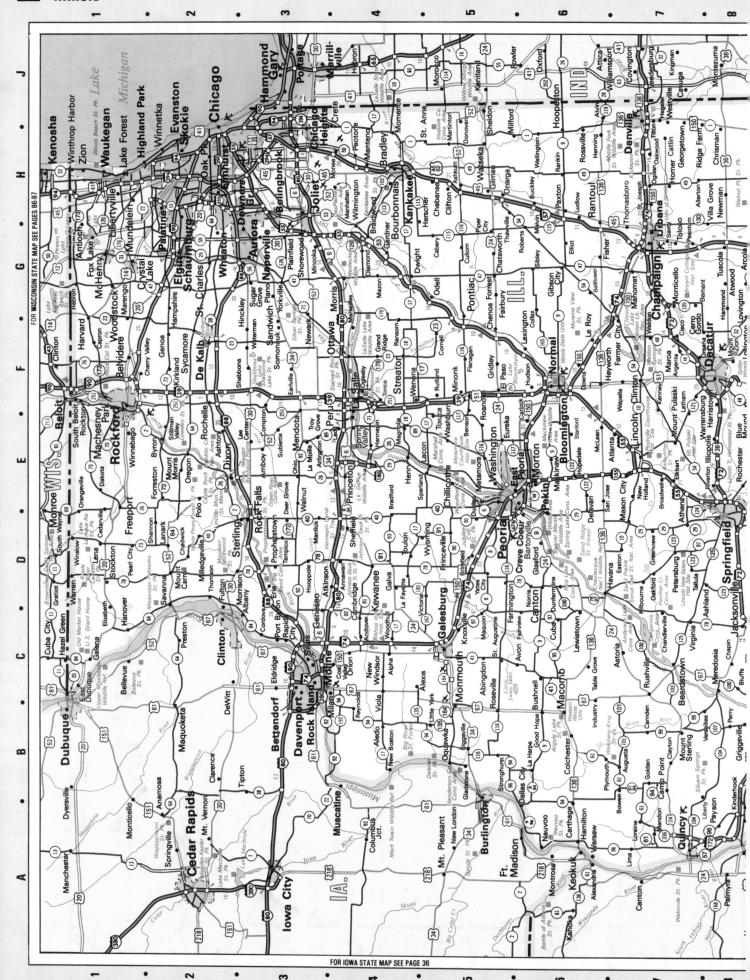

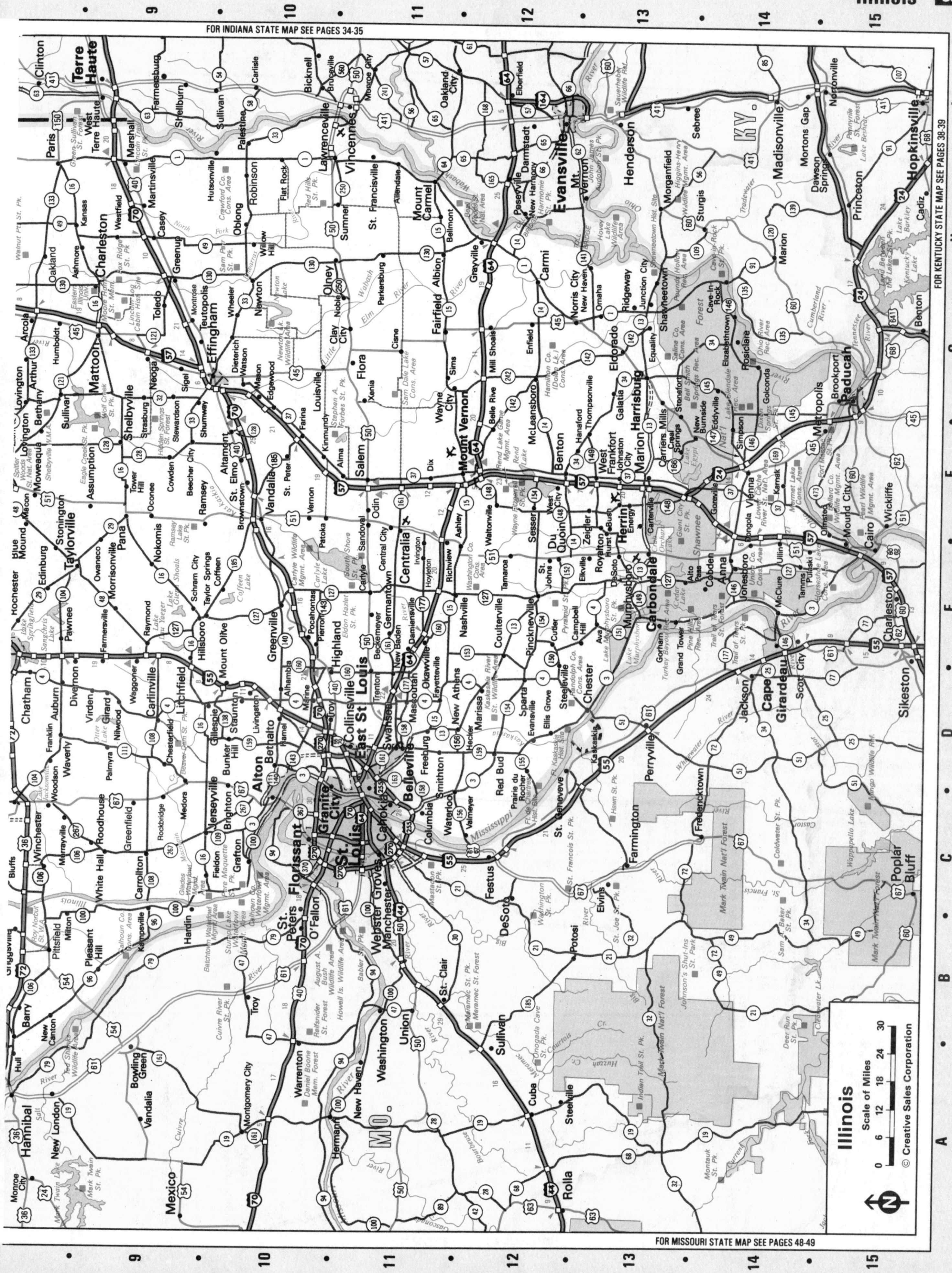
FOR INDIANA STATE MAP SEE PAGES 34-35
FOR MISSOURI STATE MAP SEE PAGES 48-49
FOR KENTUCKY STATE MAP SEE PAGES 38-39
Illinois
Scale of Miles
0 6 12 18 24 30
© Creative Sales Corporation
Terre Haute
Clinton
Paris
Charleston
Mattoon
Effingham
Olney
Vincennes
Lawrenceville
Evansville
Mt. Vernon
Henderson
Madisonville
Hopkinsville
Paducah
Metropolis
Harrisburg
Marion
Carbondale
Herrin
Du Quoin
Centralia
Salem
Vandalia
Taylorville
Pana
Litchfield
Carlinville
Alton
Granite City
Collinsville
East St Louis
St. Louis
Belleville
Florissant
St. Peters
O'Fallon
Webster Groves
Washington
Union
Sullivan
Cape Girardeau
Sikeston
Poplar Bluff
Farmington
Rolla
Mexico
Hannibal
Cairo
Jackson
Chester
Sparta
Pinckneyville
Highland
Greenville
Hillsboro
Shelbyville
Fairfield
Carmi
Flora
Benton
Anna
Vienna
Festus
Warrenton
MO.
KY.

FOR OHIO STATE MAP SEE PAGES 66-67

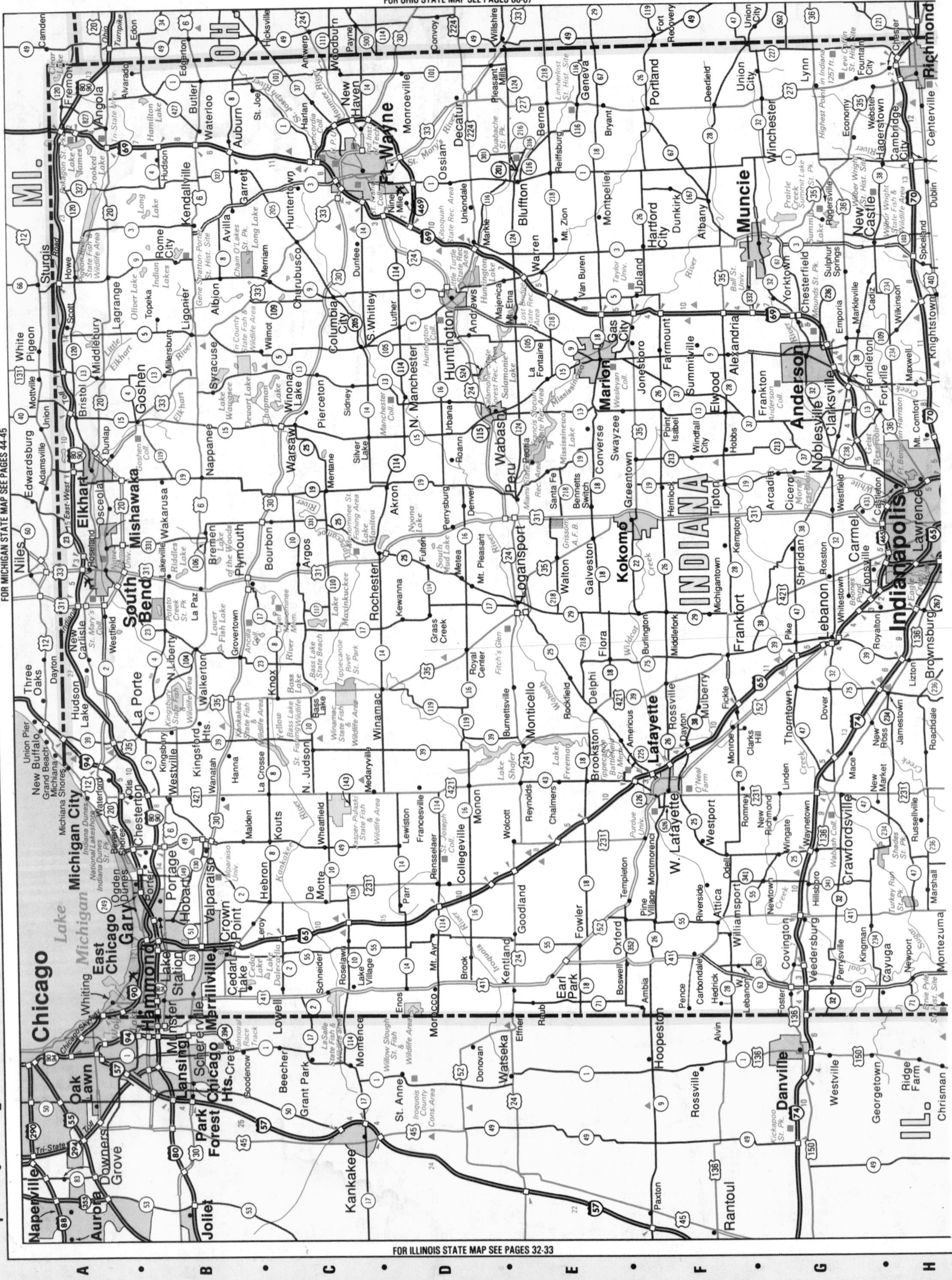

FOR MICHIGAN STATE MAP SEE PAGES 44-45

FOR ILLINOIS STATE MAP SEE PAGES 32-33

INDIANA

Major cities and places:

Chicago, Gary, Hammond, East Chicago, Whiting, Michigan City, South Bend, Mishawaka, Elkhart, Fort Wayne, New Haven, Muncie, New Castle, Richmond, Anderson, Noblesville, Indianapolis, Lafayette, W. Lafayette, Marion, Kokomo, Peru, Wabash, Huntington, Logansport, Crawfordsville, Frankfort, Lebanon, Carmel, Zionsville, Valparaiso, Crown Point, Lowell, Goshen, Warsaw, Plymouth, Rochester, Columbia City, Angola, Auburn, Kendallville, Decatur, Bluffton, Portland, Winchester, Hartford City, Gas City.

Napperville, Aurora, Joliet, Downers Grove, Oak Lawn, Park Forest, Chicago Hts., Kankakee, Rantoul, Danville.

MI. (Michigan) / OH (Ohio) / IL (Illinois)

Lake Michigan

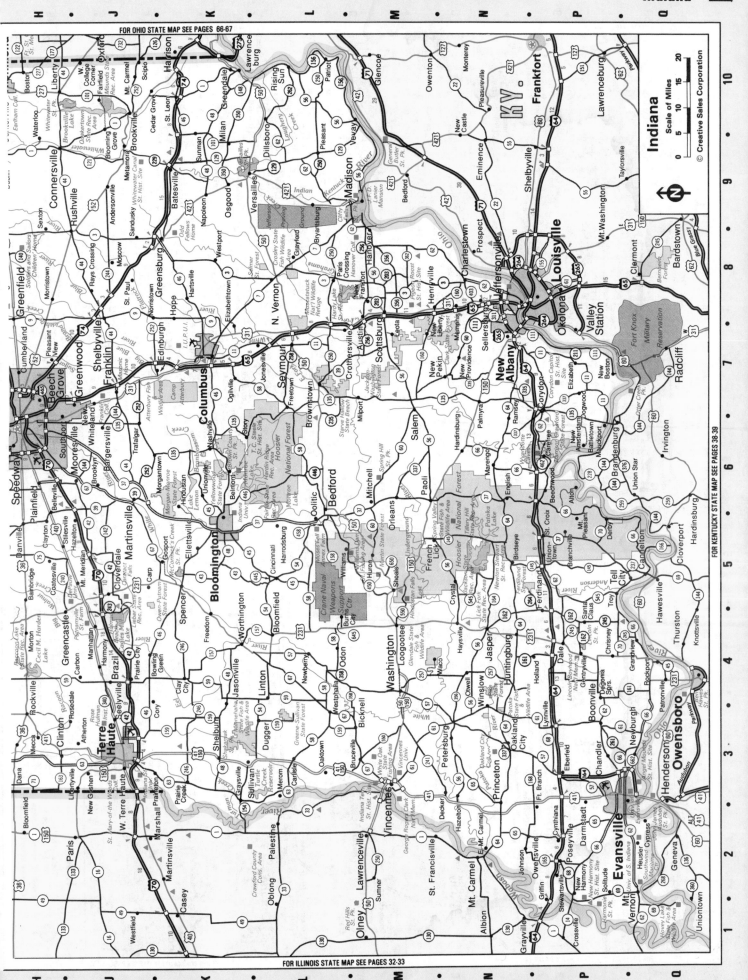

FOR OHIO STATE MAP SEE PAGES 66-67

FOR ILLINOIS STATE MAP SEE PAGES 32-33

FOR KENTUCKY STATE MAP SEE PAGES 38-39

Indiana
Scale of Miles
0 5 10 15 20
© Creative Sales Corporation

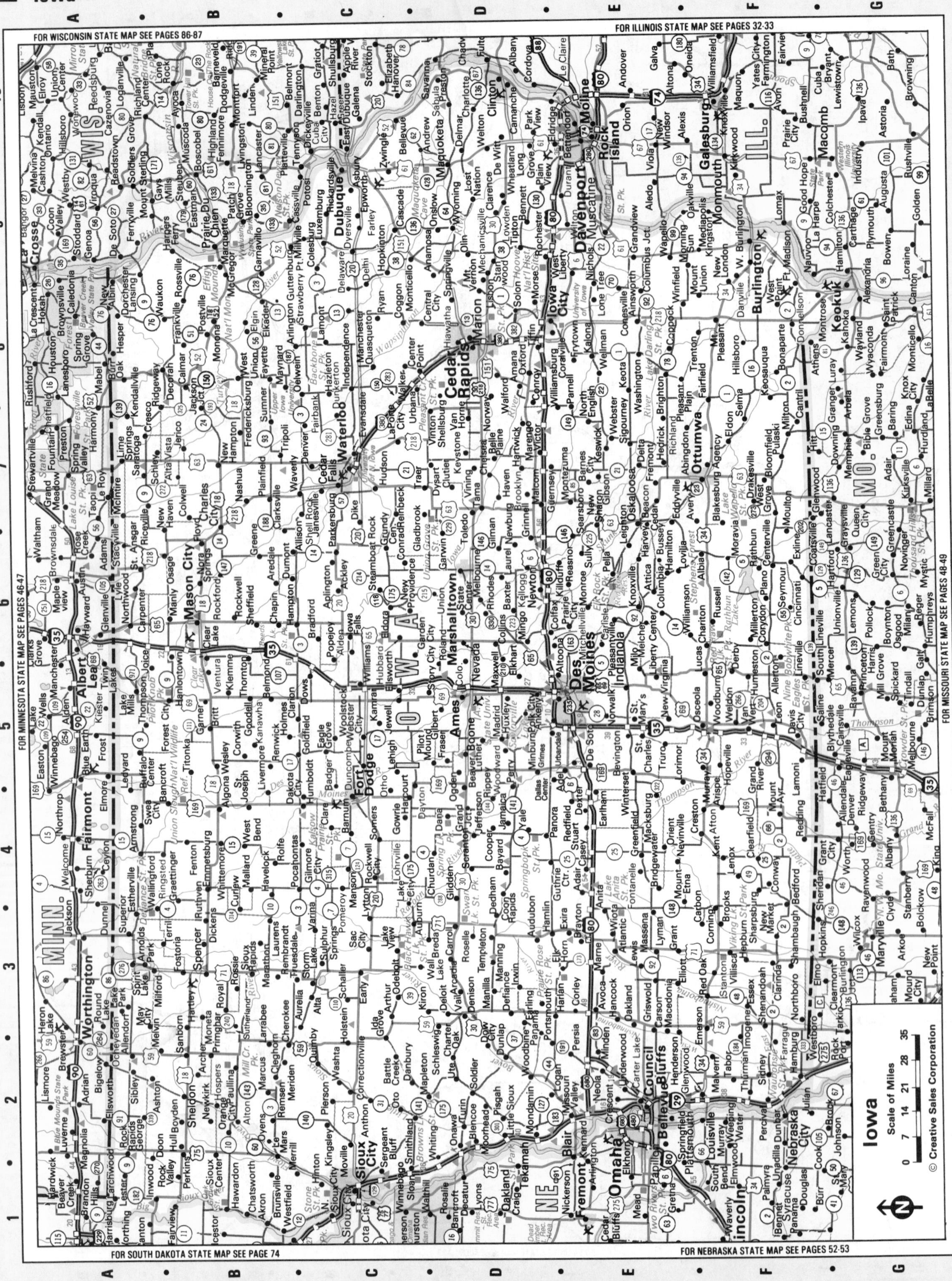

FOR WISCONSIN STATE MAP SEE PAGES 86-87
FOR ILLINOIS STATE MAP SEE PAGES 32-33
FOR MINNESOTA STATE MAP SEE PAGES 46-47
FOR MISSOURI STATE MAP SEE PAGES 48-49
FOR SOUTH DAKOTA STATE MAP SEE PAGE 74
FOR NEBRASKA STATE MAP SEE PAGES 52-53

Iowa

Scale of Miles

0 7 14 21 28 35

© Creative Sales Corporation

WIS.
MINN.
ILL.
MO.
NE.

Des Moines
Cedar Rapids
Waterloo
Davenport
Rock Island
Moline
Dubuque
Sioux City
Council Bluffs
Omaha
Mason City
Fort Dodge
Ottumwa
Burlington
Keokuk
Ames
Marshalltown
Fairmont
Worthington

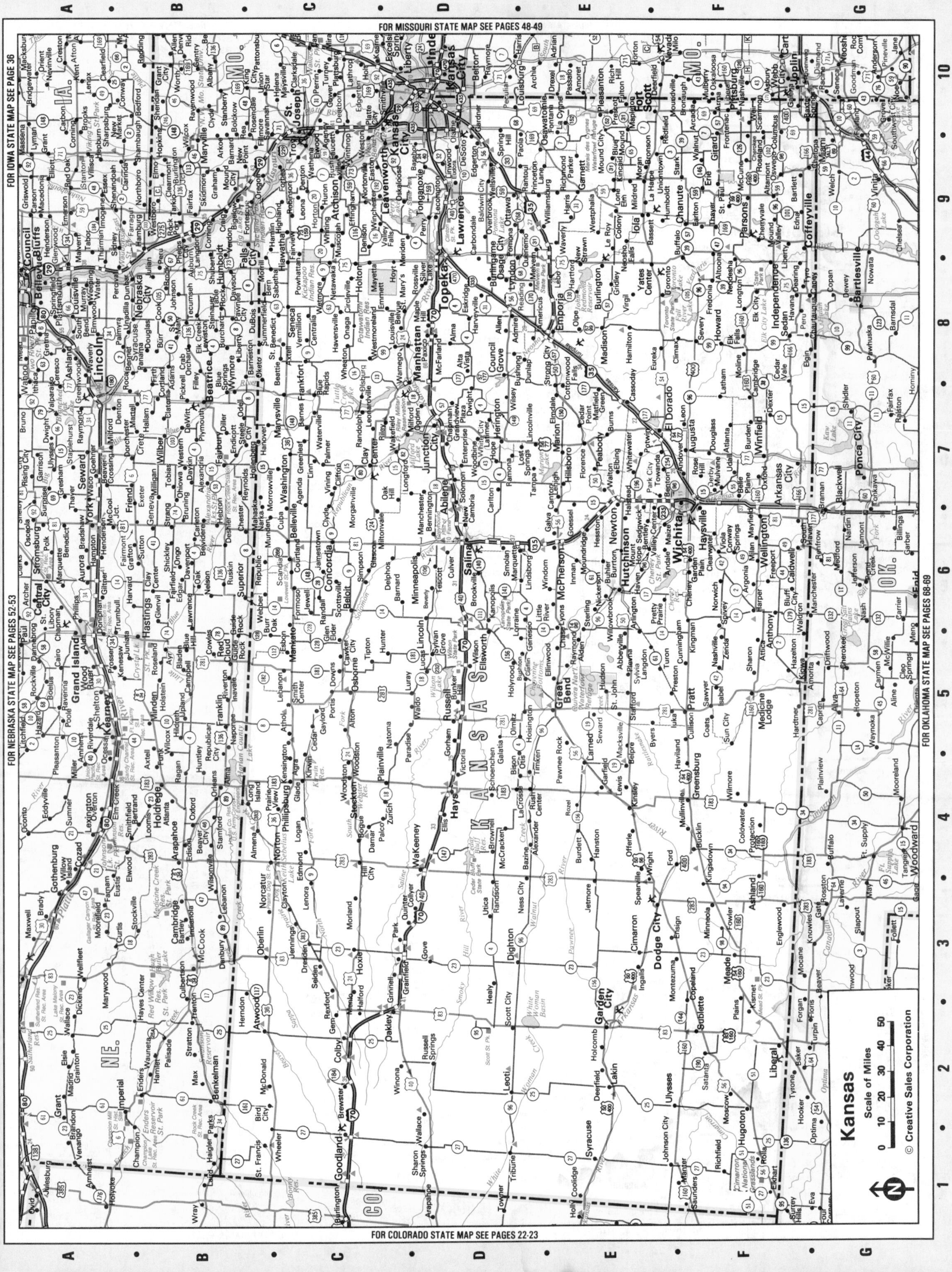

FOR MISSOURI STATE MAP SEE PAGES 48-49

FOR IOWA STATE MAP SEE PAGE 36

FOR NEBRASKA STATE MAP SEE PAGES 52-53

FOR OKLAHOMA STATE MAP SEE PAGES 68-69

FOR COLORADO STATE MAP SEE PAGES 22-23

Kansas

Scale of Miles

0 10 20 30 40 50

© Creative Sales Corporation

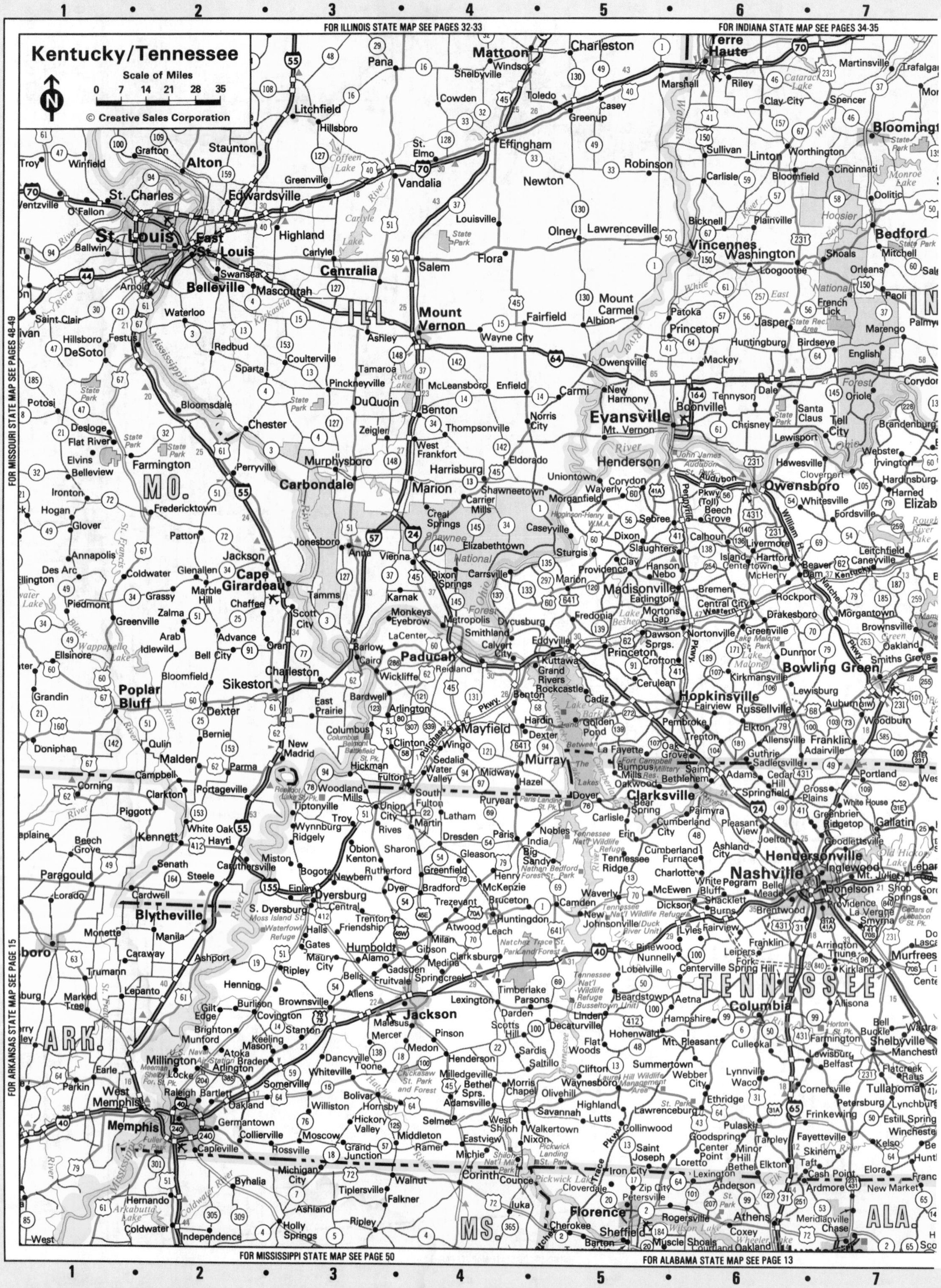

Kentucky/Tennessee

Scale of Miles

0 7 14 21 28 35

© Creative Sales Corporation

N

FOR ILLINOIS STATE MAP SEE PAGES 32-33
FOR INDIANA STATE MAP SEE PAGES 34-35
FOR MISSOURI STATE MAP SEE PAGES 48-49
FOR ARKANSAS STATE MAP SEE PAGE 15
FOR MISSISSIPPI STATE MAP SEE PAGE 50
FOR ALABAMA STATE MAP SEE PAGE 13

MO. ILL. IND. ARK. TENNESSEE MS. ALA.

St. Louis · East St. Louis · Belleville · Mattoon · Charleston · Terre Haute · Bloomington
Memphis · Nashville · Hendersonville · Murfreesboro · Bowling Green · Owensboro · Evansville
Paducah · Cape Girardeau · Poplar Bluff · Clarksville · Hopkinsville · Columbia · Florence

FOR OHIO STATE MAP SEE PAGES 66-67

FOR WEST VIRGINIA STATE MAP SEE PAGES 82-83

FOR VIRGINIA STATE MAP SEE PAGES 82-83

FOR NORTH CAROLINA STATE MAP SEE PAGES 64-65

FOR SOUTH CAROLINA STATE MAP SEE PAGES 64-65

FOR ALABAMA STATE MAP SEE PAGE 13

FOR GEORGIA STATE MAP SEE PAGES 28-29

Major labels: Cincinnati, Newport, Covington, Louisville, New Albany, Frankfort, Lexington, Richmond, Danville, Columbus, OH, Portsmouth, Ashland, Huntington, Charleston, WEST VIRGINIA, VA., Bristol, Kingsport, Johnson City, Pikeville, Middlesboro, Knoxville, Oak Ridge, Chattanooga, Asheville, N.C., Spartanburg, Greenville, KENTUCKY, GA.

Numerous town names including Shelbyville, Greensburg, Metamora, Brookville, Oxford, Hamilton, Waynesville, Washington C.H., Frankfort, Chillicothe, Athens, Marietta, Parkersburg, Glasgow, Somerset, Corbin, Williamsburg, Jellico, LaFollette, Morristown, Greeneville, Gatlinburg, Maryville, Sevierville, Cleveland, Dalton.

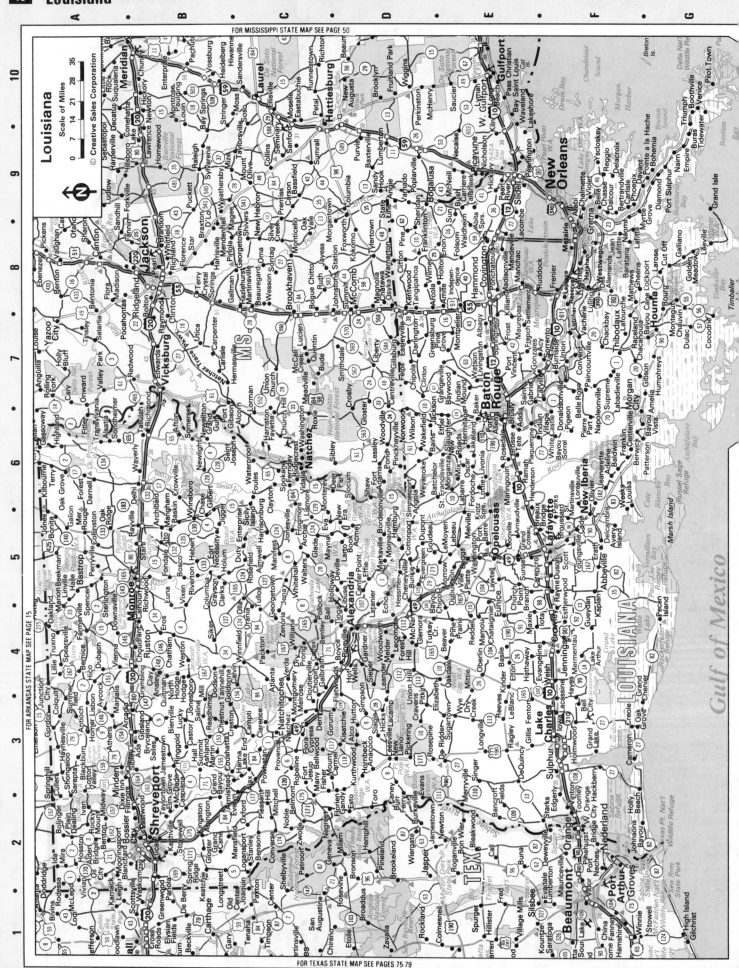

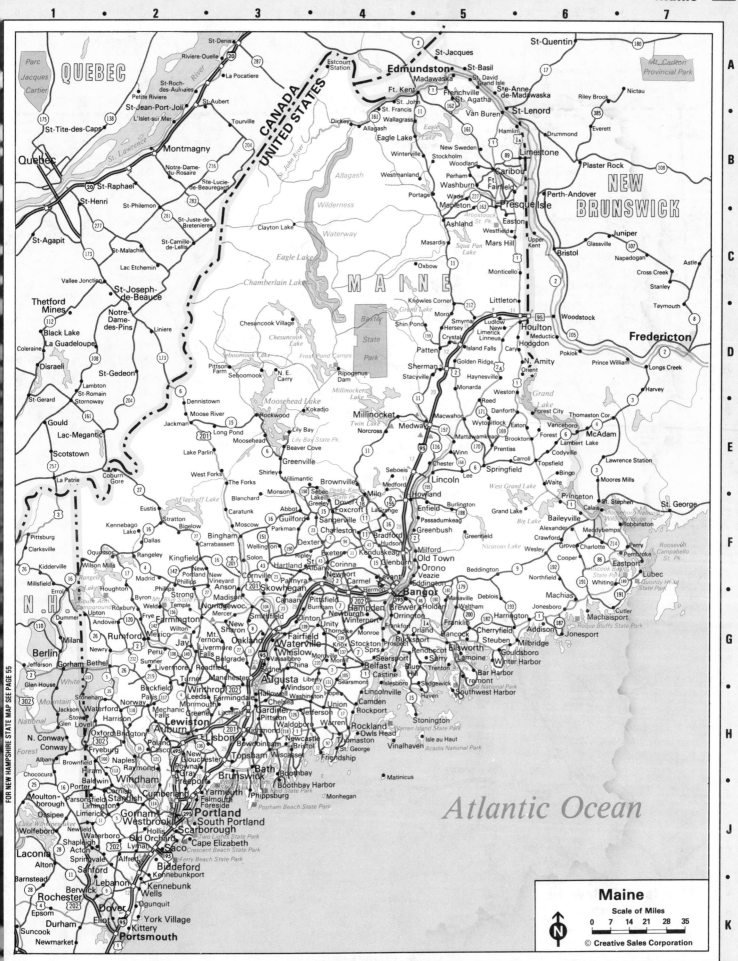

Maine

Scale of Miles

0   7   14   21   28   35

N

© Creative Sales Corporation

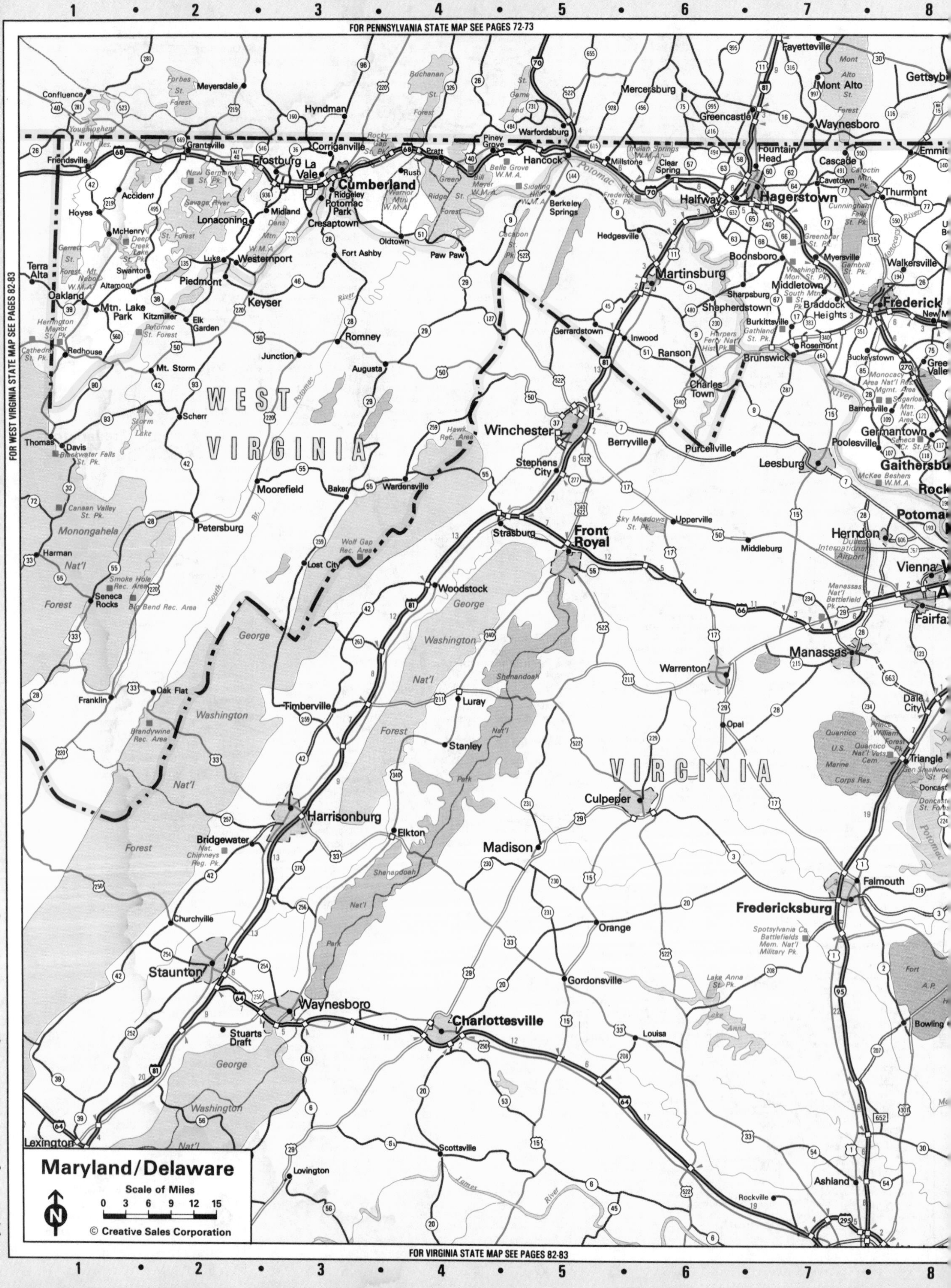

FOR PENNSYLVANIA STATE MAP SEE PAGES 72-73

1 2 3 4 5 6 7 8

A B C D E F G H J K

FOR WEST VIRGINIA STATE MAP SEE PAGES 82-83

WEST VIRGINIA

VIRGINIA

Confluence, Meyersdale, Hyndman, Grantsville, Corriganville, Pratt, Piney Grove, Warfordsburg, Mercersburg, Greencastle, Fayetteville, Mont Alto, Waynesboro, Gettysb...

Friendsville, Frostburg, La Vale, Cumberland, Rush, Hancock, Millstone, Clear Spring, Halfway, Fountain Head, Cascade, Cavetown, Emmit..., Thurmont

Accident, Ridgeley, Potomac Park, Cresaptown, Berkeley Springs, Hedgesville, Hagerstown, Boonsboro, Myersville, Walkersville

Hoyes, McHenry, Lonaconing, Midland, Oldtown, Paw Paw, Martinsburg, Sharpsburg, Shepherdstown, Middletown, Braddock Heights, Frederick, New M...

Terra Alta, Westernport, Luke, Piedmont, Fort Ashby, Gerrardstown, Inwood, Burkittsville, Rosemont, Buckeystown, Gree Valley

Oakland, Mtn. Lake Park, Kitzmiller, Elk Garden, Keyser, Romney, Ranson, Charles Town, Brunswick, Barnesville, Germantown, Poolesville

Redhouse, Mt. Storm, Junction, Augusta, Gaithersb..., Rock...

Thomas, Davis, Scherr, Winchester, Stephens City, Berryville, Purcellville, Leesburg, Potomac

Moorefield, Baker, Wardensville, Strasburg, Front Royal, Upperville, Middleburg, Herndon

Harman, Seneca Rocks, Petersburg, Lost City, Woodstock, Warrenton, Vienna, Fairfax, Manassas

Franklin, Oak Flat, Timberville, Luray, Opal, Triangle

Stanley, Culpeper, Dale City

Harrisonburg, Elkton, Madison, Falmouth

Bridgewater, Churchville, Orange, Fredericksburg

Staunton, Waynesboro, Gordonsville, Louisa

Stuarts Draft, Charlottesville, Ashland

Lexington, Lovington, Scottsville, Rockville

Maryland/Delaware

Scale of Miles
0 3 6 9 12 15

N

© Creative Sales Corporation

FOR VIRGINIA STATE MAP SEE PAGES 82-83

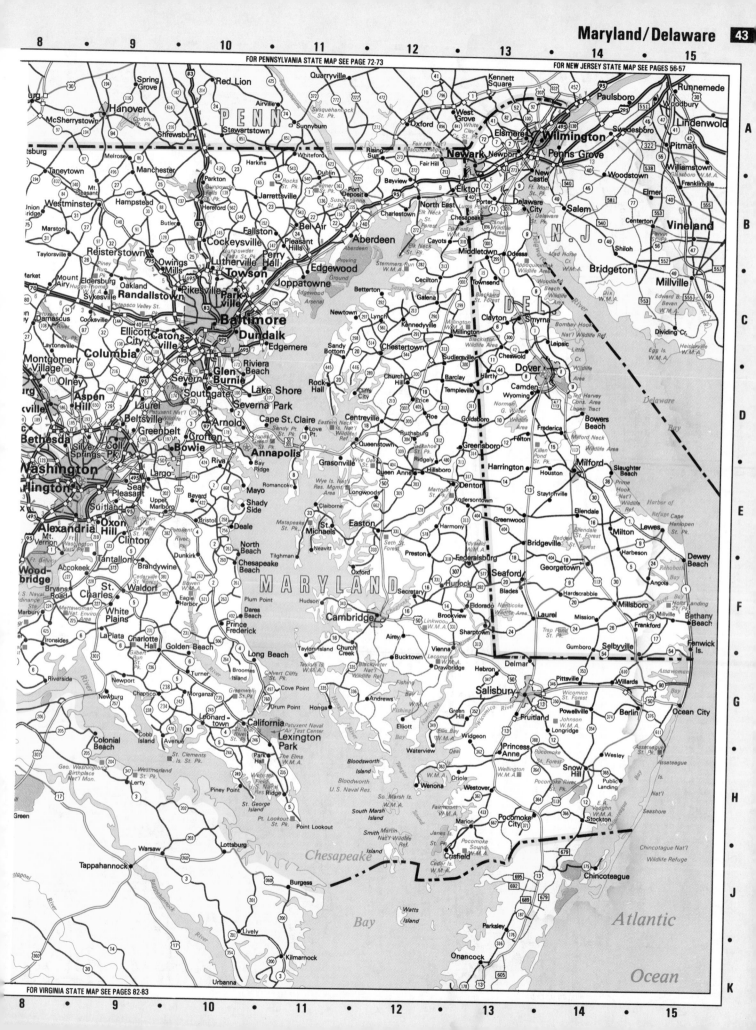

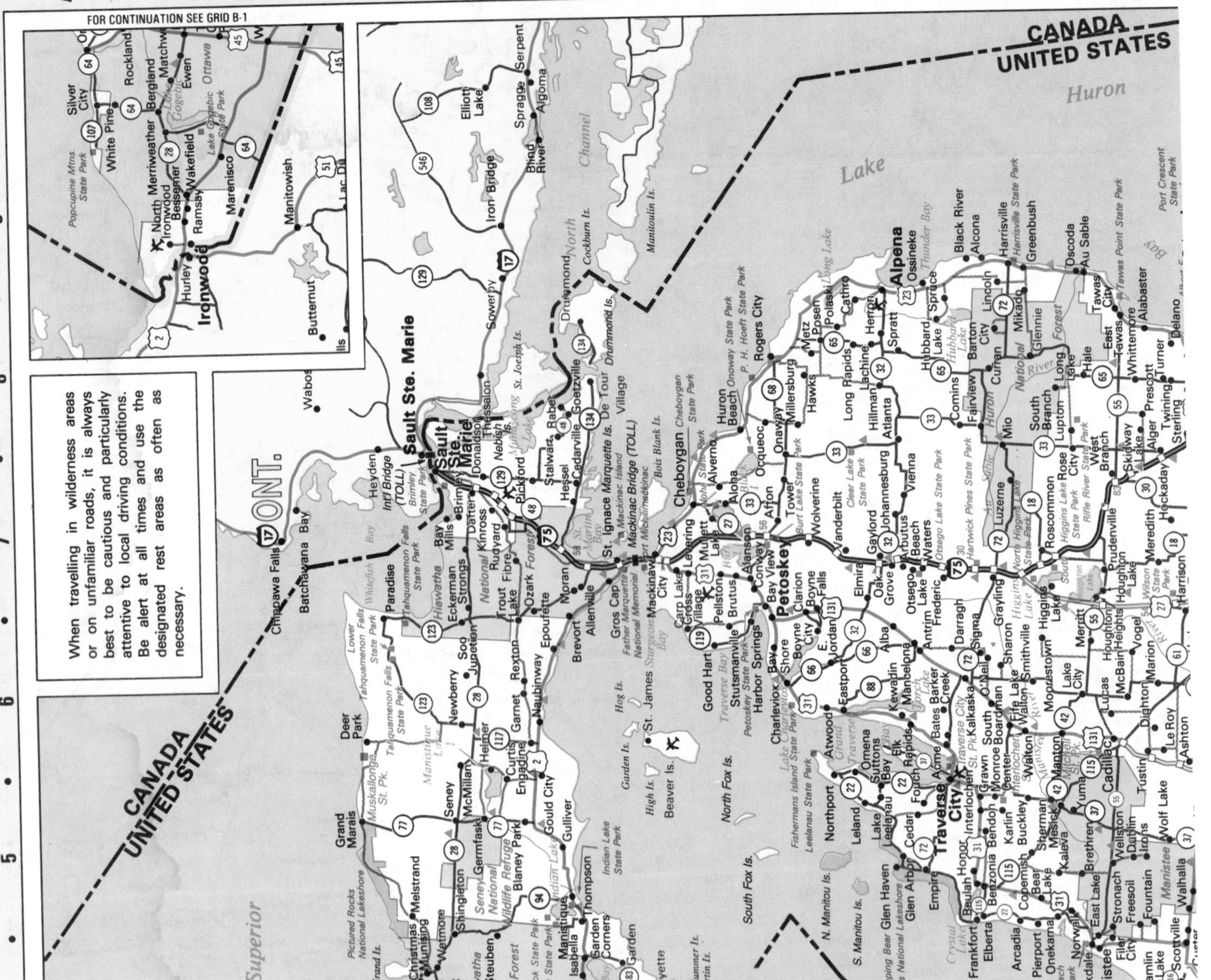

FOR CONTINUATION SEE GRID B-1

CANADA
UNITED STATES

CANADA
UNITED STATES

When travelling in wilderness areas or on unfamiliar roads, it is always best to be cautious and particularly attentive to local driving conditions. Be alert at all times and use the designated rest areas as often as necessary.

Lake Superior

Lake Huron

Lake Michigan

ONT.

Isle Royale Nat'l Park Floatplane Passenger Service

Ironwood

Sault Ste. Marie

Marquette

Negaunee

Escanaba

Petoskey

Traverse City

Cadillac

Alpena

Manistee

MICH

Green Bay

Appleton

Menasha

Neenah

Oshkosh

Manitowoc

Two Rivers

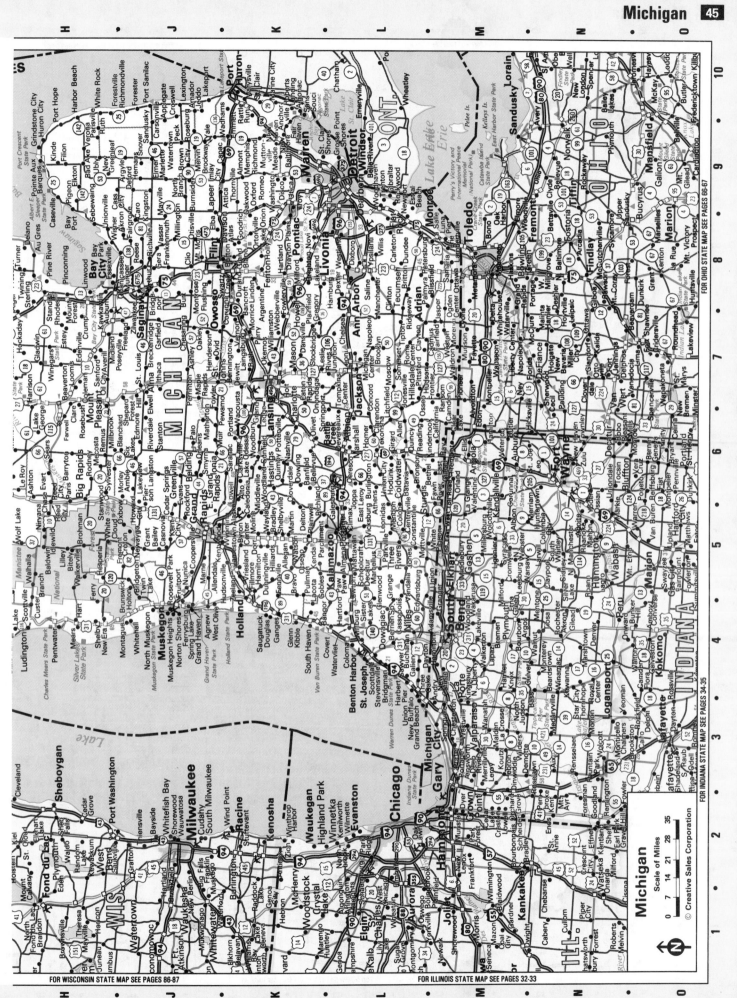

Michigan

Scale of Miles

0   7   14   21   28   35

© Creative Sales Corporation

FOR OHIO STATE MAP SEE PAGES 66-67

FOR INDIANA STATE MAP SEE PAGES 34-35

FOR CONTINUATION SEE GRID A-9
FOR WISCONSIN STATE MAP SEE PAGES 86-87
FOR CONTINUATION SEE GRID C-10

ONTARIO

CANADA

UNITED STATES

MINNESOTA

Lake Superior

Voyageurs National Park

Superior National Forest

Chippewa National Forest

Lake of the Woods

Red Lake

Upper Red Lake

Lower Red Lake

Mille Lacs

Leech Lake

Mississippi River

Red River

Selected place names:
Grand Portage, Hovland, Croftville, Grand Marais, Lutsen, Tofte, Schroeder, Taconite Harbor, Little Marais, Silver Bay, Beaver Bay, Finland, Isabella, Two Harbors, Knife River, Duluth, Superior, Ashland, Washburn, Iron River, Bayfield, Hurley, Montreal, Mellen, Hayward, Cable, Spooner, Siren, Webster

Shebandowan, Ignace, Atikokan, Seine River Village, Mine Centre, Farrington, Sioux Narrows, Nestor Falls

International Falls, Ranier, Ray, Ash Lake, Orr, Cook, Angora, Virginia, Eveleth, Gilbert, Biwabik, Aurora, Hoyt Lakes, Babbitt, Ely, Winton, Tower, Soudan, Britt, Buyck

Hibbing, Chisholm, Keewatin, Nashwauk, Coleraine, Grand Rapids, Deer River, Bovey, Calumet, Marble, Taconite

Bigfork, Effie, Marcell, Northome, Mizpah, Funkley, Blackduck, Tenstrike, Bemidji, Cass Lake, Walker, Akeley, Nevis, Longville, Remer, Outing, Emily, Crosby, Ironton, Deerwood, Aitkin, McGregor, Floodwood, Cromwell, Moose Lake, Sturgeon Lake, Willow River, Sandstone, Pine City, Hinckley, Finlayson, Askov, Bruno, Rutledge

Brainerd, Baxter, Nisswa, Pequot Lakes, Pine River, Staples, Motley, Little Falls, Swanville, Royalton, Pierz, Milaca, Mora, Isle, Onamia, Garrison, Wahkon

Thief River Falls, Red Lake Falls, Crookston, East Grand Forks, Fisher, Climax, Ada, Fertile, Twin Valley, Mahnomen, Waubun, Detroit Lakes, Frazee, Perham, New York Mills, Wadena, Sebeka, Menahga, Park Rapids, Osage, Ponsford

Moorhead, Dilworth, Glyndon, Hawley, Barnesville, Breckenridge, Wahpeton, Fergus Breckenridge, Fergus Falls, Pelican Rapids, Underwood, Battle Lake, Ashby, Dalton, Elbow Lake, Wheaton, Fargo

Roseau, Warroad, Baudette, Williams, Greenbush, Badger, Karlstad, Hallock, Lancaster, Kennedy, Donaldson, Argyle, Warren, Stephen, Oslo, Alvarado, Newfolden, Middle River, Strathcona, Viking, Holt, Goodridge, Grygla, Gatzke

Alexandria, Brandon, Garfield, Osakis, Sauk Centre, Melrose, Freeport, Long Prairie, Browerville, Eagle Bend, Clarissa, Bertha, Hewitt, Verndale

FARGO, Kindred, Sisseton, Browns Valley

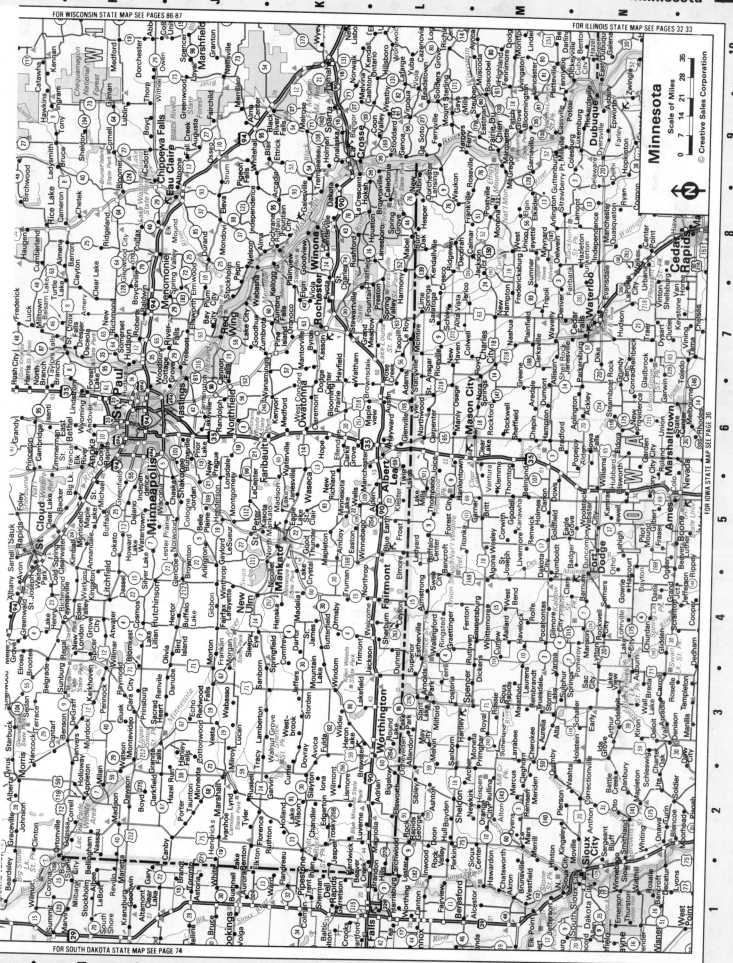

FOR WISCONSIN STATE MAP SEE PAGES 86-87

FOR ILLINOIS STATE MAP SEE PAGES 32-33

Minnesota

Scale of Miles

0   7   14   21   28   35

© Creative Sales Corporation

FOR SOUTH DAKOTA STATE MAP SEE PAGE 74

FOR IOWA STATE MAP SEE PAGE 36

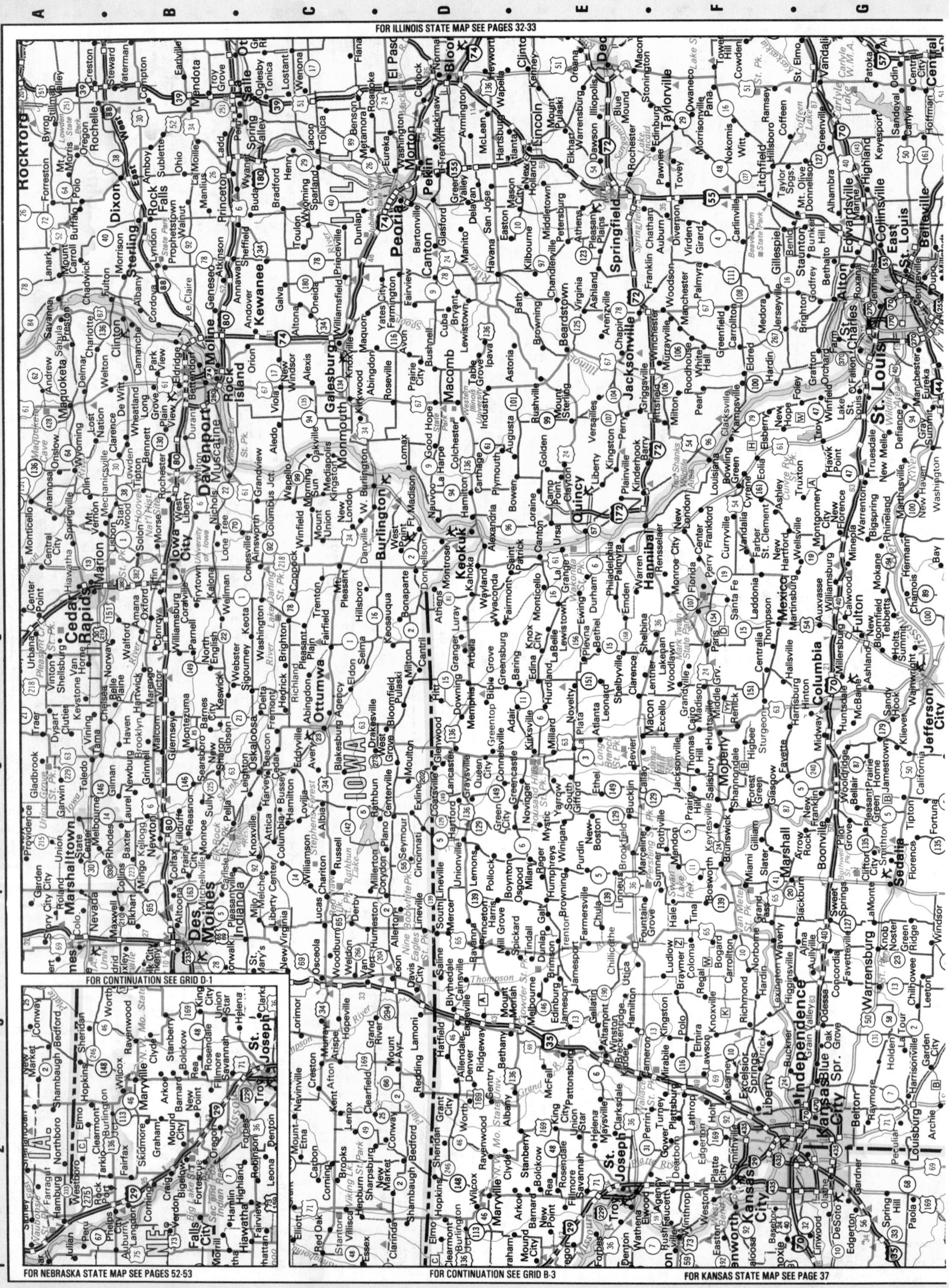

FOR ILLINOIS STATE MAP SEE PAGES 32-33
FOR CONTINUATION SEE GRID D-1
FOR NEBRASKA STATE MAP SEE PAGES 52-53
FOR CONTINUATION SEE GRID B-3
FOR KANSAS STATE MAP SEE PAGE 37

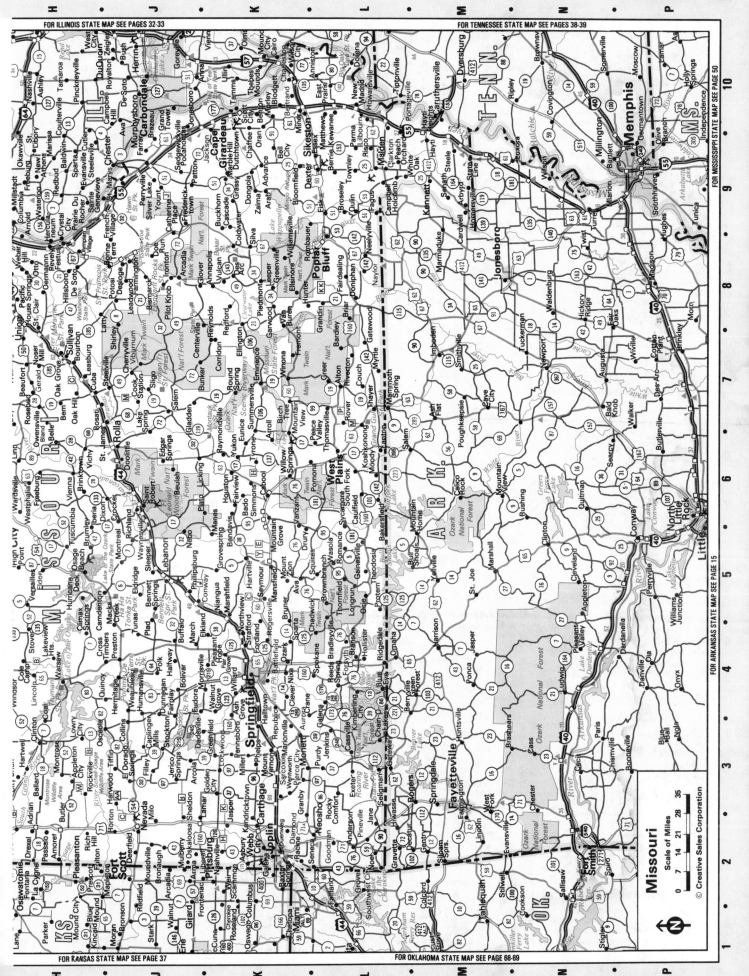

FOR ILLINOIS STATE MAP SEE PAGES 32-33
FOR TENNESSEE STATE MAP SEE PAGES 38-39
FOR MISSISSIPPI STATE MAP SEE PAGE 50
FOR ARKANSAS STATE MAP SEE PAGE 15
FOR KANSAS STATE MAP SEE PAGE 37
FOR OKLAHOMA STATE MAP SEE PAGES 68-69

Missouri

Scale of Miles

0   7   14   21   28   35

© Creative Sales Corporation

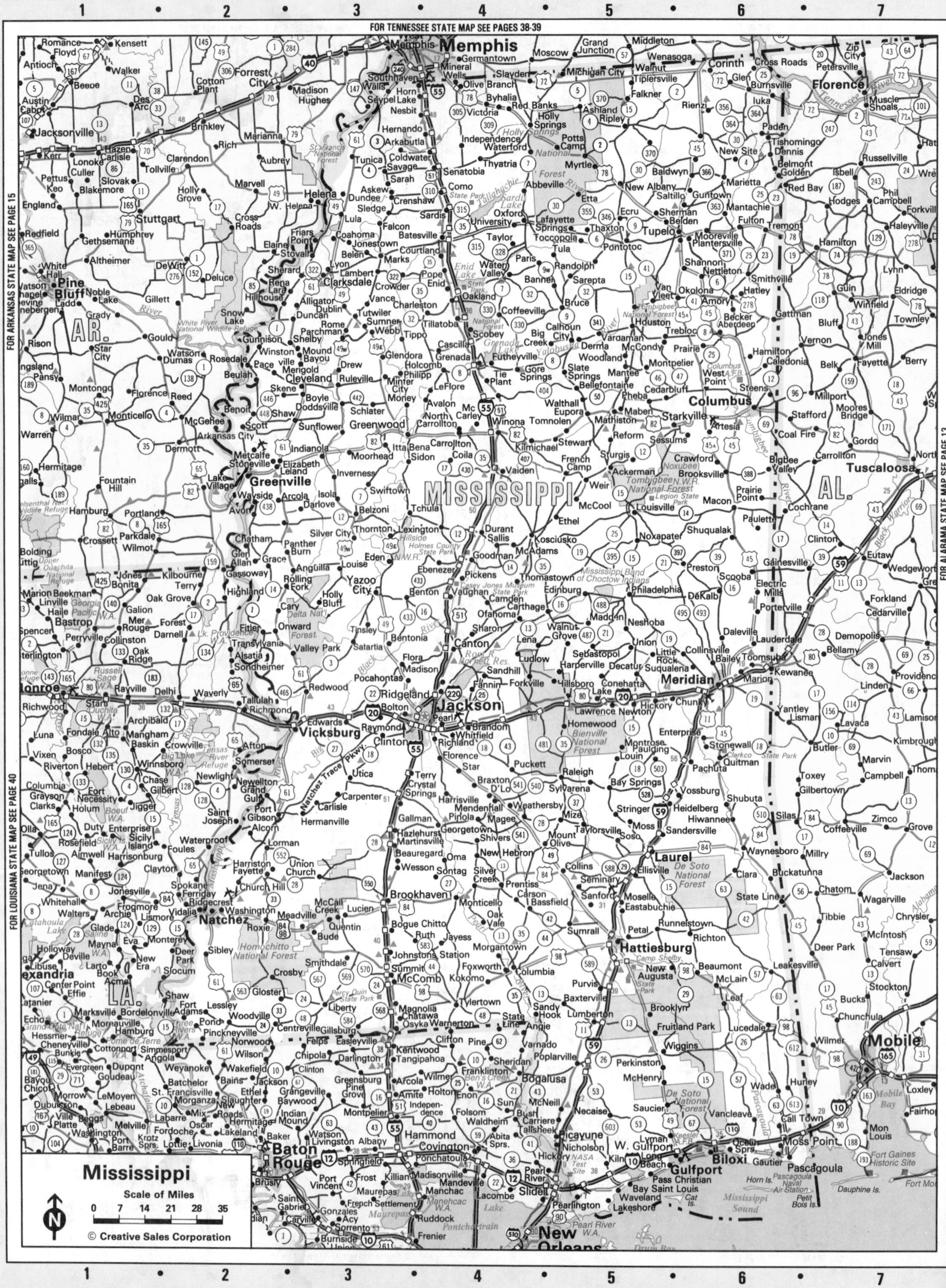
FOR TENNESSEE STATE MAP SEE PAGES 38-39
FOR ARKANSAS STATE MAP SEE PAGE 15
FOR LOUISIANA STATE MAP SEE PAGE 40
FOR ALABAMA STATE MAP SEE PAGE 13
MISSISSIPPI
AR.
AL.
LA.
Memphis
Jackson
Vicksburg
Greenville
Meridian
Hattiesburg
Columbus
Tupelo
Natchez
Gulfport
Biloxi
Mobile
Baton Rouge
New Orleans
Tuscaloosa
Mississippi
Scale of Miles
0 7 14 21 28 35
N
© Creative Sales Corporation

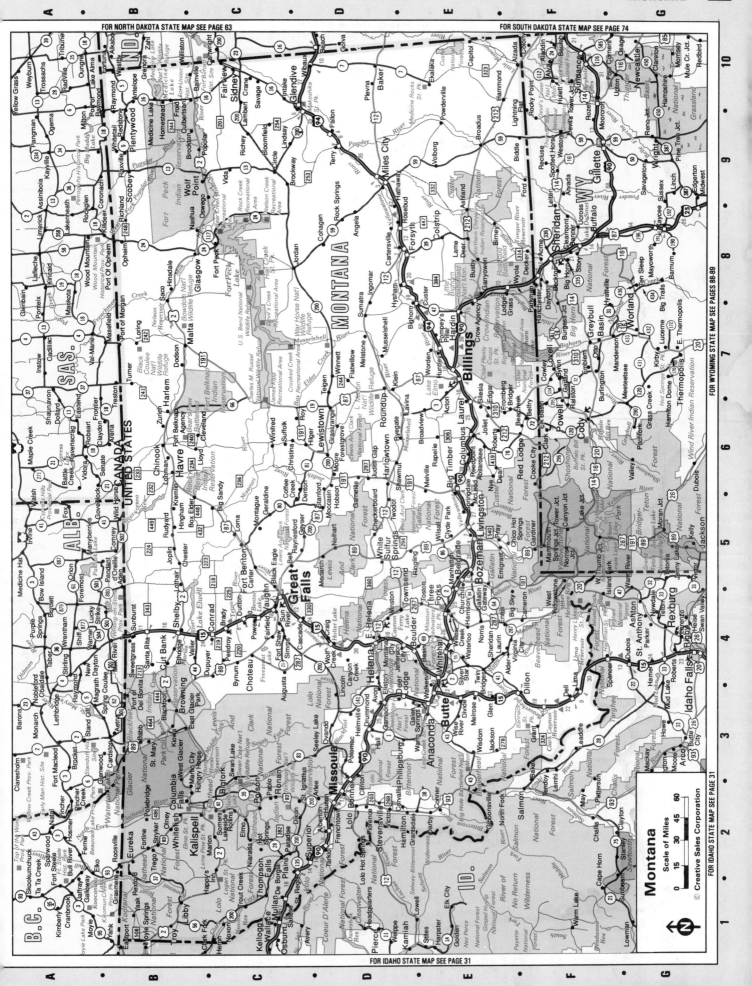

Montana

Scale of Miles

0 15 30 45 60

© Creative Sales Corporation

FOR NORTH DAKOTA STATE MAP SEE PAGE 63

FOR SOUTH DAKOTA STATE MAP SEE PAGE 74

FOR WYOMING STATE MAP SEE PAGES 88-89

FOR IDAHO STATE MAP SEE PAGE 31

FOR IDAHO STATE MAP SEE PAGE 31

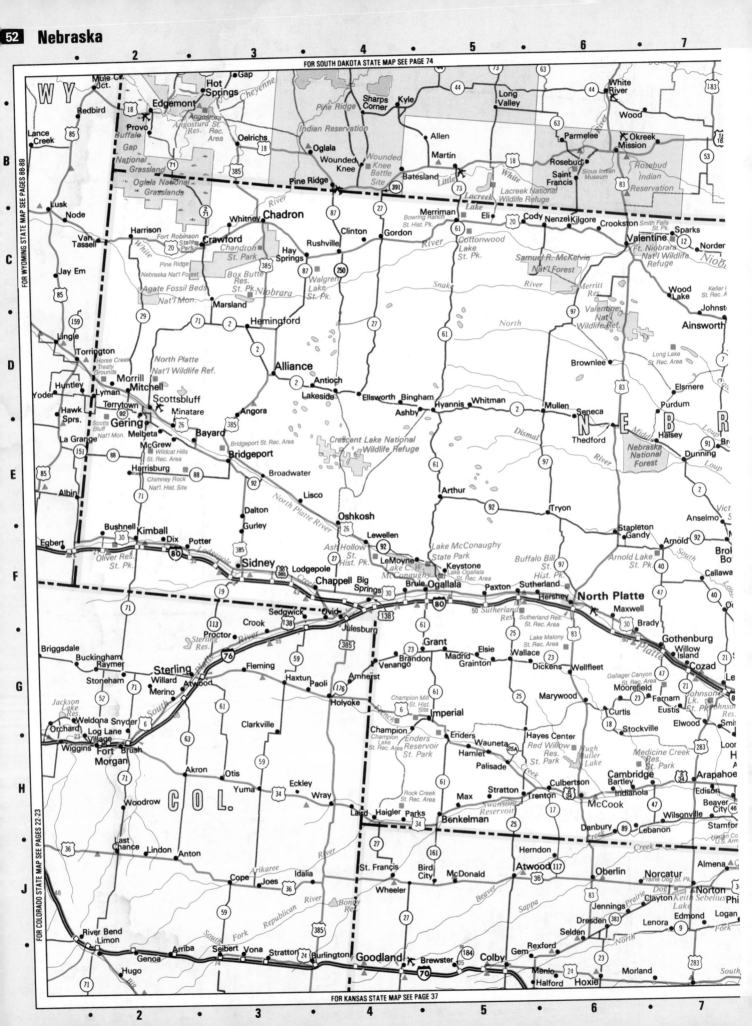

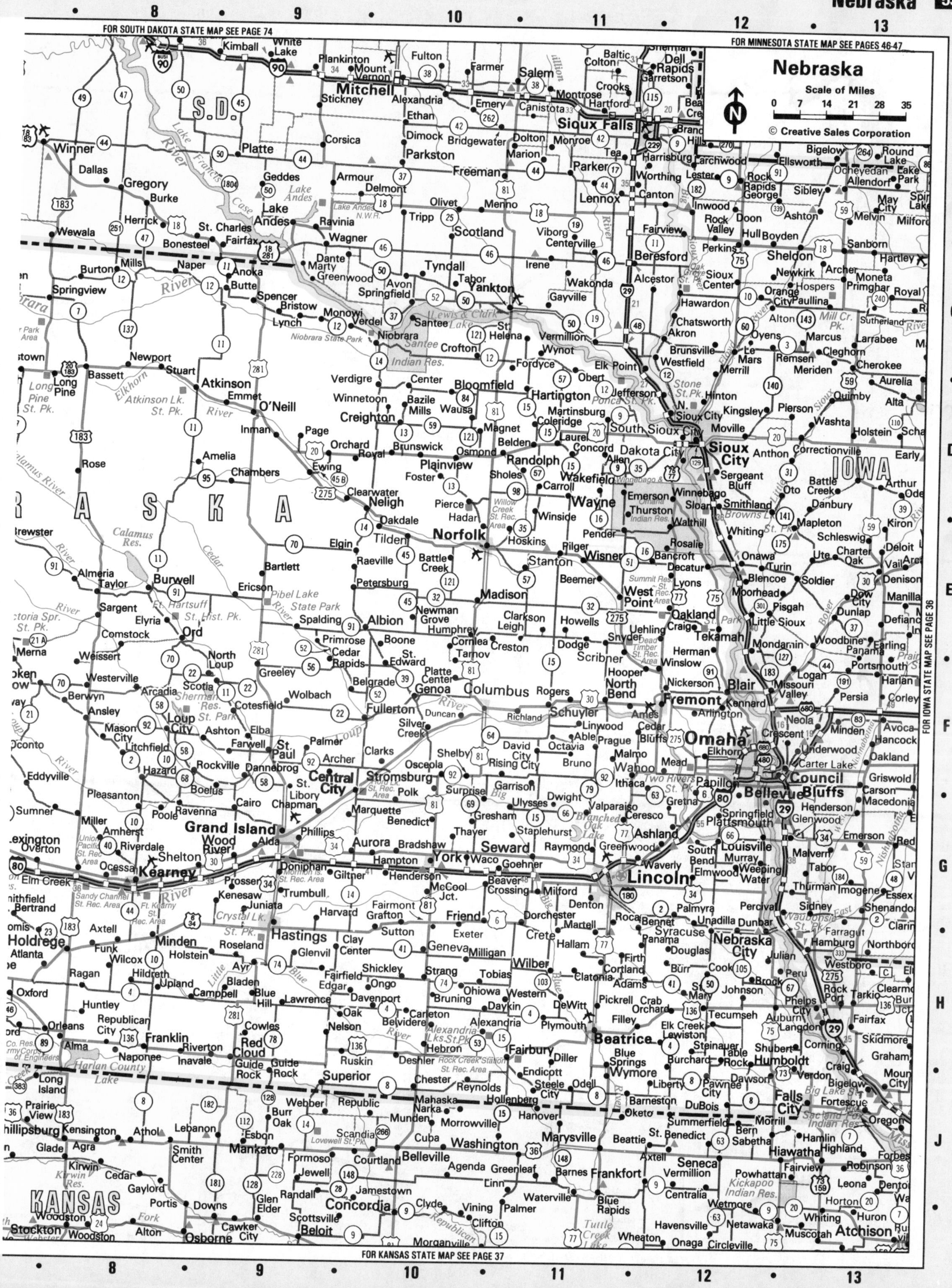

FOR SOUTH DAKOTA STATE MAP SEE PAGE 74
FOR MINNESOTA STATE MAP SEE PAGES 46-47

Nebraska

Scale of Miles

0　7　14　21　28　35

N

© Creative Sales Corporation

S.D.

IOWA

KANSAS

N E B R A S K A

Major cities: Sioux Falls, Mitchell, Winner, Yankton, Sioux City, Norfolk, Columbus, Fremont, Omaha, Council Bluffs, Bellevue, Papillion, Lincoln, Grand Island, Kearney, Hastings, Beatrice, Concordia

FOR IOWA STATE MAP SEE PAGE 36
FOR KANSAS STATE MAP SEE PAGE 37

FOR OREGON STATE MAP SEE PAGES 70-71

FOR IDAHO STATE MAP SEE PAGE 31

FOR CALIFORNIA STATE MAP SEE PAGES 18-21

FOR UTAH STATE MAP SEE PAGES 80-81

FOR ARIZONA STATE MAP SEE PAGES 16-17

FOR CALIFORNIA STATE MAP SEE PAGES 18-21

OR.
ID.
CA.
UT.
AZ.

NEVADA

Riddle • Rogerson • Three Creek • Jackpot • Contact • Montello • Wendover

McDermitt • Owyhee • Mountain City • Jarbridge • Oasis • Wells • Deeth • Halleck

Ft. McDermitt Indian Reservation • Humboldt National Forest • Duck Valley Indian Reservation

Indian Res. • Mogoc • Alkali Lake • Massacre Lake • Sheldon National Wildlife Refuge • Summit Lake Indian Reservation

Cedarville • Eagleville • Forest • Wendel • Honey Lake • Herlong • Doyle • Sutcliffe

Orovada • Paradise Valley • Midas • Tuscarora • Jack Creek • Thousand Springs

Sulphur • Winnemucca • Golconda • Valmy • Elko • Lamoille • Lee • Jiggs • Ruby Valley • Currie

Gerlach • Empire • Imlay • Mill City • Battle Mountain • Beowawe • Carlin • Te-Moak Indian Res. • Ruby Mountain Scenic Area • South Fork Indian Res.

Black Rock Desert • Rye Patch State Rec. Area • Rye Patch Reservoir • Rye Patch Dam

Pyramid Lake Indian Reservation • Eagle Picher Mine • Unionville • Beowawe Geysers • Crescent Valley • Shantytown • Lage's • Cherry Creek

Lovelock • Oreana • Ruby Lake National Wildlife Refuge • Goshute Indian Reservation

Pyramid Lake • State Park • Nixon • Wadsworth • Humboldt Wildlife Management Area • Pony Express Station Site • Trout Cr. • Gandy

Reno • Sparks • Fernley • Fallon • Austin • Eureka • McGill • Ely • Baker

Squaw Valley • Virginia City • Silver Springs • U.S. Naval Air Station • Cold Springs • Middle Gate • Ruth • Kimberly • East Ely • Lehman Caves Nat'l Mon. • Garrison

Lake Tahoe • Carson City • Weed Heights • Yerington • Schurz • Gabbs • Ione • Carver's • Duckwater • Preston • Lund • Major's Place • Great Basin National Park

Meeks Bay • Camp Richardson • Meyers • Wellington • Walker Lake • Babbitt • Hawthorne • Round Mountain • Duckwater Indian Res. • Currant • Wheeler Peak Scenic Area

Topaz • Bear Valley • Walker • Luning • Mina • Railroad Valley W.M.A. • Piochie • Caselton • Panaca • Ursine • Lund • Beryl

Bridgeport • Coaldale • Tonopah • Warm Springs • Nyala • Adaven • Hiko • Caliente • Uvada

Yosemite National Park • Lee Vining • Benton • Dyer • Silver Peak • Goldfield • Rachel • Ash Springs • Alamo • Caliente • Dixie National Forest

June Lake • Mammoth Lakes • Toms Place • Bishop • Laws • Oasis • Lida • Gold Point • Scotty's Junction • Elgin • Carp • Shivwits

Fish Camp • Sugar Pine • Round Valley • Independence • Beatty • Mercury • Indian Springs • Glendale • Moapa • Mesquite • Bunkerville

Clovis • Fresno • Tulare • Lone Pine • Keeler • Death Valley • Cactus Springs • Overton

Visalia • Hanford • Camp Nelson • Little Lake • Panamint Springs • Death Valley Jct. • Shoshone • N. Las Vegas • Las Vegas • Henderson • Boulder City

Delano • Oildale • Bakersfield • China Lake • Inyokern • Westend • Tecopa • Goodsprings • Sandy • Jean • Nelson • Cal Nev Ari • Laughlin • Kingman

Lost Hills • Mojave • California City • Johannesburg • Boron • Barstow • Yermo • Searchlight • Nipton • Cima • Baker

Nevada
Scale of Miles
0 20 40 60
© Creative Sales Corporation

N

1 • 2 • 3 • 4 • 5 • 6 • 7

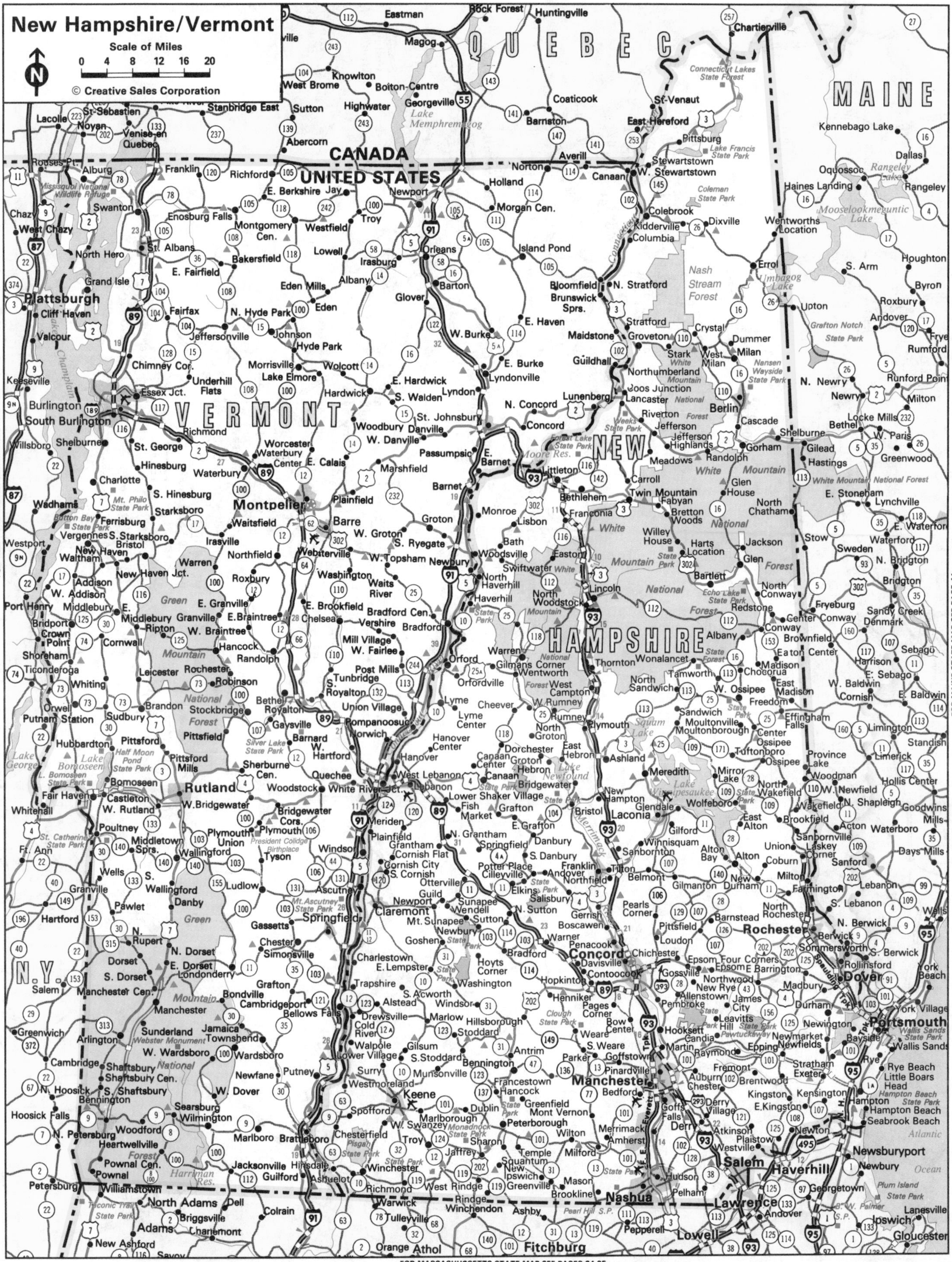
New Hampshire/Vermont
Scale of Miles
0 4 8 12 16 20
N
© Creative Sales Corporation
QUEBEC
CANADA
UNITED STATES
MAINE
VERMONT
NEW HAMPSHIRE
N.Y.
Lake Memphremagog
Lake Champlain
Green Mountain National Forest
White Mountain National Forest
Nash Stream Forest
Umbagog Lake
Mooselookmeguntic Lake
Rangeley Lake
Lake Winnipesaukee
Squam Lake
Newfound Lake
Connecticut Lakes State Forest
Atlantic Ocean
Plattsburgh
Burlington
South Burlington
St. Albans
Montpelier
Barre
Rutland
Newport
St. Johnsbury
Lyndonville
Bennington
Brattleboro
Springfield
White River Jct.
Lebanon
Hanover
Claremont
Keene
Concord
Manchester
Nashua
Laconia
Littleton
Berlin
Lancaster
Colebrook
Rochester
Dover
Portsmouth
Salem
Haverhill
Lawrence
Lowell
Fitchburg
Newburysport
Gloucester
Ipswich
North Adams
Athol
Rangeley
Rumford
Bethel
Conway
Sherbrooke
Magog
Coaticook
Eastman
Lake Francis State Park
Coleman State Park
Moore Res.
Harriman Res.

FOR NEW YORK STATE MAP SEE PAGES 66-69

FOR MAINE STATE MAP SEE PAGE 41

FOR MASSACHUSSETTS STATE MAP SEE PAGES 24-25

1 • 2 • 3 • 4 • 5 • 6 • 7

FOR NEW YORK STATE MAP SEE PAGES 58-61

FOR PENNSYLVANIA STATE MAP SEE PAGES 72-73

NEW YORK

PENNSYLVANIA

Ocean

Hudson River

Long Island Sound

Staten Is.

Palisades

Scranton · Moscow · Gouldsboro St. Pk. · Sterling · Mt. Pocono · Tobyhanna St. Pk. · Big Pocono St. Pk. · Palmerton · Macungie

Pt. Jervis · Montague · High Point St. Park · Colesville · Sussex · Hamburg · Franklin · Ogdensburg · Sparta · Newton · Fredon · Andover · Hackettstown · Blairstown · Hope · Johnsonburg · Belvidere · Oxford · Washington · Phillipsburg · Easton · Wilson · Alpha · Bethlehem · Allentown · Catasauqua · Northampton · Nazareth · Quakertown

Peekskill · Ossining · Nyack · Tarrytown · White Plains · Mt. Vernon · Yonkers · Valley Stream · Long Beach · Atlantic Beach

Spring Valley · Westwood · Norwood · Bergenfield · Englewood · Hackensack · Fort Lee · West New York · Union City · Hoboken · Jersey City · Bayonne · New York

Ringwood · Wanaque · Waldwick · Ridgewood · Pompton Lakes · Butler · Riverdale · Bloomingdale · Kinnelon · Montville · Lincoln Park · Fair Lawn · Hawthorne · Paterson · West Paterson · Passaic · Clifton · Nutley · Bloomfield · Belleville · Newark · Elizabeth · Carteret · Perth Amboy · South Amboy · Keansburg · Union Beach · Keyport · Matawan

West Milford · Newfoundland · Stockholm · Rockaway · Denville · Dover · Wharton · Netcong · Stanhope · Hopatcong · Budd Lakes · Long Valley · Chester · Mendham · Morristown · Morris Plains · Parsippany-Troy Hills · Morris Hanover · Madison · Chatham · Florham Park · New Providence · Summit · West Orange · Orange · East Orange · Irvington · Roselle · Roselle Park · Kenilworth · Linden · Rahway · Westfield · Plainfield · Dunellen · Metuchen · Highland Park · Sayreville · South River

Bernardsville · Fairmount · Peapack · Bedminster · Oldwick · Whitehouse · Readington · Flemington · Somerville · Manville · Raritan · Bound Brook · Warren · Watchung · South Plainfield · New Edison · New Brunswick · Milltown · Spotswood · Monroe · Cranbury · Jamesburg · Englishtown · Manalapan · Marlboro · Holmdel · Shrewsbury · Red Bank · Rumson · Fair Haven · Atlantic Highlands · Highlands

Sandy Hook Light Nat'l Hist. Landmark · Gateway Nat'l Rec. Area

Stroudsburg · Bangor · Broadway · Hampton · Clinton · Lebanon · High Bridge · Glen Gardner · Pittstown · Baptistown · Frenchtown · Milford · Spring Mills · Stockton · Lambertville · Pennington · Hopewell · Blawenburg · Princeton · Lawrence · Trenton · Morrisville · Levittown · Newtown · Warminster · Lansdale · Doylestown

Eatontown · Freehold · Adelphia · Farmingdale · Long Branch · West Long Branch · Asbury Park · Bradley Beach · Belmar · Neptune · Oceanport · Tinton Falls · Colts Neck · Robertsville · Roosevelt · Hightstown · Clarksville · Edinburg · Hamilton Sq. · Ewingville · Washington Crossing · Titusville

Delaware Water Gap Nat'l Rec. Area

New Berlinville · Pottstown · Evansburg St. Pk. · Pennsburg

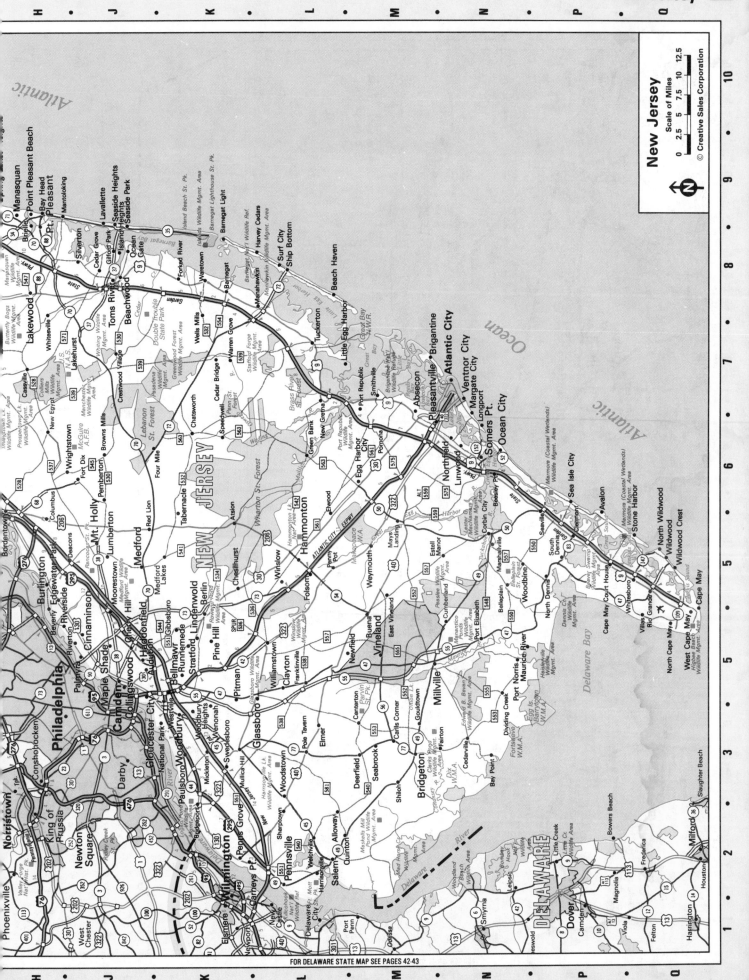

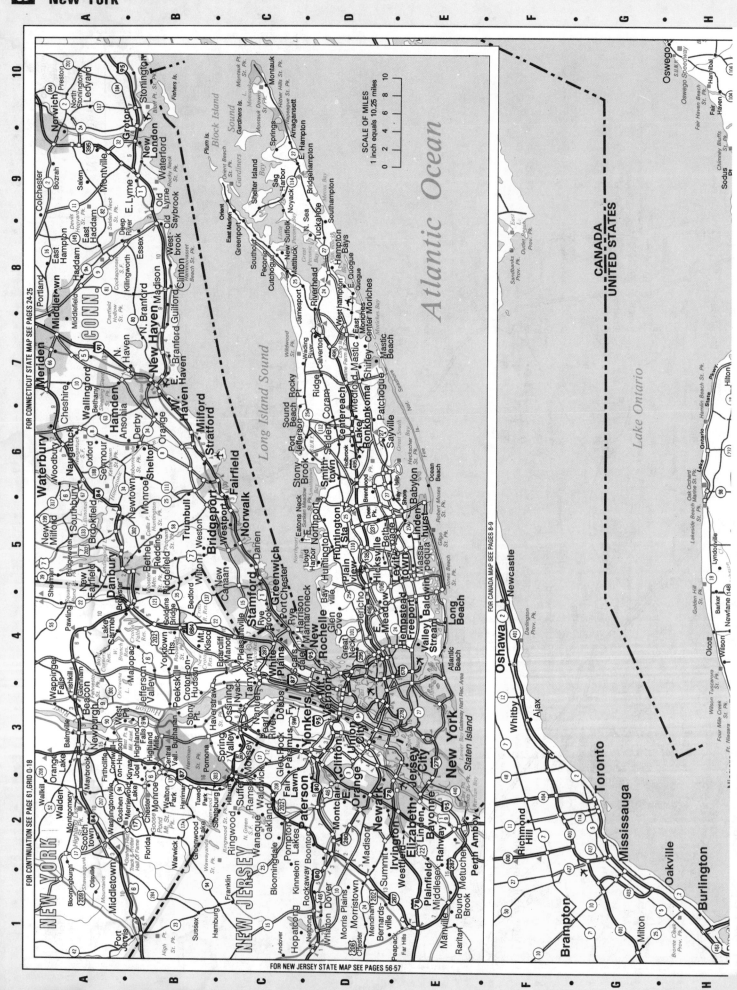

FOR CONNECTICUT STATE MAP SEE PAGES 24-25

FOR CONTINUATION SEE PAGE 61, GRID O-18

FOR CANADA MAP SEE PAGES 8-9

FOR NEW JERSEY STATE MAP SEE PAGES 56-57

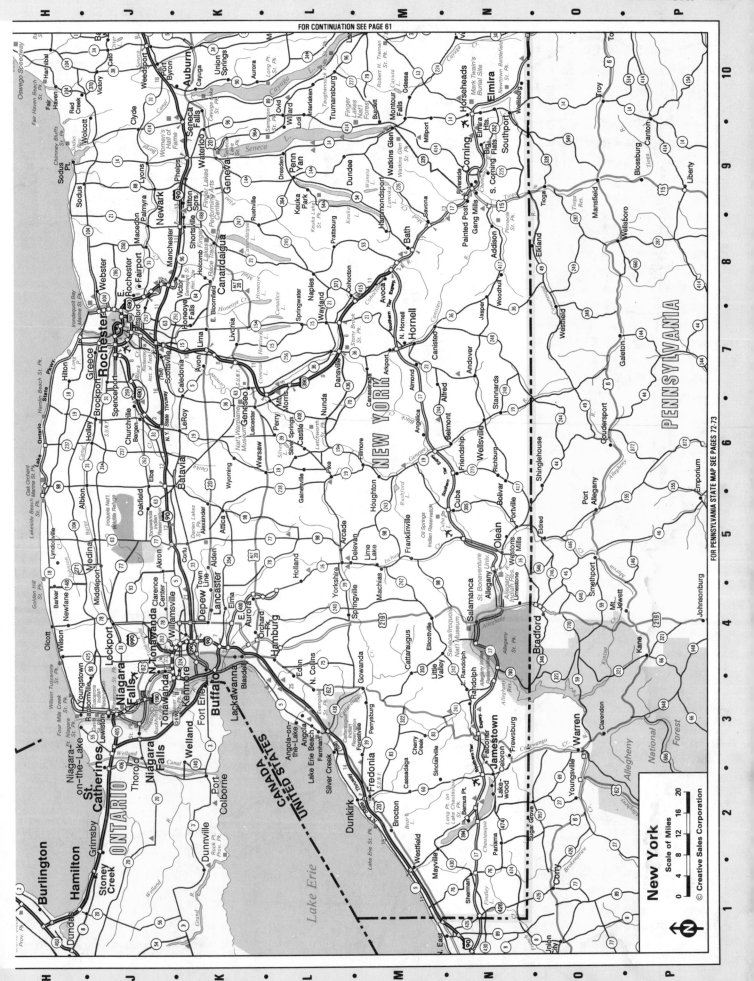

FOR CONTINUATION SEE PAGE 61

PENNSYLVANIA

NEW YORK

ONTARIO

CANADA
UNITED STATES

Lake Erie

FOR PENNSYLVANIA STATE MAP SEE PAGES 72-73

New York

Scale of Miles
0 4 8 12 16 20

© Creative Sales Corporation

FOR VERMONT STATE MAP SEE PAGE 55

New York

Scale of Miles

0 4 8 12 16 20

© Creative Sales Corporation

N

CANADA
UNITED STATES

QUEBEC

ONTARIO

VERMONT

NEW YORK

Lake Champlain

Adirondack Park

Adirondack Mountains

St. Albans · Swanton · Milton · Colchester · Essex Jct. · Burlington · Winooski · Shelburne · Hinesburg · Charlotte · Bristol · New Haven · Middlebury · Vergennes · Addison · Bridport

Venise-en-Quebec · Alburg · Grand Isle · South Hero · Champlain Park

Barrington · Lacolle · Rouses Pt. · Champlain · Mooers · W. Plattsburgh · Morrisonville · Plattsburgh · Peru · Keeseville

Ormstown · Port-Lewis · Huntingdon · Dannemora · Chateaugay · Burke · Malone · Brushton · Dundee

Westport · Port Henry · Witherbee · Mineville · Ticonderoga · Crown Pt. St. Hist. Site

Olympic Site Tour · Lake Placid · Saranac Lake · Bloomingdale · Six Nations Indian Museum · Tupper Lake · Robert Louis Stevenson Cottage

Mt. Marcy Highest Pt. in N.Y.

Warrensburg · Lake Luzerne · Hadley · Corinth · Lake George · Glens Falls · Hudson Falls · Ft. Edward · Ft. Ann · Whitehall · Fair Haven · Castleton · Poultney · Pawlet · Granville · Argyle

Northville · Speculator · Old Forge · Atwell · Enchanted Forest/Water Safari · The Nordgewock III River Boat

Remsen · Cold Brook · Barneveld · Prospect · Boonville · Port Leyden · Lyons Falls · Lowville · Croghan · Carthage · Castorland · Copenhagen · Constableville · Turin

Camden · Camp · Camp Drum · Ft. Drum Military Reserve · Philadelphia · Antwerp · Gouverneur · Edwards · Star Lake · Harrisville · Deferiet · Black River · W. Carthage · Watertown

Massena · F.D.R. St. Lawrence Power Project Visitors Center · Robert Moses St. Pk. · Eisenhower Lock · Brasher Falls · Winthrop · Norwood · Norfolk · Unionville · Potsdam · Canton · Hermon · Richville

Chesterville · Cornwall · Barnhart Is. · Waddington · Morrisburg · Iroquois · Chesterville · Winchester · Kemptville · Merrickville · Smiths Falls · Lanark · Newboro

Ogdensburg · Prescott · Heuvelton · Rensselaer Falls · Hammond · Theresa · Gouverneur · Philadelphia · Evans Mills · Glen Park · Brownville · Dexter · Sackets Harbor · Adams · Mannsville · Lacona · Pulaski · Parish · Central Square

Brockville · Athens · Morristown · Alexandria Bay · St. Lawrence Park · Clayton · Cape Vincent · Chaumont · Dexter · Sandy Creek · Ellisburg · Lakeview · Mexico · Minetto · Oswego · Fulton

Gananoque · Thousand Islands Intl. Bridge · Kingston · Wolfe Is.

Black River · Beaver River · Moose River · Raquette River · Grass River · Oswegatchie River

Mt. Macomb · Rainbow Falls Res.

FOR MASSACHUSSETTS STATE MAP SEE PAGES 24-25

FOR CONNECTICUT STATE MAP SEE PAGES 24-25

FOR CONTINUATION SEE PAGE 58, GRID A-1

FOR PENNSYLVANIA STATE MAP SEE PAGES 72-73

FOR CONTINUATION SEE PAGE 59

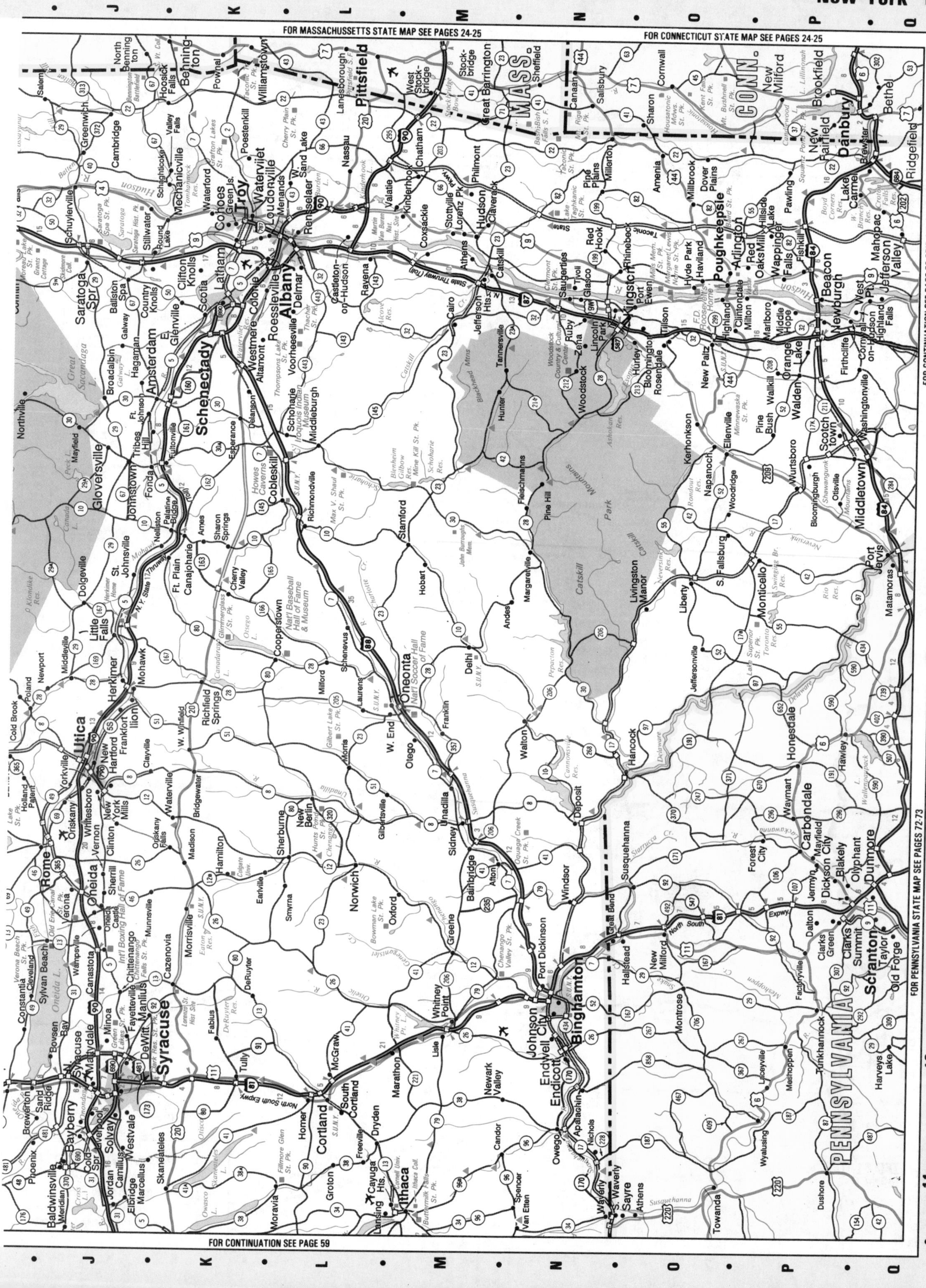

MASS

CONN

PENNSYLVANIA

Pittsfield · Troy · Albany · Schenectady · Saratoga Spr. · Amsterdam · Gloversville · Johnstown · Little Falls · Herkimer · Ilion · Mohawk · Utica · Rome · Oneida · Sherrill · Syracuse · Cazenovia · Hamilton · Norwich · Oneonta · Cooperstown · Cobleskill · Middleburgh · Catskill · Hudson · Kingston · Poughkeepsie · Newburgh · Middletown · Port Jervis · Monticello · Liberty · Margaretville · Delhi · Walton · Deposit · Hancock · Binghamton · Endicott · Endwell · Johnson City · Cortland · Ithaca · Oneonta · Sidney · Bainbridge · Afton · Greene · Oxford · Whitney Point · Marathon · Homer · Dryden · Groton · Moravia · Scranton · Carbondale · Honesdale · Waymart · Danbury · New Milford · Brewster · Carmel · Beacon · New Paltz · Ellenville · Walden · Goshen

Adirondack · Catskill Park · Catskill Mtns · Saratoga Nat'l Hist. Park · Nat'l Baseball Hall of Fame & Museum · Howes Caverns · Int'l Boxing Hall of Fame · Nat'l Soccer Hall of Fame

Hudson R. · Mohawk R. · Susquehanna R. · Delaware R. · Chenango R. · Unadilla R. · Schoharie Cr. · Oneida L. · Great Sacandaga L. · Ashokan Res. · Pepacton Res. · Cannonsville Res.

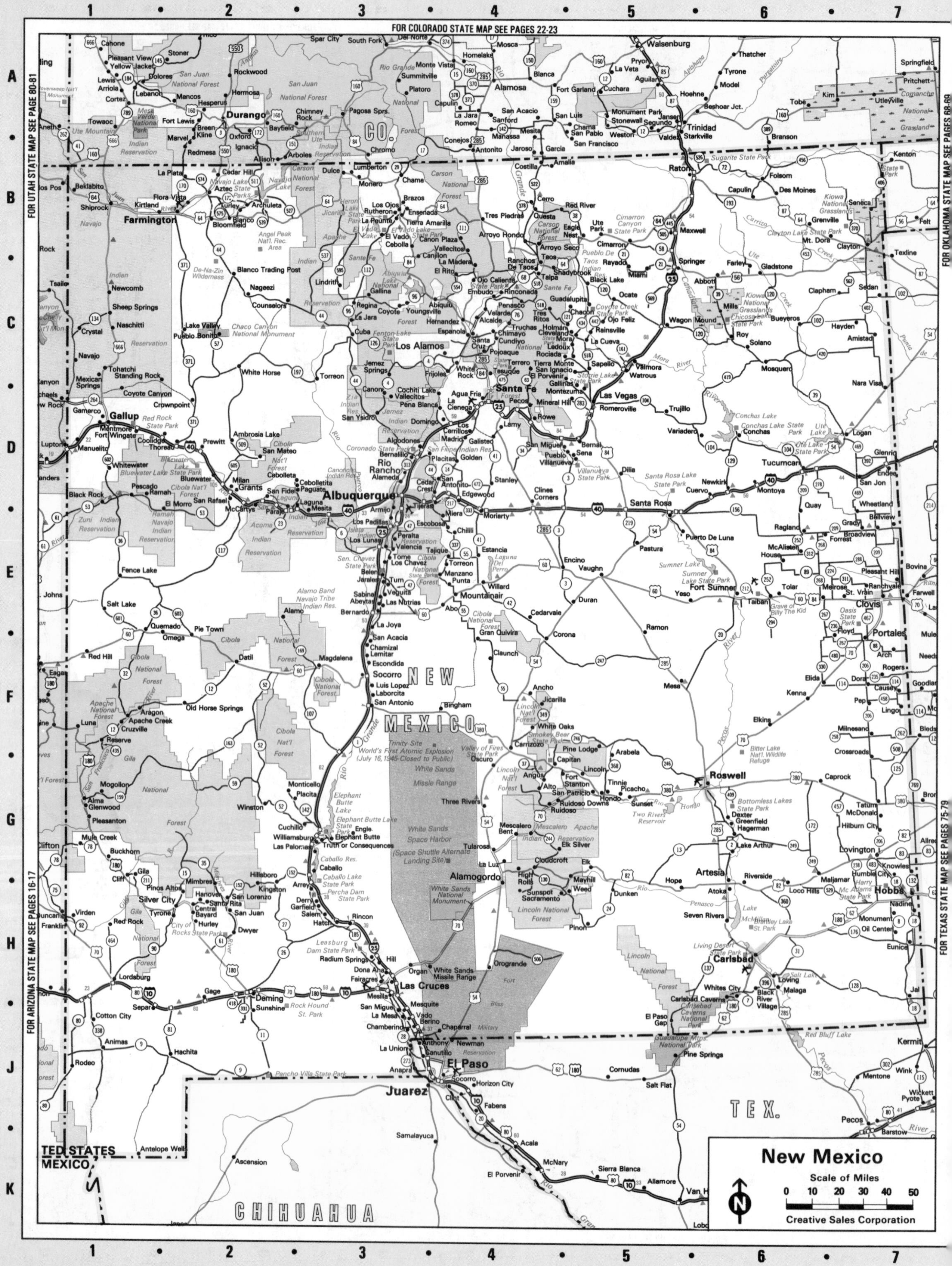

FOR COLORADO STATE MAP SEE PAGES 22-23

FOR UTAH STATE MAP SEE PAGE 80-81

FOR OKLAHOMA STATE MAP SEE PAGES 88-89

FOR ARIZONA STATE MAP SEE PAGES 16-17

FOR TEXAS STATE MAP SEE PAGES 75-79

NEW MEXICO

Major cities and places: Farmington, Durango, Gallup, Grants, Albuquerque, Rio Rancho, Santa Fe, Los Alamos, Las Vegas, Tucumcari, Clovis, Portales, Socorro, Truth or Consequences, Elephant Butte, Silver City, Deming, Las Cruces, El Paso, Juarez, Alamogordo, Roswell, Artesia, Carlsbad, Hobbs, Fort Sumner, Santa Rosa, Raton, Clayton.

CO

NEW MEXICO

TEX.

CHIHUAHUA

UNITED STATES / MEXICO

World's First Atomic Explosion (July 16, 1945-Closed to Public)

White Sands Missile Range

White Sands National Monument

Trinity Site

New Mexico

Scale of Miles

0 10 20 30 40 50

N

Creative Sales Corporation

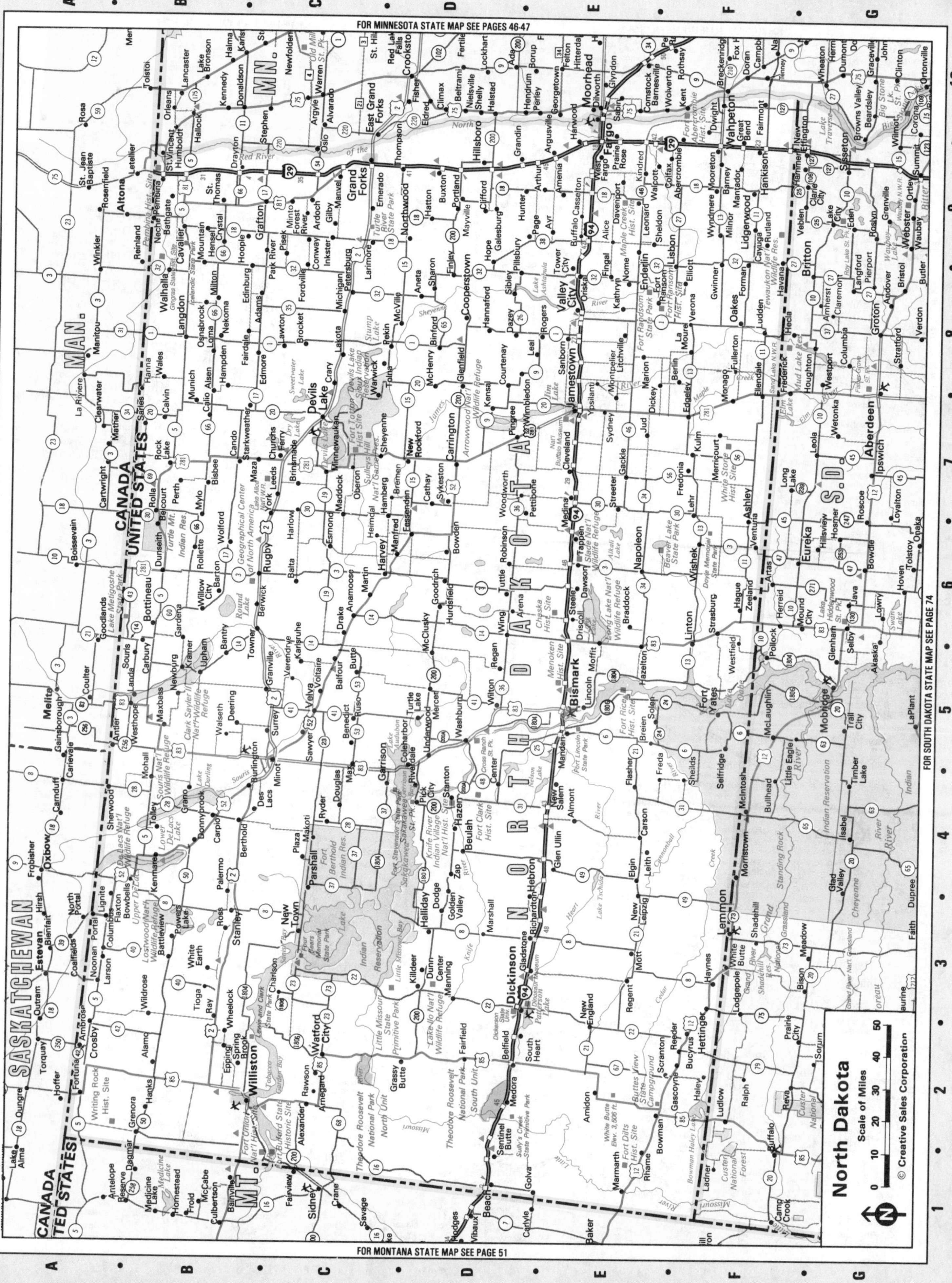

FOR MINNESOTA STATE MAP SEE PAGES 46-47

FOR MONTANA STATE MAP SEE PAGE 51

FOR SOUTH DAKOTA STATE MAP SEE PAGE 74

CANADA

UNITED STATES

SASKATCHEWAN

MANITOBA

MINNESOTA

MONTANA

SOUTH DAKOTA

NORTH DAKOTA

North Dakota
Scale of Miles
0 10 20 30 40 50

© Creative Sales Corporation

N

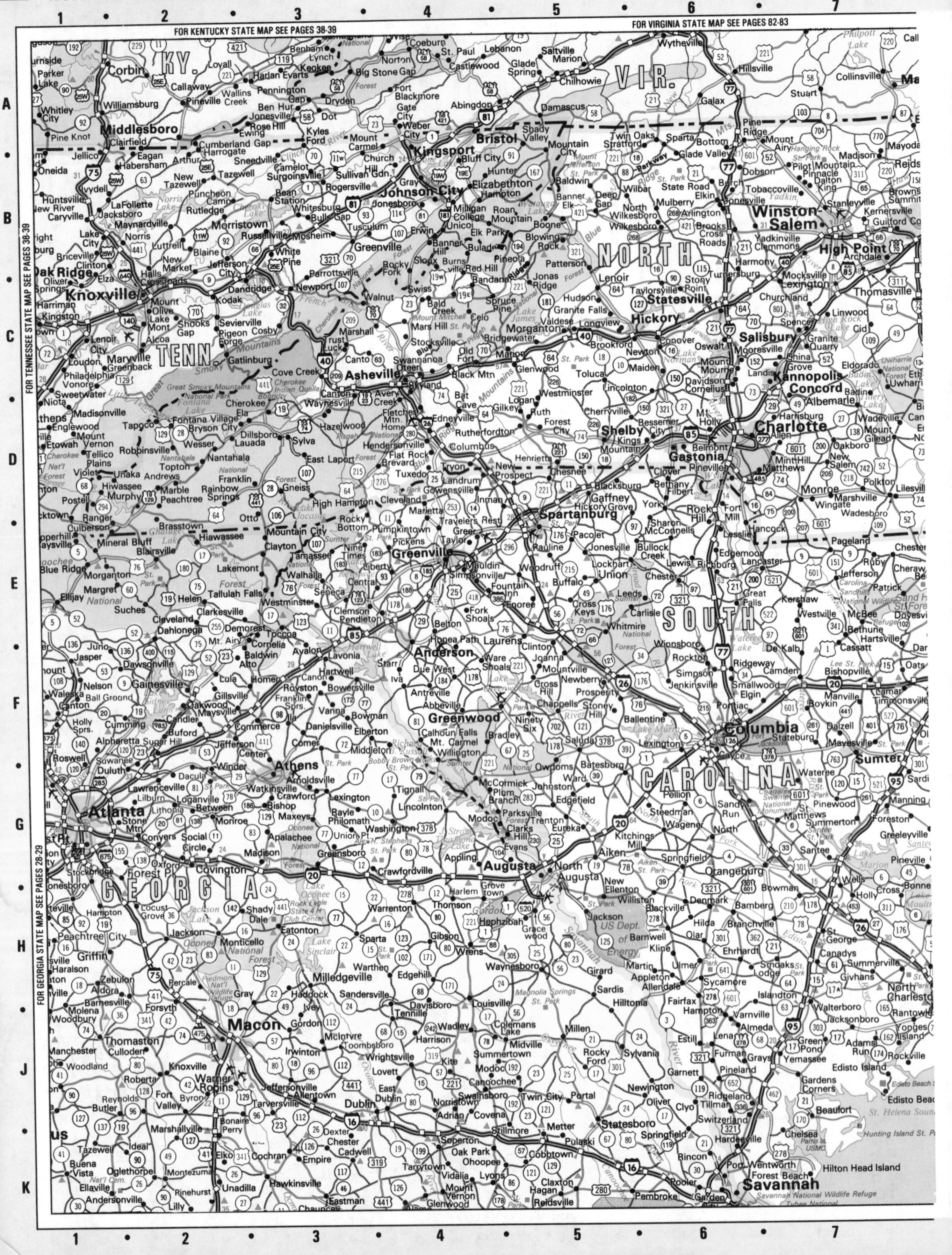
FOR KENTUCKY STATE MAP SEE PAGES 38-39
FOR VIRGINIA STATE MAP SEE PAGES 82-83
FOR TENNESSEE STATE MAP SEE PAGES 38-39
FOR GEORGIA STATE MAP SEE PAGES 28-29
KY.
VIR.
TENN.
NORTH
SOUTH
CAROLINA
GEORGIA
Knoxville
Asheville
Winston-Salem
High Point
Hickory
Charlotte
Gastonia
Greenville
Spartanburg
Columbia
Augusta
Atlanta
Athens
Macon
Savannah
Kingsport
Johnson City
Bristol
Greenwood
Anderson
Sumter
Salisbury
Kannapolis
Concord
Statesville
Dublin
Orangeburg
Great Smoky Mountains National Park
Hilton Head Island

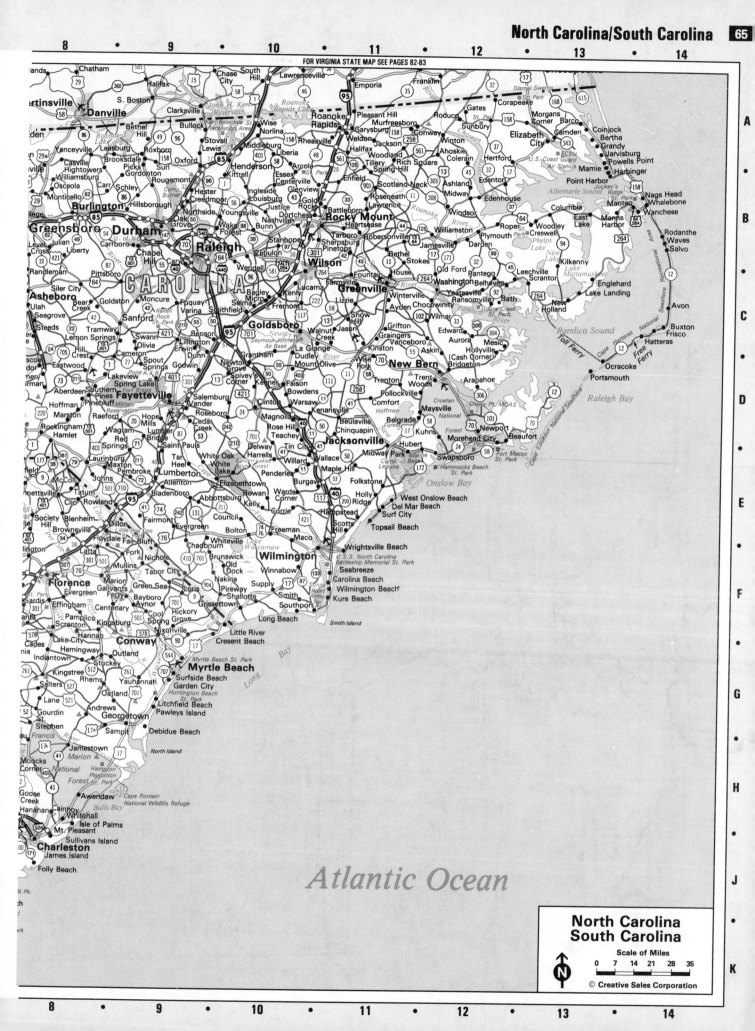

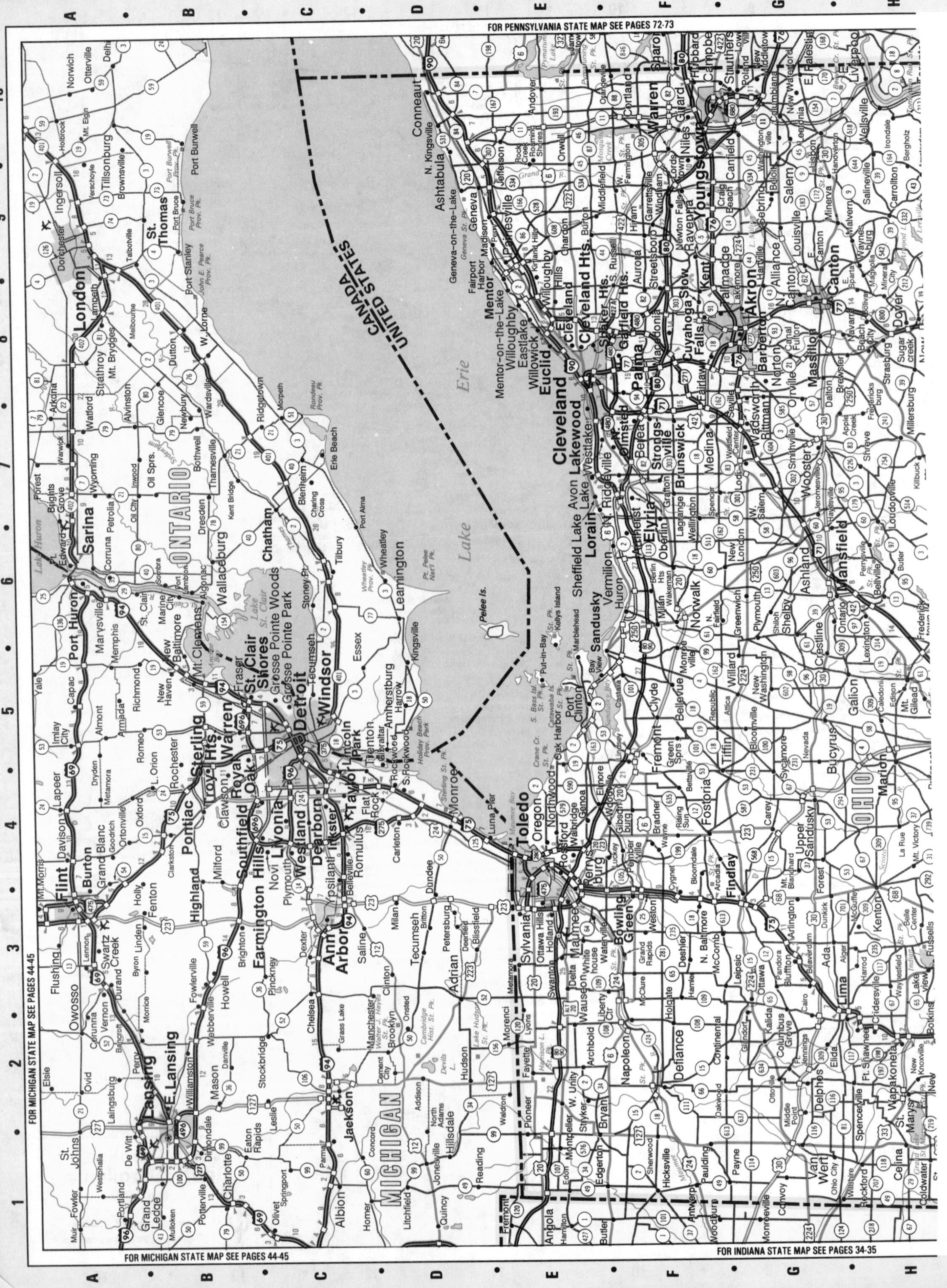

FOR PENNSYLVANIA STATE MAP SEE PAGES 72-73

FOR MICHIGAN STATE MAP SEE PAGES 44-45

FOR MICHIGAN STATE MAP SEE PAGES 44-45

FOR INDIANA STATE MAP SEE PAGES 34-35

CANADA
UNITED STATES

ONTARIO

MICHIGAN

OHIO

Lake Erie

Lake Huron

Lake St. Clair

London
Sarnia
Port Huron
Flint
Lansing
E. Lansing
Jackson
Ann Arbor
Detroit
Windsor
Warren
Sterling Hts.
Pontiac
Southfield
Livonia
Dearborn
Taylor
Westland
Farmington Hills
Highland
Chatham
Leamington
Toledo
Oregon
Bowling Green
Findlay
Lima
Van Wert
Defiance
Sandusky
Lorain
Elyria
Oberlin
Avon Lake
Sheffield Lake
Vermilion
Norwalk
Mansfield
Ashland
Wooster
Medina
Brunswick
Strongsville
Berea
Olmsted
Lakewood
Cleveland
Cleveland Hts.
Euclid
Willowick
Eastlake
Willoughby
Mentor
Mentor-on-the-Lake
Painesville
Fairport Harbor
Geneva
Geneva-on-the-Lake
Ashtabula
Conneaut
Parma
Garfield Hts.
Shaker Hts.
Cuyahoga Falls
Akron
Barberton
Wadsworth
Rittman
Canton
Massillon
Dover
Alliance
Salem
Sebring
Youngstown
Warren
Niles
Girard
Campbell
Struthers
Hubbard
Canfield
Bucyrus
Marion
Upper Sandusky
Kenton
Fremont
Tiffin
Fostoria
Port Clinton
Put-in-Bay
Pelee Is.
Kelleys Island

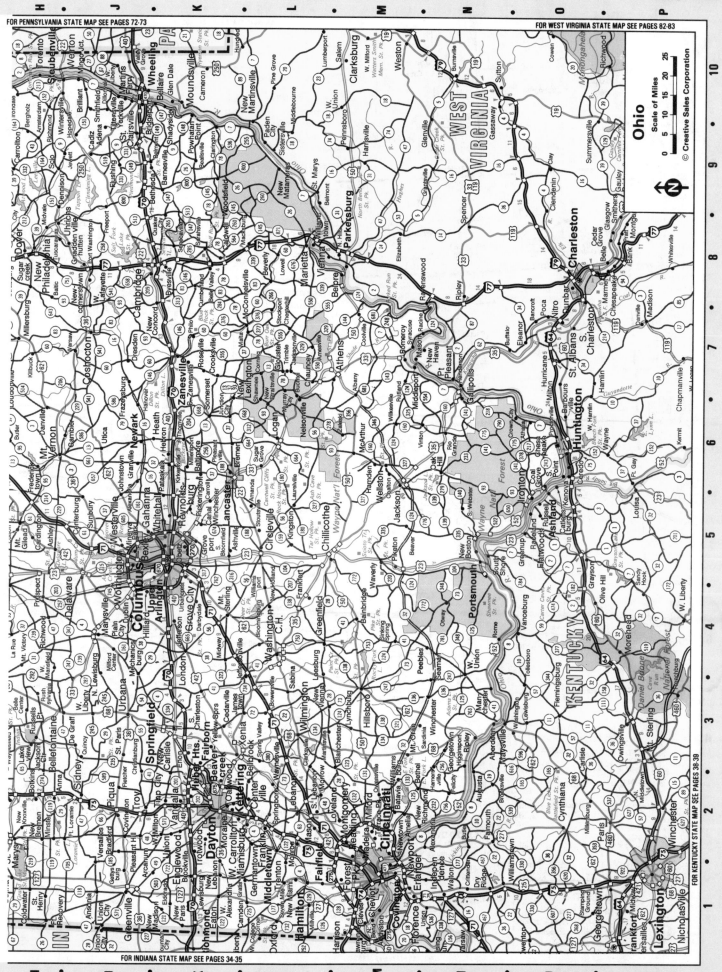

FOR PENNSYLVANIA STATE MAP SEE PAGES 72-73

FOR WEST VIRGINIA STATE MAP SEE PAGES 82-83

Ohio

Scale of Miles

© Creative Sales Corporation

FOR INDIANA STATE MAP SEE PAGES 34-35

FOR KENTUCKY STATE MAP SEE PAGES 38-39

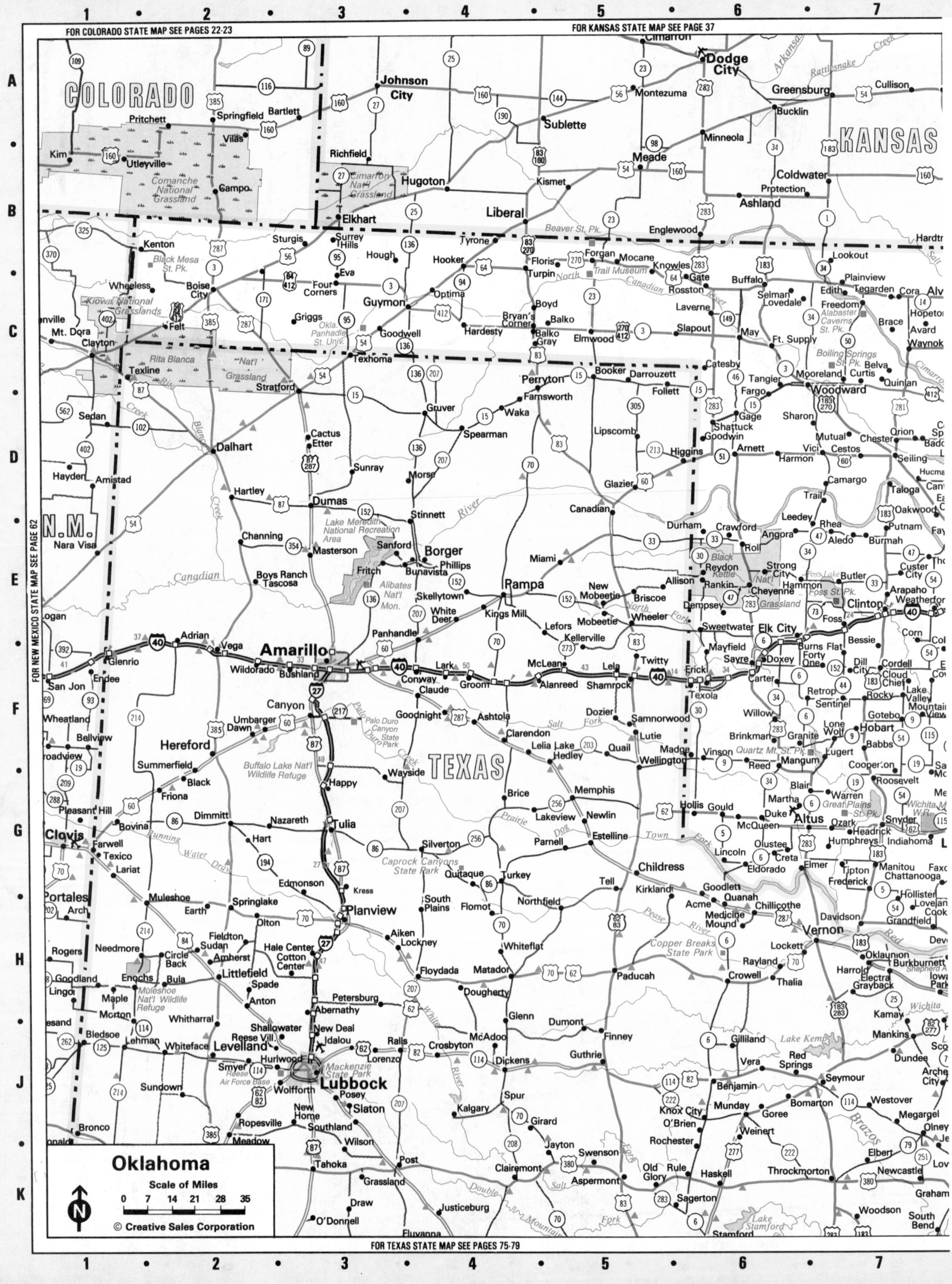
FOR COLORADO STATE MAP SEE PAGES 22-23
FOR KANSAS STATE MAP SEE PAGE 37
FOR NEW MEXICO STATE MAP SEE PAGE 62
FOR TEXAS STATE MAP SEE PAGES 75-79
COLORADO
KANSAS
N.M.
TEXAS
Oklahoma
Scale of Miles
0 7 14 21 28 35
© Creative Sales Corporation
N
Comanche National Grassland
Cimarron Nat'l Grassland
Kiowa National Grasslands
Rita Blanca Nat'l Grassland
Black Mesa St. Pk.
Okla. Panhandle St. Univ.
Lake Meredith National Recreation Area
Alibates Nat'l Mon.
Palo Duro Canyon State Park
Buffalo Lake Nat'l Wildlife Refuge
Caprock Canyons State Park
Muleshoe Nat'l Wildlife Refuge
Reese Air Force Base
Mackenzie State Park
Copper Breaks State Park
Lake Kemp
Black Kettle Nat'l Grassland
Foss St. Pk.
Quartz Mt. St. Pk.
Great Plains St. Pk.
Alabaster Caverns St. Pk.
Boiling Springs St. Pk.
Beaver St. Pk.
Trail Museum
Canadian
Red
Pease River
Prairie Dog Town Fork
Salt Fork
Double Mountain Fork
Brazos
Wichita
Cimarron
Arkansas
Springfield
Pritchett
Kim
Utleyville
Vilas
Campo
Bartlett
Richfield
Johnson City
Hugoton
Elkhart
Liberal
Sublette
Kismet
Meade
Montezuma
Dodge City
Minneola
Greensburg
Bucklin
Cullison
Coldwater
Protection
Ashland
Englewood
Kenton
Boise City
Wheeless
Felt
Clayton
Mt. Dora
Texline
Sturgis
Surrey Hills
Eva
Four Corners
Griggs
Guymon
Goodwell
Texhoma
Stratford
Hough
Hooker
Optima
Tyrone
Hardesty
Bryan's Corner
Turpin
Floris
Forgan
Mocane
Knowles
Gate
Rosston
Boyd
Balko
Balko Gray
Elmwood
Laverne
Slapout
Buffalo
May
Selman
Lovedale
Ft. Supply
Lookout
Plainview
Edith
Tegarden
Freedom
Cora
Brace
Avard
Waynoka
Woodward
Mooreland
Curtis
Belva
Quinlan
Tangier
Fargo
Gage
Shattuck
Catesby
Sharon
Mutual
Vici
Cestos
Chester
Orion
Seiling
Arnett
Harmon
Camargo
Taloga
Trail
Leedey
Rhea
Putnam
Oakwood
Aledo
Burmah
Custer City
Butler
Hammon
Strong City
Cheyenne
Rankin
Reydon
Roll
Angora
Crawford
Durham
Arapaho
Weatherford
Clinton
Foss
Elk City
Sayre
Doxey
Carter
Burns Flat
Bessie
Corn
Dill City
Cordell
Cloud Chief
Rocky
Retrop
Sentinel
Lake Valley
Gotebo
Hobart
Lone Wolf
Granite
Lugert
Willow
Brinkman
Mangum
Reed
Vinson
Babbs
Cooperton
Roosevelt
Blair
Warren
Martha
Altus
Duke
Gould
Hollis
McQueen
Ozark
Headrick
Snyder
Humphreys
Olustee
Creta
Eldorado
Elmer
Tipton
Manitou
Chattanooga
Frederick
Hollister
Loveland
Grandfield
Davidson
Vernon
Oklaunion
Harrold
Electra
Burkburnett
Kenton
Dalhart
Sedan
Hayden
Amistad
Nara Visa
Hartley
Channing
Boys Ranch
Tascosa
Dumas
Cactus
Etter
Sunray
Gruver
Spearman
Stinnett
Morse
Masterson
Sanford
Fritch
Borger
Phillips
Bunavista
Skellytown
White Deer
Panhandle
Perryton
Farnsworth
Waka
Booker
Darrouzett
Follett
Lipscomb
Higgins
Glazier
Canadian
Miami
Pampa
Kings Mill
Lefors
Mobeetie
New Mobeetie
Briscoe
Allison
Wheeler
Kellerville
McLean
Alanreed
Lela
Shamrock
Twitty
Texola
Erick
Sweetwater
Mayfield
Adrian
Vega
Glenrio
Endee
San Jon
Wildorado
Bushland
Amarillo
Canyon
Umbarger
Dawn
Conway
Claude
Lark
Groom
Goodnight
Ashtola
Clarendon
Lelia Lake
Hedley
Dozier
Samnorwood
Lutie
Quail
Madge
Wellington
Hereford
Summerfield
Black
Friona
Bovina
Dimmitt
Nazareth
Hart
Happy
Tulia
Wayside
Silverton
Quitaque
Turkey
Brice
Lakeview
Memphis
Newlin
Estelline
Parnell
Childress
Kirkland
Tell
Northfield
Clovis
Farwell
Texico
Lariat
Portales
Muleshoe
Earth
Springlake
Olton
Edmonson
Kress
Plainview
Aiken
Lockney
South Plains
Flomot
Whiteflat
Floydada
Matador
Paducah
Goodlett
Quanah
Acme
Medicine Mound
Chillicothe
Crowell
Rayland
Thalia
Lockett
Needmore
Circle Back
Sudan
Amherst
Fieldton
Littlefield
Hale Center
Cotton Center
Spade
Anton
Enochs
Bula
Maple
Morton
Whitharral
Petersburg
Abernathy
Dougherty
Shallowater
New Deal
Idalou
Ralls
Crosbyton
McAdoo
Dumont
Finney
Glenn
Guthrie
Dickens
Reese Vill.
Levelland
Whiteface
Lehman
Bledsoe
Smyer
Hurlwood
Lubbock
Wolfforth
Lorenzo
Slaton
Posey
Sundown
Ropesville
New Home
Southland
Wilson
Meadow
Tahoka
Post
Grassland
Draw
O'Donnell
Justiceburg
Kalgary
Spur
Girard
Jayton
Swenson
Clairemont
Aspermont
Old Glory
Rule
Rochester
Haskell
Sagerton
Stamford
Fluvanna
Bronco
Gilliland
Vera
Red Springs
Benjamin
Knox City
O'Brien
Munday
Goree
Weinert
Seymour
Bomarton
Westover
Megargel
Olney
Throckmorton
Elbert
Newcastle
Graham
Woodson
South Bend
Dundee
Mankins
Kamay
Archer City
Rogers
Goodland
Lingo
Wheatland
Bellview
Pleasant Hill
Logan
Clayton

FOR KANSAS STATE MAP SEE PAGE 37

FOR MISSOURI STATE MAP SEE PAGES 48-49

FOR ARKANSAS STATE MAP SEE PAGE 15

FOR TEXAS STATE MAP SEE PAGES 75-79

When travelling on highways in states where there are long stretches of open space, it is important to watch your speed. The 65 mile per hour speed limit applies only to rural areas where it is clearly marked. Drivers should always observe the posted speed limit. Remember, speed kills, so take it easy.

FOR WASHINGTON STATE MAP SEE PAGES 84-85

FOR CALIFORNIA STATE MAP SEE PAGES 18-21

FOR WASHINGTON STATE MAP SEE PAGES 84-85

Vernita Basin City Connell Hay Pullman Moscow Deary Dworshak Reservoir National Forest

U.S. Dept. of Energy Mesa Ringold Kahlotus Ayer Riparia Pendwaya Almota Troy Juliaetta Kendrick Cavendish Headquarters

Outlook Sunnyside West Richland Benton City Eltopia Clyde Pleasant View Starbuck Gould City Dodge Illia Wawawai Colton Genesee Lenore Reck Orofino Pierce

Richland Kennewick Pasco Burbank Glade Page Eureka Prescott Pomeroy Pataha Uniontown Spalding Myrtle Gifford Greer Weippe

Prosser Kiona Finley Hover Wallula Lowden Rulo Sudbury Dixie Clarkston Asotin Lapwai Mohler Kamiah

Paterson Plymouth Touchet College Place Walla Walla Cloverland Anatone Waha Craigmont Ferdinand Greencreek Kooskia Stites

Umatilla McNary Hermiston Stanfield Umapine Milton-Freewater Troy Rogersburg Keuterville Cottonwood Harpster Lowell

Boardman Helix Weston Flora Fenn Grangeville Mount Idaho Golden Elk City

Echo Adams Athena Gibbon Minam Wallowa White Bird Orogrande Dixie

Pendleton Mission Meacham Elgin Summerville Imbler Lostine Imnaha Lucile Salmon River Breaks Primitive Area

Pilot Rock Kamela Alicel Island City Enterprise Riggins Payette Gospel Hump Wilderness

Ukiah LaGrande Cove Union Joseph Pollock Burgdorf Warren

North Powder Telocaset Homestead Cuprum Tamarack New Meadows Meadows Yellow Pine Stibnite

Medical Springs Haines Halfway Starkey McCall Lake Fork IDAHO

Granite Sumpter Baker City New Bridge Richland Fruitvale Council Donnelly Warm Lake

Greenhorn Austin Durkee Pleasant Valley Cambridge Midvale Indian Valley Cascade

Prairie City Whitney Bridgeport Smiths Ferry Cape Horn Sunbeam

Mount Vernon John Day Canyon City Unity Ironside Huntington Brogan Weiser Ola Banks Crouch Garden Valley Lowman Stanley

Seneca Jamieson Payette Jct. Payette Sweet Gardena Centerville Placerville Pioneerville

Westfall Willow Creek Vale Ontario Fruitland New Plymouth Horse Shoe Bend Idaho City

Drewsey Drinkwater Pass Harper Nyssa Owyhee Letha Montour Pearl Atlanta

Burns Hines Juntura Adrian Parma Emmett Middleton Eagle Meridian Garden Valley

Riley Lawen Crane Roswell Wilder Caldwell Star Boise Ketchum

Warm Springs Valley New Princeton Homedale Nampa Mayfield Pine

Diamond Marsing Kuna Bowmont Melba Orchard Corral Fairfield

Frenchglen Sheaville The Craters Reynolds Murphy Mountain Home Hill City

Andrews Jordon Valley Silver City Oreana Hammett King Hill Bliss

Arock Lava Beds Grand View Bruneau Glenns Ferry Hagerman

Rome Triangle Bruneau Hot Sprs. Castleford Buhl Filer Twin Falls

Burns Jct. Grasmere Hollister

Fields Blue Mtn. Pass Riddle

Charles Sheldon Denio Denio Junction McDermitt Owyhee

FOR NEVADA STATE MAP SEE PAGE 54

FOR IDAHO STATE MAP SEE PAGE 31

Oregon

Scale of Miles
0 7 14 21 28 35

N

© Creative Sales Corporation

FOR NEW YORK STATE MAP SEE PAGES 58-61

Grid columns: 1 2 3 4 5 6 7
Grid rows: A B C D E F G H J K

Lake Erie

PENNSYLVANIA

OH — OHIO

WV — West Virginia

MD — Maryland

Major places:
Erie, N. East, Fairview, Lake City, Girard, McKean, Conneaut, Albion, Springboro, Conneautville, Linesville, Edinboro, Union City, Corry, Youngsville, Warren, Bradford, Smethport, Port Allegany, Coudersport, Walton

Jamestown, Frewsburg, Salamanca, Allegany, Olean, Bolivar, Portville, Shinglehouse, Eldred, Oswayo, Austin, Emporium

Meadville, Cambridge Springs, Venango, Saegertown, Blooming Valley, Townville, Centerville, Titusville, Pleasantville, Hydetown, Tidioute, Clarendon, Kane, Mt. Jewett, Sizerville, St. Marys, Johnsonburg, Wilcox, Russell City, Ridgway, Driftwood, Westport, Renovo

Cochranton, Franklin, Oil City, Rouseville, Cooperstown, Tionesta, Sugarcreek, Polk, Stoneboro, Mercer, Jackson Center, Clintonville, Emlenton, Knox, Clarion, Strattanville, Brockway, Brookville, Corsica, Falls Creek, Reynoldsville, Du Bois, Clearfield, Curwensville, Philipsburg, Osceola Mills, Houtzdale, Port Matilda, Bellefonte, Milesburg, Snow Shoe, State College

Greenville, Jamestown, New Lebanon, Sandy Lake, Sharon, Hermitage, Farrell, Wheatland, Sharpsville, Grove City, Harrisville, Slippery Rock, New Wilmington, New Castle, Bessemer, Youngstown, New Brighton, Beaver Falls, Ellwood City, Zelienople, Harmony, Evans City, Butler, Saxonburg, Freeport, Kittanning, Ford City, Rural Valley, Punxsutawney, Big Run, Grampian, Lumber City, Glen Hope, Ramey, Coalport, Irvona, Tyrone, Altoona, Hollidaysburg

Pittsburgh, Carnegie, Dormont, Bethel Park, McKeesport, Clairton, Monroeville, Murrysville, Latrobe, Greensburg, Johnstown, Windber, Ebensburg, Cresson, Portage, Gallitzin, Loretto, Patton, Carrolltown, Indiana, Homer City, Blairsville, Saltsburg, Vandergrift, New Kensington, Oakmont, Plum, Wilkinsburg, Bellevue, Aliquippa, Ambridge, Coraopolis, Monaca, Conway, Baden, Economy, Mars

Washington, Canonsburg, Monessen, Charleroi, Belle Vernon, California, Brownsville, Connellsville, Uniontown, Masontown, Point Marion, Waynesburg, Carmichaels, Mt. Pleasant, Scottdale, Everson, Ligonier, Somerset, Rockwood, Berlin, Meyersdale, Salisbury, Hyndman, Bedford, Everett, Breezewood, McConnellsburg, Mercersburg, Chambersburg, Greencastle

WV — Morgantown, Westover, Frostburg, Cumberland, Hagerstown, Williamsport, Hancock

FOR OHIO STATE MAP SEE PAGES 66-67

FOR WEST VIRGINIA STATE MAP SEE PAGES 82-83

FOR MARYLAND STATE MAP SEE PAGES 42-43

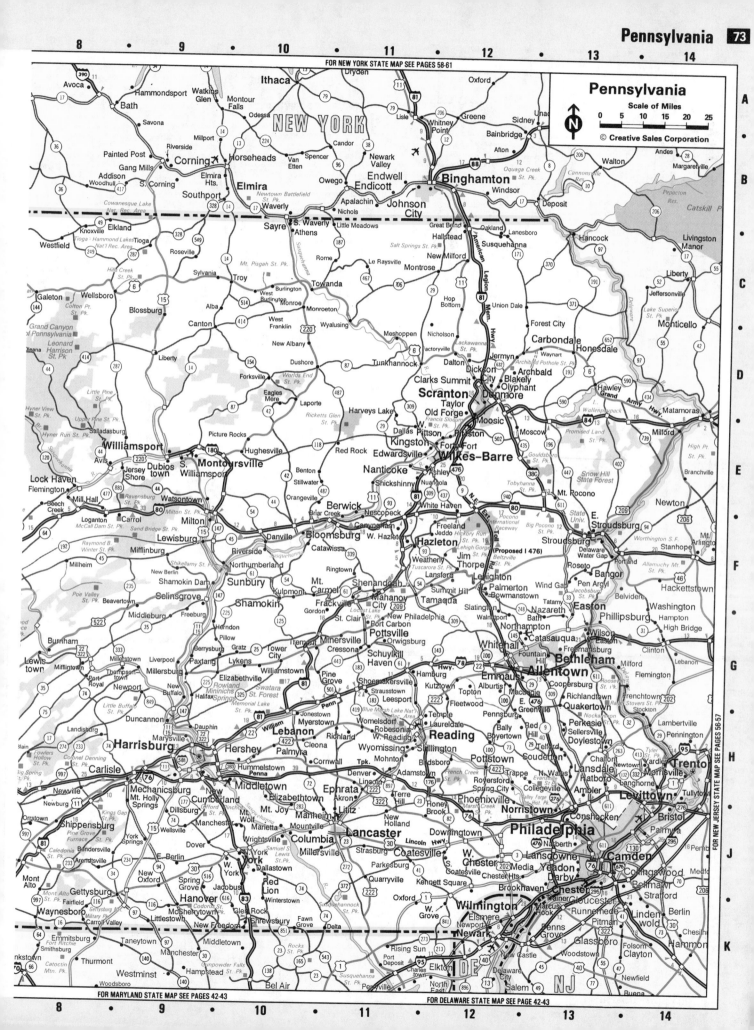

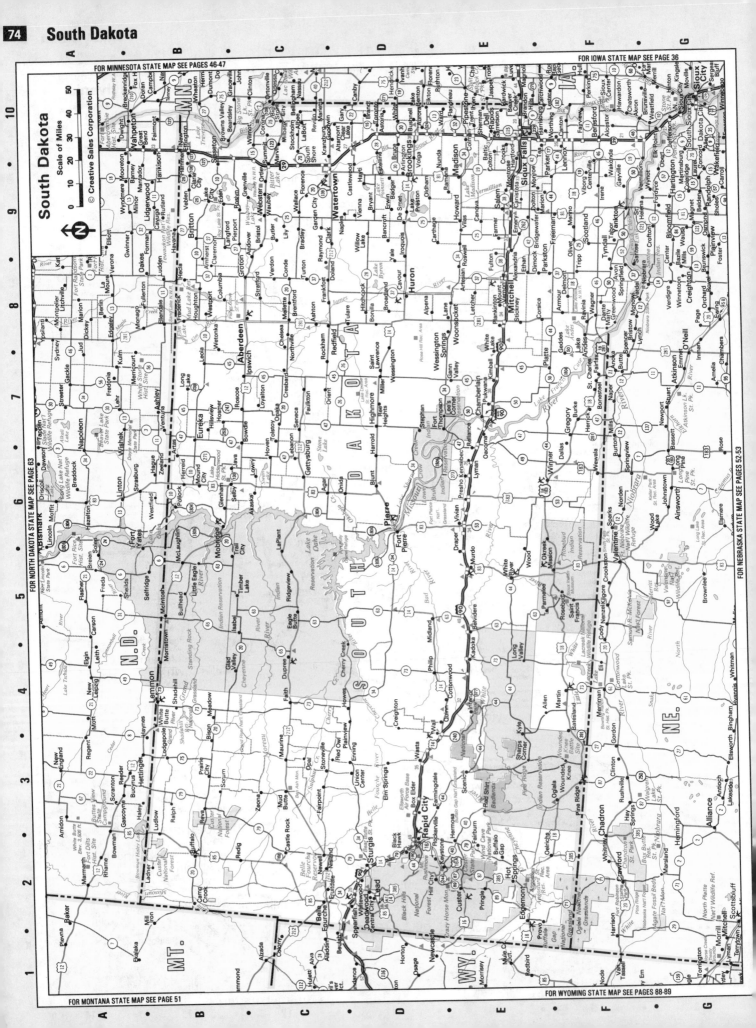

South Dakota

Scale of Miles

© Creative Sales Corporation

FOR MINNESOTA STATE MAP SEE PAGES 46-47
FOR IOWA STATE MAP SEE PAGE 36
FOR NORTH DAKOTA STATE MAP SEE PAGE 63
FOR NEBRASKA STATE MAP SEE PAGES 52-53
FOR MONTANA STATE MAP SEE PAGE 51
FOR WYOMING STATE MAP SEE PAGES 88-89

Texas

Scale of Miles

0 8 16 24 32 40

© Creative Sales Corporation

N

FOR NEW MEXICO STATE MAP SEE PAGE 62
FOR CONTINUATION SEE PAGE 76
FOR CONTINUATION SEE PAGE 78

NEW MEXICO

TEXAS

UNITED STATES

MEXICO

CHIHUAHUA

Ancho
Jicarilla
White Oaks
Carrizozo
Capitan
Lincoln
Pine Lodge
Arabela
Mesa
Elida
Rogers
Needmore
Circle Back
Fieldton
Sudan
Amherst
Littlefield
Dora
Pep
Goodland
Enochs
Bula
Spa
Lingo
Maple
Morton
Whitharral
Milnesand
Bledsoe
Lehman
Whiteface
Levelland
Reese V
Smyer
Crossroads
Sundown
Ropes
Meadow
Brownfield
Bronco
McDonald
Hilburn City
Lovington
Denver City
Wellman
Loop
Welc
Humble City
Seagraves
Knowles
Hobbs
Seminole
Monument
Nadine
Oil Center
Eunice
Frankel City
Patricia
Jal
Gardendale
Midland
Kermit
Notrees
Odessa
Wink
Monahans
Penwell
Pecos
Barstow
Wickett
Pyote
Royalty
Crane
Toyah
Coyanosa
Grandfalls
Imperial
McCamey
Girvin
Fort Stockton
Bakersfield
Iraa
Saragosa
Balmorhea
She
Valentine
Fort Davis
Alpine
Sanderson
Dryden
Marfa
Plata
Shafter
Ojinaga
Redford
Terlingua
Study Butte
Chisos Basin
Boquillas del Carmen
Big Bend National Park
Chihuahua

Roswell
Dexter
Greenfield
Hagerman
Lake Arthur
Artesia
Riverside
Loco Hills
Atoka
Maljamar
Seven Rivers
Lake McMillan
Carlsbad
Black River Village
Loving
Malaga
Whites City
Carlsbad Caverns
Jal

El Paso
Ciudad Juarez
Las Cruces
Alamogordo
Tularosa
La Luz
Mescalero
Cloudcroft
High Rolls
Sacramento
Weed
Mayhill
Dunken
Hope
Pinon
Three Rivers
Ruidoso
Ruidoso Downs
San Patricio
Hondo
Tinnie
Picacho
Sunset
Angus
Alto
Bent

White Sands Nat'l Mon.
White Sands Missile Range
Fort Bliss Military Reservation
Lincoln National Forest
Apache Mescalero Indian Reservation
Two Rivers Res.
Guadalupe Mtns. National Park
Carlsbad Caverns National Park
Davis Mountains State Park
Monahans Sandhills State Park
Balmorhea State Park
Fort Leaton State Park
Muleshoe Nat'l Wildlife Refuge
Franklin Mt. State Park
Magoffin House State Park
Hueco Tanks State Park
Mesilla
San Miguel
La Mesa
Chamberino
Anthony
Newman
Canutillo
Univ. of Texas at El Paso
Socorro
Clint
Fabens
San Elizario
Tornillo
Acala
Fort Hancock
McNary
Horizon City
Dell City
Cornudas
Salt Flat
El Paso Gap
Orla
Mentone
Sierra Blanca
Allamore
Van Horn
Lobo
Rincon
Fairacres
Dona Ana
Organ
Chaparral
Berino
Engle

Rio Grande
Big Bend National Park

Lincoln National Forest

FOR NEW MEXICO STATE MAP SEE PAGE 62

FOR CONTINUATION SEE PAGE 75

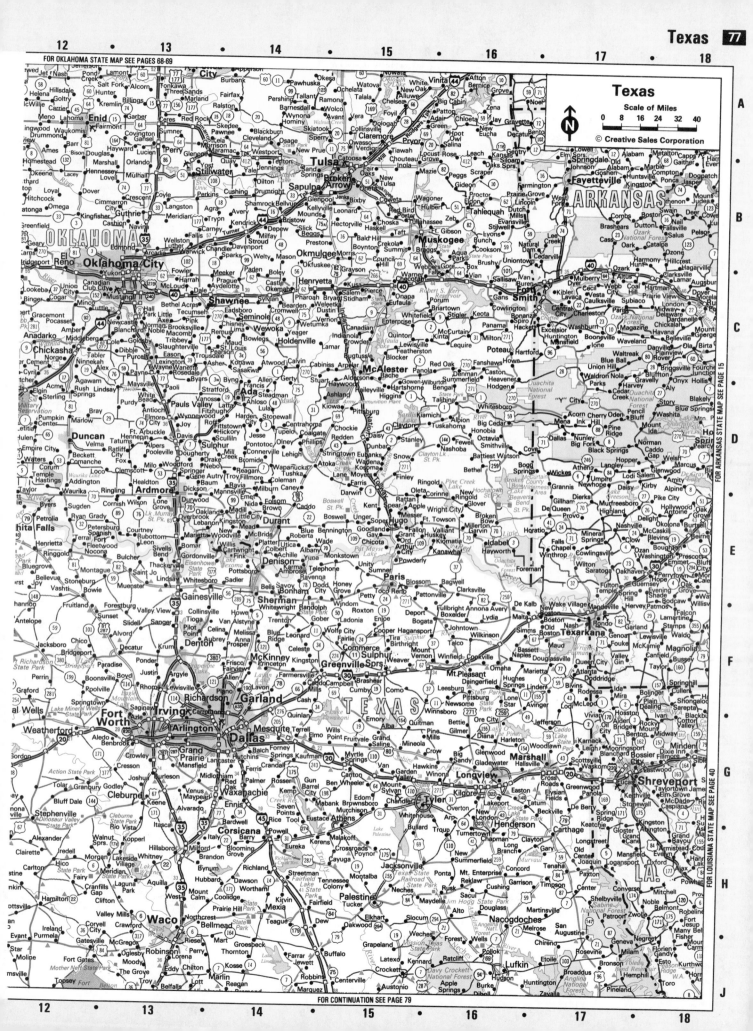

FOR CONTINUATION SEE PAGE 76

FOR CONTINUATION SEE PAGE 75

6 · 7 · 8 · 9 · 10 · 11

J
K
L
M
N
P
Q
R
S

Rankin
McCamey
Mertzon
Knickerbocker
Christoval
Big Lake
67
Barnhart
Eden
Melvin
Rochelle
Richland Springs
Lometa
Adamsville
385
Girvin
Pecos
349
18
Fort Stockton
Brady
San Saba
Cop
Lampasas
14
35
Bakersfield
Iraan
190
Calf Creek
71
Voca
Fredonia
Cherokee
Tow
Buchanan Lake
23
Menard
Hext
Katemcy
Pontotoc
Valley Spring
Bluffton
Llano
Buchanan Dam
Longh
Sheffield
42
10
Ozona
137
Eldorado
190
Fort McKavett
London
Grit
29
Mason
29
Kingsland
Lake L. B. Johnson
Marble Falls
71
290
Fort Lancaster State Park
37
Fort McKavett State Park
377
Lake Lyndon B. Johnson
285
163
Sonora
57
Roosevelt
Junction
Doss
87
Cherry Spring
Willow City
Round Mountain
Spicew
Big Canyon
Segovia
Loyal Valley
16
Enchanted Rock State Park
Sanderson
River
Juno
Telegraph
Harper
290
Fredericksburg
Johnson City
Stonewall
Hye
Lyndon B. Johnson State Park
Dryden
349
55
Rocksprings
54
Mountain Home
Hunt
Ingram
27
Luckenbach
Blanco State Park
Blanco
90
Langtry
Loma Alta
41
Kerrville
39
16
Center Pt.
33
Sisterdale
Spring Branch
S
Rio Grande
377
Kerrville State Park
Comfort
10
46
Ne
Bra
Carta Valley
Barksdale
Camp Verde
Medina
Pipecreek
Seminole Canyon State Park
Comstock
Camp Wood
Lost Maples State Park
Vanderpool
Bandera
Leon Springs
Conyers Sch
Amistad National Recreation Area
222 377
Devils Lake
Lake Walk
Garner State Park
Utopia
Tarpley
Lake Hills
Mico
16
Concan
55
Medina Lake
Universal City
San
Del Rio
127
Riomedina
Jose Antonio
Navarro
Castroville
Martinez
Ciudad Acuna
Fort Clark Springs
Brackettville
Knippa
D'Hanis
173
90
Dunlay
Kelly Air
Force Base
32
Elm
Spofford
Dabney
Blewett
90
Uvalde
Sabinal
Hondo
Natalia
Lytle
Somerset
131
Frio
Devine
16
Leming
Quemado
Normandy
Frio Town
Moore
173
Bigfoot
281
Pleasant
57
Batesville
La Pryor
57
Divot
35
22
Jourdanton
Eagle Pass
Crystal City
Pearsall
Charlotte
85
97
Christine
Piedras Negras
277
Brundage
Dilley
85
Hindes
Campbellton
Whitsett
Carrizo Springs
Big Wells
Woodward
Millett
Los Angeles
72
Tilden
Three Rivers
Asherton
Cotulla
97
Fowlerton
Calliham
George We
Catarina
16
53
83
Artesia Wells
Nueces
TEXAS
Nuevo Rosita
44
Encinal
Choke Canyon Lake
57
44
Freer
Ora
44
San Diego
339
Ben I
30
Laredo St. Univ.
35
59
COAHUILA
Benavides
16
Lake Casa Blanca State Park
359
Rio
Nuevo Laredo
Laredo
359
Oilton
Realitos
Concepcion
85
Bruni
Mirando City
Ramirez
Monclova
Hebbronville
285
San Ygnacio
Escobas
Randado
83
16
Bustamante
Falcon Res.
Lopeno
2
Falcon
La Gloria
Santa Elen
San Isidro
Nueva Guerrero
Falcon State Park
El Sauz
La Reforma
Sabinas Hidalgo
Cd. Mier
Roma
Rio Grande City
Edinbur
57
Cd. Camargo
83
La Grulla
La Joya
Mission
107
53
Sullivan City
Bentson-Rio Grande Valley State Park
NUEVO LEON
Presa De El Azucar
54
Reynosa
40
San Pedro de las Colonias
Encir
UNITED STATES
MEXICO
Rio Grande

Monterrey

6 · 7 · 8 · 9 · 10 · 11

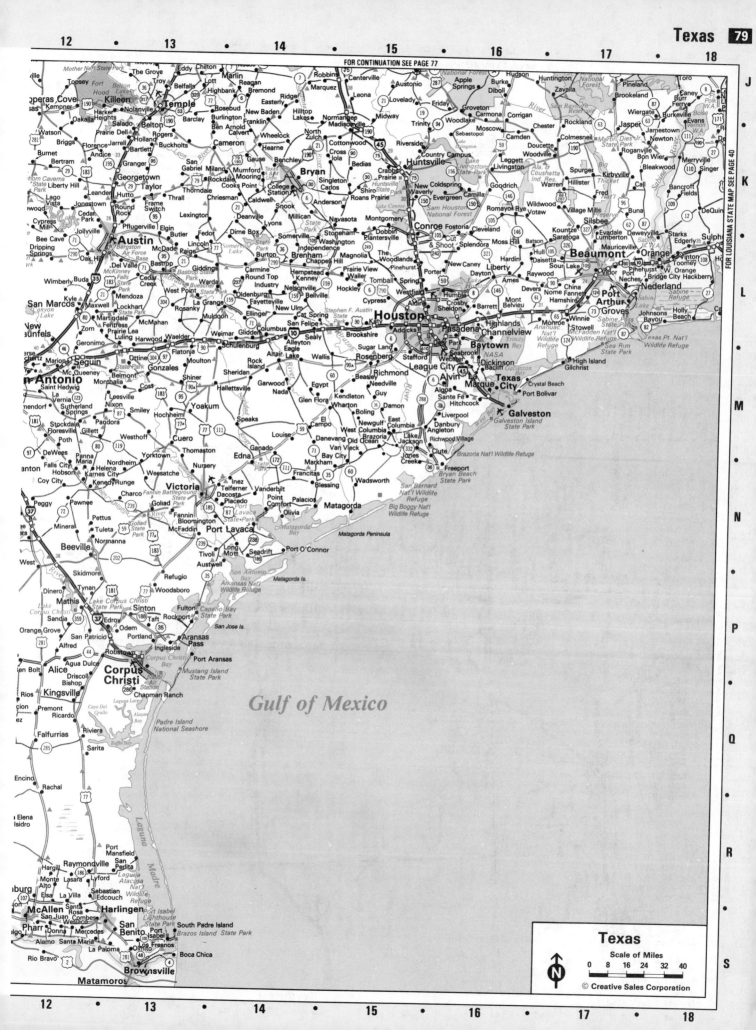

FOR CONTINUATION SEE PAGE 77

FOR LOUISIANA STATE MAP SEE PAGE 40

Gulf of Mexico

Texas

Scale of Miles

0   8   16   24   32   40

© Creative Sales Corporation

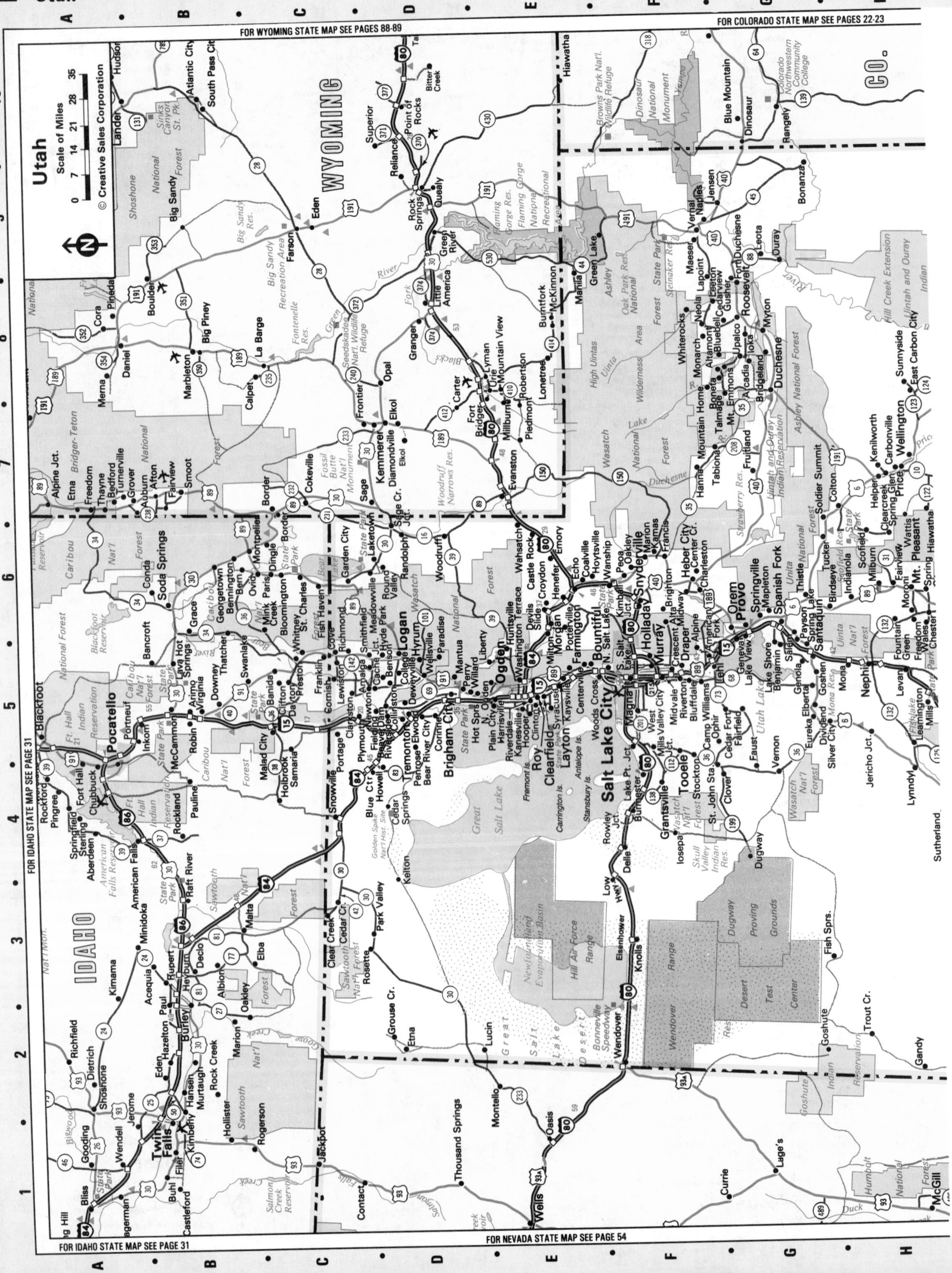

Utah

Scale of Miles
0 7 14 21 28 35
© Creative Sales Corporation

N

FOR WYOMING STATE MAP SEE PAGES 88-89
FOR COLORADO STATE MAP SEE PAGES 22-23
FOR IDAHO STATE MAP SEE PAGE 31
FOR NEVADA STATE MAP SEE PAGE 54

WYOMING

IDAHO

CO.

Salt Lake City
Provo
Orem
Ogden
Logan
Pocatello
Blackfoot
Twin Falls
Brigham City
Tooele
Nephi
Vernal
Roosevelt
Duchesne
Price
Evanston
Rock Springs
Green River
Wendover
Wells

Great Salt Lake

Wasatch National Forest
Ashley National Forest
Uinta National Forest
Caribou National Forest
Sawtooth National Forest
Dinosaur National Monument
Flaming Gorge National Recreation Area

High Uintas Wilderness

Dugway Proving Grounds
Hill Air Force Range
Desert Test Center

Uintah and Ouray Indian Reservation
Fort Hall Indian Reservation
Goshute Indian Reservation
Skull Valley Indian Res.

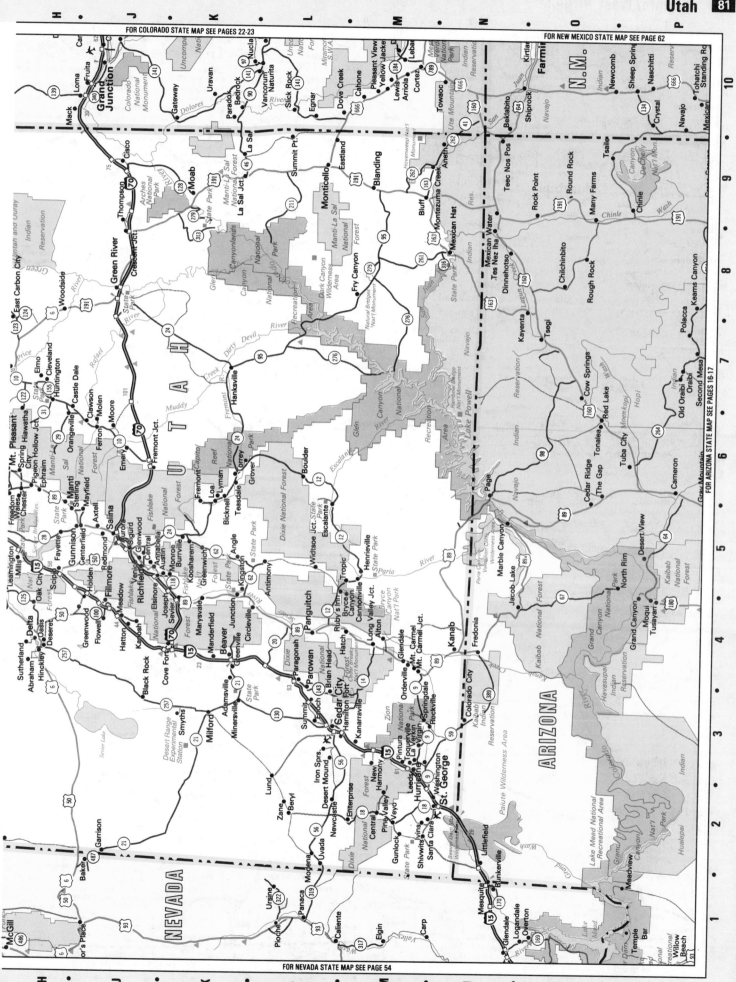

FOR COLORADO STATE MAP SEE PAGES 22-23

FOR NEW MEXICO STATE MAP SEE PAGE 62

FOR ARIZONA STATE MAP SEE PAGES 16-17

FOR OHIO STATE MAP SEE PAGES 66-67

FOR PENNSYLVANIA STATE MAP SEE PAGES 72-73

FOR OHIO STATE MAP SEE PAGES 66-67

FOR KENTUCKY STATE MAP SEE PAGES 38-39

FOR TENNESSEE STATE MAP SEE PAGES 38-39

FOR NORTH CAROLINA STATE MAP SEE PAGES 64-65

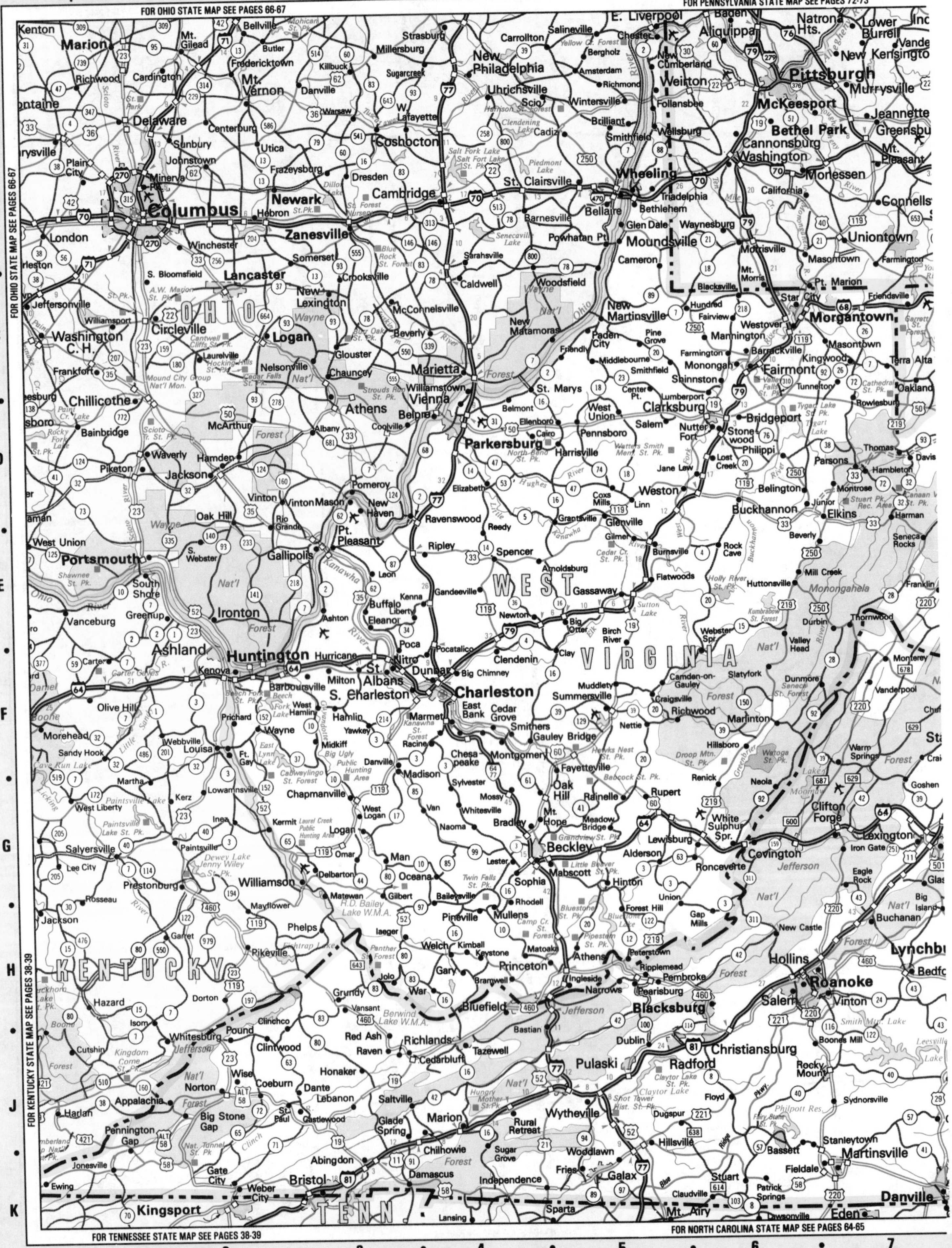

Column numbers: 1 2 3 4 5 6 7

Row letters: A B C D E F G H J K

OHIO

WEST VIRGINIA

KENTUCKY

TENN.

Columbus, Marion, Delaware, Newark, Zanesville, Lancaster, New Lexington, Logan, Nelsonville, Athens, Marietta, Vienna, Parkersburg, Chillicothe, Jackson, Portsmouth, Ironton, Ashland, Huntington, Charleston, S. Charleston, Dunbar, Nitro, St. Albans, Beckley, Bluefield, Princeton, Williamson, Logan, Pittsburgh, McKeesport, Bethel Park, Wheeling, Moundsville, Morgantown, Fairmont, Clarksburg, Bridgeport, Buckhannon, Elkins, Lewisburg, White Sulphur Spr., Covington, Roanoke, Salem, Blacksburg, Christiansburg, Radford, Pulaski, Wytheville, Marion, Abingdon, Bristol, Kingsport

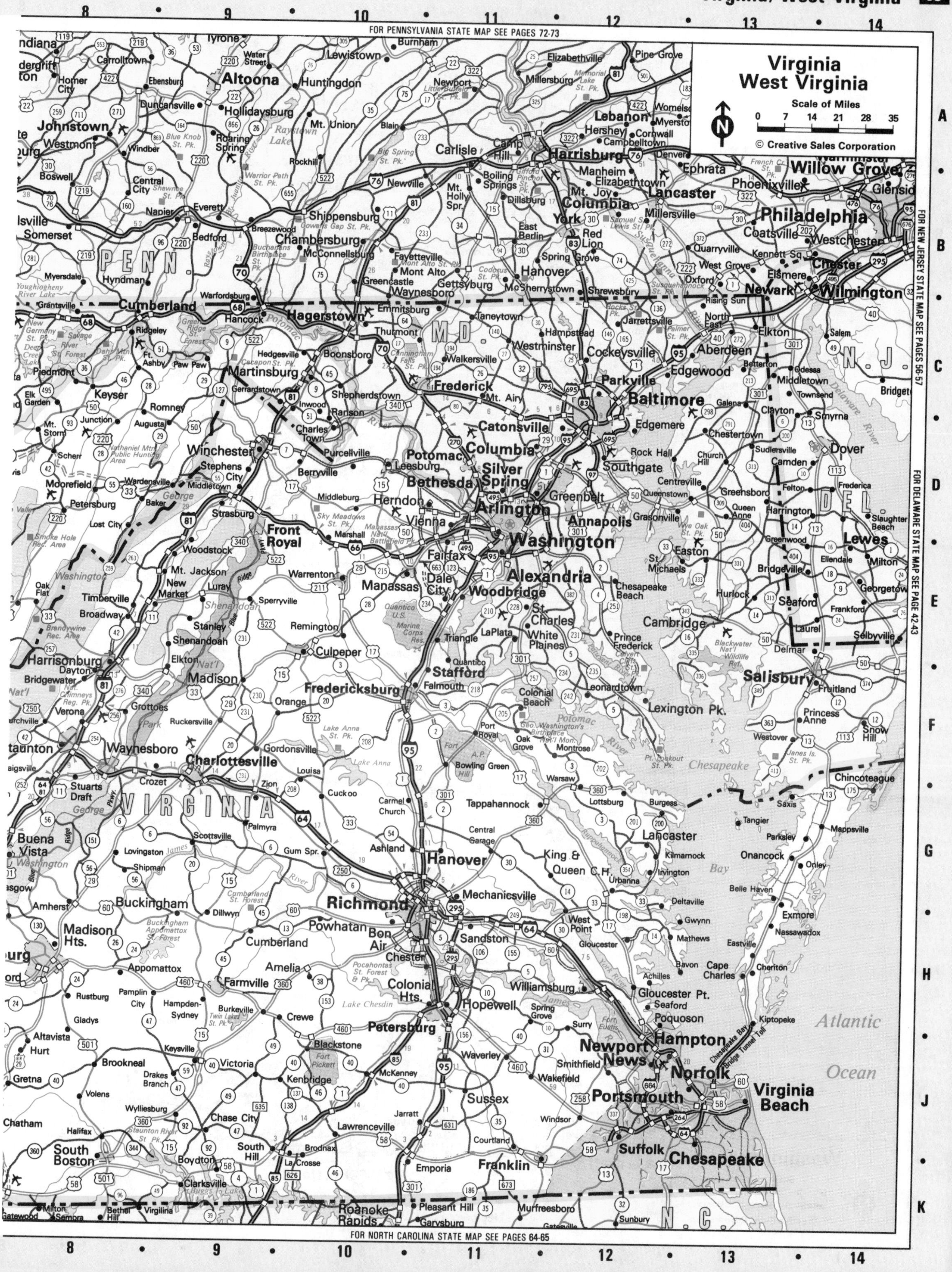
FOR PENNSYLVANIA STATE MAP SEE PAGES 72-73
Virginia
West Virginia
Scale of Miles
0 7 14 21 28 35
© Creative Sales Corporation
FOR NEW JERSEY STATE MAP SEE PAGES 56-57
FOR DELAWARE STATE MAP SEE PAGE 42-43
FOR NORTH CAROLINA STATE MAP SEE PAGES 64-65
PENN.
MD.
N.J.
DEL.
VIRGINIA
N.C.
Altoona
Johnstown
Harrisburg
Lancaster
Philadelphia
Wilmington
Baltimore
Hagerstown
Cumberland
Frederick
Washington
Arlington
Alexandria
Annapolis
Dover
Winchester
Fredericksburg
Charlottesville
Richmond
Petersburg
Newport News
Hampton
Norfolk
Portsmouth
Virginia Beach
Chesapeake
Suffolk
Salisbury
Chesapeake Bay
Atlantic Ocean

BRITISH COLUMBIA

Vancouver Island

CANADA
U.S.

Strait of Juan De Fuca

Strait of Georgia

Pacific Ocean

Olympic Nat'l Park

Olympic Nat'l Forest

Mt. Rainier Nat'l Park

Snoqualmie Nat'l Forest

Gifford Pinchot Nat'l Forest

North Cascades

Neah Bay, Ozette, Sappho, Joyce, Forks, La Push, Queets, Taholah, Pacific Beach, Copalis Beach, Ocean Shores, Ocean City St. Pk., Westport, North Cove, Ocean Park, Long Beach, Ilwaco, Seaside, Cannon Beach, Manzanita, Tillamook, Garibaldi

Port Renfrew, Sooke, Sidney, Victoria, Friday Harbor, Anacortes, Oak Harbor, Coupeville, Port Townsend, Sequim, Port Angeles, Fairholm, Port Gamble, Poulsbo, Bainbridge Island, Bremerton, Port Orchard, Eldon, Hoodsport, Union, Shelton, Neilton, Humptulips, McCleary, Elma, Montesano, Aberdeen, Hoquiam, Cosmopolis, Raymond, South Bend, Menlo, Lebam, Naselle, Rosburg, Altoona, Megler, Astoria, Warrenton, Cathlamet, Stella, Clatskanie, Kalama

Blaine, White Rock, Langley, Mission, Sumas, Lynden, Ferndale, Everson, Deming, Acme, Wickersham, Bellingham, Mount Baker, Baker Lake, Lower Baker Dam, Concrete, Rockport, Darrington, Lyman, Hamilton, Sedro-Woolley, Burlington, Mount Vernon, La Conner, Stanwood, Camano, Arlington, Granite Falls, Marysville, Lake Stevens, Everett, Mukilteo, Snohomish, Sultan, Gold Bar, Index, Lynnwood, Edmonds, Brier, Bothell, Monroe, Duvall, Seattle, Kirkland, Redmond, Carnation, Mercer Island, Bellevue, Renton, Issaquah, Snoqualmie, North Bend, Tukwila, Normandy Park, Des Moines, Kent, Black Diamond, Auburn, Pacific, Sumner, Enumclaw, Buckley, South Prairie, Wilkeson, Carbonado, Greenwater, Puyallup, Bonney Lake, Orting, Tacoma, Fircrest, Steilacoom, Gig Harbor, Olympia, Tumwater, Lacey, Yelm, Roy, Rainier, Eatonville, Elbe, Packwood, Randle, Morton, Glenoma, Trout Lake

Littlerock, Oakville, Rochester, Tenino, Bucoda, Centralia, Chehalis, Napavine, Winlock, Vader, Ryderwood, Toledo, Mossyrock, Castle Rock, Silver Lake, Kelso, Longview, Woodland, Ridgefield, La Center, Battle Ground, Yacolt, Duluth, Orchards, Camas, Washougal, Vancouver, Hillsboro, Forest Grove, Stevenson, North Bonneville, Hood River, Bingen, White Salmon, Klickitat, Husum, The Dalles, Wishram, Dufur

Portland, Gresham, Oregon City, Sandy, Newberg, Yamhill, Vernonia, Mt. St. Helens, Mt. Adams, Mt. Hood

Washington
Scale of Miles
0 6 12 18 24 30
N
© Creative Sales Corporation

8 • 9 • 10 • 11 • 12 • 13 • 14 • 15

BC
Manning Prov. Pk.
Cathedral Prov. Pk.
Ross Lake
Pasayten
Wilderness
Osoyoos
Greenwood
Grand Forks
Rossland
Trail
Montrose
Christina Lake
CANADA
U.S.
Oroville
Similkameen Dam
Osoyoos Lake Vets. Mem. St. Pk.
Danville
Colville
Boundary
Boundary Dam
Northport
Metaline Falls
Okanogan
Palmer Lk.
Colville
Orient
Metaline
Nordman
Nat'l
Tonasket
Wauconda
Curlew Lk. St. Pk.
Bossburg
Ione
Forest
Priest Lake
Conconully St. Pk.
Republic
Marcus
Kettle Falls
Kaniksu
Priest Lake
Conconully
Riverside
Colville
National
Sandpoint
Winthrop
Twisp
Omak
Disautel
Addy
Cusick
Forest
Okanogan
Omak Lake
Colville
Gifford
Chewelah
Newport
Priest River
Brewster
Pateros
Bridgeport
Chief Joseph Dam
Grand Coulee Dam
Keller
Springdale
Clayton
Deer Park
Oldtown
Round Lake St. Pk.
Spirit Lake
Bayview
Athol
Chelan
Manson
Wells Dam
Electric City
Grand Coulee
Free Ferry
Spokane Indian Res.
Little Falls Dam
Long Lake Dam
Twin Lakes
Farragut St. Pk.
Leavenworth
Waterville
Withrow
Mansfield
Dry Falls Dam
Wilbur
Creston
Davenport
Reardan
Spokane
Millwood
Coeur D'Alene
Post Falls
Rathdrum
Cashmere
Wenatchee
East Wenatchee
Rock Island
Rock Island Dam
Coulee City
Hartline
Almira
Harrington
Medical Lake
Cheney
Rockford
Plummer
Soap Lake
Krupp
Odessa
Edwall
Spangle
Fairfield
Waverly
Latah
WASHINGTON
Ephrata
Quincy
Crescent Bar
Moses Lake
Ritzville
Sprague
Rosalia
Tekoa
Oakesdale
IDAHO
Ellensburg
Kittitas
Vantage
George
Lind
Lamont
St. John
Steptoe
Garfield
Palouse
Farmington
Potlatch
Warden
Washtucna
Endicott
Colfax
Yakima
Union Gap
Wapato
Zillah
Granger
Sunnyside
Grandview
Mabton
Prosser
Royal City
Othello
Hatton
Connell
Mesa
Kahlotus
La Crosse
Dusty
Albion
Pullman
Moscow
Colton
Uniontown
Genesee
West Richland
Benton City
Richland
Pasco
Kennewick
Eureka
Dayton
Waitsburg
Prescott
Starbuck
Dodge
Pomeroy
Clarkston
Lewiston
Asotin
Anatone
Wallula
College Place
Walla Walla
Milton-Freewater
Athena
Bickleton
Goldendale
Roosevelt
Boardman
Hermiston
Stanfield
Pendleton
Elgin
Wallowa
Enterprise
Joseph
OREGON
Wasco
Moro
Arlington
Ione
Lexington
Heppner
Pilot Rock

FOR IDAHO STATE MAP SEE PAGE 31
FOR OREGON STATE MAP SEE PAGES 70-71

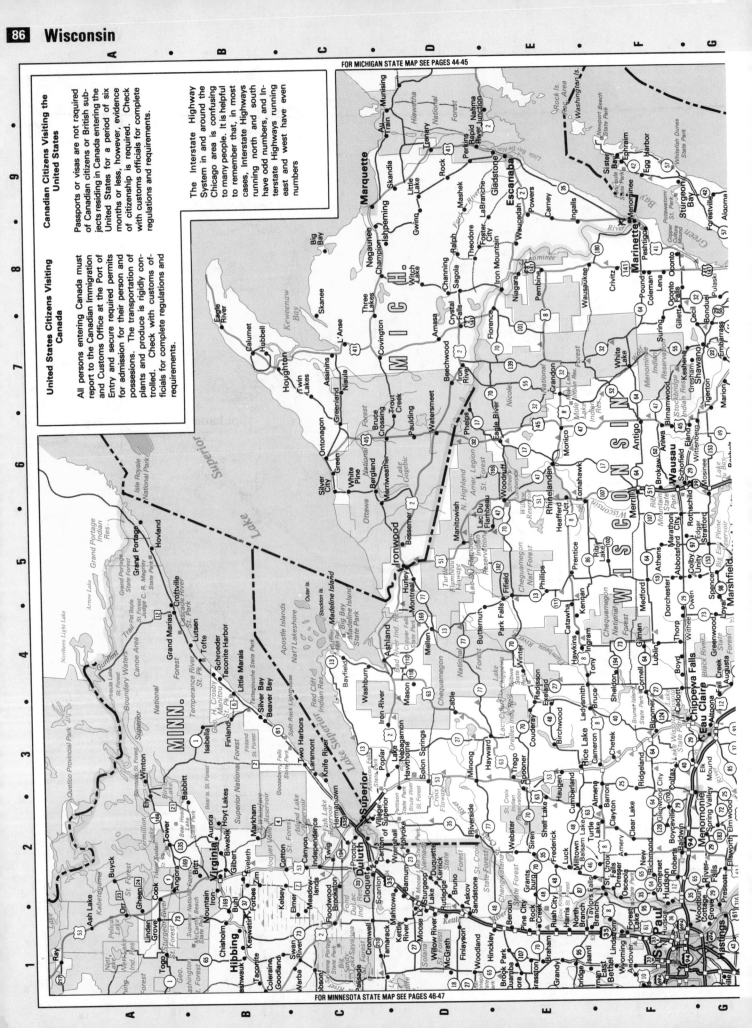

FOR MICHIGAN STATE MAP SEE PAGES 44-45

FOR MINNESOTA STATE MAP SEE PAGES 46-47

United States Citizens Visiting Canada

All persons entering Canada must report to the Canadian Immigration and Customs Office at the Port of Entry and secure required permits for admission for their person and possesions. The transportation of plants and produce is rigidly controlled. Check with customs officials for complete regulations and requirements.

Canadian Citizens Visiting the United States

Passports or visas are not required of Canadian citizens or British subjects residing in Canada entering the United States for a period of six months or less, however, evidence of citizenship is required. Check with customs officials for complete regulations and requirements.

The Interstate Highway System in and around the Chicago area is confusing to many people. It is helpful to remember that, in most cases, Interstate Highways running north and south have odd numbers, and Interstate Highways running east and west have even numbers.

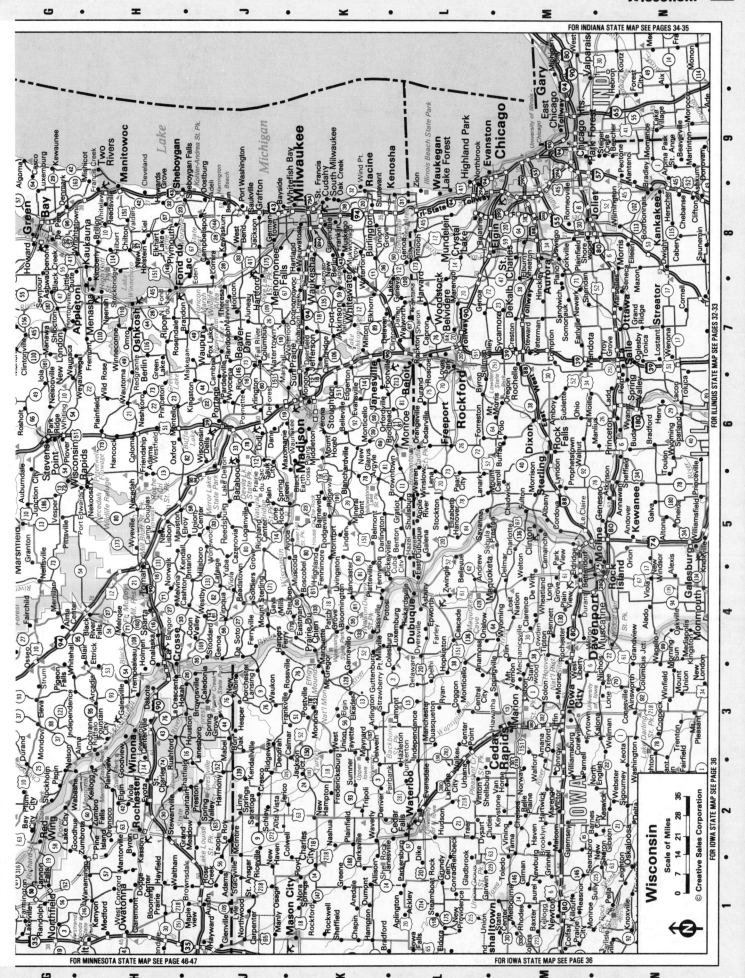

FOR INDIANA STATE MAP SEE PAGES 34-35

FOR ILLINOIS STATE MAP SEE PAGES 32-33

FOR IOWA STATE MAP SEE PAGE 36

Wisconsin

Scale of Miles

0   7   14   28   35

© Creative Sales Corporation

FOR MINNESOTA STATE MAP SEE PAGE 46-47

FOR IOWA STATE MAP SEE PAGE 36

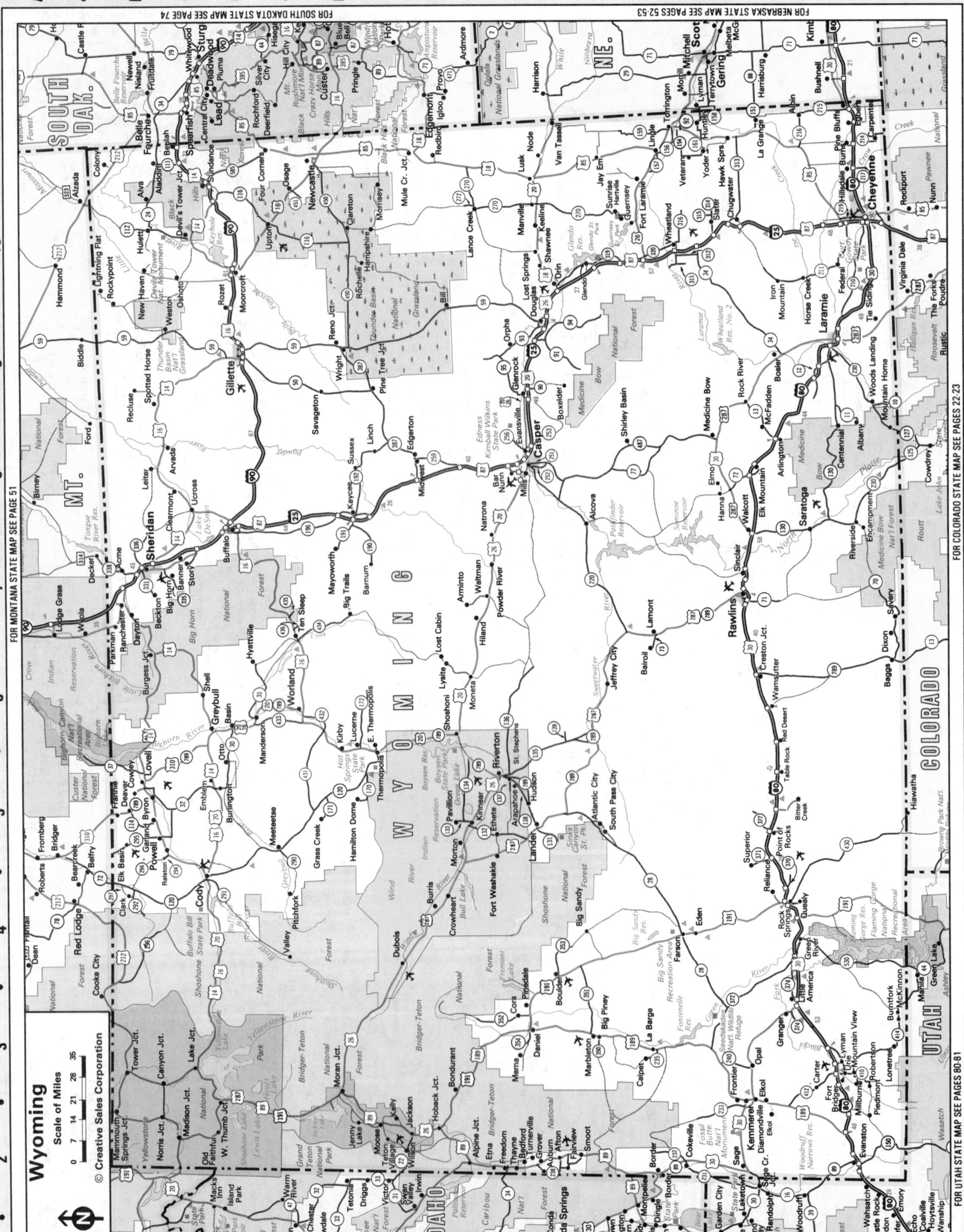

Wyoming
Scale of Miles
0 7 14 21 28 35
© Creative Sales Corporation
FOR MONTANA STATE MAP SEE PAGE 51
FOR SOUTH DAKOTA STATE MAP SEE PAGE 74
FOR NEBRASKA STATE MAP SEE PAGES 52-53
FOR COLORADO STATE MAP SEE PAGES 22-23
FOR UTAH STATE MAP SEE PAGES 80-81
FOR IDAHO STATE MAP SEE PAGE 31
W Y O M I N G
MT.
SOUTH DAK.
NE.
COLORADO
UTAH
IDAHO
Cheyenne
Casper
Laramie
Rawlins
Sheridan
Gillette
Cody
Riverton
Lander
Rock Springs
Jackson
Evanston
Worland
Douglas
Torrington
Newcastle
Buffalo
Kemmerer
Green River

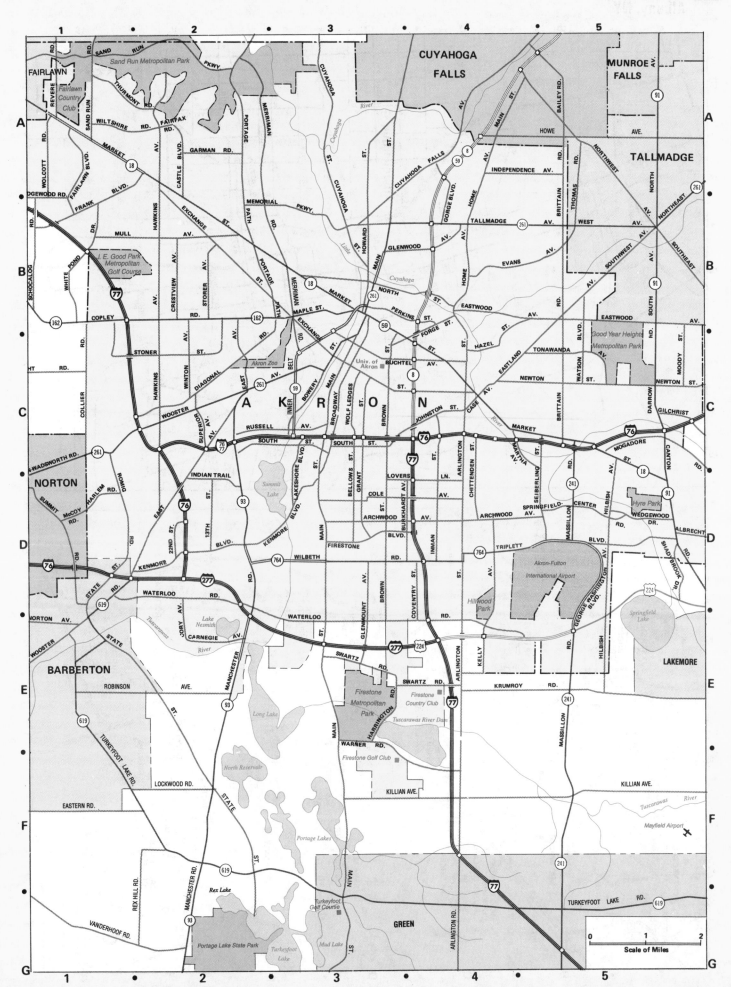

Scale of Miles

Allentown, PA

TREICHLERS
SEEMSVILLE
KREIDERSVILLE
HECKTOWN
NORTHHAMPTON
BALLIETTSVILLE
CATASAUQUA
WEST CATASAUQUA
SHOENERSVILLE
BETHLEHEM
Race St.
Muhlenburg Medical Center
Allentown-Bethlehem Easton Airport
Masada
Monocacy Park
Butztown
Oakland
STEEL CITY
Dauphin
Catasauqua Rd.
Hicks Mills Rd.
Eaton Ave.
Main Blvd.
Union Blvd.
Stefko
Pembroke Rd.
Riverside
Cedar Crest Blvd.
Chew St.
State Hospital
Broad
Spring
3rd Ave.
New
Lehigh
FOUNTAIN HILL
Lehigh University
Tilghman St.
Hamilton
Linden
Hanover
Susquehanna
QUEEN CITY
ALLENTOWN
Broadway
HELLERTOWN
Dorney Park
Penn
SUMMIT LAWN
Queen City Mun. Airport
FRIEDENSVILLE
EAST TEXAS
LEITHSVILLE
EMMAUS
CENTER VALLEY

Scale of Miles
0   1   2   3
© C.S.C.

Asheville, NC

French Broad
Riverside
Elk Mountain Scenic Highway
NEW BRIDGE
ELK MOUNTAIN
WOODFIN
Macedonia Rd.
Leicester
Stratford Rd.
Beaverdam Rd.
Webb Cove Rd.
RICEVILLE
CRAGGY
BIRMINGHAM HEIGHTS
Merrimon Av.
Lakeshore Dr.
Gracelyn
Mountain
Blue Ridge
Lower
ASHEVILLE
Eliada Rd.
Broadway
Chestnut St.
Cap Cove Rd.
Veterans Federal Hospital
EMMA
Johnson Blvd.
Patton
Av.
Merrimon Av.
Kenilworth
New
AZALEA
Dearview
Haywood
Depot St.
Tunnel
BEVERLY HILLS
Cove Rd.
Swannanoa
Fairview
Meadow
Sweeten
BILTMORE
SAND HILL
French Broad River
BUENA VISTA
Sardis
Busbee Mountain
Blue Ridge
VALLEY SPRINGS
BUSBEE
Brevard
Pinners Cove Rd.
Concord
Merrills Cove Rd.
WEST HAVEN
Shoals Rd.
SKYLAND
ROYAL PINES
Asheville Regional Airport
MIDWAY

Scale of Miles
0   1   2   3
© C.S.C.

Atlantic City, NJ

Great Bay
LEEDS POINT
Brigantine National Wildlife Refuge
BRIGANTINE
Steel Chase Pier
Central Pier
Million Dollar Pier
ATLANTIC CITY
PORT REPUBLIC
SMITHVILLE
OCEANVILLE
CONOVERTOWN
Reeds Bay
Smithville Airport
Moss Mill Rd.
Oyster Creek Rd.
Great Creek Rd.
ABSECON
Absecon Bay
VENTNOR CITY
Atlantic Ocean
Cologne Port Republic Rd.
Piney Ave.
Ebuhn Ave.
PLEASANTVILLE
Pleasantville Rd.
MARGATE CITY
LONGPORT
Clarks Landing
Wrangleboro Rd.
Leeds
White Horse Pike
Shore Rd.
NORTHFIELD
LINWOOD
OCEAN CITY
Indian Cabin Rd.
GERMANIA
COLOGNE
POMONA
Atlantic City NAFEC
CARDIFF
Zion Rd.
SOMERS POINT
Great Egg Harbor Bay
Tilton
Mordham Airport
Ocean City Airport
Schiller St.
Mannheim
Tilton Rd.
Heights
Ocean Heights
Great Egg Harbor
DEVONSHIRE
EGG HARBOR CITY
Atlantic City Expressway
Atlantic City Blvd. Racetrack
MCKEE CITY
ENGLISH CREEK
SCULLVILLE
BEESLEYS POINT
PALERMO
New York Ave.
English Creek Ave.
MARMORA
Garden State Parkway

Scale of Miles
0   1   2   3
© C.S.C.

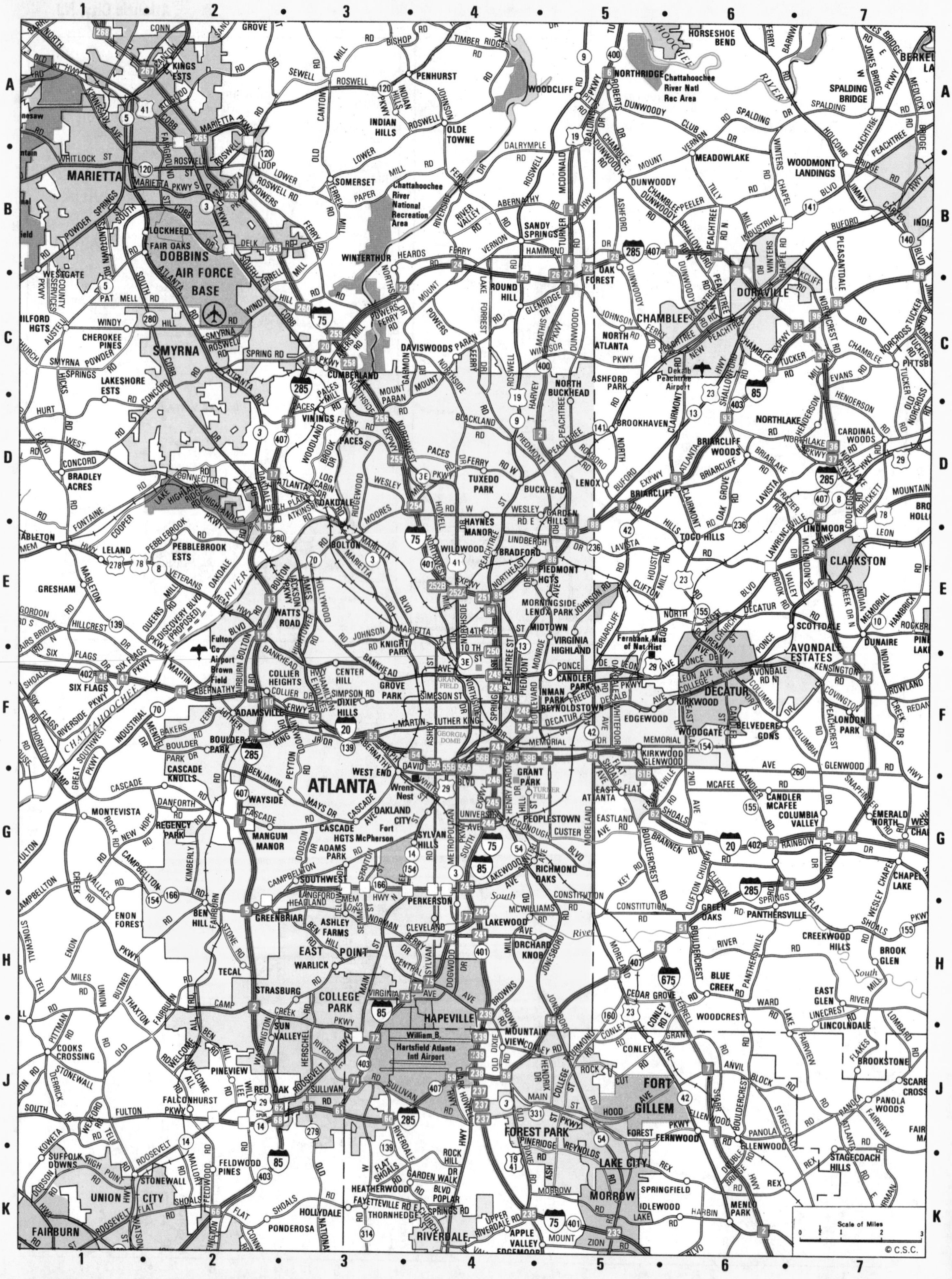
MARIETTA
KINGS ESTS
DOBBINS AIR FORCE BASE
SMYRNA
CHEROKEE PINES
LAKESHORE ESTS
VININGS
PACES
CUMBERLAND
INDIAN HILLS
OLDE TOWNE
PENHURST
SOMERSET
Chattahoochee River National Recreation Area
WINTERTHUR
SANDY SPRINGS
ROUND HILL
WOODCLIFF
NORTHRIDGE
Chattahoochee River Natl Rec Area
HORSESHOE BEND
SPALDING BRIDGE
MEADOWLAKE
WOODMONT LANDINGS
DUNWOODY
OAK FOREST
CHAMBLEE
DORAVILLE
NORTH ATLANTA
Dekalb Peachtree Airport
ASHFORD PARK
NORTH BUCKHEAD
BROOKHAVEN
NORTHLAKE
CARDINAL WOODS
BRIARCLIFF WOODS
BRIARCLIFF
TOCO HILLS
LINDMOOR
CLARKSTON
TUXEDO PARK
BUCKHEAD
LENOX
GARDEN HILLS
HAYNES MANOR
BRADFORD
WILDWOOD
PIEDMONT HGTS
MORNINGSIDE LENOX PARK
MIDTOWN
VIRGINIA HIGHLAND
Fernbank Mus of Nat Hist
SCOTTDALE
AVONDALE ESTATES
DUNAIRE
DECATUR
KIRKWOOD
BELVEDERE GDNS
LONDON PARK
WOODGATE
EDGEWOOD
CANDLER PARK
INMAN PARK
REYNOLDSTOWN
KIRKWOOD GLENWOOD
GRANT PARK
EAST ATLANTA
EASTLAND
CANDLER MCAFEE
COLUMBIA VALLEY
EMERALD NORTH
ATLANTA
WEST END
Wrens Nest
GEORGIA DOME
OAKLAND CITY
Fort McPherson
SYLVAN HILLS
PEOPLESTOWN
CUSTER
RICHMOND OAKS
LAKEWOOD
ORCHARD KNOB
PANTHERSVILLE
GREEN OAKS
CREEKWOOD HILLS
BROOK GLEN
CHAPEL LAKE
BLUE CREEK
EAST GLEN
LINCOLNDALE
BROOKSTONE
PANOLA WOODS
STAGECOACH HILLS
FORT GILLEM
CONLEY
MOUNTAIN VIEW
FOREST PARK
LAKE CITY
MORROW
ELLENWOOD
FERNWOOD
MENLO PARK
RIVERDALE
APPLE VALLEY
HAPEVILLE
William B. Hartsfield Atlanta Intl Airport
COLLEGE PARK
EAST POINT
SUN VALLEY
PERKERSON
GREENBRIAR
ASHLEY FARMS
BEN HILL
ENON FOREST
TECAL
STRASBURG
PINEVIEW
RED OAK
FALCONHURST
COOKS CROSSING
SUFFOLK DOWNS
UNION CITY
FAIRBURN
FELDWOOD PINES
PONDEROSA
HOLLYDALE
HEATHERWOOD
THORNHEDGE
MANGUM MANOR
CASCADE HGTS
ADAMS PARK
WAYSIDE
REGENCY PARK
MONTEVISTA
CASCADE KNOLLS
BOULDER PARK
ADAMSVILLE
COLLIER HEIGHTS
CENTER HILL
GROVE PARK
DIXIE HILLS
KNIGHT PARK
WATTS ROAD
BOLTON
OAKDALE
Fulton Co Airport Brown Field
SIX FLAGS
GRESHAM
LELAND
PEBBLEBROOK ESTS
BRADLEY ACRES
CHATTAHOOCHEE
RIVER
Scale of Miles
© C.S.C.

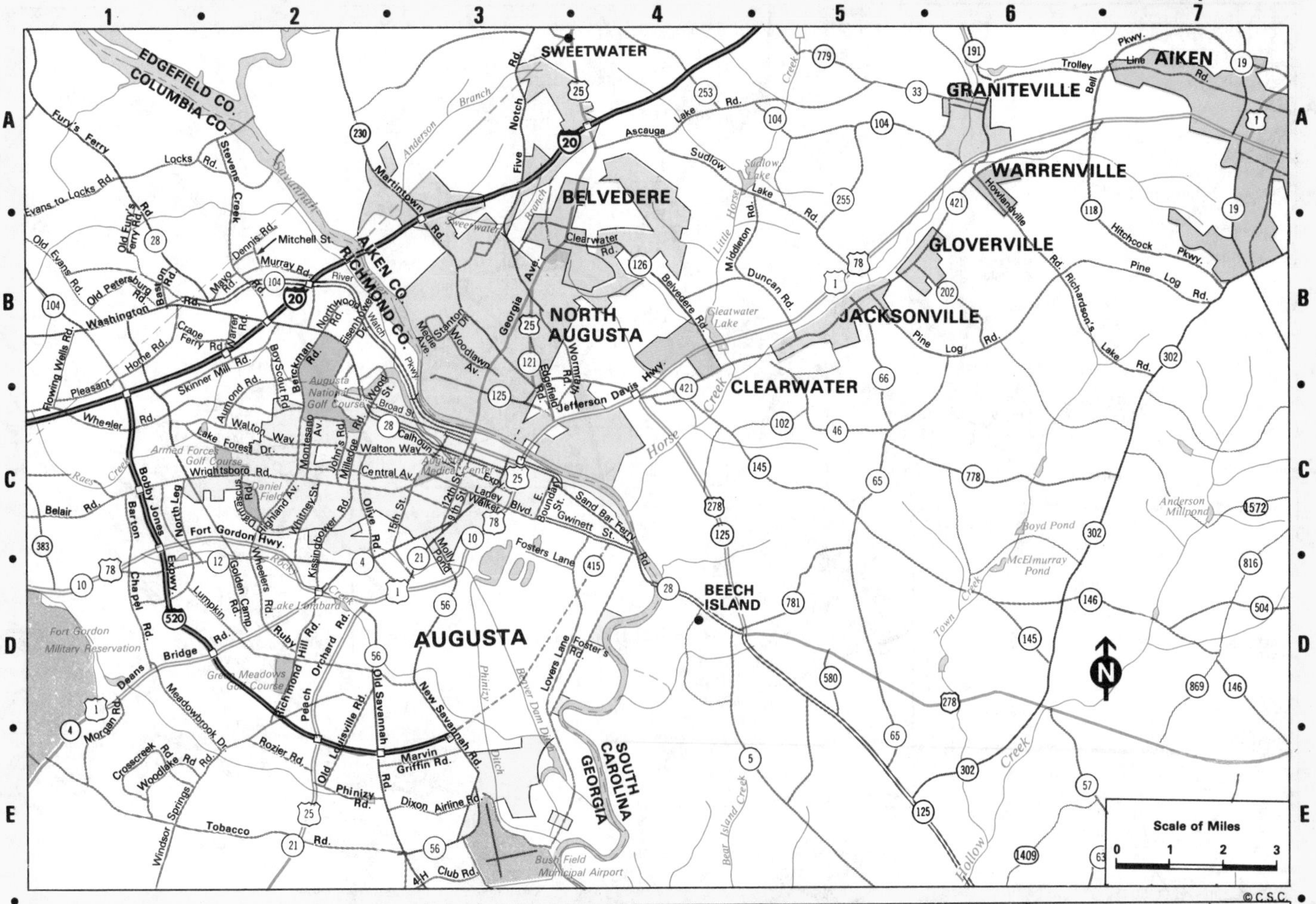

Augusta, GA (top map)

EDGEFIELD CO.
COLUMBIA CO.
RICHMOND CO.
AIKEN CO.

SWEETWATER
AIKEN
GRANITEVILLE
WARRENVILLE
BELVEDERE
GLOVERVILLE
NORTH AUGUSTA
JACKSONVILLE
CLEARWATER
AUGUSTA
BEECH ISLAND
SOUTH CAROLINA
GEORGIA

Fort Gordon Military Reservation
Augusta National Golf Course
Armed Forces Golf Course
Bush Field Municipal Airport

Scale of Miles
0 1 2 3

©C.S.C.

Austin, TX (bottom map)

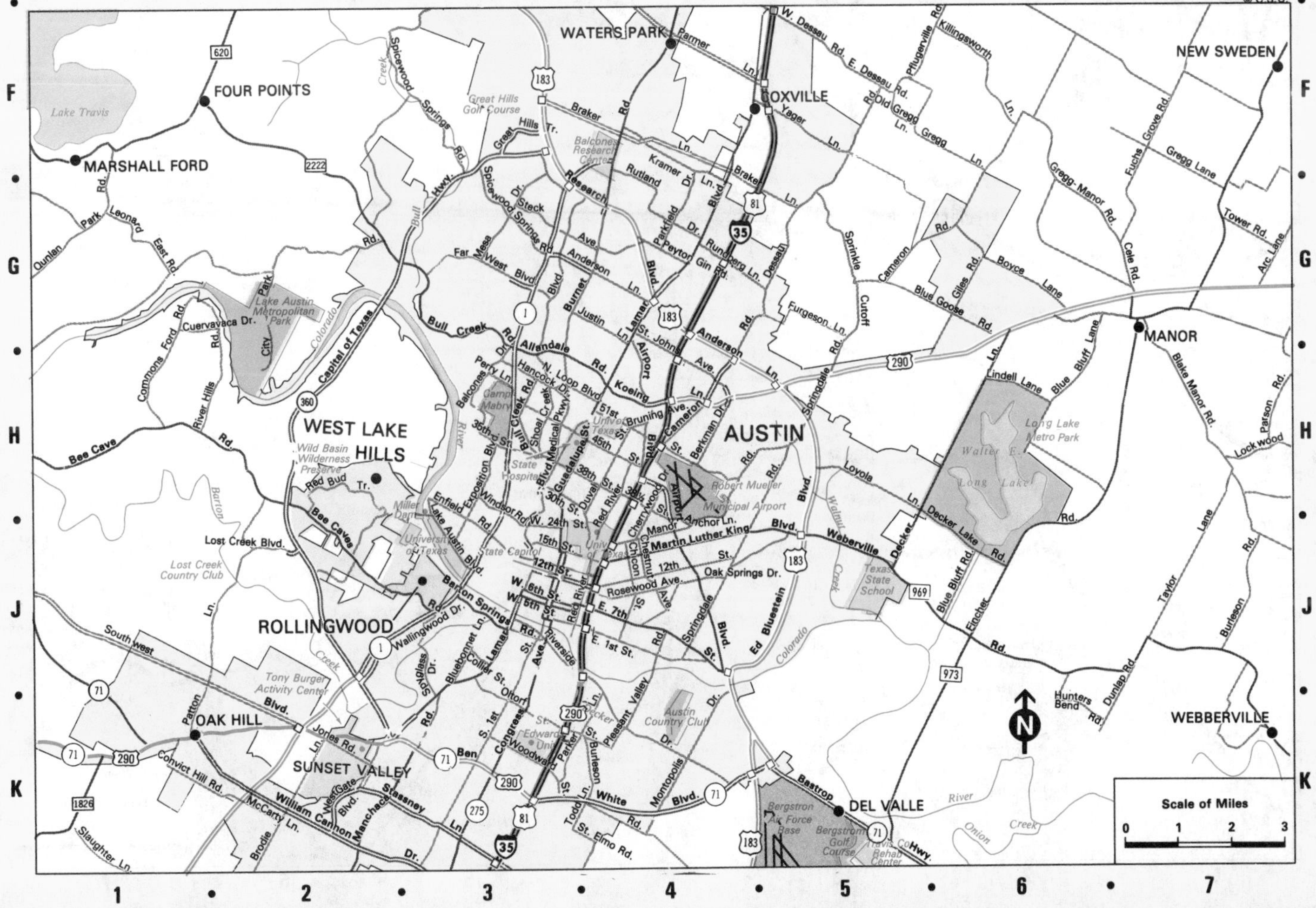

WATERS PARK
NEW SWEDEN
FOUR POINTS
FOXVILLE
MARSHALL FORD
MANOR
WEST LAKE HILLS
AUSTIN
ROLLINGWOOD
WEBBERVILLE
OAK HILL
SUNSET VALLEY
DEL VALLE

Lake Travis
Lake Austin Metropolitan Park
University of Texas
Robert Mueller Municipal Airport
Texas State School
Long Lake Metro Park
Bergstrom Air Force Base
Bergstrom Golf Course

Scale of Miles
0 1 2 3

Scale of Miles
0 1 2 3

© C.S.C.

SMITHFIELD
CHAMBERLIN
DEVALLS
CAREY
ALLENDALE
LEJEUNE
KAHNS
ANCHORAGE
BELMONT Hwy.
Airline
SUNRISE
ITHRA
PORT ALLEN
Court St.
CINCLARE
MERLIN
LUKEVILLE
ADDIS

MARYLAND
Thomas Rd.
Comite
CENTRAL
TANGLEWOOD
MAGNOLIA
COMITE
DENHAM SPRINGS
Hooper
Ford St.
Mickens Rd.
Southern University A & M College
Baton Rouge Ryan Airport
Earl K. Long Memorial Hospital
Hollywood Dr.
Evangeline St.
Prescott Rd.
Winbourne Ave.
N. Acadian West
N. Acadian East
Choctaw Dr.
Greenwell
Airline
Monterey
S. Choctaw Dr.
MILLERVILLE
Capitol Lake
North Florida Blvd.
BATON ROUGE
Broussard
Jefferson
Hwy.
Goodwood Blvd.
Sharp Rd.
Sherwood Forest Blvd.
Old State Capitol
Park Blvd.
Highland
Dalrymple Rd.
Stanford Ave.
Perkins
Hospital
Out Lady of the Lake Medical Center
Louisiana State University A & M College
Brightside Dr.
University Lake
COLLEGE HILLS
ESSEN
NESSER
WOODLAWN Bend
Tiger
Burbank
Sterling Ln.
Bluebonnet Blvd.
Essen Ln.
Jefferson Hwy.
FOREMAN
HILLSIDE
Perkins Rd.
Siegen Ln.
Pecue Ln.
Highland Rd.
GARDERE
HOPE VILLA
BURTVILLE
Intracoastal Waterway
Mississippi River
River Rd.
Bayou Fountain

Scale of Miles
0 1 2 3

N

© C.S.C.

PEVETO
Lucas St.
Folsom Dr.
South Texas Fairgrounds
Magnolia Ave.
Pine St.
VIDOR
Terry Rd.
Concord Rd.
Old Highway
ROSE CITY
Dewitt
Mansfield Ferry Rd.
BEAUMONT
Calder Rd.
11th St.
Orleans St.
College
4th St.
Washington Blvd.
Mansfield Ferry Rd.
Lamar University
Cardinal Stadium
Fannett
Highland Ave.
Major
Walden Rd.
Brooks Rd.
Tyrrell Port Rd.
Tyrrell Park
Frint Dr.
Steinhagen
Blewell Rd.
LaBelle Rd.
Hildebrandt Bayou
West Port Arthur Rd.
HEBERT
CENTRAL GARDENS
Port Arthur Rd.
Southport
NEDERLAND
27th
Beaumont Gardens Rd.
Jefferson County Airport
LOVELL LAKE
HILLEBRANDT
PORT ARTHUR
Port Neches Ave.
Grisby Ave.
Magnolia
PORT NECHES
Atlantic
Old Ferry Rd.
ORANGE CO.
JEFFERSON CO.
Neches River
Hopebloom Rd.
Main St.
Taft Ave.
GROVES
Pure
Proctor St.
Sabine Lake
Humble Is.
Sidney Is.
Stewts Is.
Old River Cove
ORANGEFIELD
Brown Airport
BRIDGE CITY
Cove Bayou
Gulley
Anderson
South Terry Rd.
Jap Lane
TEXAS
LOUISIANA
Sabine Neches Canal

Scale of Miles
0 1 2 3

N

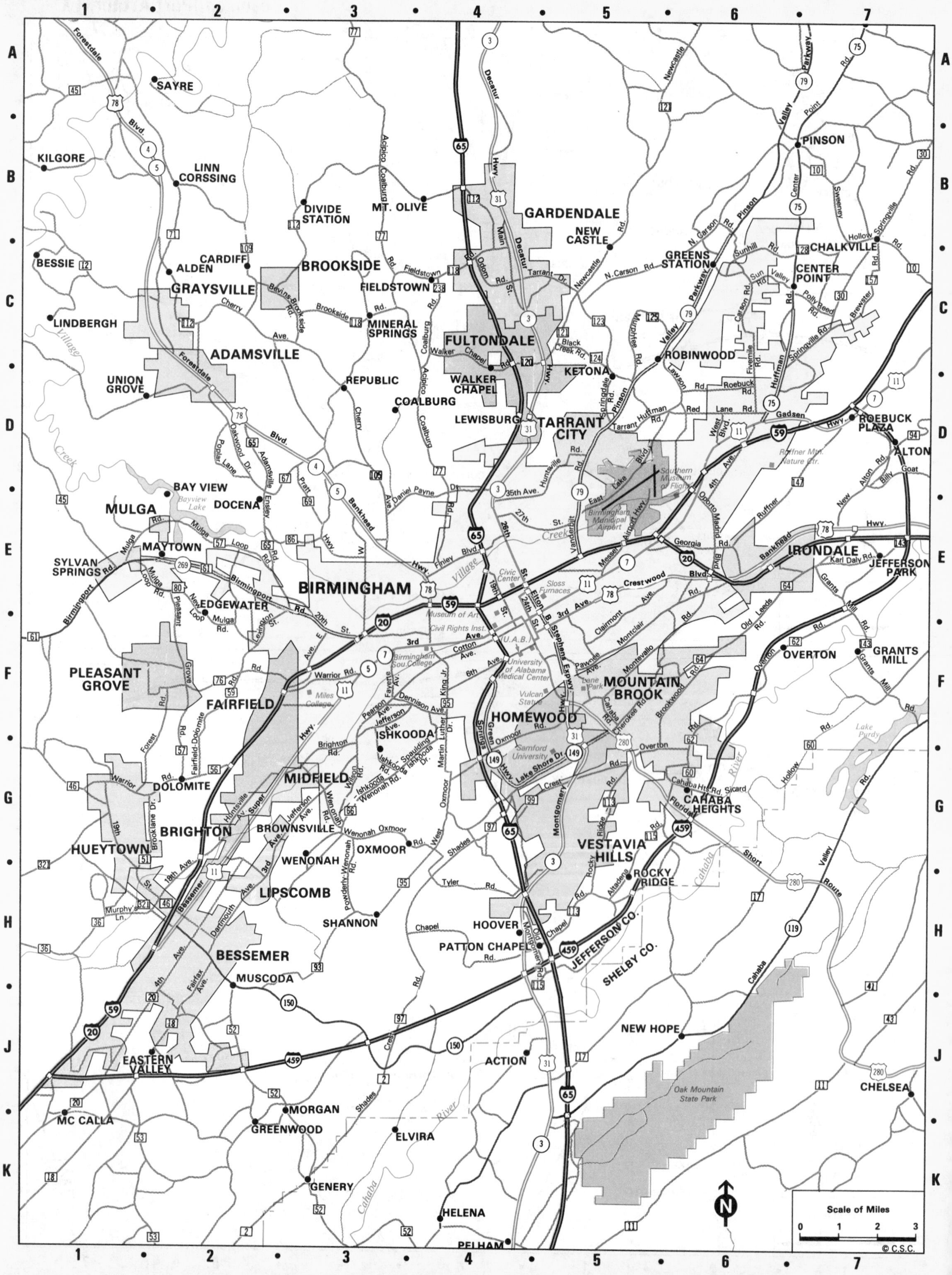

SAYRE
KILGORE
LINN CORSSING
DIVIDE STATION
MT. OLIVE
GARDENDALE
NEW CASTLE
PINSON
GREENS STATION
CHALKVILLE
CENTER POINT
BESSIE
ALDEN
CARDIFF
GRAYSVILLE
BROOKSIDE
FIELDSTOWN
MINERAL SPRINGS
FULTONDALE
ROBINWOOD
LINDBERGH
ADAMSVILLE
REPUBLIC
COALBURG
WALKER CHAPEL
KETONA
UNION GROVE
LEWISBURG
TARRANT CITY
ROEBUCK PLAZA
ALTON
BAY VIEW
DOCENA
Southern Museum of Flight
Birmingham Municipal Airport
IRONDALE
JEFFERSON PARK
MULGA
MAYTOWN
SYLVAN SPRINGS
EDGEWATER
BIRMINGHAM
Civic Center
Sloss Furnaces
Crestwood
GEORGIA
OVERTON
GRANTS MILL
Museum of Art
Civil Rights Inst.
U.A.B.
University of Alabama Medical Center
PLEASANT GROVE
FAIRFIELD
Miles College
Birmingham Sou College
Cotton Ave.
Vulcan Statue
MOUNTAIN BROOK
ISHKOODA
HOMEWOOD
Samford University
Lane Park
DOLOMITE
MIDFIELD
BROWNSVILLE
CABAHA HEIGHTS
HUEYTOWN
BRIGHTON
WENONAH
OXMOOR
VESTAVIA HILLS
LIPSCOMB
SHANNON
ROCKY RIDGE
HOOVER
PATTON CHAPEL
JEFFERSON CO.
SHELBY CO.
BESSEMER
MUSCODA
NEW HOPE
EASTERN VALLEY
ACTION
Oak Mountain State Park
CHELSEA
MC CALLA
MORGAN
GREENWOOD
ELVIRA
GENERY
HELENA
PELHAM
Lake Purdy
Bayview Lake
Ruffner Mtn. Nature Ctr.

Scale of Miles
0 1 2 3

N

© C.S.C.

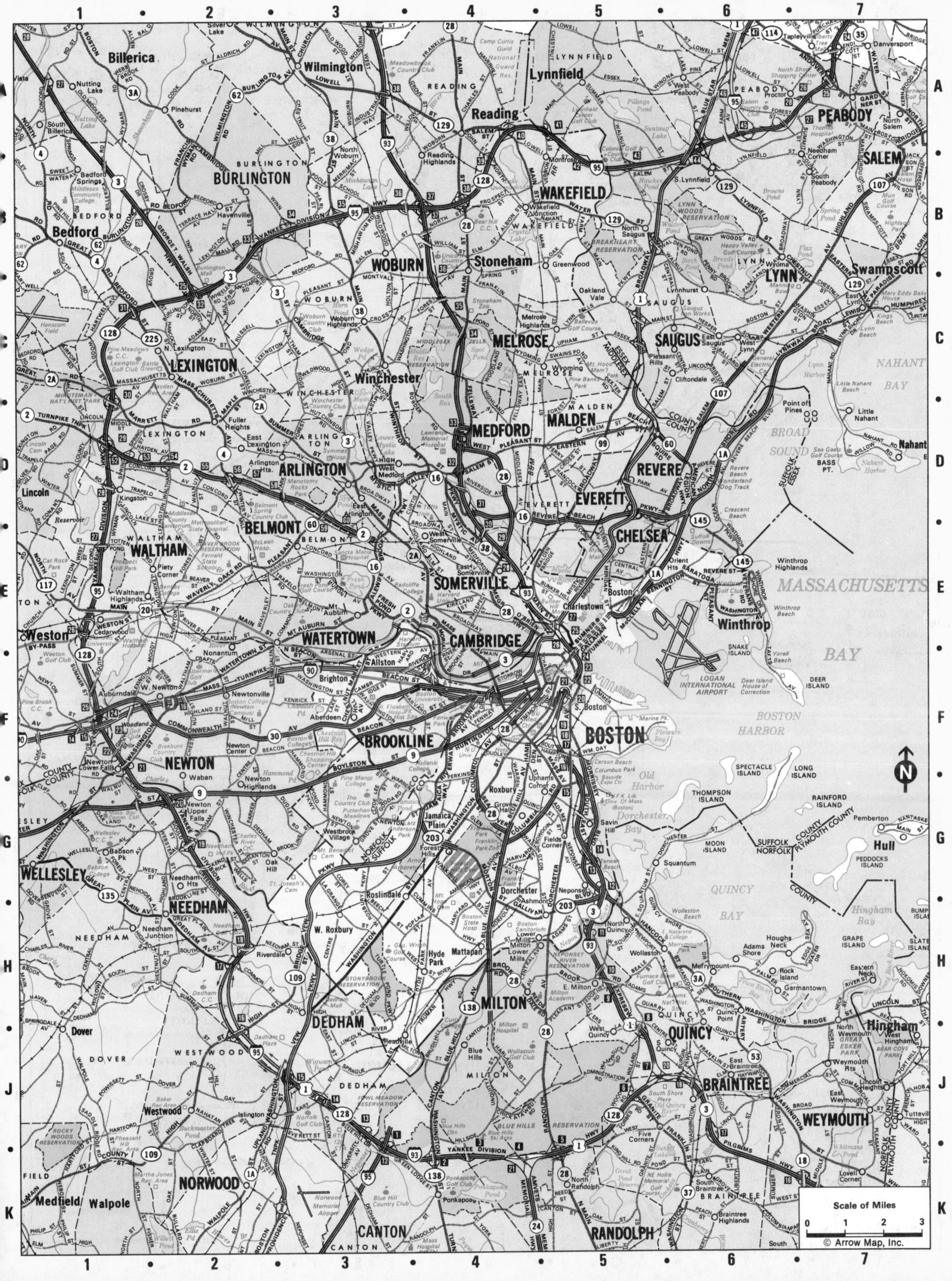
Billerica
Wilmington
Reading
Lynnfield
PEABODY
SALEM
BURLINGTON
WAKEFIELD
Bedford
WOBURN
Stoneham
Swampscott
LYNN
LEXINGTON
MELROSE
SAUGUS
Winchester
NAHANT BAY
MEDFORD
MALDEN
Nahant
ARLINGTON
REVERE
EVERETT
BELMONT
WALTHAM
CHELSEA
SOMERVILLE
MASSACHUSETTS
Winthrop
Weston
WATERTOWN
CAMBRIDGE
BAY
LOGAN INTERNATIONAL AIRPORT
BROOKLINE
BOSTON
BOSTON HARBOR
NEWTON
WELLESLEY
NEEDHAM
QUINCY BAY
Hull
MILTON
DEDHAM
QUINCY
Hingham
BRAINTREE
WEYMOUTH
NORWOOD
Medfield
Walpole
CANTON
RANDOLPH
Scale of Miles
0 1 2 3
© Arrow Map, Inc.

NIAGARA FALLS
ECHOTA
ST. JOHNSBURG
BERKHOLTZ
BEACH RIDGE
Loveland
RAPIDS
PENDLETON
MILLERSPORT
Niagara Falls International Airport
Oppenheim Zoo
NASHVILLE
HOFFMAN
WENDELVILLE
ELSERS CORNERS
NIAGARA FALLS
LA SALLE
SAWYER
SWORMVILLE
CHIPPAWA
PEACH HAVEN
WURLITZER PARK
Chippawa Battle Monument
SANDY BEACH
EDGEWATER
MARTINSVILLE
EAST AMHERST
GETZVILLE
CLARENCE CENTER
NIAGARA CO. ERIE CO.
E. ROBINSON
Big Six Mile Creek Park
Ellicott Cr. Park
S.U.N.Y. Buffalo
NORTH TONAWANDA
Grand Island
GRANDYLE VILLAGE
TONAWANDA
KENMORE
NORTH BAILEY
AMHERST
Buffalo C.C.
SNYDER
HARRIS HILL
Park C.C.
FERRY VILLAGE
Beaver Island State Park
Sheridan Park
Englewood
EGGERTSVILLE
SNYDER
WILLIAMSVILLE
BOWMANSVILLE
STEVENSVILLE
S.U.N.Y. Buffalo
Buffalo International Airport
FORT ERIE NORTH
Fort Erie Airport
Delaware Park
Buffalo Zoo
SUNY Coll Buffalo
Kensington
Kensington Expwy
DEPEW
LANCASTER
FORT ERIE
Fort Erie Race Track
Buffalo Museum of Science
E. Ferry
Walden
George
Urban
CRESCENT PARK
ERIE BEACH
War Mem. Stadium
Broadway
SLOAN
CHEEKTOWAGA
BELLEVUE
Como Park
POINT ABINO
RIDGEWAY
William
190
BLOSSOM
THUNDER BAY
CRYSTAL BEACH
Crescent Beach
Waverly Beach
Airport
Swan
South
Seneca
BUFFALO
Buffalo River
354
GARDENVILLE
WEST SENECA
EAST SENECA
ELMA
ELMA CENTER
Crystal Beach
Buffalo Harbor
Botanical Gardens
EBENEZER
SPRINGBROOK
CANADA / UNITED STATES
ONTARIO / NEW YORK
WELLAND CO. / ERIE CO.
LACKAWANNA
BLASDELL
Buffalo Air Park
Orchard Park Airport
Proner Airport
Lake Erie
WOODLAWN
WINDOM
Webster Cors.
WEBSTER CORNERS
BAY VIEW
EAST HAMBURG
ORCHARD PARK
Orchard Park C.C.
ATHOL SPRINGS
BIG TREE
DUELLS CORNERS
LOCKSLEY PARK
South Shore C.C.
ELLICOTT
ELLICOTT HEIGHTS
MT. VERNON
WANAKAH
CARNEGIE
Erie Co. Fairgrounds
ARMOR
JEWETTVILLE
GRIFFINS MILLS
CLIFTON HEIGHTS
PINEHURST
SCRANTON
Chestnut Ridge Park
JEWETTVILLE
HIGHLAND-ON-THE-LAKE
LAKE VIEW
WATER VALLEY
HAMBURG
WEST FALLS
NORTH EVANS
Lakeview Airport
Eighteen Mile Creek
JERUSALEM CORNERS
DERBY
EDEN VALLEY
NORTH BOSTON
ANGOLA-ON-THE-LAKE
EVANS
EAST EDEN
PATCHIN

Scale of Miles
0 1 2 3

© C.S.C.

N

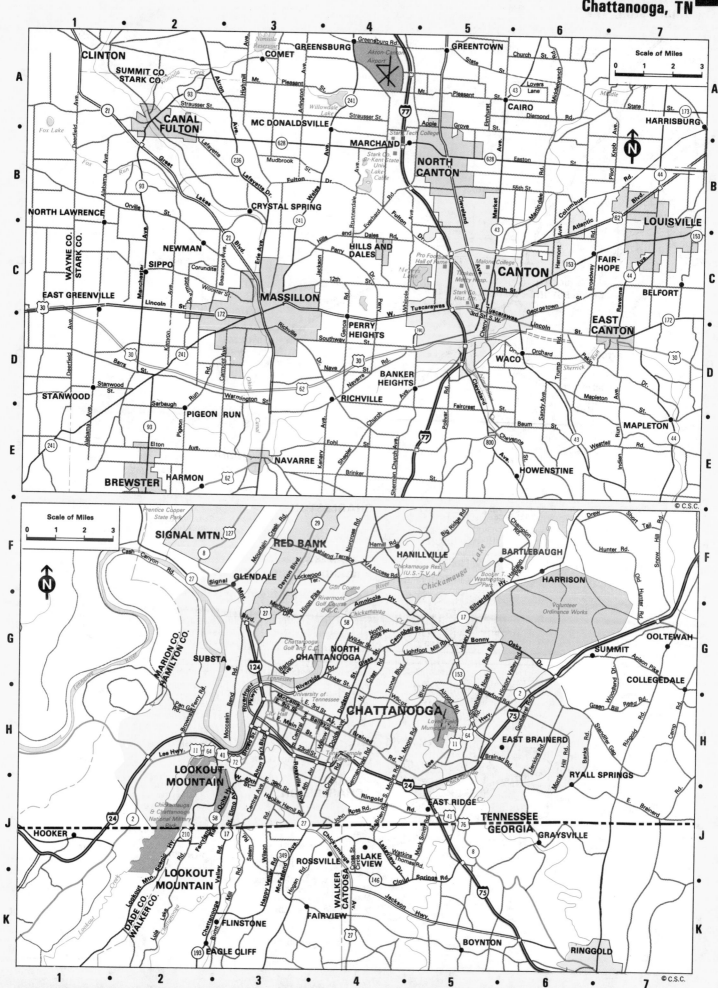

© C.S.C.

Charleston, SC (top map)

LADSON
GOOSE CREEK
DEER PARK
ASHLEY HEIGHTS
HANAHAN
U.S. Naval Reservation
Red Bank Hwy.
U.S. Naval Reservation
Goose Creek
Cooper River
CHARLESTON CO. DORCHESTER CO.
Ashley Phosphate Rd.
Eagle Dr.
Murray Ave.
Yeamans Hall Rd.
Aviation Ave.
Remount Rd.
Rhett Ave.
Charleston Air Force Base
Charleston International Airport
NORTH CHARLESTON
Montague Ave.
Fairgrounds Ave.
Dorchester Rd.
Ashley River Rd.
Leeds Ave.
Durant Ave.
Spruill Ave.
U.S. Naval Hospital
U.S. Naval Base
Clark Expwy.
Mark Clark Expwy.
DRAYTON
PIERPONT
ASHLEY HALL
Cantrell Rd.
Ferry
Paul
Savannah Hwy.
USDA Experimental Farm
Sycamore Ave.
Rutledge Ave.
Old Town Rd.
Sam Rittenberg Blvd.
Huger St.
King St.
Meeting St.
East Bay St.
Calhoun St.
Wentworth St.
Wappoo Dr.
Tradd St.
Veterans Hospital
Ashley River
CHARLESTON
RED TOP
RIVERLAND TERRACE
Riverland Dr.
Maybank Hwy.
Folly Rd.
Harbor View Rd.
Camp Rd.
Johnson Rd.
CENTERVILLE
JAMES ISLAND
Fort Sumter National Monument
Clark Sound
Lighthouse Creek
Stono River
JOHNS ISLAND
FENWICK CROSSROADS
Maybank
Charleston Executive Airport
Cut Bridge Rd.
Grimball Road
RIVERLAND
CAINHOY
Cainhoy Rd.
Beresford Creek
Nobles Creek
Wando River
Francis Marion National Forest
BERKELEY CO. CHARLESTON CO.
PHILIP
TEN MILE
Wando River
SNOWDEN
Long Point Rd.
Highway
Clements Ferry Rd.
Isle of Palms Connector
Johnnie Dodds Blvd.
W. Coleman Blvd.
MOUNT PLEASANT
USS Yorktown Aircraft Carrier Museum
Willson Memorial Airport
Intracoastal Waterway
Breach Inlet
Inlet Creek
SULLIVANS ISLAND
ISLE OF PALMS
Atlantic Ocean
Scale of Miles 0 1 2 3
N
© C.S.C.

Charleston, WV (bottom map)

BIG CHIMNEY
PINCH
COCO
Suger Creek Dr.
Falcon Dr.
Scraggs Dr.
Sisson Hwy.
GUTHRIE
CREED
BREAM
MILLIKEN
Pennsylvania Ave.
Elk River
Washington St.
Woodburn Lane
Woodford Dr.
West
Fairlawn
INSTITUTE
DUNBAR
Dutch Rd.
Rosedale Ave.
Washington St.
Kanawha Tpk.
ETOWAN
Yeager Airport
RUTLEDGE
QUICK
MacCorkle Ave.
10th St.
Dunbar Ave.
SOUTH CHARLESTON
Kanawha River
Jefferson Rd.
Patrick St.
Greenbrier St.
Bakers Rd.
CHARLESTON
Oakridge Dr.
ELK
Oakhurst Dr.
Elk Bridge Rd.
MacCorkle Ave.
RIVERVIEW
SNOW HILL
COAL FORK
Campbells Creek
FIVEMILE
TAD
CINCO
RENSFORD
BLOUNT
Spring Fork Dr.
Campbells Creek Dr.
Chestnut St.
Myrtle St.
Church Dr.
RUTH
Berry Hill Dr.
Oakhurst Dr.
Lincoln St.
SOUTH PARK
SOUTH MALDEN
Davis Creek
Park
PORT
SPRING FORK
MALDEN
RAND
Kanawha State Forest
Middle Fork
Davis Creek
W.V. Turnpike
Scale of Miles 0 1 2 3
N
© C.S.C.

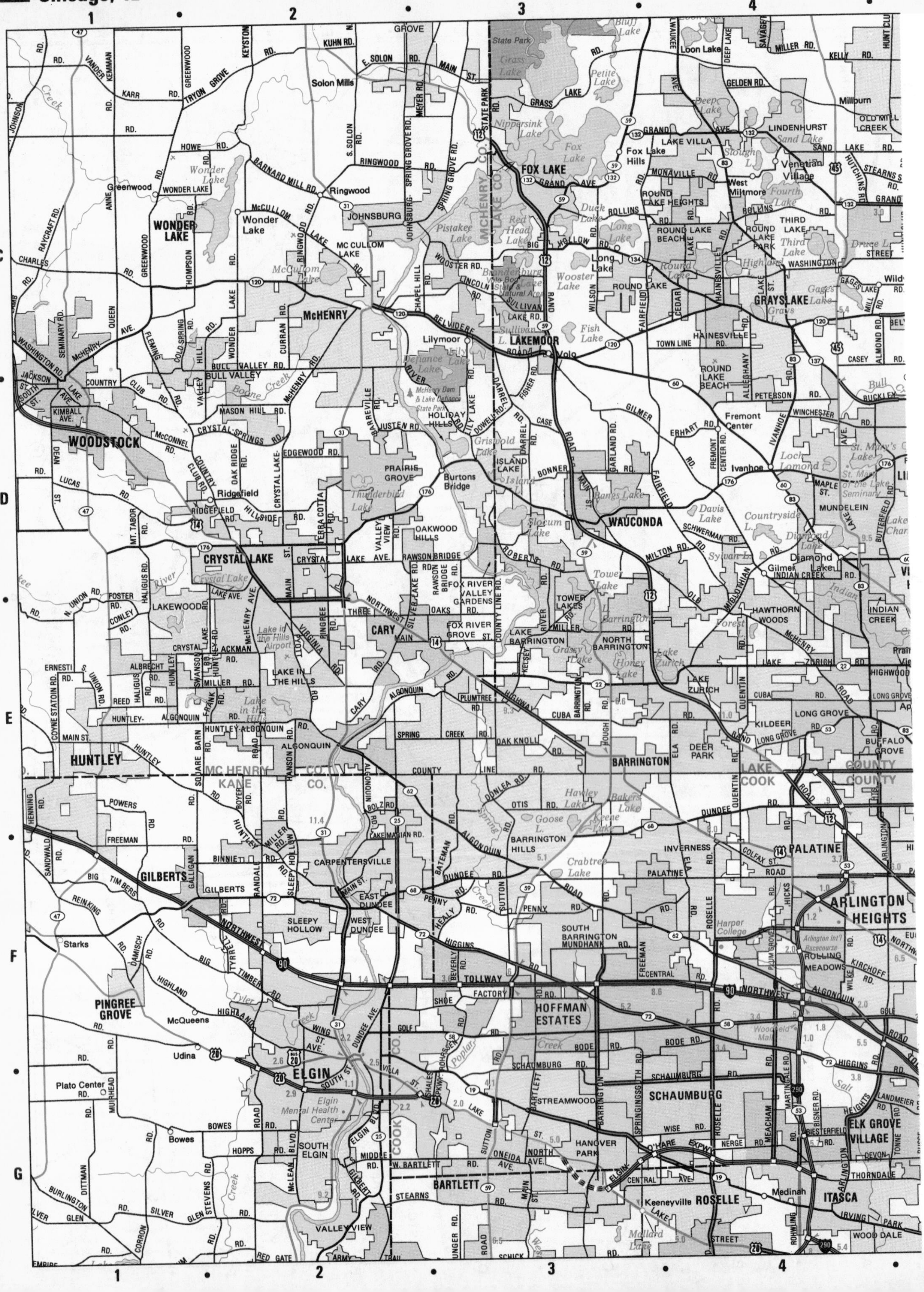

WONDER LAKE

Greenwood

Solon Mills

Ringwood

Johnsburg

Wonder Lake

McHENRY

WOODSTOCK

Lilymoor

L. LAKEMOOR

Volo

FOX LAKE

Fox Lake Hills

West Miltmore

Venetian Village

Millburn

Lindenhurst

LAKE VILLA

Round Lake Heights

Round Lake Beach

Round Lake Park

Round Lake

THIRD LAKE

GRAYSLAKE

Hainesville

Round Lake Beach

Fremont Center

Ivanhoe

MUNDELEIN

INDIAN CREEK

Ridgefield

CRYSTAL LAKE

LAKEWOOD

PRAIRIE GROVE

Burtons Bridge

OAKWOOD HILLS

HOLIDAY HILLS

Island Lake

WAUCONDA

Diamond Lake

CARY

FOX RIVER GROVE

Lake in the Hills

LAKE IN THE HILLS

TOWER LAKES

NORTH BARRINGTON

LAKE BARRINGTON

LAKE ZURICH

Hawthorn Woods

HIGHWOOD

INDIAN CREEK

LONG GROVE

KILDEER

BUFFALO GROVE

HUNTLEY

ALGONQUIN

BARRINGTON

DEER PARK

McHENRY CO.
KANE CO.

LAKE COUNTY
COOK COUNTY

PALATINE

ARLINGTON HEIGHTS

GILBERTS

CARPENTERSVILLE

BARRINGTON HILLS

Palatine

ROLLING MEADOWS

Starks

SLEEPY HOLLOW

WEST DUNDEE

EAST DUNDEE

SOUTH BARRINGTON

INVERNESS

PINGREE GROVE

McQueens

Udina

Plato Center

Bowes

ELGIN

SOUTH ELGIN

HOFFMAN ESTATES

SCHAUMBURG

STREAMWOOD

HANOVER PARK

ELK GROVE VILLAGE

ITASCA

Wood Dale

ROSELLE

Keeneyville

Medinah

BARTLETT

VALLEY VIEW

Woodfield Mall

Arlington Int'l Racecourse

Harper College

Elgin Mental Health Center

CONTINUED ON PAGE 105, GRID L-8

LAKE MICHIGAN

LAKE MICHIGAN

Scale of Miles

0   1   2   3

© A.M.C.

Lake Campton
Wasco
ELBURN
La Fox
Kane County Fairgrounds
ST. CHARLES
GENEVA
BATAVIA
Baldmond
Mooseheart
NORTH AURORA
Marywood
AURORA
Aurora University
SUGAR GROVE
MONTGOMERY
OSWEGO
YORKVILLE
Wayne
DuPAGE County Airport
WEST CHICAGO
Prince Crossing
FERMI LAB
Kress Creek
Eola
NAPERVILLE
North Central College
Frontenac
Wheatland Airfield
Wolfs
Normantown
PLAINFIELD
Lake Renwick
BLOOMINGDALE
Gloverdale
CAROL STREAM
GLENDALE HEIGHTS
ADDISON
LOMBARD
VILLA PARK
GLEN ELLYN
Wheaton College
WHEATON
WINFIELD
Flowerfield
York Center
Highland Hills
College of DuPage
Herrick Lake
Morton Arboretum
LISLE
Illinois Benedictine College
DOWNERS GROVE
WOODRIDGE
BOLINGBROOK
ARGONNE NATIONAL LABORATORY
LEMONT
ROMEOVILLE
Lewis University
Stateville Correctional Center
LOCKPORT
South Lockport
Fairmont
CREST HILL
JOLIET
College of St. Francis
SHOREWOOD
Joliet Jr. College
ROCKDALE
Preston Heights
Ridgewood
Ingalls Park
NEW LENOX
Caton Farm
Plattville
Lisbon Center
MINOOKA
KANE CO.
DU PAGE CO.
KENDALL CO.
WILL CO.
GRUNDY CO.
Scale of Miles
0 1 2 3
© A.M.C.

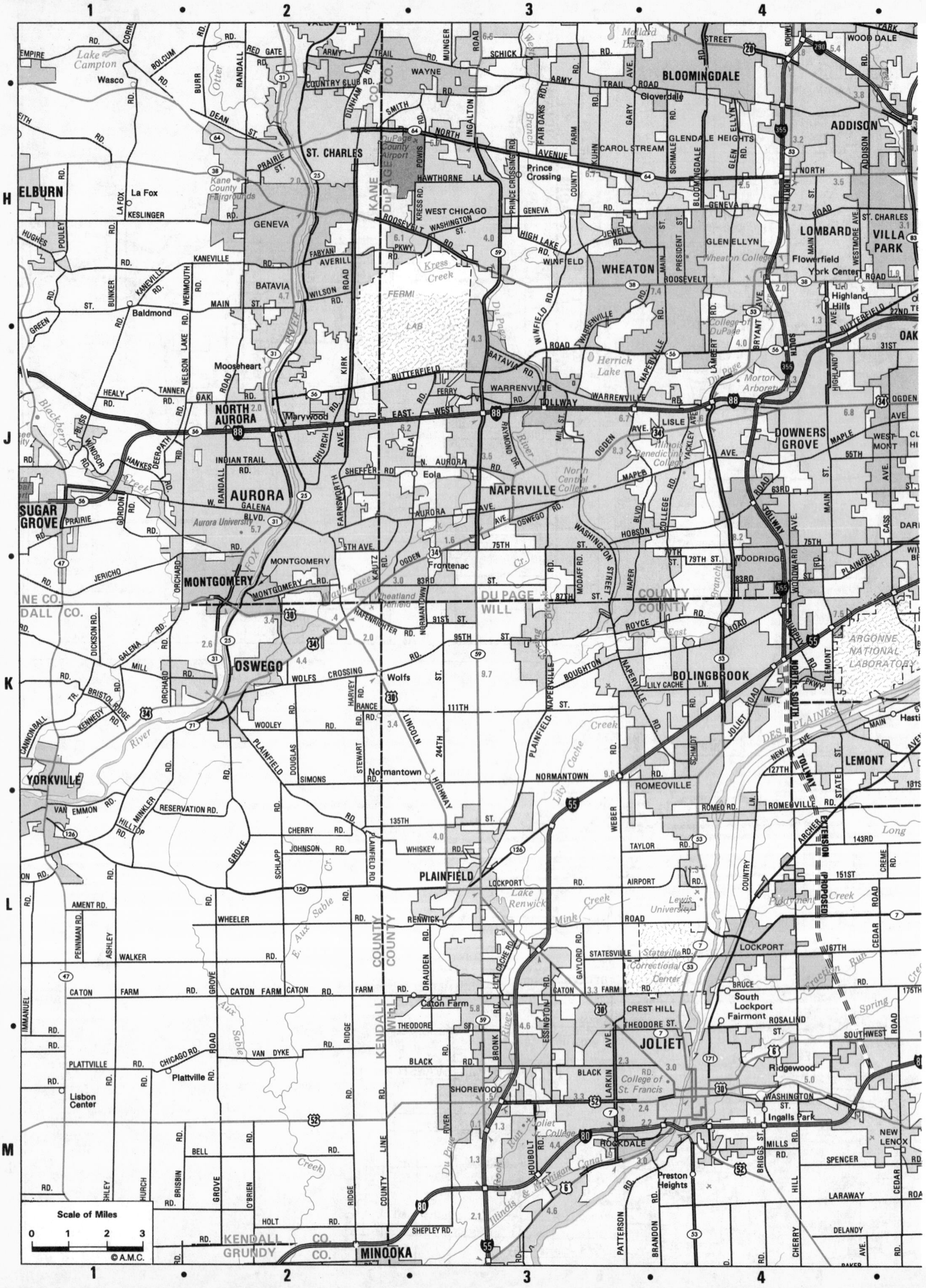

LAKE MICHIGAN

N

Major places: O'Hare Airport, Schiller Park, Elmwood Park, Oak Park, Maywood, Berwyn, Cicero, Elmhurst, Oak Brook, Oakbrook Terrace, Westchester, La Grange Park, Brookfield, River Forest, River Grove, Northlake, Melrose Park, Stone Park, Bellwood, Hillside, Broadview, North Riverside, Riverside, Stickney, Forest View, Summit, Hodgkins, Countryside, La Grange, Western Springs, Hinsdale, Clarendon Hills, Indian Head Park, Willow Springs, Justice, Bridgeview, Bedford Park, Burbank, Hometown, Evergreen Park, Oak Lawn, Chicago Ridge, Hickory Hills, Palos Hills, Palos Park, Worth, Alsip, Blue Island, Calumet Park, Robbins, Dixmoor, Posen, Midlothian, Crestwood, Orland Park, Orland Hills, Tinley Park, Oak Forest, Markham, Harvey, Phoenix, Dolton, Riverdale, Burnham, Calumet City, Hammond, Whiting, East Chicago, Columbus, South Holland, Thornton, Lansing, Munster, Dyer, Lynwood, Glenwood, Flossmoor, Homewood, Hazel Crest, East Hazel Crest, Country Club Hills, Hickory Hills, Olympia Fields, Matteson, Park Forest, Richton Park, Chicago Heights, South Chicago Heights, Ford Heights, Glenwood, Steger, Crete, Frankfort, Mokena, New Lenox, Marley, Spencer, Lincoln Estates, St. Francis, Aubury Hills

Parks / features: Lincoln Park, Humboldt Park, Garfield Park, Grant Park, Field Mus. of Natural History, Meigs Field, Burnham Park, Douglas Park, Columbus Park, Washington Park, Jackson Park, Marquette Park, Merrionette Park, Lake Calumet, William W. Powers Conservation Area, Wolf Lake, Lake Michigan, Chicago Midway Airport, Sag Bridge, McGinnis Slough, Goodings Grove, Tinley Park Mental Health Center, World Music Theater, Prairie State College, Abraham Lincoln Oasis, Wicker Memorial Park, Hickory Creek, Butterfield Creek

Roads: Adlai Stevenson Expwy (55), Eisenhower Expressway (290), John F. Kennedy Expwy (90/94), Dan Ryan Expwy (90/94), Lake Shore Drive (41), Chicago Skyway (90), Tri-State Tollway (294), Southwest Highway, Dr. Martin Luther King Jr. Dr., East-West Toll Road, Calumet Expwy, Bishop Ford Expwy (94)

COOK CO. / WILL CO. / DuPAGE CO. / ILLINOIS / INDIANA / LAKE CO.

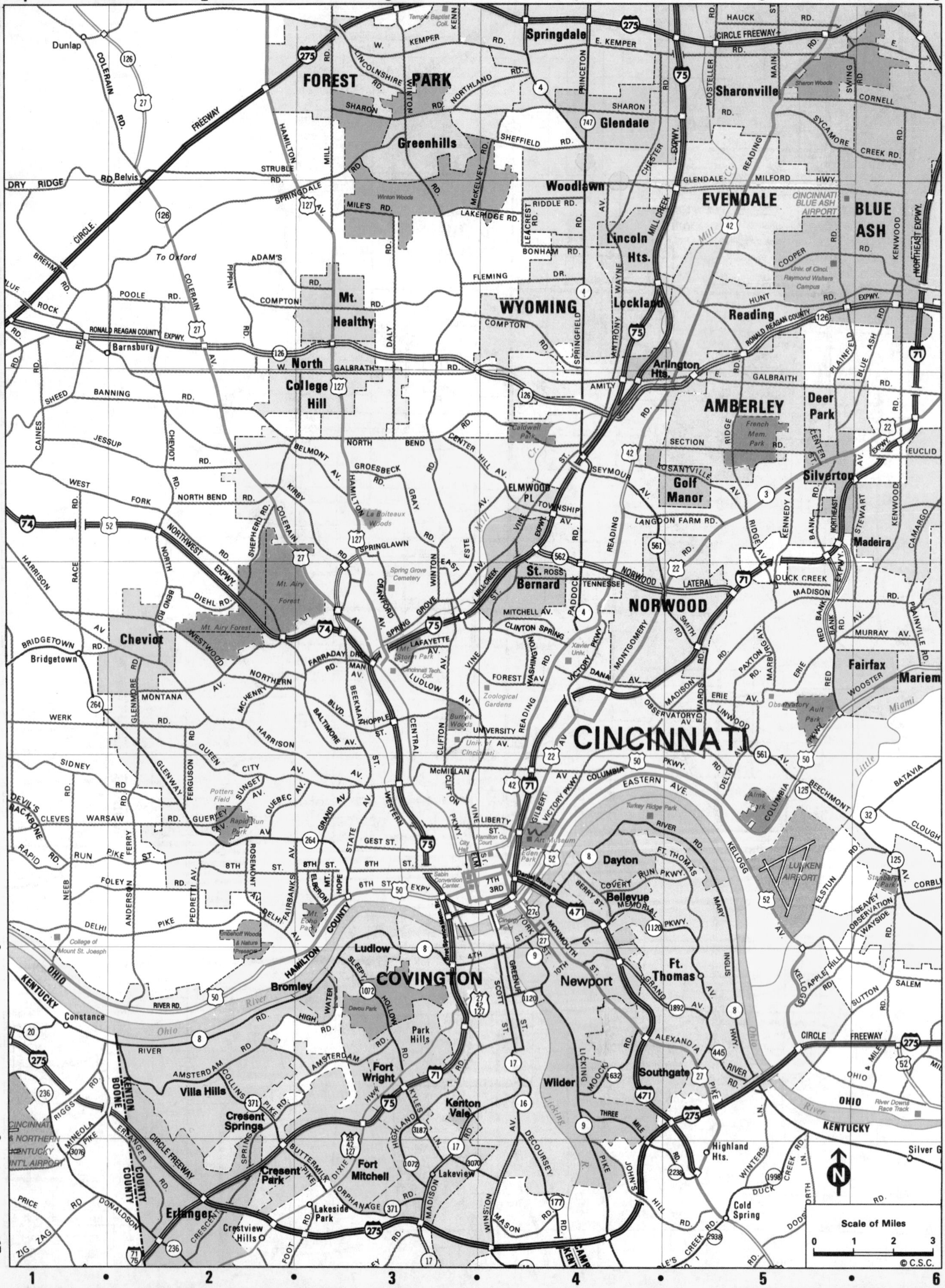

FOREST PARK

Dunlap

Belvis

Barnsburg

Greenhills

Mt. Healthy

North College Hill

Cheviot

Bridgetown

Mt. Airy Forest

Springdale

Glendale

Woodlawn

WYOMING

Lincoln Hts.

Lockland

Reading

Arlington Hts.

AMBERLEY

Elmwood Pl.

St. Bernard

NORWOOD

Golf Manor

Deer Park

Silverton

Madeira

Fairfax

Mariem

Sharonville

EVENDALE

BLUE ASH

CINCINNATI

University of Cincinnati

Zoological Gardens

Covington

Ludlow

Bromley

Newport

Dayton

Bellevue

Ft. Thomas

Southgate

Villa Hills

Cresent Springs

Fort Wright

Fort Mitchell

Cresent Park

Erlanger

Lakeside Park

Crestview Hills

Kenton Vale

Lakeview

Wilder

Constance

Cold Spring

Highland Hts.

Park Hills

Lunken Airport

Cincinnati Blue Ash Airport

Cincinnati & Northern Kentucky Int'l Airport

OHIO

KENTUCKY

Ohio River

Licking River

Little Miami River

HAMILTON COUNTY

KENTON COUNTY

BOONE COUNTY

CAMPBELL

Scale of Miles

0   1   2   3

N

© C.S.C.

Lake Erie

Lakefront State Park

WICKLIFFE
WILLOUGHBY HILLS
EUCLID
RICHMOND HEIGHTS
HIGHLAND HTS.
LYNDHURST
MAYFIELD HEIGHTS
SOUTH EUCLID
EAST CLEVELAND
CLEVELAND HEIGHTS
UNIVERSITY HEIGHTS
BRATENAHL
Gordan Park
Burke Lakefront Airport
CLEVELAND
Gund Arena
City Hall
Jacobs Field
Cleveland State University
Case Western Reserve University
John Carroll University
Notre Dame Coll. of Ohio
Ursuline College
SHAKER HEIGHTS
PEPPER PIKE
BEACHWOOD
WOODMERE
MORELAND HILLS
ORANGE
LAKEWOOD
Edgewater Yacht Club
ROCKY RIVER
FAIRVIEW PARK
BROOKLYN
Cleveland Metropark Zoo
NEWBURGH HEIGHTS
CUYAHOGA HEIGHTS
BROOKLYN HEIGHTS
WARRENSVILLE HEIGHTS
NORTH RANDALL
GARFIELD HEIGHTS
MAPLE HEIGHTS
BEDFORD HTS.
BEDFORD
SOLON
GLENWILLOW
Baldwin Wallace Coll.
Cleveland Hopkins Int'l Airport
Ford Motor Company Assembly Plant
Holy Cross Cem.
Snow
BROOK PARK
MIDDLEBURG HEIGHTS
BEREA
PARMA HEIGHTS
PARMA
Parma Comm. Hosp.
Cuyahoga Community College
SEVEN HILLS
INDEPENDENCE
VALLEY VIEW
Normandy H.S.
Chevrolet Motor Company
Midtown S.C.
WALTON HILLS
OAKWOOD
Bedford Reservation
NORTH ROYALTON
BROADVIEW HEIGHTS
BRECKSVILLE
SAGAMORE HILLS
NORTHFIELD
MACEDONIA
TWINSBURG
Macedonia H.S.
Strongsville Airport
STRONGSVILLE
City Hall
Rocky River Reservation
Brecksville Reservation
Brecksville V.A. Hosp.
Cuyahoga Valley Nat'l Rec. Area
CUYAHOGA CO. / SUMMIT CO.
Hawthornden St. Hosp.
Northfield Sq. S.C.
Four Points Airport
BOSTON
Cleveland Boys Sch.
HUDSON
CUYAHOGA CO. / MEDINA CO.
Villaain Golf Club
Pine Hills Golf Club
Ironwood Golf Course
Mattingly
Skyland Golf Club
Babcock Rd.
Hinckley Hills Golf Club
U.S. Military Res.
Brunswick Hill Golf Course
HINCKLEY
BRUNSWICK
RICHFIELD
Hinckley Lake / Hinckley Res.
PENINSULA
HEIGHTS
Furnace Run Park
Cuyahoga Valley Nat'l Rec. Area
Virginia Kendall Park
EVERETT
STOW
ABBEYVILLE
WEYMOUTH
REMSEN CORNERS
Pleasant Valley Golf Club
BATH
BATH CENTER
GHENT
GRANGER
BOTZUM
CUYAHOGA FALLS
AKRON
Rest Area

Scale of Miles
0 1 2 3

© CSC

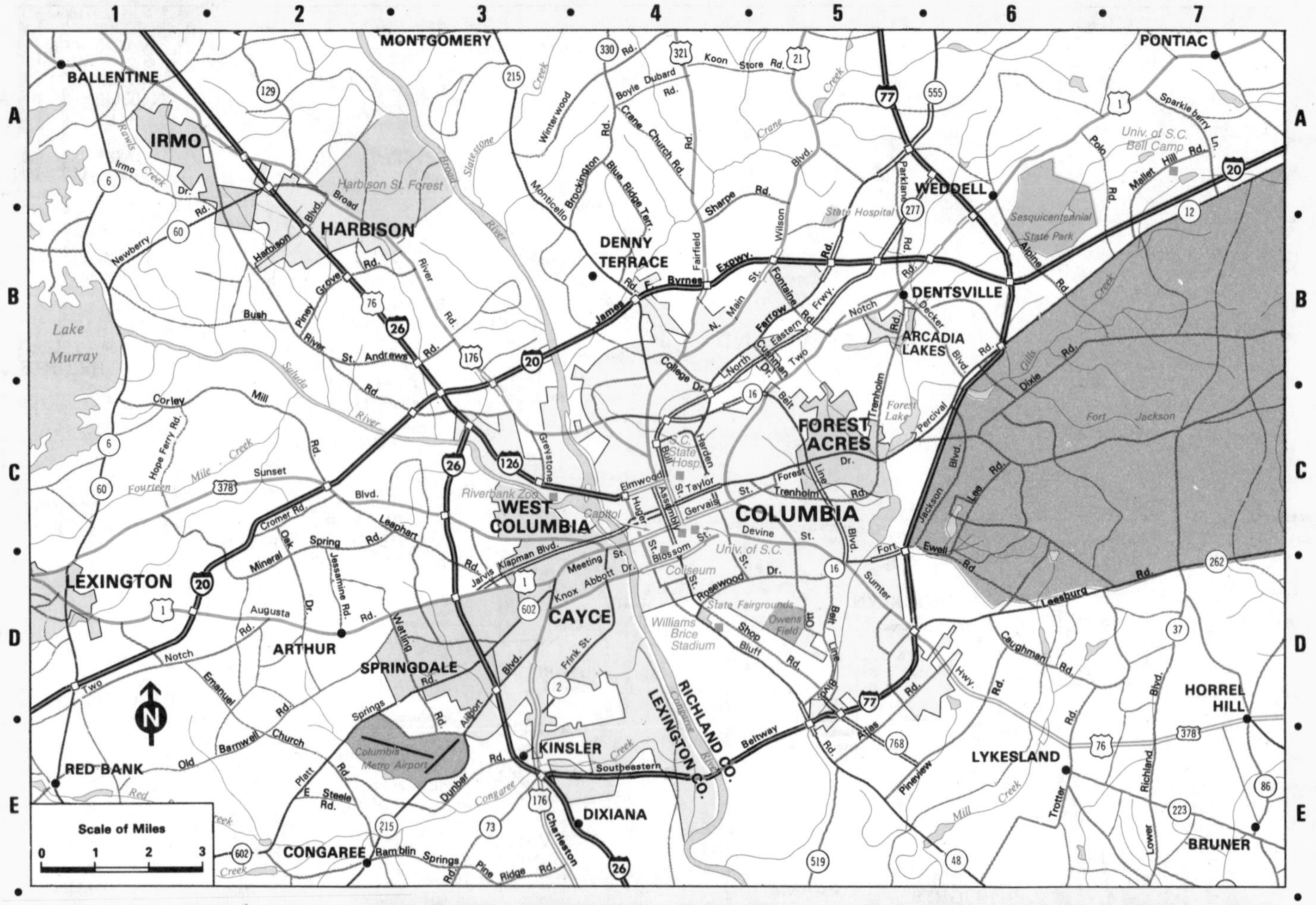
BALLENTINE
MONTGOMERY
PONTIAC
IRMO
HARBISON
Harbison St. Forest
Lake Murray
DENNY TERRACE
WEDDELL
DENTSVILLE
ARCADIA LAKES
Sesquicentennial State Park
Univ. of S.C. Bell Camp
State Hospital
FOREST ACRES
Forest Lake
Fort Jackson
WEST COLUMBIA
COLUMBIA
Riverbank Zoo
Capitol
S.C. State Hosp.
Univ. of S.C.
Coliseum
State Fairgrounds
Williams Brice Stadium
Owens Field
LEXINGTON
CAYCE
ARTHUR
SPRINGDALE
KINSLER
Columbia Metro Airport
RICHLAND CO.
LEXINGTON CO.
HORREL HILL
LYKESLAND
RED BANK
DIXIANA
CONGAREE
BRUNER
Scale of Miles
0 1 2 3

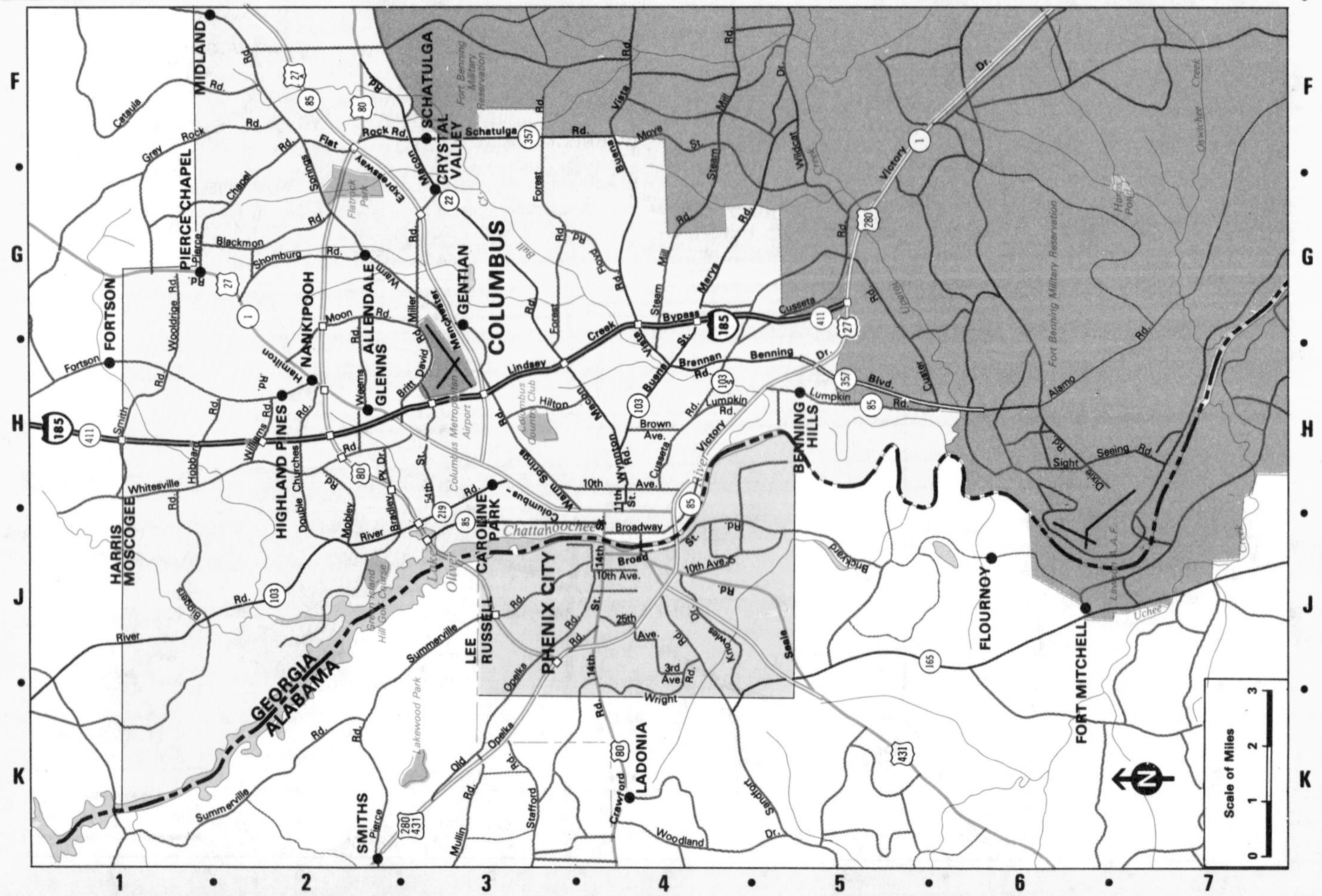
MIDLAND
SCHATULGA
CRYSTAL VALLEY
PIERCE CHAPEL
Fort Benning Military Reservation
Flatrock Park
COLUMBUS
GENTIAN
FORTSON
NANKIPOOH
ALLENDALE
GLENNS
HIGHLAND PINES
Columbus Metropolitan Airport
Columbus Country Club
BENNING HILLS
HARRIS
MOSCOGEE
CAROLINE PARK
Chattahoochee
PHENIX CITY
LEE
RUSSELL
GEORGIA
ALABAMA
Lakewood Park
FLOURNOY
FORT MITCHELL
Lawson A.A.F.
LADONIA
SMITHS
Scale of Miles
0 1 2 3

Map grid columns: 1 2 3 4 5 6 7
Map grid rows: A B C D E F G H J K

Scioto River
745 257
Hyatts
HYATTS
Moore
Duffy
Merchant
RATHBONE
Home
Cook
Harriott
Concord
42
JEROME
SHAWNEE HILLS
Powell
315
Shanahan
Hollenback
Platt
North
Columbus
Lewis Center
LEWIS CENTER
Alum Creek State Rec. Area
Rome Corners
GALENA
Vans Valley
605
37
Trenton
Rest Area
Rest Area
Lewis Center
Jaycox
AFRICA
Africa
Woodtown
Miller-Paul
Center Village
CENTER VILLAGE
Freeman
Big Walnut
Maxtown
Smothers
Hoover Reservoir
Sunbury
Red Bank
HARLEM
Gorsuch
Robins
Fancher
Bevelheimer
Peter Hoover
Green-Cook

Olentangy River
W. Orange
E. Orange
257
Carriage
Seldom Seen
Rutherford
Steitz
Taggert
Perry
Columbus
23
750 POWELL
Powell
Brand
Smoky Row
Jewett
DELAWARE CO.
FRANKLIN CO.
Summit View
745
Hard Rd.
Bright Rd.
JACK NICKLAUS FRWY.
161
Snouffer
Hanawalt
Polaris Pkwy.
Lazelle Rd.
Polaris
Polaris Amphitheatre
71
Highbanks Metro Park
Worthington-Galena
MOUNT AIR
FLINT
Flint Park
WESTERVILLE
Walnut
Schrock
Otterbein College
Sharon Woods Metro Park
Pike
Maxtown
Tussic Street
Schott
Lee
Central College
605
62
NEW ALBANY
161
Reynoldsburg-New Albany

Plain City
161
KILEVILLE
Post
Coffman
DUBLIN
Shier Rings
Avery
Wilcox
Rings
Tuttle
Coseuy
161
UNION CO.
FRANKLIN CO.
MADISON CO.
AMLIN
HAYDEN
Houchard
Hayden Run
Elliott
33
HILLARD
Davidson
Hillard-Cem.
270
Sawmill Rd.
LINWORTH
Dublin-Granville
WORTHINGTON
Antrim Park
RIVERLEA
Don Scott Airport
Case
Bethel
Henderson
Godown Rd.
R.R. Museum
Olentangy
MINERVA PARK
Minerva Lakes Rd.
Dempsey
Warner
HUBER RIDGE
GOULD PARK
Blendon Woods Metro Park
Morse
Headley Rd.
161
Hoover Dam

CLINTON
Cooke
23
Morse
Sinclair
Ferris Rd.
Kerr
Innis
Sunbury
Columbus-Wooster
270
GAHANNA
McCutcheon
McCutcheon Rd.
Clark
Havens
Haven's Corner
Mann Rd.
33
McCoy
Highland
Kenny
UPPER ARLINGTON
Fishinger
Whetstone Park
Columbus Park of Roses
N. Broadway
Oakland Park
Weber
Agler
62
Styaler
Gahanna Woods Park

315
SAN MARGHERITA
Trabue
Maryville
Lane
Trement
North Star
5th
Dublin Rd.
Hudson
71
Mock Rd.
Mock Park
Seventeenth
Ohio History Museum
Ohio State Univ.
Ohio Stadium
Summit St.
Fourth
Fifth
Ohio Dominican College
Woodland
Cassady Ave.
Sunbury
Columbus-Millersburg
670
Int'l. Gateway
Port Columbus Int'l. Airport
317
BLACKLICK
16

MARBLE CLIFF
GRANDVIEW HEIGHTS
670
McKinley
Fisher Rd.
Jack
70
VALLEYVIEW
Broad Ave.
State Capitol
33
Broad
40
Leonard
BEXLEY
WHITEHALL
Main
Big Walnut Park
40
Yearing
REYNOLDSBURG
256
70

ALTON
NEW ROME
40
Sullivant Ave.
Sullivant
62
Cooper Stadium
71
23
COLUMBUS
Livingston
33
Lockbourne
Alum
James
Champion
Capital University
Main Ave.
Blacklick Woods Metro Park

Darby Dan Airport
National Rd.
Feder Rd.
Amity
Georgesville
Big Run Park
3
Lou Berliner Park
Marion
Refugee
Winchester
Refugee Rd.
BRICE
Natzgran Park

GALLOWAY
Alkire
Bolton Field Airport
Grove City Monteney Airport
Grove Port
BRIGGSDALE
Frank
104
JAMES MOONEY HWY.
Groveport
270
Hamilton
Helser Park
Noe-Bixby
Shannon Rd.
Wright
Pickerington Ponds Wetlands Wildlife Area

GEORGEVILLE
Alkire
Battelle Darby Creek Metro Park
Johnson
URBANCREST
Home Rd.
Gantz Rd.
Beulah Park
Williams
Groveport
OBETZ
GROVEPORT
317
33
Bixby
CANAL WINCHESTER
674

DARBYDALE
665
PLEASANT CORNERS
London-Groveport
Lukens
Grove
Rensch
City
GROVE CITY
White
Stringtown
Orders
Holton
Beatty
Parson's
JACK NICKLAUS FRWY.
REESE
Rohr
London-Groveport
317
WATERLOO
Lithopolis
Gender

71
Harrisburg-London Rd.
HARRISBURG
Gay Rd.
Boyd
Opossum Run
Young
Borror
ORIENT
FRANKLIN CO.
PICKAWAY CO.
SHADEVILLE
Cols-Chillicothe
LOCKBOURNE
Rowe
Vause
U.S. Military Res.
Rickenbacker Air Force Base
Lancaster
LITHOPOLIS
Elder
62
3
762
104
23

N

Scale of Miles
0   1   2   3

© C.S.C.

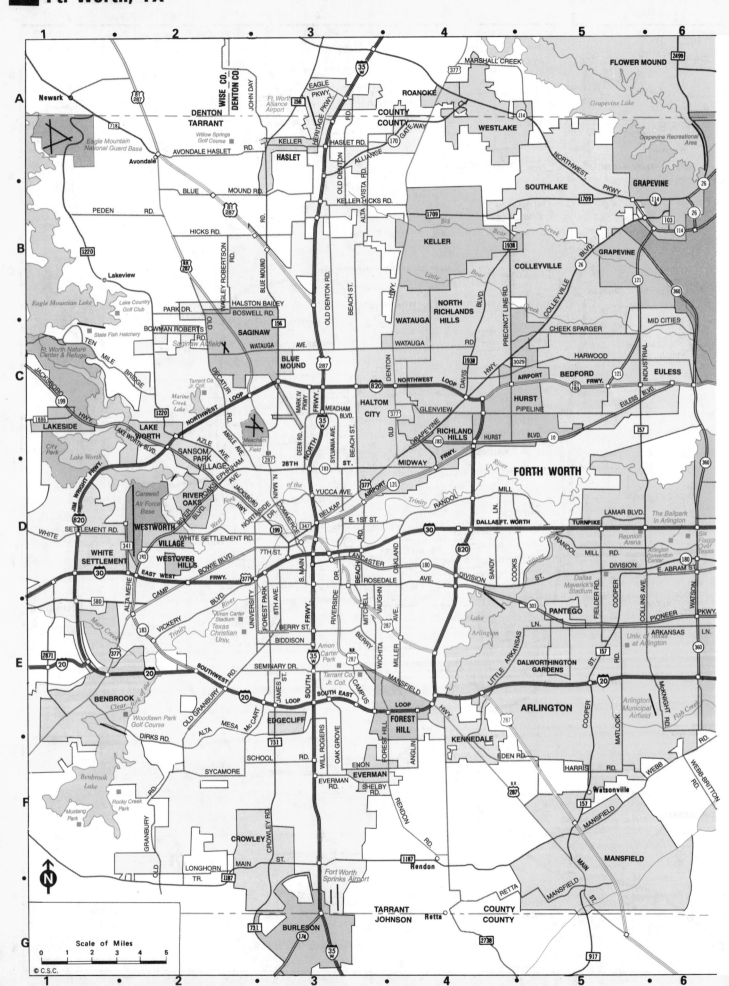

Scale of Miles
0   1   2   3   4   5

© C.S.C.

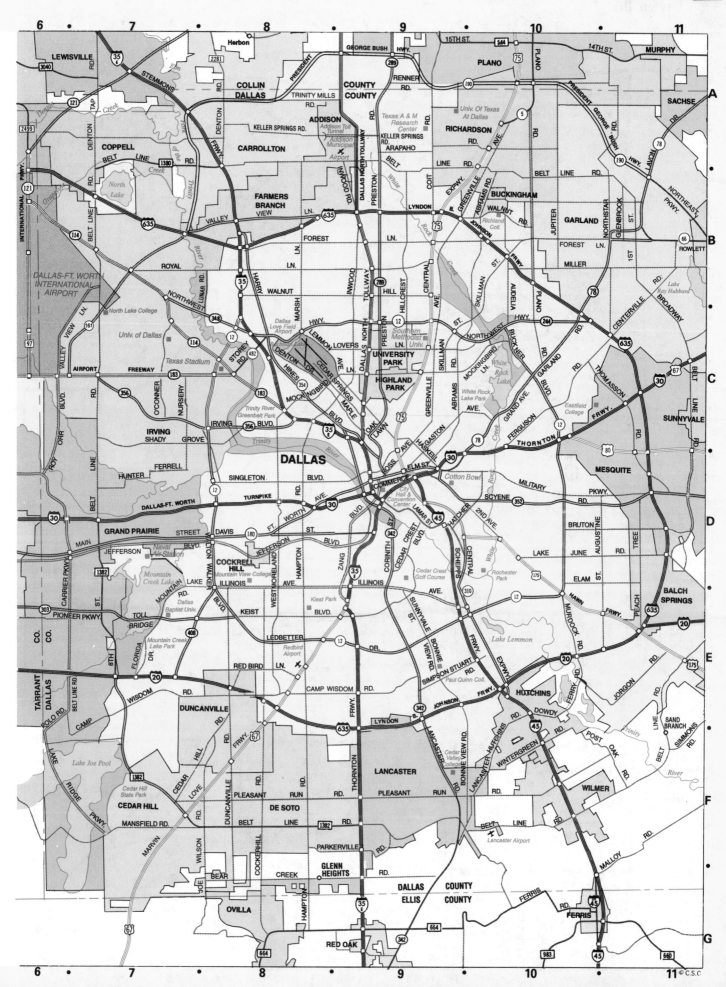

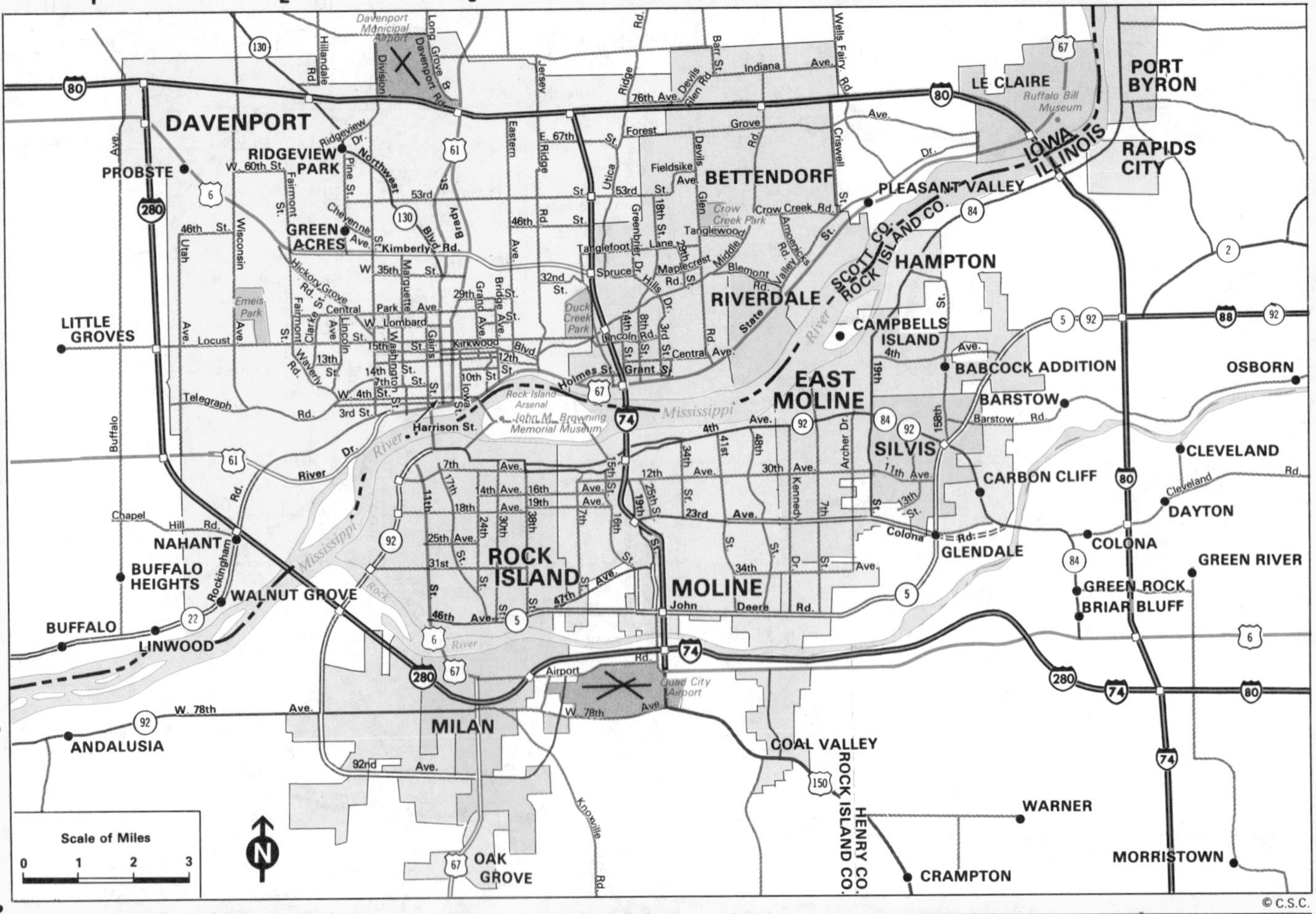

Map 1 — Davenport, IA / Quad Cities

Grid columns: 1 2 3 4 5 6 7
Grid rows: A B C D E

DAVENPORT

Davenport Municipal Airport
Long Grove Rd.
76th Ave.
Devils Glen Rd.
Indiana Ave.
Jersey Ridge Rd.
Forest Grove Ave.
LE CLAIRE
Buffalo Bill Museum
PORT BYRON
IOWA / ILLINOIS
RAPIDS CITY

PROBSTE
RIDGEVIEW PARK
W. 60th St.
Ridgeview Dr.
Northwest Blvd.
Pine St.
Fairmont
Cheyenne
53rd St.
E. 67th
Utica Ridge Rd.
Fieldsike St.
BETTENDORF
PLEASANT VALLEY
HAMPTON
OSBORN

GREEN ACRES
Wisconsin
Utah
46th St.
Hickory Grove
Kimberly Rd.
W. 35th St.
46th
Crow Creek Park
Tanglewood
Tanglefoot Dr.
Greenbelt
Maplecrest
RIVERDALE
SCOTT CO. / ROCK ISLAND CO.
CAMPBELLS ISLAND
BABCOCK ADDITION
BARSTOW
Barstow Rd.

LITTLE GROVES
Emeis Park
Central Park Ave.
W. Lombard
29th St.
Grand Ave.
Bridge Ave.
Kirkwood Blvd.
Holmes St.
Duck Creek Park
Lincoln Rd.
Grant Ave.
State St.
Middle Rd.
EAST MOLINE
SILVIS
11th Ave.
CARBON CLIFF
CLEVELAND
Cleveland Rd.
DAYTON

Locust
13th St.
14th St.
10th St.
7th St.
Harrison St.
Rock Island Arsenal
John M. Browning Memorial Museum
Mississippi River
4th Ave.
41st St.
48th Ave.
92
84
GLENDALE
COLONA
GREEN RIVER

Telegraph Rd.
3rd St.
W. 4th St.
River Dr.
7th Ave.
11th
4th Ave.
16th Ave.
18th Ave.
19th Ave.
24th St.
30th St.
38th Ave.
12th Ave.
23rd Ave.
30th Ave.
Kennedy Dr.
Colona Rd.
GREEN ROCK
BRIAR BLUFF

NAHANT
BUFFALO HEIGHTS
Chapel Hill Rd.
Rockingham Rd.
WALNUT GROVE
25th St.
31st St.
ROCK ISLAND
34th Ave.
MOLINE
John Deere Rd.

BUFFALO
LINWOOD
22
46th Ave.
47th Ave.
River Dr.
Airport Rd.
Quad City Airport
I-74
I-280
I-80

ANDALUSIA
92rd Ave.
MILAN
W. 78th Ave.
COAL VALLEY
ROCK ISLAND CO. / HENRY CO.
WARNER
MORRISTOWN

OAK GROVE
Knoxville Rd.
150
CRAMPTON

Scale of Miles 0 1 2 3
N

© C.S.C.

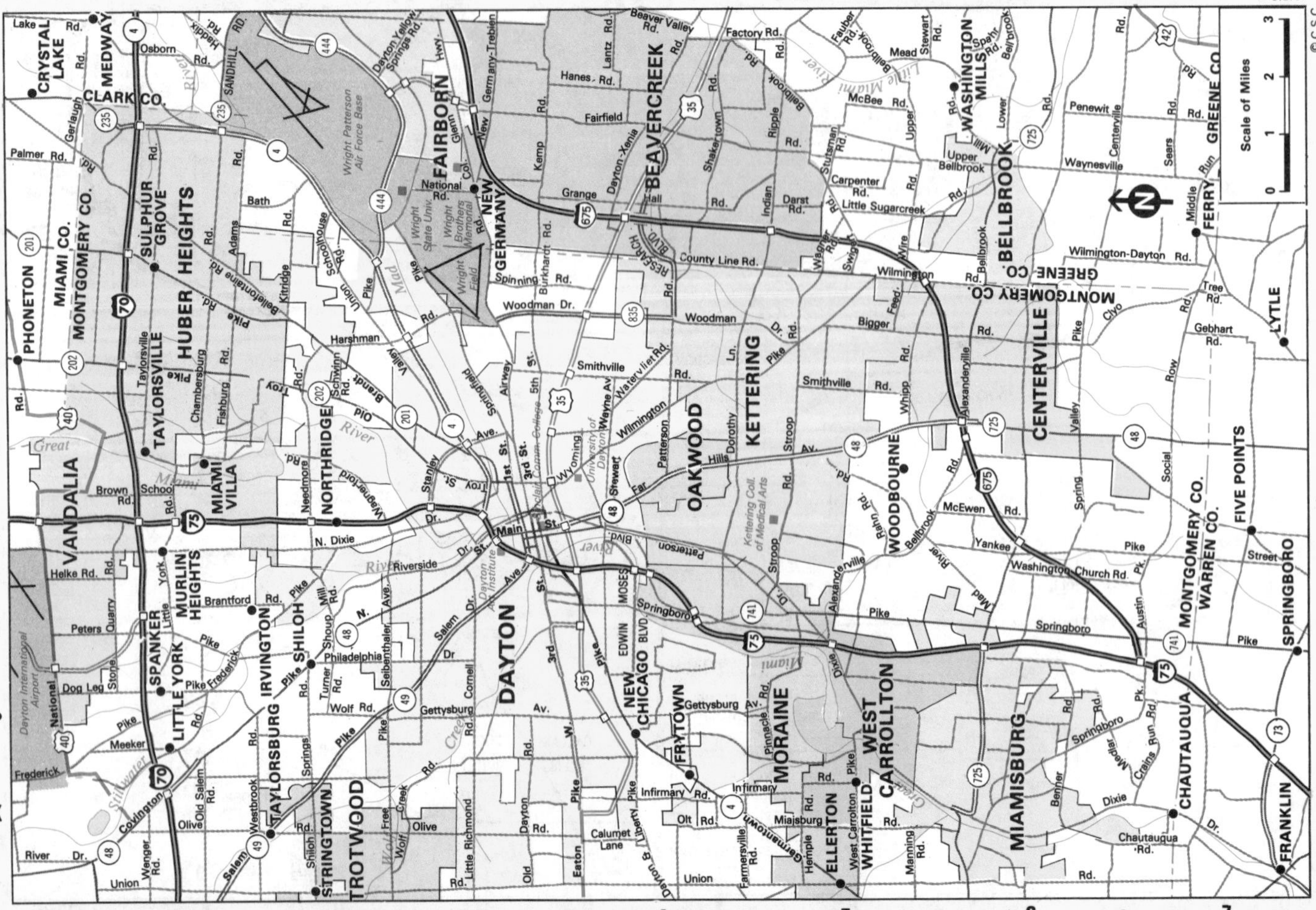

Map 2 — Dayton, OH

Grid columns: 1 2 3 4 5 6 7
Grid rows: F G H J K

CRYSTAL LAKE
MEDWAY
CLARK CO.
Osborn Rd.
Sandhill Rd.
Dayton-Yellow Springs Rd.
444
Beaver Valley Rd.
Factory Rd.
WASHINGTON MILLS
GREENE CO.

PHONETON
MIAMI CO. / MONTGOMERY CO.
201
Palmer Rd.
Gerlaugh Rd.
235
SULPHUR GROVE
Bath Rd.
Wright Patterson Air Force Base
FAIRBORN
Wright State Univ.
National Rd.
NEW GERMANY
Germany-Trebein Rd.
Hanes Rd.
Fairfield
BEAVERCREEK
35
McBee Rd.
Upper Bellbrook Rd.
Penewit Rd.
Centerville
Waynesville
Sears Rd.

202
HUBER HEIGHTS
TAYLORSVILLE
70
Chambersburg Rd.
Troy Pike
Wright Brothers Mem.
675
Grange Hall Rd.
Shakertown Rd.
Wilmington Pike
Carpenter Rd.
Little Sugarcreek Rd.
BELLBROOK
Wilmington-Dayton Rd.
MONTGOMERY CO. / GREENE CO.
LYTLE
Tree Rd.

440
Great Miami River
MIAMI VILLA
NORTHRIDGE
Harshman Rd.
Airway Rd.
Smithville Rd.
Woodman Dr.
Bigger Rd.
Smithville Rd.
CENTERVILLE
Gebhart Rd.
FIVE POINTS
48

VANDALIA
Brown School Rd.
75
MURLIN HEIGHTS
Needmore Rd.
Stanley Ave.
Valley St.
Keowee St.
3rd St.
1st St.
Wayne Ave.
Patterson Blvd.
Stroop Rd.
OAKWOOD
KETTERING
Whipp Rd.
Social Row Rd.
MONTGOMERY CO. / WARREN CO.
675
725

Dayton International Airport
Peters Pike
SPANKER
LITTLE YORK
Frederick Pike
SHILOH
IRVINGTON
N. Dixie Dr.
Salem Ave.
Main St.
DAYTON
Riverside Dr.
Great Miami River
Patterson Blvd.
Springboro Pike
WOODBOURNE
Alexandersville Rd.
McEwen Rd.
Yankee Rd.
Washington-Church Rd.
741

Helke Rd.
York St.
Philadelphia Dr.
Turner Rd.
Gettysburg Ave.
NEW CHICAGO
FAIRTOWN
MORAINE
WEST CARROLLTON
MIAMISBURG
725
SPRINGBORO

TROTWOOD
STAYLORSBURG
STRINGTOWN
Wolf Creek Pike
Gettysburg Ave.
Infirmary Rd.
ELLERTON
WHITFIELD
Dixie Dr.
CHAUTAUQUA
73
FRANKLIN
75

VANDALIA
Frederick
Dog Leg Rd.
Meeker Rd.
River Rd.
48
Union Rd.
Wenger Rd.
49
Westbrook Rd.
Shiloh Springs Rd.
Little Richmond Rd.
Olive Rd.
Dayton Rd.
Calumet Lane
Farmersville-W. Alexandria Rd.
Miaisburg
Chautauqua Dr.

Scale of Miles 0 1 2 3
Z

© C.S.C.

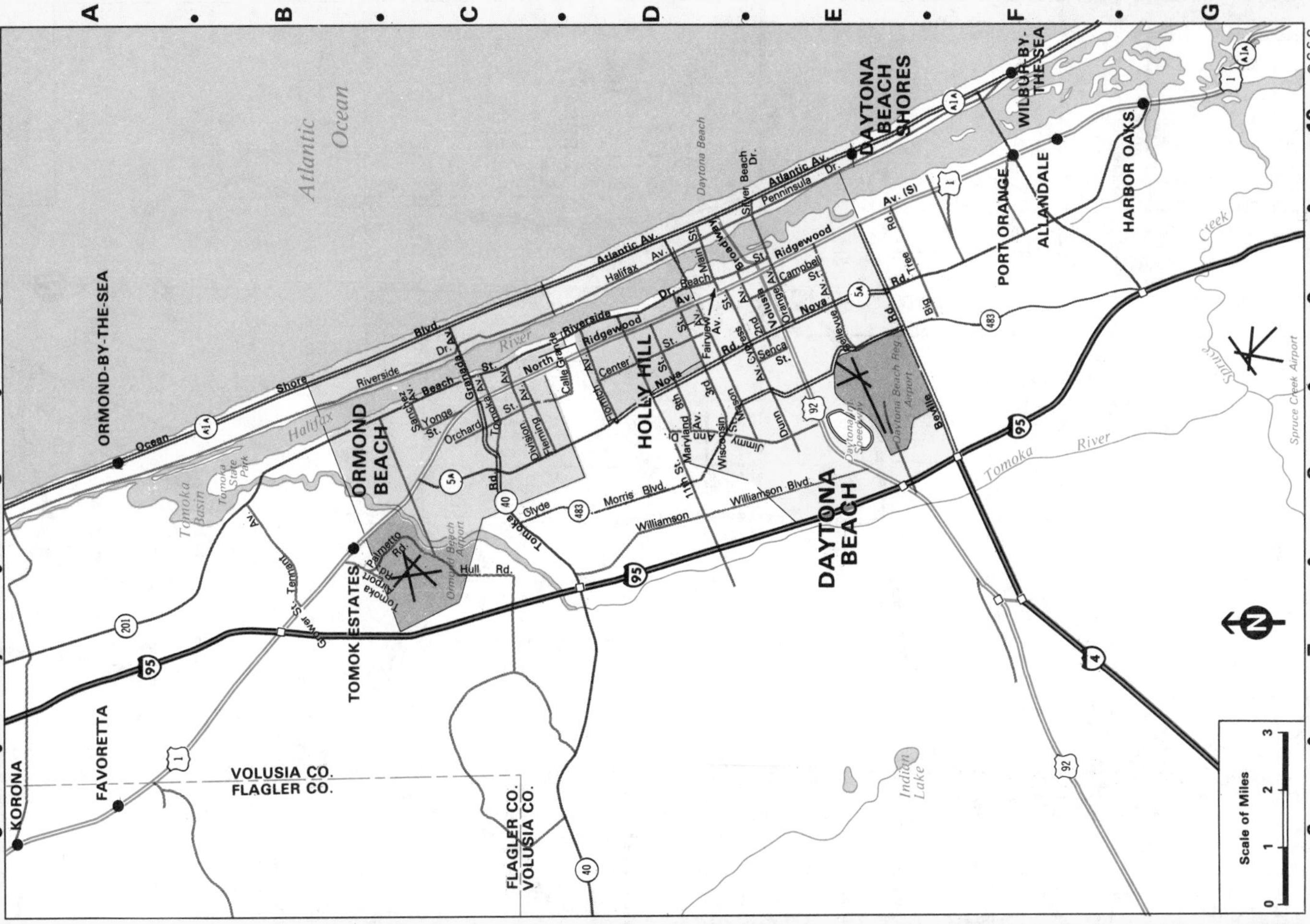

© C.S.C.

Daytona Beach, FL (map)

Atlantic Ocean

ORMOND-BY-THE-SEA

ORMOND BEACH

DAYTONA BEACH SHORES

WILBUR-BY-THE-SEA

PORT ORANGE

ALLANDALE

HARBOR OAKS

DAYTONA BEACH

HOLLY HILL

TOMOK ESTATES

Tomoka Basin

Tomoka State Park

Ormond Beach Airport

Daytona Beach Reg. Airport

Spruce Creek Airport

Tomoka River

Indian Lake

Spruce Creek

KORONA

FAVORETTA

VOLUSIA CO.
FLAGLER CO.

FLAGLER CO.
VOLUSIA CO.

Atlantic Av.
Halifax Dr.
Riverside Dr.
Ridgewood Av.
Beach St.
Shore Blvd.
Riverside Blvd.
Halifax River

Roads: 95, 4, 92, 1, A1A, 5A, 40, 483, 201, 11

Center St., North Beach St., Orchard, Yonge St., Division St., Calle Grande, Fleming, Volusia Av., Fairview, Campbell, Nova Rd., Mason Av., Williamson Blvd., Williamson, Morris Blvd., Hull Rd., Glyde, Palmetto, Tennis, Tomoka, Beville Rd., Big Tree Rd., Dunn, Jimmy Ann, Wisconsin, 3rd, Santa, Seneca, Clyde Morris Blvd., 8th St., 11th St., Mainland, Ridgewood, Atlantic Av. (S), Penninsula Dr., Daytona Beach Dr., Street Beach Dr.

Scale of Miles 0 1 2 3

N

Des Moines, IA (map)

© C.S.C.

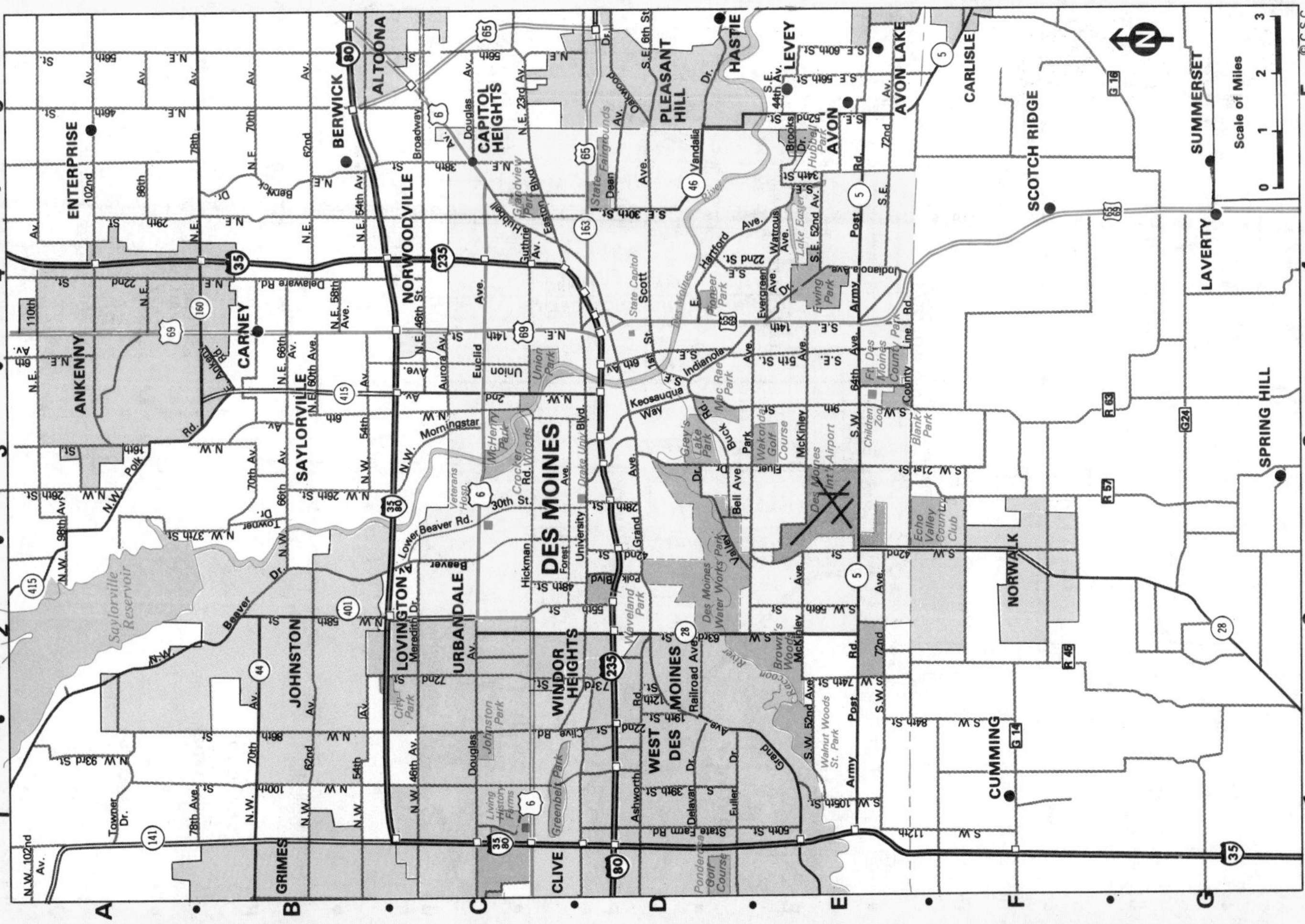

DES MOINES

WEST DES MOINES

URBANDALE

WINDSOR HEIGHTS

JOHNSTON

CLIVE

GRIMES

ENTERPRISE

ALTOONA

BERWICK

CAPITOL HEIGHTS

NORWOODVILLE

PLEASANT HILL

HASTIE

LEVEY

AVON

AVON LAKE

CARLISLE

SCOTCH RIDGE

SUMMERSET

LAVERTY

SPRING HILL

CUMMING

NORWALK

ANKENY

CARNEY

SAYLORVILLE

LOVINGTON

Saylorville Reservoir

Des Moines Int'l Airport

Fort Des Moines

Echo Valley Country Club

Waveland Golf Course

Children's Zoo

Water Works Park

Greenwood Park

Gray's Lake Park

Union Park

McHenry Park

Veterans Hosp.

Blank Park

Ewing Park

Birdland Park

Des Moines River

Raccoon River

Walnut Woods St. Park

Roads: 35, 80, 235, 65, 6, 5, 69, 160, 415, 401, 44, 46, 28, 163, 141, F 57, F 63, G 14, G 16, R 45, R 46, S 45, 316

Scale of Miles 0 1 2 3

N

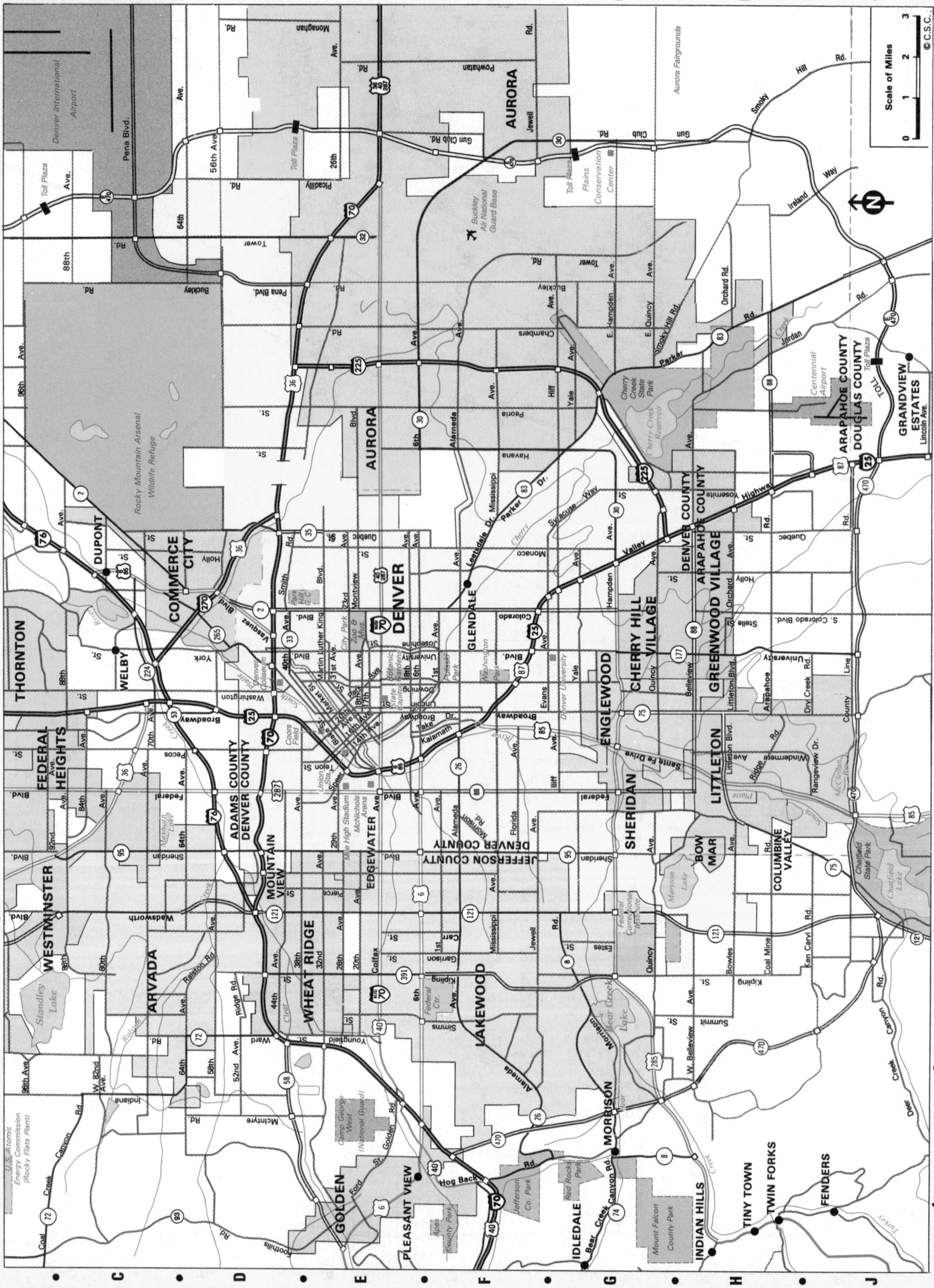

Scale of Miles

© C.S.C.

Denver International Airport

Toll Plaza

Pena Blvd.

Rocky Mountain Arsenal (Wildlife Refuge)

Monaghan Rd.

Powhatan

AURORA

Jewell

Gun Club Rd.

Buckley Air National Guard Base

Plains Conservation Center

Aurora Fairgrounds

Smoky Hill Rd.

Ireland

Way

Toll Plaza

COMMERCE CITY

THORNTON

WELBY

DUPONT

U.S. Atomic Energy Commission (Rocky Flats Plant)

FEDERAL HEIGHTS

WESTMINSTER

Standley Lake

ARVADA

WHEAT RIDGE

MOUNTAIN VIEW

ADAMS COUNTY / DENVER COUNTY

DENVER

Coors Field

Mile High Stadium

McNichols Arena

Union Sta.

City Park

Denver Zoo & Mus.

Botanic Gardens

Washington Park

GLENDALE

Cherry Creek State Park

Cherry Creek Reservoir

Centennial Airport

ARAPAHOE COUNTY / DOUGLAS COUNTY

GRANDVIEW ESTATES

Lincoln Ave.

DENVER COUNTY / ARAPAHOE COUNTY

CHERRY HILL VILLAGE

GREENWOOD VILLAGE

ENGLEWOOD

SHERIDAN

LITTLETON

BOW MAR

COLUMBINE VALLEY

Chatfield State Park

Chatfield Lake

JEFFERSON COUNTY / DENVER COUNTY

EDGEWATER

LAKEWOOD

Federal Center

GOLDEN

PLEASANT VIEW

Camp George West (National Guard)

Hog Back

Apex County Park

Red Rocks Park

Mount Falcon County Park

IDLEDALE

MORRISON

Bear Creek

INDIAN HILLS

TINY TOWN

TWIN FORKS

FENDERS

Turkey Creek

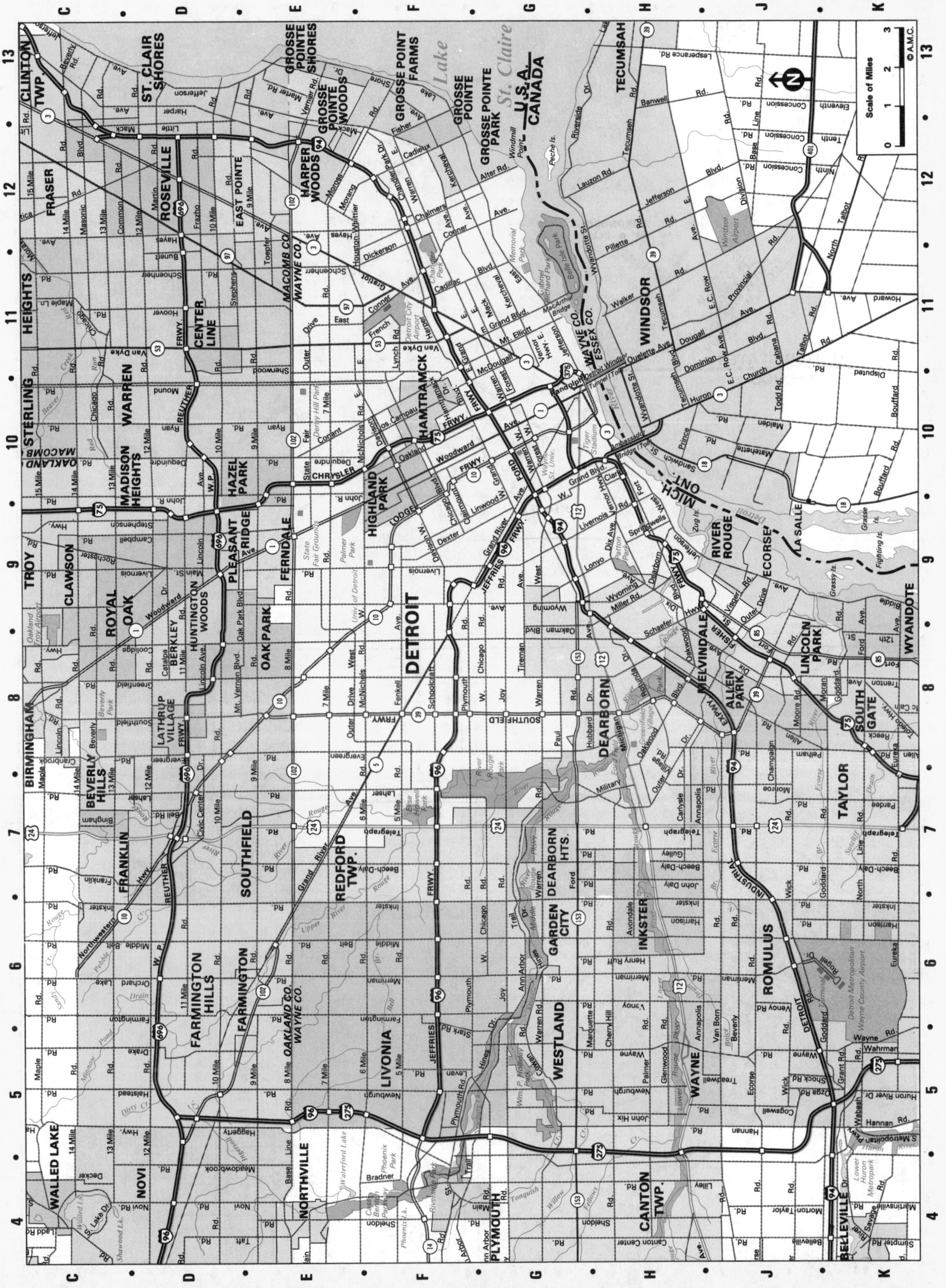

Scale of Miles
0 1 2 3
A.M.C.

CLINTON TWP.
FRASER
STERLING HEIGHTS
WARREN
CENTER LINE
MACOMB CO.
WAYNE CO.
ROSEVILLE
ST. CLAIR SHORES
EAST POINTE
HARPER WOODS
GROSSE POINTE SHORES
GROSSE POINTE WOODS
GROSSE POINT FARMS
GROSSE POINTE
GROSSE POINTE PARK
Lake St. Claire
U.S.A.
CANADA
MICH.
ONT.
WINDSOR
WAYNE CO.
ESSEX CO.
Tecumseh

MADISON HEIGHTS
HAZEL PARK
PLEASANT RIDGE
FERNDALE
HIGHLAND PARK
HAMTRAMCK
CHRYSLER
OAKLAND
MACOMB
TROY
CLAWSON
ROYAL OAK
BERKLEY
HUNTINGTON WOODS
OAK PARK
DETROIT
RIVER ROUGE
ECORSE
WYANDOTTE
LA SALLE

BIRMINGHAM
BEVERLY HILLS
FRANKLIN
SOUTHFIELD
LATHRUP VILLAGE
OAKLAND CO.
WAYNE CO.
REDFORD TWP.
GARDEN CITY
DEARBORN
DEARBORN HTS.
MELVINDALE
ALLEN PARK
LINCOLN PARK
SOUTHGATE
TAYLOR
INKSTER

WALLED LAKE
NOVI
NORTHVILLE
FARMINGTON HILLS
FARMINGTON
LIVONIA
PLYMOUTH
WESTLAND
WAYNE
ROMULUS
CANTON TWP.
BELLEVILLE
Detroit Metropolitan Wayne County Airport

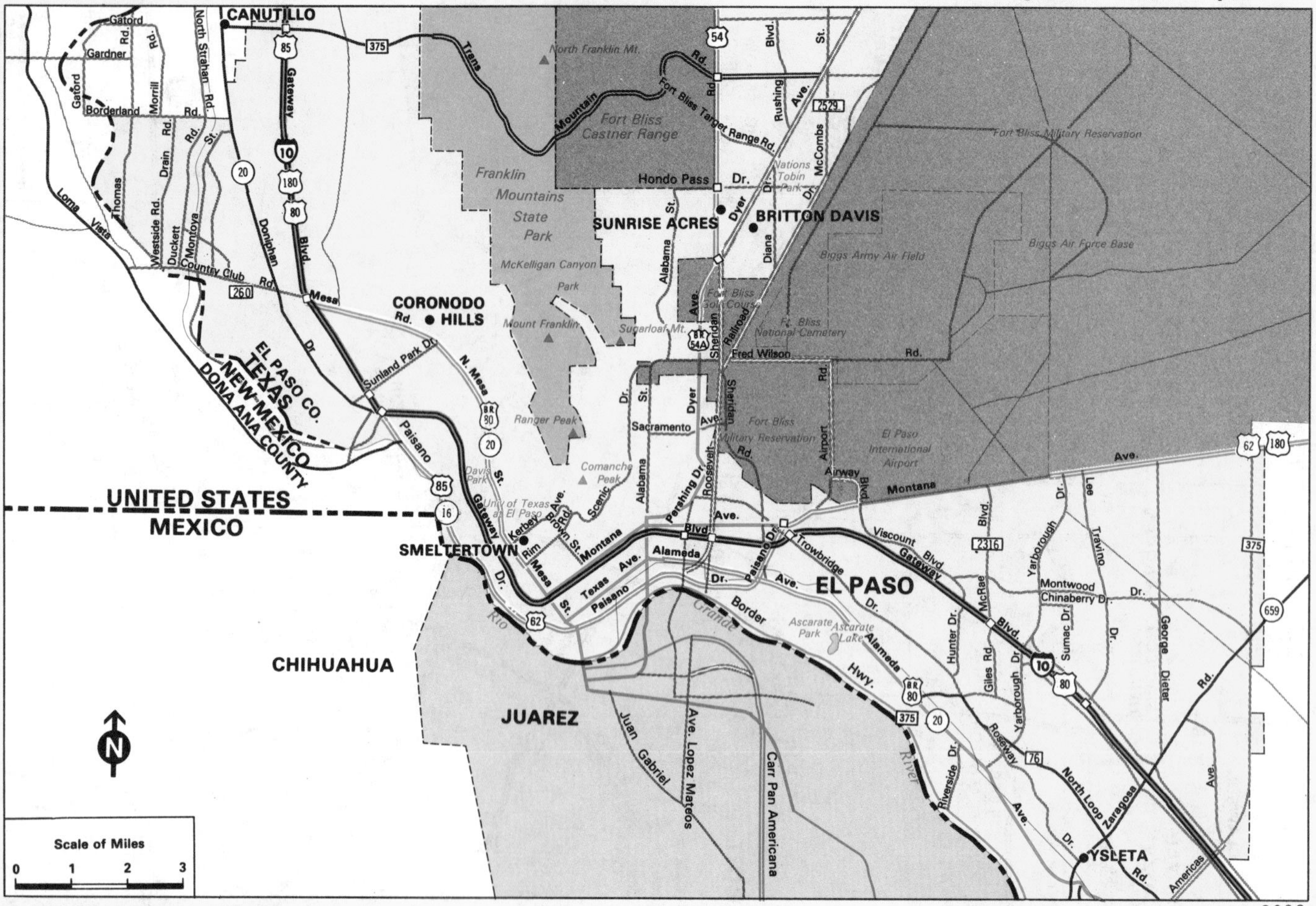

El Paso, TX (top map)

CANUTILLO

UNITED STATES
MEXICO

EL PASO CO.
TEXAS
NEW MEXICO
DONA ANA COUNTY

CHIHUAHUA

JUAREZ

SMELTERTOWN

CORONODO HILLS

SUNRISE ACRES

BRITTON DAVIS

EL PASO

YSLETA

North Franklin Mt.
Fort Bliss Castner Range
Franklin Mountains State Park
McKelligan Canyon Park
Mount Franklin
Sugarloaf Mt.
Ranger Peak
Comanche Peak
Univ. of Texas El Paso
Fort Bliss Military Reservation
Biggs Army Air Field
Biggs Air Force Base
Fort Bliss Military Reservation
Ft. Bliss National Cemetery
El Paso International Airport
Ascarate Park
Ascarate Lake
Hondo Pass
Fred Wilson
Rio Grande

Scale of Miles
0 1 2 3

N

© C.S.C.

Erie, PA (bottom left map)

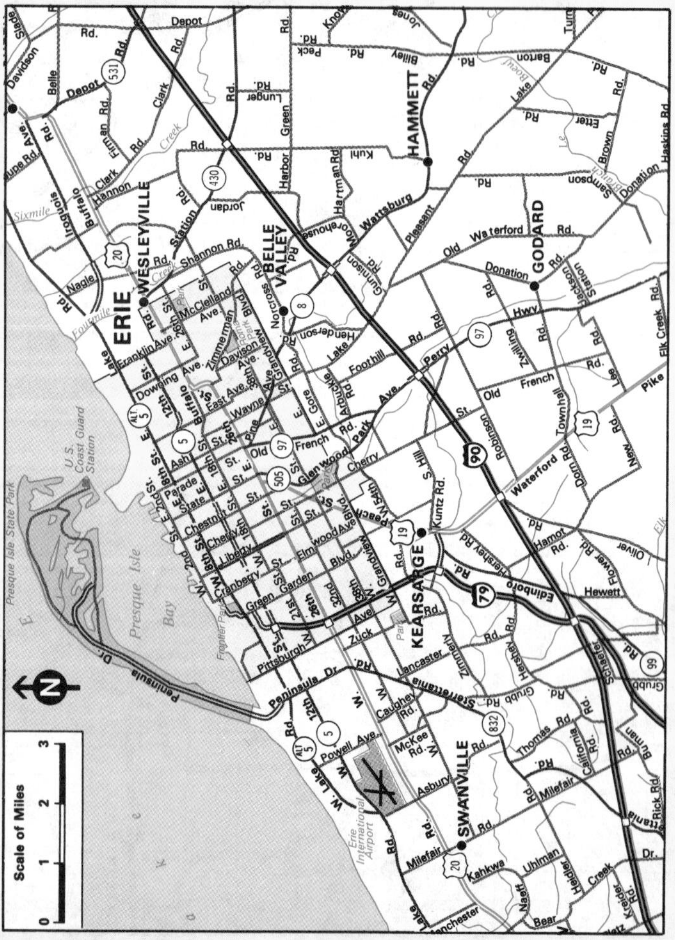

ERIE

WESLEYVILLE

BELLE VALLEY

KEARSARGE

SWANVILLE

HAMMETT

GODARD

U.S. Coast Guard Station
Presque Isle State Park
Presque Isle Bay
Lake Erie
Erie International Airport

Scale of Miles
0 1 2 3

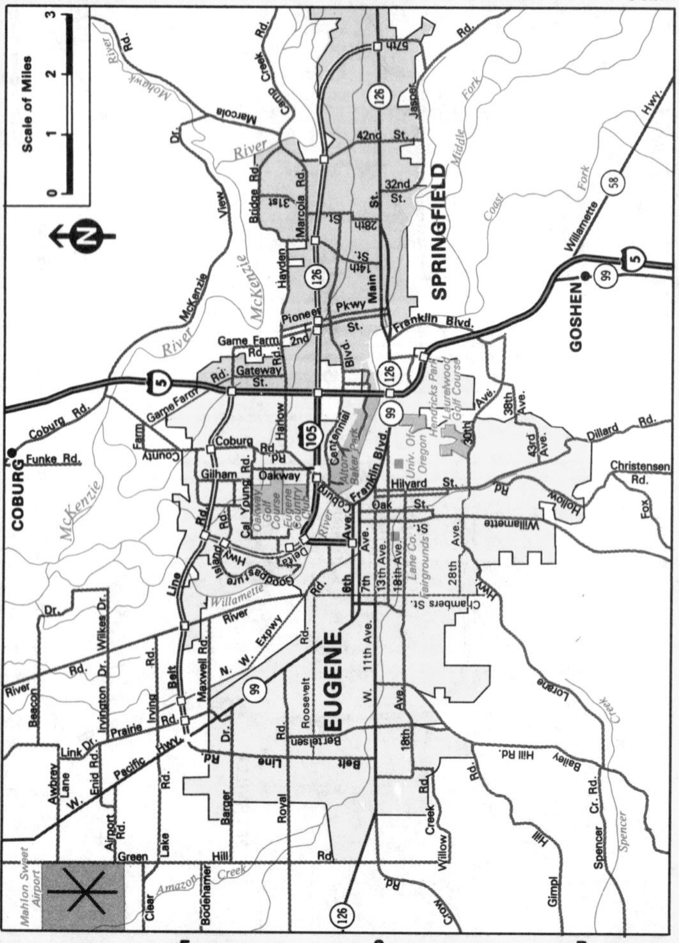

N

Eugene, OR (bottom right map)

EUGENE

SPRINGFIELD

GOSHEN

COBURG

McKenzie River
Middle Fork
Coast Fork
Willamette River
Willamette
Mahlon Sweet Airport
Lane Co. Fairgrounds
Univ. of Oregon
Hendricks Park
Amazon Creek

Scale of Miles
0 1 2 3

N

© C.S.C.

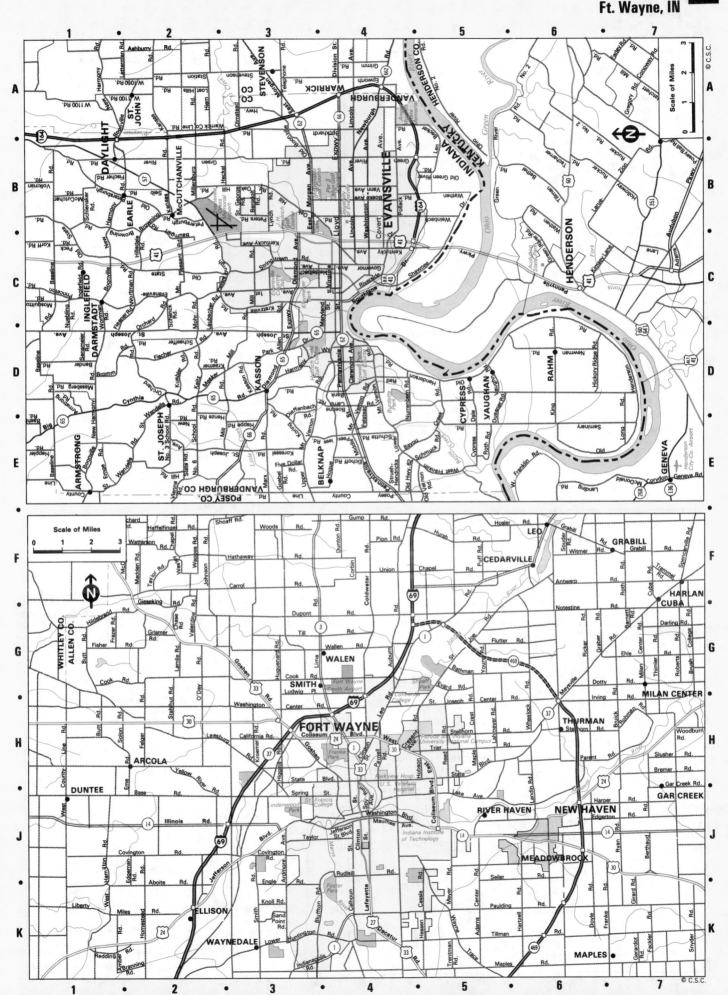

Fayetteville, NC

HARNETT CO. / CUMBERLAND CO.

Betts Rd.
MANCHESTER
Manchester Rd.
Tom Hart Rd.
McCormick Rd.
Johnson Rd.
Farm
Little River
Gilliam
401
Carvers Creek
Middle Rd.
Slocomb Rd.
SLOCOMB
Johnson Rd.
24
87
Pope Air Force Base
SPRING LAKE
McCormick
Andrews Church Rd.
Air Field
Andrews Rd.
Bragg Blvd.
Longstreet Rd.
Randolph St.
Honeycutt Rd.
Smith Lake
Callie Rd.
Fort Bragg
Honeycutt Rd.
MacArthur Rd.
Ramsey St.
Military Reservation
Gruber Rd.
Rosehill Rd.
Shaw Mill Rd.
TOKAY
Morganton
210
Country Club Dr.
Murchison Rd.
BONNIE DOONE
87
Pamalee
BYP 401
FAYETTEVILLE
CLIFFDALE
24
Morganton Rd.
Bragg Rd.
Ramsey St.
Person St.
River Rd.
Dunn Rd.
Cliffdale
401
Raeford Rd.
Hay St.
95
Skibo Rd.
Reilford
Robeson St.
24
Downing
Owen Dr.
Clinton Rd.
301
59
Southern Ave.
Eastern
Ellzabethtown Rd.
Wilkes Rd.
Legion
Sapona Rd.
53
CUMBERLAND
Field Rd.
87
210 95

© C.S.C.

Fresno, CA

Scale of Miles
0 1 2 3
N

MADERA CO. / FRESNO CO.
San Joaquin River
Sierra Airpark
HERNDON
Copper Ave.
Perrin Ave.
Shepherd Ave.
Teague Ave.
Willow Ave.
Nees Ave.
Maple Ave.
Blackstone
Alluvial Ave.
Cedar
Chestnut Ave.
Peach Ave.
West Coast Bible College
PINEDALE
Sierra Ave.
41
CLOVIS 3rd
California State University
Barstow Ave.
99
Bullard Ave.
Barstow Ave.
168
Shaw Ave.
168
Hughes Ave.
Gettysburg Ave.
Ashlan Ave.
Dakota Ave.
Shields Ave.
Clinton Ave.
McKinley Ave.
Dakota Ave.
Clovis Ave.
Marks Ave.
FRESNO
Fresno City College
Clinton
McKinley Ave.
LAS PALMAS
Olive Ave.
Olive Ave.
Belmont Ave.
180
Belmont Ave.
Nielsen Ave.
Huntington Ave.
Canyon Rd.
Kearney Blvd.
Chandler Downtown Airport
Kings Canyon Rd.
Butler Ave.
Fulton Mall
Fresno County Fairgrounds
California Ave.
Church Ave.
Orange Ave.
41
Willow Ave.
Annadale Ave.
CALWA
Cornelia Ave.
Brawley Ave.
Valentine Ave.
North Ave.
Muscat Ave.
99
MALAGA
Central Ave.
Central Canal

© C.S.C.

Ft. Lauderdale, FL

National Wildlife Refuge
Atlantic Ave.
806 DELRAY BEACH
441
Hagen Rd.
Carter Rd.
Germantown Trail
95
Line Rd.
809
Clint Moore Rd.
Yamato Rd.
794
Range Rd.
Boca Raton Airport
Military
Canal
Glades Rd.
808
UNIVERSITY PARK
809
BOCA RATON
798
Palmetto Park Rd.
Lake Boca Raton
PALM BEACH CO. / BROWARD CO.
S.E. 5th Ave.
WEST DIXIE BEND
Hillsboro Blvd.
810
DEERFIELD BEACH
Holmberg Rd.
Johnson Rd.
Deerfield
Parkway S.W. 10th St.
Sawgrass Ex-Dwy.
Florida's Turnpike (Toll)
Wilburn Rd.
Powerline Rd.
Sample Rd.
Cullum Rd.
N.W. 9th
834
Crystal Lake C.C.
Dixie Highway
1
N.E. Ocean Blvd.
Holiday Springs Golf Course
Copans Rd.
Pompano Beach Airport
PINEHURST VILLAGE
MARGATE
POMPANO BEACH
Coconut Creek Parkway
912
N.W. 15th St.
Atlantic Blvd.
814
Atlantic Blvd.
Southgate Blvd.
S.W. 6th St.
7
Pompano Park
Racetracks
Cypress Creek
W. McNab Rd.
870
CYPRESS CREEK
Ft. Lauderdale Executive Airport
Powerline Rd.
LAUDERDALE BY-THE-SEA
Rock Island Rd.
Prospect Rd.
Lockhart Stadium
Commercial Blvd.
Cypress
Federal Hwy.
OAKLAND PARK
Inverary C.C.
Woodland C.C.
816
Oakland Park Blvd.
Andrews Ave.
Decker Rd.
N.E. 26th St.
WILTON MANORS
Hugh Taylor Birch State Park
N.W. 31st St.
N.W. 19th St.
N.W. 9th St.
Bayview Dr.
838
Sunrise Blvd.
N.W. 13th St.
N.E. 13th St.
Holiday Park
PLANTATION
N.W. 6th St.
N.E. 6th St.
Atlantic Ocean
842
W. Broward Blvd.
E. Las Olas Blvd.
FORT LAUDERDALE
U.S. Dept. of Agriculture Experimental Station
Davie Blvd.
Ocean World
S.E. 17th St.
North New River Canal
595
Riverland Rd.
Port Everglades Turning Basin
84
S.W. 4th
Lauderdale/Hollywood International Airport
736
Lloyd Beach State Rec. Area
DAVIE
Griffin Rd.
48th St.
818
Dania Cut-off
DANIA
Dania Beach Blvd.
South Florida Ed. Center
441
441
848
Stirling Rd.
West Lake
822
Topeekeegee Yugnee Regional Park
Sheridan St.
A1A
Taft St.
95
HOLLYWOOD
820
Hollywood Blvd.
Dixie
Federal
North Lake C.C.
South Lake

N

Scale of Miles
0 1 2 3

© C.S.C.

Grid columns: 1 2 3 4 5 6 7

Grand Rapids, MI (top map)

HERRINGTON
MARNE
TALLMADGE
GRAND VALLEY
WALKER
GRAND RAPIDS
EAST GRAND RAPIDS
HUDSONVILLE
GRANDVILLE
WYOMING
KENTWOOD
NORTH BYRON

Roads and places: Garfield, 8th, 5 Mile Rd., Kenowa, Fruit Ridge Ave., Peach Ridge Ave., Alpine Church St., River Ave., Colfax Ave., Coit Ave., Hunsberger Ave., North Kent Mall, 5 Mile, 4 Mile, Grand River Dr., Valley, Cannonsburg State Game Area, 3 Mile, Knapp, Egypt, 2 Mile Rd., Seidman Park, Conservation St., Honey, Bailey Dr., Vergennes St., Bennett St., Buttrick, Somerville Airport, Ada Dr., Hall St., Cascade Rd., 28th St., 30th St., 36th, Cascade Rd., Kent County Airport, Whitneyville Ave., McCords Ave., Snow Ave., Johnson, Lincoln St., Leonard, Michigan, Lake, Richmond, Kinney Ave., Oakleigh Ave., Covell Ave., Bristol Ave., Alpine Ave., College Ave., Plainfield Ave., Dean, Belt St., East Beltline Ave., Fulton St., Ford Museum, Reeds Lake, Forest Hill, Burton, O'Brien, Maynard Ave., Collindale Ave., John Ball Park and Zoo, Franklin, Hall, Eastern Ave., Kalamazoo Ave., Paris, Burton, River Bend Dr., Butterworth Dr., Veterans Memorial Dr., Wilson, Johnson Park, Chicago Dr., Porter St., 28th St., Prairie St., Division Ave., 32nd St., Breton, 36th Ave., Cottonwood Dr., 24th Ave., Bauer Rd., Baldwin Dr., 20th Ave., Rosewood Dr., Main St., Port Sheldon St., 12th St., 44th, Nannest St., Center St., Clyde Park, Palmer Park, 52nd, 56th, 54th St., 60th, 68th, Quincy, Jackson, Ransom St., 64th St., Byron, 72nd St., Eastern, Kalamazoo, Patterson

Highways: 96, 11, 131, 37, 44, 45, 196, 21

Scale of Miles: 0 1 2 3

© C.S.C.

Harrisburg, PA (bottom map)

Scale of Miles: 0 1 2 3

DAUPHIN
COVE
PERDIX
HECKTON
FT. HUNTER
MARYSVILLE
SUMMERDALE
LINGLESTOWN
PAXTONIA
ENOLA
WEST FAIRVIEW
HARRISBURG
COLONIAL PARK
PENBROOK
PROGRESS
UNION DEPOSIT
GOOD HOPE
WORMLEYSBURG
CAMP HILL
PAXTANG
HUMMELSTOWN
HOGESTOWN
LEMOYNE
NEW KINGSTOWN
SHIREMANSTOWN
MECHANICSBURG
NEW CUMBERLAND
STEELTON
HIGHSPIRE
MIDDLETOWN
BOWMANSDALE
LISBURN
SIDDONSBURG
YOCUMTOWN
PLAINFIELD
GOLDSBORO

Places and roads: State Rd., Fishing Creek, State Game Lands No. 211, Valley Rd., Manada, State Game Lands No. 170, Shermansdale, Millers Gap Rd., Lambs Gap Rd., Legion Rd., Valley Rd., Mem. Hwy., Harrisburg Community Colleges, Lingleston, Progress Ave., Paxton Creek, Mountain Rd., Jonestown, Hershey, PERRY CO., CUMBERLAND CO., Wertzville Rd., New Gap Rd., Conodoguinet Creek, American Ave., Good Hope Rd., Davison St., Locust Ln., Deposit Rd., Newside Rd., Union Deposit, Enola Rd., Barnhosel, Willow Mill Rd., Carlisle Rd., Center St., Maclay St., Hert St., Rutherford Rd., Derry St., 81, Hogestown Pike, Harrisburg Pike, Talpol Bridge, Forster St., Capitol St., Cameron St., Derry St., Chambers St., Hill Rd., Main St., Carlisle Pike, St. Johns Rd., 11, 15, VFW, Harrisburg Hwy., Fiddlers Elbow Rd., Waltonville Rd., U.S. Naval Reservation, Harrisburg Expwy., Bridge St., Capitol City Airport, Highland St., 283, Oberlin, 441, St. Game Lands No. 246, Simpson Ferry Rd., Liburn Rd., Rosemary Rd., Limakin Rd., New Cumberland General Depot, Fulling Mill Rd., Union Middletown Rd., School House Rd., Trindle Rd., Market St., York St., Pennsylvania Rd., Church St., Evergreen Rd., Turnpike, Harrisburg Intl. Airport, PSU at Harrisburg, Lisburn Rd., Yellow Breeches, Old Forge Rd., Lewisberry Rd., Fishing Creek Rd., York Rd., Valley Rd., Hillsdale Church Rd., Three Mile Island, Boiling Springs Rd., Williams Rd., Grove Rd., York Rd., Main St., Cedars Rd., Andersontown Rd., Pleasant View Rd., Mem. Hwy., Pines Rd., Yocumtown Rd., Geyers Church Rd., Round Top Rd.

Highways: 11, 15, 322, 22, 81, 39, 443, 850, 944, 114, 83, 76, 230, 441, 283, 3032, 641, 174, 74, 262, 382, 177, 392

N

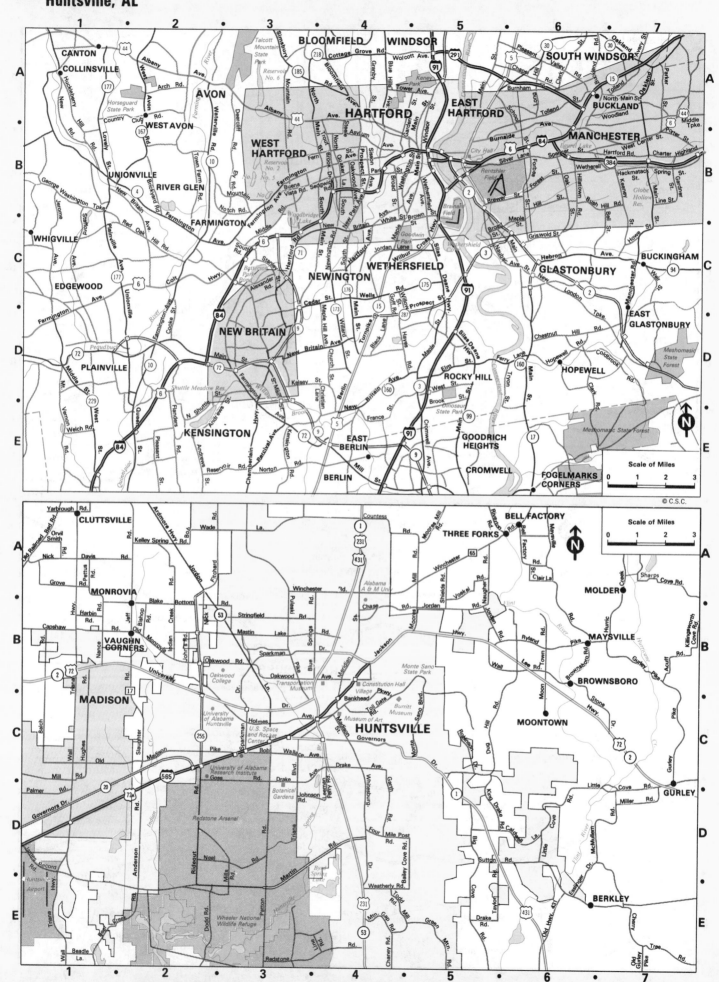

© C.S.C.

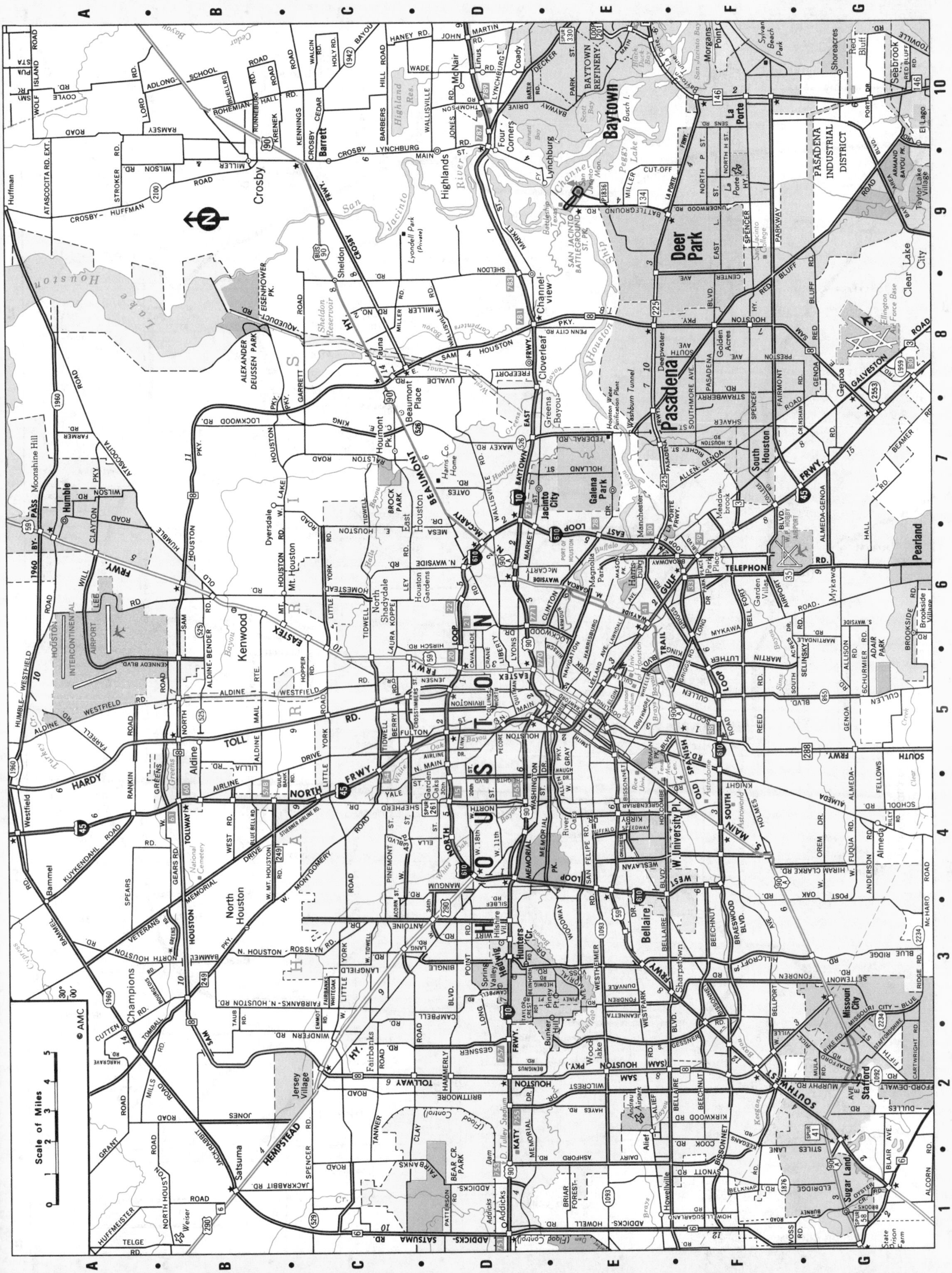

Crosby

Barrett

Highlands

Four Corners

Lynchburg

BAYTOWN REFINERY

Baytown

La Porte

PASADENA INDUSTRIAL DISTRICT

Seabrook

Clear Lake City

Deer Park

San Jacinto Battleground St. Pk.

Channelview

Pasadena

South Houston

Galena Park

Jacinto City

Beaumont Place

Humble

HOUSTON

Lake Houston

Alexander Deussen Park

Kenwood

Houston Intercontinental Airport

North Houston

Hardy

Aldine

Jersey Village

Champions

AMC

Telephone

Pearland

Bellaire

Hunters Cr.

Hedwig

Missouri City

Stafford

Sugar Land

Alief

Satsuma

Fairbanks

Scale of Miles
0 1 2 3 4 5

Grid columns: 1 2 3 4 5 6
Grid rows: A B C D E F G

116TH ST.
Eagle Village
Carmel
Fishers
White
Metropolitan Airport

A

334
Zionville
421
465
COLLEGE AVE.
WESTFIELD BLVD.
31
431
37
HAMILTON CO.
MARION CO.
96TH ST.
69
465
421

86TH ST.
Sahm Park
Allisonville
Castleton
82ND ST.
Fairbanks Hosp.
FALL CR.

65
86TH ST.
79TH ST.
79TH ST.
TOWNSHIP LINE
DITCH RD.
Williams Creek
Nora
86TH ST.
SOUTH RIVER RD.
Castleton
Square S.C.
71ST ST.
71ST ST.
ALLISONVILLE RD.
465

B

Traders Point
71ST ST.
Augusta
73RD ST.
Meridian Hills
Ravenswood
71ST ST.
85TH ST.
Hillcrest C.C.
ZIONVILLE RD.
New Augusta
62ND ST.
Shore Acres
KESSLER BLVD.
KEYSTONE AVE.
Glendale S.C.
62ND ST.
Fort Harrison State Park
Camp Belzer

Eagle Creek Pk.
LAFAYETTE RD.
Little Eagle Creek
North Westway Park
56TH ST.
FOX HILL DR.
North Crows Nest
Washington Park North Cemetery
Highland Country Club
Crows Nest
31
56TH ST.
Cathedral H.S.
Lawrence Central H.S.
Fort Benjamin Harrison
Arlington H.S.
Lawrence
Pleasant Run
State School For The Deaf
46TH ST.
46TH ST.
67
36
PENDLETON PIKE

C

Indianapolis Colts Training Facility
52
Eagle Creek Reservoir
Clermont
136
74
Eagle Creek Airport
GUION RD.
Broadmoor Country Club
Highwood
Spring Hills
Rocky Ripple
Wynnedale
Woodstock
Butler University
Crown Hill Cem.
State Fairgrounds
N. MERIDIAN ST.
COLLEGE ST.
FALL CR. PKWY.
38TH ST.
34TH ST.
MASSACHUSETTS ST.
Chrysler Corp.
SHADELAND AVE.
465
Indiana St. Police Hqts.

HIGH SCHOOL RD.
Moller RD.
34TH ST.
Marian College
Coffin G.C.
South Grove G.C.
30TH ST.
30TH ST.
25TH ST.
ARLINGTON AVE.

D

Indianapolis Country Club
21ST ST.
Camp Dellwood
GEORGETOWN RD.
Speedway H.S.
Indianapolis Motor Speedway
TIBBS RD.
16TH ST.
16TH ST.
31
Benjamin Harrison Memorial
SHERMAN DR.
21ST ST.
16TH ST.
10TH ST.
EMERSON AVE.
70
Pleasant Run G.C.
Warren Park
40
COUNTRY CLUB RD.
134
Speedway
10TH ST.
I.U.P.U.I.
War Memorial
Market Square Arena
RURAL ST.
Ford Assembly Plant
POST RD.

E

HENDRICKS COUNTY
MARION COUNTY
36
Tremont
GIRLS SCHOOL RD.
465
INDIANAPOLIS
ROCKVILLE RD.
Thatcher Golf Course
Indiana Univ. Medical Center
Central State Hosp.
Indianapolis Zoo
State Capitol
White River St. Pk.
Victory Field
RCA Dome
DELAWARE ST.
Nat'l Track & Field Hall Of Fame
Union Station Market Place
NEW WASHINGTON
Willard Park
MICHIGAN ST.
YORK ST.
ENGLISH AVE.
ENGLISH AVE.

40
Ben Davis
WASHINGTON
Bridgeport
Six Points
Indianapolis International Airport
Mickeyville
MORRIS ST.
MINNESOTA
Indiana Nat'l Guard
70
LYNHURST DR.
TIBBS AVE.
HOLT RD.
Union Stock Yards
WEST ST.
MERIDIAN ST.
MADISON AVE.
PROSPECT
SOUTHEASTERN AVE.
RAYMOND ST.
Raymond Park
Marion County Fair Grounds

Mars Hill
KENTUCKY AVE.
Maywood
HARDING ST.
White River
W. RAYMOND ST.
Sarah Shank G.C.
KEYSTONE AVE.
TROY AVE.
Five Points
FISHER RD.
74
421

E/F

40
74
37
465
HANNA AVE.
Univ. of Indianapolis
St. Francis Hospital
Beech Grove
Hanna
52
Wanamaker

F

70
67
Valley Mills
Decatur Central H.S.
HIGH SCHOOL RD.
74
465
MANN RD.
THOMPSON RD.
EPLER
37
BLUFF RD.
Edgewood
THOMPSON RD.
Edgewood
SHELBYVILLE RD.
Franklin Central H.S.
N

Camby
CAMBY RD.
MOORESVILLE RD.
Antrim
EDGEWOOD
135
EAST ST.
MADISON AVE.
Homecroft
65
Scale of Miles
0 ½ 1 2 3

G

West Newton
South Westway Park
STOP 11 RD.
Glenns Valley
SOUTHPORT RD.
31
Southport
Carl Smock Park
© C.S.C.

MARION COUNTY

N

MADISON

GREENS CROSSING RD.

US 49

Live Oak Golf Course

MAC CLEAN RD.

BILLY BELL RD.

COUNTY LINE RD.

KICKAPOO RD.

COUNTY LINE RD.

PKWY.

NATCHEZ TRACE

US 51

RIDGELAND

NATIONAL

NATIONAL PKWY.

HIGHLAND COLONY PKWY.

Ross Barnett Reservoir

SPILLWAY RD.

PINE HAVEN

NATCHEZ TRACE Rd.

Cynthie

US 49

HILDA DR.

FOREST AV.

DELTA DR.

I-220

Costas Lake

Tougaloo College

L. Larue

MADISON HINDS

LIVINGSTON DR.

WATKINS

BEASLEY RD.

MOSS ST.

HANGING

COUNTY COUNTY

COUNTY LINE RD.

Peer Orchard Dr.

ADKINS BLVD.

CANTON CLUB CIR.

OLD CANTON

SEDGWICK

Westbrook Rd.

Country Club of Jackson

HINDS RANKIN COUNTY

BRIARWOOD DR.

Woodway Dr.

I-55

US 51

MAGNOLA

OLD VICKSBURG RD.

NORTHSIDE

FLAG CHAPEL RD.

L. Higo

CALIFORNIA AV.

NORTHSIDE AV.

N. STATE ST.

MANHATTEN

MEADOWBROOK

RIDGEWOOD DR.

EASTOVER

DOGWOOD ST.

DR.

CLINTON

Lakewood Mem. Gardens

CLINTON BLVD.

SHAW RD.

Shady Oaks C.C.

Country Club Dr.

BOLING ST.

MILLS

BULLARD ST.

Hawkins Field Airport

Municipal G.C.

MAYES AV.

RIDGEWAY ST.

LIVINGSTON

BAILEY

Mem. Stadium

Univ. Of Miss. Medical Cent.

LAKELAND DR.

US 51

Lefleur's Bluff St. Pk.

Pearl R.

US 25

US 25

US 475

US 468

Jackson's Allen C. Thompson Int'l. Airport

US 80

I-20

WOODROW WILSON BLVD.

SOUTH DR.

OLD DIXON RD.

LINDSEY DR.

WHITFIELD MILLS

CAPITOL ST.

Zoological Park

JACKSON

FORTIFICATION

WILSON

N. STATE ST.

RIVERSIDE DR.

Millsaps College

HIGHLAND DR.

FLOWOOD

US 475

WIGGINS RD.

McRAVEN RD.

N. HAVEN

ROBINSON

CHARLES ST.

PRENTISS ST.

WEST ST.

State Capital

HIGH ST.

Coliseum & Fairground

FANNIN RD.

US 468

BRANDON

US 80

US 475

ROBINSON RD.

LYNCH ST.

VALLEY ST.

Jackson State Univ.

SOUTH ST.

PEARL ST.

S. STATE ST.

Pearl R.

I-55

US 49

I-20

US 80

Old Brandon Rd.

PEARL

US 20

US 18

MADDOX RD.

HIGHLAND

ELLIS

US 51

GALLATIN

US 49

CHILDRES RD.

US 468

TIMBER LAWN RD.

JACKSON RAYMOND RD.

McDOWELL DR.

BELVEDERE DR.

McDOWELL RD.

Battlefield Park

Weigh Station

Richland

US 18

BYRAM

SUNCREST DR.

COOPER

LONGWOOD DR.

WOODY DR.

DANIELS LAKE BLVD.

RAINY RD.

MEADOW LN

SAVANNA ST.

US 55

TERRY RD.

US 468

ROCKET DR.

GORE RD.

McCLUER

FOREST RD.

Jackson Mem. Gardens

Parham Bridges Park

PARKS RD.

BROADWATER RD.

SIWELL RD.

HILL

L. Catherine

Swan Lake

LAKESHORE RD.

RICHLAND

MONTEREY RD.

BIG CREEK RD.

HENDERSON RD.

Brookwood Country Club

Lake Dockery

OLD BYRAN RD.

MONTEREY RD.

DAVIS RD.

GARY RD.

SIWELL RD.

SPRING RIDGE RD.

Lake Ridge

US 55

US 51

HINDS RANKIN

BYRAN RD.

CLEARY RD.

FLORENCE

US 469

SCALE OF MILES
0   1   2   3

SCALE IN MILES
0   1½   3
0   1.5   3
SCALE IN KILOMETERS
©1999 TRAKKER MAPS, INC.

To Waycross

JACKSONVILLE INTERNATIONAL AIRPORT

NEW KINGS RD

LEM TURNER RD

ARNOLD RD

YELLOW BLUFF RD

STARRATT RD

NASSAU CO.
DUVAL CO.

Amelia Island

Atlantic Ocean

Nassau Sound

ARNOLD RD

PECAN PARK RD

OWENS RD
AIRPORT RD
TERRELL RD
DUVAL RD

DUVAL STATION RD

NEW BERLIN RD

CEDAR POINT RD

EASTPORT RD

Broward River

ANHEUSER-BUSCH BREWERY TOUR

HECKSCHER DR

Fort George River

FORT GEORGE CULTURAL CENTER

Fort George Inlet

DUNN AV

BROWARD RD

TROUT RIVER BLVD

SOUTEL DR

MONCRIEF RD

EDGEWOOD AV

Trout River

JACKSONVILLE ZOO

St Johns River

Blount Island

Little Mill Cove

MAYPORT U.S. NAVAL AIR STATION

HANNA STATE PARK

PRITCHARD RD

CSX

NEW KINGS RD

FT CAROLINE

JACKSONVILLE UNIVERSITY

MERRILL RD

GILMORE HTS RD

MONUMENT RD

MT PLEASANT RD

GRAIG MUNICIPAL AIRPORT

ATLANTIC BLVD

ATLANTIC BEACH

NEPTUNE BEACH

JACKSONVILLE BEACH

COMMONWEALTH AV

BEAVER ST

CONVENTION CENTER

CIVIC AUDITORIUM
MUSEUM OF SCIENCES

ARLINGTON RD

ALLTEL STADIUM

NORMANDY BLVD

LANE AV

CASSAT AV

PARK ST

JACKSONVILLE

ST. Johns River

Ortega River

HERLONG RD

ORTEGA BLVD

ROOSEVELT BLVD

EMERSON ST

AUGUSTINE BLVD

UNIVERSITY BLVD

ST. JOHNS BLUFF RD

BEACH BLVD

SAN PABLO RD

FOURAKER RD

WILSON BLVD

TIMUQUANA RD

JACKSONVILLE NAVAL AIR STATION

PHILLIPS HWY

J. TURNER BUTLER BLVD

RICKER RD

MORSE AV

TOWNSEND RD

BLANDING BLVD

JAMMES RD

BAY MEADOWS RD

SOUTHSIDE BLVD

SUNBEAM RD

DUVAL COUNTY
CLAY COUNTY

BUCKMAN BRIDGE

OLD ST AUGUSTINE RD

DUVAL COUNTY
ST JOHNS COUNTY

To Gainesville

To Tallahassee

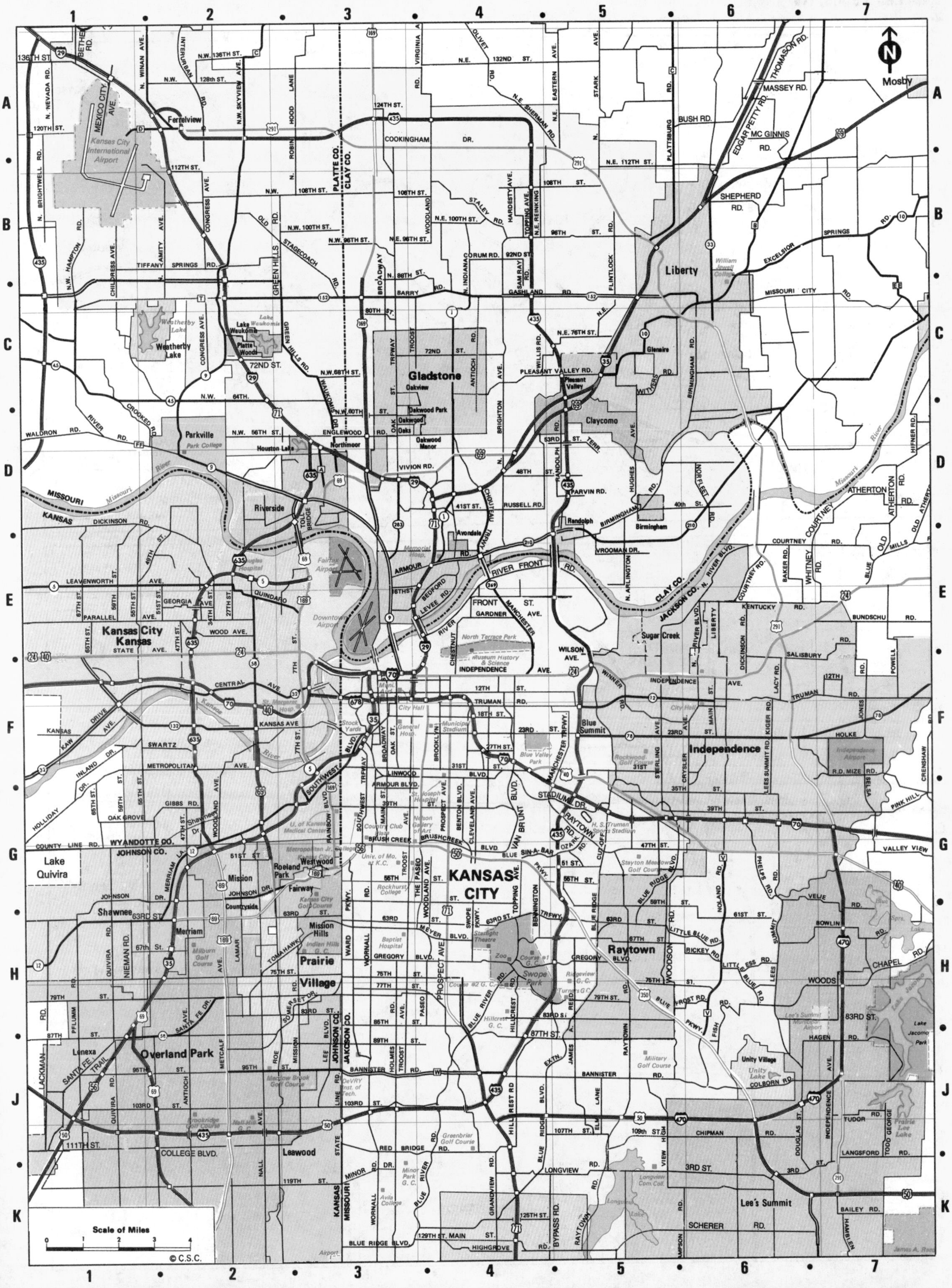

Mosby
Liberty
Glenaire
Gladstone
Oakview
Oakwood Park
Oakwood
Oaks
Oakwood Manor
Claycomo
Pleasant Valley
Ferrelview
Kansas City International Airport
Weatherby Lake
Lake Waukomis
Platte Woods
Parkville
Park College
Houston Lake
Northmoor
Riverside
Randolph
Birmingham
Avondale
MISSOURI
KANSAS
Missouri River
Kansas City Kansas
Fairfax Airport
Downtown Airport
North Terrace Park
Museum History & Science
Sugar Creek
Independence
Independence Airport
Blue Summit
Kansas River
Rockwood Golf Course
Blue Valley Park
WYANDOTTE CO.
JOHNSON CO.
Lake Quivira
Mission
Roeland Park
Westwood
Fairway
Shawnee
Countryside
Merriam
Mission Hills
Prairie Village
KANSAS CITY
Raytown
Swope Park
Overland Park
Lenexa
Leawood
Unity Village
Lee's Summit
Lake Jacomo
Prairie Lee Lake
Longview Lake
CLAY CO.
JACKSON CO.
PLATTE CO.
CLAY CO.
KANSAS
MISSOURI
JOHNSON CO.
JACKSON CO.
Scale of Miles
0 1 2 3 4
© C.S.C.

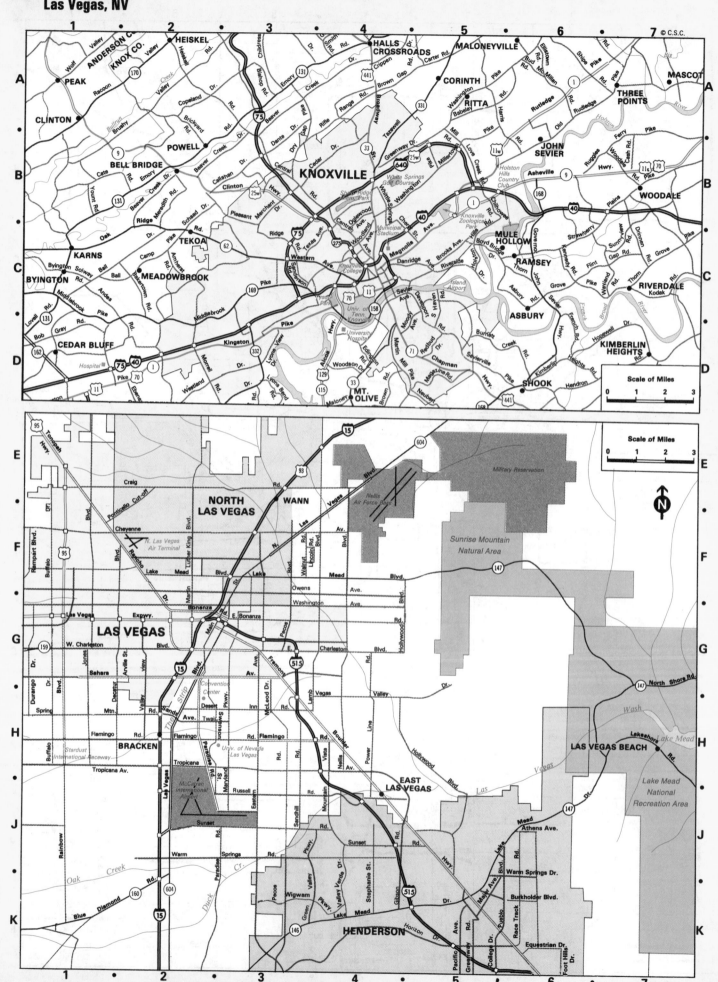

© C.S.C.

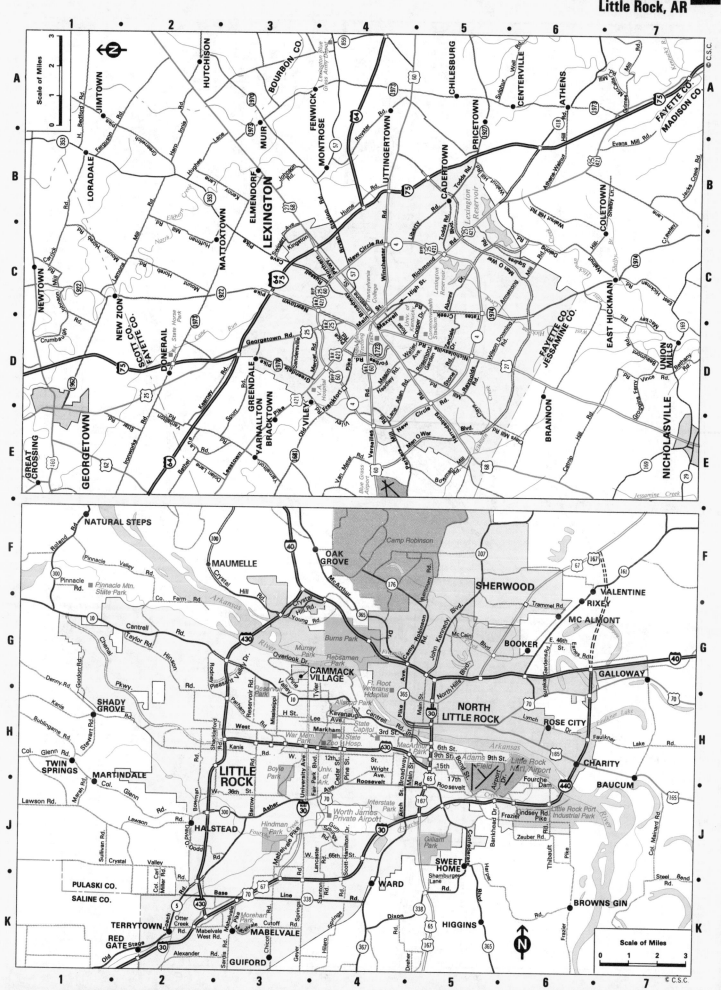

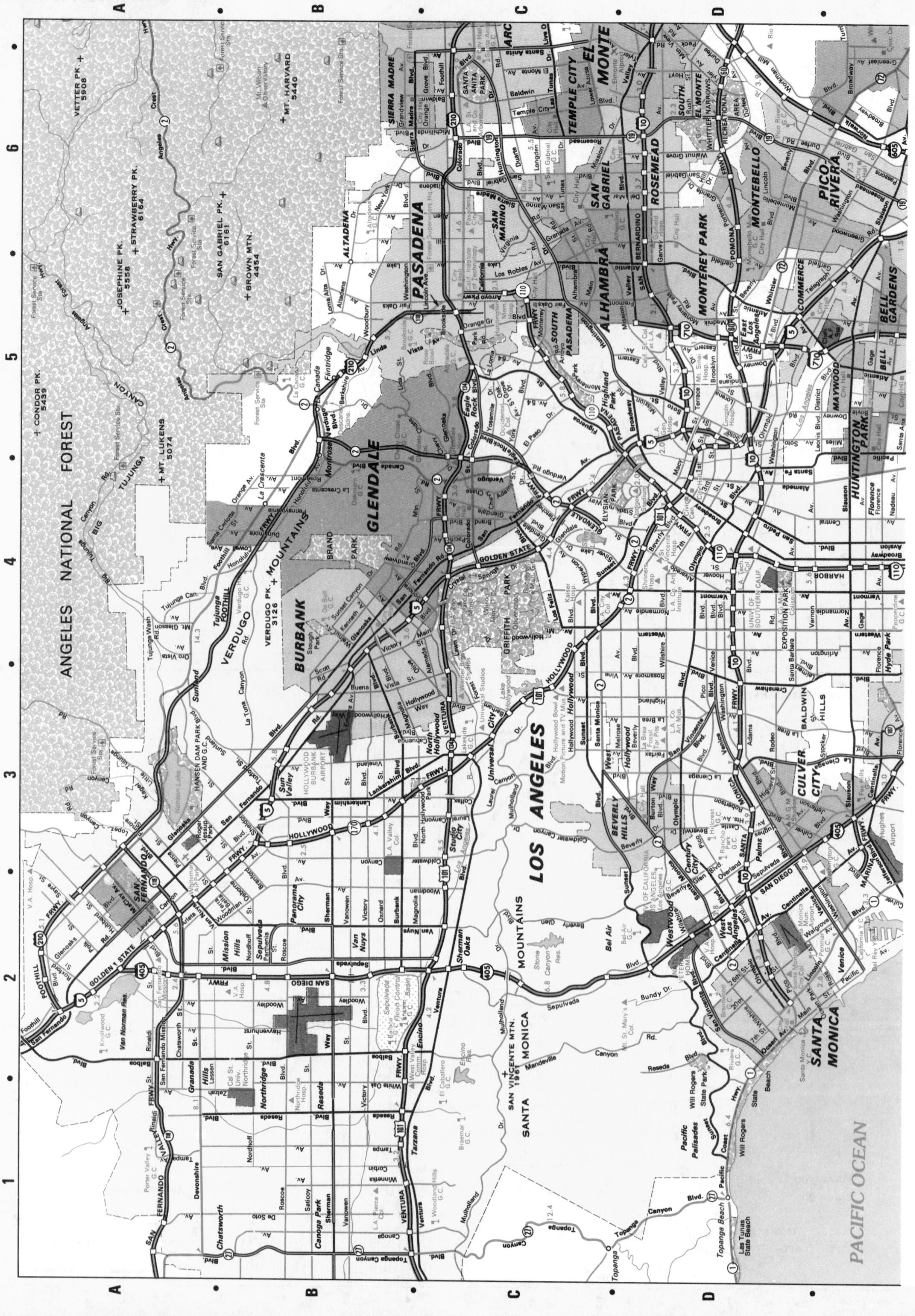

ANGELES NATIONAL FOREST

VETTER PK. + 5908

JOSEPHINE PK. + 5556

STRAWBERRY PK. + 6164

SAN GABRIEL PK. + 6161

BROWN MTN. + 4454

MT. HARVARD 5440

CONDOR PK. + 5439

MT. LUKENS 5074

BIG TUJUNGA CANYON

ALTADENA

PASADENA

SIERRA MADRE

SOUTH PASADENA

SAN MARINO

ARCADIA

TEMPLE CITY

EL MONTE

SOUTH EL MONTE

SAN GABRIEL

ROSEMEAD

ALHAMBRA

MONTEREY PARK

MONTEBELLO

PICO-RIVERA

COMMERCE

East Los Angeles

BELL GARDENS

MAYWOOD

HUNTINGTON PARK

Florence

GLENDALE

VERDUGO MOUNTAINS

VERDUGO PK. + 3126

BURBANK

GRIFFITH PARK

North Hollywood

Hollywood

LOS ANGELES

BEVERLY HILLS

Bel Air

SANTA MONICA MOUNTAINS

CULVER CITY

BALDWIN HILLS

UNIV. OF SOUTHERN CALIF.

EXPOSITION PARK

SAN FERNANDO

Mission Hills

Panorama City

Sherman Oaks

Van Nuys

Studio City

Encino

Tarzana

Reseda

Northridge

Chatsworth

Canoga Park

SANTA MONICA

Pacific Palisades

Will Rogers State Park

PACIFIC OCEAN

Topanga State Beach

Las Tunas State Beach

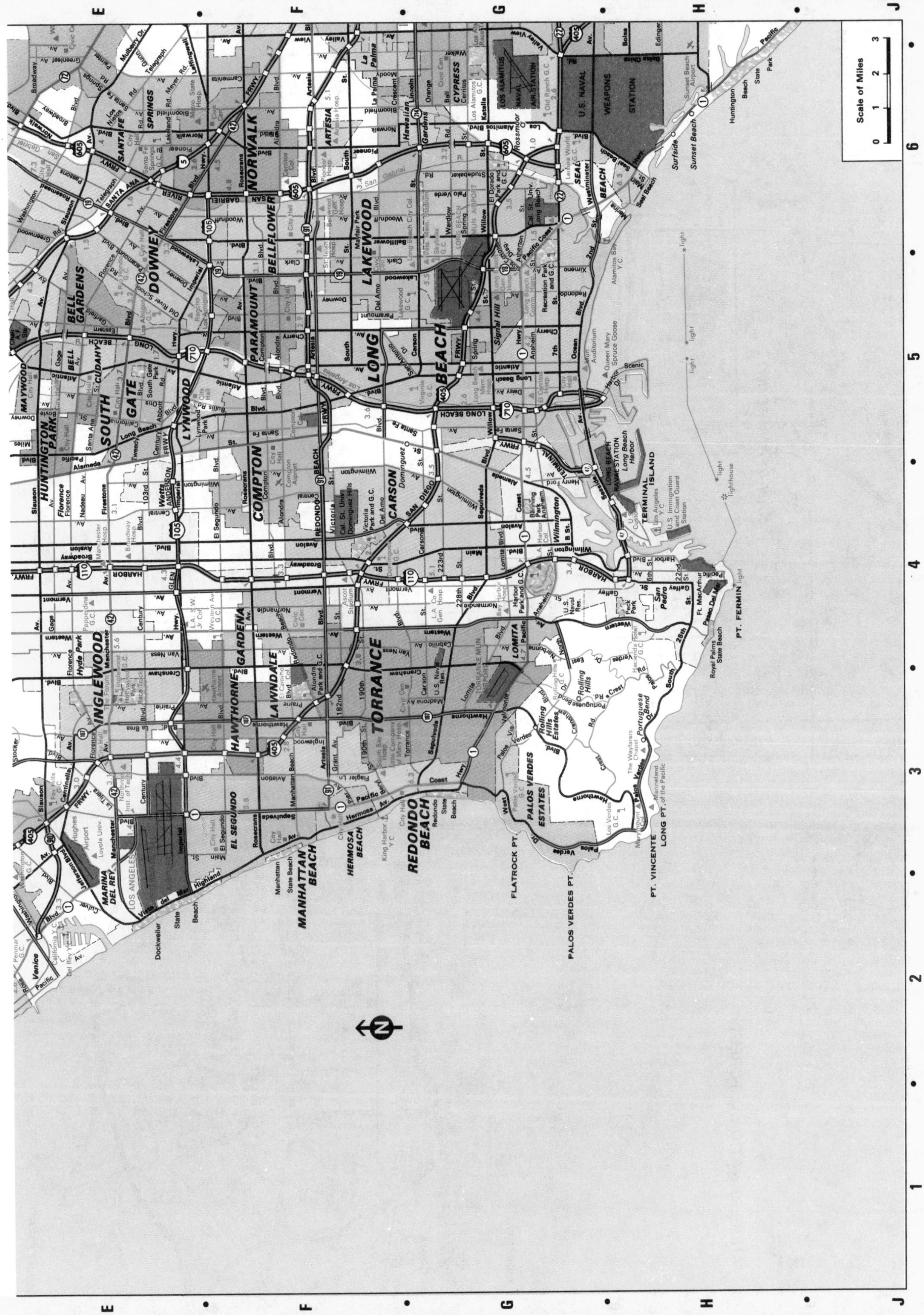

Scale of Miles

0 1 2 3

NORWALK
SANTA FE SPRINGS
BELLFLOWER
DOWNEY
BELL GARDENS
MAYWOOD
HUNTINGTON PARK
SOUTH GATE
CUDAHY
BELL
LYNWOOD
PARAMOUNT
LAKEWOOD
LONG BEACH
CYPRESS
SEAL BEACH
U.S. NAVAL WEAPONS STATION
NAVAL STATION
LOS ALAMITOS
COMPTON
ANDERSON
WATTS
CARSON
SAN DIEGO FRWY
WILMINGTON
TERMINAL ISLAND
SAN PEDRO
LONG BEACH HARBOR
LOS ANGELES HARBOR
INGLEWOOD
HAWTHORNE
GARDENA
LAWNDALE
TORRANCE
LOMITA
MANHATTAN BEACH
HERMOSA BEACH
REDONDO BEACH
PALOS VERDES ESTATES
ROLLING HILLS
ROLLING HILLS ESTATES
MARINA DEL REY
VENICE
EL SEGUNDO
FLATROCK PT.
PALOS VERDES PT.
PT. VINCENTE
LONG PT.
PT. FERMIN
PALOS VERDES
SANTA ANA FRWY
SAN GABRIEL RIVER FRWY
HARBOR FRWY
LONG BEACH FRWY

LONG BEACH

E F G H J

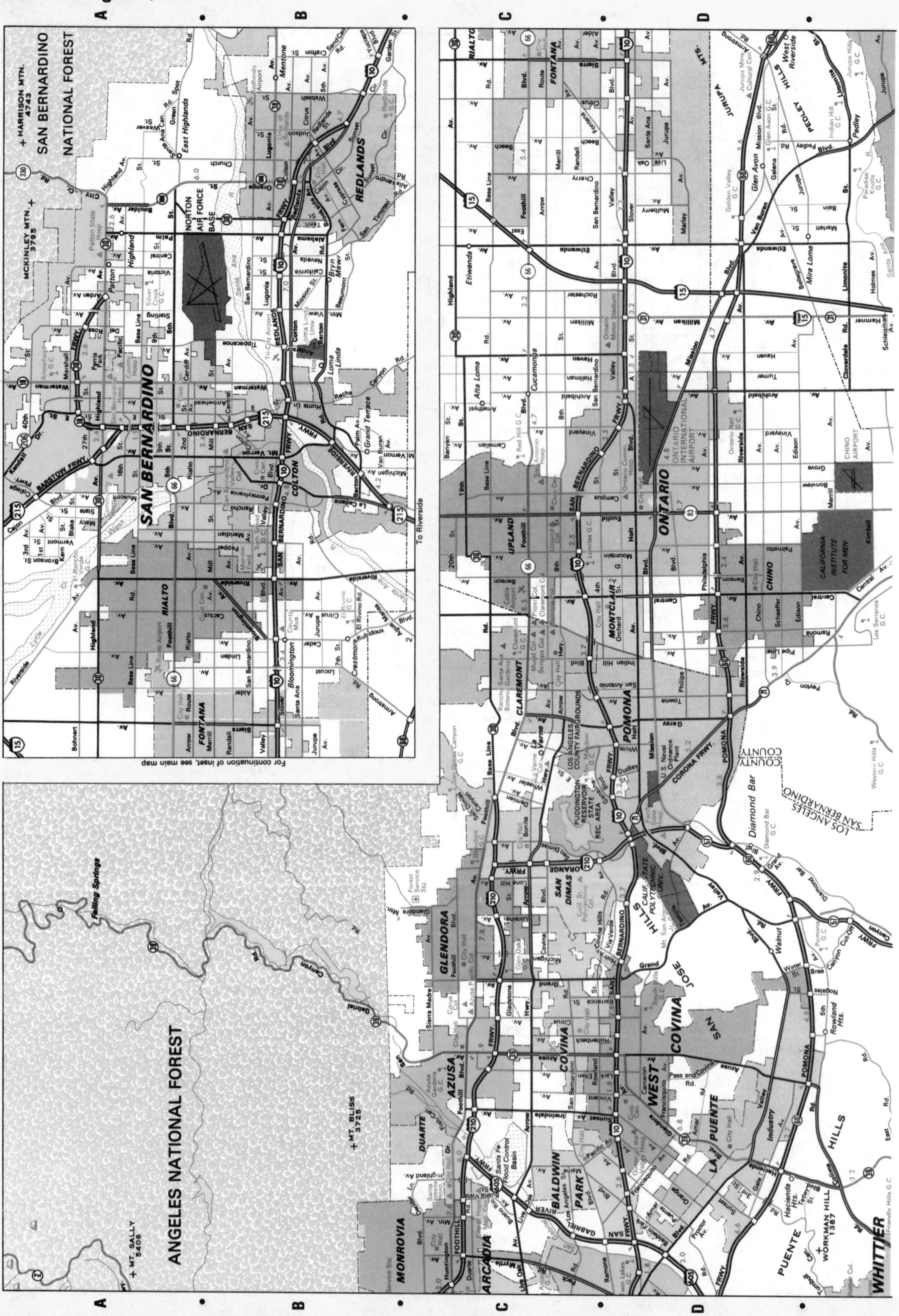

SAN BERNARDINO NATIONAL FOREST

+ HARRISON MTN. 4743

+ McKINLEY MTN. 3795

NORTON AIR FORCE BASE

REDLANDS

SAN BERNARDINO

COLTON

RIALTO

FONTANA

RIALTO

RIALTO

For continuation of inset, see main map

RIALTO

FONTANA

ONTARIO INTERNATIONAL AIRPORT

ONTARIO

UPLAND

MONTCLAIR

CHINO

CHINO AIRPORT

CALIFORNIA INSTITUTE FOR MEN

POMONA

CLAREMONT

JURUPA

ANGELES NATIONAL FOREST

+ MT. SALLY 5408

Falling Springs

+ MT. BLISS 3725

GLENDORA

SAN DIMAS

AZUSA

DUARTE

MONROVIA

ARCADIA

BALDWIN PARK

COVINA

WEST COVINA

LA PUENTE

Diamond Bar

SAN JOSE HILLS

PUENTE HILLS

WHITTIER

+ WORKMAN HILL 1387

LOS ANGELES — SAN BERNARDINO COUNTY

CALIF. STATE POLYTECHNIC UNIV.

LOS ANGELES COUNTY FAIRGROUNDS

PUDDINGSTONE RESERVOIR STATE REC. AREA

U.S. NAVAL ORDNANCE PLANT

Scale of Miles
0 1 2 3

N

Major labels

CLEVELAND NATIONAL FOREST

RIVERSIDE

CORONA

NORCO

HOME GARDENS

EL CERRITO

CHINO HILLS

CALIFORNIA INSTITUTE FOR MEN

CALIF. INST. FOR WOMEN

CHINO AIRPORT

RIVERSIDE MUNICIPAL AIRPORT

PRADO FLOOD CONTROL BASIN

U.S. NAVAL RESERVATION

SAN BERNARDINO COUNTY
RIVERSIDE COUNTY

LOS ANGELES COUNTY
ORANGE COUNTY

SAN BERNARDINO COUNTY
ORANGE COUNTY

Trabuco Canyon

Silverado Canyon

Santiago Canyon

Modjeska Canyon

Villa Park Res.

Santiago Res.

EL TORO U.S.M.C. AIR STATION

SANTA ANA U.S.M.C. AIR FACILITY

IRVINE

UNIV. OF CALIFORNIA IRVINE CAMPUS

Lake Forest

SANTA ANA

TUSTIN

ORANGE

COSTA MESA

NEWPORT BEACH

FOUNTAIN VALLEY

HUNTINGTON BEACH

WESTMINSTER

GARDEN GROVE

ANAHEIM

STANTON

BUENA PARK

LA MIRADA

LA HABRA

FULLERTON

BREA

PLACENTIA

YORBA LINDA

WORKMAN HILL 1367

ROWLAND HILLS

Rowland Hts.

Diamond Bar

Roads / Freeways

RIVERSIDE FRWY

CORONA FRWY

ORANGE FRWY

SANTA ANA FRWY

GARDEN GROVE FRWY

SAN DIEGO FRWY

Newport Blvd.

Harbor Blvd.

Beach Blvd.

Magnolia

Euclid

Brookhurst

Chapman Av.

Lincoln Av.

Katella Av.

Ball Rd.

La Palma Av.

Imperial Hwy.

Coast Hwy.

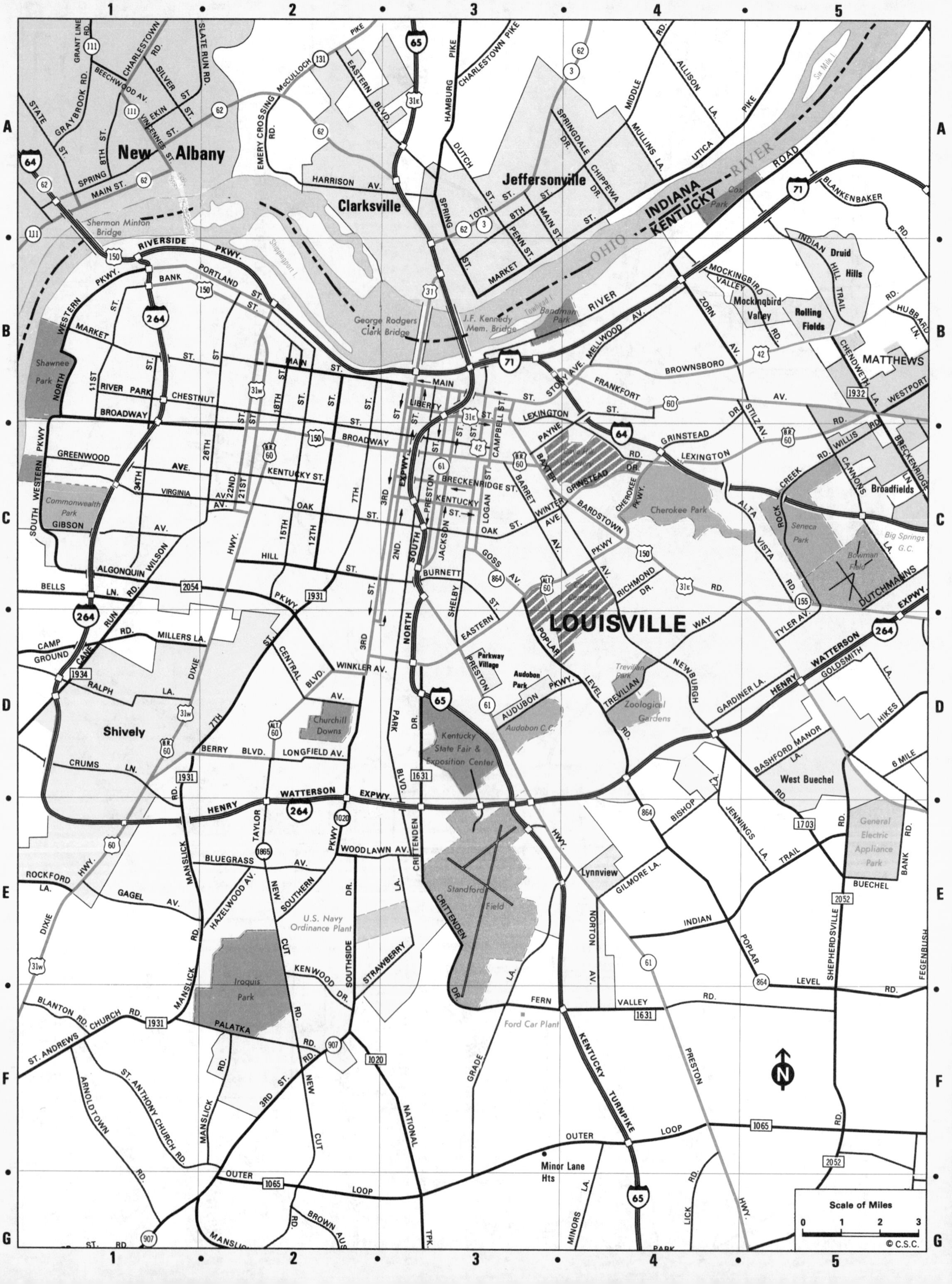

New Albany
Clarksville
Jeffersonville
Shively
West Buechel
Lynnview
Matthews
Rolling Fields
Mockingbird Valley
Druid Hills
Broadfields
Dutchmans
Minor Lane Hts

LOUISVILLE

INDIANA
KENTUCKY

OHIO RIVER

Shawnee Park
Commonwealth Park
Churchill Downs
U.S. Navy Ordinance Plant
Iroquis Park
Kentucky State Fair & Exposition Center
Parkway Village
Audobon Park
Audobon C.C.
Cherokee Park
Seneca Park
Bowman Field
Big Springs G.C.
Trevilian Park
Zoological Gardens
General Electric Appliance Park
Ford Car Plant
Standford Field
Cox Park
Bandman Park
Gibson
George Rodgers Clark Bridge
J.F. Kennedy Mem. Bridge
Sherman Minton Bridge

Scale of Miles
0   1   2   3

© C.S.C.

N

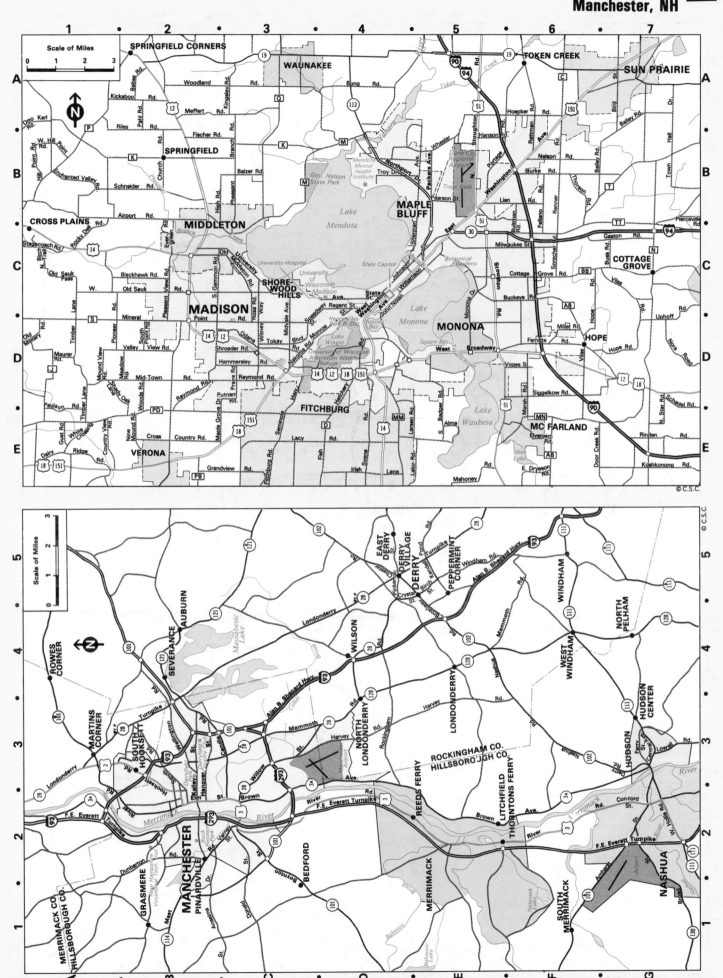

Scale of Miles

© C.S.C.

Scale of Miles

© C.S.C.

MEEKER
GERMANTOWN
COLGATE
MEQUON
MEQUON
BAYSIDE
MENOMONEE FALLS
WASHINGTON CO.
WAUKESHA CO.
BROWN DEER
RIVER HILLS
FOX POINT
Plainview
Menominee Co. Park & G.C.
LANNON
Brown Deer Park
GLENDALE
WHITEFISH BAY
SUSSEX
BUTLER
Timmerman Airport
SHOREWOOD
PEWAUKEE
BROOKFIELD
DUPLAINVILLE
Brookfield City Park
WAUWATOSA
University of Wisconsin (Milwaukee)
Lake Park
ELM GROVE
Milwaukee County Zoo
MILWAUKEE
McKinley Park
City Hall
WAUKESHA
GREENFIELD
WEST MILWAUKEE
Milwaukee County Stadium
Marquette Univ.
Lake Michigan
NEW BERLIN
WEST ALLIS
Jackson Park
SAINT FRANCIS
Greenfield Park
VERNON
HALES CORNERS
GREENDALE
General Mitchell International Airport
CUDAHY
MUSKEGO
Whitnall Park
Grobschmidt Park
Sheridan Park
BIG BEND
FRANKLIN
Rainbow Airport
Muskego Lakes G.C.
Oakwood G.C.
OAK CREEK
SOUTH MILWAUKEE
Grant Park
WAUSHEKA CO.
RACINE CO.
MILWAUKEE CO.
RACINE CO.
TICHIGAN
UNION CHURCH
CADDY VISTA
Kee Nong Go Mong Lake
Wind Lake
KNEELAND
HUSHER
Waubeesee Lake
Tichigan Lake
RAYMOND
CALEDONIA
TABOR
BUENA PARK
NORTH CAPE
THOMPSONVILLE

Scale of Miles
0 1 2 3

© C.S.C.

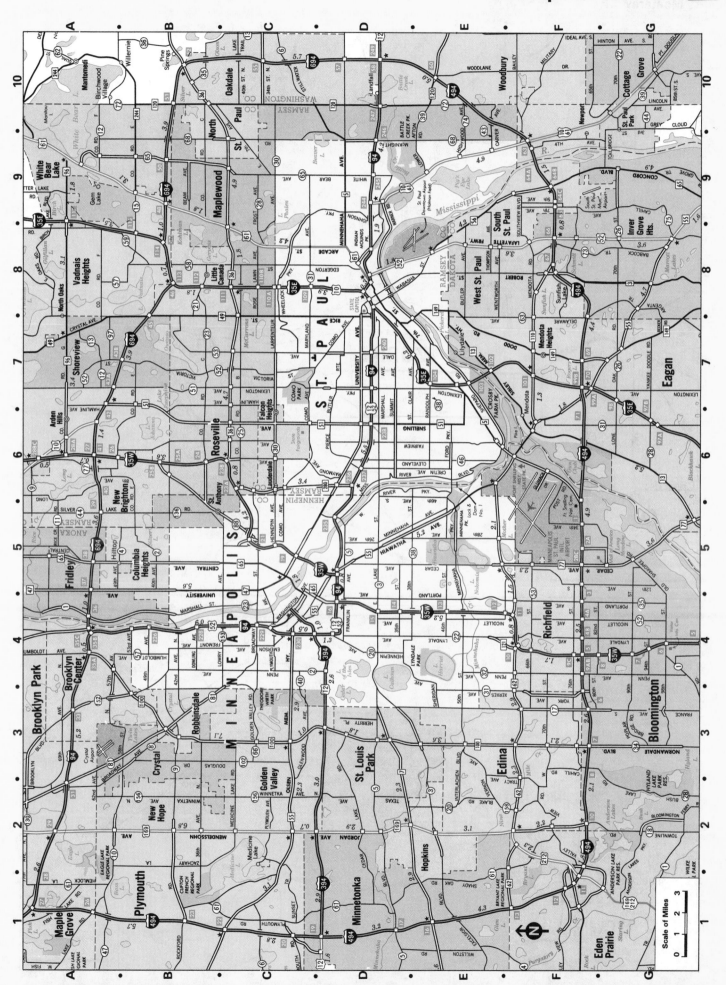

Mobile, AL

1 2 3 4 5 6 7

A

US 98

MOFFAT RD.

GREAVES

217

LOTT

ST. STEPHENS

SHELTON

WHISTLER

CHICKASAW

LEE ST.

GERONIMO ST.

43

PRICHARD

231

217

MYERS RD.

12TH AV.

SCHILLINGER RD.

JARRET RD.

BEAR FORK

BLVD.

BOAZ AV.

WASSON

45

TELEGRAPH HWY.

PAPER MILL RD.

Grand Bay

B

Millers Park

US 98

98

HIGHPOINT

Magginson Park

BEACH BLVD.

SHELTON

WOLF RIDGE

65

PRICHARD ST.

SUMMERVILLE RD.

WILSON ST.

CRAFT

43

194

165

MEAHER ST.

GLENNON

BAY BRIDGE

43

BLAKELY ISLAND

Mobile Bay

HOWELL'S FERRY

OVERLOOK RD.

MOFFAT

FOREST HILL DR.

98

Mobile ST.

ST. STEPHENS RD.

STONE ST.

45

DAVIS AV.

43

16

Delavan Bay

C

ATHEY RD.

ZEIGLER

BLVD.

SPRING HILL

3 Mile Cr.

98

OLD SHELL

GAILLARD DR.

Langan Park

AV.

STANTON ST.

31

13

98

10

90

D

Univ. Of South Alabama

UNIVERSITY BLVD.

OLD SHELL RD.

CODY RD.

AIRPORT BLVD.

McGREGOR

DAUPHIN

SAGE AV.

OLD SHELL

FLORIDA ST.

90

ANN ST.

City Hall

Battleship Park (U.S.S. Alabama)

PINTO ISLAND

MUNICIPAL AIRPORT

HIGHPOINT BLVD.

MOBILE

AZALEA RD.

MICHAEL BLVD.

GOVERNMENT

BROAD ST.

WASH AV.

VIRGINIA ST.

10

McDUFFIE ISLAND

SCHAUB AV.

GALOWAY AV.

PLEASANT VALLEY RD.

163

HOUSTON

Ladd Stadium

MICHIGAN

E

DAWES RD.

MORRISON ST.

COTTAGE HILL RD.

AZALEA BLVD.

90

DUVAL ST.

McVAY DR.

ISLAND PKWY.

DAUPHIN ISLAND

BROOKLEY FIELD

Univ. of South Alabama

MOBILE

COTTAGE HILL

SCHILLINGER RD.

MILKHOUSE CR.

CREST

DEMETROPOLIS RD.

90

HALLS MILL

65

10

163

BAY

F

N

Scale of Miles
0 1 2 3

CODY

GIRBY RD.

MILL

RIVIERE DU CHIEN Cr.

SOUTH DR.

Halls Mill Cr.

Monterey, CA

1 2 3 4 5 6 7

G

Pacific Ocean

Monterey Bay

1

MARINA

G17

GRAVES

McFADDEN

Watsonville

Cooper Rd.

183

SALINAS

Main St.

Laurel Dr.

Del Monte

California Rodeo Grounds

Hartnell A & M College East Campus

H

Indian Head Beach

WORKFIELD

1

Reservation Rd.

Blanco Rd.

River

Landing Strip

Fort Ord

Davis Rd.

Hitchcock Rd.

Foster Rd.

68

Hunters Ln.

Hartnell A & M Colleges West Campus

Main St.

Abbott St.

Blanco

Market St.

Salinas Municipal Airport

101

J

Municipal Golf Course

Spanish Bay

Pacific Grove Marine Gardens Park

SAND CITY

Mescal

Gen. Jim Moore Blvd.

FORT ORD VILLAGE

Military

SPRECKELS

Asilomar Conference Grounds

PACIFIC GROVE

Ocean View Blvd.

Lighthouse Ave.

Sunset Dr.

MONTEREY

68

SEASIDE

Del Monte

Fremont

Canyon

Hilby Ave.

Reservation

SERRA VILLAGE

68

Point Joe

Monterey Peninsula Golf Course

Presidio Of Monterey

Lighthouse

218

DEL REY OAKS

Laguna Seca

G17

Fan Shell Beach

Spyglass Hill Golf Course

17 Mile Dr.

Forest Lake

Munras Ave.

68

Old Del Monte Golf Course

Monterey Peninsula Airport

Salinas

Cypress Point

Cypress Point Golf Course

Ronda

Aguajito

Del Rey Rd.

Laguna Seca

AMBLER PARK

Monterey

K

PEBBLE BEACH

Stevenson Dr.

Serra Ave.

Carmel-Pacific Grove

Del Monte

San Benancio Rd.

N

Scale of Miles
0 1 2 3

Pebble Beach Golf Course

Stillwater Cove

CARMEL BY THE SEA

Juniper Ave.

Carmel

Carmel River

Valley

G16

Grade Rd.

Carmel De Tierra

Carmel Bay

Rancho Canada Golf Club

Laguna Seca Ranger Station

Carmel River State Beach

© C.S.C.

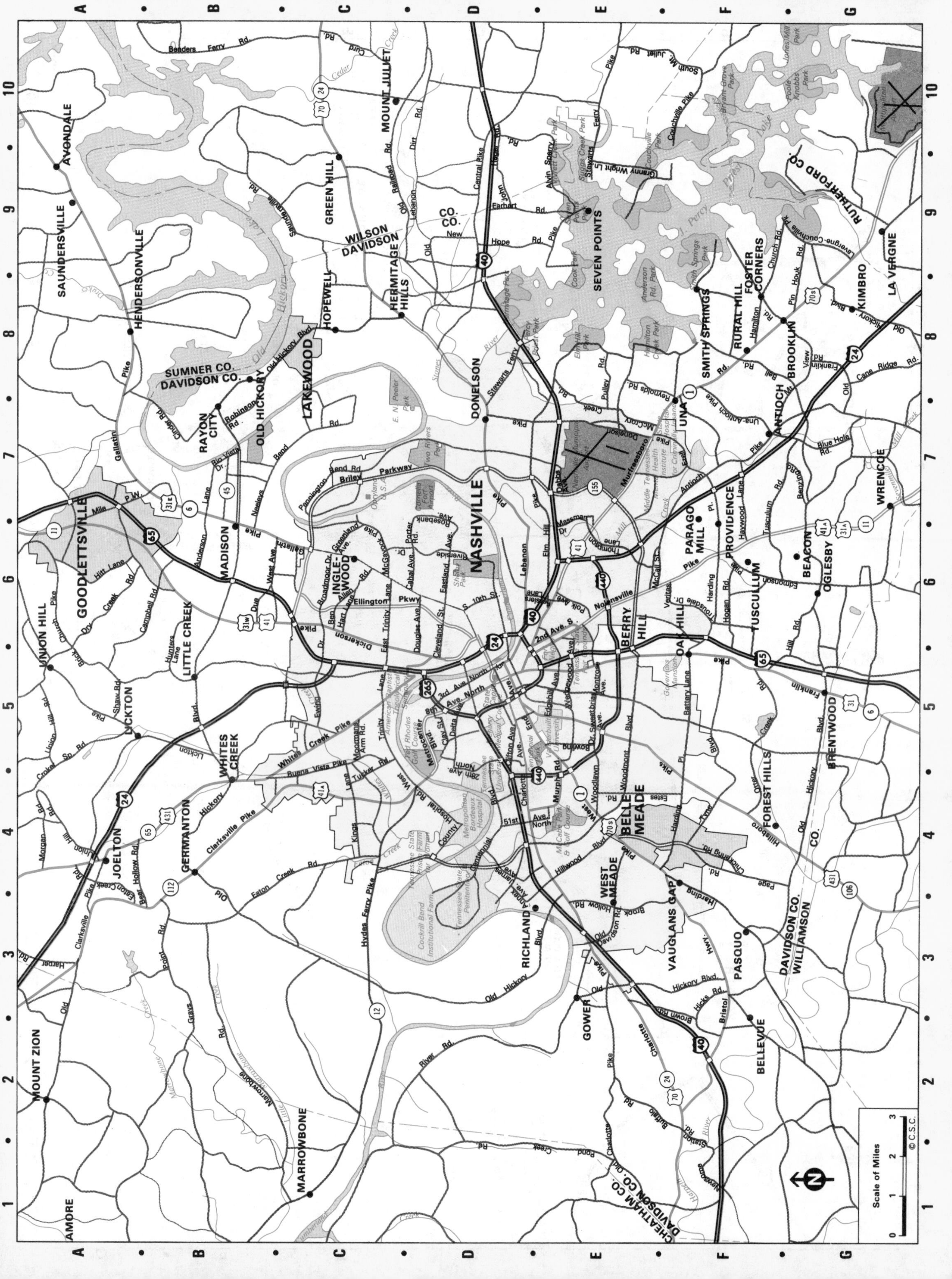

NASHVILLE

AVONDALE
SAUNDERSVILLE
HENDERSONVILLE
MOUNT JULIET
GREEN HILL
WILSON
DAVIDSON
HERMITAGE HILLS
HOPEWELL
CO. CO.
SEVEN POINTS
SMITH SPRINGS
RURAL HILL
FOSTER CORNERS
BROOKLYN
KIMBRO
LA VERGNE
RUTHERFORD CO.
SUMNER CO.
DAVIDSON CO.
LAKEWOOD
RAYON CITY
OLD HICKORY
DONELSON
UNA
ANTIOCH
WRENCOE
GOODLETTSVILLE
MADISON
INGLEWOOD
PARAGON MILL
PROVIDENCE
TUSCULUM
BEACON
OGLESBY
UNION HILL
LITTLE CREEK
BERRY HILL
OAK HILL
BRENTWOOD
WHITES CREEK
JOELTON
GERMANTON
BELLE MEADE
WEST MEADE
FOREST HILLS
MOUNT ZION
RICHLAND
VAUGHANS GAP
PASQUO
BELLEVUE
GOWER
DAVIDSON CO.
WILLIAMSON CO.
MARROWBONE
CHEATHAM CO.
DAVIDSON CO.

Scale of Miles
© C.S.C.
0   1   2   3
N

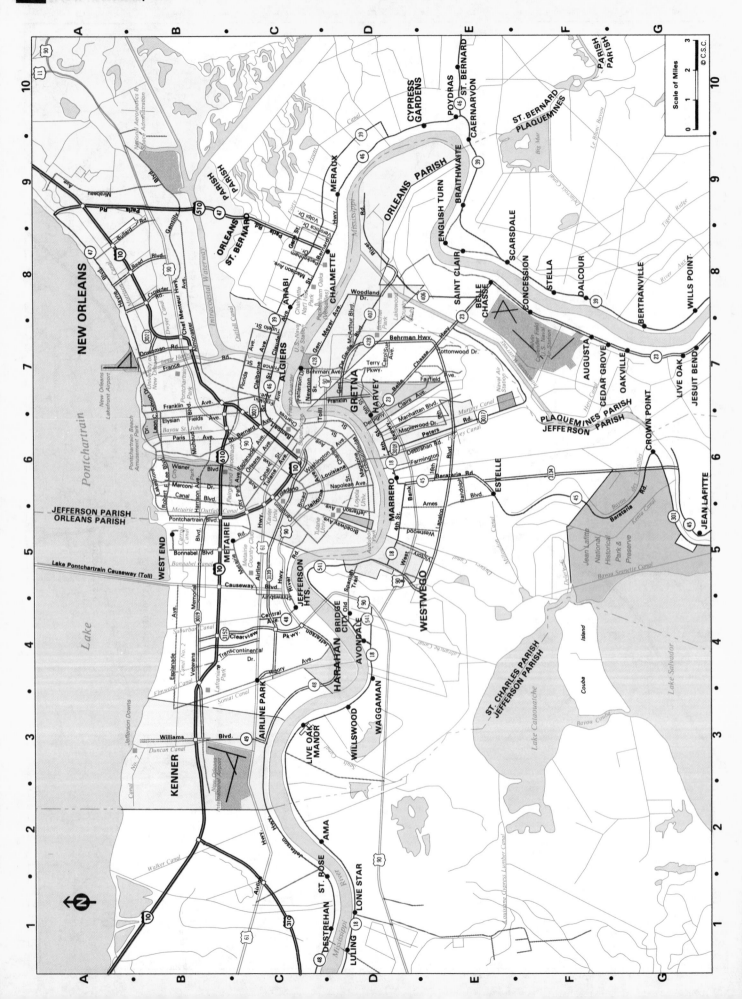

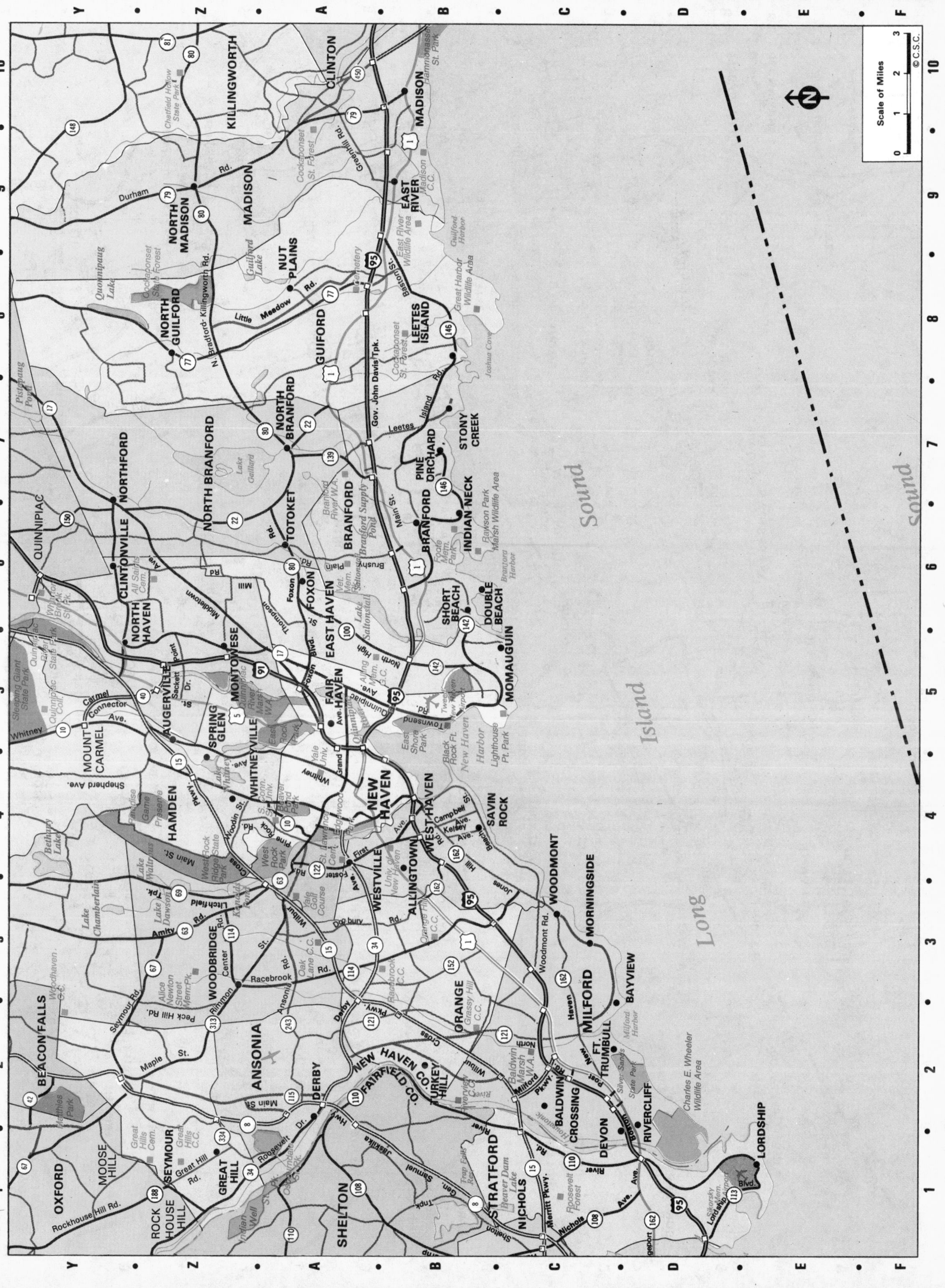

Scale of Miles
0 1 2 3
© C.S.C.

N

Long Island Sound

Sound

KILLINGWORTH
CLINTON
MADISON
EAST RIVER
NORTH MADISON
NUT PLAINS
Durham
NORTH GUILFORD
GUIFORD
LEETES ISLAND
Leetes
STONY CREEK
PINE ORCHARD
NORTHFORD
NORTH BRANFORD
TOTOKET
BRANFORD
INDIAN NECK
QUINNIPIAC
CLINTONVILLE
NORTH HAVEN
MONTOWESE
FOXON
EAST HAVEN
SHORT BEACH
DOUBLE BEACH
MOMAUGUIN
SAUGERVILLE
SPRING GLEN
WHITNEYVILLE
FAIR HAVEN
NEW HAVEN
WEST HAVEN
SAVIN ROCK
MOUNT CARMEL
HAMDEN
WESTVILLE
ALLINGTOWN
WOODMONT
MORNINGSIDE
BEACONFALLS
WOODBRIDGE
ORANGE
MILFORD
BAYVIEW
FT. TRUMBULL
MOOSE HILL
ROCK HOUSE HILL
SEYMOUR
GREAT HILL
ANSONIA
DERBY
NEW HAVEN CO.
FAIRFIELD CO.
TURKEY HILL
BALDWIN CROSSING
DEVON
RIVERCLIFF
LORDSHIP
OXFORD
SHELTON
STRATFORD
NICHOLS

Cockaponset St. Forest
Chatfield Hollow State Park
Cockaponset St. Forest
Quonnipaug Lake
Guilford Lake
Pistapaug Pond
Lake Gaillard
Branford Supply Pond
Branford River W.A.
Great Harbor Wildlife Area
Guilford Harbor
Joshua Cove
Rawson Park
Thimble Islands
Branford Harbor
Sleeping Giant State Park
Quinnipiac Golf
Sperry's Point
Lake Whitney
Yale Univ.
East Rock Park
East Shore Park
New Haven Harbor
Black Rock Ft.
Lighthouse Pt. Park
Lake Saltonstall
Bethany Lake
Lake Watrous
Lake Chamberlain
West Rock Ridge State Park
Yale Golf Course
Oak Lane C.C.
Orange Hills C.C.
Glassy Hill C.C.
Milford Harbor
Gulf Pond
Silver Sands State Park
Charles E. Wheeler Wildlife Area
Great Hills Cem.
Matthias Park
Woodhaven C.C.
Race Brook C.C.

Roads: 81, 80, 148, 79, 80, 17, 150, 40, 10, 15, 22, 139, 80, 77, 1, 146, 79, 50, 95, 1, 100, 142, 91, 5, 10, 122, 63, 69, 114, 67, 243, 313, 34, 115, 110, 8, 108, 334, 188, 110, 121, 152, 162, 1, 95, 113

NEW YORK
NEW JERSEY
ORANGE CO.
PASSAIC CO.
BERGEN CO.
ROCKLAND CO.
WESTCHESTER CO.
BRONX CO.
ESSEX CO.
Hudson River
Tappan Zee
Tappan Zee Bridge
TUXEDO PARK
SLOATSBURG
RAMAPO
HILLBURN
SUFFERN
MAHWAH
HEWITT
RINGWOOD
ERSKINE
BORO OF RINGWOOD
BORO OF WANAQUE
OAKLAND
POMPTON LAKES
BORO OF BLOOMING DALE
RIVERDALE
PEQUANNOCK
LINCOLN PARK
FAIRFIELD
WEST CALDWELL
NORTH CALDWELL
CEDAR GROVE
LITTLE FALLS TWP.
WEST PATERSON
BORO OF TOTOWA
WAYNE
WAYNE TWP.
FRANKLIN LAKES
HALEDON
NORTH HALEDON
PROSPECT PK.
PATERSON
HAWTHORNE
CLIFTON
PASSAIC
WALLINGTON
WOOD RIDGE
LODI
GARFIELD
ELMWOOD PARK
SADDLE BROOK
ROCHELLE PK.
MAYWOOD
HACKENSACK
HASBROUCK HTS.
TETERBORO
MOONACHIE
LITTLE FERRY
RIDGEFIELD PK
SOUTH HACKENSACK
BOGOTA
TEANECK
LEONIA
PALISADES PK.
FORT LEE
ENGLEWOOD CLIFFS
ENGLEWOOD
TENAFLY
BERGENFIELD
NEW MILFORD
DUMONT
CRESSKILL
DEMAREST
HAWORTH
CLOSTER
ALPINE
NORWOOD
NORTHVALE
ROCKLEIGH
OLD TAPPAN
HARRINGTON PK.
RIVER VALE
WESTWOOD
EMERSON
ORADELL
RIVER EDGE
PARAMUS
FAIR LAWN
GLEN ROCK
RIDGEWOOD
HO-HO-KUS
MIDLAND PARK
WYCKOFF
WALDWICK
ALLENDALE
SADDLE RIVER
UPPER SADDLE RIVER
RAMSEY
WOODCLIFF LAKE
PARK RIDGE
MONTVALE
HILLSDALE
WASHINGTON TWP.
PEARL RIVER
ORANGETOWN
ORANGEBURG
BLAUVELT
TAPPAN
SPARKILL
PIERMONT
PALISADES
GRANDVIEW-ON HUDSON
S. NYACK
NYACK
CENTRAL NYACK
UPPER NYACK
VALLEY COTTAGE
BARDONIA
CLARKSTOWN
NEW HEMPSTEAD
SPRING VALLEY
HILLCREST
MT. IVY
WESLEY HILLS
LADENTOWN
VIOLA
MONSEY
TALLMAN
AIRMONT
OSSINING
ARCHVILLE
BRIARCLIFF MANOR
CHAPPAQUA
PLEASANTVILLE
THORNWOOD
HAWTHORNE
MT. PLEASANT
POCANTICO HILL
N. TARRYTOWN
TARRYTOWN
EAST VIEW
ELMSFORD
GREENBURGH
IRVINGTON
DOBBS FERRY
ARDSLEY
HASTINGS-ON HUDSON
WHITE PLAINS
SCARSDALE
EASTCHESTER
TOWN OF MAMARONECK
LARCHMONT
NEW ROCHELLE
PELHAM
PELHAM MANOR
MOUNT VERNON
YONKERS
BRONX
RIVERDALE
VALHALLA

TRUMBULL · **BRIDGEPORT** · STRATFIELD · MELVILLE VILLAGE · PLATTSVILLE · EASTON · WESTON · FAIRFIELD · GREENFIELD HILL · MILL PLAIN · SOUTHPORT · WESTPORT

FAIRFIELD · Bridgeport Harbor · Seaside Park · Sherwood Island State Park · Southport Harbor

WILTON · NORTH WILTON · CANNONDALE · SOUTH WILTON · CRANBURY · WESTPORT · EAST NORWALK · SOUTH NORWALK · WINNIPAUK · NORWALK · WEST NORWALK · ROWAYTON · TONEKENE · NOROTON

RIDGEFIELD · NEW CANAAN · SPRINGDALE · GLEN BROOK · DARIEN · NORTON HEIGHTS · MIANUS · RIVERSIDE · OLD GREENWICH · COS COB · BYRAM

BOUTONVILLE · LEWISBORO · POUND RIDGE · SCOTTS CORNER · HORSESHOES HILL · SARIES CORNERS · LONG RIDGE · NORTH STAMFORD · STAMFORD · STANWICH · ROUND HILL · NORTH GREENWICH · GREENWICH · GLENVILLE · RIVERSVILLE · PEMBERWICK · PORT CHESTER · RYE BROOK

BEDFORD HILLS · BEDFORD CENTER · BEDFORD · MOUNT KISCO · ARMONK · WINDMILL FARM · RIVERSVILLE · HARRISON · RYE · VALHALLA · TOWN OF MAMARONECK · VILLAGE OF MAMARONECK · LARCHMONT

FAIRFIELD CO. / WESTCHESTER CO. · NEW YORK / CONNECTICUT · SUFFOLK CO. / NASSAU CO.

FT. SALONGA · ASHAROKEN · EATONS NECK · LLOYD NECK · EATONS NECK PT. · LLOYD NECK · Sunken Meadow St. Pk. · Long Beach · Nissequogue Golf Course · Crab Meadow Pk. · Northport Bay · Vanderbilt Museum · Caumsett St. Pk. · Lloyd Harbor · Lloyd Pt.

Long Island Sound · Long Island · Chimmons Island · Shea Is. · Sheffield Island · Scott's Cove · Cove Harbor · Stamford Harbor · Greenwich Harbor · Greenwich Point Pk. · Byram Harbor

Devils Den Nature Conservancy · Ward Pond Ridge Reservation · Mianus River · New Croton Res. · Cross River Res. · Byram Lake Res. · Kensico Reservoir

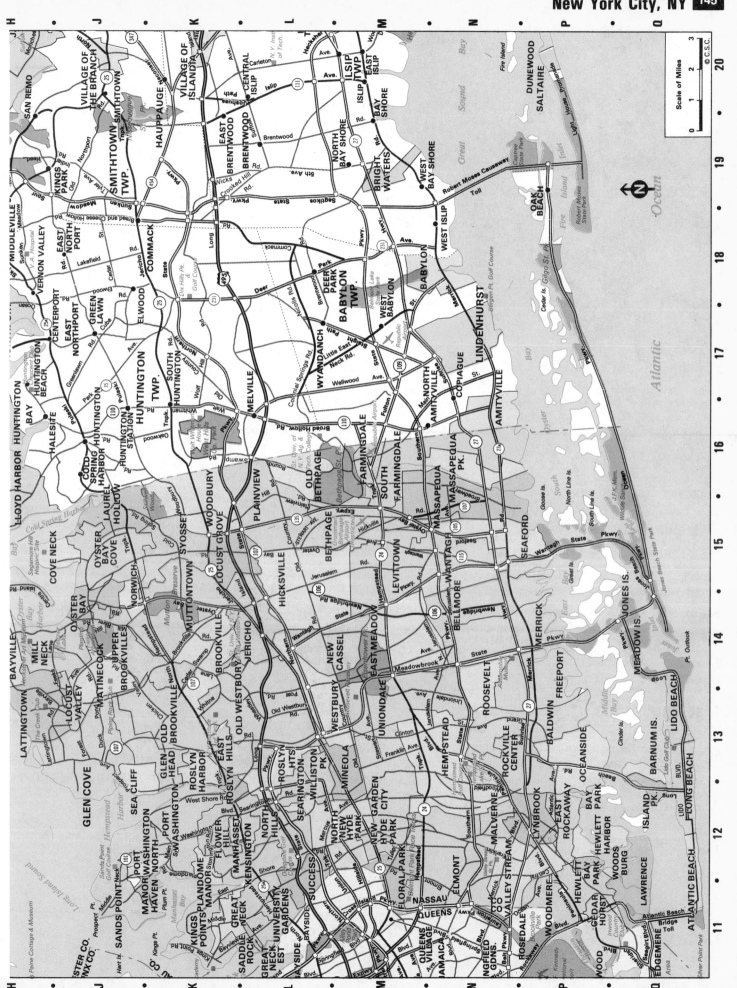

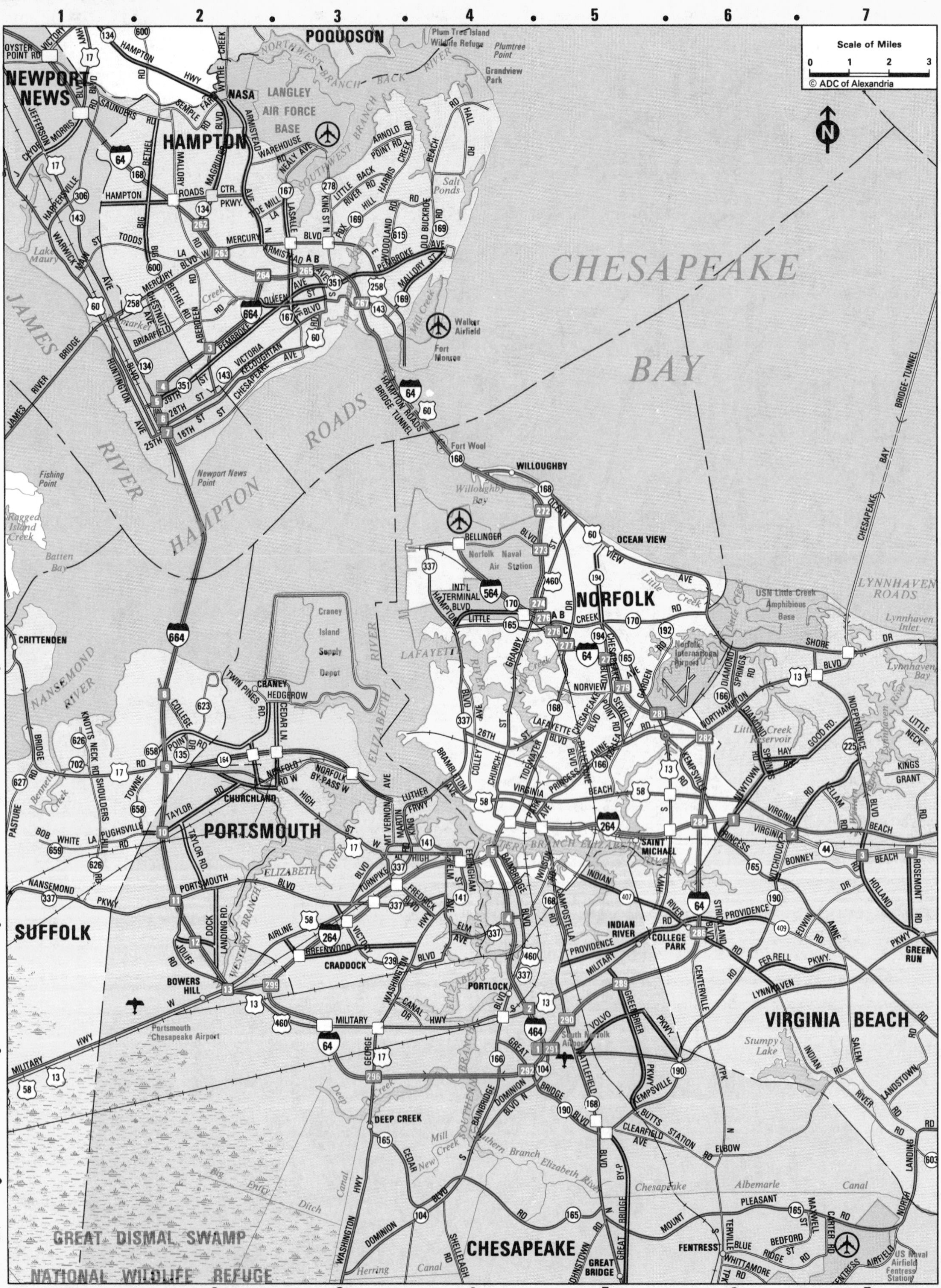

Scale of Miles
0 1 2 3
© ADC of Alexandria

N

POQUOSON

Plum Tree Island
Wildlife Refuge
Plumtree
Point

Grandview
Park

NEWPORT
NEWS

HAMPTON

LANGLEY
AIR FORCE
BASE

NASA

Salt
Ponds

CHESAPEAKE

BAY

Walker
Airfield

Fort
Monroe

HAMPTON ROADS
BRIDGE-TUNNEL

Fort Wool

WILLOUGHBY

JAMES

RIVER

Fishing
Point

Ragged
Island
Creek

Batten
Bay

Newport News
Point

HAMPTON

ROADS

Willoughby
Bay

BELLINGER

Norfolk Naval
Air Station

INT'L
TERMINAL
BLVD

OCEAN VIEW

NORFOLK

USN Little Creek
Amphibious
Base

LYNNHAVEN
ROADS

Lynnhaven
Inlet

Lynnhaven
Bay

CRITTENDEN

NANSEMOND

RIVER

Craney
Island
Supply
Depot

CRANEY
HEDGEROW
TWIN PINES

ELIZABETH

RIVER

LAFAYETTE

Little
Creek

Norfolk
International
Airport

NORVIEW

Little Creek
Reservoir

Diamond
Springs

KINGS
GRANT

LITTLE
NECK

CHURCHLAND

PORTSMOUTH

SAINT
MICHAEL

SUFFOLK

EASTERN BRANCH ELIZABETH

VIRGINIA BEACH

BOWERS
HILL

CRADDOCK

PORTLOCK

INDIAN
RIVER

COLLEGE
PARK

Stumpy
Lake

GREEN
RUN

Portsmouth
Chesapeake Airport

South Norfolk
Airport

DEEP CREEK

Chesapeake

Albemarle

Canal

GREAT DISMAL SWAMP

NATIONAL WILDLIFE REFUGE

CHESAPEAKE

FENTRESS

US Naval
Airfield
Fentress
Station

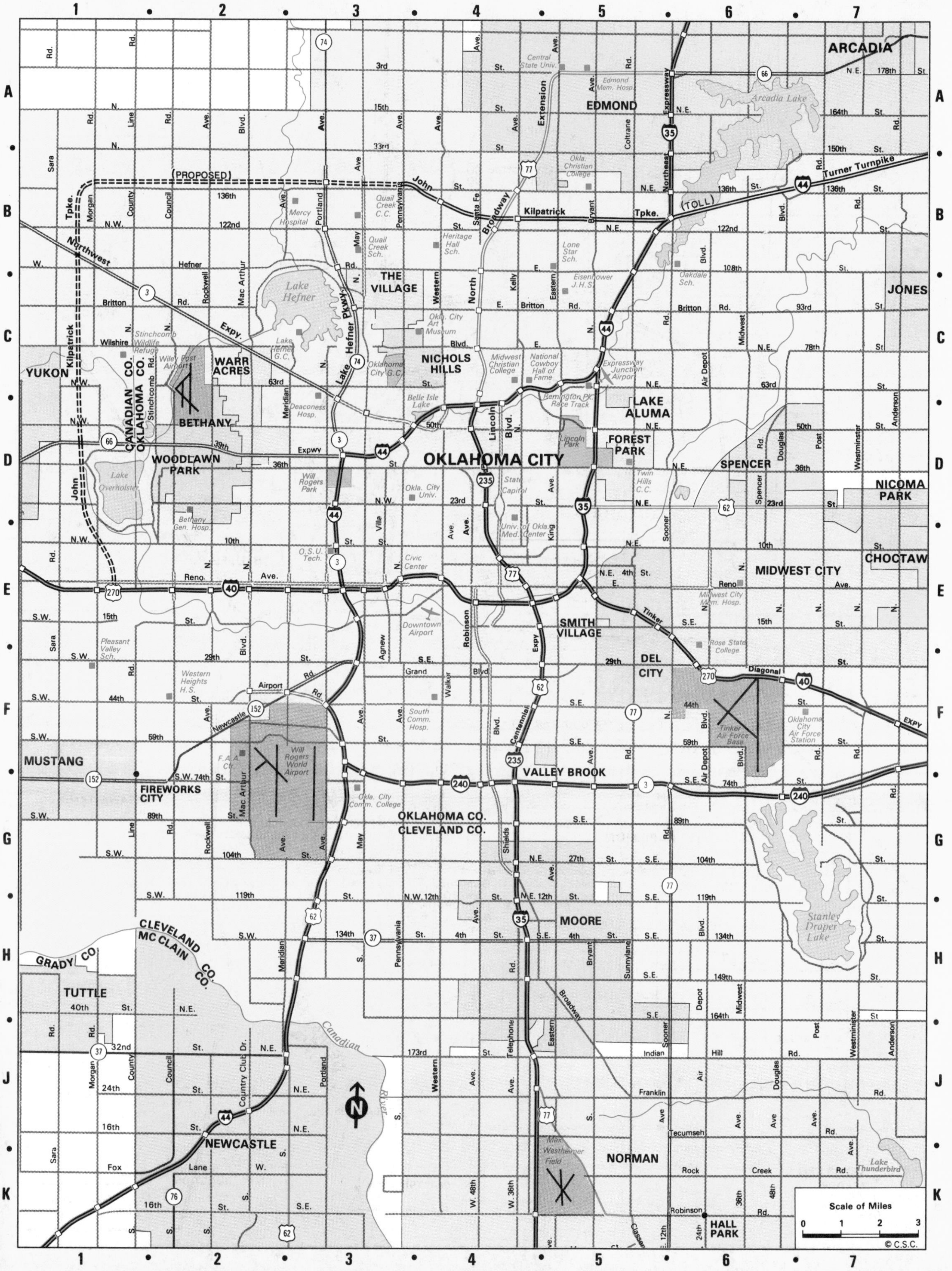

ARCADIA

Arcadia Lake

EDMOND

Central State Univ.

Edmond Mem. Hosp.

Okla. Christian College

Turner Turnpike

Kilpatrick

Mercy Hospital

Quail Creek C.C.

Heritage Hall Sch.

Lone Star Sch.

Eisenhower J.H.S.

THE VILLAGE

Oakdale Sch.

JONES

Lake Hefner

Lake Hefner G.C.

Okla. City Art Museum

NICHOLS HILLS

Midwest Christian College

National Cowboy Hall of Fame

Expressway Junction Airport

Stinchcomb Wildlife Refuge

Wiley Post Airport

WARR ACRES

Oklahoma City G.C.

Belle Isle Lake

Remington Pk. Race Track

LAKE ALUMA

BETHANY

Deaconess Hosp.

Lincoln Park

FOREST PARK

SPENCER

NICOMA PARK

YUKON

CANADIAN CO.   OKLAHOMA CO.

WOODLAWN PARK

Lake Overholser

Bethany Gen. Hosp.

OKLAHOMA CITY

Okla. City Univ.

State Capitol

Univ. of Okla. Med. Center

Twin Hills C.C.

CHOCTAW

O.S.U. Tech.

Civic Center

MIDWEST CITY

Midwest City Mem. Hosp.

Downtown Airport

Pleasant Valley Sch.

SMITH VILLAGE

Rose State College

Western Heights H.S.

South Comm. Hosp.

DEL CITY

Tinker

MUSTANG

Airport

F.A.A. Ctr.

Will Rogers World Airport

Okla. City Comm. College

Tinker Air Force Base

Oklahoma City Air Force Station

FIREWORKS CITY

VALLEY BROOK

OKLAHOMA CO.

CLEVELAND CO.

Stanley Draper Lake

GRADY CO.   MC CLAIN CO.

CLEVELAND CO.

MOORE

TUTTLE

Canadian River

NEWCASTLE

Max Westheimer Field

NORMAN

Lake Thunderbird

HALL PARK

Scale of Miles
0 1 2 3

© C.S.C.

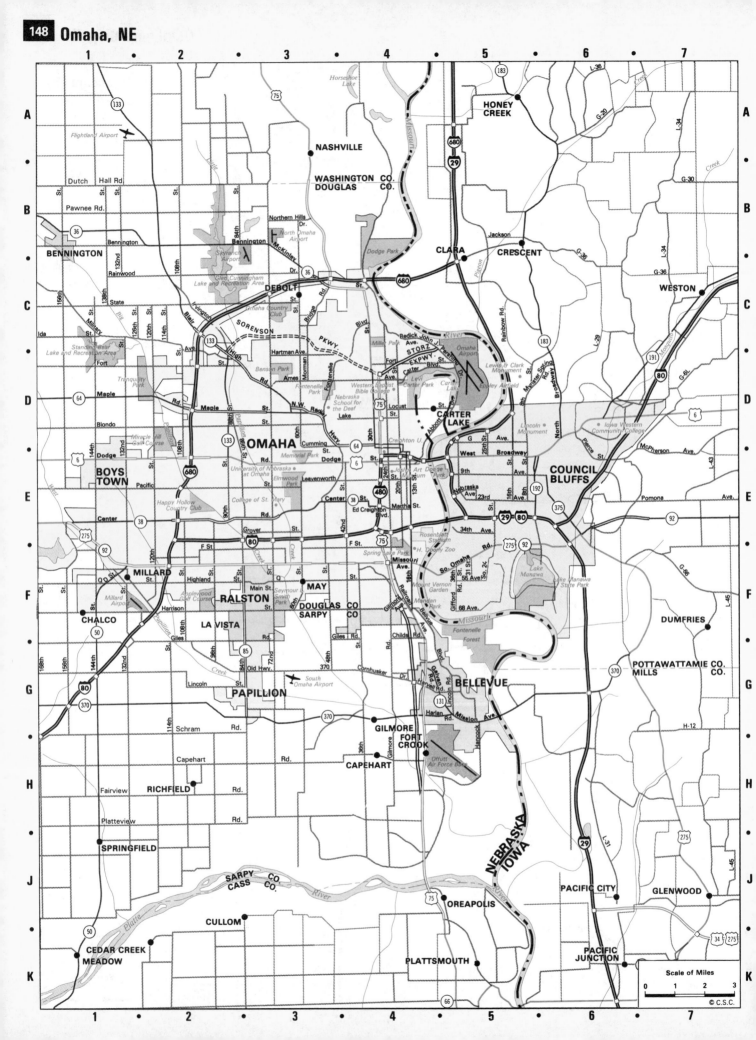

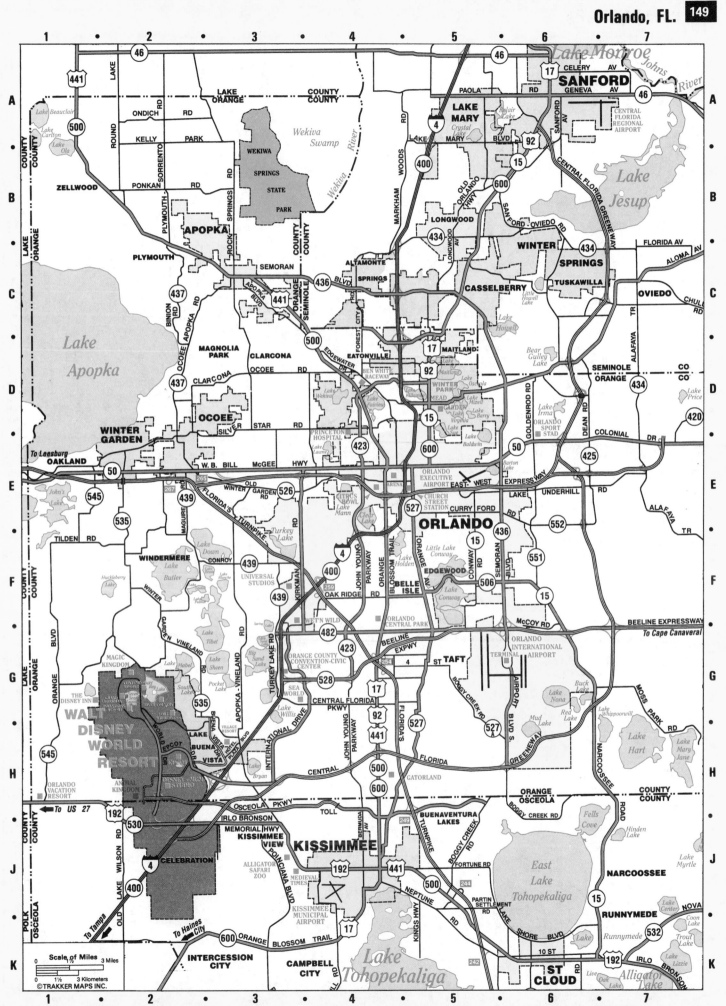

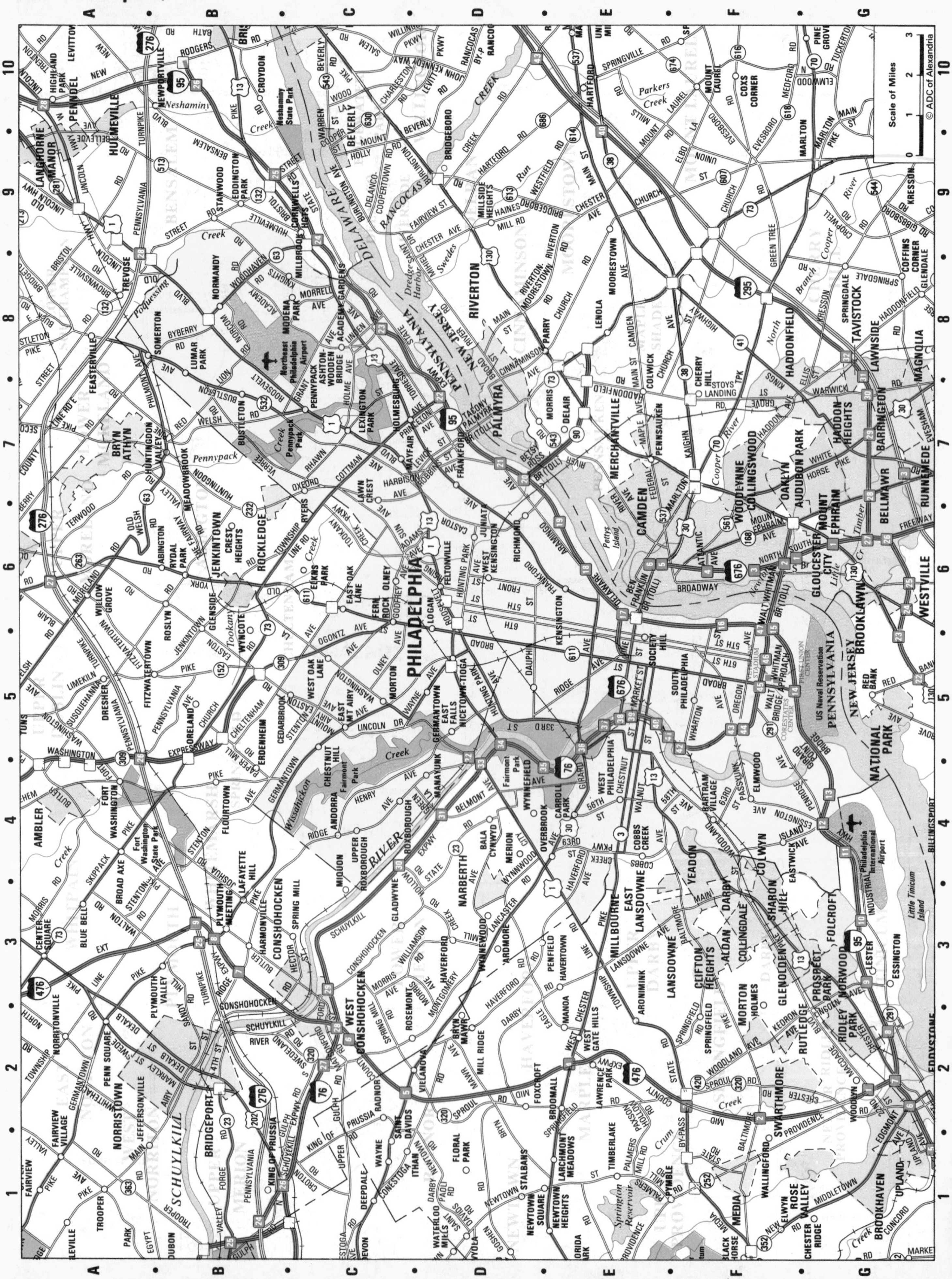
Scale of Miles
0 1 2 3
© ADC of Alexandria

PHOENIX

Grid columns: 1 2 3 4 5 6
Grid rows: A B C D E F G

Beardsley Canal
McMicken Dam Outlet Canal

Cave Creek Dam

DYNAMITE RD.
JOMAX RD.
HAPPY VALLEY RD.
PINNACLE PEAK RD.
PINNACLE PEAK RD.
Currys Corner

Peoria
Adobe
Deer Valley RD.
Deer Valley Airport
Thunderbird Regional Pk.
Arizona Veterans Mem. Cemetery

Beardsley
Suprise
Sun City West
BEARDSLEY RD.
UNION HILLS
UNION HILLS RD.
BELL
BELL RD.
Paradise City
Paradise Valley Community College
Paradise Valley Park

GREENWAY RD.
GREENWAY RD.
GREENWAY
Turf Paradise Race Track
Moon Valley C.C.
Scottsdale Mun. Airport

WADDELL RD.
BULLARD AVE.
El Mirage
Sun City
Youngstown
THUNDERBIRD
CACTUS
PEORIA AVE.
DUNLAP
American Inst. for Foreign Trade
ASU West
Cactus Pk.
Metro Center
North Mountain Park
THUNDERBIRD
CACTUS
SHEA
Century C.C.
HAYDEN
Scottsdale

OLIVE
NORTHERN
Glendale
GLENDALE
Glendale Com. Col.
Heatheaven Pk. Cem.
Royal Palm Mobile Pk.
Phoenix Mountain Preserve
Squaw Peak Park
Paradise Valley
Paradise Valley C.C.

Luke Air Force Base
MIRAGE
BETHANY HOME RD.
BETHANY
CAMELBACK
LINCOLN
MC DONALD DR.
CAMELBACK
INDIAN SCHOOL

Litchfield Park
Avondale
Holiday Pk.
Grand Canyon Col.
Mun. G.C.
INDIAN SCHOOL RD.
V.A. Hospital
Arizona Biltmore

Irrigation District
Eloso Pk.
THOMAS
MC DOWELL
Encanto Golf Course & Park
Phoenix C.C.
Heard Mus.
County Hospital
Arizona C.C.
Military Res.
Desert Botanical Garden

PAPAGO FRWY.
Goodyear
Tolleson
VAN BUREN ST.
PAPAGO FRWY.
VAN BUREN
State Fair Grounds
State Hospital
Phoenix Greyhound Pk.
Papago Park
Zoological Park

Avondale
Cashion
BUCKEYE
State Capitol
Mun. Bldg.
WASHINGTON ST.
BankOne Ballpark
SKY HARBOR BLVD.
Sun Devil Stadium

Goodyear Airfield
LOWER BUCKEYE RD.
BROADWAY
AmericaWest Arena
Sky Harbor Int'l. Airport
Tempe Stadium
UNIVERSITY
APACHE
Arizona State Univ.
Tempe

SOUTHERN AVE.
BROADWAY RD.
Manzanita Speedway
SOUTHERN
Western
Canal

Salt River
BASE LINE RD.
DOBBINS RD.
ELLIOT
ESTRELLA DR.
Laveen
Phoenix Police Academy
Thunderbird C.C.
CANYON RD.
GUADALUPE RD.
Guadalupe
ELLIOT RD.
Ahwatukee
WARNER

Casey Abbott Semi-Regional Park
ESTRELLA MOUNTAIN REGIONAL PARK
Las Ramadas Picnic Area
SAN JUAN RD.
STEPHEN
MATHER RD.
TELEGRAPH PASS
BUENA VISTA
Gila Valley Lookout
PHOENIX SOUTH MOUNTAIN PARK
International Harvester Proving Ground
RAY RD.
WILLIAMS RD.
Chandler

N

GILA
Gila River
PECOS RD.
MARICOPA CO.
PINAL CO.
RIVER
INDIAN
RESERVATION
Goodyear Air Force Mil. Field

Scale of Miles
0 1 2 3 4 5

© C.S.C.

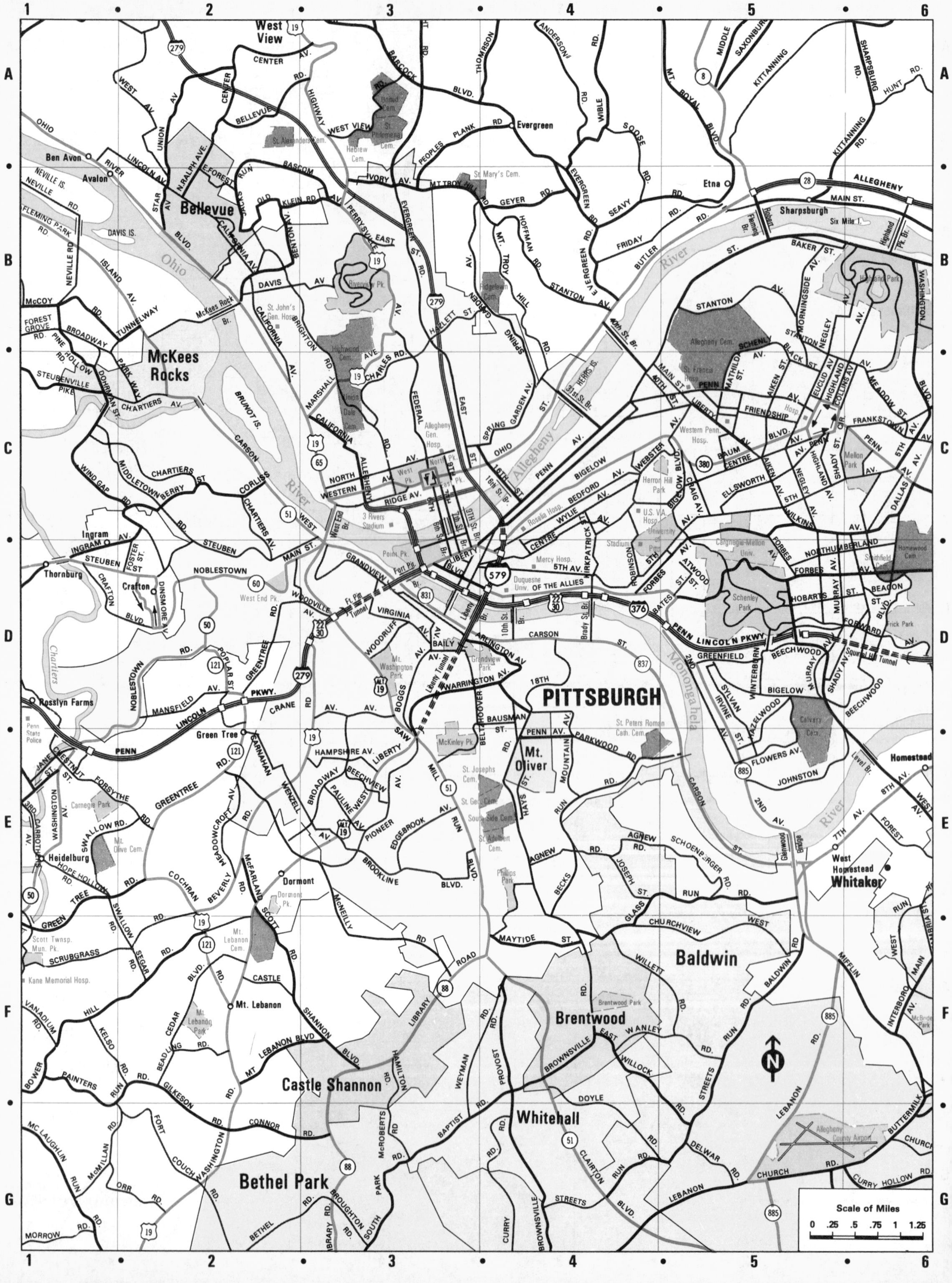

Grid columns: 1 2 3 4 5 6
Grid rows: A B C D E F G

West View

PITTSBURGH

Bellevue
McKees Rocks
Ben Avon
Avalon
Neville Is.
Davis Is.
McCoy
Forest Grove
Ingram
Thornburg
Crafton
Rosslyn Farms
Green Tree
Heidelburg
Scrubgrass
Dormont
Mt. Lebanon
Castle Shannon
Bethel Park
Whitehall
Brentwood
Baldwin
Mt. Oliver
Whitaker
West Homestead
Homestead
Sharpsburg
Etna
Evergreen
Stanton
Schenley
Friendship
Carnegie-Mellon Univ.
University
Schenley Park
Duquesne Univ.
U. OF THE ALLIES
Mercy Hosp.
Allegheny Gen. Hosp.
St. John's Gen. Hospital
Western Penn. Hosp.
Herron Hill
U.S. V.A. Hosp.
Mt. Washington Park
Grandview Park
McKinley Pk.
3 Rivers Stadium
Point Pk.
West End Pk.
West Park
Carnegie Park
Penn State Police
Scott Twnsp. Mun. Pk.
Kane Memorial Hosp.
Dormont Pk.
Mt. Lebanon Cem.
Brentwood Park
Allegheny County Airport
Phillips Park
Calvary Cem.
St. Peters Roman Cath. Cem.
Highland Park
Mellon Park
Frick Park
Homewood Cem.
Squirrel Hill Tunnel
Penn Lincoln Pkwy
Liberty Tunnel
Fort Pitt Tunnel

Rivers: Ohio River, Allegheny River, Monongahela River, Chartiers River

Scale of Miles
0 .25 .5 .75 1 1.25

N

1   2   3   4   5   6

A

SLAVE ISLAND RD.
Multnomah Channel
GILLIMAN
LOOP
MARINE DR.
Hayden Island
Columbia
MULTNOMAH COUNTY
CLARK COUNTY
VANCOUVER
E. MILL PLAIN BLVD.
Pearson Field
SKYLINE BLVD.
NEWBERRY RD.
N.W. SKYLINE BLVD. GERMANTOWN RD.
COLUMBIA BLVD.
N. FESSENDEN ST.
Slough
Columbia River
Exposition Center
Delta Park
Portland Tomahawk Island
Tomahawk Island
Tyee Yacht Club
WASHINGTON
OREGON
Rose City Yacht Club
Columbia River Yacht Club

B

N
N. LOMBARD ST.
N. WILLAMETTE BLVD.
WILLIS BLVD.
Columbia Park
N. PORTLAND AVE.
N. PENINSULAR AVE.
N. DENVER AVE.
Delta Park
Portland G.C.
N.E. COLUMBIA
Columbia Edgewater G.C.
N.E. MARINE RD.
Portland Int'l Airport
Riverside G.C.
Broadmoor G.C.
Portland Air Force Base
Colwood G.C.
BYP 30

Univ. of Portland
Swan Island
Willamette River
Forest Park
N. PORTLAND AVE.
Peninsula Park
N.E. LOMBARD
N.E. SUNDERLAND AVE.
BYP 30
Alberta Park
KILLINGSWORTH ST.
N.E. CULLY RD.

C

Columbia River
YEON AVE.
N. GREELEY AVE.
N. INTERSTATE AVE.
N. UNION AVE.
Broadway Bridge
PORTLAND
N.E. FREMONT ST.
N.E. 42ND AVE.
N.E. 33RD AVE.
N.E. 39TH AVE.
THE ALAMEDA
N. 57TH AVE.
Rose City G.C.
SR 30

BRONSON RD.
CORNELL RD.
CORNELL RD.
N.W. VAUGHN ST.
Fremont Bridge
N.E. BROADWAY
N.E. HALSEY ST.
Memorial Coliseum
405
84

D

174TH AVE.
WALKER
CORNELL RD.
MacLeay Park
N.W. SKYLINE RD.
N.W. 23RD AVE.
N.W. 19TH AVE.
N.E. SANDY
N.E. GLISAN ST.
Laurelhurst Park
E. BURNSIDE
S.E. STARK ST.
S.E. BELMONT ST.
S.E. MORRISON ST.
S.E. HAWTHORNE BLVD.
Mt. Tabor Park
WALKER RD.
BARNES RD.
26
Zoological Gardens and Museum
Portland State Univ.
MARKET
405
S.E. DIVISION ST.
Warner Pacific College
62ND
71ST
JENKINS RD.
S.W. VISTA AVE.
S.W. BROADWAY DR.
S.E. 26TH AVE.
POWELL
26
FOSTER RD.
170TH AVE.

E

West Slope
W. HUMPHREY
S.W. FAIRMONT
Council Crest
Univ of Oregon Med. Sch.
Ross Is. Bridge
Ross Island
S.E. 52ND
S.E. HAROLD
HOLGATE
Reed College
WOODSTOCK BLVD.
72ND ST.
FARMINGTON RD.
Raleigh Hills
BEAVERTON-HILLSDALE RD.
HAMILTON
SHATTUCK RD.
CAMERON RD.
Hillsdale
DOSCH RD.
SUNSET BLVD.
TERWILLIGER BLVD.
Harktack Island
Pioneer Park
BYBEE BLVD.
Eastmoreland Golf Course
STROWBRIDGE
S.E. TOLMAN ST.
WESTERN AVE.
ALLEN BLVD.
CEDAR HILLS BLVD.
CENTER RD. S.W. CANYON RD.
S.W. VERMONT ST.
Gabriel Park
Multnomah
30TH AVE.
S.E. 13TH AVE.
TACOMA
JOHNSON CREEK BLVD.
Kendall
S.E FLAVEL DR.
LINWOOD
ALBERTA
DENNEY BLVD.
HART RD.
GARDEN RD.
HOME
S.W. MULTNOMAH BLVD.
S.W. BARBUR BLVD.
MACADAM AVE.
RIVERSIDE C.C.
32ND AVE.
Milwaukie
KING RD.
BELL AVE.

F

BEAVERTON
WEIR RD.
MURRAY BLVD.
HALL BLVD.
SCHOLLS FERRY RD.
OLESON RD.
TAYLORS FERRY RD.
45TH
35TH AVE.
S.W. TAYLORS FERRY RD.
FERRY RD.
Lewis & Clark College
Tryon Creek State Park
Waverly C.C.
HARRISON ST.
WILLAMETTE BLVD.
RAILROAD AVE.
LAKE RD.
EXPWY
HARMONY RD.
TIGARD
Metzger
80TH AVE.
OAK ST.
Portland Comm. College
CAPITAL HWY.
KERR
MULTNOMAH CO.
WASHINGTON CO.
STEPHENSON ST.
BOONES FERRY RD.
ALDERCREST RD.
N. Clackamas Central Park
WEBSTER RD.
210
217
99W

G

REUSSER RD.
OLD SCHOLLS FERRY RD.
MURRAY
WEIR RD.
HALL BLVD.
PACIFIC HWY.
BONITA RD.
KRUSE WAY
CARMEN DR.
KING CITY
DURHAM RD.
Lake Grove
Waluga Park
LAKE OSWEGO
Lake Oswego C.C.
COUNTRY CLUB RD.
Oswego Lake
PORTLAND RD.
Oak Grove
OAK GROVE BLVD.
HILL RD.
CONCORD RD.
THIESSEN RD.
BEEF BEND RD.
DURHAM
TUALATIN
CLACKAMAS CO.
STAFFORD RD.
ROSE MONT
WEST LINN
Maryhurst College
5
99E
43
224

Scale of Miles
0   .5   1   1.5

© C.S.C.

Peoria, IL (top map)

1 2 3 4 5 6 7

A

EDWARDS

Dubois Rd.
Gilles Rd.
Ludolph Rd.
74
6
Charter Oak Rd.
150
Allen Rd.
Pioneer Pkwy.
Northmoor Rd.
Forest Park
Upper Peoria Lake
116 GERMANTOWN HILLS
1200N
WOODFORD CO.
TAZEWELL CO.
400E
750E
900E

Kickapoo
West Cottonwood Rd.
Kickapoo Creek
Hollow Rd.
Glen Ave.
Lake St.
Dr.
PEORIA HEIGHTS
29
Spring
100E
26
Tenmile Cr Rd.
County Line Rd.
HARVARD HILLS
Dutch Lane
2500E
Cruger Rd.
Metamora

B

Pottstown Rd.
Goetz Rd.
Church
Taylor
NORWOOD
PEORIA
EL VISTA
POTTSTOWN
8
University
Sterling Ave.
Gale Ave.
Knoxville
Nebraska
Glen Oak Park
88
24
EAST PEORIA
150
116
Highview
2400E
Guth Rd.
WASHINGTON
24
Irish Lane
2700E

C

HANNA CITY
116
McAllister
W. Greengold Rd.
North Murphy Rd.
Pinkerton Rd.
McCluggage
Plank Rd.
Farmington Rd.
Maxwell Rd.
Christ
BELLEVUE
Middle Rd.
Cameron Lane
Hager
Greater Peoria Airport
Smithville Lane
Airport Rd.
Bradley Park
Main St.
Lincoln Ave.
Griswold
Washington
8
Meadow
150
74
MORTON
2600E
Cooper Rd.
Lakeland Rd.
Farmdale Reservoir
Schuck Rd.

D

SMITHVILLE
Behrends Rd.
Smithville
Riekena
Johnson Lane
S. Riekena Rd.
Lancaster
BARTONVILLE
Tapping
Hollis
Garfield
Pfeiffer
CREVE COEUR
474
MARQUETTE HEIGHTS
Birchwood Ave.
98
Springfield Rd.
GROVELAND
Groveland Airport
Queenswood
155
Harding Rd.
98
150
74
N
Queenswood Rd.

E

GLASFORD
Todd School Rd.
Clark Rd.
Hemmerick Rd.
Cowser Rd.
McCullough Rd.
Strand
Cameron
ORCHARD MINES
Maple
Ridge
Kingston Rd.
MAPLETON
24
9
29
NORTH PEKIN
PEKIN
Parkway
Sheridan Rd.
TOWNE OAKS
Queenswood
Broadway
Tennessee Rd.

Scale of Miles
0 1 2 3

Providence, RI (bottom map)

1 2 3 4 5 6 7

E

TARKILN
PRIMROSE
5
Woonsocket Reservoir No. 3
ALBION
295
CHARTLEY
Taunton Ave.

F

N
7
Stillwater Reservoir
Geo.
Washington Hwy.
Airport Rd.
116
ASHTON
122
BERKELEY
LIME ROCK
114
ADAMSVILLE
Manchester Pond Reservoir
South St.
ATTLEBORO
DODGEVILLE
Wilmarth
BRIGGS CORNER
NORTH REHOBOTH
Glebe St.

G

SPRAGUEVILLE
HARMONY
Waterman Reservoir
44
GREENVILLE
Smith
ESMOND
GEORGIAVILLE
44
CENTERDALE
246
146
LONSDALE
VALLEY FALLS
CENTRAL FALLS
SAYLES VILLE
PAWTUCKET
95
1
Oak Hill
SOUTH ATTLEBORO
Tremont St.
Pine St.
WADES CORNER
NORTH SCITUATE
5
Moswansicut Pond
Snake Den State Park
Belfield Dr.
Hartford
NORTH PROVIDENCE
Mt. Pleasant Ave.
Providence College
PROVIDENCE
126
Charles St.
Seekonk River Res.
Slater Memorial Park
Central Pond
152
Bliss St.
Anavan St.

H

6
Oak Swamp Reservoir
SAUNDERSVILLE
6
Pike
Hartford
Broadway
George M. Cohan Blvd.
Waterman St.
EAST PROVIDENCE
44
REHOBOTH
Winthrop Ave.
County St.
Horton St.
James V. Turner Reservoir
Palmer River

J

116
Simmons Lowers Reservoir
295
14
COMSTOCK
WATERMAN GARDENS
FOUR CORNERS
Scituate Reservoir
12
THORNTON
Plainfield
10
Cranston
KNIGHTSVILLE
Olney
Arnold
CRANSTON
AUBURN
117
RIVERSIDE
103
195
MASSACHUSETTS
RHODE ISLAND
WEST BARRINGTON
NORTH SWANSEA
118
HORTONVILLE
LUTHER CORNER
SWANSEA

K

HOPE
FISKEVILLE
J. L. Curran Park
Scituate Reservoir
HARRIS
LIPPITT
5
Rhode Island Medical Center
37
WARWICK
Airport
T. F. Green Airport
Post Road
1
2
113
CONIMICUT
Providence River
BARRINGTON
136
WARREN
OCEAN GROVE
103
Wilbur
114
SOUTH SWANSEA

Scale of Miles
0 1 2 3

© C.S.C.

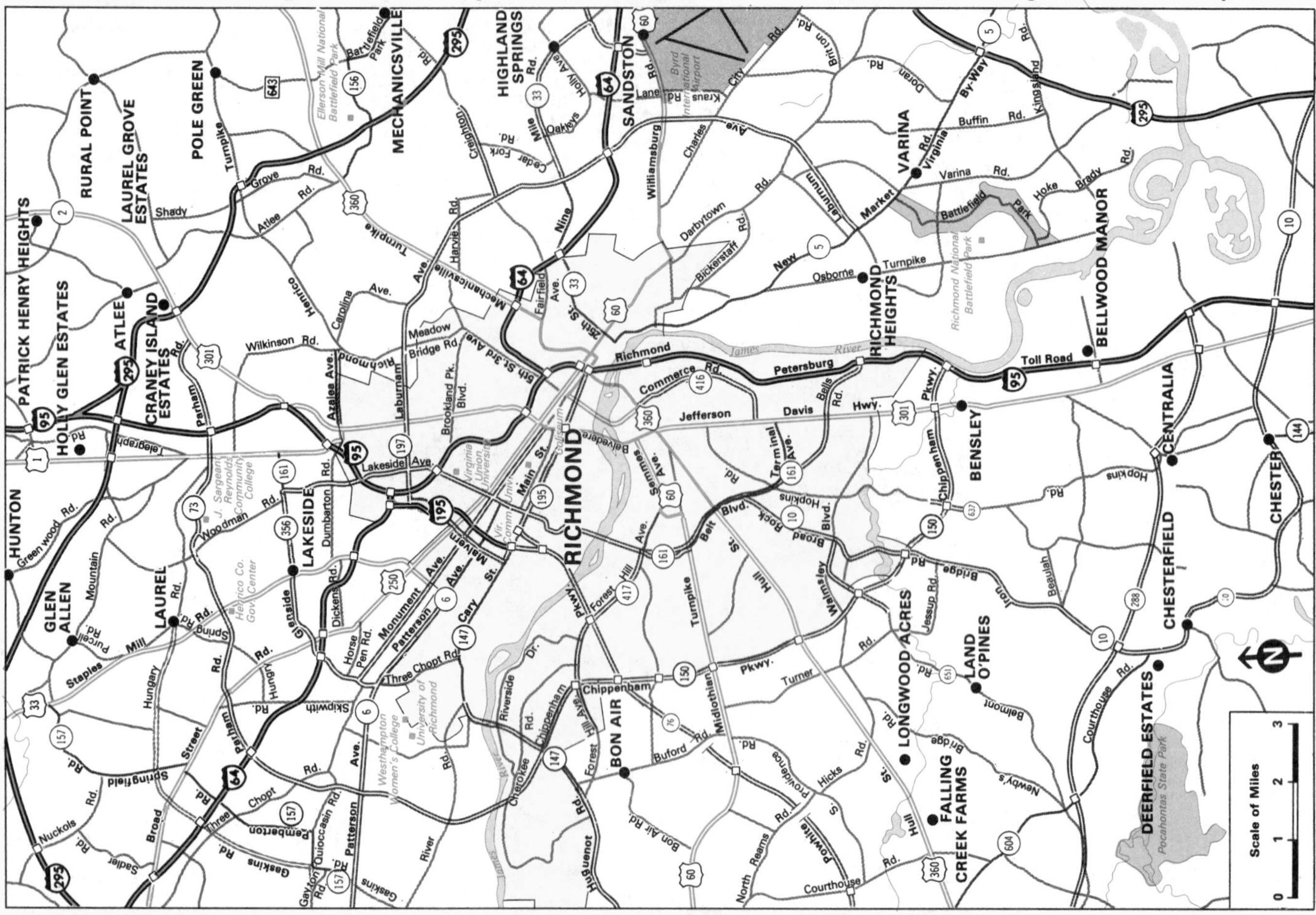

Richmond, VA

RURAL POINT · POLE GREEN · LAUREL GROVE ESTATES · MECHANICSVILLE · HIGHLAND SPRINGS · SANDSTON · Byrd International Airport · VARINA · PATRICK HENRY HEIGHTS · HOLLY GLEN ESTATES · ATLEE · CRANEY ISLAND ESTATES · RICHMOND HEIGHTS · BELLWOOD MANOR · CENTRALIA · CHESTER · HUNTON · GLEN ALLEN · LAUREL · LAKESIDE · RICHMOND · Virginia Union University · J. Sargeant Reynolds Community College · BENSLEY · CHESTERFIELD · University of Richmond · Westhampton Women's College · BON AIR · CHIPPENHAM · LONGWOOD ACRES · LAND O'PINES · DEERFIELD ESTATES · Pocahontas State Park · FALLING CREEK FARMS

James River · Richmond National Battlefield Park · Ellerson Mill National Battlefield Park

Scale of Miles 0 1 2 3

© C.S.C.

Rochester, NY

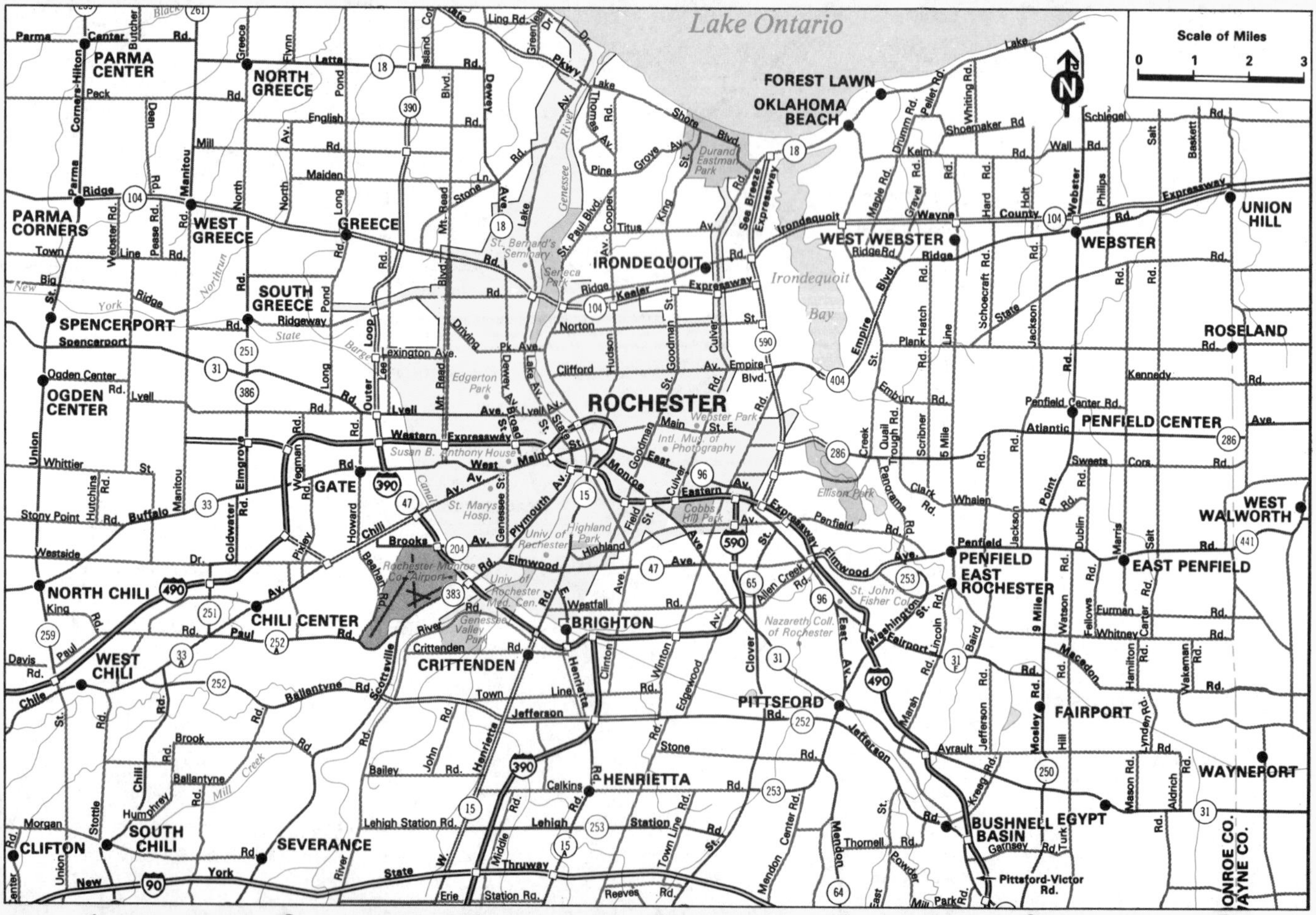

Lake Ontario · PARMA · PARMA CENTER · NORTH GREECE · FOREST LAWN · OKLAHOMA BEACH · PARMA CORNERS · WEST GREECE · GREECE · WEST WEBSTER · WEBSTER · UNION HILL · SPENCERPORT · SOUTH GREECE · IRONDEQUOIT · Irondequoit Bay · ROSELAND · OGDEN CENTER · ROCHESTER · Int. Mus. of Photography · PENFIELD CENTER · GATE · Rochester-Monroe Co. Airport · Univ. of Rochester · Highland Park · WEST WALWORTH · NORTH CHILI · CHILI CENTER · Genesee Valley Park · BRIGHTON · PENFIELD · EAST ROCHESTER · EAST PENFIELD · WEST CHILI · CRITTENDEN · FAIRPORT · PITTSFORD · WAYNEPORT · CLIFTON · SOUTH CHILI · SEVERANCE · HENRIETTA · BUSHNELL BASIN · EGYPT · MONROE CO. WAYNE CO.

Genesee River · Durand Eastman Park · Seneca Park · Ellison Park · Susan B. Anthony House · St. Mary's Hosp. · Nazareth Coll. of Rochester · St. John Fisher Coll.

Scale of Miles 0 1 2 3

1 2 3 4 5 6 7

Sacramento, CA (top map)

Sacramento Municipal Airport
Elkhorn
Del Paso Centro Rd.
RIO LINDA
Marysville
NORTH HIGHLANDS
Elkhorn Rd.
FOOTHILL FARMS
Greenback Ln.
ORANGEVALE
Madison Ave.
Hazel Ave.
Madison Ave.
VALLEY VIEW ACRES
ROBLA
Main Ave.
Ascot
Raley
McClellan Air Force Base
Roseville
Auburn
Northridge C.C.
FAIR OAK
Winding Way
Sunset
Winding Way
Bell Ave.
El Centro
San Juan
Haggin Oaks G.C.
Del Paso Country Club
ROBERTSON
CARMICHAEL
Madison Ave.
Manzanita
Sunrise Blvd.
El Dorado Hwy.
NIMBUS
50
ALDER CREEK
Highway
Discovery Park
Northgate
Carl Johnston Park
Marconi
El Camino Ave.
Fulton
Eastern
Walnut
Garfield
Ancil Hoffman Park
Coloma Rd.
CITRUS
White Rock Rd.
Del Paso Blvd.
Arden Way
Howe
Arden Fair
Watt
Arden Way
Oaks
C.M. Goethe Park
RANCHO CORDOVA
WEST SACRAMENTO
SACRAMENTO
Exposition Blvd.
California Exposition
Elvas Ave.
Fair Oaks Blvd.
American River
Folsom Blvd.
Douglas Rd.
Capitol Ave.
State Capitol
Broadway
California St. Univ. at Sacramento
Folsom Blvd.
PERKINS
Mather Air Force Base
Greens Lake
ARLINGTON OAKS
Linden Rd.
Land Park
Broadway
Tahoe Park
14th Ave.
65th St.
Power Inn Rd.
Florin
ROSEMONT
Kiefer Blvd.
Bradshaw Rd.
Excelsior Rd.
Jackson Rd.
SOUTH PORT
Gregory Ave.
Butterville Rd.
12th Ave.
Fruitridge
Stockton
Sacramento Army Depot
Perkins
Elder Creek Rd.
Rd.
RIVERVIEW
Jefferson Blvd.
Riverside
Freeport Blvd.
24th St.
Franklin Blvd.
Sacramento Executive Airport
FLORIN
Florin Rd.
Elk Grove-Florin Rd.
Meadowview Rd.
160
Mack Rd.
Florin Rd.
Gerber Rd.
Eagles Nest Rd.

Scale of Miles
0 1 2 3

Salt Lake City, UT (bottom map)

Antelope Island
WOODS CROSS
BOUNTIFUL
NORTH SALT LAKE
Orchard Dr.
Wasatch Bountiful Nat'l Forest
DAVIS COUNTY
SALT LAKE COUNTY
2400 N.
DAVIS CO.
SALT LAKE CO.
Canyon
Great Salt Lake
N. Point
Consolidated Canal
Goggin Drain
4000 W. St.
Salt Lake City International Airport
Beck St.
City Creek
Victory Rd.
SALT LAKE CITY
Riverside Park
6th N. St.
State Fair Ground
Fort Douglas Military Res.
North Temple
WEST VALLEY FREEWAY
Surplus Canal
4th St.
Salt Palace
Utah State Capitol
University of Utah
Pioneer Trail State Park
SALT LAKE CITY
172
13th South St.
Jordan Park
3rd St.
Liberty Park
California Ave.
Mount Olivet Cemetery
Hogle Zoo
Bonneville Golf Course
Foothill Dr.
ALT 50
21st South
201
2700 St.
9th St.
Fairmont Park
11th E. St.
21st South
186
WEST VALLEY CITY
154
3100 South
215
SOUTH SALT LAKE
Sugarhouse Park
Forest Dale Golf Course
Parley's Way
80
MAGNA
West
3500 South
8000 W.
7200 W.
56th St.
4100 South
171
Utah & Salt Lake Canal
68
266
9th E.
33rd South
39th South
45th South
VAN
1300 E.
23rd E.
EAST MILLCREEK
181
HOLLADAY
215

Scale of Miles
0 1 2 3

© C.S.C.

Scale of Miles
0 1 2 3 4

© C.S.C.

St. Charles
St. Charles County / St. Louis County
Florissant
Hazelwood
Bridgeton
Black Jack
Berkeley
Ferguson
Dellwood
Bellefontaine Neighbors
Riverview
Moline Acres
Jennings
St. Ann
Woodson Terr.
Breckenridge Hills
St. John
Bel-Ridge
Charlack
Sycamore Hills
Bel-Nor
Normandy
Bellerive
Cool Valley
Northwoods
Velda City
Pine Lawn
Pagedale
Wellston
Granite City
Niedringhaus
Madison
Venice
Madison County
St. Clair County
Brooklyn
National City
East St. Louis
Maryland Heights
Overland
Vinita Park
Hanley Hills
University City
Olivette
Creve Coeur
Ladue
Clayton
Frontenac
Brentwood
Richmond Heights
Maplewood
Forest Park
St. Louis
St. Louis County
Town and Country
Des Peres
Huntleigh
Warson Woods
Rock Hill
Webster Groves
Shrewsbury
Sauget
Cahokia
Kirkwood
Glendale
Crestwood
Marlborough
Wilbur Park
Bella Villa
St. George
East Carondelet
Dupo
North Dupo
Fenton
Sunset Hills
St. Louis Co. / Jefferson Co.
Columbia
Sugar Loaf Heights
Bixby
Arnold
Oakville
Missouri / Illinois
Missouri River
Mississippi River
Chouteau Island
Mosenthein Island
Gabaret Island
Lambert-St. Louis International Airport
Creve Coeur Memorial Park
Creve Coeur Lake
National Museum of Transportation
Grant's Farm
Jefferson Barracks Historical Park
Sylvan Springs Park
Veterans Hospital
Gateway Arch
Busch Stadium
Forest Park
Zoo
Art Museum
Muny Opera
Planetarium
Missouri Botanical Gardens

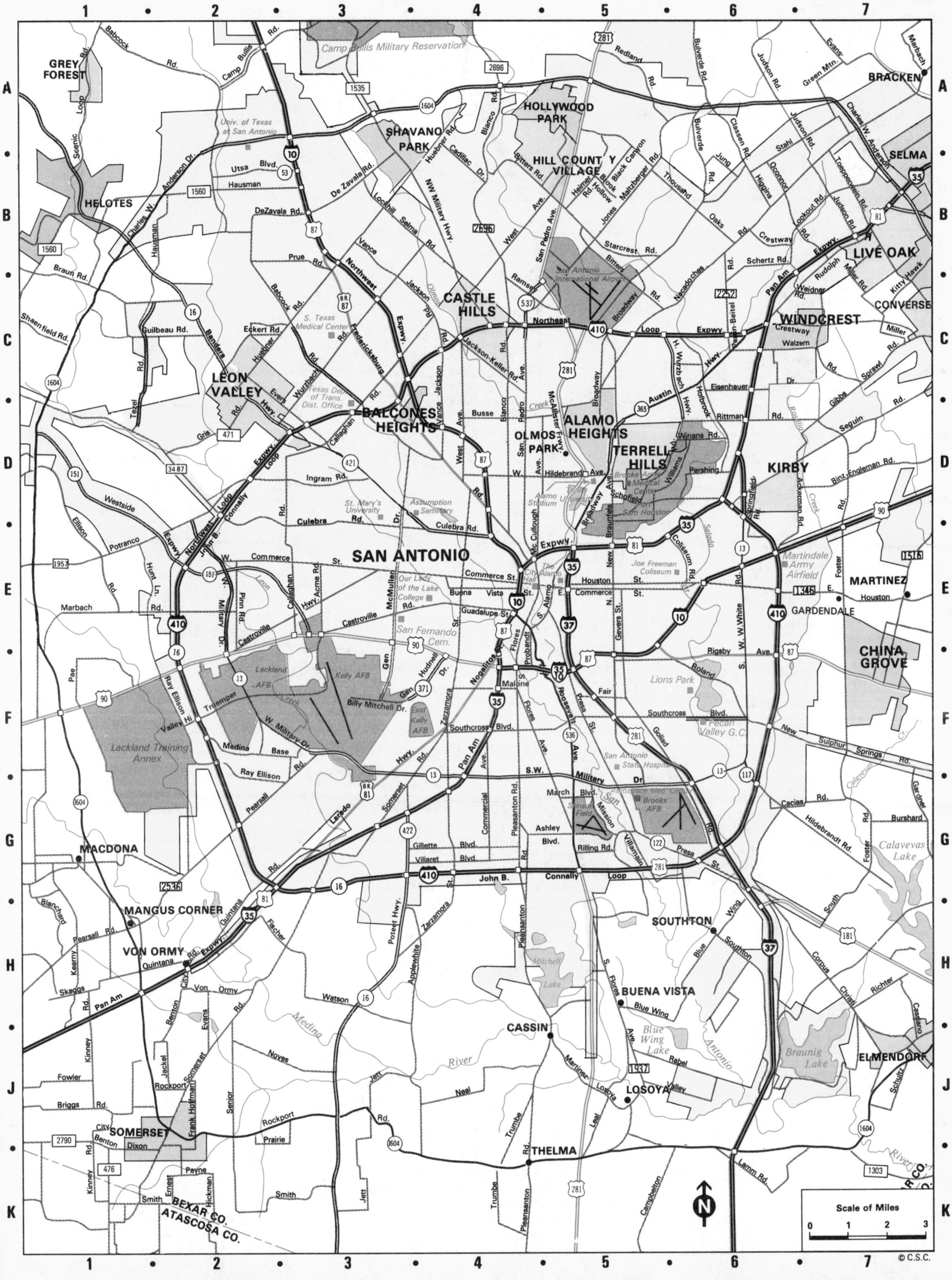

GREY FOREST

Camp Bullis Military Reservation

BRACKEN

SELMA

HELOTES

Univ. of Texas at San Antonio

SHAVANO PARK

HOLLYWOOD PARK

HILL COUNTY VILLAGE

LIVE OAK

CONVERSE

CASTLE HILLS

San Antonio International Airport

WINDCREST

LEON VALLEY

S. Texas Medical Center

Texas Dept. of Trans. Dist. Office

BALCONES HEIGHTS

OLMOS PARK

ALAMO HEIGHTS

TERRELL HILLS

KIRBY

St. Mary's University

Assumption Seminary

Brooke Army Medical Center

SAN ANTONIO

Our Lady of the Lake College

City Hall

The Alamo

Joe Freeman Coliseum

Martindale Army Airfield

MARTINEZ

GARDENDALE

San Fernando Cem.

Lackland AFB

Kelly AFB

East Kelly AFB

Lions Park

Pecan Valley G.C.

CHINA GROVE

Lackland Training Annex

Billy Mitchell Dr.

Medina Base

San Antonio State Hospital

Aerospace Med. Center

Brooks AFB

MACDONA

Stinson Field

Mission

MANGUS CORNER

SOUTHTON

VON ORMY

Quintana

Mitchell Lake

BUENA VISTA

Blue Wing

Calaveras Lake

CASSIN

Blue Wing Lake

Braunig Lake

ELMENDORF

Medina River

LOSOYA

SOMERSET

Dixon

THELMA

BEXAR CO.
ATASCOSA CO.

N

SOLANA BEACH

DEL MAR

Del Mar Heights Rd.

Torrey Pines State Park

SORRENTO

University of California San Diego Campus

Scripps Institute of Oceanography

La Jolla Caves

LA JOLLA

La Jolla G.C.

Pacific Beach

MISSION BEACH

Mission Bay G.C.

Mission Bay Yacht Club

Sea World Aquatic Park

Ocean Beach

Pointe Loma Coll.

U.S. International Univ.

Cabrillo Nat'l. Mon.

SAN DIEGO

MIRAMAR

Miramar G.C.

Miramar Naval Air Station

U.S. Air Force Reservation

Camp Elliott

Powers Airport

POWAY

FERNBROOK

EUCALYPTUS HILLS

MORENO

LAKESIDE

LAKEVIEW

JOHNSTOWN

WINTER GARDENS

GLENVIEW

SANTEE

Carlton Oaks G.C.

Fletcher Hills G.C.

Gillespie Field

EL CAJON

Clairemont General Hosp.

Montgomery Field

U.S. Naval Recreational Facilities

San Diego State Univ.

LA MESA

SPRING VALLEY

LEMON GROVE

JAMACHA JUNCTION

JAMACHA

DICTIONARY HILL

LA PRESA

Sweetwater Reservoir

Univ. of San Diego

San Diego International Airport

Naval Training Center

U.S.M.C. B.

BALBOA PARK

Zoo

CORONADO

North Island Naval Air Station

U.S. Military Reservation

San Diego Naval Station

U.S. Naval Amphibious Base

NATIONAL CITY

LINCOLN ACRES

SUNNYSIDE

LYNWOOD HILLS

Southwestern College

Upper Otay Reservoir

Lower Otay Reservoir

Pacific Ocean

San Diego Bay

Silver Strand State Beach

Imperial Beach Naval Radio Station

HARBOR SIDE

CHULA VISTA

IMPERIAL BEACH

Imperial Beach Naval Air Station

SAN DIEGO

U.S. Immigration Detention Facility

Brown Field

OTAY MESA

N

Scale of Miles
0   1   2   3

© C.S.C.

Marin Is.
San Rafael Bay
San Pablo Strait
San Pedro
U.S. Naval Fuel Depot
RICHMOND-SAN RAFAEL BRIDGE (TOLL)
Richmond
San Pablo
El Cerrito
Wildcat Canyon Regional Park
San Pablo Dam Res.
Paradise
California Pt.
Tiburon
Bluff Pt.
Tiburon Oceanographic Center
Brooks Is. Regional Park
Richmond Inner Harbor
Albany
Charles Tilden Reg. Park
Briones Regional Park
Pleasant Hill
Concord
Cowell
Clayton
Walnut Creek
Belvedere
Sausalito
Angel Island
Angel Island State Park
Blunt Pt.
University of California
Berkeley
U.C. Berkeley
Lafayette
Mt. Diablo
Moraga
St. Mary's College
Danville
Emeryville
Robert Sibley Regional Park
Fort Baker
Cavallo Pt.
Baker Beach
Golden Gate Bridge (Toll)
Presidio
Alcatraz Island
Treasure Island
Naval Res.
Yerba Buena Island
San Francisco Oakland Bay Bridge (Toll)
Oakland Army Terminal
Oakland Naval Supply Center
Piedmont
Redwood Regional Park
Las Trampas Regional Park
Bollinger Canyon
Chinatown
Civic Center
OAKLAND
SAN FRANCISCO
Kezar Stadium
Glen Canyon Park
Alameda Naval Air Station
Alameda Mem. St. Beach
Alameda
Mills College
Knowland State Park & Arboretum
Anthony Chabot Regional Park
San Leandro Res.
Cull Canyon Rec. Area
Hunters Point Naval Shipyard
Oakland Metropolitan International Airport
San Leandro
San Lorenzo
Harding Park
McLaren Park
Candlestick Park
Cow Palace
Daly City
Serramonte
Broadmoor
Brisbane
Oyster Pt.
South San Francisco
Hayward Air Terminal
Hayward
Fairview
California State College at Hayward
Glenn Reg. Park
SAN FRANCISCO BAY
San Bruno
San Francisco International Airport
Millbrae
Junipero Serra Co. Park
Pacifica
Coyote Point Park
Coyote Pt.
Whipple Rd.
Union City
Montara
Moss Beach
Burlingame
Hillsborough
San Mateo
County Fairgrounds
Foster City
Foster City
Beach Park
San Francisco Bay
Coyote Hills Reg. Park
Fremont
Newark
Princeton
El Granada
Miramar
Pillar Pt.
Half Moon Bay
San Andreas Lake
Fish and Game Refuge
Belmont
San Carlos
Redwood City
Bair Island
Ravenswood Pt.
Dumbarton Pt.
Wildlife Refuge
Calaveras Pt.
Long Pt.
PACIFIC OCEAN
Half Moon Bay
Lower Crystal Springs Lake
Upper Crystal Springs Lake
Huddart Park
San Carlos
Palo Alto Airport
Sand Pt.
Coyote Slough
Atherton
Menlo Park
Rinconada Park
Civic Center

Scale of Miles
0 1 2 3 4 5

© A.M.C.

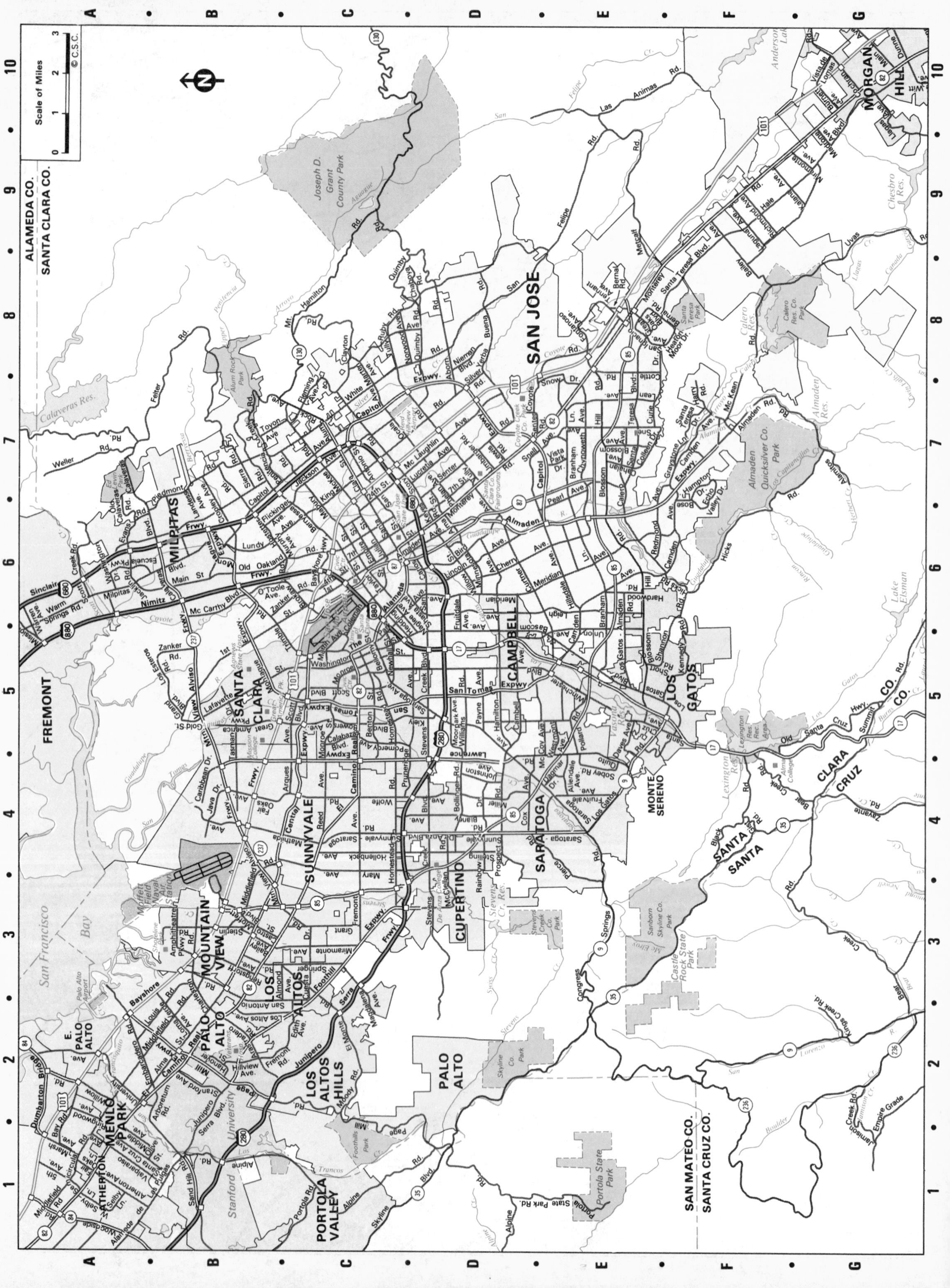
Scale of Miles
0 1 2 3
© C.S.C.
ALAMEDA CO.
SANTA CLARA CO.
SAN MATEO CO.
SANTA CRUZ CO.
SAN JOSE
SANTA CLARA
SUNNYVALE
MOUNTAIN VIEW
PALO ALTO
LOS ALTOS
LOS ALTOS HILLS
CUPERTINO
CAMPBELL
SARATOGA
LOS GATOS
MONTE SERENO
MILPITAS
FREMONT
MENLO PARK
ATHERTON
E. PALO ALTO
PORTOLA VALLEY
MORGAN HILL
San Francisco Bay
Joseph D. Grant County Park
Alum Rock Park
Calaveras Res.
Almaden Quicksilver Co. Park
Almaden Res.
Calero Res.
Calero Res. Co. Park
Santa Teresa Park
Chesbro Res.
Anderson Lake
Lake Elsman
Lexington Res.
Lexington Res. Rec. Area
Sanborn Skyline Co. Park
Castle Rock State Park
Stevens Creek Co. Park
Skyline Co. Park
Foothills Park
Portola State Park
Stanford University
Moffett Field Naval Air Station
Palo Alto Airport
Santa Clara Co. Fairgrounds
Coyote Creek Co. Park
Almaden Expwy
Capitol Expwy
San Tomas Expwy
Lawrence Expwy
Central Expwy
Foothill Expwy
Montague Expwy
Nimitz Frwy
Bayshore Frwy
Junipero Serra Frwy
Sinclair Frwy
Skyline Blvd.
Santa Cruz Hwy.
Empire Grade
Kings Creek Rd.
Zayante Rd.
Uvas Rd.
Las Animas Rd.

Scale of Miles
0 1 2 3
© C.S.C.

Grid columns: 1 2 3 4 5 6 7
Grid rows: A B C D E F G H J K

EDMONDS
LYNNWOOD
KINGSTON
WOODWAY
MOUNTLAKE TERRACE
BRIER
MALTBY
SNOHOMISH CO. KING CO.
Appletree Cove
Jefferson Pt. Rd.
Tulin Rd.
Main St.
196th St. S.W.
212th St. S.W.
220th
84th Ave. W.
9th Ave.
Richmond
Beach N.E.
Larch
Cedar Way
Swamp Creek
Maltby Rd.
Paradise Lake Rd.
Echo Lake Rd.
Lost Lake Rd.
Fales Rd.
Welch Rd.

Puget Sound
SHORELINE
LAKE FOREST PARK
KENMORE
BOTHELL
WOODINVILLE
N. 175th St.
N. 145th St.
N. 130th St.
N. 105th St.
85th
Carkeek Park
Golden Gardens Park
Holman Rd. N.W.
Greenwood Ave.
15th Ave. N.E.
North
Roosevelt
Lake City Way
170th
St. Edward State Park
Juanita Woodinville Rd. N.E.
132nd St.
N.E. 124th St.
N.E. 116th St.
Market St. N.E.
116th Ave.
Cottage Lake
Woodinville Duvall
175th Ave.
Novelty Hill Rd.
196th Ave. N.E.
208th Ave. N.E.

ROLLINGBAY
Shilshole Bay
Discovery Park
West Point
Murden Cove
Bainbridge Island
Sunrise Dr.
65th St.
Market St.
45th
N.E. 65th St.
Sand Point Way
Magnusson Park
University of Washington
KIRKLAND
REDMOND
Bridle Trails State Park
132nd Ave. N.E.
140th Ave. N.E.
148th Ave. N.E.
Union Hill Rd.
Avondale
River
Bear

Seattle-Victoria Ferry
Seattle-Winslow Ferry
Eagle Harbor
Thorndyke
15th Ave.
Gilman Ave. W.
Queen Anne Ave.
Elliott Ave. W.
U.S. Naval Supply Depot
Seattle Aquarium
Lake Union
Key Arena
Aurora
Fairview
10th Ave.
Madison
Pacific
Montlake Blvd.
Union Bay
Evergreen Point Floating Bridge (Toll)
HUNTS PT.
MEDINA
CLYDE HILL
520
76th Ave.
84th Ave.
92nd Ave.
104th Ave. N.E.
N.E. 8th St.
Bellevue-Redmond
BELLEVUE
Northrup Rd.
Lake Sammamish
Inglewood Hill Rd.

SEATTLE
Safeco Field
Elliott Bay
Bremerton-Seattle Ferry
Bainbridge Island Ferry
Alki Point
Alki Beach Park
S.W. Admiral
California Ave. S.W.
Fauntleroy Way
Beaux Arts
Lake Washington Floating Bridge
MERCER ISLAND
Seward Park
East Mercer Way
West Mercer Way
Mercer
EASTGATE
Newport Way
S.E. 40th St.
S.E. 60th St.
148th Ave. S.E.
164th Ave. S.E.
Phantom Lake
S.E. 24th St.
Pine Lake
Lake Sammamish State Park

Vashon-Southworth Ferry
Fauntleroy-Vashon Ferry
SOUTHWORTH
VASHON HEIGHTS
Lincoln Park
Country Club Rd.
Delridge Way
35th Ave. S.W.
16th Ave. S.W.
NEWCASTLE
N. 30th St.
Coalfield Way
Renton-Issaquah Rd.
ISSAQUAH
Coalfield
Creek
Issaquah-Hobart Rd.

BURIEN
West Seattle Freeway
S.W. Holden
S.W. Barton
S.W. Henderson
Ambaum Blvd. S.W.
1st Ave.
152nd St.
SKYWAY
TUKWILA
RENTON
W. Valley
900
Renton-Issaquah Rd.
148th Ave. S.E.
128th St.

NORMANDY PARK
Three Tree Point
SEA TAC
Seattle-Tacoma Int. Airport
Des Moines Wy.
Military Rd.
Pacific
S. 176th St.
S. 188th St.
S. 200th St.
S. 216th St.
KENT
S. 180th St.
212th St.
S.E. 192nd St.
Lake Desire
Otter Lake

VASHON ISLAND
PORTAGE
DES MOINES
MAURY ISLAND
Tramp Harbor
S.W. 168th St.
S.W. 176th St.
S.W. 196th St.
204th St. S.W.
220th St. S.W.
248th St.
S.W. 232nd St.
Vashon Island
91st Ave. S.W.
S. 228th St.
S.E. 240th St.
Kent-Kangley
S.E. 208th St.
S.E. 224th St.
S.E. 240th St.
116th Ave. S.E.
132nd Ave. S.E.
148th Ave.
MAPLE VALLEY
Lake Youngs
Cedar Grove Rd.
Crosson-Sweeney Rd.
Petrovitsky

Puget Sound
Lake Washington
Lake Sammamish

Route markers: 5, 405, 99, 104, 513, 520, 522, 524, 527, 9, 202, 908, 900, 516, 518, 599, 515, 509, 169, 167, 181, 18

© C.S.C.

Syracuse, NY (inset, top left)

NORTH SYRACUSE, COLLAMER, EAST SYRACUSE, DE WITT, MATTYDALE, PITCHER HILL, GATEVILLE, LIVERPOOL, COLD SPRINGS, BAYBERRY, SOLVAY, WESTVALE, SYRACUSE, SPLIT ROCK, ONONDAGA, Onondaga Lake

Cicero Swamp State Wildlife Management Area, Clay Marsh State Wildlife Management Area, Clark Reservation State Park, New York State Thruway, Thomas E. Dewey Thruway, State Fair Blvd.

Scale of Miles 0 1 2 3

Tacoma, WA (inset, top right)

MILTON, EDGEWOOD, NORTH PUYALLUP, PUYALLUP, SUMMIT, FIFE, TACOMA, HILLSDALE, MIDLAND, BROWNS POINT, KING COUNTY, PIERCE COUNTY, UNIVERSITY PLACE, FIRCREST, MANITOU, WOLLOCHET, Commencement Bay, The Narrows, Tacoma Narrows Bridge, Point Defiance Park, Western Washington State Hospital

Scale of Miles 0 1 2 3

Scranton/Wilkes-Barre, PA (main map)

OLYPHANT, THROOP, MARSHWOOD, DUNMORE, NAY AUG, SCRANTON, CHINCHILLA, CLARKS GREEN, MILWAUKEE, NEWTON, SCHULTZVILLE, MILL CITY, WEST FALLS, KEELERSBURG, VERNON, CENTER MORELAND, ORANGE, MAPLEWOOD HEIGHTS, FERN BROOK, KETCHAM, UPPER EXETER, HARDING, RANSOM, TAYLOR, OLD FORGE, MOOSIC, DURYEA, WEST PITTSTON, EXETER, PITTSTON, CORK LANE, BROWNSTOWN, DUPONT, BELIAN VILLAGE, GLENDALE, SUSCON, OLD BOSTON, WESTMINISTER, RIDGEWOOD, INKERMIN, LAFLIN, HILLDALE, WYOMING, WEST WYOMING, SWOYERSVILLE, FORTY FORT, PLAINSVILLE, HUDSON, MIDVALE, EDWARDS VILLE, LARKSVILLE, COURTDALE, LUZERNE, TRUCKSVILLE, SHAVERTON, BOULEVARD MANOR, WILKES-BARRE, GEORGETOWN, LAUREL RUN, OLIVER MILLS, NEWTON, BUTTONWOOD, ASHLEY, SUGAR NOTCH, LOOMIS PARK, WITINSKI VILLA, MOUNTAIN TOP, SOLOMON GAP, PENOBSCOT, FOREST PARK, BEAR CREEK, PLEASANT VIEW SUMMIT, SHADES GLEN

Susquehanna River, Lackawanna River, Lake Scranton, Lackawanna State Park, Pennsylvania Turnpike, North Scranton Expwy., Wilkes-Barre Scranton International Airport, U.S. Veterans Hospital, Frances Slocum State Park, Crystal Lake, Lake Louise, Meadow Pond, Mill Creek Reservoir

Scale of Miles 0 1 2 3

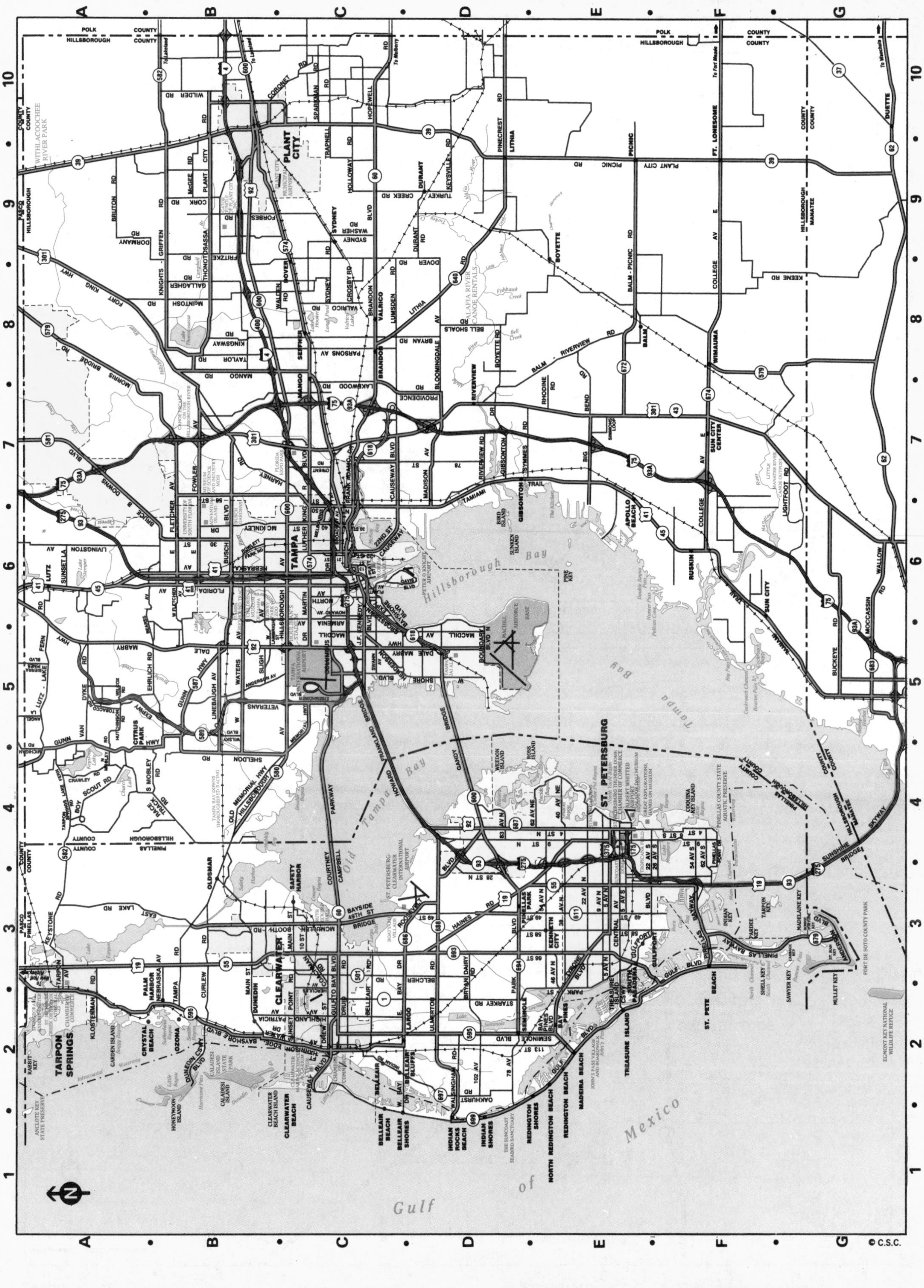
POLK COUNTY
HILLSBOROUGH COUNTY
PINELLAS COUNTY
MANATEE COUNTY
PASCO COUNTY
PLANT CITY
TAMPA
ST. PETERSBURG
CLEARWATER
TARPON SPRINGS
DUNEDIN
OLDSMAR
SAFETY HARBOR
LARGO
PINELLAS PARK
GULFPORT
ST. PETE BEACH
TREASURE ISLAND
MADEIRA BEACH
REDINGTON BEACH
NORTH REDINGTON BEACH
REDINGTON SHORES
INDIAN SHORES
INDIAN ROCKS BEACH
BELLEAIR BEACH
BELLEAIR SHORES
CLEARWATER BEACH
RUSKIN
APOLLO BEACH
SUN CITY CENTER
BRANDON
LUTZ
Hillsborough Bay
Tampa Bay
Old Tampa Bay
Gulf of Mexico
SUNSHINE SKYWAY BRIDGE
HOWARD FRANKLAND BRIDGE
GANDY BRIDGE
MACDILL AIR FORCE BASE
TAMPA INTERNATIONAL AIRPORT
FORT DE SOTO COUNTY PARK
CALADESI ISLAND STATE PARK

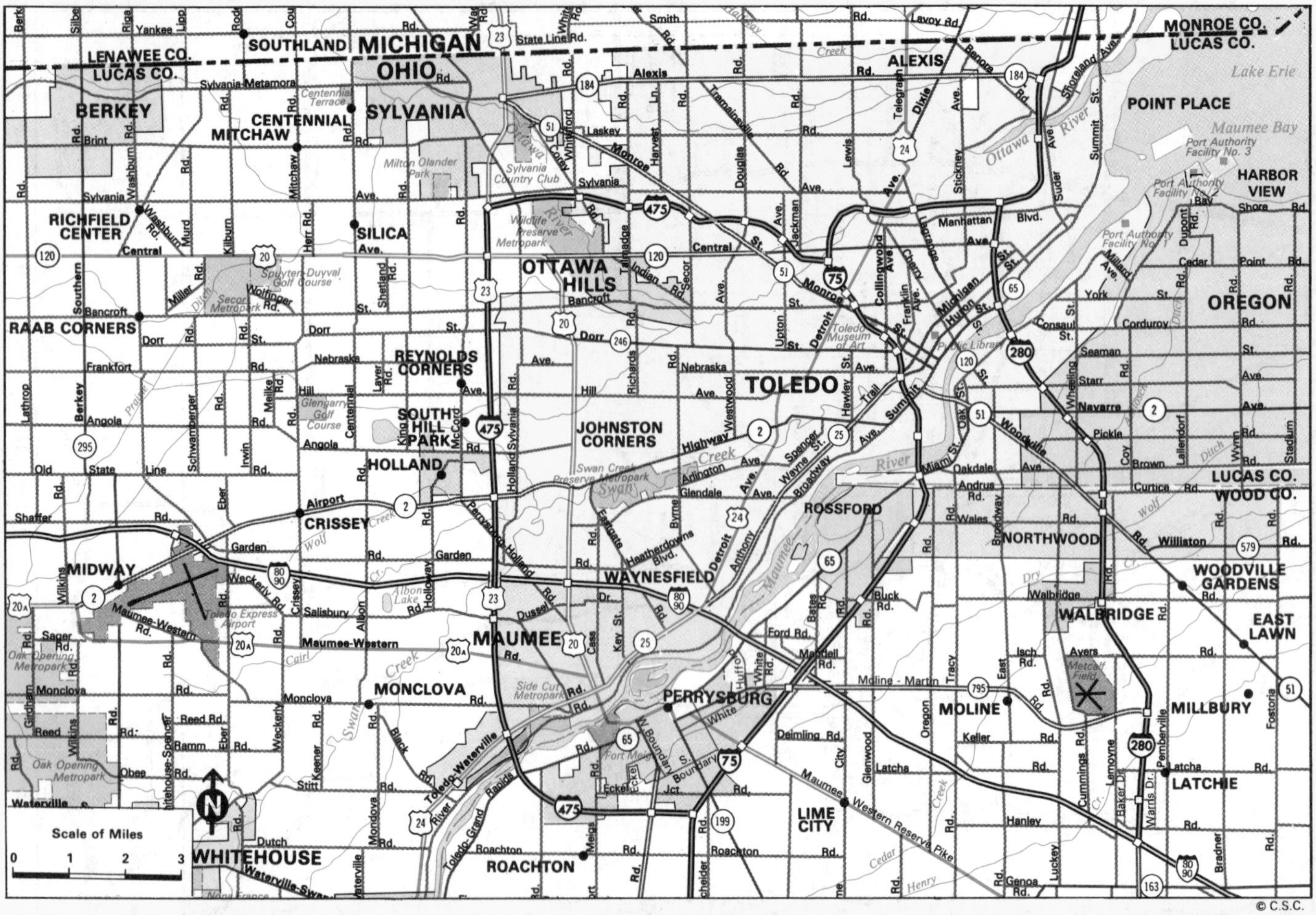

Toledo, OH (map)

MICHIGAN / OHIO — SOUTHLAND — State Line Rd.

LENAWEE CO. / LUCAS CO. — MONROE CO. / LUCAS CO.

Lake Erie — Maumee Bay

BERKEY — CENTENNIAL — MITCHAW — SYLVANIA — POINT PLACE — HARBOR VIEW

RICHFIELD CENTER — SILICA — OTTAWA HILLS — OREGON

RAAB CORNERS — REYNOLDS CORNERS — SOUTH HILL PARK — HOLLAND — JOHNSTON CORNERS — TOLEDO

CRISSEY — WAYNESFIELD — ROSSFORD — NORTHWOOD — WOODVILLE GARDENS — LUCAS CO. / WOOD CO.

MIDWAY — MAUMEE — MONCLOVA — PERRYSBURG — WALBRIDGE — EAST LAWN — MOLINE — MILLBURY — LATCHIE

WHITEHOUSE — ROACHTON — LIME CITY

Toledo Express Airport — Maumee-Western Reserve Pike — Metcalf Field

Wildlife Reserve Metropark — Swan Creek Preserve Metropark — Side Cut Metropark — Oak Opening Metropark — Secor Metropark

Scale of Miles: 0 1 2 3

N

© C.S.C.

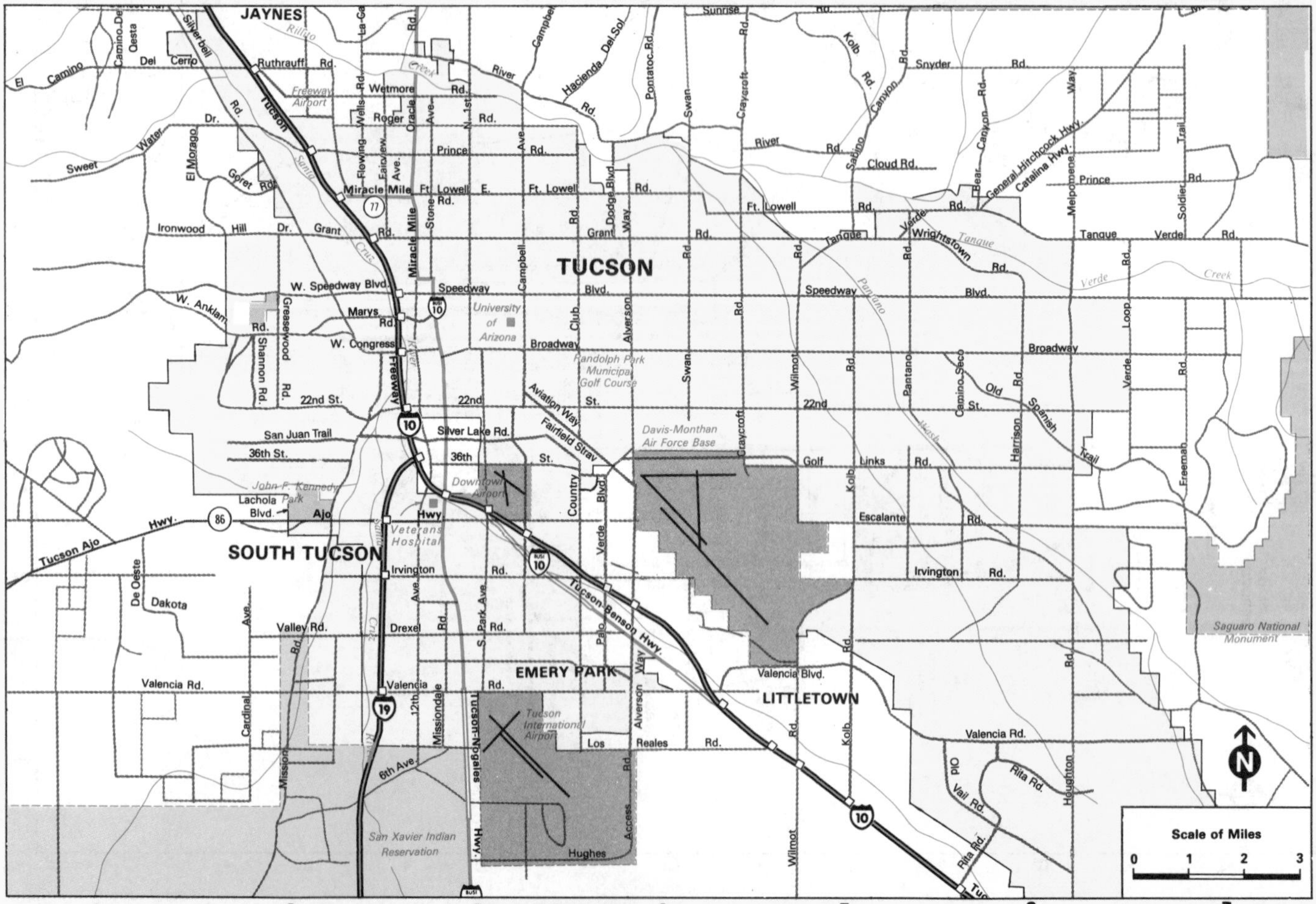

Tucson, AZ (map)

JAYNES — TUCSON — SOUTH TUCSON — EMERY PARK — LITTLETOWN

University of Arizona — Randolph Park Municipal Golf Course — Davis-Monthan Air Force Base — Saguaro National Monument

San Xavier Indian Reservation — Tucson International Airport

Miracle Mile — Speedway Blvd. — Broadway — 22nd St. — Valencia Rd. — Valencia Blvd.

Silverbell Rd. — Grant Rd. — Ft. Lowell Rd. — River Rd. — Prince Rd.

Kolb Rd. — Wilmot Rd. — Swan Rd. — Campbell — Craycroft Rd. — Pantano

Veterans Hospital — John F. Kennedy Park — Downtown Airport

Tucson-Benson Hwy. — Tucson-Nogales Hwy. — Tucson Ajo Hwy.

Scale of Miles: 0 1 2 3

N

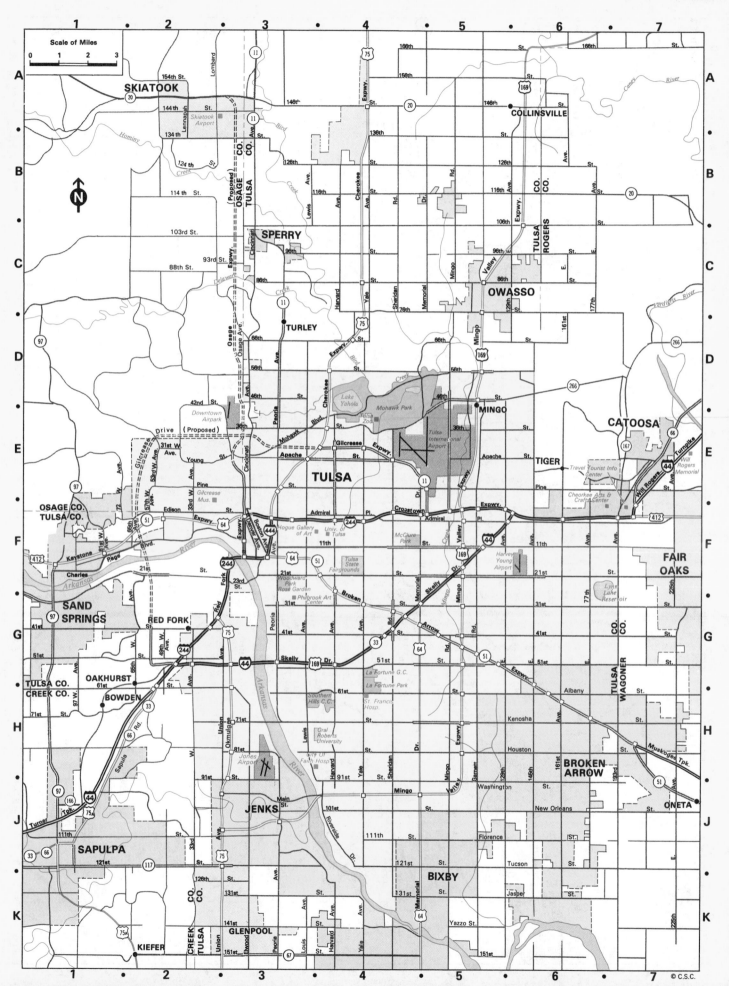

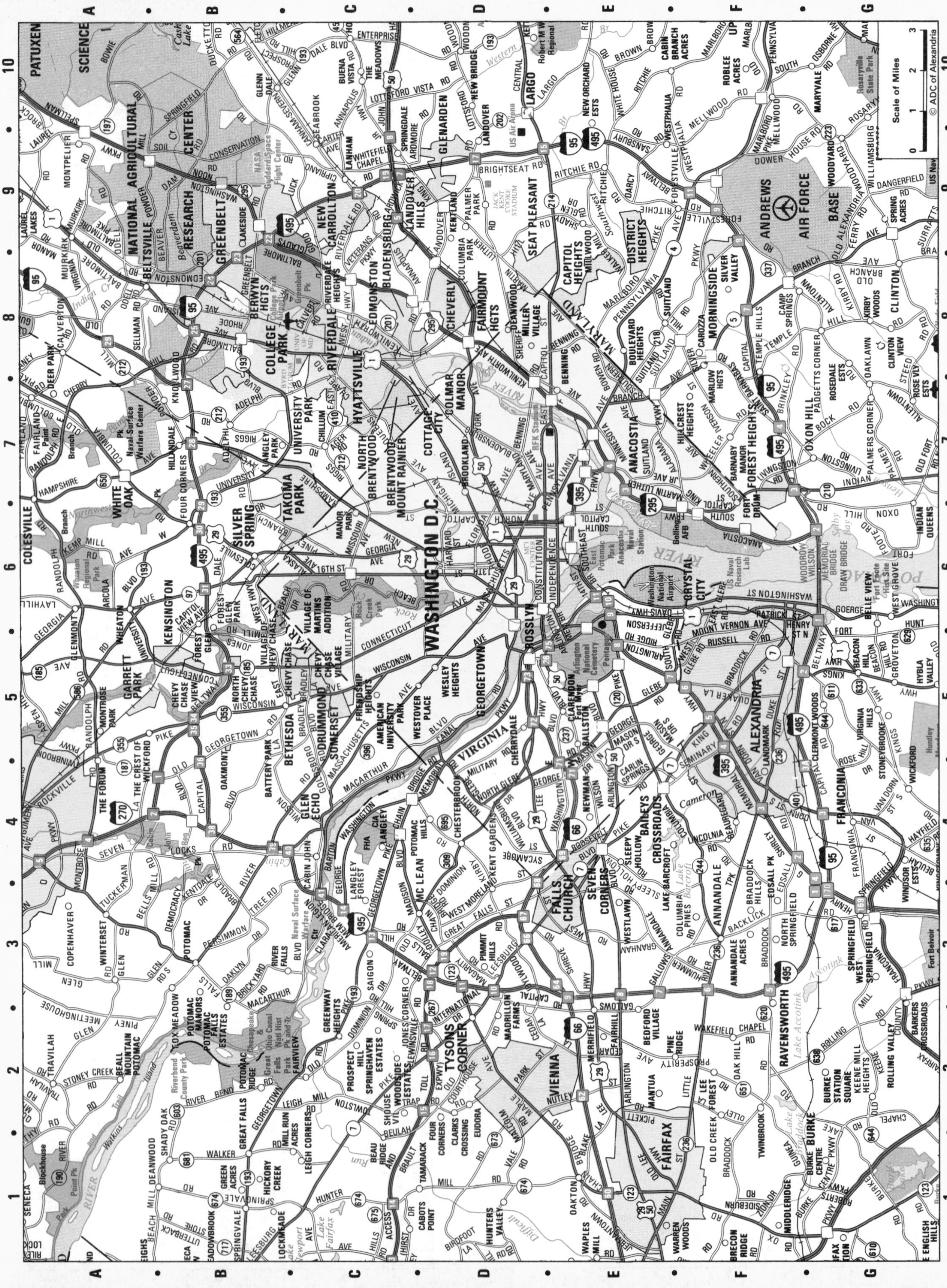

Scale of Miles
0 1 2 3
© ADC of Alexandria
WASHINGTON D.C.
MARYLAND
VIRGINIA
ALEXANDRIA
ROSSLYN
GEORGETOWN
ARLINGTON
FALLS CHURCH
BETHESDA
SILVER SPRING
TAKOMA PARK
COLLEGE PARK
GREENBELT
BELTSVILLE
HYATTSVILLE
ANACOSTIA
CAPITOL HEIGHTS
DISTRICT HEIGHTS
ANDREWS AIR FORCE BASE
TYSONS CORNER
VIENNA
FAIRFAX
ANNANDALE
SPRINGFIELD
FRANCONIA
MC LEAN
POTOMAC
KENSINGTON
WHEATON
WHITE OAK
NATIONAL AGRICULTURAL RESEARCH CENTER
LARGO
CLINTON
BURKE

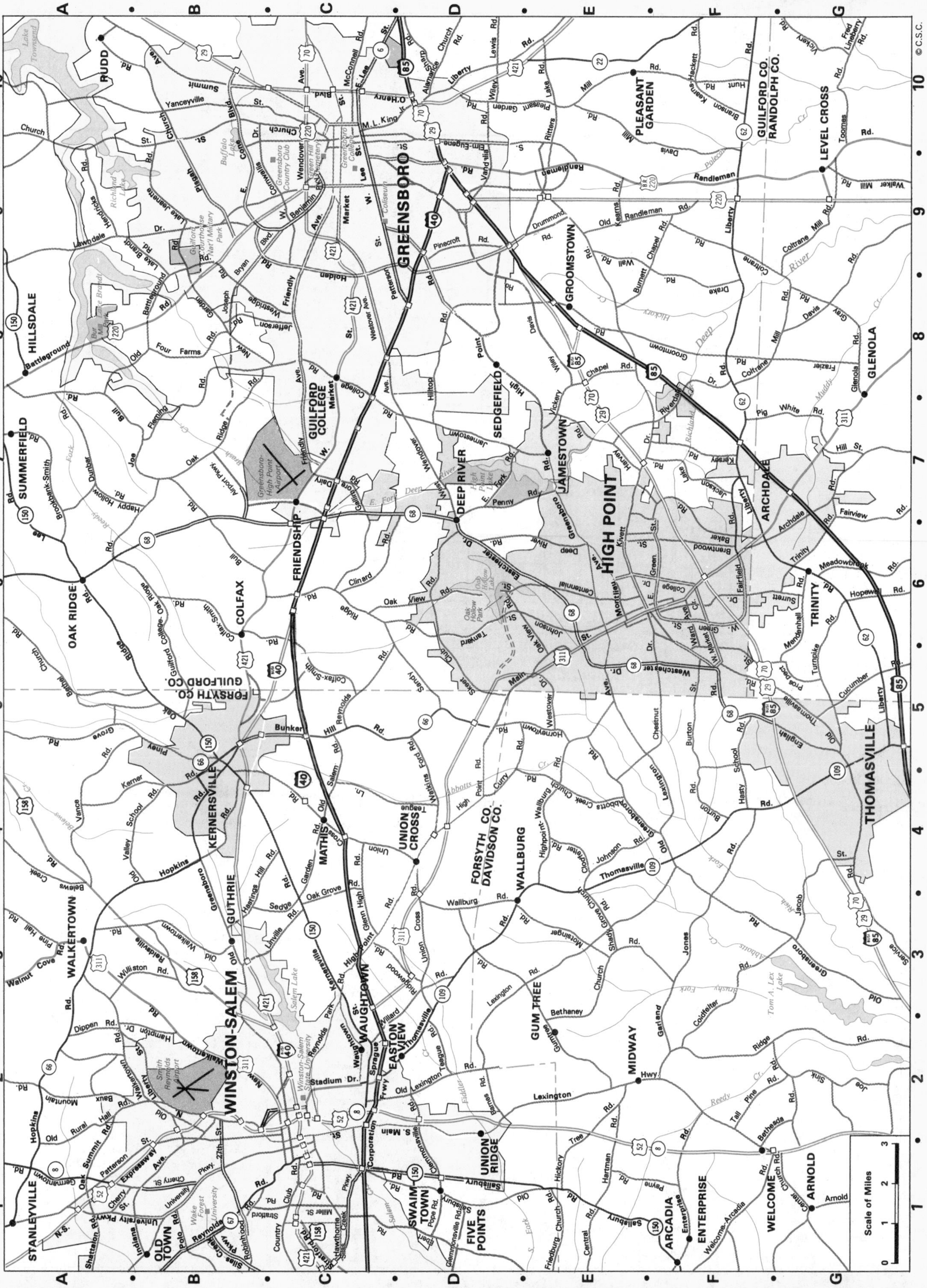

N

© C.S.C.

GREENSBORO

WINSTON-SALEM

HIGH POINT

THOMASVILLE

JAMESTOWN

ARCHDALE

TRINITY

SEDGEFIELD

DEEP RIVER

GROOMSTOWN

PLEASANT GARDEN

LEVEL CROSS

GLENOLA

GUILFORD CO.
RANDOLPH CO.

GUILFORD CO.
FORSYTH CO.

FORSYTH CO.
DAVIDSON CO.

GUILFORD COLLEGE

FRIENDSHIP

COLFAX

OAK RIDGE

SUMMERFIELD

HILLSDALE

RUDD

KERNERSVILLE

GUTHRIE

MATHIS

UNION CROSS

WALLBURG

WALKERTOWN

WAUGHTOWN

EASTON VIEW

SWAIM TOWN

FIVE POINTS

UNION RIDGE

GUM TREE

MIDWAY

WELCOME

ENTERPRISE

ARCADIA

ARNOLD

STANLEYVILLE

OLD TOWN

Greensboro High Point Airport

Smith Reynolds Airport

Guilford Courthouse Nat'l Military Park

Winston-Salem State University

Scale of Miles
0   1   2   3

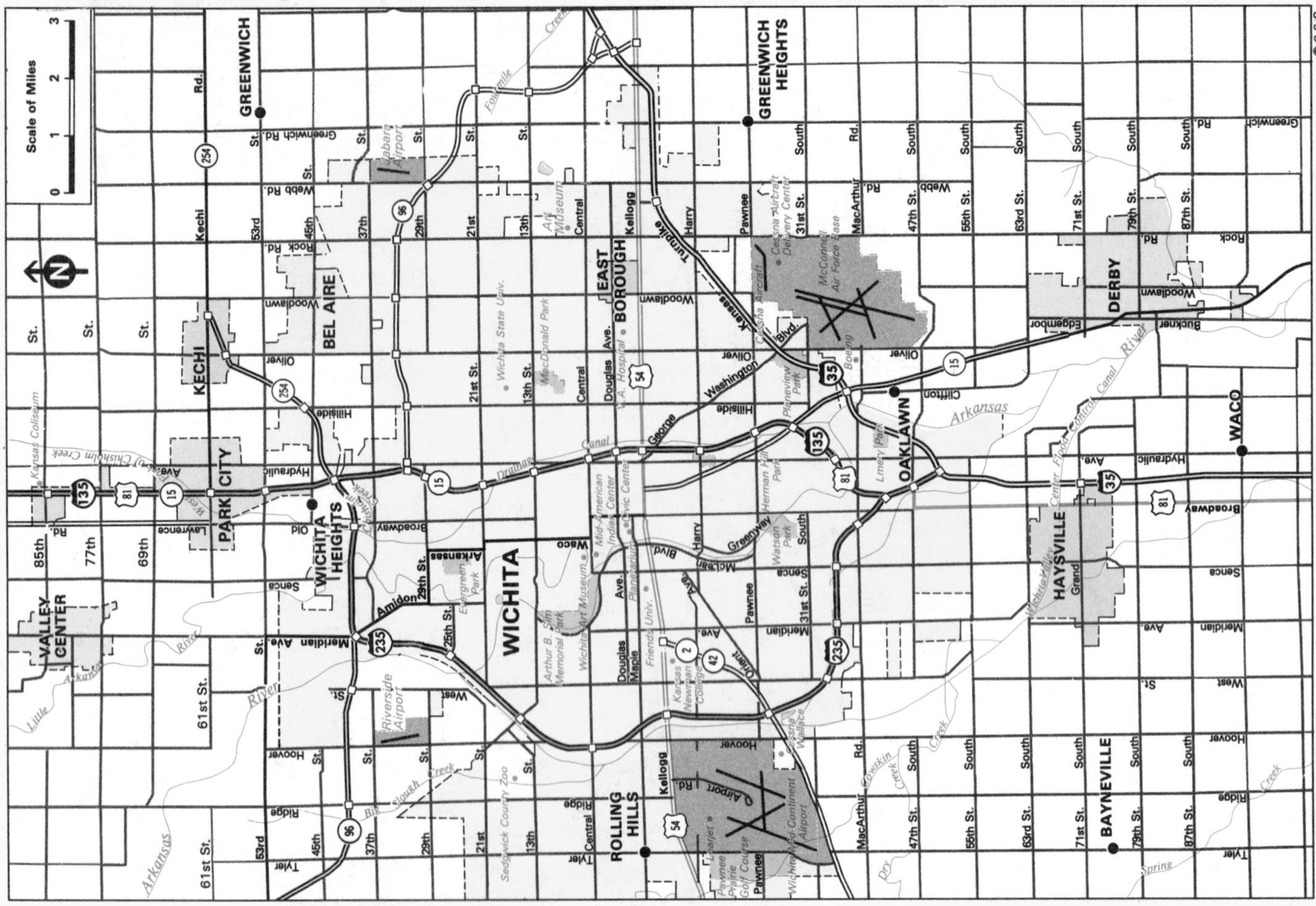

© C.S.C.

Wichita, KS

Scale of Miles

GREENWICH · GREENWICH HEIGHTS · KECHI · BEL AIRE · PARK CITY · WICHITA HEIGHTS · VALLEY CENTER · EAST BOROUGH · WICHITA · OAKLAWN · DERBY · WACO · HAYSVILLE · BAYNEVILLE · ROLLING HILLS

McConnell Air Force Base · Cessna Aircraft Delivery Center · Boeing · Mid-America All-Indian Center · Wichita State Univ. · McAdam Park · Arthur B. Sim Memorial Park · Wichita Art Museum · Friends Univ. · Kansas Newman College · Century II Civic Center · Lawrence Dumont Stadium · Sedgwick County Zoo · Pawnee Prairie Golf Course · Wichita Mid-Continent Airport · Riverside Airport · Wabaq Airport · Kansas Coliseum

Arkansas River · Little Arkansas River · Chisholm Creek · Cowskin Creek · Big Slough Creek · Gypsum Creek

US 81 · US 54 · 96 · 254 · 15 · 35 · 135 · 235 · 2 · 42

Youngstown, OH

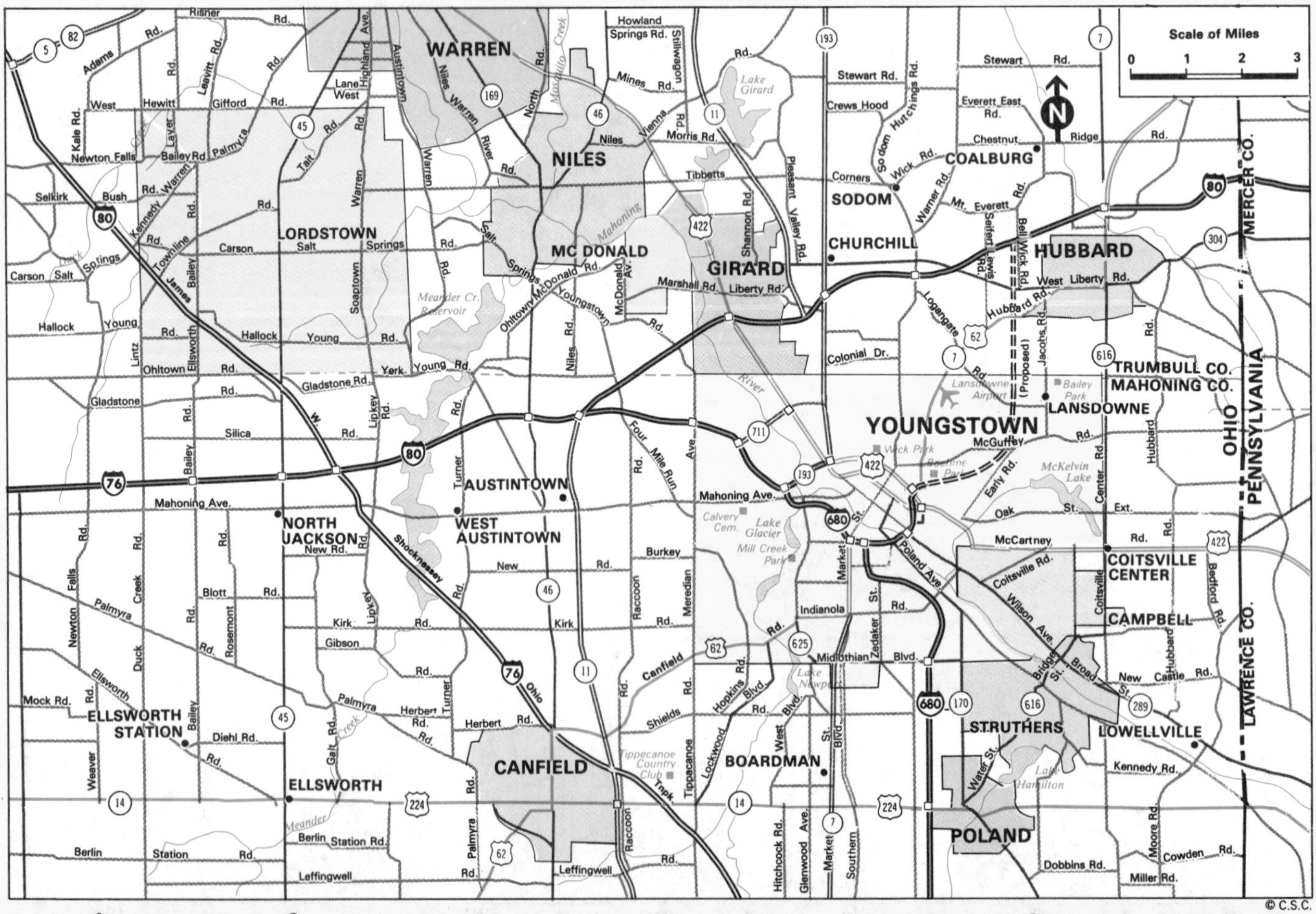

Scale of Miles

WARREN · NILES · MC DONALD · GIRARD · LORDSTOWN · AUSTINTOWN · WEST AUSTINTOWN · NORTH JACKSON · ELLSWORTH STATION · ELLSWORTH · CANFIELD · BOARDMAN · YOUNGSTOWN · STRUTHERS · POLAND · LOWELLVILLE · CAMPBELL · COITSVILLE CENTER · HUBBARD · SODOM · COALBURG · CHURCHILL · LANSDOWNE

TRUMBULL CO. · MAHONING CO. · MERCER CO. · LAWRENCE CO. · OHIO · PENNSYLVANIA

Meander Cr. Reservoir · Lake Girard · McKelvin Lake · Lake Glacier · Lake Newport · Lake Hamilton · Mill Creek Park · Mahoning River · Wick Park · Calvary Cem. · Tippecanoe Country Club · Lansdowne Airport

I-80 · I-76 · I-680 · US 62 · 11 · 45 · 46 · 169 · 193 · 422 · 711 · 304 · 616 · 625 · 14 · 224 · 170 · 289 · 7 · 5 · 82

© C.S.C.

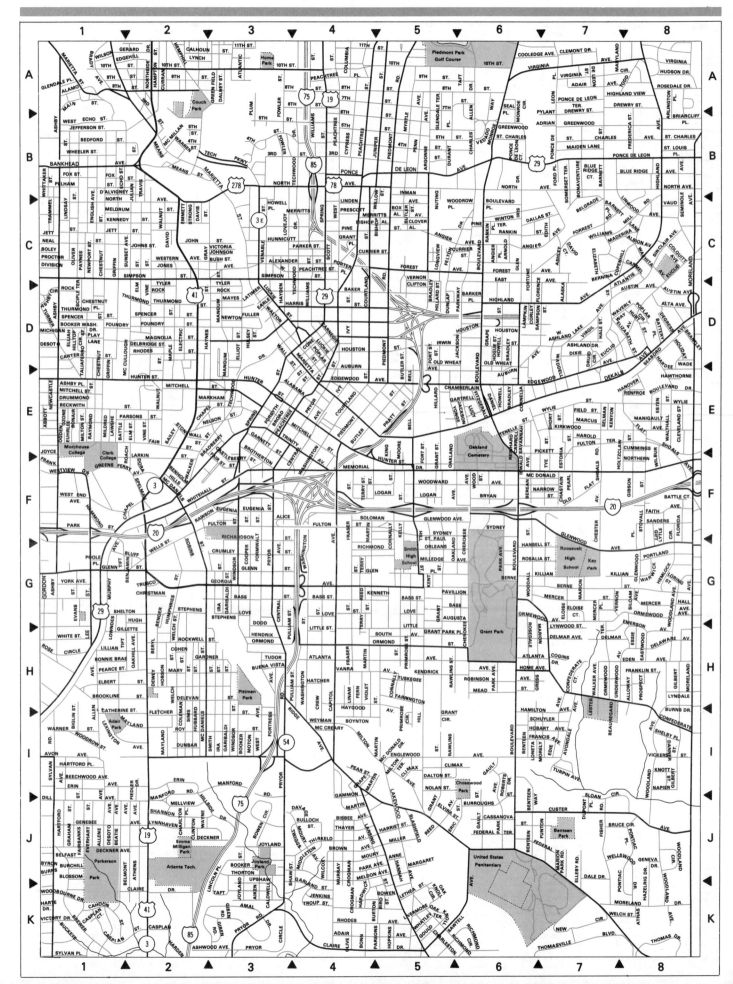

ATLANTA

Abbott E1
Adair Ave. A7,K7
Adrian B7
Aiken K3
Alabama E4
Alamo A1
Alaska D7
Albion Ave. C8
Alexander St. C3
Alice F3
Allen Ave. I1
Allene Ave. J1
Alloway H8
Alta Ave. D8
Amal Dr. K3
Angier Ave. C5,C6
Angier Pl. C6
Anne J5
Argonne Ave. B5
Arlington Pl. A8
Arnold C6
Ashby B1,D1,G1
Ashby Cir. D1
Ashby Pl. E1
Ashland Dr. D7
Ashland, W. D7
Ashley B7
Ashwood Ave. K2
Athas K8
Athens Ave. J2
Atlanta Ave. H4,H6
Atlantic A3
Atlantis C7
Auburn Ave. D4,D6
Augusta G5
Austin Ave. C8,D8
Avon Ave. I1
Avondale Ave. I7
Bailey E2
Baker D4
Bankhead Ave. B1
Barker Pl. D6
Barnett Pl. C7
Barnett St. B7
Bass St. G3,G4,G5
Battery Pl. D8
Battle E1
Battle Ct. F8
Beatie Ave. J1
Beauregard I7
Beckwith St. E1
Bedford St. B1
Beechwood Ave. I1
Belfast J1
Belgrade C7
Bell E5
Belmont Ave. J2
Bender G2
Benjamin G6
Benteen I6,J6
Benteen Way J6
Berean Ave. F6
Berne St. G6,G7
Beryl H2
Biglin St. I1
Bird St. K5
Bisbee Ave. J4
Bishop C5
Bishop Al. C5
Blashfield J5
Blossom J1
Blue Ridge Ave. B8
Blue Ridge Ct. B7
Bluff G2
Boley C1
Bonair E1
Bonaventure B7
Bonn K4
Bonnie Brae H1
Booker I3,J3
Booker T.
Washington Dr. D1
Boulevard C6,D6
Boulevard Dr. E8
Boulevard Pl. C6
Bowen K5
Bowen Cir. J3
Box Al. C5
Boynton I4
Bradberry E3
Bradley D5,D6,E5
Brady Ave. A1
Brantley D8
Brenna C7
Brewer K1
Briarcliff Pl. A8
Broad St. E3
Brookline St. H1
Brotherton St. E3
Brown Ave. J4
Bruce Cir. J7
Bryan St. F6
Buckeye K1
Buena Vista H3
Bulloch St. J4
Burchill J1
Burns J1
Burns Dr. H8
Burroughs St. J6
Burton K5
Bush St. C3
Butler St. C5,E4,E5
Byron J7
Cahoon St. K1
Caldwell K3
Capitol Ave. H4
Carmel C8
Carnegie D4
Carroll E6
Carter St. D1
Casplan Ct. K1
Casplan St. K1
Cassanova St. J6
Castleberry F3
Catherine St. H1
Central Ave. F3,G3
Chamberlain E6
Chapel St. E2,F2
Charles Allen Dr. B6
Charleston K5
Charlton Pl. J2
Chastain F7
Cherokee Ave. H6,G6
Chester Ave. F7
Chestnut Pl. D1
Chestnut St. C2,D1
Christman G2
Claire Dr. K1,K4
Clemont Dr. A7
Cleveland St. E8
Clifton D5
Climax I5
Clinton J2
Clover Al. C5
Cogins Dr. H7
Cohen H2
Coleman St. I2
Colquitt Ave. C8
Columbia A4
Cone D4
Confederate H8
Confederate Ct. H7
Connally St. G5,H5
Cooledge Ave. A6
Cooper St. G3
Copenhill C7
Corley D6
Cornelia E6
Courtland St. C4,E4
Crew St. H4
Crogman K4
Crumley St. G3
Cummings E8
Curran A2
Currier St. C4
Custer Ave. J7
Cypress B4
D'Alvigney B1
Dale Dr. J7
Dallas St. C6
Dalney St. A3
Dalton St. I5
Daniel E6
Danner st. I8
Davage J4
David C2
David Ct. C7
Davis C2
De Leon St. A7
DeKalb Ave. E7
DeSoto D1
Deckner Ave. J1,J2
Degress D8
Delaware Ave. H8
Delbridge St. D2
Delevan St. H2
Delmar Ave. H7
Desoto Ave. J1
Dewey H2
Dill Ave. J1
Division C1
Dixie D7
Dodd G3
Dora J2
Drewry St. A7,A8
Druid Cir. D7
Drummond E1
DuPont Pl. J7
Dunbar I2
Dunlap D5
Durant Pl. B5
Earle D3
East Ave. C6
Eastwood H8
Echo St. B1
Eden Ave. H8
Eden Ave. H8
Edgehill A1
Edgewood Ave. E4,E6
Edie Ave. I7
Edith C7
Elbert St. H1
Electric G2
Elijah D1
Elizabeth St. C7,D7
Elleby Rd. J7
Elliot St. D3
Elm St. D2,E2
Eloise G7
Eloise Ct. G7
Elvira St. J5
Emerson Ave. H8
Emmett C2
Englewood Ave. I5
English Ave. C1
Eric St. J6
Erin Ave. I1,I2
Essie J7
Esten E8
Estoria St. F7
Euclid Ave. C8,D7
Eugenia F3
Euhrlee E1
Evans St. G1
Everhart St. J1
Fair St. E2,E3
Fairbanks St. J1
Faith Ave. E8
Farmington H5
Federal J7
Federal Ter. J6
Felton Dr. C5
Fern St. H4
Fiedler Dr. I2
Field St. E7
Fisher Rd. J7
Fitzgerald E6
Flat Shoals Ave. E8
Fletcher St. I2
Florence D6
Florida F8
Ford Pl. B7
Forest Ave. C5,C6
Formwalt St. G3
Forrest Rd. C7
Forsyth St. E3
Fort St. D5,E5
Fortress Ave. I3
Fortune C6
Foundry St. D2
Fowler St. A3,B3
Fox St. B1
Francis Ave. I6
Frank F1
Franklin St. H8
Fraser St. F4,H4
Frederica St. B8
Fuller D3
Fulton St. F3,F4
Fulton Ter. E7
Funton J7
Gammon I4
Gardener H2
Garibaldi St. G3,I3
Garland St. K4
Garnett St. E3
Gartrell E6
Gault St. I6,J6
Genessee Ave. J1
Geneva Dr. J8
Georgia Ave. G3
Gerard A2
Giben Rd. K3
Gibson St. F8
Gift F8
Gilbert St. H8,I8
Gillette H1
Glen Iris Dr. C6
Glen Pl. G5
Glendale Pl. A1
Glendale Ter. B5
Glenn St. G1,G3
Glenwood Ave. F5,G7
Glenwood Pl. G8
Gordon G1
Gould K5
Graham St. J1
Grant Cir. I5
Grant Park Pl. H5
Grant Pl. C4
Grant St. F5,G5,J5
Grape D6,I4
Gray St. C2
Green Field A3
Greens Ferry Ave. J1
Greenwood B6,B7
Gress H6
Griffin C1,D1
Hale St. D7
Hall Ave. G8
Hamilton Ave. I6
Hammond F1
Hampton St. A2
Hannah J5
Hanover E8
Hansell St. G6
Hardee D8
Harden K2
Hardwick K4
Harold E7
Harriet St. J5
Harris St. D4
Harte Dr. K1
Hartford Ave. J1
Hartford Pl. J1
Hatcher H4
Hawthorne E8
Hayden B5
Haygood Ave. H4
Haynes St. D3
Hazelrig Dr. K8
Hemlock Cir. G8
Hemphill A2
Hendrix H3
Highland Ave. B8,D6
Highland View A7
Hill St. F5,I5
Hillard St. D5,E5
Hills F2
Hillside Dr. J2
Hilltop Cir. D1
Hobart Ave. I6
Hobson H2
Hogue St. D6
Holiday D8
Holtzclaw F8
Home Ave. F8
Hopkins K5
Houston St. D4,D6
Howell Pl. C3
Howell St. D6,E6
Hubbard St. I2
Hudson Dr. A8
Hugh G2
Hulsey St. D3
Humphries St. G2
Hunnicutt C3
Hunter St. E2,E3,F5
Hurt St. D8
Inman B5
Ira St. G3,I3
Irwin St. D5
Iswald F6
Ivy St. D4,E4
Jackson E6
Jackson Pkwy. D6
Jefferson St. B1
Jenkins K4
Jett St. C1
John St. C2
Johnson C3
Jones Ave. C2
Joyce J7
Joyland St. J3
Julian St. B2
Juniper St. B5
Kelly St. F5
Kendrick Ave. H5
Kennedy St. C1
Kenneth G5
Kent G5
Kenyon E7
Killian G7
King E5
Kirkwood Ave. E7
Knott I8
Lake Ave. D7
Lakewood Ave. J5
Lampkin D6
Lane C8
Lansing St. J4
Larkin St. E2
Latimer D3
Lawshe E1
Lee St. H1
Lester H7
Lethea St. K5
Lexington Ave. I1
Lillian H1
Linam H4
Lincoln Pl. J3
Linden Ave. C4
Lindsay St. C1
Linwood Ave. C8
Little St. H4,H5
Livermore K5
Logan F5
Loneta I6
Longview C5
Loring St. G8
Love St. G3,G4,G5
Lovejoy C3
Lowndes H1
Luckie St. D3
Lucy E6
Lynch A2
Lyndale H8
Lynnhaven J2
Lynwood St. H7
Lytle F8
Maderira C7
Magnolia St. D2
Magnum st. D3
Maiden Ln. B7
Main St. A1
Manford Rd. I2,I3
Mangault Ave. E8
Maple St. D2
Marcus E7
Margaret C5
Marietta St. A1,B3,D4
Marion G7,J7
Markham E3
Martin St. F4,J4
Mary H2
Maryland A7,I2
Mayes D3
Mayland I2
Mc Cullough D2
Mc Millan B2
McCreary I4
McDaniels St. F2,I2
McDonald Dr. F7,I5
Mead St. H6
Means St. B2
Meldon Ave. J4
Meldrum St. C1
Mellview J2
Memorial Dr. F4
Mercer Pl. G7
Mercer St. G7,G8
Merritts Ave. C3,C4
Michigan D1
Middleton J4
Mildred E1
Milledge Ave. G5
Miller J5
Milton Ave. I4
Milton St. E1
Milton Ter. I5
Mitchell St. E1,E2,E4
Monroe B6
Monroe Cir. A6
Moore E5
Moreland Ave. C8,H8
Moreland Dr. K8
Moton I3
Moury Ave. J4
Murphy Ave. G1
Murray J2
Myrtle B5
Naper I8
Narrow F6
Neal St. C1
Nelson St. E3
New Cir. K7
Newcastle E1
Newport St. C1
Newton D3
Nolan St. I5
North Ave. B1,B3,B6,B8
Northern F8
Northside Dr. A2
Nuting B5
Oak Knoll Cir. K5
Oak Knoll Ter. K5
Oakhill Ave. J4
Oakland Ave. F5,G5
Ogden E1
Old Flat Shoals Rd. F7
Old Wheat D5,D6
Olive A8
Oliver St. C1
Orleans G5
Ormewood Ave. G6,G8
Ormewood Ter. H7
Ormond St. H3,H5
Ozone E1
Park Ave. G6,H6,J6
Park Rd. J7
Park St. F1
Parker St. C4
Parsons K5
Parsons St. E2
Pavillion E5
Paynes C1
Peachtree Pl. A4
Peachtree St. B4
Peachtree St., W. E3
Pear St. I4
Pearce St. H1
Pearl St. F7
Pelham St. B1
Penn Ave. B5
Pickett E7
Piedmont Rd. B5,D5,E4
Pine St. C4,C6
Play Ln. D1
Plum A3
Plyant B7
Ponce De Leon Ave. B4
Ponce De Leon Ct. B6
Ponce De Leon Pl. B7
Ponce De Leon Ter. A7
Pontiac Pl. J8
Poole Pl. G1
Poplar D4
Poplar Cir. D8
Porter Pl. C4
Portland G8
Pratt St. E5
Prescott C4
Primrose Ccir. I5
Primrose St. H5
Proctor C1
Prospect H8
Pryor Cir. K3
Pryor Rd. I3,K3
Pryor St. E4,G3
Pullman St. H4
Rankin Pl. C6
Rankin St. C6
Rawlins St. H5,I5
Rawson F2
Raymond St. E1
Reed Ave. J5
Reed St. G4
Reinhard E6
Renfroe E8
Rhodes Ave. K4
Rhodes St. D2
Richardson St. G4
Richmond G4,K6
Richmond Cir. K6
Ridge Ave. I4
Roach F2
Roberts Dr. I6
Robins G2
Robinson Ave. I6
Rock D1,D2,D3
Rockwell St. H2
Rosalia St. G6
Rose Cir. H1
Rosedale H6
Rosedale Dr. A8
Roy St. D2
Sampson St. D7
Sanders F8
Savannah E6
Sawtell Ave. K6
Schuyler Ave. I6
Sciple Ter. D1
Scott C4
Seaboard Ave. D8
Seal Pl. A6
Selman E7
Seminole Ave. C8
Shannon J2
Shaw St. J4
Shelby Pl. I8
Shelton G1
Short E7
Siloam Ave. G8
Simpson St. C2,C3
Sims St. I2
Sinclair Ave. C8
Sloan Cir. J7
Smith St. I3
Soloman F4
Somerset Ter. B7
South Ave. H5
Spelman F2
Spencer St. D1,D2
Spring St. C4,E3
St. Charles Ave. B6,B7
St. Louis Pl. B8
St. Paul F5
Stephens G2,G3
Stonewall St. E2
Stovall St. F8
Strong C2
Sunset Ave. C2
Sydney F5,F6
Sylvan Pl. K1
Sylvan Rd. I1
Taft A6,K3
Taliaferro St. D1
Tech Pkwy. B3
Techwood Dr. B4,D4,E3
Tenelle St. E6
Terry St. F4,G4
Thayer J4
Thirkeld Ave. J4
Thomas Dr. K8
Thomasville Blvd. K7
Thornton J3
Thurmond St. D1,D2
Tift G1,H1
Todd A8
Trammel C1
Travis B2
Trenholm F2
Trinity Ave. E4
Troup St. K4
Trusco G2
Tudor D1
Turner D1
Turpin Ave. I7
Tuskegee H5
Twiggs J4
Tye St. F7
Tyler C2,C3
Underwood Ave. H7
Upshaw J3
Vanra Ave. H4
Vaud C8
Vedado Way B6
Venable St. C3
Vernon C5,G7
Vickers St. I8
Victoria C3
Victory Dr. K1
Vine St. D2,E2
Violet St. H4
Virgil D7
Virginia Ave. A6,A8
Virginia Cir. A7
Waddell D7
Wade D8
Walker Ave. H7
Walker St. F2
Wall St. D3
Walnut St. C2,E2
Walthall St. E8
Walton St. D3
Warner St. I1
Warren B2
Warwick G8
Washington E4
Washington St. F4,G4,H4
Washita Ave. C8
Waverly Way D7
Wayne J2
Welch St. H2,K8
Wells St. G2
Wellswood Dr. J8
West Ave. I3
West Echo St. B1
West End Ave. F1
Western Ave. C2
Westview Dr. F1
Weyman I4
Whatley K5
Wheeler St. B1
White St. H1
Whitehall St. F2
Whittaker St. B1
Wilbur F8
Wilcox J4
Williams Mill Dr. C7
Williams St. B4,D4
Willow St. B4,D4
Wilson A1
Windsor St. G3,I3
Winton Ter. C6
Wood St. F6
Woodall St. G6
Woodbourne Dr. K1
Woodland Ave. G8,I8,K8
Woodland Cir. J8
Woodrow Pl. C5
Woodrow St. I1
Woodward Ave. F5
Wylie St. E7,E8
Yonge E6
York Ave. G1
3rd St. A2,B3,B4
4th St. B2,B3,B5
5th St. B2,B3,B4,B5
6th St. A4
7th St. A4,A5
8th St. A3,A4,A5
9th St. A1,A2,A5
10th St. A1,A2,A3,A6
11th St. A3,A4

BALTIMORE

Abbotson St. A8
Abbott St. E8
Abell A5
Aiken St. B8
Aisquith St. B7,C7,E7,G7
Albermarle H7
Aliceanna I7
Alluvion St. J3
Amity St. H2
Ann St. I8
Annapolis Rd. K3
Argeant St. I2
Argyle Ave. E2
Arlington Ave. G2,H2
Art Museum Dr. A4
Ashland Ave. E8
Atkinson St. B4
Baker St. D1
Baltimore St. G7,H4
Bank St. H7
Barclay St. B5,D5
Barnes St. E8
Barney St. K5,K6
Barre St. I3
Bartlett Ave. B6
Battery Ave. I-K6
Bayard Rd. J3
Bayard St. J2
Beason St. K8
Belt St. K6
Belvidere St. D6
Bennett Pl. G2
Bethel St. D8,I8
Bevan J5
Biddle St. E6,F3
Block St. I7
Bloom St. D1
Bolton Pl. E4
Bolton St. E4
Bonaparte Ave. C7
Bond St. F8,G8,I8
Boone St. B6,C6
Booth St. H1,H2
Boyle St. K7
Bradley F3
Brantley F2
Brentwood Ave. B5,E6
Broadway D8,H8
Brookfield Ave. C2
Brooks Ln. C2
Brunt St. E2
Bush St. J2
Byrd St. K5
Calender St. H2
Calhoun St. I1
Callow Ave. C2
Calvert St. B5,H5
Camden St. H4
Carey St. D1,I2
Carlton St. G2,H2
Caroline St. I7
Carroll St. I3,J2
Carrollton Ave. H2
Carswell St. A8
Carter D6
Cathedral St. E4
Cecil Ave. B7,C6
Central Ave. F7
Centre St. F4
Chapel St. D8,F8
Charles St. H5,J5
Chase St. E4
Chauncey Ave. C2
Chestnut Ave. A3
Clarkson St. K5
Clay St. F4
Clement St. J5,J6,K7
Clendenin Ave. D2
Cleveland St. J2
Cliftview Ave. C7
Cloverdale Rd. C1
Cokesbury Ave. C6
Colvin St. F6
Commerce St. H6
Constitution St. F6
Conway St. I3,I5,J3
Cooksie St. K8
Covington St. J6
Cresmont Ave. A4
Cross St. I2,J4,J5
Cuba K8
Cumberland D1
Curtain Ave. C7
Dallas St. F7,G8,I8
Darley Ave. B7,C8
Davis St. G5
Decatur K8
Dexter St. I3
Division St. D1
Dock St. I8
Dolphin St. E3,E4
Dorn St. F3
Druid Hill Ave. C1,F3
Druid Park Lake Dr. C1
Ducatel St. C2
Durham St. D8,F8,I8
Eager St. E5
East St. F6
Eastern Ave. H7
Eden St. E7,H7
Edmonson Ave. F1,F2
Edythe St. F7
Eislen St. I3
Ellerslie Ave. A6
Ellsworth St. D8
Elm St. A2
Etting St. D1,E3
Eutaw Pl. C1,E4
Eutaw St. H4,J4,K3
Exeter Hall Ave. A6
Exeter St. F6,H7
Fairmount Ave.
G4,G7,H1,H2
Faith La. E8
Falls Rd. B3
Fallscliff Rd. A2
Fawcett C4
Fawn St. H6
Fayette St. G1,G4,G7
Federal St. D5,D7
Fenwick Ave. A8
Filmore A7
Fleet St. I7
Fort Ave. K5,K7
Francis St. C1
Franklin St. G4
Frederick St. H6
Freindship B7
Fremont Ave. E2,G3
Frisby St. A6
Front St. F6,G6
Garrett Ave. B7
Gay St. F7,H6
George St. F3
Germania C7
Gilbert St. F2
Gilmore St. I1
Gittings St. J5,J6
Glyndon St. I2
Gold St. D1
Gorsuch Ave. A7
Gough St. H7
Granby St. H6
Graves St. F6
Greene St. H4
Greenmount Ave. E6
Guilford Ave. B5,F5
Gutman Ave. B6
Haines St. K3
Hamburg St. I3,I4,J5
Hamilton St. F5
Hampden Ave. B4,C4
Hanover St. H5,K5
Harford Rd. B8
Harlem Ave. F1
Hartford Ave. E7
Harvey St. K7
Haubert St. K8
Heath St. K5,K6
Henneman Ave. E7
Henrietta I5
Henry St. K6
Herkimer St. I2
High St. F6,H7
Hill St. I5
Hillen St. F6
Hillman St. E6
Hoffman St. D6,E4,F3
Holbrook St. E7
Holiday G6
Hollins St. H1
Holy Cross La. C8
Homestead St. A7
Homewood Ave.
A7,C6,E6
Hope St. D7
Hopkins Pl. H4
Howard St. B4,H4,J4
Hughes St. I5
Hull St. K8
Hunter St. E5,F5
Huntingdon C4
Huntingdon Ave. B4
Ilchester Ave. A5
Independence St. A6
Irvine Pl. G8
Jackson St. K6
James St. I2
Jasper St. F4
Jefferson St. F8
John St. D4
Johnson St. K6
Jones Falls Expy. A2
Josephine St. G3
Kennedy B8
Kennedy Ave. C6
Kensett C1
Keswick Rd. A3
Key Hwy. I6,J6,K7
Kirk Ave. B7,C6
Lafayette Ave.
D4,D8,E3,F1
Lakeview Ave. C2
Lamont Ave. E8
Lamont St. D7
Lancaster I7
Lanvale St. D5,D8,E3,F1
Latrobe St. D5
Laurens St. E1,E2
Lawrence St. K7
Leadenhall St. J4
Lee St. I5
Lemmon St. H1
Lennox St. C3
Lexington St. G4,G4
Liberty St. G5
Light St. H5,K5
Linden Ave. C2,D3,F4
Llewelyn Ave. D8
Lloyd G7
Lo Dr. C8
Loch Raven Rd. B6
Lombard St. H1,H4
Lorraine Ave. B4,B5
Lovegrove St. A5,C5
Low St. G6
Lowman K8
Ludlow St. K7
Madison Ave. C1
Madison St. E3,F4
Market J5
Market Pl. H6
Marriott K8
Mary St. F3
Maryland Ave. B4,E4
Mathews St. B6
May G7
McAllister St. D5
McCulloh St. C1,E3
McDonogh St. F8
McElderry St. F8
McHenry St. H2
McKim St. F6
McMechen St. E2
Miles Ave. B4
Mill Rd. A3
Miller St. F8
Millman St. F8
Monroe St. J1
Montgomery St. I4,I6
Montpelier St. A6,B7
Monument St. F4
Mosher St. D3,F1
Mount St. I1
Mt. Clare H2
Mt. Royal Ave. D4
Mt. Royal Ter. C3
Mt. Vernon Pl. F5
Mulberry St. G4
Mullikin St. G8
Mura St. E6
Myrtle Ave. F2,G3
Nanticoke St. J2
Newington Ave. C2
Normal Ave. C8
Norris St. I1
Oler St. K3
Olive St. J,K5
Oliver St. D4,D5,D7
Orchard St. F3
Orleans St. G7
Ostend St. I2,J3,J5
Oxford F3
Paca St. I3,J3
Pacific St. A3
Park Ave. E4,F4
Parkin St. H3
Parrish St. F1,G1,I1
Patapsco St. J5,K5
Pearl St. G3
Penn St. H3
Pennsylvania Ave. C1,F3
Perry St. H5
Philpot St. I7
Pierce St. G3
Pine St. G3
Pitcher E2
Pleasant G5
Polk St. B8
Poppleton St. G2,H2
Portland St. H3
Poultney J5
Pratt St. H4,H7,H8
President St. I7
Presstman St. D2
Preston St. E6,F3
Proctor E6
Race St. J5
Ramsay St. I3
Randall St. K5
Read St. E4,F5
Redwood St. H3,H5
Reese St. A6,B6
Regester St. D8,I8
Remington Ave. A3
Reservoir St. C3
Retreat St. D1
Richardson St. K8
Ridgley I3,K3
Riggs Ave. E1
River St. J6
Riverside Ave. K6
Robb St. B7
Robert St. E2
Russell St. K3
Rutland Ave. D8,F8
Ryan I2
Sarah Ann St. G2,G3
Saratoga St. G4
School St. E1
Schroeder St. H2
Scott St. J3
Severn St. J2
Shakespeare St. I8
Sharp St. H4,J4
Sheilds Pl. F2
Shuter St. F8
Sinclair La. C8
Sisson St. B3,C4
Smithson E2
Somerset St. E7
South St. H5
Spring St. D7,E7,F7,G7,I7
St. Ann's B6
St. James St. F7
St. Paul Pl. G5
St. Paul St. B5,E5,G5
Stanford Pl. D1
Sterrett St. I3
Stevenson St. K7
Stiles St. H6
Stirling St. F7
Stockton St. E1,H2
Stricker St. F1,I1
Thames St. I8
The Alameda A8
The Fallsway G6
Tilden Dr. A3
Tivoly Ave. A8
Towson St. K8
Tyler B7
Tyson St. F4,G4
Upton St. F2
Valley St. E6
Vincent St. F1,G1,I1
Vine St. G1,G2,G3
Vineyard La. A5
Wards St. J2
Warner St. K3
Warren Ave. I5
Washington Blvd. J1,I3
Washington St. D8
Water St. H6
Watson St. G7
Webb St. E7
Webster St. K6
Welcome I5
West St. J3,J4
Whatcoat St. F1
Wheeling J5
Whitelock St. C2
Whitridge B5
Wicomico St. J2
William St. K6
Wills St. I7
Wilmer Ct. E2
Wilson E2
Winchester St. E1
Wirton St. E6
Wolfe St. D8,I8
Woodall K7
Woodbrook Ave. C1
Woodyear St. E1,I1
Worchester St. J3
Wyeth H3,I3
Wyman Park Dr. A3
Wyman Pl. A4
York St. I5
20th St. C4,C8
21st St. C4
22nd St. C4
23rd St. C4
24th St. C4
25th St. B4,C8
26th St. B4
27th St. B4
28th St. A8,B3,B4,B6
29th St. A4,A6,A8,B3
30th St. A4,A5,A6,A8
31st St. A3,A5,A8
32nd St. A3

Scale of Miles
0 .1 .2 .3 .4

N

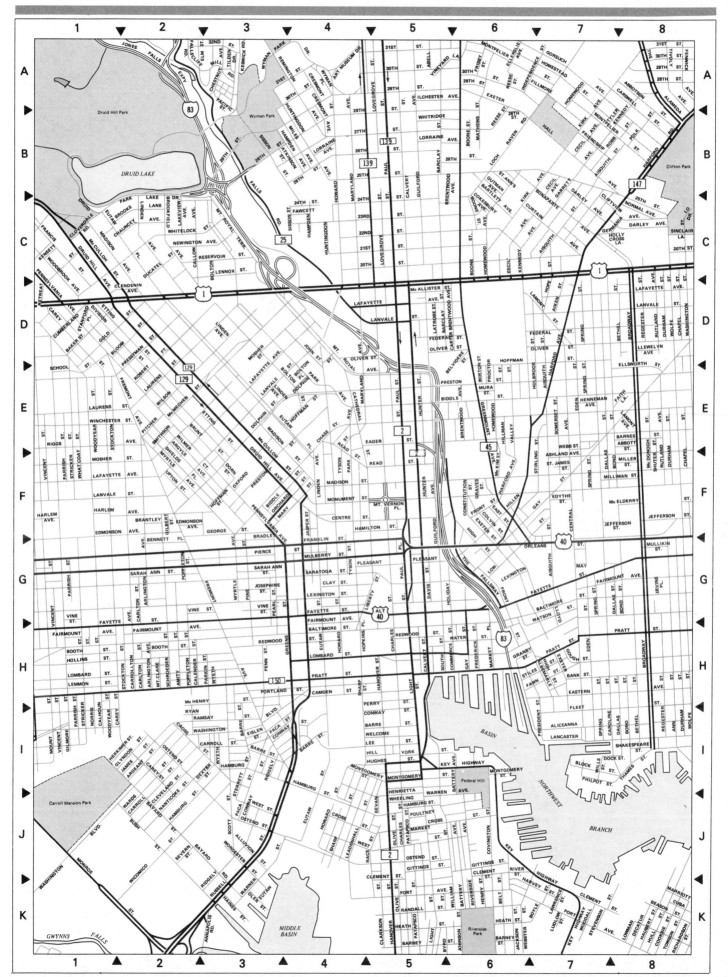

Scale of Miles

0 .1 .2 .3 .4 .5

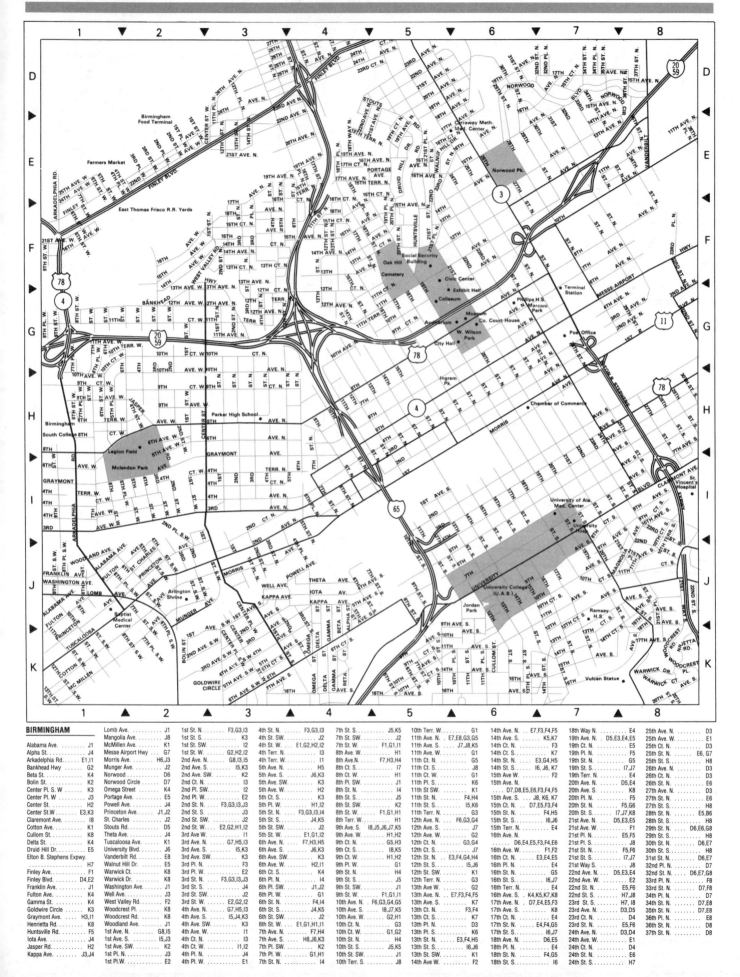

BIRMINGHAM

Alabama Ave.	J1
Alpha St.	J4
Arkadelphia Rd.	E1,I1
Bankhead Hwy	G2
Beta St.	K4
Bolin St.	K2
Center Pl. S. W	K3
Center Pl. W	J3
Center St.	H2
Center St.W	E3,K3
Claremont Ave.	I8
Cotton Ave.	K1
Cullom St.	K8
Delta St.	K4
Druid Hill Dr.	E5
Elton B. Stephens Expwy.	
	H7
Finley Ave.	F1
Finley Blvd.	D4,E2
Franklin Ave.	J1
Fulton Ave.	K4
Gamma St.	J3
Goldwire Circle	K3
Graymont Ave.	H3,I1
Henrietta Rd.	K8
Huntsville Rd.	F5
Iota Ave.	J4
Jasper Rd.	H2
Kappa Ave.	J3,J4

Lomb Ave.	J1
Mangolia Ave.	J8
McMillen Ave.	K1
Messe Airport Hwy	G7
Morris Ave.	H6,J3
Munger Ave.	J2
Norwood	D6
Norwood Circle	D7
Omega Street	K4
Portage Ave.	E5
Powell Ave.	J4
Princeton Ave.	J1,J2
St. Charles	J2
Stouts Rd.	D5
Theta Ave.	J4
Tuscaloosa Ave.	K1
University Blvd.	J6
Vanderbilt Rd.	E8
Walnut Hill Dr.	E5
Warwick Ct.	K8
Warwick Dr.	K8
Washington Ave.	J1
Well Ave.	J3
West Valley Rd.	F2
Woodcrest Pl.	K8
Woodcrest St.	K8
Woodland Ave.	J1
1st Ave. N.	G8,I5
1st Ave. S.	I5,J3
1st Pl. N.	J3
1st Pl.W.	E2

1st St. N.	F3,G3,I3
1st St. S.	K3
1st St. SW.	I2
2nd Ave. N.	G8,I3,I5
2nd Ave. S.	I5,K3
2nd Ave. SW.	K2
2nd Ct. N.	I3
2nd Pl. SW.	I2
2nd Pl. W.	I2
2nd St. N.	F3,G3,I3,J3
2nd St. S.	J3
2nd St. SW.	J2
3rd Ave N.	I3
3rd Ave. N.	G7,H5,I3
3rd Ave. S.	I5,K3
3rd Ave. SW.	K3
3rd Pl. N.	F3
3rd Pl. W.	E2
3rd St. N.	F3,G3,I3,J3
3rd St. S.	J4
3rd St. SW.	J2
4th Ave. N.	G7,H5,I3
4th Ave. S.	I5,J4,K3
4th Ave. SW.	I1
4th Ct. N.	I3
4th Pl. N.	J4
4th Pl. W.	E1

4th St. N.	F3,G3,I3
4th St. SW.	J2
4th St. W.	E1,G2,H2,I2
4th Terr. W.	I1
5th Ave. N.	H5
5th Ave. S.	J6,K3
5th Ave. SW.	K3
5th Ct. S.	K3
5th Pl. N.	J6
5th St. N.	F3,G3,I3,I4
5th St. S.	J4,K5
5th St. SW.	J2
5th St. W.	H1
6th Ave. N.	F7,H3,H5
6th Ave. S.	J6,K3
6th Ave. SW.	K3
6th Ct. N.	I4
6th Pl. N.	I4
6th Pl. S.	J5
6th St. N.	G1
6th St. W.	E1,G1,H1,I1
7th Ave. N.	H8,J6,K3
7th Ave. S.	J6
7th Ct. N.	G5,H3
7th Pl. N.	J5
7th St. N.	I4
8th Ave. N.	I1,I2
9th Ave. S.	J8
9th Ct. N.	H4
9th Pl. W.	G1
9th St. N.	J5

7th St. S.	J5,K5
7th St. SW.	J2
7th St. W.	F1,G1,I1
8th Ave. W.	H1
8th Ct. S.	I7
8th Ct. W.	H1
8th Pl. SW.	J1
8th St. N.	I4
8th St. S.	J5
8th St. SW.	K1
8th Terr. W.	H1
8th St. W.	F1,G1,H1,I1
9th Ave. N.	I8,J5,J6,J7,K5
9th Ct. S.	G5,H3
9th Pl. W.	G1
9th St. N.	H1,H2
9th St. W.	G1
9th St. S.	J5,K5
9th St. SW.	J1
10th Ave. N.	G2,H1
10th Ave. S.	I8,J7,K5
10th Ct. N.	K7
10th Ct. S.	K1
10th St. S.	J5,K5
10th St. SW.	J1
10th Terr. S.	J8
14th Ave W.	F2

10th Terr. W.	G1
11th Ave. N.	E7,E8,G3,G5
11th Ave. S.	J7,J8,K5
11th Ct. N.	G5
11th Ct. S.	J8
11th Pl. SW.	K6
11th Pl. S.	K1
11th St. S.	I5,K6
11th Terr. S.	G3
12th Ave. S.	J7
12th Ave. S.	J7
12th St. N.	G3,G4
12th St. S.	I5,J6
12th Terr. S.	J7
13th Ave. N.	E7,F3,F4,F5
13th Ave. S.	F3,F4
13th Pl. N.	D3
13th Pl. S.	E3,F4,H5
13th St. N.	I6,J6
13th St. SW.	K1
13th Terr. S.	I6,J6
14th Ave W.	F2

14th Ave. N.	E7,F3,F4,F5
14th Ave. S.	K5,K7
14th Ct. N.	F3
14th Ct. S.	K7
14th Pl. N.	E3,G4,H5
14th St. N.	G5
14th St. S.	I6,J6,K7
15th Ave. N.	
	D7,D8,E5,E6,F3,F4,F5
15th Ave. S.	J8,K6,K7
15th Ct. N.	D7,E5,F3,F4
15th Ct. S.	F4,H5
15th Pl. S.	F5,G6
15th St. N.	I7,J7,K8
15th Terr. N.	E4
16th Ave. N.	I6,J6
16th Ave. W.	F1,F2
16th Ct. N.	E3,E4,E5
16th Pl. N.	E4
16th Pl. W.	F2
16th St. N.	G5
16th St. S.	K4,K5,K7,K8
17th Ave. N.	D7,E4,E5,F3
17th Ave. S.	K8
17th Ct. N.	E4,F4,G5
17th St. N.	I6,J7
18th Ave. N.	D6,E5
18th St. N.	F4,G5
18th St. S.	I6

18th Way N.	E4
19th Ave. N.	D5,E3,E4,E5
19th Ct. N.	E5
19th Pl. N.	F5
19th St. N.	G5
19th St. S.	I7,J7
19th Terr. N.	E4
20th Ave. N.	D5,E4
20th Pl. N.	K8
20th St. N.	F5
20th St. S.	I7,J7,K8
21st Ave. N.	D5,E3,E5
21st Pl. N.	E5,F5
21st St. N.	F1
21st St. S.	I7,J7
21st Way S.	J8
22nd Ave. N.	D5,E3,E4
22nd Ave. S.	E2
22nd St. N.	E5,F5,G6
22nd St. S.	H7,J8
23rd St. N.	H7,I8
23rd Pl. S.	E4
23rd St. N.	D3,D5
23rd St. S.	E5,F6
24th Ave. N.	D3,D4
24th Ct. N.	D4
24th Ct. S.	E6
24th St. S.	H7

25th Ave. N.	D3
25th Ave. W.	E1
25th Ct. N.	D3
25th St. N.	E6, G7
26th Ave. N.	D3
26th St. N.	E6
27th Ave. N.	D3
27th St. N.	E6
28th St. N.	E5,B6
29th St. N.	D6,E6,G8
30th Pl. N.	D6,F7
30th St. N.	H8
31st St. N.	D6,F7
32nd Pl. N.	D7
32nd St. N.	D6,E7,G8
33rd Pl. N.	F8
33rd St. N.	D7,F8
34th Pl. N.	D7
34th St. N.	H8
35th St. N.	D7,E8
36th St. N.	E8
37th St. N.	D8

Scale of Miles

0   .1   .2   .3   .4

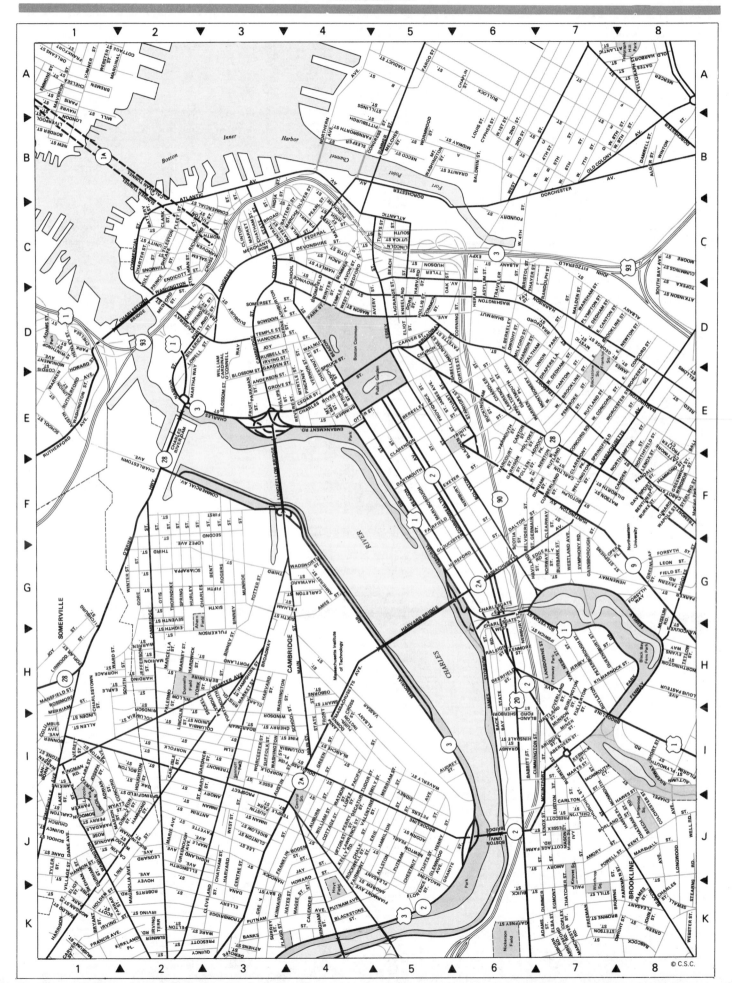

BOSTON

A St. B6
Abbotsford Rd. K7
Aberdeen St. I7
Acorn St. J5
Adams St. D1
Adams St. K7
Adrian St. I1
Albany St. C6,D8
Albany St. I4
Alger St. B8
Allen St. I1
Allston St. J5
Ames St. G4
Amherst St. G4
Amory St. J7
Amory St. I3
Anderson St. E3
Andrews St. K5
Antrim St. J3
Appleton St. E6
Arch St. C4
Arundel St. I7
Ashburton Pl. D3
Asylum St. D6
Athens St. K3
Atkinson St. D8
Atlantic Ave. B2,C5
Atlantic St. A7
Auburn St. J4
Audrey St. I5
Austin St. E1
Austin St. J3,I3
Autumn St. I8
Avery St. D5
Avon St. C4
B St. A5,B7
Babbit St. I6
Babcock St. K7
Back St. I6
Baldwin St. B6
Ball E8
Banks St. K3
Battery St. C2,C3
Bay St. K3
Bay State Rd. I6
Beach St. C5
Beacon St. K8
Beacon St. D4,F5
Bedford St. C4
Beech Rd. J8
Belvidere St. G6
Bent St. G3
Benton St. F8
Berkeley St. E5
Berkeley St., E. D6
Berkshire St. H3
Bigelow St. J3
Billerical St. D2
Binney St. G3,H3
Blackstone St. K4
Blagden St. E6
Blanche St. I4
Blandford St. I6
Blossom St. E3
Boardman St. I3
Boden St. J4
Bolton St. I2
Bolyston St. F6,G7,H7
Bonner Ave. I1
Border St. B1
Borland St. J7
Boston Univ. Bridge J6
Bowdoin J1
Bowdoin St. D3
Braddock Pl. E7
Bradford St. D7
Branch St. E4
Bremen St. A1
Brimmer St. E4
Bristol St. H3
Bristol St. C6
Broad St. C3
Broadway D5,H3
Bromfield St. D4
Brookline Ave. I8
Brookline St. J5
Brookline St., E. D7
Brookline St., W. E7
Brownie St. K7
Bryant St. K1
Buckingham St. E6,J2
Buick St. K6
Bullock St. A6
Burbank St. G7
Burke St. F8
Burlington St. H7
Buswell St. I7
Byron St. E4
C St. B7
Cabot St. F8
Calahan Tunnel B2
Calendar St. K4
Calvin St. J1
Cambridge St. D3,H2
Camden St. E8
Canal St. D2
Canton St. E6
Canton St., E. D7
Canton St., W. E7
Carleton St. G4
Carlisle St. I2
Carlton St. F7,J1,J7
Carver St. D5,K1
Causeway St. D2
Cedar St. E4
Central St. C3
Centre St. J3
Chalk St. J4
Chandler St. E6
Chapel St. J8
Chaplin St. J8
Charles River Dam E2
Charles St. E3,E4,G2,K8
Charlesgate East G6
Charlesgate West G6
Charlestown Ave. F2
Charlestown St. H1
Charter St. C2
Chatham St. C3,J3,J8
Chelsea St. A1,D1
Cherry St. I3
Chestnut St. E4,J5
Chilton St. J7
Church J1
Church St. D5
Churchill St. J7
Claremont Pk. F7
Clarendon St. E5
Clark St. C2,H3,I1
Clearway St. F7
Cleveland St. K3
Clinton St. C3,J3
Colchester St. J8
Columbia St. I2,I4
Columbus Ave. I1
Commercial Ave. F3
Commercial St. C2,C3
Common St. D5
Commonwealth Ave. F6
Concord Ave. I1
Concord Sq. E7
Concord St., E. D8
Concord St., W. E7
Congress St. B5,C3
Copley St. K7
Cordis St. D1
Corning St. D6
Cortes St. E6
Cottage Farm Road J7
Cottage St. A2,J4
Court St. C3
Cross St. C3
Cumberland St. F7
Cummings St. C8
Cummington St. I7
Cunard St. F8
Cypher St. B6
D St. B7
Dalton St. G6
Dana St. K3
Dane Ave. J1
Dane St. J1
Darnell St. B8
Dartmouth St. F6
Dartmouth Pl E6
Davenport St. F8
Decatur St. J4
Dedham St., E. D7
Dedham St., W. E7
Deerfield St. H6
Devonshire St. C4
Dewolee St. K3
Dilworth St. F8
Dimick St. J2
Dorchester Ave. B5,B7,B8
Douglass Ct. I4
Drapers Ln. E7
Dummer St. K7
Durham St. F7,J1
Dwight St. D6,K8
E St. B7
Earle St. H1
Edgerly Rd. G7
Egmont St. K7
Eighth St. G2
Elba St. K7
Eliot Kneeland St. D5
Eliot St. K1
Ellery St. K3
Ellisworth Ave. J2
Elm St. I3
Embankment Rd. E4
Emily St. I5
Emmons St. A1
Endicott St. C2
Erie St. J5
Essex St. D5,I3,J7
Euston St. J7
Evans Way H8
Everett St. I1
Exeter St. F5
F St. A8
Fairfield F5
Fairmont St. J4
Fargo St. A5
Farnsworth St. B4
Farrar St. K1
Fay St. D6
Fayette St. D5,J3
Federal St. C4
Fellows St. E8
Felton St. K2
Fenway H8
Fiarmont Ave. K5
Field St. G8
Fifth St. G3
First St. F3
Fisk Pl. I3
Fitchburg St. G1
Flagg St. K3
Fleet St. C2
Florence St. K5
Follen St. F6
Forsyth St. G8
Forsyth Way G8
Foundry St. C6
Francis Ave. K1
Frankfort St. A1
Franklin St. C4,J3
Freeman St. K7
Friend St. D2
Front I4
Fruit St. E3
Fulkerson St. H3
Fullerton St. H7
Fulton St. C2
Gaffney St. K6
Gainsborough St. G7
Garden St. D3
Gardener St. I2
Garrison St. F6
Gates St. A8
Glenwood Ave. J5
Gloucester St. G5
Gore St. A1,G2
Granby St. I6
Granite St. B6,J5
Green St. I4,K3,K8
Greenleaf St. G8
Greenough Ave. J2
Greenwich St. F8
Grove St. E3
Hamilton St. J5
Hammond St. F8,J2
Hampshire St. H3
Hancock St. D3,J3
Hanover C3
Hanson St. D6,J1
Harcourt St. F6
Harding St. H2
Hardwick St. H2
Harrison Ave. D7
Harrison St. K1
Harvard St. D5,H3,J3
Haviland St. G6
Havre St. A1
Hawes Pl. J8
Hawes St. J8
Hawkins St. I1
Hawley St. C4
Hayes St. K3
Hayward St. G4
Hemenway St. G7
Henley St. D1
Henry St. J5
Herald St. D6
Hereford St. G6
High St. C4
Highland Ave. J2
Hingham St. K4
Hinsdale St. I6
Holden St. K1
Hollis St. C5
Holyoke St. E6
Horrace St. H1
Houghton St. I2
Hovey Ave. J2
Howard St. D1,J4
Hudson St. C5
Hull St. C2
Huntington Ave. F7
Hurley St. G2
Ilavado St. K1
India St. C3
Inman St. J3
Ipswich St. H7
Irving St. D3,K1,K2
Irving Terr K2
Isabella E6
Ivy St. J7
James St. E8,K8
James Storrow H6
Jay St. J4
Jefferson St. H2
Jersey St. H7
John Fitzgerald Expwy. C7
John St. K8
Joseph St. I1
Joy St. D3,H1
Kelly Rd. J4
Kendall St. F8
Kenmore St. H6
Kent St. J8
Keswick St. I7
Kilmarnock St. H7
Kingman Rd. I2
Kinnaird St. K3
Kirkland Pl. K2
La Grange St. D5
Lake St. J1
Lansdowne St. H7,I4
Lattmore Ct. E8
Lawrence St. E6,J4
Lee St. J3
Lenox St. F8,J7
Leon St. G8,J2
Leonard Ave. J2
Lime St. E4
Lincoln Pkwy J1
Lincoln St. C5,I1,I2
Line St. J1
Linwood St. H1
Liverpool B1
London St. B1
Longfellow Bridge F3
Longwood Ave. J8
Lopez Ave. F2
Lopez St. J4
Louis Pasteur Ave. H8
Louis St. B6
Lowell St. D2
Magazine St. J5
Magee St. K4
Magnolia Ave. K2
Magnus J1
Main St. H4,I4
Maitland St. I7
Malden St. D7
Manchester Rd. K7
Mansfield St. H1
Maple Ave. J2
Marceila St. H2
March Oliver St. C4
Marginal A1
Marion St. H2,J2
Market St. C3,H3
Marlborough St. F5
Marle Ave. J2
Marney St. H2
Marshall St. J8
Martha Way E2
Marys St. I7
Mason St. D4,J7
Massachusetts Ave. F7,G6,H4
Matthews St. C4
Maverick St. A1
Medford St. D6
Melcher St. B5
Melrose St. D5
Memorial Dr. G5,H5
Mercer St. A8
Merchants Row C3
Merriam St. H1,I5
Midway St. B6
Milford St. D6
Milk St. C4
Mill St. A1
Miner St. I7
Monmouth Ct. I7
Monmouth St. I7
Montgomery St. E7
Monument Ave. D1
Moore St. C8
Morgan St. K1
Mountfort St. I7
Mt. Vernon St. E3
Mt. Washington St B5
Munroe St. G3
Munson St. I7
Museum Rd. G8
Museum St. K1
Myrtle St. E4
Mystic St. D7
Nashua St. E2
Necco St. B5
New St. B1
Newbury St. F6,H6
Newton J5
Newton St. I1
Newton St., E. D8
Newton St., W. F7
Norfolk St. I2,I3
North St. C3
Northern Ave. B4
Northfield St. F8
Northhampton St. E8
Norway St. G7
O'Brian Hwy F2
Oak St. D5,I2
Old Colony Ave. B7
Old Harbor St. A8
Opera Pl. G7
Orleans St. A1
Osborn St. H4,K7
Otis St. C4,G2
Otter St. E4
Overland St. H7
Pacific Street I4
Palermo St. H2
Paris St. A1
Park Dr. H8
Park St. D1,D4,J3,K1
Parkdale J1
Parker J1
Parker St. G8
Parkman St. E3,K8
Paul Street K7
Pearl St. C4,J5
Pelham St. G4
Pembroke St. E7
Perry St. J1,J4
Peterborough St. H7
Peters J5
Phillips St. E3
Pilgrim Rd. I8
Pinckney St. E4
Pine St. I4
Pittsburgh St. B5
Pleasant St. J5,K8
Plymouth H3
Plymouth St. I8
Plympton St. D7
Poplar St. H1
Portland St. D2,H3
Portsmouth H3
Potter St. G3
Powell St. J7
Prescott St. J7,K3
Prince St. C2
Prospect St. I3
Providence St. E5
Province St. C4
Purchase St. C4
Purrington I4
Putnam Ave. J5,K3,K4
Queensbury St. H7
Quincy St. J1,K3
Raleigh St. H6
Randolph St. D7
Reed St. E8
Revere St. E4
Richmond St. C2
River St. E4
Riverway I8
Roberts Rd. K2
Rockwell St. J4
Rodgers St. G3
Rose J1
Rossmore H1
Ruggles St. G8
Russell St. D3
Rutherford Ave. E1
Rutland St. E7
Rutland St., W. F7
Salem C2
Sanborn I1
School St. C4,E1,I4,J1
Sciarappa St. G2
Scotia St. G6
Scott St. K1
Seckel H3
Second St. F3
Seventh St. G2
Sewall Ave. K8
Shawmut Ave. D6
Sheafe St. C2
Sherborn St. I6
Short Street I8
Sidney Street I5
Sixth Street G3,G4
Skehan St. J1
Sleeper St. B4
Smart St. H4
Snowhill St. C2
Somerset St. D3
Somerville Ave. J1
South Bay Ave. D8
South St. C5,H2
Spring St. G2
Springfield St. F7,I2
Spruce St. D4
St. Botolph F7
St. George St. D7
St. Germain St. F6
St. James Ave. E5
St. Mary St. I2
St. Stephens St. G7
Stanhope St. E6
State St. C3,I4
Stearns Rd. J8
Sterling St. F8
Stetson St. K7
Still St. J7
Stillings St. A5
Stillman St. C2
Stone St. I1
Stuart St. E6
Sudbury St. D3
Suffolk St. I3
Summer Rd. K2
Summer St. B5,C4
Sumner St. A1
Sumner Tunnel B2
Surrey St. K3
Symphony Rd. G7
Tavern Rd. G8
Telegraph St. A8
Temple Pl. D4
Temple St. D3,J3
Tetlow St. H8
Thatcher St. K7
Thayer St. C6
Third St. G2,G3
Thorndike St. G2
Tileston C2
Topeka St. D8
Traveler St. D6
Traverse St. D3
Tremont St. E7,F8,I3
Tremont St. I3
Trinity Pl. E6
Trotter Ct. E8
Trowbridge K3
Tudor St. D1
Tufts St. C5,J5
Tyler St. C5,J1
Union Park Street D7
Union St. E1,I3
Unity St. C2
Upton St. J4
Utica St. C5
Valentine St. J4
Van Ness St. H7
Vancouver St. G8
Vassar St. I5
Viaduct St. A5
Village St. J1
Vine St. K1
Wadsworth St. G4
Waldo St. J2
Walnut St. D4
Waltham St. D6
Wapole St. F8
Ward St. H1
Ware St. K3
Wareham St. D7
Warren Ave. E6
Warren St. E1,H2,I1
Washington St. D2,D6,E1,E8,H3,I3,J1
Water St. C3
Watson St. F7,J4
Waverly St. I5
Webster Ave. H3
Webster St. A1,K8
Well Rd. J8
Wellington St. F7
West St. B6,D4,J3
Westland Ave. G7
William Cardinal O'Connell Way D3
William St. J4
Willow St. H2
Windsor St. F8,H2,I3
Winter St. D4,G2
Winthrop St. D1
Winton St. B8
Worcester St. E8,I3
Worcestor Sq. E8
Wormwood St. B5
Worthington St. H8
Wyatt J1
Yarmouth St. E6
York St. H2
1st St. W. B6
2nd St. W. B7
3rd St. W. B7
4th St. W. B7,C6
5th St. W. B7
6th St. W. B7
7th St. W. B7
8th St. W. B7
9th St. W. B8

BUFFALO

A St. F7
Abbotsford B2
Ada Pl. C5
Adams St. H5
Addison H6
Alabama St. K4
Alexander Ave. C5
Amity St. C7
Amsterdam St. C7
Anderson Pl. D2
Appenheimer Ave. C7
Archer J8
Archie St. G4
Ardmore Pl. C2
Argyle C3
Arkansas St. D1
Arlington E2
Ash St. G4
Ashland Ave. E2
Ashland Ave.,N. B2,E2
Ashley St. G8
Atlantic D3
B St. F7
Babcock St. J7
Bailey J8,K8
Baitz Ave. I8
Balcom St. C4
Baltimore I3
Barker St. E3
Barryrees B1
Barton St. C1
Beach St. F5
Beck St. F7
Bender I7
Bennett St. G4
Berkley B3
Bertha K7
Best St. E4
Beverly Rd. C5
Bidwell Pkwy. C2
Birch C7
Bird Ave. B1
Bissell Ave. E8
Blaine Ave. B5
Bolton J5
Bond I6
Box Ave. D7
Boyd St. C1
Bradford St. J7
Bradley St. A1
Brantford C3
Bremen D2
Bristol St. H6
Broadway St. G5,H3
Brooklyn D5
Brown St. F5
Brunswick Blvd. C5
Bryant St. F5
Buell Ave. C6
Buffalo Skyway J2,K3
Burton F3
Bushnell St. I8
Butler Ave. C5
C St. F7
California D1
Cambridge Ave. B8,D8
Carl St. D8
Carlton St. F3
Carolina St. G1
Carroll St. H3,I4,I6
Cayuga St. F5
Cedar I4
Cedar St. G4
Central Park Ave. A7
Chaplin Pkwy. B3
Charles H2
Chelsea C7
Chenango St. D2
Cherry G4
Chester St. C4,D4
Chicago St. J3
Childs St. K4
Chippewa St.,E. G3
Chippewa St.,W. G2
Church St. H2
Claredon B3
Claremont Ave. B2
Clarence A8
Clark St. G7
Clemo St. I7
Cleveland Ave. C3
Clifford J6
Clinton St. H3,H4
Clyde A8
Colfax Ave. B8
College St. F2
Colt St. H6
Columbia I3
Commercial I2
Como St. F5
Concord G7
Congress St. C1
Connecticut St. E1
Cornelia I6
Cornwall Ave. B8,D8
Cory St. G2
Cottage F2
Court St. H3
Crescent Ave. B5
Curtiss St. G7
Cypress G4
Daisy C6
Dart St. B1
Davis St. F5
Deerfield Ave. B8
Delaware Ave. D3,G3
Delgvan Ave. C1
Delgvan Ave.,E. C5
Depot H8
Detroit St. H6
Dewey Ave. A7
Dillon I6
Division St.,N. H3,H5
Division St.,S. H3,H4
Dodge St. E4
Dole St. J7
Donaldson Rd. C5
Dorchester Rd. B2
Dorothy St. I7
Dover G7
Drexel St. B7
Dunbar K8
Duncan St. J8
Dupont St. D5
Durham Ave. B8,C8
Dutton C7
Eagle St. H2,H5
Earl Pl. F5
Eastwood Pl. B5
Eaton St. E4
Edna Pl. E4
Edward St. F2
Efner St. G1
Eighteenth St. D2
Elk St. J5
Ellicott H3
Elm St. H3
Elmwood Ave. C3,F2,G2
Emerson D4
Emslie St. H5,I5
Erie H2
Essex D2
Eureka G4
Exchange St. I3,I4
Farnhill Ave. B8
Federal A8
Ferguson Arnold St. C1
Ferry St.,E. D4
Fifteenth St. D1
Fillmore Ave. B7,C7,H6
Fitzgerald J5
Fleming St. H7
Florence Ave. A5
Florida St. C5
Forrest Ave. B2
Fougeron St. E7
Fourteenth St. D1
Fourth St. F1,G2
Fox St. G6
Frankfort Ave. D8
Franklin Ave. G3
French St. D7
Fritz Ave. H6
Fulton St. I4,J5
Galveston F5
Ganson St. J3
Garner Ave. B1
Genesee St.,W. F6,H2
Geneva G7
George G5
Georgia G2
Gerhardt St. E5
Gibson St. G7
Gilbert St. I8
Girard Pl. E6
Gittere St. E8
Glendale B5
Glenny Dr. B7
Glenwood Ave. D4,D7
Goodell F4
Goodrich St. E3
Goodyear Ave. F8
Goulding Ave. D5
Granger Penhurst Pl. B3
Grant St. C1
Grape St. F5
Gray St. G5
Greenwood Pl. C1
Gridar St. D8
Grimes St. G8
Guilford St. G6
Gurham St. J7
Hadley Pl. C5
Halbert St. A6
Hamburg K4
Hamlin Rd. C5
Hannah St. H8
Hardwood I6
Harmonia St. F7
Harrison St. J7
Harvey J5
Hayes Pl. J8
Helen C1
Hermann St. G6
Hickory St. G4,H4
High St. F3
Highland Ave. D2
Hill St. A7
Hobart St. I8
Hodge Ave. D3
Holland E4
Holt St. H7
Houf D5
Houghton G7
Howard St. H5
Howlett E8
Hubbard St. J8
Hudson F1
Hughes Ave. B5
Humber Ave. B8,C8
Humboldt Pkwy. B5
Hurlock D8
Huron St.,E. G3
Huron St.,W. G2
Illinois I3
Indiana I3
Inwood Pl. B3
Iroquois H5
Irving Pl. F3
Ivy St. E8
James St. H6
Jefferson Ave. D5,H5
Jewett Ave. A5,A7
Johnson St. G6
Jones St. I7
Josephine E7
Kahr St. E7
Kane St. F5
Keating St. J8
Kellogg St. J8
Kenova Pl. B7
Kensington Ave. B6
Kensington Pkwy. D6
Kent St. G7
Kentucky St. J4
Ketchum E2
Kingsley St. E5
Kirkover St. I8
Kisfer St. E7
Klaus H7
Koons Ave. E8,F8
Kosciuszko St. F7
Krettner St. H6
Krupp Ave. G8
Lafayette Ave. C1
Lakeview Ave. F1
Lancaster Ave. C3
Landsdale Rd. D5
Lark St. C6
Larkin St. I5
Latchworth St. A1
Lathrop St. F7
Laurel St. D4
Laux St. I7
Lawrence D1
Leddy J5
Lee St. K6
Lemon St. F4
Leroy Ave. A7
Lester St. J8
Letour E7
Lewis St. I7
Lexington Ave. D2
Lincoln Pkwy. B3
Linwood Ave. D3
Litchfield Ave. B8
Littell J8
Livingston St. C2
Locust St. F4
Loepers St. F7
Lombard St. G7
London St. D5
Longview Ave. C7
Loring Ave. B6
Louisiana St. J4
Lowell D2
Lyman St. H7
Madison St. H5
Main St. B5,E3,H3
Makinaw St. J3,J4
Manchester B2
Manhattan Ave. A8
Manitoba St. I8
Maple G4
Marigold Ave. A8
Marina St. H2
Mariner St. F2
Market,E. I3
Market,W. I3
Marshall E7
Maryland St. F2
Masten Rd. E4
McKibbon E8
Melvin Keppel K8
Memorial Dr. H7
Miami St. H4
Michigan Ave.,S. I3,J2
Milburn St. G8
Miller Ave. F8
Mills St. F7
Milnor St. G4
Milton St. J7
Minton J6
Mississippi I3
Mohawk St. G2
Monroe St. H5
Montclair Ave. A8
Montgomery St. H6,I6
Monticello Pl. B6
Morley Pl. C4
Mortimer St. G5
Moselle St. D8,E8
Mulberry St. F4
Myers E6
Myrtle Ave. I4
Nash St. H4
Nevada Ave. D8
New Babcock St. H8,I8
New Jersey F1
Newell H7
Newton G7
Nineteenth St. D2
Normal Ave. D1
North St. E2
North St.,E. E4,E6
Northampton St. E4
Northland Ave. C5
Norwood Ave. E2
Nottingham Rd. A3
O'Connell St. J4
Oak H3
Oak Grove C6
Oak St.,N. G3
Oakland Pl. E3
Oakwood Pl. A5
Oberlin St. F8
Ohio St. J3,K3
Old Bailey K8
Olga H6
Oneida St. H6
Orange St. F4
Orlando St. J7
Owahn Pl. J6
Oxford Ave. C4
Paderewski Dr. G6
Palos A8
Parade Ave.,E. E7
Parade Ave.,N. E7
Park St. F3
Parkdale Ave. C1
Parkridge A8
Parkside Ave. A5
Pauline B6
Peabody St. J6
Peach St. F5
Pearl St. H2
Pearl St.,N. F3
Peck St. G8
Peckham G5
Pembroke Ave. B8
Pennsylvania F1
Perkins B1
Perry St. I2,J5
Pershing Ave. F5
Persons St. G8
Peterson E7
Phelps St. A6
Pine St. G4,H4
Playter St. G7
Plymouth Dewitt St. C1
Pomeroy K8
Poolay Pl. B1
Porter E1,F1
Pratt St. G4
Prenatt J6
Purdy St. C5
Putnam St. C2
Quincy St. G8
Quinn St. J7
Red Jacket J5
Reed St. G6
Republic St. J4
Rich St. E6
Richlawn Ave. A7
Richmond Ave. B2,E2
Rickert Ave. C6
Riley St. D4
Ripley D2
Robie St. A5
Rodney Ave. A7
Roehrer E5
Rohr St. E7
Rommel Ave. F8
Rose St. F5
Roseville St. I5
Rostzor St. E8
Rother Ave. F7
Ruhland St. F8
Rumsey Rd. B3
San Domingo Ave. H6
Sanford B6
Saybrook Pl B3
Scajaquada Ave. C8
Scajaquada Expy. A4
Schmarbeck St. F8
Schuehle St. D8
Scott St. I3
Scoville Ave. I8
Sears St. G7
Selkirk St. J6
Seneca St. I4,I6
Seventeenth St. D2
Seymour St. I5
Shawnee Ave. A8
Sheridan Ave. C7
Sherman H6
Shumway St. H6
Sidney St. C6
Sidway St. J4
Sixteenth St. D2
Smith St. H6,K5
Sobieski St. F7
South Park St. I3,K6
South St. J3
Southhampton St. E4
Spillman Pl. C5
Spring St. G4,H5
Spruce St. G4
St. Clair K4
St. James Pl. C3
St. Johns F2
St. Louis St. E8
Stanislaus St. F7
Stannard St. I4
Stanton St. H6
Stephens Pl. J5
Stetson St. H7
Stortz D5
Strauss St. G6
Summer St. E2
Sussex St. B8
Swan St. H4
Sweet Ave. G7
Swinburne St. G8
Sycamore Ave. F7,G3
Tennessee J4
Tenth St. F2
Thomas St. H7
Timon St. F5
Titus Ave. F8
Tonoyanda A1
Townsend St. H6
Tracy St. G2
Tremont B2
Trenton Ave. G1
Trinidad Pl. B6
Trinity F2
Tudor Pl. C3
Tupper St.,E. G3
Tupper St.,W. F3
Urban St. D7
Utical St.,E. D4
Utical St.,W. D2
VanRensselaer I5
Vandalia St. K4
Vangarder St. B7
Verdun B7
Vermont St. E1
Victoria Ave. A7
Vincennes K4
Virginia St. F2,F4,G1
Wakefield Ave. A7
Walker St. D5
Walnut G4
Walter St. J6
Warren Ave. G7
Warwick Ave. B8
Washington St. H3
Wasmuth St. E8
Wasson St. J7
Watson St. H5
Waverly St. C5
Wells I3
Wescott J7
Whitney Pl F2
William St. H3,H4,H7
Willow D5,E5
Willow Lawn A6
Wilson St. H6
Winchester Ave. D7
Windsor Pl. B3
Winona St. J7
Winslow Ave. D5,D6
Winter St. D1
Woepoel St. D6
Wohlers Ave. E6
Woltz Ave. F7
Woodlawn Ave. D4,D6,D8
Woodward Ave. B5
Wyoming St. B8,D8
York St. E1
Young Ave. G8

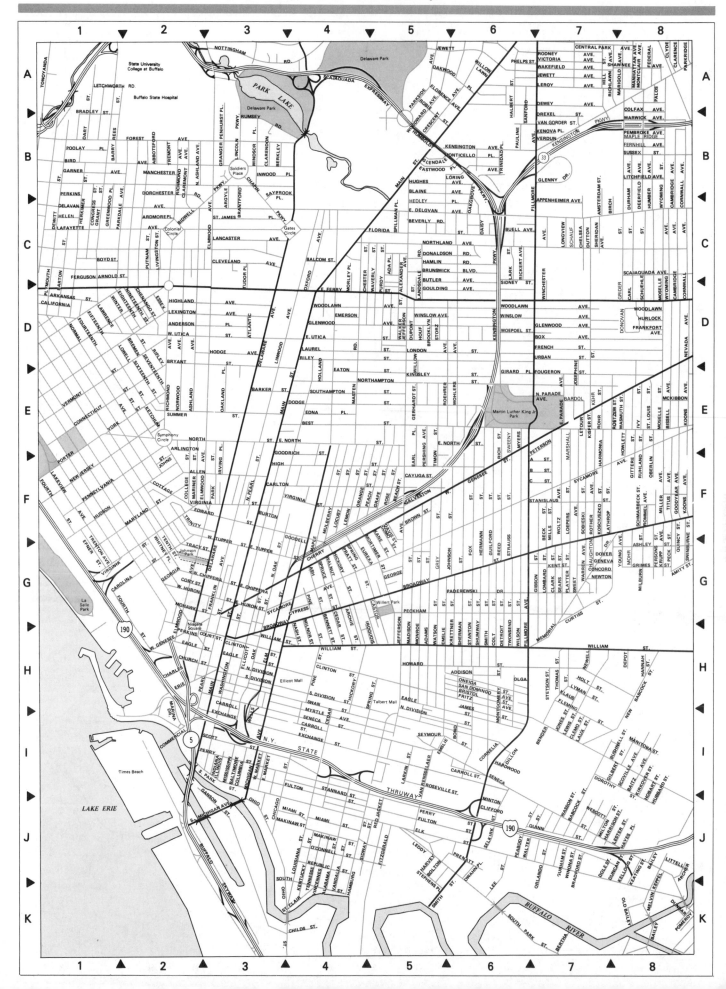

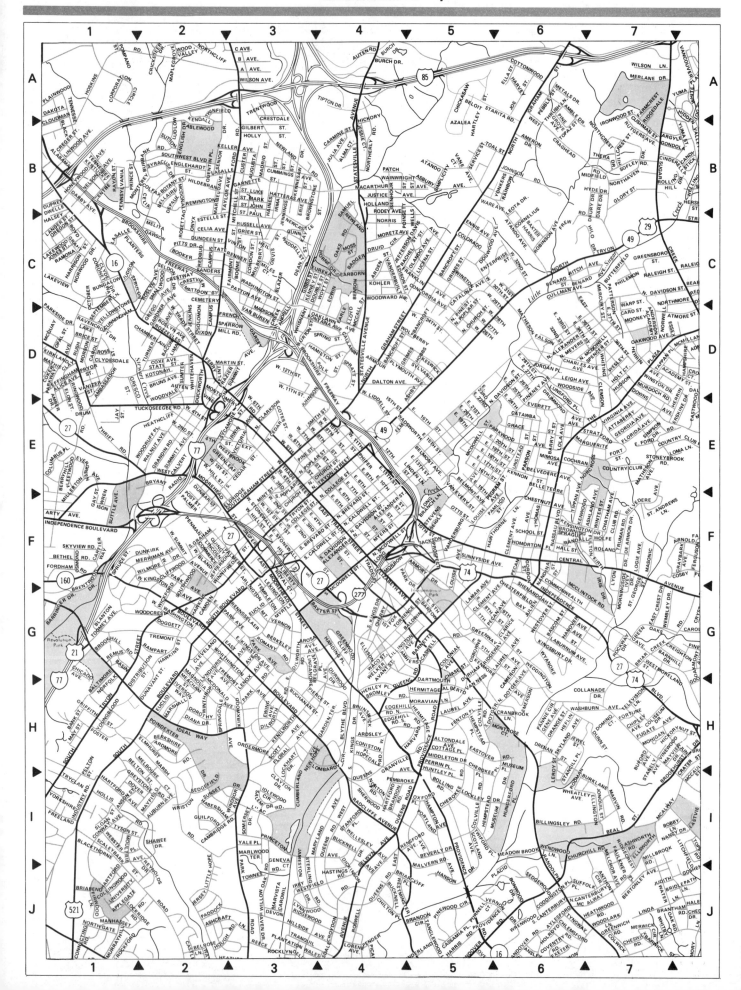

Scale of Miles

0 .2 .4 .6 .8

N

CHARLOTTE

A Ave. A3
Ablewood B2
Academy D7
Academy St. D7
Alabama B1
Alberto H5
Alexander,N. D6,F4
Alexander,S. F4
Alice Ave. D1
Alma Ct. B4
Altondale Ave. H5
Ambassador D1
Amber Dr. D1
Amble Dr. A6
Ameron Dr. B6
Amherst G5
Anderson St. D7
Andover Rd. J6
Andrill D3
Ansley J6
Anson St. I1
Anthony Circle J7
Applegate J1
Arden St. C4
Ardmore H2
Ardsley H4
Argyle B7
Arlington F3
Armour D4
Armoury Dr. F5
Arosa Ave. G3
Arty Ave. F1
Asbury Ave. B5
Ashby D5
Ashcraft Ln. J2
Ashland Ave. F7
Ashworth Rd. I7
Atando Ave. B5,C6
Attaberry E7
Auburn Ave. I2
Augusta B3
Auten Rd. A4,D2
Avant St. G4
Aylesfora J6
Azalea B5
B Ave. A3
Bacon D2
Badger C4
Baldwin G5
Baltimore H1
Bancroft St. C5,D4,D5
Bank St. H1
Barnette G5
Barnhill Dr. G7
Barnhill Dr. G7
Barringer Dr. G1
Barringer Dr. G1
Barry St. E6
Barry St. E6
Bartow G5
Bartow G5
Barwick J7
Bascom St. G6
Basin G1
Baxter St. G4
Bay St. G6
Beal St. I7
Bellaire B2
Belleterre E6
Belmont Ave. E5
Beloit A5
Belrose Ln. J2
Belton St. H1
Belvedere Ave. E6,F7
Benard C6
Benson C4
Berkeley Ave. G3
Berkshire H2
Berryhill E1
Bertonley Ave. J7
Bethel Rd. F1
Beverly Dr. I5
Billingsey Rd. I6
Black B1
Blackthorne Rd. I1
Bland, W. F2
Blanton G1
Blazer C3
Blythe Blvd H4
Bobby Ln. I7
Bolling Rd. I5
Bonwood Dr. J6
Booker C2
Boone St. C3
Botony St. B2
Boyd C1
Brandon Cir. J5
Brandon Rd. I4
Brentwood Dr. F1
Brevard St., N. F4
Brevard St., S. F3
Briabend J1
Briar Creek Rd. G7
Briarcliff Pl. J4
Brice St. D1
Bromley Rd. H4
Brook Hill Rd. G1
Brookhurst Dr. I7
Brookshire Frwy C2,D3
Browning Sprague F6
Brownstone B3
Bruns Ave. D2
Brunswick Ave. H4
Bryant E2
Buchanan St. H3
Bucknell I4,J4
Bulford Ave. H7
Bungalow C1
Burbank Rd. B2
Burch Dr. A4
Burklane I7
Burton D3
Butterfield C7
C Ave. A3
Caldwell St., N. F4
Caldwell St., S. F4
Callahan D4
Calvert E2
Cambridge Rd. I2
Camden G2
Cameron G6
Campus C2,D2
Canterbury, N. J7
Canterbury, S. J6
Card D7
Carmine St. B4
Carol D1
Carowil J3
Cartier Way F1
Cassamia Pl. J5
Castlewood J2
Caswell Rd. G5
Catalina Ave. C5
Catawba E6
Cedar St., S. E3
Cedar,N. E3
Celia B2,C2
Cemetary C2
Central Ave. F6
Centre B1
Chamberland D2
Charles Ave. D6
Chase St. G5
Chatman Ave. F7
Cherokee Pl. H5
Cherokee Rd. I5
Cherry G4
Chesterfield Ave. G6
Chestnut Ave. F6
Cheswick Rd. J7
Chicago Ave. G1
Chilton Pl. J4
Chipley Ave. H7
Chlemsford Rd. J6
Church St., N. D5,E4
Church St., S. F3
Churchill Rd. I6
Clarkson,N. E3
Clay D1
Clayton Dr. I3
Clement Ave. F6,G5
Clemson D7
Cleveland G2
Clifford F2
Cloudman A1
Club Rd. F7
Clyde Dr. C1
Clydesdale Rd. D1
Cochran E6
Coddington Pl. J6
Coker D1
Colfax B2
Collanade Dr. H7
College St., N. E4
College St., S. F3
Collingwood J1
Colliseum Dr. H7
Colonial Ave. G5
Columbus Pl. E1
Colville Rd. H5,I5
Colwick J7
Commerce F2
Commonwealth Ave. G6
Concordia C5
Concordia Ave. C5
Condon St. C3
Coniston Pl. H4
Connecting Rd. J1
Conway Ave. I1
Cornelius C6
Cornell Ave. J6
Coronet Way C1
Corporation Circle A1
Cotes St. E3
Cottage Pl. H5
Cottonwood A6
Country Club Rd. E7
Coventry Rd. J6
Coxe Ave. D2
Craighead Rd., W. B6
Cranbrook Ln. H6
Creek D3
Creger St. B1
Crest Dr., E. G7
Crestdale A3
Crestview C2
Crestway C2
Cricketeer Dr. A2
Croydon Rd. J4
Cullman Ave. C6
Cumberland Ave. I3
Cummings Ave. B3
Cunningham D1
Cushman St. B7
Custer B3
Dakota A1
Dalton Ave. D4
Darby Ave. B1
Dare Dr. B7
Darsey D3
Dartmouth H5
Davidson St., N. C7,D6,F4
Davidson St., S. F4
Dawson C2
DeArmon Dr. F7
DePaul B2
Dean St. C3
Dearborn C4
Devon J3
Diana Dr. H2
Dickinson I4
Dilworth Rd. H3
Dilworth, E. G3
Distribution St. G2
Dixon D2
Doggett G2
Dogwood Ave. C5
Domino Ct. H7
Dorothy H2
Dotger Ave., N. H6
Dotger Ave., S. H6
Double St. C4
Dover I1
Downs Ave. D7
Druid Circle C4
Drum E1
Drummond Ave. E6
Drury Dr. B7
Duckworth D2
Dunavant St. H2
Dunbar St. E2
Dundeen St. C2
Dunkirk F2
Dunn St. H7
Dupree B1
Durham G5
Durwood Dr. G4
Dwelle B1
Earle D4
East Boulevard H3
Eastover Rd. H5
Edgehill Rd., N. H4
Edgehill Rd., S. H4
Edison St. C4
Edwin C4
Effingham D1
Eldridge F3
Elizabeth Ave. F4
Ella St. A6
Ellington I7
Ellison G4
Ellsworth I7
Elm E4
Elmhurst Rd. H2
Elon St. D1
Emerson H6
Englehardt St. B2
English Dr. B2
Ennis Ave. C5
Enterprise St. C6
Erie St. B3
Estelle St. C2
Euclid G3,H2
Eureka C4
Everett E6
Evergreen E1
Ewing Ave. H3
Exeter J6
Fairmont C3
Falson D6
Fannie Circle H6
Farmcrest A7
Faulkner I7
Fenton Pl. H5
Firth F7
Firwood Ln. J1
Fleetwood Rd. E1
Flint D2
Floral Ave. H3
Florida Ave. E7
Fontana Ave. D4
Ford Rd. B3
Ford Rd., E. E7
Fordham Rd. F1
Fort St. E7
Fortune H7
Foster H1
Fox G4
Franklin C5
Frazier D3
Freeland I1
French D3
Frew Rd. C6
Fugate Ave. H7
Fulton F7
Gardenter H4
Gardner Ave. D2
Garnette B3
Gay St. F1
Gene Ave. H6
Geneva Ct. I3
Georgia Ave. E7
Gibbs St. C3
Gilbert St. B3
Glory St. B7
Gondola B7
Goodwin Ave. H6
Gordon St. F6
Grace E6
Graham St. F2
Graham St., N. A6,D4
Graham St., S. F2
Grandin Rd. E2
Grant C1
Granville Rd. H4
Green Oaks G7
Greenleaf E2
Greensboro St. C7
Greenway Ave. G5
Greenwich Rd. J7
Greenwood Cliff G4
Gregg Ave. D2
Greystone Rd. I1
Grier St. C3
Griffith St. H1
Grimes St. C5,D5
Guilford I2
Gunn A1
Habersham I2
Haines B3
Hall St. F6
Halsey C1
Hamilton St. D4
Hampton Ave. I5
Hanover G6
Hanson Dr. J5
Harding Pl. D4
Harris Rd. J5
Harrison St. C1
Hartford I4
Hartford Ave. I1,J1
Hartley St. B5
Harvard H5
Harvey A6
Hasting J4
Hatteras Ave. B3
Haven Dr. J3
Hawkins St. G2
Hawthorne Lane F6
Heathcliff E2
Heather Lane J2
Heathwood Rd. J7
Heflin H6
Heil C3
Hempstead Pl. H5,I5
Henley Pl. H4
Hermitage Rd. H5
Herrin D7
Hickory A4
Hildebrand B2
Hill St., E. F3
Hill St., W. E2,F3
Hillcrest St. B7
Hillsdale J4
Hillside Ave. J3
Hilo Dr. C7
Hobbs D5
Holland B4
Hollis Rd. I1
Holly St. B3
Holroyd J6
Holt Ct. D7
Homorton Pl. F6
Honeywood Ave. B1
Hope Dale H4
Horne Dr. C4
Hoskins Rd. A1
Hough Rd. J2
Hudson D7
Hungerford Pl. I6
Huntley Pl. H5
Hyde Dr. B7
Ideal Way H2
Idlewood Circle I3
Independence Blvd. F1,G6
Industry Rd. I1
Irby J3
Iris Dr. F7
Irma B3
Ironwood St. B7
Irwin E3
Isenhour B4
Ison F1
Iverson Way H2
Ivey Dr. G7
Jackson F5
Jameston Sr. I3
Jasper F3
Jay St. E1
Jefferson F2
Jefferson Davis C4
Jenkins D2
Jennings B3
Jersey J2
Jessie Court B4
Jewel St. H6
Joe St. A6
Johnson D4
Johnson Rd. B6
Jones St. C1
Jonquil St. I7
Jordan Pl. D6
Judith J7
Judson C1
Julia Ave. B4
Julien St. G6
Justice Ave. B4
Kasaw A5
Kay C3
Keller Ave. B3
Kendall A2
Kenilworth H3
Kenmore G5
Kennesaw Dr. B3
Kenney St. C3
Kennon St. E6
Kensington Dr. F6
Kentucky B1
Kenwood F6
Keswick D5
Kings Dr., S. G4,H4
Kingsbury Dr. G6
Kingston Ave., E. G3
Kingston Ave., W. F2
Kirkland D1
Kirkwood H3
Kohler C4
Kotonah D2
LaSalle C1
LaSalle St. B2
Laburnum Ave. G6
Lake D1
Lakeview C1
Lakewood C1
Lamar Ave. G5
Lander St. C1
Laurel Ave. G6,H5
Leigh Ave. D6
Lenox Ave. G3
Leota Dr. B6
Leroy St. I6
Lexington G3
Liberty F3
Liddell St., W E4
Lilac Rd. I3
Lilington Ave. G4
Lima D2
Lincoln F2
Linda Ln. J7
Linden Ln. E5
Linganore G3
Linwood Ave. B1
Little Hope J2
Lloyd D4
Lockhart Dr. H3
Lockley Dr. I5
Lockridge Rd. J1
Logle Ave. F7
Lombardy Circle H4
Long F4
Long Branch F5
Lorene Ave. J4
Louise Ave. F5
Lucena St. C5
Ludlow B2
Lundhurst Ave. G2
Lunsford Place D6
Lynnwood J3
Lyon F7
Macathur Ave. B4
Madison D3
Madrid Rd. B3
Magnolia Ave. G2
Malvern Rd. I5
Manhasset J1
Maple Grove A2
Marguerita E7
Maribe Ave. B2
Marlwood Terr. I3
Marsh Rd. H2
Marshall H2
Martin St. D3
Marvin Rd. I7
Marvista J3
Maryland Ave. I4
Masonic F7
Matheson Ave. D6,E7
Mathis D1
Mattoon C2
May St. H1
May View Dr. H7
Mayfield I2
McAlway 17,J7
McCall St. J5
McClintock Rd. G6
McDonald B2,H2
McDowell St. E5
McDowell St., N. D7,F4
McDowell St., S. F4
McQuay D1
Meacham St. H2
Meadow Brook I6
Melbourne Ct. H2
Melchor Ave. I7
Melita C2
Mercury St. C7
Merlane Dr. A7
Merriman Ave. F2
Merwick Cir. J7
Metals Dr. A6
Meyer,N. D6
Middleton Dr. H5
Midfield B7
Miles Ct. C3
Millbrook Rd. I7
Millerton Ave. E1
Mimosa Ave. E6
Mint St. F3
Mitchell St. B3
Mohigan H7
Monterey B2
Montgomery D2
Montrose Ct. H6
Mooney D7
Moorehead St., E. F3
Moorehead St., W. E2
Moravian Ln. H5
Moretz Ave. C4
Morningside Dr. G7
Morrow F4
Morson D1
Moss St. C4
Moultrie St. I1
Mt. Vernon G3
Mulberry C3
Murdoch Rd. D7
Murray Hill Rd. J1
Museum Dr. I6
Museum Pl. H6
Myers St. F4
Myrtle G3
Nandina St. F6
Nassau Blvd. F6
Nelson Ave. B1
New Castle C3
New Castle C3
New Hope H3
New Hope H3
Newland Rd. B3
Norcross E7
Norfolk H1
Norris Ave. C4
North Gate J1
Northcliffe A2
Northcrest B7
Northerly Rd. B4
Northhaven Dr. B7
Northmore C7
Norton Rd. I4
Norwell D7
Norwood Dr. C1
Oaklawn Ave. D4
Oaks Rd. C4
Oakwood Ave. D7
October C1
Onyz C2
Opal St. D1
Orange St. H6
Ordermore H3
Oregon St. C1
Orvis St. C3
Osborne G5
Osmond F1
Otts St. F5
Oxford Pl I5
Paddock J2
Palmer F2,F3
Pamlico St. F6
Park Ave., E. G3
Park Ave., W. F2
Park Dr. F5
Park Rd. J3,H3
Parkside Dr. D1
Parkway Dr. D1
Parkwood Ave. E6
Patch B4
Patterson C7
Patton Ave. C3
Pearson St. E6
Pebble St. A6
Pecan Ave. F6,G5
Pelton St. H1
Pembroke I4
Pender J4
Penman F2
Pennsylvania B1
Perrin Place H5
Phifer E4
Philemon C7
Picaroy J4
Pierce St. H3
Pine Grove Ave. B6
Pine St. E3
Pine St., N. D5
Pinewood Circle J5
Pinkney Ave. D6
Pitts Dr. C2
Placid I6
Plainwood A1
Plantation J3
Planters C1
Plymouth Ave. D4
Poindexter Dr. H2
Polk St. D4
Pompano St. A1
Poplar St., N. D5,E3
Poplar,S E3
Portland I5
Post St. F2
Prince St. B1
Princeton Ave. I3
Prospect F5
Providence J5
Providence Rd. H5,I5
Pryor St. D1
Purnell Ct. J5
Queens I4
Queens Rd. H4
Queens Rd., E. J4
Queens Rd., W. I4
Quentin Pl. B2
Quincy F2
Rachel St. C5
Radcliffe Ave. I4
Radio E2
Rainbow B2
Raleigh St. C7
Ramona C1
Rampart G2
Randolph Rd. I6
Ravencroft Dr. D1
Rayon St. B1
Redbud C2
Reece J3
Remington B2
Remus G1
Renner C3
Rennsselaer G3
Rensford Ave. I5
Reynolds Dr. J2
Ridgecrest I7
Ridgedale A7
Ridgeway Ave. G5
Ridgewood J3
Ringwood D1
Ritch Ave. C6
Robinson Ave. C6
Rockford J1
Rocklyn J3
Rockway Dr. G7
Rodman I6
Roland F7
Romany Rd. G3
Rose D1
Rosetta C2
Rosewell Ave. J4
Roslyn Ave. C2,D2
Royal Ct. F3
Rozzelles Ferry Rd. D2
Rush D1
Russell Ave. C3
Rutgers Ave. B7
Salem Dr. I3
Samuel B4
Sandalwood Rd. H6
Sanders C2
Scaleybark I1
School St. F6
Scotland Ave. I5
Scott Ave. H3
Sedgefield I2
Sedgewood J6
Seldon Dr. D2
Selwyn Ave. I4
Senior B2
September Ln. B2
Service St. B5
Shawee Dr. I2
Shenandoah Ave. G6
Sherwood I4
Simplicity B5
Simpson Dr. E7
Skyland Ave. H6
Skyview Rd. F1
Sloan St. I1
Smallwood C2
Smith St. E4
Sofley Rd. B7
Solomon D2
Somerset Dr. I3
South Blvd. G2,H2
Southwest Blvd. B2
Southwood F2
Sparrow Mill Rd. D3
Spencer D7
Spratt St. D4
Spring St. D4
Springdale H2
Spruce St. F1
St. Andrews Ln. F7
St. Bernard C6
St. George St. G7
St. John B3
St. Luke B3
St. Mark B3
St. Paul B3
Stancill Pl. I6
Stanford Pl. I4
Stanley Ave. H7
Starita Rd. A6
State St. D2
Statesville Ave. B4,D4
Sterling Rd. J3
Stevens Seigle F5
Stonewall, E. F3
Stonewall, W. F3
Stoneybrook Rd. E7
Stratford E7
Suffolk Pl. J6
Sugar Creek C7
Summit Ave. D3,E2
Summit Ave., W. F2
Sumter D2
Sunderland J5
Sunnyside Ave. F5
Sunset Dr. I2
Suttle Ave. F1
Sutton B2
Sycamore E3
Sylvania D5
Syracuse Dr. B2
Tanglewood Ln. J5
Tappan Pl. D7
Tate C2
Taylor Ave. B3
Television Ln. H7
Templeton G3
Tennessee B1
The Plaza D7
Thera Dr. B7
Thomas F6
Thrift Rd. E1
Thrush Ln. A6
Tippan Ave. F6
Toal St. B5
Toomey Ave. G1
Topaz St. B6
Torrence St. G4
Townes Rd. J3
Trade St. D2,F4
Trade St., E. F4
Trade St., W. E3
Tranquil J3
Tremont G2,G3
Trentwood A3
Truman Rd. F7
Tryclan I1
Tryon St., N. C7,E4
Tryon St., S. F3,H1
Tuckoseegee Rd. E2
Turner Ave. D2
Twiford Pl. I5
Twinfield A2
Tyngway J6
Tyson St. I1
University J7
Unstead St. E6
Van Buren D3
Van Every St. F5
Van Ness H5
Vance, E. F3
Vance, W. F3
Vanderbuilt C4,F5
Vane Ct. B5
Vanizer D1
Vernon Dr. J6
Victoria E3
Vine D2
Vinewood H7
Vinton C3
Virginia Ave. E7
Waco St. G4
Waddell St. C3
Wadsworth E5
Wainwright B4
Wales J3
Walnut Ave. E2
Walter Oak Rd. J7
Ware St. B5
Warp St. C7
Washburn Ave. H7
Washington St. C3
Washington, W. G2
Waterbury J2
Webster Pl. I1
Weddington Dr. G6
Welker G4
Wellesley Ave. I4
Wells St. C5
Wembley Dr. G7
Wendover Rd. J5
Wendwood Ln. I6
Wesley D7
Westbrook E3
Westfield Rd. J3
Westminster J4
Westmoreland St. G7
Westover St. G6
Wheatley Ave. I6
Whisnant D3
Whitby Ln. J7
Whitehaven D2
Whiting D7
Wickford G2
Willow Oak Rd. J3
Wilmore Dr. F2
Wilson Ave. A3
Wilson Ln. A7
Windsor Ave. I3
Winnifred F2
Winston C5
Winston Dr. D7
Winter St. F7
Winthrop H2
Wolfberry D5
Wolfe F7
Wood Valley A2
Woodcrest G2
Woodlark Ln. J7
Woodruff Pl. E2
Woodside Ave. D6
Woodvale D2
Woodward Ave. C4
Worthington Ave. G3
Woyt St. C4
Wren F1
Wrenwood J6
Wrinston B3
Wyanoke G6
Yale Pl. I3
Yellowstone D1
Yonkers B6
Yorkshire I1
Youngblood H1
1st G4
1st St., W. E2,F3
1st, E. F3
2nd St., E. F3
2nd St., W. E2,F3
3rd St., E. F3
3rd,W. E3
4th St. Ext. E2
4th St., E. F4
4th St., W. E2,E3
5th St., E. F4,G5
5th W. E3
6th St., E. F4
6th W. E3
7th St. G5
7th St., E. E4
7th,W. E3
8th St., E. E4,G5
8th St., W. E4
9th St., E. E4,G6
9th St., W. E4
10th St. F5
10th St., E. E4
10th St., W. E4
11th St., E. E4
11th St., W. D3,E4
12th St. E4
12th St., W. D3
13 St., E. E5
15th St. E4
15th St., E. E5
16th St., E. E5
17th St., E. E5
18th St., E. E6
19th E. E5
19th St., E. E6
20th E. E5
20th St., E. E6
21st E. E5
22nd E. E5
23rd,E. D5
24th E. E6
24th St., W. D5
25th, E. D6
26th E. D5
26th, W. D5
27th, E. D6
27th, W. D5
28th St., E. D6
28th, W. D6
29th, W. C6
30th St., W. C6
31st, W. C6
32nd St. D6
32nd St., W. C6
33rd St., E. D6
34th St., E. D6
35th St., E. D7
36th St., E. D7
37th St.,E. D7

CHICAGO

Aberdeen K13-16
Ada K12-16
Adams J-L14
Albany J12-16
Alexander L15
Allport K15
Almond J14
Alta Vista Ter. K11
Altgeld J-L12
Anacona K13
Anson Pl. J13
Arbour Pl. K14
Arcade Pl. K14
Arch K16
Archer L15
Arlington Pl. L12
Armitage J-K12
Armour K13
Artesian J12-16
Arthington J-L14
Ashland K12-16
Astor L13
Attrill J12
Augusta Blvd. J-K13
Avondale J-K12
Balbo Dr. L-M14
Banks L13
Barber L15
Barry J-L11
Bauwans K13
Beach J-K13
Beaubien Ct. L14
Belden J-K12
Bell J12-16
Bellevue Pl. L13
Benson K16
Besly Ct. K12
Bingham J12
Bishop K13-16
Bissell K-L12
Blackhawk K-L13
Blanchard Ct. L16
Bliss K13
Bloomingdale J-K12
Blue Island J-K15
Bonaparte K16
Bonfield K16
Bosworth K12
Boulevard Way J16
Bowler J14
Broad K16
Bross J16
Browning M16
Burling L12
Burton Pl. L13
Cabrini K-L14
California J12-16
Calumet M15-16
Cambridge L12-13
Campbell J12-16
Canal L14-16
Canalport K-L15
Carpenter K13-16
Carroll J-L14
Caton J12
Cedar L13
Cermak Rd. J-M15
Chanay J12
Charleston J12
Cherry K13
Chestnut K-L13
Chicago J-M13
Churchill J12
Claremont J12-16
Clark St. L12-15
Cleaver K13
Cleveland L13
Clifton K12
Clinton L14-15
Clybourn K12
Commonwealth L12
Concord Pl. J-L12
Congress Pkwy. J-L14
Corbett K15-16
Cortez Dr. J-K13
Cortland J-K12
Couch Pl. L14
Court Pl. L14
Crilly L12
Crosby L13
Crowell K16
Crystal J-K13
Cullerton J-L15
Damen K12-16
Dayton K12
Dean K13
Dearborn L13-16
Dekoven L14
Delaware Pl. L13
Deming Pl. J-L12
Denvir J14
Depot Pl. L15
Des Plaines L13-15
Dewitt Pl. L13
Dickens J-L12
Division J-L13
Dominick K12
Dr. M. L. King Dr. M15-16
Draper K12
Drummond Pl. J-L12
Eastman K-L13
Eberhart M16
Edward Ct. L12
Eleanor K16
Elias Ct. K16
Elizabeth K13-16
Elk Grove K12-13
Ellen K13
Ellis M16
Elm L13
Elston J12,K13
Emerald L16
Erie J-L13
Ernst Ct. L13
Eugenie L12
Evans Ct. L13
Evergreen J-L13
Fair Pl. L13
Fairbanks Ct. L13
Fairfield J12-16
Farrell K16
Federal L14-16
Felton Ct. L13
Ferdinand J13
Fern Ct. L12
Field Plaza Dr. M15
Fifth J14
Fillmore J-K14
Financial L14
Flournoy J-K14
Ford L15
Francis Pl. J12
Francisco J12-16
Franklin L14
Franklin Blvd. J13
Fremont K12-13
Fry K13
Fuller K16
Fullerton J-L12
Fulton J-L14
Garland Ct. L14
Geneva Ter. L12
Germania Pl. L13
Giles M16
Gladys J-L14
Goethe L13
Grady Ct. K16
Grand J-L13
Grant Pl. L12
Gratten K16
Green L14-16
Greenview K12-13
Grenshaw J-L15
Grove L15
Haddon J-K13
Haines L13
Halsted L12-16
Hamilton J12-16
Hampden Ct. L12
Harrison J-L14
Hartland Ct. K16
Hastings J-K15
Haynes Ct. K16
Heath J15
Henry Ct. J12
Hermitage K12-16
Hickory K13
Hill L13
Hillock K16
Hirsch J13
Hobbie L13
Hobson K12
Hoey K16
Holly K13
Homer J-K12
Honore K12-16
Hooker K13
Horner J12
Howe L12-13
Hoyne Ave. J12-16
Hoyt J16
Hubbard J-L13
Hudson L12-13
Huguelet Pl. L13
Humboldt Blvd. J12
Humboldt Dr. J13
Huron J-M13
Illinois L13
Indiana L15-16
Institute Pl. L13
Iowa G-K13
Iron K16
Jackson Blvd. J-L14
Jackson Dr. L-M14
Jasper Pl. K16
Jefferson L14-15
Jenssen Blvd. K11
Jessie Ct. J13-14
Jones J12
Jourdan Ct. L15
Julia Ct. J12
Julian K13
Justine K14-16
Kedzie Ave. J12-16
Kedzie Blvd. J12
Keeley K16
Kemper Pl. L12
Kenmore K12
Kingsbury K12-14
Kinzie J-L14
Laflin K14-16
Lake J-L14
Lake Park M16
Lake Shore Dr. L13
Lake View L12
Lakewood K12
Larrabee L12-13
Le Moyne J-K13
Leavitt J12-16
Lee Pl. J-K13
Lessing K13
Levee K16
Lexington J-L14
Liberty K-L15
Lill K12
Lincoln L12
Lincoln Park W. L12
Linden Pl. J12
Lister K12
Lituanica K16
Lloyd K16
Lock K16
Locust L13
Logan Blvd. J12
Loomis K14-16
Loomis Pl. K16
Louis Munoz Marin Dr J13
Lowe L15-16
Lumber K-L15
Luther Pl. J16
Lyman K16
Lyndale J-J12
Lytle K14-15
Madison J-L14
Magnolia K12
Mansfield K15
Maple L12
Maplewood J12-16
Marcey K12
Marion Ct. K13
Marshall Blvd. J-K16
Marshfield K12-16
Mary K16
Maud K12
Mautene Ct. K13
Maxwell K-L15
May K13-16
Maypole J-K14
McClurg Ct. M13
McFetrige Dr. M15
McLean J-K12
Medill J-K12
Meis Van Der Rohe L13
Mendell K12
Menominee L12
Meyer L12
Michigan L13-16
Miller K14-15
Milwaukee K13
Moffat J-K12
Mohawk L12
Monroe J-L14
Monroe Dr. L-M14
Montana J-K12
Moore L13
Moorman K13
Morgan K14-16
Mozart J12-16
Nada K13
New M13-14
Newberry L15
Newburg L15
Noble K12-13
Normal L15-16
North J-L12
North Branch K13
North Park L12-13
North Water M13
Norton K14
Nursery K12
O'Brien L15
Oak Pl. K13
Oakley Blvd. J13
Ogden Blvd. K14,L12
Ohio J-M13
Ontario J-M13
Orchard L12-13
Orleans L12-13
Oswego K13-14
Palmer J12
Palmer Blvd. J12
Park M13
Parnell L16
Paulina K12-16
Pearl Ct. L12
Pearson L13
Peoria L13-16
Peshtigo Ct. M13
Pierce J-K13
Pine G13-14
Pitney Ct. K16
Plymouth Ct. L14-15
Poe K12
Point J12
Polk J-L14
Poplar K16
Potomac J-K13
Prairie L15-16
Princeton L16
Prindiville J12
Quincy J-L14
Quinn K-L16
Race J-K13
Racine K12-16
Randolph Dr. J-M14
Rhodes M16
Rice J-K13
Richmond J12-16
Ridge Dr. L12
Ritchie Ct. L13
River E. M14
Robinson K16
Rockwell J12-16
Roosevelt Rd. J-L15
Roslyn Pl. L12
Ruble L15
Rundell Pl. K14
Rush L13
Sacramento Blvd. J12-16
Sacramento Dr. J15
Sacramento Sq. J13
Sangamon K13-16
Schick Pl. L13
Schiller J-L13
Scott L13
Sedgwick L13
Seeley K12-16
Seminary K12
Seneca L13
Senour K16
Shakespeare J-L12
Sheffield K12
Shelby Ct. K15
Sherman L14
Shields L16
Short K16
Siebens Pl. L13
Solidarity Dr. M15
Southport K12
St. Clari L13
St. Georges Ct. J12
St. Helen J12
St. James Pl. L12
St. Mary J12
St. Michaels Ct. L12
St. Paul J-L12
Stark K16
State L13-16
Stave J12
Stetson L14
Stewart L15-16
Stockton Dr. L12
Stone L13
Streeter Dr. M13-14
Sullivan L13
Superior J-M13
Surrey Ct. K12
Talman J12-16
Taylor J-L14
Terra Cotta Pl. K12
Thomas J-K13
Throop K12-16
Troy J12-16
Union L13-16
Van Buren J-M14
Vernon M16
Vernon Pk. Pl. K-L14
Viaduct Dr. M15
Vine L12
Wabansia J-K12
Wabash L13-16
Wacker Dr. L14
Waldron Dr. M15
Wallace L15-16
Walnut J-L14
Walton J-L13
Warren Blvd. J-L14
Washburne J-K15
Washington Blvd. J-L14
Washtenaw Ave. J12-16
Water North M14
Water South L14
Wayman J-L14
Wayne K12
Webster J-L12
Weed K-L13
Wells L12-16
Wendell L13
Western Ave. J12-16
Whipple J12-16
Wicker Park K13
Wieland L13
Wilcox J14
Willard Ct. K13-14
Willets Ct. J12
Willow K12
Wilmot J12
Winchester K12-16
Winnebago J12
Wisconsin K-L12
Wolcott K12-16
Wood K12-16
Wrightwood J-L12
8th L14
9th L14
10th K-L14
11th Pl. L15
12th Pl. H-L15
13th J-L15
13th Pl. J-L15
14th G-L15
14th Blvd. M15
14th Pl. K-L15
15th J-L15
15th Pl. J-L15
16th J-L15
17th J-L15
17th Pl. K-L15
18th J-L15
18th Pl. J-L15
19th J-L15
19th Pl. J-L15
20th Pl. J-L15
21st J-M15
21st Pl. J-K15
22nd L15
22nd Pl. J-L15
23rd J-M15
23rd Pl. J-L15
24th J-M15
24th Blvd. J16
24th Pl. J-L16
25th J-M16
25th Pl. J-L16
26th J-M16
26th Pl. L16
27th J-M16
28th J-L16
28th Pl. L16
29th K-M16
29th Pl. L-M16
30th J-M16
30th Pl. L16
31st J-M16
31st Pl. K-M16
32nd J-M16
32nd Pl. K-M16
33rd J-M16
33rd Pl. K-M16
34th J-L16
34th Pl. J-L16
35th J-M16
35th Pl. J-L16
36th J-M16

Scale of Miles

N

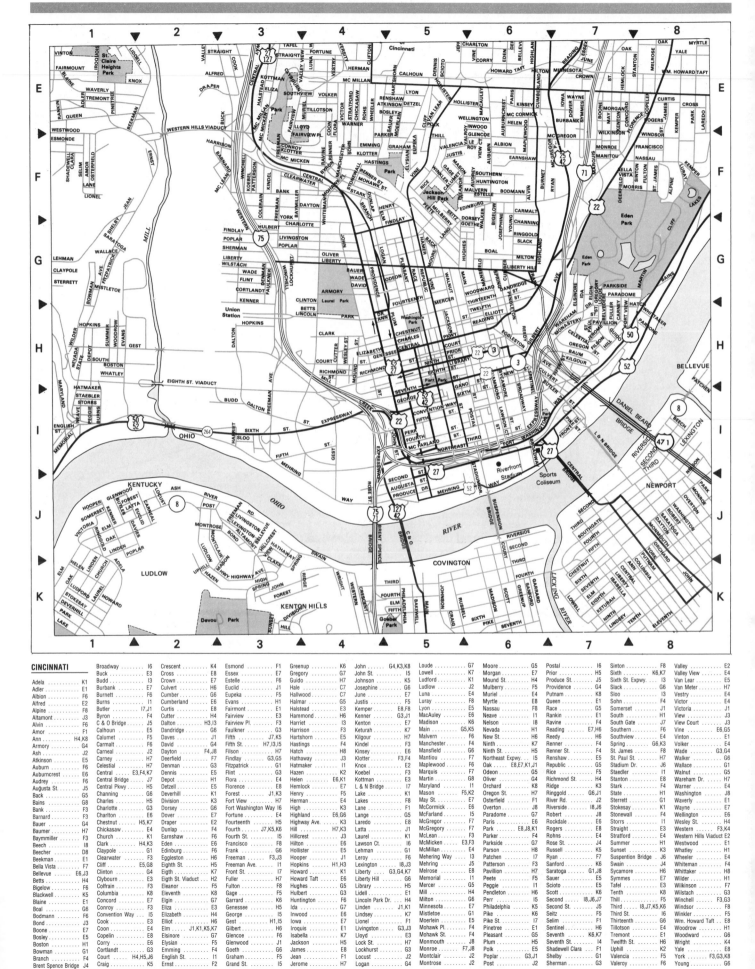

Scale of Miles
0 .1 .2 .3 .4 .5

CINCINNATI

Adela ... K1
Adler ... E1
Albion ... F6
Alfred ... E2
Alpine ... F8
Altamont ... J3
Alvin ... F4
Amor ... F1
Ann ... H4,K8
Armory ... G4
Ash ... J2
Atkinson ... E5
Auburn ... F6
Auburncrest ... F6
Audrey ... F5
Augusta St. ... J5
Back ... G5
Bains ... G8
Bank ... F3
Barnard ... G4
Bauer ... G4
Baumer ... H7
Baymiller ... E4
Beech ... I8
Beecher ... D8
Beekman ... E1
Bella Vista ... E6,J3
Bellevue ... E6,J3
Betts ... H4
Bigelow ... F6
Blackwell ... K5
Blaine ... E1
Boal ... G6
Bodmann ... F6
Bond ... J3
Boone ... E7
Bosley ... F5
Boston ... H1
Bowman ... G1
Branch ... F4
Brent Spence Bridge ... J4

Broadway ... I6
Buck ... E3
Budd ... I3
Burbank ... E7
Burnett ... F6
Burns ... I1
Butler ... I7,J1
Byron ... F4
C & O Bridge ... J5
Calhoun ... E5
Calumet ... F5
Carmalt ... F6
Carneal ... J2
Carney ... H7
Celestial ... H7
Central ... E3,F4,K7
Central Bridge ... J7
Central Pkwy ... H5
Channing ... G6
Charles ... H5
Charlotte ... F3
Charlton ... E6
Chestnut ... H5,K7
Chickasaw ... E4
Church ... H4
Clark ... H4,K3
Claypole ... G1
Clearwater ... F3
Cliff ... E5,G8
Clinton ... G4
Clybourn ... F5
Colfrain ... F3
Columbia ... K8
Concord ... E7
Conroy ... F4
Convention Way ... I5
Cook ... E4
Coon ... E4
Copelin ... E6
Corry ... E6
Cortlandt ... F5
Court ... H4,H5,J6
Craig ... K5

Crescent ... K4
Cross ... E8
Crown ... E7
Culvert ... H6
Cumber ... G6
Cumberland ... E6
Curtis ... E8
Cutter ... H4
Dalton ... H3,I3
Dandridge ... G6
Daves ... J1
David ... G4
Dayton ... F4,J8
Deerfield ... F7
Denman ... G3
Dennis ... E5
Depot ... H1
Detzell ... E5
Deverhill ... K1
Division ... K3
Dorsey ... G6
Dover ... E7
Draper ... F4
Dunlap ... F4
Earnshaw ... F6
Eden ... E6
Edinburg ... F6
Eggleston ... H6
Eighth St. ... H5
Eigth ... K7
Eighth St. Viaduct ... H7
Eleanor ... K8
Eleventh ... K8
Elgin ... G7
Eliza ... E3
Elizabeth ... H4
Elliot ... E6
Elm ... J1,K1,K5,K7
Elsinore ... G7
Elysian ... F5
English St. ... I1
Ernst ... F2

Esmond ... F1
Essex ... E7
Estelle ... F6
Euclid ... J1
Eupeka ... F5
Evans ... H1
Fairfax ... E3
Fairmont ... F5
Fairview ... E3
Fairview Pl. ... F5
Faulkner ... G3
Fifth ... J7,K5
Fifth St. ... H7,I3,I5
Filson ... H7
Findlay ... F3,G5
Fitzpatrick ... G1
Flint ... G3
Flora ... F5
Florence ... E8
Forest ... J1,K3
Fort View ... H7
Fort Washington Way ... I6
Fortune ... E5
Fourth ... J7,K5,K6
Fourteenth ... G5
Frank ... E5
Freeman ... F3,J3
Freeman Ave. ... I1
Front St. ... H7
Fuller ... H7
Fulton ... F5
Gage ... F5
Garrard ... K6
Genessee ... H5
George ... H5,I5
Gest ... H1,I5
Gilbert ... F5
Glencoe ... F6
Glenwood ... J1
Goeth ... G6
Graham ... F5
Grand St. ... I5

Greenup ... K6
Gregory ... G7
Guido ... E7
Hale ... C7
Hallwood ... C7
Halmar ... G5
Halstead ... E3
Hammond ... H6
Harriet ... I3
Harrison ... F3
Hartshorn ... E5
Hastings ... F4
Hatch ... H8
Hathaway ... J3
Hatmaker ... I1
Hazen ... K2
Helen ... E6,K1
Hemlock ... E7
Henry ... F5
Herman ... E4
High ... E6
Highland ... E6,G6
Highway Ave. ... K3
Hill ... H7,K3
Hillcrest ... J3
Hilton ... E6
Hollister ... E5
Hooper ... J1
Hopkins ... H1,H3
Howard ... K1
Howard Taft ... E6
Hughes ... G5
Hulbert ... F6
Huntington ... F6
Ida ... G7
Inwood ... E6
Iowa ... E5
Iroquois ... E1
Isabella ... K7
Jackson ... H5
James ... H5
Jean ... F1
Jerome ... H7

John ... G4,K3,K8
John St. ... I5
Johnson ... K5
Josephine ... G6
June ... E7
Justis ... F5
Kemper ... E8,F8
Kenner ... G3,J1
Kenton ... E7
Keturah ... K7
Kilgour ... H7
Kindel ... F4
Kinsey ... F6
Klotter ... F3,F4
Knox ... E2
Koebel ... F4
Kottman ... E3
L & N Bridge ... J6
Lake ... K1
Lakes ... F8
Lane ... F1
Lange ... G5
Laredo ... E6
Latta ... J1
Laurel ... K1
Lawson ... H6
Lawson Ct. ... H6
Leroy ... G1
Lexington ... I3,J3
Liberty ... G3,G4,K7
Liberty Hill ... G6
Library ... H5
Lincoln Park Dr. ... H4
Linden ... J1,K1
Lindsey ... K7
Lionel ... F1
Livingston ... G3,J3
Lloyd ... H5
Lock St. ... H7
Lockhurst ... H7
Locust ... J2
Logan ... G4

Loude ... G7
Lowell ... K7
Ludford ... K1
Ludlow ... J2
Luna ... E7
Luray ... F8
Lyon ... E5
MacAuley ... E6
Madison ... K7
Main ... G5,K5
Malvern ... F6
Manchester ... F4
Mansfield ... F6
Mantiou ... F7
Maplewood ... F6
Marquis ... F7
Martin ... G8
Maryland ... I1
Mason ... F5,K2
May St. ... E7
McCormick ... E6
McFarland ... I5
McGregor ... E6
McGregory ... F7
McLean ... F4
McMicken ... E3,F3
Mehering Way ... I3
Melrose ... E8
Memorial ... G5
Mercer ... G5
Mering ... I3
Milton ... G6
Minnesota ... E6
Mistletoe ... G1
Mohawk Pl. ... F4
Monmouth ... J8
Monroe ... F7,J8
Montclair ... J2
Montrose ... J2

Moore ... G5
Morgan ... E7
Mound St. ... H4
Mulberry ... F5
Muriel ... E4
Myrtle ... E1
Nassau ... F7
Neave ... I1
Nelson ... I8
Nevada ... H1
New St. ... H6
Ninth ... K7
Ninth St. ... H5
Northeast Expwy. ... I5
Oak ... E8,E7,K1,J1
Odeon ... G5
Oliver ... G4
Orchard ... K8
Oregon St. ... H7
Osterfield ... F1
Overton ... J8
Paradome ... G7
Paris ... E6
Park ... E8,J8,K1
Parker ... F4
Parkside ... G7
Parson ... H8
Patchen ... I7
Patterson ... F3
Pavillion ... G7
Peete ... F5
Peggie ... I1
Pendleton ... H5
Perr ... H6
Philadelphia ... K5
Pike ... K6
Pike St. ... I7
Pinetree ... E1
Pleasant ... G5
Plum ... H5
Polk ... F5
Poplar ... G3,J1
Post ... J2

Postal ... I6
Prior ... H5
Produce St. ... I5
Providence ... G4
Putnam ... K8
Queen ... E1
Race ... F5
Rankin ... E1
Ravine ... F4
Reading ... E7,H6
Reedy ... H6
Renner ... E5
Renner St. ... F5
Renshaw ... E5
Republic ... F5
Rice ... F5
Richmond St. ... H4
Ridge ... K3
Ringgold ... G6,J1
River Rd. ... J2
Riverside ... I8,J6
Robert ... J8
Rockdale ... E6
Rogers ... E8
Rohns ... E8
Rose St. ... J4
Russell ... K5
Ryan ... F7
Sanford ... K6
Saratoga ... G1,J8
Sauer ... E5
Scioto ... E5
Scott ... K5
Second ... I8,J6,J7
Selim ... F1
Sentinel ... E4
Seventh ... K6,K7
Seventh St. ... I4
Shadewell Clara ... E6
Shelby ... G1
Sherman ... G3

Sinton ... F8
Sixth ... K6,K7
Sixth St. Expwy. ... I3
Slack ... G6
Sloo ... I3
Sohn ... F4
Somerset ... J1
South ... H1
South Gate ... J7
Southern ... F6
Southview ... E4
Spring ... G6,K3
St. James ... F8
St. Paul St. ... H7
Stadium Dr. ... J6
Stanton ... E8
Stark ... F4
State ... H1
Sterrett ... G1
Stokesay ... K5
Stonewall ... F4
Storrs ... H1
Straight ... E3
Stratford ... E2
Summer ... H1
Sunset ... K3
Suspension Bridge ... J6
Swain ... J4
Sycamore ... H6
Symmes ... E5
Tafel ... E3
Thill ... F5
Third ... I8,J7,K5,K6
Third St. ... I6
Thirteenth ... G6
Tillotson ... E4
Tremont ... E1
Twelfth St. ... H6
Uphill ... K2
Valencia ... F5
Valeroy ... F6

Valley ... E2
Valley View ... E4
Van Lear ... E5
Van Meter ... H7
Vestry ... E5
Victor ... E4
Victoria ... J1
View ... J3
View Court ... J3
Vine ... E6,G5
Vinton ... E1
Volker ... E1
Wade ... G3,G4
Walker ... G6
Wallace ... G1
Walnut ... H5
Warner ... F4
Washington ... J8
Waverly ... E1
Wayne ... E6
Wellington ... E6
Western ... F3,K4
Western Hills Viaduct ... E2
Westwood ... E1
Wheeler ... F4
Whatley ... H1
Whiteman ... E4
Whittaker ... H7
Wilder ... H1
Wilkinson ... F7
Winchell ... F3,G3
Windsor ... F8
Winkler ... F6
Woodrow ... H1
Woodward ... G4
Wright ... K4
Yale ... E8
York ... F3,G3,K8
Young ... G6

Scale of Miles

0 .1 .2 .3 .4

CLEVELAND

Abbey	G3
Apple	H1
Auburn	H4
Bailey	H1
Barber	H2
Bolivar	D5
Bradford	F3
Brayton	H5
Brevier	G3
Bridge	G2
British	E2
Broadway	F6,G7
Buckley	H1
Burwell	F8
Canal	E4
Carnegie	D8
Carroll	G2
Carter	E3
Castle	I3
Cedar	D8
Center	E1
Central	D7
Chatham	G2
Chester	C7,D5
Church	F1
Cleveland Memorial Shoreway	C3,D3
Clinton	F1
Cloud	I1
Clyde	H5
College	G5
Columbus	G3
Community College Ave.	E7,E8
Cooper	B8
Crayton	G8
Croton	F8
Crown	G4
Cuyahoga	F5
Czar	I8
Davenport	B5
Dille	H7,H8
Division	E1
Dodge	C5
Douse	H8
Drylock	F5
Eagle	E4
Elm	D1
Erie	D5
Erieside	B3,C3
Fall	E3
Fairfield	G4
Film	H3
Frankfort	D2
Franklin	F1,F2
Freeman	G3
French	E2
Front	D2
Fruit	H5
Fulton	H2
Gallup	H8
Gehring	G3
Hamilton	B5
Hancock	H2
Harrison	F5
Hemlock	E2
Houston	H6
Howard	H4
Huron	D5
Independence	G6
Jefferson	G5
Jewett	I8
John	G1
Johnson	D3
Katy	F3
Kelly	B8
Kenilworth	H4
Kenlworth	H4
King	A7
Lakeside	A6,A7,C4
Lakeview Loop Terr.	E1
Leonard	F3
Literary	G5
Longwood	E8
Mable	F2
Mahoning	G3
Marginal,N.	B4
Marginal,S.	B5
Marquard	H5
Martin	H8
Mary	H6
Mayflower	F7
Mentor	I4
Merwin	E2
Miller	G5
Minkton	E5
Monroe	H2
Moore	F3
Mulberry	E1
Northwest Frwy	H1
Old River Road	D2
Ontario	D4
Orange	E6,F8
Orchard	H1
Parafine	G3
Payne	C6
Perkins	C8
Pittsburgh	F6
Professor	G5
Prospect	D4,D8
Quigley	I5
Railroad	G4
Randall	G1
Richner	I1
River	E1
Riverbed	F2
Rockwell	B6,C5
Roseville	H8
Scotham	H6
Scranton	E4
Senora	B7
Severn	H6
Seymour	I2
Siam	H1
Smith	F3
Spruce	E2
St. Clair	C4
St. Olga	H5
St. Tikhon	H5
Stone Levee	E4
Summer	D5
Superior	C4
Terretto	F1
Tom	F3
Train	H2
Transport Rd.	F6,F7
Tremont	H5
Trumbul	G7,G8
University	F4
Vega	H2
Vermont	F1
Vestry	F2
Vincent	D4
Walnut	C4,C5
Washington	E1,E2
Webster	E5
Whitman	G1
Willey	G3
Willow Freeway	G8
Winslow	E2
Woodbine	G1
Woodland	E7
3rd West	D4
4 West	E4
4th East	D4,E5
4th West	D3
5 West	G5,H6
6th East	C4
6 West	D3,G5
7 West	G5
8th West	C2,D3
9th West	C2,D3
9th East	C4
10th West	D2,G4
11 West	I4
11th Pl. West	D2
12 West	I4
12th East	C5
14 West	I4
14th East	C5
15 West	G4
16 West	I4
16th	B5
17 West	G3,I3
17th East	C5
18 West	F3,H3,I3
18th East	B5,C6
19 East	C6,D6
19 West	F3
20 East	C6
20 West	G3
20th East	B5
21 East	C6
22 East	C6,D6,E6
23 East	B6,C6
24 East	E7
25 East	B6
25 West	E2,F2,G3
26 East	B6
26 West	G2
27 East	B7
28 East	D7
29 West	G2
30 East	B7,E7
30 West	G2,I3
31 East	B7
32 East	B7,F7
32 West	F1,G2,I2
33 East	B7,D8,E7,G7
33 West	G2
34 East	B7,E8,F7,G7
35 East	D8,E8,F7
36 West	H1
36 East	J1
37 East	B8,D8,E8,F8,G7
37 West	H1
38 East	A7,B8,D8,E8
38 West	F1,H1,I1,G1
39 East	A8,B8,D7
40 East	A8,F8
40 West	H1
41 East	A8
41 West	H1
42 East	H1
43 East	A8
43 West	J1
44 West	G1,I1
45 East	A8,H8
48 East	I8

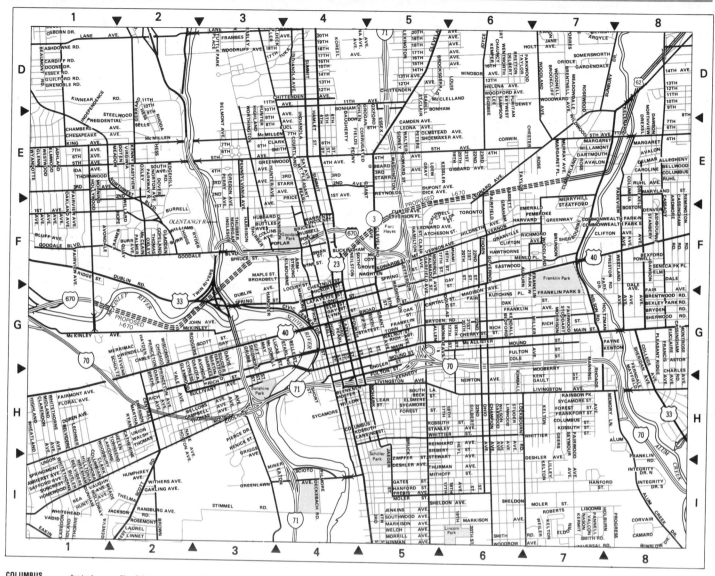

COLUMBUS

Allegheny ... E8
Allen ... G5
Alum ... H8
Alum Creek Dr. ... I8
Amherst Ave. ... I1
Ardmore Rd. ... F8
Argyle ... D7
Armstrong ... F4
Ashbourne ... G5
Ashdowne Rd. ... D1
Ashland Ave. ... E1
Astor ... G8
Atcheson St. ... F5
Auburn ... F6
Avalon ... E7,E8
Avonddale ... F1,G3
Bassett ... E6
Beaumont Rd. ... D1
Beck St. ... H5
Bedford ... F8
Belle St. ... G4
Bellows Ave. ... H2
Bellwood ... E8
Belmont Ave. ... D3
Belvidere ... I1
Bexford ... F8
Bexley Park Rd. ... G8
Blenkner ... H4
Bluff Ave. ... F1
Bonham ... D4,D5
Boston ... F8
Brehl Ave. ... H2
Brentnell Ave. ... D7
Brentwood Rd. ... G8
Bretton ... D6
Brickel ... F4
Broad St. ... G5
Broadbelt ... F3
Brookcliff ... D7
Brooksgerald ... D5
Brown Rd. ... I2
Bruck ... H5
Brunson ... F4
Bryden Rd. ... G5,G8
Buckingham ... F4
Burr ... F2
Burrell ... F2
Butler ... I1
Buttles Ave. ... F3
Cable ... G2
Caldwell Ct. ... F5
Camaro ... I8

Camden Ave. ... E5
Campbell Ave. ... H2
Capital St. ... G5
Cardiff Rd. ... D1
Caroline ... E8
Cassady ... F8
Cassingham Rd. ... E8,G8
Catherine ... H2
Central ... H2
Chambers Ave. ... E1
Champion Ave. ... H6
Charles ... G8
Chauncy ... D6
Cherry St. ... G6
Chesapeake Ave. ... E1
Chester ... E8
Chestnut St. ... F4
Chicago ... G2
Chittenden Ave. ... D4
Clarendon Ave. ... H1
Clarendon Dr. N. ... J1
Clark ... E3,I1
Cleveland Ave. ... D5,F5
Clifton Ave. ... F6,F7
Cole St. ... G6
College Ave. ... F3
Collins Ave. ... F3
Columbia Ave. ... E4
Columbian ... F1
Columbus ... E8,H4
Columbus ... S.H7
Commonwealth Park N. ... F7
Commonwealth Park S. ... F7
Coolidge ... H3
Copeland ... G2
Corrugated ... E4
Corvair ... I8
Corwin ... D7
Courtland ... H4
Cumberland ... E7
Curtis Ave. ... G8
Cypress ... G2
Dakota ... G3
Dale Ave. ... F8
Dana Ave. ... F8
Dartmouth ... E7
Daugherty ... H2
Davis Ave. ... G3
Dawson ... E8,F8
Deckebach Rd. ... I4

Delbert ... D6
Delmar ... E8
Dennison ... F4
Denver ... F8
Deporres ... F2
Dewey ... F2
Dick Ave. ... E5
Doone Dr. ... D1
Doren ... H1
Doten ... H1
Douglas ... G6
Dover ... E4
Dow ... E4
Drexel ... E8
Drexel Ave. ... E8
DuPont Ave. ... E8
Dublin Dr. ... G3
Dublin Rd. ... G3
Dunham ... I1
Durham Dr. ... I1
Eakin Rd. ... I1
Eastview ... E2
Eastwood ... F5
Eaton ... I4
Edgehill Rd. ... E3
Edwards ... F5
Elda St. ... F2
Eldhorn ... I7
Elm St. ... G4
Elmwood Ave. ... E1
Elsmere ... H5
Emerald ... F6
Emerson ... H1
Essex ... E5
Essex Rd. ... D1
Euclaire Ave. ... G8
Euclid ... F2
Eureka ... J1
Fair ... G8
Fair Ave. ... G8
Fairfield ... H7
Fairfield Ave. ... G8
Fairmont Ave. ... H1
Fairwood Ave. ... H7
Ferndale ... E4
Fields ... E4
Filmore ... I7
Floral Ave. ... H1
Forest St. ... H5,H7
Frambes ... D3

Francis Ave. ... G8
Frankfort St. ... H7
Franklin Ave. ... G5
Franklin Park S. ... G7
Franklin Park W. ... F7
Franklin Rd. ... I8
Frebis Ave. ... H6
Front St. ... G4
Gardendale ... D7
Garfield Ave. ... F5
Garling Ave. ... I2
Gates St. ... I5
Gault St. ... H7
Gay ... G3
Gay St. ... F6,G4
Geers ... H7
Geneva ... I1
Gerrard ... F2
Gibbard ... E2
Gibbard Ave. ... E6
Gift St. ... G3
Gilbert St. ... H6
Gladden ... G3
Glenn Ave. ... E1
Glenwood ... G3
Goodale Blvd. ... F1,F2
Governor ... G8
Graham ... F5
Grant ... E5
Grant Ave. ... G5
Granville ... F6
Gray ... G4
Greenlawn Ave. ... I3
Greenway ... F7
Greenwood ... E3
Grenoble Dr. ... D1
Griggs Ave. ... H3
Grove ... G5
Grubb St. ... G3
Guilford Rd. ... D1
Hamilton ... F5
Hamlet St. ... E4
Hanford ... I5,I7
Hanover ... F3
Harrison ... F3
Hartford ... H7
Harvard ... F6
Hawkes ... G3
Hawthorne ... F6
Hayden ... H1
Helen ... H2
Helena Ave. ... D6

Hess ... E2
Heyl Ave. ... H6
Hickory St. ... G4
Higgs ... G4
High St. ... E5
Highland ... E3,H1
Hildreth Ave. ... F6
Hilltonia ... I1
Holburn ... I7
Holloway ... H6
Hollywood ... E1
Holt Ave. ... D7
Holton Ave. ... H2
Holtzman ... H5
Home ... F2
Homewood ... I1
Hope ... F2
Hoster ... H4
Howard St. ... E5
Hubbard ... F3
Humphrey Ave. ... I1
Hunt Ave. ... I5
Hunter ... D3
Ida Ave. ... E5
Independence ... E1
Indianola ... H6
Indianola Ave. ... E4
Ingleside ... F3
Integrity Dr. N. ... I8
Integrity Dr. S. ... I8
Isabell ... D4
Iuka ... E5
Jackson Rd. ... I2
Jaeger St. ... H5
Jane ... D7
Jefferson ... F5
Jefferson Pl. ... F5
Jenkins Ave. ... I5
John Ave. ... G2
Joyce Ave. ... D7
Karon ... D7
Kelenard ... D8
Kelton ... H7,I7
Kemper ... D6
Kendall ... H2
Kennedy ... H5
Kenny ... E2
Kent St. ... H7
Kenton ... H7
Kermit ... I7
Keswet ... D6
Keywest ... D6
Kilbourne ... G5
Kimball ... H6
King Ave. ... E1

Kingston ... J5
Kinnear Rd. ... D1
Korbel ... D6
Kossuth ... G4
Kossuth St. ... H5,H7
Kramer ... D7
Kutchins Place ... G6
Lane Ave. ... D1,D3
Lansing St. ... H5
Larcomb ... H1
Laurel ... I2
Lazelle St. ... G4
Lechner ... H1
Lee ... D6
Leona Ave. ... E5
Leonard Ave. ... E6,F5
Lexington ... D5
Lilley ... I7
Lincoln St. ... F4
Linden ... C6
Linnet ... I2
Linwood Ave. ... H6
Liscomb ... I7
Livingston Ave. ... H5,H7
Lockbourne Rd. ... H6
Locust St. ... G4
Loew ... E5
Long St. ... G5
Louis ... D6
Lucas St. ... G3
Lynn St. ... G4
Madison Ave. ... H5
Main St. ... G5,G7
Manning ... H7
Maple St. ... F3
Marconi ... F4
Margaret ... E7,E8
Margaret Pl. ... E7
Markinson Ave. ... I6
Martha ... G3
Martin ... G3
Maryland St. ... E7
May ... H8
Mayfield ... H8
McAllister ... G6
McClain ... E4
McClelland ... D5
McCoy ... G5
McDowell ... H3
McKinley ... G2
McKinley Ave. ... G1
McMillen ... E2,E3

Meade ... I1
Meadow ... E2
Meadowdale ... D7
Memory Ln. ... H8
Menlo Pl. ... F6
Meredith ... D7
Merrimac ... G2
Merryhill ... F7
Michigan ... E3
Midland ... I1,J1
Midland Ave. ... H1
Midway ... K7
Miller Ave. ... G7
Miner ... I3
Mithoff St. ... I5
Mohawk ... H5
Moler St. ... I5,I7
Monroe Ave. ... F5,G6
Montrose Ave. ... G8
Mooberry ... D6
Morning ... E1
Morrison ... G3
Mound ... H3
Mound St. ... G5,G6
Mt. Pleasant ... E4
Mt. Vernon Ave. ... F5
Murray Ave. ... E2
Nace Ave. ... H2
Naghten ... G5
Nashoba ... I1
Nason ... I7
Neilston ... F4
Nelson Rd. ... E6
Newton Ave. ... H6
Northwest Blvd. ... D2
Norton Ave. ... E2
Oak St. ... G5,G6
Oakland Ave. ... F1
Oakwood Ave. ... H5
Ohio Ave. ... H5
Ohlen ... D4
Oregon Ln. ... E3
Oriole ... D1
Osborn Dr. ... D1
Osceola Ave. ... B4
Oxford ... D4
Oxley ... E2,F2
Palmer Ave. ... F2
Pannell ... I7
Park Dr. ... I7
Parkview Ave. ... E8

Parkway N. ... E2
Parkwood ... D6
Payne ... G8
Pearl ... G4
Pearl St. ... G4
Peasley ... D3
Pembroke ... F7
Pennsylvania Ave. ... E3
Penny ... I4
Perry Ave. ... E3
Peters ... E5
Pleasant Ridge ... G8
Poplar ... F6
Powell ... F8
Presidential ... E1
Preston Rd. ... F8
Price ... E5
Princeton ... G2
Princeton Ave. ... H2
Puritan ... D6
Quay ... G3
Rainbow Park ... H7
Ransburg Ave. ... D7
Rea Ave. ... I1
Reeb ... A8
Reinhard Ave. ... H5
Remington ... F8
Renick St. ... H3
Reynolds ... E5
Rhoads Ave. ... H7
Rhoda ... G5
Rich ... H2
Rich St. ... G5,G7,H3
Richmond ... E7
Ridge St. ... F1
Roberts ... I7
Rodgers ... G2
Rose ... E7
Rosemont ... I1
Rosewood ... D7
Ross ... E8
Ruhl ... E8
Russell ... F4
Ryan ... F4
Ryder ... F2
Safford Ave. ... H1
Sampson ... D6
Say Ave. ... E5
Schultz ... G3
Scioto ... I5
Scott Rd. ... I2
Scott St. ... G3

Sells ... E2
Seneca Park Pl. ... F8
Seymour Ave. ... H7
Shady Hill ... C1
Shadywood ... C1
Sheldon ... I6
Sheldon Ave. ... I5
Sherbourne ... F7
Sheridan Ave. ... G8
Sherwood Rd. ... G8
Shoemaker Ave. ... E5
Short St. ... H4
Sidney ... H5
Siebert St. ... H5
Sigsbee ... D6
Skidmore St. ... G3
Smith ... E3
Smith Rd. ... I6,I7
Somersworth ... D7
Souder Ave. ... G3
South Ave. ... E2
South Ln. ... I1
Spring St. ... F5,G3
Springmont ... I1
Spruce St. ... F1
St. Claire Ave. ... D5
St. Claire ... D5
Stanbery ... F8
Stanley Ave. ... H5
Starling ... G3
Starr ... E4,E5
State St. ... G5
Steelwood ... D1
Stevens ... G3
Stewart Ave. ... H5
Stimmel Rd. ... I3
Stoddart ... I7
Stratford ... F7
Studer Ave. ... H5
Sullivant Ave. ... G3
Summit ... D4,E4
Suncrest ... D7
Swan St. ... G4
Sycamore ... H4,H5
Sycamore St. ... H5
Talmadge St. ... F7
Taylor ... E5
Thelma ... I2
Thomas Ave. ... H3
Thorn ... E7
Thornwood ... E1
Thurber ... F3

Thurman Ave. ... I5
Toronto ... F6
Town St. ... G5
Townsend ... H2
Tuttle Park Pl. ... D3
Twin Rivers ... G4
Union ... H2,I1
Valcon ... I1
Vaughn ... I1
Vernon St. ... F6
Vine St. ... F4
Virginia ... E3
Wall St. ... G4
Walnut St. ... G5
Walters ... F4
Warren St. ... F4
Washington Ave. ... G5
Weiler ... I1
Wendell ... G2
Wentworth ... D6
Westland Ave. ... E7
Westwood Ave. ... E1
Wheatland ... H1
Whitehead ... I1
Whitehorne ... H1
Whitehorne Ave. ... H1
Whittier St. ... H5,H7
Wildwood ... E7
Willamont ... E7
Willard ... E7
Williams ... F2
Willow ... H5
Wilson Ave. ... H6
Windsor Ave. ... D5
Wisconsin ... G2
Withers Ave. ... I2
Woodbury ... H1
Woodford Ave. ... G8
Woodland ... F7
Woodland Ave. ... F7
Woodnell ... D7
Woodrow ... D7
Woodward ... D7
Worthington ... E3
Wrexham ... I3
Wyandotte ... E1
Yale Ave. ... H2
Zimpher St. ... I5
1st Ave. ... E4,F1,F3
2nd ... E2
2nd Ave. ... E3,E4
3rd ... E4

3rd Ave. ... E1,E3,E5
3rd ... G4,I5
4th ... E6,E8
4th Ave. ... E3,E4,E5
4th St. ... E4,G4,I5
5th Ave. ... E1,E3,E5,E7
5th ... E4,E5
6th ... E3,E4,E8,E4
6th Ave. ... E1
6th St. ... E1
7th ... E3,E4,E8
7th Ave. ... E1
8th ... D8,E5
8th Ave. ... E3
9th Ave. ... E3
9th St. ... G5
10th ... D2,D8
11th ... D5
11th St. ... D3,D4
12th ... D4,D6,D8
12th Ave. ... D5
13th ... D5
13th St. ... D4,D5
14th ... D4
15th St. ... D4
15th Ave. ... H5,H7
16th ... D4,D6
16th Ave. ... D3,D5
17th ... D3,H6,I6
17th St. ... F5,G6
18th ... D3,D4,D5
18th Ave. ... C5
18th St. ... F6,E8,I6
19th ... D4,E6,I6
19th Ave. ... C5
20th ... D4
20th Ave. ... C5
20th St. ... E7
21st St. ... E6,F6,I6
22nd ... C5
22nd Ave. ... C5
23rd ... C6,E6
23rd Ave. ... C5
24th ... C5
24th Ave. ... C5
25th Ave. ... C5
26th Ave. ... C5

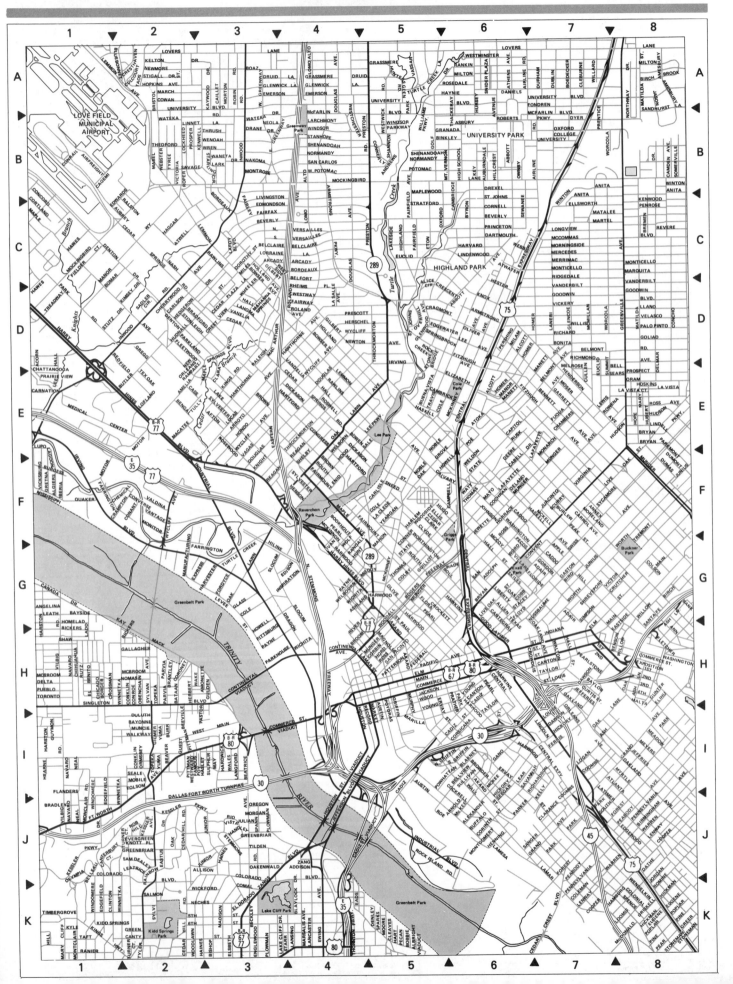

DALLAS

Abbott ... B6
Abbott Ave. ... D6
Acorn ... D1
Adair ... G7
Addison ... J4
Adolph ... G6
Afton ... E3
Air Line Rd. ... A7,B7
Airfreight ... B1
Akard ... H5
Akard St. ... I6
Albright ... A5
Alcott ... D6,E6
Alexander ... J6
Algiers ... F1
Alice Circle ... C5
Allen ... G6
Allison ... A2
Amelia ... E2
Amesbury ... A8
Amonette ... H3
Andrews ... B5
Angelina ... G1
Anita ... B7,B8
Ann ... H8
Annex ... F7
Apple ... G8
Arcady ... C3,C4
Armstrong ... D6
Armstrong Pkwy. ... C5
Arnold ... J6
Arroyo ... J3
Asbury ... B6
Ash ... I7
Ash Ln. ... H8
Ashland ... G4
Athens Ave. ... A6
Atlanta ... I7
Atoka ... E6
Atwater ... C6
Atwell ... C2
Aubrey ... C2
Auburndale ... B6
Austin ... H5,I5
Bank ... G8
Bataan ... H3
Baylor ... H7
Bayonne ... J2
Bayside ... G1
Beatrice ... I3
Beaver ... A3
Beckley Ave. ... K3
Beeville ... I2
Belclaire ... C3,C4
Belfort ... C4
Bell ... E8
Belleau ... J1
Bellview ... F6
Belmont Ave. ... E7
Belmont Rd. ... D7
Bengal ... E2
Bennett Ave. ... E7
Benson ... H8
Beverly ... C3,C6
Bickers ... G1,H2
Binkley ... B6
Birch ... A8,G8
Bird ... G7
Birmingham Ave. ... J8
Bishop ... K3
Blakney ... I6
Blaylock Dr. ... A3
Bluebonnet ... A2
Boaz ... A3
Bobbie ... A5
Boedecker ... A7
Boll ... E8
Bomar ... C1
Bonita ... D7
Bookhout ... F4
Bordeaux ... B3,C4
Borger ... H1
Bowen St. ... C4
Bowser ... D4
Bowser Ave. ... C3
Bradford ... D7
Bradley ... J1
Brantley ... C8
Bremen ... C8
Bristol ... A2
Brook ... A8
Broom ... H4
Browder ... I6
Brown ... E3,F4
Bryan ... E8,G6
Bryan Pkwy. ... E8
Buena Vista ... E5
Buffalo ... J6
Burgess ... F1
Burlew ... F7
Burr ... I2
Butler ... C6
Byron ... C6
Cabell Dr. ... F6
Caddo ... F6
Cadis St. ... G1
Cadiz ... H6,I5
Cadiz St. Viaduct ... J4
Cagemi ... B1
Caillet ... A3
Calvary ... E5
Cambrick ... E5
Cambridge ... F4
Camden Ave. ... B8
Campbell ... F6
Canada Dr. ... G1
Cantegral ... G6
Canterbury Ct. ... J1
Canton ... H6,H7
Canty St. ... K2
Capitol Ave. ... G6
Carlson ... D2
Carnation ... E1
Carrol Ave. ... G6
Cass ... H3
Cedar ... D3,F5
Cedar Crest Blvd. ... K7

Cedar Hill Rd. ... J2,K2
Cedar Plaza Ln. ... D3
Cedar Springs Rd. ... C2,E2
Central ... H6
Central Expwy. ... E6,G6,I7
Chambers ... E7
Chattanooga ... D1
Chemical ... F2
Cherrywood Ave. ... D2
Chicago ... H1
Chihuahua ... H1
Clara ... E3
Clarance ... J7
Clark ... F5
Cleaves ... K5
Cleburne ... A7
Clinton ... K1
Clyde ... F5
Cobb ... G6
Cochran ... F6
Cockrell ... I6
Colby ... G5
Cole ... F5,G3
Cole Ave. ... E5
Coleman ... K7
College ... B7
Colonial ... A7
Colorado Blvd. . J1,J3
Colson ... G8
Comal ... K3
Glencoe ... D7
Glenwick Ln. ... A3,A4
Glenwood Ave. ... E5
Commerce St. ... H5,H8
Commerce St. Viaduct ... I3
Conant ... F2
Concho ... D8
Concord ... B1
Congress ... E4
Conklin ... H2,I2
Conner ... F5
Connerly ... B5
Conrail ... B1
Conroe ... H2
Continental Ave. ... H4
Continental Viaduct ... H3
Convent ... G7
Converse ... F2
Coombs ... H1
Cooper ... J8,K7
Corbin ... H5
Corinth St. ... J6
Cornell ... C6
Coronet ... H2
Corsicana ... H1
Cortland ... B1
Cowan ... A2
Cragmont ... D5
Crampton ... F2
Crescent ... D6
Crest ... D3
Cresthaven ... A2
Crockett ... G5
Crossman ... H1
Crowdlis ... H7
Crutcher ... G8
Culcourt ... A2
Cullen ... E7
Curtis St. ... H7
Dallas-Ft. Worth Tpk. ... I2
Daniels ... A6
Dartmouth ... C6
Dathe ... J8
Dawson ... H7,I7
Deere ... F6
Delano ... F6
Delmar Dr. ... E8
Delta ... H1
Denley ... K5
Denton ... D2
Denton Dr. ... C1
Dickason ... E4
Dorothy St. ... C3
Douglas ... E3,E4
Douglas Ave. ... A4,C4
Dragon ... G4
Drane Dr. ... B3
Drexel ... B6
Driskell ... K8
Druid ... A5
Druid Ln. ... A3
Dublin ... A7
Dumas ... F8
Dumont ... F8
Durham ... A7
Dyer ... B7
Eads ... K4
Eastern ... E3
Eastside ... H8
Eastus Dr. ... J2
Edgefield ... I1
Edgefield Dr. ... K1
Edgewater ... D5
Edgewood ... J8
Edison ... G4
Edmondson ... C3
Edwards ... B2
El Benito ... H1
El Dorado ... K3
Elihu ... H8
Elizabeth ... E6
Ellis ... F5
Ellsworth ... C7
Elm St. ... H5,H7
Elsbeth ... K3
Emerson ... A3,A4
Englewood Ave. ... E3
Enid ... F1
Ervay St. ... H5,I6
Eton ... C5
Euclid ... C5,E7
Evergreen ... H6,J2
Exeter ... K2
Exposition ... H8
Express ... G2
Fairfax ... C3

Fairfield ... C5
Fairfield Ave. ... C5
Fairley ... C3
Fairmount ... F4
Fairway ... D4
Famous ... C4
Farrington ... F1,G3
Federal ... H5
Ferris ... I7
Fielder Ct. ... C1
Fitzhugh Ave. ... D6,E6
Flanders ... I1
Fleetwood ... D2
Fletcher ... H8
Flora ... G5
Floride ... E7
Floyd ... G6
Folsom ... J2
Fondren ... A7
Fordyce ... D2
Forest ... J7,J8
Fox ... I2
Ft. Worth Ave. ... J1
Fuqua ... E7
Gallagher ... K7
Gano ... I6
Garrett ... E7
Gaston Ave. ... G7
Gilbert ... C3,D4
Gilmer ... I2
Glass ... G3
Glencoe ... D7
Glenwick Ln. ... A3,A4
Glenwood Ave. ... E5
Golf ... D8
Goliad ... D8
Good Latimer Ave. ... G7
Goodwin ... D7,D8
Gordon ... I3
Granada ... B6
Grand Ave. ... I8,J7
Grassmere ... A4,A5
Green ... K2
Greenbriar ... J2,J3
Greenville Ave. ... D8
Greenway ... A4
Greenway,W. ... A3
Greer ... K8
Gregg ... D2
Gretna ... F1
Griffin ... G4
Griffin,N. ... I5
Griffin,S. ... I6
Guest ... H3
Guilden ... H3
Guillot ... G4
Gunter ... H8
Guymon ... I1
Haggar ... D5
Haines ... J3,K2
Hall ... D1,D3,E4
Hall St. ... G6,H7
Hamburg ... K7
Handley ... J3
Hardwick ... I3
Harlem ... F5
Harry Hines Blvd. ... E2,G4
Harston ... G1,I1
Hart ... K5
Hartford ... E4,F4
Harvard ... C6
Harvester ... K3
Harwood ... G4,G5,H6,I8
Haskell Ave. ... A1,E4
Haskill ... E5
Haslet ... I2
Hawes ... C1
Hawkins ... G6,H6
Hawthorne ... E3
Hawthorne Ave. ... D4
Haynie ... A6
Hearne ... I1
Hedgerow Dr. ... D2
Henderson Ave. ... E7
Henning ... J6
Henson ... F2
Herbert ... H2
Herschel ... H2
Hester ... D5
Hickman ... K8
Hickory ... I6,I7
High School ... B6
Highland ... I1
Hill ... G7,K1
Hillcrest Ave. ... B6
Hilline ... G3
Holland ... D4
Holland Ave. ... C3
Homeland ... C3
Homer ... D7,E6
Hondo ... E4
Hood ... F4
Hope ... C7
Hopkins Ave. ... A2
Hord ... H5
Horrace ... F6
Hoskins ... I4
Houston ... I4
Houston St. Viaduct ... J4
Howell ... F6,H3
Hubert ... E6
Hudnall St. ... D2
Hudson ... D3
Hugo ... F5
Hunt ... F6
Hunters Glen Rd. ... A6
Hursey ... A6
Iberia ... F1
Indiana ... H7
Industrial Blvd. ... F3,J5
Inspiration ... G4
Inwood Rd. ... B3,D2
Irving ... D5
Irving Blvd. ... F1
Ivan ... G4
Jackson ... H5

Jefferies ... H7,I8
Jefferson Blvd. Viaduct ... J4
Jewette ... F6
Johnson ... F6
Jordan ... J8
Julian ... J3
Junior ... J2,J3
Junius ... F8,G7
Kay ... G2
Kaywood Dr. ... A3
Kelly ... J7
Kelton Dr. ... A2
Kenwell ... B3
Kenwood ... C8
Kessler Ave. ... J2
Kessler Pkwy. . J1,J2
Key ... B6
Kidd Springs ... K1
Kimsey Dr. ... D2
Kings Hwy. ... K1
Kings Rd. ... E3
Knight ... F3
Knott Pl. ... J2
Knox ... D6
Kyle ... K1
La Clede ... F5
La Salle Ave. ... D4
La Vista ... E8
La Vista Ct. ... E8
Ladd ... H1
Lafayette ... F6,F7
Lafoy Blvd. ... C3
Lagoon ... E1
Lahoma ... D3
Lake ... E3
Lake Cliff Dr. ... K3
Lakeside ... C5
Lamar St. ... H4
Lamesa ... j6
Lancaster ... K4
Lane ... I7
Langford ... I3
Lansing ... K4
Larchmont ... B4
Lark Dr. ... B3
Latimer ... I7
Lear ... I6
Leath ... G1
Leatrice ... J2
Lee ... E1
Lee Ave. ... d6
Lee Pkwy. ... E5
Lemmon ... C3
Lemmon Ave. .. A1,E4
Lenway ... J8,K7
Levee St. ... G3
Lewis ... E7
Liberty ... G6
Lincoln ... I7
Lindell ... E8
Lindenwood ... C6
Linnet Ln. ... B2
Live Oak St. ... F7,G6
Livingston ... B3
Llano ... D8
Lockheed ... B2
Lofland ... E2
Logan ... I7
Lomo Alto ... A4,C4
Longview ... C4
Loomis ... K8
Lorraine Ln. ... C3
Louise ... I7
Lovers Ln. ... A2,A6
Lucas Ave. ... E3
Lupo ... E1
Mabel ... B2
MacArthur ... D3
Macatee ... E2
Mack ... H2
Madison ... K3
Magnolia ... H5
Mahanna Springs . D3
Main ... G8
Main St. ... H5
Manett ... E6
Mannet Ave. ... D7
Manor ... E6
Manor Way ... C1
Manufacturing ... G2
Maple ... E5
Maple Ave. ... C1,F4
Maplewood ... B5
March ... A2
Marilla ... H5
Market ... H5
Marquita ... C8
Marsalis Ave. ... K4
Martel ... C7
Mary ... E8
Mary Cliff ... K1
Matalee ... C7
Matilda ... D8
Matilda St. ... A8
Matton ... F6
May ... I3
Mayo ... F6
McBroom ... H1,H2
McCommas Blvd. ... C7
McCoy ... G6
McDonald ... K8
McFarlin Blvd. .. A4,B7
McKee ... I6,J6
McKinney ... G5
McKinney Ave. ... E5
McKinnon ... F4
McMillan ... C7
Meadow ... I8
Medical Center ... E1
Melrose ... E7
Mercedes ... C7
Merrimac ... C7
Meyers ... H8
Milam ... D6
Miles ... C3

Milton ... A6,A8
Mississippi ... F1
Mobile ... I2
Mockingbird ... C1
Mockingbird Ln. ... B4
Monarch ... E7
Monitor ... F2
Montclair ... K1
Montclair Rd. ... J1
Montgomery ... J6
Monticello ... C7,C8
Montrose ... B3
Moody ... B3
Moore ... K5
Moreland ... F7
Morgan ... J3
Morningside ... C7
Morton ... A3
Moser ... E2,F1
Mt. Vernon ... B6
Muncie ... I2
Munger . F6,F8,G5,H5
Murphy ... H5
Myrtle ... H5
Nakoma ... B3
Nash ... C2
Navaro ... H1,I1,J1
Neal ... I1,J1
Neches ... K2
Neola ... B3
New Orleans ... G3,G4
Newmore ... A2
Newton Ave. ... D4
Nob Hill ... J2
Nokomis ... E5,F5
Nomas ... H1
Normandy ... B4,B5
Northway Dr. ... A8
Nusbaume ... G7
Oak ... G6,H8,I7,J2
Oak Grove ... F5
Oak Lawn ... G3
Oak Lawn Ave. ... E4
Oakenwald ... J3
Oakland ... H7
Oakland Ave. ... H7,I8
Obenchain ... H4
Olive ... G5
Oliver ... D6
Olympia ... J1
Oram ... E8
Oregon ... J3
Orleans Ave. ... I7
Ormsbey ... J2
Overhill ... H1
Ownby ... B6
Oxford ... B7,C8
Pacific Ave. ... H5
Palo Pinto ... D8
Park ... A5,H6,J8,I7
Park Rd. ... D1
Parker ... J6
Parkhouse ... H3
Parkland ... D2
Parkmont ... E8
Parvia ... H2
Pastor ... I2
Patterson ... H5
Payne ... G4,H3
Peabody ... J7
Peabody Ave. ... J8
Peak St. ... F7
Pear ... K8
Pearl ... F4,G5,H6
Pearlstone ... H7
Pecan ... K5
Pecos ... G7
Pennsylvania .. J7,K7
Penrose ... C8
Pershing ... D6
Pine ... H8
Pittman ... I2
Pittsburg ... H3
Plowman ... J3,K3
Poe ... H8
Poplar ... K8
Potomac ... B5
Potomac,W. ... B4
Powhattan ... I5
Poyldras ... E1
Prairie View ... E1
Prentice ... B7
Prescott ... D4
Preston ... B5
Preston Rd. ... C5
Princeton ... C4
Prospect ... E8
Prosper ... B7
Pueblo ... H1
Quaker ... F1
Rainbow ... J2
Raleigh ... D3
Ralston ... C2
Rampart ... E4
Randell ... G4
Ranier ... K1
Rankin ... A6
Rawlins ... C3,E4
Reagan ... E4,F3
Record ... I5
Redfield ... C8
Revere ... C8
Rheims Pl. ... B5
Richard ... D7
Richardson ... C7
Richmond Ave. ... C7
Ridgedale ... C7
Rio Vista ... J3
River ... H1
Roberts Pkwy. ... B6
Robin Rd. ... A3
Rock Creek ... D5
Rock Island Rd. ... J5
Roe ... J5
Roland Ave. ... D4
Romaine ... K8
Roper ... D2
Rosedale ... A6

Rosewood ... E3
Ross ... H5
Ross Ave. ... E8,F6
Roswell ... E4
Routh ... F4,G5
Rowens ... E7
Rusk ... E6
Rutz ... H1
Sadler Circle ... D2
Sale ... E5
Salmon ... K2
Sam Desly ... J2
San Carlos ... B4
San Jaucinto .. G6,H5
Sandhurst Ln. ... B8
Sanger ... J6
Santa Fe ... H8
Savage ... B2
Savannah ... I6
Scurry ... F7
Seale ... I2
Sears ... E8
Seager ... J6
Sewanee ... C6
Shannon ... B5
Shaw ... H1
Shelby ... C2
Shenandoah .. B4,B5
Shreveport ... G7
Simpson ... G7
Singleton Blvd. ... H1
Skiles ... G6
Slocum ... G3,G4
Sneed ... F5
Snider Plaza ... A6
Somerville ... B8
South ... J7
Spann ... J3
Sparks ... K5
Spence ... K8
Springbrook ... D5
Springs Blvd. ... D3
St. John ... D5
St. Johns ... C6
St. Joseph ... G7
St. Louis ... H7
St. Paul ... G5
Stacey ... G6
Stanhope ... B4
Starling Cir. ... B3
Starr ... K3
State ... F6,G5
Stemmons ... J3
Stemmons Frwy.,N.
Stigall Dr. ... A2
Stone Bridge ... D5
Stoneman ... K8
Stoneleigh ... D2
Stratford ... C5
Stutz Dr. ... D1
Sullivan ... I6
Sulphur ... I3
Summit ... E7
Swiss ... G7
Sycamore ... F7
Sylvan Ave. ... H2
Sylvester ... E3,E4
Sylvi ... K2
Taft ... K1
Taos ... H8
Taylor ... H7,I6
Tex Oak ... I3
Texas ... G8
Thackery ... B6
Thedford ... B2
Thomas ... F6,G5
Thorton Frwy. ... K4
Throckmorton .. D5,E4
Thrush ... B3
Tilden ... J3
Timbergrove ... K1
Topeka ... H2,I2
Toronto ... H1
Travis ... D1
Treadway ... D1
Tremont ... E8
Tully ... E2
Turner Ct. ... J2,K2
Turtle Creek ... A3
Turtle Creek Ln. ... A5
Tyler ... K2
Tyree ... B2
University ... E4
University Blvd. ... A2,A5,A7
Vagas ... C7
Valdina ... E2
Vanderbilt ... D7,D8
Vanelia ... D3
Vantage ... C7
Vassar ... A4
Velasco ... D8
Versailles ... C4
Versailles,N ... C4
Vickery Blvd. ... D7
Vicksburg ... F1
Victor ... B2
Victoria ... B2
View ... D3
Vilbig Rd. ... H1,J1
Villars ... G6
Virginia ... F7
Wade ... A3
Wake ... H2
Waketa ... I3
Wall ... H7
Walton ... H7
Wanetka ... J3
Warren ... J7,J8
Washington ... F6,H8
Wateka Rd. ... B2,B3
Watt ... H6
Webb ... F6
Webster ... J2
Welborn ... E4
Welbourn ... G4

Weldon ... F6
Wendelkin ... K8
Wenoah ... B3
West Side ... A7
Westchester ... A6
Westward ... I2
Westway ... D4
Westwick Rd. ... B5
Wheeler ... B2
Wichita ... G4,H4
Wickford ... K2
Willard ... A7
Williams Dr. ... A7
Williams Pkwy. ... B5
Willis ... D7
Willow ... G8,H8
Windomere ... J1,K1
Windsor ... B4
Windsor Pkwy. ... B5
Winnetak .. H2,I1,K1
Winton ... B8,C7
Wolf ... F4
Wood ... H5
Woodall Rogers Frwy. ... D6
Woodlawn ... k2
Woodside ... F5
Worcola ... B8,D7
Word ... G6
Worth ... G7,G8
Worthington ... F5
Wren ... B3
Wyclift ... H2
Wyclift Ave. .. D4,E3,F2
Yeargan ... F5
Young ... H5,H6
Yuma ... I2
Zang ... J4
Zangs Blvd. ... K3
1st ... H7,H8
2nd ... H8
3rd ... H8
4th ... H8
5th St. ... K2
6th St. ... K2

DAYTON

Acorn Dr. ... J6
Addison ... F1
Agnes ... F1
Agricola Ave. ... B7
Air ... E5
Aircity Ave. ... C5
Alaska. Ave. ... C5
Albany ... H2,H3
Alberta Ave. ... H4,I5
Alice ... H7
Allen ... G6
Alpine Way ... C1
Alton ... F5
Amelia ... F5
Amherst Blvd. ... G1
Antioch ... G1
Apple,E ... H4
Apple,W. ... H4
Arbor ... H7
Argyle ... H7
Ashwood Ave. ... B1
Auburndale ... A3
Avondale Rd. ... B6
Bacon ... F5
Bainbridge ... G5
Baltimore ... H1
Bancroft ... H1
Banker ... F1
Bannock ... D4
Basswood Ave. ... C4
Bates ... F5
Bayard ... H4
Beardshear Rd. ... A5
Beatrice Dr. ... A7
Beckel ... F5
Beckman ... I6
Beechwood Ave. ... C2
Belfonte Ave. ... B4
Bell ... H2
Bellaire Ave. ... J7
Bellefontaine Ave. ... D6
Berm St. ... F2
Berwick ... H4
Beverly Pl. ... J6
Bickmore Ave. ... D6
Bierce ... F7
Bluefield ... G3
Bolander ... H3
Boltin ... G5
Bond ... E3
Bowen ... H1
Boyer ... H1
Brandt Pike ... B7
Brandt St. ... D6
Brennan Dr. ... D4
Broadvie Blvd. ... J7
Broadway ... F2,G2,H2,I2
Brooklands Rd. ... J4
Brookline ... H7
Brooks ... H7
Brown ... G4,G5
Bruce Ave. ... C1
Bryan Ave. ... F5
Bryant ... A3
Buchanan Ave. ... H6
Burns ... H4
Burton ... G2
Caldwell St. ... I5
Calvery Ave. ... E5
Cambridge ... J7
Camden ... C7
Campbell ... A4
Canfield ... F6
Carillon blvd. ... C7
Carl Ave. ... I5
Carlisle Ave. .. G7,H7
Carlton Dr. ... B3
Carroll ... B2

Cass ... G4
Castlewook Ave. ... B1
Catalpa Dr. .. C1,E1,F1
Central ... F2
Chambers ... H5
Chapel ... E5
Charles ... G7
Cherry Dr. ... C1,D1
Church ... G6
Cincinnati ... H3,D1
Clarence ... H7
Clement Ave. ... I1
Cleveland ... H7
Herman ... E5
Cliff ... C1
Clinton ... F5
Clover ... G6
College ... H1
College Park ... I5
Collingwood ... J6
Columbia ... G3
Colwick Dr. ... J7
Commerce Park ... B5
Commercial ... E2
Community ... J7
Connecticut ... H6
Conover ... G2
Constantia Ave. ... I4
Coronett Ave. .. A3,A4
Cory Dr. ... E1
Crane ... F5
Creighton ... D3
Cromwell Pl ... B1
Croyden Dr. ... J7
Cumberland ... E1
Dakota ... G2
Dale View ... B1
Davis Ave. ... C7
Dayton Towers ... G5
Deanwood ... H7
Deeds Ave. .. D5,E5
Delware Ave. ... E2
Demphile ... H6
Detrick ... E4
Detzen ... I2
Deweese Pkwy. ... B3
Diamond ... E7
Dixon Ave. ... J6
Dogson Ct. ... D6
Dona Ave. ... I2
Douglas ... F6
Dover ... H6
Dow ... F1
Drake ... D3
Drill Ave. ... C3
Drummer ... G6
Dryden Rd. ... J2
Dunbar ... F5
East River Rd. ... J2
East View Ave. ... D2
Edgar ... H6
Edgemont ... I2
Edgewood Ave. ... F2
Edgeworth ... C3
Edison ... G1
Edmund ... D5
Elliot ... H7
Embley Ave. ... C3
Embury Park ... C2
Emerson Ave. ... D1
Erie ... H6
Ernest Ave. ... D2
Euclid Ave. ... E1,F1,H1,I1
Fair Oaks Dr. ... A1
Fairfield Ave. ... A2
Fairview Ave. .. D1,D2
Far Hills Ave. ... J5
Faulkner ... F1
Ferdon Rd. ... B2
Ferguson ... F1
Ferndale Ave. ... D2
Fifth ... F6,G2
Fifth, E. ... F7,G3
Filmore ... G6
Findlay ... H7
Firwood Dr. ... J6
Fitch ... G1
Five Oaks Ave. ... I2
Foraker ... H4
Forest ... G2
Forest Park Dr. ... A1
Foundry ... F4
Fourth ... F5,F7,G2,G4
Fourth,E. ... G3
Franklin ... G3
Gaddis Blvd. ... I7
Gale ... H2
Garden Ave. ... C5
Garland Ave. ... F7
Garst ... H2
Gates ... G4
Germantown ... H1
Geyer ... E7
Glencoe ... H5
Glendale ... F1
Glenous Ave. ... D2
Gold ... H1
Graf ... H7
Grafton ... F2
Grand Ave. ... E2,E3,F1,F2
Greenmount Blvd. . K6
Grove Ave. ... H6
Gunckel ... H6
Hall ... J7
Hamilton ... G6
Hamlin ... F6
Hampshire Ave. ... J7
Harbine Ave. .. E7,F7
Harker ... H6
Harmon Blvd. ... A4
Harriet ... I3
Harshman ... F6
Hart ... E5
Hartford ... H2

Harvard Blvd. .. D1,E1
Haskins Ave. ... I7
Haver Rd. ... J5
Haviland ... E5
Hawkes ... G6
Hawthorn ... G2
Haynes ... D4
Heaton ... H6
Heck Ave. ... I2
Hedges ... E7,F7
Heid Ave. ... B5
Helena ... D4,E3
Herman ... E5
Hess ... E5
Hiawatha ... C4
Hickory ... G6
High Noch ... G5
Highland ... H6
Highland Hills ... G7
Hill Point Ln. ... D4
Hill Rose Ave. ... D4
Hillcrest Ave. ... I1
Hilldale Ave. ... B3
Hillmont ... B3
Hochwalt Ave. ... I1
Hodapp ... G7
Holly Ave. ... H7
Holt ... F2
Home Ave. ... H1
Homestead ... H2
Homewood Ave. ... E2
Hopeland ... H3
Horton ... E1
Howe Ave. ... C7
Howell Ave. ... G1
Hudson Ave. .. D1,D2
Huffman Ave. ... F6
Huffman Ave.,E. ... F6
Hunter Ave. ... E4
Huntor ... D4
Illinois ... B7
Imo ... C1
Indiana ... H4
Ingleside Ave. ... I2
Irving Ave. .. I5,I6
Irwin ... E7,F7
Jacobs ... D2
Janney Rd. ... C5
Jasper ... H4
Jefferson ... F4
Jergens Rd. ... C6
Jersey ... D3
Jessie ... I6
Jones ... G4
Joseph's ... G6
Josie ... G5,G6
K St. ... I5
Karen ... G3
Kathleen Ave. ... I7
Kearns ... C3
Keenan Ave. .. A3,A4
Kelly Ave. .. C5,C6
Kendall Ave. ... B3
Kenilworth Ave. ... E2
Kenwood Ave. ... E1
Kiefaber ... I5
King Ave. ... I7
King Tree Ct. ... A2
Kinnard ... H1
Kirkham ... H3
Kling Ave. ... J6
Kling Dr. ... J6
Knecht ... C2
Koehler Ave. ... A3
Koeing Ct. ... H1
Kolping Ave. .. G7,H7
Kramer Rd. ... J4
Kumler Ave. .. E1,G1
Kuniz Rd. ... C2
Kurtz ... C1
La Belle ... G5
La Crosse ... B3
Lakeview ... H1
Lamar ... F5
Laura Ave. ... C2
Leo ... D3,D4,D5
Leonard ... D4,D5
Leroy ... H1
Lexington Ave. .. F1,F2
Light ... E5
Lincoln ... H4
Linda Vista ... D1
Linden Ave. ... H3
Lindorph Dr. ... C2
Little ... G5
Livingston ... G7
Locust ... G6
Lodell Ave. ... C3
Lodge Ave. ... C4
Lombard ... F6
Longworth ... B8
Lonoke ... E7
Lookout Dr. ... J5
Lorain Ave. ... H7
Lorella Ave. ... H2
Louie ... G3
Lowes ... B3
Lucille Dr. ... C4
Ludlow ... G2
Lytle Ln. ... J4

Maryland Ave. ... E5
Master ... G7
Mathison ... G1,H1
Mawr Dr. ... F1
McCall ... H1
McClure ... F5
McDonough ... F5
McGee ... F3
McLain ... G5,G6
McPherson ... F3
Mead ... G3
Medford ... H6
Meigs ... F5
Melbeth ... C5
Melford Ave. ... B1
Mello ... I6
Merger Ave. ... G2
Meridian ... G7
Merrimac Ave. ... B2,C2
Miami Blvd. ... E3
Miami Blvd.,W. ... I3
Miami Chapel ... I1
Milburn ... E4
Monmouth ... F7
Monte Video Dr. ... B4
Monument Ave. ... E7
More Ave. ... E7
Morse ... I7
Mound ... G2
Mumma ... E3
Nassau ... H6
Neal ... E3
Neff Ave. .. B3,B4
Nellie Ave. ... C6
Neva Ave. ... B4
Neva Dr. ... C3
Niagara Ave. ... B3
Nicholas Rd. .. J1,J2
Nill Ave. ... I8
Noble Pl. ... I2
Nordale Ave. ... J7
Norledge Dr. ... B4
Norman Ave. .. D1,D2
North Ave. ... C3
North Bend Blvd. ... D3
North Dixie ... J5
Northview ... J5
Northwood ... B1
Norwood ... G2
Notre Dame Ave. ... I5
Nottingham Rd. ... A1
Oak ... H5
Oakridge Dr. ... G1
Obell ... H5
Oberer Dr. ... C5
Odlin Ave. ... C1
Ohio ... E5
Old Orchard ... E2
Old Troy Pike ... B6
Ome Ave. ... C4
Onaoto Ave. ... B3
Ontario Ave. ... C3
Oneida Ave. ... B4
Orchard ... G1,H1
Ottawa ... F5
Ottello Ave. ... A3
Otterbelli ... D1
Oxford ... E2,F1
Park Dr. ... H5
Parks Ave. ... C2
Parkwood Dr. ... C1
Parnell ... G7
Parrot ... G6
Patterson Blvd. ... F4,G4,I4,J6
Pennsylvania Ave. ... E3
Perry ... F3,H4
Phillips Ave. ... H7
Pierce St. ... G6
Pilgrim ... B3
Pinecrest Dr. ... B3
Pinehurst Ct. ... C1
Pioneer ... C3
Pleasant ... F7
Pleasant Valley Rd. B7
Plymouth ... F7
Pointview Ave. ... C2
Pompano Ct. ... C3
Pontiac ... H2
Prince Albert Blvd. ... I7
Princeton Dr. ... E1
Pritz ... G7,H7
Protzman Ave. ... E2
Quitman ... G5
Randolph ... I1
Ravenwood ... D3
Ray ... D4
Red Haw ... C3
Reddar Ave. ... B1
Redwood Ave. ... B1
Revere Ave. .. I7,J7
Reynolds ... G5
Richard ... G7
Richley Ave. ... I1
Richmond ... E2
Ridge Ave. .. C3,D3
Ridgewood Ave. ... J5
Ringgold ... F6
Riverdale ... F3
Riverside Dr. ... A2,B2,C2
Riverview Ave. .. F2,F3
Rocce ... H6
Rockcliff Circle ... C1
Rockford Ave. ... H4
Rockwood Ave. ... E2
Rondows ... C7
Rosemary ... A1
Rott ... A7
Rubicon ... H4
Rugby Rd. .. C1,D1
Rustic Ave. ... D1

Ryburn Ave. ... B5
Rydale Wentz ... A2
Sabina ... B2
Sacamore ... C3
Salem Ave. .. D1,F2
Samuel ... G6
Sandal ... C4
Sandhurst Dr. ... B2
Santa Clara Ave. ... D2
Santa Cruz ... H7
Schaefer ... D5
Schantz ... J4,J5,J6
Schenck Ave. ... J5
Sears ... F4
Second ... E1,F1,F5,G1,G2
Semier ... G6
Shaddy Side ... C2
Shadowlawn Ave. ... J7
Shafor Blvd. ... J6
Shannon ... G2
Shaw ... E3
Shelton ... D1
Sherer Ave. .. A3,A4
Sherman ... G6
Shoap Mill Rd. ... A1
Shroyer Rd. ... J6
Siedenthaler Ave. ... B1,B3
Sixth ... G4
Smith ... I3
Southshore Dr. ... B6
Southview ... J5
Sprague ... G2
Springfield Pike .E7,F6
St. Adalbert ... B2
St. Brown ... I5
St. Clair ... F4
St. Louis ... B1
St. Mary's Dr. ... I1
St. Paul ... C6
Stafford ... B2
Stainton ... F6
Staley ... I2
Stanley Ave. ... D3
Stanview ... D6
Steele ... G6
Stegman ... D5
Stewart ... I3,I1
Stewart Wayne Ave. ... I5,I6
Styles Ave. ... A3
Sue Ann Blvd. ... C1
Summit ... F1,G1,H2
Sumter ... A4
Superior ... F1,G2
Susannah Ave. ... C4
Tacoma ... G7
Tampa ... I1
Taylor ... E4,F5
Terry ... F5
Theodore Ave. ... C2
Third ... F4,G1,G2
Third,E. ... F7
Thurston Blvd. ... A7
Thurston Blvd.,E. .. J3
Torrence ... C7
Trieschman ... I1
Trinity Ave. ... I5
Troy St. .. D5,E5
Urbana ... D6
Utah Ave. ... H6
Valley St. .. C7,E5
Valleycrest Dr. ... C1
Valleyview ... C1
Van Buren ... D5
Van Lear ... C7
Victor Ave. ... D2
Vincent ... E3
Virginia ... G6
Volusia Ave. ... C5
Vull ... C7
Wabash Ave. ... D1
Wagner Ford Rd. ... A1
Walbrook ... B2
Waldo ... E5
Walnut ... G5
Wampler Ave. ... G5
Warner Ave. ... D5
Warren ... H4
Washington ... G3
Watterson ... H3
Watts ... F7
Waverly ... B1
Wayne Ave. .. G4,H5
Weakely ... H2
Weaver ... I1
Webb ... C6
Webster ... A4,D4,E4
Weller ... H1
Wellmier ... E2
Wesley ... F7
West River Rd. ... A4
West Schantz ... J4
Western ... G1,H1
Wheatley Ave. ... E2
Wilford ... F3
Wilkinson ... F3
Williams ... C5
Willow Grove ... J4
Willow Wood Dr. ... J5
Wilmington Ave. .. H7
Wilmington Pike ... J7
Windham ... D4
Windsor ... A4
Wire Dr. ... A7
Wisconsin Blvd. ... C5
Wisteria Dr. ... B2
Wonderview ... C4
Wood Dr. ... C1
Woodland Hills Blvd. ... A4
Woodley Dr. ... J3
Woodsdale Rd. ... A2
Woodway ... C7
Wyoming .. H5,H7
Xenia Ave. ... F1
Yale ... D1
York ... E5
Zephyer Dr. ... B3

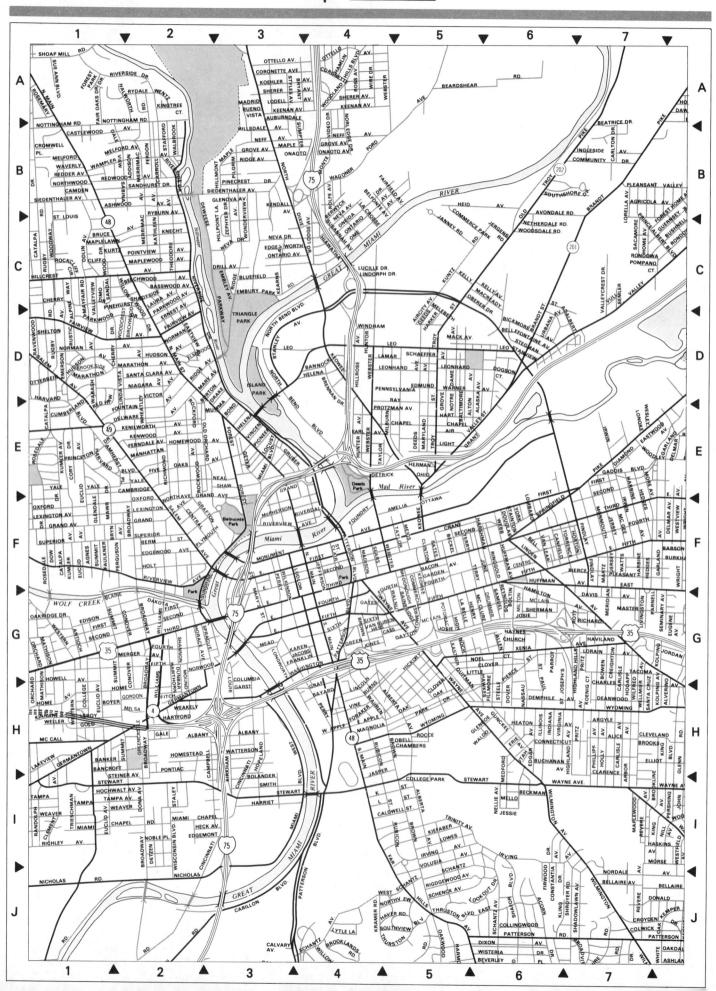

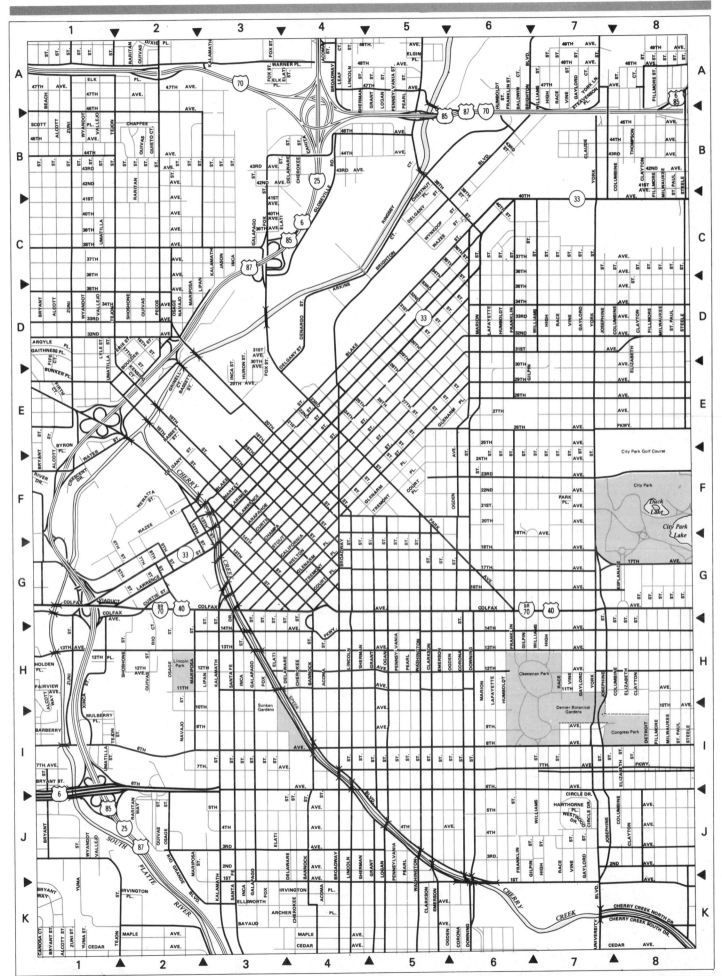

DENVER

Acoma St. A4,H4,K4
Alcott St. B1,F1,K1
Arapahoe St. F3
Archer Pl. K3
Argyle Pl. D1
Arkins Ct. D4
Baldwin Ct. A6
Bannock St. H4,J4
Barberry I1
Bassett St. E2
Bayaud Ave. K3
Beach St. A1
Blake St. D4,F3
Boulder St. D1
Brighton Blvd. A7,C5
Broadway A4,G4,J4
Bryant St. D1,F1,I1
Bryant Way K1
Bryon Pl. E1
Bunker Pl. E1
Cahita B4
California St. G4
Cedar Ave. K1,K8
Chaffee B2
Champa St. F3
Cherokee St. B4,H4,K4
Cherry Creek North Dr. K8
Cherry Creek South Dr. K8
Chestnut Pl. C5
Circle Dr. J7
Clarkson St. H5,K5
Claude B7
Clayton St. B8,H8,J8
Colfax Ave. G1,G6
Columbine St. B8,H8,J8
Corona St. H6,K6
Court Pl. F5,G4
Crescent Dr. F1
Curtis St. F3,G2
Delaware St. B4,H4,J4
Delgany St. C5,D4,F2
Denargo St. D4
Detroit St. I8
Dixie Pl. A2
Downing St. H6,K6
Elati St. A4,C4,H4,J4
Elgin Pl. A5
Elizabeth St. E8,I8
Elk Pl. A1,A3
Ellsworth Ave. K3
Emerson St. H5,K5
Erie St. D2
Explande G8
Fairway Ave. H1
Fife Ct. D1
Fillmore St. A8,D8,I8
Firth Ct. E1
Fox St. A3,C3,E3,K3
Franklin St. A6,H6,J6
Gaithness Pl. D1
Galapago St. C3,K3,H3
Gaylord St. A7,H7,J7
Gilpin St. E7,H6,J7
Glenarm Pl. E5,F5,G4
Globeville Rd. C4
Grant St. A5,H5,J5
Grinell Ct. E2
Hawthorne Pl. J7
High St. A7,H7,J7
Holden Pl. H1
Humboldt St. A6,D6,H6
Inca St. C3,E3,K3
Irvington Pl. K2
Jason St. C3
Josephine St. D7,H7,J7
Kalamath St. A3,C3,H3,K3
Kensing Ct. E2
Lafayette St. H6
Larimer St. F3
Lawrence St. F3,G2
Leaf Ct. A4
Lincoln St. A4,H4,J4
Lipan St. D3,H3
Logan St. A5,H5,J5
Lyle St. D1
Maple Ave. K2,K3
Marion St. H6
Mariposa St. D2,H2,J2
Market St. F3
MilwaukeeSt. B8,D1,I8
Mulberry Pl. I1
Navajo St. D2,I2
Ogden St. H6,K5
Osage St. D2,H2,J2
Park Ave. F5
Park Pl. F7
Pearl St. A5,H5,J5
Pecos St. D2,H2
Pennsylvania St. A5,H5,J5
Quieto Ct. B2
Quivas St. A2,B2,D2,J2
Race St. A7,H7,J7
Raritan A2,B2
Raritan Way J2
Ringsby Ct. C5
Rio Ct. H2
River Dr. F1
Santa Fe St. H3,K3
Scott Pl. B1
Sheer Blvd. H4
Sherman St. A4,H4,J4
Shoshone St. D2,H2
St. Paul St. B8,D8,I8
Steavenson Pl. A7
Steele St. B8,D8,I8
Stout St. G3
Tejon St. B1,I1,K1
Thompson Ct. B8
Tremont Pl. F5,G4
Umatilla St. C1,E1,I1
Vallejo St. B1,D1,J1
Viaduct G1
Vine St. A7,H7,J7
Warner Pl. A3
Washington St. H5,K5
Water St. F1
Watzee St. C5,F2
Welton St. G4
Westwood Dr. J7
Wewatta St. F2
Williams St. A7,D7,J7
Wyandot St. B1,D1,J1
Wynkoop St. C5
Xinca St. H1
York Ln. A7
York St. B7,D7,H7
Yuma St. K1
Zuni St. B1,H1,K1
1st Ave K6
2nd Ave. J3,J8
3rd Ave. J3,J6
4th Ave. J3,J6
5th Ave. J3,J6
5th St. J2
6th Ave. I2,I6
6th St. G2
7th Ave. I2,I7
7th St. G2
8th Ave. I2,I6
8th St. G2
9th Ave. I2,I6
9th St. G2
10th Ave. H2,H8
11th Ave. H2,H7
12th Ave. H2,H6
12th Place H1
12th St. F2
13th Ave. H1,H3,H6
13th St. F3,G3
14th Ave. H3,H6
14th St. G3
15th St. E2
16th Ave. G6
16th St. E2
17th Ave. G6,G8
17th St. D2,F3
18th Ave. G6
18th St. D2,E3
19th Ave. F6
19th St. E3
20th Ave. F6
20th St. E3
21st Ave. F6
21st St. E4
22nd Ave. F6
22nd St. E4
23rd Ave. F6
23rd St. E4
24th Ave. F6
24th St. E4
25th Ave. E6
25th St. E4
26th Ave. E6
26th St. E5
27th Ave. E6
27th St. E5
28th Ave. E6
29th Ave. E3,E6
29th St. D5
30th Ave. D3,E6
30th St. D5
31st Ave. D3,D6
31st St. D5
32nd Ave. D1,D6
32nd St. D5
33rd Ave. D1,D6
33rd St. D5
34th Ave. D1,D6
34th St. C5
35th Ave. D1,D6
35th St. C6
36th Ave. C1,C6
36th St. C6
37th Ave. C1,C6
38th Ave. C1
38th St. B5
39th Ave. C1,C3
39th St. B5
40th Ave. C1,C3,C6
40th St. C6
41st Ave. B1,B3,B8
42nd Ave. B1,B3,B8
43rd Ave. B1,B4,B8
44th Ave. B1,B4,B8
45th Ave. B1,B4,B8
46th Ave. A1
47th Ave. A1,A5,A7
48th Ave A4,A7,A8
49th Ave. A4,A7,A8

DETROIT

Abbott J6
Ackley C8
Adams E. I7
Adams W. I6
Adelaide H7,I6
Adele D6
Alexandrine H4
Alexandrine E. F7,G6
Alfred H7,H8
Alger C5,D4
Alice C6
Alpena A7
Amsterdam F4
Andrus C6
Anna C5
Antietam I7
Antoinette G2
Arden Park C3
Ash I3,I4,J2
Atkinson C3,D1
Atlas A4
Atwater E. J8
Austin K4
Avalon A1,B1
Avery F3,G3
Avery Terr. G3
Bagley J5,J6,K2
Baltimore E4
Bangor H1
Bates J7
Beaublen J7
Beech J6
Belmont A5,B3
Benham C7
Bernard B5
Berres B6
Bethune D4,E2
Blaine D3,E2
Boston Blvd.E C3
Boston Blvd.W. D1
Brainard I4
Brandon K1
Brewster G8,H6
Broadway I7
Brockton A7
Brooklyn G4,K6
Brush A3,D4,J7
Bryanston H8
Bryant G3
Buchanan H3,I1
Buena Vista A1
Buffalo A7
Burger A5
Burlingame C2
Burroughs F4
Butler B7
Butternut I3,J2
Byron D2,E3
California A3
Calumet H3
Calvert C2
Cameron B4
Campbell K1
Canfield E. F7
Canfield W. G5,H3
Caniff A5,B4
Canton C8
Cardoni B4
Carrie B8,C8
Carter E1
Casmer A5
Cass I6,J6
Centre I7
Chandler D4
Charest A6
Charlotte I5
Chateaufor Pl. I8
Chene F7
Cherboneau Pl. I8
Chicago Blvd. D1
Chipman K4
Christopher B7
Church J5
Churchill E2
Civic Center Dr. K6
Clairmount D1,D3
Clark K2
Clarkdale K2
Clay C6,D5
Clifford I6
Clinton I7
Cochiane I4
Collingwood A3
Colorado A3
Columbus F1
Columbus E. I7
Columbus W. I6
Commonwealth F3,G4
Commor A4
Comstock A7,B6
Conant C7
Concord B8,C8
Congress E. J7
Connecticut B3
Cortland B2
Cromwell K4
Custer E4
Cymbal C7
Daizelle J4
Dallas C5
Dane D7
Danforth C6
Davenport H5
Davison Expwy. A1
Deleware E2,E3
Delmar B4
Deming K2
Denton C6
Dequindre G7
Dodge B7
Domine B7
Doremus A6,A7
Dorothy B7
Dubois B5,C6
Dunderin F2
Dunn Rd. C7
Dwyer B7
Dyar A4
East Grand Blvd. D6,D8
Eastern Pl. G1
Edison C3,D1
Edsel Ford Frwy. E6,G3
Edwin A6,A7,B5
Elijah McCoy Dr. F3
Eliot H6
Elizabeth J5
Elizabeth E. I7
Elizabeth W. I6
Ellery A6,D8,E8
Elm I4
Elmhurst B2,C1
Elmwood F8
Endicott E4
Englewood B3
Erskine G8,H6
Euclid E. D4
Euclid W. D3,E2
Evaline A5,A7
Faber B6
Farmer I6
Farnsworth E7,F5
Farr C8
Farrand A3
Ferry E. E7,F5
Ferry Park F2
Field C8
Filer B8
Finley D6
Fisher Frwy. I6,J3
Fleming A5
Florian B5
Ford A1
Fordyce C6
Forest Ct. G4
Forest E. F7,G5
Forest W. G5,H3
Fort W. K6
Foster B8
Franklin J8
Frederick E7,F5
Frontenac C8
Gage F3
Gallagher A6
Garfield F7,G5
Geimer B6
Georgia B7,B8
Gibson H4
Gillett C5
Girardin B8
Gladstone D3,E1
Glendale A4,B1
Glynn Ct. C2
Goldner J1
Goodson B6
Goodwin B4,C4
Grand A1
Grand Haven A4
Grand River G1,I6
Grandy C6,F8
Gratiot G8,I7
Grayling C6
Greenley C5
Griffin C7
Grinnell A8
Griswold J7
Guthrie A8
Hague C5,D4
Hale G8
Hamilton B2
Hammond K1
Hancock H3,I1
Hancock E. F7
Hancock W. G5
Hanley B6
Hanover F2
Harmon B3
Harper E5
Harrison I4
Hartwick C5
Hastings E5
Hawthorne B4
Hazelwood D1,D3
Heck Pl. E8
Hecla F3,G3
Hedge A7
Heintz B7
Helen B8,C8
Hendricks H8
Hendrie E7
Henry I5
Hewitt B6
Highland B2
Hindle B4
Hobart F4
Hobson I5
Hogarth F1
Holborn D8
Holbrook B6,C4
Holmes A5
Hooker G2
Hope Pl. G1
Horatio I1
Horton D6,E4
Howard J6,K4
Hubbard K2
Huber A8
Hudson G2
Hughes Terr. F2
Humboldt I3
Hunt G8
Huron I3
Hyde H8
Illinois G6,G8
Jacob B6
Jay H8
Jefferies I5
Jefferies Frwy. I2
Jefferson W. K6
John C. Lodge Service Dr. D3,J6
John R. E4,I6
Joliet Pl. I8
Jos Campau A6,F8
Josephine C4
Junction K1
Kanter D7
Kenilworth C4
King C4
Kingsley D4
Kipling E3
Kirby F5,F6,G4
Kirby E. E7,F5
Kirby W. H1
Klein C7
Knox C5
Konkel K1
Kopernick J1
LaBelle A1
LaBrosse J5
LaSalle E1,F2
LaSalle Gds.N. F1
LaSalle Gds.S. F1
Lafayette E. I8
Lafayette W. J6
Lambert D8
Lambie Pl. K3
Lamothe F2
Lanman I1
Larned E. J7
Lawrence C2
Lawton E1,I3
Ledyard I5
Lee Pl. E2
Legrand C7
Lehman B6
Leicester Ct. C4
Leland G6,G8
Leverette J5
Liberty C6
Lincoln B1,F3,G4
Linwood E1,G2
Lockwood J1
Lodi D8
Longfellow C3,D1
Loraine G2
Lothorp E3,F1
Lovett I1
Lumpkin A5,C5
Lyman D6
Lynn B4
Lysander H3
Mack G6,H8
Macomb I7
Madison I7
Magnolia I2,I3,J1
Manhattan B7
Manson K1
Mansur E5
Manuel B7
Maple I7
Marantette J4
Marcus B8
Marjorie A8
Mark G3
Marquette G2
Marston D4,D6
Massachusetts A3
McDougall A6,F8
McGraw G2
McGregor K1
McKinley I2
McLean A3
Mechanic I7
Medbury D8,E7
Melbourne D4
Melrose D5
Merrick G4,H1
Merrill E3
Merritt K1
Michigan J2,J6
Middle J6
Milford H1
Miller B7,B8,C6
Milwaukee D7,E4
Missouri G2
Mitchell A5,A6,F3
Monning Ct. E6
Monroe I7
Montclam E. I7
Monterey B2
Montgomery F1
Moore Pl. G1
Moran E8
Morrow C5
Mt. Elliott B7,D8
Mt. Vernon D4
Mulberry I3
Myrtle H5,I3,J2
Nagle B8
Nall I1
Nebraska F2
Newark K1,K4
Newhall B7
Newton C6
Nicolet Pl. I8
Northwestern F1
Norwalk A6,A7,B5
Oakland A3
Oliver B7
Orleans D6,G7,I8
Osborne Pl. E6
Otis J1
Owen C4
Pallister E2,E3
Palmer E. E7,F5
Palmer W. F4
Palms K2
Park Dr. H8
Parks H3
Parsons H5
Pasadena A1
Pease B8
Perry I5,J3
Peterboro I5
Philadelphia E. D4
Philadelphia W. D3,E2
Pierce G8
Pine I5
Pingree D3,E2
Piquette D7,E5,E6
Plaza Dr. J6
Plum J5
Plumer K1
Poe E3
Poland B5
Poplar I2,I3
Porter K5
Prentis G5
Preston G8
Pulaski A5
Putnam G5
Randall K3
Randolph J7
Reed Pl. G4
Rhode Island A3
Rich I1
Richardson B8
Richton B2
Riopelle C5,D6,H7,J8
Risdon J2
Rivard H7,J8
Roby E6
Rockwood B7
Roland A8
Roosevelt B6,G1,I2
Rosa G3
Rosa Parks Blvd. B1
Rose J3
Rosedale B3
Rugg B8
Ruskin K3
Russell F7
Saginaw D8
Sallan B7
Sampson K4
Sargent D7
Schewitzer Pl. J8
Scott G8
Scotten I1,K2
Scovel Pl. G1
Second B2,E4
Selden H4,H5
Selkirk B7
Service H8
Seward E2,E3
Sheehan A8
Shelby J7
Sherwood B8
Sibley I6
Sloman B4
Smith C6,D4
Sproat I6
Spruce I5
St. Antone D5,F6
St. Aubin A4,C5,F7,I8
St. Cyril B8
St. Hedwig J1
St. Joseph G8
St. Thomas C8
Stanley G2
Sterling F3
Stimson H6
Stroh Dr. I7
Strong C8
Sturtevant B1
Superior F7,G6
Sycamore I4
Taylor D1,D3
Temple I5
Tennyson B3
Theodore F5,F7
Third B2,E3
Times Square J6
Toledo K1
Torrey J1
Torrey Ct. I1
Trombly D6
Trowbridge A5,B3
Trumbull A1,F3,G4,K5
Tuscola H5
Tuxedo B2
Tyler A1
Varney C7
Vermont I4,K4
Vernor Hwy.,E. H8
Vernor Hwy.,W. K2
Vicksburg F1
Vincen B7
Vinewood K2
Virginia Park D3,E2
Walter P. Chrysler Frwy. B5,F6
Warren E. F7
Warren W. G4,H1
Washington J7
Washington Blvd. J6
Watson G8,H6
Waverly A1
Webb B2
Weitzel Ct. D8
Wellington C5
West Grand Blvd. F1,G1,J2
Westminster C3
Whalin A5
Whitney F1
Widman Pl. D6
Wildemere E1
Wilkins G8,H7
Willis G6,H5
Willis E. F7
Winder H7,I6
Winfield B8
Wing Pl. K4
Winkleman B7
Winona A1
Witherell I6
Woodbridge J8
Woodland B3
Woodrow Wilson B1,D2,E2
Woodward B2,F5,J7
Wreford G2
Wyandotte B6
Yemans A5
Zinow A5
3rd G5,J6
4th H4,J5
5th J5
6th K6
8th H4,J5,K5
10th K5
14th E2,I3,K4
15th I3
16th I3,K4
17th I3,K4
18th I3,K4
20th K3
21st K3
22nd I2
23rd I2
24th I2
25th I2,K3
26th I2
28th I1
29th I1
30th I1,J1
31st J1
32nd J1

Scale of Miles

0   .2   .4   .6

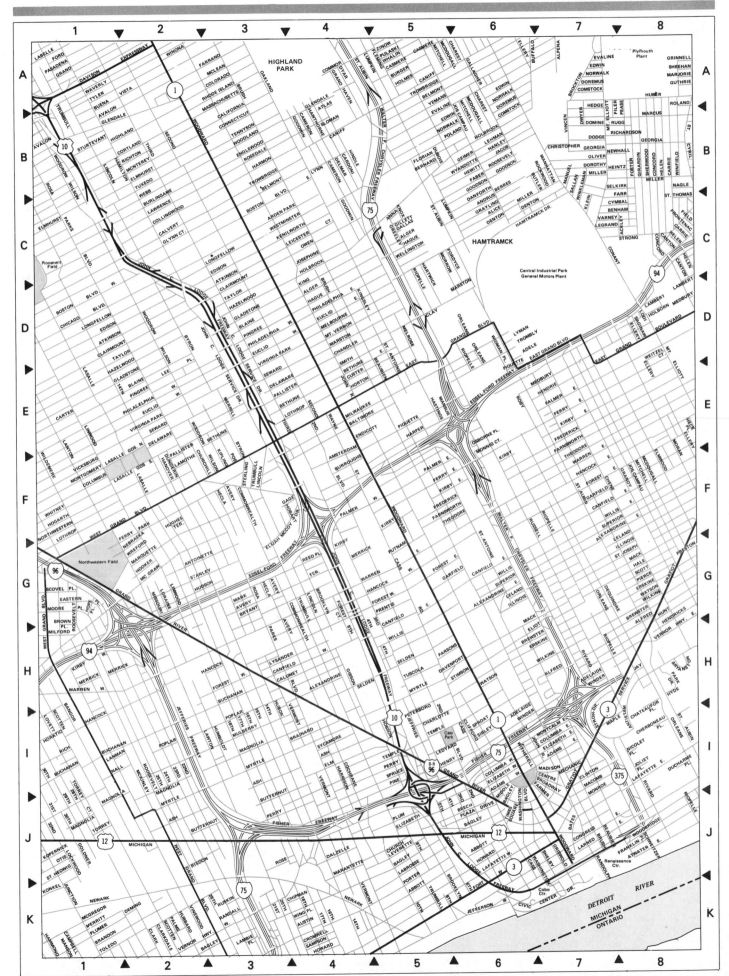

Scale of Miles

0 .2 .4 .6 .8

N

FT. LAUDERDALE

Acacia...H-7
Agua Vista Blvd...G-7
Alamanda...H-7
Algiers...A-8
Alhambra...G-7
Allenwood...B-8
Andrews Ave...D-4
Andrews Ave., N...G-4
Andrews Ave., S...H-4,I-4
Atlantic Blvd...D-8
Aurama...G-7
Aureila...H-7
Banyan...H-7
Barcelona...G-7
Basin Dr...A-8
Bayshore...G-7
Bayview Dr...C-7,E-7
Belmar...G-7
Birch Rd...F-7,G-7
Bombay...A-8
Bontona...H-6
Breakers Ave...F-8
Brickell...H-5
Broward Blvd...G-4
Capri...A-8
Castle Harbor...B-8
Castillia Pl...G-7
Castillo...G-7
Center Ave., N.E...D-8
Chateau Park Dr...F-3
Clematus...H-7
Coconut Dr...H-3
Codrington...B-8
Commercial Blvd....A-1,A-5
Cook St...J-2
Coral Gardens Dr....C-6,D-6
Coral Shore Dr....C-6,D-6
Cordon...H-6
Cordova...I-5
Corsair...A-8
Cortez...H-7
Datura...A-8
Datura Ct...H-7
Decker Rd...B-2
Del Lago Dr...I-6
Delmar Pl...H-7
Desota Dr...G-7
Dixie Hwy...E-5
East Lake Dr...I-7
Eisenhower Blvd...K-6
Eller Dr...K-6
El Mar Dr...B-8
Federal Hwy...D-7
Flagler Ave...H-4
Flagler Dr...F-5
Floranda Rd...B-6
Fryer Pl...D-7
Galt Ocean Dr...C-8
Garden Dr...D-6
Grace...J-7
Granada...G-7
Grand Dr...H-3
Harbor...A-8,I-7
Harborage Dr...I-6,I-7
Harbor Beach Pkwy...I-7
Hibiscus...B-8,H-7
Holiday Dr...I-7
Holly Heights Dr...E-5
Imperial Ln...B-8
Intracoastal Dr....E-7,G-7
Islo Babia Dr...I-6
Kensington Dr...E-5
Kensington St...E-5
Laguna...I-6
Las Clas Blvd...H-3,H-6
Las Olas Cir...H-7
Marion...J-7
McIntosh Rd...K-6
Miami Rd...J-5
Middle River Dr...D-7,F-6
Miramar...A-8
Neptune...A-8
New River...H-4
Oakland Park Blvd....C-1,C-2,C-6,C-7
Ocean Dr...A-8,I-7
Oceanic...A-8
Ocean Ln...J-7
Old Dixie Hwy...A-5,B-5
Palm...B-8
Pelican Dr...G-7
Perry...J-2
Poinciana Bougainvillas...A-8
Poinciana Dr...H-7
Poinsettia...H-7
Poinsettia St...D-6,E-5
Ponce De Leon Dr...I-5
Private...A-2
Private Rd...I-3
Prospect Rd...B-2
Ravenswood Rd...K-2
Riomar...G-7
Rio Vista Blvd...H-5
Riverland Dr...J-1
Riverland Rd...J-1
Riverland Ter...J-1
River Reach Dr...I-5
Riverside Dr...H-2
Rose Dr...I-4
Royal Isles...B-8
Seabreeze Blvd....H-7,I-7
Sebastian...G-7
Seminole Dr...F-7
Seville...G-7
Sliphead Rd...J-6
Slocum St...J-2
Sunrise Blvd...F-6
Sunrise Blvd, W...F-1
Sunrise Key Blvd...G-6
Sunset...H-7
Terra Mar St...G-7
Toledo Blvd...G-7
Tradewinds Ave...A-8
Tropic...A-8
Valencia...G-7
Victoria Park Rd....E-6,G-6
Vistamar St...F-7
Waverly Rd...H-3
West Lake Dr...I-7
Wilton Blvd...D-5
Windamar...G-7
Yacht Club Blvd...F-7
1st Ave. N.E...A-4,D-4,G-4
1st Ave. N.W...F-4,G-4
1st Ave. S.E...H-4,I-4
1st Ave. S.W...H-4,I-4
1st Ct...H-2
1st Key...G-6
1st St. S.E...G-4,G-5
1st St. S.W...G-1,G-3
1st St. N.E...G-4
1st St. N.W...G-2,G-3
1st Ter. N.E...A-4
2nd Ave. N.E...A-4,B-4,D-4,F-4,G-4
2nd Ave. N.W...D-4,E-4,G-4
2nd Ave. S.E...H-4,I-4
2nd Ave. S.W...H-4
2nd Ct...G-5
2nd Ct. S.E...H-5
2nd Ct. S.W...H-1,H-3
2nd Key...G-6
2nd St. N.E...G-4
2nd St. N.W...G-1,G-2,G-3
2nd St. S.E...H-5
2nd St. S.W...H-1,H-2,H-3,K-4
2nd Ter. N.E...A-4,B-4
3rd Ave. N.E...A-4,B-4,C-4,D-4,F-4,G-4
3rd Ave. N.W...D-4,G-4
3rd Ave. S.E...I-4
3rd Ave. S.W...H-4,I-4
3rd Ct...H-1
3rd Ct. N.W...G-2,G-3
3rd Key...G-6
3rd St. N.E...G-4
3rd St. N.W...G-3
3rd St. S.W...H-1,J-4
3rd Ter. N.E...A-4,B-4
4th Ave. N.E...A-4,B-4,C-4,F-4,G-4
4th Ave. N.W...F-4,G-4
4th Ave. S.E...H-4,I-4
4th Ave. S.W...H-4,K-4
4th Ct...G-1,H-1
4th Ct. N.E...G-5
4th Ct. S.W...H-2,H-3
4th Key...G-7
4th Pl...H-1,H-3
4th Pl. N.E...G-5
4th St...G-1,G-2,H-1
4th St. N.E...G-4
4th St. N.W...G-1,G-2
4th St. S.E...H-4,H-5
4th St. S.W...H-2,H-3
4th Ter. N.E...A-4
5th...H-5
5th Ave...D-4,H-4
5th Ave. N.E...A-5,B-4,D-5,F-4,G-5
5th Ave. N.W...D-4,G-4
5th Ct...H-1
5th Ct. N.E...G-5
5th Ct. N.W...G-3
5th Ct. S.E...H-5
5th Ct. S.W...H-2
5th Key...G-7
5th Pl...H-2
5th Pl. S.W...H-2
5th St...H-1
5th St. N.E...G-4
5th St. N.W...G-1,G-2
5th St. S.W...H-2
5th Ter...C-5,H-5
5th Ter. N.E...B-5,F-5
6th Ave. N.E...B-5,C-5,D-5,F-5,G-5
6th Ave. N.W...D-4,F-4,G-4
6th Ave. S.E...H-5,I-5
6th Ave. S.W...H-4,J-4
6th Ct...G-3,G-7
6th Ct. N.W...G-1,G-2
6th Ct. S.E...H-4
6th Ct. S.W...H-1
6th Pl. N.W...G-2
6th St...H-3
6th St. N.E...G-4
6th St. N.W...G-1,G-2
6th St. S.E...H-4
6th St. S.W...H-1
6th Ter...B-5
7th S.W...H-3
7th Ave...D-3
7th Ter. N.W...F-3,G-3
7th Ave. N.E...A-5,F-5,G-5
7th Ter...B-5,E-5
7th Ave. N.W...F-3,G-3
7th Ct...F-6
7th Ct. N.W...F-1,F-2
7th Pl...F-6,F-7
7th Pl. N.W...F-2
7th St. N.E...G-4
7th St. N.W...F-1,G-1,G-2,G-3
7th St. S.E...H-4,H-6
7th St. S.W...H-1,H-3
8th Ave...D-3
8th Ave. N.E...A-5,C-5,D-5,F-5,G-5
8th Ave. N.W...F-3,G-3
8th Ave. S.W...H-3,I-3,K-3
8th Ct...F-1,F-2,H-3
8th Ct. N.W...F-1
8th Pl...F-1,F-2
8th Pl. N.W...F-1
8th Rd...F-1
8th St. N.E...F-6,F-7
8th St. N.W...F-1,F-2
8th St. S.E...H-5,H-6
8th St. S.W...H-1,H-3
9th...F-3
9th Ave...H-3
9th Ave. N.E...B-5,D-5,E-5,F-5,G-5
9th Ave. N.W...G-3
9th Ave. S.E...H-5
9th Ave. S.W...J-3
9th Ct...F-7,H-3
9th Ct. N.W...F-1,F-2
9th Pl...F-6
9th Pl. N.W...F-1
9th Pl. S.W...H-1
9th St...F-7
9th St. N.E...F-5,F-7
9th St. N.W...E-3,F-3,F-1,F-2
9th St. S.E...H-5
9th St. S.W...H-1,H-2,H-4
9th Ter...A-5
9th Ter. N.W...A-3,D-3
10th Ave. N.E...B-5,C-5,D-5,E-5,H-5
10th Ave. N.W...B-3,D-3,E-3,F-3,G-3
10th Ave. S.E...I-5
10th Ave. S.W...J-3
10th Ct...I-2
10th Ct. N.W...F-1,F-2
10th Pl...F-1
10th Pl. N.W...F-2,F-3
10th St...H-3
10th St. S.E...I-4,I-6
10th St. S.W...I-1,I-2,I-4
10th Ter...B-3,D-5,I-3
10th Ter. N.W...F-3,G-3
10th Way...B-3
11th Ave...B-3
11th Ave. N.E...B-5,D-5,F-5,G-5
11th Ave. N.W...G-3
11th Ave. S.E...H-5
11th Ave. S.W...H-3
11th Ct...F-7
11th Ct. N.W...F-1,F-2,F-3
11th Ct. S.E...I-5
11th Ct. S.W...I-1,I-2,I-4
11th Pl. N.W...F-1,F-2,F-3
11th St...F-7,I-4
11th St. N.E...F-5
11th St. N.W...F-1,F-2,F-3,F-4
11th St. S.E...I-5,I-6
11th St. S.W...I-2,I-4
11th Way...E-3
12th...C-5,K-3
12th Ave...B-3,D-3,E-3
12th Ave. N.E...A-5,C-5,F-5,G-5
12th Ave. N.W...D-3,G-3
12th Ave. S.W...H-3,J-3
12th Ct...F-7
12th Ct. N.W...F-1,F-2,F-3
12th Ct. S.E...I-5,I-6
12th Ct. S.W...I-2,I-3
12th Rd...D-5
12th St. N.E...F-4,F-5,F-7
12th St. N.W...F-1,F-2,F-3,F-4
12th St. S.E...I-5,I-6
12th St. S.W...I-1,I-3,K-3
12th Ter...B-3,C-2,E-3,H-5
12th Ter. N.E...B-5,E-5
13th...C-5
13th Ave...B-3
13th Ave. N.E...G-5
13th Ave. N.W...G-3
13th Ave. S.E...I-6
13th Ave. S.W...H-3,J-3
13th Ct...E-7
13th Ct. N.W....E-1,E-2,E-3
13th Ct. S.W...I-1,I-2
13th St...F-7
13th St. N.E...F-4,F-5
13th St. N.W...E-1,E-3
13th St. S.E...I-5,I-6
13th St. S.W...I-1,I-2,I-3
13th Ter...A-5,B-5,I-5
14th...C-5,E-5
14th Ave. N.E...E-5,G-5
14th Ave. N.W...E-3,G-3
14th Ave. S.W...H-3,I-3,J-3
14th Ct...E-5
14th Ct. N.W...E-1,E-2,E-3
14th Ct. S.E...I-5
14th Ct. S.W...I-1,I-2,I-3
14th Pl...E-5
14th St...E-5
14th St. N.E...E-6,E-7
14th St. N.W...E-1,E-2,E-3,E-4
14th St. S.E...I-5,I-6
14th St. S.W...I-1,I-2,I-3
14th Ter. N.W...G-3
14th Way...A-6
14th Way N.W...G-3
15th S.W...I-3
15th Ave...I-1
15th Ave. N.E...B-6,E-5,F-5,G-5
15th Ave. N.W...A-3,B-3,E-3,G-3
15th Ave. S.W...J-3
15th Ct...I-1
15th Ct. N.W...E-1,E-2,E-3
15th Ct. S.W...I-3
15th Pl. N.W...E-2,E-3
15th St. N.E...E-6,E-7,E-8
15th St. N.W...E-1,E-2,E-3,E-4
15th St. S.E...I-4,I-5,I-6
15th St. S.W...I-3
15th Ter. N.E...B-6,D-6
15th Ter. N.W...E-2,G-2
15th Ter. S.W...I-2
15th Way...G-2
15th Way N.E...B-6
16th...E-3
16th Ave...I-2
16th Ave. N.E...C-6,D-6
16th Ave. N.W...G-2
16th Ct...I-1
16th Ct. N.E...E-4,E-5,E-6
16th Ct. N.W...E-1,E-2
16th Ct. S.E...I-5
16th Ct. S.W...I-3
16th Pl. N.E...E-4
16th St. N.E...E-4,E-5,E-6
16th St. N.W...E-1,E-2,E-3,E-4
16th St. S.E...I-5
16th St. S.W...I-2,I-3
16th Ter. N.E...B-6,F-6,G-6
16th Way...F-2
17th...E-8
17th S.E...H-6
17th Ave...D-6,G-6
17th Ave. N.E...A-6,B-6,C-6,D-6,F-6
17th Ave. N.W...F-2,G-2
17th Ct...E-6
17th Ct. N.E...E-4,E-5
17th Ct. N.W...E-3,E-4
17th St...E-5
17th St. N.E...E-5,E-6,E-7
17th St. N.W...E-1,E-3,E-4
17th St. S.E...I-5
17th St. S.W...J-1,J-3
17th Ter. N.E...A-6,B-6,D-6,F-6
17th Ter. N.W...C-2
17th Way N.E...F-6,G-6
17th Way S.E...H-6
18th...D-6,E-8,G-6
18th Ave...B-2
18th Ave. N.E...B-6,C-6,D-6,E-5,E-6,F-6,G-6
18th Ave. N.W...E-2,G-2
18th Ave. S.E...H-6,J-6,K-6
18th Ave. S.W...H-2,I-2
18th Ct. N.W...E-1,E-2,E-3
18th Ct. S.E...J-4,J-6
18th Ct. S.W...J-3
18th St...E-1,E-2
18th St. N.E...E-5,E-7
18th St. N.W...E-3,E-4
18th St. S.E...J-4
18th St. S.W...J-1,J-3
18th Ter...D-2,I-2
18th Ter. N.E...A-6
18th Ter. S.W...J-2
19th...G-6
19th Ave. N.E...A-6,C-6,D-6,G-6
19th Ave. N.W...B-2,D-2,E-2,G-2
19th Ave. S.E...H-6,K-6
19th Ave. S.W...H-2,J-2
19th Ct...E-3
19th Ct. N.W...E-3
19th St...E-6,E-7,E-8,J-1
19th St. N.W...E-1,E-2,E-3
19th St. S.E...J-4,J-6
19th St. S.W...J-3
19th Ter. N.W...B-2,G-2
20th...D-2
20th N.E...D-4
20th Ave...I-2
20th Ave. N.E...B-6,C-6,E-6,G-6
20th Ave. N.W...E-2,F-2,G-2
20th Ave. S.E...H-6
20th Ct...D-3,E-7
20th Dr. N.E...D-5
20th St...D-3,E-7,J-1
20th St. N.E...E-6
20th St. N.W...D-1,D-3,E-1
20th St. S.E...J-5,J-7
20th St. S.W...J-3
20th Ter...A-7,I-2
21st...A-7,D-5
21st Ave...D-6
21st Ave. N.E...B-6,G-6
21st Ave. N.W...G-2
21st Ave. S.E...H-6
21st Ct...J-1
21st Ct. N.E...D-4,E-7
21st Ct. N.W...D-1,D-4
21st Dr...D-5
21st St...D-3,D-6,E-6,E-7
21st St. N.E...D-4,D-8,E-7
21st St. N.W...D-1
21st St. S.W...J-3,J-4
21st Ter...D-2
21st Ter. N.E...D-6
21st Ter. N.W...G-2
21st Ter. S.E...H-6
21st Ter. S.W...H-2,I-2
21st Way...H-2
22nd...D-5
22nd Ave...I-2
22nd Ave. N.E...B-6,C-6,E-6,G-6
22nd Ave. N.W...G-2
22nd Ave. S.E...H-6,J-7
22nd Ave. S.W...H-2,I-2,J-2
22nd Ct...D-3,J-1
22nd Dr. N.E...D-5
22nd Rd. N.W...F-1
22nd St...D-3,D-8,E-7,J-1
22nd St. N.E...D-4
22nd St. N.W...D-1,E-2
22nd St. S.E...J-4
22nd St. S.W...J-2,J-4
22nd Ter...H-2,I-2
22nd Ter. N.E...A-7,E-6
23rd...C-6,D-5,G-7
23rd Ave. N.E...G-6
23rd Ave. S.W...G-2,I-2,J-2
23rd Dr. N.E...D-5
23rd Ln...D-1
23rd St...D-7,J-1
23rd St. N.E...D-4,D-8
23rd St. N.W...D-1,D-4
23rd St. S.E...J-4
23rd St. S.W...J-2,J-4
23rd Ter. N.W...F-2
23rd Ter. S.W...J-2,K-2
23rd Way...F-2
24th...C-6
24th Ave. N.W...D-1,E-1
24th Ave. S.E...H-7,J-7
24th Ave. S.W...J-1
24th St...D-2
24th Ct. N.E...D-7
24th Ct. N.W...D-1
24th Pl. N.E...D-7
24th St. N.E...D-4,D-7
24th St. N.W...D-1,D-3,D-4
24th St. S.W...J-2
24th Ter...F-1
24th Ter. N.E...A-7
24th Ter. N.W...E-1
25th...C-7
25th Ave...E-1,G-1,H-1,I-1
25th Ave. N.E...B-7,E-7
25th Ave. S.E...H-7,J-7
25th Ct. N.E...D-7
25th Pl...D-7
25th St...D-8
25th St. N.E...D-4,D-7
25th St. N.W...D-1,D-3,D-4
25th St. S.W...J-2,J-4
25th Ter...C-7,E-1,G-1,H-1,I-1,K-1
25th Way...F-1
26th...D-8,H-7
26th Ave...H-1
26th Ave. N.E...A-7,C-7,D-7,E-7,F-7
26th Ave. N.W...D-1,E-1
26th Ave. S.W...I-1
26th Ct. N.E...D-7
26th Dr. N.E...D-4,D-5,D-6
26th Pl. N.E...D-7
26th St. N.E...D-4,D-5
26th St. N.W...D-3
26th St. S.W...J-2,J-3,J-4
26th Ter...E-1,I-1
26th Ter. N.E...D-7
26th Ter. S.W...K-1
27th...J-3
27th Ave...C-7
27th Ave. N.E...A-7,B-7
27th Ave. N.W...E-1
27th Ave. S.W...H-1,J-1
27th Ct...D-7,J-2
27th Dr. N.E...D-4,D-5
27th Ln...D-1
27th St...D-8
27th St. N.E...D-4,D-5,D-6,D-7
27th St. N.W...D-1,D-2,D-3
27th St. S.E...J-4
27th St. S.W...J-4
27th Ter...D-7,H-1,I-1,J-1
27th Ter. N.W...G-1
28th Ave. N.E...A-7,B-7
28th Ave. N.W...D-1,E-1,F-1,G-1
28th Ave. S.W...H-1,I-1,J-1
28th Ct...D-2
28th Ct. N.W...D-3,D-4
28th Rd...I-1
28th St. N.E...D-4,D-5,D-6,D-7,D-8
28th Dr...D-6
28th St. N.W...D-1,D-2,D-3,D-4
28th St. S.E...K-4,K-6
28th St. S.W...K-2,K-3
28th Ter. N.W...D-1,G-1
28th Ter. S.W...H-1,I-1,J-1
28th Way N.W...G-1
28th Way S.W...I-1,J-1
29th S.E...K-4
29th Ave...D-1,F-1,G-1
29th Ave. N.E...A-7,B-7
29th Ave. N.W...D-1
29th Ave. S.W...H-1,I-1
29th Ct...C-6,D-3
29th Ct. N.E...C-7
29th Dr. N.E...D-4,D-5
29th St...C-6,D-8
29th St. N.E...C-7,D-8
29th St. N.W...D-2,D-3,D-4
29th St. S.W...K-2,K-4
29th Ter. N.W...D-1,G-1
29th Ter. S.W...H-1,I-1
29th Way...F-1,I-1
30th Ave. N.W...D-1,F-1,G-1
30th Ave. S.W...H-1,I-1
30th Ct. N.E...C-5
30th Ct. N.W...C-1,C-3
30th Pl. N.E...C-7
30th St...C-1,C-3,C-4,C-6
30th St. N.E...C-7
30th St. S.E...K-4,K-6
30th St. S.W...K-2,K-3,K-4
30th Ter. N.W...B-1,E-1
30th Ter. S.W...J-1
31st S.E...K-4
31st Ave...A-7,E-8
31st St. S.W...K-1,K-2,K-3,K-4
32nd Ave...A-8,C-8
32nd Ave. N.E...D-8
32nd Ct. S.E...K-4
32nd Ct. S.W...K-2,K-4
32nd Pl...K-2
32nd St. N.E...C-5,C-7
32nd St. S.E...K-4,K-6
32nd St. S.W...K-1,K-3,K-4
33rd Ave...A-8
33rd Ave. N.E...D-8
33rd Ct...C-2
33rd St...C-2
33rd St. N.E...C-5,C-7
33rd St. N.W...C-3,C-4
33rd St. S.W...K-4
34th...C-2
34th Ave. N.E...C-8,D-8
34th Ct. N.E...C-5
34th St. N.E...C-5,C-7
34th St. N.W...C-3,C-4
35th Ct...C-4
35th Ct. N.E...C-7
35th Dr. N.E...C-7
35th St. N.E...C-5,C-7
35th St. N.W...C-3,C-4
36th Ct...C-4
36th Ct. N.W...C-2
36th St...C-6,C-7
36th St. N.E...C-5,C-7,C-8
36th St. N.W...C-3,C-4
37th Ct...C-7
37th Dr. N.E...C-7
37th St...C-7
37th St. N.E...C-5
37th St. N.W...C-2,C-3,C-4
38th...C-8
38th St...B-7
38th St. N.W...C-1,C-2,C-4,C-5
39th...B-8
39th St...B-4,B-5,B-7
39th St. N.E...B-5,B-6
39th St. N.W...B-2,B-3,B-4
40th...B-8
40th Ct...B-4,B-5,B-6,B-7
40th Ct. N.W...B-4
40th St...B-5,B-5,B-7,B-8
40th St. N.E...B-5,B-6
40th St. N.W...B-3,B-4
41st St...B-3,B-4,B-5,B-6
41st St. N.W...B-3,B-4
42nd Ct...B-3,B-8
42nd St...B-2,B-3,B-5
42nd St. N.E...B-4,B-5,B-8
42nd St. N.W...B-3,B-4
43rd Ct. N.E...B-4,B-5
43rd Ct. N.W...B-3,B-4
43rd St...B-3
43rd St. N.E...B-4,B-6,B-7
43rd St. N.W...B-3,B-4
44th Ct...B-5
44th St...B-6
44th St. N.E...B-7
45th Ct...B-3
45th Ct. N.W...B-4
45th St...B-3,B-4,B-5,B-7,B-8
45th St. N.W...B-4
46th Ct...B-4,B-5
46th St...A-1,A-2,B-2,B-4,B-7
46th St. N.E...B-5,B-6
46th St. N.W...B-2
47th Ct...A-4,A-5,A-7
47th St...B-3,B-4
47th St. N.E...A-7,B-6
48th Ct...A-4
48th Ct. N.E...A-4,A-5,A-6
48th St...A-1,A-3,A-4,A-5,A-7
49th St...A-3,A-4
49th St. N.E...A-4,A-6,A-7
50th Ct. N.E...A-5,A-6,A-7
51st Ct...A-4
51st Ct. N.E...A-6
51st Pl...A-1,A-3
51st St...A-3,A-4,A-6
51st St. N.E...A-4,A-6,A-7
52nd Ct...A-1,A-4,A-6
52nd St...A-3,A-4,A-6,A-7
52nd St. N.E...A-6
53rd Ct...A-4,A-5
53rd St...A-3,A-4
53rd St. N.E...A-5,A-6,A-7
54th St...A-1,A-3
54th St. N.E...A-6,A-7
55th St...A-1

POINTS OF INTEREST

Ft. Lauderdale Executive Airport...A-2
Holiday Park...F-5,G-5
Hugh Taylor Birch State Park...E-7,E-8,F-7,F-8
Osswald Park...D-2
S.P. Snyder Park...K-3,K-4
Sunland Park...F-2,F-3

FORT WORTH

A Ave...G-7
Abney...J-5
Ada St...H-7
Adams St...G-3,I-3,K-3
Adolph...E-2
Adrian...E-1
Akers...D-5
Alabama...F-3
Alcannon St...K-7
Alice St...K-3
Allen Ave...H-3,H-5
Alloway...J-6
Alston Ave...G-3
Alta View...A-6
Alvin...K-7
Alvord...E-6
Amont...J-4
Amspoker...K-5
Amy...H-6
Andy Ave...F-8
Angle...B-1
Ann...G-6
Anna St...J-6
Annabell...J-6
Annglenn...J-6
Annie St...G-4,G-5
Arch St...G-8,H-8
Arch Adams...E-1
Arizona...G-4,H-4
Arlington...H-3,H-5,H-6
Armour...C-4
Arnold...D-7
Arthur...E-2
Ash Crescent...G-6,I-6
Aster...B-5,B-6
Atkins St...J-5
Aurline...E-5
Austin...D-6,E-2
Aval...F-8
Avenue...B-3
Avondale...H-1
Ayers Ave...F-8,G-8
Azalea...E-1
B Ave...G-6,G-7
Bailey...E-1
Baker Lane...B-8
Baker St...I-4
Baldwin St...J-3,K-3
Ballinger...F-3
Balsam...B-5
Baltimore Ave....H-3,H-5
Barbella...B-6
Barclay...C-6
Barden...E-1
Baylor St...J-7
Beach St...A-6,D-6,D-7,E-7,G-7
Beckham...G-2
Bedsoe...F-1
Belford Ct...F-8
Belknap...A-8,D-5,E-3
Belmead St...K-4
Belmont...C-1
Belzise...G-6
Belzise Terr...I-6
Benbrook Dr...J-1,J-2
Benhal Ct...H-2
Benjamin...C-2
Berke Rd...K-5
Berner...A-5
Bernice...B-7
Berry St...I-7,I-8,J-3,J-4
Berryhill...H-6
Bessie...F-5
Betty...C-7
Beverly Ave...H-5
Bewick...J-1,J-3
Biddison...J-1,J-2,J-4
Bideker Ave...H-7
Binkley St...G-7,H-7,I-7
Bird...C-5
Birdville...C-8
Bishop...I-8
Blanch...E-1
Blandin...B-5,C-5
Blalock Ave...K-4,K-5
Blevins...D-6
Blitton...K-5
Blodgett Ave...K-5
Blue...C-5
Bluebird...B-4
Blue Grove...D-6
Blue Smoke Ct...F-6
Boland...E-1
Bolt...K-1
Bomar...F-6,F-7
Bonnett...B-5,C-5
Bonnie Brae...B-6,C-6
Booker...E-5
Boston Ave...F-8,G-8
Bowie St...I-1,I-3,I-4
Boyd Ave...I-1,K-1
Brady...K-1
Brandies...E-6
Bransford...G-5
Braswell...A-4
Brenning...B-3
Brents...D-4
Bright...I-8
Bristol...E-4
Brittian...B-6
Broadway...F-2,F-3,F-5,F-6
Brookshire...E-4
Brown...D-6
Bruce...A-5
Bryan Ave...G-4,I-4,K-4
Buck St...G-2
Bundie St...K-7
Burchill...H-7
Burchill Ct...H-7
Burnett...E-3,F-3
Burson...J-4
Burton St...I-8
Buster Ct...C-6
Butler...J-1,J-2,K-2,K-4,K-5
Buxton...G-5
Calhoun...B-2,D-3,E-3,F-4
Calvert...E-2
Calvin...I-6
Camilla...G-6
Campbell St...G-8,H-8,I-8
Canberra...H-6
Cannon...G-3,G-5
Cantey...I-1,I-3,I-4,I-5
Canyon Ct...G-8
Capps St...I-3
Cardinal...B-4
Carlock St...H-3
Carnation...B-5,B-6
Carnes...K-5
Carrol...E-2
Carter...F-6
Carter Park Dr...K-5
Carver...C-4
Casablanca...E-1
Castleman...I-8
Catalpa...B-8,C-7
C Ave...G-6,G-7
Cedar...F-5
Central...C-2
Chambers...E-4
Chandler...C-5,E-6
Chandler Dr...B-6
Chenault...D-5
Cherry...F-3
Cheryl...B-6
Chase Ct...H-3
Chester...B-4,F-6
Chester Boyer Rd...A-6
Chestnut...B-1
Chicago Ave...F-8,G-8
Chickasaw Ave...J-8
Childress...J-7
Christin...H-7
Circle...D-7
Circle Park. Blvd...C-2
Circle Pkwy...H-1
Clairemont Ave...F-8,G-8
Clara St...G-1
Clarence...C-7,D-7
Clary...C-6
Clearview...K-6
Cleckler...C-6
Clement...G-6,G-7
Cleveland...F-4
Cleyburn...J-2
Clinton...A-2,B-2,C-2
Cloer...K-1
Cobb...F-5
Cobb Park Dr...H-6
Cockerell Ave...I-1,J-1,K-1
Cole St...K-4
Cole Spring Rd....C-4,D-4
Collard...I-7
College St...G-3,I-3,J-3
Collier...F-3
Collin...J-7,J-8
Collins...H-1
Colonial...D-6
Columbus...B-1
Colvin Ave...I-4,I-5
Comanche...I-7
Commerce...B-2
Commercial...E-2
Concord...C-6
Congress...E-2
Conkling...A-7
Conway...D-6,D-7
Cook...D-4
Cooper...G-2
Corner Ave...G-7
Corpus Ct...J-3
Cosgrove Ct...A-8
Cottonwood...D-6
Court...G-7
Covella...D-6
Coventry...E-1
Crawford St...G-4
Creach Rd...B-7
Crenshaw St...H-7
Crest...J-6
Crockett...E-1
Cromwell...F-6
Crump...E-4
Cullen...D-2
Cummings...E-3
Currie...E-1
Cutter St...K-7
Cypress...F-5
D Ave...G-6,G-7
Daggett...F-2-4
Dakota...E-2
Daisy La...B-5
Dalford...C-5
Dallas-Ft. Worth Tpk...F-5
Damon...D-6
Darby...H-8
Darcy...E-1
Dashwood...G-3,G-4
David...B-6
Davis Blvd...H-5
Dayton...B-8,C-5
Debbie St...K-5
Decatur...A-3
Decosta...D-6,E-6
Degar...G-1
Delaware St...H-5
Delga...C-4
Dell...B-7,C-5
Denair...E-6
Denman St...K-7
Denver...C-1
Devitt...J-2,J-4,J-5
Dewey...A-3,A-4
Dickson...K-1,K-2,K-4
Donalee St...H-8,I-8
Donna St...J-4
Dooling...A-5
Dowell...J-8
Drew St...K-1,K-2,K-4
Duell St...H-6
Dundee...B-4
Dunford...I-6
Dunlap dr...K-6
E Ave...G-6,G-7
E Dr...F-1
Eagle...B-6,C-6
Earl...B-6
Eastland...I-7
Eastline Dr...J-6,K-6
East Ridge...A-7,B-7
Eden Ave...B-8
Edith...A-7
Edwin...H-2
Elinor...A-6
Elizabeth Blvd...I-3
Ella...E-4
Elliot...D-7
Ellis...A-2,B-2,C-2
Elm...A-2,E-4
Elmwood Ave...H-5,H-6
El Paso...F-3
El Rancho Rd...K-6
Elsie...G-7
Elton...B-8
Elva Warren St...K-5
Embry...C-5
Emerson...I-7
Enneca...F-2
Ennis...E-6
Eoch...E-1
Erath St...K-8
Ernst...G-6
Essex...G-6
Esthill...I-7
Etsie...C-8
Eugene...K-5
Evans St...H-4,I-4,J-4
Exchange...B-2
Exeter...F-5,G-5
Faett Ct...J-6
Fain...C-7
Fairfax...K-8
Fairline...K-8
Fairmont Ave...I-3
Fair Park Blvd...K-5
Fair View...A-6,B-6,C-6,D-6
Fairway...J-7
Fairway Rd...J-7
Felcher-Andrews...A-8
Field...A-8
Fincher...B-8
Finley...E-5
First Ave. East...D-5
First St. East...D-7
Fisher...E-6
Fitzhugh...I-7,I-8
Flint...K-1,K-2
Florence...F-3
Foard...K-7
Fogg...K-3,K-4
Forbes...I-8
Forby Ave...F-8
Forest Blvd...H-2,I-2
Forest Park Blvd....F-2
Fossil...A-8
Fouriner...F-2
Fox...C-7
Frazier Ave...I-2,K-2
Freddie...I-8,J-8
Freman...G-5
Fry St...K-4
Fulton...F-3
G Ave...H-7,H-8
Gage...B-8
Galves...D-5,D-6
Galveston...H-4
Gardina St...K-7
Garvey...D-4
Gibson...C-7,E-5
Gilcrest...C-6
Gillis...D-5
Gilmore...D-7
Glen...J-6
Glencoe Terr...H-2
Glenda...A-7
Glendale...B-3
Glengarden Dr...I-4
Glenhaven...B-8
Glenmore...C-4
Goldenrod...B-5
Goldie...B-7
Goddard...D-7
Gorden Ave...I-2,K-2
Gould...B-1,C-1
Gounah...D-5
Grace...B-5
Grainge...G-3
Grand...D-1,D-2
Grant...D-4
Grapewood...D-5
Grayson...J-7
Greene Ave...I-1,J-1
Greenfield...D-4
Greenleaf...E-2
Greer...D-3
Gross...D-7
Grover...A-4,B-4
Grove St...C-2,E-4,J-4,K-4
Gunther...B-3
H Ave...H-7,H-8
Hale...A-4,B-3
Hall...G-6
Haltom Rd...A-8,B-8
Hampshire...G-8
Hampton...A-3,D-4,E-4
Hanger Ave...H-7
Harding...A-3,D-4,E-4
Hardy...A-3
Harper...C-7
Harrington...D-1
Harris...G-2
Harris Lane...B-7
Harrison...G-2
Harrold...E-2
Harrow...A-8
Harvey...H-5
Harwent Terr...J-1
Harwood St...F-7
Hathcox...K-5
Hattie...G-5
Hawthorne...H-2,H-3
Haynes Ave...F-8,G-8
Hazeline...G-8
Heath Ct. E...E-5
Hedrick...A-6
Hemlock...C-8
Hemphill St...G-3,I-3,K-3
Henderson St...F-3,G-3,J-3
Hendricks...G-6
Hickory...C-8
Higgens...B-7
Highcrest...A-5
Highland...C-1
High Point Rd...J-6
Hill Dr...I-2
Hill Place...C-1
Hillview...J-6
Hoffman...E-5
Hollis St...B-7
Holmes...G-6
Holtzer...H-1
Homan...D-1
Honey Suckle...B-5,B-6
Houston...B-2,C-2,D-2,D-3,F-3
Howard...A-8,J-7
Hudgins...D-6
Humboldt...G-2,G-4
Hunting Dr...K-7
Huntington...H-2
Hutchinson...A-3
I Ave...H-7,H-8
Illinois...F-5,J-5
Inderly...H-2
Inderly Pl...H-2
Industrial Blvd...F-4
Irion...B-4,E-7
Irma...G-4
Irwin...G-2
Ivey...B-5,B-7
J Ave...H-7,H-8
Jackson...J-7
Jamaica...F-6,G-8
James Ave...J-2,K-2
Jane Ln...K-7
Janis St...F-3
Jarvis St...F-2
Jeanette...J-1,K-1
Jefferies...A-7
Jefferson Ave...H-3,H-5
Jennings Ave...F-3,G-3,H-3,I-3
Jerome...F-2,G-2
Jessamine St...H-3,H-5
Jones St...C-2,D-2,I-4,K-4
Joplin...C-7
Juanita...D-5
Judd St...I-4,I-6
Juniper...B-8
K Ave...H-7,H-8
Kansas...E-2
Karnes...C-6,D-6
Kearby...B-7
Kellis...K-8
Kennedy St...F-5
Kent...I-1
Kentucky Ave...G-4
Kerry...A-8
Killian...J-8
Kimble St...H-6
Kimbo Ct...A-6
King...B-8,C-7,D-7
King Oaks...D-7
Kingsdale...J-6
Knoll...B-7
Knox Dr...K-8
L Ave...H-7,H-8
Lagonia...C-1
Lake...F-3,G-3
Lakeland...A-6
Lames...J-1
Lancaster Ave...F-1,F-3,F-4,F-6
Lane...A-7
Lasalle...E-5
Laughton...J-3
Lawnwood...E-6
Layton...B-7
Lee...B-1,C-2
Leming...A-4
Leona...B-7
Leon Ave...G-5
Leota...C-4
Leslie...G-2
Leuda...G-3,G-5
Lewis St...F-8
Lexington...E-3,F-3
Lilac St...H-3
Lillian...C-5
Lincoln...B-1,C-2
Linda Ln...K-6
Lipscomb St...G-3,I-3,K-3
Lisbury...B-4
Little St...H-8,I-8
Little John St...H-7,H-8
Live...D-4
Livingston...I-2,J-2,K-2
Locust...D-3
Loeton Terr...H-1
Logan...H-6
Lois St...I-8
Lola...B-6
Lollita Ct...J-6
Lomita...J-7
Lomo...K-4
Loney St...G-5
Loraine...A-1,A-4,A-7
Lotus...B-5
Louisiana...H-4
Loving...B-1
Lowden...I-1,I-3,I-4
Lowe St...J-3
Lower Birdville Rd...B-8,C-7,E-7
Lowriemore...I-6
Lucinda...K-7
Lucy...G-4
Ludell...F-6
Lulu...A-3
Lynch...D-7
Lynfield...G-8
M Ave...H-7,H-8
Macon...F-3
Maddox Ave...H-3,H-5
Magnolia Ave...G-2-4
Main St...D-3,E-3,J-4,K-4
Malone...B-3
Malta St...K-3,K-4
Malvern...I-6
Mandell...F-7
Mansfield Ave...G-5
Maple...D-4
Maple Leaf...B-5
Marigold...C-6
Marion Ave...I-5
Market...B-1
Marsalis...C-7
Marshall...D-5
Martin St...K-8
Mason St...K-3,K-4
Maurice...C-6
Maxine St...C-7
May St...H-3,J-3,J-3,K-4
Mayfield...D-3
McCart...I-2,K-2
McComas...H-6
McCurdy...G-6,H-6
McIvey...E-5
McKenzie St...G-7,H-7
McLean St...F-7
McLemore Ave...C-5
McLennon...B-3
McNutt...C-7
McPherson Ave...I-1,I-2
Meadowbrook Dr...F-7
Mecca St...J-7
Medford Ct...H-1
Menzer...E-8
Menzer Ct...E-8
Mercedes...E-1
Mercury...B-7
Merida Ave...I-1,J-1
Meriwether...K-5
Merrimac...E-1
Mesquite...A-6
Midland...G-7
Millet Ave...H-7
Mills...E-3
Milton...F-6
Minden...J-2,J-5
Minnie...B-7
Mission...J-1
Mississippi Ave...H-5
Missouri Ave...G-4,H-4
Mistletoe...G-1
Mistletoe Ave...G-2
Mistletow Blvd...G-2
Mitchell Blvd...H-6,I-7
Mitchell St...H-3
Moberly St...K-8
Moline...B-8
Monda St...J-2
Montague...J-7
Moore...B-4
Moreby...I-6
Morgan...E-4
Morning Glory...B-4
Morningside Dr....I-3,I-4
Morphy...G-3,G-5
Morrison...D-3
Morton...F-1
Mt. Vernon St...F-7,F-8
Mt. View...F-8
Mulke St...I-3,I-5
Murphy...C-5
Myrtle St...H-3,H-5
N Ave...H-7,H-8
Nashville...G-7
Neal...B-3
Nebraska...E-2
Nelson...B-5
Newman...A-7
Newton...B-8
New York...F-5,J-4
New York Ave...H-5,I-4
Nichols...A-3,E-4
Nixon...C-4
Noble...D-5,D-6
Noe St...I-8
Nolan St...K-8
Normandy...F-8
North...C-2
North Glen Dr...J-6
Northside Dr...C-2
Norwood...E-1
Oak...C-7,D-4
Oak Grove St...G-4
Oak Hurst Scenic Dr...C-4,E-5
Oak Ridge...B-8
Oak View...C-7
Oakwood...B-7
Odessa Ave...J-1
Old Mansfield Rd...J-6
Oleander...G-3
Ollie St...K-7
Orange St...J-2,J-3
Orr...G-2
Oscar...A-3
Otto St...H-8
Owens...B-8
Oxford...B-4
Pafford St...K-1,K-2,K-3
Page St...I-3
Panola...G-8
Paradise...E-5
Park...C-1,C-3,I-1
Parkdale...G-7
Park Dr...D-1
Parkins St...F-8
Park Place Ave...H-3
Park Place Dr...H-2
Park Ridge Blvd...J-1
Parrish...C-7
Patton Ct...H-2
Pavillion...C-3
Peach...E-3
Peak...B-3
Pearl...B-1
Pecan St...A-2,E-4,J-4
Pecos...K-6-8
Pembroke Dr...H-2
Penn...F-2
Pennsylvania Ave...G-3
Perry...A-7
Petersmith...F-2,F-3
Pharr...D-4
Photo St...G-1
Pine...F-5
Pioneer...K-7,K-8
Pittsburgh...D-5
Plumwood...D-5
Poindexter...C-3
Poplar...F-4
Porter St...G-6
Portland...C-4
Post...B-7
Powell Ave...H-3,H-5
Prairie...B-1
Pratcher...K-6
Premier...A-6
Presidio...F-3,F-5
Prince...J-6
Primrose...C-5
Prospect...B-1
Pruitt...G-2,G-3
Pulaski...G-3,G-4
Quentin Ct...A-4
Quinn...H-7
Race...C-5
Ramey...H-8,I-8
Ramsey...H-4,I-6
Ranch Ter...J-6
Rapurt...A-4
Rattikin...I-6
Ravin...G-7
Ray...K-7
Raynor...D-5
Reaford...A-7
Refugid...B-1
Retta...E-5
Riardale Rd...J-6
Richmond...H-3,H-5,H-6
Ridgeview...J-6
Riley St...J-5
Rio Grand...F-3
Ripy St...J-2,J-3,J-4,J-5
Riverridge...C-6
Riverside Dr...G-6,I-5,K-6
Roberts...I-2-5
Robert Burns Dr...J-6
Robinwood...B-6
Rodeo St...K-7
Rogers Ave...H-1,I-1
Rolling Hills Dr...J-6
Roosevelt...B-1
Rosedale St...G-3,G-5,G-7
Ross...A-2,B-2
Rouse...D-5
Rufus...I-8
Runnels...A-4
Rupert...E-2
Rusty...B-6
Rutan...K-8
Ryan Ave...J-2,K-2
Ryan Place Dr...I-3
St. Louis Ave...J-4,K-4
St. Louis St...G-4
Samuels...C-3
Sanborn...F-7
Sandage...I-1
Sanders...B-7
Sanderson St...F-8
Sandgate...I-6
Santa Rosa...B-8
Sarah...K-6
Sargent...E-7
Seaman...C-6,D-6
Seaman Ave...D-6
Selk...B-6
Selma...B-5,B-6
Scenery Hill Ct...E-8
Scenic Ct...C-5
Schadt...A-3
Schwartz...A-3
Scott...E-4,F-6
Shackelford...K-8
Shadow...C-7
Shamrock...D-2
Shane...A-7
Shaw St...J-2-5
Shirley Way...I-1
Shotts...E-1
Shropshire...I-6
Simpson...F-5
Smilay...C-4
South Freeway...I-4
South Hill...J-1
Southland St...G-2
Spiller...I-6
Spring St...G-1
Springdale Rd...B-6
Stadium Dr...I-1,J-1
Stanley...H-2,I-2,J-2,K-2
Stephen Lee...J-6
Stardust...J-6
Stayton...E-2
Stearnes...G-6
Stella...F-5
Stephenson...F-4
Stratford Dr...F-8
Strong...I-7
Stuart Dr...I-4,K-4
Summit...F-2
Sunday...A-7
Sunset...F-2
Surrey...K-1
Swayne...E-6
Swift...C-4
Sycamore...G-6
Sydney...I-8
Sylvania...D-5
Tallman St...K-8
Taylor...E-3
Templeton...E-1
Tennessee...G-5
Terrace...D-1
Terrell...G-2,G-3,G-4
Terry...A-2,E-4
Thanntson...I-7
Thockmorton...D-3,E-3
Thrall St...G-7,H-7,I-7
Tillar...E-1
Timberline Dr...K-5,K-6
Todd Ave...J-5
Tom Ellen...A-6
Townshend Dr...I-2,K-2
Transcontinental Cutoff...A-5
Travis St...G-3,I-3,K-3
Troost...G-5
Trueland Dr...J-7,K-7
Tucker St...G-5
Ubbock Ave...I-1,J-1,K-1
University Dr...F-1,I-1,J-1
Uvalde...H-6
Vacek...E-2
Valley...E-3
Vance...C-7
Van Horn...E-5
Vaughn Blvd...I-7
Vaughn St...J-8
Vera Cruz...A-4
Verben E...G-4
Vickery Blvd...F-3,F-6
Vicki Ln...I-4
View...F-7
Vinetta...K-8
Viola...E-2
Virginia...C-5,G-5
Vogt St...H-8
W Dr...F-1
Wabash...I-1
Wabash Ave...J-1
Waggoman St...K-1,K-3,K-4
Waits Ave...I-1,J-1
Waldemar...B-7,B-8
Walker...B-4
Wall...D-4
Wallace St...E-7,H-8
Ward Pkwy...H-2
Ward St...F-7
Warner...H-2
Warwick...B-4
Washington Ave...G-3
Watauga Rd...B-5
Waterman...D-4
Wathal...A-8
Wayne...B-7,C-7,D-7
Wayside Dr...I-2,K-2
Weatherbee St...H-2
Weatherford...E-3
Weber...A-3
Weisenberger St....E-1,J-5
Wesley...A-6
Wesleyan Dr...G-7,H-7
Westbrook...C-5
Westchester...B-8
Wheeler...C-7
White Ave...G-5
White Settlement Rd...E-1
Whitmore...E-1
Wichita St...K-7
Wilbarger St...J-7
Wilkinson...F-7
William...F-4
Williams...A-6
Williams Pl...B-6
Willing Ave...J-2,K-2
Wilshire...H-2
Wimberly...E-1
Windham...F-6
Windmill...C-4
Winfield...K-1
Wingate...E-1
Winslow Pl...H-2
Winston Rd...J-1
Winston Terr...H-1
Withers St...G-6
Woodland...J-3
Woodrow St...G-6
Woods...B-8
Woodward...E-2
Worth St...G-2
Worthills...J-1
Wyatt Ct...J-6
Wynne...C-6
Young...F-7
Yucca...C-6
Yuma St...H-5,I-5,J-5
Zelma...B-8
1st St...D-5,E-3
2nd...E-3
3rd...E-3
4th St...D-3,D-5,D-6,E-1,E-3
5th St...D-3,E-1-3
5th Ave...D-3,E-1-3,I-3,K-3
6th...D-3,E-1-3
6th Ave...I-3,K-3
7th...D-3,E-1,E-3
8th...E-3
8th Ave...H-2,J-2,K-2
9th...D-3,E-3
10th...C-2,C-3
11th St...C-3,F-2,G-2
12th St...E-5,G-2
13th St...C-3,G-2
14th St...C-1,F-2,F-4
15th...C-1,F-4
16th...C-1,C-3,F-4
17th...C-3,F-4
18th...C-1,C-3,F-5
19th St...C-1,F-4
20th...C-1,C-2
21st...C-1,C-2
22nd...B-1,B-2
23rd...B-1,B-2
24th...B-1
25th...B-1
26th...B-1
27th...B-1,B-2
28th...A-1,A-2,A-5
29th...A-1,A-3,A-6
30th...A-1,A-2,A-3
31st...A-1,A-2,A-3
32nd...A-1,A-2,A-3

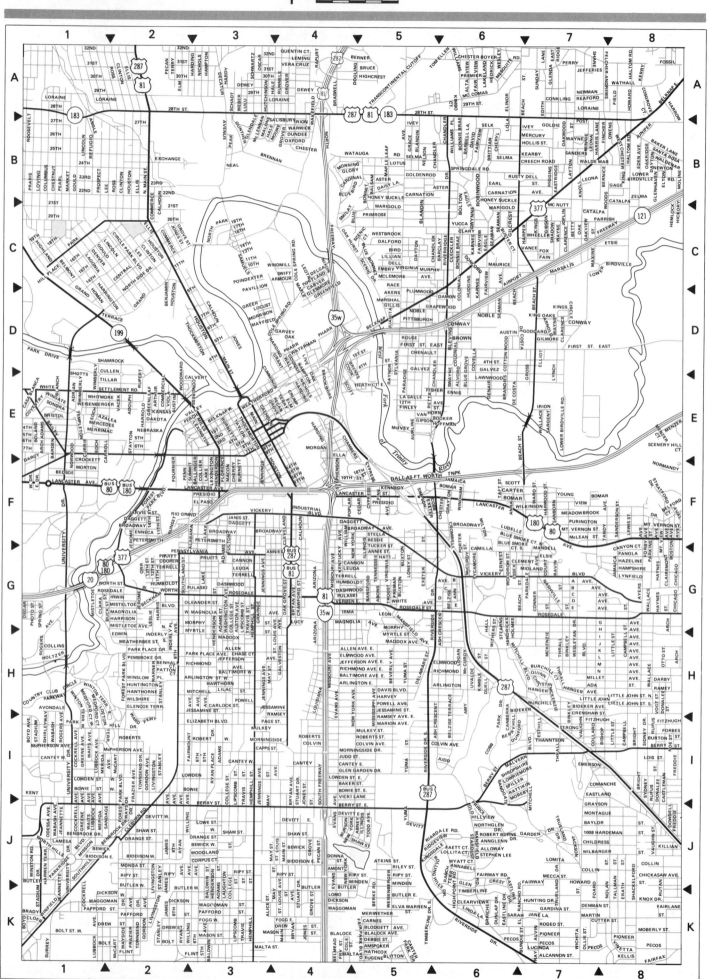

Scale of Miles

0   .2   .4   .6

N

HARTFORD

Affleck St.	F5	
Albany Ave.	B1,C6	
Allen Pl.	G5	
Allyn St.	D6	
Ann St.	E6	
Arch St.	E7	
Ashley St.	D5	
Asylum Ave.	C3	
Asylum Pl.	D6	
Asylum St.	E6	
Ath Sq. N.	E7	
Atlantic St.	D5	
Atwood St.	D5	
Auburn St.	D1	
Babock St.	D7	
Bainbridge Rd.	D1	
Ballard Dr.	C2	
Barbour St.	B6	
Barker St.	H6	
Bartholomew Ave.	F5,G4	
Beacon St.	E3	
Bedford St.	C6,D6	
Beldeno St.	D6	
Belknap Rd.	C2	
Bellevue St.	C7	

Bishop Rd.	F1	
Bond St.	H6	
Bonner St.	G4	
Bouanger Ave.	G2	
Brainard Rd.	B1,H8	
Brentwood Rd.	H1	
Brewster Rd.	B1	
Broad St.	G6	
Brook St.	D6	
Brookfield St.	H4	
Brown St.	I6	
Buckingham St.	E6	
Burton St.	C5	
Bushnell St.	H6	
Cabot St.	C5	
Campfield Ave.	H6	
Canton St.	C7	
Capen St.	C5	
Capitol Ave.	E5,F3	
Case St.	C6	
Catherine St.	G4	
Cedar St.	F6	
Center St.	C6	
Chandler St.	H4	
Charter Oak Ave.	F7	
Charter Oak Pl.	F7	
Chester St.	I6	
Chestnut St.	D6	

Church St.	D6	
Clark St.	B6	
Clinton St.	E6	
Cogswell St.	D6	
Collins St.	D5	
Colony Rd.	B2	
Columbia St.	E7	
Columbus Blvd.	E7	
Commerce St.	E7	
Congress St.	F7	
Connecticut Blvd.	D8	
Cromwell St.	I6	
Crestwood Rd.	G1	
Cumberland Rd.	D1	
Dart St.	I4	
Donald St.	D7	
Douglas St.	I6	
Earle St.	E1	
East St.	C6	
Edgewood St.	C6	
Edwards St.	D6	
Ely St.	F6	
Elizabeth	D3	
Enfield St.	C6	
Essex	G6	
Fairfield Ave.	I5	
Haynes Rd.	C1	

Fairmount St.	C6	
Farmington Ave.	E2	
Federal St.	I1	
Fern St.	D1,D3	
Fishery	A8	
Flatbush Ave.	H2,H4	
Florence St.	C6,I1	
Flower St.	E6	
Ford St.	E7	
Forest St.	E6	
Foxcroft Rd.	D2	
Francis Ave.	F4	
Franklin Ave.	H7	
Fraser Pl.	D6	
Freeman St.	I4	
Garden St.	B6,D6	
Gold St.	E7	
Governor St.	E1	
Grand St.	F6	
Grant St.	I3	
Green St.	D6	
Greenfield St.	B5	
Griswold Dr.	D2	
Groton St.	G2	
Grove St.	E7	
Hamilton St.	F7	
Hawthorn St.	E5	
Haynes St.	E6	

Haynes St.	E6	
Hebron St.	B4	
Hicks	E7	
High St.	D6	
Hillside Ave.	I5	
Highland St.,S.	F3	
Hollywood Ave.	I3	
Homestead Ave.	C5	
Hudson St.	F6	
Hungerford St.	D5	
Huntington St.	D5	
Huntley Pl.	F6	
Huyshope Ave.	F8	
Imlay St.	E5	
Irving St.	D6	
Jefferson St.	F6	
Jewell St.	E7	
John St.	F6	
Keney Park	B5	
Kinsley St.	E7	
Lafayette St.	F6	
Laurel St.	E5	
Lawler Rd.	C1	
Lawrence St.	F5	
Laxton St.	F7	
Ledgewood Rd.	H1	
Lewis St.	E7	

Lexington Rd.	F2	
Liberty	D6	
Lincoln St.	F6	
Linnmore St.	I4	
Lisbon St.	F7	
Madison St.	F6	
Magnolia St.	C5	
Main St.,N.	B7,D7	
Maple Ave.	I5	
Maplewood Ave.	F2	
Marion St.	J3	
Market St.	E7	
Marshall St.	E4	
Martin St.	B4	
Mather St.	C6	
Maxim Rd.	H8	
May St.	D5	
Mechanic St.	E7	
Miamis Rd.	B1	
Middlebrook Rd.	B1	
Milton St.	E7	
Mohawk Dr.	B1	
Morris St.	G7	
Mortson St.	F5	
Myrtle St.	D6	
New Britian Ave.	H5,I1,I3	

New Park Ave.	G3,I2	
Niles St.	D5	
Norwich St.	F7	
Norwood Rd.	B2	
Oak St.	F6	
Oakbrook Rd.	G1	
Oakland Ave.	G2	
Oakwood Ave.	G2	
Overlook Terr.	H3	
Oxford St.	E3	
Park Rd.	F3,F5	
Park Terr.	F5	
Pearl St.	E6,E7	
Penn Dr.	D1	
Pilgrim Rd.	B2	
Pleasant St.	D7	
Pope Park Dr.	F5	
Potter St.	E7	
Pratt St.	E7	
Preston St.	H6	
Prospect Ave.	B3	
Prospect St.	E7,F7	
Putnam Hts.	F5	
Putnam St.	F5	
Quaker Lane N	D2,E2	
Quaker Lane,S.	F2,G2	
Reserve Rd.	G8	

Retreat Ave.	F6	
Richard St.	F2	
Robin Rd.	E1	
Rockledge Dr.	G1	
Rockledge Dr.	G1	
Roger St.	I4	
Rowe Ave.	F3	
Russ St.	E5	
Sargeant St.	D5	
Saybrook St.	G4	
Scarborough St.	C3	
Sequassen St.	F8	
Seymour St.	F6,G6	
Seyms St.	C6	
Sharon St.	B4	
Sherbrook Ave.	H4	
Sidney Ave.	G2	
Sigourney St.	E5	
Sisson Ave.	E3	
Somerset St.	I1	
South St.	G6	
Spring St.	D6	
Square St.	F6	
St. Augustine St.	G2	
St. Charles St.	G2	
State St.	E7	
Steele Rd.	F2	
Sterling St.	C5	
Stonnington St.	F7	

Sumner St.	D5	
Sycamore Rd.	C3	
Talcott St.	E7	
Taylor St.	E7	
Temple St.	E7	
Terry Rd.	E1	
Townley	D5	
Trinity St.	E6	
Trout Brook Rd.	E1,H1	
Trumbull St.	E7	
Union Pl.	E7	
Union St.	F7	
Van Block Ave.	F8	
Van Dyke	F8	
Vern St.	F1	
Vine	C5	
Vrendale Ave.	G2	
Wadsworth St.	F7	
Walnut St.	D6	
Ward St.	E7	
Warrenton Ave.	E3	
Washington St.	F6,G6	
Weehasset St.	F8	
Wells St.	E7	
West Blvd.	E3,F1	
West St.	E6	
Westbourne Pkwy.	B4	

Westbrook Rd.	G1	
Westland St.	A6	
Weston St.	B8	
Westphal St.	G2	
Wethersfield Ave.	G7	
White Ave.	G1	
White St.	I5	
Whitney St.	D3	
Whitney St.,S.	E3	
Willard St.	D5	
Williams St.	C7,D7	
Windsor St.	C6	
Winter St.	C6	
Winthrop St.	D7	
Wolcott St.	F6	
Woodland St.	C5	
Wooster St.	C6	
Wyllys St.	F7	
Yale St.	I5	
York St.	F5	
Zion St.	H5	

HOUSTON

Alabama St. J5,J7
Alabama St.,W. H1
Alamo C4
Albany G3
Alber St. A7
Allen D1
Allen Parkway E2
Allston St. B1
Alpha St. F1
Andrews St. F3
Angella F1
Anita St. H4,I7
Ann St. F8
Arbor St. J4,K6
Arch E7
Archer A4
Arlington St. B2
Arthur St. F4
Ashby J1
Attucks J7
Audobon H3
Austin J3
Austin St. G5,J3
Autrey I2
Averill A6
Avondale St. G3
Baer D8
Bagby St. F5,G4
Bailey G3
Baker E6
Baldwin F4
Banks I2
Banks St. J1
Barbee St. J5
Bardwell A7
Barkdull J2
Barnes D1
Bass St. D1
Bastrop St. G6,H6,J5
Bayard J2
Bayland St. B3
Beach D5
Bell H8
Bell Ave. G6
Bell,W. F3
Bering F8
Berry I5
Berthea J2
Beverly St. B2
Bigelow St. A7
Billingsley St. A6
Bingham St. D4
Binz St. J3,K4
Bishop C5
Bissonnet St. J1
Blair St. A1
Blodgett St. J5,K6
Bolsover K1
Bomar G2
Bonnie Brae I1
Boone B8
Booth St. B6
Boswell St. A7
Boundary B6
Bradley B4
Brailsfort St. I6
Branard St. I1
Brandt I3
Brazos St. F5
Bremond G4
Bremond St. I7
Briley St. I6
Brooks Pl. C8
Brooks St. D6
Bruce A4
Buckner St. F4
Buel G3
Buffalo Terrace E3
Bunton St. A7
Burkett J6
Burkett St. K6
Burnett St. D6
Bute St. I3
Butler St. E2
Calendar A5
Calhoun Ave. G5
California H2
Calle J8
Calumet St. J3
Campbell St. C7
Canal F8
Canfield St. I7
Capitol E4
Capitol Ave. F5
Carl C5
Caroline St. G5,J3
Carr A8
Castle Ct. I2
Catherine A5
Cetti B6
Chapman C7
Chartres K3
Chase St. C7
Chelsea I3
Chenevert St. G6,J4
Cherokee J1
Cherry A8
Churchill B5
Clay Ave. G6
Clay St. H7
Clay,W. F3
Cleburne St. J5
Cleveland F3
Cline St. E8
Clinton Dr. E7
Cobb St. K6
Cochran St. B6
Collingsworth St. A7
Collins D6
Colorado St. D4
Colquitt I1
Columbia St. B2
Columbus F2
Commerce St. E6
Common B6
Common St. C6
Congress Ave. E6
Conti D8
Cook G4
Cordell A4
Cordier F7
Cortland St. B2
Cottage A3
Court St. D2
Courtland Pl. H3
Coyle St. H7
Cranberry C2
Crawford J4
Crawford St. F6
Crocker St. F3
Crockett D4
Crosby St. F4
Cullen St. K7
Cushing St. F4
D'Amico St. F1
Dallas Ave. F5
Dallas,W. F2
Daly D6
Damon G2
Dart St. D4
Davis St. C8
Day I3
De George A4
De Pel C4
DeLano St. H7,I6
Decatur E4
Dell A4
Dennis Ave. H5
Denver H8
Dewey D4
Diesel D3
Dora J2
Douglas St. I7
Dowling St. G7,J4
Drew G4,H5
Drew St. G4
Driscoll St. G1,I1
Dunlavy St. H1
Dunstan K1
Eagle St. J5
Eberhard F2
Edison St. A6
Edmundson St. I8
Edwards St. D4
Elder D4,D5,E5
Elgin H4
Eli St. D1
Elmen St. G1
Elser B6
Elysian C7,E7
Embry B6
Emerson H3
Engeike St. F8
Enid A4
Ennis St. H7,J6
Ennis,N. F8
Erin St. A7
Euclid St. B3
Eunice B5
Evella A8
Ewing St. J3
Fairview St. G1
Fannin St. G5,I3
Fargo St. G3
Fletcher St. C6
Flora H3
Florence St. B4
Flynn F8
Foote E8
Fowler E1
Fox F8
Francis H4,J7
Franklin Ave. E6
Frasier C2
Freund E8
Fugate St. A3
Fulton St. A5,B6
Gano C7
Gardner,W. A3
Gargan C5
Garrott I3
Garrow St. G8
Garvin Ct. D4
Genese St. G3
Gilette G3
Gillespie E8
Givens D2
Gladys C4
Glaser D6
Goldenrod B5
Golf Links F3
Goliad St. D5
Grant G2
Graustark J2
Gray Ave.,W. F3
Gray St. G4,G5
Grayson E8
Greeley St. I3
Greenle C8
Grigsby B8
Gross F1
Gulf Freeway I8
Haddon Ave. G1
Hadley Ave. G4
Hain A5
Hamilton St. G6,H5
Hammock B6
Hardy C7
Harold St. H1
Harrington St. D6
Harrisburg G8
Harvard St. B2,D2
Hathaway St. H3
Hawkins G8
Hawthorne St. H2
Hays St. B6
Hazard St. H1
Hazel F2
Heights Blvd. B2,D2
Helen St. B4
Helena G3
Hemphill St. E4
Henderson St. E4
Herkimer St. B1
Hermann St. K3
Hickory D5
Hiensley D5
Highland St. B3
Hill St. E1
Hogan St. C6
Hogg C8
Holman Ave. H4,J7
Holy D5
Home D2
Honsin D2
Hopkins St. G3
Hopson F3
Houston St. D5
Howe F4
Hussion St. I8
Hutcheson St. H8
Hutchins St. G6,J4
Hyacinth B5
Hyde St. G3
Ideal B5
Indiana Ave. G1
Ingborg I8
Institute J2
Isabella St. J5
Jack St. I3
Jackson J4
Jackson St. F6
James St. C6
Jasmine F1
Jefferson Ave. G5
Jensen E8
Jensen St. C8
Jessamine A5
Joe Anne St. F2
Johnson St. D4
Jones B8
Joseph St. H8
Julian C3
Kane E4
Karnes A5
Keating St. H8
Keene C6
Kennedy F8
Kent J1
Key St. A3
Kipling St. H1
Koehler St. D1
Kolb St. C1
Kuester H1
Kyle I2
La Branch J4
La Branch St. F6
La Rue F2
Lamar F2
Lamar Ave. F5
Lamar,W. F3
Larkin D2,E2
Lee St. C7
Leek St. J8
Leeland Ave. G6,H8,I8
Leona D8
Leonidas St. F1
Leverkuhn E4
Lewis St. D6
Lexington I1
Lincoln F2
Live Oak St. G7,K4
Live Oak,N. F8
Loretto St. I2
Lorraine St. C7
Lottmann St. E8
Louisiana St. F5,H4
Lovett St. H2
Lubbock E4
Lucinda St. J7
Luzon St. B7
Lyle E7
Lyons Ave. D7,D8
MacGregor K4
Maggie B6
Main St. G5,I3
Main St. W. I1
Main St.,N. A4
Mandell H1,J1
Marconi St. F2
Marie St. C5
Marigold B5
Marina C1
Marshall St. H1
Marstow F1
Mary St. C8
Maryland Ave. G1
Mason St. G3
Matthews F4
Maury St. C7
Maverick A5
Maylor D6
McGowen G4
McGrower St. I7
McKee C7
McKenney,W. F3
McKinney Ave. F5
McLlhenney G4
McLlhenney Ave. I7
McMillan St. E2
McNeil St. B7
Melwood St. A3
Menefee C1
Merrill St. B3
Michaux B3
Michigan Ave. G1
Milam St. F5
Milby St. I8
Milford St. J1
Miller St. I8
Mills C8
Mills St. C7
Mirimar I2
Missouri G2
Montana St. D1
Montrose I2
Moore B6
Mop C7
Morgan G3
Morris B6,B8
Morrison St. B4
Morse G1
Moss St. A4
Mt. Vernon St. I2
Mulberry St. H2
Nagle Alley F8
Nagle St. G7,I6
Nagle St.,N. F8
Nance St. D7
Napoleon St. J7
Nettletor J6
Nevada G1
Newhoff B8
Newhouse F1
Nicholson B1
Noble St. C7
Norfolk I1
Norhill A3
North B3
North Blvd. J1
Northwood B4
O'Neil St. F4
Oak Ct. G4
Oak Dr. C4
Oak Ridge St. B3
Oakdale J3
Oakley I3
Odin D8
Olive St. D1
Omar St. B3
Opelousas St. D7
Orr St. B7
Ovid C4
Oxford B2
Pacific G3
Paige F8
Paige St. H7,I6
Palm J3
Palmer H7,K5
Palmer,N. F8
Panama St. B6
Park B6,G1
Parkview B5
Paschall C6
Patterson E1
Payne B5
Pease H7
Pease Ave. G5
Peden Ave. F2
Peveto F2
Pierce,W. F3
Pierre Ave. G5
Pincknery St. C6
Pinedale J3
Pineridge B3
Polk F5
Polk Ave. G6
Polk,W. F3
Portland J3
Portsmouth I1
Praire Ave. E6
Preston Ave. E6,G8
Prospect St. J3
Providence D7
Quinn A4
Quitman C6
Race E7
Railey A4
Rains E7
Ralph H1
Raymond D2
Reagan B4
Redan B4
Reeves J7
Rein B6
Reisner E5
Renfro F1
Renner Ct. E4
Reynolds B6
Rice Blvd. K1
Richmond Ave. I1
Ridge St. B4
Ridgewood G1
Riverside Dr. K4
Roanoke E7
Roberts H8
Robertson B6
Robila St. F3
Robin St. F3
Rochow F1
Rockwood St. K8
Rosalie St. H4,I7
Rose D1
Rosedale J3,K5
Roseland I3
Rosewood J5
Rosine F2
Rossmoyne St. I2
Ruiz St. E7
Rusk Ave. F5
Ruth St. J5,K7
Ruthven F3
Rutland Pl. C1
Rylis F2
Ryon St. B7
Sabine St. C4,E4
Sachs St. E2
Saltus F8
Sampson H8,K5
Sampson St. K6
San Jacinto St. G5,I3
Sanders j7
Sauer St. I5,K5
Saulnier,W. F3
Sawyer St. D3
Schulan St. D1
Schwartz D8,E8
Scott K7
Scott St. J7
Searle A5
Sellers D2
Semmes St. C7
Shaw F5
Shearn St. D4
Shelby St. A6
Shelley A4
Sherman St. F8
Shiloh E8
Silver St. E4
Simmons J7
Sledge C3
Smith St. F5
Snover E1
South Blvd. J1
Southmore St. J3
Southwest Freeway I1
Spencer C1
Spring C4
Spruce St. E7
St. Charles St. G7,I6
St. Charles St.,N. F8
St. Emmanuel St. G6,J4
Stalker D2
Stanford St. I3
State St. E4
Stevens St. C8
Stout B7
Stuart H4,J7
Stude C3
Studenmont D3
Studewewood D3
Sul Ross St. H1
Summer D4
Sumpter St. C7
Sun Ct. F7
Sunset Blvd. K2
Sutton St. G3
Sweetwood F1
Sydnor D8
Tabor A4
Tackaberry B6
Taft St. G3
Taylor St. E3
Temple A4
Temple St.,W. A3
Terrell F1
Terry C7
Texas Ave. E6,G8
Thelma C4
Thomas C5
Thompson D1
Threlkeld C3
Tierwester St. K6
Top E7
Travis I3
Travis St. G5,I3
Tretham D6
Trimble A5
Trinity E4
Trulley H6
Truxillo J5
Tuam St. H4,I5
Tulane St. B1
Union St. D3
Usener Blvd. C3
Valentine St. F4
Van Buren F2
Varsity K8
Vassai I2
Velasco G8,K5
Vermont Ave. G1
Vick E1
Victor F3
Vincent A4
Violet F1
Voight C3
Wagner St. D2,E2
Walker Ave. F5
Walker,W. F3
Walton A4
Watson A3
Waugh Dr. F2
Waverly Ct. J2
Waverly St. B1
Weber C4
Weber Ave. G4
Webster G4,H6
Welch Ave. G1
Wendel C3
Wentworth St. J4,K6
West Blvd. J2
West St. C8
Westmoreland H3
Wheeler Ave. J5,K7
White Oak Dr. C2
White St. E4
Whitney H3
Wichita St. J3
Wilkenson St. F2
Wilkes B6
Willard Ave. G2
Wilson G4
Winbern J5
Winnie C5
Wood Leigh H8
Wood Row I3
Woodhead St. H1
Woodland St. B3
Wrightwood A5
Yale St. B1,D1
Yoakum G2,J2
York H8
Yupon St. G2,H2
2nd D2
4 1/2 E. C2
4th St.,E C2
4th W. C2
5th W. C2
5th,E. C2
6 1/2 St., B2
6th St.,W. C2
7 1/2 St.,E. B2
7th St.,E B2
8 1/2 St.,E. B2
8th St.,E. B2
8th St.,W. B2
9 1/2 E. B2
9th St.,E. B2
9th St.,W. B2
10 1/2 St.,E. A2
10 1/2 St.,W. A1
10th St.,W. B2
10th,E. B2
11 1/2 St.,E. A2
11th St.,E A2
11th St.,W. A2
12th St.,E A2
12th St.,W. A1
13 1/2 St.,E. A2
13th St.,E. A2
13th St.,W. A1
14th St.,E. A2
14th St.,W. A1

INDIANAPOLIS

Alabama St. B4,F4,I4
Alford St. A7
Allegheny St. E2
Anderson St. B2
Arch St. D5
Arsenal St. A8,F8,H8
Barth Ave. K7
Bates St. H7
Bell St. E7
Bellefontaine St. A6
Bicking St. J4
Blackford E1,G1
Brighton Blvd. A1
Broadway B5,D5
Brookside Ave. C7
Broom G1
Buchanar St. J5
California D1,G1
Capitol Ave. B2,F2,I2
Carollton Ave. A6,D6
Cedar St. I6
Center D1
Central Ave. B5
Chadwick St. J1
Charles St. K3
Chesapeake St. G3
Church St. J2
Cleveland St. F5
College Ave. B6,F6
Columbia Ave. B7,C7
Commerce Ave. B8
Cora St. B2
Cornell Ave. A6
Court St. G4
Cruse St. G7
Dakota St. K1
Davidson St. E6
DeLoss St. H7
Delaware St. B4,G4,I4
Detroit St. H8
Dickson F7
Dorman St. D7,E7
Drake St. B1
East St. F5,I5
Edison Ave. D6
Elm St. I6
Empire St. H1
English Ave. H6,I7
Evison St. K8
Fayette D2
Fletcher Ave. H6,I7
Fort Wayne Ave. E4
Fulton St. E6
Gardeners Ln. H1
Georgia St. G3,H5
Greer St. J5
Grove Ave. J6
Hall Pl. B3
Harrison St. H6
Hartford St. K6
Henry H1,I3
High St. J4
Highland Ave. E7,F7
Home Pl. I4
Hosbrook St. J6
Hoyt Ave. I7
Hudson St. C4,F4
Illinois St. B3,E3,J3
Indiana Ave. E2
Ingram St. A8
Joseph St. C3
Kansas St. K2
Kentucky Ave. G3,I1
Kenwood Ave. J3
Laurel St. J8,K8
Leonard St. K6
Leota St. H7
Lewis St. B7,C7
Lexington Ave. I6,J7
Linden St. K7
Lockerbie St. F5
Lord St. H5,H6
Louisiana St. H3,H6
Lynn Dr. B1
Madison St. K4
Market St. F3,F7
Marlowe Ave. F7
Martindale Ave. B7
Maryland St. G3,G5,G7
Massachusetts Ave. C7,E4
McCarty St. I2,I4
McKim St. H8
Meikel St. J2
Meridian St. E3,J3
Merrill St. I3
Miami St. F2
Michigan Ave. E3
Michigan Pl. E7
Missouri St. B2,F2,J2
Mobile St. H2
Monument Cir. F3
Morris St. K2,K5
Muskigum St. E3,G3
New Jersey St. B5,F5,I5
New York St. F3,F7
Newman St. B8
Nobel St. J5
North St. E3,E7
Northwestern A1
Norwood St. I1,I4
Ogden St. E4,F4
Ohio St. F3,F7
Olive St. J7,K7
Orange St. K2,K5,K7
Oriental St. E8,H8
Paca D1
Park Ave. B5,C5,F5,G5,I5
Pearl St. G1,G3
Pennsylvania St. B4,G3,J4
Pierson St. E3
Pine St. G6,I6
Pleasant St. J7
Polk St. C7
Prospect St. J6
Rankin St. B2
Ransom St. B1
Ray St. J1
Reno St. K1
Ringgold St. K6
Roanoke St. E2
Roosevelt A8,B7
Sanders St. K4
Senate Ave. B2,F2,I2,K2
Shelby St. G7,J7
Sheldon St. A8
Smith St. B2
South St. H3
Spann Ave. I7
Spruce St. J8
St. Clair St. D2,D7
Stevens St. I5
Stillwell C7
Sturm Ave. E8
Summit St. F8,H8
Sycamore St. J3
Talbot St. A4,G4,K4
Terrace Ave. K8
Toledo St. F2
Union St. I3,K3
Vermont St. E3,E7
Virginia Ave. G4
Wabash St. F3
Walnut St. D2,D5
Washington St. G2
West Ave. C1
West St. F1,K1
Wilkins St. J1,J2
Williams St. G8
Wisconsin St. K2
Woodlawn Ave. J6
Woodruff Pl. D8
Wright St. J6,K6
Wyoming St. J4
Yandes St. B7,C7
9th St. D2,D5,D7
10th St. C2,C7
11th St. C2,C5,C8
12th St. C1,C3,C8
13th St. B1,B2,B4
14th St. B2,B4
15th St. B2,B4,B5,B7
16th St. A1,A2,A7
17th St. A1,A5
18th St. A1,A3

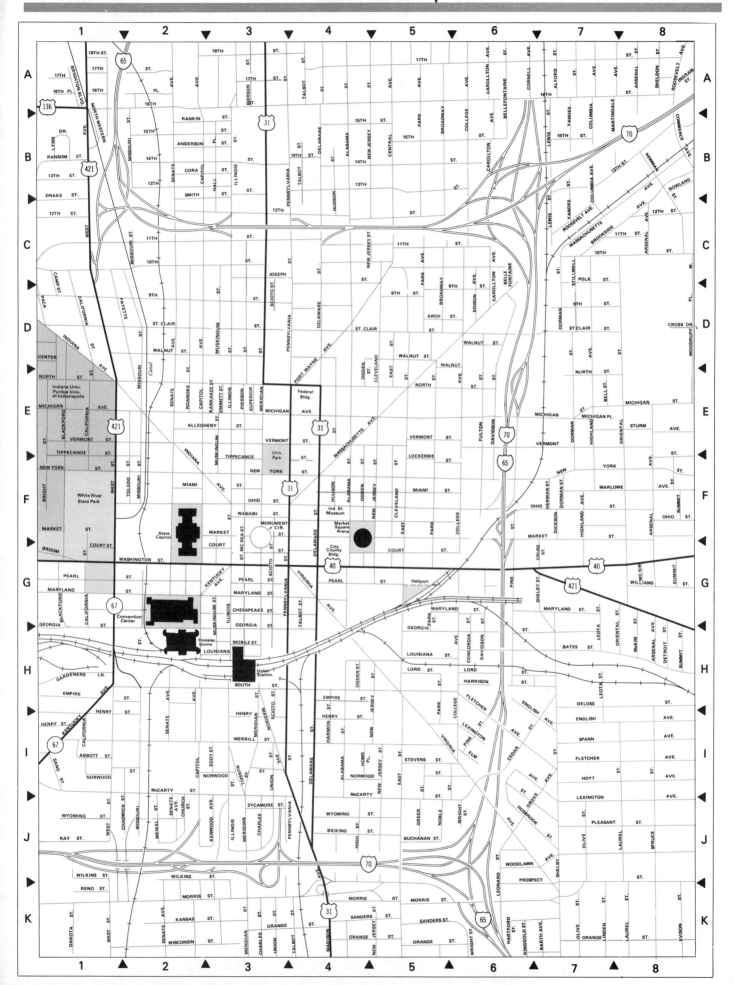

Scale of Miles
0 .2 .4 .6 .8

N

KANSAS CITY

Admiral E3
Agnes,N. C5
Allen St. F1
Amie E3
Anderson D6,D8
Armour Rd. A3
Askew B6,D6
Bales D6
Baltimore E4
Bank E2
Beacon D8
Beley D6
Bellaire Ave. D8
Bellefontaine,N. . . D5
Belleview E4
Belmont E8
Belmont Ave. D8
Bennington E8
Benton Blvd. . . D5,F5
Brighton D7,E7
Brighton Ave. G7
Broadway Bridge . . D2
Broadway,N. B2
Brownell D4
Campbell D3
Central Ave. H2

Charlotte E3
Chelsea D7
Chelsea Ave. G7
Cherry E3
Cherry St. E3
Chestnut C5
Chouteau B7,C8
Chouteau Bridge . . A6
Clay St. B3
Cleveland C6
Cleveland Ave. . . . C6
Cliff Dr. D5
Clinton C5
Collins E7
Colorado C7,D7
Corporate Dr. . . . B8
Cypress G7
Cypress Ave. G7
Denver C7,E7,G7
Deramus A7
Dowden Pl. B6
Drury F7,G7
Drury Ave. F6
Elma D5
Elmwood D7,G7
Erie St. B3
Executive Dr. A8

Fayette St. B3
Flora E4
Forest . . . D4,E4,F4
Fremont F8
Front D4
Front St. B6
Fuller E8
Funston Rd. B1
Gardner Ave. C6
Garfield D5
Garland C5
Garner D6
Genesee E1,F1
Gentry St. B3
Gillis D4
Gladstone D5
Gladstone Blvd. . . C7
Grand D4
Grand St. E3
Guinotte Ave. . . . D4
Hanley D4
Hardesty Ave. . D7,F8
Harlem Rd. D2
Harrison D3
Highland F4
Holmes D3
Holmes St. E3
Howell St. A3

Independence Ave. . E5
Indiana Ave. D6
Iron St. A3
Jackson Ave. . . B6,D6
Jarboe E2,F2
Jefferson D4
Jefferson Ave. . . . H2
June C6
Kansas Ave. F1
Kansas,N. F1
Kensington G6
Kenworth Ave. . . . B7
Knox St. B3
Lawn D7,G7
Lawndale G8
Lawndale Ave. . . . D8
Lexington . . D5,D6,D8
Liberty E1,F1
Linn St. A4
Linwood Blvd. . . . H4
Lockridge G5
Locust D3
Locust St. E3
Lorene C5
Lydia D4,F4
Lyon D7
Macon A4

Madison E2,F2
Main D3
Main St. E3,F3
Maple D4
Martin C5
McGee E3,H3
Mercier F2
Mersington D6
Minnie D5
Missouri D4
Monroe D6
Monroe Ave. B6
Montgall D6
Montgall Ave. . . . F5
Morrell D6
Mulberry D2
Myrtle B6
Myrtle Ave. D6
Nero E1
Newton C5
Nicholson Ave. . . . C5
Nodaway A4
Norledge Ave. . D6,D7
Norton Ave. D6
Oak D3
Oak St. E3
Oakley G8
Oakley Ave. . . . D8,F8

Olive C5
Owen C5
Ozark A7
Pacific D4
Paseo Bridge C4
Peery Ave. . . . E5,E8
Pendleton D5
Pennsylvania E2
Pennsylvania Ave. . H2
Perimeter Rd. . . . C1
Pine D3
Polk A4
Poplar Ave. G7
Prospect C5
Quebec St. A4
Quincy C7,D7
Quincy Ave. G7
Quindaro B1
Rickel Rd. B1
Ripley A4
River Front Rd. . . . C4
Roberts D6
Rochester C5
Royal Dr. F1
Salida Ave. C7
Saline A4
Sante Fe St. E2
Scarritt D6

Smart Ave. D6
Southeast Freeway . F6
Southern Rd. A7
Southwest Trway. . H2
Spruce G6
Spruce Ave. D6
St. John D5
St. John Ave. D7
St. Louis E1,E2
Stillwell A7
Summit F2
Sunrise Dr. C7
Swift St. B3
Taney A4
Thompson Ave. . . . G7
Topping Ave. . . C8,D8
Topping Rd.,N. . . . A8
Tracy D4,E4,G4
Troost E4,G4
Truman Rd. E1
Union E1
Universal Ave. . . . B8
Van Brunt Blvd. . C7,G7
Victor H5
Virginia E4
Wabash C5
Walnut H3
Walnut St. E3

Walrond,N. B5
Warner C5
Washington . . . E2,F2
Washington Ave. . . H2
Westport Rd. J1
Wheeling Ave. . . . D8
White E8,F8
White Ave. D8
Wilburn D7
Wilson Ave. E8
Windsor Ave. D6
Winner Rd. E8
Woodswether Rd. . F2
Wyandotte D2,F3
Wyandotte Ave. . . H3
Wyoming E1,F1
2nd St. B6,D3,D4
3rd St. D4
4th D3,D4
5th D3,E2
6th St. E5,E7
7th . . . E2,E3,E5,E7,E8
8th St. . . . E2,E3,E5,E7
9th St. E3,E5,E8
10th E3,E5
11th . . . C3,E1,E3,E5,E8
12th St. B3,E3
13th St. . B3,E1,E3,E5,E8

14th St. . . B3,E1,E3,F5,F8
15th B3,F4
16th St. . . . B3,F1,F3,F4,F6
17th St. . . . B3,F1,F3,F6
18th St. . . . A3,F2,F3,F6
19th A3,F2,F6
20th St. . . . A3,F2,F6
21st St. . . . A3,A4,F2,F5
22nd St. . A4,F2,F3,F6,G5
23rd St. . A3,A4,G3,G5,G6
24th St.
. . . . . A3,A4,G2,G3,G5,G6
25th St.
. . . . . A4,G2,G3,G5,G6,G7
26th St. . . A3,G3,G5,G6,G7
27th St. . G2,G3,G4,G6,G6,G8
28th St. . A3,G2,G4,G6,G6,G8
29th St. . . . H2,H4,H7
30th St. . . H2,H4,H7,H8
31st St. H2,H8
32nd St. H3,H8
33rd St. . . H1,H3,H4,H7
34th St. . . H1,H3,H4,H7

Scale of Miles

0   .2   .4   .6   .8

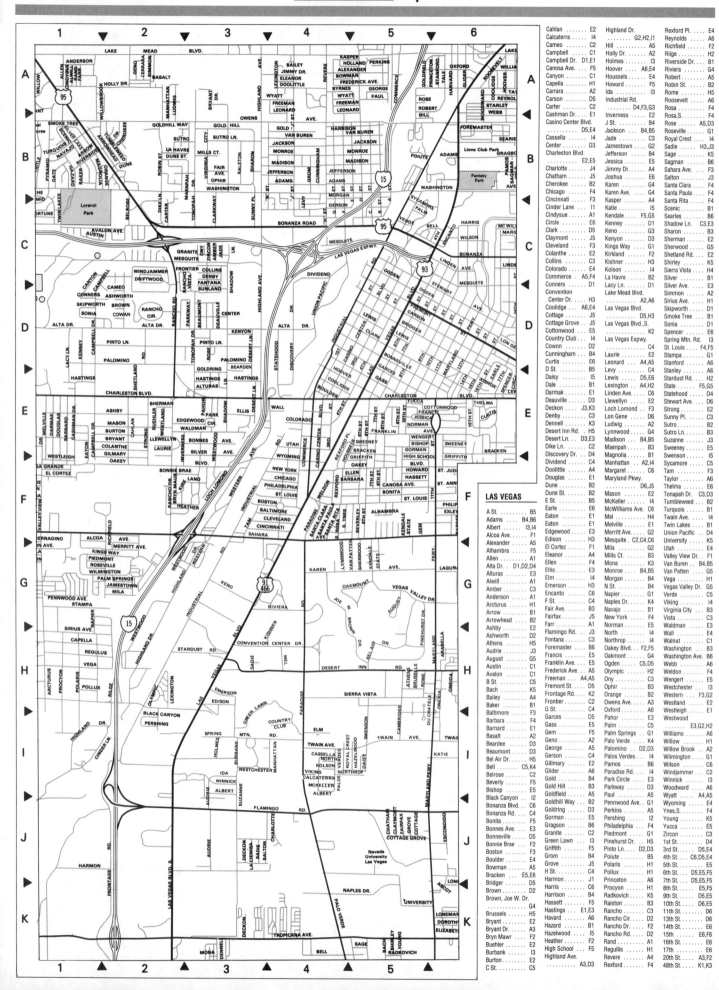

Scale of Miles

N

LOS ANGELES

Aaron St. ... C-6
Academy ... D-7
Adair St. ... K-6
Adams Blvd. ... J-1,J-3
Agatha St. ... I-7
Alameda St. ... H-8,K-8
Albany St. ... I-4
Alexandria Ave. ... B-2, C-2,E-2
Allesandro St. ... C-5,D-5
Allison Ave. ... D-6
Alpine St. ... F-8
Alvarado St. ... D-5,F-4,H-3
Altman St. ... B-8
Angelina St. ... F-6
Angelus Ave. ... C-5
Apex Ave. ... B-6
Arapahoe St. ... H-3,I-3
Ardmore Ave. ... B-1,C-1, E-1,H-1,I-1
Ashmore Pl. ... C-6
Avon Terr. ... B-7
Avon Pk. Ter. ... B-7
Azusa ... H-8
Banning St. ... H-8
Bard St. ... B-7
Bates Ave. ... A-3
Baxter St. ... B-6
Bay St. ... J-8
Beaudry Ave. ... E-7,F-6,G-6
Bellevue Ave. ... D-3,E-6
Belmont ... F-5
Benedict St. ... A-7
Berendo St. ... B-2, E-2,H-2,I-2
Benton Way ... C-5,D-4,F-3
Berkeley Ave. ... C-5
Beverly Blvd. ... D-1,E-4
Bimini Pl. ... E-2
Birch St. ... J-7
Birkdale ... B-8
Bixel St. ... G-5,H-5
Blackstone Ct. ... I-6
Blake Ave. ... A-7
Blimp St. ... A-8
Bonniebrae ... E-5,H-4,I-3
Bonsallo Ave. ... J-4
Boston St. ... F-7
Boyd St. ... H-7
Boylston Dr. ... D-7
Boylston St. ... F-6,G-6
Branden St. ... C-6
Brighton Ave. ... J-1
Broadway ... G-7,I-6,K-4
Broadway, N. ... F-8
Brooks Ave. ... D-8
Bruce Ct. ... D-6
Budlong Ave. ... I-2,J-2,K-2
Burlington Ave. ... F-5, H-4,I-3
Burns Ave. ... C-3
Byram ... H-5
Cabot ... B-8
Calumet Ave. ... E-6
Cambridge St. ... H-1
Cambria St. ... G-5
Camero Ave. ... A-3
Cameron Ln. ... I-5
Carroll Ave. ... E-6
Carondelet St. ... E-4,G-3
Catalina St. ... A-2,E-2, H-2,J-2,K-2
Catsby Ln. ... I-5
Cecelia St. ... I-7
Centennial St. ... E-7
Central Ave. ... I-8,K-6,K-7
Ceres Ave. ... I-7
Cerro Gordo St. ... B-7
Cherry ... I-4
Clayton Ave. ... A-3
Cleveland ... F-8
Clifford St. ... C-6
Clinton St. ... C-1,C-2,D-5
College St. ... E-7
Colton St. ... F-6
Columbia Ave. ... G-5
Colyton St. ... I-8
Commercial ... G-8
Commonwealth Ave. ... B-3,F-3
Congress Ave. ... J-1
Connecticut St. ... H-4
Constance St. ... H-4
Cordova St. ... I-2
Coronado St. ... C-5, D-5,F-3
Corralitas Dr. ... A-6
Cortez St. ... E-6
Cottage Pl. ... H-5
Council St. ... D-1-3,5
Court St. ... E-5,F-6
Cove Ave. ... B-6
Crandall St. ... E-4
Crestmont St. ... B-4
Crocker St. ... I-7,J-7
Crownhill Ave. ... F-5
Cumberland Ave. ... A-3
Curran St. ... B-7
Dahlia ... B-4
Dallas ... B-8
Dalton Ave. ... J-1
Dawson ... F-5
Deacon Ave. ... H-4
Delong St. ... I-4
Delongpre Ave. ... A-1,A-2
Denby ... A-7
Denker Ave. ... K-1
Descanso ... C-4
Dewey Ave. ... H-2
Diamond St. ... F-6
Dillon St. ... B-5,D-4,E-3
Donaldson St. ... B-7
Douglas St. ... D-7,F-6
Dorris Pl. ... B-8
Duane St. ... B-6
Ducommun ... G-8
Eads ... B-8
Earl St. ... B-6
East Edgeware ... E-6
Echo Park Ave. ... C-7,D-6
Edgecliffe Dr. ... B-4,C-4
Edgemont Ave. ... C-2
Edgemont St. ... E-2
Effie St. ... C-6
Ellendale ... J-3
Ellwood St. ... K-8
Elsinore ... D-5
Elyian Park Dr. ... C-7,C-8,D-7
Essex St. ... J-7
Everett St. ... E-7
Ewing St. ... B-6
Factory Pl. ... I-8
Fairbanks Pl. ... D-6
Fargo St. ... B-6,B-7
Fedora St. ... H-2
Figueroa Pl. ... E-7
Figueroa St. ... I-5,K-3
Figueroa Ter. ... F-7
Firmin St. ... F-6
Florida St. ... H-5
Flower St. ... H-5,I-5
Forney ... B-8
Fountain Ave. ... B-1,B-3
Francis Ave. ... G-3
Francisco ... H-5
Frank Ct. ... H-7
Fremont Ave. ... F-7
Gail ... B-8
Garey St. ... H-8
Garland Ave. ... H-5
Gateway Ave. ... B-3
Georgia St. ... H-5,I-4
Glassell St. ... E-4
Gladys Ave. ... I-8
Glendale ... B-6
Glendale Blvd. ... A-6
Glover Pl. ... B-8
Golden Gate Ave. ... B-4
Grand Ave. ... H-6,K-4
Grandview St. ... G-3
Grattan St. ... H-4
Green Ave. ... H-4
Griffith Ave. ... K-6
Griffith Park Blvd. ... A-4
Halldale Ave. ... J-1
Harbor Frwy. ... H-5
Harlem Pl. ... H-7
Harold Way ... A-1
Hartford Ave. ... G-5
Harvard ... B-1
Harvard Blvd. ... C-1, D-1,E-1,I-1,J-1
Heliotrope ... D-2
Hemlock St. ... J-7,J-8
Hewitt St. ... H-8,I-8
Hidalgo Ave. ... A-6
Hill St. ... F-8,I-6,K-4
Hobart Blvd. ... A-1, B-1,E-1,I-1
Hobart Pl. ... D-1
Hollywood Blvd. ... A-1,A-2,A-3
Hooper Ave. ... K-7
Hoover St. ... A-3,F-3, H-3,K-3
Hope St. ... G-6,I-5, J-4,J-5,K-4
Hunter St. ... J-8
Huntley Dr. ... F-6
Hyans St. ... E-4
Hyperion Ave. ... A-4,C-3
Imogen Ave. ... C-3
Industrial St. ... I-8
Ingraham St. ... G-5
Irolo St. ... H-1
Jaunita Ave. ... C-2
Jefferson Blvd. ... K-1-3
Juliet St. ... J-2
Kellam Ave. ... E-6
Kenilworth Ave. ... A-5
Kenmore Ave. ... B-2, E-2,H-2
Kensington Rd., E. ... E-7
Kensington Rd., W. ... E-6
Kent St. ... D-4,D-5
Kenwood Ave. ... J-1
Kinglsey Dr. ... B-1,C-1, E-1,H-1,I-1
Kingswell Ave. ... A-2
Knox ... A-7
Kodak Dr. ... C-3
Kohler St. ... I-7
Lafayette Park Pl. ... F-3
Lake St. ... F-4,G-3
Lakeshore Ave. ... C-6,D-6
Lake View Ave. ... A-6
La Mirada Ave. ... B-2
Landa St. ... B-4,B-7
Larissa Dr. ... C-4
Lasalle Ave. ... I-1,J-1
Laveta Terr. ... D-6,E-6
Lawrence St. ... K-8
Lebanon St. ... H-6,I-5
Leeward Ave. ... F-2
Lemoyne Ave. ... B-7
Lemoyne St. ... C-6,D-6
Lexington Ave. ... B-2
Lilac Ter. ... E-8
Lily Crest Ave. ... C-2
Lindley Pl. ... H-7
Little St. ... G-4
Lockwood Ave. ... B-3
Logan St. ... D-6
Loma Dr. ... G-5
Loma Pl. ... F-5
Loma Vista Pl. ... B-6
London St. ... D-3,D-4
Long Beach Ave. ... K-8
Los Angelos St. ... I-7,J-5,J-6
Lucas Ave. ... G-5
Lucille Ave. ... A-4,C-3
Lucretia ... C-6
Macy St. ... G-8
Madison Ave. ... D-2,E-3
Magnolia Ave. ... I-3,J-3
Main St. ... H-6,I-6,K-5
Maltman Ave. ... C-3
Malvern Ave. ... H-3
Manzanita St. ... B-3
Maple Ave. ... I-7,J-6,K-5
Mar Ave. ... B-3
Marathon St. ... C-3,C-4
Mariposa Ave. ... C-1, E-1,H-1,I-1
Margo ... I-5
Marview Ave. ... E-7
Maryland St. ... F-4,G-6
Mayberry St. ... C-5
McClintock Ave. ... K-3
McCollum Pl. ... C-5
McCready Ave. ... A-6
McGarry St. ... K-8
Meadow ... A-4
Melrose Ave. ... C-1,C-3
Melrose Hill ... C-1
Menlo Ave. ... H-2
Merwin St. ... D-5
Micheltonena ... B-4,C-4
Middlebury St. ... D-3
Mignonette Ct. ... F-6
Miramar St. ... F-4
Modjeska St. ... A-7
Mohawk St. ... C-5
Moore St. ... B-6
Monroe Ave. ... C-2
Montana St. ... C-5
Morton Ave. ... C-6
Montrose St. ... D-5
Mountainview Ave. ... E-5,F-5
Myra Ave. ... A-3,B-3
Myrtle St. ... J-6
Naomi Ave. ... J-7,K-7
New England St. ... I-3
New Hampshire Ave. ... B-2,E-2,H-2
New High ... F-8
Newell St. ... A-7
Newton St. ... K-7
Normal Ave. ... C-3
Normandie Ave. ... C-1, E-1,H-1,K-1
Normandie Pl. ... D-1
North Main St. ... G-8
North Spring ... F-8
Norwood ... I-4
Oak St. ... H-4,I-4
Oakwood Ave. ... D-1,D-3
Occidental Blvd. ... C-5,D-4,E-3
Oceanview Ave. ... F-4
Olive St. ... H-6,J-5,K-4
Olympic Blvd. ... G-2, H-4,J-7
Omar ... H-8
Orchard Ave. ... I-3,K-3
Ord St. ... F-8
Oxford Ave. ... G-1,H-1
Palm Dr. ... J-4
Palmetto St. ... I-8
Paloma St. ... J-7
Panorama ... A-4
Park Dr. ... C-7
Park Pl. ... D-4
Parkman Ave. ... D-4
Parkview St. ... G-3
Park Grove Ave. ... J-4
Patton St. ... E-6
Pembroke Ln. ... I-5
Pico Blvd. ... H-1,H-2,I-4
Pirtle St. ... A-7
Plata St. ... D-3,D-4
Portland St. ... J-3
Preston Ave. ... C-6
Princeton St. ... B-7
Prospect Ave. ... A-2,A-3
Queen St. ... A-7
Quintero St. ... D-7
Rampart Blvd. ... D-4,F-3
Raymond Ave. ... I-2,J-1
Reno St. ... E-3
Reservoir St. ... C-5
Rich St. ... A-7
Ridgeway ... E-6
Riverdale ... B-8
Robinson St. ... D-3,D-4
Rockwood St. ... F-5
Rosalia Rd. ... A-3
Rose St. ... H-8
Roselake Ave. ... E-4
Rosemont Ave. ... D-5,E-4
Roosevelt Ave. ... I-1
Sacremento St. ... J-8
St. James Pk. ... J-4
St. Paul Ave. ... G-6
St. Paul Pl. ... G-5
Sanborn Ave. ... A-4,B-3
San Julian St. ... I-6, I-7,J-6
San Marino St. ... G-1,G-2
San Pedro ... I-7,K-6
Santa Ana Frwy. ... F-7,G-8
Santa Monica Blvd. ... B-1
Santa Monica Frwy. ... I-2,I-3,I-5,K-7,K-8
Santa Ynez St. ... D-5
Santee St. ... I-6
Sargent Pl. ... D-6
Scarff St. ... J-3
Scott Ave. ... C-5,D-6
Scott Pl. ... C-5
Scout Way ... E-5
Seaton St. ... I-8
Sentous St. ... H-4
Serrano Ave. ... B-1,E-1,H-1
Severance St. ... J-3
Shatto Pl. ... F-2
Shatto St. ... G-5
Shoreland Dr. ... D-8
Shrine Pl. ... K-3
Silverlake ... D-4
Silver Ridge Ave. ... A-6
Spring St. ... H-6
Stadium Way ... D-7,E-7,E-8
Stanford Ave. ... I-7, I-8,J-7,K-6
Staunton ... K-8
Sunbury Ct. ... H-5
Sunflower ... A-7
Sunset Dr. ... A-3
Sunset Blvd. ... A-1, C-4,D-6,F-7
Sunset Pl. ... F-3
Sutherland St. ... D-6
Sunvue Pl. ... E-7
Swansea Pl. ... B-1
Talmadge St. ... A-3
Tarleton ... K-7
Teed St. ... F-8
Temple St. ... G-7
Terminal St. ... J-8
Teviot St. ... A-6
Toberman St. ... I-4
Toluca St. ... F-6
Towne Ave. ... I-7,J-7
Traction ... H-8
Trenton St. ... I-5
Trinity St. ... K-5
Tularosa Dr. ... C-3,C-4
Turner St. ... H-8
Union ... F-5
Union Ave. ... G-4
Union Dr. ... G-5
Union Pl. ... F-5
University Ave. ... K-3
Valencia St. ... I-4,H-4
Valentine ... B-7
Van Buren Pl. ... J-2
Vendome ... D-4,E-3
Venice Blvd. ... H-2,I-4
Vermont Ave. ... H-2,K-2
Vestal Ave. ... B-7,C-6
View St. ... E-4
Virgil Ave. ... C-3,F-3
Virgil Pl. ... A-3
Virginia ... B-3
Wall St. ... I-6,J-6,K-5
Wallace ... E-6
Walnut St. ... K-7
Walton Ave. ... I-2,K-2
Warehouse St. ... J-8
Washington Blvd. ... I-1,I-2,K-5
Waterloo St. ... B-6,D-5
Welcome ... F-6
Weller ... H-8
Werdin Pl. ... H-7,I-5
West Edgeware ... E-6
Westmoreland Ave. ... B-3,D-3,F-3
Westmoreland Blvd. ... I-1
Westerly Ter. ... C-4
Westlake Ave. ... F-5
Westlake St. ... H-3
West Silver Lake Dr. ... A-5,B-5
White Knoll Dr. ... E-7
Whitmore Av. ... B-7
Wilde St. ... I-8
Willowbrook Ave. ... B-2
Wilshire Blvd. ... F-2,G-4
Wilshire Pl. ... F-3
Wilson ... K-8
Winona Blvd. ... A-1
Winslow Dr. ... C-4
Winston St. ... H-7
Witmer St. ... G-5
Wright St. ... I-4
1st St. ... D-1,D-2,G-7
2nd St. ... E-1,E-3,E-4, F-5,G-7
3rd St. ... E-1,E-3,F-5,G-7
4th Pl. ... H-8
4th St. ... E-1,E-3,F-4, F-5,G-6,H-7,H-8
5th St. ... E-1,E-3,F-4,G-6
6th St. ... E-1,F-4,H-6,I-8
7th Pl. ... J-8
7th St. ... F-1,F-2, G-4,H-6,J-8
8th St. ... F-2,G-4,H-6,J-8
9th Pl. ... I-7
9th St. ... G-1,G-4,H-6
10th Pl. ... H-5
10th St. ... G-3,I-7,J-8
11th Pl. ... H-4
11th St. ... G-3,I-6,J-7
12th St. ... H-4,I-5,J-7
14th Pl. ... I-5,J-6,J-7
14th St. ... H-1,H-3, I-4,I-5,J-7,K-8
15th St. ... H-1,H-3, I-5,J-6,K-7
16th St. ... J-6,K-8
17th St. ... H-2,I-3
18th St. ... I-3,I-4
20th St. ... I-1,I-3, J-4,J-6,K-7
21st St. ... I-3,J-4,J-5,K-7
22nd Pl. ... I-2
22nd St. ... I-1,I-3 J-4, K-6, K-7
23rd St. ... I-1,I-3,J-3,J-5
24th St. ... I-1,J-3,J-5
25th Pl. ... J-3
25th St. ... J-1,J-2,J-3,K-5
27th St. ... J-1,J-3, J-4,K-4,K-5
28th St. ... J-2,J-3,K-4,K-5
29th St. ... J-1,J-2, J-3,K-4,K-5
30th Pl. ... K-2
30th St. ... J-1,J-3,K-5
31st St. ... K-2,K-4
32nd St. ... K-3,K-4
34th St. ... K-3
35th Pl. ... K-1,K-2
35th St. ... K-1,K-2
36th Pl. ... K-1,K-2
36th St. ... K-1
37th St. ... K-1

POINTS OF INTEREST

Barnsdale Park ... A-2
Bellevue Park ... C-3
Dodger Stadium ... E-8
Lafayette Park ... F-3
MacArthur Park ... F-4
Rosedale Cemetery ... I-1,I-2
St. James Park ... J-4
Terr Park ... H-3

LOUISVILLE

Abraham ... B-6
Adams St. ... A-8
Adelia Ave. ... F-2
Adair St. ... I-6
Airview Dr. ... J-8
Algonquin Pkwy. ... E-2
Alley ... A-3
Alleycourt Pl. ... B-5
Alliston Ave. ... E-1
Alma Ave. ... J-2
Almond Ave. ... J-5
Anna Lane ... J-1
Ann Ct. ... F-2
Appleton Ct. ... G-1
Appleton Ln. ... G-1
Arcade Ave. ... G-3
Ardmore Dr. ... F-7
Argonne Ave. ... G-1
Arling Ave. ... K-3
Arling Ct. ... K-2
Armory ... B-5
Ash St. ... E-7
Ashbury Rd. ... K-4
Ashland Ave. ... I-3,I-5
Ashton Ave. ... I-6
Auburndale Ave. ... K-4
Audobon Parkway ... G-7
Auery Ave. ... E-5
Bachman Dr. ... H-1
Badger Ave. ... J-5
Ballard Ct. ... B-7
Bancroft St. ... C-6
Bank St. ... A-4
Barbee Ave. ... F-6
Barbee Way ... F-6
Barkwood Rd. ... H-2
Baroness St. ... D-7
Barret Ave. ... C-7
Bardstown ... C-8
Barret ... C-8
Barrowdale Dr. ... K-1
Barton Ave. ... I-7
Bates Ct. ... D-8
Baxter St. ... B-8
Beacher St. ... I-3
Becker Ct. ... F-1
Beech Ave. ... I-2
Beech St. ... E-1
Beecher St. ... I-3
Beeler ... K-4
Bedgravia Ct. ... E-5
Bellevue ... J-4
Bellevue Ave. ... I-4
Belmar Ave. ... H-8
Bergman St. ... E-6
Berkley Sq. ... J-8
Bernheim Ave. ... E-2
Berry Blvd. ... H-2
Bicknell Ave. ... J-3
Bloom ... E-5
Blue Grass ... J-3
Bobolink Rd. ... F-8
Bohannon St. ... G-3
Bolling Ave. ... D-2
Bourban Ave. ... H-8
Boxley Ave. ... G-6
Boyle St. ... D-7
Brandies ... F-5
Breckinridge St. ... C-4,C-7
Brent St. ... D-8
Brentwood Ave. ... H-3
Briden Ave. ... I-8
Broadway ... B-1,C-6
Brook ... C-6,F-5,I-5
Brookline Ave. ... J-3
Buchanan ... A-7
Buckner Ave. ... K-4
Burnett Ave. ... D-2,E-5,E-7
Burwell ... E-1
Byrne Ave. ... G-5
Cable St. ... A-8
Caldwell ... C-7
Camden Ave. ... I-2
Campbell St. ... C-7
Camp St. ... D-6
Cardinal Dr. ... H-8
Carl Ct. ... I-1
Carlisle Ave. ... H-2
Carrico ... I-3
Cassin Ave. ... E-5
Castlevale Dr. ... E-8
Castlewood Ave. ... D-8
Catalpa St. ... D-1
Cawthan St. ... C-4
Cayuga ... I-2
Cedar St. ... A-2
Center Cliff ... I-4
Central Ave. ... G-3
Chalmer ... F-2
Chapel St. ... A-4
Charles St. ... D-7
Cherokee ... C-8
Chester Rd. ... H-1
Chestnut ... B-1,B-4,B-7
Cheyenne Ave. ... H-6
Chickadee Rd. ... G-8
Chicopee ... I-5
Christopher Pl. ... J-4
Churchman Ave. ... J-2
Clara Ave. ... H-2
Clarks Lane ... F-7
Clay ... C-7
Clay St. ... E-6
Cliff Ave. ... J-4
Clover Hills Dr. ... J-1
College St. ... C-5
Colgan St. ... B-3
Collins Ct. ... H-5
Colorado Ave. ... G-3
Columbia St. ... A-2
Compton St. ... F-4
Concord Dr. ... G-6
Conestoga Ave. ... E-1
Congess ... A-2,A-5
Conlin Ave. ... F-7
Conn St. ... H-2
Conrad ... C-6
Cooper St. ... B-8
Cornette Way ... J-1
Craig Ave. ... I-2
Crittenden Dr. ... G-6,J-6
Crop St. ... A-2
Crossbill Rd. ... G-8
Crown St. ... D-8
Cumberland Ave. ... K-4
Curry Dr. ... I-7
Cypress St. ... D-2,E-1
Dahlia Dr. ... E-8
Dakota Ave. ... H-6
Dale Ave. ... G-3,K-4
Dana Dr. ... I-1
Dandridge ... D-7
Date St. ... C-2
Davies Ave. ... E-4
Dearcy ... H-3
Dellwood Dr. ... J-1
Del Mar Ave. ... K-1
Delmar Ct. ... J-1
Delmar Ln. ... J-1
Delor Ave. ... F-7
Del Park ... B-1
Dena Dr. ... I-1
Denmark Ave. ... H-3
Dixdale Ave. ... E-1
Dixie St. ... F-8
Dixie Hwy. ... E-2,H-1
Dixon St. ... E-7
Doerr Dr. ... H-1
Dove Ln. ... G-8
Dove Rd. ... G-8
Dresden Ave. ... H-3
Dubourg Ave. ... G-1
Dumesnil ... D-2
Durrett Lane ... I-8
Duvall ... G-6
Eagan Ave. ... J-6
Eagle Pass ... F-8
Earl Ave. ... G-3
Eastern Pkwy. ... F-7
Edward St. ... C-8
Eicher Rd. ... H-1
Eigelbach Ave. ... E-8
Elderwood Way ... I-1
Elliot Ave. ... B-2
Ellison Ave. ... D-8
Elm St. ... A-8
Emil Ave. ... G-6
English Ave. ... G-8
Estate Dr. ... K-1
Euclid ... F-4
Euclid Ave. ... F-4
Evelyn Ave. ... H-4
Expressway St. ... B-6
Fairmount Ave. ... H-5
Falcon Dr. ... G-8
Farmdale Ave. ... I-8
Farmington Ave. ... H-5
Farnsley Rd. ... H-1
Fayette Ave. ... H-8
Faywood Way ... G-2
Federal Pl. ... B-5
Fern Dr. ... G-8
Finzer St. ... C-6
Fischer Ave. ... D-7
Fitzgerald Dr. ... G-1
Flexner Way ... B-6
Floral Terr. ... D-5
Florence Ave. ... I-4,I-5
Floyd ... C-6,G-5
Fontaine Ave. ... H-7
Forest Ave. ... E-7
Forum Ave. ... K-4
Foster St. ... G-6
Fountain Ct. ... E-5
Francis Ave. ... J-5
Franklin Ave. ... H-8
Franklin St. ... A-8
Fust Ave. ... F-2
Gagel Ave. ... K-1
Garden Row ... J-8
Garey Ln. ... G-2
Garland Ave. ... C-2,C-4
Garrett St. ... H-4
Garvey Ct. ... J-1
Garvey Dr. ... J-1
Garvin Pl. ... D-5
Gaulbert Ave. ... D-2,E-5
Geiger St. ... A-7
Georgetown Ave. ... H-2
Gillette Ave. ... G-1,I-5
Glenafton Ln. ... G-7
Glendale Ave. ... H-2
Glenrock Rd. ... K-1
Glenview Rd. ... F-2
Goddard Ave. ... D-8
Goss St. ... D-7
Grand Ave. ... C-1,C-2
Grant ... H-5
Gray ... B-6
Greenleaf Rd. ... G-7
Green St. ... A-2
Greenup ... F-7
Greenwood Ave. ... C-2
Gregg St. ... E-2
Guthrie St. ... B-5
Hale ... C-2
Hamilton Ave. ... A-7
Hancock St. ... C-6,E-6
Hannah Ln. ... I-8
Hardesty Ave. ... F-1
Harding Ave. ... I-6
Harold Ave. ... F-2
Harrison Ave. ... F-6
Hartwell ... K-5
Harwell ... G-6
Haskin Ave. ... K-3
Hathaway Ave. ... H-3
Hawes Ln. ... I-6
Hawthorne ... E-8
Hazel St. ... D-1
Hazelwood Ave. ... J-2
Hazelwood Ct. ... K-2
Hdertz Ave. ... E-7
Helm St. ... G-6
Hemlock St. ... D-1
Hepburn Ave. ... C-8
Herbert Ave. ... I-1
Herr ... F-4
Hess Lane ... G-8
Heywood Ave. ... G-4
Hickory St. ... E-7
Highland Ave. ... C-8
Highway ... H-8
High Pine Dr. ... K-1
Hill Ave. ... D-2,E-4
Hill Top Ct. ... I-4
Hobart Dr. ... J-1
Homeview Dr. ... F-3,G-4
Hopkins Ave. ... F-4
Howard St. ... C-2
Hull St. ... B-8
Huntoon Ave. ... K-3
Huron Dr. ... H-5
Innis Ct. ... C-8
Inverness ... K-4
Iowa Ave. ... G-4
Iroquois Ave. ... K-3,K-4
Ivy Ct. ... A-1
Jackson St. ... C-6,E-6
Jacob St. ... C-5,C-6
Jefferson ... A-1,A-4
Jefferson Ct. ... G-7
Johnson St. ... B-7
Jordan ... E-4
Joseph St. ... I-1
Julia Ave. ... D-8
Kahlert Ave. ... I-3
Kathleen Ave. ... I-4
Kelland Way ... H-1
Keller Ave. ... I-7
Kennedy Dr. ... F-2
Kenton St. ... H-5
Kentucky St. ... C-1,C-4,C-6
Kenwood Way ... J-4
Keswick ... F-7
Kings ... K-2
Kingston ... K-4
Knight Ave. ... J-2
Knight Rd. ... K-1
Krieger St. ... E-7
Lafayette ... H-2
Lammers ... D-8
Lampton St. ... C-6
Lancaster Ave. ... K-2
Lance Dr. ... J-1
Lansing Ave. ... I-5
Larchmont Ave. ... G-3
Larue Ave. ... H-8
La Salle Ave. ... J-2
Lawrence ... H-2
Lawrie Ln. ... K-2
Lee Dr. ... J-8
Lee St. ... E-5,E-6
Lehigh Ave. ... J-3
Lennox St. ... H-5
Lentz Ave. ... I-3
Leroy Ave. ... H-1
Lester ... H-3
Lewis Ave. ... B-2
Lexington Rd. ... B-8
Libertybell ... H-2
Liberty St. ... B-5
Lillian Ave. ... F-3
Lily Ave. ... F-6
Lindberg ... G-2
Lindberg Dr. ... F-3
Lincoln Ave. ... F-4
Linnet Rd. ... G-8
Linwood Ave. ... E-1
Livingston Ave. ... I-4
Locust Lane ... G-7
Logan St. ... C-7
Lone Oak Ave. ... K-4
Loney Ln. ... F-2,G-2
Longfield ... H-2
Loretta Ave. ... H-2
Lou Gene Way ... J-1
Louisville ... J-6
Lucas Ave. ... I-8
Lukin Dr. ... H-1
Lupino Ct. ... H-8
Lydia St. ... E-7
Lynnhurst Ave. ... J-3
Lynn St. ... F-6
Lyttle ... A-4
Madelon St. ... B-1
Madison St. ... B-1,B-6
Magazine ... B-1
Magnolia Ave. ... D-2,D-4
Main ... A-1,A-4
Malcom Rd. ... J-1
Malcome Pl. ... J-2
Manitau Ave. ... I-3
Mann Ave. ... J-2
Manning Rd. ... H-7
Manor Rd. ... H-7
Manslock Ct. ... I-1
Maple ... B-2
Maple Ct. ... I-4
Mapleton ... I-3
Market St. ... A-1,A-4
Marrett Ave. ... D-6
Mary St. ... D-7
Mary Catherine Dr. ... H-1
Mason Ave. ... C-7
Mathias Ln. ... H-1
Mayer Ave. ... E-8
May Lawn Ave. ... G-6
McAtee ... B-1
McCloske Ave. ... F-1
McCoy ... G-3
McKinley Ave. ... F-8
Meade St. ... F-8
Meadowlark ... G-8
Mellwood Ave. ... B-8
Merhoff St. ... G-6
Merriweather St. ... E-6
Merwin ... G-6
Mill St. ... A-7
Millers Lane ... F-1
Milton Ave. ... E-7
Mission Dr. ... H-7
Mitscher Ave. ... K-4
Mix Ave. ... E-4
Model Dr. ... F-2
Mohawk Ave. ... I-5
Molter Ave. ... G-7
Montana Ave. ... G-3
Morgan Ave. ... E-7
Morgan St. ... H-8
Morrison Ave. ... K-3
Morton Ave. ... C-8
Mulberry Ave. ... E-7
Myrtle St. ... D-4
Nancy Lee Dr. ... J-8
Naneen Dr. ... J-1
Narraganset Dr. ... E-1
Navaho Ave. ... I-3
Nelson Ave. ... F-1
New High St. ... G-6
Nichols Dr. ... H-2
Nobel ... H-1
Nobel Pl. ... H-1
North-South St. ... B-6
Oak St. ... C-2,D-5,D-7
Oakwood Ave. ... J-3
Oehrle Dr. ... H-1
Ohio St. ... A-8
Oldham St. ... D-4
Oleanda Ave. ... G-3,H-3
Oleanda Ct. ... G-3
Olenda Ave. ... G-1
Olive St. ... D-1
Oneida Ct. ... I-2
Oregon Ave. ... E-1
Oriole Dr. ... G-8
Ormsby Ave. ... D-3,D-6
Osage Ave. ... C-2
Ottawa Ave. ... I-5
Packard Ave. ... G-7
Park Ave. ... D-5,H-1
Park Rd. ... H-1
Parkway Dr. ... F-7
Parthenina ... I-2
Parthenina Ave. ... I-2
Paul Ave. ... H-3
Payne St. ... B-8
Peachtree ... H-3
Peachtree St. ... I-3
Peck Ave. ... I-3
Peerless Ct. ... D-3
Penquin ... G-6
Penway Ave. ... E-1
Phillips Lane ... I-6
Phyllis Ave. ... G-3
Picadilly Ave. ... J-3
Pidgeon Ave. ... G-8
Pikeview Rd. ... H-7
Pindell Ave. ... F-7
Pine St. ... B-8
Piper Ct. ... G-7
Place St. ... B-5
Plantation Dr. ... F-1
Plover ... F-8
Plymouth Ct. ... B-2
Pocahantis ... A-7
Poplar Level Rd. ... F-8
Powell Ave. ... I-2
Preston ... C-6,G-7
Prosperity Ct. ... B-1
Pylon Ct. ... I-7
Queen Ave. ... G-3
Quincy St. ... A-8
Racine Ave. ... G-4
Ralph Ave. ... G-1
Rammers ... D-7
Ramser Ave. ... G-1
Ratcliffe Ave. ... E-2
Rawlings Ave. ... E-6
Reasor Ave. ... E-7
Reutlinger St. ... D-7
Rhonda Dr. ... J-1
Rhonda Way ... J-1
Rice Ave. ... H-6
River Rd. ... A-6
Robin Dr. ... H-1
Robin Rd. ... G-7
Rochester Dr. ... K-4
Rodman St. ... G-4
Rondean Dr. ... J-1
Roosevelt ... H-8
Rosa Ter. ... H-1
Roselane Ave. ... C-6
Rosemary Dr. ... G-7
Rowan ... A-2,A-4
Royal Ave. ... E-8
Rubel Ave. ... C-8
Ruffer Ave. ... D-8
Rutland ... I-3
Sadie Ave. ... J-1
St. Bertand St. ... D-5
St. Catherine ... C-4,D-7
St. James Ct. ... E-5
St. Louis Ave. ... D-2
St. Michael ... D-7
St. Paul St. ... D-6
Sale Ave. ... H-3
Samuel St. ... D-7
Sanders Ln. ... K-1
Scanlon St. ... G-5
Schaffner ... F-3
Schiley St. ... J-2
Schiller ... C-7
Schneiter Ave. ... G-3
School ... K-2
School Way ... K-4
Seelbach Ave. ... I-2,I-3
Seneca ... I-5
Sharp Ave. ... F-3
Shelby St. ... C-7
Sherry Dr. ... G-6
Shingo Ave. ... K-3
Short ... H-8
Sioux Ave. ... H-6
Skyway Dr. ... J-8
Sonne Rd. ... F-2,F-3
Southcrest Dr. ... J-4
Southern Ave. ... D-1
Southern Pkwy. ... K-3
Southern Heights ... I-2,I-4
Southgate Ave. ... H-3
Southland Blvd. ... K-3
South St. ... F-3
Speckert Ct. ... C-7
Spratt St. ... E-7
Spring St. ... B-8
Springdale ... I-8
Squires Dr. ... I-3
Standard Ave. ... D-2
Stanford Ave. ... J-8
Stanford Lane ... J-8
Stanley Ave. ... I-3
Stephan Lane ... K-1
Story Ave. ... B-7
Strader ... I-2
Strader Ave. ... I-2
Stratter Alley ... C-6
Summit Ave. ... E-8
Swako Ln. ... K-1
Swan St. ... C-7
Sylvia Ave. ... E-7
Tallulah Ave. ... I-6
Talmadge Way ... J-1
Taylor Ave. ... J-3
Teal Ave. ... G-8
Tennessee Ave. ... F-3
Tenny Ave. ... J-4
Terry ... K-5
Texas Blvd. ... F-7
Theresa ... K-5
Theresa Ave. ... H-1
Thornberry Ave. ... G-4
Thrush Rd. ... G-8
Thruston Dr. ... F-7
Tokay Ave. ... G-6
Towne Way ... J-5
Tuberose Ave. ... K-8
Tuscarora Way ... J-3
Utah ... G-3
Valley Forge ... H-2
Valley Rd. ... D-8
Valley View Dr. ... I-1
Vine ... C-7
Virginia Ave. ... C-1
Vorster Ave. ... E-2
Wabasso Ave. ... J-6
Wagner Ave. ... E-7
Wainwright ... F-6
Wallie ... F-2
Walnut St. ... A-1,B-4
Walter Ave. ... J-3
Wampum Ave. ... I-5
Warnock ... F-5
Warren Ave. ... H-4,I-3
Washington St. ... A-7
Wathens Ln. ... F-2
Watkins Ave. ... C-8
Wawa ... I-5
Weaver Ct. ... D-1
Webster ... A-8
Weyler ... G-3
Weller Ave. ... F-3
Wellington Ave. ... J-5
Wenatchee ... E-1
Wenona Ave. ... I-6
Wenzel St. ... B-7
Wetterau ... E-7
Wheeler ... J-2
Wheeler Ave. ... I-2
Whitewood Dr. ... I-6
Whitney Ave. ... H-5
Wilson ... E-1
Wilson Ave. ... D-3
Wingfield ... F-1
Wingfield Ave. ... E-3
Winkler Ave. ... F-4
Winter St. ... D-8
Wirth ... G-7
Wolfe Ave. ... H-8
Woodbine ... D-5
Woodlawn Ave. ... D-1, D-2,J-4,J-6
Woodruff ... I-3
Woody Ave. ... J-3
Wren Rd. ... G-7
Wue St. ... F-2
Wurtele Ave. ... Fp3,G-1
Wyandotte Ave. ... E-1
Yolanda Dr. ... J-1
York St. ... C-4
Youngland Ave. ... F-1
Zane St. ... C-5
Ziegler ... E-6
1st St. ... C-5,E-5,J-5
2nd St. ... C-5,E-5,J-5
3rd St. ... C-5,G-5,J-4
4th St. ... C-5,G-4,J-4
5th St. ... C-5,G-4,I-4,J-4
6th St. ... C-5,E-5,G-4,J-4
7th St. ... C-5,G-2
8th St. ... C-4,E-4,I-4
9th St. ... C-4,E-4,G-4
10th St. ... B-4,E-4
11th St. ... D-4,E-4
13th St. ... B-4,E-3
14th St. ... B-4,E-3
15th St. ... B-4,E-3
16th St. ... B-3,D-3,E-3
17th St. ... B-3,D-3,E-3
18th St. ... B-3
19th St. ... B-3
20th St. ... B-3,E-2
22nd ... C-2,E-2
23rd ... A-2,B-2,C-2,E-2
24th St. ... A-2,B-2,C-2,E-2
25th St. ... A-2,C-2,E-2
27th St. ... B-2
28th St. ... A-2,C-1,D-1
29th St. ... A-2,B-1,E-1
30th St. ... A-1,B-1,C-1
31st St. ... B-1,D-1
32nd ... D-1
33rd St. ... C-1
34th St. ... C-1
35th St. ... B-1
36th St. ... A-1

POINTS OF INTEREST

Standiford Field Airport ... J-6
Algonquin Park ... E-1
Boone Park ... A-3
Central Park ... D-5
Elliot Park ... B-1
George Rogers Clark Park ... F-8
Iroquois Park ... K-3
Shelby Park ... D-6
Sheppard Park ... B-3
South Central Park ... F-3
Victory Park ... C-2
Westonia Park ... A-1
Wyandotte Park ... I-3

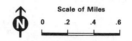

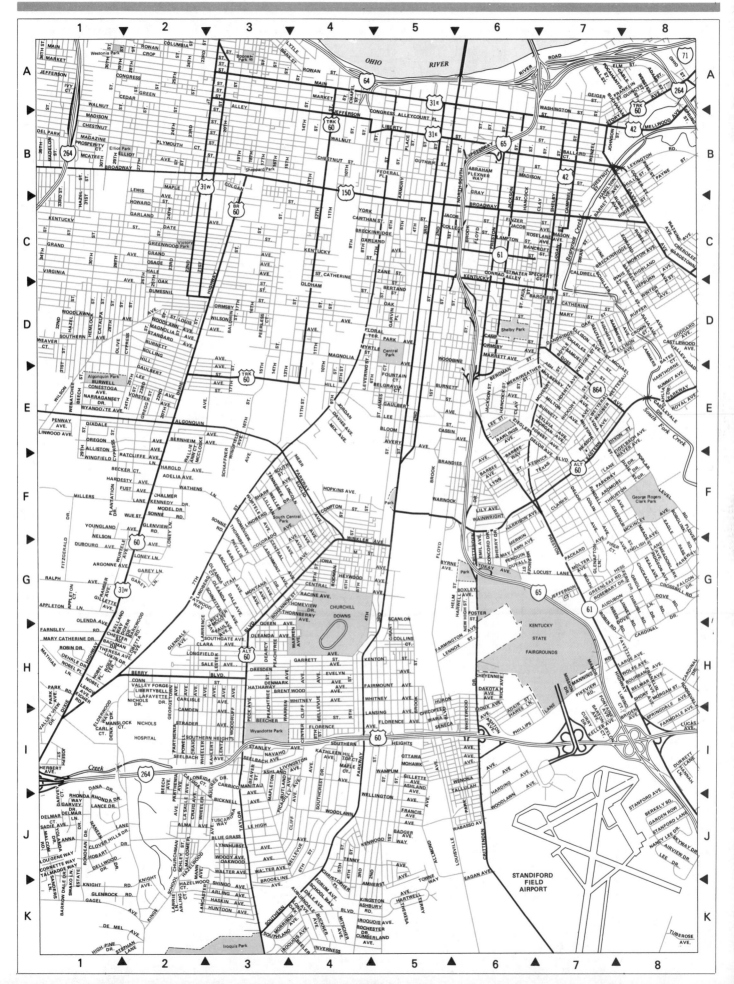

Scale of Miles

0 .1 .2 .3 .4

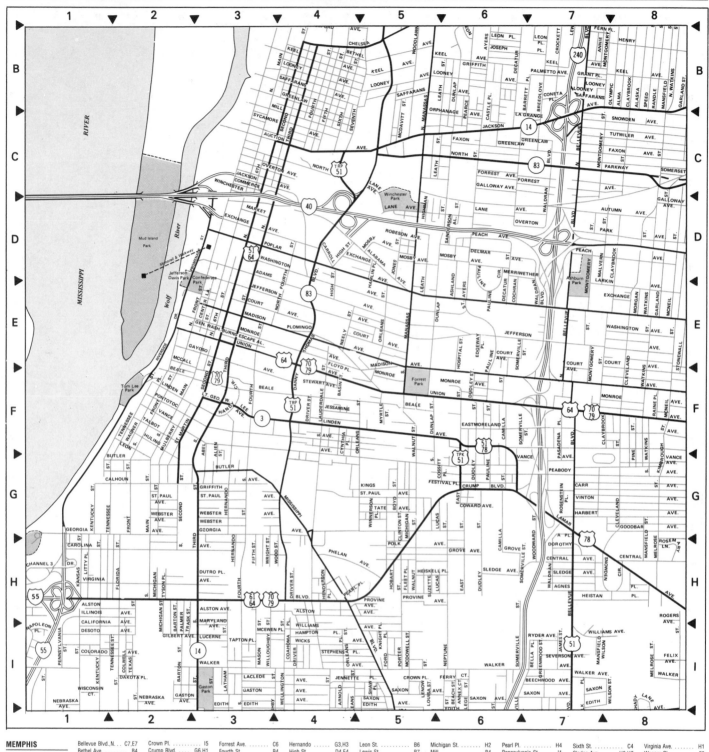

MEMPHIS

A Pl. G7
Abel F3
Adams Ave. D3
Agnes Pl. H7
Alabama Ave. D5
Alaska St. B8
Alien St. F3
Alma St. B8
Alston Ave. H1,H4
Annex Ct. I6
Annie Pl. B7
Arkansas Riverdale Dr.
. . . . E2
Arnold Pl. I4
Ashburn Park D7
Ashland St. D6
Auction Ave. B6,E6
Autumn Ave. D8
Ayers St. B6,E6

Barboro E3
Barrett St. B7
Barton St. H2
Basin St. F4
Beach St. I6
Beachwood Ave. . . . I7
Beale F2,F3,F5
Bellevue Blvd. H7

Bellevue Blvd.,N. . . C7,E7
Bethel Ave. B4
Boyd St. G5
Breedlove St. B7
Butler G1,G3
Calhoun Ave. G1
California Ave. H1
Camilla St. F6,r,i6
Carolina Ave. H1
Carr Ave. G7
Carroll E3
Castle Pl. B6
Center La E3
Central Ave. H7,H8
Channel 3 Dr. H1
Chelsea Ave. B4
Claybrook St. D8,F7
Cleveland St. D7
Clinton St. I5
Coahoma Ave. I4
Cochran D5
College St. I6
Colorado Ave. H1
Colwell I2
Commerce C4
Coneta Ave. B7
Cossitt Pl. G6
Court Ave. . . . E3,E6,E8
Coward Ave. G6

Crown Pl. I5
Crump Blvd. G6,H1
Cynthia Pl. F4
Dakota Pl. I2
Danny Thomas Blvd. . E4
Decatur St. B6,E6
Delmar Ave. D6
Desoto Ave. I1
Dorothy H7
Driver St. F4,H4
Dudley St. F6,H6
Dunlap St. B6,E5
Dunlap St.,S. F5
Dutro Pl. H3
East St. G6
Eastmoreland Ave. . . F5
Edgeway Pl. E6
Edith Ave. I3,I7
Escape Al. E3
Exchange Ave. D3,D5,E8
Faxon Ave. C6,C8
Felix Ave. I8
Fern Pl. I4
Ferry Ct. I6
Festival St. G6
Fifth St. C4,H3
Fleet St. G7
Flordia St. H1
Floyd St. F4
Ford St. I5

Forrest Ave. C6
Fourth St. B4
Fourth St.,N. B7
Fourth St.,S. F3,H3
Front St. G2
Front St.,N. E3
Front St.,S. F2
Galloway Ave. C6,D8
Garland St. B8,E8
Gaston Ave. I2,I3
Gayoso Ave. E5
Gen Wash.-Burns . . . E5
Georgia Ave. G1,G3
Gilbert Ave. I2
Goodbar Ave. D7
Grant Pl. B7
Greenlaw B4,C6
Greenwood St. I1
Griffith B6,G3
Grove Ave. H6
Hamlin St. D5,E5
Hampton Pl. I4
Handy Circle F3
Harbert Ave. G7
Heiskell St. H5
Heistan Pl. H7
Henderson Pl. H6
Henry Ave. B8

Hernando G3,H3
High St. D4,E4
Highman D5
Hobart H5
Hospital St. F2
Illinois Ave. H1
Jackson Ave. . . . C3,C6
James St. I7
Jefferson Ave. . . E3,E6
Jennette St. I4
Jessamine F4
Jones D5
Joseph Pl. B7
Kansas St. H1
Keel Ave. B4,B8
Kentucky St. G1,I1
Kings G5
LaGrange Ave. . . C6,C7
Laclede Ave. I3
Lamar Ave. G7
Lane Ave. C5,D6
Larkin Ave. D8
Latham St. I3
Lauderdale St.,S. . . . F4
Leath St. B6,E5
Lenow St. I5
Leon F3
Leon Pl. B6,B7

Leon St. B6
Lewis St. B7
Linden Ave. F2,F4
Litty St. H1
Looney Ave. B4,B7
Louisa St. I5
Lt. Geo. W. Lee Ave. . F3
Lucas St. G5,H5
Lucerne I3
Madison Ave. . . . E3,E5
Main St.,N. B4
Main St.,S. F2,G2
Malvern St. D7
Manassas St.,N. C5
Manassas St. D5
Mansfield St. . B8,H8,I7
Market D3
Mars Hall Ave. . . . E4,E5
Maryland Ave. H3
Mason I4
McCall E4
McDavitt St. C5
McDowell St. I6
McLenmore Ave.,E. . . I1
McNeil St. E8,E8
Mcwen Pl. I3
Melrose St. H8
Merriwether D6
Michigan G5

Michigan St. H2
Mill B4
Mississippi Blvd. G4
Monroe Ave. . . E3,E5,F8
Montgomery St. . . . . .
. . . . B7,C7,E7
Morgan E8
Mosby Ave. D5
Mulberry F2
Myrtle St. F5
Napoleon Pl. I1
Nebraska Ave. . . . I1,I2
Neeley St. E4
Neptune St. I6
North C4
Olympic St. B8
Orleans St. E5,F5
Orphanage Ave. . . B5,C6
Overton St. C3,D6
Palmer I2
Palmetto Ave. B7
Park Ave. C6,C7
Parkway C7
Pasadena Pl. F7
Pauline Cir D6
Pauline St. F6,G6
Peabody Ave. G7
Peach Ave. D6,D7
Pearce St. C6

Pearl Pl. H4
Pennsylvania St. I1
Phelan Ave. H4
Pine St. C8
Plomingo E4
Polk Ave. H5
Pontotoc Ave. F2
Poplar Ave. D3,D8
Porter St. I5
Promenade St. C3
Provine Ave. H5
Raine St. E4
Randle St. B8
Robeson Ave. D5
Rogers Ave. H8
Rosemary Ln. G7
Rosenstein St. G7
Ryder Ave. I7
Sanderson Al. I2
Saxon Ave. I5,I7
Second St. F3
Second St.,N. C4
Second St.,S. G2
Seventh St. C4
Severson Ave. I7
Shady Ln. I2
Shaw Pl. I5

Sixth St. C4
Sledge Ave. H6,H7
Snowden Ave. C8
Snowden Circle H8
Somerset C8
Somerville St. . . . .
. . . . E6,F6,H6,I6
Speed St. B8
St. Kimbrough St. . . . G8
St. Martin F2
St. Paul Ave. G2,G5
Stephens Pl. I4
Stonewall E8
Suzette H5
Sycamore Ave. C3
Talbot F2
Tapton Pl. I3
Tate Ave. G5
Tennessee St. . . F2,G1,I2
Texas St. I1
Third St.,N. C4
Third St.,S. E3,I3
Trask St. I2
Tutwiler Ave. C8
Tyson St. H2
Union Ave. E3,F5
Vance Ave. . . . F2,G6,G8
Vinton Ave. G7

Virginia Ave. H1
Wagner Pl. F2
Waldran Blvd. . . D7,E7,H7
Walk Pl. I7
Walker Ave. I3,I8
Walnut St. F5,H5
Washington Ave. . . . . .
. . . . D3,D4,E8
Watkins E8,F8
Watkins St.,N. B8
Watkins,S. F8,G8
Webster Ave. G2,G3
Wellington St. I4
Wicks Ave. I4
Williams Ave. I4,I7
Wilson St. I7,I8
Winchester C3
Winnerson Pl. G5
Wisconsin Ct. I1
Wood St. H4
Woodlawn St. B5
Woodward St. H7
Wright St. H3
6th St.,N. C3,E3

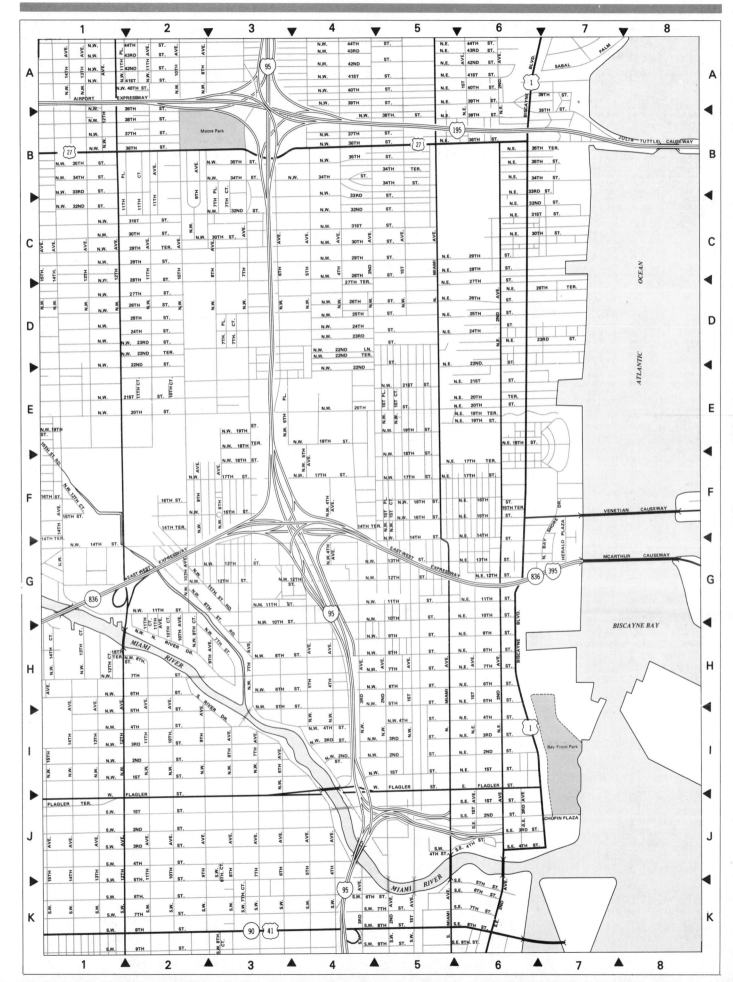

MIAMI

Airport Expwy.	A1
Bay Shore Sr.,N.	F7,G7
Biscayne Blvd.	A6,B6,H6
Chopin Plaza	J7
East-West Expwy.	G2,G5
Flagler St.,E	I6
Flagler St.,W.	I2,I5
Flagler Terr.	J1
Herald Plaza	F7,G7
Julia Tuttle Causeway	B8
McArthur Causeway	G7,G8
Miami Ave.,N.	C5,H5
Miami Ave.,S.	K5
Palm	A7
River Dr. N.W.	H2
River Dr. S.	H2
Sabal	J7
Venetian Causeway	F7,F8
1st Ave. N.E.	A6,H6
1st Ave. N.W.	C5,H5
1st Ave. S.E.	J6
1st Ave. S.W.	K5
1st Ct. N.W.	E5,F5
1st Pl. N.W.	E5,F5
1st St. N.E.	I6
1st St. N.W.	I2,I5
1st St. S.E.	J6
1st St. S.W.	J2
2nd Ave.N.E.	A6,D6,H6
2nd Ave.N.W.	C4,H5
2nd Ave.S.E.	K6
2nd Ave.S.W.	K5
2nd St.N.E.	I6
2nd St.N.W.	I2,I4,I5
2nd St.S.E.	J6
2nd St.S.W.	J2
3rd Ave. N.W.	H4
3rd Ave.S.E.	J6
3rd Ave.S.W.	K4
3rd St.N.E.	I6
3rd St.N.W.	I2,I4,I5
3rd St.S.E.	J6
3rd St.S.W.	J2
4th Ave.N.W.	C4,F4,G4,H4
4th Ave.S.W.	J4
4th St.N.E.	I6
4th St.N.W.	I2,I4,I5
4th St.S.E.	J6
4th St.S.W.	J2,J5
5th Ave.N.W.	C4,F4,G4
5th Ave.S.W.	J4
5th Pl.N.W.	E3
5th St.N.E.	H6
5th St.N.W.	H3,H5,I2
5th St.S.E.	K6
5th St.S.W.	J2
6th Ave.N.W.	C3,I3
6th Ave.S.W.	J3
6th St.N.W.	H2,H3,H5
6th St.S.E.	K6
6th St.S.W.	K2,K4
7th Ave.N.W.	C3,H3,I3
7th Ave.S.W.	J3
7th Ct.	C3,D3
7th Ct.S.W.	J3
7th Pl.	C3,D3
7th St.N.E.	H6
7th St.N.W.	H2,H3,H5
7th St.S.E.	K6
7th St.S.W.	K2,K5
8th Ave.N.W.	A2,C3,F3,I3
8th Ave.S.W.	J3
8th Ct.S.W.	J3,K3
8th St.N.E.	H6
8th St.N.W.	H2,H3,H5
8th St.Rd. N.W.	G2
8th St.S.E.	K6
8th St.S.W.	K2,K5
9th Ave.	H3
9th Ave.N.W.	B2,F2,I2
9th Ave.S.W.	J2
9th Ct.N.W.	H2
9th St.N.E.	H6
9th St.N.W.	H5
9th St.S.E.	K6
9th St.S.W.	K2,K5
10th Ave.	H2
10th Ave. N.W.	A2,C2,G2,I2
10th Ave. S.W.	J2
10th Ct.	E2,H2
10th St. N.W.	G3,G5
11th Ave.N.W.	C2,I2
11th Ave.S.W.	J2
11th Ct.	C2,E2,H2
11th Pl.	C2
11th St.N.E.	G6
11th St.N.W.	G2,G3,G5
11th St.Rd.N.W.	G3
12th Ave.N.W.	B1,C1,I1
12th Ave.S.W.	J1
12th Ct.	H1
12th St.	G6
12th St.N.W.	G3,G4,G5
13th Ave.N.W.	A1,C1,I1
13th Ave.S.W.	J1
13th St.N.E.	G6
13th St.N.W.	G3,G5
14th Ave. NW	A1,C1,F1,I1
14th Ave.S.W.	J1
14th Ct.N.W.	H1
14th St.N.E.	G6

14th St.N.W.	G1,G5
14th Terr.	F1,F2,F4
15th Ave.N.W.	C1,I1
15th Ave.S.W.	J1
15th St.	F1
15th St.N.E.	F6
15th St.N.W.	F3,F5
15th St.Rd.	E1
15th Terr.	F6
16th St.	F1,F2
16th St.N.E.	F6
16th St.N.W.	F5
17th St.N.E.	F6
17th St.N.W.	F3,F5
17th Terr.N.E.	F6
18th St.N.E.	E6
18th St.N.W.	F3,F5
18th Terr.	H1
18th Terr.N.W.	E3
19th St.	E6
19th St.N.W.	E1,E3,E5
19th St.N.E.	E6
20th St. NE	E6
20th St.N.W.	E2,E4
20th Terr. NE	E6
21st St.	E6
21st St.N.W.	E2,E5
22nd Ln.N.W.	D4
22nd St.N.E.	E6
22nd St.N.W.	D2,E4
22nd Terr.N.W.	D2,D4
23rd St.	D7
23rd St.N.W.	D2,D4
24th St.N.E.	D6
24th St.N.W.	D2,D4
25th St.	D6
25th St.N.W.	D2,D4
26th St.N.E.	D6
26th St.N.W.	D2,D4
27th St. NE	D6
27th St. NW	D2
27th Terr.	D4
28th St.N.E.	C2,C4
28th St.N.W.	C2,C4
29th St.N.E.	C2,C4
29th St.N.W.	C2
29th Terr.N.W.	C2
30th St.N.E.	C6
30th St.N.W.	C2,C4
31st St.N.E.	C6
31st St.N.W.	C2,C4
32nd St.N.E.	C6
32nd St.N.W.	C1,C3,C4
33rd St.N.E.	B7
33rd St.N.W.	B1,C4
34th St.N.E.	B7
34th St.N.W.	B1,B3,B5
34th Terr.	B5
35th St.N.E.	B7
35th St.N.W.	B1,B3,B4
35th Terr.N.E.	B6
36th St.N.W.	B6
36th St.N.E.	B2,B4
37th St.N.E.	B6,B7
38th St.N.E.	B2,B5
38th St.N.W.	B2,B5
39th St.N.E.	A6,A7
39th St.N.W.	A2,A4
40th St.N.E.	A6
40th St.N.W.	A2,A4
41st St.N.E.	A6
41st St.N.W.	A2,A4
42nd St.N.E.	A6
42nd St.N.W.	A2,A4
43rd St.N.E.	A6
43rd St.N.W.	A2,A4
44th St.N.E.	A6
44th St.N.W.	A2,A4

MILWAUKEE

Adams Ave.,S.	H6,J6
Ahmedi Ave.,S.	I7,K7
Alabama Ave.,S.	I7
Albany Pl.,W.	A4
Aldrich St.,S.	G6
Allerton Ave.,W.	J1,J5
Allis St.,S.	G6
Alois St.	C1
Amy Pl.,S.	F4
Andover Rd.,W.	G1
Anthony Dr.,W.	I2
Archer Ave.,E.	G6
Arizona St.,W.	H1
Arlington	B7
Armour Ave.,E.	K6
Armour Ave.,W.	J1,K1,K5
Arthur Ave.,W.	G4
Arthur Ct.,W.	G2
Artic Ave.	I8
Astor St.,N.	A7
Austin St.,S.	H6,I6,J6
Backbay,E.	B8
Barland Ave.,E.	J8
Barland Ave.,W.	K2,K3,K4
Bartlett,E.	A7
Bay St.,E.	G6,G7
Becher St.,E.	E6
Becher St.,W.	F4,G4
Belleview,E.	E4
Beloit Rd.	F1
Bennett Ave.,E.	H8
Betz.	J8
Blue Mound Rd.,W.	D2
Boddenhagen Pl.,W.	D1
Bolivar Ave.,W.	J3
Bombay Ave.,S.	I8
Booth St.,N.	A6
Bottsford Ave.,E.	J1,J3,J5
Bottsford St.,W.	J6,J8
Bradford Ave.,E.	A7
Bradley Ave.,E.	I6
Brady St.,E	B6
Branting Ln.,W.	F2
Bremen St.,N.	A6
Broadway St.,N.	C6
Brown St.,E.	B6
Brown St.,W.	B4
Bruce St.,E.	E6
Bruce St.,W.	E5
Brust Ave.,S.	I7,J7
Buffalo St.,E.	D6
Buffum St.,N.	A6
Burnham St.,W.	F3
Burrell St.,S.	H6,J6
Bush Ln.N.	A7
California St.,S.	H7
Cambridge,N.	B7
Canal St.,W.	D3
Carferry Dr.,S.	F6,G7
Carol St.,E.	I7
Carpenter Ave.,E.	K6
Carpenter Ave.,W.	K3,K5
Cass,N.	C6
Center St.,E.	A6
Center St.,W.	A4
Chase Ave.,S.	E6
Cherry St.,W.	C1,C4
Chicago St.,E.	D6
Clarence St.,E.	G6
Clark St.,E.	A6
Clark St.,W.	A4
Clement Ave.,E.	H7
Cleveland Ave.,W.	G1,H4
Clifford St.,E.	G6
Clybourn St.,E.	D6
Clybourn St.,W.	D4
Comstock Ave.,S.	F4
Congo Ave.	F4
Conway St.,E.	G6
Cora Ave.,E.	I7
Corcoran St.,E.	K6
Crawford Ave.,E.	I7,I8
Crawford Ave.,W.	I1,I4
Cudahy Ave.,E.	K6,K7
Dakota Ave.,W.	H1,H5
Dakota St.,E.	H7
Dana Ct.,S.	D1
Dayfield St.,S	I7
Deer Pl.,E.	G6
Delaware Ave.,S.	H7,H8,J8,K8
Denton Ave.,E.	H8
Dewey Pl.,E.	H6
Dorothy Pl.,W.	E2
Doty Pl.,E.	J7
Dover St.,E.	G6
Downer,N.	A8
Drury Ln.	H3
Eden Pl.,E.	I5
Eden Pl.,W.	I5
Edison,N.	C5
Elecric Ave.,W.	G1
Elgin Ln.,W.	E4
Elizabeth	B3
Ellen St.,S.	H7,I7
Erie St.,E.	E6
Estes St.,E.	H8
Euclid Ave,E.	H6,H7
Euclid Ave.,W.	H1,H4
Falling Heath,E.	H8
Fardale Ave.,W.	I3

Farwell Ave.,N.	C7
Fernwood Ave.,E.	H8
Fillmore Dr.,W.	G1
Florida St.,E.	E6
Florida St.,E.	E5
Fond Du Lac Ave.	A3
Forest Home Ave.,W.	F4,G4
Franklin,N.	C6
Fratney St.,N.	A6
Frederick Pl.,E.	E2
Frederick,N.	A7
Front St.,N.	D6
Fulton St.,S.	H7
Galena Pl.	C6
Galena St.,W.	B1,B4
Garfield Ave.,E.	B6
Garfield Ave.,W.	B4
Gauer Cir.,E.	H6
Gladstone,S.	H6
Gordon Ct.,N.	A7
Gordon Pl.N.	A7,B7
Graham St.,S.	D6,G6
Grant St.,W.	G4
Greeley St.,S.	H6
Greenfield Ave.,E.	F6
Greenfield Ave.,W.	F4
Greenwich Ave.,E.	A7
Griffin Ave.,S.	I6,J6
Hackelt,N.	A8
Hadley Ave.,E.	A6
Hadley St.,W.	A4
Halsey Ave.,W.	K3,K4
Hamilton,E.	B6
Hansen Ave.,S.	H7
Harbor Dr.,S.	F7
Harbor Pl.,E.	E6
Harbor,N.	D6
Harrison Ave.,W.	G4
Hawley Rd.	D1
Hayes Ave.,E.	G6
Hayes Ave.,W.	G1,G4
Herman St.,S.	H7
Highland Blvd.	C2,C4
Hilbert St.,S.	F6
Hilda Pl.,W.	E2
Hill Ave.	D1
Hillcrest Ave.,E.	H7
Holmes Ave.,E.	K8
Holmes Ave.,W.	K2,K3,K4
Holt Ave.,W.	I1,I2,I4,I6
Holton St.,N.	A6
Homer St.,E.	G6
Hopkins,W.	A4
Howard Ave.,E.	I6
Howell Ave.,S.	H6
Hubbard St.,N.	F6
Humbolt Blvd.,N.	A6,B6,C6
Illinois Ave.,S	K8
Indiana Ave.,S.	I8
Iowa Ave.,S.	I7,J7
Iron St.,S.	H7
Irving Ave.,N.	B7
Ivanhoe Pl.	B8
Jackson Park Dr.,W.	G1
Jackson St.,N.	C6
Jasper Ave.,S	J6
Jefferson St.,N.	C6
Jerelyn Pl.	G1
Jones St.,E.	E6
Juneau Ave.,E.	C6
Juneau Ave.,W.	C2,C3
Kaine Pl.,E.	B7
Kane,E.	B6
Kansas Ave.,S.	J7
Kenilworth Pl.,E.	B7,B8
Kentucky Ave.,S.	J4
Kewaunee	B6
Kilbourn Ave.,E	C6
Kilbourn Ave.,W.	C3,C4
Kinnickinnic River Pkwy.,W.	G1,H3
Kinnikinnic Ave.,S.	G7,H7
Knapp St.,E.	C6
Koenig Ave.,E.	I8
La Fayette Pl.,E.	B7
Lake Dr.,N.	B8
Lake Freeway	D6
Lakefield Dr.,W.	H3
Land Pl.,E.	A2
Lapham St.,E.	F1,F3,F5
Laurel Pl.,W.	B3
Layton Ave.,E.	K7
Layton Blvd.	F3
Leeds Pl.,W.	G2
Legion St.,E.	F3
Lenox St.,S.	H6,J6
Leroy Ave.,E.	J7
Leroy Ave.,W.	J1,J3
Lincoln Ave.,E.	G6
Lincoln Ave.,W.	G4
Lincoln Memorial Dr.,N.	C6
Lincoln Memorial Dr.,S.	F7
Linden Pl.,W.	C2
Linebarger Terr.,S.	H7
Linus St.,E.	G6
Lloyd Ave.,N.	B4
Lloyd St.,E.	B6
Logan Ave.,S.	H7,J7
Loomis,S.	K2
Louisinana Ave.,S	J4
Lynndale Ave.,W.	J4

Lyon St.,E.	C6
Mabbett Ave.,S.	H7,H8
Madison St.,N.	F5
Malvern Pl.,E.	I6,I8
Manitoba St.,E.	H6,H7
Manitoba St.,W.	H2,H5
Maple St.,E.	F6
Maple St.,W.	F3,F5
Marietta,N.	A8
Market St.,N.	C6
Marshall St.,N.	C6
Martin Dr.,W.	C1,C2
Martin Ln.,W.	J5
Mason St.,E.	C6
McKinley Ave.,W.	C1
McKinley Blvd.,W.	C3,C4
Meinecke Ave.,E.	B6
Meinecke Ave.,W.	A4
Meinecke St.,E.	A6
Menomonee St.,E.	D6
Meredith St.,E.	H8
Merrill St.,W.	F3
Michigan St.,E.	D6
Michigan St.,S.	D3,D5
Middlemass,W.	G4
Midland Dr.,W.	H2,I1
Milwaukee St.,N.	C6
Miner St.,S.	I3
Mineral St.,E.	E6
Mineral St.,W.	E1,E4
Mitchell St.	F3
Mobile St.	G1
Monarch Pl.,W.	C2
Montana St.,E.	H6
Montana St.,W.	H1,H5
Morgan Ave.,W.	I4,I6
Mound,S.	C6
Mt.Vernon Ave.,W.	D3,D4
Murray N.	A7
Muskego Ave.,S.	E4,F4
National Ave.	E4
National Ave.,E.	E6
Nevada St.,S.	H7,J7
New Hall St.,W.	A7
New York,S.	I8,J8
Newberry Blvd.,E.	A7
Nicholas St.,W.	E5
Nicholson,S.	K8
Nock St.,S.	H7
North Ave.,E.	B6
North Ave.,W.	B4
North-South Frwy.	J5
Norwich Ave.,E.	J1
Norwich Ct.,W.	J1
Norwich Pl.,S.	J6
Norwich St.,W.	J1,J5
Oak Park Ct.,S.	E1
Oakland,N.	A7
Ogden St.,E.	C6
Ohio Ave.,E.	I6
Ohio Ave.,W.	H1,H2,H4
Oklahoma Ave.,E.	H6
Oklahoma Ave.,W.	H4
Ontario St.,E.	G7
Orchard St.,E.	F6
Orchard St.,W.	F3,F5
Oregon St.,E.	E6
Oregon St.,W.	E5
Otjen St.,E.	G6
Pabst Ave.,S.	G3
Palmer St.,N.	A6
Park Hill Ave.,W.	D2
Park Pl.,E.	A7
Pearl St.,S.	F4
Pearson,E.	B6
Pennsylvania Ave.,S	J8
Petibone Pl.,W.	D3
Pier St.	E6
Pierce St.	A6
Pierce St.,N.	A6
Pine St.,S.	H6,J6
Pine Crest,N.	D1
Pittsburgh Ave.,W.	D5,D6
Placid Dr.,S.	J1
Plainfield Ave.,E.	J6
Plainfield Ave.,W.	J1,J3,J4,J5
Plankinton,N.	D6
Pleasant St.,E.	C6
Poe St.,W.	I3
Point Terr.,S.	I3
Polk,E.	E6
Potter Ave.,E.	G6
Price Ave.,E.	K7
Princeton Ave.,S.	I2
Prospect Ave.,N.	B7
Pryor St.	H7
Pryor St.,E.	G7
Pulaski St.,N.	B6
Quincy Ave.,S.	H6,J6
Reservoir Ave.,E.	B6
Reservoir Ave.,N.	B5
Reservoir Ave.,W.	B4
Richards St.,N	A6
Rita Dr.,W.	G1
Robinson,E.	B6
Rogers St.,W.	F1,F3
Rosedale,E.	H6
Royale Pl.,E.	B7
Rusk Ave.,E.	H7
Ruskin St.	I3
Ruskin St.,W.	H3
Russell,E.	H6

Rutland,S.	I8
Sarnow Ave.	A1
Saveland Ave.,E.	I7
Saveland Ave.,W.	I6
Schiller St.,E.	H6
Scott St.,E.	E6
Scott St.,W.	E1,E4
Seeboth St.,W.	D5
Seeley St.,E.	G7
Shea Ave.,S.	E3
Sheppard,N.	A8
Smith St.,E.	G6
Somers Ave.,E.	K8
Spaulding Pl.	B2
Springfield,S.	I8
St. Clair St.,S.	G7
St. Francis Ave.	I7
St. Francis Ave.,W.	I1,I2
St. Paul Ave.,W.	D1,D4
Stadium Frwy.	C1,E2
Stark Dr.,W.	H1
State St.,E.	C6
State St.,W.	C2,C4
Stewart St.,E.	F6
Story Pkwy.	D1
Sumac St.,W.	G2
Summit Ave.,N.	A8,B7
Sunbury Ct.,W.	I3
Sunnyside Dr.,W.	D1
Superior St.,S.	H8
Taylor St.,S.	H6,J6
Tennessee Ave.,S.	J4
Terrace Ave.,N.	B8
Tesch Ave.,E.	J7
Tesch Ave.,W.	J1
Teutonia St.,N.	A4
Texas Ave.,E.	H8
Thomas Ave.,E.	B7
Tripoli Ave.,E.	I7
Tripoli Ave.,W.	I1,I3,I6
Trowbridge St.,E.	H7
Union St.,S.	F4
Valley Forge Dr.,W.	C1
Van Beck Ave.,E.	J6
Van Beck Ave.,w.	J1,J3
Van Buren St.,N.	C6
Van Norman Ave.,E.	J6
Van Norman Ave.,W.	J4,J5
Vermont,S.	H8,I8,J8
Verona Ct.,W	I3
Vieau Pl.,W.	E3
Vilet St.,W.	C2,C4
Vilter Ln.,W.	F4
Vine St.,E.	B6
Vine St.,W.	B1,B4
Virginia St.,W.	H7
Vogel Ave.,E.	K8
Vogel Ave.,W.	K3
Vollmer,E.	I8
Wahl Dr.	B8
Walker St.,E.	E6
Walker St.,W.	E1,E5
Walnut St.,W.	B4
Ward St.	G6
Warnimont Ave.,E.	I6
Warnimont Ave.,W.	I3,I6
Warren N.	B7
Washington Blvd.,W.	B1
Washington St.,E.	E6
Washington St.,W.	E1,E4
Water St.,N.	C6
Water St.,S.	E6
Waterford Ave.,E.	J6
Waterford Ave.,W.	J5
Webster Pl.,E.	J6
Wells St.,E.	A7
Wells St.,E.	A6
Wells St.,W.	C3,C4
Wentworth Ave.,S.	H8
Whitaker Ave.,E.	J6,J8
Whithall Ave.,S	J7
Wilbur St.,S.	I6
Wilbur Ave.,W.	I1,I4,I6
Wilson St.	G6
Winchester,S.	G6
Windlake Ave.,W.	G4
Windsor,E.	B7
Winona Ln.,S.	F4
Wisconsin Ave.,E.	D6
Woodlawn Ct.,W.	D1
Woodstock Pl.,E.	B7
Woodward St.,S.	G6
Wright St.,E.	A6
Wright St.,W.	A4
Wyoming Pl.	B8
1st Pl.,S.	J6
1st St.,N.	A6
1st St.,S.	E6
2nd St.,N.	A5,D5
2nd St.,S.	E5,J6,K5
3rd St.,N.	A5,C4
3rd St.,S.	A5,J5
4th St.,N.	E5
4th St.,S.	A5,G5
5th Pl.,S.	G5,J5
5th St.,N.	A5,C5
5th St.,S.	G5,J5
6th St.,N.	A5,C5
6th St.,S.	D5,G5
7th Pl.,S.	G5,K5
7th St.,N.	A5,C5
8th St.,S.	A5,C5

8th St.,N.	G5
9th Pl.,S.	G5
9th St.,N.	A5,C5
9th St.,S.	G5,K5
10th St.,N.	A5,C5
10th St.,S.	G5,K5
11th Ln.,N.	A5
11th St.,N.	A5,C5
11th St.,S.	D5,G5
12th St.,N.	A4
12th St.,S.	C4
12th St.,S.	G5
13th St.,S.	G4,J4
14th St.,N.	A4,C4
14th St.,S.	G4,J4
15th St.,N.	A4,C4
15th St.,S.	G4
16th St.,N.	A4,C4
16th St.,S.	G4
17th St.,N.	A4,C4
17th St.,S.	G4
18th St.,N.	A4,C4
18th St.,S.	G4,K4
19th St.,N.	A4,C4
19th St.,S.	D4,G4
20th St.,N.	A4,C4
21st St.,N.	A4,C4
21st St.,S.	F4,I4
22nd St.,N.	A4,C4
22nd St.,S.	F4,I4
23rd St.,N.	A4,C3
23rd St.,S.	F3,I3
24th Pl.,N.	C3
24th St.,N.	A3,C3
24th St.,S.	F3,I3
25th St.,N.	A3,C3
25th St.,S.	F3
26th St.,N.	B3
26th St.,S.	F3
27th St.,N.	B3
28th St.,N.	B3
29th St.,N.	B3
29th St.,S.	G3
30th St.,N.	B3
30th St.,S.	G3
31st St.,N.	B3
31st St.,S.	G3
32nd St.,N.	B3
32nd St.,S.	G3
33rd St.,N.	B3
33rd St.,S.	G3
34th St.,N.	B3
34th St.,S.	G3,I3
35th St.,N.	B2
35th St.,S.	G2,K2
36th St.,N.	B2
36th St.,S.	G2,J2
37th St.,N.	B2
37th St.,S.	G2,K2
38th St.,N.	B2
38th St.,S.	F2,G2
39th St.,N.	B2
39th St.,S.	H2
40th St.,N.	B2
40th St.,S.	H2,J2,K2
41st St.,N.	B2
41st St.,S.	H2,J2
42nd St.,N.	A2
42nd St.,S.	H2
43rd St.,N.	A2
43rd St.,S.	G2
44th St.,N.	A2
44th St.,S.	E2,F2,H2
45th St.,N.	A2
45th St.,S.	E2,H2
46th St.,S.	E2,H2
47th St.,N.	E1,H1,K1
47th St.,S.	E1,H1,K1
48th St.,N.	B1
48th St.,S.	E1
49th St.,N.	B1
49th St.,S.	E1,H1
50th St.,N.	B1
50th St.,S.	E1,H1
51st St.,N.	B1
51st St.,S.	F1,H1,K1
52nd St.,N.	B1
52nd St.,S.	F1,H1,K1
53rd St.,N.	B1
53rd St.,S.	F1,H1
54th St.,N.	B1
54th St.,S.	F1,H1
55th St.,N.	B1
55th St.,S.	F1,H1
56th St.,N.	B1
56th St.,S.	F1,H1
57th St.,N.	B1
57th St.,S.	F1,H1
58th St.,N.	B1
58th St.,S.	F1,I1
59th St.,N.	B1
59th St.,S.	F1

Scale of Miles

N

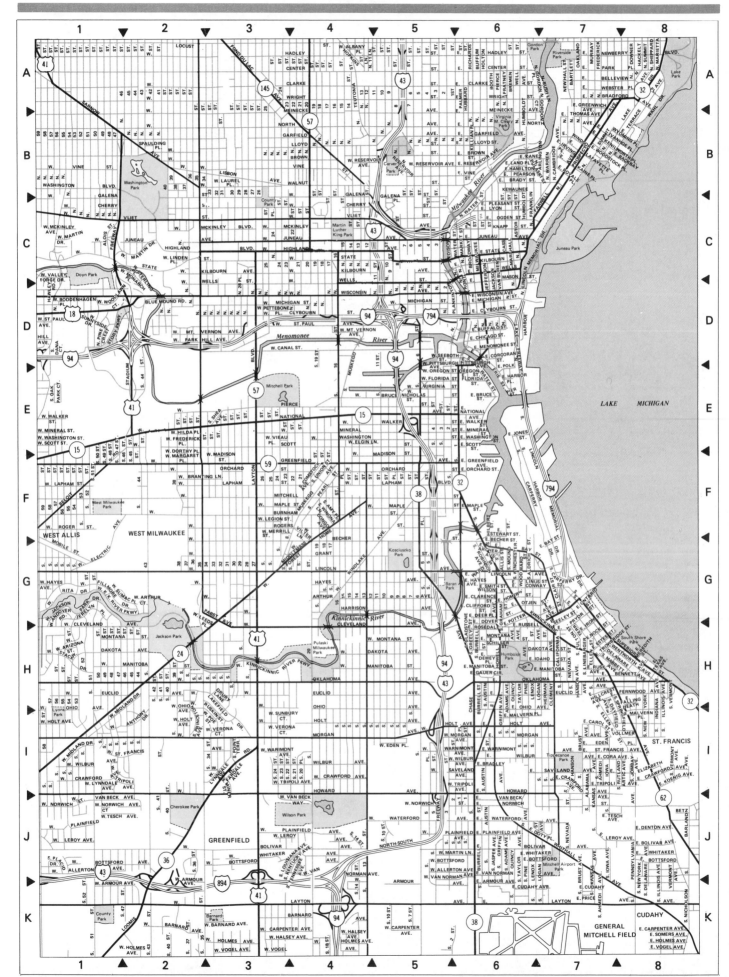

Scale of Miles

N

0   .2   .4   .6   .8

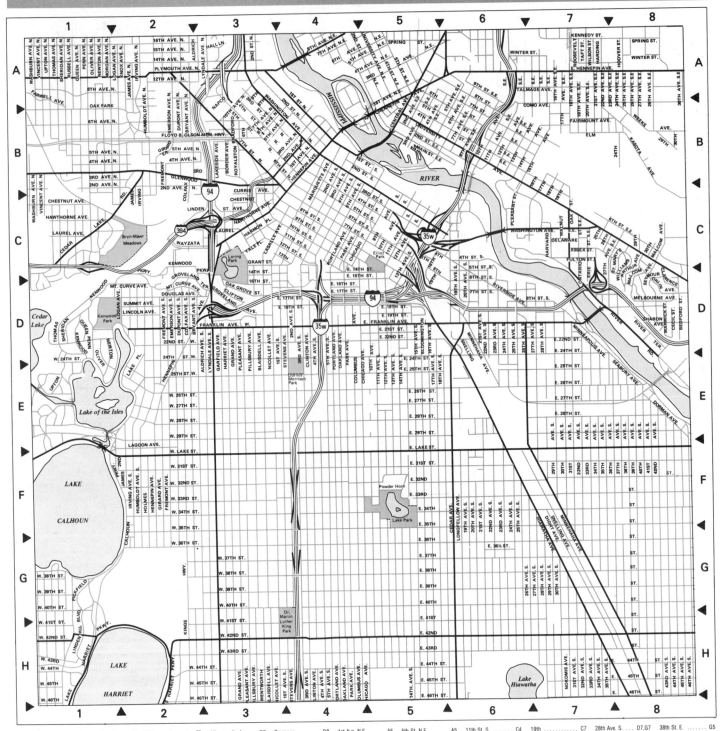

MINNEAPOLIS

Aldrich	B3	Dupont Ave., N.	B2
Aldrich Ave., S.	E3	Dupont Ave., S.	D2
Arthur Ave.	D8	Elm Ave.	B7
Batavia St.	F1,F2	Emerson Ave., N.	B2
Bedford St.	D8	Emerson Ave., S.	D2
Bellwood	H2	Erie St., S.E.	D7
Blaisdell Ave.	E3,H3	Essex St., S.E.	C7
Bloomington	E5	Fairmount Ave.	B7
Border Ave.	B3	Floyd B. Olsen	
Bradford	B3	Memorial Hwy.	B2
Bryant Ave., N.	B2	Franklin Ave.	E,D5
Bryant Ave., S.	D2	Franklin Ave. W.	D3
Calhoun Pkwy.	G2	Fremont Ave.	F2
Cecil St.	D8	Fremont Ave., N.	B2
Cedar Ave.	H4	Fremont Ave., S.	D2,F2
Cedar Lake Rd.	C1	Fulton St.	C7
Central Ave.	C1,C3	Garfield Ave.	F2
Chicago	C4	Girard Ave.	D2
Chicago Ave.	E5,H4	Girard Terr.	B2
Clarence	D8	Glenwood Ave.	C3
Clifton	C2	Grand Ave.	E3,H3
Clinton Ave.	D4,H4	Groveland Ave.	D3
Colfax	C2	Groveland Terr.	H1
Colfax, S.	D2	Harding	A7
Columbus Ave.	E4,H4	Harmon Pl.	C3
Como Ave.	B7	Harriet Ave.	E3
Currie Ave.	B3	Harvard	C7
Delaware	C7	Hawthorne Ave.	C1,C3
Dight Ave.	F7	Hennepin Ave.	
Dorman Ave.	E8		B4,E2,F2
Douglas Ave.	D2	Hennepin Ave., E.	A7,B5
		Hiawatha Ave.	G7

Holmes	F2	Minneapolis Ave.	D7
Hoover St.	A8	Minnehaha	D6,D7
Humboldt Ave., N.	A1	Mt. Curve Ave.	D2
Humboldt Ave., S.	F2	Newton Ave. N.	A1
Irving Ave. N.	A2,C2	Newton Ave.	D1
Irving Ave. S.	F2	Nicollet Ave.	B4,E3,H3
James Ave. N.	A2,C2	Nokomis Ave.	H7
James Ave. S.	F2	Oak Grove St.	D3
Kasota Ave.	B8	Oak Park	A7
Kennedy St.	A7	Oak St.	C7
Kenwood	D1	Oakland Ave.	E4,H4
Kenwood Pkwy.	C2,D1	Oliver Ave. N.	A1
Knox Ave.	A2	Oliver Ave. S.	D1
Lagoon Ave.	E2	Ontario St. S.E.	D7
Lake Pl.	E2	Orlin Ave.	D7
Lake St. E.	F5	Park Ave.	C4,E4,H4
Lake St. W.	F2	Pshury Ave.	D3,H3
Lakeside Ave.	B3	Pleasant Ave.	E3,H3
Lasalle Ave.	C3	Pleasant Ave., S.	E3
Laurel Ave.	C1,C3	Pleasant St.	C6
Lincoln Ave.	D2	Plymouth Ave. N.	A2
Linden Ave.	C3	Portland Ave.	C4,E4,H4
Linden Hill Blvd.	H1	Queen Ave. N.	A1
Logan Ave. N.	A1	Queen Ave. S.	D1
Logan Ave. S.	D2	River Rd.	D8
Longfellow Ave.	G8	River Terr.	D8
Lyndale Ave. N.	A3	Riverside Ave.	D6
Lyndale Ave. S.	E3	Roosevelt	A7
Main St. E.	B5	Royalston	A7
Malcom	C8,D8	Russell Ave. N.	A1
Marquette Ave.	C4	Seabury Ave.	E8
Melbourne Ave.	D8	1st Ave. N.	B4

Seymour	D8	1st Ave. N.E.	A5
Sharon Ave.	D8	1st Ave. S.	E3,H3
Sheridan Ave. N.	A1	1st St. N.	A4
Sheridan Ave. S.	D1	1st St. S.	B5
Snelling	D6	6th	B3,C5
Snelling Ave.	F7	6th Ave. N.	B1,B3
Spring St.	A5,A8	6th Ave. N.E.	A4
St. Mary's	C8	6th Ave. S.	B6
Stevens	D4,D4,H4	6th St. N.	B3,B4
Summit Ave.	D2	6th St. S.	C4,D6
Taft St.	A7	7th Ave.	E5
Talmadge Ave.	A7	7th Ave. N.	A4
Thomas Ave. N.	A1	7th Ave. S.	B3
Thomas Ave. S.	D1	7th St. N.	A4
University Ave.	B5	7th St. S.	C4,D7
University Ave. N.E.	A5	7th St. E.	B6
Upton Ave. N.	A1	8th Ave.	A1
Upton Ave. S.	E1	8th Ave. N.E.	A4
Vincent Ave. N.	A1,C1	8th Ave. S.	B6
Walnut	C7	9th Ave. N.	C5
Warwick St.	D8	9th Ave. S.	A7
Washburn Ave. N.	A1	9th St. S.	C5
Washington Ave. N.	A3	10th Ave. N.	B5
Washington, S.E.		10th Ave. S.	B6
	C6	10th St. S.	C5
Wayzata	C2	11th Ave.	C3
Weeks	B8	11th Ave. S.E.	B6
Wentworth	H3	11th St. S.	C4
Williams	D8	12th Ave.	E5
Wilson St.	A7	12th Ave. N.	A2
Winter St.	A6,A8	12th Ave. S.	C4
Yale Pl.	C3	12th Ave. S.E.	B6
1st Ave.	F2	13th	E5

5th N.E.	A5	11th St. S.	C4
5th St. S.	C4,C6	12th Ave.	E5
12th Ave. N.	A2	19th	C7
12th Ave. S.	C4	19th Ave.	D6,F6
12th Ave. S.E.	B6	19th Ave. S.E.	B8
13th	E5	19th E.	D5
13th Ave.	E5	20th Ave.	D6,F6
13th Ave. S.E.	B6	20th Ave. N.	A3
14th Ave.	E5,H5	20th Ave. S.E.	B8
14th Ave. N.	B7	21st Ave.	D6,F6
14th St. E.	D5	21st Ave. S.E.	B7
15th	D5	21st St. E.	D5
15th Ave.	D5	22nd Ave.	D6,F6
15th Ave. S.E.	B6	22nd Ave. N.	A3
16th	D5	22nd Ave. S.E.	B8
16th Ave. N.	A2	22nd St. E.	D5,D7
16th Ave. S.	D4	23rd Ave.	D6,F6
17th	C7	23rd Ave. N.	A3
17th Ave. N.	A3	24th	B8
17th Ave. S.	D4	24th Ave. S.	D7,E5
17th St. W.	D4	24th Ave. N.	A3
18th	C7	24th Ave. S.E.	B8
18th Ave. S.	D4,D5	24th St. W.	D1,D2
18th St. E.	D5	25th	B8
27th St. E.	E2	25th Ave. N.	A3
		25th Ave. S.	E5,E7
		25th St. W.	D2
		26th	C7
		26th Ave.	D6,G6
		26th Ave. N.	A3
		26th Ave. S.E.	B8
		26th St. E.	D7,G7

28th Ave. S.	D7,G7	38th St. E.	G5
28th Ave.	E5,E7	38th St. W.	G1,G5
28th St. W.	D2	39th Ave. S.	F8
29th	B8,C8	39th St. E.	G5
29th Ave. S.	F7,G7	39th St. W.	G1,G3
29th Ave. S.E.	B8	40th Ave. S.	F8
29th St. E.	E5	40th St. E.	G5
29th St. W.	E5	40th St. W.	G1,G3
30th	B8,C8	41st Ave. S.	F8
30th Ave. S.	F7,G7	41st E.	G5
30th Ave. S.E.	B8	41st St. W.	H1,H3
31st Ave. S.	F7,H7	42nd Ave. S.	F8
31st St. E.	F5	42nd E.	H5
31st St. W.	F2	42nd St. W.	H1,H3
32nd Ave. S.	F7,H7	43rd Ave. S.	H8
32nd St. E.	F5	43rd St. E.	H8
32nd St. W.	F2	43rd W.	H1
33rd Ave. S.	F7,G7	44th Ave. S.	H8
33rd St. E.	F5	44th St. E.	H5,H8
33rd W.	F2	44th W.	H1
34th Ave. S.	F7,H7	45th Ave. S.	H8
34th St. W.	F2	45th St. E.	H5,H8
35th Ave. S.	E5,E7	45th W.	H1
35th St. E.	G5	46th Ave. S.	H8
35th St. W.	F2	46th St. E.	H5,H8
36 1/2 St. W.	G6	46th W.	H1
36th Ave. S.	F8		
36th St. E.	G5		
37th Ave. S.	F8		
37th St. E.	G5		
37th St. W.	F2		
38th St. S.	F8		

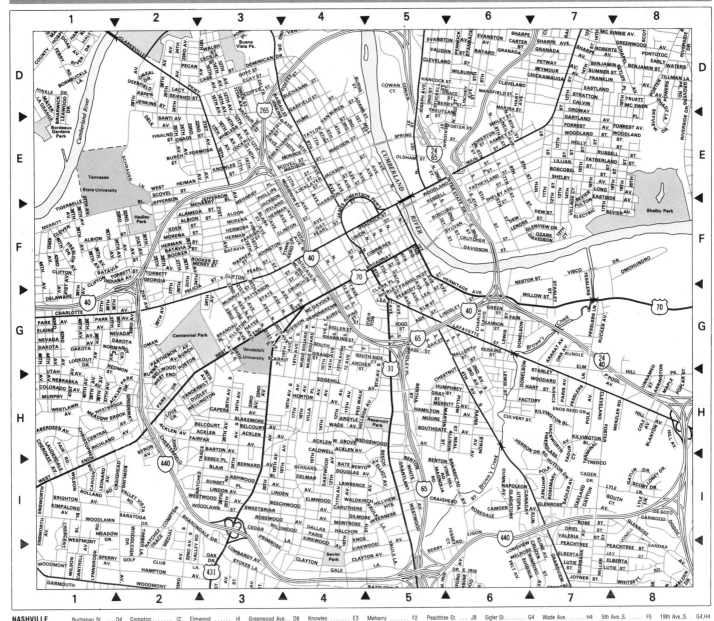

NASHVILLE

Aberdeen Ave. ... H1	Buchanan St. ... D4	Compton ... I2	Elmwood ... I4	Greenwood Ave. . D8	Knowles ... E3	Meharry ... F2	Peachtree St. ... J8	Sigler St. ... G4	Wade Ave. ... H4	5th Ave..S. ... F5	19th Ave..S. . G4,G1
Acklen Ave. .. H2,H4	Burbank Ave. ... J7	County Hospital Rd.	Ensworth Ave. .. I1	Grove,W. ... H4	Knox ... G4	Meharry Pl. ... F2	Pearl St. ... F3,F4	Skyview St. ... D8	Waldkirch ... I4	5th ... D6	19th St. ... E8
Acklen Park Dr. .. H1	Burch ... G2	D1	Essex Pl. ... H3	Grovers Pk.Rd. ... D8	Lacy ... D2	Melrose ... J6	Pecan ... D2	Smiley St. ... E6	Walsh St. ... D3	5th St. ... E6	20th Ave. ... I3
Adams St. ... D4	Burns St. ... E2	Cowan St. ... D5	Eugenia Ave. ... J6	Hackworth ... H7	Lafayette St. ... G6	Menzler Rd. ... H8	Pennock ... D6	South St. ... I7	Warner St. ... F3	6th Ave. ... F4	20th Ave..N. ... F3
Alameda St. ... F2	Burns St. ... D4	Craighead ... I1	Evanston Ave. . D5,D6	Halcyon ... I4	Lauderdale ... H1	Meridian St. ... E5	Perkins St. ... G6	South Side Ct. ... G4	Waters ... D8	6th Ave..S. ... F5	20th Ave..S. ... G3
Albion St. .. F1,F2	Byron Ave. .. H2,H6	Craighead St. ... I5	Eastwood ... D6	Halcyon ... I4	Laurel St. ... G4	Merritt Ave. ... H5	Petway Ave. ... D7	South St. ... G4	Wedgewood ... H4	6th Ave..N. ... E6	20th St. ... E8
Aldon ... F3	Caden Dr. ... I1	Crescent ... I3	Fadur Ct. ... H7	Hampton Ave. ... J2	Lawrence ... I4	Merry St. ... E3	Phillips St. ... E3	Southgate Ave. ... H5	Wellington ... H2	6th St.N. ... E6	21st Ave. . E3,F3
Allison ... H5	Caldwell ... H6	Crutcher St. ... F6	Fair Rd. ... H1	Harrison St. ... E4	Lea St. ... G5	Mill St. ... E4	Pillow St. ... H6	Sperry ... J1	West End Ave. ... G3	7th Ave. ... E4	21st Ave..N. ... F3
Ararat Ave. ... G6	Calvin ... D7	Cruzen St. ... J7	Fair Rd. ... H1	Hart Ave. ... D6	Leawood Dr. ... D1	Miller St. ... J7	Pine St. ... G4	Spring St. ... E5	West End Dr. ... I1	7th Ave..S. ... E4	21st Ave..S. ... G3
Archer St. ... I6	Camden ... I6	Culvert St. ... H6	Fairfax Ave. ... H2	Hart St. ... H6	Lenore St. ... D4	Montrose ... J6	Polk Ave. ... H7	Stanback Ave. ... D6	West Heiman St. .. E2	7th Ave..S. ... E4	22nd Ave. .. E2,F3
Argyle ... H4	Canaday ... I1	Dakota Ave. ... G1	Fatherland St. E6,E7	Hawkins St. ... G4	Leonard St. ... I1	Moore ... H5	Poplar St. ... F7	Stanley St. ... F7	Westend ... H2	7th St.S. ... E6	22nd Ave..N. ... F3
Arrington ... I7	Cannon St. ... G6	Dakota Pl. ... G1	Felicia St. ... G2	Haynes St. ... G3	Lewis St. ... G6	Morena ... F3	Poston ... G2	State St. ... G3	Westlawn . H1,I2	8th Ave. .. E4,E6	22nd Ave..S. ... G2
Arthur Ave. ... D3	Cantrell Ave. ... J1	Dallas ... J6	Felt Ave. ... J6	Herman ... F3	Ligon ... I6	Morena St. ... F3	Powell Ave. ... G2	Stockell St. ... D5	Westmont ... I1	8th Ave..S. ... E6	23rd Ave. ... G3
Ash St. ... G5	Carden Ave. ... I7	Darmouth ... J1	Fessey Ct. ... I6	Herman St. .. F2,F3)	Lillian St. ... I2	Morrison St. ... G4	Powers ... D8	Stratton ... D7	Westwood ... I2	9th Ave. ... I4	23rd Ave..N. ... G3
Ashwood Ave. .. I3	Caruthers ... I5	Davidson ... G4	Fesslers ... F7	Hermitage Ave. . F6	Linden Ave. ... I3	Murphy Rd. F1	Preslor Dr. ... F1	Strokes Ln. ... J3	Westwood Ave. . I2	9th St. ... I4	23rd Ave..S. ... F3
Aspen ... I2	Cass ... D3	Davidson St. ... F6	Finland St. ... E2	Hermosa ... F3	Lindon Ave. .. I3	Murphy St. ... G3	Primrose ... I3	Sunset Pl. ... I3	Whitney ... I7	10th Ave. ... I4	24th Ave. . D2,E2,G3
Barton Ave. ... H3	Cecilia St. ... D3	Dayton ... J7	Fisk St. ... F3	Herron Dr. ... H6	Lindsley St. ... G5	Music Square,E. . G4	Rains Ave. ... H6	Sunset Pl. ... I3	Wilburn ... D6	10th St. ... I7	24th Ave..N. .. E2
Bass St. ... F5	Cedar Ln. ... I3	Deadrick St. .. F4	Forest Ave. . E7,E8	Hill Ave. ... H8	Lischey Ave. ... D6	Music Square,W. . F2	Ramsey St. ... I3	Sweetbriar Ave. . I3	Wilbur ... D6	11th Ave. . D3,H4,I4	24th Ave..S. . G3,H3
Batavia ... F3	Centennial Blvd. .. F1	Deerfield ... G1	Formosa ... E2	Hillside Ave. ... H4	Lockaver St. ... D5	Napoleon ... I6	Red Walk ... H4	Sylvan St. ... F6	Willow St. ... G6	11th Ave..S. ... E7	25th ... F2
Batavia St. .. F1,F2	Central Ave. .. H1	Delta ... D3	Foss St. ... G5	Hillview Heights . H5	Lombardy Ave. .. I3	Nassau St. ... D3	Redmon St. ... G1	Tanksley ... J7	Wilson Bl. ... I1,J1	11th St. ... E7	26th Ave. . D2,H3,I3
Bate ... I4	Chapel Ave. ... G1	Delk Ave. ... G5	Foster St. ... E6	Holly St. ... E7	Loney Ct. ... I8	Neal ... H6	Richland Ave. .. H1	Taylor St. ... E4	Winford Ave. ... J6	12th Ave. . D3,E3,H4	27th ... F2,G2
Bayard ... D6	Charlotte Ave. .. G1	Demonbrenn St. . G4	Foster St. ... E6	Home St. ... H4	Long Ave. ... G7	Neil Ave. ... H5	Ridley St. ... G5	Terminal Blvd. .. H7	Wingate Ave. ... J8	12th Ave..S. ... E7	28th Ave. D2,G2,G3
Beechwood Ave. . H3	Cheatham Pl. ... E3	Dew ... F6	Franklin Dr. .. D7	Horton Ave. ... H4	Longview ... J6	Nelson ... I3	River Dr. ... D1	Tigerbelle ... F1	Woodland ... I7	12th St. ... E7	28th ... F2
Belcourt Ave. ... H3	Cherokee Ave. .. H1	Dew St. ... F6	Franklin St. ... F5	Howerton St. .. G6	Lookout Dr. ... G1	Nevada ... G1	Riverside Dr. . D8,E8	Tillmania ... D8	Woodward ... H7	13th Ave. .. E7	29th ... F1
Bellwood ... H2	Chesterfield ... H2	Doak Ave. ... E6	Fulton ... F7	Humphrey ... H5	Louise Ave. ... G1	Nevada ... G1	Roberts ... E3	Timber Ln. ... I2	Woodleigh Dr. .. I2	13th Ave..S. ... G4	30th ... F1
Benjamin ... D7	Chestnut St. ... G6	Dobbs Ave. ... E6	Gale St. ... J4	Hutton Ct. ... I7	Louise Dr. ... G1	Nevada Ave. ... G1	Rolland Rd. ... I1	Torbett ... F2	Woodmont Blvd.	13th Ct. ... G4	31st Ave. ... F2,G2
Benton ... I5	Chickamauga ... D7	Dodge ... I8	Garfield St. .. D4,E3		Love Circle ... H2	Normandy Circle . H4	Roscobel St. ... F5	Town Send Dr. .. H2	J1,J2,J4	13th St. ... G4	32nd Ave. ... F2
Benton Ave. ... I4	Christopher ... H1	Dominican Dr. .. D3	Gatlin Dr. ... I8	Indiana Ave. .. F7	Lutie St. ... I7,I8	Oakland ... E5	Rose St. ... I7	Trace ... H2		14th Ave. .. E7	33rd Ave. ... G3
Bernard Ave. .. I3	Church St. ... F4	Donelson ... G6	Gay ... F4	Interstate Dr. .. E6	Lyle Ln. ... I5	Oldham St. .. E5	Rosedale Ave. .. I6	Tredco ... I7	Woodward ... H7	14th Ave..S. ... G4	34th Ave. ... F1
Berry St. ... D5	Clay St. ... G5	Douglas Ave. C5,C7,I4	Georgia ... F2	Inverness ... I5	Lynnbrook Rd. .. J1	Oldham St. ... E5	Rosemary ... I7	Treutland St. ... D5		14th St. . D3,E3,H4	35th Ave. ... F1
Bertha St. ... F4	Clayton Ave. ... J4	Dudley ... G4	Gilmore ... H4	Iris Dr.,W. ... J5	Madison St. ... E4	Oman ... G2	Rosewood Ave. . I3	Truett ... D8	1st Ave.N. ... D7,E7	14th St. .. D3,E3,H4	36th ... F1
Blair ... I3	Clayton Ave. ... J4	Dudley ... G4	Gladstone ... I6	Iris Rd.,E. ... J6	Magnolia Rd. .. I5	Omohundro ... E1	Rucker Ave. ... G6	Tuggle Ave. ... I8	1st Ave.S. ... F5	15th Ave..S. ... G4	37th Ave. E1,G1,H1
Blakemore ... H3	Cleveland ... D6	Early ... D8	Glenrose Ave. . I7,I8		Main St. ... E6	Oneal Dr. ... D2	Russell St. .. E5,E7	Union St. ... E4	1st St..N. ... E4	15th St. ... G4	38th Ave. E1,G1,H1
Blank St. ... F3	Cleveland St. ... D5	Eastdale Ave. .. E7	Glenview Dr. .. I7	Jane St. ... E3	Malden Dr. ... D6	Oriel St. ... I7	Sadler Ave. .. H7	Utah Ave. ... G1	1st St..N. ... E4	15th St. ... G4	39th ... F1
Blanton ... H3	Clifton ... F1,F3	Eastland Ave. .. D7	Goff St. ... D3	Jefferson St. .. E2	Mallory St. ... G5	Orr Ave. ... G6	Santi Ave. ... D2	Utopia ... I6	1st St..N. ... E4	16th Ave. .. F5,G6	42nd Ave. ... F1
Booker ... F2	Clinton St. ... D3	Eastside Ave. .. D7	Golf Club Ln. .. J2	Jefferson Blvd. .. E2	Mansfield St. ... D6	Osage ... D4	Saratoga ... I2	Valeria St. ... I7	2nd Ave. ... F5,G6	16th St. ... G4	43rd Ave. ... F1
Booker St. .. F1,F3	Clover ... F1	Eastwood ... D7	Grace ... D3	Jenkins St. ... D2	Maple ... D8	Overton ... G5	Scarrt St. ... G4	Valley Vista Rd. .. I1	2nd Ave..S. ... F5,G6	17th Ave. .. E4	44th ... F1
Bornbuckle Ln. . D1	Cockrill St. ... G6	Eden St. ... E2	Granada ... D5	Johnston Ave. .. J3	Marina St. ... D6	Owen St. ... E5	Scovel St. . E2,E4	Van Buren St. ... D4	2nd Ave..S. ... F5,G6	17th Ave..S. ... G3	44th ... F1
Boscobel St. ... E6	Coffee St. . D3,D4	Eletric Ave. .. E7	Granada Ave. .. D7	Joseph Ave. .. D3	Marion St. ... J4	Ozark ... F3	Sevier ... E7,F7	Vanderbilt ... G2	3rd Ave. ... F1	17th St. ... E8	45th Ave. ... G1
Bowling Ave. .. I2	Cole Ave. ... H8	Elberta ... J7	Grand St. ... G4	Joyner St. ... J7	Martin St. ... H5	Paris Ave. ... H7	Seymour Ave. .. D7	Vaughn St. ... D5	3rd Ave..N. ... D4	18th Ave. D3,E3,H4	
Brandau Pl. .. G3	Collier ... J8	Elliot Ave. .. I5	Grandview Ave. . J7		Mayer ... D1	Paris Ave. ... H7	Shady Ln. ... D8	Vaughn St. ... D5	3rd Ave..S. .. F5,G6	18th Ave..N. .. F3	
Bransford Ave. .. I6	Colorado Ave. .. H1	Elliston St. .. G3	Gray St. ... H5	Kilvington Blvd. . H7	McGavock St. ... G4	Park Ave. ... G1	Sharondale Dr. .. I1	Village Ct. .. E7	4th Ave. ... G4,H4	18th St. . D3,E3,H4	
Briarwick ... H2	Commerce St. .. F5	Elm Hill ... G6	Green St. ... G6	Kimpalong Ave. .. I1	McMinn ... F6	Parthenon Ave. .. F3	Sharpe Ave. . D6,D7	Villa Pl. ... H4	4th Ave..N. ... E6	19th Ave. .. G4,G1	
Brighton Ave. .. I1		Elm St. ... G5	Greenway ... H2	Kirkwood Ave. I4,J4	Meadow Dr. .. I1	Patterson St. .. G3,I6	Shelby Ave. .. E6,E7	Vine Hill Rd. .. I5	4th St..S. ... E6	19th St. ... H3	
Broadway ... F5				Kline Ave. ... I7	Medial ... I2	Peachtree ... I7	Shifried St. .. D2	Visco Dr. .. I5	5th Ave. ... E4	19th Ave..N. .. F3	

NEWARK

Abington Ave.,E. B6
Abington Ave.,W. A4
Academy St. F5
Adams St. H7
Afton C8
Alexander St. E1
Algea H8
Alpine St. J1,K1
Alpine St.,E. I4
Alpine St.,W. I4
Amherst St. C1
Ampere Pkwy. B4
Ann St. H8
Argyle G1
Arlington G6
Arlington Ave.,S. D2
Arlington,N. B3
Ashland B2
Astor St. I5
Austin St. I5
Avenue A I5
Avenue B I6
Avenue C I6
Avon Ave. H2
Badger Ave. I3
Baldwin Ave. H3
Ballantine B6
Bank St. F6
Barclay St. H5
Bayview Ave. J1
Beacon St. G5
Beardsley Ave. A4
Bedford C1,G4
Beech St. C2
Belgrove Dr. D8
Belmont A5
Bergen Ave. C8
Bergen St. F8,G4,K2
Berkeley G1
Berkeley Ave. A5
Berwyn B1
Beverley St. H1
Bigelow St.,E. I4
Bigelow St.,W. I3
Bleeker St. F6
Bloomfield Ave. C6
Bock Ave. I2
Boston St. F5
Boyd St. H4
Boyden St. E6
Boylan E6
Bragaw Ave. I1
Branford I4
Branford Pl. G6
Breckenridge F1
Brenner St. G3
Bridge St. E7
Brighton C8,G1
Briley Ave. K1
Broad St. D7,G6
Broadway C7
Brockside G1
Brookwood St. E1
Broone St. G5
Bruce St. F4
Bruen St. G7
Brunswick St. H5
Burnet St.,S. C1
Burnet,N. B2
Cabinet St. E4
Calumet I7
Camden G4
Camp St. H6
Carlton St. B2
Carnegie Ave. C1
Center St. A1,F7
Central Ave. C1,E4,E8
Chadwick Ave. J3
Chancellor Ave. J1
Charlton St. H4
Chelsea Pl. A1
Chester Ave. B7
Chestnut C2
Chestnut St. H6
Clark Ave. D8,K1
Clark St. D7
Clay St. E7
Clifford St. I7
Clifton Ave. D6
Clifton St. I4
Clinton Ave. H2,H4
Clinton Pl. J1
Clinton St. F6
Clinton St.,N. B2
Clinton St.,S. C1
Clover St. G8
Columbia St. G7
Commerce St. F7
Concord St. J4
Congress St. H7
Conklin Ave. K1
Court G5
Crane St. D6
Crawford C1
Crawford St. H5
Crescent Ave. J1
Cross St. E8
Custer Ave. J2
Cutler St. D6
Cypress St. H1
Davenport Ave. A5
Davis D8
Dawson St. I6
DeLancy St. I7
Delavan Ave. A7
Delmar G1
Devon D8
Dewey St. J1
Dickerson St. E4
Division St. E7
Dorer Ave. K1
Downing St. G8
Duryea E5
Eagles E6
Earl St. I5
Eastwood A2
Edger St. D1
Edgerton Terr. A3
Edison A3,A5
Edison Pl. G6
Elizabeth Ave. I4,K2
Ellington St. B4
Elliot A8
Ellis Ave. G1,H1
Elm St. A1,G6
Elmwood Ave. D1
Elwood Ave.,E. A7
Emmet St. I5
Empire J4
Essex St. F8
Evergreen C1
Fabyan Pl. I1
Fairmount G4
Fairmount Terr. E1
Fairview Ave. G4
Farley Ave. H3
Ferguson St. H8
Ferry St. G7
Franklyn G6
Freeman Ave. E1
Frelinghuysen Ave. K4
Fuller Pl. G1
Fulton F7
Garden H7
Garden State Pkwy. C3,D2,E2
Garrison St. I8
Garside St. D6
Gillett H5
Glenwood Ave. B1
Goble St. I6
Goldsmith Ave. J1
Goodwin Ave. J2
Gotthart St. I8
Gould Ave. D4
Gouverneur D7
Grafton Ave. A7
Grand Ave. E1
Grant E7
Grant Ave. D8
Gray St. D4
Green St. G6
Greenwood Ave. C3
Grove St. F2,H1
Grove St.,N. A4,C3
Grove St.,S. D3
Grove Terr. F1
Grumman Ave. K1
Halleck St. A8
Halsey St. G6
Halstead St. C1
Hamilton Ave. A2
Hamilton St. G7
Hampton Terr. B1
Harding Terr. J2
Harper St. I6
Harrison Ave. E8
Harrison Pl. H1
Harrison St.,S. C1
Hartford St. E5
Harvey St. C7
Hawthorne D2
Hawthorne Ave. I1,J4
Hayes St. F4
Heckel St. D1
Hecker St. E5
Hedden Terr. I3
Heller Pkwy. A7
Hensler H8
Herbert Pl. B7
Hickory St. B1
High St. D6,F6,H5
Highland G1
Highland Ave. C6,D8
Hill St. G6
Hillside Ave. I4
Hinsdale Pl. B7
Hobson St. J1
Hoffman Blvd. A4
Holland St. G3
Hollywood D3
Hopkins Pl. H1
Hose D8
Houston St. I8
Howard St. G5
Hoyt St. D8
Hudson St. K5
Humboldt D4
Hunter St. I4
Hunterdon St. J3
Huntington Terr. J2
Irving J2
Irving Turner Blvd. H4
Isabella Ave. F1
Jabez St. I8
Jacob St. G3
James St. E6
Jay St. E5
Jefferson St. H7
Jelliff Ave. I3
Jersey St. E8
John St. E8
Johnston Ave. D8,I4
Jones St. F5
Kearney Ave. D8
Kearney St. C6
Keer Ave. J1
Kellor St. F7
Kent St. G3
Kinney St.,E. H6
Kinney St.,W. G4
La France A4
Lafayette St. G6,H7
Lake St. C6
Lang St. H8
Lehigh Ave. J2
Lenox Ave. C2
Leslie St. B4,J1
Liberty St. G7
Lincoln Ave. B7
Lincoln St. B2,G5
Linden Ave. D1,G1
Littleton Ave. G3
Livingston St. H4
Lock St. F5
Lombardy F7
Longworth H5
Lyons Ave. J1
Madison G8
Madison Ave. G1
Magnolia St. G3
Main St. B1,C3
Malvern St. H7
Mapes Ave. J2
Maple Ave. H1,K1
Maple Ave.,N. A4,C3
Maple Ave.,S. D3
Market St. F6
Market St.,W. E4,F5
Marshall D8
May St. B7
McCarter Hwy. D7,H6
McNary D8
McWhorter St. H7
Meeker Ave. J3
Melmore Gardens B2
Melrose F1
Mercer St. G5
Merchant St. H8
Middlesex St. F8
Milford Ave. I4
Miller St. B1,I5
Millington Ave. I2
Milton St. E8
Mohammad Ali Ave. H5
Monroe H8
Montgomery G5
Montgomery Ave. H1
Montrose F2
Morris A3,E5,F4
Morton G5
Moutainview Ave. E1
Mt.Prospect Ave. D6
Mulberry St. H6
Munn Ave.,N. C3
Munn Ave.,S. E2
Murray St. H5
Myrtle D4
Myrtle Ave. F1
Nairin Pl. I2
Napoleon St. I8
Nesbitt Ave. E6
Nevada St. G6
New St. A1,E5,F6
New York Ave. H7
Newark St. F5
Newfield St. B4
Nobel K4
Norfolk St. F5
Norwood St. D1
Nursery C7
Nye Ave. H1
Oak Ave. F2
Oak St. D1
Oakwood Ave. B1
Oakwood Pl. B1
Oliver St. H7
Orange Ave.,S. E1,F4
Orange St. D4,E6,E7
Oraton St. B7
Oriental St. C7
Osbourne Terr. J2
Park Ave. A5
Park Pl. A1,F7
Park St. A1
Parker St. C6
Parkhurst St. H6
Parkview Terr. K1
Patterson H8
Peabody B8
Peddle St.,E. J4
Peddle St.,W. I3
Pennington St. H6
Peshine Ave. J3
Poinier St. I5
Polk St. H8
Pomona Ave. J1
Prince St. H4
Prospect St. B2,H7
Pulaski St. I8
Quitman St. H5
Randolph H2
Rankin G5
Raymond Blvd. F6,G8
Raymond Plaza,E. G7
Raymond Plaza,W. G7
Renner Ave. J2
Rhode Island Ave. D1
Richmond F5
Ridge St. D6
Ridgewood Ave. I4
Roosevelt Ave. A4
Rose St. G3,H4
Rose Terr. H3
Roseville Ave. D4
Runyon St.,E. I4
Runyon St.,W. I3
Rutledge Ave. A3
Sanford St. C1
Saybrook F7
Scheerer Ave. J2
Schley St. J1
Seymour Ave. J2
Shanley Ave. H3
Shepard D1
Shepard Ave. J2
Sherman Ave. D8,I5
Shipman G5
Snyder A1
Somerset St. F8,H5
South St. H6
Springdale Ave. A2
Springfield Ave. G2
Spruce St. G4
St. Agnes Lane D2
Standard G2
Stanton St. I5
State St. A1,E6
Stengel J2
Sterling St. F5
Stockton C3
Stockton Pl. F1
Stone St. D6
Stratford Pl. F1
Stueben D3
Summit B2
Summit St. F6
Sunnyside E1
Sunset Ave. E1
Sussex E8
Sussex Ave. D4
Taylor C6
Telford St. D1
Thomas St. H6
Tichenor F1
Tichenor St. H6
Tillinghast St. I2
Treacy Ave. H3
Tremont D1,G1
Union St. G7
University F1
University Ave. G6
Van Buren St. H8
Vanderpool St. I5
Vanness I2
Vassar Ave. J1
Vermont Ave. F1
Vernon H2
Vernon Terr. C3
Victoria J4
Wainwright St. J1
Wall H8
Wallace A1
Walnut St. G6
Walnut St.,N. A3,B2
Ward St. A1
Warren St. E8,F5
Warrington Pl. B3
Warwick St. B4
Washington St. A1,F6,G6
Washington Terr. B2
Watson J3
Watson Ave. D2
Waverly Ave. G3
Webster Pl. B1
Webster St. D6
White Terr. I2
Wickliffe St. F5
William St. B1,E8,G5
Williamson Ave. K1
Willow St. J1
Wilsey St. F5
Wilson H8
Wilson Ave. C8
Winans Ave. G3,K1
Winans St. C2
Woodland G2
Woodland Ave. A2,D8
Woodside B7,C7
Wright St. I5
Yates Ave. I3
1st Ave.,W. B5
1st St. D5,F8
2nd Ave.,E. C6
2nd Ave.,W. B5
2nd St. D5,F8
2nd St.,N. E8
3rd Ave.,E. C6
3rd Ave.,W. B4
3rd St. B6,D5,F8
4th Ave. B3
4th Ave.,E. D6
4th St. C5,D5,F8
5th St. F8
5th St.,N. C5
6th Ave.,E. D6
6th Ave.,W. C3
6th St.,N. B5
7th Ave.,E. D6
7th Ave.,W. D4
7th St.,N. B5
8th H1
8th Ave. E6,E7
9th A5
9th Ave. D3
10th St.,N. B5
10th St.,S. H3
11th Ave. E4
12th Ave. E3
12th St.,N. B4
13th Ave. E2,E3,E5
14th Ave. F3
14th St.,S. D4,H2
15th Ave. F3
15th St.,N. A5,C4
15th St.,S. H2
16th Ave. F3
16th St.,N. A5,C4
16th St.,S. H2
17th Ave. F2,G4
17th St. H2
17th St.,N. A4,C4
18th Ave. G3
18th St. F1
18th St.,N. C4
19th Ave. G2
19th St.,N. C3
20th St. B4
21st St. B4,H1
22nd St. B4,G1

NEW ORLEANS

Abundance A2
Adele J8
Agriculture A2
Alix E8
Allen C3
Almonaster Ave. A5
Alvar C7
Annette C4
Annunciation K7
Anthony C4
Arts A4
Aubry C3
Banks G3
Baronne K5
Barracks D2,D4
Bartholomew A7
Basin F4
Bayou Rd. D2
Belfort Ave. C1
Bell E1
Bellechase E1
Bermuda E7
Bertrand G3
Bienville F3,F5
Bolivar G3
Bouny E7
Bourbon E5
Bradish G2
Brainard J6
Broad Ave.,N. E2
Broad Ave.,S. G2
Brooklyn F8
Bruxelles B1
Burgandy B7,D5,F5
Cadiz K2
Calhoun K1
Calliope H7
Callipest H5
Camp K6,G6
Canal Blvd. F4
Carondelet H5,H6,K5
Castiglione C1
Celeste J8
Chartres C7,D6,F5
Chestnut K6
Chippewa K7
Claiborne Ave.,S. H4,J3
Claiborne,N. A6
Clairborne Ave. C4
Clara I4
Clay F6
Cleveland G3
Clio I4
Clio Pl. I2
Clouet A6
Coliseum K6
Colombus D3
Commerce G6
Common G5
Conery K6
Congress A7
Conti F3,F5
Crete C1
Crossman F6
Croza F4
Dabadie C2
Danneel J5
Dauphine C7,D5,E5
De Armas F8
De Lachaise J2
De Laronde D7,E7
De Soto D1
Decatur D5,D6
Delta G6
Derbigny,N. A6,C4,F3
Derbigny,S. G3,I3,K2
Diamond,N. H6
Diamond,S. H6
Diana F8
Division K8
Dixon H1
Dorgenois,N. B3,F2
Dorgenois,S. J2
Dryades I5
Dugue B1
Dumaine E3,E4
Dupre,N. C1,E1
Dupre,S. G1
Earhart Blvd. I3
Eden J1
Elba J1
Elk Pl. G4
Elysian Fields Ave. C5
Elza E8
Erato H7,I4
Esplanade Ave. D4
Euphbosine I1
Euterre Ave. I5,I7
Eve J1
Evelina E8
Exchange Pl. F5
Felciana A6
Felicity J6
First J5
Florida Ave. B1
Fontainblau Dr. J1
Fortin D1
Foucher K4
Fourth K5
France A8
Franklin Ave. A4,C6
Frenchmen C4
Freret G4
Front,N. F6
Front,S. G6
Fulton G6
Gaiennie H7
Gallier A7
Galvez,N. C3,F3
Galvez,S. H3,I3,K2
Gayoso,N. C1,E1
Gayoso,S. G1
Gen.Pershing J1,J2
Gen.Taylor K2
Gentilly Blvd. A1
Girod H5
Gov. Nicholls E2,E4
Grand Route St. John D1
Gravier G2,G4
Hagan F1
Harmony K4
Hastings J7
Havana B1
Henderson I8
Hewes J1
Homer E8
Howard Ave. H6
Humanity A2
Iberville F5
Independence A7
Industry B2
Jackson Ave. I4,J6
Jane Pl. G2
Japonia A8
Jeff Davis Pkwy. I1
Jefferson K1
Jena J1
Johnson, S. H3,K2
Johnson,N. B3,F3
Joseph K1
Josephine J6
Julia H3,H5
Kentucky A8
Kerlerac D4,D5
Lafayette G5,H2
Lafreniere A1
Laharpe D3
Lamarouse F8
Lapeyrouse D3
Lasalle G4,K4
Laurel K7
Lavergne E7
Lesseps A8
Liberty,N. E4
Liberty,S. H4,J5
London Ave. C3
Lopez,N. E1
Lopez,S. H1
Louisa A6
Louisiana Ave.Pkwy. J2
Loyola J5
Madison St. E5
Magazine G6
Man Pl. G2
Mandeville C5
Manuel A8
Marais B7,C5,E4
Marengo K3
Marigny C5
Market J7
Maurepas D1
Mazant A8
McKenna K1
Melpomene I5
Milan K3
Miro,N. B3,F3
Miro,S. G3,K2
Mississippi River Bridge H8
Montegut A6
Morgan E7
Music A4
Napoleon Ave. K2
Nashville K1
Natchez G6
New Orleans B2
Newton F8
Notre Dame G6
Nuns J8
O'Keefe G5
O'Reilly C1
Octavia K1
Oliver E7
Onzaga C3
Opelousas Ave. E8
Orange I7
Orchid E1
Orleans Ave. E3,E5
Painters A4
Palmetto H1
Palmyra G3
Paris Ave. B1
Patterson E7
Pauger C4
Pauline A7
Paulmorphy C1
Pelican Ave. E7
Peniston K3
Perdido G4,H2
Peters F6
Peters,N. D6
Peters,S. G6,I8
Philip J5,J6
Piety A6
Pleasure A1
Poeyfarre H6
Poland A8
Ponce De Leon D1
Pontchartrain Expy. H1
Port C6
Powder F7
Poydas G4
Prieur Pl. K2
Prieur, S. H3,I3
Prieur,N. C3,F3
Prytania H6,K6
Ptolemy G8
Race I7
Rampart,N. B7,D5,E4
Rampart,S. I5,G5
Religious I8
Rendon,N. E1
Rendon,S. H1
Republic B1
Richard J7
River F8
Robert K2
Robertson,N. A7,C4,E4
Robertson,S. G4,I4
Rocheblave,N. B3,F2
Rocheblave,S. K2
Romain,N. C4,F3
Romain,S. G3,I3,K2
Rosiere C1
Rousseau J8
Rousselin C2
Royal C7,D5,E5
Salcedo,N. E1
Salcedo,S. G1
Saratoga G4
Saratoga,S. K5,I5
Scraparu K8
Second J5
Seguin E7
Serantine B1
Sere A1
Seventh K4
Simon I5
Sixth K5
Slidell E8
Socrates G8
Spain C5
St. Andrews I5,J6
St. Ann E3,E4
St. Bernard Ave. D4
St. Charles Ave. G5
St. Claude B7,C5
St. Ferdinand B6
St. James J8
St. Joseph H5
St. Louis F5
St. Mary J6
St. Peter E1,E5
St. Philip E5
St. Roch Ave. C5
St. Thomas J8
State St.Dr. K1
Tchoupitoulas G6,I8,K8
Teche F8
Terpsichore I4,I7
Thalia H7,I4
Third J5
Toledano J3,K4
Tonti,N. B3,F2
Tonti,S. K2
Toulouse F1,F5
Touro C4
Treasure A2
Tulane Ave. G3
Union G5
University Pl. G5
Upper Line K2
Urquhart B7,C4
Ursulines Ave. E5
Vallette F8
Vendome Pl. J1
Verret E8
Villere,N B7,C4,E4
Villere,S. G4
Vincennes Pl. J1
Washington K5
Washington Ave. I1
Water G7
Wells F6
White,N. E1
White,S. G1
Wilkinson St. E5
Willow I4
Wright J7
York K1

Scale of Miles

0   .1   .2   .3   .4

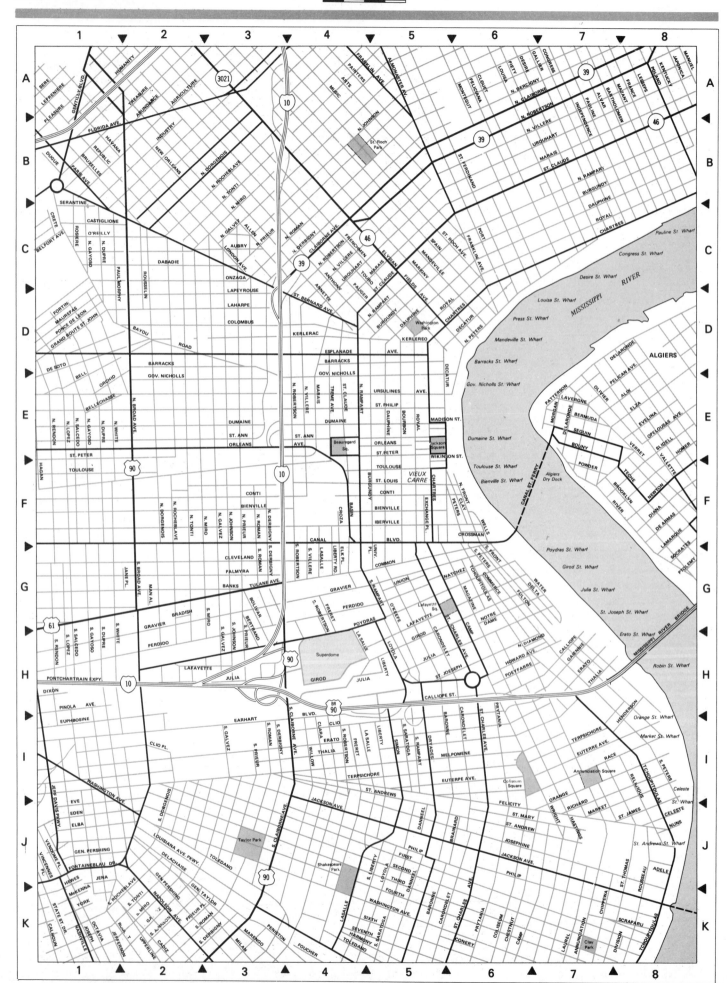

NEW YORK

Adams St. A1
Albany I1
Allen H3
Amsterdam Ave. B4,C3
Ann H2
Anslie St. H6
Ash F5
Ashland Pl. J4
Astor G3
Astoria Blvd. C7,C8
Atlantic Ave. J2,K4,K6
Attorney H3
Auburn Pl. J4
Ave. A G3
Ave. B G3
Ave. C G3
Ave. D G4
Avenue of the Americas D3
Bainbridge St. K7
Baltic St. K3
Bank St. F2
Banker St. G5
Barclay St. H1
Barrow G2
Baruch H4
Baxter H2
Bayard St. H6
Beach H1
Beadle St. H6
Beaver I1,I6
Bedford Ave. H5,I4,I5,J5
Beekman E4,I2
Bergen St. K3
Bergenline Ave. A1
Bergenwood A1
Berry I4
Bethune St. F2
Bleecker St. G2,J7
Bonn C1
Borden Ave. F5
Bowery H2
Bridge St. J3
Broad I1
Broadway A2,B1
Broadway A4,D3,E3,H3
Broadway D7,E8
Broadway I4,I6,K8
Broadway St. G2
Brooklyn Bridge I2
Brooklyn Queens Connecting Hwy. J4
Broome G2
Buchanan B1
Bushwick Ave. J7,I6
Butler St. K3
Calyer G5
Cambridge K5
Canal H2
Cardinal H2
Carlisle I1
Carlton Ave. J4
Carmine G2
Carroll St. K2
Cedar I1
Central C3,J8
Central Park South D3
Central Park West C4
Centre H2
Chambers St. H1
Charles F2
Charlton G2
Chauncey K7,K8
Cherry H3,I2
Christopher St. F2
Chrystie H2
Clark St. J2
Clarkson G2
Classon Ave. J5
Clay St. F5
Clermont Ave. J4
Clifton C1
Clifton Pl. J5
Clinton H3,I4
Clinton Ave. J4
Clinton St. K2
Clymer I4
Coenties I1
Columbia C1,H3
Columbus B4,C3
Commercial F5
Conimer St. G5
Conselyea St. H6
Cook St. I6
Cooper C1
Cooper St. K8
Cornelia G2
Cornelia St. J8
Cortlandt H1,I1
Cour St. K2
Covert St. K8
Cranberry St. I2
Crescent St. C7,E6
Crosby St. G2
Cuylers I1
De Bevoise St. I6
De Kalb St. J5,J7
Dean St. K4
Decatur St. K6,K8
Degraw St. K2,K3
Delancey St. H3
Des Brosses G2
Devoe St. H6
Dey H1
Diamond St. G6
Ditmars Blvd. B8
Division H2,I4
Division Pl. H6
Dobbin St. G5
Dominick G2
Doughty I2
Douglass St. K3
Downing G2
Driggs Ave. G6,H5,I5
Duane H1,H2
Duer Pl. C1
Durham A1
Eckford St. G6
Eldert St. K8
Eldorado C1
Eldridge H3
Elizabeth H2
Emerson J5
Engert Ave. H6
Entrance St. E4
Essex St. H3
Evergreen St. J7
Fairview I8
Flatbush Ave. J3
Fletcher I2
Forsyth H2
Franklin H1,H2
Franklin Ave. J5
Franklin Roosevelt Dr. F4,H4
Franklin St. F5
Freedon Pl. C3
Front I2
Front St. I3
Frost H6
Frost St. H5
Fulton C1
Fulton St. H1,I2,J3,K5
Gansevoort St. F2
Gardner G7
Gates Ave. J6,J8,K4
George I7
Gerry I6
Gould I2
Gouveneur H3
Graham Ave. H6
Grand G2
Grand Ave. K5
Grand St. H5,H6,H7
Grandview I8
Green St. K4
Greene G2
Greene Ave. J7,K7
Greenpoint Ave. F6,G5
Greenwich F2,G1
Grove G2
Grove St. J7
Guernsey St. G5
Hall St. J4
Halsey St. J8,K5,K7
Hamill H2
Hamilton C1
Hancock St. J8,K5,K7
Hansman G6
Hanson Pl. K4
Harman St. J7
Harrison A1,H1
Harrison Ave. I5
Hart St. I7,J5
Havemeyer H5
Henry H2
Henry Hudson C3
Henry St. J2,K2
Hester H3
Hewes I5
Hewes St. I5
Heyward St. I5
Hicks St. J2
Highland C1
Himrod St. J7
Hobart Ave. D8
Honeywell St. E7
Hooper St. I5
Hope St. H5
Hopkinson Ave. K8
Horatio St. F2
Houston St. G2,H3
Howard H2
Howard Ave. K7
Hoyte Ave. C7
Hubert H1
Hudson C1
Hudson Ave. A2,B1
Hudson Blvd. B1
Hudson Blvd.,E. B1
Hull St. K8
Humboldt St. G6,H6
Hunter St. E6
Huron St. G5
Imlay St. K1
India St. G5
Irving K5
Irving Ave. I7
Irving St. K2
Jackson H3
Jackson Ave. E6
Jackson St. H6
James H2
Jane St. F2
Java St. G5
Jay St. H1
Jefferson H3
Jefferson Ave. I7,J8,K5,K7
Jefferson St. A1
Jewel St. G6
John I2
John St. I3
Johnson Ave. I6,I7
Jones G2
Kane St. J2
Keap St. I5
Kent I4
Kent Ave. H4,J5
Kent St. G5
King C1
King St. G2,K1
Kings Island Ave. G6
Knickerbocker Ave. I7,J7
Kosciusko St. J5
Lafayette H2
Lafayette Ave. J6,K4
Laight G1
Lawrence J3
LeRoy St. G2
Lee Ave. I5
Leonard H2
Leonard St. G5,H6
Lewis H3
Lewis Ave. J5
Lexington Ave. C5,F3,J6,K5
Liberty C1,I1
Lincoln Tunnel D1
Linden St. J7
Lispenard H2
Livingston St. J3
Lombardy St. G6
Lonimer St. I5,I6
Ludlow St. H3
Lynch St. I5
Macdougal St. G2,K8
Macon St. K6
Madison H2,I8
Madison Ave. C5,F3,K7
Madison St. J8,K5
Mangin H4
Manhatten Ave. F5,H6
Manhatten Bridge I3
Marcy H5
Marcy Ave. I5,H5
Marion St. K7
Marshall I3
Maspeth Ave. H6
Mavjer St. I6
McKibbin St. I6
Meadowview A1
Meeker Ave. G6
Melrose St. I7
Menahan St. J7
Mercer St. G2
Messerole H7,I6
Messerole Ave. G6
Metropolitan Ave. H4,H6,H8
Middagh I3
Miller Hwy. D2,G1
Milton St. G5
Mitchell E4
Monitor St. G6
Monroe B1,H2
Monroe St. K5,K7
Montagomery H3
Montague St. J2
Montrose Ave. I6
Moore St. I6,I7
Moore St.,N. H1
Morgan I7
Morgan Ave. G6,H6
Morton G2,I4
Mott H2
Moultrie G6
Mt.Guiness Blvd. F5
Mulberry H2
Murray St. H1
Myrtle Ave. J5,J6,J7
Nassau I1
Nassau Ave. G5
Navy St. J3
New I1
Newel St. G6
Newkirk A1
Newton Ave. C7
Noble St. G5
Norfolk St. H3
Norman Ave. G5
North Henry St. G6
Northern Blvd. E7
Nostrand Ave. J5
Oak St. G5
Old I2
Onderdonk I8
Pacific St. J3,K4
Page Pl. H8
Paidge Ave. F5
Palisade Ave. A2,B1
Palmetto St. J8
Park H3
Park Ave. A2,B1,C5,D4,F3
Park Row H2
Park Row East H2
Park St. H1
Patchen Ave. J7
Pearl H2,I2
Peck I2
Pell H2
Penn St. I5
Perry St. F2
Pierrpont St. J2
Pilling K8
Pitt St. H3
Platt I2
Pleasant Ave. A7
Pleasent C1
Plymouth St. I3
Poplar I3
Porter G6,I7
Powers St. H6
President St. K2
Prince St. G2
Prospect I3
Provost St. F6
Pulaski St. J5,J6
Putnam Ave. J8,K5,K7
Quay St. G5
Queens Blvd. E6,E7
Queens Midtown Tunnel E5
Quincy St. J6,K5
Ralph Ave. J7
Randolph St. I7
Rector St. I1
Reid Ave. J7
Remsen St. J2
Renwick G2
Review Ave. F6
Richardson St. H6
Ridge H3
River H4
Riverside Dr. A4,B3
Rivington H3
Rockaway K8
Roebling H5
Ross St. I5
Russell St. G6
Rutgers H3
Rutledge St. I5
Sackett St. K2,K3
Sands I3
Sanford J5
Saratoga Ave. K8
Schermephorne St. J3
Scholes H7,I6
Seigel St. I6
Seneca Ave. I8
Shaefer St. K8
Skillman Ave. E7,F6,H6
Skillman St. J5
Slip H3
Smith Ave. A1,K2
Somers St. K8
South I2
South Ave. E4
Spencer St. J5
Spring G2
Spruce H2
St. James Pl. J4
St. Marks Ave. K4
St. Nicholas Ave. I8
Stagg St. H7,I6
Stanhope St. J7
Stanton H3
Starr St. I7
Sterling C1
Stewart Ave. I7
Stockholm St. I7
Stone K8
Stuyvesant Ave. J7
Suffolk H3
Sullivan St. G2,K1
Summitt St. K2
Sumner Ave. J6,J7
Sumpter St. K8
Sutton Pl. D5
Sutton St. G6
Suydam St. I7
Taaffee Ave. J5
Taylor St. I4
Thomas St. H2
Thompson Ave. E6
Thompson St. G2
Throop Ave. I6,J6,K6
Tillary J3
Tompkins Ave. J6
Tonsor H8
Trinity I1
Troutman St. I7,I8
Tudor City Pl. E4
Tunnel Exit St. E4
Union I5
Union St. K2
University G2
Van Brunt St. K1
Van Buren J6
Van Dam St. F7
Vandam G2
Vanderbilt E4
Vanderbilt Ave. J4
Vandervoort H6
Varet St. I6
Varick H2
Varick Ave. H7
Vernon Ave. J5
Vernon Blvd. D6,E5
Vessey St. H1
Vestry G2
Vine I2
Walker H2
Wall I1
Wallabout I5,I6
Walton St. I5
Walworth Pl. J5
Warren St. H1,K3
Warsoff Pl. J5
Washington G1,J3
Washington Ave. J4
Water I2
Water St. I3
Watts G2
Waverly J4
Weirfield St. J8
West H2
West St. F4,G2
Westend C3
White Hall I1
Willett H3
William I2
Williamsburg Bridge H4
Willoughby Ave. J4
Willoughby St. I7
Wilson Ave. J8
Wolcott K1
Woodbine I8
Woodbine St. J8
Woodside E8
Woodward Ave. I8
Wooster St. G2
Worth St. H2
Wyckoff Ave. I7
Wyckoff St. K3
Wythe H4
York I3
York Ave. C6,D5
Zold Pl.,S. G4
1st Ave. C5,F4,G3
1st Pl. K2
1st St. C6,H5
2nd Ave. C5,F3,G3
2nd Pl. K2
2nd St. C6,F5,H5
2nd St.,E. G3
3rd Ave. C5,E4,G3
3rd Pl. K2
3rd St. C7,H5
3rd St.,E. G3
3rd St.,W. G2
4th Ave. G3
4th Pl. K2
4th St. H4,H5
4th St.,E. G3
4th St.,W. G2
5th Ave. B5
5th St. E5,H4,H5
5th St.,E. G3
6th Ave. K4
6th St. H5
6th St.,E. G3
7th Ave. F2,K2
7th St. H5
7th St.,E. G3
8th I4
8th Ave. D3,F2
8th St. H5
8th St.,E. G3
8th St.,W. F2
9th Ave. E2
9th St. C7,D6,H5
9th St.,E. G3
9th St.,W. F2
10th Ave. E2
10th St. D6,E5,E6,H5
10th St.,E. G3
10th St.,W. F2
11th Ave. E2
11th St. D6,E5,E6,H5
11th St.,E. G3
11th St.,W. F2
12th St. D6,E5,G6
12th St.,E. G3
12th St.,W. F2
13th St. E6
13th St.,W. F2
14th St. C7,D6
14th St.,E. F3
14th St.,W. F2
15th St. H5
15th St.,E. F3
15th St.,W. F2
16th St.,E. F3
16th St.,W. F2
17th St.,E. F3
17th St.,W. F2
18th St.,E. G3
18th St.,W. F2
19th St. C7
19th St.,E. F3
20th Ave. B8
20th St. B8
20th St.,E. F3
20th St.,W. F2
21st Ave. B8
21st St. B8,C7,D7,E6,F6
21st St.,E. F3
21st St.,W. F2
22nd Rd. B8
22nd St. E6
22nd St.,E. F3
23rd St. C7,D7,E6
23rd St.,E. F3
23rd St.,W. E2
24th St. C7,E6
25th Ave. D8
25th Rd. C7
25th Rd.,W. E2
25th St.,E. F3
26th Ave. C7
26th St. C8
26th St.,E. F3
26th St.,W. E2
27th Ave. C7
27th St. C8,E6
27th St.,E. F3
27th St.,W. E2
28th St. C8,E6
28th St.,W. E2
29th Ave. C7,D8
29th St. C8,E6
29th St.,W. E2
30th Ave. D8
30th Dr. C7
30th Pl. F6
30th Rd. C7
30th St. C7,D7,E6,F6
30th St.,E. F3
30th St.,W. E2
31st Ave. C7
31st Dr. D7
31st Pl. F6
31st St. F6
31st St.,E. F3
31st St.,W. E2
32nd Pl. F7
32nd St. D7,E7
32nd St.,E. E3
32nd St.,W. E3
33rd St. C8,D7,E6,F7
33rd St.,E. E3
33rd St.,W. E2
34th St., E. E4
34th Ave. D7
34th St. F7
34th St.,W. E2
35th Ave. D6
35th St. C1,C8,E7,F7
35th St.,E. E4
35th St.,W. E2
36th Ave. D6
36th St. C1,C8,E7,F7
36th St.,E. E4
36th St.,W. E2
37th Ave. D6,E8
37th St. C1,C8,E7,F7,G6
37th St.,E. E4
37th St.,W. E3
38th E8
38th Ave. D6
38th St. C8,E8,F7
38th St.,E. E4
38th St.,W. E3
39th Ave. E6,E8
39th Pl. F7
39th St. C1,F7
39th St.,E. E4
39th St.,W. D3
40th Ave. E6
40th St. F7
40th St.,E. E4
40th St.,W. D3
41st Dr. E8
41st St. C1,C8,E7,F7
41st St.,E. E4
41st St.,W. D3
42nd Pl. E7
42nd St. C8,E7,F7
42nd St.,E. F4
42nd St.,W. D3
43rd Ave. E5,E7
43rd Rd. E5
43rd St. C1,E8,F7,G7
43rd St.,E. F4
43rd St.,W. D3
43th St.,E. E4
44th Ave. E5
44th Dr. E5
44th Rd. E5
44th St. E8,F7,G7
44th St.,E. E4
44th St.,W. D3
45th B1
45th Ave. E5
45th Rd. E5
45th St. E8,F7
45th St.,E. E4
45th St.,W. D7
46th Ave. E5
46th Rd. E5
46th St. C1,E8,F7
46th St.,E. E4
46th St.,W. D3
47th Ave. E5,F6
47th Rd. E5
47th St. C1,E8,F8,H7
47th St.,E E4
47th St.,W. D3
48th Ave. F5,F6
48th St. B1,E8,F8,G7
48th St.,E. E4
48th St.,W. D3
49th Ave. F5
49th St. B1,D8,E8,F8
49th St.,E. D4
49th St.,W. D3
50th B1
50th Ave. D8,E8,F5
50th St. B1,E8,F8,G8
50th St.,E. D4
50th St.,W. D3
51st B1
51st Ave. F5
51st St. B1,F8
51st St.,E. D4
51st St.,W. D3
52nd Ave. F8
52nd Rd. F8
52nd St. B1,E8
52nd St.,E. D4
52nd St.,W. D3
53rd H8
53rd St. B1,F8
53rd St.,E. D4
53rd St.,W. D3
54th Ave. F5,G7,G8
54th Dr. G7
54th Pl. H8
54th Rd. G7
54th St. B1,E8,F8,H8
54th St.,E. D4
54th St.,W. D3
55th Ave. F5,G7
55th Dr. G7
55th St. B1,E8,F8,H8
55th St.,E. D4
55th St.,W. D3
56th Rd. G7,G8
56th St. B1,E8,F8,H8
56th St.,E. D4
56th St.,W. D3
57th Ave. G7
57th Dr. H8
57th Rd. G8
57th St. B1,E8,F8
57th St.,E. D4
57th St.,W. C3
58th Ave. H8
58th Ln. F8
58th Rd. H8
58th St. B1,E8,F8
58th St.,E. D4
58th St.,W. C3
59th Dr. H8
59th Pl. H8
59th St. A1,G8
59th St.,E. D4
59th St.,W. C3
60th St. A1
60th St.,E. D4
60th St.,W. C3
61st St. A1
61st St.,E. D4
61st St.,W. C3
62nd St. A1
62nd St.,E. D4
62nd St.,W. C3
63rd St. A1
63rd St.,E. D4
63rd St.,W. C3
64th St. A1
64th St.,E. D4
64th St.,W. C3
65th St. A1
65th St.,E. D4
65th St.,W. C3
66th St. A1
66th St.,E. D4
66th St.,W. C3
67th St. A1
67th St.,E. C4
67th St.W. C3
68th St. A1
68th St.,E. C4
68th St.,W. C3
69th St. A1,C4
69th St.,E. C4
69th St.,W. C4
70th St. A1
70th St.,E. C4
71st St. A2,C3
71st St.,E. C4
72nd St. A2,B3
72nd St.,E. C5
73rd St. A2,B3
73rd St.,E. C5
74th St. A2,B3
74th St.,E. C5
75th St. A2,B3
75th St.,E. C5
76th St. A2
76th St.,E. C5
76th St.,W. B4
77th St. A2,B3
78th St. A2,B3,C5
79th St. A2,B3,C5
80th St. B3,C5
81st St. B3,C5
82nd St. B3,C5
83rd St. B3,C5
84th St. B4,C5
85th St. C4,C5
86th St. B4,B5
87th St. A4,B5
88th St. B4,B5
89th St. A4,B5
90th St. A4,B5
91st St. A4,B5
92nd St. A4,B5
93rd St. A4,B5
94th St. A4,B5
95th St. A4,B4
96th St. A4,B5
97th St. A4,B5
98th St. A4,B5
99th St. A4,B6
100th St. A4,B6
101st St. B6
102nd St. A4,A5,B6
103rd St. A4,A6
104th St. A4,A6
105th St. A4,A6
106th St. A6
107th St. A6
108th St. A6
109th St. A6
110th St. A6
111th St. A6
112th St. A6
113th St. A6
114th St. A6
115th St. A6
116th St. A6
117th St. A6
118th St. A6
119th St. A6

NORFOLK

A Ave. F3
Abbey Rd. C5
Abingdon Cir. B7
Alabama Ave. E7
Alsace Ave. B4,C5
Amelia St. F3
Amherst St. C7
Anderson St. F4
Anne St. F3
Arden Circle A3
Arden Circle,S. A3
Argonne Ave. C6,E5
Arizona Ave. D6
Arkansas Ave. E7
Arlington J5,J6
Armistead Ave. F2
Ashland Ave. C4
Ashland Cicle C4
Ashton Ave. J3
Atlantic I1
Atterbury St. D7
Atwater Circle B5
Augusta F3
Avon Rd. A6
B Ave. F3
Bagnall Rd. G3
Baldwin Ave. F1
Ballentine Blvd. E6
Bank St. H2
Bankhead Ave. C7
Bapume Ave. D5
Barney F4
Barraud Ave. F4
Barre St. E3
Bayne Ave. G6,G7
Beach Ave. C3
Beachland St. J6
Beachmont Ave. G6,G7
Beckner St. B6
Bellamy Ave. J3
Bellevue Ave. D5
Bellmore Ave. H6
Belvedere Rd. A3
Belvedere Rd.,W. A2
Bickel St. I6
Billings St. F4
Blair Ave. D4
Blanch Dr. B5
Bland St. B7
Blow F1
Bonner Dr.,E. D7
Bonner Dr.,W. D7
Booth H4
Botetourt St. H1
Botherys Ln. I1
Botton St. F4,G4
Bourbon D4
Boush St. H1
Bower F3
Bower F3
Boyce Dr. C4
Brambleton Ave. H3
Brest Ave. D5
Brightley Rd. A5
Broadway D2
Brooke St. H1
Brown Ave. I4
Buckingham St. C7
Bucks Rd. G5
Burks Wide St. G3
Burruss H3
Bute St. H1,H2
Bute St. Ext. H3
C Ave. F3
Cabona Ave. F4
Calt St. F4
Campostella Rd. J5
Cape Henry Ave. F6,F7
Cape Henry Ave.,S. F6,F7
Carolina Ave. C1
Carr St. H3
Cary Ave. G5
Cecelia St. H4
Central Ave. B7
Channel St. I3
Chapel St. G3,H2,H3
Charlotte St. H2
Chase St. F3
Chatham Circle B6
Chesapeake Blvd. D6
Chesterfield I5
Chicazola St. G3
Church St. D2,H2
City Hall Ave. H2
Clare St. A7
Clay Ave. I3,I4
Clayborne Ave. I4
Clifton St. J2
Coburn Cres. B4
College Pl. H1
Colley Ave. D1
Colonial Ave. D1
Columbia Ave. C5
Columbus Ave. C3
Commerce I1
Concord I1
Connecticut Ave. B1
Cooke Ave. H3
Corprew Ave. H4
Cottage Ave. F4
County St. C6
Cour St. H2
Courtney Ave. F4,G4
Covenant St. H5
Cromwell Dr. C5
Cromwell Rd. E6
Cumberland St. G2,H2
Dana St. F6
Dare Circle B6
Davis St. E6,E7
De Bree Ave. D2,F1
Delaware Ave. C1
Denby G3
Denhart St. F3
Denver Ave. E7
Devonshire Rd. A7
Dogan St. G6
Dora Circle C7
Douglas B6
Dove St. A7
Dover Circle A3
Drain I3
Druid Circle D3
Drummond Rd. G7
DuPont Circle D4
Dubious H5
Duke St. H1
Dunbar St. G4
Dungee H3
Dunkirk Ave. D5
Dunmore St. H1
Earlscourt I6
East End I7
East St. I2
Eden F3
El Mere C4
Elmore Pl. C5
Elmwood Ave. F3
Emmett Pl. J2
Emory Pl. A4
Enterprise Rd. F7
Essex Circle B7
Ethel C3
Fairfax Ave. G1
Farragut E4
Fawn St. F3
Fayette St. I1
Fearer Ave. E5
Febian Ave. H6
Fenchurch St. H2
Fielding I5
Filer St. I5
Flanders Ave. D6
Flordia Ave. E7
Fontainebleau Cres. C4
Forbes St. I5
Forge St. F5
Fox H2
Freemason St. I1
Galts Ct. H1
Garden St. B7
Gay Pl. E4
Gazel St. E3
Georgia Ave. C1
Glen Ave. D7
Glenoak Dr. A6
Glenrock St. B5
Godfrey Ave. H6
Goff St. G3,G4
Gondola Rd. G7
Goochland F3
Gordon St. F4
Gornto E5
Gosnold Ave. D1
Gowrie Ave. E4
Grace St. G1
Granby St. C2,F2,H1
Grandy Ave. E6
Granville Ave. I4
Green St. A7
Greenwood St. A7
Hadlock B4
Hale St. E3
Hampshire Ave. B7
Hanbury St. D6
Hancock Ave. E4
Hanson Ave. F4,H4
Hardy Ave. J2
Harmott Ave. B4
Harrell Ave. E6
Hayes St. E3
Henrico St. D7
Henry St. G3
Highland Ave. I5
Holland C4
Hollister Ave. G6,G7
Holly Ave. C3
Holt St. I3
Hood Rd. D7
Horton Circle A7
Hough Ave. J3
Hugo St. B6,B7
Hunter St. F3
Huntington C4
Huntington Pl. B4
Hurley Ave. D7
Hydro St. I4
Illinois D6
Indian River Rd. J2
Ingleside Rd. E6,G8
Inventors Rd. G7
Ivaloo St. A7
Jackson I1
Jacob St. I4
Jamaica Ave. G5
Jason Ave. E4
Jersey Ave. C7
Johnson Ave. F3
Jones Pl. H3
Kansas Ave. D6
Keller Ave. E6,F6
Kelley I1
Kenosha Ave. A5
Kenton Ave. H5
Kimball Ct. I6
Kimball Terr. I6,I7
Kirkland Ave. D5
Kitchner Ave. D5
Knox A6
La Salle Ave. D4
Lafayette Blvd. D4,D5,D6
Lakewood Dr. B4
Lamberts Point Rd. D1
Lamont St. E4
Landing St. H3
Lanvale G3
Larkin St. E7
Latimer B7
Laxalette C3
Lead St. F5,G5
Lenoir Circle B7
Lens Ave. E5
Leo St. E3
Lexington St. F3
Liberia Dr. G5
Lincoln St. G2
Lindenwood Ave. E3
Lindsay F2
Link St. G4
Llewellyn Ave. E2,G1
Lombard St. F3
Lorraine Ave. D4
Lovitt I2
Low H3
Lowell Ave. A6
Lucile Ave. C3
Ludlow St. E4
Luxenbourg Ave. D4
Lyons Ave. D6
Main St. I1,I2
Majestic Ave. H5,I5
Maltby Ave. F4,H4
Mangrove Ave. H7
Manteo St. F1
Mapleton Ave. G6,G7
Mapole Ave. H5
Marathon H5
Mariner St. H2
Market H2
Marlboro Ave. I5
Marne Ave. E6
Marshall Ave. F5,G4,H4
Martins I1
Maryland Ave. C1
Masi St. E4
Massachusetts Ave. B1
Mathews I1
Maury Ave. F1
May Ave. H3
Mayflower Rd. B1,C1,C2
Maymont Ave. A6
Maysville F3
McKann Ave. E6
McLemore St. F6
Memphis St. H7
Merrill Ave. C7
Merrimac G6
Merrimac Ave. H6,I6
Michigan Ave. C1
Middle E3
Mihiel Ave. D5
Minnesota Ave. E7
Monrovia Dr. G5
Montana Ave. D7
Montclair Ave. J5,J6
Montgomery St. C7
Monticello Ave. E2,H1
Montserrado Pl. G6
Morris Ave. D4
Moultrie Ave. D4
Mowbray Arch G1
Muskogee Ave. A5
Myrtle Ave. H6
Nansemond Circle B7
National Magazine Ln. G1
Natrona A5
Nevada Ave. E7
New Hampshire Ave. B1
New Jersey Ave. B1
New York Ave. B1
Newport Ave. A2,D1
Newport Cres. A2
Newport Pt. A2
Nicholson St. G2
Norchester St. H6,I6
Norfolk G1
Norland Circle C6
Norland Ct. C7
Norview Ave. B6
Norway B4,C4
Nottaway St. C6
O'Keefe St. F3
Oaklawn Ave. H5
Odell I4
Oklahoma Ave. D7,E7
Olney Rd. G1,G2,H3
Omohundro Ave. E2
Orange St. C7
Orchard B3
Orleans Circle D4
Outten F3
Overbrook Ave. D7
Palem Rd. A7
Palmetto St. E7
Pamela Pl. A4
Pamlico Circle B7
Parish Rd. G6
Park Ave. H4
Partridge St. A7
Pearl St. J1
Pendleton St. J2
Pennsylvania Ave. C1
Percy St. G4
Peronne Ave. D5
Pershing Ave. C5
Peterson St. D8,E6
Pine St. J1
Pioneer Ave. H6
Plume Ln. I2
Plume St. I1
Plymouth Cres. B2
Pollard St. E3
Pomroy Ave. C5
Pope Ave. D4
Poplar Ave. K2
Posey Ln. H2
Preston G3
Princess Anne Rd. F1,G5
Princeton Ave. K5,K6
Production Rd. F7
Proescher F3
Pulaski H3
Quail St. A7
Quail St.,S. A7
Racine C5
Racine Ave. D4
Radford St. C7
Radis C6
Railroad Ave. G5
Raleigh Ave. G1
Randolph St. H1
Redgate Ave. F1
Reeves Ave. I4
Regent Rd. A2
Reilly St. I2
Reivelle Ave. J3
Reservoir Ave. F5,G4,H4
Rhode Island Ave. B1
Ridgeley A2
Ridgeley ,S. A2
Ridgeley Pt. A2
River Rd. A2
River Rd. Pt. A1
River Rd.,S. A2
River Rd.,W. A1
Riviera St. I6
Roberts Rd. G5
Roland Dr. A5
Roscoe G3
Rose Ave. I4
Ruffin St. E4
Ruffin Way E3
Rugby St. E3,F4
Rush St. E7
Sangamon A5
Schooley Ave. H6
Scott St. H7
Sedgefield Dr. A6
Sedgewick I5
Severn Rd. A3
Shanks St. G5
Shenandoah Ave. A4
Shipp Ave. H4
Shirley Ave. E1
Shoop Ave. E5
Silbert Rd. B6
Sinde Pl. G6
Smith St. G2,G3
Somme Ave. C5,D5
South Ave. C7
Spotwood Ave. E1
Springfield Ave. J5
Square G1
St. Denis Ave. D5
St. Julian Ave. F4
St. Louis D4
St. Pauls Blvd. I2
Standard St. G5
Stanhope Ave. I6
Stansbury Ave. F2
Stapleton St. I7
Starke St. G2
Strathmore Ave. I7
Strickler St. F3
Summit Ave. E3
Sunshine Ave. A6
Sutton St. F3
Sweet Briar Ave. B4
Tabb St. H3
Taft Terr. E6
Tait E4,E5
Talbot I1
Tappahannock A5
Tarrall Ave. B4
Tarran St. F6
Thayor St. I5
Thistle St. F4
Thomas H1
Tidewater Dr. C5,I3
Tiller Ave. E5
Trant Ave. H7
Tulip Ln. H2
Tunstall H3
Tyler St. G3
Upshur St. D6
Vendome Terr. D4
Verdun Ave. E5
Versailles Ave. D4
Vick St. G3
Vicoria Ave. I6
Villa Circle D3
Vimy Ridge Ave. D5
Vincent Ave. E6,F6
Virginia Ave. C1
Virginia Beach Blvd. G4,H7
Vista St. E4
Voss St. G1
Wake Circle B6
Walker St. H3
Wall St. F4
Washington Ave. F3
Washington Park E1
Water St. I2
Waterfield St. J1
Waterfront Dr. I1
Waverly Way D3
Waylon Ave. B4
Wayne Circle B7
Webster E4
Websters Ct. H1
Weiss Ln. H7
West Ave. E3
Westminster I5
Westover Ave. F1
White Oak Ave. H6
Whitechapel Rd. C5
Whittier Dr. A6
Wide St. H3
Wiley Dr. I7
Willard Pl. C5
Willoughby I3
Willow Grove Ct. B3
Willow Wood Dr. B4,C5
Wilson Ave. G1
Winckley Ave. J3
Winder Dr. C4
Windham A3
Windsor I4
Windsor Point Rd. B3
Winter St. G3
Winward Rd. A7
Withers Ave. E5
Wood St. H2
Woodland Ave. G7,H6
Wyoming Ave. E7
Yarmouth H1
9th St. G2
10th St. G1
11th St. F2
12th St. F2
13th St. F2
14th St. F2
15th St. F1,F2
16th St. F2
17th St. E1,F2
18th St. F2
19th St. E2
20th St. E1,F2
21st St. E1
22nd St. E1
23rd St. E1,E3
24th St. E1
25th St. E1,E3
26th St. D1,E3
27th St. D1,E3
28th St. D1,E3
29th St. D1,E3
30th St. D2,E3
31st St. D2
32nd St. D2
33rd St. D2
34th St. D1
35th St. D1
36th St. D1
37th St. C1
38th St. C1
39th St. C1,C3
40th St. C1,C2
41st St. C1
42nd St. C1,C2
43rd C1
44th C1
45th St. C1
46th B1
47th B1
48th St. B1
49th B1
50th B1
51st St. B1
52nd St. B1

Scale of Miles
0 .1 .2 .3 .4 .5

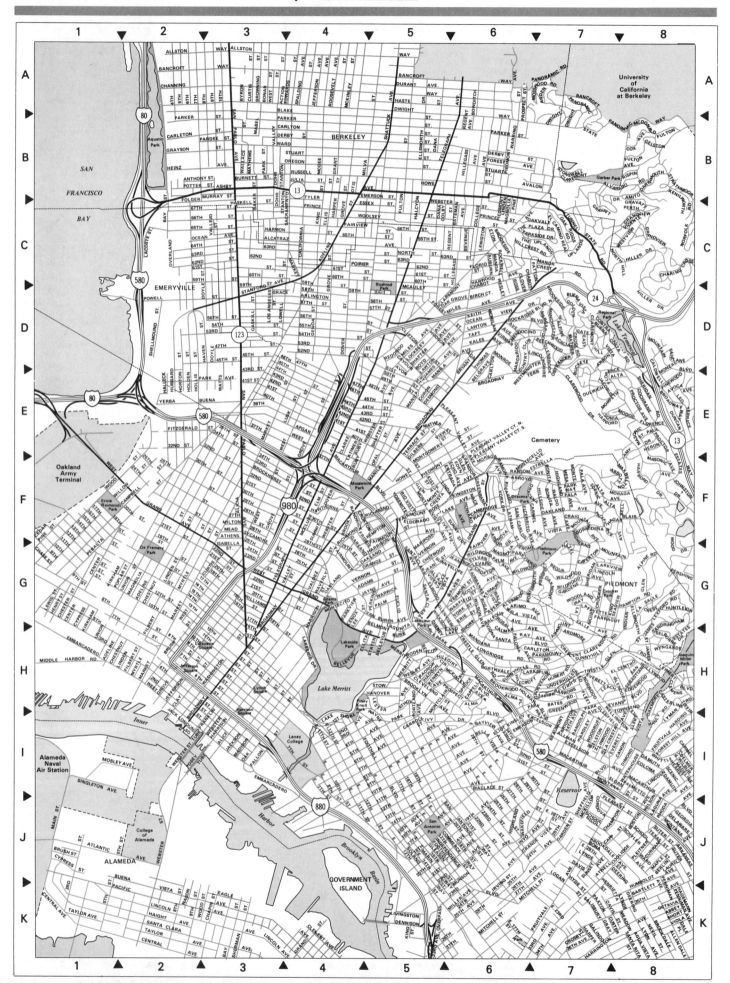

OAKLAND

Abbey K8
Abbott F8
Acacia D7
Action St. A4
Ada D6
Adams St. G5
Adeline St. ... C4,G2,H1
Alcatraz Ave. C3
Alice St. I3
Alicia F3
Allen Dale K8
Allman I7
Allston Way A3,A5
Alma H6
Alma Pl. H6
Alpine D7
Alpine Rd. G8
Alta E8
Alta Ave. F7
Alta Vista G5
Alvarado G6
Alvarado Rd. B8
Amito B8
Amy Dr. E8
Anthony St. B2
Apgar E4
Aqua Vista G5
Arbon D7
Arbor Dr. F6
Arden A7
Ardley I7
Ardmore H7
Arimo Ave. G6
Arkansas J8
Arlington D4
Arroyo Plwy. F6
Ashby Ave. B3
Ashmount H7
Athens F3
Athol Ave. H5
Atwell J7
Auburn C6
Avalon B7
Avoca Ave. E8
Avon D5
Baker St. B3
Balfour Ave. G6
Bancroft A7
Barrows H7
Bartlett Ave. K8
Bateman C6
Bates Rd. H7
Bay K3
Bay St. C2
Bayview Ave. I6
Beacon H5
Beaumont I7
Beechwood D7
Belgrave D6
Bell F8
Bella Vista I6
Bellevue H4,H5
Belmont G5
Benvenue Ave. C6
Bequa G7
Berlin J8
Birch Ct. D6
Blair F8
Blake Way A4
Bonar St. A3
Bonita Ave. F7
Boston Ave. J8
Bowditch A6
Boyd Ave. D5
Brandon F6
Brighton I7
Broadway E5,G3,H2
Broadway Terr. E6
Brook F4
Brookdale K8
Brookdale Ave. J7
Brookhurst F3
Brooklyn Ave. H5
Brookside C6,D7
Brookwood H6
Browning St. A3
Brush St. H2
Bryant D6
Buckeye D7
Buena Vista D7
Buena Vista Ave. K2
Burk H5
Burnett St. B3
Byron A3
Caldwell E8
California St. C4
Calmar Ave. H6
Cambridge Way F6
Campbell St. F2
Canon I8
Caperton G7
Capp St. J8
Cappell H6
Carleton St. B2
Carlston H7
Carlton D6
Carlton St. B4
Carmel F7,I8
Carroll St. I5
Casterline H8
Castro G3
Cavour St. D5
Cedar F1
Center G1
Central State Hwy. Ave. K2
Chabot C6
Chabot Rd. C6
Champion St. J8
Channing Way A2
Chapin K3
Charing Cross C8
Chase St. G1
Cherry G5
Chester St. G1
Chestnut St. G2
Chetwood G5
Claremont B7
Claremont Ave. D6
Claremont Hill D7
Clarewood Dr. E7
Clarke E4
Clay St. H2
Clemens H8
Clement Ave. K4
Cleveland St. H5
Clifton St. D5
Clover C6
Cochrane E8
Colby C5
College Ave. C6
Colma H7
Commerce Way J6
Contra Costa Rd. D7
Coolidge J8
Cordova J7
Coron E5
Country Club D6
Cox Ave. B8
Craig F7
Creed H7
Crescent Clarendon H7
Crest Rd. G8
Crocker G7
Crofton F4,G6
Crosby K7
Cross Rd. D6
Curran J8
Curtis G3
Curtis St. A3
Custer K8
Cypress G1
Dale Pl. K8
Damuth I8
Dana C5
Dana St. B5
Dartmouth B8
Davis St. J7,K8
Deering K8
Deleware J8
Delmer I8
Dennison K5
Denoa St. D4
Derby St. B4,B6
Desmond E5
Diamond I8
Dohr B3
Dona St. J7
Dormidera F7
Dover F4
Dover St. D4
Doyle St. D3
Dracena F6
Dulwich E7
Duncan Way E8
Durant Ave. A5
Dwight B7
Eagle Ave. K3
East D7
Echo Ave. F6
Edgewood H8
Edwards St. A4
El Camino Real C7
El Centro H8
Elcerrito Ave. F6
Eldorado F5
Eliot I6
Ellis St. C4
Ellita H5
Ellsworth G8
Ellsworth Dr. B5
Elm St. F4
Elmwood G5
Elston I7
Embarcadero West H1
Emerson I6
Emerson St. B5
Entrada F6
Erie St. G6
Essex St. C5
Estates E8
Estates Dr. H8
Estrander D7
Estrella F7
Eton C6
Euclid G5
Evans Blvd. H8
Everett H7,I8
Excelsior Ave. I7
Fairbanks G6
Fairlane D6
Fairmount F5,G4
Fairview Ave. F6
Fairview St. C4
Fallon St. I3
Farracut G7
Filbert St. G2
Fitzgerald St. E2
Fleet H7
Florence E7
Florio St. C6
Folger C2
Foothill J6
Foothill Blvd. I5
Forest D5
Forest Ave. B6
Forest Hill Ave. I8
Franklin St. I3
Frisbie F4
Fruitvale Ave. I8,K7
Fulton B8
Fulton St. C5
Galindo K7
Garden St. J7
Garland G4
Gaskill St. D3
Gelston B8
Georgia J8
Gilbert St. E5
Gleason J5
Glen G8
Glen Ave. F5
Glen Eden F8
Glenbrook D7
Glendora H8
Glenfield I7
Glenview G5
Golden Gate Vista D7
Grace D3
Grand G4
Grand St. F6,K4
Grand Vista J7
Grandview C8
Grant St. B4
Gravatt C7,C8
Gray K7
Grayson St. B2
Greenbank Ave. F6
Greenwood H7
Grosvenor H7
Grove St. C4,E4,F3,H2
Hadoon H5
Hagar F7
Hagemann K8
Halcyon C5
Hampton Rd. G8
Hanly Rd. I8
Hanover Ave. H5
Harboad Dr. E7,F8
Harding I8
Harmon St. C3
Harper K7
Harper St. C4
Harrington Ave. K7
Harrison G4,G5
Harrison St. I3
Harwood Ave. C6
Haskell St. C3
Haste A5
Haven St. D3
Hawthorne F4
Hazel G7
Hearst I8
Heinz Ave. B2
Henrietta K8
Henry St. G1
Heron E8
Highland J6
Highland Ave. F7
Hillcrest Rd. C7,C8
Hillcroft H6
Hillegass B6
Hillegass Ave. C6
Hiller Dr. C8,D8
Hillgrit Circle H6
Holden St. E2
Hollis St. E2
Hollywood H8
Holman H7
Horton St. E2
Howard F6
Howe B5
Howe St. F5
Hubbard E2
Hubert Rd. H7
Hudson St. D5
Humboldt Ave. J8
Huntleigh G8
Hyde St. K7
Independence J6
Indiana G8
Inyl Ave. J6
Irving St. K6
Isabella St. G3
Ivy Dr. I5
Jack London Square I2
Jackson St. I3
Jacobus E7
James Ave. E5
Jayne Ave. G5
Jean Blvd. G6
Jean St. G5
Jefferson Ave. A4
Jefferson St. H2
Johnston Dr. F8
Julia St. B4
Kales D6
Keith Ave. D6
Kempton F5
Kenilworth B8
Kenmore G6
Kenwyn H5
King St. C4,K5
Kingston F6
Kinsley I6
Kirkham G1
La Cresta Ave. I7,I8
La Guna Ave. J8
La Salle Ave. G7
Lacoste St. C2
Lafayette G7
Lagunita H5
Lake Ave. F6
Lake Park H5
Lake Shore I4
Lake Shore Ave. H6
Lakeside Dr. H4
Larkspur H6
Larkview G7
Latham St. F6
Latimer E4
Laurel J8
Lawton D6
Leach H7
Lee St. G4
Leimert Blvd. H8
Lenox G4
Leo Terrace E8
Lester H5
Lewis St. G1
Lewiston C6
Lexford Rd. G8
Lincoln G7,I8
Lincolnshire D7
Linda Ave. F6
Linden C6
Linden St. G2
Linwood I7
Livingston K5
Locksley Ave. D5
Logan St. J7
Longridge Rd. H6
Los Angeles St. D3
Lowell St. D4
Lusk St. E4
Lyman Rd. I8
Lynde J7,K8
Lyon Ave. K8
Mabel B3
MacArthur Blvd. H6,I7,I8
Madeline I8
Madison St. I3
Magnolia Ave. C6,G2,G6
Manchester D7
Manila Ave. E5,F5
Manoa C6
Manor Crest C7
Maple Ave. J8
Margarido D6,D7
Marin Way J5
Mariposa F5
Market C4
Market St. E3,G2
Masonic F8
Mather D6
Mather St. E5
Mathews B3
Max Welton F8
McAuley D5
McClure F4
McDonald B8
McGee Ave. B4
McKillop J7
McKinney St. A4
McMilan D6
Mead F3
Meadow K8
Medocino D6
Merritt H5
Mesa Ave. F7
Middle Harbor Rd. H1
Miles Ave. D5,D6
Miller Ave. K6
Milton F3
Milva St. B5
Mitchell St. K6
Modoc E8
Mondana Blvd. H6
Monroe D6
Montana J8
Montana St. I8
Monte F7
Monte Cresta F5
Monte Vista Ave. F5
Montecello Ave. F6
Montecito G4
Montgomery St. E5
Monticlair H5
Monzale E8
Moraga F6
Moraga Ave. F8
Morpeth E7
Mosswood Rd. A7
Mountain Ave. F7
Mountain Blvd. D8
Muir G7
Munson J6
Murray St. B3
Myrtle St. G2
Nace F6
Nason K2
Nevil St. K8
Nicol Ave. J8
Nimitz Frwy. G1
Norfolk Rd. C8
North Hill C8
North St. C5
Northvale H6
Nova F6
Oak Grove D6
Oak Ridge Rd. C7
Oak St. I3
Oakland Ave. F7,G5
Oakmont G7
Oakmore H8
Oakvale C7
Ocean Ave. C3
Ocean View Dr. D6
Octavia K8
Olive Ave. F5
Opal St. F5
Orange St. G5
Oregon St. B4
Overland C2
Pacific Ave. F7,K2
Pala Ave. F7
Palm G5
Palmetto I8
Paloma H6
Panoramic Rd. A7
Panoramic Way B8
Paramount Rd. H7
Pardee St. B3
Park Ave. E3,H7
Park Blvd. H7,I5
Park St. B3
Parker St. B2,B4,B6
Parkside Dr. C7
Parkview G4,G6
Patton C7
Paxton K7
Penniman Ave. K8
Peralta St. G1
Perkins G5
Pershing G8
Perth C8
Piedmont C6
Piedmont Ave. B6,F5
Pine C6
Pine St. F1
Pinewood E8
Pleasant St. J8
Pleasant Valley Ave. E6
Pleasant Valley Ct.,N. E6
Pleasant Valley Ct.,S. E6
Poirer St. C4
Poplar St. G2
Portland Ave. H5
Portsmouth G7
Posey Tube I2
Potter St. B2
Powell St. D2
Prince C4
Prince St. C6
Proctor Ave. E8
Prospect G7,H6
Ramona Ave. F6
Rand H6
Randolph I7
Randwick F4
Ransom Ave. F6
Raonor H5
Redondo D5
Regent Ave. B6
Regent St. C6
Rhoda Ave. J8
Ricardo F6
Richmond F4
Rio Vista F5
Rispin B8
Rockridge Blvd.,N. D6
Rockridge Blvd.,S. D6
Rockwell C6
Roden H5
Roosevelt Ave. A4
Rosal G6
Ross C6
Ross Ave. F5
Ruby E4
Russell St. B4
Sacramento St. C4
Salisbury K7
San Antonio Way J6
San Carlos F6
San Pablo Ave. B3,E3
San Sebastian H8
Sandringham H8
Santa Clara Ave. G5,K2
Santa Ray Ave. H6
Santa Ray St. K8
Scenic F7,I8
School St. J8
Schyler J8
Scott St. G6
Selborne H8
Shafter Ave. D5,E5
Shatuck Ave. B5
Sheffield Ave. J7
Shellmound St. D2
Sheridan G7
Sheridan Rd. E8
Sherman K3
Short K8
Sloan I8
Soland Way J5
Sonia E7
Spalding Ave. A4
Spruce H6
St. James H8
St. Paul E8
Stanford Ave. D3
Stanton B3,B4
State B7
Staten H5
Stonewall B7
Stow H5
Strathmoor B8
Stuart St. B4,B6
Summit F4
Sunny Side F6
Sunnyhills Rd. H6,H7
Sunnyslope G6
Sunset Ave. J7
Suter St. J8
Sycamore St. F3
Sylvan Ave. G6
Taft D6
Telegraph Ave. B5,G3
Terrace St. E5
Texas St. J8
The Plaza Dr. C7
The Uplands C7
Thomas D6
Tiffin D6
Townsend H8
Trestle Glen Rd. H6,H7
Tunnel State Rd. C7
Tyler B4
Underhills H7
Union G1
Union St. G2
Uplands C7
Valdez St. G4
Vallejo St. C3
Valley St. B3,G4
Valley Vista G5
Van Buren Ave. G5
Vermont St. G6
Vernon G5
Vicente C8
View St. E5
Viola K8
Viona H6
Virmar Ave. D6
Vista F7,I8
Wakefield J6
Waldo F7
Waldo F7
Walker G6
Walla Vista G6
Wallace E2
Wallace St. B3,I6
Ward J8
Ward St. B4
Warfield Ave. G6
Warring Ave. B6
Warwick G5
Washington St. H3
Waterhouse I8
Watts E3
Waverly St. G4
Wayne I5
Webster Ave. E5
Webster St. C5,F4,I3,J2
Webster St. Tube I2
Wellington I7
Wesley D6
Wesley Ave. H5
West Grand Ave. F2
West MacArthur Blvd. F4
West St. A3,E4,F3
Westminster D7
Westview C8
Whittle Ave. I8
Wickson G5
Wilbur I8
Wildwood Ave. G7
Wildwood Gardens G7
Wildwood Palm Ave. G6
Williams G3
Willow St. F2
Wilson J8
Wilson Ave. G6
Wood F8,K2
Wood St. F1
Woodland Way G7
Woodruff I7
Woolsey St. C5
Wyngarde H8
Yerba Buens E2
York Dr. F6
York St. G6
Yosemite F5
1st I4
2nd Ave. I4
2nd St. H2
3rd Ave. I4
3rd St. H1
4th A2
4th Ave. I4
4th St. H2
5th A2
5th Ave. I4
6th A2
6th Ave. I4
6th St. H2
7th A2
7th Ave. I4
7th St. G1,H2,I4
7th St.,E. I4
8th A3,K2
8th Ave. I5
8th St. G1,H2
8th St.,E. I4
9th A3,K2
9th Ave. I5
9th St. G1,H2
10th A3
10th Ave. I5
10th St. G1,G2,H2
10th St.,E. I4
11th Ave. J5
11th St. F1,H2
11th St.,E. I4
12th Ave. J5
12th St. F1,G2
12th St.,E. I4,J5
13th Ave. J5
13th St. F1,G3
14th Ave. I7,J5
14th St. F1,G3
14th St.,E. J5
15th Ave. J5
15th St. F1,G3
15th St.,E. J5
16th Ave. J5
16th St. F1,G3
17th Ave. J5
17th St. F1,G3
17th St.,E. I5,J6,K6
18th Ave. J5
18th St. F2,G3
18th St.,E. I5,J6
19th Ave. J6
19th St. F2,G3
19th St.,E. I5
20th Ave. J5
20th St. F2,G3
20th St.,E. I5
21st Ave. J5
21st St.,E. I5
22nd Ave. J5
22nd St. G3
22nd St.,E. J6
23rd Ave. K6
23rd St. G3
23rd St.,E. J6,K7
24th Ave. K6
24th St. F2,G3
24th St.,E. J6
25th G4
25th Ave. J7,K6
25th St. F3
25th St.,E. J6
26th G4
26th Ave. K6
26th St. F2,F3
26th St.,E. J6
27th G4
27th Ave. K6
27th St. F3
27th St.,E. I6
28th St. F2,F3,G4
28th St.,E. J7
29th St. F3
29th,E. J7
30th St. F3
30th St.,E. I7
31st St. F3
31st St.,E. I6
32nd F3,F4
32nd St. E2
32nd St.,E. I6
33rd Ave. K7
33rd St. F3
33rd St.,E. I6
34th Ave. K7
34th St. E3
34th St.,E. I6
35th Ave. K8
35th St. E3
36th Ave. K7
37th E3,F4
38th St.,E. I7
39th E3
40th E3
40th St. E4
41st E3
41st St. E4,E5
42nd E3,E5
43rd E3,E5
43rd St. D3
44th St. E3,E5
45th D3
45th St. D3,E5
46th D4,E4
47th D4,E4
47th St. D3
48th E5
49th St. E5
50th St. E5
51st St. E5
52nd St. D4
53rd St. D3,D4
54th St. D3,D4
55th St. D4
56th St. D3,D4
57th St. D4,D5
58th St. D4,D5
59th St. C3,D3,D4,D5
60th St. C3,C4,C5
61st St. C2,C4,C5
62nd C5
62nd St. C3
63rd C3
63rd St. C2,C5
64th St. C2
65th St. C2,C4,C5
66th St. C2,C5
67th St. C2

OKLAHOMA CITY

Agnew Ave. H3,K3
Agnew Pl. J3
Allen E3
Aurora A3
Avenida J4
Barnes Ave. A3,C3,G3,K3
Barnes Pl. J3
Beals Pl. G5
Beatrice Ave. F2
Billen Ave. B3
Binkley I3
Birch F4
Blackwelder Ave. A5,E4,I4,K5
Brauer Ave. B5,C5
Broadway F7,H7,J7
Broadway Pl. C7
Broadway,E. I7
Broadway,W. I7
Brookline Ave. B1,I1,J2,K1
Byers Ave. I8
California Ave. E6
Carey Pl. B4
Cedar Ave. F1
Central Ave. D8
Chestnut Dr. K4
Classen Blvd. D6
Classen Dr. C6
Clegern I5
College B5
Compress E7
Concord Dr. D6
Couch Dr. D6
Cross Ave. B3
Dale Ave. C7
Daugherty G4
Dewey Ave. B6,F6,K6
Doffing E2
Douglas Blvd. K5
Douglas Ave. B5,C5,I5
Douglas Ave.,N. D5
Drexel Ave. J1,K1
Drexel Blvd. B1
Durland D8
Ellison Ave. B5,C5,E5,J5
Exchange St. F1
Flordia Ave. A4
Flynn Ave. B3
Francis Ave. B6,D6,K6
Gatewood Ave. B4
Grand Blvd. J3
Gurnsey Ave. B6
Harrison Ave. D8
Harvey Ave. B7,F7,G7,J7
Heyman G4
Hudson Ave. B7,F7,J7
Independence Ave. C1,J1
Indiana Ave. A4,E4,F4,G4,I4
James St. J4
Johnson Dr. J4,K4
Kentucky Ave. A4,E4,I4
Kinkaid Dr. J4
Klein Ave. C5,D5,E5,J5,K5
Lafayette Dr. K4
Land Ave. C1,K1
Lee Ave. B6,F6,J6
Lincoln Blvd. B8
Linden F4
Lindley E2
Linn Ave. A2,C2,E2,I2
Linwood Blvd. D5
Madison St. A8
Magdelena K4
Main St. E6
May Ave. D2,J2
McKinley Ave. C5,E5,J5,K5
McRae F2
Mehl H5
Melrose Ln. K7
Miller Ave. C2,E2,J2
Miller Blvd. C2
Miltary Ave. A5
Morton Ave. J2
Murray Dr. K1,K2
Noble E2
North Pl. B1,B2
Oak St. G1
Oklahoma Ave. A8,C7,D8,J8
Olie Ave. B6,J6,K6
Park Dr. I3
Park Pl. C7
Park St. C1
Parkview Ave. I1
Pennsylvania Ave. C4,K4
Pettee AVe. G4
Pioneer St. A1
Pott F2
R.S. Kerr Ave. D6
Rancho Dr. J4,K4
Reding Dr. J4
Reno Ave. E1,E4,E8
Reno Ave.,E. E8
Robinson Ave. B7,F7,J7
Ross Ave. A2,C2,E2,K2
Rotary D. G4
Sage Ave. K7
Santa Fe Ave. A7,J7,K7
Schuneman St. G1,G2
Shartel Ct. C1
Sheridan Ave. E6
Sherwood Ave. J2
Shields Blvd. H8,K8
South Dr. K4
Stanford H4
Stiles Ave. A8,D8,I8
Sullivan St. F1,F2
Suzberger G4
Texoma Dr. K2
Thomas Pl. B1
Tuttle E3
Villa Ave. A3,B3,E3,K3
Virginia Ave. B4,D4,I4
Walker Ave. B6,F6,K6
Walnut Ave. A8,D8,E8,H8
Watson Ave. J2
Western Ave. B5,E5,K5
Westwood Ave. H4
Williams Dr. K4
Woodward C1
Woodward Ave. H1,J1
Youngs Ave. G3,K3
Youngs Blvd. A3,C3
Youngs Pl. J3
1st St. D2,D4,D8
1st St.,NW. E3
2nd St. D2,D4,D6,E2,E6
3rd St. D3,D4,D6,E2,E6
4th St. D4,D6
5th St. D4,D6
6th St. D4,D6
7th St. C4,C6
8th St. C4,C6,F3
9th St. C4,C6,F3,F6
10th St. C1,C6,F3,F7,F8
11th St. C1,C6,F3,F5,F7,F8
12th St. C1,C2,C6,F3,F5,F7
13th St. B1,C2,C6,G3,G5,G7
14th Pl. G5
14th St. B1,B2,B6,G3,G5,G7
15th St. B1,B2,B6,G1,G4,G7,G8
16th St. B1,B4,B6,G1,G4,G8
17th St. B1,B4,B6,G1,G4,G8
18th St. B1,B4,B6,G1,G4,G8
19th St. B1,B4,B6,G1,G4,G8
20th St. B1,B4,B6,G1,G8,H4
21st St. A1,A4,A6,H1,H4,H7
22nd St. A1,A4,A6,H1,H3,H7
23rd St. A1,A5,H1,H2,H6
24th St. A1,A5,A8,H1,H2,H6
25th St. A1,A5,A8,H1,H6
26th St. A1,A5,A6,A7,A8,H1,H6
27th St. A1,A5,A6,A7,H1,H6
28th St. I1,I6
29th St. I1,I6
30th St. I2,I7
31st St. I2,I7
32nd St. I2,I7
33rd St. I2,I7
34th St. I2,I7
35th St. I2,I7
36th St. J7
37th St. J1,J4,J8
38th St. J1,J2,J8
39th Pl. J1
39th St. J2,J8
40th St. J1,J3,J6,J8
41st St. J1,J3,J6,J8
42nd St. J1,J2,J6,J8
43rd St. J1,J3,J6,J8
44th St. K3,K7
45th St. K1,K5,K8
46th Pl. K2
46th St. K1,K5,K8
46th Terr. K2
47th St. K1,K3,K5,K8
48th St. K1,K2,K3,K5,K8
49th Pl. K7
49th St. K1,K2,K3,K5,K8
50th St. K2,K3,K5,K8

Scale of Miles

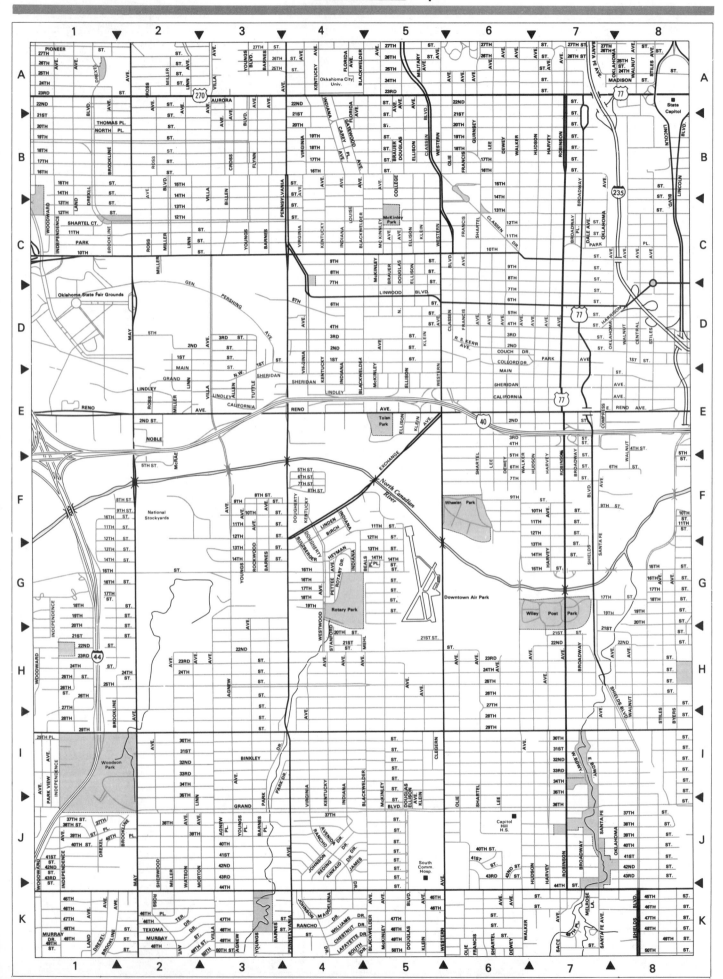

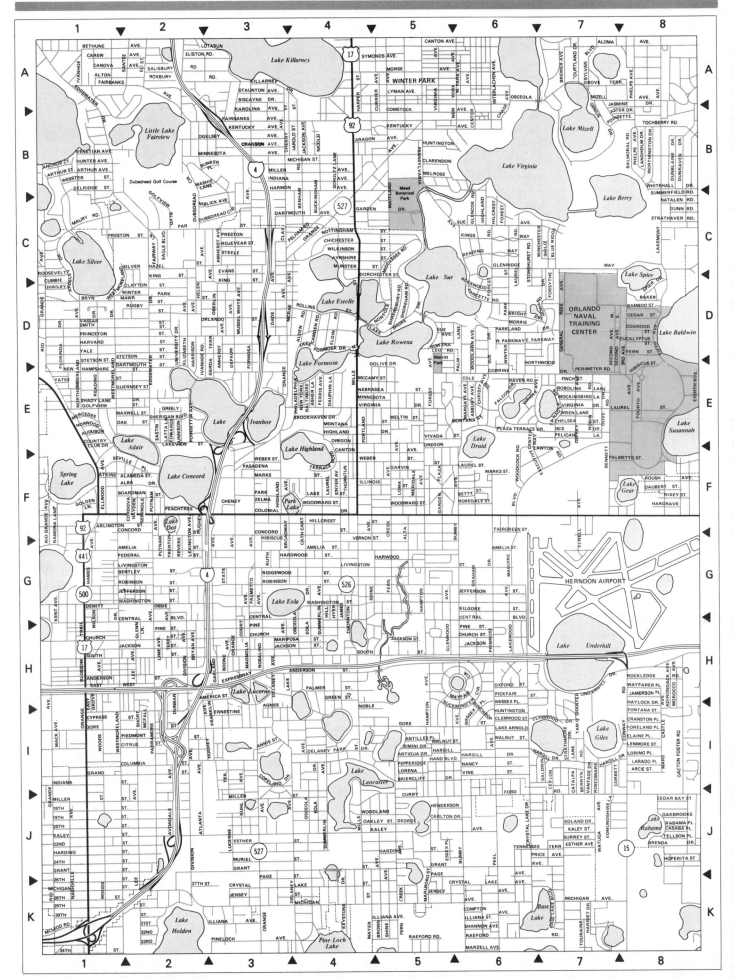

ORLANDO

Adanson Ave........A-1
Adirondack Ave.....H-8
Agnes..............H-3
Alameda St.........F-2
Alba Dr............F-2
Alden Rd...........D-4
Alta Loma Ave......F-5
Alton..............A-1
Amelia St....G-1,G-4,G-6
America St.........H-3
Amherst Ave....C-3,D-3
Anchor Ct..........B-1
Anderson St.....H-1,H-4
Annie St...........I-3
Antigua Dr.........I-5
Antilles Pl........I-5
Aragon Ave.........B-4
Ardsley Dr.........C-1
Arlington St.......F-1
Arthur Ave.........B-1
Arthur St..........B-1
Asbury Ave.........E-6
Asher Ln...........E-4
Aster Dr...........A-7
Atkins.............F-1
Atlanta Ave........J-2
Audobon............E-1
Avondale Ave.......J-2
Ayrshire St........C-4
Baker..............D-8
Baldwin............I-7
Balmoral Rd........B-8
Baltimore..........E-4
Bass Lake Blvd.....K-7
Benham Rd..........C-4
Bennett Rd.........F-7
Bentley St.........G-2
Berwyn Rd..........I-7
Bethune Ave........A-1
Betty St...........F-6
Bimini Dr..........I-5
Biscayne Dr........A-3
Blossom Trail......H-1
Blueridge..........C-7
Boardman St........F-2
Bobolink Lane......E-7
Boone Ave..........H-3
Brenda Dr..........J-8
Brewer Ave.........A-7
Briarcliff Dr......I-5
Broadway Ave.......F-3
Brookhaven Dr......E-4
Brown Ave..........K-5
Bryan Ave..........H-2
Bryn Mawr St.......D-1
Buckingham.........C-4
Buckminster Cir....H-5
Bumby Ave.....F-6,J-6
Bunker Pl..........B-3
Camden Rd..........D-4
Canova Ave.........A-1
Canton Ave.........E-4
Carew Ave..........A-1
Carlton Dr.........J-5
Casaba Pl..........J-8
Catalpa Lane.......I-7
Cathcart...........F-4
Cedar Bay St.......J-8
Cedar St...........D-8
Center Ave.........B-6
Central Blvd.G-2,G-3,G-6
Ceylon.............I-7
Chanson Ave........B-3
Chase Ave..........B-6
Chelsea............E-7
Cheny..............F-3
Cherry St..........B-3
Chichester St......C-4
Christy Ave........E-6
Church St...H-1,H-3,H-6
Citrus St..........I-2
Clarendon..........B-5
Clay...............C-3
Clayton St.........D-2
Clemwood Dr........I-7
Clemwood St........I-6
Cole Rd............E-6
Colonial...........F-3
Columbia St........I-2
Compton............K-6
Comstock Ave.......A-5
Concord.......F-2,F-3
Conway Rd..........I-8
Copeland Dr........I-3
Corbett............I-7
Cordova............F-2
Corrine Dr.........E-6
Country Club Dr....E-1
Court..............H-3
Cranston Pl........I-8
Crystal Lake St...K-3,K-6
Cumbie.............C-1
Currier Ave........A-5
Curry..............J-5
Cypress............I-1
Dade Ave...........D-3
Dartmouth Ave......C-4
Dartmouth St.......D-2
Daubert St.........F-8
Dauphin Ln.........E-4
Delaney Ave.....H-3,K-3
Delaney Park Dr....I-4
Delridge St........B-1
De Pauw Ave........D-3
Dewitt.............G-1
Division Ave.......J-2
Dogwood St.........D-8
Dolive Dr..........D-5
Dorchester St....C-4,C-5
Dove Dr............E-7
Dubsdread Cir......C-3
Dunbar.............H-2
Dunblaine Dr.......B-8
Dunraven Dr........B-8
East...............H-1
Easy Grove.........H-1
Edgewater..........E-2
Edgewater Dr.......A-1
Edland Dr..........J-7
Edmundshire Ln.....J-7
Edwards............E-2
Eighth Ave.........E-8
Elaine Pl..........I-8
Elgin Rd...........D-4
Elizabeth Ave......D-2
Ellwood Ave........F-1
Eola Dr............H-4
E. Parkway.........D-7
Ernestine..........I-3
Essex Pl...........J-5
Esther St..........J-3
Eucalyptus St......D-8
Evans St...........C-3
Executive Center Way..........F-7
Fairbanks Ave......B-3
Fairgreen St.......F-6
Falcon Dr..........E-6
Fawcette Rd........D-6
Federal St.........G-2
Fern St............D-8
Fern Creek Ave. F-5,G-5
Ferris Ave.........E-4
Fifth Ave..........D-8
Florinda Dr........D-1
Fontana St.........I-8
Ford Rd............J-6
Foreland Pl........I-8
Forest Ave.........E-5
Forest Rd.......C-6,D-6
Formosa St.........D-3
Forsythe...........D-7
Fourth Ave.........E-8
Franklin...........I-3
Garden Dr..........C-4
Garden Plaza.......F-5
Garland............H-3
Garvin St..........F-5
General Reed Ave...D-7
Genius Dr..........B-7
George Ave.........J-5
Gerda Terr.........D-3
Glencoe Rd.........C-6
Glenn Ln...........H-2
Glenridge Way......C-6
Glenwood Ave.......H-5
Golden Lane........F-1
Golfview Blvd......B-2
Golfview St........E-1
Gore...............I-1
Gore St............I-5
Graham.............G-6
Grand St...........I-1
Grant Ave.......J-3,J-5
Grant St........J-1,J-3
Green St...........H-4
Grove Terr.........A-7
Guernsey St........E-2
Gunn Rd............C-8
Hames Ave..........G-1
Hampton Ave....G-5,I-5
Hand Blvd..........I-5
Harding St......J-1,J-5
Hardwood St....G-3,G-5
Hargill............I-5
Hargill Dr.........I-6
Hargrave...........F-8
Harmon Ave.........B-3
Harper St..........A-4
Harriet Dr.........K-7
Harrison Ave.......D-2
Harvard St.........D-1
Hayden.............F-2
Haylock Dr.........H-8
Hazel St...........C-2
Helen Ave..........D-2
Henderson..........J-5
Hibiscus...........F-3
Hibiscus St........E-8
Highland.......C-6,E-4,F-3
Hill...............G-4
Hillcrest..........C-6
Hillcrest St.......F-4
Hoperita St........J-8
Howard Dr..........D-7
Hughey.............I-3
Hunter Ave.........B-1
Huntington......B-5,I-6
Hyer...............G-4
Ibis Dr............E-7
Illiana Ave.....K-3,K-5
Illiana St.........K-6
Illinois...........F-4
Indiana Ave........B-3
Indiana St.........I-1
Ivanhoe............A-1
Ivanhoe Rd.........D-2
Jackson St..H-2,H-3,H-5
James..............G-4
Jasmine Dr.........A-8
Jefferson St. G-1,G-2,G-6
Jersey Ave......K-3,K-5
Kaley Ave..........J-5
Kaley St...........J-1
Karolina Ave.......A-3
Kent Ave...........G-1
Kentucky Ave....B-3,B-5
Keystone Dr........K-4
Kilgore St.........G-6
Killarney Dr.......A-3
King St.........C-2,C-3
Kings Way..........C-6
Kuhl Ave...........J-3
Lake Ave...........H-3
Lake St.........F-4,K-4
Lake Arnold........I-6
Lake Formosa Dr. N. D-4
Lakefront Ave......C-8
Lake Shore Dr......D-5
Lakeview St........E-2
Lakewood Ave.......H-6
Langholm Dr........B-8
Lattala............E-2
Laurel.............F-4
Laurel Rd.......C-6,D-6
Laurel St.......E-7,F-6
Lawson Dr..........I-7
Lawton.............E-7
Lawton Rd..........E-7
Lee Ave.........H-2,K-2
Lenmore St.........I-8
Leu Rd.............D-5
Lexington Ave......G-2
Lime Ave...........H-2
Livingston.........G-4
Livingston St. G-2,G-4
Lorena.............I-5
Loring Pl..........I-8
Lucerne Ter........J-3
Mack Ave...........I-1
Magnolia...........H-3
Maguire Blvd.......G-6
Maitland Ave.......C-5
Margate Ave........E-6
Mariposa St........H-3
Marks St........F-3,F-6
Marlboro St........K-5
Mars Castle Rd.....I-8
Marzell Ave.....A-7,K-6
Mashie Lane........B-3
Maxwell St.........E-1
Mayer St...........K-4
McCamy St..........E-4
McFall.............I-2
McRae Ave.......D-3,D-4
Melrose............B-5
Mercedes...........E-1
Meridale Ave.......F-5
Merritt Park.......D-5
Michigan...........K-4
Michigan Ave.......K-7
Miller Ave.........B-3
Miller St.......J-1,J-3
Mills..............E-4
Mills St...........J-4
Minnesota..........E-4
Minnesota Ave......B-3
Mockingbird Ln.....E-7
Montana St......E-4,E-6
Morocco Ave........H-8
Morris Dr..........D-6
Morse Ave..........A-5
Munster St.........C-4
Muriel St..........J-3
Mussel White Ave...D-3
Nancy St...........I-6
Nashville Ave......K-1
Natalen Rd.........C-8
Nebraska...........E-4
New Hampshire St. E-1
New York...........E-4
New York AVe.......A-6
Niblick Ave........C-3
Noble..............H-4
Norfolk............D-5
Northumberland.....E-1
Northwood..........D-6
Norwood............E-1
Nottingham St......C-4
Oak St.............E-2
Oakbrook...........J-8
Oakley St..........J-4
Oberlin Ave........D-3
Ogelsby Ave........B-3
Orange.......C-4,H-3,I-1
Orange Ave.........E-3
Oregon..........E-4,E-5
Oriole Ave.........E-6
Orlando St.........D-3
Osceola.........A-6,H-4
Osceola Ave........J-4
Osceola Dr.........J-4
Osprey Ave.........E-7
Ossie..............G-2
Oxford St..........H-6
Page Ave........J-3,J-5
Palm Ln............D-6
Palmer St..........H-4
Palmetto St.....F-7,G-3
Par................C-2
Park...............F-3
Parkland Dr........D-6
Parramore..........I-2
Pasadena...........F-3
Peachtree..........F-2
Peel Ave...........J-6
Pelican La.........E-7
Pennsylvania.......B-5
Pepperidge.........I-5
Perimeter Rd.......E-7
Phelps Ave......A-8,B-8
Philadelphia.......E-4
Pickfair St........H-6
Piedmont St........I-2
Pine St.....H-2,H-3,H-6
Pineloch Ave.......K-3
Plaza Terrace Dr...E-6
Poinsette..........B-7
Poinsettia Ave.....E-2
Portland...........E-4
Preston.........C-1,C-3
Price Ave..........J-6
Primrose Dr........H-6
Princeton St.......D-1
Putnam..........F-2,G-2
Quailey............D-1
Rabama Pl..........J-8
Raeford Rd......K-5,K-6
Ramona Lane........F-1
Raven Rd...........E-6
Reading............E-1
Reading Way........C-6
Revere.............G-2
Ridgewood St.......G-3
Rio Grande Ave. D-1,F-1,K-1
Rixey St...........F-8
Robin Rd...........E-7
Robinson St.....G-1,G-3
Rockledge Rd.......H-8
Rockwood...........D-6
Roosevelt..........C-1
Rosalind...........H-3
Roscomare..........I-7
Rosedale St........F-6
Rosevear St........C-3
Roush Ave..........F-8
Rowena Rd..........D-5
Rugby St...........D-2
Ruth...............G-3
Schultz Lane.......B-4
Second Ave. E......D-7
Second Ave. W......D-7
Seminole...........F-2
Seville Pl.........F-1
Shady Lane Dr......E-1
Shannon Ave........K-6
Sheridan Blvd......E-2
Shilo..............C-7
Shine Ave.......G-4,K-5
Shoreham Rd........D-5
Short..............I-2
Shrewsbury Rd......D-5
Silver.............C-2
Smith St...........D-1
South St........H-1,H-4
Spier Dr...........D-8
Staunton Ave.......A-3
Steele.............C-3
Stetson St......D-1,D-2
Strathaver Rd......C-8
Strathmore Dr......I-7
Summerfield Rd.....C-8
Sue Ave.........C-6,D-5
Sue Dr.............D-6
Summerlin Ave..H-4,J-4
Surrey St..........J-7
Tam O'Shanter......I-7
Tanager Dr.........E-7
Tellson Pl.........J-8
Tennessee Terr.....J-6
Terrace Blvd.......F-4
Thornton...........H-4
Touraine...........K-7
Trenton............G-2
Underhill Dr.......H-7
Vantage Dr.........I-7
University Dr......D-2
Vassar St..........D-1
Venetian Ave.......B-1
Vine St............I-6
Virginia...........E-4
Virginia Ave.......A-5
Virginia Dr........E-7
Vision Ave.........H-2
Vivada St..........E-5
Walnut St.......I-5,I-6
Washington St......G-2
Wayfarer Pl........H-8
Weber St........F-3,F-4
Webster St.........B-1
Weltin St..........E-5
Wessex Pl.......H-6,I-6
West...............H-2
W. Park Ave........A-6
W. Parkway.........D-6
Westmoreland Dr. E-1,I-1
Whitehall Dr.......B-8
Wilkinson St.......C-4
Wilson Ave.........G-1
Winchester.........C-7
Winter Park St. D-2,D-6
Winthrop St........I-6
Woodcock Rd........F-6
Woodland...........J-4
Woodlawn Ave.......D-6
Woods..............I-1
Woods St...........K-1
Woodward St.....F-4,F-5
Worthington Dr.....B-8
Wren Lane..........E-7
Wright Ave.........D-6
Yale St............D-1
Yates St...........E-1
Zelma..............F-3
18th St............J-1
19th St............J-1
20th St............J-1
22nd St............J-1
24th St............J-1
26th St............J-1
27th St.........K-1,K-2
28th...............K-1
29th St............K-1
30th St............K-1
31st...............K-2
32nd...............K-2
33rd...............K-2

POINTS OF INTEREST

Herndon Airport....G-7
Mead Botanical Park..........B-5
Merritt Park.......D-5
Orlando Naval Training Center.....D-7

PHILADELPHIA

Abigail............A-8
Addison............I-6
Alder..............A-5
Allen..............D-8
Alter..............J-1
Alter St...........J-2
Amber..............A-8
American........F-7,I-7
Annin..............J-1
Annin St........J-1,J-3
Appletree..........G-3 ....G-5,G-6
Arch...............G-1
Arch St.....G-2,G-3,G-6
Arizona............A-8
Arlington..........A-3
Aspen St...........E-2
Bailey St.......C-1,K-1
Bainbridge St......I-2
Bambrey.........D-2,K-2
Bancroft........A-4,I-4
Baring.............F-1
Beach..............E-8
Belgrade...........C-8
Benjamin Franklin Bridge..........F-7
Benjamin Franklin Parkway..........G-3
Berks...........A-3,A-6
Beulah.............K-6
Bodine.............F-7
Bodine St..........A-7
Bolton.............C-2
Boston.............A-8
Bouvier St......A-3,C-4 ....J-3,K-3
Bowers.............D-4
Brandywine St......E-2
Bread..............G-7
Broad St.....C-4,G-4,I-4
Brown..............D-1
Brown St...........D-4
Bucknell........B-2,E-2
Burns..............G-4
Butler..........H-5,I-5
Buttonwood St...F-3,F-4
Cabot St...........C-3
Cadwallader........C-7
Callowhill St......F-3
Camac...........D-5,K-5
Camac St...........H-5
Cambridge.......D-5,D-7
Cambridge St.......D-3
Cameron............D-3
Canal St...........E-8
Capitol............K-3
Capitol St.........E-3
Carlisle........I-4,K-4
Carlisle St.....A-4,C-4
Carlton............F-3
Carlton St.........F-5
Carpenter St.......J-3
Catharine.......I-1,I-2
Catharine St.......I-7
Chadwick........A-4,I-4
Chancellor..H-2,H-3,H-7
Chancellor St. H-3,H-5
Chang..............D-1
Chelton............F-7
Cherry.............G-1
Cherry St.......G-3,G-6
Chestnut St........H-3
Christian St...J-1,J-3,J-5
Church St..........G-7
Clarion............K-5
Clarion St.........G-5
Clay...............E-3
Clay St............E-5
Cleveland St....J-3,K-3
Clifton......F-5,G-5,I-5
Clinton............H-5
Clover.............G-5
Clymer.............I-3
Colona.............A-5
Colorado...........A-4
Colorado St.....J-4,K-4
Columbia....B-1,B-6,C-8
Commerce St....G-3,G-5
Cooper.............D-8
Coral..............A-8
Corinthian Ave.....E-3
Crease.............C-8
Croskey......B-2,G-2,I-2
Cross...........K-2,K-5
Cuthbert........G-4,G-7
Cuthbert St........G-3
Cypress St......H-2,H-3 ....H-4,H-6
Dakota.............A-8
Darien..........I-6,J-6
Dauphin.........A-3,A-8
Day St.............C-8
DeGray..........G-4,G-5
Delancey St........H-2 ....H-3,H-7
Delaware Ave....G-8,I-8
Diamond.........A-3,A-6
Dickinson.......K-1,K-5
Dondill Pl.........C-5
Dorrance St.....J-3,K-3
Dover.......A-1,C-1,K-1
Dreer..............A-8
Earl...............C-8
Edgley.............A-2
Edgley St..........A-2
Elfreth's Al.......G-7
Ellsworth..........J-1
Ellsworth St.......J-2
Emerald............A-8
Etting.............K-1
Eyre...............B-1
Fairhill.....A-6,I-6,K-6
Fairmount Ave...E-2,E-5
Fawn...............A-5
Federal St.........J-2
Filbert............G-7
Filbert St.........G-5
Fitzwater St....I-2,I-7
Fletcher........A-1,A-8
Flora..............D-4
Fountain...........A-4
Francis............D-4
Frankford Ave......C-8
Franklin........E-6,K-6
French..........A-1,A-4
Front..............C-8
Front St...........H-7
Fulton St..........I-7
Garnet.............K-3
Gaskill............I-7
George.............D-3
George St..........D-7
Germantown Ave.....B-6
Gerritt......K-1,K-3,K-6
Girard Ave......D-1,D-6
Glenwood........A-2,B-1
Green St........E-3,E-7
Greenwich..........K-2 ....K-5,K-7
Hamilton...........F-1
Hamilton St.....F-3,F-4
Hancock.........B-7,C-7 ....F-7,I-7
Harlan..........C-2,C-3
Harper.............D-5
Harper St..........D-3
Hicks...........F-4,K-4
Hicks St...........I-4
Hollywood..........C-1
Hope...............C-8
Howard..........B-8,K-7
Hutchinson St......A-5 ....D-5,G-5,I-5
Ingersoll.......C-2,C-3
Ingram St..........J-1
Ionic...........H-2,H-6
Iseminger.......A-5,K-5
Jefferson.......C-1,C-6
Jessup.............I-5
John F. Kennedy Blvd...........G-1,G-3
Judson.............B-2
Judson St..........E-2
Juniper.........I-4,K-4
Kater St........I-3,I-4
Kenilworth.........I-4
Kershaw............C-3
Kimball St......J-2,J-5
Lambert.........B-3,K-3
Latimer St......H-2,H-4
Latona..........J-1,J-3
Laurel.............D-7
Lawrence........A-7,C-7 ....E-7,F-7,H-7
League St.......J-3,J-6
Lee................D-8
Leithgow St........A-7 ....D-7,H-7,I-7
Lemon St...........E-5
Leopard............D-8
Letitia............G-7
Locust St..........H-3
Lombard St......I-2,I-7
Ludlow St.......G-3,G-5
Manning St.........H-2 ....H-3,H-4
Manton St.......J-1,J-3
Market St.......G-3,G-6
Marlborough........C-8
Marshall........C-6,J-6
Marston.....A-1,C-1,K-1
Martha.............A-8
Mascher.........C-7,G-7
Master..........C-2,C-6
Melon St...........E-4
Melvale............D-8
Meredith St........E-2
Milford.........I-6,J-6
Mole.........F-4,I-4,K-4
Monroe.............I-7
Montgomery......B-1,B-6
Montrose...........J-6
Montrose St........J-3
Moravian........H-3,H-5
Morse..............B-6
Mott...............J-4
Mt. Vernon.........E-2
Moyamensing Ave. J-7,K-7
Myrtle.............D-5
Myrtlewood.........C-1
Nassau.............C-2
Natrona............F-1
Naudian St.........I-2
Nectarine.......E-3,F-4
Nevada.............A-5
New St.............F-7
Newkirk.........A-1,C-1
Newson.............B-6
Nicholas...........B-2
Noble St...........F-4
Norris.......B-3,B-6,B-8
North...........E-3,E-5
N. College Ave.....D-2
Oakford............J-1
Ogden..............D-5
Ogden St...........D-3
Olive St...........E-2
Opal...............K-3
Opal St............I-3
Orianna.........A-7,D-7 ....F-7,G-7
Orkney.............A-6
Oxford.......C-1,C-6,C-8
Page............A-2,A-4
Palmer.............B-8
Palsthrop..........B-7
Panama.......H-2,H-3,H-5
Park...............C-4
Parrish.........D-1,D-5
Passyunk Ave.......K-5
Pearl...........F-1,F-3
Pearl St...........F-5
Peltz..............J-1
Pemberton St....I-2,I-7
Penn St............E-8
Pennock............D-1
Percy...........D-5,I-5
Perkiomen..........D-3
Perot..............E-2
Perth...........H-6,I-6
Philip..........C-7,H-7
Pine St............I-2
Point Breeze Ave. K-2,K-3
Pollard............D-7
Poplar St.......D-2,D-6
Potts..............E-4
Powelton Ave.......F-1
Quarry St.......G-5,G-7
Queen St...........J-7
Quince St..........H-5
Race St.........G-3,G-7
Ramp A.............F-2
Ramp B.............F-3
Ramp C.............F-2
Ramp D.............F-2
Randolph........F-6,I-6
Ranstead St........G-2 ....G-3,G-6
Redner.............C-2
Reed............K-1,K-6
Reese...........A-6,H-6 ....I-6,K-6
Reno...............D-4
Richmond...........D-8
Ridge Ave.......B-2,F-5
Ringgold........B-2,K-2
Ringgold St........E-2
Rodman St..........I-2 ....I-3,I-5
Rosewood........H-4,I-4
St. James St.......H-6
Sansom St..........H-3
Schell.......G-6,H-6,I-6
Schuylkill Ave.....I-1
Schuylkill Expwy. H-1,I-1
Sears..............K-1
Sedgley............B-1
Seybert.........C-2,C-3
Shackamaxon........C-8
Sharswood.......C-2,C-3
Shirley............E-3
Smedley.........H-4,I-4
South St...........I-2
S. College Ave.....D-2
Spring..........F-4,F-5
Spring Green St. E-4,E-5,F-1
Spruce St.......H-2,H-7
Stamper............I-7
Starr Garden.......I-6
Stewart............C-2
Stiles St..........D-3
Stilman............K-2
Stockbeck..........H-3
Strawberry......G-7,H-7
Summer..........F-1,F-5
Summer St..........F-4
SusquehannaA-3,A-6,A-8
Swain..............E-2
Sydenham St........A-4 ....C-4,H-4
Taney St.....E-1,I-2,K-1
Tasker..........K-2,K-5
Taylor St....B-2,E-2,K-2
Thompson........C-2,C-8
Titan..............K-1
Titan St...........K-3
Tulip..............B-8
Turner.............C-2
Uber St............B-3
Van Horn...........D-7
Van Pelt........G-3,I-3
Van Pelt St........H-3
Vine St.........F-2,F-4
Walden.............G-3
Wallace............E-6
Wallace St.........E-3
Walnut St.......H-3,H-7
Warnock.........H-5,I-5
Washington Ave..J-1,J-5
Waterloo...........B-7
Watts...........A-4,E-4 ....G-4,I-4,K-4
Waverly St......I-2,I-5
Webster St......I-1,I-3
Westmont...........A-4
Wharton St......K-1,K-6
Wilcox St..........E-3
Wilder..........K-1,K-3 ....K-6,K-7
Wildey..........D-7,D-8
Willington.........C-4
Willow St..........F-6
Winter..........F-1,F-5
Winter St..........F-3
Wood............F-3,F-6
Wood St............F-5
Woodstock.......B-3,K-3
York...............A-8
2nd St..........B-7,I-7
3rd St..........B-7,I-7
4th St..........C-7,I-7
5th St..........C-6,I-6
6th St..........C-6,I-6
7th St..........C-6,I-6
8th St..........C-6,I-6
9th St..........C-6,I-6
10th St.........C-5,I-5
11th St.........C-5,I-5
12th St.........C-5,I-5
13th St.........C-5,I-5
15th St.........B-4,I-4
16th St.........B-4,I-4
17th St.........B-4,I-4
18th St.........B-3,I-3
19th St.........B-3,I-3
20th St.........B-3,I-3
21st St.........B-3,I-3
22nd St.........B-2,I-2
23rd St.........C-2,E-2 ....H-2,J-2
24th St.........C-2,E-2 ....F-2,H-2,J-2
25th St......C-2,I-2,J-2
26th St.........C-1,I-2 ....J-1,K-1
27th St.........A-1,C-1 ....I-2,K-1
28th St......A-1,C-1,K-1
29th............C-1,K-1
30th St.........B-1,C-1 ....H-1,K-1
31st St............H-1
32nd............G-1,H-1
33rd St.........G-1,H-1

POINTS OF INTEREST

Fairmount Park.....E-1
Franklin Field.....H-1
Franklin Square....F-6
Independence Square..........H-6
Independece Square Mall..........G-6
Jefferson Square...J-7
Logan Circle.......F-3
Norris Square......A-7
Passyunk Square....K-5
Rittenhouse Square..........H-3
Vine St. Bridge....F-2
Washington Square..H-6
Wharton Square.....K-2

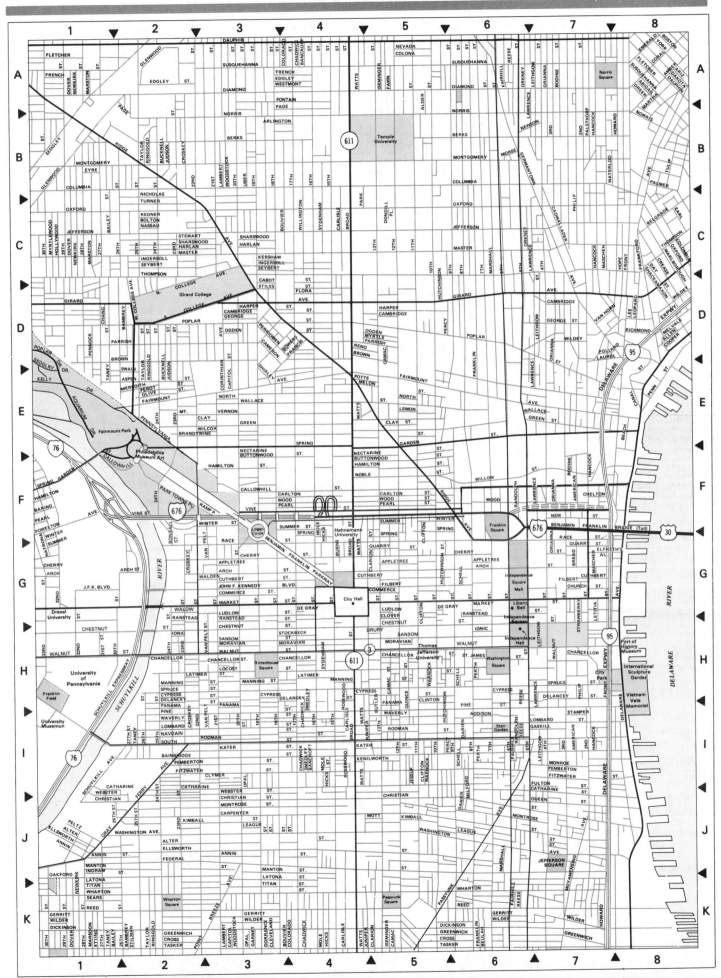

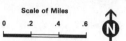

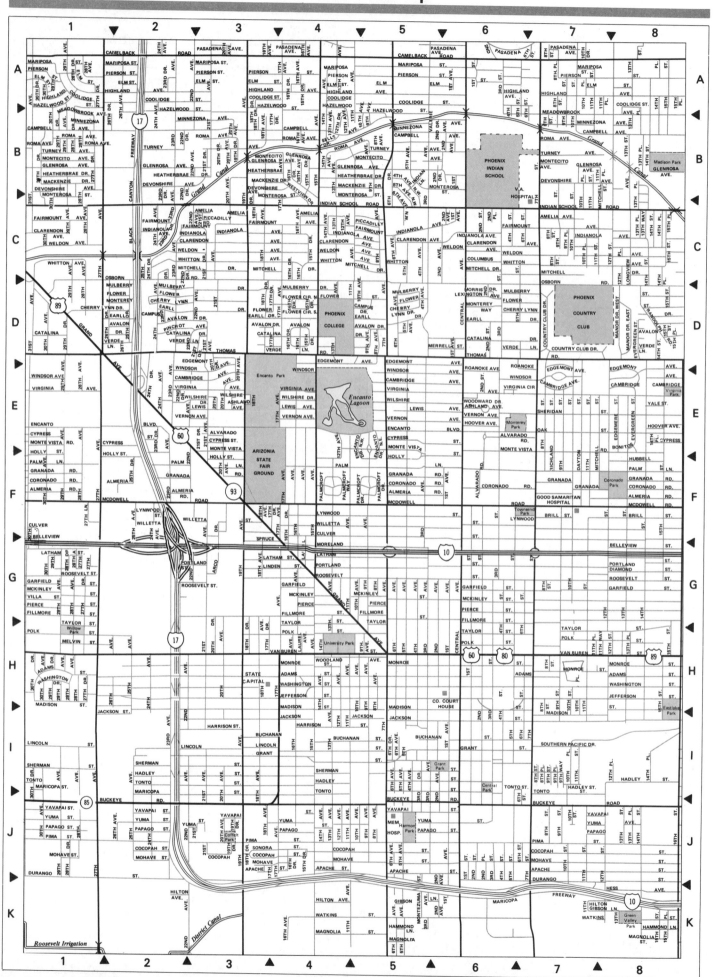

PITTSBURGH

Abstract ... J-5
Adams ... C-1
Addison ... D-7
Admiral ... A-6
Agnew ... K-7,K-8
Ajax ... C-8
Albany ... G-1
Alcor ... D-4
Alice ... I-6
Allegheny ... C-3
Allen ... G-6
Allequippa ... E-7
Alplaus ... J-7
Alries ... K-7
Altaview ... K-4
Alton ... I-3
Alturia ... J-3
Alverado ... I-2
Amabell ... F-3
Amanda ... H-6,J-6
Anderson ... D-5
Anthony ... I-7
Arcena ... D-7
Arch ... C-4,D-4
Arion ... H-4
Arlington ... G-5,H-7
Armandale ... B-3
Arthur ... D-6
Atmore ... B-1
Attica ... E-1
Augusta ... F-2
Avery ... C-5
Badger ... A-6
Bailey ... G-5
Bank ... D-4
Banksville ... H-2,J-1
Bark ... A-4
Barker ... D-5
Barlton ... J-7
Basin ... B-6
Bausman ... I-6
Bayonne ... I-2
Bealty ... J-3
Beaufort ... K-3,K-4
Beaver ... C-1
Becks Run ... J-8
Bedford ... D-6
Beech ... C-3
Beechview ... I-2
Beelen ... E-7
Behan ... C-3
Belasco ... I-2
Belinda ... D-7
Belham ... I-2
Belle Isle ... K-3
Bellingham ... J-1
Belmont ... D-2
Belonda ... G-3
Beltzhoover ... G-5
Bensonia ... K-2
Bentley ... E-7
Berg ... H-8
Berwin ... K-3
Bexley ... I-1
Biatto ... A-6
Bidwell ... C-2
Bigelow ... D-6,E-5
Bigger ... I-4
Biggs ... A-4
Bigham ... F-3
Bingham ... F-6
Birmingham ... J-7
Birtley ... K-3
Bloom ... I-4
Bluff ... F-6
Boggs ... G-4,I-4
Boggston ... H-4
Blvd. of the Alles ... E-5,F-6
Bon Air ... I-5
Bonifay ... I-8
Boustead ... J-2
Bowmore ... J-2
Boyd ... E-6
Boyle ... B-4
Brabec ... B-6
Brackenridge ... D-8
Bradley ... E-2
Brady ... F-8
Brahm ... B-5
Branchport ... B-1
Breed ... G-7
Brenham ... E-7
Brent ... H-8
Brereton ... C-7
Brighton ... B-2,C-3
Brighton Pl. ... B-3
Brightridge ... B-3
Broadway ... J-2,K-2
Brook ... J-6
Brookside ... I-3
Brosville ... G-6
Brownsville ... J-6
Bruner ... J-7
Buchanan ... B-6
Buena Vista ... B-3
Buente ... A-5
Burgess ... A-3
Burham ... G-8
Burrows ... E-7
Butler ... A-8
Cadet ... I-4
Cagwin ... J-2
Cairo ... G-3
Calhoun ... J-6
California ... B-1,B-2
Calle ... J-5
Campfield ... J-5
Candace ... J-2
Canton ... I-2
Caperton ... I-5
Capital ... J-3
Carl ... I-6
Carnahan ... I-1
Carrie ... B-4
Carrington ... B-3
Carson ... F-6
Casement ... A-1
Cassatt ... D-6
Cathedral ... I-7
Catoma ... B-4
Cecl Pl. ... E-4
Cedar ... C-4
Cedarhurst ... H-5
Cedricton ... J-6
Celtic ... K-6
Centre ... D-7,D-8,E-6
Chalfont ... H-5
Chancery ... E-4
Chaplotte ... A-8
Chappel ... I-1
Charles ... A-3,B-3,H-5
Chateau ... C-2
Chauncey ... C-8,D-8
Chautaugua ... B-3
Cherryhill, E. ... K-7
Cherryhill, W. ... K-6
Cherry Way ... E-5
Chester ... A-3
Church ... I-7
Claim ... A-6
Clarance ... F-2
Clark ... E-6
Clayton ... B-3
Cliff ... D-6
Clifferty ... D-3
Climax ... H-5
Clinton ... G-7
Clover ... H-8
Cloverdale ... J-6
Coast ... J-3
Cobden ... H-8
Coffey ... E-5
Cohasset ... F-3
Colerain ... K-6
Colfax ... B-2
Cologne ... H-8
Colorado ... B-1
Columbus ... C-2
Colwell ... E-6
Commonwealth ... E-4
Compton ... I-1
Concordia ... K-7
Conkling ... C-8
Connecticut ... K-1
Conniston ... J-5
Copperfield ... K-6
County ... J-5
Cowan ... G-4
Cowley ... A-6
Craighead ... G-5
Crailo ... K-7
Crane ... H-3
Crawford ... E-6
Creswell ... I-8
Crispen ... A-3
Crosby ... J-2
Crysler ... J-4
Curtin ... H-5
Curtis ... H-4
Cushman ... G-4
Cuthbert ... G-4
Dagmar ... I-3
Daleland ... I-1
Dalemount ... J-1
Damas ... A-6
Danbury ... A-2
Dasher ... D-4
Davenport ... D-7
Dawes ... H-7
Dawn ... I-4
Daytona ... I-6
Dell Ave. ... K-2
Dellrose ... K-6
Delray ... E-4
Denham ... B-4
Devilliers ... D-7
Diamond ... C-4
Dickson ... A-1
Dilworth ... G-3
Dinwiddie ... E-7
Divinity ... B-3
Dobson ... B-8
Dodds ... K-1
Donora ... A-5
Dowling ... K-7
Drum ... B-3
Drycove ... J-5
Duff ... D-8
Dunster ... J-4
Durham ... J-1
East ... G-6
Eathan ... K-3
Edenvale ... B-4
Edgebrook ... K-4
Edgemont ... G-5
Edith ... F-2
Edle ... D-7
Eccles ... H-8
Elba ... D-8
Eldora ... I-5
Eleanor ... H-8
Elkton ... D-1
Ellers ... E-7
Elliott ... E-1
Elmbank ... K-4
Elmira ... A-4
Elmore ... D-7
Elsdon ... A-3
Engstler ... I-8
Enoch ... D-7
Erie ... C-4
Erin ... D-7
Estella ... G-5
Etna ... D-5
Eureka ... G-5
Eutaw ... G-4
Fairacres ... J-3
Fairview ... E-1
Fallowfield ... I-2
Federal ... B-4
Ferncliff ... K-4
Fernhill ... K-4
Fiat ... K-5
Fifth ... E-5,E-6
Fingal ... E-2
First ... E-5
Firth ... B-6
Fisher ... I-8
Fitler ... H-8
Flach ... H-8
Fontella ... C-2
Forbes ... E-5,E-6
Fordyce ... I-5
Foreland ... C-5
Forsythe ... A-1
Fort Duquesne Blvd. ... E-4
Fort Pitt Blvd. ... E-4
Fort Pitt Tunnel ... F-2
Fountain ... B-4
Fourth ... E-5
Francis ... C-8
Franklin ... C-2
Fredell ... J-7
Freeland ... H-5
Freemont ... K-2
Freyburg ... G-6
Frontier ... A-5
Fulton ... C-2,D-2
Galveston ... C-3
Garden ... A-6
Gardner ... B-6
Garrison ... D-5
Gearing ... H-5
General ... D-4
Georgia ... I-6
Gibson ... E-1,E-6
Giffin ... I-6,I-7
Gifford ... A-1
Giller ... J-6
Gist ... E-7
Glade ... K-6
Gladys ... H-2
Glenrose ... A-4
Goebel ... D-2
Goering ... B-5
Goettmann ... B-6
Goldbach ... H-8
Goldstrom ... I-2
Grace ... G-3
Grandview ... F-4
Granite ... C-8
Grant ... E-5
Grape ... I-6
Gray ... G-4
Graymore ... I-2
Green ... D-7
Greenbush ... G-4
Greenside ... I-1
Greenleaf Pl. ... F-2
Greentree ... F-1
Greenleaf ... E-1,E-2
Griffin ... G-4
Grimes ... H-6
Grogan ... I-6
Grove ... D-7
Haberman ... G-5
Hackstown ... G-7
Hallett ... D-8
Hallock ... F-3,G-2
Hallowell ... K-5
Halsey ... B-1
Hampshire ... I-2
Hanover ... G-6
Harbor ... A-6
Harlen ... A-3
Harmony ... K-5
Harpster ... A-6
Hartford ... G-6
Hartranft ... K-4
Harwood ... G-5
Haslage ... B-5
Haug ... A-6
Hays ... I-6
Hazelton ... A-4
Hechkleman ... A-7
Heinz ... C-6
Hemans ... D-7
Hemlock ... B-4
Henderson ... B-4
Henger ... I-8
Herman ... B-6
Herndon ... E-1
Herron ... B-8
Hestor ... G-1
Hetzel ... A-6
Hibbs ... H-3
High ... B-6
Highwood ... A-1
Hodgkiss ... A-1
Holbrook ... A-1
Hollace ... C-8
Holyoke ... A-3
Homer ... B-6
Hooper ... E-6
Hornaday ... K-7
Horner ... E-2
Horton ... C-8
Howard, East ... A-4
Iberia ... G-5
Independence ... F-1
Industry ... H-5
Ingham ... A-1
Institute ... I-5
Irwin ... B-3
Isabella ... D-4
Island ... B-1,B-2
Itan ... B-5
Jacksonia ... C-3
Jacob ... I-7
James ... C-4
Jane ... G-7
Jasper ... H-4
Jefferson ... B-3
Jessie ... J-1
Jonquil ... H-7
Josephine ... G-8
Jucunda ... H-5
Jumonville ... E-7
Juniata ... C-2,C-8
Kambach ... G-5
Kathleen ... G-5
Kenberma ... I-3
Kenwood ... A-3
Kingsboro ... H-5
Kiraley ... J-3
Kirkbridge ... B-2
Kirkpatrick ... D-8
Kirsopp ... I-1
Knapp ... A-1
Knoll ... B-5
Knox ... B-1,H-6
Kunkle ... B-2
Kuth ... G-4
Labella ... F-3
Lacock ... D-4
Lacona ... J-7
Lafayette ... A-4
Lafferty ... H-4
Lager ... B-6
Lampe ... G-1
La Marido ... K-4
La Moine ... K-4
Lanark ... B-4
Lander ... E-1
Langley ... B-3
Laplace ... D-8
Lappe ... A-5
La Rose ... J-4
Laughlin ... J-6,J-7
Lawson ... D-7
Leavitte ... J-4
Leech ... A-8
Leister ... B-5
Lelia ... H-4
Leolyn ... K-7
Leticoe ... G-8
Letsche ... B-4
Liberty ... C-7
Liberty, West ... K-3
Lighthill ... D-2
Ligonier ... A-8
Lilian ... H-5
Lincoln, N. ... C-3
Linda ... J-4
Linial ... I-4
Linneview ... J-7
Linton ... D-7
List ... A-5
Lithgow ... B-4
Liverpool ... C-2
Lockhart ... C-5
Locust ... E-7
Lofink ... A-7
Loleta ... K-6
Lombard ... E-7
Lonergan ... J-3
Longmore ... I-3
Los Angeles ... K-2
Louisiana ... K-1
Lovelace ... E-1
Lowen ... G-4
Lowenhill ... H-3
Lowrie ... B-6
Lupton ... F-2
Lyceum ... A-4
Lynnbrook ... K-4
Lyzell ... A-4
Mackinaw ... K-2
Maddock ... D-5
Maginn ... A-3
Mahon ... D-8
Main ... E-1
Manhattan ... C-2
Manilla ... D-6
Marena ... D-1
Marengo ... H-7
Margaret ... I-6,I-7
Marion ... E-7
Market St. ... E-4
Marloff ... K-4
Marlow ... D-1
Marquis ... C-3
Marvista ... B-2
Mary ... G-7
Maryland ... I-6
Mathews ... I-6
Mathias ... A-5
May ... I-3
Maydell ... J-1
Mayville ... K-4
Maywood ... A-3
McClintock ... B-3
McCullough ... B-3
McIntyre ... A-3
McKean ... F-5
McKeever ... A-2
McKinley ... I-6
McKinney Ln. ... G-8
McLain ... G-6
Meadville ... B-4
Medhurst ... I-1
Melrose ... B-3
Mercer ... D-6
Merchant ... C-4
Meredith ... K-7
Meridan ... F-3
Merrimac ... F-3
Merriman ... F-7
Meta ... F-3
Metcalf ... B-3
Methyl ... I-2
Metropolitan ... C-1
Meyer, E. ... J-7
Meyers, W. ... K-6
Michigan ... H-5
Millbridge ... G-6
Miller ... E-7
Minooka ... J-6
Minsinger ... H-4
Mission ... G-8
Mohawk ... E-7
Monastery ... G-7
Monterey ... C-3
Moore ... I-6
Moredale ... K-5
Morgan ... C-8
Morrison ... B-2
Moultrie ... E-7
Mt. Joseph ... K-6
Mt. Oliver ... H-6
Mountain ... I-8
Mountford ... A-4
Moye ... H-7
Mullins ... A-1
Muriel ... F-6
Napoleon ... I-2
Natchez ... G-4
Neeld ... J-2
Neff ... G-4
Neidell ... E-1
Neptune ... E-1
Neville ... B-8
New Hampshire ... B-2
Newton ... G-6
New York ... G-1
Niggel ... A-7
Nixon ... B-1
Nobles ... J-6,K-6
Noblestown ... F-1
Norman ... B-3
North ... C-2
Northcrest ... I-4
North Shore Dr. ... D-4
Norton ... G-3
Noster ... A-6
Oakhurst ... K-6
Oakville ... H-1
O'Hern ... B-3
Ohio, E. ... B-6
Ohio, W. ... C-4
Ohio River Blvd. ... D-3
Oliver ... E-5
Olympia ... F-3
Oneida ... F-3
Onyz ... I-6
Orangewood ... I-3
Orchard ... H-5
Oriana ... B-2
Ormsby ... I-7,I-8
Orr ... E-7
Osgood ... A-4
Ottillia ... I-7
Overbeck ... A-5
Page ... C-2
Palisade ... A-2
Palm Beach ... K-2
Palo Alto ... C-3
Parallel ... J-7
Parkhurst ... C-4
Park Low ... I-5
Parkwood ... I-8
Pasadena ... G-5
Patterson ... H-8
Paul ... H-4
Pauline ... J-2
Paulowna ... B-8
Pawnee ... F-3
Peekskill ... A-4
Penn ... C-7,D-5,I-7,J-8
Penn-Lincoln Parkway ... F-6
Pennsylvania ... C-2
Peralta ... C-5
Perrilyn ... K-3
Perry ... D-7
Perrysville ... B-3
Petunia ... K-5
Phineas ... C-5
Piermont ... F-3
Pioneer ... I-4,K-3
Pitler ... A-1
Pius ... G-7
P. J. McArdle ... F-4
Plainview ... K-3
Platt ... I-3
Plough ... A-1
Plunkett ... G-2
Plymouth ... F-3
Pocono Dr. ... H-1
Popargrove ... K-7
Potomac Ave. ... K-1
Preble ... C-1
Pressley ... C-5
Pride ... E-6
Princess ... I-3
Progress ... C-5
Prospect ... G-4
Protectory ... D-6
Province ... B-6
Pynchon ... A-4
Quarry ... H-6
Queen ... B-5
Quincy ... J-6
Ravine ... H-4
Rectenwald ... I-7
Reddour ... C-4
Redlyn ... I-6
Redrose ... K-7
Reed ... D-8
Reedsdale ... D-2
Reese ... E-2
Regina ... G-6
Reifert ... I-6
Republic ... F-2
Resaca ... C-3
Rescue ... A-6
Rhine ... A-6
Rhode Island ... G-1
Ridge ... D-2
Ridgemont ... G-1
Ridgeway ... C-7,D-6
Ridgewood ... B-3
Ringwalt ... J-3
Risby ... H-2
Rising Main ... B-4
River ... C-6
River Blvd. ... D-4
Robinson ... D-5,D-8
Rochelle ... I-6
Rockland ... I-3
Rockledge ... A-6
Romanhoff ... A-5
Rose ... E-7
Roseanne ... J-1
Roseberry ... I-1
Rosegarden ... J-1
Roseton ... I-5
Ross ... E-5
Rothman ... H-8
Royal ... A-5
Rubicon ... G-3
Rugraff ... H-6
Russell ... A-3
Ruth ... G-4
Rutherford ... I-2
Rutledge ... E-2
Ruxton ... G-5
St. Ives ... B-2
St. Joseph ... I-7
St. Lucas ... I-7
St. Paul ... G-7
St. Thomas ... G-7
Salerna ... G-1
Salisbury ... H-8
Sampsonia ... C-3
Sanctus ... G-1
Sarah ... G-7
Saranac ... K-2
Saw Mill Run ... H-3,J-5
Schuler ... I-8
Scott Pl. ... D-5
Schafer ... H-8
Scripway ... E-5
Seabright ... A-4
Sebring ... I-3
Sedgewick ... C-2
Seneca ... E-7
Seventh ... E-5
Seward ... E-2
Shadycrest ... G-2
Shaler ... F-2
Sharon ... G-6
Sheffield ... C-2
Sherman ... C-4
Shiras ... J-2
Shulze ... H-7
Sidney ... F-7,F-8
Sigel ... B-2
Simms ... H-4
Sixth ... E-5
Smallman ... C-7
Smith Field ... E-5
Soffel ... H-4
Soho ... D-8
Somers ... D-7
Sophia ... B-5
Sorrell ... A-1
Southcrest ... J-4
Southern ... H-4
Spahrgrove ... G-3
Spring ... B-6,H-8
Springfield ... F-1,G-1
Spiral ... A-4
Sprucewood ... K-7
Square ... D-7
Stamm ... H-7
Stanwik ... E-4
Stayton ... A-2
Steil ... I-8
Stetson ... J-3
Steuben ... E-1
Stevenson ... E-6
Stockholm ... C-8
Stockton ... D-4
Strachan ... K-1
Stranmore ... B-2
Strauss ... A-2
Stromberg ... G-8
Success ... B-2
Suffolk ... A-4
Suismon ... C-5
Sulgrove ... F-3
Summer ... G-8
Suncrest ... I-6
Sunderman ... A-7
Superior ... A-1
Sweetbriar ... F-2,G-3
Sycamore ... F-2,F-3
Sylvania ... H-4,H-5
Taft ... H-4
Tarragunna ... J-6
Taylor ... C-3
Terrace ... E-8
Texdale ... J-3
The Boulevard ... J-7
Thelma ... A-1
Thielman ... K-6
Third ... E-5
Timberland ... J-5
Tinsbury ... A-6
Tippet ... J-1
Tonapah ... J-2
Topeka ... I-8
Transverse ... I-7,J-7
Traymore ... I-4
Trent ... D-7
Triana ... J-7
Tripoli ... C-5
Tropical ... H-2
Trost ... J-6
Troy Hill ... B-6
Tucker ... G-1
Tumbo ... A-1
Tuscola ... G-4
Tyrone ... C-7
Ulysses ... F-4
Valonia ... D-1
Van Bram ... E-7
Varley ... A-5
Vaughn ... E-2
Venango ... A-5
Vincent ... H-5
Vickroy ... E-6
Vine ... E-7
Vinial ... B-6
Virginia ... F-3
Vista ... B-5
Vodeli ... K-2
Voskamp ... B-6
Wabash ... E-1
Wade ... G-4
Wadsworth ... E-7
Wagner ... J-7
Walde ... I-7
Walden ... G-4
Walnut ... H-7
Walter ... H-6,I-7
Wandless ... C-8
Warden ... F-1
Warfield ... C-5
Warning ... D-8
Warren ... B-4
Warrington ... H-4
Washington ... E-6
Watson ... E-6
Watt ... C-8
Weaver ... F-1
Webster ... D-7
Well ... F-2
Wenke ... H-8
Wentworth ... I-2
Wenzell ... K-2
Western ... D-2
Westfield ... I-3
Westmont ... K-6
Westwood ... G-4
Wharton ... F-7,F-8
White ... C-8
Whited ... K-5
Whiteside ... D-7
Wick ... E-7
Wiese ... H-8
Wiggins ... B-8
Wilber ... J-6
Wilbert ... G-3
Wilhelm ... E-1
William ... G-4
William Penn ... E-5
Wilmar ... F-2
Wilmerding ... G-2
Wilson ... A-3
Winfield ... B-2
Wingate ... J-7
Winton ... G-5
Wisdom ... G-6
Woessner ... A-5
Wolford ... K-3
Wood ... E-5
Woodcover ... J-1
Woodland ... A-1
Woodruff ... G-2,G-3
Woodward ... K-3
Woodville ... F-1
Wooster ... D-7
Wurzell ... A-4
Wyandotte ... E-7
Wylie ... D-7,E-5
Wynoka ... J-7
Wyola ... F-2
Wyoming ... G-4
Yetta ... B-5
Younger ... J-1
Zara ... H-5
Zimmerman ... K-5
1st St. ... K-8
1st St., S. ... F-5
3rd, S. ... F-5
4th, S. ... F-5
5th, S. ... F-6
6th ... D-5
6th, S. ... F-6
7th ... D-5
7th, S. ... G-6
8th ... D-5
8th, S. ... F-6
9th ... D-5
9th, S. ... F-6
10th ... D-5
10th, S. ... G-6
11th, S. ... G-6
12th ... D-6
12th, S. ... G-6
13th ... D-6
13th, S. ... G-7
14th ... D-6
14th, S. ... G-7
15th ... D-6
15th, S. ... G-7
16th ... D-6
16th, S. ... G-7
17th ... C-6
17th, S. ... G-7
18th ... C-6,F-7
18th, S. ... F-7,G-7,H-7
19th ... C-6,F-7
19th, S. ... F-7
20th ... C-6,F-7
20th, S. ... F-7
21st ... C-6
21st, S. ... G-8
22nd ... C-6
22nd, S. ... G-8
23rd ... C-6
24th ... C-7
24th, S. ... G-8
25th ... C-7
25th, S. ... G-8
26th ... B-7
26th, S. ... G-8
27th ... B-7
28th ... B-7
29th ... B-7
30th ... B-8
31st St. ... B-8
32nd ... B-8
33rd ... A-8
34th ... A-8
35th ... A-8
36th ... A-8
38th ... A-8

POINTS OF INTEREST

Brady St. Bridge ... F-8
East Park ... C-5
Fort Duquesne Bridge ... D-4
Fort Pitt Bridge ... E-4
Grandview Park ... G-5
Herr's Island ... A-7
Liberty Bridge ... F-5
McKinley Park ... I-5
Melon Square Park ... E-5
Mt. Washington Park ... G-3
Ninth St. Bridge ... D-5
North Park ... C-4
Olympia Park ... F-3
Point State Park ... E-4
Roberto Clemente Memorial Park ... D-3
Seventh St. Bridge ... D-5
Sixteenth St. Bridge ... C-6
Sixth St. Bridge ... D-4
Smithfield St. Bridge ... F-5
Southside Park ... H-7
Tenth St. Bridge ... F-6
West Park ... C-3,C-4
Westend Bridge ... D-2
31st St. Bridge ... A-7

PHOENIX

Adams ... H-7
Adams St. ... H-1-8
Almeria ... F-2
Almeria Rd. ... F-1-8
Alvarado ... E-3
Alvarado Rd. ... E-6,F-6
Amelia ... C-3,C-4
Amelia Ave. ... C-7
Apache St. ... J-3-7
Arco Dr. ... G-3
Ashland ... E-3
Ashland Ave. ... E-6
Avalon ... D-2,D-4,D-8
Avalon Dr. ... D-2-5
Belleview St. ... F-1,G-8
Black Canyon Frwy. ... B-2-C-2
Bonitos ... E-8
Brill St. ... F-7,F-8
Buchanan ... I-3
Buchanan St. ... I-4,I-5
Buckeye Rd. ... J-1-7
Cambridge ... E-8
Cambridge Ave. ... E-2-7
Camelback Rd. ... A-2,A-5
Campbell Ave. ... B-1-7
Campus ... D-2
Campus Dr. ... D-5
Catalina Dr. ... D-1-6
Central Ave. ... D-6-H-6
Cherry Lynn ... D-2
Cherry Lynn Dr. ... D-1-6
Clarendon Ave. ... C-1-6
Cocopah ... J-3
Cocopah St. ... J-2-7
Columbus Ave. ... C-6
Coolidge ... A-4
Coolidge St. ... A-1-8
Coronado Rd. ... F-1-8
Country Club Dr. ... D-7
Culver St. ... F-1,F-4,G-3
Cypress ... E-1,E-8
Cypress St. ... E-1,E-5
Dayton St. ... F-7
Devonshire Ave. ... B-1-7
Diamond St. ... G-8
Durango St. ... J-1-7
Earll ... D-2
Earll Dr. ... D-2-6
Edgemere St. ... E-8
Edgemont ... D-2,D-3
Edgemont Ave. ... D-4-8
Elm St. ... A-1-8
Encanto Blvd. ... E-1,E-5
Encanto Dr. N.E. ... E-5
Encanto Dr. N.W. ... E-5
Evergreen St. ... E-8,E-8
Fairmount ... C-2-5
Fairmount Ave. ... C-1-7
Fillmore St. ... G-1-6
Flower ... D-2-6
Flower cir. N. ... D-4
Flower Cir. S. ... D-4
Flower St. ... D-4
Garfield ... G-4
Garfield St. ... G-1-8
Glenrosa ... B-4
Glenrosa Ave. ... B-1-8
Gibson Ln. ... K-5-7
Granada ... F-7
Granada Rd. ... F-1-8
Grand Ave. ... D-1,G-4
Grant St. ... I-3-6
Hadley St. ... I-2-8
Hammond Ln. ... K-5,K-8
Harrison St. ... I-3,I-4
Hazelwood ... A-4
Hazelwood St. ... A-1,A-4
Hazelwood St. ... A-2,A-5
Heatherbrae ... B-3
Heatherbrae Dr. ... B-1-4
Hess Ave. ... K-8
Highland ... A-1
Highland Ave. ... A-2-7
Hilton ... K-7
Hilton Ave. ... K-2,K-3
Holly St. ... E-1,F-3,F-5
Hoover Ave. ... E-6,E-8
Hubbell ... F-8
Indian Ln. ... B-5
Indianola ... C-2,C-3
Indianola Ave. ... C-2-7
Indian School Rd. ... C-4-7
Jackson ... I-4,I-5
Jackson St. ... I-1-5
Jefferson St. ... H-4-8
Latham St. ... G-1-4
Laurel Ave. ... G-4,H-4
Lewis Ave. ... E-3-5
Lexington Ave. ... D-6
Lincoln ... I-3
Lincoln St. ... I-1-3
Linden St. ... G-3,G-4
Longview Ave. ... C-8
Lynwood ... F-6
Lynwood St. ... F-2-4
Mackenzie Dr. ... B-1-4
Madison ... H-7
Madison St. ... H-1-5
Magnolia ... K-5
Magnolia St. ... K-4,K-8
Manor Dr. East ... D-8
Manor Dr. West ... D-8
Maricopa Frwy. ... K-6
Maricopa St. ... I-1,I-2
Mariposa ... A-1,A-4
Mariposa St. ... A-2,A-5
McDowell Rd. ... F-2-8
McKinley ... G-4
McKinley St. ... G-1-6
Meadowbrook Ave. ... A-1,A-7
Melvin St. ... H-1
Merrell St. ... D-5,D-6
Minnezona ... B-1
Minnezona Ave. ... B-2-7
Mitchell Dr. ... C-2-7
Mitchell St. ... B-7,F-7
Mohave ... J-3
Mohave St. ... J-1-7
Monroe St. ... H-4-8
Montecito ... B-3
Montecito Ave. ... B-1-7
Monterey ... D-2
Monterey Way ... D-6
Monterosa St. ... B-1-6
Monte Vista ... E-3,E-5
Monte Vista Rd. ... E-1,E-6
Montezuma St. ... K-5
Moreland ... G-3
Moreland St. ... G-1-8
Morris Dr. ... D-6
Mulberry ... D-2,D-5
Mulberry Dr. ... D-2,D-4
Mulberry St. ... D-6
Oak St. ... E-7
Osborn Rd. ... C-2-7
Palm Ln. ... F-1-8
Palmcroft ... F-4
Palmcroft Dr. ... F-5
Palmcroft Way ... F-4
Papago ... J-4,J-7
Papago St. ... J-1-5
Pasadena ... A-6
Pasadena Ave. ... A-3-7
Piccadilly ... C-5
Piccadilly Rd. ... C-3
Pierce ... G-4,G-5
Pierce St. ... G-1,G-6
Pierson ... A-4
Pierson St. ... A-1-8
Pima St. ... J-1-7
Pinchot Ave. ... D-2
Polk St. ... H-1-7
Portland St. ... G-2-8
Randolph Rd. ... D-8
Richland St. ... F-7
Roanoke ... D-6
Roanoke Ave. ... D-6
Roma Ave. ... B-1-7
Roosevelt St. ... G-1-8
Sells Dr. ... B-4
Sheridan St. ... E-7
Sherman St. ... I-1-4
Sonora St. ... J-3
Southern Pacific Dr. ... I-7
Spruce ... F-3
Taylor ... G-5
Taylor St. ... G-1,G-4,H-6,H-7
Thomas Rd. ... D-3-6
Tonto ... I-1-4
Tonto St. ... I-2-7
Turney Ave. ... B-1-7
Valerie ... B-5
Van Buren St. ... H-4-8
Verde Ln. ... D-2-8
Vernon Ave. ... E-2-6
Villa St. ... G-1
Virginia Ave. ... E-1-5
Virginia Cir. ... E-6
Washington Dr. ... H-1
Washington St. ... H-4-8
Watkins St. ... K-4-7
Weldon Ave. ... C-1-6
Westview Dr. ... B-4
Whitton ... C-5,C-6
Whitton Ave. ... C-1-4
Willetta ... F-2
Willetta St. ... F-2-4
Wilshire ... E-3,E-5
Wilshire Dr. ... E-2,E-4
Windsor Ave. ... E-1-6
Woodland Ave. ... H-4
Woodward Dr. ... E-6
Yale St. ... E-8
Yavapai ... J-7
Yavapai St. ... J-1-5
Yuma Ave. ... J-7
Yuma St. ... J-1-5
1st Ave. ... A-5-K-5
1st St. ... A-6-J-6
2nd Ave. ... B-6-K-6
2nd Dr. ... B-5,B-6
2nd Pl. ... C-6,J-6
2nd St. ... C-6-J-6
3rd Ave. ... B-5-K-5
3rd Dr. ... I-5
3rd St. ... A-6-J-6
4th ... A-6
4th Ave. ... C-5-I-5
4th Ave. N.W. ... B-5
4th St. ... C-6-J-6
5th ... C-5,I-5
5th Ave. ... B-5-K-5
5th Ave. N.W. ... B-5
5th St. ... A-6-J-6
6th Ave. ... C-5-K-5
6th Ave. N.W. ... B-5,C-5
6th Dr. ... B-5,I-5
6th St. ... A-6-J-6
7th Ave. ... D-5-I-5
7th St. ... B-7-J-7
8th ... G-5
8th Ave. ... B-5-J-5
8th Pl. ... A-7,I-7
8th St. ... A-7-J-7
9th Ave. ... B-5-J-5
9th Pl. ... C-7,I-7
9th St. ... B-7-J-7
9th Way ... I-7
10th Ave. ... B-5-J-5
10th Dr. ... A-7
10th Pl. ... A-7-I-7
10th St. ... B-7-J-7
11th ... B-7,K-8
11th Ave. ... B-4-K-4
11th Pl. ... A-7,H-7
11th St. ... A-7-J-7
11th Way ... H-8
12th Ave. ... B-4-J-4
12th Dr. ... B-4
12th Pl. ... C-8,I-8
12th St. ... C-8,J-8
13th ... C-4,K-8
13th Ave. ... A-4-J-4
13th Pl. ... B-8,C-8,H-8,J-7
13th St. ... A-8-J-8
13th Way ... C-8
14th ... H-4
14th Ave. ... B-4-J-4
14th Pl. ... A-8-I-8
14th St. ... B-8-J-8
15th Ave. ... B-4-I-4
15th Dr. ... A-4-J-4
15th Pl. ... A-8,D-8,K-8
15th St. ... A-8-K-8
16th ... C-4,D-4
16th Ave. ... A-4-K-4
16th Dr. ... A-4-J-4
16th St. ... J-8
17th ... J-3
17th Ave. ... A-4-J-4
17th Dr. ... B-3-H-3
18th Ave. ... A-3-J-3
18th Dr. ... B-3-J-3
19th Ave. ... B-3-J-3
19th Dr. ... B-3,J-3
20th ... E-3
20th Ave. ... A-3-J-3
20th Dr. ... B-3-H-3
21st ... C-3,J-3
21st Ave. ... A-3-J-3
21st Dr. ... B-3-E-3
22nd ... B-2-E-2
22nd Ave. ... A-2-K-2
23rd Ave. ... B-2-I-2
23rd Dr. ... A-2-E-2
24th ... J-2
24th Ave. ... A-2-H-2
24th Dr. ... C-2,E-2
25th ... C-2
25th Ave. ... F-2-J-2
25th Dr. ... D-2-F-2
26th ... D-2
26th Ave. ... B-2,H-2,J-2
26th Dr. ... B-1,D-1
27th ... G-1
27th Ave. ... D-1-J-1
27th Dr. ... A-1,G-1,H-1
27th Ln. ... F-1,G-1
28th ... B-1,C-1,H-1
28th Ave. ... A-1-J-1
28th Dr. ... A-1-J-1
29th ... A-1-G-1
29th Ave. ... A-1-J-1
29th Dr. ... B-1-H-1
30th ... A-1-G-1
30th Ave. ... D-1-J-1
30th Dr. ... A-1,B-1,H-1,I-1
31st Ave. ... B-1-D-1

POINTS OF INTEREST

Central Park ... I-6
Coffeit Park ... J-3
Coronado Park ... F-8
Eastlake Park ... H-8
Encanto Park ... E-3
Grant Park ... I-6
Green Valley Park ... K-8
Harmon Park ... J-5
Madison Park ... B-8
Monterey Park ... E-6
Townsend Park ... G-7
University Park ... H-4
Virginia Park ... E-8
Willow Park ... H-1

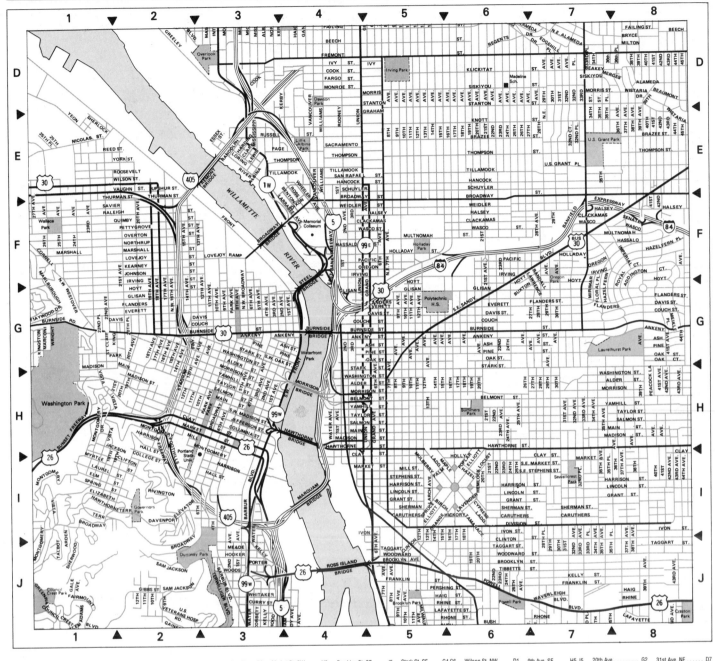

N

Scale of Miles

0 .2 .4 .6

RICHMOND

Abington G5
Accommodation St.
.... F7
Adams St. F5
Addison St. F3
Admiral St. E5
Alder E7
Allen Ave. F5
Allison St. E3
Alpine C7
Althea D7
Altmont C7
Alvis Ave. C7
Ambler St. C7
Ambrose E8
Amelia G3
Ancestor Rd. D5
Anniston Ave. ... C1
Antrim Ave. C1
Appomattox St. .. G5
Arch St. G5
Archer St. G3
Arlington Rd. C3
Arnold C7
Auburn Ave. E2
Augusta Ave. ... C1
Bacon St. ... E5,E6
Baker St. F6
Balding St. G7
Bancroft C7
Barton Ave. D6
Bates F6
Bath St. D4
Battery D4
Beaumont Ave. .. E1
Bedford I6
Beech St. E8
Belevidere St. ... G5
Beleville St. G5
Bellvue St. C2
Belmont Ave. . E2,F1
Berkley G2
Bethell E8

Birch St. F4
Blacker St. C1
Blair St. G3
Blanton Ave. F2
Blue Shingles Ln. . G1
Boscobel I2
Botetour St. D4
Boulevard C3,E2
Boulevard Bridge . H1
Bowe St. E4
Bowling Green ... E7
Boyd F4
Bragg G5
Brandon Ln. F2
Brang F8
Bravers Ln. F8
Brenton St. B6
Broad St. . D3,F6,H8
Brook Rd. ... E5,F5
Brookfield C7
Brookland Pkwy. . C5
Brunswick St. ... F4
Bryan F7,F8
Burns St. C8
Burton G7
Bute Lake F1
Byrd St. G5
Byron St. C8
Caledonia Rd. ... C7
Calhoun E6
Call St. E6
Cameron St. D1
Canal St. E8
Carillon Ct. G1
Carlton F4
Carmine St. C4
Carolina Ave. ... C7
Carrington St. ... G4
Carroll St. G4
Carrolton St. F1
Carter St. H3
Carver St. H3
Cary St. E6
.... E1,E2,G5,H7
Cathedral Pl. F4

Catherine E5
Cecil C1
Cedar Ln. I1
Chamberlayne ... E5
Charity F6
Charlotte E1
Cherry St. G4
Chesterfield I3
Chestnut E7
China St. G4
Church St. G5
Claiborne St. ... G3
Clarence I1
Clay St. .. C2,F6,H8
Cleveland St. ... E2
Cliff Ave. C7
Clifton D7
Coalter St. G6
College St. G6
Colonial D2,F2
Colorado St. G3
Commerce St. ... I6
Commonwealth Ave.
.... C1
Condie St. F2
Conrad E8
Coutts E6
Cowardin Ave. .. I4
Crafton La. C7
Craigie C7
Crawford St. ... C6
Crenshaw E1
Crump St. E8
Cumberland F4
Cummings St. ... C4
Custer St. D8
Cutshaw Ave. C1,D2
Cypress St. B6
D.M.U. Dr. D3
Dakota Ave. G3
Daniel E7
Davis Ave. E7
.... C1,D2,E4,G5
Dawn St. D6
Decatur St. I5

Deforest St. E8
Denny St. C8
Detroit Ave. D8
Devonshire Rd. .. I1
Dinneen D4
Dobson St. G4
Dock St. H7
Dooley Ave. C2
Douglasdale Ave. F1
Dove St. D6
Dubois St. C4
Dunn Ave. C7
Dunston Ave. ... I1
Dupont Circle ... C1
Durham St. D4
Edgehill D5
Eggleston St. ... G4
Elizabeth G3
Ellen St. E1
Ellwood St. E1
Endicott C4
Enslow St. C8
Essex St. .. C6,C7
Evelyn Byrd ... H1
Everett St. I5
Exeter Ave. E1
Fairmont Ave. ... C4
Federal St. E6
Fells E5,E6
Fendell Ave. C8
Fifth E7
First St. C8
Floyd St. ... D1,E2
Ford St. F7
Forest Circle ... I2
Forest Hill Ave. . I1
Forestview Dr. ... I1
Forquean Ln. ... D7
Fourth D7
Foushee St. F5
Franklin St. E6
.... C1,D2,E4,G5
Freeman St. F2
French F1,F2

Fritz E5
Front St. C8
Garland D6
Garrett St. F1
Gate St. G3
Gay St. G8
Georgia H2
Gilbert St. G3
Giles C7
Gilmer St. G4
Gladstone Ave. . C7
Gleniea I5
Goshen St. F5
Grace St. ......
.... C1,D3,F6,G7
Graham D5,D6
Granby St. F3
Grant St. F3
Graveland G2
Green Alley G4
Green St. F4
Greenville Ave. .. D6
Greenwood Ave. . D2
Grove Ave. ... D1,E3
Groveland D7
Gun Club Road .. D1
Hamilton St. D1
Hammond Ave. . C5
Hampton St. ... H2
Hancock St. E5
Hanes Ave. C6
Hanover Ave. . D1,E3
Harold D7
Harrison St. E4
Harry St. C4
Harvey Ave. ... D6
Harvie St. E4
Hawthorne D6
Henry St. F5
Herbert St. H1
Hermitage Rd. .. C4
Hickory St. E4
High D5
Highland St. C8
Highland View .. C8

Highpoint D2
Hildreth H7
Hill St. E6
Hillcrest ... I1,I3
Hills Blvd. I1
Holly St. G4
Home St. D6
Hooper C6
Hospital St. D4
Howe G5
Hull St. I5
Huxley St. F1
Idlewood Ave. ..
.... E1,F3,G4
Jackson St. F6
Jacquelin F3
Jefferson Ave. .. G7
Jefferson St. ... E6
Jessanine G8
Joshua St. E6
Juniper D7
Kemper St. F3
Kensington Ave. ..
.... D1,D2
Kent Rd. D1
King St. G8
King William Rd. . H1
Kinney St. E4
Ladies Mile Rd. . C6
Lafayett St. D1
Lakeview St. ... D2
Lamb Ave. .. C6,D6
Lamont D3
Langston Ave. .. D4
Lanvale C3
Laurel St. E5
Lebanon E7
Leigh St. .. C2,D3,F6
Letcher D7
Libby Terrace ... I8
Lindel St. E4
Lipscomb J3
Littlejohn St. ... I5
Lodge St. E4

Lombardy St. ...
..... E4,F4,G3
Louisa St. D4
Louisiana St. ... I8
Loxley Rd. C7
Lunenburg St. .. C7
M St. G8
Mactavish D2
Maddox F5
Madison St. F5
Magnolia D8
Maiden G5
Main St. .. E2,G5,H7
Malvern C1
Manchester Bridge
.... H5
Maplewood Ave. ..
.... E1,F2
Marshall Rd. ...
.... D3,E4,F6,H8
Marston Ln. E1
Maryland Ave. .. C7
Maury I5
Mayo's Bridge .. H6
McCloy St. F1
McDonough St. . I3
Meade G3
Meadow St. . F3,H2
Mechanicville Tnpk.
.... C3
Melbourne F8
Melklenburd ... C7
Meredith C6
Meyers St. D3
Middlesex St. .. D4
Miller Ave. D6
Milton St. .. C6,C8
Mitchell E5
Monroe St. F5
Monterio G8
Montvale C7
Monument Ave. C1,E3
Moody Ave. ... J3
Moore St. .. C2,D4,E5
Morris F4

Mulberry St. ... F2
Munford F5
Myrtle D7
N St. G8
Nansemond St. E1,F1
Napolean St. ... C7
Nevada G3
New Kent . H1,I2,I3
New York Ave. .. H3
Ninemile G8
Nicholson St. ... I8
Norfolk C3
North Ave. D6
North Umbrella Ave.
.... C5
North Umbrella Ln.
.... D5
Northside Ave. .. C7
Norton St. D6
Norwood St. ... G8
O St. G8
Oak E5
Overbrook Rd. D4,D5
Oz Ave. I1
Park Ave. ... C1,D2
Parkwood Ave. E2,F3
Patterson Ave. . D1,D2
Patton C3
Peach St. I7
Pear St. H7
Pelham D7
Pennsylvania Ave.
.... C4
Perry St. I5
Peterborough ... H1
Phaum St. H1
Pine St. G8
Pink G8
Pleasants St. ... I7
Plum St. F4
Poe E6
Pollock St. . C7,C8
Porter I5
Portland F1

Powhatan G3
Preble I6
Preston St. F6
Prince Arthur Rd. . I1
Prince Edward .. H1
Prince George .. I1
Pulaski St. D8
Pumphouse Dr. G1,G2
Q St. G8
Queen E1
Quickshall E6
Sharon Ct. C1
R St. G8
Randolf St. G5
Raven F7
Redd E6
Redwood E8
Reedy Ave. I6
Rendale F1
Renelle St. C7
Rennie Ave. ... C4
Reserve St. C4
Rhoadmiller ... D4
Richmond & Henrico
Trpk. D7
Richmond Petersburgs
Trpk. E5
Richmond St. .. E7
Riverside Dr. ... H1,I2
Robert E. Lee
Bridge H4
Roberts ... D4,D5,D6
Robin Hood Rd. . C4
Robinson St. ... F2
Rock Ridge C3
Rockingham ... E7
Rogers St. H8
Rose E8
Rosedale C7
Rosenath Rd. .. C2
Rosewood Ave. F4,F5
Rothesay Circle . F1
Rowen E7
Rowland St. ... F3
Rugby Rd. F1

Russell G8
Ryland E4
S St. G8
Saver Ave. C1
School St. I1
Schuttle Ave. .. I1
Second Ave. ... D7
Semmes Ave. .. I3
Sewell E7
Shafer St. E4
Shenandoah St. . C1
Sheppard St. ... E2
Sherwood Ave. . C4
Shields Ave. ... F8
Shipley G2
Shockoeslip H6
Sledd St. C8
Smith St. F5
Smithdeal I2
South Hampton . H3
Southcliff Rd. .. I1
Spotsylvania St. F7,F8
Spottswood Dr. . E7
Spring St. G4
Springhill Ave. . I2,I3
Spruce St. D7
St. James ... E6,F6
St. John E6
St. Peter E6
Stafford Ave. ... F5
Sterl St. D1
Stockton St. ... H3
Stonewall Ave. . I2,I3
Stony Run E3
Strawberry St. . E3
Stuart Ave. . D1,D2,E3
Summit Ave. ... D3
Sumpter C5
Sunset F1
Sussex Ln. G1
Sussex St. I2
Sylvan Rd. I1
T St. F8
Taylor Ave. I1

Tazewell D5
Terminal Rd. ... D3
Texas Ave. H3
Third Ave. D7
Thompson St. .. E1
Thoms D4
Tilden St. E2
Tomacee Rd. .. I1
Trigg G4
Tulip G8
Tuskegee F8
Tyler E6
U St. F8
Utah Pl. C8
Valley Rd. G7,H7
Venable C7
Vine F3
Virginia St. H6
W St. F8
Walker G3
Wall G8
Wallace G4
Walpol E3
Waverly C8
Wayne H7
Wellford E7
Wellington St. .. C4
West Ave. E4
Westbridge Rd. . C4
Westove Rd. ... G2
Whatley D1
Whitby Rd. C5
Whitcomb E7
Wickham D6
Willow St. H8
Winber Dr. G3
Wood St. .. E7,E8
Woodbine Rd. . I2
Woodcliff ... C7,D7
Woodrow Ave. . C1
Wormley G4
Wythe Ave. . C1,D2
X St. F8
Yancy E6

1st St. G5,I6
2nd St. G5,I6
3rd St. G5,I6
4th St. .. G5,I5,H6
5th St. G6,I5
6th St. .. G6,H5,I5
7th St. G6,H5
8th St. G6,H6
9th St. G6,H5
10th St. G6,I5
11th St. G6
12th St. .. G6,I5,I6
13th St. G6,I6
14th St. G6,I5
15th St. H6,I5
17th St. G7,H7
18th St. G7
19th St. .. F8,G8,H7,I4
20th St. . G7,G8,H7,I4
21st St. . G7,G8,H7,I4
22nd St. H8,I4
23rd St. G8,H7
24th St. . G8,H7,I4
25th St. I4
26th St. H7,I4
27th St. H7,I3
28th St. H8,I3
29th St. I3
30th St. I3
31st St. I3
32nd St. I3
33rd St. I3
34 1/2 St. I8
34th St. I3
35 1/2 St. I8
35th St. . H8,I4
36 1/2 St. I8
37th St. I4
45th St. I2
46th St. I1
47th St. G4
48th St. I2
49th St. ......

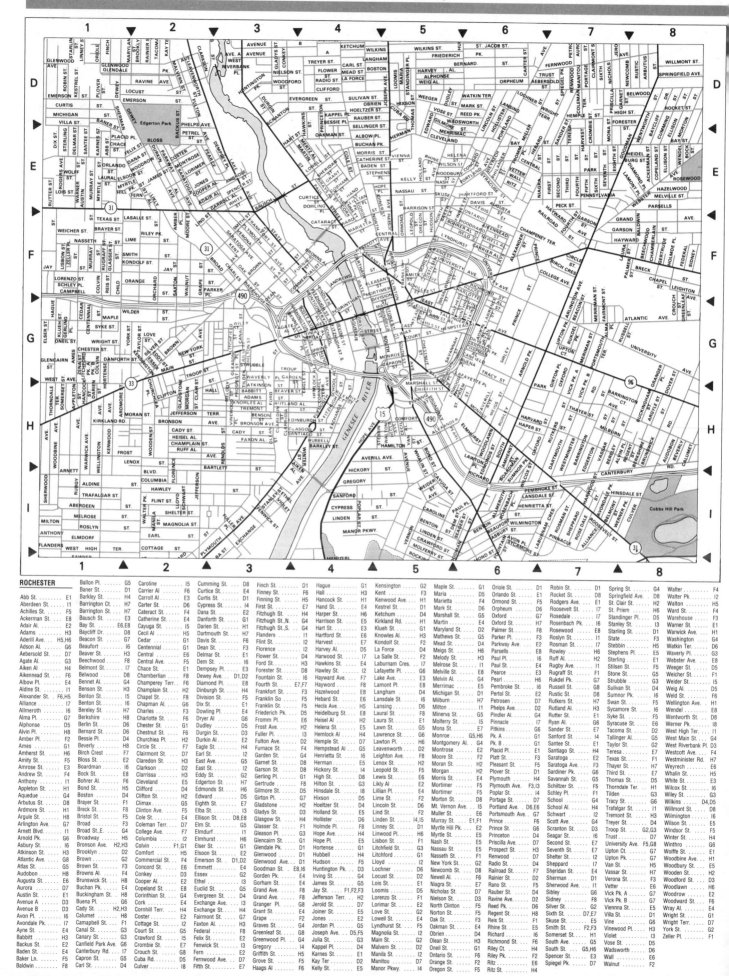

Scale of Miles
0 .2 .4 .6

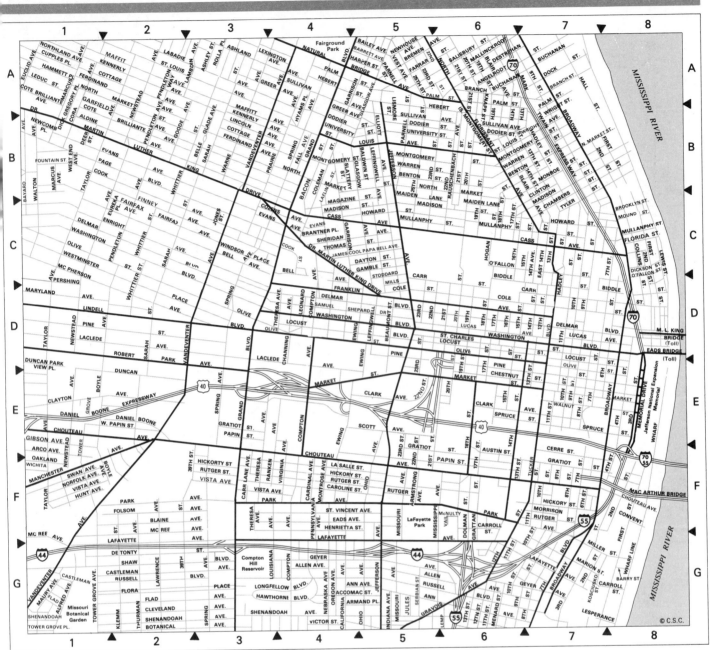

ST. LOUIS

Accomac St. G4
Aldine Ave. B1
Alfred Ave. G1
Allen Ave. G4,G5
Angelrodt St. A6
Ann Ave. G5,G6
Arco Ave. E1
Armand Pl. G4
Armstrong Ave. f5
Ashland Ave. A3
Ashley St. A3
Austin St. E6
Bacon St. B4
Bailey Ave. A5
Baldwin St. B5
Beaumont St. D5
Bell Ave. C3,C4
Belle Glade Ave. B3
Benton St. B5,B6
Biddle St. C6,D8
Blaine Ave. F2
Blair Ave. A6,B7
Botanical Ave. G2
Boyle Ave. F1,G2
Branch St. A6
Brantner St. C4
Bremen Ave. A5
Broadway A7,E8,G7
Buchanan A6,A7
Caerre St. F7
California Ave. G4
Cardinal Ave. F4
Carr St. C5,D7
Carrlane Ave. F3

Carroll St. F6,G8
Cass Ave. C4,C7
Castleman Ave. G2
Chambers St. C7
Channing Ave. D4
Chestnut St. E6
Chouteau Ave. E1,F4
Clark Ave. E5,E6
Clayton Ave. E1
Cleveland Ave. G2
Clinton St. B7
Cole St. D5,D6
Coleman Ave. B4
Collins St. C8
Compton Ave. . . D4,E4,G4
Convent F8
Cook Ave. B1
Cora Ave. B2
Cote Brilliante Ave. . A1,B2
Cottage Ave. A2,B3
Cupples Pl. A1
Daniel Boone E2
Dayton St. C5
Deer St. B1
Delmar Blvd. . . C1,D4,D7
Destrehan A6
Detony St. G2
Dick Gregory Pl. A1
Dickson St. C4
Dock St. A7
Dodier St. B4,B5,B6
Dolman St. F6
Dr. Martin Luther King Dr.
Duncan E2

Duncan Park View Pl. . . D1
Eads Ave. F4
Eads Bridge D8
Elliott Ave. B5
Enright Ave. C2
Euclid Ave. A1
Eureka Pl. C2
Evans Ave. B2,C3
Ewing D5,E4
Ewing Ave. D5
Fairfax Ave. C2
Fall Ave. B4
Farrar St. A5
Ferdinand Ave. A1,B3
Finney Ave. B2
First St. B8,C8,G8
Flad Ave. G2
Flora G2
Flordia St. C8
Folsom Ave. F2
Franklin Ave. D4
Gamble St. C5
Garrison Ave. A4,C4
Gayer Ave. G4,G7
Gibson Ave. E1
Glasgow Ave. B5
Goode Ave. B2
Grand Blvd. . . . B4,E3,G3
Gratiot St. E3,E5,F7
Grattan St. F6
Gravois Ave. G5
Greer Ave. A4
Hadley St. B7,D7
Hall St. A7

Hammett Pl. A1
Harper St. A5
Hawthorne Blvd. G3
Henrietta St. F4
Herbert St. A4,A6
Hickory St. F3,F4,F7
Hogan St. C6
Howard St. C5,C7
Hunt Ave. F1
Hyams Pl. A4
Indiana Ave. G5
Jefferson Ave. B5,G5
Jones St. C3
Jules G5
Kennerly Ave. A2,B3
Klemm St. G2
Knapp St. A6
LaSalle Ave. F1,F2
Labadie Ave. A2
Laclede Ave. E6
Lafayette Ave. . . F2,F4,G7
Lambdin Ave. A3
Lawrence Ave G3
Leduc St. A1
Leffingwell D5
Lenard D4
Lesperance G7
Lewis St. C8
Lexington Ave. A4
Lincoln Blvd. B3
Lindell Blvd. D1
Lismore St. A5
Locust St. D6,D7
Longfellow Blvd. F3
Louisiana Ave. G3

Lucas Ave. D4,D7
MacArthur Bridge F8
Madison St. C4,C5,C7
Maffitt Ave. A2,A3
Magazine St. C4
Maiden Lane B5,C6
Mallinckrodt A6
Manchester Ave. F1
Marcus Ave. A1,B1
Marion St. G7
Market Ave. A2
Market St. E4,E6
Martin Luther King D8
Maryland Ave. D1
Maury Ave. G1
McNair Ave. G5
McPherson Ave. C1
McRee Ave. F1,F2
Memorial Dr. E8
Menard St. G6
Mississippi Ave. F5
Missouri Ave. F5,G5
Monroe St. B7
Montgomery St.
. . . . B4,B5,B6
Montgomery St.,S. B6
Montrose Ave. F4
Morrison St. F7
Mullanphy St. . . . C5,C6,C8
Natural Bridge Ave. . . . A4
Nebraska Ave. G4
Newcomb Pl. A1
Norfolk Ave. F1
North Florissant Ave. . . B6

North Market St. . A2,B4,B6
Northland Ave. A1
O'Fallon St. C6
Oakland Ave. E1
Ohio Ave. F5,G5
Olive St. C1,D3,D6
Oregon Ave. G4
Page Ave. B1
Palm St. A4,A6,A7
Papin St. E3,E6
Papin St.,W. E1
Park Ave. F2,F3
Parnell St. A5,B5
Pendleton Ave. B2,C2
Pendleton Way A2
Pennsylvania F4
Pershing C1
Pine D1,E6
Pine St. D1,E6
Place G3
Prarie Ave. B4
Ranken Ave. F3
Rauschenbach Ave. . . . D2
Robert Park Ave. D2
Rolla Pl. B1
Russell Blvd. G2,G5
Rutger St. F3,F4,F5,F7
Salisbury St. A5
Sarah St. B3,C2,D2
Scott Ave. E5
Shaw Blvd. G2
Shenandoah Ave. . . . G2,G3
Sheridan Ave. C4
Slattery St. B4
Spring Ave. . . . B4,D3,E3,G3
Spruce St. E6,E7

St. Charles D6
St. Louis Ave. A2,B5,B6
St. Vincente Ave. F4
Sullivan Ave. . . . A4,B5,B6
Swan Ave. F1
Taylor Ave. B1,D1,F1
Theresa Ave. D4,F3
Thomas St. C4
Thurman Ave. G2
Tower Grove Ave. G1
Tyler St. C7
University St. B4,B5
Vandeventer
. . . . B3,D2,G1
Vest Ave. A5
Victor St. G4
Virginia Ave. F4
Vista Ave. F1,F3
Walton Ave. B1
Warne Ave. B3
Warren St. B5,B6
Washington Blvd.
. . . . C1,D4,D6
West End Ave. B1
Westminster Pl. C1
Wharf Line E8,G8
Whittier St. B2,C2
Windsor Pl. C3
Wright St. B7
2nd St. B7,C8,F8,G7
3rd St. E8,G7
4th St. E8,F8
6th St. E7,F7
7th Blvd. G7
7th St. C8,E7,F7
8th St. E7,F7,G6

9th St. . . A7,D7,E7,F7,G6
10th St. . . D7,E7,F7,G6,G7
11th St. D7,E7,F7,G6
12th St. E7,G6
13th St.
. . . . B7,C7,D7,E7,F6,G6
14th Ave. C7
14th St. B6,B7,D7,E6
15th St. C7,D6,E6
16th D6
16th St. C6
17th D6
17th St. C6,D6,E6,E6
18th St. C6,D6,E6,F6
19th D6
19th St. A6,B6,C6,G6
20th St. A6,B6,E6
21st D5
21st St. A6,B6,B6,F5
22nd D5
22nd St. B6,E5,F5
23rd D5
23rd St. A5,B5,E5
25th St. A5,B5,B5
39th St. F2,G2

© C.S.C.

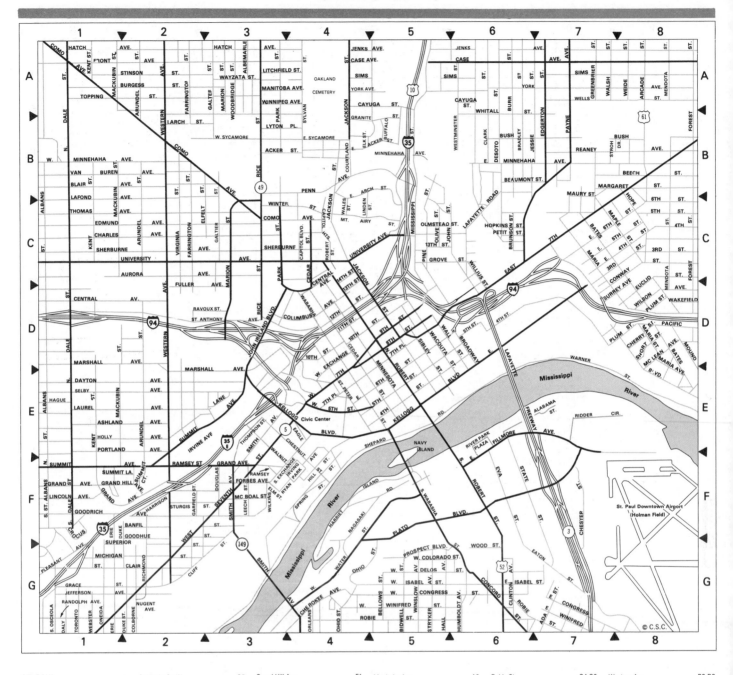

ST. PAUL

Acker St. ... B3	Colorado St.,W. ... G5	Grand Hill Ave. ... F1
Ada St. ... G7	Columbus Ave. ... D4	Greenbrier St. ... A7
Albemarie ... A3	Como Ave. ... A1,B2,C3	Grove St. ... C5
Arcade St. ... A8	Concord St. ... G6	Hall Ave. ... G5
Arundel St. ... A2,C2	Congress St.,W. ... G5	Hatch Ave. ... A1,A3
Arundel St. ... E2	Congress,E. ... G7	Holly Ave. ... E1
Ashland Ave. ... E1	Conway St. ... D7	Hopkins St. ... C6
Aurora Ave. ... C2	Crocus ... F1	Humboldt Ave. ... G5
Banfil St. ... F2	Dale St.,N. ... B1,E1	Irvine Ave. ... E2
Bates Ave. ... C7,D8	Dale St. ... F1	Isabel St.,E. ... G6
Beaumont St. ... B6	Daly St. ... G1	Isabel St.,W. ... G5
Beech St. ... B8	Dayton Ave. ... E1	Jackson St. ... B4,C4
Bidwell St. ... G5	Delos St.,W. ... G5	Jefferson Ave. ... G1
Blair Ave. ... B1	Desoto St. ... B6	Jenks Ave. ... A4
Bradley St. ... B6	Edgerton St. ... B7	Jessie St. ... B6
Brinson St. ... C6	Edmund Ave. ... C1	John Ireland Blvd. ... D3
Broadway ... D6	Elfelt St. ... C2	John St. ... C5
Burgess St. ... A2	Euclid St. ... D8	Kellogg Blvd. ... E3
Burr St. ... A6	Eva St. ... F6	Kellogg Blvd.,E. ... E5
Bush ... B8	Exchange,W. ... E4	Kent St. ... A1,C1,E1
Case Ave. ... A5,A6	Farrington St. ... A2,C2	Lafayette Frwy. ... D6
Cayuga St. ... A4,A6	Fillmore Ave.,E. ... E6	Lafayette Rd. ... A6
Cedar St. ... C4,D4	Forbes Ave. ... F3	Lafond Ave. ... B1
Central Ave. ... C4	Forest St. ... B8,C8	Larch St. ... B2
Charles Ave. ... C1	Front Ave. ... A1	Laurel Ave. ... E1
Cherokee Ave. ... G4	Fuller Ave. ... C2	Lincoln Ave. ... F1
Cherry St. ... F7	Galter St. ... A3,C3	Litchfield St. ... A3
Clark St. ... B6	Gelby St. ... E1	Lyton Pl. ... B3
Clinton Ave. ... G6	Goodhue St. ... F2	Mackubin St. ... A1,C1,E1
	Goodrich Ave. ... F1	Maiden Lane ... E2
	Gran St. ... B4	

Manitoba Ave. ... A3	Robie St. ... G4,G6	Western Ave. ... B2,D2
Maple St. ... C7	Seventh St.,W. ... F2	Willius St. ... C6
Margaret St. ... B7	Sherburne Ave. ... C1,C3	Wilson Ave. ... D8
Maria Ave. ... C7,D8	Short St. ... D8	Winifred St.,W. ... G5
Marion St. ... A3,C3	Sibley St. ... D5	Winifred,E. ... G7
Marshall Ave. ... D1,E2	Sims ... A4,A5,A7	Winnipeg Ave. ... A3
Maury St. ... B7	Smith Ave. ... E3,G3	Winslow Ave. ... G5
McBoal St. ... F3	St. Albans ... C1	Winter St. ... C3
McLean Ave. ... D8	St. Albans,N. ... F1	Wood St. ... G6
Michigan St. ... G1	St. Albans,S. ... F1	Wood St. ... G6
Minnehaha Ave.,E. ... B6	St. Clair ... E2,F1	Woodbridge St. ... A3
Minnehaha Ave.,W. ... B1	State St. ... F6	3rd St. ... C7,C8
Minnesota ... D5	Stinson St. ... A2	4th ... C8
Mississippi St. ... C5	Stryker Ave. ... G5	4th St.,E. ... C7
Ohio St. ... G4	Summit Ave. ... E2,F1	5th St. ... C8,E4,E5
Olive St. ... C5	Summit Ct. ... F2	5th St.,E. ... C7
Olmstead St. ... C5	Summit Ln. ... F1	6th St. ... C8
Pacific ... D8	Superior St. ... F1	6th St.,E. ... C7,E4
Park St. ... B3	Surrey Ave. ... D7	7th Pl. ... D5
Penn Ave. ... B4	Thomas Ave. ... C1	7th Pl.,W. ... E4
Petit St. ... C6	Topping St. ... A1	7th,E. ... C6
Pine St. ... C5	University Ave. ... C2,C4	7th,W. ... E4
Plato Blvd. ... F5	Van Buren Ave. ... B1	8th St. ... D5
Plum St. ... D7,D8	Virginia St. ... C2	9th St. ... D5
Portland Ave. ... E1	Wacouta St. ... D5	10th St. ... D5
Prospect Blvd. ... G5	Wakefield ... D8	11th St. ... D4
Ramsey St. ... F2	Wall St. ... D5	12th St. ... D4
Reaney Ave. ... B7	Walsh St. ... A7	13th St. ... C5,D4
Rice St. ... B3,D3	Wazata ... A3	
Robert St.,S. ... F6	Weide St. ... A8	
Robert,N. ... D5	Weide St. ... A8	

© C.S.C.

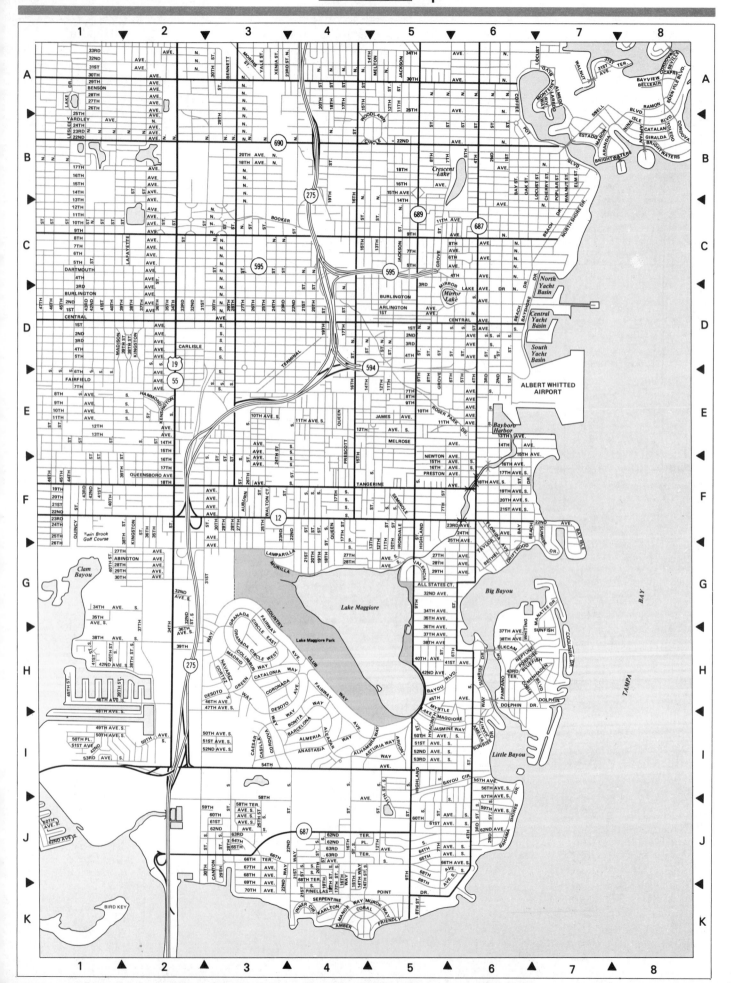

ST. PETERSBURG

Abington Ave. G1
Alcazar Way I4
Alhambra Way I4
All States Ct. G5
Almedo A7
Almeria I4
Amber K4
Amelia I6
Anastasia Way I4
Appian B8
Aranda B7
Argon I5
Arlington Ave. D5
Asturia Way I5
Auburn F3
Bahama Shores Dr. J6
Barcelona I4
Bay Isle F7
Bay St. B6,F6
Bayou Blvd. H5
Bayou Cir. I5
Bayshore Dr. D6
Bayview A8
Beach Dr. C7,D6,F6
Bellaire A8
Bennett A3
Benson Ave., N. A1
Bethel G6
Bluefish H6
Bonita Way I4
Booker C3
Brightwaters B7,B8
Burlington Ave., N. D1,D5
Caesar Way I3
Canton J3
Capri A8
Carlisle D2
Casilla I3
Catalan B8
Catalonia Way H3
Central Ave. D1,D6
Cherry St. B7
Cobia H6
Coffee Pot Blvd. A6
Columbus Way H3
Coquin Dr. H7
Coral K4
Cordova A8,B8,I3
Coronada H3
Cortez H3
Country Club Way G3
Dartmouth Ave.,N. C1
Desoto Ave. H3
Desoto Way H3
Dolphin H7
Dolphin Dr. H6
Driftwood Dr. G6
Eden Isle Blvd. A8
Elkham Blvd. A6
Elm St. B7
Estado B7
Fairfield Ave. E1
Fairway Ave. G3,H4
Flordia Ave. F6
Friendly K5
Giralda B8
Granada Circle East G3
Granada Circle West H3
Green Way H3
Grove St. C5,E5
Hammond E2
Highland St. G5,I5
Hyacinth St. I5
Inner Circle K4
Irondale G5
Isle Blvd. B8
James Ave. E5
Jasmine Way I5
Juanita Way I6
Karlton K4
Kensington E2
Kingston D2,F2
Lafayette St. C2
Lake Maggiore I5
Lamparilla G3
Laredo A7
Leslie Lake Dr. B1
Locust A7
Locust St. B7
Madrid H3
Manatee Dr. G7
Manor Way K4
Maron B7
Melrose Ave. E5
Melton A5
Mentladen H6
Mirrow Lake Ave.N. D6
Monterey Blvd. A7
Morris St. A3
Murilla G3
Murok Way K5
Myrtle H5
Naryarez H3
Neptune H6
Newton Ave. F5
Nina B8
North Shore Dr. C7
Oak St. B6
Pampano Sr. H6
Pinellas Point Dr. K4
Poplar St. B7
Porpoise H6
Prescott F4
Preston Ave. F5
Queen E4,F4
Queensboro Ave. F2
Quincy St. F1
Ramon A8
Riv Way A7
Roser Park Dr. E5
Seminole F5
Serpentine K4
Seville A8
Snell Blvd. A7
Sunfish H7
Sunrise Dr. F7,H6,I6
Tangerine Ave. F4
Taylor G6
Terminal D4
Toledo B8
Valencia G5
Walnut A7
Walnut St. B7
Walton Ct. F3
Way,S. H3
Whiting H6
Woodlawn Circle B5
Xenia St. A3
Yale St. A3
Yardley Ave.,N. B1
1st Ave.,N. D1,D5
1st Ave.,S. D1,D5
1st St.,N. B6
1st St.,S. E6
2nd Ave.,N. D1
2nd Ave.,S. D1,D5
2nd St.,N. B6
2nd St.,S. E6,J6
3rd Ave.,N. C1,D5
3rd Ave.,S. D1,D5
3rd St.,S. E6,J6
4th Ave.,N. C1,C6
4th Ave.,S. D1,D5
4th St.,N. B6
4th St.,S. E6,J6
5th Ave.,N. C1,C5
5th Ave.,S. D1
5th St.,N. B6
5th St.,S. E6
6th Ave.,N. C1,C6
6th Ave.,S. D1
6th St.,S. E6,H6
7th Ave.,N. C1,C5
7th Ave.,S. E1,D5
7th St. F5
7th St.,N. B5
7th St.,S. J5
8th Ave.,N. C1,C6
8th Ave.,S. E1,E5
8th St.,N. B5,E5
8th St.,S. K5
9th Ave.,N. C1,C5
9th Ave.,S. E1,E5
9th St.,N. E5
9th St.,S. G5,J5
10th Ave. E5
10th Ave.,N. C1
10th Ave.,S. E1,E3
10th St.,S. G5
11th Ave.,N. C1,C5
11th Ave.,S. E1,E4,E5
11th St.,N. A5,E5
11th St.,S. G5,J5
12th Ave.,N. C1
12th Ave.,S. E1,E4
12th St.,N. A5,C5,E5
12th St.,S. J5
13th Ave. E1,E6
13th Ave.,N. B1
13th St.,N. C5
13th St.,S. G5
14th Ave.,N. B1,C5
14th Ave.,S. E2,E6
14th St.,N. A5,E5
14th St.,S. K4
14th Way J4
15th F4
15th Ave. E6
15th Ave.,N. B1,B5
15th Ave.,S. E2,F5
15th St.,N. A4,C4
15th St.,S. J4
16th Ave. F6
16th Ave.,N. B1,B5
16th Ave.,S. F2,F5
16th St.,N. C4,E4
16th St.,S. J4
16th Way J4
17th Ave.,N. B1
17th Ave.,S. F2,F6
17th St. F4
17th St.,N. A4,D4
17th St.,S. K4
18th Ave.,N. B3,B5
18th Ave.,S. F2,F6
18th St., N. A4
18th St.,S. G4,K4
19th Ave.,S. F1,F6
19th St. D4
19th St.,N. B4
19th St.,S. G4,J4
20th Ave.,N. B3
20th Ave.,S. F1,F6
20th St.,N. A4,D4
20th St.,S. G4,J4
21st Ave.,S. F1,F6
21st St.,N. D4
21st St.,S. G4,K4
21st Way J4
22nd Ave. F7
22nd Ave.,N. B1,B5
22nd Ave.,S. F1
22nd St.,N. D4
22nd St.,S. F4,J4
22nd Way K4
23rd Ave. F1,F6
23rd Ave.,N. B1
23rd St. F3
23rd St.,N. A4,D3
24th Ave. F1,F6
24th Ave.,N. B1
24th St. F3
24th St.,N. D3
25th Ave.,N. A1
25th Ave.,S. F1,F6
25th St.,N. D3
25th St.,S. F3,J3
26th Ave.,N. A1,A5
26th Ave.,S. F1
26th St.,N. D3
26th St.,S. F3
27th Ave. G1,G5
27th Ave.,N. A1
27th Ave.,S. G4
27th St.,N. D3
27th St.,S. F3
28th Ave. G1,G5
28th Ave.,N. A1
28th Ave.,S. G4
28th St.,N. D3
28th St.,S. F3,J3
29th Ave. G1,G5
29th Ave.,N. A1
29th St. B3
29th St.,N. D3
29th St.,S. F3,J3
30th Ave. G1
30th Ave.,N. A1,A5
30th St. A3
30th St.,N. D3
30th St.,S. F3,J3
31st Ave. A7
31st Ave.,N. A1
31st St.,N. D3
31st St.,S. G3
31st Terr. A7
32nd D2
32nd Ave. G5
32nd Ave.,N. A1
32nd Ave.,S. G2
32nd St.,S. G2
33rd Ave.,N. A1
33rd St. D2
34th Ave. G5
34th Ave.,N. A5
34th Ave.,S. G1
34th St.,N. D2
34th St.,S. G2
35th Ave. G5
35th Ave.,S. G1
35th St.,N. D2
35th St.,S. F2
36th Ave. H5
36th Ave.,S. H2
36th St. D2
36th St.,S. F2
37th Ave. H5,H6
37th St.,N. D2
37th St.,S. G2
38th Ave. H5,H6
38th Ave.,S. H1
38th St. D2,F2
38th St.,S. H2
39th H2
39th St. D2,F2,H1
39th St.,N. D2
40th Ave. H5
40th St. G1
40th St.,N. D1
40th St.,S. F1,H1
41st Ave. H6
41st St.,N. D1
41st St.,S. F1,H1
42nd I1
42nd Ave. H5
42nd Ave.,S. H1
42nd St.,N. D1
42nd St.,S. F1
43rd St.,N. D1
43rd St.,S. F1
43rd Terr. H6
44th St.,S. F1
45th Ave. H5
45th St. H1
45th St.,N. D1
45th St.,S. F5
46th Ave.,S. H1
46th St.,N. D1
46th St.,S. F1
47th Ave.,S. H3
47th St.,N. D1
48th Ave.,S. H1
49th Ave.,S. I1
50th Ave.,S. I1,I3,I5
50th PL. I1
51st Ave.,S. I3,I5
53rd Ave.,S. I1,I5
54th Ave. I3
55th Ave. I6
56th Ave.,S. I6
57th Ave.,S. I6
58th Ave.,S. I3
58th Terr. J3
59th Ave.,S. J3,J6
60th Ave.,S. J1,J3,J5
61st Ave.,S. J3,J5
62nd Ave. J6
62nd Ave.,S. J1,J3
62nd Pl. J4
62nd Terr. J4
63rd J3
63rd Ave.,S. J4
63rd Terr. J4
64th J3
64th Ave.,S. J5
65th J3
65th Ave.,S. J5
66th Ave.,S. J3,J5
66th Terr. J3
67th Ave.,S. J3
68th Ave.,S. J3,J5
68th Terr. J4
69th Ave.,S. J3,J5
70th Ave. K3

SALT LAKE CITY

A St. C5
Acadia Pl. F6
Acorn Ct. G6
Adams Pl. C3
Aiken Ct. D4
Alameda Ave. D6
Albermarle Ave. I3
Almond St. C4
Aloha Rd. A7
American Ave. G1,G3
Amos Villa E6,I4
Andrew Ave. I3,I4
Apricot Ave. C4
Arapahoe Ave. F2
Ardmore Pl. C4
Arnold Pl. D6
Artic Ct. B4
Aspen Ave. G3
Athletic Park H7
Atlantic Ct. C4
Autumn Ave. B1
B St. C6
Baddley Pl. E8
Baltic St. B4
Beaumont Ct. B3
Beldon Pl. F6
Bellhaven Ct. F7
Belmont Ave. G7
Bishop Pl. B4
Blaine Ave. J6,J8
Blair St. E6,G6,K6
Bonneville Blvd. A5
Bonneville Dr. A8
Bothwell St. F1
Braewick Rd. A5
Briarcliff Ave. B1
Brixten Ct. F8
Broadway E5
Brooklyn Ave. G1,G4
Browning Ave. I5,I7
Brunswick Pl. E5
Bryan Ave. I6,I7
Bueno Ave. D7
Burns St. E6
Butterwood Ct. C7
C St. C6
California Ave. H1,H4
Canyon Rd. C5
Capitol St., E. C5
Capitol St., W. A4
Carson St. E4,F4
Center St. C4
Chamberlain Ct. F5
Chase Ave. G7
Chesney Ct. E4
Chicago St. B1
Citizens Ct. E3
Clayton Ct. C4
Cleveland Ave. I6
Clinton Ave. B4
Coatsville Ave. J6
Cody Pl. E6
Colmar Ave. J1
Coloney Ct. B4
Commonwealth Ave. K5,K6,K7
Conway Ct. F6
Cottage Ave. F6
Crane St. E4
D St. C6
Dallmore Ct. G5
Dalton H1
Delmar Ct. E4
Denver St. E6,G6
Depot Ct. E2
Deseret Ave. D3
Dine Ct. J5
Dooley Ct. D7
Dorchester A5
Downington Ave. J5,J8
Dresden Pl. F8
Dubec Ct. E6
Duncan Pl. E7
E St. C6
Eardley Pl. F5
Edgecombe Dr. A5
Edgehill Rd. A8
Edgemont Ave. C4
Edison St. E5,G5,I5,J5
Edith Ave. H5
Egli Ct. F7
Elm Ave. K6,K8
Ely Pl. F7
Emerson Ave. I6
Erie St. B3
Euclid Ave. D1
Exchange Pl. E5
F St. C6
Fayette Ave. G2,G4
Findlay Ct. F4
Fletcher Ct. E8
Folsom Ave. D1,D4
Formosa Pl. C3
Foulton Pl. E3
Fremont Ave. H1,H4
Fuller Ave. E7,E8
G St. C7
Gale St. D3,F3,H3
Gallagher Pl. F6
Gardena Ct. C2
Garfield Ave. J6,J8
Gemmill D6
Genesee Ave. G2
Girard Ave. B1,B3,B4
Glen St. F1
Glendale St. H1
Goltz Ave. H4
Goodard Ct. D5
Gordon Pl. C5
Goshen St. F1
Goss Ct. F3
Grace Ct. G6
Grand Pl. F8
Grant St. B2,J2
Green St. G7,H7,K7
Greenlawn Pl. C3
Gregory Pl. F5
Grove Ave. J4
Gudgell Ct. F6
H St. C7
Hammer Pl. D6
Hampton Ave. H5
Hanover Pl. D7
Hansen Ave. I3
Harmony Ct. D7
Harris Ave. I4
Harrison Ave. I6,I8
Hartwell Ave. J3,J4
Harvard Ave. H5,H8
Hawkes Ct. D7
Hawthorne Ave. F5,F7
Haxton Ct. D8
Hayes Ave. G1
Hazel St. E6
Heather St. D7
Herbert Ave. G5,G6,G8
High Ave. I4
Hills Dr. A8
Hilltop Rd. A7
Hollywood Ave. K6,K8
Holmer Ct. E5
Hope Ave. I3
Hoyt Pl. C1
Hubbard Ave. G5
I St. C7
Iowa St. E8
Ivan Ct. E7
Iverson St. F8
J St. C7
Jackson Ave. C2,C4
James Ct. G6
James St. J1
Jefferson Ave. J4
Jefferson St. G4
Jeremy St. D2,F2,H2
Jewell Ave. J1
Juniper Ct. F6
K St. C7
Kelsey Ave. H5
Kensington Ave. I6,I8
Kilbourne Ct. G6
Kimball Ct. C4
L St. C7
Laconio Ct. F6
Lafayette Dr. A1
Laird Ave. H8
Lake St. G7,J7
Laker Ct. E7
Lanark Ct. F6
Langton Pl. C4
Laxon Ct. C1
Layton Ave. J2,J4
Lerned Ave. D1,D3
Lester Ct. G3
Lexington Ave. H1
Liberty Ave. H7
Lincoln St. D8,G8
Linden Ave. E7,E8
Little Valley Dr. A8
Logan Ave. I7
Long Ave. J1
Los Angeles St. A1
Lowell Ave. F5,F6
Lucy Ave. H2,H4
Lyman Ct. H8
M St. C8
MacArthur Ave. J4
MacFarland Dr. A1
Main St. E5,J5
Main St., N. B4
Major St. F5,K5
Margaret Ave. J1
Margett Pl. E6
Marion St. B1
Markea Ave. E6,E8
Markell Ct. F4
Maryland Pl. E5
McClelland St. D8,I8
McDonald Pl. F7
Mead Ave. G2,G4
Mendon Ct. G7
Menlo Ave. E7
Meredith Ct. D2
Merriman Ave. I4
Milton Ave. I6,I7
Montague Ave. G2
Montclair Ct. E7
Montrose Ave. F4
Mordivall Ct. D6
Mortem Ct. F5
Mortenson Ct. F5
N St. C8
Naylor Ct. H8
Newman Ct. F4
Nocturne Dr. A1
Norris Pl. E8
North Temple St. C3
Northcliffe Dr. A8
Northcrest Dr. A8
Northhills Dr. A7
Northmont Way A6
O St. C8
Orchard Pl. F4
Orpheum Ave. D5
Ouray Ave. B1,B2
Owen Pl. E6
P St. C8
Pacicic Ave. E2,E4
Pacific Pl. E3
Paramount Ave. I4
Park St. E6,F6,J6
Paxton Ave. H2,H3,H4
Penna Pl. E8
Pershing Pl. E4
Pierpoint E3,E4
Pleasant Ct. E4
Plum Alley D5
Poinsettia Dr. A1
Poplar Ct. E4
Post Office Pl. E4
Post St. E1
Princeton Ave. H7
Prosperity Ave. A1
Pugsley St. B3
Q St. C8
Quayle Ave. J1,J4
Queen St. I2
Quince St. C4
Ramona Ave. J6,J8
Redondo Ave. K6
Reed Ave. A3
Regent St. D5,K5
Remington Way H2
Richards St. D4,G4,J4,K4
Rio Grande St. E3,G3
Roberts St. I5
Roosevelt Ave. I6
Rosewood Ave. K5
Rustic Pl. C3
Sandberg Pl. F5
Sego Ave. F6,F7
Seward Ave. C2
Sherman Ave. H6,H7
Shotline Ave. C3
Signora Dr. A1
Simondi Ave. C1,C2
Slade Pl. E6
Smith Pl. D7
Social Hall Ave. D5
South Temple St. D1,D4
Stanton Ave. F6
State St. E5,J5
Strongfellow Ct. F5
Strongs Ct. E8
Sunrise Ave. A7
Talisman Dr. A1
Temple Ave. D5
Temple St. C4
Temple St., W. C4,D4,J4
Thorn Ct. F4
Tiffany Ct. B4
Tribley Pl. F6
Trinidad Pl. F4
Trisler Pl. D3
Turtle Ct. B3
Tyler St. H7
Utahna Cir. I1
Utahna Dr. I1
Utopia Ave. K5
Van Buren Ave. I4
Van Ct. F5
Victory Rd. A4
Vine St. C4
Vissing Pl. F4
Volney Ct. F4
Voyles Pl. E8
Vulcan Ct. D2
Walker Pl. E4
Wall St. B5
Walton Ct. D5
Wasatch K4
Wasatch Pl. F4
Washington St. G4
Wayne Ct. E4
Webster St. I2
Welton Ct. D5
Wenco Cir. I1
Wenco Dr. I1
Wentworth Ave. K5
Werner Pl. E6
Westminster Ave. J6
Westwood Ave. K4
Whitecloud Ct. E6
Whitmore Ct. D4
Whitney Ave. I3
Willard Ct. F4
Williams Ave. G5,G8
Wilmington Ave. K6
Wilshire Pl. F8
Wilson Ave. J6,J8
Windsor St. D8,F7,H7,J7
Winthrop Ct. E6
Wood Ave. I5,I8
Woodbine St. D3,F3
Yale Ave. H5,H7
Zane Ave. B5
1st Ave. D6
1st South St. D1
2nd Ave. C6
2nd East St. E5,J5
2nd South St. D1,E4
3rd Ave. C6
3rd East St. E6,J6
3rd South St. E1,E7
4th Ave. C6
4th East St. E6,J6
4th South St. E1,E4
5th Ave. C6
5th East St. J6
5th South St. F1,F4
6th Ave. C6
6th East St. J7
6th South St. F1,F4
7th Ave. C6
7th East St. J7
7th South St. F1,F4
8th Ave. B6
8th East St. E7,J7
8th South St. G1,G4
9th Ave. B7
9th East St. E8,J8
9th South St. G1,G4
10th Ave. B7
10th East St. J8
11th Ave. B7
11th East St. J8
12th Ave. B7
13th Ave. A7
13th South St. H2,H6
14th Ave. A7
14th South St. I1,I4
15th South St. I3
16th Ave. A7
16th South St. I3
17th Ave. A7
17th South St. J1,J6
18th Ave. A7
21st South St. K1,K6
1000 West St. D1,I1
1045 West St. J1
1100 West St. D1
1355 South St. H2
1390 South St. I2
200 North St. C3
200 West St. D4,J4
2155 South St. K5
2170 South St. K4
2205 South St. K6
300 North St. C3
300 West St. D3,J3
400 East St. K6
400 North St. B3
400 West St. D3
500 North St. B1,B4
500 West St. D3,J3
600 North St. B3
600 West St. D2
700 North St. A3
700 West St. C2,J2
800 North St. A1,A3
800 West St. D2,H2
900 North St. A3
900 West St. D1,J1

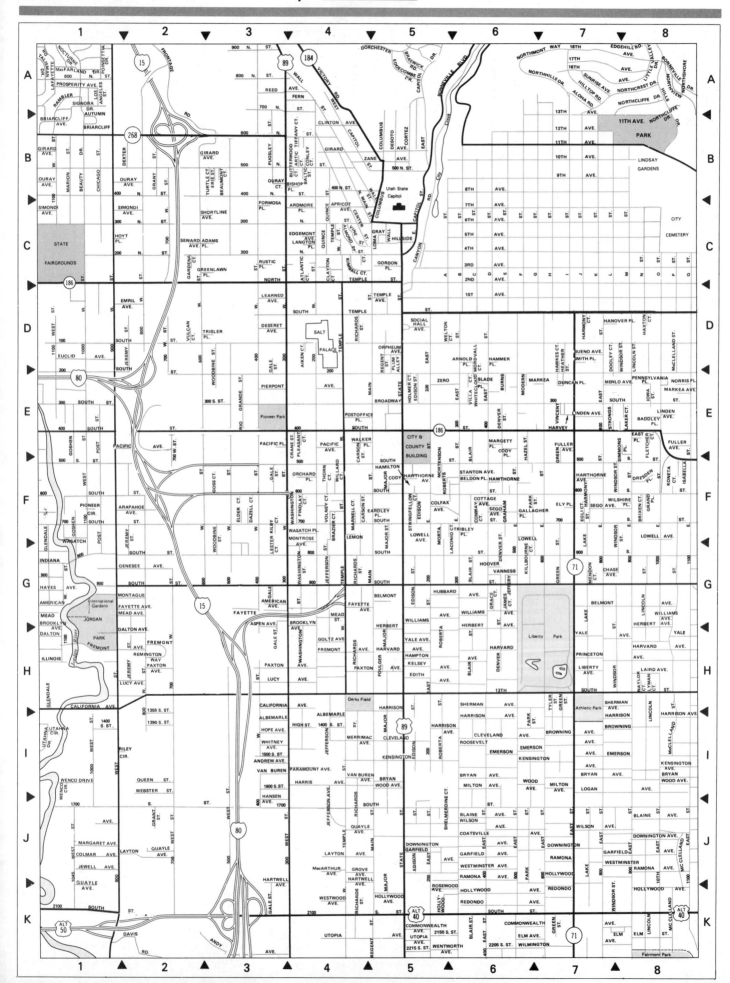

Scale of Miles
N
0 .2 .4 .6

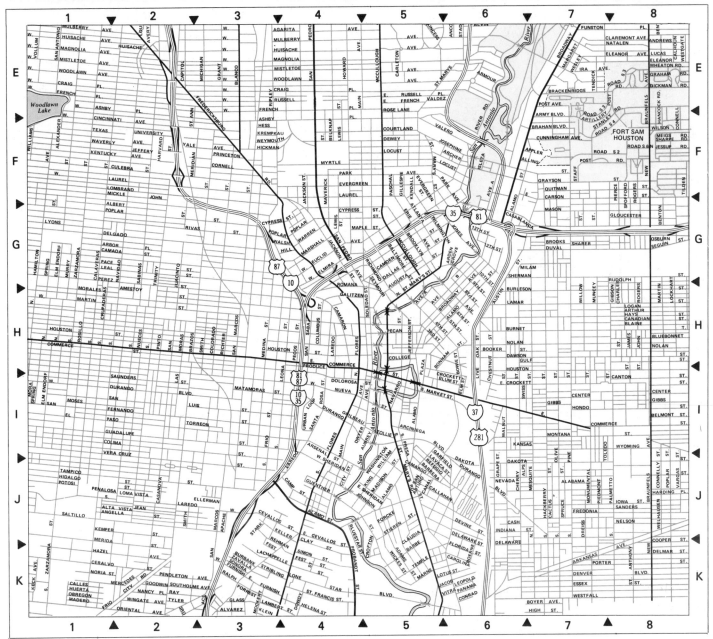

SAN ANTONIO

Ace	K3	
Adams St.	K5	
Agarita Ave.	E4	
Alabama St.	J7	
Alamo Plaza	I5	
Alamo St.	G6,H6,J4,J5	
Albert	G1	
Alexander	F1	
Alling	F7	
Alps	J6	
Alta Vista	J1	
Alvarez	K3	
Amestoy	H2	
Ancona	E6	
Andrews	E8	
Angella St.	J1	
Apache	J3	
Appler	F7	
Arbor Pl.	G1	
Archer	F6	
Arcinega	I5	
Arden Grove	G6	
Arkansas Ave.	K7	
Armour	E6	
Army Blvd.	F7	
Arsenal St.	I4	
Arthur	H8	
Artillery	F7	
Ashby Pl.	F3	
Ashby Pl., W.	E1	
Atlanta	G5	
Aubrey	I5	
August St.	G5	
Austin	H6	
Ave. A	F6,H5	
Ave. B	H5	
Avery	E2	
Baltimore St.	G5	
Barbe	K5	
Barrera	J5	
Belknap	F4	
Belmont St.	I8	
Benton	E8,G8	
Blaine	H8	
Blanco Rd.	E3	
Blue Star St.	J4	
Blum St.	I6	
Boerne	K6	
Bonham St.	H5	
Booker St.	H6	
Boyer Ave.	E7	
Brackenridge Rd.	E7	
Brahan Blvd.	F7	
Brazos St.	H2	
Broadway Ave.	E7,H6	
Brooklyn Ave.	G5	
Brooks	G7	
Burbank	K3	
Burleson St.	H6	
Burnet St.	H6	
Cactus St., S.	J7	
Calaveras St., S.	G1	
Calhoun	E8	
Callahan	J5	
Calles	K1	
Camada St.	G1	
Camargo	J5	
Camaron	H4	
Camden St.	G5	
Camp St.	J4	
Canadian St.	H8	
Canal	J5	
Canton St.	I8	
Capitol	E2	
Carleton	E5	
Carolina	K6	
Carson St.	E7	
Casablanca	G6	
Casanova	J2	
Cash	J6	
Center	I7,I8	
Ceralvo St.	K1	
Cevallos St., E.	J4	
Cevallos St., W.	J3	
Cherry St.	J6	
Chestnut St.	I6	
Cincinnati Ave., W.	F1	
City St.	J4	
Claremont Ave.	E8	
Claudia	J5	
Clay St.	J4	
Colina St.	I1	
College	H5	
Colorado St.	H3	
Columbus St.	H4	
Commerce St., E.	H1,H4,I7	
Connell	F8	
Connelly St.	J8	
Conrad	K6	
Cooper St.	K8	
Courtland	F5	
Craig Pl., W.	E1,E4	
Crockett	I6	
Crockett St., E.	I6	
Crofton	K5	
Crupaderas St.	H1	
Culebra	F2	
Cunningham Ave.	F7	
Cypress St.	G3,G4	
Dakota	J6	
Dakota St.	J6	
Dallas St.	G5	
Dawson St.	H6	
Delaware	K6,J6	
Delgado	G1	
Delmar St.	K8	
Denver Blvd.	K7	
Devine St.	J6	
Dewey	F5	
Dickman Rd.	E8	
Dolorosa St.	I4	
Dowdy St.	K4	
Dreiss St.	J7	
Durango Blvd.	I2,I4,J6	
Duval	G7	
Dwyer Ave.	I4	
El Paso	I1	
Eleanor	E8	
Eleanor Ave.	E8	
Ellerman	J3	
Elm Endorf	I1	
Elm Endorf St.	G1	
Elm St.	I6	
Elmira, W.	G4	
Elwood	E8	
Erie Ave.	G5	
Essex St.	K7	
Euclid Ave., W.	G4	
Evergreen	F4,F5	
Fest	K3	
Fest St.	K4	
Flores, N.	H4	
Flores, S.	H4	
Florida St.	K6	
Forck	J5	
Forrest	K3	
Fredonia	J7	
French Pl., W.	E1,E3	
Frio City Rd.	K1	
Frio St., S.	I3	
Funston Pl.	E7	
Furnish	K3	
Furnish, E.	K3	
Galitzen St.	H5	
Garfield	J5	
Gibbs	I7,I8	
Gibson	H8	
Gillespie	F5	
Glass	K1	
Glouchester St.	G8	
Goodwin	J5	
Graham Rd.	E8	
Grant	E3	
Grape St.	J6	
Grayson St.	F7	
Guadalupe St.	I1	
Guenther	J4	
Guilbeau	I4	
Hackberry St., S.	J7	
Hamilton Ave., N.	G1	
Hancock Rd.	F8	
Harding Pl.	J8	
Harvard	F2	
Hays St.	H8	
Hazel Ave.	K1	
Helena St.	K4	
Hess	F3	
Hickman	F3	
High St.	K7	
Hill	G4	
Hondo St.	I7	
Houston St.	H1,H3,I6	
Howard St.	I4	
Huerta	K1	
Huisache Ave.	E2	
Huisache Ave., W.	I6	
Indiana St.	J6	
Iowa St.	J8	
Ira Ave.	E7	
Isleta	F6	
Jackson St.	F4,G4	
Jacob	K6	
Jefferson St.	H5	
Jeffery	F2	
Jessup Rd., N.	F7	
Johnson	J5	
Jones Ave.	G5	
Josephine St.	F6	
Kansas	J1	
Keck Ave.	K1	
Keller	K3	
Kemper St.	J1	
Kendall	F8	
Kentucky Ave.	F1	
King William	J5	
Klein	K3	
Krempkau	F3	
Lachappelle St.	K3	
Lamar St.	H6	
Lambert St.	J4	
Laredo	H4,J2,J4	
Las Moras	H2	
Laurel	F2,F4	
Leal St.	G1	
Leona St., S.	I4	
Leopold	J6	
Lewis St.	F4,G4	
Live Oak St.	H8	
Lockhart	H8	
Locust	F5,F6	
Logan	H8	
Loma Vista	J2	
Lombrand	F2	
Lone Star Blvd.	J4	
Lotus St.	K6	
Louise	E8	
Lucas	E8	
Lyons	G5	
Madero	K1	
Madison	J5	
Magnolia, W.	E1,E4	
Mann Ave.	I4	
Maple St.	G5	
Margaret	E7	
Marine	J6	
Market St., E.	I5	
Marshall	G4	
Martin	H8	
Martin, W.	H4	
Mason	G7	
Matamoras	I3	
Maverick St.	H4	
McCullough St.	E5,G5	
Medina St.	H4	
Meigs Rd.	F8	
Mercedes	K2	
Merida St.	J1	
Meridian	F2	
Mesquite, N.	J7	
Michigan	E3	
Mickle John	F2	
Milam	G6	
Milam St.	G4	
Mistletoe Ave., W.	I6	
Mockert	K3	
Montana St.	I7	
Monumental St.	I7	
Mora	I1	
Morales St.	H2	
Moses	I1	
Mulbery Ave., W.	E4	
Muncey St.	H7	
Murry	G1	
Myrtle	F4	
Nancy Pl.	K3	
Natalen	E8	
Navarro St.	I5	
Navidad	G2	
Nelson	J6	
Neuva St., W.	I4	
Nevada St.	J6	
New Braunfels Ave.	F8,J8	
Nolan	H6,H8	
Noria St.	K1	
Nueces St.	H4	
Obregon	K1	
Olive St., S.	J7	
Oriental Ave.	K2	
Osburn	G1	
Pace St.	G1	
Palmetto, S.	K6	
Panama	K6	
Park Ave.	F4,F6	
Paschal	F5	
Pecan	H4	
Pecos St.	H4	
Pendelton Ave.	K2	
Perez St.	J6	
Piedmont	J7	
Pierce	F8	
Pine St., S.	H2	
Pinto	H2	
Poplar St.	G1	
Popular	G3	
Popular St.	G4,G8	
Porter	K7	
Post Ave.	F7	
Post Rd.	F7	
Potosi St.	I5	
Presa St., S.	I5	
Princess	E5	
Princeton	F3	
Probandt St.	J4	
Produce	H4	
Quitman St.	F7	
Ralph	K3	
Ray	K1	
Refugio	J5	
Rehman	K3	
Richmond	G5	
Richter	K6	
Rivas St.	G2	
River Rd.	J6	
Road S 2	F7	
Road S 3	E8,F7	
Road S 4	F7	
Road S 6	F7	
Rogers	F8,H8	
Roman	J6	
Rose Lane	E5	
Rosillo	H1	
Rudolph	G8	
Russell Pl., E.	H8	
Russell, W.	E4	
Sabinas St.	J4	
Saltillo	J1	
San Antonio	E5,G5	
San Antonio Ave.	E1	
San Fernando St.	H2	
San Juacinto St.	H2	
San Luis St.	I4	
San Marcos	J3	
San Marcos St.	J3	
San Pedro	G4	
San Pedro Ave.	E4	
San Saba	H4	
Sanders	J8	
Santa Rosa St.	I5	
Saunders	I2	
Seguin St.	G5	
Seymour	G5	
Sharer	K2	
Sharpe Rd.	F8	
Sheridan, E.	J5	
Sheridan, W.	J4	
Sherman St.	G6	
Simon St.	K4	
Smith	H3,J2	
Soledad St.	H4	
Sonora	K3	
Southolme Ave.	K3	
Spofford	K6	
Spring	I1	
Spring St.	G1	
Spruce St.	J7	
St. Ann	K8	
St. Anthony	K8	
St. Charles	H8	
St. Francis St.	H8	
St. James	H8	
St. John	H8	
St. Mary's Rd., N.	F5,H5	
St. Mary's St.	J5	
St. Marys	H5	
Stadium	E6	
Staff	F7	
Stanley Rd.	F7	
Stark	J5	
Stieren St.	J5	
Stribling	J4	
Swiss	I6	
Tampico St.	I5	
Temple	J6	
Tendick	F8	
Texas	F1	
Tilden	F8	
Toledo St.	I5	
Tolle	I5	
Torreon	I2	
Trinity St.	G2	
Tyler	K2	
University	F2	
Urban Loop	I4	
Valdez	E5	
Valero	F5	
Vargas St.	J8	
Vera Cruz St.	I1	
Vitra	K6	
Vollum Ave.	E1	
Walnut St.	I6	
Walsh	F1	
Warren	G4	
Washington	J5	
Waverly	F1	
Welhausen	E7	
Wesley	E8	
Westfall	K7	
Westgate	E8	
Weymouth	F3	
Wheaton Rd.	E8	
Wickes St.	K5	
Williams	F1	
Willow St.	H7	
Wilmington	F5	
Wilson	F8	
Wingate Ave.	K2	
Woodlawn Ave., W.	E1,E4	
Wyoming	I8	
Yale Ave.	F7	
Zarzamora St., S.	G1,K1	
Zavalla	K2	
3rd	K2	
3rd St.	H5	
4th St.	H5	
5th St.	H5	
6th St.	H6	
8th St.	H6	
9th St.	G6	
10th St.	G6	
12th St.	G6	
13th St.	G6	

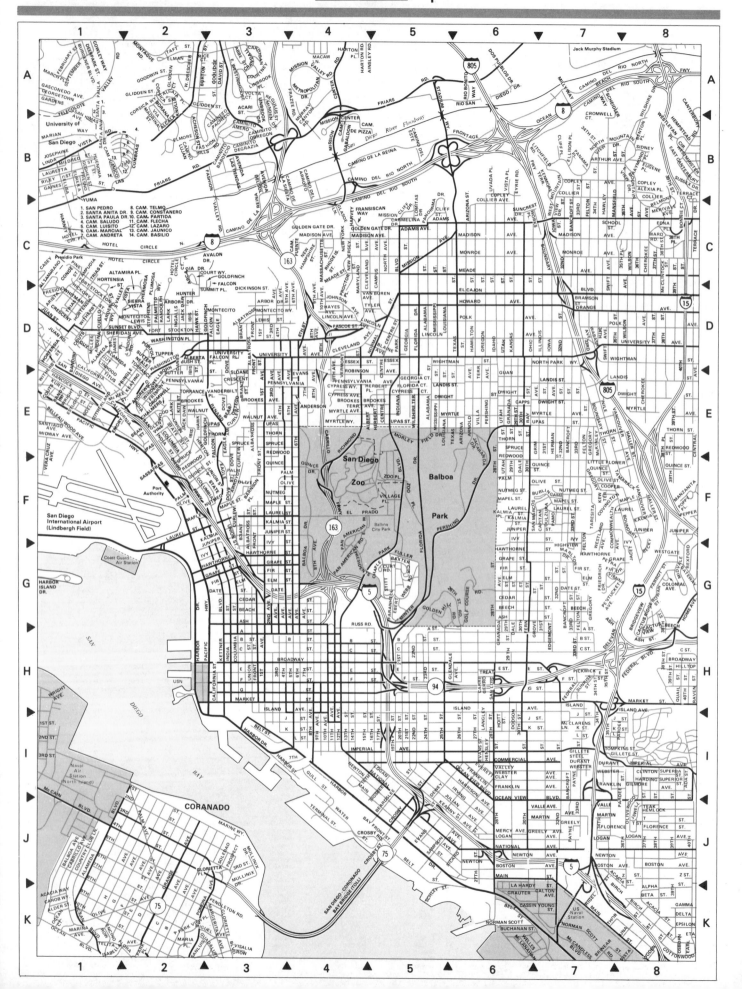

SAN DIEGO

A Ave....K-2
A St....H-3,H-4,H-5,H-7
Abbe St....A-3
Acacia St....J-8,K-8
Acacia Way....K-1
Acar St....A-3
Acheson St....B-2
Adams Ave....C-5
Ada St....I-8
Ainsley Rd....A-4
Alabama St....D-5,E-5
Alameda....D-1
Alameda Blvd....J-1
Albatross St..D-3,E-3,F-3
Alcala Ct....B-2
Alder St....K-1
Alexia Pl....B-8
Alpha St....K-8
Altamirano....C-1
Ampudia....C-1
Arbor Dr....D-3
Arcadia Dr....C-2
Arch....C-4
Arden....D-1
Arden Wy....D-1
Arista Ct....C-1
Arista St....D-1
Arizona Ave....E-6
Arnold Ave....E-6
Arroyo....F-3
Arthur Ave....B-7
Ash St....G-3,G-6
Avalah Dr....C-2
B Ave....K-2
B St....H-3,H-4,H-5,H-7
Balboa Ave....J-1
Balboa Dr....G-4
Bancroft St...E-7,G-7,I-7
Barnson Pl....F-3
Baxter Cir....G-5
Bay Front St....J-5
Beach St....G-3,G-6
Bean St....E-2
Beardslee St....J-5
Becky....G-8
Belmont....B-8
Belt St....J-5,K-6
Benton Pl....B-8
Berana....A-2
Beta St....K-8
Birch St....K-8
Blaine Ave....D-5
Bonnie Ct....C-8
Boston Ave....J-6-8
Boundary....F-8
Boundary St....E-7
Bramson St....D-7
Brant St....D-3,E-3,F-3
Brinear St....K-7
Broadway....H-3,H-8
Brookes Ave..E-2,E-3,E-5
Brookes Terr....E-4
Buchanan St....K-6
Burgener Blvd....A-1
Burgener Dr....A-1
Burlingame....F-7
C Ave....K-2
C St....H-3-5,H-7-8
Cabrillo Ave....J-1
California St.
....D-1,E-1,H-3
Calton Ave....K-7
Cam Andreta....B-2
Cam Basilio....B-1
Cam Costanero....B-2
Cam Estoban....B-1
Cam Flecha....B-2
Caminito Amero....B-3
Caminito Bardecio..B-3
Caminito Cantti....B-2
Caminito Degrazia..B-3
Camino de la Reina
....B-4,C-3
Camino Del Arroyo..B-4
Camino de la Siesta..B-4
Camino del Este....B-5
Camino del Rio North
....A-7,A-8,B-4,B-5
Camino Del Rio South
....A-7,A-8,B-5
Caminito Mangana..B-3
Caminito Obregon...B-3
Camineto Pacheco..B-3
Cam Juanico....B-1
Cam Lazaro....B-2
Cam Luisito....B-2
Cam Marcial....B-2
Cam Partido....B-2
Campus Ave....D-5
Cam Saludo....B-2
Cam Talmo....B-2
Canterbury Dr....B-8
Canterbury, E....B-8
Capps....E-6
Captain....F-7
Cardigan....A-3
Cardinal....A-4
Carmelina....C-5
Carob Wy....K-1
Carre Gerro....H-6
Casey....C-1
Cassin Young St....K-7
Cedar St....G-3,G-6
Celusa....B-1
Central Ave....E-8
Centre St....D-5
Chaple....G-5
Cherokee Ave....C-8,E-8
Clay Ave....I-6
Cleveland Ave....C-4,D-4
Cliff Pl....B-7
Cliff St....C-5
Clinton....I-8
Collier Ave...B-7,B-8,C-6
Columbia St..E-2,F-2,H-3
Commercial Ave....I-6
Commonwealth Ave.F-7
Coolidge St....B-2
Cooper....F-7
Copley Ave..B-7,B-8,C-6
Corsica St....A-2
Corsica Wy....A-2
Cottonwood....K-8
Country Club Ln....J-1
Court Way....C-2
Courtney....A-3
Couts....E-1
Covington....F-7
Crescent....E-3
Crescent Dr....D-1
Cromwell Ct....A-7
Crosby St....J-5
Crowell....E-2
Curlew....E-3
Curlow....F-3
Curt Rd....G-5
Cypress Ave....E-4
Cypress Ct....E-5
Cypress Wy....E-4
D Ave....K-2
Dale St....F-6,G-6
Dane....D-2
Date St....G-3,G-7
Delta....K-8
Dewey....I-5
Dickinson St....D-3
Dodson....I-6
Douglas....D-2
Dove....E-3
Drescher St....A-2
Drescher, W....A-2
Duluzura....F-7
Durant....I-7
Dwight St....E-6,E-8
E Ave....K-2
E St....H-3-7
Eagle....D-3,E-3,F-3
Earl....K-8
Edna Pl....C-8
El Cajon Blvd....D-6
Ellison Pl....B-7
Elman....A-2
Elmore St....B-2
Elm St....G-3,G-6,G-7
El Prado....F-4,F-5
Emery....E-1
Encino Row....K-1
Epsilon....K-8
Essex St....D-4
Estudillo....E-1
Eta....K-8
Eugene Pl....B-8
Eureka....B-1
Evans St....E-4,I-6,J-5
Everett....I-6
Eyrie Rd....B-6
F Ave....K-2
F St....H-3-5,H-7
Falcon....D-3
Falcon Pl....D-3
Faranhell Ebert....G-5
Fashion Valley Rd...B-3
February St....A-1
Federal Blvd....H-7,H-8
Felton St....E-7,G-7
Fern St....G-6
Fir Dr....G-7
Fir St....G-3,G-6,G-7
Flora....K-2
Florence St....J-8
Florida Ct....E-5
Florida Dr....D-5,F-5
Fort Stockton Dr.D-1,D-2
Franciscan Wy....C-5
Franklin Ave....I-6,I-7
Frazee Rd....A-4
Fremont....E-2
Fresno....B-1
Friars Rd....A-5,B-2
Friedrich Dr....G-7
Frontage....B-6
Front St....D-3,F-3,H-3
Fuller....G-5
G Ave....K-1
G St....H-3,H-6
Gaines St....B-1
Gamma....K-8
Gardens Ave....A-1
Gasconedo Ave....A-1
Gateway....G-8
Georgetown....A-1
Georgia Ct....E-5
Georgia St....D-5
Gillete St....I-7
Gilmore....I-8
Glasoe Ln....C-4
Glendale Ave....H-6
Glenwood....E-2
Glidden Ct....A-2
Glidden St....A-2
Gloriette Blvd....K-3
Gloriette Pl....J-2,J-3
Golden Gate Dr....C-4
Golden Mill Rd....G-5
Golf Course Rd....G-6
Goodwin St....A-2
Goshawk Ave....A-4
Goshen St....B-1
Granada Ave....E-6,H-6
Grape St....G-3,G-6,G-7
Grauter....K-6
Greenly Ave....J-7
Gregory....E-7,F-7,G-7
Grim Ave....E-7
Grove St....G-7
Guadalupe....K-3
Guan St....E-6
Gull St....I-4
Guy....D-1,E-2
H Ave....K-1
Haller St....F-8
Hamilton St....D-6
Hancock St....E-1
Harbor Dr....H-2,I-4
Harding....I-8
Harrison Ave....I-6
Harton Pl....A-4
Harton Rd....A-4
Harvey Rd....C-4
Hawk....E-2
Hawley....C-7
Hawthorne St.
....G-3,G-6,G-7
Haydon....D-1
Hayes Ave....D-4
Heitt St....I-6
Hemlock....J-8
Hempstead, N....B-8
Hensley....I-6
Herbert Pl....E-5
Herman Ave....E-7
Hertensia St....C-1,D-1
Herton....E-2
Hickory St....D-1
Highview....G-7
Hilldale....B-8
Hilltop....H-8
Hoffman St....C-4
Hortensia....D-1
Hotel Circle Ct....C-2
Hotel Circle N....C-2
Hotel Cir. Pl....C-1
Hotel Circle S....C-2
Howard Ave....D-6
Huenoma St....B-1
Ibis St....D-2,E-2
Idaho St....D-6
Illinois St....D-7
Impasse....D-1
Imperial Ave....I-4,I-8
India St....Ep2,H-2
Ingalls....D-2
Inland Fwy....A-6
Iowa....D-7
Irving Ave....I-6
Isabella Ave....K-1
Island Ave...H-3,H-6,H-8
Ivy St....F-6,F-8,G-3
J St....I-4,I-6,I-7
Jacaranda Dr....E-6
Jacet....G-8
Jack Daw....D-2,E-2
Jewell....J-8
Johnson Ave....D-4
Josephine....B-1
Juan....D-1
Julian Ave....J-6
Juniper St....F-3,F-6,F-8
K St....I-4,I-6-8
Kalmia Pl....F-6
Kalmia St....F-3,F-6,F-8
Kansas St....D-6
Kearny Ave....J-6
Keating....E-2
Kenmore Terr....B-7
Kettner Blvd....H-3
Kew Ter....F-7
Kurtz St....E-1
L St....I-4,I-7,I-8
Las Cumbras....B-1
LaHardy St....K-6
Lake Ct....A-2
Landis St....E-6,E-8
Langley....I-6
Lark....D-2,E-2
Laurel St....F-2,F-3
....F-6,F-7,F-8
Lauretta St....B-1
Lewis St....D-2,D-3
Linbrook Pl....A-3
Lincoln Ave....D-4,D-5
Linda Vista Rd....B-1
Linwood....D-1
Litchfield Rd....B-7
Little Flower....F-7
Logan Ave....I-5,J-6,J-8
Lomitas Dr....C-5
Louisiana St....E-5
Lyndon Rd....D-2
Macaw Ln....A-4
Madison Ave.C-4,C-6,C-7
Main St....I-4,J-6,K-7
Manzanita....F-8
Maple St....F-3,F-6-8
March Pl....A-1
Margerita Ave....K-3
Marian Way....B-1
Marina Ave....K-1
Marine Wy....J-3
Market St....H-3,H-8
Marlton Dr....G-7
Maryland St....C-4
McCain Blvd....I-1,J-1
McCandless Blvd....K-7
McClarens Ln....I-7
McClintock St....C-8
McKee St....E-1
McKinley....E-7
McLanahan....K-6
Meade Ave....C-6
Mercy Ave....J-6
Merivale Ave....C-8
Midvale....G-8
Midway Ave....E-1
Miguel Ave....K-3
Mildred St....B-1
Miller....D-1
Minden Dr....A-3
Minter....G-5
Mission Ave....C-5
Mission Center Ct....B-4
Mission Center Rd.
....A-4,B-4
Mission Cliff Dr....C-5
Mississippi St....E-5
Monroe Ave....C-6,C-7
Montecito....D-2,D-3
Montecito Wy....D-3
Morgha....D-1
Morley Field Dr....E-5
Morse Ct....A-3
Mountain View Dr.,E.B-8
Mountain View Dr., N.
....B-7,B-8
Mullinix Dr....J-3
Murray Canyon Rd...B-4
Myrtle Wy....E-4
Myrtle Ave...E-4,E-7,E-8
National Ave....I-5,J-6
New Hampshire St...C-4
New Jersey....C-4
Newton Ave...I-4,J-6,J-7
New York....C-4
Nile St....E-7
Noell....E-1
Normal St....D-5
Norman Scott Rd.
....K-6,K-7
North Ave....C-5
North Park Wy....D-7
Nutmeg St....F-3,F-6,F-7
Ocean Beach Fwy...A-7
Ocean Blvd....K-1
Ocean Ct....K-1
Ocean View Blvd....I-6
Ohio St....D-6
Old Town....D-1
Olive Ave....K-1
Olive St....F-3,F-7
Olivewood....J-8
Orange Ave.D-7,J-2,ZK-2
Oregon St....D-6
Osborn....K-8
Otis....A-3
Pacific Hwy....E-1,H-3
Palm....F-3,F-6
Palm Ave....J-2
Palmetta....D-2
Pamo....F-7
Panama Pl....B-7
Pan American Rd. E..G-4
Pan American W....F-4
Panorama Dr....C-5
Pardee....I-8
Park Blvd....D-5,G-5
Park Pl....K-2
Parrot St....G-8
Pascoe St....D-4
Payne....I-7,J-7
Pendleton Rd....K-3
Pennsylvania Ave.
....E-2,E-3,E-4
Pentucket Ave....G-7
Pepper....F-8
Pershing Ave....E-6
Pershing Dr....F-5,F-6
Petra....G-7
Pickwick....H-7
Pine St....C-1
Plumosa Wy....D-2
Polk Ave....D-6,D-7
Pomona Ave....K-2
Poplar Pl....D-2
Poppy Pl....F-8
Presidents....G-4
Presidio....D-1
Pringle....E-2
Procter Pl....D-4
Prospect....J-3
Quail St....H-8
Quince Dr....F-3,F-4
Quince St....F-2,F-7,F-8
Quine....A-3
Randolph....D-2
Raven St....H-8
Raymond Pl....B-8
Ray St....E-6
Redwood St..E-3,E-6,E-8
Regulus St....A-3
Renard....E-3
Rexford....G-8
Rhode Island St....C-4
Rice Ct....A-2
Richmond St....E-4
Rigel St....K-7
Riley St....B-1
Robinson Ave....E-4
Rowan St....G-8
Russ Rd....G-4
Sampson St....J-5
San Diego Ave...D-1,E-1
San Luis....H-6,K-2
San Marcos....F-7
Santa Anita Dr....A-1
Santa Paula Dr....A-1
Santiago Ave....E-1
San Pedro St....A-1
San Rimas Ave....B-1
Schley St....K-5
School St....C-7
September....A-1
Sheridan Ave....D-1
Sicard St....J-6
Sidney....B-8
Sigsbee....I-5
Slean....E-3
Soledad....J-3
Spruce....E-3,E-6,F-2
Stadium Wy....A-5
State St....E-2
Steel....I-7
Stephens....D-2
Stitt....G-5
St. James Pl....D-1
Summit Pl....D-2,D-3
Suncrest Dr....C-6
Sunrise St....H-7
Sunset Blvd....D-1
Superba St....I-8
Superior St....I-8
Sussex Dr....B-8
Sutherland....E-1
Sutter St....E-2
Swift Ave....C-7,D-7
Switzer St....J-4
T St....J-8
Taft St....A-2
Tamarack....F-8
Taresita....F-7
Teak....J-8
Telita....K-1
Terminal St....J-4
Terrace Ct....B-8
Terrance....D-2,E-2
Texas St....D-6,E-6
Thorn....E-2,E-3,
....E-6,E-7,E-8
Thorn St....E-8
Thor St....K-8
Titus....E-1
Tompkins St....I-7
Trent....H-6
Trias St....D-1
Tyler Ave....D-5
Una St....H-3
Union St....E-2,F-3,H-3
University Ave...D-3,D-8
Upas St....E-2,E-3,E-7
Utah St....E-6,F-6
Uvada Pl....B-6
Valla....J-7
Valley....I-6
Van Buren Ave....D-5
Vancouver Ave...E-8,F-8
Vanderbilt Pl....E-3
Vermont....E-4
Via Madrina St....A-2
Vienna....G-7
Village Pl....F-5
Villa Terr....E-6
Vine....E-2
Visalia Row....K-3
Vista Pl....B-6
Vista St....K-8
Volta Ct....A-3
Wabash Ave....D-7
Wade Dr....G-5
Water St....I-3,J-4
Wallas....K-6
Walnut Ave....E-2,E-3
Ward Rd....C-8
Washington St....D-2
Webster Ave....I-6,I-7
Wedan St....K-8
Wellborn....E-2
Westgate....G-8
Westinghouse, E....A-3
Westland Ave....G-7
Westlayan Pl....B-8
Westminster....B-8
West Mountain View
Dr....B-7
Wightman St....D-5,D-8
Wilshire Dr....A-8
Wilson....C-8
Winder....E-2
Witherby St....D-1,E-1
Works Pl....C-6
Wright Ave....E-1,H-1
Yuma St....B-1
Z St....J-8
Zoo Dr....F-5
Zoo Pl....F-5
1st Ave....D-3,H-3
1st St....I-1,J-2
2nd Ave....G-3
2nd St....I-1,J-2
3rd Ave....D-3,H-3
3rd St....I-1,J-2,J-3
4th Ave....D-3,E-3,H-3
4th St....J-2
5th Ave....D-3,E-4,H-4
5th St....J-1
6th Ave....D-4,E-4,H-4
6th St....J-1
7th Ave....E-4,H-4
7th St....J-1
8th Ave...D-4,E-4,G-4,I-4
8th St....J-1
9th Ave....D-4,I-4
9th St....K-1
10th Ave....D-4,I-4
10th St....K-1
11th Ave....I-4
12th Ave....I-4
13th St....I-4
14th St....I-4
15th St....I-4
16th....I-4
16th St....I-5
17th St....I-5
19th St....I-5
20th St....I-5
21st St....G-5,H-5,I-5
22nd St....H-5,I-5
23rd St....H-5
24th St....I-5
25th St....I-5
26th St....I-6
27th St....I-6,J-6
28th St...F-6,G-6,I-6,J-6
28th St. Rd....G-6
29th St....F-6,H-6
30th St....E-6,F-6,G-6
....I-6,J-6
31st St....E-7,G-7,J-7
32nd St....E-7,G-7,J-7
33rd St...C-7,E-7,G-7,J-7
34th St...B-7,C-7,H-7,J-7
35th Pl....C-8
35th St....H-7,I-7,J-7
36th St....J-8
37th St....J-8
38th St....B-8,C-8
....G-8,H-8,J-8
39th St....F-8,H-8,J-8
40th St....H-8,J-8

POINTS OF INTEREST

Balboa City Park....F-5
Coast Guard Air Station....G-1
Naval Air Station (North Island)....I-1
San Diego International Airport (Lindbergh Field)....F-2
San Diego Stadium..A-7
U.S. Naval Station....K-7

SAN FRANCISCO

Abbey St....I-2
Alabama St....K-4
Alameda St....H-5
Albion St....I-3
Alpine Ter....H-1
Alvardo....K-1
Ames St....K-2
Annie St....E-6
Anthony St....E-6
Arkansas St....J-5
Ash St....F-2
Austin St....E-2
Balmy St....K-4
Bartlett St....K-3
Battery St....C-6
Bay St....B-2
Beach St....A-3,B-1
Beale St....D-7
Beaver St....I-1
Bedwood Gate Ave...F-3
Belcher St....H-2
Bernice St....H-4
Berry St....G-7
Birch St....G-2
Bird St....I-3
Boardman Pl....G-6
Brady....H-3
Brannon St....G-6
Broadway....C-5,D-2
Brosnan....H-3
Bryant St....F-7,G-6,K-5
Buchanan....D-2,H-2
Buena Vista Ter....I-1
Bush St....E-2,E-4
Caledonia....I-3
California St....D-3
Camp St....I-3
Capp St....K-3
Carolina St....K-6
Casa Way....B-1
Castro....K-1
Cedar St....E-3
Center Pl....F-7
Cervantes Blvd....V-1
Channel....H-6
Chattanooga St....K-2
Chestnut....B-3
Chula Ln....I-2
Church St....K-2
Clara St....F-6
Clarence Pl....F-7
Clay St....D-3
Clementina St....F-5
Cleveland St....G-5
Clinton Park St....H-2
Collingwood St....K-1
Collin P. Kelley Jr.
St....F-7
Colton St....H-3
Columbia Square....G-5
Columbus Av....B-4
Connecticut St...J-5,K-6
Croft St....G-5
Cumberland St....J-1
Dagget St....I-6
Dakota....K-7
Davis....D-6
Dearborn St....I-3
De Boom....F-7
Deharo St....K-6
Diamond St....K-1
Divisadero....H-1
Division St....H-5
Dolores St....K-2
Dore St....G-4
Dorland St....I-2
Drumm....D-7
Duboce Ave....H-1
Ecker St....E-6
Eddy St....F-1,F-4
Elgin Park St....H-3
Elizabeth....K-1
Ellis St....E-4
Elm St....F-3
Embarcadero St....C-7
Erie St....H-3
Essex St....E-7
Eureka St....K-1
Fair Oaks St....K-2
Falmouth St....F-5
Federal St....F-7
Fell St....G-2
Fern St....E-2
Filbert St....C-1,C-3
Fillmore St....D-1,G-1
Flint St....I-1
Florida St....K-4
Folsom St....F-6,K-4
Ford St....I-1
Francisco....B-3
Franklin St....D-3
Freelon St....G-6
Fremont St....D-7
Front St....D-6
Fulton St....G-1
Geary....E-2
Germania St....H-1
Gilbert St....G-6
Gough....H-3
Gough St....D-2,G-2
Grace St....G-4
Grant St....D-5
Green St....C-1,C-3
Greenwich St....C-1,C-3
Grove St....G-2
Guerrero St....K-3
Guy....E-7
Haight St....H-1
Hampshire St....K-5
Hampton Pl....F-6
Hancock St....J-1
Harriet St....F-5
Harrison St....G-6,K-4
Hartford St....J-1
Hawthorne St....E-6
Hayes St....G-2
Hemlock St....E-3
Hermann St....H-1
Hickory St....G-3
Hidalgo Ter....I-2
Hill....K-1
Hoff St....I-3
Holly St....C-5
Hooper St....I-6
Howard St....G-4
Hubbell St....I-6
Hunt St....E-6
Hyde St....C-3,F-4
Indiana St....K-7
Irwin St....I-6
Isis St....H-4
Ivy St....G-2
Jackson St....D-1,D-3
James Lick Frwy....K-5
Jefferson St....A-4
Jessie Otis....H-3
Jessie St....F-5
Jones St....C-4,E-4
Julian Ave....I-3
Juniper St....H-4
Kansas St....J-6
Kearny St....C-5
Kenneth St....B-6
King Av....G-7
Kissling St....H-4
Lafayette St....G-3
Laguna....D-2
Landers St....I-2
Lansing....E-7
Lapidge St....J-3
Larch St....F-3
Larkin St....C-3,F-3
Laskie St....G-4
Laussat St....H-1
Leavenworth St..C-4,E-4
Leslie St....C-5
Lexington St....J-3
Liberty St....J-1
Lily St....G-2
Linda St....J-3
Linden St....G-2
Lombard....B-3
Lucerne St....G-6
Lucky St....K-4
Lusk....G-7
McAllister....F-1
McCoppin St....H-3
Main St....D-7
Mallorca Way....B-1
Marina Blvd....A-1
Mariposa St....I-4
Market Ave....I-2
Market St....F-5
Mason St....C-4,E-5
Masset....E-6
Mersey....K-2
Middle St....E-1
Midway....B-5
Minna St....G-4,I-3
Mint Mary....F-5
Mission St....G-4,K-3
Mississippi St....J-5
Missouri St....J-5
Montgomery St..D-6,E-6
Moss St....G-5
Myrtle St....E-3
Natoma St....G-4,I-3
Nellie St....K-2
Noe St....J-1
Norfolk St....H-4
Northpoint St....B-3
Oak St....G-3
Oakwood St....J-2
Octavia St....D-2
O'Farrell St....E-4,F-1
Olive St....E-3
Orosemont St....H-2
Owens St....H-7
Pacific Av....D-1,D-3
Page St....G-1
Paul St....G-5
Pearl....H-3
Pennsylvania Ave....K-7
Pfeiffer....B-5
Pierce St....E-1,H-1
Pine St....D-4,E-2
Plum....H-3
Polk St....C-3,F-3
Pond St....I-1
Post St....E-2,E-4
Potrero Ave....J-5
Powell St....B-4
Prosper St....I-1
Quane St....K-2
Ramona....I-2
Reservoir St....H-2
Retiro Way....B-1
Rhode Island St....K-6
Robert St....B-6
Rondel....I-3
Rose St....G-2
Russ St....F-5
Sacramento St....D-3
San Bruno Ave...J-5,K-5
San Carlos St....J-3
Sanchez....H-1,K-2
San Francisco-Oakland Bay Bridge (Toll)....E-8
San Jose Ave....K-3
Sansome St....C-6
Scott St....H-1
Severn St....K-2
Seymour St....F-1
Sharon St....I-2
Sheridan....H-4
Sherman....G-5
Shirley St....F-6
Shotwell St....K-4
S. Park Ave....F-7
South Van Ness Ave.
....K-4
Spear St....D-7
Stanford St....F-7
States St....I-1
Steiner St....E-1,F-1
Steuart....D-7
Stevenson St....E-5,H-3
Stockton St....D-5
Sutter St....E-2,E-3
Sycamore St....I-3
Taber Pl....F-7
Taylor St....C-4,E-4
Tehama St....F-7
Texas St....J-5,J-7,K-7
Toledo Way....B-1
Townsend St....G-7
Trainor St....H-4
Treat Ave....I-4,K-4
Tubbs St....K-7
Turk St....F-2
Union St....C-1,C-3
Utah St....J-5,K-5
Valencia....K-3
Vallejo St....C-1,C-4
Vandewater St....B-4,
Van Ness Ave....E-3
Varney Pl....F-7
Vermont St....K-5
Verona Pl....F-6
Vicksburg St....K-2
Waller St....H-1
Water St....B-4,H-1
Washburn St....G-4
Washington St....D-3
Webster St....D-1,G-2
Welsh St....G-6
Wiesse St....I-3
Willow St....F-3
Wilmot St....E-1
Wisconsin St....K-6
Woodward St....H-3
York St....K-5
Zoe St....F-7
1st St....E-7
3rd St....F-6,J-5
4th St....F-6
5th St....F-5
6th St....F-5,H-7
7th St....F-7
8th St....G-4
9th St....G-4
10th St....G-4
11th St....G-4
12th St....G-3,H-3
14th St....H-1
15th St....I-1,I-5
16th St....I-2,I-6
17th St....I-1,I-4
18th St....J-1,J-4
19th St....J-1,J-4
20th St....J-1,J-4
21st St....J-1
22nd St....J-6,K-1
23rd St....K-1,K-6
24th St....K-1,K-8
25th St....K-6,K-8

POINTS OF INTEREST

Alamo Sq....G-1
Alta Plaza....D-1
Aquatic Park....A-3
Duboce Park....H-1
Franklin Sq....I-5
Ft. Mason (U.S. Mil. Res.)....B-2
Jackson Park....I-6
Jefferson Sq....F-2
Marine Park....A-1
Mission Dolores Park....J-2
Union Sq....E-5

Scale of Miles

0 .1 .2 .3 .4

N

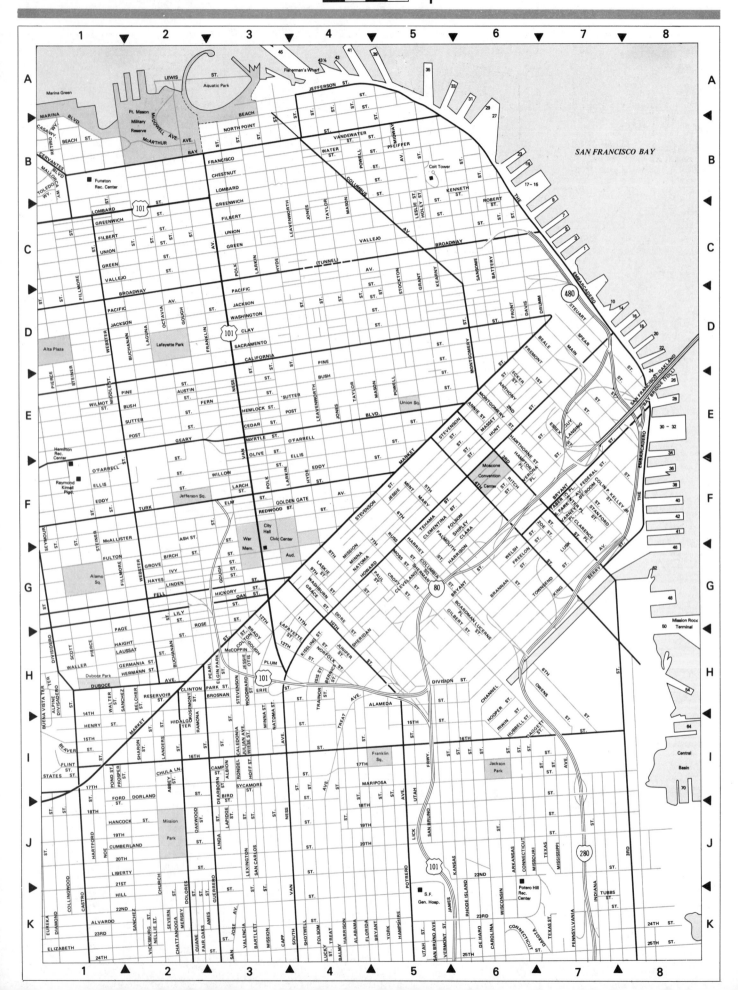

SAN FRANCISCO BAY

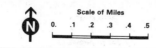

SEATTLE

Airport Way S. J5
Alaskan Way H4
Alaskan Way S. . . . I4
Alder H8
Alder St. H5
Alder St.,E. H8
Aloha St. F6
Aloha St. E. F6
Aloha St. N. F3
Arboretum Dr. E8
Arlington H8
Arthur Pl. F7
Atlantic St. S. . . . J4,J6
Auburn Pl. H6
Aurora Ave. E4
Barclay Ct. H6
Battery St. G3
Bay St. G3,J7
Bell St. G4
Bellevue Ave. F5
Bellevue Ave. E. F5
Belmont F5
Belmont Ave. E. F5
Belmont Pl. F5
Bigelow Ave. E3
Birch St. D3
Blaine St. D7
Blaine St. E. E3
Blaine St. W. E1
Blanchard St. G4
Blenheim Dr. E8
Borden Ave. G5
Boren Ave.,N. F4
Boston St
. . . . D1,D5,D7
Boston St. E. D5

Boston St. N. D3
Bothwell St. D1
Boyer Ave. E. D7
Boylston Ave. G5
Boylston Ave. E. . . . G5
Broad St. G3
Broadmoor Dr. . . D8,G8
Broadway Ave. . . . F5
Broadway Ct. . . F6,G6
Bush Pl. J7
Calhoun St. E. D7
Cedar St. G3
Charles St. J6
Charles St. S. J7
Cherry St. H5
Cherry St. E. H6
Clay St. G3
Columbia St. H5
Columbia St. E. . . . H6
Comstock St. W. . . E2
Connecticut St. S. . J4
Corwin Pl. J6
Crawford Pl. J6
Crescent Dr. E7
Crockett D6
Crockett St. D3
Crockett St. W. . . . D2
Davis Pl. J7
Dean J6
Dearborn Pl. J6
Dearborn St. I4
Dell Alder St. H8
Delmar Dr. D6
Denny Way F4,G6
Denny Way E. G6
Dewey Pl. J7
Dexter D4
Dexter Ave. N. . . . F4
Dexter Way D3

Dravus St. W. C1
Eastlake Ave. E.
. . . . D5,F5
Edgar St. D7
Eaton Pl. D7
Edgar St. E. D5
Elliot Ave. E1
Elmwood Pl. J7
Empire Way I7
Empire Way S. J7
Erie I8
Euclid Ave. I8
Fairview Ave. E. . . . D5
Fairview Ave. N. . . . F4
Federal Ave. E. . . D6,F6
Fir St. E. I6
Florence G8
Frink Park Dr. J7
Galer E5
Galer St. E. E7
Galer St. N. E3
Galer St. W. E1
Garfield E6
Garfield St. E1
Garfield St. N. E3
Garfield St. W. E2
Gilman Dr. W. D1
Glen G7
Golf Dr. J5
Grandview Pl. E6
Halladay St. D2,D3
Harbor Ave. SW . . . J1
Harrison St. F4
Harrison St. E. . . F5,F6
Harrison St. N. F4
Harvard Ave. E.
. . . . F5,G5
Hayes St. N. E3
Helen St. E. E7
Hiawatha Pl. J6

Highland Dr.
. . . . E2,E5,E7
Highland Dr. N. E3
Holgate St. J4
Howe E4
Howe St. E5
Howe St. N. E3
Howe St. W. E1
Howell St. G5
Howell St. E. G8
Ingersoll Pl. J7
Interlaken Blvd. . . . D6
Interlaken Dr. E7
Interlaken Pl. E7
Irving St. J7
Jackson Pl. I6
Jackson St. I4
James St. H5,H7
James St. E. H8
James Way H6
Jansen E. H7
Jefferson St. H5
Jefferson St. E. . . . H8
John St. F4
John St. E. F5,F7
John St. N. F2
John St. W. F4
Judkins Pl. J7
Judkins St. J6
Judkins St. E. J6
Kinnear Pl. W. E2
Lake J8
Lake Washington
Blvd.
Lane St. S. I5
Lee St. E. E7
Lee St. N. E3
Lee St. W. E2
Lenora St. G4
Pike Pl. H4

Lesch Pl. I8
Loretta Pl. F5
Louisa St. D7
Lynn St. E. D5,D7
Lynn St. N. D3
Madison St. E. H5
Main St. I4
Main St. S. I6
Malden Ave. E. F6
Marion St. H5
Marion St. E. H6
Massachusetts
St. S. J4,J5
McGraw Pl. D2
McGraw St. D7
McGraw St. N. D3
McGraw St. W. D2
Melrose Ave. E. . . . G5
Mercer St. F8
Mercer St. E. F5
Miller St. E. D7
Minor Ave. D5,G5
Montlake D7
Morley Way E8
Nagle Pl. G6
Newell St. D1
Newton St. D5,D7
Newton St. N. D3
Norman St. J7
Nye Pl. J7
Olga St. K1
Olive St. E. G6
Olive Way G4
Olympic Pl. W. F2
Olympic Way E2
Orange St. E3
Parkside Dr. E8
Peach Ct. E7
Pike Pl. H4

Pike St. H4
Pike St. E. G5,G6
Pine St. G4
Pine St. E. G5
Pleasant Pl. D2
Pontius Ave. N. . . . F5
Poplar Pl. S. J6
Post Ave. H4
Prospect St.
. . . . E2,E5,E7
Prospect St. E. . . . E6
Prospect St. N. . . . E3
Queen Anne Ave. N.
. . . . E3
Rainer Ave. I6
Raye St. W. D2
Republican St. F8
Republican St. N . . . F4
Republican St. W . . . F2
Roanoke St. E
. . . . D5,D7
Roy St. N. F3
Roy St. W. F2
Royal D7
Sander Rd. J6
Schubert St. G8
Seneca St. G6,H4
Shenandoah Dr. . . . E8
Shore Dr. D7
Short Pl. I8
Smith St. W. D2,D3
Spring St. H5
Spring St. E. H6
Spruce St. H5
Spruce St. E. . . . H6,I8
St. Andrews E8
State St. S. J6
Stewart St. G4

Sturgus Ave. S. . . . J6
Summit Ave. . . . E5,G5
Summit Ave. E. . . . G5
Superior I8
Taylor Ave. N. E3
Temple Pl. H7
Terrace I5
Terrace St. E. . . H6,H8
Terry Ave. G5
Terry Ave. N. F4
Thomas St. E. . . F5,F6
Thomas St. N. F4
Thomas St. W. F7
Union St. H4
Union St. E. G5
University St. G5
Valley St. F6,F8
Valley St. E. F5
Valley St. N. . . . F3,F4
Vine St. G3
Virginia St. G4
W. Mercer Pl. F3
Wall St. G3
Ward E5
Ward St. F8
Ward St. N. F3
Warren Ave. E2,F2
Washington Blvd. . . J8
Washington Pl. F8
Washington Pl. S
Washington St. S
. . . . I4,I6
Waverly D4
Waverly Ave. D4
Wellar St. I5
Western Ave. G3
Westlake Ave. N . . D4,F4

Westview Ave. W . . D1
Wheeler St. N . . . D3
Wheeler St. W. . . D1
Willard Ave. E2
Windermer E8
Yakima Ave. J8
Yakima Pl. J8
Yale Ave. E5
Yale Ave. N. F5
Yesler Way I4
1st Ave. G4
1st Ave. N. F3
1st Ave. S. I4
1st Ave. W. . . . E2,F2
2nd Ave. D3,G4
2nd Ave. N. . . . E3,F3
2nd Ave. S. I4
2nd Ave. W. . . . E2,F2
3rd Ave. G4
3rd Ave. N. F3
3rd Ave. S. I4
3rd Ave. W. . . . E2,F2
4th Ave. G4
4th Ave. N. F3
4th Ave. S. I5
4th Ave. W. . . . E2,F2
5th Ave. G4
5th Ave. N. F3
5th Ave. S. I5
6th Ave. G4
6th Ave. N. F3
6th Ave. S. I5
6th Ave. W. . . E1,E2,F7
7th Ave. G4
7th Ave. N. F3
7th Ave. W. E2
8th Ave. F4,G4
8th Ave. N. . . . D4,F4

8th Ave. S. I5
8th Ave. W. E2
9th Ave. G5
9th Ave. N. D4
9th Ave. W. D2
10th Ave. D6
10th Ave. E. D6
10th Ave. W. D2
11th Ave. H6
11th Ave. E. . . . D6,G6
11th Ave. S. I6
11th Ave. W. E1
12th Ave. D6,H6
12th Ave. S. G1
13th Ave. D6
13th Ave. E. D6
13th Ave. W. E1
14th Ave. D6
14th Ave. E. D6
14th Ave. W. E1
15th D1
15th Ave. E6,H6
15th Ave. E. D6
15th St. S. K6
16th Ave. D6
16th Ave. E. . . . E6,H6
16th Ave. S. I6
17th Ave. H6
18th Ave. I6
18th Ave. S. . . . H6,H7
19th Ave. I6
19th Ave. E. . . . F7,H7
19th Ave. S. I6
20th Ave. D7,J7
20th Pl. I6

22nd St. E. F7
23rd Ave. D7
23rd Ave. E. H7
23rd Ave. S. J7
23rd St. E. F7
24th Ave. D6
24th Ave. S. J7
25th Ave. E. . . E7,F7
25th Ave. S. J7
26th Ave. E. . . E7,H7
26th Ave. S. I7
27th Ave. E7
28th Ave. H8
29th Ave. S. J8
30th Ave. J8
30th Ave. S. J8
31st Ave. F8,J8
31st Ave. S. J8
32nd Ave. E. J8
32nd St. J8
33rd Ave. E. H8
33rd Ave. S. J8
34th Ave. E. . . F8,H8
35th Ave. J8
35th Ave. E. . . . I8,J8
35th Ave. S. H6
36th Ave. J8
36th Ave. S. J8
37th Ave. E. . . F8,H8
37th Ave. S. H8

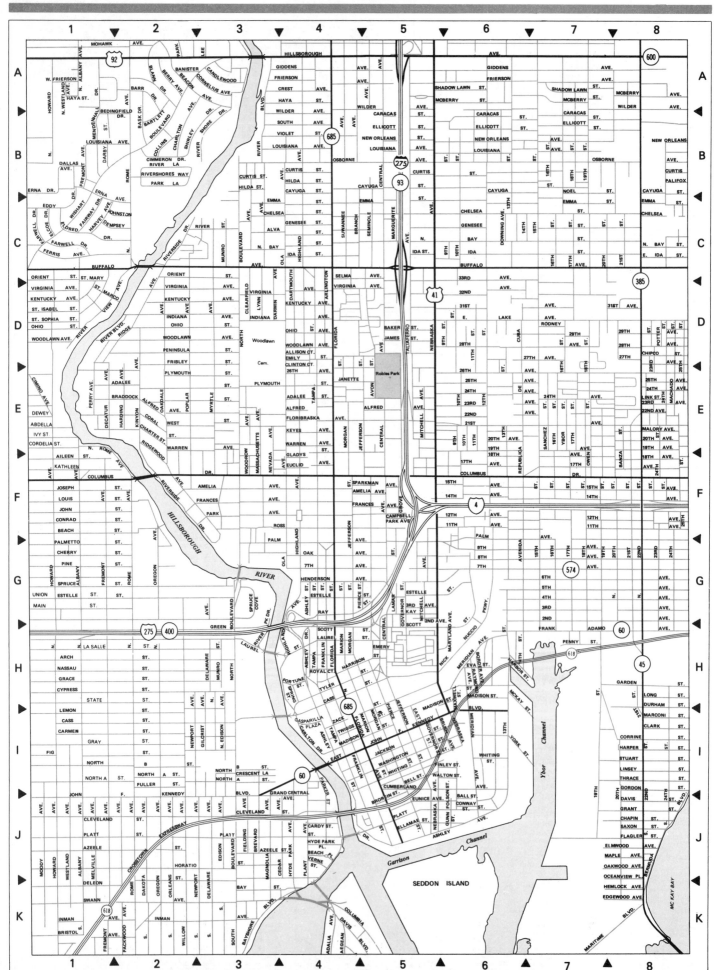

TAMPA

Adalee St.	E2,E4
Adalia Ave.	K4
Aegean	K4
Aileen St.	F1
Albany Ave., N.	A1,G1
Albany Ave., S.	J1
Alfred Ave.	E2,E4,E5
Allison Ct.	D4
Alva St.	D3
Amelia Ave.	F3,F4
Arch St.	H1
Ashley Ave.	J5
Ashley Dr.	H4,I4
Ashley St.	G4
Avenida Republica de Cuba	D5,E6,F6,G6
Avon St.	E5
Azeele St.	J1,J3
Baker St.	D5
Ball St.	J6
Banister	A2
Banza St.	F8
Barr Dr.	A2
Bartlett	B2
Bay St.	K3
Bay St., N.	C3,C4,C6,C8
Bayshore Blvd.	K3
Beach Pl.	J4
Beach St.	F1
Beacon Ave.	A2
Bedingfield Dr.	A1
Bell St.	I5
Berry Ave.	A2
Blann Dr.	A2
Border Ave.	H6
Braddock St.	E2
Branch Ave.	C4
Brevard	J3
Bristol Ave.	K1
Brorein St.	J5
Brush Ave.	I6
Buffalo Ave.	C1,C6
Campbell Grove	F5
Candlewood	A3
Caracas St.	B5,B7
Cardy St.	J4
Carlton Dr.	I4
Carmen St.	I1
Casparilla Plaza	I4
Cass St.	H4,I1
Cayuga St.	B4,B5,B6,B8
Cedar Ave.	J4
Central Ave.	B5,E5,H5
Chapin St.	J8
Charlton Ave.	B2
Charter St.	E2
Chelsea St.	C3,C6,C8
Cherry St.	G1
Chipco St.	D8
Cimino Ave.	E1
Cimmeron Dr.	B2
Clark St.	I8
Clearfield Ave.	D3
Cleveland St.	J1,J3
Clinton Ct.	D4
Collins	B2
Columbia	K4
Columbus Dr.	F1,F6
Conrad St.	F1
Conway	J6
Coral St.	E2
Cornelius Ave.	A3
Corrine St.	I8
Crescent La.	I3
Crest Ave.	A4
Crosstown Expwy.	J2
Cumberland Ave.	I5
Curtis St.	B3,B4,B5,B8
Cypress St.	H1
Dakota Ave., S.	K2
Dallas Ave.	B1
Dartmouth	D4
Davis Blvd.	K4
Davis St.	J8
Decatur Ave.	E1
Delaware Ave., N.	H3
Delaware Ave., S.	K3
Deleon St.	K1
Dempsey	C1,C2
Downing Ave.	C6
Durham St.	I8
Eddy Dr.	C1
Edgewood Ave.	K8
Edison Ave., N.	I3
Edison Ave., S.	J3
Elcoe Dr.	C1
Eldred Dr.	C1
Ellamae St.	J5
Elliscott St.	B5,B7
Elmwood Ave.	J8
Emery	H5
Emily St.	D4
Emma St.	C3,C5,C7,C8
Erna Dr.	B1
Estelle St.	G1,G4,G5
Euclid Ave.	F4
Eunice Ave.	J5
Eva St.	H6
Fairway Dr.	C1
Farwell Dr.	C1
Ferris Ave.	C1
Fielding Ave.	J3
Fig St.	I1
Finley St.	I6
Flagler St.	J8
Floribraska Ave.	E4
Florida Ave.	D4,H4
Florida Ave., N.	I4,I5
Folson St.	J6
Fortune St.	H4
Frances Ave.	F3,F5
Frank Adamo Ave.	H7
Franklin St.	H4,I4
Fremont Ave.	B1,K1
Fremont Ave., N.	G1
Fribley St.	D2
Frierson Ave.	A4,A6
Frierson Ave., W.	A1
Fuller St.	I2
Garden St.	H8
Genesee St.	C4,C6
Giddens Ave.	A4,A6
Gilcrist Ave.	I3
Gladys St.	F4
Gordon St.	I8
Governor St.	G5,I5
Grace St.	H1
Grand Central Ave.	I3
Grant St.	J8
Green	H3
Gunn St.	J6
Harbor St.	H6
Harding Ave.	E1
Harper St.	I8
Harrison St.	H4
Harvey Ave.	C1
Haya St.	A1,A4
Hemlock Ave.	K8
Henderson Ave.	G4
Highland Ave.	C4,F4,G4,H4
Hilda St.	B3,B4
Hillsborough Ave.	A4
Horatio St.	J2
Howard Ave., N.	A1,G1,J1
Hyde Park Ave.	J4
Hyde Park Pl.	J4
Ida St.	C4,C6
Ida St., E.	C8
Indiana Ave.	D2,D3
Inman Ave.	K1,K2
Jackson St.	I5
James St.	D5
Janette	E4,E5
Jefferson St.	E5,F5,I5
John F. Kennedy Blvd.	J1,J3
John F. Kennedy Blvd., E.	I4,I5
John St.	F1
Johnston	C2
Joseph St.	F1
Kay	G5
Kentucky Ave.	D1,D2,D4
Keyes Ave.	E4
Kinyon Ave.	E2
Lake Ave., E.	D6
Lamar St.	G5
Laurel St.	H1,H5
Lee	A3
Lemon St.	I1
Link St.	E8
Linsey St.	I8
Long St.	H8
Louis St.	F1
Louisiana Ave.	B1,B4,B6
Lynn Ave.	D3
Machado St.	E8
Madison St.	H5,H6,I4
Magnolia Ave.	J3
Malory Ave.	E8
Maple Ave.	J8
Marconi St.	I8
Marguerite	C5
Marion St.	H5,I5
Maritime Blvd.	K7
Maryland Ave.	H6
Massachusetts Ave.	E3,F3
McBerry St.	A6,A8
McKay St.	H6
Melville Ave.	J1
Mendenhall Dr.	B1
Meridian Ave.	H6,I6
Mitchell Ave.	E5,G5
Mohawk Ave.	A1
Moody Ave.	J1
Morgan St.	E4,H4,I5
Munro St.	C3,H3
Myrtle Ave.	E3
Nassau St.	H1
Nebraska Ave.	D5,J5,I6
Nevada Ave.	F3
New Orleans Ave.	B6,B8
New Orleans St.	B5
Newport Ave.	I2
Newport Ave., S.	K2
Nick Nuccio Pkwy.	H6
Noel St.	B7
North A St.	I2,I3
North B St.	I1,I3
North Blvd.	C3,D3,H3
Oak Ave.	G4
Oakdale Ave.	E2
Oakwood Ave.	J8
Oceanview Pl.	J8
Ohio St.	D1,D2,D4
Ola Ave.	C4,G4
Oregon Ave.	G2
Oregon Ave., N.	G2
Orient St.	C1,C2
Orleans Ave., S.	K2
Osborne Ave.	B4,B7
Owen St.	F7
Packwood Ave.	K2
Palm Ave.	G3,G6
Palmetto St.	G1
Park	A2
Park Ave.	F3
Park La.	B2
Peninsula St.	D2
Penny St.	H7
Pierce St.	I5
Pine St.	G1
Plant Ave.	J4
Platt St.	J1,J3,J5
Plymouth St.	E2,E3
Poplar Ave.	E2
Potter	D8
Ray St.	G4
Raymond Ave.	H6
Ridge Ave.	D2
Ridgewood	E2
River Blvd.	B3,D1
River La.	B2
River Park Dr.	H3
River Shore Dr.	B3
River St.	C3,I4
River View Ave.	D1
Rivershores Way	B2
Riverside Dr.	C2,F2
Rodney	D7
Rome Ave.	K2
Rome Ave., N.	B2,E1,G2
Ross	F3,F4
Royal Ct.	H4
Sanchez St.	E7
Saxon St.	J8
Scott St.	H4,H5
Selma Ave.	C4
Seminole Ave.	C5
Shadow Lawn St.	A6,A7
Shirley Dr.	B2
South Ave.	B4
South Blvd.	K3
Sparkman Ave.	F4,F5
Spring St.	H4
Spruce Cove	G3
Spruce St.	G1
St. Isabel St.	D1
St. Marco	D1
St. Mary	C1
St. Sophia St.	D1
Stuart St.	I8
Suwannee Ave.	C5
Swann Ave.	K1
Tampa St.	D4,E4,H4,I4
Thrace St.	I8
Twiggs St.	I4
Tyler St.	H4
Verne St.	J4
Violet St.	B4
Virginia Ave.	D1,D4
Walton St.	I6
Warren Ave.	E2,E4
Washington St.	I5
West St.	E2
Westland Ave.	J1
Westland Ave., N.	A1
Whiting St.	I5,I6
Wilder Ave.	A4,A5,A8
Willow Ave.	K2
Wishart	C1
Woodlawn Ave.	D1,D2,D4
Woodrow Ave.	F3
Ybor St.	E7
York St.	I6
Zack St.	I4
2nd Ave.	G7
3rd Ave.	G5,G7
4th Ave.	G7
5th Ave.	G7
6th Ave.	G7
7th Ave.	G4,G6
8th Ave.	G6
9th Ave.	G6
9th St.	C6,D6,E6
10th St.	C6,E6
11th Ave.	F6,F7
11th St.	D6,E6
12th Ave.	F6,F7
12th St.	E6
13th St.	C6,E6,I6
14th Ave.	F6,F7
14th St.	C7,H6
15th Ave.	F6,F7
15th St.	C7,G7
16th St.	B7,C7,E7,G7
17th Ave.	F6,F7
17th St.	C7,F7,G7
18th Ave.	F6,F8
18th St.	B7,D7,G7
19th Ave.	E6,E8
19th St.	B7,G7,I7,J7
20th Ave.	E6,E8
20th St.	C7
20th St., N.	F8,J8
21st Ave.	E6
21st St.	C8
22nd Ave.	E6,E8
22nd St., N.	G8,H8,I8
23rd Ave.	E6,E8
23rd St.	D8,G8
24th Ave.	E6,E8
24th St.	E8,F8,G8,J8
25th Ave.	E6,E8
25th St.	E8,F8
26th Ave.	E4,E6
27th Ave.	D7,D8
28th Ave.	D6,D8
29th Ave.	D7,D8
31st Ave.	D5,D6,D8
32nd Ave.	D6
33rd Ave.	D6

WASHINGTON,D.C.

A St., N.E.	F8
A St., S.E.	F8
Adams Dr.	F4
Army Navy Dr.	J1
Bancroft Pl.	A1
Bates St.	B6,B7
Belmont Rd.	A1
C St., N.E.	E8
C St., N.W.	E2, E6
C St., S.W.	F4,F6
California Pl.	A1
California St.	A2,A3
Canal St.	F7,I7
Capitol St.	E7,H7
Caroline St.	A3
Carroll St.	F8
Carrollburg Pl.	H7
Church St.	B3
Columbia St.	B5
Connecticut Ave.	B2
Constitution Ave.	E2
Corcoran St.	B3
Cushing Pl.	H7
D St., N.E.	E8
D St., N.W.	E5
D St., S.W.	G6
Decatur Pl.	B1
Defrees	D7
Delaware Ave.	H6
DuPont Circle	B2
Duddington Pl.	G8
E St., N.E.	E8
E St., N.W.	E4
E St., S.E.	G8
Eads St.	K1
East Capitol St.	F8
Eaton Rd.	K8
Eckington Pl.	B8
Elm St.	A6
F St., N.E.	E8
F St., N.W.	E2,E4
Fenton Pl.	C7
Fern St.	K1
Firth Rd.	K8
Flager St.	A6
Florida Ave.	A2,A6,B6
Franklin St.	B6
French St.	B5
G Pl.	D7
G St., N.E.	D8
G St., N.W.	D2,D4
G St., S.E.	G8
G St., S.W.	G5
George Washington Memorial Pkwy.	H1,J3
H St., N.E.	D8
H St., N.W.	D2,D4
H St., S.W.	G6
Half St.	J7
Howard Rd.	J8
Howison Pl.	H7
I St., N.E.	D8
I St., N.W.	D2,D5
I St., S.E.	H8
I St., S.W.	H6
Independence Ave.	F5
Indian St.	E5
Ivy St.	G7
Jefferson Davis Hwy.	K1
Jefferson Dr.	F4
K St., N.E.	D8
K St., N.W.	D2,D6
K St., S.E.	H7
K St., S.W.	H6
Kalorama Rd.	A1
Kirby St.	C6
L St., N.E.	C8
L St., N.W.	D2,D5
L St., S.E.	H7
L St., S.W.	H6
Lafayette Square	D3
Lincoln Rd.	B7
Logan Circle	B4
Louisiana Ave.	E7
M St., N.E.	C8
M St., N.W.	C2,C5
M St., S.E.	H8
M St., S.W.	H6
Madison Dr.	F4
Maine Ave.	H5
Marion St.	B5
Maryland Ave.	E8,F6
Massachusetts Ave.	C3,D6
Morris St.	C8
Mt. Vernon Pl.	D5
Myrtle St.	D7
N St., N.W.	C2,C5
N St., S.W.	H6
Neal Pl.	B8,C6
New Hampshire Ave.	B3,C2
New Jersey Ave.	C6,G7
New York Ave.	C6
North Carolina Ave.	G8
O St., N.W.	C1,C2,C5
O St., S.W.	I6
Oakdale Pl.	A6
Ohio Dr.	G2,I4
P St., N.W.	B2,B5
P St., S.W.	I6
Patterson St.	C7
Pennsylvania Ave.	D2,E5
Phelps Pl.	A2
Pierce St.	C7
Portner Pl.	A4
Potomac Ave.	I7
Q St., N.W.	B2,B5
Q St., S.W.	I6
Quincy St.	B7
R St., N.E.	B8
R St., N.W.	B3,B7
R St., S.W.	I-7
Randolph Pl.	B7
Rhode Island Ave.	B6,C3
Ridge St.	C6
Riggs Pl.	B3,B4
Rock Creek and Potomac Pkwy.	E1
S St., N.E.	B8
S St., N.W.	B3,B7
S St., S.W.	J7
Scott Circle	C3
Seaton Pl.	A7
Sheridan Circle	B1
South Carolina Ave.	G8
Stanton Square	E8
Stevens Rd.	K8
Swann St.	A3
T St., N.E.	A8
T St., N.W.	A3,A7
T St., S.W.	J7
Tenton Pl.	A1
Thomas Circle	C4
Todd Pl.	A7
Tracey Pl.	A1
U St., N.E.	A8
U St., N.W.	A3,A6,A7
V St., N.E.	A8
V St., N.W.	A3,A6,A7
V St., S.W.	J7
Van St.	H7
Vermont Ave.	C4
Virginia Ave.	E2,G6
Wallach Pl.	A4
Warner St.	B6
Washington Circle	D1
Washington Dr.	F4
Water St.	J7
Waterside Dr.	B1
Westminster St.	A5
Willard St.	A3
Wyoming Pl.	A2
1st St., N.E.	C7
1st St., N.W.	E7
1st St., S.E.	I7
1st St., S.W.	J7
2nd St., N.E.	F8
2nd St., N.W.	B6
2nd St., S.E.	H8
2nd St., S.W.	G6,J8
3rd St., N.E.	A8,E8
3rd St., N.W.	D6,E6
3rd St., S.E.	H8
4th St., N.E.	A8,E8
4th St., N.W.	A6,E6
4th St., S.E.	H8
4th St., S.W.	F6,G6
5th St., N.E.	A8,E8
5th St., N.W.	A6,E6
5th St., S.E.	H8
6 1/2 St., N.W.	C5
6th St., N.W.	E6
6th St., S.W.	H6
7th St., N.W.	E5
7th St., S.W.	H5
8th St., N.W.	E5
9th St., N.W.	E5
9th St., S.W.	G5
10th St., N.W.	E5
10th St., S.W.	G5
11th St., N.W.	E5
11th St., S.W.	G5
12th St., N.W.	E4
12th St., S.W.	G4
13th St., N.W.	E4
13th St., S.W.	G4
14th St., N.W.	E4
15th St., N.W.	E4
16th St., N.W.	D3
17th St., N.W.	E3
18th St., N.W.	E3
19th St., N.W.	E2
20th St., N.W.	E2
21st St., N.W.	E2
22nd St., N.W.	D2
24th St., N.W.	D1
25th St., N.W.	D1
26th St., N.W.	D1
27th St., N.W.	C1

Scale of Miles

0 .1 .2 .3 .4

N

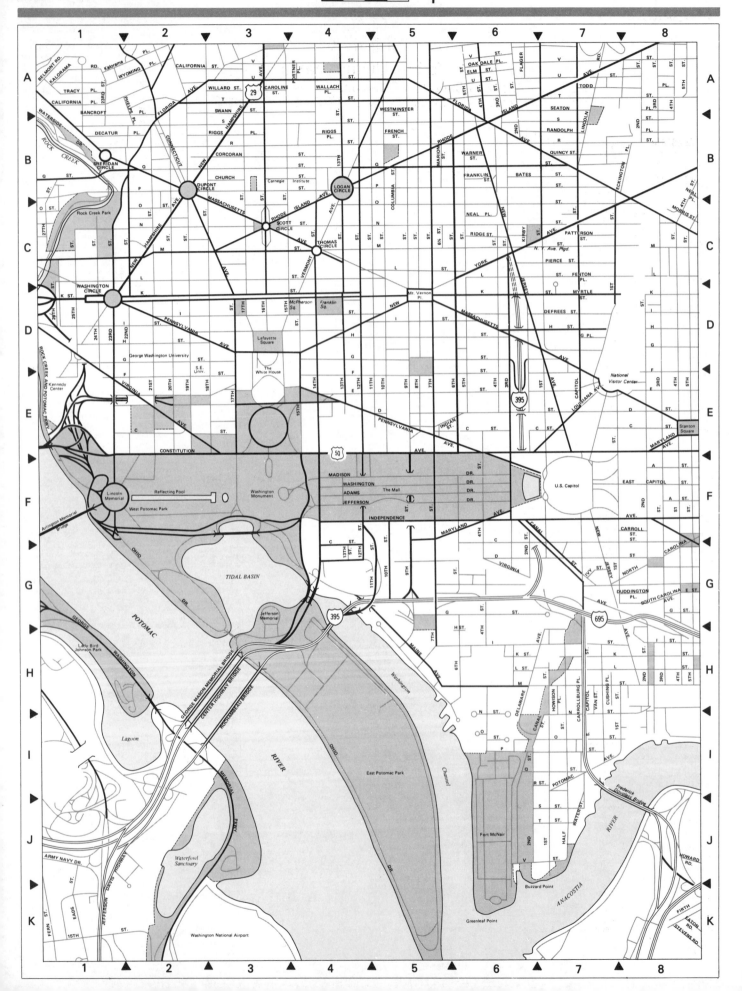

INDEX
To The United States
Index to Canadian Cities and Towns on Page 8-9.
Index to Mexican Cities and Towns on Page 11.

ALABAMA
Page 13
Population: 3,893,888
Capital: Montgomery
Land Area: 50,767 sq. mi.

Abanda E-6
Abbeville H-6
Action . . . . Pg. 96, J-4
Ada G-5
Adamsville . Pg. 96, C-2
Addison B-4
Akron E-3
Alabaster D-4
Albertville B-5
Alden . . . . Pg. 96, C-2
Aldrich D-4
Alexander City E-5
Aliceville E-2
Allgood C-5
Almond E-6
Altoona C-5
Andalusia H-4
Anderson A-4
Anniston C-5
Arab B-5
Arcus H-5
Ardilla H-6
Ardmore A-4
Argo D-5
Arkadelphia C-4
Arley C-4
Ashbury C-6
Ashford H-7
Ashland D-6
Ashville C-5
Athens A-4
Atmore J-3
Attalla C-5
Auburn F-6
Awin G-4
Axis J-2
Babbie H-5
Bailyton B-4
Bakerhill G-6
Ballplay C-6
Bangor C-4
Banks G-5
Bankston C-3
Barfield D-6
Barton A-3
Bass A-6
Batesville G-7
Bay Minette J-3
Bay View . . Pg. 96, D-2
Bayou LaBatre K-2
Bear Creek B-3
Beatrice G-3
Belgreen B-3
Belk D-3
Bell Factory Pg. 120, A-6
Bellamy F-2
Belleville H-4
Benton F-4
Berkley . . . . Pg. 120, E-7
Berry C-3
Bessemer D-4
Vicinity . . . Pg. 96, H-2
Bessie . . . . Pg. 96, C-1
Big Cove B-5
Billingsley E-4
Birmingham D-4
Vicinity . . . . Pg. 96
Detailed City . Pg. 209
Blacksher H-3
Blount Springs C-4
Blountsville C-4
Blue Mountain D-5
Bluff C-3
Boaz C-5
Bolinger G-2
Bon Secour K-3
Borden Springs . . . C-6
Boyd F-2
Braggs G-4
Brantley H-5
Bremen C-4
Brent E-4

Brewton J-4
Bridgeport A-6
Brighton . . . Pg. 96, G-2
Brilliant C-3
Brinn B-3
Brooklyn H-4
Brookside . . Pg. 96, C-3
Brookwood D-3
Browns F-4
Brownsboro Pg. 120, B-7
Brownsville . Pg. 96, G-3
Brundidge G-6
Bryant A-6
Butler G-2
Bynum D-5
Cahaba Heights
. . . . Pg. 96, G-6
Calera E-4
Calvert H-2
Camden G-4
Campbell G-3
Camphill E-6
Carbon Hill C-3
Cardiff . . . . Pg. 96, C-2
Carrollton D-2
Carrville F-6
Castleberry H-4
Catalpa G-6
Catherine F-3
Cedar Bluff B-6
Center Point Pg. 96, C-6
Centre C-6
Centreville E-4
Chalkville . . Pg. 96, B-7
Chastang J-2
Chatom H-2
Chelsea D-5
Vicinity . . . Pg. 96, J-7
Cherokee A-3
Chickasaw J-2
Vicinity . . Pg. 138, A-5
Childersburg D-5
Chrysler H-3
Citronelle H-2
Claiborne H-3
Clanton E-4
Claud F-5
Clayton G-6
Cleveland C-5
Clinton E-2
Clio G-6
Clopton H-6
Cloverdale A-3
Cluttsville . . Pg. 120, A-1
Coalburg . . . Pg. 96, D-3
Cochrane E-2
Coden K-2
Coffeeville G-2
Collinsville B-6
Columbia H-7
Columbiana D-5
Consul F-3
Cooper E-5
Cordova C-4
Cottonwood J-6
Courtland B-4
Coxey A-4
Creola J-2
Crossville B-6
Cuba F-2
Cullman C-4
Cullomburg G-2
Dadeville E-6
Damascus H-4
Dancy E-2
Danville B-4
Daphne J-3
Dauphin Island K-2
Davenport G-5
Daviston E-6
Davisville F-6
Dawes J-2
Dayton F-3
Deans H-4
Deatsville F-5
Decatur B-4
Deer Park H-2
Dees K-2
Delta D-6

Demopolis F-3
Dill H-6
Divide Station Pg. 96, B-3
Dixie J-4
Dixons Mill G-2
Dixonville H-4
Docena . . . . Pg. 96, E-2
Dolomite . . . Pg. 96, G-2
Dora C-4
Dothan H-7
Double Springs . . . C-3
Dry Forks G-3
Dublin G-5
Duke C-6
Duncanville E-3
E. Brewton J-4
Eastern Valley Pg. 96, J-2
Easton E-6
Echola D-3
Eclectic F-6
Edgewater . . Pg. 96, E-2
Eight Mile J-2
Elamville H-6
Elba H-6
Elberta K-3
Elias E-5
Eliska H-3
Elmore F-5
Elrod D-3
Elvira . . . . . Pg. 96, K-3
Emelle E-2
Enterprise H-5
Eoline E-4
Epes E-2
Equality E-5
Ethelsville D-2
Eufaula G-7
Eunola J-6
Eutaw E-3
Evergreen H-4
Ewell H-6
Fairfax E-7
Fairfield D-4
Vicinity . . . Pg. 96, F-2
Fairhope K-2
Falkville B-4
Fatama G-4
Fayette D-3
Fieldstown . Pg. 96, C-4
Flat Rock A-6
Flint City B-4
Flomaton J-4
Florala J-5
Florence A-3
Flournoy . . Pg. 108, J-6
Foley K-3
Forkland F-2
Forkville B-3
Fort Mitchell F-7
Fort Payne B-6
Fountain H-3
Francisco A-5
Frisco City H-3
Fruitdale H-2
Fulton G-3
Fultondale C-4
Vicinity . . . Pg. 96, C-4
Gadsden C-6
Gainesville E-2
Gallant C-5
Gallion F-3
Gantt H-5
Gardendale C-4
Vicinity . . . Pg. 96, B-5
Geiger E-2
Genery . . . . Pg. 96, K-3
Geneva J-5
Georgiana G-4
Geraldine B-5
Glencoe C-6
Goodwater E-6
Gordo D-3
Grand Bay K-2
Grants Mille . Pg. 96, F-7
Graysville . . Pg. 96, C-4
Green Bay H-5
Green Pond D-4
Greens Station
. . . . Pg. 96, C-6
Greensboro E-3

Greenville G-5
Greenwood . Pg. 96, K-2
Grove Hill G-3
Guin C-2
Gulf Shores K-3
Guntersville B-5
Gurley B-5
Vicinity . . . Pg. 96, C-7
Hackleburg B-3
Haleyville B-3
Halsell F-2
Halsos Mill G-5
Hamilton B-2
Hammondville B-6
Hanceville C-4
Harpersville D-5
Harrisburg E-3
Hartford J-6
Hartselle B-4
Hatton B-3
Havana E-3
Hawk D-6
Hayneville F-4
Hazel Green A-5
Hazen F-4
Headland H-7
Helena D-4
Vicinity . . . Pg. 96, K-4
Henagar B-6
Hobson City D-6
Hodges B-3
Hokes Bluff C-6
Hollis E-5
Hollywood A-6
Holt D-3
Holy Trinity F-7
Homewood D-4
Vicinity . . . Pg. 96, F-4
Hoover . . . . Pg. 96, H-4
Hueytown D-4
Vicinity . . . Pg. 96, G-1
Hulaco B-5
Hunter F-5
Huntsville A-5
Vicinity . . . . . Pg. 120
Hurtsboro F-6
Huxford H-3
Hybart G-3
Ider B-6
Ino H-5
Intercourse F-2
Irondale D-4
Vicinity . . . Pg. 96, E-7
Ishkooda . . Pg. 96, G-3
Isney G-2
Jachin F-2
Jack H-5
Jackson H-3
Jacksonville C-6
Jasper C-4
Jefferson F-2
Jefferson Park Pg. 96, E-7
Jemison E-4
Jenkins Crossroads . G-6
Jones F-4
Jones Chapel C-4
Kellerman D-4
Kelly's Crossroads . . E-5
Kellyton E-5
Kennedy D-2
Ketona . . . . Pg. 96, D-5
Kilgore . . . . Pg. 96, B-1
Kimberly C-4
Kimbrough G-3
Kinsey H-7
Kinston H-5
Knoxville E-3
Koenton H-2
La Place F-6
Ladonia . . . Pg. 108, K-4
Lafayette E-6
Lanett E-6
Langdale E-7
Lawrenceville H-6
Leeds D-5
Leighton A-3
Letohatchee F-5
Lewisburg . . Pg. 96, D-4
Lexington A-3
Lillian K-3

Lincoln D-5
Lindbergh . . Pg. 96, C-1
Linden F-3
Lineville D-6
Linn Crossing Pg. 96, B-2
Lipscomb . . Pg. 96, H-3
Littleville B-3
Livingston F-3
Lockhart J-5
Lottie H-3
Louisville G-6
Lowndesboro F-5
Loxley K-3
Luverne G-5
Lyefflon H-4
Lynn C-3
Madison . . . Pg. 120, D-1
Magnolia F-3
Malvern J-6
Maplesville E-4
Marbury E-5
Marion E-3
Marvyn F-6
Maysville . . Pg. 120, B-7
Maytown . . Pg. 96, E-2
McCalla . . . Pg. 96, J-1
McDade F-5
McIntosh H-2
McKenzie H-5
Mentone B-6
Meridianville A-5
Vicinity . . Pg. 138, A-4
Midfield . . . Pg. 96, G-3
Midland City H-6
Midway G-4
Midway G-5
Millerville E-5
Millport D-2
Millry G-2
Mineral Springs
. . . . Pg. 96, C-3
Mitchell F-6
Mobile J-2
Vicinity . . Pg. 138, D-4
Molder . . . Pg. 120, A-7
Monroeville H-4
Monrovia . . Pg. 120, A-1
Montevallo E-4
Montgomery F-5
Montrose K-2
Moontown . . Pg. 120, C-6
Mooresville B-4
Morgan . . . Pg. 96, J-3
Morgan City B-5
Morris C-4
Morvin G-3
Moulton B-4
Moundville E-3
Mount Andrew G-6
Mount Olive E-5
Vicinity . . . Pg. 96, B-4
Mount Vernon J-2
Mount Willing G-4
Mountain Brook D-4
Vicinity . . . Pg. 96, F-5
Mulberry F-4
Mulga . . . . . Pg. 96, E-1
Munford D-6
Muscle Shoals A-3
Muscoda . . Pg. 96, H-2
Nanafalia G-2
Natural Bridge C-3
New Brockton H-5
New Hope B-5
Vicinity . . . Pg. 96, J-6
New Lexington D-3
New Market A-5
Newburg B-3
Newsite E-6
Newton H-6
Newtonville D-3
Newville H-6
Northport D-3
Oak Grove D-4
Oakland B-4
Oakman C-3
Oakwood F-5
Odenville D-5
Ohatchee C-5
Omaha G-7
Oneonta C-5

Opelika E-6
Opp H-5
Owens Crossroads . . B-5
Oxford D-6
Ozark H-6
Palmerdale C-4
Parrish C-4
Patton Chapel Pg. 96, H-5
Pelham . . . Pg. 96, K-4
Pell City D-5
Pennington F-2
Perdido J-3
Peterman H-3
Peterson D-3
Petersville A-3
Phenix City F-7
Phil Campbell B-3
Pickensville D-2
Piedmont C-6
Pine Apple G-4
Pine Grove C-6
Pine Hill G-3
Pinson . . . . Pg. 96, B-7
Pisgah B-6
Plantersville F-4
Pleasant Grove D-2
Vicinity . . . Pg. 96, F-1
Prattville F-5
Priceville B-4
Prichard J-2
Vicinity . . Pg. 138, A-4
Pt. Clear K-2
Rabun J-3
Rainbow City C-5
Rainsville B-6
Ranburne D-6
Range H-3
Red Bay B-2
Red Level H-4
Reece City C-5
Reform D-3
Repton H-3
Riley G-4
River Falls H-5
River View J-4
Roanoke E-6
Robertsdale K-3
Rockdale D-6
Rockford E-5
Rogersville A-3
Rome H-5
Romulus E-3
Russellville B-3
Rutledge G-5
Saco G-6
Safford F-3
Saint Elmo K-2
Salitpa G-2
Samson H-5
Sanford H-5
Santuck E-5
Saraland J-2
Sardis G-4
Satsuma J-2
Scottsboro B-5
Seale F-7
Section B-5
Selma F-4
Shawmut E-7
Sheffield A-3
Shelby E-5
Shepardville E-6
Shorter F-6
Silver Hill K-3
Simcoe B-4
Sipsey C-4
Sledge F-3
Slocomb J-6
Smith . . . . Pg. 108, K-2
Smut Eye G-6
Snead B-4
Snowdoun F-5
Somerville B-4
Southside C-5
Spring Hill H-6
Springville C-5
Sprott E-4
Spruce Pine B-3
Stafford D-2
Steele C-5

Stevenson A-6
Stewartville E-5
Stockton J-3
Sulligent C-2
Sumiton C-4
Summerdale K-3
Sunflower H-2
Suttle F-4
Sweet Water G-3
Sylacauga E-5
Sylvan Springs
. . . . Pg. 96, E-1
Sylvania B-6
Talladega D-5
Tallassee E-6
Tarrant City . Pg. 96, D-5
Tensaw H-3
Terese G-7
Theodore K-2
Thomaston F-3
Thomasville G-3
Thorsby E-4
Three Forks Pg. 120, A-5
Three Notch H-2
Tibbie H-2
Town Creek B-4
Toxey G-2
Trinity B-4
Troy G-5
Trussville D-5
Tuscaloosa D-3
Tuscumbia A-3
Tuskegee F-6
Union Grove E-5
Vicinity . . . Pg. 96, D-1
Union Springs G-6
Uniontown F-3
Uriah H-3
Valley Head B-6
Vance E-3
Vaughn Corners
. . . . Pg. 120, B-2
Vernon C-2
Vestavia Hills H-4
Vicinity . . . Pg. 96, G-5
Victoria H-6
Vidette G-5
Village Springs C-5
Vineland B-4
Vinemont B-4
Wadley E-6
Wagarville H-2
Walnut Grove C-5
Walnut Hill E-4
Warrior C-4
Weaver C-6
Wedowee D-6
West Blockton D-4
West Point B-4
Wetumpka F-5
Whatley G-3
Whiteoak B-2
Whitson D-3
Wicksburg H-6
Wilburn C-2
Wilmer J-2
Wilton E-4
Windham Springs . . D-3
Winfield C-2
Wing J-4
Winterboro D-5
Woodville B-5
Wren B-3
Yantley F-2
Yarbo H-2
York F-2
Zip City A-3

ALASKA
Page 14
Population: 401,851
Capital: Juneau
Land Area: 570,883 sq. mi.

Akhiok F-5
Akolmiut D-4
Akulurak D-4
Akutan F-2

Alakanuk C-4
Alaktak A-7
Aleknagik E-4
Alice Arm H-10
Allakaket C-6
Ambler B-6
Anartuvuk Pass . . . B-7
Anchorage E-6
Anderson D-7
Angoon G-9
Aniak D-4
Anvik D-5
Arctic Village C-8
Atka H-8
Atkasuk A-6
Attu H-5
Baranof G-9
Barrow A-7
Beaver C-7
Beechey Pt. A-7
Bethel D-4
Bettles C-7
Big Delta D-7
Big Port Walter G-9
Black D-7
Brevig Mission B-4
Buckland C-5
Candle C-5
Cantwell D-7
Cape Romanzof . . . D-3
Cape Yakataga . . . F-8
Caro C-7
Chalkyitsik C-8
Chatanika D-7
Chenik F-5
Chevak D-4
Chickaloon E-7
Chicken D-8
Chignik F-4
Chitina E-7
Christian C-8
Christochina E-7
Chugiak B-2
Circle C-8
Circle Hot Springs . . D-8
Clarks Pt. E-5
College D-7
Copper Center E-7
Cordova E-7
Craig H-9
Crooked Creek D-5
Deadhorse B-7
Deering B-5
Delta Junction D-7
Dillingham E-4
Donnelly D-7
Dot Lake D-8
Douglas G-9
Dutch Harbor F-2
Eagle D-8
Eagle River E-6
Edna Bay H-9
Eek E-4
Egavic C-5
Elfin Cove G-9
Emmonak C-4
English Bay F-6
Eureka D-7
Fairbanks D-7
False Pass F-3
Farewell D-6
Flat D-5
Fort Yukon C-8
Gakona E-7
Galena C-6
Gambell C-3
Glen Alps E-6
Glennallen E-7
Golovin C-5
Goodnews Bay E-4
Gordon B-8
Grayling D-5
Gulkana E-7
Gustavus G-9
Haines F-9
Hawk Inlet G-9
Healy D-7
Homer F-6
Hoonah G-9
Hooper Bay D-3

ALASKA

Hope E-6
Houston A-2
Hughes C-6
Huslia C-6
Hydaburg H-9
Ituilick E-5
Juneau G-9
Kachemak E-6
Kake G-9
Kaktovik B-8
Kalla C-6
Kaltag C-5
Karluk F-5
Kashegelok E-5
Kasilof E-6
Kaskanak E-5
Katalla F-7
Kenai B-1
Ketchikan H-10
Kiana B-5
Kinegnak E-4
King Cove F-3
King Salmon F-5
Kipnuk E-4
Kivalina B-5
Klawock H-9
Knik B-2
Kobuk C-6
Kodiak F-6
Kokrines C-6
Koliganek E-5
Kotlick C-4
Kotzebue B-5
Koyuk C-5
Koyukuk C-5
Kuliuk F-5
Kwethluk D-4
Kwigillingok E-4
Larsen Bay F-5
Latouche F-7
Levelock E-5
Lime Village E-5
Livengood C-7
Long A-5
Lower Tonsina E-7
Manley Hot Springs D-6
Manokotak E-5
McCarthy E-8
McGrath D-5
McKinley Park D-7
Medfra D-6
Mekoryuk D-3
Mentasta Lake E-7
Metlakata H-10
Minto D-7
Moose Pass B-2
Mount Edgecumber G-9
Mountain Village D-4
Naknek F-5
Napakiak E-4
Napaskiak E-4
Nenana D-7
New Stuyahok E-5
Newhalen E-5
Nikolai D-6
Nikolski F-1
Noatak B-5
Nogamut E-5
Nome C-4
Nondalton E-5
Noorvik C-5
North Pole D-7
Northeast Cape C-4
Northway C-5
Nulato C-5
Old Harbor F-5
Ooliktok A-7
Ouzinkie F-5
Palmer E-7
Pedro Bay G-9
Pelican G-9
Perryville F-4
Petersburg E-6
Pilgrim Springs C-4
Pilot Point F-4
Platinum F-4
Point Hope A-5
Point Lay A-5
Porcupine F-9
Port Alexander G-9
Port Lions F-5
Portlock F-5
Prudhoe Bay B-8
Quinhagak E-4
Rampart C-7
Rampart House C-8
Richardson D-7
Ruby C-6
Russian Mission D-4
Sagwon B-7

Salchaket D-7
Sand Pt F-4
Saroonga C-3
Selawik B-5
Seward E-6
Shageluk D-5
Shaktoolik C-5
Shishmaref B-4
Shungnak B-6
Sinuk C-4
Sitka G-9
Skagway F-9
Sleetmute D-5
Soldotna E-6
Squaw Harbor G-3
St. George E-2
St. Marys D-4
St. Michael C-5
St. Paul E-2
Stebbins C-4
Stevens Village C-7
Stony River D-5
Stuyahok D-5
Susitna B-2
Takotna D-5
Talkeetna E-7
Tanalian Pt E-5
Tanana C-6
Tatitlek E-7
Teller C-4
Tetlin E-8
Tetlin Junction E-8
Togiak E-4
Tok D-8
Toksook Bay D-4
Tonsina E-7
Tuluksak D-4
Tununak D-4
Tyonek E-6
Ugashik F-5
Umiat B-7
Unalakleet C-5
Unalaska F-2
Valdez E-7
Venetie C-8
Wainwright A-6
Wales B-4
Wasila A-2
Wasilla E-7
White Mountain C-5
Whittier B-2
Willow E-6
Wiseman C-7
Wrangell G-10
Yakutat F-8

ARIZONA
Pages 16-17
Population: 2,718,215
Capital: Phoenix
Land Area: 113,508 sq. mi.

Aguila J-3
Ahwatukee Pg. 151, F-5
Ajo L-4
Ak Chin K-5
Alpine J-10
Amado N-7
Anegam L-5
Angell F-7
Apache Jct. K-6
Arivaca Jct. N-7
Arizona City L-6
Arlington K-4
Artesa M-6
Ash Fork F-5
Ashurst K-9
Avondale K-5
 Vicinity Pg. 151, E-2
Bagdad G-4
Bapchule K-6
Beardsley Pg. 151, B-1
Beaverhead J-10
Bellemont F-6
Benson M-8
Bisbee N-9
Black Canyon City H-5
Bonita L-9
Bouse J-2
Bowie M-10
Brenda J-2
Buckeye K-5
Bullhead City F-2
Bylas K-9
Cameron E-7
Camp Verde H-6
Carefree J-6
Carmen N-7
Carrizo J-8

Casa Grande K-6
Cashion Pg. 151, E-2
Catalina L-7
Cave Creek J-6
Cedar Creek J-9
Cedar Ridge D-7
Cedar Springs F-8
Central L-9
Chambers F-9
Chandler K-6
 Vicinity Pg. 151, F-6
Chandler Heights K-6
Chilchinbito D-9
Childs L-4
Chinle E-10
Chino Valley G-5
Chloride F-2
Christmas K-8
Chuichu L-6
Circle City J-4
Clarkdale G-5
Clay Spring H-8
Claypool K-7
Clifton K-10
Cochise M-9
Colorado City C-4
Concho H-9
Congress H-4
Continental M-7
Coolidge K-6
Cordes Jct. H-5
Cornville G-6
Cortaro L-7
Cottonwood G-6
Covered Wells M-5
Cow Springs D-8
Cross Canyon E-10
Curtis M-8
Dateland K-3
Desert View E-6
Dewey H-5
Dilkon F-8
Dinnehotso D-9
Dolan Springs F-2
Dome L-2
Dos Cabezas M-10
Douglas N-10
Dragoon M-9
Dudleyville L-8
Duncan L-10
Eager H-10
Eden K-9
Ehrenberg J-2
Elfrida N-9
Eloy L-6
Fairbank N-8
Flagstaff F-6
Florence K-7
Florence Jct. K-7
Fort Apache J-9
Fort Defiance E-10
Fort Grant L-9
Fort McDowell J-6
Fort Thomas K-8
Fountain Hills J-6
Francisco Grande K-5
Franklin L-10
Fredonia C-5
Gadsden L-1
Ganado F-9
Gila Bend K-4
Gilbert K-6
Glendale J-5
 Vicinity Pg. 151, C-3
Globe K-8
Golden Shores G-2
Goldroad F-2
Goodyear K-5
 Vicinity Pg. 151, E-1
Grand Canyon E-5
Gray Mountain E-7
Greasewood (Lower) F-9
Green Valley M-7
Greer J-10
Guadalupe K-6
 Vicinity Pg. 151, F-5
Hackberry F-3
Hannigan Meadow K-10
Harcuvar J-3
Hawley Lake J-9
Hayden K-7
Heber H-8
Higley K-6
Hillside H-4
Holbrook G-8
Hope J-3
Hotevilla E-8
Houck F-10
Huachuca City N-8

Humboldt H-5
Indian Wells F-8
Jacob Lake D-5
Jerome G-5
Johnson M-8
Joseph City G-8
Katherine F-2
Kayenta D-8
Keams Canyon E-9
Kearney K-7
Kelvin K-7
Kingman F-2
Kirkland H-4
Kirkland Jct. H-5
Kohls Ranch H-7
La Palma L-6
Lake Havasu City G-2
Lake Montezuma G-6
Lakeside H-9
Laveen K-5
 Vicinity Pg. 151, F-3
Leupp F-7
Litchfield Park J-5
 Vicinity Pg. 151, D-1
Littlefield C-3
Littletown Pg. 166, J-5
Lukeville M-4
Lupton F-10
Mammoth L-8
Many Farms D-10
Marana L-6
Marble Canyon D-6
Maricopa K-5
Mayer H-5
McGuireville G-6
McNeal N-9
Meadview E-2
Mesa J-6
Mexican Water C-9
Miami K-7
Moenkopi E-7
Moqui E-5
Morenci K-10
Morristown J-4
Mountainaire G-6
Mt. View M-7
Munds Park G-6
Naco N-9
Navajo G-10
Nelson F-3
New River J-5
Nicksville N-8
Nogales N-7
North Rim E-6
Nutrioso J-10
Oatman G-2
Ocotillo K-6
Old Oraibi E-8
Olberg K-6
Oracle L-7
Oracle Jct. L-7
Oraibi E-8
Oro Valley L-7
Overgaard H-8
Page C-7
Palm Springs K-6
Palo Verde K-4
Palominas N-8
Pantano M-8
Paradise City
 Pg. 151, B-5
Paradise Valley J-6
 Vicinity Pg. 151, C-5
Parker H-2
Parks F-6
Patagonia N-7
Paul Spur N-9
Paulden H-5
Payson H-6
Peach Springs F-3
Peeples Valley H-4
Peoria J-5
 Vicinity Pg. 151, B-2
Peridot K-8
Phoenix J-6
 Vicinity Pg. 151, ..
 Detailed City Pg. 272
Picacho L-6
Pima L-9
Pine H-6
Pine Springs F-5
Pinedale H-8
Pinetop H-8
Pirtleville N-9
Polacca E-8
Pomerene M-8
Prescott G-5
Prescott Valley G-5
Punkin Center J-7
Quartzite J-2

Queen Creek K-6
Quijotoa M-5
Randolph K-6
Red Lake D-7
Red Rock L-7
Rillito K-8
Riverside K-7
Riviera F-2
Rock Point D-10
Rock Springs J-5
Roosevelt J-7
Rough Rock D-9
Round Rock D-10
Rye H-7
Sacaton K-6
Safford L-9
Sahuarita M-7
Saint David M-9
Saint Johns H-10
Saint Michaels F-10
Salome J-3
San Carlos K-8
San Luis (Yuma Cty) L-1
San Luis (Pima Cty) L-5
San Manuel L-8
San Simon M-10
Sanders F-10
Sasabe N-6
Scottsdale J-6
 Vicinity Pg. 151, D-6
Seba Dalkai E-8
Second Mesa E-8
Sedona G-6
Seligman F-4
Sells M-5
Sentinel K-3
Shonto D-8
Show Low H-9
Shumway H-9
Sierra Vista N-8
Silver Bell L-7
Snowflake H-9
Solomon L-9
Somerton L-1
Sonoita N-7
South Tuscon M-7
 Vicinity Pg. 166, J-2
Springerville H-10
Stanfield L-6
Star Valley H-7
Stargo K-10
Strawberry H-6
Sun City J-5
 Vicinity Pg. 151, C-2
Sun City West J-5
 Vicinity Pg. 151, B-1
Sun Lake K-6
Sun Valley G-9
Sunizona M-9
Sunsites M-9
Superior K-7
Surprise J-5
Surprise F-7
 Vicinity Pg. 151, B-1
Tacna L-2
Taylor H-9
Teec Nos Pas D-10
Tempe K-6
 Vicinity Pg. 151, E-6
Tes Nez Iha D-10
Thatcher L-9
The Gap D-7
Three Points (Robles) M-6
Tolleson Pg. 151, C-4
Tombstone N-9
Tonalea D-7
Tonopah J-4
Topock G-2
Tortilla Flat J-7
Tracy M-5
Truxton F-3
Tsaile D-10
Tsegi D-7
Tuba City E-7
Tubac N-7
Tucson M-7
 Vicinity Pg. 166
Tumacacori N-7
Tusayan E-5
Vail M-8
Valentine F-3
Valle H-9
Vernon H-9
Vicksburg J-2
Wellton L-2
Wenden J-3
Whiteriver J-9
Why M-4
Wickenburg J-4

Wikieup G-3
Wilhoit H-5
Willcox M-9
Williams F-5
Window Rock F-10
Winkelman K-8
Winona F-7
Winslow H-7
Wintersburg K-4
Wittmann J-4
Yampai F-4
Yarnell H-4
Young H-7
Youngtown J-5
 Vicinity Pg. 151, C-2
Yucca G-2
Yuma L-1

ARKANSAS

ARKANSAS
Page 15
Population: 2,286,435
Capital: Little Rock
Land Area: 52078 sq. mi.

Alpena A-4
Altheimer E-6
Amity E-4
Arkadelphia E-4
Arkansas City F-7
Ash Flat A-7
Ashdown F-3
Athens E-3
Atkins C-4
Augusta C-7
Bald Knob C-7
Banks F-5
Barling C-2
Batesville B-6
Baucum Pg. 127, H-7
Bay B-8
Bearden F-5
Beebe D-6
Benton D-5
Bentonville A-3
Bergman A-4
Berryville A-3
Bismark E-4
Black Rock B-7
Blue Springs D-4
Bluff City F-4
Blytheville B-9
Booker Pg. 127, G-6
Booneville C-3
Boxley B-4
Bradley G-3
Brashears B-3
Brinkley D-7
Browns Gin Pg. 127, K-7
Bryant D-5
Bull Shoals A-5
Cabot D-6
Calico Rock B-6
Calion F-5
Camden F-4
Cammack Village
 Pg. 127, G-4
Carlisle D-6
Carthage E-5
Cash B-8
Caulksville C-3
Cave City B-7
Cedarville C-2
Centerville C-4
Charity Pg. 127, H-7
Charleston C-3
Cherry Valley C-8
Clarksville C-4
Clinton C-5
Conway C-5
Corning A-8
Cotton Plant D-7
Cove E-2
Crossett G-6
Crossroads E-7
Crows D-5
Cushman B-6
Dalark E-4
Damascus C-5
Danville D-4
Dardanelle C-4
DeQueen E-2
DeWitt E-7
Decatur A-2
Delight E-3
Deluce E-3
Dermott F-7
Des Arc D-7
Dierks E-3
Dodridge G-3

Dover C-4
Dumas F-7
Earle C-8
El Dorado G-5
Elaine E-8
Emerson G-4
England D-6
Eudora G-8
Eureka Springs A-3
Falcon F-4
Fallsville B-4
Farmington B-2
Fayetteville B-3
Fisher C-7
Flippin A-5
Florence F-6
Fordyce F-5
Foreman F-2
Forrest City D-8
Fouke G-3
Fountain Hill F-6
Ft. Smith C-2
Galloway Pg. 127, G-7
Garland G-3
Gentry A-2
Gillett E-7
Gilmore C-8
Glenwood E-3
Gosnell B-9
Gould E-7
Grady E-6
Grapevine E-5
Gravette A-2
Green Forest A-4
Greenbrier C-5
Greenwood C-2
Greers Ferry C-6
Guilford Pg. 127, K-3
Gurdon E-4
Hackett C-2
Hagarville C-4
Halstead Pg. 127, J-2
Hamburg G-6
Hampton F-5
Hardy A-7
Harrisburg C-8
Harrison A-4
Hartford D-2
Haskell E-5
Hazen D-7
Heber Springs C-6
Helena D-8
Hermitage F-5
Higgins Pg. 127, K-5
Holly Grove D-7
Hope F-3
Horatio E-2
Horseshoe Bend A-6
Hot Springs D-4
Hoxie B-7
Hughes D-8
Humnoke E-6
Humphrey E-6
Huntsville B-3
Huttig G-5
Jacksonville D-6
Jasper B-4
Jonesboro B-8
Judsonia C-6
Junction City G-5
Keiser B-9
Kensett C-7
Kingsland F-5
Lake City B-8
Lake Village F-7
Lavaca C-3
LePanto C-8
Lead Hill A-5
Leslie B-5
Lewisville F-3
Lincoln B-2
Little Rock D-5
 Vicinity Pg. 127, H-3
Lockesburg E-3
Lonoke D-6
Lowell B-2
Luxora B-9
Mabelvale Pg. 127, K-3
Madison D-8
Magnolia G-4
Malvern E-5
Mammoth Spring A-7
Manila B-9
Mansfield C-2
Marianna D-8
Marion C-9
Marked Tree C-8
Marmaduke A-8
Marshall B-5

Marvell D-8
Maumelle C-5
 Vicinity Pg. 127, F-3
Maynard A-7
McAlmont Pg. 127, G-6
McCrory C-7
McGehee F-7
Melbourne B-6
Mena D-2
Mineral Springs F-3
Monette B-9
Monticello F-6
Montrose G-8
Morrilton C-5
Mountain Home A-5
Mountain View B-6
Mt. Ida D-3
Mt. Pleasant G-3
Murfreesboro E-3
Nashville E-3
Natural Steps Pg. 127, F-1
Needmore C-7
Newport C-7
Nola E-3
Norman E-3
Oak Grove Pg. 127, F-4
Oark B-3
Ola D-4
Onyx D-4
Osceola C-9
Oxford B-6
Ozark C-3
Pansy F-6
Paragould B-8
Paris C-3
Parkdale G-8
Parkin C-8
Pea Ridge A-3
Pelsor B-4
Perryville D-5
Piggot A-9
Pine Bluff E-6
Pleasant Plains C-7
Pocahontas A-7
Pollard A-8
Ponca B-4
Portland G-8
Poughkeepsie E-5
Prairie Grove B-2
Prattsville E-5
Prescott F-4
Princeton E-5
Quitman C-6
Rector A-8
Red Gate Pg. 127, K-2
Reed F-7
Rison E-6
Rixey Pg. 127, F-6
Rogers A-3
Rose Bud C-6
Rose City Pg. 127, H-6
Rosston F-4
Rushing B-6
Russelville C-4
Salem A-6
Salesville A-5
Scranton C-4
Searcy C-6
Shady Grove Pg. 127, H-1
Sherdian E-5
Sherwood Pg. 127, F-5
Shirley C-5
Siloam Springs A-2
Smackover F-5
Snow Lake E-7
Springdale A-2
St. Francis G-4
Star City E-6
Stephens F-4
Story D-3
Strawberry B-7
Strong G-5
Stuttgart D-7
Success A-8
Sweet Home Pg. 127, J-5
Taylor G-4
Terrytown Pg. 127, K-2
Texarkana F-3
Timbo B-5
Trumann B-8
Tupelo C-7
Turrell C-9
Twin Springs Pg. 127, H-1
Valentine Pg. 127, F-7
VanBuren C-2
Vilonia C-5
Waldo F-4
Waldron D-2

ARKANSAS (continued)

Walker ... C-6
Walnut Ridge ... B-8
Ward ... Pg. 127, K-4
Warren ... F-6
Washington ... F-3
Watson ... F-7
West Fork ... B-2
West Helena ... D-8
West Memphis ... C-9
Western Grove ... B-4
White Hall ... E-6
Wickes ... E-2
Williams Jct. ... D-5
Willisville ... F-6
Wilmar ... F-6
Wilmot ... G-8
Wilson ... C-9
Winslow ... B-3
Witt Springs ... B-4
Wynne ... C-8
Y City ... D-3
Yellville ... B-5

CALIFORNIA
Pages 18-21
Population: 23,667,902
Capital: Sacramento
Land Area: 156,299 sq. mi.

Acton ... S-10
Adelanto ... S-11
Adin ... C-7
Agoura Hills ... S-9
Ahwahnee ... L-8
Alameda ... Pg. 161, E-3
Alamorio ... V-15
Albany ... Pg. 161, C-3
Albion ... G-2
Alder Creek Pg. 157, F-6
Alder Springs ... F-3
Alderpoint ... E-2
Alhambra ... Pg. 128, C-5
Alleghany ... F-6
Almanor ... E-6
Alpaugh ... P-8
Alpine ... V-12
Alta Loma ... Pg. 130, C-11
Altadena ... Pg. 128, B-6
Altaville ... J-6
Alton ... D-1
Alturas ... C-7
Ambler Park ... Pg. 138, J-5
Amboy ... S-15
Anaheim ... T-11
  Vicinity ... Pg. 131, G-7
Anderson ... D-4
Angels Camp ... J-7
Angwin ... H-3
Annapolis ... H-2
Antioch ... J-4
Apple Valley ... S-12
Aptos ... L-4
Arbuckle ... G-4
Arcadia ... Pg. 130, C-7
Arcata ... C-1
Arlington Oaks
  ... Pg. 157, D-2
Arnold ... J-7
Arroyo Grande ... Q-6
Artesia ... Pg. 129, F-6
Artois ... F-4
Arvin ... Q-9
Atascadero ... P-6
Atherton ... Pg. 162, A-1
Atwater ... L-6
Auberry ... L-8
Auburn ... H-6
Avalon ... U-10
Avenal ... N-7
Azusa ... Pg. 130, C-8
Badger ... M-9
Baker ... Q-14
Bakersfield ... Q-9
Balboa Park ... Pg. 160, F-3
Baldwin Park
  ... Pg. 130, C-7
Balsa Knolls Pg. 129, A-7
Banning ... T-13
Barstow ... R-12
Bartlett Sprs. ... G-3
Bass Lake ... L-8
Baxter ... G-6
Baywood Park ... P-6
Bear Valley ... K-7
Beaumont ... T-12
Beckwourth ... F-7
Bel Air ... Pg. 128, C-2
Belden ... E-6
Bell ... Pg. 129, E-5

Bell Gardens Pg. 129, E-5
Bella Vista ... D-4
Bellflower ... Pg. 129, F-6
Bells Station ... L-5
Belmont ... Pg. 161, J-3
Belvedere ... Pg. 161, D-1
Ben Lomond ... L-4
Bend ... E-4
Benton ... K-10
Berenda ... L-7
Berkeley ... J-4
  Vicinity ... Pg. 161, D-3
Berry Creek ... F-6
Bertsch Terr. ... A-1
Beverly Hills ... S-10
  Vicinity ... Pg. 128, D-3
Bieber ... C-6
Big Bar ... D-3
Big Bear Lake ... S-13
Big Bend ... C-5
Big Creek ... L-8
Big Oak Flat ... K-7
Big Pine ... L-10
Big Sur ... N-4
Biggs ... G-5
Bishop ... L-10
Blackwells Corner ... P-7
Blairsden ... F-7
Bloomington
  ... Pg. 130, B-10
Blue Lake ... C-2
Blythe ... U-16
Bodega Bay ... H-2
Bodfish ... P-10
Bolinas ... J-3
Boonville ... G-2
Boron ... R-11
Borrego Springs ... U-13
Boulder Creek ... L-4
Boulevard ... V-13
Bow Mar ... Pg. 114, H-4
Bowman ... G-6
Bradley ... P-6
Brawley ... V-15
Brea ... Pg. 131, F-6
Brentwood ... J-5
Bridgeport ... J-9
Bridgeville ... D-2
Broderick ... H-5
Browns Valley ... G-5
Brownsville ... G-5
Bryn Mawr Pg. 130, B-12
Buellton ... R-6
Buena Park ... Pg. 131, F-7
Burbank ... Pg. 128, B-4
Burlingame ... Pg. 161, H-2
Burney ... D-5
Burnt Ranch ... C-3
Butte City ... F-4
Butte Meadows ... E-5
Buttonwillow ... Q-8
Cabazon ... T-13
Cahuilla ... U-13
Calavo Gardens
  ... Pg. 160, F-6
Calexico ... V-15
Caliente ... Q-10
California City ... Q-11
California Hot Sprs. ... P-9
Calipatria ... V-15
Calistoga ... H-3
Callahan ... C-4
Calpella ... G-2
Calpine ... F-7
Calwa ... Pg. 118, K-3
Cambria ... P-5
Cameron Park ... H-6
Camino ... H-6
Camp Nelson ... N-10
Camp Richardson ... H-8
Campbell ... Pg. 162, E-6
Campo ... V-13
Camptonville ... G-6
Canby ... C-7
Canoga Park
  ... Pg. 128, B-1
Cantil ... Q-10
Canyon Dam ... E-6
Capay ... H-4
Capetown ... D-1
Capitola ... L-4
Carlotta ... D-1
Carlsbad ... U-11
Carmel By The Sea
  ... Pg. 138, K-1
Carmel Valley ... M-4
Carmichael ... Pg. 157, B-5
Carnelian Bay ... G-8
Carpinteria ... S-8
Carson ... Pg. 129, F-4

Carson Hill - Cartago

Caruthers ... N-11
Casmalia ... R-6
Caspar ... F-1
Castaic ... S-9
Castella ... C-4
Castroville ... M-4
Cayucos ... P-5
Cedar Grove ... M-10
Cedarville ... C-8
Century City Pg. 128, D-3
Ceres ... K-6
Chalfant ... L-10
Challenge ... F-6
Chatsworth ... Pg. 128, B-1
Chester ... E-6
Chico ... E-5
China Lake ... P-11
Chino ... Pg. 130, D-10
Cholame ... P-7
Chowchilla ... L-7
Chula Vista ... V-12
  Vicinity ... Pg. 160, J-5
Cima ... Q-15
Citrus ... Pg. 157, B-6
Claremont Pg. 130, C-10
Clarksburg ... H-5
Clay ... J-6
Clearlake ... G-3
Clovis ... M-8
  Vicinity ... Pg. 118, G-4
Coachella ... U-14
Coalinga ... N-6
Coarsegold ... L-8
Cobb ... G-3
Colfax ... H-6
Coloma ... H-6
Colton ... Pg. 130, B-11
Colusa ... F-4
Commerce ... Pg. 128, D-5
Compton ... Pg. 129, F-4
Copperopolis ... J-6
Corcoran ... N-8
Corning ... E-4
Corona ... Pg. 131, F-11
Coronado ... V-12
  Vicinity ... Pg. 160, H-2
Costa Mesa ... Pg. 131, H-8
Cottonwood ... D-4
Coulterville ... K-7
Courtland ... J-5
Covelo ... E-3
Covina ... Pg. 130, C-8
Crannell ... C-1
Crescent City ... B-1
Crescent Mills ... E-6
Crestmore ... Pg. 130, B-10
Cucamonga
  ... Pg. 130, C-11
Cudahy ... Pg. 129, E-5
Culver City ... Pg. 128, D-3
Cummings ... E-2
Cupertino ... Pg. 162, D-4
Cutler ... N-9
Cutten ... C-1
Cuyama ... R-8
Cypress ... Pg. 129, G-6
Daggett ... R-12
Dairyville ... E-4
Dales ... E-4
Daly City ... K-3
  Vicinity ... Pg. 161, G-1
Dana Point ... U-10
Danville ... Pg. 161, D-6
Darwin ... N-11
Davis ... H-5
Davis Creek ... B-8
Death Valley Jct. ... N-13
Del Mar ... V-11
Del Rey Oaks
  ... Pg. 138, J-4
Delano ... P-9
Desert Center ... T-15
Desert Hot Springs ... T-13
Desert Shores ... U-14
Devils Den ... P-7
Diamond Bar ... Pg. 130, D-8
Diamond Sprs. ... H-6
Dillon Beach ... J-2
Dinkey Creek ... L-9
Dixon ... H-5
Dobbins ... G-6
Dominguez Pg. 129, F-5
Dorris ... B-7
Dos Palos ... L-6
Dos Rios ... F-2
Douglas City ... D-3

Downey ... Pg. 129, E-5
Doyle ... F-8
Duarte ... Pg. 130, C-7
Ducor ... P-9
Dulzura ... V-12
Dunsmuir ... C-4
Durham ... F-5
Eagle Rock Pg. 128, C-5
Eagleville ... C-8
Earlimart ... P-9
Earp ... T-17
East Highlands
  ... Pg. 130, A-12
East Los Angeles
  ... Pg. 128, D-5
East Palo Alto
  ... Pg. 162, A-2
Edison ... Q-9
El Cajon ... V-12
  Vicinity ... Pg. 160, E-6
El Centro ... V-15
El Cerrito ... Pg. 161, C-3
El Granada ... Pg. 161, J-1
El Monte ... Pg. 128, C-6
El Nido ... L-7
El Portal ... K-8
El Segundo Pg. 129, F-3
Elk Creek ... F-4
Elk Grove ... J-5
Elmira ... J-4
Emeryville Pg. 161, D-3
Encinitas ... V-11
Encino ... Pg. 128, C-2
Enterprise ... D-4
Escalon ... K-6
Escondido ... U-11
Esparto ... H-4
Essex ... R-15
Etiwanda ... Pg. 130, C-12
Etna ... B-4
Eucalyptus Hills
  ... Pg. 160, C-7
Eureka ... C-1
Exeter ... N-9
Fair Oak ... Pg. 157, A-5
Fairfield ... J-4
Fall River Mills ... C-6
Fallbrook ... U-12
Farmersville ... N-9
Farmington ... J-6
Fawnskin ... S-12
Feather Falls ... F-6
Fellows ... Q-8
Fenner ... R-15
Ferndale ... D-1
Fields Landing ... D-1
Fillmore ... S-9
Firebaugh ... M-6
Fish Camp ... L-8
Fish Rock ... G-2
Five Points ... N-7
Flintridge ... Pg. 128, B-5
Florence ... Pg. 129, G-6
Florin ... H-5
  Vicinity ... Pg. 157, E-4
Floriston ... G-8
Flournoy ... E-4
Folsom ... H-6
Fontana ... Pg. 130, C-12
Foothill Farms
  ... Pg. 157, A-5
Forbestown ... F-5
Ford City ... Q-8
Forest Glen ... D-3
Forest Ranch ... F-5
Foresthill ... G-6
Forks Of Salmon ... C-3
Fort Ord Village
Fortuna ... D-1
Foster City ... Pg. 161, H-4
Fountain Valley
  ... Pg. 131, H-7
Fowler ... M-8
Frazier Park ... R-9
Fredericksburg ... H-8
French Gulch ... D-4
Fresno ... M-8
  Vicinity ... Pg. 118, H-3
Ft. Bidwell ... B-8
Ft. Bragg ... F-1
Ft. Dick ... A-1
Ft. Jones ... B-4
Ft. Ord Village
  ... Pg. 129, C-3
Fullerton ... T-11
  Vicinity ... Pg. 131, F-7
Furnace Creek Ranch
  ... N-13
Galt ... J-5

Garberville ... E-2
Garden Grove
  ... Pg. 131, G-7
Gardena ... Pg. 129, F-4
Gasquet ... A-2
Gaviota ... R-7
Gazelle ... B-4
Georgetown ... H-6
Gerber ... E-4
Geyserville ... H-3
Giant Forest Village N-10
Gilroy ... L-5
Glamis ... V-16
Glen Avon Pg. 130, D-12
Glen Ellen ... H-3
Glendale ... Pg. 128, C-4
  Vicinity ... Pg. 128, B-4
Glendora ... S-11
Glenn ... F-4
Glennville ... P-10
Goffs ... R-16
Goleta ... S-7
Gonzales ... M-5
Gorman ... R-9
Goshen ... N-8
Graeagle ... F-7
Granada Hills
  ... Pg. 128, A-1
Grand Terrace
  ... Pg. 130, B-11
Graniteville ... G-7
Grass Valley ... G-6
Graves ... Pg. 138, G-5
Green Acres ... Q-9
Greenfield ... N-5
Greenview ... B-4
Greenville ... E-6
Grenada ... B-4
Gridley ... G-5
Grimes ... G-4
Groveland ... K-7
Grover City ... Q-6
Guadalupe ... Q-6
Gualala ... G-2
Guerneville ... H-2
Guinda ... H-4
Gustine ... L-6
Hacienda Heights
  ... Pg. 130, D-7
Half Moon Bay ... K-3
  Vicinity ... Pg. 161, J-2
Hallelujah Jct. ... F-8
Hamburg ... B-3
Hamilton City ... F-4
Hanford ... N-8
Happy Camp ... B-3
Harborside ... Pg. 160, J-4
Harden Flat ... K-7
Hawaiian Gardens
  ... Pg. 129, G-6
Hawthorne ... Pg. 129, F-3
Hayfork ... D-3
Hayward ... K-4
  Vicinity ... Pg. 161, G-6
Healdsburg ... H-3
Heber ... V-15
Helena ... D-3
Helendale ... R-12
Hemet ... T-12
Herald ... J-6
Herlong ... E-8
Hermosa Beach
  ... Pg. 129, F-3
Herndon ... M-7
  Vicinity ... Pg. 118, G-1
Hesperia ... S-12
Highland ... Pg. 130, A-12
Highland Park
  ... Pg. 128, C-5
Hillsborough Pg. 161, H-2
Hilmar ... L-6
Hilt ... A-4
Hinkley ... R-12
Hobart Mills ... G-7
Hollister ... L-5
Hollywood Pg. 128, C-3
Holtville ... V-15
Homewood ... H-8
Honcut ... G-5
Honeydew ... D-1
Hoopa ... C-2
Hopland ... G-2
Hornbrook ... B-4
Hornitos ... K-7
Hume ... M-9
Huntington Beach ... T-10
  Vicinity ... Pg. 131, H-7
Huntington Park
  ... Pg. 128, E-5
Huron ... N-7

Hyde Park ... Pg. 129, E-4
Idyllwild ... T-13
Igo ... D-4
Imperial ... V-15
Imperial Beach ... V-12
  Vicinity ... Pg. 160, K-3
Independence ... M-10
Indio ... T-14
Industry ... Pg. 130, D-7
Inglewood ... Pg. 129, E-3
Ingot ... D-5
Inverness ... J-3
Inyokern ... P-11
Ione ... J-6
Irvine ... Pg. 131, H-9
Isleton ... J-5
Ivanpah ... Q-15
Jackson ... J-6
Jamestown ... K-7
Jamul ... V-12
Janesville ... E-7
Johannesburg ... Q-11
Johnstonville ... E-7
Jolon ... N-5
Joshua Tree ... S-13
Julian ... V-13
Junction City ... D-3
June Lake ... K-9
Keddie ... E-6
Keeler ... N-11
Keene ... Q-10
Kelseyville ... G-3
Kelso ... R-15
Kenwood ... H-3
Kerman ... M-7
Kernville ... P-10
Kettleman City ... N-7
King City ... N-5
Kings Beach ... G-8
Kingsburg ... N-8
Kirkwood ... H-8
Kit Carson ... H-7
Klamath Glen ... B-2
Klamath River ... B-4
  Vicinity ... Pg. 138, G-4
Kneeland ... D-2
Knights Ferry ... K-6
Knights Landing ... H-5
Kyburz ... H-7

La Canada ... Pg. 128, B-5
La Crescenta
  ... Pg. 128, B-4
La Grange ... K-7
La Habra ... Pg. 131, E-7
La Honda ... L-3
La Jolla ... V-11
  Vicinity ... Pg. 160, D-1
La Jolla Mesa
  ... Pg. 160, D-1
La Mesa ... Pg. 160, F-5
La Mirada ... Pg. 131, F-7
La Palma ... Pg. 129, F-6
La Presa ... Pg. 160, G-5
La Puente ... Pg. 130, D-7
La Quinta ... U-14
Lafayette ... Pg. 161, C-5
Laguna Beach ... U-10
Lake City ... B-8
Lake Elsinore ... T-12
Lake Forest ... T-11
Lakehead ... D-4
Lakeport ... G-3
Lakeside Farms
  ... Pg. 160, D-6
Lakewood ... Pg. 129, F-5
Lamont ... Q-9
Lancaster ... R-10
Las Palmas ... Pg. 118, J-3
Lawndale ... Pg. 129, F-3
Laytonville ... F-2
Lee Vining ... K-9
Leggett ... E-2
Lemon Grove
  ... Pg. 160, G-5
Lemoore ... N-7
Lenwood ... R-12
Leucadia ... V-11
Likely ... C-7
Lincoln ... H-5
Linda ... G-5
Linden ... J-6
Lindsay ... N-9
Litchfield ... E-7
Little Lake ... P-11
Live Oak ... G-5
Livermore ... K-4
  Vicinity ... Pg. 138, J-2
Livingston ... L-6
Lockeford ... J-6
Lockwood ... N-5
Lodi ... J-5
Loleta ... D-1

Loma Linda Pg. 130, B-11
Lomita ... Pg. 129, G-4
Lompoc ... R-6
Lone Pine ... N-10
Long Beach ... T-10
  Vicinity ... Pg. 129, G-5
Longvale ... F-2
Lookout ... C-6
Loomis ... H-6
Los Alamos ... R-7
Los Altos ... Pg. 161, C-3
Los Altos Hills
  ... Pg. 162, C-2
Los Angeles ... T-9
  Vicinity ... Pg.128-131
  Detailed City ... Pg. 247
Los Banos ... L-6
Los Gatos ... L-4
  Vicinity ... Pg. 162, F-5
Los Molinos ... E-4
Los Olivos ... R-7
Lost Hills ... P-8
Lower Lake ... G-3
Loyalton ... F-7
Lucerne ... G-3
Lucerne Valley ... S-12
Ludlow ... R-14
Lynwood ... Pg. 129, E-5
Macdoel ... B-5
Mad River ... D-2
Madeline ... D-7
Madera ... M-7
Malaga ... M-8
Malibu ... Pg. 118, K-3
Mammoth Lakes ... K-9
Manchester ... G-2
Manhattan Beach
  ... Pg. 129, F-3
Manteca ... K-5
Manton ... D-5
Maricopa ... Q-8
Marina ... M-4
  Vicinity ... Pg. 138, G-4
Markleeville ... H-8
Marysville ... G-5
Maxwell ... G-4
Maywood ... Pg. 128, E-5
McArthur ... C-6
McCloud ... C-5
McFarland ... P-9
McKinleyville ... C-1
McKittrick ... Q-8
Meadow Valley ... F-6
Meadow Vista ... G-6
Mecca ... U-14
Meeks Bay ... H-8
Mendocino ... F-2
Mendota ... M-7
Menlo Park ... Pg. 162, A-2
Merced ... L-6
Mercy Hot Springs ... M-6
Meridian ... G-5
Meyers ... H-8
Mi-wuk Village ... K-7
Middletown ... H-3
Midpines ... K-7
Milford ... E-7
Millbrae ... Pg. 161, H-2
Millville ... D-4
Milpitas ... K-4
  Vicinity ... Pg. 162, B-6
Mineral ... D-5
Mira Loma Pg. 130, E-12
Miramar ... Pg. 161, C-4
Miranda ... E-2
Mission Beach
  ... Pg. 160, F-1
Mission Hills Pg. 128, B-2
Mission Viejo ... T-11
Modesto ... K-6
Mokelumne Hill ... J-7
Mono Hot Springs ... L-9
Mono Lake ... K-9
Monrovia ... Pg. 130, C-7
Montague ... B-4
Montara ... Pg. 161, H-1
Montclair ... Pg. 130, D-10
Monte Rio ... H-2
Monte Serena
  ... Pg. 162, E-4
Montebello ... Pg. 128, D-6
Montecito ... R-7
Monterey ... M-4
  Vicinity ... Pg. 138, J-2
Monterey Park
  ... Pg. 128, D-5
Montgomery Creek ... C-5
Montrose ... Pg. 128, B-5

Moorpark ... S-9
Moraga ... Pg. 161, D-5
Moreno
Moreno Valley ... T-12
Morgan ... Pg. 162, G-10
Morgan Hill ... L-5
Mormon Bar ... L-8
Morongo Valley ... T-13
Morro Bay ... Q-5
Moss Beach Pg. 161, J-1
Moss Landing ... M-4
Mountain View
  ... Pg. 162, B-3
Mt. Bullion ... K-7
Mt. Laguna ... V-13
Mt. Shasta ... C-4
Mugginsville ... B-4
Murphys ... J-7
Murrieta ... U-12
Napa ... H-3
Nashua ... Pg. 129, A-4
National City Pg. 160, H-4
Natividad ... Pg. 129, A-4
Navarro ... G-2
Needles ... R-16
Neponset ... Pg. 129, A-4
Nevada City ... G-6
New Cuyama ... R-7
New Idria ... N-6
Newark ... Pg. 161, J-6
Newberry Springs ... R-13
Newell ... B-6
Newport Beach ... T-10
  Vicinity ... Pg. 131, J-8
Nice ... G-3
Niland ... U-15
Nimbus ... Pg. 157, B-7
Nipomo ... Q-6
Nipton ... Q-15
Norco ... Pg. 131, E-11
Nord ... F-5
North Edwards ... R-11
North Fork ... L-8
North Highlands
  ... Pg. 157, A-4
North Hollywood
  ... Pg. 128, C-3
Northridge ... Pg. 128, B-1
Norwalk ... Pg. 129, F-6
Novato ... J-3
Noyo ... F-2
Nubieber ... C-6
O'Neals ... L-8
Oakdale ... K-6
Oakhurst ... L-8
Oakland ... K-4
  Vicinity ... Pg. 161, E-4
  Detailed City ... Pg. 265
Oasis ... L-11
Oceano ... Q-6
Oceanside ... U-11
Ocotillo ... V-14
Ocotillo Wells ... V-14
Ojai ... S-8
Olancha ... N-11
Old Station ... D-6
Olema ... J-3
Olinda ... D-4
Ono ... D-4
Ontario ... T-11
  Vicinity ... Pg. 130, D-10
Onyx ... P-10
Orange ... Pg. 131, G-8
Orange Cove ... M-9
Orangevale ... Pg. 157, A-6
Orcutt ... R-6
Ordbend ... F-5
Orick ... B-1
Orland ... E-4
Orleans ... C-2
Oro Grande ... R-12
Orosi ... N-9
Oroville ... F-5
Oxnard ... S-8
Pacific Grove ... M-4
  Vicinity ... Pg. 138, H-1
Pacific Palisades
  ... Pg. 128, D-1
Pacifica ... K-3
  Vicinity ... Pg. 161, G-1
Paicines ... M-5
Pala ... U-12
Palermo ... G-5
Palm Desert ... T-13
Palm Springs ... T-13
Palmdale ... S-10
Palms ... Pg. 128, D-3
Palo Alto
  Vicinity ... Pg. 162, B-2
Palo Verde ... U-16

CALIFORNIA

Palomar Mountain . . U-13
Palos Verdes Estates
. . . . . . Pg. 129, G-3
Panamint Sprs. N-12
Panoche M-6
Panorama City
. . . . . . Pg. 128, B-2
Paradise F-5
Paramount . Pg. 129, F-5
Parker Dam S-17
Parkfield P-6
Pasadena S-10
Vicinity . . Pg. 128, C-5
Paskenta E-4
Paso Robles P-6
Patterson K-6
Patton . . . . Pg. 130, A-12
Pauma Valley U-12
Pearblossom S-11
Pebble Beach M-4
Vicinity . . Pg. 138, K-1
Pedley . . . . Pg. 131, E-12
Penn Valley G-6
Perkins . . . . Pg. 157, D-4
Perris T-12
Petrolia D-1
Phelan S-11
Philo G-2
Pico Rivera . Pg. 128, E-6
Piedmont . . Pg. 161, D-4
Piercy E-2
Pine Grove J-6
Pine Valley V-13
Pinecrest J-8
Pinedale M-8
Vicinity . . Pg. 118, G-3
Pioneer Station J-7
Pismo Beach Q-6
Pixley P-9
Placentia . . Pg. 131, F-8
Placerville H-6
Planada L-7
Plymouth H-6
Point Arena G-2
Pollock Pines H-7
Pomona T-11
Vicinity . . Pg. 130, D-9
Pondosa C-5
Poplar P-9
Port Hueneme S-8
Porterville N-9
Portola F-7
Portola Valley
. . . . . . Pg. 162, C-1
Portuguese Bend
. . . . . . Pg. 129, H-3
Potter Valley F-3
Poway V-12
Vicinity . . Pg. 160, B-5
Pozo Q-6
Princeton G-4
Vicinity . . Pg. 161, J-1
Project City D-4
Pulga F-6
Pumpkin Center . . . Q-9
Quincy F-6
Raisin M-7
Raisin City
Ramona V-12
Rancho Cordova
. . . . . . Pg. 157, C-6
Randsburg Q-11
Ravendale D-7
Red Bluff E-4
Red Mountain Q-11
Redcrest D-1
Redding D-4
Redlands . Pg. 130, B-12
Redondo Beach . . . T-9
Vicinity . . Pg. 129, G-3
Redway E-2
Redwood City
. . . . . . Pg. 161, J-4
Redwood Valley . . . G-2
Requa B-1
Reseda . . Pg. 128, B-1
Rialto . . . Pg. 130, A-10
Richmond . . Pg. 161, C-2
Richvale F-5
Ridgecrest Q-11
Rio Dell D-1
Rio Linda H-5
Vicinity . . Pg. 157, A-3
Rio Oso H-5
Rio Vista J-5
Ripley U-16
Ripon K-5
River Pines H-6
Riverdale N-7

Riverside T-12
Vicinity . . Pg. 131, E-12
Riverview . . Pg. 157, E-1
Robla . . . . Pg. 157, A-3
Rock Haven Pg. 160, A-6
Rocklin H-5
Rockport F-2
Rohnert Park J-3
Rolling Hills Pg. 129, G-3
Rolling Hills Estate
. . . . . . Pg. 129, G-3
Romoland T-12
Rosamond R-10
Rosemead . Pg. 128, D-6
Rosemont . Pg. 157, C-5
Roseville H-5
Rough And Ready . . G-6
Round Mountain . . . D-5
Rovana L-10
Rowland Heights
. . . . . . Pg. 130, E-8
Rutherford H-4
Sacramento H-5
Vicinity . . . . . Pg. 157
Salinas M-5
Vicinity . . Pg. 138, G-7
Salton City U-14
Salyer C-2
San Andreas J-7
San Ardo N-6
San Bernardino . . T-12
Vicinity . . Pg. 130, A-11
San Carlos . Pg. 161, J-3
San Clemente U-11
San Diego V-12
Vicinity . . . . . Pg. 160
Detailed City . Pg. 286
San Dimas . Pg. 130, C-9
San Fernando . . . S-10
Vicinity . . Pg. 128, A-2
San Francisco K-3
Vicinity . . . . . Pg. 161
Detailed City . Pg. 288
San Gabriel Pg. 128, C-6
San Jacinto T-12
San Joaquin M-7
San Jose L-5
Vicinity . . . . . Pg. 162
San Juan Bautista . M-5
San Juan Capistrano
. . . . U-11
San Leandro Pg. 161, F-5
San Lorenzo Pg. 161, G-6
San Lucas N-5
San Luis Obispo . . Q-6
San Marcos U-12
San Marino . Pg. 128, C-6
San Martin L-5
San Mateo K-3
Vicinity . . Pg. 161, H-3
San Miguel P-6
San Pablo . . Pg. 161, B-3
San Pedro . Pg. 129, H-4
San Simeon P-5
Sand City . Pg. 138, H-3
Sanger M-8
Santa Ana T-11
Vicinity . . Pg. 131, H-8
Santa Barbara S-7
Santa Clara L-4
Vicinity . . Pg. 162, C-5
Santa Clarita S-9
Santa Cruz L-4
Santa Fe Springs
. . . . . . Pg. 129, E-6
Santa Margarita . . . Q-6
Santa Maria Q-6
Santa Monica T-9
Vicinity . . Pg. 128, E-2
Santa Nella L-6
Santa Paula S-8
Santa Rita . Pg. 129, A-6
Santa Rosa H-3
Santa Ysabel V-13
Santee V-12
Vicinity . . Pg. 160, D-6
Saratoga L-4
Vicinity . . Pg. 162, E-4
Saticoy S-9
Sattley F-7
Sausalito J-3
Vicinity . . Pg. 161, D-1
Sawyers Bar C-3
Scotia D-1
Scotts Valley L-4
Scottys Castle . . . M-12
Seaside . . . Pg. 138, J-3
Seeley V-14
Selma M-8
Serra Village Pg. 138, J-6
Shafter Q-8

Shandon P-6
Shasta D-4
Shaver Lake L-8
Shelter Cove E-1
Sherman Oaks
. . . . . . Pg. 128, C-2
Shingletown D-5
Shoshone P-14
Sierra City F-7
Sierra Madre Pg. 128, B-6
Sierraville F-7
Signal Hill . Pg. 129, G-5
Simi Valley S-9
Simmler Q-7
Sisquoc R-7
Sites G-4
Sloat F-7
Smith River A-2
Snelling K-7
Soda Springs G-7
Solana Beach
. . . . . . Pg. 160, A-1
Soledad N-5
Solvang R-7
Somerset H-7
Somes Bar B-3
Sonoma J-3
Sonora K-7
Soquel L-4
Sorrento . . Pg. 160, C-1
South El Monte
. . . . . . Pg. 128, D-6
South Gate . Pg. 129, E-5
South Lake Tahoe . . H-8
South Pasadena
. . . . . . Pg. 128, C-5
South Port . Pg. 157, D-1
South San Francisco
. . . . . . Pg. 161, G-2
Spreckels . Pg. 138, H-6
Springville N-9
Squaw Valley G-7
St. Helena H-3
Standish E-7
Stanton . . Pg. 131, G-7
Stewarts Point . . . H-2
Stirling City F-5
Stockton K-5
Stonyford F-4
Stovepipe Wells . . N-12
Stratford N-8
Strathmore N-9
Studio City . Pg. 128, C-3
Suisun City J-4
Summerland S-8
Summit City D-4
Sun City T-12
Sun Valley . Pg. 128, B-3
Sunland . . Pg. 128, A-3
Sunnyvale K-5
Vicinity . . Pg. 162, C-4
Surf R-6
Susanville E-7
Sutter G-5
Sutter Creek J-6
Taft Q-8
Tahoe City G-7
Talmage G-3
Tarzana . . Pg. 128, C-1
Taylorsville E-7
Tecopa P-14
Tehachapi Q-10
Temecula U-12
Temple City Pg. 128, C-6
Templeton P-6
Terminous J-5
Termo E-7
Terra Bella P-8
Thornton J-5
Thousand Oaks . . . S-9
Thousand Palms . . T-13
Three Rivers N-9
Tiburon . . Pg. 161, D-1
Tipton N-8
Tomales J-3
Toms Place L-10
Topanga . . Pg. 128, D-1
Topanga Beach

Turlock K-6
Tustin . . . Pg. 131, G-9
Tuttletown K-7
Twain F-6
Twain Harte K-7
Twentynine Palms . S-14
Ukiah G-3
Union City . Pg. 161, H-6
Universal City
. . . . . . Pg. 128, C-3
Upland . . . Pg. 130, C-10
Upper Lake G-3
Vacaville H-4
Vallejo J-4
Valley Springs . . . J-6
Valley View Acres
. . . . . . Pg. 157, A-2
Van Nuys . . Pg. 128, B-2
Venice . . . Pg. 128, E-2
Ventura S-8
Victorville S-12
Vidal T-17
Vina E-4
Vinton F-8
Visalia N-8
Vista U-12
Walker J-8
Walnut . . . Pg. 130, D-8
Walnut Creek K-4
Vicinity . . Pg. 161, C-6
Walnut Grove J-5
Wasco P-8
Washington G-7
Waterford K-6
Waterloo J-6
Watsonville L-4
Watts . . . Pg. 129, E-4
Wawona K-8
Weaverville D-3
Weed H-8
Weitchpec C-2
Wendel E-8
Weott D-1
West Covina Pg. 130, D-8
West Hollywood
. . . . . . Pg. 128, D-3
West Los Angeles
. . . . . . Pg. 128, D-2
West Point J-7
West Riverside
. . . . . . Pg. 130, D-12
West Sacramento
. . . . . . Pg. 157, C-2
Westley K-6
Westminister
. . . . . . Pg. 131, G-7
Westmorland . . . V-14
Westport F-2
Westwood E-6
Wheatland G-5
Whitmore D-5
Whittier . . Pg. 131, E-7
Williams G-4
Willits F-2
Willow Creek C-2
Willow Ranch B-8
Willow Springs . . . R-10
Willows F-4
Wilmington Pg. 129, G-4
Winterhaven V-16
Winters H-4
Winton L-6
Wofford Heights . . P-10
Woodfords H-8
Woodlake N-9
Woodland H-4
Woodville N-9
Woody P-9
Workfield . . Pg. 138, H-3
Wrightwood S-11
Yermo R-12
Yolo H-5
Yorba Linda Pg. 131, F-9
Yorkville G-2
Yosemite Village . . K-8
Yreka B-4
Yuba City G-5
Yucaipa T-12
Yucca Valley S-13

COLORADO
Pages 22-23

Population: 2,889,964
Capital: Denver
Land Area: 103,595 sq. mi.

Abarr C-12
Agate D-10
Aguilar J-9

COLORADO

Akron C-11
Alamosa J-7
Allison J-5
Alma E-7
Almont F-6
Amherst B-12
Antero Jct. F-6
Anton D-11
Antonito J-7
Arapahoe E-12
Arboles J-5
Arlington G-11
Aroya F-11
Arriba E-11
Arriola J-3
Arvada H-10
Vicinity . . Pg. 114, C-3
Aspen E-6
Atwood B-11
Ault B-9
Aurora D-9
Vicinity . . Pg. 114, E-7
Austin F-4
Avon D-6
Avondale G-9
Bailey E-8
Barnesville B-9
Bartlett H-12
Basalt E-6
Baxter G-9
Bayfield J-5
Bedrock G-3
Bellvue B-8
Bennett D-9
Berthoud C-8
Beshoar Jct. J-10
Bethune D-12
Black Hawk D-8
Blue Mountain . . . C-3
Blue River E-7
Bond D-6
Boone G-10
Boulder C-8
Bowie F-4
Boyero E-11
Brandon F-12
Breckenridge D-7
Breen J-4
Briggsdale B-9
Brighton C-8
Vicinity . . Pg. 157, C-2
Bristol G-12
Broomfield D-8
Brush C-10
Buckingham B-9
Buena Vista F-7
Buford D-5
Burlington D-12
Byers D-9
Cahone H-3
Calhan E-10
Cameo E-4
Campo J-12
Canon City F-8
Capulin J-7
Carbondale E-5
Carlton G-12
Carr B-8
Castle Rock E-9
Cedaredge F-4
Center H-7
Chama J-8
Cheney Center . . . G-12
Cheraw G-11
Cherry Hill Village
. . . . . . Pg. 114, G-5
Cheyenne Wells . . F-12
Chimney Rock . . . J-5
Chipita Park F-9
Chivington F-12
Chromo J-6
Cimarron G-5
Clarkville B-12
Clifton E-4
Climax E-7
Coaldale G-7
Coalmont C-6
Collbran E-4
Colorado City . . . G-8
Colorado Springs . F-9
Columbine Valley
. . . . . . Pg. 114, J-3
Commerce City . . D-9
Vicinity . . Pg. 114, D-6
Como E-7
Conejos J-7
Conifer D-8
Cope D-11
Cortez J-3
Cotopaxi G-8

Cowdrey B-6
Craig B-5
Crawford F-5
Creede H-6
Crested Butte F-6
Cripple Creek F-8
Crook B-11
Crowley G-10
Cuchara J-9
Dailey B-11
DeBeque E-4
Deckers E-8
Deer Ridge C-7
Deer Trail D-10
Del Norte H-7
Delhi H-10
Delta F-4
Denver D-9
Vicinity . . . . . Pg. 114
Detailed City . Pg. 227
Dillon D-7
Dinosaur C-3
Divide F-8
Dolores H-4
Dotsero D-5
Dove Creek H-3
Dowd D-6
Doyleville F-6
Drake C-8
Dunton H-4
Dupont . . Pg. 114, C-6
Durango J-5
Eads F-12
Eagle D-6
Eaton B-9
Echo Lake D-7
Eckley C-12
Edgewater . Pg. 114, E-3
Edwards D-6
Egnar H-3
Eldorado Springs . . D-8
Elizabeth E-9
Elk Springs C-4
Ellicott F-9
Empire D-7
Englewood D-8
Vicinity . . Pg. 114, G-5
Estes Park C-7
Evans C-9
Fairplay E-7
Falcon E-9
Farisita H-8
Federal Heights
. . . . . . Pg. 114, B-4
Fenders . . Pg. 114, J-1
Firstview E-11
Flagler E-11
Fleming B-11
Florence G-8
Florissant F-8
Ford G-10
Fort Collins B-8
Fort Garland J-8
Fort Lewis J-4
Fort Lupton C-9
Fort Lyon G-11
Fort Morgan C-10
Fountain F-9
Fowler G-10
Franktown E-9
Fraser D-7
Frederick C-8
Frisco D-7
Fruita E-3
Galatea F-11
Garcia J-8
Gardner H-8
Garfield F-7
Garo Park E-7
Gateway F-3
Genoa E-11
Georgetown D-7
Gilcrest C-9
Gilman D-7
Gladstone H-5
Glendale . . Pg. 114, F-5
Glenwood Springs . D-5
Golden D-8
Vicinity . . Pg. 114, E-1
Goodrich C-10
Gould B-7
Granada G-12
Granby C-7
Grand Junction . . . E-3
Grand Lake C-7
Grandview Estates
. . . . . . Pg. 114, J-7
Granite E-7
Grant E-7
Greeley C-9

Greenwood Village . D-8
Vicinity . . Pg. 114, H-5
Guffey F-8
Gunnison F-6
Gypsum D-6
Hamilton C-5
Hartsel E-7
Hasty G-11
Haswell F-11
Hawley G-10
Haxtun B-12
Hayden C-5
Hermosa J-5
Hesperus J-4
Hiawatha B-3
Hillrose C-10
Hillside G-8
Hoehne J-9
Holly G-12
Holyoke B-12
Homelake H-7
Hooper H-7
Hot Sulphur Springs . C-7
Hotchkiss F-5
Howard G-7
Hudson C-9
Hugo E-11
Idaho Sprs. D-8
Idalia D-12
Idledale . . Pg. 114, G-1
Ignacio J-5
Iliff B-11
Indian Hills . Pg. 114, H-1
Jansen J-9
Jaroso J-8
Jefferson E-7
Joes D-12
Johnson Village . . F-7
Julesburg A-12
Keenesburg C-9
Kersey C-9
Kim J-11
Kiowa E-9
Kit Carson F-12
Kline J-4
Komman E-9
Kremmling C-7
La Jara J-7
La Junta G-11
La Salle C-9
La Veta H-9
Lafayette C-8
Laird C-12
Lake City G-5
Lake George F-8
Lakewood D-8
Vicinity . . Pg. 114, F-2
Lamar G-12
Larkspur E-9
Las Animas G-11
Last Chance D-10
Lay C-4
Lazear F-5
Leadville E-7
Lebanon J-3
Lewis J-3
Limon E-10
Lindon D-11
Littleton D-8
Vicinity . . Pg. 114, H-4
Lochbule C-9
Log Lane Village . . C-10
Loma E-3
Longmont C-8
Loveland C-8
Lucerne B-9
Lycan H-12
Lyons C-8
Mack E-3
Maher F-5
Malta E-6
Manassa J-7
Mancos J-4
Manitou Springs . . F-8
Manzanola G-10
Marble E-5
Marvel J-4
Masters C-9
Matheson . . Pg. 114, E-1
Maybell B-4
McClave G-11
McCoy D-6
Meeker C-4
Meeker Park B-8
Merino B-10
Mesa E-4
Mesita J-7
Milliken C-9
Milner B-5
Mineral Hot Springs . G-7

Minturn D-6
Model J-10
Moffat G-7
Molina E-4
Monte Vista H-7
Montrose G-4
Monument E-9
Monument Park . . J-9
Morrison . . Pg. 114, G-2
Mosca H-7
Mount Princeton
Hot Springs . . F-7
Mountain View
. . . . . . Pg. 114, D-3
Nathrop F-7
Naturita G-3
Nederland D-7
New Castle D-5
Northglenn D-8
Norwood G-4
Nucla G-4
Nunn B-9
Oak Creek C-6
Olathe F-4
Olney Springs . . . G-10
Ophir H-4
Orchard C-9
Orchard City F-4
Ordway G-10
Otis C-11
Ouray G-4
Ovid A-12
Oxford J-5
Pagosa Sprs. J-6
Palisade E-4
Palmer Lake E-8
Paoli B-12
Paonia F-4
Parachute E-4
Paradox G-3
Park F-9
Parkdale F-8
Parker D-9
Parlin F-6
Parshall C-7
Peetz A-11
Penrose F-8
Peyton E-9
Phippsburg C-6
Pierce B-9
Pinewood Springs . C-8
Placerville G-4
Platoro J-6
Platteville C-9
Pleasant View . . . H-3
Poncha Springs . . F-7
Poudre Park B-8
Powderhorn G-6
Pritchett H-12
Proctor B-11
Prospect Valley . . C-9
Pryor H-9
Pueblo G-9
Pueblo West G-9
Punkin Center . . . F-10
Ramah E-9
Rand C-7
Rangely C-3
Raymer B-10
Raymond C-8
Red Mountain . . . H-5
Redcliff E-6
Redmesa J-4
Redstone E-5
Redvale G-4
Rico H-4
Ridgway G-4
Rifle D-4
Rio Blanco D-4
Rockport B-9
Rockwood H-5
Rocky G-10
Roggen C-9
Rollinsville D-7
Romeo J-7
Royal Gorge G-8
Rush F-10
Rustic B-7
Rye H-8
Saguache G-7
Salida F-7
San Acacio J-8
San Francisco . . . J-8
San Luis J-8
San Pablo J-8
Sanford J-7
Sapinero G-5
Sargents G-6
Saw Pit G-4

COLORADO

Security-Widefield . . F-9
Sedalia E-8
Sedgewick A-11
Segundo J-9
Seibert E-11
Shawnee E-8
Sheridan F-12
Vicinity . . Pg. 114, G-4
Sheridan Lake . . . F-12
Silt D-5
Silver Cliff G-8
Silverthorne D-7
Silverton H-5
Simla E-10
Skyway E-4
Slick Rock G-3
Snow Mass E-6
Snow Mass Village . . E-6
Snyder C-10
Somerset F-5
South Fork H-6
Spar City H-6
Springfield H-12
Starkville J-9
State Bridge D-6
Steamboat Springs . . B-6
Sterling B-11
Stoneham B-10
Stoner H-4
Stonewall J-9
Strasburg D-9
Stratton D-12
Sugar City G-11
Summitville H-6
Sunbeam B-4
Swink G-10
Tabernash D-7
Telluride H-5
Texas Creek G-8
Thatcher H-10
The Forks B-8
Thornton D-8
Vicinity . . Pg. 114, B-5
Timpas H-10
Tiny Town . . Pg. 114, H-1
Tobe J-10
Toonerville H-11
Toponas C-6
Towaoc J-3
Towner F-12
Trinidad J-9
Twin Forks . Pg. 114, H-1
Twinlakes E-6
Two Buttes H-12
Tyrone H-10
Uravan G-3
Utleyville J-11
Vail D-7
Valdez J-9
Vancorum G-3
Victor F-8
Vilas H-12
Villa Grove G-7
Vineland G-9
Virginia Dale B-8
Vona E-11
Wagon Wheel Gap . . H-6
Walden B-6
Walsenburg H-8
Walsh H-12
Watkins D-9
Welby . . . . Pg. 114, C-5
Weldona C-10
Westcliffe G-8
Westcreek E-8
Westminster D-8
Vicinity . . Pg. 114, B-3
Weston J-9
Wetmore G-8
Wheat Ridge D-8
Vicinity . . Pg. 114, E-3
Whitewater F-4
Wiggins C-10
Wild Horse F-11
Wiley G-12
Windsor B-8
Winter Park D-7
Wolcott D-6
Woodland Park E-8
Woodrow C-10
Woody Creek E-6
Wray C-12
Yampa C-6
Yellow Jacket H-3
Yoder F-9
Yuma C-12

CONNECTICUT
Page 24

Population: 3,107,576
Capital: Hartford
Land Area: 4,872 sq. mi.

Allingtown . . Pg. 141, B-3
Andover F-6
Ansonia H-3
Vicinity . . Pg. 141, Z-2
Ashford F-6
Augerville . . Pg. 141, Z-5
Avon F-4
Vicinity . . Pg. 120, A-2
Baldwin Crossing
. . . . Pg. 141, C-2
Barkhamsted E-4
Bayview . . . Pg. 141, D-3
Beacon Falls Pg. 141, Y-2
Berlin F-5
Vicinity . . Pg. 120, E-4
Bethel H-2
Bethlehem G-3
Bloomfield F-4
Vicinity . . Pg. 120, A-3
Branford J-4
Vicinity . . Pg. 141, B-6
Bridgeport J-2
Vicinity . . Pg. 144, A-19
Bristol F-4
Brookfield G-2
Brooklyn F-7
Buckingham Pg. 120, C-7
Buckland . . Pg. 120, A-6
Burlington F-4
Byram . . . . Pg. 144, F-13
Canaan E-2
Cannondale Pg. 144, B-16
Canterbury F-7
Canton F-4
Vicinity . . Pg. 120, A-1
Chaplin F-7
Cheshire G-4
Chester H-5
Clinton J-5
Vicinity . . Pg. 141, A-10
Clintonville . . Pg. 141, Y-6
Colchester G-6
Colebrook E-3
Collinsville . Pg. 120, A-1
Columbia F-6
Cornwall F-2
Cornwall Bridge . . . F-2
Cos Cob . . Pg. 144, E-13
Coventry F-6
Cranbury . . Pg. 144, C-17
Cromwell G-5
Vicinity . . Pg. 120, E-5
Danbury H-1
Darien J-2
Vicinity . . Pg. 144, D-15
Dayville F-8
Deep River H-6
Derby H-3
Vicinity . . Pg. 141, A-2
Devon . . . Pg. 141, C-1
Double Beach
. . . . Pg. 141, B-6
Durham G-5
E. Hartland E-4
East Berlin . Pg. 120, E-4
East Glastonbury
. . . . Pg. 120, C-7
East Granby F-4
East Hampton G-5
East Hartford F-5
Vicinity . . Pg. 120, A-5
East Haven J-4
Vicinity . . Pg. 141, A-6
East Lyme H-3
East Norwalk
. . . . Pg. 144, D-16
East River . . Pg. 141, B-9
Eastford E-7
Easton . . . Pg. 144, A-18
Edgewood . . Pg. 120, C-1
Ellington E-5
Enfield E-5
Essex H-6
Fairfield J-3
Vicinity . . Pg. 144, B-18
Fairhaven . . Pg. 141, A-5
Falls Vill. E-2
Farmington F-4
Vicinity . . Pg. 120, C-2
Fogelmarks Corners
. . . . Pg. 120, E-6
Foxon . . . Pg. 141, A-6
Franklin G-7
Ft. Trumbull . Pg. 141, C-2
Georgetown J-2
Glastonbury F-5
Vicinity . . Pg. 120, C-6
Glen Brook Pg. 144, D-15
Glenville . . Pg. 144, E-12
Goodrich Heights
. . . . Pg. 120, E-5
Goshen F-3
Granby E-4
Great Hill . . Pg. 141, Z-1
Greenfield Hill
. . . . Pg. 144, B-18
Greenwich K-1
Vicinity . . Pg. 144, E-12
Groton H-7
Guilford J-5
Vicinity . . Pg. 141, A-8
Haddam H-5
Hamden H-4
Vicinity . . Pg. 141, Z-4
Hampton F-7
Hartford F-5
Vicinity . . Pg. 120
Detailed City . Pg. 235
Harwinton F-3
Hebron G-6
Hopewell . . Pg. 120, D-6
Indian Neck Pg. 141, B-6
Kensington . Pg. 120, E-2
Kent F-2
Killingworth H-5
Vicinity . . Pg. 141, Z-10
Lebanon G-7
Ledyard Ctr. H-7
Leetes Island
. . . . Pg. 141, B-8
Litchfield F-3
Long Ridge Pg. 144, C-13
Lordship . . Pg. 141, E-1
Madison J-5
Vicinity . . Pg. 141, B-10
Manchester F-5
Vicinity . . Pg. 120, B-6
Marlborough G-6
Melrose E-5
Meriden G-4
Mianus . . . Pg. 144, E-14
Middlefield G-5
Middletown G-5
Vicinity . . Pg. 141, C-2
Mill Plain . . Pg. 144, C-18
Momauguin Pg. 141, C-5
Monroe H-2
Montowese . Pg. 141, Z-5
Morningside . Pg. 141, C-3
Morris G-3
Mount Carmel
. . . . Pg. 141, Y-4
N. Canton E-4
Naugatuck G-3
New Britain G-4
Vicinity . . Pg. 120, D-3
New Canaan J-1
Vicinity . . Pg. 144, C-15
New Fairfield G-2
New Hartford F-3
New Haven H-4
Vicinity . . Pg. 141, A-4
New London H-7
New Milford G-2
Newington F-4
Vicinity . . Pg. 120, C-4
Newtown H-2
Nichols . . . Pg. 141, C-1
No. Stonington H-8
Norfolk E-3
Noroton . . . Pg. 144, E-15
Noroton Heights
. . . . Pg. 144, E-15
North Branford H-4
Vicinity . . Pg. 141, A-7
North Guilford
. . . . Pg. 141, Z-8
North Haven H-4
Vicinity . . Pg. 141, Z-6
North Madison
. . . . Pg. 141, Z-9
North Mianus
. . . . Pg. 144, E-14
North Stamford
. . . . Pg. 144, C-14
North Wilton
. . . . Pg. 144, B-15
Northford . . Pg. 141, Y-7
Norwalk J-2
Vicinity . . Pg. 144, D-16
Norwich G-7
Nut Plains . . Pg. 141, A-8
Old Greenwich
. . . . Pg. 144, F-14
Old Saybrook J-6
Orange . . . Pg. 141, B-2
Oxford . . . Pg. 141, Y-1
Pine Orchard
. . . . Pg. 141, B-7
Plainfield F-7
Plainville . . Pg. 120, D-1
Plymouth F-3
Pomfret E-7
Prospect H-3
Putnam E-8
Quinnipiac . Pg. 141, Y-6
Redding H-1
Ridgefield H-1
Vicinity . . Pg. 144, A-15
River Glen . Pg. 120, B-2
Rivercliff . . Pg. 141, D-2
Riverside . . Pg. 144, F-14
Rocky Hill G-5
Vicinity . . Pg. 120, D-5
Round Hill Pg. 144, D-12
Rowayton . . Pg. 144, D-16
Salem G-6
Salisbury E-2
Savin Rock . Pg. 141, B-4
Scotland F-7
Seymour H-3
Vicinity . . Pg. 141, Z-1
Sharon E-2
Shelton H-3
Vicinity . . Pg. 141, A-1
Short Beach Pg. 141, B-6
Simsbury F-4
Somers E-6
South Norwalk
. . . . Pg. 144, D-16
South Wilton
. . . . Pg. 144, B-16
South Windsor F-5
Vicinity . . Pg. 120, A-16
Southbury G-2
Southington G-4
Southport . . Pg. 144, C-18
Spring Glen Pg. 141, Z-5
Springdale . Pg. 144, D-14
Stafford E-6
Stamford K-1
Vicinity . . Pg. 144, D-14
Sterling F-8
Stony Creek Pg. 141, B-7
Stratford J-3
Vicinity . . Pg. 141, C-1
Suffield E-5
Thomaston G-3
Thompson E-8
Tolland E-6
Torrington F-3
Totoket . . . Pg. 141, A-6
Trumbull J-2
Vicinity . . Pg. 144, A-19
Turkey Hill . . Pg. 141, B-5
Union E-7
Unionville . . Pg. 120, B-2
Vernon F-5
Voluntown G-8
Wallingford H-4
Warren F-2
Washington G-2
Waterbury G-3
Waterford H-7
Watertown G-3
West Avon . Pg. 120, A-2
West Hartford F-4
Vicinity . . Pg. 120, B-3
West Haven H-4
Vicinity . . Pg. 141, B-4
West Norwalk
. . . . Pg. 144, D-15
Westbrook H-5
Westchester G-6
Weston J-2
Vicinity . . Pg. 144, A-17
Westport J-2
Vicinity . . Pg. 144, C-17
Westville . . Pg. 141, A-3
Wethersfield F-5
Vicinity . . Pg. 120, C-4
Whigville . . Pg. 120, C-1
Whitneyville Pg. 141, Z-4
Willington F-6
Wilton J-2
Vicinity . . Pg. 144, B-16
Windsor F-5
Vicinity . . Pg. 120, A-4
Windsor Locks E-5
Winnipauk . Pg. 144, D-16
Wolcott G-4
Woodbridge H-3
Vicinity . . Pg. 141, Z-3
Woodbury G-2
Woodmont . Pg. 141, C-3
Woodstock E-7

DELAWARE
Page 43

Population: 594,338
Capital: Dover
Land Area: 1,932 sq. mi.

Angola F-15
Bethany Beach . . . F-15
Blades F-13
Bowers Beach . . . D-14
Bridgeville F-13
Camden D-13
Cheswold C-13
Clayton C-13
Delaware City B-13
Dewey Beach E-15
Dover C-13
Ellendale E-14
Elsmere A-13
Felton D-13
Fenwick Is. F-15
Frankford F-15
Frederica D-14
Georgetown F-14
Greenwood E-13
Gumboro F-14
Harbeson F-15
Hardscrabble F-14
Harrington E-13
Hartly D-13
Houston E-14
Laurel F-14
Leipsic C-14
Lewes E-15
Middletown B-13
Milford D-14
Millsboro F-14
Millville F-15
Milton E-14
Mission F-15
New Castle A-13
Newark A-13
Newport A-13
Odessa B-13
Porter B-13
Seaford F-13
Selbyville F-15
Slaughter Beach . . . E-15
Smyrna C-14
Staytonville E-14
Townsend C-13
Wilmington A-14
Wyoming D-13

DIST. OF COLUMBIA
Page 43

Population: 638,333
Capital: Washington
Land Area: 63 sq. mi.

Washington E-8
Vicinity . . . . . Pg. 168
Detailed City . Pg. 300

FLORIDA
Pages 26-27

Population: 9,746,324
Capital: Tallahassee
Land Area: 58,560 sq. mi.

Alachua C-5
Allandale . . Pg. 113, F-10
Altamonte Springs
. . . . Pg. 149, C-4
Apalachicola Q-6
Apollo Beach H-5
Vicinity . . Pg. 165, E-7
Apopka F-7
Vicinity . . Pg. 149, B-3
Arcadia J-6
Archer D-5
Atlantic Beach B-7
Vicinity . . Pg. 124, C-4
Avon Pk. H-7
Baldwin B-6
Bartow H-7
Bay Harbor Is.
. . . . Pg. 135, E-5
Bay Pines . . Pg. 165, E-2
Bellair . . . Pg. 124, H-2
Belle Glade K-9
Belle Isle . . Pg. 149, E-5
Belleair . . . Pg. 165, C-2
Belleair Beach
. . . . Pg. 165, C-1
Belleair Bluffs
. . . . Pg. 165, C-2
Belleair Shores
. . . . Pg. 165, C-1
Belleview E-6
Biscayne Park
. . . . Pg. 135, B-4
Blountstown P-6
Bloxham P-6
Boca Raton L-10
Vicinity . . Pg. 118, C-6
Bonifay N-5
Bonita Spr. L-6
Boynton Beach . . . K-10
Bradenton H-5
Brandon G-5
Branford C-4
Bristol P-6
Brooksville F-5
Buenaventura Lakes
. . . . Pg. 149, J-5
Bunnell D-7
Bushnell F-6
Callahan B-6
Callaway P-5
Campbell City
. . . . Pg. 149, K-4
Cantonment N-2
Cape Coral K-6
Carrabelle C-6
Casselberry F-7
Vicinity . . Pg. 149, C-5
Cedar Key D-4
Celebration . Pg. 149, J-2
Chattahoochee . . . A-1
Chiefland D-4
Chipley N-5
Citrus Spr. E-5
Clarcona . . Pg. 149, D-3
Clearwater . Pg. 165, B-3
Clearwater Beach
. . . . Pg. 165, B-2
Clermont F-6
Clewiston K-8
Cocoa Beach F-8
Cooper City L-9
Coral Gables M-9
Vicinity . . Pg. 135, F-2
Crawfordsville C-2
Crescent City D-7
Crestview N-3
Cross City D-4
Crystal River E-5
Cutler Ridge M-9
Dade City F-5
Dania . . . . Pg. 118, J-6
Davie . . . . Pg. 118, J-4
Daytona Beach . . . E-8
Vicinity . . . . . Pg. 113
Daytona Beach Shores
. . . . Pg. 113, E-10
DeBary E-7
DeFuniak Springs . . N-4
DeLeon Springs . . . E-7
Deerfield Beach
. . . . Pg. 118, D-6
Delray Beach K-10
Vicinity . . Pg. 118, A-6
Deltona E-7
Dover G-5
Dunedin H-4
Vicinity . . Pg. 165, B-2
Dunnellon E-5
East Palatka D-7
Eastpoint C-5
Eatonville . . Pg. 149, D-4
Edgewater E-8
Edgewood . . Pg. 149, E-5
El Portal . . Pg. 135, C-4
Ellenton H-5
Englewood J-5
Ensley N-2
Eustis E-6
Everglades City . . . M-8
Favoretta . . Pg. 113, A-6
Fellsmere H-9
Fernandina Beach . . B-7
Flagler Beach D-7
Florida City M-9
Fort Basinger H-8
Fort Lauderdale . . . L-9
Vicinity . . Pg. 118, H-6
Fort Myers Beach . . K-6
Fort Pierce H-9
Fort Walton Beach . . N-3
Fort White C-5
Freeport N-4
Frost Proof H-7
Gainesville D-5
Gibsonton . . Pg. 165, D-7
Gifford H-9
Graceville M-5
Green Cove Spr. . . . C-6
Greenville B-3
Gretna B-1
Grove City J-5
Gulfport . . Pg. 165, E-3
Haines City G-7
Harbor Oaks
. . . . Pg. 113, G-10
Hastings D-7
Havana B-2
Hawthorne D-6
Hialeah . . . Pg. 135, C-2
High Springs C-5
Hilliard A-6
Hobe Sound J-10
Holly Hill . . Pg. 113, D-8
Hollywood L-10
Vicinity . . Pg. 118, K-5
Holmes Beach H-5
Homestead M-9
Homosassa E-5
Hosford P-6
Hudson F-5
Indian Creek Pg. 135, B-5
Indian Harbour Beach G-8
Indian Rocks Beach
. . . . Pg. 165, D-1
Indian Shores
. . . . Pg. 165, D-1
Indiantown J-9
Inglis E-5
Intercession City
. . . . Pg. 149, K-3
Inverness E-5
Islamorada P-9
Jacksonville B-7
Vicinity . . . . . Pg. 124
Jacksonville Beach . B-7
Vicinity . . Pg. 124, C-4
Jasper B-4
Jay M-1
Kenneth City Pg. 165, E-3
Key Biscayne
. . . . Pg. 135, G-5
Key Largo N-9
Key West P-6
Keystone Hts. C-6
Kissimmee F-7
Vicinity . . Pg. 149, J-4
Kissimmee View
. . . . Pg. 149, J-3
Korona . . . Pg. 113, A-6
LaBelle K-7
Lacoochee F-6
Lake Buena Vista . . F-7
Vicinity . . Pg. 149, H-2
Lake City C-5
Lake Mary . . Pg. 149, A-5
Lake Park K-9
Lake Wales G-7
Lakeland G-6
Lantana K-10
Largo . . . . Pg. 165, C-2
Vicinity . . Pg. 165, C-2
Lauderdale-By-The-Sea
. . . . Pg. 141, F-7
Leesburg E-6
Lehigh Acres K-7
Live Oak B-4
Longboat Key H-5
Longwood . . Pg. 149, B-5
Lynn Haven P-5
Macclenny B-6
Madeira Beach
. . . . Pg. 165, E-2
Madison B-3
Magnolia Park
. . . . Pg. 149, D-3
Maitland . . Pg. 149, D-5
Marathon P-8
Marco Island L-6
Margate . . . Pg. 118, E-5
Marianna N-5
Mayo C-4
Medley . . . Pg. 135, C-1
Melbourne G-9
Merritt Island F-8
Miami M-9
Vicinity . . . . . Pg. 135
Detailed City . Pg. 252
Miami Beach M-10
Vicinity . . Pg. 135, D-6
Miami Shores
. . . . Pg. 135, D-1
Miami Springs M-9
Vicinity . . Pg. 135, D-1
Milton N-2
Mims F-8
Monticello B-3
Moore Haven K-8
Mount Dora E-7
Naples L-6
Naples Pk. L-6
Narcoossee Pg. 149, J-7
Neptune Beach . . . B-7
New Port Richey . . . G-5
New Smyrna Beach . E-8
Niceville N-3
North Bay Village
. . . . Pg. 135, E-5
North Lauderdale . . L-9
North Miami Pg. 135, B-4
North Miami Beach
. . . . Pg. 135, A-4
North Palm Beach . . K-10
North Port J-6
North Redington Beach
. . . . Pg. 165, E-2
Oakland . . . Pg. 149, E-1
Oakland Park L-10
Vicinity . . Pg. 118, G-6
Ocala E-6
Ocoee . . . Pg. 149, D-3
Okeechobee J-8
Oldsmar . . Pg. 165, B-3
Opa-Locka L-9
Vicinity . . Pg. 135, B-2
Orange Pk. C-6
Orlando F-7
Vicinity . . . . . Pg. 149
Detailed City . Pg. 269
Ormand by the Sea . D-8
Ormond Beach . . . D-8
Osprey J-5
Oviedo . . . Pg. 149, C-7
Pace N-2
Palatka D-6
Palm Bay G-9
Palm Beach . Pg. 118, A-2
Palm Beach Shores
. . . . Pg. 120, C-3
Palm Harbor Pg. 165, A-2
Panama City P-5
Pembroke G-6
Pembroke Pines . . . L-9
Pensacola N-2
Perrine M-9
Perry C-3
Pinehurst Village
. . . . Pg. 118, E-7
Pinellas Park
. . . . Pg. 165, D-3
Plant City G-6
Vicinity Pg. 165, B-10
Plantation . . Pg. 118, H-5
Plymouth . . Pg. 149, C-2
Pompano Beach . . . L-10
Vicinity . . Pg. 118, E-6
Port Charlotte J-6
Port St. Joe Q-5
Port St. Lucie H-9
Punta Gorda L-6
Quincy B-1
Reddick D-5
Redington Beach
. . . . Pg. 165, E-2
Redington Shores
. . . . Pg. 165, D-2
Richmond Hts. M-9
Ridge Manor F-6
Riviera Beach K-10
Rockledge F-8
Rotonda K-6
Runnymede Pg. 149, K-7
Ruskin . . . Pg. 165, F-6
Safety Harbor
. . . . Pg. 165, B-3
Sanford E-7
Vicinity . . Pg. 149, A-6
Sanibel K-6
Sarasota J-5
Satellite Beach . . . G-8
Sebastian H-9
Sebring H-7
Seminole . . Pg. 165, D-2
Semoran . . Pg. 149, C-3
Sneads N-6
Sopchoppy C-1
South Bay K-8

FLORIDA

South Miami . Pg. 135, G-1
South Pasadena
. . . . Pg. 165, E-3
South Venice J-5
Spring Lake H-7
Springfield P-5
St. Augustine C-7
St. Augustine Beach H-4
St. Cloud G-7
Vicinity . . Pg. 149, K-6
St. Pete Beach . . . H-4
Vicinity . . Pg. 165, F-3
St. Petersburg G-4
Vicinity . . Pg. 165, E-4
Detailed City . . Pg. 280
Stuart J-10
Sun City . . Pg. 165, F-6
Sun City Ctr. H-5
Vicinity . . Pg. 165, F-7
Taft . . . . . . Pg. 149, G-6
Tallahassee B-2
Tampa G-5
Vicinity . . Pg. 165, B-6
Detailed City . . Pg. 295
Tarpon Springs G-4
Vicinity . . Pg. 165, A-2
Temple Terrace G-5
Tennille C-3
Thomas City J-9
Tice K-6
Titusville F-8
Tomack Estates
. . . . Pg. 113, B-7
Treasure Island H-4
Vicinity . . Pg. 165, G-4
Trenton D-4
Tuskawilla . Pg. 149, C-6
Umitilla E-6
University Park
. . . . Pg. 118, C-6
Valparaiso N-3
Venice J-5
Vero Beach H-9
Virginia Gardens
. . . . Pg. 135, D-1
Warrington N-2
Watertown E-6
Wauchula H-6
Wausau N-5
Waverly G-7
West Dixie Bend
. . . . Pg. 118, D-5
West Melbourne . . . G-8
West Miami . Pg. 135, F-1
Westwood Lake . . . M-9
Wewahitchka P-5
White City Q-5
Wilbur-By-The-Sea
. . . . Pg. 113, F-10
Wildwood E-6
Williston D-5
Wilma P-6
Wilton Manors
. . . . Pg. 118, G-6
Windermere Pg. 149, F-2
Winter Garden F-7
Vicinity . . Pg. 149, D-2
Winter Park F-7
Vicinity . . Pg. 149, D-5
Winter Springs F-7
Vicinity . . Pg. 149, C-6
Woodville B-2
Zellwood . . Pg. 149, B-1
Zephyrhills G-5
Zolfo Spr. H-4

GEORGIA

Pages 28-29
Population: 6,478,216
Capital: Atlanta
Land Area: 54,153 sq. mi.

Abbeville K-5
Acworth F-3
Adairsville E-2
Adams Park Pg. 92, G-3
Adamsville . Pg. 92, F-2
Adel M-5
Adrian J-7
Alamo J-6
Alapaha L-5
Albany L-3
Aldora H-4
Allendale . Pg. 108, G-2
Allentown J-5
Alma L-6
Alpharetta E-4
Alston K-7
Alto E-5

Alvaton H-3
Ambrose L-6
Americus K-4
Amsterdam N-3
Andersonville K-3
Apalachee F-5
Apple Valley Pg. 92, K-4
Appling G-7
Arabi K-4
Aragon F-2
Arlington L-3
Arnoldsville F-6
Ashburn L-4
Ashford Park Pg. 92, C-5
Ashley Farms Pg. 92, H-3
Athens F-5
Atlanta F-3
Vicinity . . . . . . Pg. 92
Detailed City . Pg. 205
Attapulgus N-3
Augusta G-7
Vicinity . . . . . . Pg. 93
Austell F-3
Avalon E-6
Avondale Estates
. . . . Pg. 92, E-7
Axson M-7
Baconton M-4
Bainbridge N-3
Baldwin E-5
Ball Ground E-4
Barnesville H-4
Barney M-5
Barwick N-5
Baxley L-7
Bellview L-2
Belvedere Gardens
. . . . Pg. 92, F-6
Ben Hill . . . Pg. 92, H-2
Benevolence K-3
Benning Hills
. . . . Pg. 108, H-5
Berkeley Lake Pg. 92, A-7
Berlin M-5
Berryton E-1
Between F-5
Bishop F-5
Blackshear L-8
Blakely L-2
Blue Creek . Pg. 92, H-6
Blue Ridge D-3
Bluffton L-2
Bonaire J-5
Boston N-4
Boulder Park Pg. 92, F-2
Bowden G-2
Bowersville E-6
Bowman E-6
Boykin J-9
Boynton . . Pg. 99, K-5
Bradley Acres Pg. 92, D-1
Bremen F-2
Briarcliff Woods
. . . . Pg. 92, D-6
Bridgeboro L-4
Bristol L-7
Bronwood L-3
Brook Glen . Pg. 92, H-7
Brook Hollow Pg. 92, D-7
Brookhaven . Pg. 92, D-5
Brookstone . Pg. 92, J-7
Broxton L-6
Brunswick M-9
Buchanan F-2
Buckhead . . Pg. 92, D-4
Buena Vista J-3
Buford E-4
Butler J-3
Byron J-4
Cadwell J-6
Cairo N-4
Calhoun E-2
Calvary N-3
Camilla M-3
Candler E-4
Canon E-6
Canoochee H-7
Canton E-3
Cardinal Woods
. . . . Pg. 92, D-7
Carnegie L-2
Caroline Park
. . . . Pg. 108, J-3
Carrollton G-2
Cartersville F-2
Cascade Knolls
. . . . Pg. 92, G-1
Cave Spring E-2
Cecil M-5
Cedar Springs M-2

Cedartown F-2
Center F-5
Center Hill . Pg. 92, F-3
Centerville M-2
Chamblee . Pg. 92, C-5
Chatsworth D-2
Chauncey K-5
Cherokee Pines
. . . . Pg. 92, C-1
Chester J-6
Chickamauga D-2
Cisco D-3
Clarkesville D-5
Clarkston . . Pg. 92, C-7
Claxton K-8
Clayton D-5
Cleveland D-4
Climax N-3
Clyattville N-5
Clyo J-9
Cobbtown J-8
Cochran J-5
Cogdell M-6
Cohutta D-2
Colemans Lake H-7
College Park Pg. 92, H-3
Collier Heights
. . . . Pg. 92, F-2
Colquitt M-3
Columbia Valley
. . . . Pg. 92, G-6
Columbus J-2
Vicinity . . Pg. 108, G-3
Comer E-6
Commerce E-5
Conley . . . . Pg. 92, J-5
Coolidge M-4
Cordele K-4
Cornelia E-5
Cotton M-4
Covena J-7
Covington G-5
Crandall D-3
Crawford F-5
Crawfordville G-6
Creekwood Hills
. . . . Pg. 92, H-7
Crystal Valley Pg. 108, F-3
Culloden H-4
Cumberland Pg. 92, C-3
Cumming E-4
Cusseta J-2
Cuthbert L-2
Dacula F-4
Dahlonega D-4
Dallas F-3
Dalton D-2
Damascus M-3
Danielsville E-6
Darien L-9
Dasher N-6
Davis Woods Pg. 92, C-4
Davisboro H-7
Dawson L-3
Dawsonville E-4
Decatur . . . Pg. 92, F-6
Demorest D-5
Dexter J-6
Doerun M-4
Donalsonville M-2
Doraville . . Pg. 92, C-6
Douglas L-6
Douglasville F-3
Dublin J-6
Duluth F-4
Dunaire . . . Pg. 92, E-7
Dunwoody . . Pg. 92, B-5
Dupont M-6
East Atlanta Pg. 92, G-5
East Dublin J-6
East Point F-3
Vicinity . . Pg. 92, H-3
Eastglen . . Pg. 92, H-7
Eastman K-6
Eatonton G-5
Edgehill H-7
Edgewood . Pg. 92, F-5
Edison L-3
Elberton E-6
Elko J-5
Ellaville K-3
Ellenton M-5
Ellenwood . Pg. 92, J-6
Ellijay D-3
Emerson E-3
Empire J-5
Enigma L-5
Enon Forest Pg. 92, H-1
Evans F-8

Faceville N-3
Fair Oaks . . Pg. 92, B-1
Fairburn . . . Pg. 92, K-1
Fairmount E-3
Fairview . . . Pg. 99, K-4
Falconhurst . Pg. 92, J-2
Fargo N-7
Fayetteville G-3
Feldwood Pines
. . . . Pg. 92, K-2
Fernandina Beach . N-9
Fernwood . . Pg. 92, B-1
Finleyson K-5
Fitzgerald L-5
Flairsville D-4
Flemington K-9
Flintstone . . Pg. 99, K-4
Folkston N-8
Forest Park G-4
Vicinity . . Pg. 92, J-4
Forsyth H-4
Fort Gaines L-2
Fort Gillem . Pg. 92, J-5
Fort Oglethorp D-2
Fort Valley J-4
Fortson . . . Pg. 108, G-3
Franklin G-2
Franklin Springs . . . E-6
Gainesville E-4
Garden City K-9
Geneva J-3
Gentian . . . Pg. 108, G-3
Georgetown K-2
Gibson G-7
Gillsville E-5
Girard H-9
Glenns . . . Pg. 108, H-2
Glennville K-8
Glenwood K-7
Gordon H-5
Gracewood G-8
Grant Park . Pg. 92, G-4
Grantville G-2
Gray H-5
Graysville . . Pg. 99, J-4
Green Oaks Pg. 92, H-6
Greenbriar . Pg. 92, H-2
Greensboro F-6
Greenville H-3
Gresham . . Pg. 92, E-1
Griffin G-3
Grovania J-5
Grove Park . Pg. 92, F-3
Grove Town G-7
Haddock H-6
Hagan K-8
Hahira M-5
Hamilton H-2
Hampton G-4
Hapeville . . Pg. 92, H-4
Haralson H-3
Harlem G-7
Harrison H-6
Hartwell E-6
Hawkinsville K-5
Haynes Manor
. . . . Pg. 92, E-4
Hazelhurst K-7
Heatherwood Pg. 92, K-3
Helen D-5
Helena K-6
Hephzibah G-7
Herod L-3
Hiawassee D-5
Hickox M-8
Highland Pines
. . . . Pg. 108, H-2
Hilltonia H-9
Hilton M-2
Hinesville K-9
Hoboken M-8
Hogansville G-2
Holly Springs E-4
Hollydale . . Pg. 92, K-3
Homeland M-8
Homer E-5
Homerville M-7
Hooker . . . Pg. 99, J-1
Horseshoe Bend
. . . . Pg. 92, A-6
Ideal J-4
Idlewood . . Pg. 92, F-7
Ila E-6
Indian Crossing
. . . . Pg. 92, B-7
Irwinton H-5
Irwinville L-5
Ivey H-6
Jackson G-4
Jacksonville K-6

Jasper E-3
Jefferson E-5
Jeffersonville J-5
Jesup L-8
Jonesboro G-3
Juno D-4
Kingsland N-9
Kingston E-2
Kirkwood . . Pg. 92, F-5
Kite H-7
Knight Park . Pg. 92, E-3
Knoxville H-4
La Grange H-2
LaFayette D-2
Lake City . . Pg. 92, K-5
Lake Park N-6
Lakeland M-6
Lakemont D-5
Lakeshore Estates
. . . . Pg. 92, D-1
Lakeview . . Pg. 99, J-4
Lavonia E-6
Lawrenceville F-4
Leary L-3
Leesburg L-4
Leland . . . . Pg. 92, E-1
Lenox M-5
Vicinity . . Pg. 92, D-5
Lenox Park . Pg. 92, E-4
Leslie K-4
Lexington F-6
Liburn F-4
Lilly K-4
Lincolndale . Pg. 92, J-6
Lincolnton F-7
Lindmoor . . Pg. 92, E-7
Lithonia F-4
Lockheed . . Pg. 92, B-1
Locust Grove G-4
Loganville F-5
London Park . Pg. 92, F-7
Lookout Mountain
. . . . Pg. 99, K-2
Louisville H-7
Lovett J-6
Ludowici L-8
Lula E-5
Lumber City K-6
Lumpkin K-3
Luthersville G-3
Lyons J-7
Macon H-5
Madison F-5
Manchester H-2
Mangum Manor
. . . . Pg. 92, G-2
Manor M-7
Margret D-4
Marietta F-3
Vicinity . . Pg. 92, B-1
Marshallville J-4
Maxeys F-5
Maysville E-5
McCaysville D-3
McIntire H-5
McRae K-6
Meadow Lake Pg. 92, B-5
Meigs M-4
Menlo Park D-3
Merrillville M-4
Metcalf N-4
Metter J-8
Middleton F-6
Midland . . Pg. 108, F-1
Midtown . . Pg. 92, F-4
Midville H-7
Milan K-6
Milledgeville H-5
Millen H-8
Mineral Bluff D-4
Modoc H-3
Molena H-3
Moncrief N-4
Monroe F-5
Montevista . Pg. 92, G-1
Montezuma J-4
Monticello G-4
Morgan L-3
Morningside . Pg. 92, E-4
Morris K-2
Morrow . . . Pg. 92, K-5
Morven M-6
Moultrie M-4
Mountain City D-5
Mountain View Pg. 92, J-6
Mt. Airy D-5
Mt. Vernon K-7
Mt. Zion F-2
Nahunta M-8

Nankipooh Pg. 108, G-2
Nashville M-6
Naylor N-6
Nelson E-4
Newington J-9
Newnan G-2
Newton M-3
Nicholls L-7
Norcross . . Pg. 92, B-7
Norman Park M-4
Norristown J-7
North Atlanta Pg. 92, C-5
Northlake . . Pg. 92, D-6
Northridge . Pg. 92, A-5
Oak Park J-7
Oakfield L-4
Oakland City Pg. 92, G-3
Oakman D-3
Oakwood E-5
Ochlocknee M-4
Ocilla L-6
Odum L-8
Offerman L-8
Oglethorpe J-4
Ohoopee J-7
Oliver J-9
Omaha K-2
Omega L-5
Orchard Knob Pg. 92, H-4
Oxford F-5
Palmetto G-3
Panola Woods Pg. 92, J-7
Panthersville Pg. 92, H-6
Parrott K-3
Patterson L-8
Pavo M-4
Peachtree City G-3
Pearson M-6
Pebblebrook Estates
. . . . Pg. 92, E-2
Pelman M-4
Pembroke K-9
Penhurst . . Pg. 92, A-3
Percale L-8
Perkerson . . Pg. 92, H-4
Perry J-5
Philomath F-6
Piedmont Heights
. . . . Pg. 92, E-4
Pierce Chapel
. . . . Pg. 108, G-1
Pine Lake . . Pg. 92, E-7
Pine Park N-4
Pinehurst K-4
Pineview K-5
Vicinity . . Pg. 92, J-2
Pitts K-5
Pittsburg . . Pg. 92, C-7
Plains K-3
Ponderosa . Pg. 92, K-4
Pooler K-9
Portal J-8
Poulan L-5
Preston K-3
Pulaski K-8
Quitman N-5
Radium Springs L-4
Raleigh H-3
Ranger D-3
Ray City M-6
Rayle F-6
Red Oak . . Pg. 92, J-2
Regency . . Pg. 92, G-1
Reidsville K-8
Resaca D-2
Revecca K-5
Rex K-6
Reynolds J-3
Richland K-3
Richmond Hill K-9
Richmond Oaks
. . . . Pg. 92, G-4
Rincon J-9
Ringgold . . Pg. 99, K-6
Riverdale . . Pg. 92, K-4
Roberta H-4
Robins J-4
Rochelle K-5
Rockmart F-2
Rocky Ford H-8
Rome E-2
Roopville G-2
Rossville . . Pg. 99, J-4
Roswell F-3
Round Hill M-5
Saffold M-2
Sale City M-4
Sandersville H-6
Sandy Springs
. . . . Pg. 92, B-4

Sardis H-9
Sasser L-3
Savannah K-10
Schatulga . Pg. 108, F-3
Scottdale . . Pg. 92, E-6
Screven L-8
Senoia G-3
Seville K-5
Shady Dale G-5
Shellman L-3
Shiloh H-3
Six Flags . . Pg. 92, F-1
Smithville K-4
Smyrna . . . Pg. 92, C-2
Social Circle F-5
Somerset . . Pg. 92, B-3
Soperton J-7
Southwest . Pg. 92, G-2
Spalding Bridge
. . . . Pg. 92, A-7
Sparks M-5
Sparta G-6
Springfield J-9
Vicinity . . Pg. 92, K-5
St. George N-8
St. Marys N-9
St. Simons Island . . . M-9
Stagecoach Hills
. . . . Pg. 92, K-7
Statenville N-6
Statesboro J-8
Stillmore J-7
Stockbridge G-4
Stockton M-6
Stone Mountain F-4
Stonewall . . Pg. 92, H-2
Strasburg . . Pg. 92, H-2
Suches D-4
Sugar Hill E-4
Summertown H-7
Summerville E-2
Sumner L-4
Sun Valley . . Pg. 92, J-2
Surrency L-8
Suwanee F-4
Swainsboro J-7
Sycamore L-4
Sylvan Hills Pg. 92, G-3
Sylvania H-9
Sylvester L-4
Talbotton J-3
Tallulah Falls D-5
Talmo L-7
Tarrytown J-6
Tarversville J-5
Tazewell J-3
Tecal . . . . . Pg. 92, H-2
Tenille H-7
Tennga D-3
Thomaston H-4
Thomasville N-4
Thomson G-7
Thornhedge . Pg. 92, K-3
Thunderbolt K-10
Tifton L-5
Tignall F-7
Toccoa D-5
Toco Hills . . Pg. 92, E-5
Toombsboro H-6
Towns K-7
Toyston E-6
Trenton D-1
Trion D-2
Turin G-3
Tuxedo Park Pg. 92, D-4
Twin City J-8
Ty Ty L-5
Unadilla K-5
Union City F-3
Vicinity . . Pg. 92, K-1
Union Point F-6
Uvalda K-7
Valdosta N-6
Van Wert F-2
Vanna E-6
Vidalia J-7
Vienna K-4
Villa Rica G-2
Vinings . . . Pg. 92, D-3
Wadley H-7
Waleska E-3
Waresboro M-7
Warlick . . . . Pg. 92, H-2
Warner H-5
Warrenton G-7
Warthen H-6
Warwick L-4
Washington F-6
Watkinsville F-5

Watts Road . Pg. 92, E-2
Waycross M-7
Waynesboro H-8
Wayside . . . Pg. 92, G-2
Wesley Chapel
. . . . Pg. 92, G-7
West End . . Pg. 92, G-3
West Point H-2
Whigham N-3
White E-3
Whitesburg G-2
Wildwood . . Pg. 92, E-4
Willacoochee L-6
Winder F-5
Winterthur . . Pg. 92, B-3
Woodbine M-8
Woodbury H-3
Woodcliff . . Pg. 92, A-4
Woodcrest . . Pg. 92, J-6
Woodland H-3
Woodmont Landings
. . . . Pg. 92, B-6
Wrens G-7
Wrightsville H-6
Zebulon H-4

HAWAII

HAWAII

Page 30
Population: 964,691
Capital: Honolulu
Land Area: 6,425 sq. mi.

Aiea G-6
Anahola D-3
Apole Pt C-9
Apua Pt G-10
Barbers Pt G-4
Cape Halawa A-6
Cape Hanamanioa . C-8
Captain Cook F-9
Eleele F-2
Ewa G-5
Glenwood F-9
Haena D-2
Haena Pt D-2
Haiku A-9
Hakalau F-10
Halawa A-6
Haleiwa F-4
Hana B-10
Hanalei D-2
Hanamalo Pt G-8
Hanamaulu E-3
Hanapepe F-1
Hauula F-6
Hawaii Kai G-6
Hawi E-9
Hekili Pt B-7
Hilo F-10
Honaunau F-8
Honohina E-10
Honokaa E-9
Honokahau F-8
Honokahua A-7
Honolulu G-5
Honuapo G-9
Hookena F-8
Ka Lae G-9
Kaalualu G-9
Kaena Pt G-10
Kahakuloa Pt A-8
Kahaluu F-6
Kahana F-6
Kahlu Pt A-4
Kahuku E-5
Kahuku Pt. E-5
Kahului A-8
Kailua (Hawaii) F-8
Kailua (Oahu) G-7
Kaimu F-10
Kainaliu F-8
Kaka Pt E-7
Kalae A-5
Kalaheo F-2
Kalahu Pt B-10
Kalalau D-2
Kalaoa F-8
Kalapana G-10
Kamalo A-5
Kamiloloa A-5
Kaneohe G-6
Kapaa E-3
Kauna Pt G-8
Kaunakakai A-5
Kaupo B-9
Kawahae E-8
Keaau F-10
Keahole Pt F-8

Kealia E-3
Keauhou F-8
Kekaha E-1
Keokea B-8
Keomuku D-7
Kepuhi Pt F-4
Kihei B-8
Kikipua Pt A-5
Kilauea D-2
Kipahulu B-10
Koele D-6
Koheo Pt F-2
Koko Head G-7
Kolo A-4
Koloa F-2
Kualapapa A-4
Kualapuu A-4
Kualoa Pt F-6
Kukaiau E-9
Kukuihaele E-9
Kurtistown F-10
Laau Pt A-3
Lahaina A-7
Laie E-6
Lamaloa Head A-6
Lanai City D-6
Lawai F-2
Lihue E-3
Lilo Pt A-3
Maalaea B-8
Mahukona E-8
Maili G-4
Makaha F-4
Makaha Pt D-1
Makahuena Pt F-3
Makakilo City G-4
Makanalua Pen A-5
Makapuu Pt G-7
Makawao A-9
Makena B-8
Mana E-1
Mauna Loa A-4
Mililani Town F-5
Milolii G-8
Mokapuu Pt. F-7
Moloaa D-3
Mopua B-7
Mountain View F-9
Muolea Pt. B-10
Naalehu G-9
Nakalele Pt. A-7
Nanakuli G-4
Napoopoo F-8
Nawiliwili E-3
Ninini Pt. E-3
Niulii E-9
Nukuele Pt. C-8
Olowalu B-7
Ookala E-9
Opihikao F-10
Pahala G-9
Pahoa F-10
Paia A-8
Papa G-9
Papaaloa E-10
Papaikou F-10
Paukaa F-10
Pauwalu A-6
Pauwela A-8
Pauwela Pt. A-8
Pearl City F-5
Pearl Harbor G-5
Pepeekeo F-9
Pepeekeo Pt. F-10
Pohoiki F-10
Port Allen F-2
Puako E-8
Puhi E-2
Pukaulua Pt. A-10
Pukoo A-5
Puunene A-8
Puuwai B-1
Sprecklelsville A-8
Sunset Beach E-5
Ulapue A-5
Ulupalakua B-9
Upola Pt. E-8
Wahiawa F-5
Waiahukini G-9
Waiaka E-9
Waiakea F-10
Waialua (Molokai) . . A-6
Waialua (Oahu) . . . F-5
Waianae F-4
Waihee Pt. A-8
Waikiki G-6
Wailea B-8
Wailua (Kauai) E-3
Wailua (Maui) A-9
Wailuku A-8
Waimanalo G-7
Waimea (Hawaii) . . E-9
Waimea (Kauai) . . . E-1
Waiohinu G-9
Waipahu G-5

IDAHO

Page 31
Population: 943,935
Capital: Boise
Land Area: 82,413 sq. mi.

Ahsahka D-2
American Falls J-5
Arco H-5
Arimo J-6
Ashton G-7
Atlanta H-3
Atomic City H-5
Avery C-3
Bellevue H-4
Bigby H-6
Blackfoot H-6
Bliss J-4
Blue Dome G-5
Boise H-3
Bonners Ferry A-2
Bovill D-2
Bruneau J-3
Burley J-4
Butte City H-5
Caldwell H-2
Cambridge G-2
Cape Horn G-3
Carey H-4
Cascade G-3
Cataldo C-2
Challis G-4
Chubbuck J-6
Coeur D'Alene C-2
Colburn B-2
Cottonwood E-2
Craigmont D-2
Deary D-2
Declo J-5
Downey J-6
Dubois G-6
Eagle H-2
Eastport A-3
Elba K-5
Elk City E-3
Elk River D-3
Emmett H-2
Fairfield H-4
Fernan Lake B-2
Garden City H-2
Gibbonsville E-4
Golden E-3
Gooding J-4
Grand View J-2
Grangeville E-3
Hagerman J-4
Hailey H-4
Hamer G-6
Harpster E-3
Harvard C-2
Headquarters D-3
Hill City H-3
Holbrook K-6
Hollister J-4
Homedale H-2
Hope B-3
Horseshoe Bend . . . G-2
Howe H-5
Idaho City H-3
Idaho Falls H-6
Jerome J-4
Kamiah D-3
Kellogg C-3
Ketchum H-4
King Hill J-3
Kooskia E-3
Kuna H-2
Lamb Creek A-2
Leadore F-5
Lemhi F-5
Lewiston D-2
Lowell D-3
Lowman G-3
Mackay G-5
Malad City K-6
Malta K-5
May G-4
McCall F-3
Meridian H-2
Middleton H-2
Minidoka J-4
Montpelier J-7
Moreland H-6
Moscow D-2
Mountain Home . . . H-3
Moyie Springs A-3
Mud Lake H-6
Mullan C-3
Murphy H-2
Myrtle D-2
Nampa H-2
Naples A-3
New Meadows F-2
New Plymouth G-2
North Fork E-4
Orofino D-2
Osburn C-3
Patterson G-5
Payette G-2
Pierce D-2
Plummer C-2
Pocatello J-6
Pollock F-2
Porthill A-2
Portneuf J-6
Preston J-7
Rexburg H-6
Ririe H-6
Roberts H-6
Rock Creek J-4
Rockland J-5
Salmon F-4
Samaria J-6
Sandpoint B-2
Shoshone J-4
Silver City J-2
Soda Springs J-7
Spencer G-6
Spirit Lake J-7
Springfield B-2
St. Joe C-3
Sunbeam G-4
Troy D-2
Twin Falls J-4
Victor H-7
Wallace C-3
Weiser G-2
White Bird E-2
Woodland D-3
Worley C-2

ILLINOIS

Page 32-33
Population: 11,426,518
Capital: Springfield
Land Area: 55,645 sq. mi.

Abingdon C-5
Addison . . . Pg. 104, H-4
Albany D-3
Albion H-11
Aledo B-4
Alexis C-4
Algonquin . . Pg. 102, E-2
Alhambra D-10
Allendale H-11
Allerton H-7
Alma F-11
Alpha C-4
Alpine . . . . Pg. 105, L-5
Alsip . . . . Pg. 105, K-6
Altamont F-10
Alto Pass E-14
Alton D-10
Alvin J-6
Amboy E-3
Andalusia . . Pg. 112, E-1
Andover C-4
Anna E-14
Annawan D-4
Antioch G-1
Aptakisic . . Pg. 103, E-5
Arcola G-8
Argenta F-7
Arlington E-3
Arlington Heights
. . . . Pg. 102, F-4
Arthur G-8
Ashland D-8
Ashley F-12
Ashmore H-8
Ashton E-2
Assumption F-9
Astoria C-7
Athens D-7
Atkinson D-3
Atlanta E-7
Atwood G-8
Auburn D-8
Aubury Hills Pg. 105, M-6
Augusta B-7
Aurora G-3
Vicinity . . Pg. 104, J-2
Ava E-13
Avon C-6
Babcock Addition
. . . . Pg. 112, B-5
Baldmond . . Pg. 104, H-1
Bannockburn
. . . . Pg. 103, E-5
Barrington . Pg. 102, E-3
Barrington Hills
. . . . Pg. 102, F-3
Barry B-8
Barstow . . . Pg. 112, C-5
Bartlett . . . Pg. 102, G-3
Bartonville D-6
Vicinity . . Pg. 154, D-2
Batavia . . . Pg. 104, H-2
Beach Park Pg. 103, C-6
Beardstown C-7
Beckemeyer E-11
Bedford Park Pg. 105, J-6
Beecher City F-9
Belle Rive F-12
Belleville D-11
Bellevue . . Pg. 154, C-2
Bellflower G-6
Bellmont H-11
Bellwood . . Pg. 105, H-5
Belvidere F-1
Bement G-7
Bensenville Pg. 103, G-5
Benson E-5
Benton F-12
Berkeley . . . Pg. 105, H-5
Berwyn H-2
Vicinity . . Pg. 105, H-6
Bethalto D-10
Bethany F-8
Biggsville B-5
Bloomingdale
. . . . Pg. 104, G-4
Bloomington E-6
Blue Island . Pg. 105, K-7
Blue Mound E-8
Bluffs C-8
Bolingbrook H-2
Vicinity . . Pg. 104, K-4
Bourbonnais H-4
Bowen B-7
Bradford E-4
Bradley H-4
Braidwood H-4
Briar Bluff . . Pg. 112, D-6
Bridgeview . Pg. 105, J-6
Brighton C-10
Brimfield D-5
Broadview . Pg. 105, H-5
Brookfield . . Pg. 105, J-6
Brooklyn . . . Pg. 158, E-7
Brookport G-15
Brownstown F-10
Buckley H-6
Buffalo Grove
. . . . Pg. 102, E-4
Bull Valley . Pg. 102, D-2
Bunker Hill D-10
Burbank . . . Pg. 105, K-6
Burnham . . Pg. 105, L-8
Burr Ridge . Pg. 105, J-5
Burtons Bridge
. . . . Pg. 102, D-3
Bush F-13
Bushnell C-6
Byron E-2
Cabery G-5
Cahokia C-11
Vicinity . Pg. 158, G-7
Cairo F-15
Calumet City Pg. 105, L-8
Calumet Park Pg.105, K-7
Cambridge C-4
Camden B-7
Camp Point B-7
Campbell Hill . . . E-13
Campbells Island
. . . . Pg. 112, B-5
Canton D-6
Capron F-1
Carbon Cliff Pg. 112, C-6
Carbondale E-13
Carlinville D-9
Carlyle E-11
Carmi G-12
Carol Stream Pg. 104, H-3
Carpentersville
. . . . Pg. 102, F-2
Carriers Mills F-13
Carrollton C-9
Carterville F-13
Carthage A-6
Cary . . . . . Pg. 102, E-2
Casey H-9
Caton Farm Pg. 104, L-3
Cave-In-Rock H-14
Cedarville D-1
Central City F-11
Centralia E-11
Cerro Gordo F-7
Chadwick D-2
Champaign G-7
Chandlerville C-7
Channel Lake
. . . . Pg. 102, B-3
Chapin C-8
Charleston H-9
Chatham D-8
Chatsworth G-5
Chebanse H-5
Chenoa F-5
Cherry Valley F-1
Chester D-13
Chesterfield D-9
Chicago J-2
Vicinity . . . Pg. 102-105
Detailed City . Pg. 215
Chicago Heights J-3
Vicinity . Pg. 105, M-7
Chicago Ridge
. . . . Pg. 105, K-6
Chillicothe E-5
Chrisman H-8
Cicero . . . . Pg. 105, H-6
Cisco F-7
Cisne G-11
Clarendon Hills
. . . . Pg. 105, J-5
Clay City G-11
Clayton B-7
Cleveland . . Pg. 112, C-7
Clifton H-5
Clinton F-7
Coal Valley . Pg. 112, E-5
Coal Village C-4
Cobden E-14
Coffeen E-10
Colchester B-6
Colfax G-6
Collinsville D-11
Colona . . . . Pg. 112, C-6
Columbia C-11
Vicinity . . Pg. 158, J-5
Compton E-3
Cordova C-3
Cornell F-5
Coulterville E-12
Country Club Hills
. . . . Pg. 105, L-6
Countryside Pg. 105, J-5
Cowden F-9
Crampton . . Pg. 112, E-6
Creal Springs F-13
Crest Hill . . Pg. 104, L-3
Crestwood . Pg. 105, L-6
Crete F-9
Vicinity . Pg. 105, M-7
Creve Coeur E-6
Vicinity . . Pg. 154, C-4
Crystal Lake G-1
Vicinity . . Pg. 102, D-2
Cuba C-6
Cullom G-5
Cutler E-12
Dakota E-1
Dallas City B-6
Damiansville E-11
Danville J-7
Darien . . . . Pg. 105, J-5
Dayton . . . . Pg. 112, C-7
De Kalb F-2
De Soto E-13
Decatur F-8
Deer Grove E-3
Deer Park . . Pg. 102, E-4
Deerfield . . Pg. 103, E-5
Delavan E-6
Des Plaines Pg. 103, F-5
Diamond Lake G-4
Vicinity . . Pg. 102, D-4
Dieterich G-10
Divernon E-9
Dix F-11
Dixmoor . . . Pg. 105, L-7
Dixon E-2
Dolton . . . . Pg. 105, L-7
Donovan H-5
Downers Grove H-3
Vicinity . . . Pg. 104, J-4
Du Quoin E-12
Dunfermline D-6
Dunlap D-5
Dupo . . . . Pg. 158, H-6
Dwight G-4
Earlville F-3
East Carondelet
. . . . Pg. 158, H-5
East Dubuque C-1
East Dundee Pg. 102, F-2
East Hazelcrest
. . . . Pg. 105, L-7
East Moline Pg. 112, C-5
East Peoria E-5
Vicinity . . Pg. 154, B-5
East St. Louis D-11
Vicinity . . Pg. 158, E-7
Easton D-7
Eddyville G-14
Edgewood G-10
Edinburg E-8
Edwards . . . Pg. 154, A-1
Effingham G-10
El Paso F-5
El Vista . . . Pg. 154, B-3
Elburn . . . . Pg. 104, H-1
Eldorado G-13
Elgin G-2
Vicinity . . Pg. 102, F-2
Elizabeth C-1
Elizabethtown G-14
Elk Grove Village
. . . . Pg. 102, G-4
Elkhart E-7
Elkville E-13
Elliot G-6
Ellis Grove D-12
Elmhurst H-2
Vicinity . . Pg. 105, H-5
Elmwood Park
. . . . Pg. 105, H-6
Enfield G-12
Eola . . . . . Pg. 104, J-3
Equality G-13
Erie D-3
Eureka E-5
Evanston J-2
Vicinity . Pg. 103, G-7
Evansville D-12
Evergreen Park
. . . . Pg. 105, K-7
Fairbury G-5
Fairfield G-11
Fairmont . . . Pg. 104, L-4
Fairview C-6
Farina F-10
Farmer City F-7
Farmersville E-9
Farmington D-5
Fayetteville D-11
Fieldon C-10
Fisher G-6
Flanagan F-5
Flat Rock H-10
Flora G-11
Flossmoor Pg. 105, M-7
Flowerfield . Pg. 104, H-4
Ford Heights Pg. 105, M-7
Forest Park . Pg. 105, H-6
Forest View Pg. 105, J-6
Forrest G-5
Forreston E-2
Fox Lake G-1
Vicinity . . Pg. 102, C-3
Fox Lake Hills
. . . . Pg. 102, C-3
Fox River Grove
. . . . Pg. 102, E-3
Fox River Valley Gardens
. . . . Pg. 102, D-3
Frankfort . . Pg. 105, M-5
Franklin D-8
Franklin Park Pg. 105, H-5
Freeburg D-11
Freeport D-1
Fremont Center
. . . . Pg. 102, D-4
Frontenac . . Pg. 104, K-3
Fulton D-2
Gages Lake Pg. 102, C-4
Galatia G-13
Galena C-1
Galesburg C-5
Galva D-4
Gardner G-4
Geneseo C-3
Geneva G-2
Vicinity . . Pg. 104, H-2
Genoa F-2
Georgetown H-7
Germantown E-11
Germantown Hills
. . . . Pg. 154, A-6
Gibson City G-6
Gilberts . . . Pg. 102, F-1
Gillespie D-10
Gilman H-5
Gilmer . . . . Pg. 102, D-4
Girard D-9
Gladstone B-5
Glasford D-6
Vicinity . . Pg. 154, E-1
Glen Ellyn . Pg. 104, H-4
Glencoe . . . Pg. 103, E-6
Glendale . . Pg. 112, C-6
Glendale Heights
. . . . Pg. 104, H-4
Glenview . . Pg. 103, F-6
Glenwood . Pg. 105, M-7
Golconda G-14
Golden B-7
Golf . . . . . Pg. 103, F-6
Good Hope B-6
Goodings Grove
. . . . Pg. 105, L-5
Goreville F-14
Gorham E-13
Grafton C-10
Grand Ridge F-4
Grand Tower E-13
Granite City D-11
Vicinity . . Pg. 158, C-7
Grayslake . . Pg. 102, C-4
Grayville H-12
Green Oaks Pg. 103, D-5
Green River Pg. 112, D-7
Green Rock Pg. 112, D-6
Greenfield C-9
Greenup H-9
Greenview D-7
Greenville E-10
Greenwood Pg. 102, C-1
Gridley F-5
Griggsville B-8
Groveland . Pg. 154, D-5
Gurnee . . . Pg. 103, C-5
Hainesville . Pg. 102, C-4
Half Day . . . Pg. 103, E-5
Hamel D-10
Hamilton A-6
Hammond G-8
Hampshire G-2
Hampton . . Pg. 112, B-5
Hanaford F-13
Hanna City . Pg. 154, B-1
Hanover C-1
Hanover Park
. . . . Pg. 102, G-3
Hardin B-9
Harrisburg G-13
Harristown F-8
Harvard F-1
Harvard Hills Pg. 154, B-6
Harvey . . . . Pg. 105, L-7
Harwood Heights
. . . . Pg. 103, G-6
Hastings . . . Pg. 104, K-5
Havana D-6
Hawthorn Woods
. . . . Pg. 102, E-4
Hazel Crest Pg. 105, L-7
Hebron G-1
Hecker D-12
Hennepin E-4
Henning H-6
Henry E-4
Herrin F-13
Herscher H-5
Heyworth F-6
Hickory Hills Pg. 105, K-6
Highland E-11
Highland Hills
. . . . Pg. 104, H-4
Highland Park H-1
Vicinity . . Pg. 103, E-6
Highwood . . Pg. 103, E-6
Hillsboro E-9
Hillside . . . . Pg. 105, H-5
Hinckley G-3
Hinsdale . . . Pg. 105, J-5
Hodgkins . . Pg. 105, J-5
Hoffman Estates
. . . . Pg. 102, F-3
Holiday Hills Pg. 102, D-3
Homer H-7
Hometown . Pg. 105, K-6
Homewood . Pg. 105, L-7
Hoopeston J-6
Hooppole D-3
Hopedale E-6
Hoyleton E-11
Hudson F-6
Hull A-8
Humboldt G-8
Huntley . . . Pg. 102, E-1
Hurst E-13
Hutsonville H-10
Illiopolis E-8
Imbs Station Pg. 158, H-7
Indian Creek Pg. 102, E-4
Indian Head Park
. . . . Pg. 105, J-5
Industry B-6
Ingalls Park Pg. 104, M-4
Inverness . . Pg. 102, F-4
Irvington F-11
Island Lake . Pg. 102, D-3
Itasca . . . . Pg. 102, G-4
Ivanhoe . . . Pg. 102, D-4
Jacksonville C-8
Jerseyville C-9
Johnsburg . Pg. 102, C-2
Joliet H-3
Vicinity . Pg. 104, M-4
Jonesboro E-14
Junction City H-13
Justice . . . . Pg. 105, J-6
Kampsville B-9
Kankakee H-4
Kansas H-8
Karnak F-14
Kaskaskia D-13
Keeneyville Pg. 102, G-3
Kenilworth . Pg. 103, F-7
Kenney F-7
Kewanee D-4
Kilbourne D-7
Kildeer . . . . Pg. 102, E-4
Kinderhook B-8
Kingston F-2
Kinmundy F-10
Kirkland F-2
Knollwood . Pg. 103, D-5
Knoxville C-5
La Fayette D-4
La Fox . . . . Pg. 104, H-1
La Grange Park
. . . . Pg. 105, J-5
La Harpe A-6
La Moille E-3
La Salle F-4
Lacon E-5
Lake Barrington
. . . . Pg. 102, E-3
Lake Bluff . . Pg. 103, D-6
Lake Forest H-1
Vicinity . . Pg. 103, D-6
Lake Villa . . Pg. 102, C-4
Lake Zurich Pg. 102, E-4
Lake in the Hills
. . . . Pg. 102, E-2
Lakemoor . . Pg. 102, C-3
Lakewood . . Pg. 102, E-1
Lanark D-2
Lansing . . . Pg. 105, L-8
Latham E-7
Lawrenceville J-10
Le Roy F-6
Lee Center E-3
Lemont . . . . Pg. 104, K-4
Lena D-1
Lewistown C-6
Lexington F-6
Liberty A-8
Libertyville H-1
Vicinity . . Pg. 103, D-5
Lilymoor . . Pg. 102, C-3
Lima A-7
Lincoln E-7
Lincoln Estates
. . . . Pg. 105, M-6
Lincolnshire Pg. 103, E-5
Lincolnwood Pg. 103, G-6
Lindenhurst Pg. 102, C-4
Lisle . . . . . Pg. 104, J-4
Litchfield D-9
Little York B-5
Livingston D-10
Lockport . . . Pg. 104, L-4
Lombard . . . Pg. 104, H-4
Long Grove Pg. 102, E-4
Long Lake . Pg. 102, C-3
Loon Lake . Pg. 102, B-4
Loraine A-7
Louisville G-10
Lovington F-8
Ludlow H-6
Lynwood . . Pg. 105, M-8
Lyons . . . . . Pg. 105, J-6
Machesney Park . . . E-1
Mackinaw E-6
Macomb B-6
Madison . . . Pg. 158, D-6

ILLINOIS

Magnolia E-4
Mahomet G-7
Manlius D-3
Manteno H-4
Mapleton . . . . Pg. 154, E-2
Maquon C-5
Marengo G-1
Marine D-10
Marion F-13
Marissa D-12
Markham . . . Pg. 105, L-7
Marley . . . . Pg. 105, M-5
Maroa F-7
Marquette Heights
. . . . Pg. 154, D-4
Marseilles G-4
Marshall J-9
Martinsville H-9
Martinton H-5
Marywood . . . Pg. 105, J-2
Mascoutah D-11
Mason G-10
Mason City D-7
Matteson . . . Pg. 105, M-6
Mattoon G-9
Maywood . . . Pg. 105, H-6
Mazon F-5
McClure E-14
McCook . . . Pg. 105, J-6
McCullom Lake
. . . . Pg. 102, C-2
McHenry G-1
Vicinity . . . Pg. 102, C-2
McLean E-6
McLeansboro G-12
McQueens . . . Pg. 102, F-1
Medinah . . . Pg. 102, G-4
Medora C-9
Melrose Park Pg. 105, H-5
Melvin G-6
Mendon A-7
Mendota E-3
Meredosia C-8
Merrionette Park
. . . . Pg. 105, K-7
Metamora E-5
Metropolis G-15
Mettawa . . . Pg. 103, D-5
Midlothian . . . Pg. 105, L-6
Milan B-4
Vicinity . . . Pg. 112, E-3
Milford H-5
Mill Shoals H-12
Millburn . . . Pg. 102, B-4
Milledgeville D-2
Milton B-8
Minonk F-5
Minooka . . . Pg. 104, M-2
Mokena . . . Pg. 105, M-5
Moline C-3
Vicinity . . . Pg. 112, D-4
Momence J-4
Monmouth C-5
Montgomery Pg. 104, K-2
Monticello G-7
Montrose G-9
Mooseheart . . . Pg. 104, J-2
Morris F-4
Morrison D-2
Morrisonville E-9
Morristown F-2
Vicinity . . . Pg. 112, E-7
Morton E-6
Vicinity . . . Pg. 154, C-6
Morton Grove Pg. 103, F-6
Mound City F-15
Mount Carmel H-11
Mount Carroll D-2
Mount Morris E-2
Mount Olive D-10
Mount Prospect
. . . . Pg. 103, F-5
Mount Pulaski E-7
Mount Sterling B-7
Mount Vernon F-12
Mount Zion F-8
Moweaqua F-8
Mundelein G-1
Vicinity . . . Pg. 102, D-4
Murphysboro E-13
Murrayville C-8
Naperville G-2
Vicinity . . . Pg. 104, J-3
Nashville E-12
National City Pg. 158, E-7
Nauvoo A-6
Neoga G-9
New Athens D-12
New Baden E-11
New Boston B-4

New Burnside F-14
New Canton B-8
New Haven H-13
New Holland E-7
New Lenox Pg. 104, M-5
New Windsor C-4
Newark F-3
Newman H-8
Newton G-10
Niles . . . Pg. 103, G-6
Nilwood D-9
Noble G-11
Nokomis E-9
Normal F-6
Normantown Pg. 104, K-2
Norridge . . . Pg. 105, G-6
Norris D-6
Norris City G-13
North Aurora Pg. 104, J-2
North Barrington
. . . . Pg. 102, E-3
North Chicago
. . . . Pg. 103, D-5
North Pekin Pg. 154, D-3
North Riverside
. . . . Pg. 105, H-6
Northbrook E-9
Vicinity . . . Pg. 103, F-5
Northfield . . . Pg. 103, F-6
Northlake . . . Pg. 105, H-5
Norwood . . . Pg. 154, B-2
Oak Brook . . . Pg. 105, J-5
Oak Forest . . . Pg. 105, L-6
Oak Grove . . . Pg. 112, E-3
Oak Lawn . . . Pg. 105, K-6
Oak Park . . . Pg. 105, H-6
Oakbrook Terrace
. . . . Pg. 105, H-5
Oakford D-7
Oakland H-8
Oakwood H-7
Oakwood Hills
. . . . Pg. 105, D-3
Oblong H-10
Oconee F-9
Odell G-5
Odin F-11
Ogden H-7
Ohio E-3
Old Mill Creek
. . . . Pg. 102, B-4
Olmsted F-15
Olney H-10
Olympia Fields
. . . . Pg. 105, M-7
Omaha G-13
Onarga H-5
Oquawka B-5
Orangeville E-1
Orchard Mines
. . . . Pg. 154, D-2
Oreana F-7
Oregon E-2
Orion C-4
Orland Hills Pg. 105, L-6
Orland Park Pg. 105, L-5
Osborn . . . Pg. 112, C-7
Oswego F-2
Vicinity . . . Pg. 104, K-2
Ottawa F-3
Owaneco F-9
Palatine G-2
Vicinity . . . Pg. 102, F-4
Palestine J-10
Palmyra D-9
Palos Heights
. . . . Pg. 105, K-6
Palos Hills . . . Pg. 105, K-6
Palos Park . . . Pg. 105, K-6
Pana E-9
Paris J-8
Park City . . . Pg. 103, C-5
Park Forest J-3
Vicinity . . . Pg. 105, M-7
Park Ridge Pg. 103, G-6
Parkersburg H-11
Patoka F-10
Pawnee E-8
Paxton H-6
Payson A-8
Pearl City D-1
Pekin D-6
Vicinity . . . Pg. 154, E-3
Peoria D-5
Vicinity . . . Pg. 154, B-3
Peoria Heights
. . . . Pg. 154, A-4
Peotone H-4
Perry B-8

Pesotum G-7
Petersburg D-7
Phoenix . . . Pg. 105, L-7
Pierron E-10
Pinckneyville E-12
Pingree Grove
. . . . Pg. 102, F-1
Piper City G-5
Pittsfield B-8
Plainfield G-3
Vicinity . . . Pg. 104, L-3
Plano G-3
Plato Center Pg. 102, G-1
Plattville . . . Pg. 104, M-1
Pleasant Hill B-9
Plymouth B-6
Pocahontas E-10
Polo E-2
Pontiac G-5
Port Byron C-3
Vicinity . . . Pg. 112, A-7
Posen . . . Pg. 105, L-7
Pottstown . . . Pg. 154, B-3
Prairie Grove Pg. 102, D-2
Prairie View Pg. 102, E-5
Prairie du Rocher . . . F-12
Preston Heights
. . . . Pg. 104, M-4
Prince Crossing
. . . . Pg. 104, H-3
Princeton E-4
Princeville D-5
Prophetstown D-3
Prospect Heights
. . . . Pg. 103, F-5
Pulaski E-15
Quincy A-7
Ramsey F-9
Rankin H-6
Ransom F-4
Rantoul H-6
Rapids City C-3
Vicinity . . . Pg. 112, A-7
Raymond E-9
Red Bud D-12
Reynolds C-4
Richton Park Pg. 105, M-6
Richview E-11
Ridge Farm H-7
Ridgefield . . . Pg. 102, D-2
Ridgeway G-13
Ridgewood Pg. 104, M-4
Ringwood . . . Pg. 102, C-2
River Forest Pg. 105, H-6
River Grove Pg. 105, H-6
Riverdale . . . Pg. 105, L-7
Riverside . . . Pg. 105, J-6
Riverwoods Pg. 103, E-5
Roanoke E-5
Robbins . . . Pg. 105, L-7
Roberts G-6
Robinson H-10
Rochelle E-2
Rochester E-8
Rock Falls D-3
Rock Island B-3
Vicinity . . . Pg. 112, D-3
Rockbridge D-9
Rockdale . . . Pg. 104, M-3
Rockford D-1
Rockton E-1
Rolling Meadows
. . . . Pg. 102, F-4
Romeoville G-3
Vicinity . . . Pg. 104, J-1
Rondout . . . Pg. 103, D-5
Roodhouse C-9
Roselle . . . Pg. 102, G-4
Rosemont Pg. 103, G-5
Roseville C-5
Rosiclare G-14
Rossville H-6
Round Lake Pg. 102, C-3
Round Lake Beach
. . . . Pg. 102, D-4
Round Lake Heights
. . . . Pg. 102, C-4
Round Lake Park
. . . . Pg. 102, C-4
Royalton E-13
Rushville C-7
Rutland F-5
Sag Bridge Pg. 105, K-5
Salem F-11
San Jose E-6
Sandoval E-11
Sandwich F-3
Sauget . . . Pg. 158, F-6
Sauk Village Pg. 105, M-8
Savanna D-2

Schaumburg G-2
Vicinity . . . Pg. 102, G-4
Schiller Park Pg. 105, G-5
Schram City E-9
Sesser F-12
Shabbona F-2
Shannon D-2
Shawneetown G-13
Sheffield D-4
Shelbyville F-9
Sheldon J-5
Shorewood G-3
Vicinity . . . Pg. 104, M-3
Shumway C-12
Sibley G-6
Sigel G-9
Silvis C-3
Vicinity . . . Pg. 112, C-5
Simpson F-14
Sims G-11
Skokie H-2
Vicinity . . . Pg. 103, F-6
Sleepy Hollow
. . . . Pg. 102, F-2
Smithton D-11
Smithville . . . Pg. 154, C-1
Solon Mills . . . Pg. 102, B-2
Somonauk F-3
South Barrington
. . . . Pg. 102, F-3
South Beloit E-1
South Chicago Hts.
. . . . Pg. 105, M-7
South Elgin Pg. 102, G-2
South Holland
. . . . Pg. 105, L-7
South Lockport
. . . . Pg. 104, L-4
Sparland E-4
Sparta D-12
Spencer . . . Pg. 105, M-5
Spring Grove Pg. 102, B-2
Spring Valley E-4
Springfield D-8
St. Anne H-4
St. Augustine C-5
St. Charles H-2
Vicinity . . . Pg. 104, H-2
St. Elmo F-10
St. Francisville H-11
St. Johns E-12
St. Peter F-10
Stanford E-6
Starks . . . Pg. 102, F-1
Staunton D-10
Steeleville D-12
Steger F-9
Vicinity . . . Pg. 105, M-7
Sterling D-2
Stewardson F-9
Stickney . . . Pg. 105, J-6
Stillman Valley E-2
Stockton D-1
Stone Park . . . Pg. 105, H-5
Stonefort G-13
Stonington F-8
Strasburg F-9
Streamwood Pg. 102, G-3
Streator F-4
Stronghurst B-5
Sublette E-3
Suburban Heights
. . . . Pg. 158, J-6
Sugar Grove G-3
Vicinity . . . Pg. 104, J-1
Sugarloaf Hts.
. . . . Pg. 158, J-6
Sullivan G-8
Summit . . . Pg. 105, J-6
Sumner H-11
Swansea D-11
Sycamore G-2
Table Grove C-6
Tallula D-7
Tamaroa E-12
Tampico D-3
Taylor Springs E-9
Taylorville F-8
Teutopolis G-9
Thawville G-5
Third Lake . . . Pg. 102, C-4
Thompsonville G-13
Thomson D-2
Thornton . . . Pg. 105, L-7
Tinley Park . . . Pg. 105, L-6
Toledo G-9
Tolono G-7
Toluca F-5
Tonica F-4
Toulon D-4

Tower Hill F-9
Tower Lakes Pg. 102, E-3
Towne Oaks Pg. 154, E-5
Trenton E-11
Troy D-11
Troy Grove F-4
Tuscola G-8
Udina . . . Pg. 102, F-1
Ullin E-14
University Park
. . . . Pg. 105, M-6
Urbana H-7
Valley View Pg. 102, G-2
Valmeyer C-12
Vandalia F-10
Venetian Village
. . . . Pg. 102, C-4
Venice . . . Pg. 158, D-7
Vernon F-9
Vernon Hills Pg. 103, D-5
Versailles B-8
Victoria D-4
Vienna F-14
Villa Grove H-8
Villa Park . . . Pg. 104, H-5
Viola C-4
Virden D-9
Virginia C-8
Volo . . . Pg. 102, C-3
Wadsworth B-5
Vicinity . . . Pg. 103, B-5
Waggoner D-9
Walnut E-3
Waltonville F-12
Wapella F-7
Warner . . . Pg. 112, E-6
Warren D-1
Warrensburg F-7
Warrenville Pg. 104, J-3
Warsaw A-6
Wasco . . . Pg. 104, G-1
Washburn E-5
Washington E-5
Vicinity . . . Pg. 154, B-7
Waterloo C-12
Waterman F-3
Watseka H-5
Watson G-10
Wauconda Pg. 102, D-3
Waukegan H-1
Vicinity . . . Pg. 103, C-6
Waverly D-8
Wayne . . . Pg. 104, G-3
Wayne City G-11
Weldon F-7
Wellington H-6
Wenona F-4
West Chicago
. . . . Pg. 104, H-3
West City F-12
West Dundee
. . . . Pg. 102, F-2
West Frankfort F-13
West Miltmore
. . . . Pg. 102, C-4
Westchester Pg. 105, H-5
Western Springs
. . . . Pg. 105, J-5
Westfield H-9
Westmont . . . Pg. 104, J-5
Westville J-7
Wheaton G-3
Vicinity . . . Pg. 104, H-3
Wheeler G-10
Wheeling . . . Pg. 103, F-5
White Hall C-9
Wildwood . . . Pg. 103, C-5
Willow Hill H-10
Willow Springs
. . . . Pg. 105, K-5
Willowbrook Pg. 105, J-5
Wilmette . . . Pg. 103, F-7
Wilmington H-4
Winchester C-8
Winfield . . . Pg. 104, H-3
Winnebago E-1
Winnetka H-2
Vicinity . . . Pg. 103, F-6
Winslow F-1
Winthrop Harbor H-1
Vicinity . . . Pg. 103, B-6
Wolfs . . . Pg. 104, K-2
Wonder Lake
. . . . Pg. 102, C-2
Wood Dale . . . Pg. 102, C-4
Woodhull C-4
Woodridge Pg. 104, K-4
Woodson C-8
Woodstock G-1
Vicinity . . . Pg. 102, D-1

Worth . . . . . Pg. 105, K-6
Wyoming D-5
Xenia G-11
Yates City D-5
York Center Pg. 104, H-4
Yorkville G-3
Vicinity . . . Pg. 104, K-1
Zeigler F-13
Zion H-1
Vicinity . . . Pg. 103, B-6

INDIANA
Pages 34-35
Population: 5,490,224
Capital: Indianapolis
Land Area: 35,932 sq. mi.

Ainsworth . . Pg. 103, D-8
Akron D-7
Albany F-9
Albion B-8
Alexandria F-8
Allisonville . . . Pg. 122, B-5
Alton K-7
Alvarado B-10
Ambia F-3
Americus F-4
Anderson G-8
Andersonville J-9
Andrews D-7
Angola A-10
Antrim . . . Pg. 122, F-2
Arcadia F-6
Arcola . . . Pg. 117, H-2
Argos C-6
Armstrong . . . Pg. 117, E-1
Atherton J-3
Attica F-3
Auburn B-10
Augusta . . . Pg. 122, B-3
Austin M-7
Avilla B-9
Bainbridge H-4
Bargersville J-6
Bass Lake C-5
Batesville K-9
Battletown P-6
Bedford L-5
Beech Grove H-6
Vicinity . . . Pg. 122, E-5
Beechwood P-6
Belknap . . . Pg. 117, E-6
Belleview H-6
Belmont K-5
Ben Davis . . . Pg. 122, E-2
Bennett Switch E-7
Berne E-10
Beverly Shores B-4
Bicknell M-3
Birdseye N-5
Bloomfield L-4
Blooming Grove J-9
Bloomington K-5
Bluffton E-9
Boonville P-3
Boston H-10
Boswell E-3
Bourbon C-6
Bowling Green K-4
Branchville P-5
Brazil J-4
Bremen C-6
Bridgeport . . . Pg. 122, E-1
Bristol A-7
Brook D-3
Brooklyn J-6
Brookston E-5
Brookville J-10
Brownsburg H-6
Brownstown L-6
Bruceville M-3
Bryant E-10
Bryantsburg L-8
Burlington F-6
Burnettsville E-5
Burns City M-5
Butler B-10
Cadiz G-8
Cambridge City H-10
Camby . . . Pg. 122, F-4
Cannelton Q-5
Carbon J-4
Carbondale F-3
Carefree P-6
Carlisle L-3
Carmel G-6
Vicinity . . . Pg. 122, A-4
Carp J-5

Castleton G-7
Vicinity . . . Pg. 122, B-5
Cayuga H-3
Cedar Grove J-10
Cedar Lake B-3
Cedarville . . . Pg. 117, F-6
Centerville H-10
Chalmers E-4
Chandler P-3
Charlestown N-8
Chester H-10
Chesterfield G-8
Chrisney P-4
Churubusco C-9
Cicero G-7
Cincinnati L-5
Clarks Hill F-5
Clarksville G-7
Clay City K-4
Clayton H-5
Clermont . . . Pg. 122, C-1
Clinton H-3
Clive . . . Pg. 113, C-1
Cloverdale J-5
Coatesville H-5
Collegeville D-4
Columbia City C-8
Columbus K-7
Connersville H-9
Converse E-7
Cory J-3
Corydon P-7
Covington G-3
Crawfordsville G-4
Crothersville M-7
Crown Point B-3
Vicinity . . . Pg. 103, E-7
Crows Nest . . . Pg. 122, C-3
Crystal N-5
Cuba . . . Pg. 117, G-7
Cumberland H-7
Cynthiana P-2
Cypress Q-2
Dale P-4
Dana H-1
Danville H-5
Darmstadt P-2
Daylight . . . Pg. 117, B-7
Dayton F-4
Decatur D-10
Decker N-3
Deep River . . . Pg. 103, D-8
Deerfield F-10
Degonia Springs N-4
Delphi E-5
Demotte C-4
Denver D-7
Derby P-5
Dillsboro L-9
Dogwood P-7
Dover G-5
Dublin H-9
Dugger L-3
Dunfee C-9
Vicinity . . . Pg. 117, J-1
Dunkirk F-9
Dunlap A-7
Dyer . . . Pg. 105, M-8
E. Mt. Carmel N-2
Earl Park E-3
Earle . . . Pg. 117, B-2
East Chicago
. . . . Pg. 103, B-7
Economy G-9
Edgewood . . . Pg. 122, F-4
Edinburgh K-7
Effner E-3
Elberfeld P-3
Elizabeth P-7
Elizabethtown K-7
Elkhart A-7
Ellettsville K-5
Ellison . . . Pg. 117, K-2
Elwood F-7
Emporia G-8
English N-6
Enos D-3
Evansville P-2
Vicinity . . . Pg. 117, B-4
Fairfield J-10
Fairmount F-8
Ferdinand P-5
Fickle F-5
Fishers . . . Pg. 122, A-5
Five Points . . . Pg. 122, E-5
Flora E-6
Fort Branch P-2

Fort Wayne C-9
Vicinity . . . Pg. 117, H-4
Fortville H-7
Foster G-6
Fountain City G-10
Fowler E-3
Francesville D-4
Frankfort F-6
Franklin J-7
Frankton G-7
Freedom K-4
Freetown L-6
Fremont A-10
French Lick M-5
Fulton D-6
Galveston E-6
Gar Creek . . . Pg. 117, J-7
Garrett B-9
Gary B-3
Vicinity . . . Pg. 103, C-7
Gas City E-8
Geneva E-10
Gentryville P-4
Glenns Valley
. . . . Pg. 122, G-3
Goodland E-3
Goshen B-7
Gosport K-5
Grabill . . . Pg. 117, F-7
Grandview Q-4
Grass Creek D-6
Grayford M-8
Graysville K-3
Greencastle H-4
Greendale K-10
Greenfield H-7
Greensburg K-8
Greentown E-7
Greenwood J-7
Griffin P-2
Griffith . . . Pg. 103, D-7
Grovertown B-5
Hagerstown H-9
Hammond B-3
Vicinity . . . Pg. 105, L-8
Hanna B-5
Hanover M-8
Hardinsburg D-9
Harlan C-10
Vicinity . . . Pg. 117, F-7
Harmony J-4
Harrodsburg L-5
Hartford City F-9
Hartsville K-8
Haysville N-4
Hazelwood D-6
Hazleton N-2
Hebron C-4
Hedrick F-3
Hemlock F-7
Henryville M-8
Heusler Q-2
Highland . . . Pg. 103, C-7
Highwood . . . Pg. 122, C-3
Hillsboro G-4
Hindustan K-5
Hobart B-3
Vicinity . . . Pg. 103, D-8
Hobbs F-7
Holland P-4
Homecroft . . . Pg. 122, F-4
Hope K-7
Howe A-9
Hudson B-9
Hudson Lake A-5
Huntertown C-9
Huntingburg N-4
Huntington D-8
Huron M-5
Indianapolis H-6
Vicinity . . . Pg. 122
Detailed City . . Pg. 238
Inglefield . . . Pg. 117, C-1
Jamestown H-5
Jasonville K-3
Jasper N-4
Jeffersonville N8
Vicinity . . . Pg. 132, A-2
Johnson N-2
Jonesboro F-8
Jonesville L-7
Kasson . . . Pg. 117, D-3
Kempton F-6
Kendallville B-9
Kentland D-3
Kewanna C-6
Kingman G-3
Kingsbury B-5
Kingsford Hts. B-4
Knightstown H-8

INDIANA

INDIANA

Knox C-5
Kokomo E-6
Kouts C-4
La Crosse B-5
La Fontaine E-8
La Paz B-6
La Porte B-5
Lafayette F-5
Lagrange A-8
Lake Station B-3
Vicinity . . Pg. 103, C-8
Lake Village C-3
Lakeville B-6
Lawrence H-6
Vicinity . . Pg. 122, C-5
Lawrenceburg L-10
Lebanon G-6
Leo . . . Pg. 117, F-6
Leota M-7
Leroy B-3
Lewistown D-4
Liberty H-10
Libertyville J-3
Ligonier B-8
Linden G-5
Linton L-4
Lizton H-5
Logansport E-6
Loogootee M-4
Lowell C-3
Luther D-8
Lynn G-10
Lynnville P-3
Mace G-5
Madison L-9
Majenica D-8
Malden B-4
Manhattan J-4
Maples . . . Pg. 117, K-6
Marengo N-6
Marion E-8
Markle D-9
Markleville G-8
Mars Hill . . Pg. 122, B-4
Marshall H-4
Martinsville J-5
Mauckport P-6
Maxwell H-8
Maywood . . Pg. 122, E-3
McCutchanville
. . . . . Pg. 117, B-2
Meadowbrook
. . . . . Pg. 117, J-6
Mecca H-3
Medaryville C-5
Memphis N-7
Mentone C-7
Meridian Hills
. . . . . Pg. 122, B-3
Merom L-3
Merriam C-8
Merrillville B-3
Vicinity . . Pg. 103, D-7
Metamora K-9
Metea D-6
Michiana Shores . . A-5
Michigan City . . . A-4
Michigantown . . . F-6
Mickeyville . . Pg. 122, E-2
Middlebury A-8
Middlefork F-6
Milan K-9
Milan Center . Pg. 117, G-7
Millersburg M-7
Milport M-7
Mishawaka B-7
Mitchell M-6
Monon D-4
Monroe F-5
Monroeville D-10
Montezuma H-3
Monticello E-5
Montmorenci . . . F-4
Montpelier E-9
Mooresville J-6
Morgantown K-6
Morocco D-3
Morristown H-8
Morton H-4
Moscow J-8
Mt. Ayr D-3
Mt. Carmel J-10
Mt. Comfort H-7
Mt. Etna D-8
Mt. Meridian J-5
Mt. Pleasant (Cass Cty)
. . . . D-6
Mt. Pleasant (Perry Cty)
. . . . P-5
Mt. Vernon Q-2
Mt. Zion E-9

Mulberry F-5
Muncie G-9
Munster B-3
Vicinity . . Pg. 105, M-8
N. Liberty B-6
N. Manchester . . . D-7
N. Vernon L-8
Napoleon K-9
Nappanee B-7
Nashville K-6
New Albany N-7
New Amsterdam . . P-6
New Augusta
. . . . . Pg. 122, B-2
New Boston P-7
New Carlisle A-6
New Castle G-9
New Chicago
. . . . . Pg. 103, C-8
New Frankfort . . . J-9
New Goshen J-3
New Harmony . . . P-2
New Haven C-10
Vicinity . . Pg. 117, J-6
New Liberty M-7
New Market G-5
New Pekin M-7
New Providence . . N-7
New Richmond . . . G-4
New Ross G-5
New Whiteland . . . J-6
Newberry L-4
Newburgh Q-3
Newport H-3
Newtown G-4
Nine Mile D-9
Nobelsville G-7
Nora . . . . Pg. 122, B-4
Norristown K-7
North Crows Nest
. . . . . Pg. 122, B-3
North Judson . . . C-5
Oakland City N-3
Oaktown C-3
Odell F-4
Odon L-4
Ogilville K-7
Oolitic C-5
Orleans M-5
Osceola A-7
Osgood K-9
Ossian D-9
Otis A-4
Otwell N-4
Owensville P-2
Oxford E-3
Palmyra N-6
Paoli M-6
Paris Crossing . . . L-8
Parr D-4
Patriot L-9
Patronville E-11
Pence F-3
Pendleton G-8
Peoria E-7
Perrysburg D-7
Perrysville G-3
Peru E-7
Petersburg N-3
Pierceton C-8
Pike G-6
Pine Village F-3
Plainfield H-5
Pleasant L-9
Pleasant Mills . . . D-10
Pleasant View . . . H-7
Plymouth B-6
Point Isabel F-7
Portage B-4
Porter B-4
Portland F-10
Poseyville P-2
Prairie City J-4
Prairie Creek K-3
Prairieton K-3
Princeton N-2
Rahm . . . . Pg. 117, D-6
Ramsey N-6
Raub E-3
Ravenswood . . Pg. 122, B-4
Rays Crossing . . . J-8
Reiffsburg E-9
Rensselaer D-4
Reynolds D-4
Richmond H-10
Rising Sun L-10
River Haven . . Pg. 117, J-5
Riverside F-3
Roachdale H-5

Roann D-7
Rochester C-6
Rockfield E-5
Rockport Q-4
Rockville H-3
Rocky Ripple
. . . . . . Pg. 122, C-3
Rogersville G-9
Rome City B-9
Romney F-4
Rosedale J-3
Roseland A-6
Roselawn C-3
Rosston G-6
Rossville F-5
Royal Center D-5
Royalton H-6
Rushville J-8
Russellville H-4
Salem M-6
Sandusky J-8
Santa Claus P-4
Santa Fe E-7
Schererville B-3
Vicinity . . Pg. 103, D-7
Schneider C-3
Scipio J-10
Scott A-8
Scottsburg M-7
Seelyville J-3
Sellersburg N-7
Sexton H-8
Seymour L-7
Shelburn K-3
Shelbyville J-7
Sheridan G-6
Shoals M-5
Shore Acres . . Pg. 122, B-4
Sidney C-7
Silver Lake C-7
Smith . . . . Pg. 117, G-3
Solitude P-2
South Bend A-6
South Whitley . . . C-8
Southport H-6
Vicinity . . Pg. 122, G-4
Speedway H-6
Vicinity . . Pg. 122, D-2
Spencer K-5
Spiceland H-8
Spring Hills . . Pg. 122, C-4
St. Croix P-5
St. Joe C-10
St. John . . . Pg. 103, D-6
St. John . . . Pg. 117, A-2
St. Joseph . . Pg. 117, E-2
St. Leon A-7
St. Paul J-8
Stevenson . . Pg. 117, A-3
Stewartsville P-2
Stilesville H-5
Story K-6
Sullivan K-3
Sulphur Springs . . G-8
Summitville F-8
Sunman K-9
Swayzee E-7
Syracuse B-8
Tell City Q-5
Templeton E-4
Terre Haute J-3
Thorntown G-5
Thurman . . . . Pg. 117, H-6
Tipton F-7
Topeka B-8
Traders Point . Pg. 122, B-1
Trafalgar K-6
Tremont . . . Pg. 122, D-1
Troy P-5
Union City G-10
Uniondale D-9
Uniontown Q-1
Unionville K-6
Upland F-8
Urbana D-7
Valparaiso B-4
Van Buren E-8
Vaughan . . . Pg. 117, D-5
Veedersburg G-3
Versailles L-9
Vevay M-9
Vincennes M-3
W. College Corner . J-10
W. Lebanon F-3
W. Terre Haute . . . J-3
Wabash D-7
Waco M-4
Wakarusa B-6
Walen . . . . Pg. 117, G-4
Walkerton B-6

Walton E-6
Wanatah B-4
Warren E-8
Warsaw C-7
Washington M-4
Waterford A-8
Waterloo H-9
Waterloo B-10
Waynedale . . Pg. 117, K-3
Waynetown G-4
Webster H-10
West Lafayette . . . F-5
West Newton
. . . . . Pg. 122, G-2
West Point F-4
Westfield G-7
Westphalia L-3
Westport K-8
Westville B-4
Wheatfield C-4
Whitestown G-6
Whiting B-3
Vicinity . . Pg. 105, M-8
Wilkinson H-8
Williams L-5
Williams Creek
. . . . . Pg. 122, B-4
Williamsport F-3
Wilmot C-8
Winamac C-4
Winchester G-10
Windfall City F-7
Wingate G-4
Winona Lake C-7
Winslow N-3
Wolcott D-4
Woodburn C-10
Woodstock . . Pg. 122, C-3
Worthington K-4
Wynnedale . . Pg. 122, C-3
Yorktown G-8
Zionsville G-6
Vicinity . . Pg. 122, A-2

IOWA

IOWA
Page 36
Population: 2,913,808
Capital: Des Moines
Land Area: 55,965 sq. mi.

Abingdon F-7
Ackley C-6
Adair E-4
Adel E-4
Afton F-4
Agency E-6
Ainsworth E-8
Akron C-1
Albia F-6
Alden C-5
Algona B-4
Allendorf B-2
Allerton F-5
Allison C-6
Alta C-3
Alta Vista A-7
Alton B-1
Altoona D-5
Vicinity . . Pg. 113, C-5
Amana D-8
Ames D-5
Anamosa D-9
Anderson F-2
Andrew D-10
Anita E-3
Ankeny D-5
Vicinity . . Pg. 113, A-3
Anthon C-2
Aplington C-6
Arcadia D-3
Archer B-2
Aredale C-6
Arispe F-4
Arlington C-8
Armstrong B-4
Arnolds Park A-3
Arthur D-3
Asbury C-9
Ashton B-2
Athelstan G-4
Atkins D-7
Atlantic E-3
Attica E-6
Auburn D-3
Audubon D-3
Aurella C-3
Avery F-7
Avoca E-3
Avon . . . . Pg. 113, E-5

Avon Lake . Pg. 113, E-5
Badger C-4
Baldwin D-9
Bancroft B-4
Barnes City E-7
Barnum C-4
Bartlett F-2
Battle Creek D-2
Baxter D-6
Bayard D-4
Beacon E-6
Beaver D-5
Bedford F-4
Beech E-6
Belle Plaine D-7
Bellevue D-9
Belmond C-5
Bennett E-9
Berwick . . . Pg. 113, B-5
Bettendorf E-10
Vicinity . . Pg. 112, A-4
Bevington E-5
Blakesburg F-7
Blencoe D-2
Bloomfield F-7
Bonaparte F-8
Boone D-5
Boyden B-2
Bradford C-6
Brayton E-3
Breda C-3
Bridgewater F-4
Brighton F-8
Britt B-5
Brooklyn D-6
Brooks F-3
Brunsville C-1
Bryant D-10
Buffalo . . . Pg. 112, D-1
Buffalo Center . . . A-5
Buffalo Heights
. . . . . Pg. 112, D-1
Burlington F-8
Burr Oak A-8
Burt B-4
Bussey E-6
Calmar B-8
Calumet B-2
Camanche D-9
Cantril G-7
Capitol Heights
. . . . . Pg. 113, C-5
Carbon F-3
Carlisle . . . Pg. 113, F-5
Carney . . . Pg. 113, B-4
Carpenter B-6
Carroll D-3
Carson F-3
Carter Lake E-1
Cascade D-9
Casey E-4
Cedar F-7
Cedar Falls C-7
Cedar Rapids D-8
Center Point D-8
Centerville F-6
Central City D-8
Chapin C-6
Chariton F-6
Charles City B-6
Charlotte D-10
Charter Oak D-2
Chatsworth B-1
Chelsea D-7
Cherokee C-2
Churdan D-4
Cincinnati G-6
Clara . . . . Pg. 148, C-5
Clare C-4
Clarence D-9
Clarinda F-3
Clarion C-5
Clarksville C-7
Clear Lake B-6
Clearfield F-4
Cleghorn C-2
Clinton D-10
Clive . . . . Pg. 113, C-1
Clutier D-7
Coggon D-8
Colesburg C-9
Colfax E-6
Collins D-6
Colo D-5
Columbia F-6
Columbus Jct. . . . E-8
Colwell B-7
Conesville E-8
Conrad D-6
Conroy E-8

Conway F-4
Coon Rapids D-3
Cooper D-4
Coppock F-8
Coralville E-8
Corning F-3
Correctionville . . . C-2
Corwith B-5
Corydon F-6
Council Bluffs . . . F-2
Vicinity . . Pg. 148, E-6
Crescent E-1
Vicinity . . Pg. 148, E-6
Cresco B-7
Creston F-4
Cumming . . Pg. 113, F-1
Curlew B-4
Dakota City C-4
Dana D-4
Danbury D-2
Danville F-8
Davenport E-9
Vicinity . . Pg. 112, A-2
Davis City G-5
Dayton C-4
De Soto E-5
De Witt D-9
Decorah B-8
Dedham D-4
Defiance D-3
Delhi C-8
Vicinity . . Pg. 113, B-1
Delmar D-9
Deloit D-3
Delta E-7
Denison D-3
Denver C-7
Derby F-5
Des Moines E-5
Vicinity . . . Pg. 113
Dexter E-4
Dickens B-3
Dike C-7
Dolliver B-4
Donnellson F-8
Doon B-1
Dorchester B-8
Dow City D-2
Dows C-5
Drakesville F-7
Dubuque C-9
Dumfries . . Pg. 148, G-7
Dumont C-6
Duncombe C-4
Dunkerton C-7
Dunlap D-2
Durant D-9
Dyersville C-9
Dysart D-7
Eagle Grove C-5
Earlham E-4
Earling E-3
Early C-3
Eddyville E-7
Edgewood C-8
Eldon F-7
Eldora C-6
Eldridge E-10
Elgin B-8
Elk Horn E-3
Elkader C-8
Elkhart D-5
Elliott F-3
Ellsworth D-5
Emerson F-2
Emmetsburg B-4
Enterprise . . Pg. 113, A-5
Epworth C-9
Essex F-3
Estherville B-4
Evansdale C-7
Everly B-2
Exira E-3
Fairbank C-7
Fairfax D-8
Fairfield F-8
Farley C-8
Farnhamville D-4
Farragut F-2
Fayette C-8
Fenton B-4
Floyd B-6
Fonda C-3
Fontanelle E-3
Forest City B-5
Fort Dodge C-4
Fort Madison F-9
Fostoria B-3
Frankville B-8
Fraser D-5
Fredericksburg . . . B-7

Fremont E-7
Froelich B-8
Frytown E-8
Fulton D-9
Garden City C-6
Garnavillo C-9
Garner B-5
Garwin D-6
George B-2
Gibson E-7
Gilbert D-5
Gilman D-6
Gilmore City C-4
Gladbrook C-6
Glenwood F-2
Vicinity . . Pg. 148, J-7
Glidden D-4
Goldfield C-5
Goodell B-5
Gowrie C-4
Graettinger B-4
Grafton B-6
Grand Jct. D-4
Grand River F-5
Grandview E-9
Grant F-3
Green Acres . Pg. 112, B-2
Green Mountain . . D-6
Greene C-6
Greenfield E-3
Grimes D-5
Vicinity . . Pg. 113, B-1
Grinnell E-7
Griswold F-3
Grundy Center . . . C-6
Guernsey E-7
Gunder B-8
Guthrie Center . . . E-4
Guttenburg B-8
Hamburg G-2
Hamilton F-6
Hamlin E-3
Hampton C-6
Hancock E-3
Hanlontown B-5
Harcourt D-4
Harlan E-3
Harper's Ferry . . . B-9
Hartley B-2
Hartwick D-7
Harvey E-6
Hastie . . . Pg. 113, D-5
Havelock C-4
Haven D-7
Hawarden B-1
Hawkeye B-8
Hazleton C-8
Hedrick F-7
Henderson F-2
Hepburn F-3
Hesper B-8
Hiawatha D-7
Hillsboro F-8
Hinton C-1
Holmes C-5
Holstein C-2
Honey Creek Pg. 148, A-5
Hopeville F-5
Hopkinton C-8
Hospers B-1
Hubbard C-5
Hudson C-7
Hull B-1
Humboldt C-4
Humeston F-5
Huxley D-5
Ida Grove C-2
Imogene F-3
Independence . . . C-8
Indianola E-5
Inwood B-1
Iowa Center D-6
Iowa City E-8
Iowa Falls C-6
Ireton B-1
Irwin E-3
Jackson Jct. B-7
Jamaica D-4
Janesville C-7
Jefferson D-4
Jerico B-7
Jesup C-7
Jewell D-5
Johnston . . Pg. 113, B-2
Joice B-5
Kalona E-8
Kamrar C-5
Kanawha B-4
Kellogg D-6

Kendallville B-8
Kent F-4
Keokuk G-8
Keosauqua F-8
Keota E-7
Keswick E-7
Keystone D-7
Killduff E-6
Kingsley C-2
Kirkman E-3
Kiron D-3
Klemme B-5
Knoxville E-6
La Porte City D-7
Lake City C-3
Lake Mills B-5
Lake Park B-3
Lake View D-3
Lamoni G-4
Lamont C-8
Lansing B-8
Larchwood A-1
Larrabee C-2
Laurel D-6
Laurens C-3
Laverty . . . Pg. 113, G-4
Le Claire D-9
Vicinity . . Pg. 112, A-6
Le Mars C-2
Ledyard B-4
Lehigh D-5
Leighton E-7
Lenox F-4
Leon F-5
Lester B-1
Levey . . . . Pg. 113, E-5
Lewis E-3
Liberty Center . . . F-6
Lime Springs B-7
Linderwood E-2
Lineville G-5
Linwood . . Pg. 112, D-1
Lisbon D-8
Little Groves Pg. 112, B-1
Little Rock B-2
Little Sioux D-2
Livermore C-5
Logan E-2
Lohrville C-3
Long Grove D-9
Long Tree E-8
Lorimor F-5
Lost Nation D-9
Lovilia F-6
Lovington . . Pg. 113, C-2
Lowden D-9
Lucas F-5
Luther D-5
Luxemburg C-9
Lyman F-3
Lytton C-3
Macedonia F-2
Macksburg F-4
Madrid D-5
Malcom E-7
Mallard B-4
Malvern F-2
Manchester C-8
Manilla D-3
Manly B-6
Manning D-3
Manson C-4
Mapleton D-2
Maquoketa D-10
Marathon C-3
Marcus C-2
Marengo E-7
Marion D-8
Marne E-3
Marquette B-9
Marshalltown D-6
Mason City B-6
Massena E-4
Matlock B-2
Maxwell D-5
May City B-3
Maynard C-8
McGregor B-8
McIntire B-7
Mechanicsville . . . D-8
Mediapolis F-9
Melbourne D-6
Melcher E-6
Melrose F-5
Melvin B-2
Meriden C-2
Merrill C-1
Milford B-3
Millerton F-5
Millville C-9
Milo E-5

IOWA

Milton . . . G-7
Minburn . . . E-5
Minden . . . E-2
Mingo . . . E-6
Missouri Valley . . . E-2
Mitchellville . . . D-5
Mondamin . . . E-2
Moneta . . . B-3
Monona . . . B-8
Monroe . . . E-6
Montezuma . . . E-7
Monticello . . . D-8
Montrose . . . G-8
Moorhead . . . D-2
Moravia . . . F-6
Morning Sun . . . F-9
Morse . . . E-8
Moulton . . . G-7
Mount Ayr . . . F-4
Mount Etna . . . F-4
Mount Sterling . . . G-8
Mount Union . . . F-8
Moville . . . C-1
Mt. Pleasant . . . F-8
Mt. Vernon . . . D-8
Murray . . . F-4
Muscatine . . . E-9
Nahant . . . Pg. 112, C-1
Nashua . . . B-7
Neola . . . E-2
Nevada . . . D-5
Nevinville . . . F-4
New Albin . . . A-8
New Hampton . . . B-7
New Haven . . . B-7
New London . . . F-9
New Market . . . F-3
New Providence . . . D-6
New Sharon . . . E-7
New Virginia . . . F-5
Newburg . . . D-7
Newkirk . . . B-2
Newton . . . E-6
Nichols . . . E-9
Nora Springs . . . B-6
North English . . . E-7
Northboro . . . G-3
Northwood . . . B-6
Norwalk . . . E-5
  Vicinity . . . Pg. 113, F-2
Norway . . . D-7
Norwoodville Pg. 113, C-4
Oakland . . . E-3
Ocheyedan . . . A-2
Odebolt . . . D-3
Oelwein . . . C-8
Ogden . . . D-4
Olin . . . D-9
Onawa . . . D-2
Onslow . . . D-9
Orange City . . . B-2
Orient . . . F-4
Osage . . . B-6
Osceola . . . F-5
Oskaloosa . . . E-7
Otho . . . D-5
Oto . . . D-2
Ottumwa . . . F-7
Oxford . . . E-8
Oyens . . . C-2
Pacific City . . . Pg. 148, J-6
Pacific Junction
  . . . Pg. 148, K-6
Panama . . . E-3
Panora . . . E-4
Park View . . . E-10
Parkersburg . . . C-7
Parnell . . . E-7
Paullina . . . B-2
Pella . . . E-7
Percival . . . F-2
Perkins . . . B-1
Perry . . . D-5
Persia . . . E-2
Pierson . . . C-2
Pilot Mound . . . D-4
Pisgah . . . D-2
Plain View . . . E-9
Plainfield . . . C-7
Plano . . . F-6
Pleasant Hill Pg. 113, D-5
Pleasant Plain . . . F-7
Pleasant Valley
  . . . Pg. 112, A-5
Pleasantville . . . E-6
Pocahontas . . . C-4
Polk City . . . E-5
Pomeroy . . . C-4
Popejoy . . . C-6
Portsmouth . . . E-3

Postville . . . B-8
Prairie City . . . E-6
Preston . . . D-10
Primghar . . . B-2
Probstei . . . Pg. 112, A-1
Prole . . . E-5
Pulaski . . . F-7
Quasqueton . . . C-8
Quimby . . . C-2
Rathbun . . . F-6
Reasnor . . . E-6
Red Oak . . . F-3
Redding . . . G-4
Redfield . . . E-4
Reinbeck . . . D-7
Rembrandt . . . C-3
Remsen . . . C-2
Renwick . . . C-5
Rhodes . . . D-6
Riceville . . . B-6
Richland . . . E-7
Rickardsville . . . C-9
Ridgeview Park
  . . . Pg. 112, A-2
Ridgeway . . . B-8
Ringsted . . . A-3
Rippey . . . D-4
Riverdale . . . Pg. 112, B-4
Rochester . . . E-9
Rock Rapids . . . A-2
Rock Valley . . . B-1
Rockford . . . B-6
Rockwell . . . B-6
Rockwell City . . . C-4
Roland . . . C-5
Rolfe . . . C-4
Roselle . . . D-3
Rossie . . . B-3
Rossville . . . B-8
Royal . . . B-3
Russell . . . F-6
Ruthven . . . B-3
Ryan . . . C-8
Sabula . . . C-10
Sac City . . . C-3
Sanborn . . . B-2
Saratoga . . . B-7
Saylorville . . . Pg. 113, B-3
Schaller . . . C-3
Schleswig . . . D-2
Schley . . . B-7
Scotch Ridge
  . . . Pg. 113, F-5
Scranton . . . D-4
Searsboro . . . E-7
Selma . . . F-7
Sergeant Bluff . . . C-2
Seymour . . . F-5
Shambaugh . . . G-3
Sharpsburg . . . F-3
Sheffield . . . B-6
Sheldon . . . B-2
Shell Rock . . . C-7
Shellsburg . . . D-8
Shenandoah . . . F-3
Sibley . . . A-2
Sidney . . . F-2
Sigourney . . . E-7
Sioux Center . . . B-1
Sioux City . . . C-1
Sioux Rapids . . . B-3
Sloan . . . D-1
Smithland . . . D-2
Soldier . . . D-2
Solon . . . D-8
Somers . . . C-4
Spencer . . . B-3
Spirit Lake . . . A-3
Springhill . . . Pg. 113, G-3
Springville . . . D-8
St. Ansgar . . . B-6
St. Charles . . . E-5
St. Joseph . . . B-4
St. Marys . . . E-5
Stacyville . . . A-6
Stanton . . . E-2
Stanwood . . . D-8
State Center . . . D-6
Steamboat Rock . . . C-6
Storm Lake . . . C-3
Story City . . . D-5
Stout . . . C-7
Strawberry Point . . . C-8
Stuart . . . E-4
Sully . . . E-6
Sulphur Springs . . . C-3
Summerset Pg. 113, G-5
Sumner . . . C-7
Superior . . . B-3
Sutherland . . . B-2

Swea City . . . B-4
Tabor . . . F-2
Tama . . . D-7
Templeton . . . D-3
Terril . . . B-3
Thompson . . . B-5
Thornton . . . B-5
Thurman . . . F-2
Tiffin . . . E-8
Tipton . . . D-9
Titonka . . . B-5
Toledo . . . D-6
Traer . . . D-7
Trenton . . . F-8
Tripoli . . . C-7
Truesdale . . . C-3
Truro . . . F-5
Ulmer . . . D-3
Underwood . . . E-2
Union . . . C-5
Urbana . . . D-7
Urbandale
  Vicinity . . . Pg. 113, C-2
Ute . . . D-2
Vail . . . D-3
Valeria . . . E-6
Van Horne . . . D-7
Van Wert . . . F-5
Varina . . . C-3
Ventura . . . B-5
Victor . . . E-7
Villisca . . . F-3
Vining . . . D-7
Vinton . . . D-7
W. Burlington . . . F-8
Walford . . . D-8
Walker . . . D-8
Wall Lake . . . C-2
Wallingford . . . B-4
Walnut Grove
  . . . Pg. 112, D-2
Wapello . . . F-9
Washington . . . E-8
Washta . . . C-2
Waterloo . . . C-7
Waukee . . . D-4
Waukon . . . B-8
Waverly . . . C-7
Webster . . . E-7
Webster City . . . C-5
Weldon . . . F-5
Wellman . . . E-7
Welton . . . D-10
Wesley . . . B-5
West Bend . . . B-4
West Des Moines . . . D-4
  Vicinity . . . Pg. 113, D-1
West Grove . . . F-7
West Liberty . . . E-9
West Point . . . F-8
West Union . . . B-8
Westfield . . . C-1
Weston . . . Pg. 148, C-7
Wheatland . . . D-9
Whiting . . . D-2
Whittemore . . . B-4
Wick . . . E-5
Willey . . . D-3
Williams . . . C-5
Williamsburg . . . E-8
Williamson . . . F-6
Wilton . . . D-8
Windsor Heights
  . . . Pg. 113, C-2
Winfield . . . F-8
Winterset . . . E-4
Wiota . . . E-3
Woodbine . . . E-2
Woodburn . . . F-5
Woodward . . . D-4
Woolstock . . . C-5
Wyoming . . . D-9
Yale . . . E-4
Zwingle . . . C-9

KANSAS
Page 37
Population: 2,363,679
Capital: Topeka
Land Area: 81,781 sq. mi.

KANSAS

Abbeyville . . . E-5
Abilene . . . D-7
Admire . . . D-8
Agenda . . . C-7
Agra . . . C-4
Alden . . . E-5
Alexander . . . D-4

Allen . . . D-8
Alma . . . D-8
Almena . . . B-4
Alta Vista . . . D-8
Altamont . . . F-9
Alton . . . C-5
Altoona . . . F-8
Americus . . . D-8
Andale . . . E-6
Andover . . . F-7
Anthony . . . F-6
Arcadia . . . F-9
Argonia . . . F-6
Arkansas City . . . F-7
Arlington . . . E-5
Ashland . . . F-4
Atchison . . . C-9
Athol . . . C-5
Atlanta . . . F-7
Attica . . . F-5
Atwood . . . B-2
Augusta . . . F-7
Axtell . . . C-8
Baldwin City . . . D-9
Barnard . . . D-6
Barnes . . . C-7
Bartlett . . . F-9
Basehor . . . D-9
Bassett . . . E-9
Baxter Springs . . . F-9
Bazine . . . D-4
Beattie . . . C-8
Bel Aire . . . Pg. 170, B-2
Belle Plaine . . . F-7
Belleville . . . C-6
Beloit . . . C-6
Belpre . . . E-4
Belvue . . . D-8
Benedict . . . C-8
Bennington . . . D-6
Bentley . . . E-6
Benton . . . E-7
Bern . . . C-8
Beverly . . . D-6
Bird City . . . B-2
Bison . . . D-4
Blue Mound . . . E-9
Blue Rapids . . . C-7
Bluff City . . . F-6
Bogue . . . C-4
Brewster . . . C-2
Bronson . . . E-9
Brookville . . . D-6
Brownell . . . D-4
Bucklin . . . F-4
Buffalo . . . F-9
Buhler . . . E-6
Bunker Hill . . . D-5
Burden . . . F-7
Burdett . . . E-4
Burlingame . . . D-8
Burlington . . . D-8
Burns . . . E-7
Burr Oak . . . C-5
Burrton . . . E-6
Bushong . . . D-8
Bushton . . . D-5
Byers . . . E-5
Caldwell . . . F-6
Cambridge . . . F-7
Caney . . . F-8
Canton . . . E-7
Carbondale . . . D-9
Carlton . . . D-7
Cassoday . . . E-7
Cawker City . . . C-5
Cedar . . . C-5
Cedar Point . . . E-7
Cedar Vale . . . F-8
Centralia . . . C-8
Chanute . . . F-9
Chapman . . . D-7
Chase . . . E-5
Chautauqua . . . F-8
Cheney . . . F-6
Cherokee . . . F-9
Cherryvale . . . F-9
Chetopa . . . F-9
Cimarron . . . E-3
Circleville . . . C-8
Claflin . . . D-5
Clay Center . . . C-7
Clayton . . . C-3
Clearwater . . . F-6
Clifton . . . C-7
Climax . . . D-8
Clyde . . . C-6
Coats . . . F-5
Coffeyville . . . F-9
Colby . . . C-2

Coldwater . . . F-4
Collyer . . . C-3
Colony . . . E-9
Columbus . . . F-9
Concordia . . . C-6
Conway Springs . . . F-6
Coolidge . . . E-1
Copeland . . . F-3
Cottonwood Falls . . . E-7
Council Grove . . . D-8
Countryside Pg. 125, G-2
Courtland . . . C-6
Cuba . . . C-6
Cullison . . . F-5
Culver . . . D-6
Cunningham . . . F-5
Damar . . . C-4
  Vicinity . . . Pg. 170, D-6
De Soto . . . D-9
Dearing . . . F-8
Deerfield . . . E-2
Delphos . . . C-6
Denison . . . C-9
Denton . . . C-9
Derby . . . F-7
  Vicinity . . . Pg. 170, B-6
Dexter . . . F-7
Dighton . . . D-3
Dodge City . . . E-3
Douglass . . . F-7
Downs . . . C-5
Dresden . . . C-3
Dunlap . . . D-8
Dwight . . . D-7
Earlton . . . F-9
Eastborough Pg. 170, B-4
Easton . . . D-9
Edgerton . . . D-9
Edmond . . . C-4
Edna . . . F-9
Effingham . . . C-9
El Dorado . . . E-7
Elbing . . . E-7
Elgin . . . F-8
Elk City . . . F-8
Elk Falls . . . F-8
Elkhart . . . F-1
Ellinwood . . . E-5
Ellis . . . D-4
Ellsworth . . . D-5
Elmdale . . . E-7
Emmett . . . C-8
Emporia . . . D-8
Englewood . . . F-3
Ensign . . . E-3
Enterprise . . . D-7
Erie . . . F-9
Esbon . . . C-5
Eskridge . . . D-8
Eudora . . . D-9
Eureka . . . E-8
Fairview . . . C-9
Fairway . . . Pg. 125, G-3
Florence . . . E-7
Fontana . . . E-9
Ford . . . E-4
Formoso . . . C-6
Fort Scott . . . E-9
Fowler . . . F-3
Frankfort . . . C-8
Fredonia . . . F-8
Freeport . . . F-6
Frontenac . . . F-9
Fulton . . . E-9
Galatia . . . D-5
Galena . . . F-9
Galesburg . . . F-9
Galva . . . E-6
Garden City . . . E-2
Garden Plain . . . F-6
Gardner . . . D-9
Garfield . . . E-4
Garnett . . . E-9
Gaylord . . . C-5
Gem . . . C-2
Geneseo . . . D-5
Girard . . . F-9
Glade . . . C-4
Glasco . . . C-6
Glen Elder . . . C-5
Goessel . . . E-6
Goodland . . . C-1
Gorham . . . D-5
Gove . . . D-3
Grainfield . . . D-4
Grandview Plaza . . . D-7
Great Bend . . . E-5
Greenleaf . . . C-7
Greensburg . . . F-4
Gridley . . . E-8
Grinnell . . . C-2

Halstead . . . E-6
Hamilton . . . E-8
Hamlin . . . C-8
Hanover . . . C-7
Hanston . . . E-4
Hardtner . . . F-5
Harper . . . F-6
Harris . . . E-9
Hartford . . . D-8
Harveyville . . . D-8
Havana . . . F-8
Haven . . . E-6
Havensville . . . C-8
Haviland . . . E-4
Hays . . . D-4
Haysville . . . F-6
Hazelton . . . F-5
Healy . . . D-3
Herington . . . D-7
Herndon . . . B-2
Hesston . . . E-6
Hiawatha . . . C-9
Highland . . . C-9
Hill City . . . C-3
Hillsboro . . . E-7
Hoisington . . . D-5
Holcomb . . . E-2
Hollenberg . . . C-7
Holton . . . C-8
Holyrood . . . D-5
Hope . . . D-7
Horton . . . C-9
Howard . . . F-8
Hoxie . . . C-3
Hoyt . . . C-8
Hudson . . . E-5
Hugoton . . . F-2
Humboldt . . . F-9
Hunter . . . C-5
Huron . . . C-9
Hutchinson . . . E-6
Independence . . . F-8
Ingalls . . . E-3
Inman . . . E-6
Iola . . . E-9
Isabel . . . F-5
Jamestown . . . C-6
Jennings . . . C-3
Jetmore . . . E-3
Jewell . . . C-6
Johnson City . . . E-1
Junction City . . . D-7
Kanapolis . . . D-6
Kansas City . . . D-9
  Vicinity . . . Pg. 125, G-2
Kechi . . . Pg. 170, B-2
Kensington . . . C-4
Kincaid . . . E-9
Kingman . . . F-5
Kinsley . . . E-4
Kiowa . . . F-5
Kirwin . . . C-4
Kismet . . . F-2
La Crosse . . . D-4
La Cygne . . . E-9
La Harpe . . . E-9
Lake Quivira Pg. 125, G-1
Lakin . . . E-2
Lane . . . E-9
Langdon . . . E-5
Larned . . . E-4
Latham . . . F-7
Latimer . . . D-7
Lawrence . . . D-9
Le Roy . . . E-9
Leavenworth . . . D-9
Leawood . . . Pg. 125, J-2
Lebanon . . . C-5
Lebo . . . D-8
Lecompton . . . D-9
Lehigh . . . E-7
Lenexa . . . Pg. 125, J-1
Lenora . . . C-4
Leon . . . D-8
Leona . . . C-9
Leonardville . . . C-7
Leoti . . . D-2
Lewis . . . E-4
Liberal . . . F-2
Lincoln . . . D-6
Lincolnville . . . D-7
Lindsborg . . . D-6
Linn . . . C-7
Linwood . . . D-9
Little River . . . E-6
Logan . . . C-4
Lone Elm . . . E-9
Long Island . . . B-4
Longford . . . D-7

Longton . . . F-8
Lorraine . . . D-5
Lost Springs . . . D-7
Louisburg . . . E-9
Louisville . . . C-8
Lucas . . . D-5
Luka . . . F-5
Luray . . . D-5
Lyndon . . . D-8
Lyons . . . E-6
Macksville . . . E-4
Madison . . . D-8
Maize . . . E-6
Manchester . . . D-7
Manhattan . . . D-8
Mankato . . . C-5
Manter . . . E-1
Maple Hill . . . D-8
Mapleton . . . E-9
Marion . . . E-7
Marquette . . . D-6
Marysville . . . C-7
  . . . Pg. 125, H-3
Matfield Green . . . E-7
Mayetta . . . C-8
Mayfield . . . F-6
McCracken . . . D-4
McCune . . . F-9
McDonald . . . B-2
McFarland . . . D-8
McPherson . . . E-6
Meade . . . F-3
Medicine Lodge . . . F-5
Melvern . . . D-8
Meriden . . . C-9
Milan . . . F-7
Mildred . . . E-9
Milford . . . D-7
Miltonvale . . . C-6
Minneapolis . . . D-6
Minneola . . . F-3
Mission . . . Pg. 125, H-3
Mission Hills Pg. 125, H-3
Moline . . . F-8
Montezuma . . . E-3
Moran . . . E-9
Morganville . . . C-7
Morland . . . C-3
Morrill . . . C-8
Morrowville . . . C-7
Moscow . . . F-2
Mound City . . . E-9
Mound Valley . . . F-9
Moundridge . . . E-6
Mount Hope . . . E-6
Mullinville . . . F-5
Mulvane . . . F-7
  Vicinity . . . Pg. 125, G-2
Munden . . . C-6
Muscotah . . . C-9
Narka . . . C-6
Nashville . . . F-5
Natoma . . . C-4
Neodesha . . . F-8
Neosho Falls . . . E-9
Ness City . . . D-3
Netawaka . . . C-8
New Cambria . . . D-6
New Strawn . . . D-8
Newton . . . E-6
Nickerson . . . E-5
Norcatur . . . C-3
Norton . . . C-4
Nortonville . . . C-9
Norwich . . . F-6
Oak Hill . . . C-7
Oakland . . . Pg. 170, C-5
Oakley . . . C-2
Oberlin . . . C-3
Offerle . . . E-4
Ogden . . . D-7
Oketo . . . C-7
Olmitz . . . D-5
Olpe . . . D-8
Olsburg . . . C-8
Onaga . . . C-8
Osage City . . . D-8
Osawatomie . . . E-9
Osborne . . . C-5
Oskaloosa . . . C-9
Oswego . . . F-9
Ottawa . . . D-9
Overbrook . . . D-8
Overland Park
  . . . Pg. 125, J-2
Oxford . . . F-7
Palco . . . C-4
Palmer . . . C-7
Paola . . . E-9
Paradise . . . D-5
Park . . . C-3

Park City . . . E-7
  Vicinity . . . Pg. 170, C-2
Parker . . . E-9
Parsons . . . F-9
Pawnee Rock . . . E-4
Paxico . . . D-8
Peabody . . . E-7
Perry . . . D-9
Peru . . . F-8
Phillipsburg . . . C-4
Pittsburg . . . F-10
Plains . . . F-3
Plainville . . . C-4
Pleasanton . . . E-9
Plevna . . . E-5
Pomona . . . D-9
Portis . . . C-5
Potwin . . . E-7
Powhattan . . . C-8
Prairie View . . . C-4
Prairie Village
  . . . Pg. 125, H-3
Pratt . . . F-5
Prescott . . . E-9
Preston . . . F-5
Pretty Prairie . . . E-6
Princeton . . . E-9
Protection . . . F-4
Quenemo . . . D-8
Quinter . . . C-3
Ramona . . . D-7
Randall . . . C-6
Randolph . . . C-8
Ransom . . . D-3
Rantoul . . . E-9
Raymond . . . E-5
Reading . . . D-8
Redfield . . . E-9
Republic . . . C-6
Rexford . . . C-3
Richfield . . . F-1
Richmond . . . D-9
Riley . . . C-7
Robinson . . . C-9
Roeland Park . . . F-9
  Vicinity . . . Pg. 125, G-2
Rolla . . . F-1
Rose Hill . . . F-7
Rossville . . . D-8
Rozel . . . E-4
Rush Center . . . D-4
Russell . . . D-5
Russell Springs . . . D-2
Sabetha . . . C-8
Salina . . . D-6
Satanta . . . F-2
Sawyer . . . F-5
Scandia . . . C-6
Schoenchen . . . D-4
Scott City . . . D-2
Scottsville . . . C-6
Sedan . . . F-8
Sedgwick . . . E-6
Selden . . . C-3
Seneca . . . C-8
Severy . . . E-8
Seward . . . E-5
Sharon . . . F-5
Sharon Springs . . . D-1
Shawnee . . . Pg. 125, H-1
Silver Lake . . . D-8
Simpson . . . C-6
Smith Center . . . C-5
Smolan . . . D-7
Solomon . . . D-7
South Haven . . . F-6
Spearville . . . E-4
Spivey . . . F-6
Spring Hill . . . D-9
St. Francis . . . B-1
St. John . . . E-5
St. Marys . . . D-8
St. Paul . . . F-9
Stafford . . . E-5
Stark . . . F-9
Sterling . . . E-6
Strong City . . . E-8
Sublette . . . F-2
Summerfield . . . C-8
Sun City . . . F-5
Sylvan Grove . . . C-5
Sylvia . . . E-5
Syracuse . . . E-1
Tampa . . . D-7
Tescott . . . D-6
Thayer . . . F-9
Timken . . . D-4
Tipton . . . C-5
Tonganoxie . . . D-9
Topeka . . . D-8

KANSAS

LOUISIANA

Toronto D-8
Towanda E-7
Tribune D-1
Troy C-9
Turon E-5
Tyro F-8
Udall F-7
Ulysses E-2
Uniontown F-9
Utica D-3
Valley Center E-6
Vicinity . . Pg. 170, D-1
Valley Falls C-9
Vermillion C-8
Victoria D-4
Vining C-7
Virgil D-8
WaKeeney D-4
Wakefield C-7
Waldo D-5
Waldron F-5
Wallace D-2
Walnut F-9
Walton E-7
Wamego D-8
Washington C-6
Waterville C-7
Wathena C-9
Waverly E-9
Webber C-6
Weir Scammon F-9
Wellington F-6
Westmoreland C-8
Westphalia E-9
Westwood . Pg. 125, G-3
Wetmore C-8
Wheaton C-8
White City D-7
Whitewater E-7
Whiting C-9
Wichita F-6
Vicinity . . Pg. 170, D-3
Williamsburg E-9
Willowbrook E-6
Wilmore F-4
Wilsey D-7
Wilson D-5
Winchester C-9
Windom E-6
Winfield F-7
Winona C-2
Woodbine D-7
Woodston C-4
Yates Center E-8
Zenda F-5
Zurich C-4

Breckinridge C-10
Bremen E-6
Broadfields . Pg. 132, C-5
Brodhead E-10
Bromley E-6
Vicinity . . Pg. 106, F-3
Brooksville B-10
Brownsville E-7
Buckhorn E-11
Buffalo E-8
Burgin D-9
Burkesville F-8
Burnside F-10
Burton E-12
Butler B-10
Cadertown . . Pg. 127, B-5
Cadiz F-5
Calhoun D-6
Callaway F-11
Calvert City E-4
Campbellsburg B-8
Campbellsville E-8
Campton D-11
Caneyville E-7
Carlisle C-10
Carrollton B-9
Carrsville E-4
Carter C-11
Caseyville D-4
Catlettsburg C-12
Cave City E-8
Centertown C-8
Centerville . . Pg. 127, A-6
Central City E-6
Cerulean F-5
Chilesburg . . Pg. 127, A-5
Clairfield F-10
Clay E-5
Clay City D-10
Clearfield C-11
Clinton F-3
Cloverport D-7
Cold Spring . Pg. 106, G-5
Coletown . . . Pg. 127, B-6
Columbia E-8
Columbus F-3
Concord D-9
Constance . . Pg. 106, F-1
Corbin F-10
Corydon D-5
Covington B-9
Vicinity . . Pg. 106, F-3
Crab Orchard E-9
Crescent Park
. . . . Pg. 170, C-5
Crescent Springs
. . . . Pg. 106, F-2
Crestview Hills
. . . . Pg. 106, G-2
Crestwood C-8
Crittenden B-10
Crofton E-5
Cumberland E-12
Cynthiana C-10
Danville D-9
Dawson Springs . . . E-5
Dayton . . . Pg. 106, E-4
Dexter F-4
Dixon D-5
Donerail . . . Pg. 127, D-2
Dover B-11
Drakesboro E-6
Druid Hills . Pg. 132, B-5
Dry Ridge B-10
Dunmor E-6
Dycusburg E-4
Earlington E-5
East Hickman
. . . . Pg. 127, C-7
Eddyville E-4
Edmonton F-8
Ekron D-7
Elizabethtown D-7
Elkhorn City E-13
Elkton F-6
Elmendorf . . Pg. 127, B-3
Elsmere B-10
Eminence C-9
Erlanger . . . Pg. 106, G-2
Eubank E-9
Evarts F-12
Fairdale D-8
Fairfield D-8
Fairview F-6
Falmouth C-9
Fenwick . . . Pg. 127, A-3
Ferguson E-10
Flatwoods C-12
Fleming-Neon E-12
Flemingsburg C-11

Florence B-10
Fordsville D-7
Fountain Run F-8
Frankfort C-9
Franklin F-6
Fredonia E-5
Freeburn D-13
Frenchburg D-11
Frogue F-8
Ft. Mitchell . Pg. 106, G-3
Ft.Thomas . Pg. 106, F-5
Ft.Wright . . Pg. 106, F-3
Fulton F-3
Gamaliel F-8
Geneva . . . Pg. 117, E-7
Georgetown C-10
Vicinity . . Pg. 127, E-1
Ghent B-9
Glasgow E-8
Golden Pond F-5
Goshen C-8
Grand Rivers E-4
Gratz C-9
Grayson C-12
Great Crossing
. . . . Pg. 127, E-1
Greendale . . Pg. 127, D-3
Greensburg E-8
Greenup B-12
Greenville E-6
Guthrie F-6
Hanson E-5
Hardin F-4
Hardinsburg D-7
Harlan F-11
Harned D-7
Harrodsburg D-9
Hartford E-6
Hawesville D-6
Hazard E-12
Hazel F-4
Hazel Green D-11
Hellier E-12
Henderson D-5
Vicinity . . Pg. 117, C-6
Hickman F-3
Highland Hts.
. . . . Pg. 106, G-5
Hindman E-12
Hodgenville D-8
Hopkinsville F-6
Horse Cave E-8
Hustonville E-9
Hutchinson . . Pg. 127, A-2
Hyden E-11
Independence B-10
Inez D-12
Irvine D-10
Irvington D-7
Island E-6
Jackson D-11
Jamestown E-9
Jeffersontown C-8
Jenkins E-12
Jimtown . . . Pg. 127, A-1
Junction City D-9
Kenton Vale . Pg. 106, G-3
Kirkmansville E-6
Knob Creek D-8
Kuttawa E-4
La Fayette F-5
La Grange C-8
LaCenter E-3
Lackey E-12
Lakeside Park
. . . . Pg. 106, G-3
Lakeview . . Pg. 106, G-3
Lancaster D-10
Lawrenceburg C-9
Leatherwood E-12
Lebanon D-9
Lebanon Jct. D-8
Lee City D-11
Leitchfield D-7
Lewisburg C-11
Lewisport D-6
Lexington D-10
Vicinity . . Pg. 127, B-3
Liberty E-9
Livermore D-6
Livingston E-10
Lockport C-9
London E-11
Loradale . . . Pg. 127, B-1
Loretto D-8
Lothair E-11
Louisa C-12
Louisville C-8
Vicinity . . . . . Pg. 132
Detailed City . Pg. 249

Loyall F-11
Lucas F-8
Ludlow . . . Pg. 106, F-3
Lynch F-12
Lynnview . . Pg. 132, E-4
Madisonville E-5
Manchester E-10
Marion E-4
Martin D-12
Mason B-10
Mattoxtown . . Pg. 127, C-3
Mayfield F-4
Maysville B-11
McCreary D-10
McHenry E-6
McKee E-10
McRoberts E-12
Middlesboro F-10
Middletown C-8
Midway C-9
Midway F-4
Millersburg C-10
Milton C-9
Mockingbird Valley
. . . . Pg. 132, B-5
Monkeys Eyebrow . . E-3
Monroe E-8
Monterey C-9
Monticello F-9
Montrose . . . Pg. 127, B-4
Morehead C-11
Moreland D-9
Morgan B-10
Morganfield D-5
Morgantown E-7
Mortons Gap E-5
Mount Olivet B-10
Mount Sterling C-11
MountVernon E-10
MountWashington . . C-8
Muir . . . . . Pg. 127, B-3
Muldraugh D-8
Munfordville E-8
Murray F-4
Nebo E-5
New Castle C-9
New Haven D-8
New Zion . . . Pg. 127, D-2
Newport A-10
Vicinity . . Pg. 106, F-4
Newtown . . . Pg. 127, C-1
Nicholasville D-9
North Middletown . . . C-10
Nortonville E-6
Oak Grove F-5
Oakland E-7
Olive Hill C-11
Owensboro D-6
Owenton C-9
Owingsville C-10
Paducah E-4
Paintsville D-12
Paris C-10
Park City E-8
Park Hills . . Pg. 106, F-3
Parkers Lake F-10
Parkway Village
. . . . Pg. 132, D-3
Pembroke F-5
Perryville D-9
Phelps D-13
Pikeville E-13
Pine Knot F-9
Pineville F-11
Pleasureville C-9
Prestonsburg D-12
Prestonville B-8
Pricetown . . Pg. 127, A-5
Princeton E-5
Prospect C-8
Providence E-5
Raceland B-12
Radcliff D-7
Ravenna D-11
Reidland E-4
Renfro Valley E-10
Richmond D-10
Rockcastle F-5
Rockport E-6
Rolling Fields
. . . . Pg. 132, B-5
Russell B-12
Russell Springs . . . E-9
Russellville F-6
Sadieville C-10
Salt Lick C-11
Salyersville D-12
Sanders B-9
Sandy Hook C-12

Sardis C-11
Science Hill E-9
Scottsville F-7
Sebree D-5
Seco E-12
Sedalia F-4
Sharpsburg C-11
Shelby City D-9
Shelbyville C-9
Shepherdsville C-8
Shively C-8
Vicinity . . Pg. 132, D-1
Silver Grove Pg. 106, G-6
Simpsonville C-8
Slaughters D-5
Smithland E-4
Smiths Grove E-7
Somerset E-10
Sonora D-7
South Shore B-12
South Williamson . . . D-13
Southgate . . Pg. 106, F-4
Springfield D-9
St. Matthews Pg. 132, B-5
Stamping Ground . . . C-9
Stanford D-10
Stanton D-11
Stearns F-9
Sturgis D-5
Taylorsville D-9
Tompkinsville F-8
Trenton F-6
Trimble E-9
Tyner E-11
Union B-9
Union Mills . Pg. 127, D-7
Uniontown D-5
Upton D-8
Uttingertown Pg. 127, B-4
Valley Station C-8
Van Lear D-12
Vanceburg B-11
Vancleve D-11
Versailles C-9
Viley . . . . . Pg. 127, E-3
Villa Hills . . Pg. 106, F-2
Vine Grove D-7
Wallins Creek F-11
Walton B-10
Warfield D-13
Warsaw B-9
Washington B-11
Water Valley F-4
Waverly D-5
Wayland E-12
Webster D-7
West Beauchel
. . . . Pg. 132, D-5
West Liberty D-11
West Point D-8
Wheatley B-9
Wheelwright E-12
Whitesburg E-12
Whitesville D-6
Whitley City F-10
Wickliffe E-3
Wilder . . . . Pg. 106, F-4
Willard C-12
Williamsburg F-10
Williamstown B-10
Wilmore D-9
Winchester D-10
Wingo F-4
Woodburn F-7
Yarnallton . . Pg. 127, E-3

LOUISIANA
Page 40

Population: 4,205,9000
Capital: Baton Rouge
Land Area: 44,521 sq. mi.

Abbeville F-5
Abington B-2
Abita Springs E-8
Acme D-5
Acy E-7
Ada B-3
Addis E-6
Vicinity . . Pg. 95, E-2
Adeline F-6
Afton B-6
Aimwell C-5
Airline Park Pg. 140, C-4
Ajax C-3
Albany D-7
Alco D-3
Alden Bridge A-2
Alexandria D-4

Algiers . . . Pg. 140, C-7
Allendale . . Pg. 95, B-2
Alsatia A-6
Alto B-5
Ama . . . . . Pg. 140, C-2
Amelia G-7
Amite E-8
Anacoco D-3
Anchorage . . Pg. 95, B-3
Angie D-9
Angola D-5
Ansley B-4
Antioch A-3
Arabi D-9
Vicinity . . Pg. 140, C-8
Archibald B-5
Archie C-5
Arcola D-8
Armistead B-3
Arnaudville E-5
Ashland B-3
Athens A-3
Atlanta C-4
Augusta . . . Pg. 140, F-7
Avery Island F-5
Avondale . . Pg. 140, D-4
Aycock A-3
Bains D-6
Baker E-6
Baldwin F-6
Ball C-4
Bancroft E-2
Barataria F-8
Basile E-4
Baskin B-5
Bastrop A-5
Batchelor D-6
Baton Rouge E-7
Vicinity . . . . . Pg. 95
Bayou Cane G-7
Bayou Chicot D-5
Bayou Sorrel F-6
Bayou Vista G-6
Baywood E-7
Beaver E-4
Beekman A-5
Beggs E-5
Bell City F-3
Belle Chasse F-9
Belle Rose F-7
Bellwood C-3
Belmont C-3
Vicinity . . Pg. 95, B-2
Benson C-2
Bentley C-4
Benton A-2
Bernice A-4
Bertrandville F-9
Vicinity . . Pg. 140, G-7
Berwick F-6
Bienville B-3
Blackburn A-3
Blanchard A-2
Bogalusa D-9
Bohemia G-9
Bolinger A-2
Bonita A-5
Book D-5
Boothville G-10
Bordelonville D-5
Bosco B-5
Bossier City A-2
Bourg G-8
Boyce D-4
Braithwaite . Pg. 140, E-9
Branch E-5
Breaux Bridge E-5
Bridge City . Pg. 140, D-4
Broussard E-5
Brusly E-6
Bryceland B-3
Bunkie D-5
Buras G-9
Burnside F-7
Burr Ferry D-2
Burtville . . . Pg. 95, E-4
Bush E-9
Cade F-5
Caernarvon Pg. 140, E-9
Calhoun B-4
Calvin B-3
Cameron F-3
Campti C-3
Caney C-5
Carencro E-5
Carey . . . . . Pg. 95, B-1
Carlisle B-2
Carville E-7
Caspiana B-2

Castor B-3
Cedar Grove Pg. 140, F-7
Center Point D-5
Centerville F-6
Central . . . Pg. 95, A-6
Chacahoula G-7
Chackbay F-7
Chalmette F-9
Vicinity . . Pg. 140, D-8
Chamberlin . Pg. 95, A-1
Chase B-5
Chataignier E-4
Chatham B-4
Chauvin G-8
Cheneyville D-5
Chestnut B-3
Chipola D-7
Chopin C-4
Choudrant B-4
Church Point E-5
Cinclare . . Pg. 95, D-3
Clarence C-3
Clarks B-5
Clay B-4
Clayton C-6
Clifton D-7
Clinton D-7
Cloutierville C-4
Cocodrie G-7
Colfax C-4
College Hill . Pg. 95, D-4
Collinston A-5
Colquitt A-3
Columbia B-5
Comite . . . . Pg. 95, B-6
Concession . Pg. 140, F-8
Convent F-7
Converse C-2
Vicinity . . . . . Pg. 95
Cotton Valley A-3
Cottonport D-5
Coushatta B-3
Covington E-8
Cravens D-3
Creole F-3
Creston B-3
Crowley F-4
Crown Point Pg. 140, F-8
Crowville B-6
Cullen A-3
Cut Off G-8
Cypress C-3
Cypress Gardens
. . . . Pg. 140, D-10
Dalcour F-9
Vicinity . . Pg. 140, F-8
Darlington D-7
Darnell A-6
Davant F-9
De Quincy E-3
De Ridder D-3
Deer Park C-6
Delacroix F-9
Delcambre F-5
Delhi A-6
Denham Sprs.
. . . . Pg. 95, B-7
Derry C-3
Des Allemands F-7
Destrehan . . Pg. 140, D-1
Devalis . . . Pg. 95, A-1
Deville D-5
Diamond G-9
Dixie Inn A-2
Dodson B-4
Donaldsonville F-7
Downsville A-4
Dry Creek E-3
Dry Prong C-4
Dubach A-4
Dubuisson E-5
Dulac G-8
Dupont D-5
Duson F-5
Duty C-5
Easlyville D-7
Eastwood B-2
Echo D-5
Edgerly F-2
Effie D-5
Elizabeth D-4
Elm Grove B-2
Elton E-4
Empire G-9
Englishturn Pg. 140, E-8
Enon E-8
Enterprise C-5
Erath F-5
Eros B-5
Essen . . . . Pg. 95, D-5
Estelle . . . Pg. 140, E-6

Estherwood F-4
Esto D-2
Ethel E-6
Eunice E-4
Eva C-5
Evangeline E-4
Evans D-3
Evelyn B-2
Evergreen D-5
Farmerville A-4
Felps D-7
Fenton E-3
Ferriday C-6
Fields E-3
Fillmore A-2
Fisher C-3
Flatwoods D-4
Flora C-3
Florien D-2
Folsom E-8
Fondale B-5
Fordoche D-6
Foreman . . Pg. 95, E-6
Forest A-6
Forest Hill D-4
Fort Jesup C-3
Fort Necessity B-5
Foules C-6
Franklin F-6
Franklinton D-8
French Settlement . . E-7
Frenier E-7
Frogmore C-5
Frost E-7
Galbraith C-4
Galion A-5
Galliano G-8
Gandy D-2
Gardere . . Pg. 95, E-4
Gardner D-4
Georgetown C-4
Gheens F-8
Gibsland B-3
Gibson G-7
Gilbert B-6
Gillis E-3
Glade C-5
Glenmora D-4
Gloster B-2
Golden Meadow G-8
Goldonna B-4
Gonzales E-7
Gordon A-3
Gorum C-3
Goudeau D-5
Grambling A-4
Grand Bayou B-3
Grand Cane B-2
Grand Chenier F-4
Grand Coteau E-5
Grand Isle G-9
Grand Lake F-3
Grangeville E-7
Grayson B-5
Greensburg D-7
Gretna F-8
Vicinity . . Pg. 140, D-7
Grosse Tete E-6
Gueydan F-4
Hackberry F-3
Haile A-5
Hall Summit B-3
Hamburg D-5
Hammond E-7
Hanna C-3
Harahan F-8
Vicinity . . Pg. 140, D-7
Harrisonburg C-5
Harvey . . . Pg. 140, D-6
Hathaway E-4
Hayes F-4
Haynesville A-3
Hebert B-5
Henderson E-6
Hermitage D-5
Hessmer D-5
Hickory E-9
Hicks D-3
Hico A-4
Highland A-6
Hillside . . . Pg. 95, E-5
Hodge B-4
Holloway D-5
Holly Beach F-2
Holmwood F-3
Holton E-8
Holum B-5
Homer A-3
Hope Villa . Pg. 95, E-7
Hornbeck D-3

KENTUCKY
Pages 38-39

Population: 3,660,777
Capital: Frankfort
Land Area: 39,669 sq. mi.

Adairville F-6
Albany F-9
Alexandria B-9
Allen D-12
Allensville F-6
Arlington F-3
Ashland C-12
Athens . . . . Pg. 127, A-6
Auburn F-7
Audubon Park
. . . . Pg. 132, D-3
Augusta B-10
Barbourville F-11
Bardstown D-8
Bardwell F-3
Barlow E-3
Beattyville D-11
Beaver Dam E-6
Bedford B-8
Beech Grove D-6
Bellefonte C-12
Bellevue . . . Pg. 106, E-4
Benham E-12
Benton F-4
Berea D-10
Berry B-10
Bloomfield D-9
Bonnieville E-7
Boone D-10
Boonesboro D-10
Booneville E-11
Bowling Green E-6
Bracktown . Pg. 127, E-3
Bradfordsville D-9
Brandenburg C-7
Brannon . . . Pg. 127, E-6

LOUISIANA

Hosston A-2
HotWells D-4
Houma G-7
Humphreys G-7
Hutton D-3
Ida A-2
Independence . . . E-8
Indian Mound . . . E-7
Indian Village . . . F-6
Iota F-4
Iowa F-3
Ithra . . . Pg. 95, C-2
Ivan A-2
Jackson D-6
Jamestown B-3
Jean Lafitte F-8
　Vicinity . Pg. 140, G-5
Jeanerette F-6
Jefferson Hts.
　. . . . . Pg. 140, C-4
Jena C-5
Jennings F-4
Jesuit Bend Pg. 140, G-7
Jigger B-5
Johnsons Bayou . F-2
Jones A-5
Jonesboro B-4
Jonesville C-5
Kahns . . . Pg. 95, B-2
Kaplan F-5
Keatchie B-2
Keithville B-2
Kenner F-8
　Vicinity . Pg. 140, B-3
Kentwood D-8
Kilbourne A-6
Killian E-8
Kinder E-4
Kingston B-2
Kisatchie D-3
Krotz Springs . . . E-5
Kurthwood D-3
La Place F-8
Labadieville F-7
Labarre E-6
Lacamp D-3
Lacassine F-4
Lacombe E-8
Lafayette F-5
Lafitte F-8
Lafourche F-7
Lake Arthur F-4
Lake Charles . . . F-3
Lake End C-3
Lake Providence . A-6
Lakeland E-6
Larose G-8
　Vicinity . . . . Pg. 140
　Detailed City . Pg. 260
Larto D-5
Latanier D-4
Lawtell E-5
Le Blanc E-3
LeMoyen E-5
Leander D-4
Lebeau E-5
Lecompte D-4
Leesville D-3
Leeville G-8
Lejeune . . Pg. 95, B-1
Leonville E-5
Libuse D-5
Lillie A-4
Linville A-5
Lisbon A-3
Lismore C-5
Live Oak . . Pg. 140, G-7
Live Oak Manor
　. . . . . Pg. 140, C-3
Livingston E-7
Livonia E-6
Lockport F-8
Logansport C-2
Lone Star . Pg. 140, D-1
Longstreet B-2
Longville E-3
Lottie E-6
Louisa G-6
Lucas D-4
Lucky B-3
Lukeville . . Pg. 95, B-3
Luling . . Pg. 140, D-1
Luna B-5
Lutcher F-7
Madisonville E-8
Magnolia . . Pg. 95, A-7
Mamou E-4
Manchac E-8
Mandeville E-8
Mangham B-5
Manifest C-5
Mansfield C-2

Many C-3
Maringouin E-6
Marion A-5
Marksville D-5
Marrero . . Pg. 140, D-6
Marsalis A-3
Martin B-3
Maryland . . Pg. 95, A-4
Mathews F-8
Maurepas E-7
Maxie E-4
Mayna C-5
McDade B-2
McNary D-4
Melder D-4
Melrose C-3
Melville E-6
Mer Rouge A-5
Meraux . . Pg. 140, D-9
Merlin . . . Pg. 95, D-1
Mermentau F-4
Merryville E-2
Metairie F-8
　Vicinity . Pg. 140, C-5
Midland D-5
Midway A-2
Mill B-4
Millerville . Pg. 95, C-6
Minden A-3
Mira A-2
Mitchel C-2
Mittie E-4
Mix E-6
Monroe A-5
Montegut G-8
Monterey C-6
Montgomery . . . C-3
Montpelier E-7
Mooringsport . . . A-2
Moreauville D-5
Morgan City F-7
Morganza E-6
Morrow E-5
Mount Carmel . . C-4
Myrtle Grove . . . G-8
Nairn G-9
Naomi F-8
Napoleonville . . . F-7
Natchez C-3
Natchitoches . . . C-3
Negreet C-2
Nesser . . . Pg. 95, D-6
New Era D-5
New Iberia F-6
New Llano D-3
New Orleans . . . E-8
　Vicinity . . . . Pg. 140
　Detailed City . Pg. 260
New Roads E-6
Newellton B-6
Newlight B-6
Noble C-2
North Hodge . . . B-4
Norwood D-6
Oak Grove
　(Cameron Cty) . F-3
Oak Grove
　(West Carroll Cty) A-6
Oak Ridge A-5
Oakdale E-4
Oakland A-4
Oakville . Pg. 140, G-7
Oberlin E-4
Oil City A-2
Olivier F-6
Olla C-4
Opelousas E-5
Oscar E-6
Oxford C-2
Packton C-4
Paincourtville . . . F-7
Parks F-5
Patterson F-6
Pearl River E-9
Pecan Island . . . G-4
Perryville A-5
Phoenix F-9
Pickering D-3
Pierre Part F-6
Pigeon F-6
Pilot Town G-10
Pine D-8
Pine Grove E-7
Pine Prairie E-4
Pineville D-4
Pitkin D-3
Plain Dealing . . . A-2
Plaquemine E-6
Pleasant Hill . . . C-2
Pointe a la Hache . G-9

Pollock C-4
Port Allen E-6
　Vicinity . . . Pg. 95, C-2
Port Barre E-5
Port Sulphur . . . G-9
Port Vincent . . . E-7
Powhatan C-3
Poydras . . Pg. 140, E-10
Provencal C-3
Quitman B-4
Raceland F-7
Ragley E-3
Ramah E-6
Rayne F-5
Rayville A-5
Readhimer B-3
Reddell E-4
Reeves E-3
Reggio F-9
Reserve F-8
Richmond B-6
Richwood B-5
Ridgecrest C-6
Ringgold B-3
Riverton B-5
Robeline C-3
Robert E-8
Rocky Mountain . A-2
Rodessa A-1
Rosedale E-6
Rosefield C-5
Rosepine D-3
Ruddock E-8
Ruston B-4
Sailes B-3
Saint Bernard
　. . . . . Pg. 140, E-10
Saint Clair . Pg. 140, E-8
Saint Francisville . E-6
Saint Gabriel . . . E-7
Saint Joseph . . . B-6
Saint Martinville . F-6
Saint Rose . Pg. 140, D-1
Saline B-4
Sarepta A-3
Scarsdale . Pg. 140, E-8
Scott F-5
Shaw D-6
Sheridan D-9
Shongaloo A-3
Shreveport B-2
Sibley B-3
Sicily Island C-5
Sieper D-4
Sikes B-4
Simmesport D-5
Simpson D-3
Singer E-3
Slagle D-3
Slaughter E-6
Slidell E-9
Slocum C-4
Smithfield . . . Pg. 95, A-1
Somerset B-6
Sondheimer B-6
Sorrento F-7
Spearsville A-4
Spencer A-4
Spokane C-6
Spring Ridge . . . B-2
Springfield E-7
Springhill A-3
Stanley C-2
Starks F-3
Start B-5
State Line D-9
Stella . . . Pg. 140, F-8
Sterlington A-5
Stonewall B-2
Sugartown E-3
Sulphur F-3
Summerfield . . . A-3
Sun E-8
Sunrise . . Pg. 95, B-3
Sunset E-5
Supreme F-7
Talisheek E-8
Tallulah B-6
Tangipahoa D-8
Tanglewood Pg. 95, A-5
Tannehill B-4
Taylortown B-2
Terry A-6
Tete E-6
Thibodaux F-7
Tidewater G-9
Tioga D-4
Toomey F-2
Toro D-2

Transylvania . . . A-6
Triumph G-10
Truxno A-4
Tullos C-5
Turkey Creek . . . D-4
Union F-7
Union Hill C-4
Urania C-4
Vacherie F-7
Varnado D-9
Venice G-10
Verda C-4
Vidalia C-6
Vienna A-4
Ville Platte E-5
Vinton F-2
Violet F-9
Vivian A-2
Vixen B-5
Waggaman . Pg. 140, D-3
Wakefield D-6
Waldheim E-8
Walters C-5
Warnerton D-8
Washington E-5
Waterproof C-6
Watson E-7
Waverly B-6
Weeks F-6
Welsh F-4
West End . . Pg. 140, B-5
Weston B-4
Westwego F-8
　Vicinity . . . Pg. 140, E-4
Weyanoke D-6
White Castle . . . F-7
Whitehall C-5
Williana C-4
Wills Point . Pg. 140, G-8
Willswood . Pg. 140, D-3
Wilmer D-8
Wilson D-6
Winnfield C-4
Winnsboro B-5
Woodlawn . Pg. 95, D-6
Woodworth D-4
Worden D-6
Wye E-3
Youngsville F-5
Yscloskey F-9
Zenoria C-4
Zwolle C-2

MAINE
Page 41
Population: 1,124,660
Capital: Augusta
Land Area: 30,995 sq. mi.

Acton J-2
Addison F-6
Albion G-3
Alexander E-6
Allagash B-4
Andover G-2
Anson F-3
Appleton G-4
Ashland C-4
Athens F-3
Auburn H-3
Augusta G-3
Avon F-2
Bailey Island . . . H-3
Balleyville E-6
Bangor F-5
Bar Harbor G-5
Baring E-6
Bath H-3
Beddington F-5
Belfast G-4
Belgrade G-3
Benton F-3
Berwick J-2
Bethel G-2
Biddeford J-3
Bigelow F-2
Bingham F-3
Blaine C-5
Blanchard F-3
Blue Hill G-5
Boothbay Harbor . H-4
Bradford F-4
Bradley F-5
Brewer F-5
Bridgewater C-5
Bridgton H-2
Brighton F-3
Bristol H-4
Brooks G-4

Brownfield H-2
Brownville E-4
Brownville Jct. . . E-4
Brunswick H-3
Buckfield G-3
Bucks Harbor . . . F-6
Bucksport G-5
Burlington E-5
Burnham F-4
Buxton J-2
Byron G-2
Calais E-6
Cambridge F-3
Camden G-4
Canton G-2
Cape Elizabeth . . J-3
Cape Porpoise . . J-2
Caratunk F-3
Caribou B-5
Carmel F-4
Carrabassett . . . F-3
Carroll E-5
Cary D-5
Casco H-2
Castine G-4
Charleston F-4
Cherryfield G-6
Chester E-5
Chisolm G-2
Clayton Lake . . . C-3
Clinton G-4
Coburn Gore . . . E-2
Colby E-6
Columbia F-6
Conner B-5
Cooper F-6
Corea G-6
Corinna F-4
Cornish H-1
Costigan F-5
Crawford F-6
Crouseville B-5
Cumberland Center H-2
Cutler F-7
Daigle B-4
Dallas F-2
Damariscotta . . . H-4
Danforth D-5
Deblois F-5
Dedham F-4
Deer Isle G-5
Dennistown E-2
Dennysville F-6
Dickey B-4
Dixfield G-2
Dixmont G-4
Dover Foxcroft . . E-4
Durham H-3
Eagle Lake B-4
East Hampden . . F-4
East Machias . . . F-6
East Millinocket . E-4
East Sumner . . . G-2
East Wilton G-3
Eastbrook F-5
Easton C-5
Eastport F-7
Eaton E-6
Eddington F-4
Ellsworth G-5
Estcourt Sta. . . . A-4
Eustis F-2
Fairfield F-3
Farmingdale G-3
Farmington G-2
Fort Fairfield . . . B-5
Fort Kent A-4
Franklin G-5
Freeport H-3
Frenchville A-4
Friendship H-3
Frye G-2
Fryeburg H-2
Gardiner G-3
Gilead G-2
Glenburn Center . F-4
Gorham J-2
Gouldsboro G-5
Grand Isle A-5
Grand Lake Stream E-5
Gray H-3
Greenville E-3
Grindstone D-4
Grove F-6
Guerette B-4
Guilford F-3
Hallowell G-3
Hamlin B-5
Hampden F-4
Hancock G-5

Hanover G-2
Harrington F-5
Harrison H-2
Hartford Center . . G-2
Hartland F-3
Haven F-5
Haynesville D-5
Hersey D-5
Hinckley G-3
Hiram H-2
Hogdon C-5
Houghton F-2
Houlton C-5
Howland E-4
Island Falls D-5
Jackman E-2
Jay G-3
Jefferson G-3
Jemtland B-5
Jonesboro F-6
Jonesport F-6
Keegan B-5
Kenduskeag F-4
Kennebago Lake . E-2
Kennebunk J-2
Kennebunkport . . J-3
Kingfield F-2
Kingman E-5
Kingsbury F-3
Kittery K-2
Kittery Point K-2
Knowles Corner . C-4
Kokadjo E-4
Lagrange F-4
Lake Parlin E-2
Lambert Lake . . . E-5
Larone G-3
Lee E-5
Lewiston H-2
Liberty G-4
Lille A-5
Lily Bay E-3
Limerick J-2
Limestone B-5
Limington J-2
Lincoln E-5
Lincolnville G-4
Linneus D-5
Lisbon H-3
Lisbon Falls H-2
Littleton C-5
Livermore Falls . . G-3
Long Pond E-3
Lovell H-2
Lubec F-7
Ludlow D-5
Lynchville G-2
Machias F-6
Macwahoc D-5
Madawaska A-4
Madison F-3
Madrid F-2
Manchester G-3
Mapleton B-5
Marion F-6
Mars Hill C-5
Masardis C-4
Mattawamkeag . . D-4
Mayfield F-3
Medford E-4
Medway E-4
Mexico G-2
Milbridge G-5
Milford F-5
Millinocket E-4
Milo E-4
Molunkus E-5
Monarda D-5
Monroe G-4
Monson E-3
Monticello C-5
Moose River . . . E-2
Morrill G-4
Moscow F-3
Naples H-2
New Gloucester . H-2
Newcastle H-4
Newfield J-2
Newport F-4
Newry G-2
Nobleboro G-4
Norcross E-4
Norridgewock . . . F-3
North Amity D-6
North Anson . . . F-2
North Berwick . . J-2
North Lovell H-2
North Lyndon . . . B-5
Northeast Carry . D-3
Northeast Harbor . G-5

Northfield F-6
Norway H-2
Oakland G-3
Ogunquit J-2
Old Orchard Beach . J-2
Old Town F-5
Oquossoc F-2
Orient D-5
Orland G-4
Orono F-5
Orrington F-4
Ouelette B-4
Oxbow C-4
Oxford G-2
Palmyra F-3
Paris G-2
Parkman F-3
Patten D-4
Pittston H-3
Poland H-2
Portage B-4
Portland J-3
Presque Isle . . . B-5
Princeton E-6
Quimby B-4
Randolph G-3
Rangeley F-2
Raymond H-2
Readfield G-3
Red Beach E-7
Reed D-5
Richmond H-3
Ripley F-3
Ripogenus Dam . D-4
Robbinston E-7
Robinsons C-5
Rockland H-4
Rockport H-4
Rockwood E-3
Rome G-3
Roxbury G-2
Rumford G-2
Sabattus H-3
Saco J-3
Saint Albans . . . F-3
Saint David A-5
Saint Francis . . . B-4
Saint George . . . G-4
Saint John B-4
Salem F-2
Sanford J-2
Sangerville F-4
Saponac E-5
Scarborough . . . J-2
Seal Harbor G-5
Searsmont G-4
Searsport G-4
Sebago H-2
Sebec Lake E-4
Seboeis E-4
Seboomook D-3
Sedgewick G-4
Selden D-5
Sheridan B-5
Sherman D-4
Sherman Mills . . D-5
Sherman Sta. . . . C-4
Shin Pond D-4
Shirley Mills E-3
Sidney G-3
Skowhegan F-3
Smyrna Mills . . . C-5
Soldier Pond . . . B-4
Solon F-3
South Arm G-2
South Bancroft . . D-5
South China G-4
South Hope G-4
South Paris H-2
South Portland . . J-3
Southwest Harbor . G-5
Springfield E-5
Springvale J-2
Squa Pan C-4
Stacyville D-4
Standish J-2
Starboard F-6
Stetson F-4
Steuben G-6
Stockton Springs . G-4
Stonington G-5
Stow H-2
Stratton F-2
Strong F-2
Sweden H-2
The Forks E-3
Thomaston H-4
Topsfield E-6
Topsham H-3
Tremont G-5

MARYLAND

Turner H-2
Union G-3
Unity G-4
Upton G-2
Van Buren B-5
Vanceboro E-6
Vienna G-4
Vinalhaven G-4
Waite E-6
Waldoboro H-4
Waltham F-5
Warren H-4
Washburn B-5
Washington G-3
Waterboro J-2
Waterford H-2
Waterville G-4
Wells J-2
Wesley F-6
West Enfield E-5
West Forks E-3
West Newfield . . J-2
West Paris G-2
Westbrook J-3
Weston D-5
Whiting F-6
Williamantic E-3
Wilsons Mills . . . F-1
Wilton G-2
Winn E-5
Winslow G-3
Winter Harbor . . . G-5
Winterport G-4
Winterville B-4
Winthrop G-3
Wiscasset H-3
Woodland B-5
Woolwich H-3
Wytopitlock D-5
Yarmouth H-3
York Beach K-2
York Village K-2

MARYLAND
Pages 42-43
Population: 4,216,975
Capital: Annapolis
Land Area: 9,837 sq. mi.

Aberdeen B-12
Accident B-1
Accokeek F-9
Airy F-12
Altamont B-1
Altoona Beach
　. . . . . Pg. 94, H-5
Andersontown . . E-13
Andrews G-12
Annapolis D-11
Annapolis Junction
　. . . . . Pg. 94, J-1
Arbutus . . Pg. 94, F-3
Arnold D-10
Aspen Hill D-9
Avenue G-10
Baltimore C-10
　Vicinity . . Pg. 94, D-4
　Detailed City . Pg. 208
Barclay D-13
Barnesville C-7
Bay Ridge E-11
Bayard E-10
Bayview B-12
Bel Air B-11
Belair Edison Pg. 94, D-5
Belltown . . Pg. 94, B-1
Benfield . . Pg. 94, J-4
Berlin G-15
Berwyn Heights
　. . . . . Pg. 168, B-8
Bethesda D-8
　Vicinity . . Pg. 168, C-5
Betterton C-12
Bladensburg Pg. 168, C-9
Blenheim . . Pg. 94, B-1
Bloomsbury Pg. 94, F-2
Bonaparte Estates
　. . . . . Pg. 94, A-7
Boonsboro B-7
Bowie D-10
Braddock Hts. . . C-7
Brandywine F-9
Brentwood . Pg. 168, C-7
Bristol E-10
Broadwater Beach
　. . . . . Pg. 94, K-6
Brooklyn . . Pg. 94, F-4
Brookview F-13
Broomes Island . G-10

MARYLAND

Brunswick C-7
Bryans Road F-8
Buckeystown C-7
Bucktown G-12
Burkittsville C-7
Butler B-10
California G-11
Cambridge F-12
Cape St. Claire D-11
Capitol Heights
. . . . Pg. 168, E-8
Carney . . . Pg. 94, C-6
Cascade A-7
Catonsville C-10
Vicinity . . . Pg. 94, F-2
Caves Park . . Pg. 94, B-2
Cavetown B-7
Cayots B-13
Cecilton C-12
Centreville D-12
Chaptico G-9
Charlestown B-12
Charlotte Hall F-9
Chesapeake B-13
Chesapeake Beach . F-10
Chestertown C-12
Cheverly . . . Pg. 168, D-8
Chevy Chase
. . . . Pg. 168, C-5
Church Creek F-12
Church Hill D-12
Clear Spring B-8
Cliffs City D-12
Clinton E-9
Vicinity . . Pg. 168, G-8
Cobb Island G-9
Cockeysville B-10
Vicinity . . Pg. 94, A-4
Colesville . Pg. 168, A-6
College Park D-9
Vicinity . . Pg. 168, B-8
Colmar Manor
. . . . Pg. 168, D-7
Columbia C-9
Columbia Hills
. . . . Pg. 94, F-1
Cooksville C-9
Corriganville A-3
Cottage City Pg. 168, D-7
Cove Point G-11
Cresaptown B-3
Crisfield J-13
Crofton D-10
Cronhardt . . Pg. 94, B-3
Cub Hills . . Pg. 94, B-6
Cumberland B-3
Damascus C-8
Dares Beach F-11
Deale E-10
Delight . . . Pg. 94, B-1
Delmar G-13
Denton E-13
District Heights
. . . . Pg. 168, E-9
Doncaster F-8
Dorsey . . . Pg. 94, H-2
Drawbridge G-13
Drum Point G-11
Drummond . Pg. 168, C-5
Dublin A-11
Dunbrook . . Pg. 94, J-6
Dundalk C-10
Vicinity . . Pg. 94, F-6
Dunkirk F-10
Eagle Harbor F-10
East Point . . Pg. 94, E-6
Easton E-12
Edgemere C-11
Vicinity . . Pg. 94, F-7
Edgewood C-11
Edmonston Pg. 168, C-8
Eldersburg C-9
Eldorado F-12
Elkridge . . Pg. 94, G-2
Elkton B-13
Ellicott City C-9
Vicinity . . Pg. 94, F-1
Elliott G-12
Elmhurst . . Pg. 94, H-4
Emmitsburg A-8
Essex . . . . Pg. 94, E-7
Fair Hill A-12
Fairmont Heights
. . . . Pg. 168, D-8
Fallston B-11
Federalsburg E-13
Ferndale . . Pg. 94, G-4
Fishtown . . Pg. 94, C-2
Font Hill . . Pg. 94, G-2
Foremans Corner
. . . . Pg. 94, G-5

Forest Heights
. . . . Pg. 168, F-7
Fork . . . . . . Pg. 94, A-7
Fort Howard Pg. 94, G-7
Fountain Head A-7
Foxridge . . Pg. 94, C-1
Frederick C-8
Friendship Heights
. . . . Pg. 168, C-5
Friendsville A-1
Frostburg B-3
Fruitland G-14
Fullerton . . Pg. 94, C-6
Furnace Branch
. . . . Pg. 94, G-4
Gaithersburg D-8
Galena C-12
Gambrills . . Pg. 94, K-3
Garrett Park Pg. 168, A-5
Germantown D-8
Vicinity . . Pg. 94, B-7
Gittings . . . Pg. 94, A-6
Glen Burnie D-10
Vicinity . . Pg. 94, H-4
Glen Echo . Pg. 168, C-4
Glen Morris . Pg. 94, A-1
Glenarden . Pg. 168, D-9
Glenarm (Baltimore Cty)
. . . . Pg. 94, A-6
Glenmar (Howard Cty)
. . . . Pg. 94, D-7
Glenn Dale Pg. 168, F-8
Glenmar . . Pg. 94, F-1
Glyndon . . Pg. 94, A-1
Golden Beach F-10
Goldsboro D-13
Grantsville A-2
Grasonville E-11
Green Haven Pg. 94, H-5
Green Hill G-13
Green Valley C-8
Green Valley North
. . . . Pg. 94, A-3
Greenbelt D-9
Vicinity . . Pg. 168, B-9
Greengate . Pg. 94, C-3
Greensboro D-13
Guilford . . . Pg. 94, H-1
Hagerstown B-7
Halethorpe . Pg. 94, F-3
Halfway B-6
Hampstead B-9
Hampton . . Pg. 94, B-5
Hancock A-5
Hanover . . . Pg. 94, H-3
Hanover Woods
. . . . Pg. 94, G-2
Harkins A-11
Harmans . . Pg. 94, H-3
Harmony E-13
Harrisonville Pg. 94, C-1
Harundale . Pg. 94, H-4
Hebbville . . Pg. 94, D-2
Hebron G-13
Hereford B-10
Hillsboro D-13
Hollifield . . Pg. 94, E-1
Honga G-11
Hoyes B-1
Hurlock F-13
Hyattsville Pg. 168, C-7
Hyde Park . Pg. 94, E-7
Hydes . . . . Pg. 94, A-6
Ilchester Landing
. . . . Pg. 94, F-2
Jacobsville . Pg. 94, J-6
Jarrettsville B-11
Jenkins . . . Pg. 94, A-7
Jessup . . . . Pg. 94, H-2
Joppatowne C-11
Josenhans Corner
. . . . Pg. 94, D-7
Kennedyville C-12
Kensington . Pg. 168, B-6
Kenwood . . Pg. 94, D-6
Kingsville . . Pg. 94, A-7
Kitzmiller C-2
Kraft Corner Pg. 94, D-1
LaPlata F-9
LaVale B-3
Lake Shore . Pg. 94, J-6
Landover Hills
. . . . Pg. 168, C-8
Lansdowne . Pg. 94, F-3
Largo E-10
Laytonsville C-8
Leonardtown G-10
Lexington Pk. G-11
Liberty Manor Pg. 94, D-1
Linthicum . . Pg. 94, G-3
Lipins Corner Pg. 94, J-5

Lochearn . . . Pg. 94, D-2
Lonaconing B-2
Lonaconing B-2
Long Beach G-11
Long Green . Pg. 94, A-6
Longridge G-14
Longwoods E-12
Luke B-2
Lutherville B-10
Vicinity . . Pg. 94, B-4
Lynch C-12
Maceys Corner
. . . . Pg. 94, K-6
Manchester B-9
Manor Woods Pg. 94, A-6
Marbury F-8
Marion H-13
Marston B-8
Maryland City Pg. 94, K-1
Mayo E-11
Mays Chapel Pg. 94, A-4
McHenry B-1
Meadowcliff Pg. 94, A-6
Melrose A-9
Vicinity . . Pg. 94, H-4
Middle River Pg. 94, D-7
Middleborough
. . . . Pg. 94, E-7
Middletown B-7
Midland B-3
Milford . . . Pg. 94, A-6
Millington C-13
Millstone A-5
Morganza G-8
Morningside Pg. 168, F-8
Mt. Airy C-8
Mt. Pleasant B-8
Mt. Rainier . Pg. 168, C-7
Mtn. Lake Park C-1
Myersville B-7
New Carrollton
. . . . Pg. 168, C-9
New Market C-8
Newburg G-9
Newport G-9
Newtown C-11
Nordeau . . Pg. 94, H-1
North Beach E-10
North Brentwood
. . . . Pg. 168, C-7
North Chevy Chase
. . . . Pg. 168, B-5
North East B-12
Oakland (Garrett Cty) C-1
Oakland (Carroll Cty) B-9
Ocean City G-15
Odenton . . Pg. 94, K-3
Olde Mill . . Pg. 94, J-4
Olney D-9
Orchard Beach
. . . . Pg. 94, H-6
Oriole H-13
Overlea . . . Pg. 94, D-6
Owings Mills C-10
Vicinity . . Pg. 94, B-2
Oxford F-12
Oxon Hill G-7
Vicinity . . Pg. 168, G-7
Park Hill H-11
Parkton B-10
Parkville C-10
Vicinity . . Pg. 94, C-5
Pasadena . . Pg. 94, J-5
Pasadena Beach
. . . . Pg. 94, H-7
Patapsco . . Pg. 94, G-3
Perry Hall B-11
Vicinity . . Pg. 94, C-6
Perryville . . Pg. 94, C-7
Pfeiffer Corner
. . . . Pg. 94, G-1
Pikesville C-10
Vicinity . . Pg. 94, C-5
Pine Ridge . Pg. 94, G-2
Pinehurst on the Bay
. . . . Pg. 94, J-7
Piney Grove A-4
Piney Point H-11
Pittsville G-14
Pleasant Hills B-11
Plum Point F-11
Pocomoke City H-13
Point Lookout H-11
Poolesville C-8
Port Deposit B-12
Pot Spring . Pg. 94, B-4
Potomac Park B-3
Powellville G-14
Pratt A-4
Preston E-13
Price D-12
Prince Frederick . . . F-10

Princess Anne . . . G-13
Providence . Pg. 94, B-5
Queen Anne E-12
Queenstown D-12
Randallstown C-9
Vicinity . . Pg. 94, C-1
Redhouse C-11
Reisterstown B-9
Vicinity . . Pg. 94, A-1
Relay . . . . . Pg. 94, F-3
Ridge H-11
Ridgely D-12
Ridgeway . . Pg. 94, J-3
Rising Sun A-12
Riva E-10
Riverdale . . Pg. 168, C-8
Riverside G-8
Riviera Beach D-11
Vicinity . . Pg. 94, H-6
Rock Hall D-11
Rockdale B-10
Rockville D-8
Vicinity . . Pg. 168, A-4
Rodgers Forge
. . . . Pg. 94, C-4
Roe D-12
Rolling Ridge Pg. 94, E-1
Rosedale . . Pg. 94, D-6
Rosemont C-7
Vicinity . . Pg. 94, E-3
Rush B-4
Ruthsburg D-12
Ruxton . . . . Pg. 94, C-4
Salisbury G-13
Sandy Bottom C-1
Savage . . . . Pg. 94, H-1
Seat Pleasant E-9
Vicinity . . Pg. 168, D-9
Secretary F-12
Seven Oaks . Pg. 94, J-2
Severn D-10
Vicinity . . Pg. 94, J-3
Severna Park D-10
Vicinity . . Pg. 94, K-5
Shady Side E-11
Sharonville Pg. 94, J-6
Sharpsburg C-7
Sharptown F-13
Silver Spring D-9
Vicinity . . Pg. 168, B-6
Snow Hill H-14
Solley . . . . Pg. 94, H-5
Somerset . . Pg. 168, C-5
Southgate D-10
Sparrows Point
. . . . Pg. 94, G-6
Springbrook Pg. 94, C-1
St. Charles F-9
St. Michaels E-11
Stevenson . Pg. 94, B-3
Stockton H-14
Stonecrest Hills
. . . . Pg. 94, F-1
Suburbia . . Pg. 94, A-1
Sudlersville C-13
Sunrise Beach
. . . . Pg. 94, K-4
Swanton B-1
Sykesville C-9
Takoma Park Pg. 168, C-7
Taneytown B-8
Taylors Island F-11
Taylorsville C-8
Templeville D-13
Texas . . . . Pg. 94, A-4
The Oaks . . Pg. 94, E-1
The Provinces Pg. 94, J-2
Thurmont B-8
Timonium . . Pg. 94, B-4
Towson C-10
Vicinity . . Pg. 94, C-4
Turner G-10
Union Bridge B-8
University Park
. . . . Pg. 168, C-7
Upper Marlboro E-9
Valleywood . Pg. 94, B-4
Venice on the Bay
. . . . Pg. 94, H-7
Ventnor . . . Pg. 94, J-7
Vienna F-13
Waldorf F-9
Walkersville B-8
Warren . . . . Pg. 94, A-4
Waterloo . . Pg. 94, H-1
Waterview G-13
Wenona H-12
Wesley G-14
Westerlee . . Pg. 94, E-2
Westernport B-2

Westminster B-9
Westover H-13
White Marsh Pg. 94, C-7
White Oak . Pg. 168, A-7
White Plains F-9
Whiteford A-11
Widgeon G-13
Willards G-15
Windemere . Pg. 94, A-5
Woodlawn . Pg. 94, D-2
Woodmoor . Pg. 94, D-2

MASSACHUSETTS
Pages 24-25
Population: 5,737,037
Capital: Boston
Land Area: 7,824 sq. mi.

Abington D-11
Acton B-9
Acushnet F-11
Adams B-3
Adamsville . Pg. 154, F-4
Agawam E-5
Amesbury A-11
Amherst C-4
Andover B-11
Arlington . . Pg. 97, D-3
Ashburnham B-8
Ashfield B-4
Athol B-7
Attleboro E-10
Vicinity . . Pg. 154, F-6
Auburn D-8
Avon D-11
Ayer B-9
Baldwinville B-7
Barnstable F-13
Barre C-7
Becket C-3
Bedford B-10
Vicinity . . Pg. 97, B-1
Belchertown C-6
Bellingham E-9
Belmont . . . Pg. 97, D-3
Berkley F-11
Bernardston B-5
Beverly B-12
Billerica B-10
Vicinity . . Pg. 97, A-1
Blackstone E-9
Blanford D-4
Bolton C-8
Boston C-11
Vicinity . . . . . Pg. 97
Detailed City . Pg. 211
Bourne F-13
Boxborough C-9
Boxford B-11
Boylston C-8
Braintree D-11
Vicinity . . Pg. 97, J-6
Brewster F-14
Bridgewater E-11
Briggs Corner
. . . . Pg. 154, F-6
Brimfield D-7
Brockton E-11
Brookfield D-7
Brookline . . Pg. 97, F-3
Buckland B-4
Burlington . Pg. 97, B-2
Buzzards Bay F-12
Cambridge . Pg. 97, E-4
Canton D-11
Vicinity . . Pg. 97, K-3
Carlisle B-10
Carver E-12
Centerville G-13
Charlemont B-4
Charlton D-7
Chartley . . . Pg. 154, E-7
Chatham F-15
Chelmsford B-10
Chelsea C-11
Vicinity . . Pg. 97, E-5
Cheshire B-3
Chesterfield C-4
Chicopee D-5
Chilmark H-12
Clarksburg A-3
Cliftondale . Pg. 97, C-6
Clinton C-8
Cochituate C-9
Colrain A-5
Concord C-10
Vicinity . . Pg. 97, K-1
Conway B-5
Cummington C-4
Dalton B-3

Danvers B-11
Dartmouth G-11
Dedham . . . Pg. 97, H-3
Deerfield B-5
Dennis F-14
Dennis Port G-14
Dighton F-11
Dodgeville . Pg. 154, F-6
Dover . . . . . Pg. 97, J-1
Dracut B-10
Dudley E-7
Duxbury E-12
East Bridgewater . E-11
East Falmouth G-13
East Longmeadow . E-6
Eastham F-15
Easthampton C-4
Easton E-11
Edgartown H-13
Essex B-12
Everett . . . . Pg. 97, D-5
Fairhaven F-11
Fall River F-10
Falmouth G-12
Fitchburg B-8
Framingham D-9
Freetown F-11
Gardner B-7
Gay Head H-12
Georgetown A-11
Gilbertville C-6
Gill B-5
Gloucester B-13
Grafton D-9
Granby D-5
Granville E-4
Great Barrington . . . D-2
Greenfield B-5
Groton B-9
Groveland A-11
Hadley C-5
Halifax E-12
Hamilton B-12
Hampden E-6
Hanover D-12
Hardwick C-6
Harvard B-9
Harwich F-15
Hatfield C-5
Haverhill A-11
Hawley B-4
Heath B-4
Hingham D-11
Vicinity . . Pg. 97, J-7
Holbrook D-11
Holden C-8
Holland E-7
Holyoke D-5
Hopedale D-9
Hopkinton D-9
Hortonville Pg. 154, J-7
Hudson C-9
Hull C-11
Huntington D-4
Hyannis G-14
Ipswich B-11
Kingston E-12
Lee C-3
Leicester D-8
Lenox C-2
Leominster B-8
Leverett C-5
Lexington C-10
Vicinity . . Pg. 97, C-2
Leyden A-5
Lincoln C-10
Vicinity . . Pg. 97, D-1
Littleton B-9
Longmeadow D-5
Lowell B-10
Ludlow City D-6
Lunenburg B-8
Luther Corner
. . . . Pg. 154, K-6
Lynn C-11
Vicinity . . Pg. 97, B-6
Lynnfield B-11
Vicinity . . Pg. 94, A-5
Malden . . . . Pg. 97, D-4
Manchester B-12
Mansfield E-10
Marblehead B-12
Marion F-12
Marlborough C-9
Marshfield D-12
Mattapoisett G-12
Maynard C-9
Medfield D-10
Vicinity . . Pg. 97, K-1
Medford . . . Pg. 97, D-4
Medway D-10

Melrose . . . Pg. 97, C-5
Mendon D-9
Merrimac A-11
Methuen A-10
Middleborough F-11
Middlefield C-3
Middleton B-11
Milford D-9
Millbury D-8
Millers Falls B-6
Millis D-10
Milton D-11
Vicinity . . Pg. 97, H-6
Monson D-6
Montague B-5
Monterey D-3
Nahant C-11
Vicinity . . Pg. 97, D-7
Nantucket H-14
Natick D-10
Needham . . Pg. 97, G-2
New Bedford G-11
New Braintree C-7
New Marlborough . . D-3
Newbury A-12
Newton B-7
Vicinity . . Pg. 97, F-2
Norfolk D-10
North Adams A-3
North Brookfield . . . C-7
North Reading B-11
North Rehoboth
. . . . Pg. 154, G-7
North Swansea
. . . . Pg. 154, J-6
Northampton C-4
Northborough C-8
Northbridge D-9
Northfield A-6
Norton E-10
Norwood D-10
Oak Bluffs H-13
Oakham C-7
Ocean Grove
. . . . Pg. 154, K-7
Orange B-6
Orleans F-15
Osterville G-13
Otis D-3
Oxford D-8
Palmer D-6
Paxton C-8
Peabody B-11
Peabody . . Pg. 97, A-7
Pepperell B-9
Peru C-3
Petersham B-7
Pinehurst . . Pg. 97, A-2
Pittsfield C-3
Plainfield B-4
Plymouth E-12
Plympton E-12
Princeton C-8
Provincetown E-14
Quincy D-11
Vicinity . . Pg. 97, J-6
Randolph D-11
Vicinity . . Pg. 97, K-5
Raynham E-11
Reading B-11
Vicinity . . Pg. 94, A-4
Rehoboth F-10
Revere . . . . Pg. 97, D-5
Richmond C-2
Rochester F-12
Rockland D-11
Rockport B-13
Rowley A-12
Royalston A-7
Rutland C-7
Sagamore F-13
Salem B-12
Vicinity . . Pg. 97, B-7
Salisbury A-12
Sandisfield D-3
Sandwich F-13
Saugus C-11
Vicinity . . Pg. 97, C-6
Savoy B-4
Scituate D-12
Seekonk F-10
Sharon D-11
Sheffield D-2
Shelburne B-5
Shirley B-9
Shrewsbury C-9
So. Yarmouth G-14

Somerset F-10
Somerville . Pg. 97, E-4
South Hadley C-5
South Swansea
. . . . Pg. 154, K-7
Southbridge E-7
Spencer D-7
Sterling C-8
Stockbridge C-2
Stoneham . . Pg. 97, B-4
Stoughton D-11
Stow C-9
Sturbridge D-7
Sunderland C-5
Sutton D-8
Swampscott C-12
Vicinity . . Pg. 97, B-7
Swansea F-10
Vicinity . . Pg. 154, K-7
Taunton F-11
Templeton B-7
Tewksbury B-10
Three Rivers D-6
Tisbury H-12
Topsfield B-11
Townsend B-9
Truro E-15
Tyngsborough A-10
Upton D-9
Uxbridge E-9
Vineyard Haven . . . H-13
Wades Corner
. . . . Pg. 154, G-7
Wakefield C-11
Vicinity . . Pg. 97, B-5
Wales D-6
Walpole D-10
Vicinity . . Pg. 97, K-1
Waltham . . . Pg. 97, E-2
Ware D-6
Wareham F-12
Warren D-7
Warwick A-6
Washington C-3
Watertown . Pg. 97, E-3
Wayland C-10
Webster E-7
Wellesley C-10
Vicinity . . Pg. 97, G-1
Wellfleet E-14
Wendell B-6
Wenham B-11
West Boylston C-8
West Brookfield . . . D-7
West Dennis G-14
West Newbury A-11
West Springfield . . . D-5
West Stockbridge . . C-2
West Tisbury H-12
Westborough D-8
Westfield D-4
Westford B-9
Westhampton C-4
Westminster B-7
Weston . . . Pg. 97, E-1
Westport G-11
Westwood D-10
Vicinity . . Pg. 97, J-2
Weymouth D-11
Vicinity . . Pg. 97, J-7
Whately C-5
Whitinsville D-8
Whitman E-11
Wilbraham D-6
Williamstown C-3
Wilmington B-10
Vicinity . . Pg. 97, A-3
Winchendon A-7
Winchester . Pg. 97, C-3
Windsor B-3
Winthrop C-11
Vicinity . . Pg. 97, E-6
Woburn C-10
Vicinity . . Pg. 97, B-3
Worcester C-7
Worthington C-5
Wrentham D-10
Yarmouth F-14

MICHIGAN

MICHIGAN
Pages 44-45
Population: 9,262,078
Capital: Lansing
Land Area: 56,954 sq. mi.

Acme F-6
Adamsville L-4
Adrian L-8
Afton E-7

MICHIGAN

Agnew J-4
Ahmeek A-2
Akron H-8
Alabaster G-8
Alanson E-7
Alaska J-5
Alba F-6
Alberta B-2
Albion L-6
Alcona F-9
Alger G-8
Algonac K-10
Allegan K-5
Allen L-7
Allen Park . . Pg. 115, J-8
Allendale J-5
Allenville D-7
Allouez A-2
Alma J-7
Almena L-5
Almont K-9
Aloha E-7
Alpena F-9
Alpha D-2
Alston B-2
Alto K-6
Alverno E-7
Amador J-10
Amasa C-2
Amble H-6
Anchorville K-10
Ann Arbor L-8
Antrim F-6
Applegate J-10
Arbutus Beach . . . F-7
Arcadia G-4
Argentine K-7
Argyle H-9
Arnheim B-2
Arnold D-3
Arthur J-8
Ashley J-7
Ashton H-6
Assinins B-2
Athens L-6
Atlanta F-8
Atlantic Mine B-2
Attica J-9
Atwood E-6
Au Gres H-8
Au Sable G-9
Au Train C-4
Auburn H-8
Austin C-3
Averill H-7
Bad Axe H-9
Bailey J-5
Baldwin H-5
Banat D-3
Bancorft K-8
Banfield K-6
Bangor K-4
Baraga B-2
Bark River D-3
Barker Creek F-6
Barryton H-6
Barton City F-8
Batavia L-6
Bates F-6
Bath K-6
Battle Creek K-6
Bay City H-8
Bay Mills C-7
Bay Park H-8
Bay Port H-8
Bay View E-7
Beacon C-2
Bear Lake G-5
Beaverton H-7
Beechwood C-2
Belding J-6
Belleville . . Pg. 115, K-4
Bellevue K-6
Bendon F-5
Bennington J-7
Benton Harbor . . . L-4
Benzonia F-5
Bergland A-10
Berkley . . . . Pg. 115, D-8
Berrien Sprgs. . . . L-4
Bessemer B-9
Bethel L-6
Beulah F-5
Beverly Hills . Pg. 115, C-7
Big Bay B-3
Big Rapids H-6
Birch Creek E-3
Birch Run J-8
Birmingham . Pg. 115, C-8
Bitley H-5

Black River F-9
Blanchard H-6
Blaney Park D-5
Blissfield L-8
Boyne City E-6
Boyne Falls E-7
Bradley K-5
Brampton D-3
Branch H-5
Bravo K-5
Breckenridge J-7
Brethren G-5
Brevort D-6
Bridgeport J-8
Bridgeton J-5
Bridgman L-4
Brighton K-8
Brimley C-7
Britton L-8
Brockway J-9
Brohman H-5
Bronson L-6
Brooklyn L-7
Brown City J-9
Bruce Crossing . . . C-1
Brunswick H-5
Brutus E-7
Buchanan L-4
Buckley G-5
Burlington L-6
Burnside J-9
Burt J-8
Burton J-8
Byron Center J-5
Cadillac G-6
Cadmus L-7
Caledonia K-6
California K-8
Calumet A-2
Camden M-6
Capac K-9
Carbondale E-3
Carleton L-8
Carney D-3
Caro J-9
Carp Lake E-7
Carsonville J-9
Caseville H-9
Casnovia J-5
Cass City J-9
Cassopolis L-4
Cathro F-8
Cedar F-5
Cedar River E-3
Cedar Springs . . . J-6
Cedarville D-8
Center Line . Pg. 115, D-11
Centreville L-5
Cereso L-6
Channing C-2
Charlevoix E-6
Charlotte K-6
Chase H-6
Chatham C-4
Cheboygan E-7
Chelsea L-7
Chesaning J-7
Christmas C-4
Cilo J-8
Clare H-6
Clarendon L-7
Clarion E-7
Clarksville K-6
Clawson . . . . Pg. 115, C-9
Clayton L-7
Cliff A-2
Climax K-5
Clinton L-8
Cloverdole K-6
Coldwater L-5
Coleman H-7
Coloma L-4
Colon L-5
Comins F-8
Concord L-7
Constantine L-5
Conway E-7
Coopersville J-5
Copemish G-5
Copper Harbor . . . A-3
Cornell D-3
Corunna J-8
Covert K-4
Covington C-2
Cross Village E-7
Croswell J-10
Croton H-5
Crump H-7
Crystal Falls C-2
Cunard D-3

Curran F-8
Curtis D-6
Custer H-4
Dafter C-7
Daggett E-3
Dansville K-7
Darragh F-6
Davison J-8
Dayton L-4
DeTour Village . . . D-8
Dearborn L-9
  Vicinity . . . Pg. 115, H-8
Dearborn Heights
  . . . . Pg. 115, G-7
Decatur L-5
Deer Park C-6
Deerton C-4
Deford J-9
Delano G-8
Delton K-5
Denton L-8
Detroit L-9
  Vicinity . . . Pg. 115, H-8
  Detailed City . Pg. 230
Devereaux L-6
Dewitt K-7
Dexter L-8
Dighton G-6
Disco K-9
Dixboro L-8
Donaldson C-8
Donken B-1
Dorr K-5
Douglas K-4
Dowagiac L-4
Dowling K-6
Drayton Plains . . . K-8
Drummond D-8
Dublin G-5
Dundee L-8
Dunningville K-5
Durand K-8
Eagle Habor A-3
Eagle River A-2
East Gilead L-6
East Grand Rapids . . J-5
  Vicinity . . . Pg. 119, B-5
East Jordan E-6
East Lake G-5
East Leroy L-6
East Tawas G-8
Eastpointe . Pg. 115, D-12
Eastport F-6
Eaton Rapids K-7
Eckerman C-7
Ecorse . . . . Pg. 115, J-9
Edenville H-7
Edmore J-6
Edwardsburg L-5
Elba J-8
Elberta F-5
Elk Rapids F-6
Elkton H-9
Elmer J-9
Elmira F-7
Elwell J-7
Emmett K-9
Empire F-5
Engadine D-6
Ensign D-4
Epoufette D-7
Erie M-8
Escanaba D-4
Essexville H-8
Estey H-7
Estral Beach L-9
Evans J-6
Evart H-6
Ewen C-1
Fair Haven K-9
Fairfield L-7
Fairgrove J-8
Fairview F-8
Farmington . Pg. 115, D-6
Farmington Hills
  . . . . Pg. 115, D-6
Farwell H-6
Fawn River L-6
Fayette D-4
Felch D-3
Felch Mountain . . . D-3
Fennville K-5
Fenton K-8
Ferndale . . . Pg. 115, E-9
Ferry H-5
Ferrysburg J-4
Fibre D-7
Fife Lake G-6
Filer City G-4
Filion H-9

Filmore K-5
Flat Rock L-8
Flint J-8
Flushing J-8
Ford River D-4
Forest Hill J-7
Forest Lake C-4
Forester J-10
Forestville H-10
Foster City D-3
Fouch F-5
Fountain G-5
Fowler J-7
Fowlerville K-8
Frankenmuth J-8
Frankfort F-5
Franklin . . . . Pg. 115, C-7
Fraser . . . . . Pg. 115, C-12
Frederick F-7
Freeland H-7
Freesoil G-5
Fremont H-5
Frontier L-7
Fruitport J-5
Galesburg K-5
Galien L-4
Ganges K-4
Garden D-4
Garden City Pg. 115, G-6
Garden Corners . . . D-5
Gardendale J-10
Garfield J-7
Garnet D-6
Gaylord F-7
Gera J-8
Germfask C-5
Gibraltar L-9
Girard L-6
Gladstone D-4
Gladwin H-7
Glen Arbor F-5
Glen Haven F-5
Glenn K-4
Glennie F-7
Glenwood L-5
Gobles K-5
Goetzville D-8
Good Hart E-6
Goodrich K-8
Goodrich K-8
Gould City D-5
Gourley D-3
Grand Beach L-4
Grand Blanc K-8
Grand Haven J-4
Grand Ledge K-6
Grand Marais C-5
Grand Rapids J-5
  Vicinity . . . Pg. 119, B-4
Grand Valley Pg. 119, B-1
Grandville . . Pg. 119, D-2
Grange L-5
Granite Bluff D-2
Grant J-5
Grawn F-6
Grayling F-7
Greenbush G-9
Greenland B-1
Greenville J-6
Gregory K-7
Grindstone City . . . H-9
Gros Cap D-7
Grosse Pointe
  . . . . Pg. 115, F-13
Grosse Pointe Farms
  . . . . Pg. 115, F-13
Grosse Pointe Park
  . . . . Pg. 115, G-12
Grosse Pointe Shores L-9
  Vicinity . . . Pg. 115, E-13
Grosse PointeWoods
  . . . . Pg. 115, E-13
Gulliver D-5
Gwinn C-3
Hale G-8
Hamburg K-8
Hamilton K-5
Hamlin Lake G-4
Hamtramck Pg. 115, F-10
Hancock B-2
Harbert L-4
Harbor Beach H-10
Harbor Springs . . . E-6
Hardwood D-3
HarperWoods
  . . . . Pg. 115, E-12
Harris D-3
Harrison H-7
Harrisville F-9
Hart H-4
Hartford L-4

Hartland K-8
Harvey C-3
Hastings K-6
Hawks E-8
Hazel Park Pg. 115, D-10
Helmer C-6
Hemans J-9
Henderson J-7
Hermansville D-3
Herrington . Pg. 119, A-1
Herron F-8
Hesperia H-5
Hessel D-7
Higgans Lake G-7
Highland Park
  . . . . Pg. 115, F-9
Hilliards K-5
Hillman F-8
Hillsdale L-7
Hockaday G-7
Hodunk L-6
Holland K-4
Holly K-8
Holt K-7
Holton H-5
Homer L-6
Honor F-5
Horton L-7
Houghton B-1
Houghton Heights . . G-7
Houghton Lake . . . G-7
Howard City J-5
Howell K-8
Hubbard Lake F-8
Hubbell B-2
Hudson L-7
Hudsonville J-5
  Vicinity . . . Pg. 119, E-1
Huntington Woods
  . . . . Pg. 115, D-9
Huron Beach E-8
Huron City H-9
Hyde D-4
Idlewild H-5
Imlay City J-9
Ingalls E-3
Inkster . . . . Pg. 115, H-6
Interlochen F-5
Ionia J-6
Iron Mountain D-2
Iron River C-1
Irons G-5
Ironwood B-9
Isabella D-4
Ishpeming C-3
Ithaca J-7
Jackson L-7
Jamestown J-5
Jasper M-8
Jeddo J-10
Johannesburg F-7
Jones L-5
Jonesville L-7
Joppa L-6
Kalamazoo K-5
Kaleva G-5
Kalkaska F-6
Karlin F-6
Kawkawlin H-8
Kearsarge A-2
Kendall K-5
Kent City J-5
Kenton C-1
Kentwood J-5
  Vicinity . . . Pg. 119, E-5
Kewadin F-6
Keweenaw Bay . . . B-2
Kibbie K-4
Kinde H-9
Kinderhook L-6
Kingsford D-2
Kingston J-9
Kinross C-7
Kiva C-4
L'Anse B-2
La Salle L-8
LaBranche D-3
Lachine F-8
Lacota K-5
Laingsburg K-7
Lake City G-6
Lake George H-6
Lake Leelanau E-5
Lake Linden A-2
Lake Odessa K-6
Lake Orion K-9
Lake Roland B-1
Lakeland K-8
Lakeport J-10
Lakeview J-6

Lambertville M-8
Langston J-6
Lansing K-7
Lapeer J-9
Laporte J-7
Lathrop C-4
Lathrup Village
  . . . . Pg. 115, D-8
Laurium A-2
Lawton L-5
Le Roy G-6
Leland F-5
Leoni L-7
Leonidas L-5
Leslie K-7
Levering E-7
Lexington J-10
Liberty L-7
Lilley H-5
Lincoln F-9
Lincoln Park Pg. 115, J-8
Linden K-8
Linwood H-8
Litchfield L-7
Little Lake C-4
Livonia K-8
  Vicinity . . . Pg. 115, F-5
Long Lake G-8
Long Rapids F-8
Longrie E-3
Loomis H-7
Loretto D-3
Lowell J-6
Lucas G-6
Ludington G-4
Luna Pier M-8
Lupton G-7
Luzerne G-7
Mackinaw City . . . D-7
Madison Heights
  . . . . Pg. 115, D-10
Mancelona F-6
Mandan A-3
Manistee G-4
Manistique D-5
Manton G-6
Maple Rapids J-7
Marcellus L-5
Marenisco B-10
Marine City K-10
Marion G-6
Marlette J-9
Marne J-5
  Vicinity . . . Pg. 119, A-1
Marquette C-4
Marshall L-6
Martin K-5
Marysville K-10
Mashek D-3
Mason K-7
Masonville D-4
Mass City B-1
Matchwood B-1
Matherton J-6
Mattawan L-5
Mayville J-9
McBain G-6
McFarland C-3
McMillan C-6
Meade K-9
Mears H-4
Mecosta H-6
Melstrand C-5
Melvin J-9
Melvindale . Pg. 115, H-8
Memphis K-9
Mendon L-5
Menominee E-3
Meredith G-7
Merriman D-2
Merritt G-6
Merriweather A-10
Mesick G-5
Metz E-8
Michigamme C-3
Michigan Center . . . L-7
Middleville K-6
Midland H-7
Mikado G-8
Milburg L-4
Milford K-8
Millbrook H-6
Millersburg E-7
Millington J-8
Mineral Hills C-2
Mio F-8
Mohawk A-2
Moline K-5
Monroe L-8
Monroe Center . . . F-6

Montague H-4
Montrose J-8
Moorestown G-6
Moran D-7
Morley H-6
Morneci M-7
Morrice K-7
Moscow L-7
Mottville L-5
Mt. Forest H-8
Mt. Morris J-8
Mt. Pleasant H-6
Muir J-6
Mullett Lake E-7
Munger H-8
Munising C-5
Muskegon J-4
Muskegon Heights . . J-4
Muttonville K-9
Napoleon L-7
Nashville K-6
Nathan D-3
Naubinway D-6
Negaunee C-3
New Baltimore K-9
New Buffalo L-4
New Era H-4
New Greenleaf . . . H-9
New Haven K-9
Newaygo J-5
Newberry C-6
Newport L-9
Niles L-4
Nirvana H-5
Nisula B-1
North Branch J-9
North Byron Pg. 119, E-3
North Ironwood . . . A-9
North Muskegon . . J-4
Northland D-3
Northport E-5
Northville . . Pg. 115, F-6
Norton Shores J-4
Norwalk G-5
Norway D-2
Novi K-8
  Vicinity . . . Pg. 115, D-4
Nunica J-5
O'Neil F-6
Oak Grove F-7
Oak Park . . . Pg. 115, E-8
Oakley J-7
Oakwood K-9
Ocqueoc E-8
Ogden Center M-8
Oil City H-7
Okemos K-7
Olivet K-6
Omena F-6
Onaway E-8
Onekama G-4
Onondaga K-7
Ontonagon B-1
Orleans J-6
Ortonville K-8
Oscoda G-8
Osseo L-7
Ossineke F-9
Otisville J-8
Otsego K-5
Otsego Lake F-7
Ottawa Lake M-8
Ovid J-7
Owosso J-8
Oxbow H-5
Oxford K-9
Ozark D-7
Painesdale B-2
Palmer C-3
Palmyra L-8
Palo J-6
Paradise C-7
Parchment K-5
Paris H-6
Parisville H-9
Parkdale G-4
Parkville L-5
Paulding C-1
Paw Paw L-5
Peck J-9
Pellston E-7
Pentwater H-4
Perkins D-4
Perrinton J-6
Perronville D-3
Perry K-7
Petersburg L-8
Petoskey E-7
Pewamo J-6

Phoenix A-2
Pickford D-7
Piconning H-8
Pierport G-4
Pierson J-6
Pigeon H-9
Pine River H-8
Pittsford L-7
Plainfield K-8
Plainwell K-5
Pleasant Ridge
  . . . . Pg. 115, D-9
Plymouth . . Pg. 115, G-4
Pointe Aux Barques H-9
Polaski F-8
Pontiac K-8
Port Hope H-10
Port Huron K-10
Port Sanilac J-10
Portage K-5
Portland J-6
Posen E-8
Poseyville H-7
Potterville K-6
Powers D-3
Prescott G-8
Princeton C-3
Prudenville G-7
Pullman K-5
Quanicassee H-8
Quimby K-6
Quincy L-6
Quinnesec D-3
Raber D-8
Ralph C-3
Ramsay B-9
Randville D-2
Ransom M-7
Rattle Run K-10
Ray L-6
Reading L-6
Reed City H-6
Reese J-8
Remus H-6
Republic C-2
Rexton D-6
Rhodes H-8
Richland K-5
Richmond K-9
Richmondville H-10
Richville J-8
Ridgeway L-8
River Rouge Pg. 115, J-9
Riverdale J-6
Rives Junction K-7
Roberts Landing . . . K-10
Rochester K-9
Rock D-4
Rockford J-6
Rockland B-1
Rockwood L-9
Rodney H-6
Rogers City E-8
Rome Center L-7
Romeo K-9
Romulus . . . Pg. 115, J-6
Roosevelt Park . . . J-4
Roscommon G-7
Rose City G-7
Roseburg J-9
Rosebush H-6
Roseville . . . Pg. 115, D-12
Rothbury H-4
Royal Oak . . Pg. 115, C-9
Rudyard D-7
Rumely C-4
Ruth H-9
Saginaw J-7
Sagola D-2
Saline L-8
Samaria M-8
Sands C-3
Sandusky J-9
Sans Souci K-10
Saranac J-6
Saugatuck K-4
Sault Ste. Marie . . . C-8
Sawyer L-4
Schaffer D-3
Schoolcraft L-5
Scottdale L-3
Scottville G-4
Sears H-6
Sebewaing H-9
Seney C-5
Sharon G-6
Shelby H-4
Shelbyville K-5
Shepherd H-7

MICHIGAN

Sherman G-5
Shingleton C-5
Shore E-6
Sidnaw C-2
Sigma F-6
Silver City A-10
Sister Lakes L-4
Six Lakes J-6
Skandia C-3
Skidway Lake G-8
Smithville G-6
Smyrna J-6
Snover J-9
Somerset L-7
Soo Junction C-6
South Boardman F-6
South Branch G-8
South Haven K-4
South Range B-1
Southfield Pg. 115, E-7
Southgate Pg. 115, K-8
Spratt F-8
Spring Lake J-5
Springport K-7
Spruce F-9
St. Clair K-10
St. Clair Shores K-9
   Vicinity Pg. 115, D-13
St. Ignace D-7
St. James D-6
St. Johns J-7
St. Louis J-7
Stager D-2
Stalwart D-7
Standish H-8
Stanton J-6
Stanwood H-6
Stephenson E-3
Sterling G-8
Sterling Hts.
   Pg. 115, C-10
Steuben C-4
Stevensville L-4
Stockbridge K-7
Stronach G-5
Strongs C-7
Sturgis L-5
Stutsmanville E-6
Sundell C-4
Sunfield K-6
Suttons Bay F-6
Swanson E-3
Swartz Creek J-8
Sylvester H-6
Tallmadge Pg. 119, B-1
Tawas City H-8
Taylor Pg. 115, K-7
Tecumseh L-8
Tekonsha L-6
Theodore D-2
Thompson D-5
Thornville J-9
Three Lakes C-2
Three Oaks L-4
Three Rivers L-5
Tiovola B-1
Tipton L-7
Tower E-7
Traunik C-4
Traverse City F-5
Trenary C-4
Trenton L-9
Triangle Ranch C-2
Trout Creek C-1
Trout Lake D-7
Troy K-9
   Vicinity Pg. 115, C-9
Turner G-8
Tustin G-6
Twin Lakes J-4
Twin Lakes B-2
Twining G-8
Ubly H-9
Union L-5
Union City L-6
Union Pier L-4
Unionville H-9
Utica K-9
Vandalia L-5
Vanderbilt F-7
Vassar J-8
Vernon K-7
Verona H-9
Vicksburg L-5
Vienna F-7
Vogel Center G-6
Vriesland K-5
Vulcan D-3
Wacousta K-7
Wadhams J-9

Wakefield B-10
Waldron M-7
Walhalla G-5
Walker Pg. 119, C-2
Walkerville H-5
Wallace E-3
Walled Lake Pg. 115, C-4
Walton G-6
Warren K-9
   Vicinity Pg. 115, D-10
Washington K-9
Waterloo K-7
Waters F-7
Watersmeet C-1
Watertown J-9
Watervliet L-4
Watson (Marquette Cty)
   D-3
Watson (Allegan Cty) K-5
Watton C-2
Waucedah D-3
Wayland K-5
Wayne Pg. 115, H-5
Webberville K-7
Wells D-4
Wellston G-5
West Branch G-7
West Olive J-5
Westland K-7
   Vicinity Pg. 115, G-5
Weston M-7
Wetmore C-4
White L-5
White Cloud H-5
White Pine A-10
White Rock H-10
Whitehall J-4
Whitney D-3
Whittemore G-8
Williamston K-7
Willis L-8
Winegars H-7
Winona B-2
Wisner H-8
Wolf Lake G-5
Wolverine E-7
Woodbury K-6
Woodhaven L-9
Woodland K-6
Wyandotte Pg. 115, K-9
Wyoming J-5
   Vicinity Pg. 119, D-3
Yale J-9
Yalmer C-4
Ypsilanti L-8
Yuma G-5
Zeeland J-5
Zilwaukee J-8

MINNESOTA

MINNESOTA
Pages 46-47
Population: 4,075,970
Capital: St. Paul
Land Area: 79,548 sq. mi.

Ada D-2
Adams L-6
Adrian L-2
Ah-gwah-ching E-4
Aitkin F-5
Akeley E-4
Albany G-4
Albert Lea L-5
Alberta G-2
Alden L-5
Alexandria G-3
Alvarado C-1
Alwood D-5
Amboy K-5
Andover H-6
Angle Inlet A-3
Angora C-7
Annandale H-5
Anoka H-6
Appleton H-2
Arden Hills Pg. 137, A-6
Argyle C-1
Arlington J-4
Ashby F-2
Askov F-7
Atwater H-4
Audubon E-2
Aurora D-7
Avoca L-2
Avon G-4
Austin L-6
Babbitt D-8
Backus E-4
Badger B-2

Bagley D-3
Ball Club D-5
Barnesville F-1
Barnum F-7
Barrett G-2
Barry G-1
Battle Lake F-3
Baudette B-4
Baxter F-4
Beardsley G-1
Beaver Bay D-9
Beaver Creek L-1
Becker H-5
Bejou D-2
Belgrade H-3
Belle Plaine J-5
Bellingham H-1
Beltrami D-1
Bemidji D-4
Bena D-5
Benedict E-4
Benson H-3
Beroun G-6
Bertha F-3
Big Falls C-5
Big Fork C-5
Big Lake H-5
Bigelow L-2
Bird Island J-4
Biwabik D-7
Blackduck D-4
Blomkest J-3
Blooming Prairie K-6
Bloomington Pg. 137, G-3
Blue Earth L-5
Bluffton F-3
Bock G-5
Borup D-2
Bovey D-5
Bowstring D-5
Boy River E-5
Boyd J-2
Braham G-6
Brainerd F-4
Branch H-6
Brandon G-3
Breckenridge F-1
Brewster L-2
Britt D-7
Brook Park G-6
Brooklyn Center
   Pg. 137, A-4
Brooklyn Park
   Pg. 137, A-3
Brooks C-2
Brookston E-7
Brooten H-3
Browerville F-4
Browns Valley G-1
Brownsdale L-6
Brownsville L-8
Brownton J-4
Bruno F-7
Buffalo H-5
Buffalo Lake J-4
Buhl D-6
Burnsville J-6
Burtrum G-4
Butterfield K-4
Buyck C-7
Byron K-6
Caledonia L-8
Callaway E-2
Cambridge H-6
Campbell F-2
Canby J-1
Cannon Falls J-6
Canyon E-7
Carlos G-3
Carlton E-7
Cass Lake D-4
Cedar Mills J-4
Centerville K-8
Ceylon L-4
Chandler K-2
Chaska J-5
Chatfield L-7
Chickamaw Beach E-4
Chisholm D-6
Clara City H-3
Claremont K-6
Clarissa F-3
Clarkfield J-2
Clarks Grove L-6
Clear Lake H-5
Clearbrook D-3
Clearwater H-5

Clementson B-4
Climax D-1
Clinton H-1
Clitherall F-3
Clontarf H-3
Cloquet E-7
Cokato H-5
Cold Spring H-4
Coleraine D-6
Cologne J-5
Columbia Heights
   Pg. 137, B-5
Comfrey K-4
Comstock E-1
Cook C-7
Coon Rapids H-6
Correll H-2
Cosmos J-4
Cottage Grove J-6
   Vicinity Pg. 137, G-10
Cotton E-7
Cottonwood J-2
Croftville D-10
Cromwell E-6
Crookston C-2
Crosby F-5
Crystal Pg. 137, B-3
Currie K-2
Cushing F-4
Cuyuna F-5
Cyrus G-2
Dakota K-8
Dalton F-2
Danube J-3
Danvers H-2
Darfur K-4
Dassel H-4
Dawson J-2
De Graff H-3
Deer River D-5
Deerwood F-5
Delano H-5
Dent F-2
Detroit Lakes E-2
Dilworth E-1
Dodge Center K-6
Donaldson B-1
Donnelly G-2
Doran F-2
Dovray K-3
Duluth E-7
Dumont G-2
Dundell L-4
Duquette F-7
Eagan Pg. 137, G-7
Eagle Bend F-3
Eagle Lake K-5
East Bethel H-6
East Grand Forks C-1
East Gull Lake F-4
Easton L-5
Echo J-3
Eden Prairie Pg. 137, G-1
Eden Valley H-4
Edgerton K-2
Edina Pg. 137, E-3
Effie C-5
Elbow Lake G-2
Eldred D-1
Elgin K-7
Elizabeth F-2
Elk River H-6
Ellendale K-6
Ellsworth L-2
Elmer E-6
Elmore L-5
Elrosa G-3
Ely C-8
Emily E-5
Erhard F-2
Ericsburg B-6
Erskine D-2
Evansville G-3
Eveleth D-7
Eyota K-7
Fairfax J-4
Faribault K-6
Fairmont L-4
Falcon Heights
   Pg. 137, C-6
Farmington J-6
Farwell G-2
Felton E-1
Fergus Falls F-2
Fertile D-2
Finland D-8
Finlayson F-6
Fisher C-1
Flom E-2
Floodwood E-6

Florence K-2
Foley G-5
Forbes D-7
Forest Lake H-6
Fort Ripley F-4
Fosston D-3
Fountain L-7
Fox Home F-2
Franklin J-3
Frazee E-2
Freeport G-4
Fridley Pg. 137, A-5
Frost L-5
Fulda K-3
Funkley C-4
Garfield G-3
Garrison F-5
Garvin K-2
Gary D-2
Gatzke B-3
Gaylord J-5
Gem Lake Pg. 137, A-9
Geneva L-6
Georgetown E-1
Gheen C-7
Gibbon J-4
Gilbert D-7
Gilman G-5
Glencoe J-5
Glenville L-6
Glenwood G-3
Gluek H-3
Glyndon E-1
Golden Valley
   Pg. 137, C-2
Gonvick D-3
Good Thunder K-5
Goodhue K-7
Goodland E-6
Goodridge C-3
Goodview K-8
Graceton B-4
Graceville G-2
Granby G-6
Grand Falls C-5
Grand Marais D-9
Grand Meadow L-7
Grand Portage C-10
Grand Rapids D-5
Granite Falls J-2
Grasston G-6
Greenbush B-2
Greenfield H-5
Grey Eagle G-4
Grove City H-4
Grygla C-3
Gully D-3
Guthrie D-4
Hackensack E-4
Hallock B-1
Halma B-2
Halstad D-1
Ham Lake H-6
Hancock H-2
Hanley Falls J-3
Hanska K-4
Harding F-5
Hardwick L-1
Harmony L-7
Harris G-6
Hastings J-6
Hawley E-2
Hayfield K-7
Hayward L-6
Hazel Run J-2
Hector J-4
Heidelberg J-5
Henderson J-5
Hendricks J-2
Hendrum D-1
Henning F-3
Herman G-2
Hermantown E-7
Heron Lake L-3
Hewitt F-3
Hibbing D-6
Hill City E-5
Hills L-1
Hilltop Pg. 137, A-5
Hinckley G-6
Hines D-4
Hitterdal E-2
Hoffman G-2
Hokah L-8
Holland K-2
Holloway H-2
Holt C-2
Holyoke F-7
Hope K-6
Hopkins Pg. 137, E-2

Houston L-8
Hovland C-10
Howard Lake H-5
Hoyt Lakes D-7
Humboldt B-1
Hutchinson J-4
Ihlen K-1
Independence H-5
Indus B-5
Inver Grove Hts.
   Pg. 137, G-8
Iona K-2
Ironton F-5
Isabella D-8
Isanti H-6
Isle F-5
Ivanhoe J-2
Jackson L-4
Jacobson E-6
Janesville K-5
Jasper K-1
Jeffers K-3
Jenkins E-4
Johnson G-2
Jordan J-5
Karlstad B-2
Kasota K-5
Kasson K-7
Keewatin D-6
Kelliher C-4
Kellogg K-7
Kelsey E-7
Kennedy B-1
Kensington G-2
Kent F-1
Kenyon K-6
Kerkhoven H-3
Kerrick F-7
Kettle River F-6
Kiester L-5
Kimball H-5
Kingston H-4
Knife River E-8
La Crescent L-8
La Prairie E-6
Lafayette J-4
Lake Benton K-2
Lake Bronson B-1
Lake City J-7
Lake Crystal K-4
Lake George D-3
Lake Henry H-4
Lake Lillian J-4
Lake Park E-2
Lake Shore F-4
Lake Wilson K-2
Lakefield L-3
Lakeville J-6
Lamberton K-3
Lancaster A-1
Landfall Pg. 137, D-10
Lanesboro L-8
Laporte E-4
Larsmont E-8
Lastrup G-5
Lauderdale Pg. 137, C-6
Le Center K-5
LeRoy L-7
LeSueur J-5
Lengby D-3
Leonard D-3
Lester Prairie J-5
Lewiston K-8
Lilydale Pg. 137, E-7
Linden Grove C-6
Lindford B-5
Lindstrom H-6
Lismore L-2
Litchfield H-4
Little Canada
   Pg. 137, B-8
Little Falls G-4
Little Fork B-5
Little Rock G-5
Lockhart D-2
Loman B-5
Long Prairie F-4
Longville E-5
Lonsdale J-5
Lowry G-2
Lucan J-3
Lutsen D-9
Luverne K-2
Lyle L-6
Lynd K-2

Magnolia L-2
Mahnomen D-2
Mahtowa F-6
Malmo F-6
Manchester L-5
Mankato K-4
Mantomedi Pg. 137, A-10
Mantorville K-7
Maple Grove Pg. 137, A-1
Maple Lake H-5
Mapleton K-5
Mapleview L-6
Maplewood Pg. 137, B-9
Marcell D-5
Margie C-5
Marietta H-1
Markham D-7
Marshall J-2
McGrath F-6
McGregor F-6
McIntosh D-2
Meadowlands E-7
Medford K-6
Meire Grove G-3
Melrose G-4
Menagha E-3
Mendota Pg. 137, F-7
Mendota Heights
   Pg. 137, F-7
Mentor D-2
Middle River B-2
Milaca G-5
Milan H-2
Millville K-2
Miltona G-3
Minneapolis J-5
   Vicinity Pg. 137, C-3
   Detailed City Pg. 255
Minneota J-2
Minnesota Lake K-5
Minnetonka Pg. 137, D-1
Mizpah C-5
Montevideo H-3
Montgomery J-5
Monticello H-5
Mora G-6
Morgan J-3
Morris G-2
Morton J-4
Motley F-4
Mound Pg. 137, D-1
Mountain Iron D-7
Mountain Lake K-3
Murdock H-3
Myrtle L-6
Nashua G-2
Nashwauk D-6
Nassau H-1
Nay-Tah-Waush D-3
Nevis E-4
New Brighton
   Pg. 137, B-5
New Hope Pg. 137, B-2
New London H-4
New Prague J-5
New Richland K-5
New Ulm K-4
New York Mills F-3
Newfolden B-2
Newport Pg. 137, F-10
Nicollet K-4
Nielsville D-1
Nimrod F-3
Nisswa F-4
Norcross G-2
North Branch H-6
North Mankato K-5
North Oaks Pg. 137, A-8
North St. Paul
   Pg. 137, B-9
Northfield J-6
Northome C-5
Northrop L-4
Norwood J-5
Noyes A-1
Oak Island A-4
Oakdale Pg. 137, C-10
Odessa H-1
Ogema E-2
Ogilvie G-5
Oklee C-2
Olivia J-3
Onamia F-4
Orleans A-1
Ormsby K-4
Oronoco K-7
Orr C-6
Ortonville H-1
Osage E-3

Osakis G-3
Oslo C-1
Ottertail F-3
Outing E-5
Owatonna K-6
Palisade E-6
Park Rapids E-3
Parkers Prairie F-3
Paynesville H-4
Pelican Rapids F-2
Pencer B-3
Pennock H-3
Perley E-1
Pierz G-5
Pine City G-6
Pine Island K-7
Pine River E-4
Pine Springs
   Pg. 137, B-10
Pinewood D-4
Pipestone K-1
Pitt B-4
Plainview K-8
Plummer C-2
Plymouth Pg. 137, B-1
Ponemah C-4
Ponsford E-3
Porter J-2
Preston L-7
Princeton G-5
Prinsburg J-3
Prior Lake J-6
Proctor E-7
Quamba G-6
Randall F-4
Randolph J-6
Raudette B-4
Ray B-6
Raymond H-3
Red Lake C-3
Red Lake Falls C-2
Red Wing J-7
Redby C-4
Redwood Falls J-3
Regal H-4
Remer E-5
Renville J-3
Rice G-5
Richfield Pg. 137, F-4
Richmond H-4
Richville F-2
Robbinsdale Pg. 137, B-3
Rochester K-7
Rock Creek G-6
Roosevelt B-4
Rose Creek L-6
Roseau B-3
Roseville Pg. 137, B-6
Ross B-2
Rothsay F-1
Round Lake L-3
Round Prairie G-4
Royalton G-4
Rush City G-6
Rushford L-8
Russell K-2
Ruthton K-2
Rutledge F-7
Sabin E-1
Sacred Heart J-3
Saint Anthony
   Pg. 137, B-6
Saint Charles K-7
Saint Clair K-5
Saint Cloud H-5
Saint Francis H-6
Saint Hilaire C-2
Saint James K-4
Saint Joseph G-4
Saint Louis Park
   Pg. 137, D-3
Saint Michael H-5
Saint Paul H-6
   Vicinity Pg. 137, D-7
   Detailed City Pg. 282
Saint Paul Park
   Pg. 137, G-10
Saint Peter K-5
Saint Vincent A-1
Salol B-3
Sanborn K-3
Sandstone G-7
Sartell G-4
Sauk Centre G-4
Sauk Rapids H-5
Saum C-4
Sawyer F-6
Scanlon E-7
Schroeder D-9
Sebeka E-3

MINNESOTA

Sedan G-3
Shakopee J-5
Shelly D-1
Sherburn L-4
Shevlin D-3
Shoreview . Pg. 137, A-7
Silver Bay D-9
Silver Lake J-4
Slayton K-2
Sleepy Eye K-4
Solway D-3
South International . B-6
South St. Paul
. . . . Pg. 137, E-9
Spicer H-4
Spring Grove L-8
Spring Lake D-5
Spring Valley L-7
Springfield K-4
Squaw Lake D-5
Staples F-4
Starbuck G-3
Stephen B-1
Stewartville K-7
Storden K-3
Strandquist B-2
Strathcona B-2
Sturgean Lake F-7
Sunberg H-3
Sunfish Lake Pg. 137, F-8
Swan River E-6
Swanville G-4
Swatara E-5
Swift B-3
Taconite D-6
Taconite Harbor . . . D-9
Talmoon D-5
Tamarack F-6
Taunton J-2
Taylors Falls H-7
Tenney F-1
Tenstrike D-4
Terrace H-3
Thief River Falls . . . C-2
Togo C-6
Tommald F-5
Toopi L-7
Tower C-7
Tracy K-3
Trail C-3
Trimont L-4
Trosky K-2
Truman L-4
Turtle River D-4
Twig E-7
Twin Lakes L-5
Twin Valley D-2
Two Harbors E-8
Tyler K-2
Ulen E-2
Underwood F-2
Vadnais Hts. Pg. 137, A-8
Verdi K-1
Vergas E-2
Verndale F-4
Vesta J-3
Viking C-2
Villard G-3
Vining F-3
Viola K-7
Virginia D-7
Wabasha K-7
Wabasso J-3
Waconia J-5
Wadena F-3
Wahkon F-5
Waite Park H-4
Walker E-4
Walnut Grove K-3
Waltham L-6
Wanamingo K-6
Warba E-6
Warraska B-3
Warren C-1
Warroad B-3
Waseca K-5
Waskish C-4
Watertown J-5
Waterville K-5
Watkins H-4
Watson H-2
Waubun E-2
Wawina E-6
Welcome L-4
Wells L-5
West Concord K-6
West St. Paul
. . . . Pg. 137, E-8
Westbrook K-3
Wheaton G-1

Whipholt E-4
White Bear Lake
. . . . Pg. 137, A-9
White Earth E-2
Wilder L-3
Willernie . . Pg. 137, B-10
Williams B-4
Willmar H-4
Willow River F-6
Wilton D-3
Windom K-3
Winger D-2
Winnebago L-5
Winona K-8
Winthrop J-4
Winton C-8
Wirt D-5
Wolf Lake E-3
Wolverton F-1
Woodbury J-6
. . . . Vicinity . Pg. 137, E-10
Woodland G-6
Worthington L-3
Wrenshall F-7
Wyoming H-6
Zemple D-5
Zim D-7
Zimmerman H-6
Zumbro Falls K-7
Zumbrota K-7

MISSISSIPPI
Page 50
Population: 2,520,638
Capital: Jackson
Land Area: 47,233 sq. mi.

Abbeville B-5
Aberdeen C-6
Ackerman D-5
Alcorn G-2
Algoma B-5
Alligator C-3
Amory C-6
Anguilla E-3
Arcola D-3
Arkabutla A-4
Artesia D-6
Ashland A-5
Askew B-3
Avalon C-4
Avon D-2
Bailey F-6
Baird D-3
Baldwyn B-6
Banner B-5
Bassfield H-4
Batesville B-4
Baxterville H-4
Bay Saint Louis . . . K-5
Bay Springs G-5
Beaumont H-6
Beauregard G-3
Becker C-6
Belden B-6
Belen B-3
Bellefontaine C-5
Belmont A-6
Belzoni D-3
Benoit D-2
Benton E-4
Bentonia E-3
Beulah C-2
Big Creek C-4
Bigbee Valley D-6
Biloxi K-6
Blue Mountain A-5
Bogue Chitto H-3
Bolton F-3
Booneville A-6
Boyle C-3
Brandon F-4
Braxton G-4
Brookhaven H-3
Brooklyn H-5
Brooksville D-6
Bruce C-5
Buckatunna G-6
Bude H-3
Burnsville A-6
Byhalia A-4
Caledonia C-6
Calhoun City C-5
Call Town J-6
Camden E-4
Canton E-4
Carlisle G-3
Carpenter G-3
Carriere J-5

Carrollton D-4
Carson H-4
Carthage E-4
Cary E-3
Cascilla C-4
Cedarbluff C-5
Centreville J-3
Charleston C-4
Chatawa J-4
Chatham E-2
Chunky F-6
Church Hill G-2
Clara G-6
Clarksdale B-3
Cleveland C-3
Clifftonville D-6
Clinton F-3
. . . . Vicinity . Pg. 123, C-1
Coahoma B-3
Coffeeville C-4
Coila D-4
Coldwater A-4
Collins G-5
Collinsville E-6
Columbia H-4
Columbus C-6
Como B-4
Conehatta F-5
Corinth A-6
Courtland B-4
Crawford D-6
Crenshaw B-3
Crosby H-2
Cross Roads A-6
Crowder B-3
Crystal Springs . . . G-3
D'Lo G-4
Daleville E-6
Darling B-3
Darlove D-3
DeKalb D-5
Decatur F-5
Dennis A-6
Derma C-5
Doddsville D-3
Dorsey B-6
Drew C-3
Dublin C-3
Duck Hill C-4
Dumas A-5
Duncan C-3
Dundee B-3
Durant D-4
Eastabuchie H-5
Ebenezer E-4
Ecru B-5
Eden E-4
Edinburg E-5
Edwards F-3
Electric Mills E-6
Elizabeth D-3
Ellisville G-5
Enid B-4
Enterprise F-6
Ethel D-5
Etta B-5
Eupora D-5
Falcon B-3
Falkner A-5
Fannin F-4
Fayette G-2
Fitler E-2
Flora F-3
Florence F-4
. . . . Vicinity . Pg. 123, G-4
Flowood . . Pg. 123, D-5
Forest F-5
Forkville F-5
Fort Adams H-2
Foxworth H-4
French Camp D-5
Friar's Point B-3
Fruitland Park A-4
Fulton B-6
Futheyville C-4
Gallman G-3
Gattman C-6
Gautier K-6
Georgetown G-3
Gillsburg J-3
Glen A-6
Glen Allan E-2
Glendora C-3
Gloster H-2
Golden B-6
Goodman E-4
Gore Springs C-4
Grace E-3
Grand Gulf G-2
Greenville D-2

Greenwood D-4
Grenada C-4
Gulfport K-6
Gunnison C-2
Guntown B-6
Hamilton C-6
Harperville F-5
Harriston G-2
Harrisville G-4
Hatley B-6
Hattiesburg H-5
Hazlehurst G-3
Heidelberg G-6
Helena B-3
Hermanville G-3
Hernando A-4
Hickory F-5
Hickory Flat A-5
Hilhouse C-2
Hillsboro F-5
Hiwannee G-6
Holcomb C-4
Hollandale D-3
Holly Bluff E-3
Holly Springs A-5
Homewood F-5
Horn A-3
Houston C-5
Hurley J-6
Independence A-4
Indianola D-3
Inverness D-3
Iuka A-6
Isola D-3
Itta Bena D-3
Jackson F-4
. . . . Vicinity . . . . Pg. 123
Jayess H-4
Johnstons Station . . H-4
Jonestown B-3
Kewanee F-6
Kilmichael D-4
Kiln K-5
Kokomo H-4
Kosciusko E-5
Lafayette Springs . . B-5
Lake F-5
Lake View . . Pg. 134, G-2
Lakeshore K-5
Lambert B-3
Lauderdale E-6
Laurel G-5
Lawrence F-5
LeFlore C-4
Leaf H-6
Leakesville H-6
Leland D-3
Lena E-4
Lessley H-2
Lexington D-4
Liberty H-3
Little Rock F-5
Long Beach K-5
Lorman G-2
Louin F-5
Louise E-3
Louisville D-5
Lucedale J-6
Lucien H-3
Ludlow F-4
Lula B-3
Lumberton J-5
Lyman K-5
Lyon B-3
Maben D-5
Macon D-6
Madden E-5
Madison F-4
. . . . Vicinity . Pg. 123, A-5
Magee G-4
Magnolia H-3
Mantachie B-6
Mantee C-5
Marietta B-6
Marion F-6
Marks B-3
Martinsville G-3
Mathiston D-5
McAdams E-4
McCall Creek H-3
McCarley D-4
McComb H-3
McCondy C-5
McCool D-5
McHenry J-5
McLain H-6
McNeill J-5
Meadville H-3
Mendenhall G-4
Meridian F-6

Merigold C-3
Metcalfe D-2
Michigan City A-5
Mineral Wells A-4
. . . . Vicinity . Pg. 134, G-7
Minter City C-3
Mize G-5
Money C-3
Monticello H-4
Montpelier C-5
Montrose F-5
Mooreville B-6
Moorhead D-3
Morgan City D-3
Morgantown H-4
Morton F-4
Moselle H-5
Moss G-5
Moss Point K-6
Mound Bayou C-3
Mount Olive G-5
Myrtle A-5
Natchez H-2
Necaise J-5
Nesbit A-3
Neshoba E-5
Nettleton B-6
New Albany B-5
New Augusta H-5
New Hebron G-4
New Houlka C-5
New Site A-6
Newton F-5
Nicholson K-5
Nitta Yuma E-3
North Carrollton . . . D-4
Noxapater E-5
Oak Vale H-4
Oakland C-4
Ocean Springs K-6
Ofahoma E-4
Okolona B-6
Olive Branch A-4
Oma G-4
Onward E-3
Osyka J-3
Oxford B-4
Pace C-2
Pachuta F-6
Paden A-6
Panther Burn E-3
Parchman C-3
Paris B-4
Pascagoula K-7
Pass Christian K-5
Paulding F-5
Paulette D-6
Pearl F-4
. . . . Vicinity . Pg. 123, E-5
Pearlington K-4
Pelahatchie F-4
Perkinston J-5
Petal H-5
Pheba C-5
Philadelphia E-5
Philipp C-3
Picayune K-5
Pickens E-4
Pinkneyville J-2
Pinola G-4
Plantersville B-6
Plum Point Pg. 134, G-5
Pocahontas F-3
Pond J-2
Pontotoc B-5
Pope B-4
Poplarville J-5
Port Gibson G-2
Porterville E-6
Potts Camp A-5
Prairie C-6
Prairie Point D-6
Prentiss G-4
Preston E-6
Puckett F-4
Pulaski F-5
Purvis H-5
Quentin H-3
Quitman F-6
Raleigh G-5
Randolph B-5
Raymond F-3
Red Banks A-4
Redwood F-3
Reform D-5
Rena Lara B-2
Richland F-4
. . . . Vicinity . Pg. 123, D-5
Richton H-6
Ridgecrest H-2

Ridgeland F-4
. . . . Vicinity . Pg. 123, A-4
Rienzi A-6
Ripley A-5
Robinsonville A-3
Rolling Fork E-3
Rome C-3
Rosedale C-2
Roxie H-2
Ruleville C-3
Runnelstown H-6
Ruth H-3
Sallis E-4
Saltillo B-6
Sandersville G-6
Sandhill F-4
Sandy Hook H-5
Sanford H-5
Sarah B-3
Sardis B-4
Sarepta A-4
Satartia E-3
Saucier J-5
Savage D-2
Schlater D-3
Scobey C-3
Scooba E-6
Scott D-2
Sebastopol E-5
Seminary G-5
Senatobia A-4
Sessums D-6
Seypal Lake F-4
Shannon B-6
Sharon E-4
Shaw D-2
Shelby C-3
Sherard B-3
Sherman B-6
Shivers G-4
Shubuta G-6
Shuqualak D-6
Sibley H-2
Sidon D-4
Silver City E-3
Silver Creek G-4
Skene C-2
Slate Springs C-5
Slayden A-4
Sledge B-3
Smithdale H-3
Smithville B-6
Sontag G-4
Soso G-5
Southhaven A-3
Star F-4
Starkville D-6
State Line H-6
Steens D-6
Stewart D-5
Stoneville D-2
Stonewall F-6
Stovall B-3
Stringer G-5
Sturgis D-5
Summit H-3
Sumner C-3
Sumrall H-5
Sunflower D-3
Suqualena F-5
Swan Lake D-3
Swiftown D-3
Sylvarena G-5
Taylor B-4
Taylorsville G-5
Tchula D-4
Terry G-3
Thaxton B-5
Thomastown E-4
Thorn C-5
Thornton D-3
Thyatria A-4
Tie Plant C-4
Tillatoba C-4
Tinsley E-3
Tiplersville A-5
Tippo C-4
Tishomingo A-6
Toccopola B-5
Tomnolen D-5
Toomsuba F-6
Trebloc C-5
Tremont B-6
Tula B-5
Tunica A-3
Tupelo B-5
Tutwiler C-3
Tylertown H-4
Union E-5
Union Church G-3

University B-4
Utica G-3
Vaiden D-4
Valley Park E-3
Van Vleet C-5
Vance C-3
Vancleave J-6
Vardaman C-5
Vaughan E-4
Verona B-5
Vicksburg F-3
Victoria A-4
Vossburg G-6
Wade J-6
Walls A-3
Walnut A-5
Walnut Grove E-5
Walthall C-5
Washington H-2
Water Valley B-4
Waterford A-4
Waveland K-5
Waynesboro G-6
Wayside D-2
Weathersby G-4
Webb C-3
Weir D-5
Wenasoga A-6
Wesson G-3
West Gulfport J-5
West Point C-6
Wheeler A-6
Whitfield F-4
Wiggins J-6
Winona D-4
Winstonville C-3
Woodland C-5
Woodville J-2
Yazoo City E-3

MISSOURI
Pages 48-49
Population: 4,916,686
Capital: Jefferson City
Land Area: 68,945 sq. mi.

Adair D-5
Adrian H-2
Advance K-9
Agency F-2
Albany D-2
Alexandria D-7
Allendale D-3
Alma G-4
Altamont E-3
Alton L-7
Amoret H-2
Anderson L-2
Annapolis K-8
Anniston K-10
Appleton City H-3
Arab K-9
Arbela D-6
Arbyrd M-9
Arcadia J-8
Archie H-2
Arcola J-3
Arkoe E-2
Arnold H-8
. . . . Vicinity . Pg. 158, K-3
Arroll K-6
Arrow Rock G-4
Asbury K-2
Ash Grove K-3
Ashland G-5
Ashley F-7
Athens D-6
Atlanta E-5
Aullville G-3
Aurora K-3
Auxvasse G-6
Ava K-5
Avalon F-4
Avondale . . Pg. 125, E-4
Bado K-6
Bakersfield L-6
Ballard H-3
Bardley L-7
Baring E-6
Barnard E-2
Battlefield K-4
Bay H-7
Beaufort H-7
Bel Nor . . . Pg. 158, C-4
Bel Ridge . Pg. 158, C-3
Bell City K-10
Bella Villa . Pg. 158, H-4
Bellair G-5
Belle H-6

Bellefontaine Neighbors
. . . . Pg. 158, B-5
Bellerive . Pg. 158, C-4
Belton G-2
Bem H-7
Bendavis K-5
Bennett Springs . . . J-5
Benton K-10
Berkeley . . Pg. 158, B-3
Bernie L-9
Bertrand K-10
Bethany D-3
Bethel E-6
Beulah J-6
Beverly Hills Pg. 158, D-4
Bevier E-5
Bible Grove D-6
Bigelow E-1
Bigspring G-7
Birch Tree K-7
Birmingham Pg. 125, D-5
Bismark J-8
Bixby J-7
Black Jack . Pg. 158, A-5
Blackburn G-4
Blodgett K-10
Bloomfield K-9
Blue Eye L-4
Blue Springs G-3
Blue Summit Pg. 125, F-5
Blythedale D-3
Bogard F-3
Bolckow E-2
Bolivar J-4
Bonne Terre J-8
Boonesboro G-5
Boonville G-4
Bosworth F-4
Bourbon H-7
Bowling Green F-7
Boynton D-4
Bradleyville L-4
Branson L-4
Braymer F-3
Brazeau J-10
Breckenridge E-3
Breckenridge Hills
. . . . Pg. 158, C-3
Brentwood . Pg. 158, F-3
Briar L-8
Bridgeton . Pg. 158, B-2
Brighton K-4
Brimson E-3
Brinktown H-6
Bronaugh J-2
Brookfield F-4
Broseley L-9
Brownbranch L-5
Browning E-4
Brumley H-5
Bruner K-5
Brunswick F-4
Buckhorn J-6
Bucklin E-5
Buckner G-3
Buffalo J-4
Bunker J-7
Burlington Jct. D-1
Butler H-2
Cabool K-6
Cainsville D-3
Cairo F-5
California G-5
Callao E-5
Calverton Park
. . . . Pg. 158, B-4
Calwood G-6
Camdenton H-5
Cameron E-3
Campbell L-9
Canton E-7
Cape Girardeau . . . K-9
Caplinger Mills J-3
Cardwell M-9
Carrington G-6
Carrollton F-3
Carsonville . Pg. 158, C-4
Carthage K-2
Caruthersville M-10
Cascade K-9
Cassville L-3
Catherine Place . . . J-9
Caulfield L-6
Center F-7
Centerville J-8
Centralia F-6
Chadwick L-4
Chaffee K-10
Chain-O-Lakes L-3
Chamois G-6

MISSOURI

MISSOURI

MONTANA

Champ . . . . Pg. 158, B-1
Charlack . . . . Pg. 158, C-3
Charleston K-10
Cherryville J-7
Chilhowee G-3
Chillicothe E-4
Chula E-4
Clarence E-6
Clarksdale E-2
Clarksville F-7
Clarkton L-9
Claycomo . . Pg. 125, D-5
Clayton . . . . Pg. 158, E-3
Clearmont D-1
Clever K-4
Clifton City G-4
Climax Springs H-4
Clinton H-3
Clyde D-2
Coal H-4
Coatsville D-5
Coldwater K-8
Cole Camp H-4
Collins J-3
Coloma F-4
Columbia G-3
Concordia G-3
Connelsville D-5
Conway J-5
Cook Station J-7
Cool Valley . Pg. 158, C-4
Corning D-1
Corridon K-7
Couch L-7
Country Club Hills
. . . . Pg. 158, C-5
County Life Acres
. . . . Pg. 158, E-1
Craig E-1
Crane K-4
Crestwood . . Pg. 158, G-2
Creve Coeur Pg. 158, E-1
Crocker J-6
Cross Timbers H-4
Crystal Lake Park
. . . . Pg. 158, E-1
Cuba H-7
Curryville F-7
Cyrene F-7
Dadeville J-3
De Soto H-8
Dearborn F-2
Deerfield J-2
Defiance G-8
Dellwood . . Pg. 158, B-4
Denver D-3
Des Arc K-8
Des Peres . Pg. 158, F-1
Desloge J-8
Dexter K-9
Diamond K-2
Dixon H-6
Doe Run J-8
Dongola K-9
Doniphan L-8
Doolittle J-6
Dorena L-10
Downing D-5
Drexel H-2
Drury K-5
Duenweg K-2
Duncans Bridge F-5
Dunlap E-4
Dunnegan J-4
Durham E-6
Dutchtown K-9
Eagleville D-3
East Prairie L-10
Edgar Springs J-6
Edgerton F-2
Edina E-6
Edinburg E-3
Edmundson Pg. 158, B-3
El Dorado Springs . . . J-3
Eldon H-4
Eldridge J-5
Elkland J-4
Ellington K-7
Ellsinore K-8
Elmira F-3
Elmo D-1
Elsberry F-8
Elwood E-2
Emden E-6
Eminence K-7
Eolia F-7
Essex L-9
Ethel E-5
Eudora J-4
Eunice K-6

Eureka H-8
Everton K-3
Ewing E-6
Excello F-5
Excelsior Springs . . . F-2
Exeter L-3
Fagus L-9
Fair Grove K-4
Fair Play J-4
Fairdealing L-8
Fairfax D-1
Fairmont D-6
Fairmount G-3
Fairview K-6
Farber F-6
Farley F-2
Farmersville E-4
Farmington J-9
Farrar J-9
Faucett F-2
Fayette F-5
Fayetteville G-3
Fenton . . . . Pg. 158, H-1
Ferguson . . . Pg. 158, B-4
Ferrelview . . Pg. 125, A-2
Festus H-8
Filley J-3
Fillmore E-2
Fisk L-9
Flordell Hills Pg. 158, C-5
Florence G-4
Florida F-6
Florissant . Pg. 158, A-4
Foley G-8
Forbes E-1
Fordland K-4
Forest City E-1
Forest Green F-5
Foristell G-8
Forsyth L-4
Fortescue E-1
Fortuna H-5
Fountain Grove E-4
Frankford F-7
Fredericktown J-9
Freeburg H-6
Fremont K-7
French Village J-9
Frontenac . . Pg. 158, E-2
Fulton G-6
Gainesville L-5
Galena L-3
Gallatin E-3
Galt E-4
Garden City H-3
Garwood K-8
Gatewood L-7
Gentry D-2
Gerald H-7
Gilliam F-4
Gladden J-7
Gladstone . . Pg. 125, C-4
Glasgow F-5
Glen Echo Park
. . . . Pg. 158, C-4
Glenaire . . Pg. 125, C-5
Glendale . . Pg. 158, F-2
Glenwood D-5
Glover J-8
Golden City K-3
Goodman L-2
Gower F-2
Graham D-1
Grain Valley G-3
Granby K-3
Grand Pass F-4
Grandin L-8
Granger D-6
Grant City D-2
Grantwood Village
. . . . Pg. 158, G-3
Granville F-6
Grassy K-9
Gray Summit H-8
Graysville D-5
Green City D-4
Green Ridge G-4
Greencastle D-5
Greendale . . Pg. 158, D-4
Greenfield K-3
Greensburg D-6
Greentop D-5
Greenville K-8
Greer L-7
Grovespring K-5
Halfway J-4
Hallsville F-6
Halltown K-3
Hamilton E-3
Hanley Hills Pg. 158, D-4
Hannibal E-7

Hardin F-3
Harris D-4
Harrisburg G-5
Harrisonville G-3
Hartford D-5
Hartville K-5
Hartwell H-3
Harwood J-3
Hatfield D-3
Hawk Point G-7
Hayti M-9
Hayti Heights M-10
Hazelwood . Pg. 158, A-3
Helena E-2
Hermann G-7
Hermitage J-4
Higbee F-5
Higginsville G-3
High Point H-5
Hillsboro H-8
Hillsdale . . Pg. 158, D-4
Hinton G-5
Hitt D-5
Holcomb L-9
Holden G-3
Hollister L-4
Holt F-2
Holts Summit G-6
Hopkins D-2
Hornersville M-9
House Springs H-8
Houston K-6
Houston Lake
. . . . Pg. 125, D-2
Houstonia G-4
Humansville J-4
Humphreys E-4
Hunter K-7
Huntleigh . . Pg. 158, F-2
Huntsdale G-5
Huntsville F-5
Hurdland E-6
Hurricane Deck H-5
Iberia H-6
Idlewild K-9
Independence G-3
Vicinity . . . . Pg. 125, F-6
Ironton J-8
Jackson J-10
Jacksonville F-5
Jameson E-3
Jamesport E-3
Jamestown G-5
Jane L-2
Jasper K-2
Jefferson City H-5
Jenkins L-3
Jennings G-9
Vicinity . . . . Pg. 158, C-5
Jerico Springs J-3
Joplin K-2
Kahoka D-6
Kansas City G-2
Vicinity . . . . . Pg. 125
Detailed City . . Pg. 241
Kearney F-2
Kendricktown K-3
Kennett M-9
Kewanee L-10
Keytesville F-5
Kidder E-3
Kimberling City L-4
King City E-2
Kingston F-3
Kinloch . . . . Pg. 158, B-3
Kirksville E-5
Kirkwood . . . Pg. 158, F-2
Kliever G-5
Knob Noster G-3
Knox City E-6
Knoxville F-3
Koshkonong L-6
La Grange E-7
La Plata E-5
La Tour G-3
LaBelle E-6
LaMonte G-4
Laddonia F-6
Ladue . . . . Pg. 158, E-2
Lake Lotawana G-2
Lake Saint Louis . . . G-8
Lake Spring J-7
Lake Waukomis
. . . . Pg. 125, C-2
Lakenan E-6
Lakeshire . Pg. 158, H-3
Lamar J-3
Lancaster D-5
Lanton L-6
Lathrop F-2
Latty J-8

Lawson F-3
Leadwood J-8
Leasburg H-7
Lebanon J-5
Lee's Summit
. . . . Pg. 125, K-6
Leeper K-8
Leeton G-3
Lemons D-4
Lentner F-6
Leonard E-5
Lewistown E-6
Lexington F-3
Liberal J-2
Liberty F-2
Vicinity . . . Pg. 125, B-6
Licking J-6
Lilbourn L-10
Lincoln H-4
Linn H-6
Linneus E-4
Lockwood K-3
Lone Jack G-3
Long Lane J-5
Longrun L-5
Longwood G-4
Louisiana F-7
Lowry City H-3
Ludlow F-4
Luray D-6
Macks Creek J-5
Macon F-5
Madison F-6
Malden L-9
Manchester G-8
Vicinity . . . Pg. 158, G-1
Manes K-5
Mansfield K-5
Maplewood . Pg. 158, F-3
Marble Hills K-9
Marceline E-4
March J-4
Marionville K-4
Marlborough Pg. 158, G-3
Marshall F-4
Marshfield K-5
Marthasville G-8
Martinsburg G-6
Maryland Heights
. . . . Pg. 158, C-1
Maryville D-1
Matthews L-10
Maysville E-2
McBaine G-5
McFall E-2
Melbourne H-2
Memphis D-5
Mercer D-4
Mexico F-6
Miami F-4
Miami Station F-4
Middle Grove F-5
Midway G-5
Milan E-4
Milford J-3
Mill Grove D-4
Millard E-5
Miller K-3
Millersburg G-6
Milo J-2
Mineola G-7
Miner K-10
Mirabile F-3
Moberly F-5
Mokane G-6
Moline Acres Pg. 158, B-5
Monett K-3
Monroe City F-6
Montevallo J-3
Montgomery City . . . G-7
Monticello E-6
Montreal J-5
Montrose H-3
Moody L-6
Morley K-10
Morrisville J-4
Mosby . . . . Pg. 125, A-7
Mound City E-1
Moundville J-2
Mount Moriah D-3
Mount Vernon K-3
Mount Zion K-5
Mountain Grove K-5
Mountain View K-7
Myrtle L-7
Mystic E-4
Nashville K-2
Naylor L-8
Nebo J-5
Neelyville L-8

Neosho L-2
Nevada J-2
New Bloomfield G-6
New Boston E-4
New Florence G-7
New Franklin G-5
New Hartford F-7
New Haven G-7
New Hope F-8
New London F-7
New Madrid L-10
New Market F-2
New Melle G-7
New Point E-1
Newburg J-6
Niangua K-5
Nixa K-4
Noel L-2
Norborne F-3
Normandy . . Pg. 158, C-4
North Kansas City
. . . . Pg. 125, E-3
Northmoor . Pg. 125, D-3
Northview K-4
Northwoods Pg. 158, C-4
Norwood Court
. . . . Pg. 158, C-4
Noser Mill H-7
Novelty E-5
Novinger E-5
O'Fallon G-8
Oak Grove G-3
Oak Hill H-7
Oakland . . Pg. 158, G-2
Oaks . . . . . Pg. 125, D-3
Oakview . . . Pg. 125, C-3
Oakville . . . Pg. 158, K-4
Oakwood . . Pg. 125, D-4
Oakwood Park
. . . . Pg. 125, D-4
Ocie L-5
Odessa G-3
Oermann H-8
Olivette . . . Pg. 158, D-3
Olympian Village . . . H-8
Oran K-10
Orchard Farm G-8
Oregon E-1
Orrick F-3
Osage Beach H-5
Osceola H-3
Osgood E-4
Oskaloosa J-2
Otto H-8
Overland . . Pg. 158, D-3
Owensville H-6
Ozark K-4
Pacific H-8
Pagedale . . Pg. 158, D-4
Palmyra E-7
Paris F-6
Parkville . . Pg. 125, D-2
Parma L-9
Pasadena Hills
. . . . Pg. 158, C-4
Pasadena Park
. . . . Pg. 158, C-4
Passaio H-2
Patton J-9
Pattonsburg E-2
Peace Valley L-6
Peach Orchard L-9
Peculiar G-2
Pennsboro K-3
Perrin E-2
Perry F-6
Perryville J-9
Pevely H-8
Phelps K-3
Philadelphia E-6
Phillipsburg J-5
Piedmont K-8
Pierce City K-3
Pilot Grove G-4
Pilot Knob J-8
Pine Lawn . Pg. 158, D-4
Pineville L-2
Plad J-4
Plato J-6
Platte Woods
. . . . Pg. 125, C-2
Plattsburg F-2
Pleasant Green G-5
Pleasant Valley
. . . . Pg. 125, C-5
Plevna E-6
Pocahontas J-9
Polk J-4
Pollock D-4
Polo F-3

Pomona L-6
Poplar Bluff L-8
Portageville L-10
Potosi J-8
Prairie Hill F-5
Prairie Home G-5
Preston J-4
Princeton D-4
Protem L-5
Purdin E-4
Purdy L-3
Puxico K-9
Queen City D-5
Quincy H-4
Qulin L-9
Racine K-2
Randolph . . Pg. 125, D-4
Ravanna D-4
Ravenwood D-2
Raymondville K-6
Raymore G-2
Raytown . . . Pg. 125, H-5
Rea E-2
Redford K-8
Reeds Spring L-4
Regal F-3
Reger E-4
Renick F-5
Rensselaer F-7
Republic K-4
Reynolds K-8
Rhineland G-7
Rich Hill H-2
Richland J-5
Richmond F-3
Richmond Heights
. . . . Pg. 158, E-3
Ridgedale L-4
Ridgeway D-3
Risco L-9
Riverside . . Pg. 125, D-2
Riverton L-7
Riverview . . Pg. 158, B-6
Rock Hill . . Pg. 158, F-2
Rock Port D-1
Rockville H-3
Rocky Comfort L-3
Rogersville K-4
Rolla J-6
Romance L-5
Rombauer K-8
Rosati H-7
Rosebud H-7
Rosendale E-2
Rothville F-4
Round Spring K-7
Rover L-7
Rushville F-1
Saint Ann . . Pg. 158, C-2
Saint Charles G-8
Vicinity . . . Pg. 158, A-1
Saint Clair H-8
Saint Clement F-7
Saint George
. . . . Pg. 158, H-4
Saint James H-6
Saint John . Pg. 158, C-3
Saint Joseph E-2
Saint Louis G-8
Vicinity . . . Pg. 158
Detailed City . . Pg. 281
Saint Marys J-9
Saint Patrick E-7
Saint Robert J-6
Sainte Genevieve . . . H-8
Salem J-7
Saline D-3
Salisbury F-5
Sandy Hook G-5
Santa Fe F-6
Sarcoxie K-3
Savannah E-2
Scott City K-10
Sedalia G-4
Sedgewickville J-9
Seligman L-3
Senath M-9
Seneca L-2
Seymour K-5
Shannondale F-5
Shelbina E-6
Shelbyville E-6
Sheldon J-3
Sheridan D-2
Shirley J-7
Shrewsbury Pg. 158, F-3
Sikeston K-10
Silva K-8
Silver Lake J-9
Simmons K-6

Skidmore D-1
Slater F-4
Sleeper J-5
Sligo J-7
Smithton G-4
Smithville F-2
South Fork L-6
South Gifford E-5
South Lineville D-4
Southwest City L-2
Sparta K-4
Spickard D-4
Spokane L-4
Springfield K-4
Squires L-5
Stanberry D-3
State Line M-9
Steele M-9
Steelville J-7
Stockton J-3
Stoutsville F-6
Stover H-5
Strafford K-4
Strasburg G-3
Sturgeon F-5
Sugar Creek Pg. 125, E-5
Sullivan H-7
Summersville K-7
Sumner F-4
Sunset Hills Pg. 158, H-2
Sweet Springs G-4
Sycamore L-6
Sycamore Hills
. . . . Pg. 158, C-3
Tarkio D-1
Tebbetts G-6
Thayer L-7
Theodosia L-5
Thomas Hill F-5
Thomasville L-6
Thompson F-6
Thornfield L-5
Tiffin J-3
Tina F-4
Tindall E-4
Tipton G-5
Town & Country
. . . . Pg. 158, F-1
Townley L-9
Trenton E-4
Troy G-8
Truesdale G-7
Truxton G-7
Tunas J-4
Turney F-2
Tuscumbia H-5
Tyrone K-6
Union H-7
Union Star E-2
Unionville D-4
Unity Village Pg. 125, J-6
University City
. . . . Pg. 158, D-3
Uplands Park
. . . . Pg. 158, D-4
Urich H-3
Utica E-3
Van Buren K-8
Vandalia F-7
Vanzant K-6
Velda City . . Pg. 158, D-4
Velda Village Hills
. . . . Pg. 158, D-4
Versailles H-5
Viburnum J-7
Vichy H-6
Vienna H-6
Vinita Park . Pg. 158, D-3
Vinita Terrace
. . . . Pg. 158, D-3
Vulcan K-8
Wainwright G-6
Walnut Grove K-4
Wardsville H-6
Warren E-6
Warrensburg G-3
Warrenton G-7
Warsaw H-4
Warson Woods
. . . . Pg. 158, F-2
Washington G-7
Wasola L-5
Waverly F-4
Wayland D-6
Waynesville J-6
Weatherby Lake
. . . . Pg. 125, C-2
Weaubleau J-4
Webb City K-2
Weber Hill H-8

Webster Groves
. . . . Pg. 158, F-3
Wellston . . . Pg. 158, D-4
Wellsville G-7
Wentworth K-3
West Plains L-6
Westboro D-1
Weston F-2
Westphalia H-6
White Oak L-9
Wilbur Park Pg. 158, G-4
Wilcox D-2
Willard K-4
Williamsburg G-6
Williamsville K-8
Willow Springs L-6
Wilson City K-10
Windsor H-4
Winfield G-8
Winigan E-5
Winona K-7
Winston E-3
Winthrop F-1
Woodlawn F-6
Woods Heights F-3
Woodson Terrace
. . . . Pg. 158, C-3
Wooldridge G-5
Worth D-2
Wyaconda D-6
Yarrow E-5
Yount J-9
Yukon K-6
Zalma K-9

MONTANA
Page 51
Population: 786,690
Capital: Helena
Land Area: 145,398 sq.mi.

Absarokee E-6
Acton E-7
Alberton D-2
Alder E-4
Alzada D-10
Anaconda E-3
Angela D-8
Antelope B-10
Arlee D-2
Ashland E-8
Augusta C-4
Avon D-3
Babb B-3
Bainville B-10
Baker D-10
Basin E-4
Bearcreek F-6
Belfry F-6
Belgrade E-5
Belt C-5
Biddle E-9
Big Fork C-2
Big Sandy C-5
Big Sky E-4
Big Timber E-6
Bighorn E-7
Billings E-7
Birney E-8
Black Eagle C-5
Blackfoot B-3
Bloomfield C-9
Bonner D-2
Boulder E-4
Box Elder F-4
Bozeman E-5
Brady C-4
Bridger F-6
Broadus E-9
Broadview E-6
Brockton C-9
Brockway C-9
Browning B-3
Busby E-8
Butte E-3
Bynum C-4
Cameron F-4
Canyon Creek D-4
Capitol D-10
Carter C-5
Cartersville D-8
Cascade C-4
Checkerboard D-5
Chester F-4
Chico Hot Springs . . . F-5
Chinook B-6
Choteau C-4
Christina C-6
Churchill E-4

MONTANA

Circle — C-9
Cleveland — C-6
Clinton — D-2
Clyde Park — E-5
Coffee Creek — C-5
Cohagen — D-8
Colstrip — E-8
Columbia Falls — B-2
Columbus — E-6
Conner — E-2
Conrad — C-4
Cooke City — F-6
Corvallis — D-2
Craig — D-4
Crane — C-10
Crow Agency — E-7
Culbertson — B-9
Custer — E-7
Cut Bank — B-4
Darby — E-2
DeBorgia — C-1
Dean — E-6
Decker — F-8
Deer Lodge — D-3
Dell — F-3
Denton — C-5
Dillon — E-3
Divide — E-3
Dixon — C-2
Dodson — B-7
Drummond — D-3
Dupuyer — C-4
Dutton — C-4
East Glacier Park — B-3
East Helena — D-4
Edgar — E-7
Ekalaka — D-10
Elliston — D-3
Elmo — C-2
Emigrant — E-5
Ennis — E-4
Ethridge — B-4
Eureka — B-2
Fairfield — C-4
Fairview — C-10
Fallon — D-9
Flatwillow — D-7
Flaxville — B-9
Florence — D-2
Ford — E-9
Forestgrove — D-6
Forsyth — E-8
Fort Belknap Agency — C-6
Fort Benton — C-5
Fort Peck — C-8
Fort Shaw — C-4
Fortine — B-2
Frenchtown — D-2
Froid — B-9
Fromberg — E-6
Galen — D-3
Gallatin Gateway — E-4
Gardiner — F-5
Garneill — D-6
Garrison — D-3
Garyowen — E-7
Geraldine — C-5
Geyser — C-5
Glasgow — C-8
Glen — E-3
Glendive — D-10
Grant — F-3
Grantsdale — D-2
Grassrange — D-6
Great Falls — C-4
Hall — D-3
Hamilton — D-2
Hammond — D-10
Happy's Inn — C-1
Hardin — E-7
Harlem — B-6
Harlowton — D-6
Harrison — E-4
Hathaway — D-9
Havre — B-6
Helena — D-3
Helmville — D-3
Heron — C-1
Hilger — D-6
Hingham — F-4
Hinsdale — B-8
Hobson — D-6
Homestead — B-9
Hot Springs — C-2
Hungry Horse — B-2
Huntley — E-7
Huson — D-2
Hysham — D-8
Ingomar — D-8
Jackson — E-3

Jefferson City — D-4
Joliet — E-6
Joplin — F-4
Jordan — C-8
Judith Gap — D-6
Kalispell — B-2
Kiowa — B-3
Klein — D-7
Kremlin — F-4
Lakeside — C-2
Lambert — C-9
Lame Deer — E-8
Laurel — E-6
Laurin — E-4
Lavina — D-6
Lewistown — D-6
Libby — B-1
Lima — F-3
Lincoln — D-3
Lindsay — C-9
Livingston — E-5
Lloyd — B-6
Lodge Grass — E-7
Lohman — B-6
Lolo — D-2
Lolo Hot Springs — D-2
Loma — C-5
Loring — B-7
Lothair — F-4
Malta — B-7
Manhattan — E-4
Marion — B-2
Martin City — B-2
McLeod — E-5
Medicine Lake — B-9
Melrose — E-4
Melstone — D-7
Melville — D-6
Miles City — E-9
Missoula — D-2
Moccasin — D-5
Monarch — C-5
Montague — C-5
Montana City — D-4
Moore — D-6
Musselshell — D-7
Nashua — C-8
Neihart — D-5
Niarada — C-2
Norris — E-4
Noxon — C-1
Nye — E-6
Olney — B-2
Opheim — B-8
Oswego — C-9
Ovando — D-3
Pablo — C-2
Paradise — C-2
Pendroy — C-4
Philipsburg — D-3
Plains — C-1
Plentywood — B-9
Plevna — D-10
Polebridge — B-2
Polson — C-2
Pompeys Pillar — E-7
Poplar — C-9
Port of Del Bonita — B-3
Port of Morgan — B-7
Port of Opheim — B-8
Port of Raymond — B-9
Potomac — D-3
Powderville — E-9
Power — C-4
Pray — E-5
Rapelje — E-6
Raymond — B-9
Raynesford — C-5
Red Lodge — F-6
Redstone — B-9
Reedpoint — E-6
Rexford — B-1
Richey — C-9
Richland — B-8
Ringling — E-5
Roberts — E-6
Rock Springs — D-8
Rollins — C-2
Ronan — C-2
Rosebud — E-8
Roundup — D-6
Roy — D-7
Rudyard — B-5
Ryegate — D-6
Saco — B-7
Saint Ignatius — C-2
Saint Mary — B-3
Saint Regis — C-1
Saltese — C-1
Santa Rita — B-4

Savage — C-10
Scobey — B-9
Seeley Lake — D-3
Shawmut — D-6
Shelby — B-4
Sheridan — E-4
Sidney — C-10
Silesia — E-6
Silver Star — E-4
Simms — C-4
Somers — C-2
Springdale — E-5
Stanford — D-5
Stevensville — D-2
Stryker — B-2
Suffolk — C-6
Sumatra — D-7
Sun River — C-4
Sunburst — B-4
Superior — C-2
Swan Lake — C-2
Sweetgrass — B-4
Tarkio — D-2
Teigen — D-7
Terry — D-9
Thompson Falls — C-2
Three Forks — E-4
Toston — E-4
Townsend — E-4
Trego — B-2
Trout Creek — C-1
Troy — B-1
Turner — B-7
Twin Bridges — E-4
Twodot — D-5
Valier — B-4
Vaughn — C-5
Victor — D-2
Vida — C-9
Virginia City — E-4
Volborg — E-9
Walkerville — E-3
Warmsprings — D-3
Waterloo — E-4
West Glacier — B-3
West Yellowstone — F-4
Westby — B-10
White Hall — E-4
White Sulphur Springs — D-5
Whitefish — B-2
Whitetail — B-9
Wibaux — D-10
Willow Creek — E-4
Wilsall — E-5
Winifred — C-6
Winnett — D-7
Winston — E-4
Wisdom — E-3
Wise River — E-3
Wolf Creek — D-4
Wolf Point — C-9
Worden — E-7
Wyola — F-8
Yaak — B-1
Zurich — B-6

NEBRASKA
Pages 52-53
Population: 1,569,825
Capital: Lincoln
Land Area: 76,664 sq. mi.

Abie — F-11
Adams — H-12
Ainsworth — D-7
Albion — E-10
Alda — G-9
Alexandria — H-11
Allen — D-11
Alliance — D-3
Alma — H-8
Almeria — E-8
Amelia — D-9
Ames — F-12
Amherst — G-8
Angora — D-3
Anoka — C-9
Anselmo — E-7
Ansley — F-8
Antioch — D-4
Arapahoe — H-7
Arcadia — F-8
Archer — F-10
Arlington — F-12
Arnold — F-7
Arthur — E-5
Ashby — D-4
Ashland — G-12

Ashton — F-9
Atkinson — D-9
Atlanta — H-8
Auburn — H-12
Aurora — G-10
Axtell — H-8
Ayr — H-9
Bancroft — E-12
Barneston — J-12
Bartlett — E-9
Bartley — H-6
Bassett — D-8
Battle Creek — E-10
Bayard — E-3
Bazile Mills — D-10
Beatrice — H-11
Beaver City — H-7
Beaver Crossing — G-11
Beemer — E-11
Belden — D-11
Belgrade — F-10
Bellevue — G-12
Vicinity — Pg. 148, G-5
Belvidere — G-10
Benedict — G-10
Benkelman — H-5
Bennet — G-12
Bennington — Pg. 148, B-1
Bertrand — H-7
Berwyn — F-8
Big Springs — F-4
Bingham — D-4
Bladen — H-9
Blair — F-12
Bloomfield — D-10
Blue Hill — H-9
Blue Springs — H-11
Boelus — G-9
Boone — F-10
Boys Town — F-12
Vicinity — Pg. 148, C-1
Bradshaw — G-10
Brady — F-6
Brandon — G-4
Brewster — E-7
Bridgeport — E-3
Bristow — C-9
Broadwater — E-3
Brock — H-12
Broken Bow — F-7
Brownlee — D-6
Brule — F-4
Bruning — H-10
Bruno — F-11
Brunswick — D-10
Burchard — H-12
Burr — H-12
Burton — C-8
Burwell — E-8
Bushnell — F-2
Butte — C-9
Cairo — G-9
Callaway — F-7
Cambridge — H-6
Campbell — H-8
Capehart — Pg. 148, H-4
Carleton — H-10
Carroll — E-11
Carter Lake — Pg. 148, D-4
Cedar Bluffs — F-12
Cedar Creek — Pg. 148, K-1
Cedar Rapids — F-9
Center — D-10
Central City — G-9
Ceresco — G-12
Chadron — C-3
Chalco — Pg. 148, E-1
Chambers — D-9
Champion — G-5
Chapman — G-9
Chappell — F-4
Chester — J-10
Clarks — F-10
Clarkson — E-11
Clatonia — H-11
Clay Center — H-10
Clearwater — D-10
Clinton — C-4
Cody — C-6
Coleridge — D-11
Columbus — F-11
Comstock — F-8
Concord — D-11
Cook — H-12
Cornlea — F-11
Cortland — H-11
Cotesfield — F-9
Cowles — H-9
Cozad — G-7
Crab Orchard — H-12

Craig — E-12
Crawford — C-3
Creighton — D-10
Creston — E-11
Crete — H-11
Crofton — C-10
Crookston — C-6
Culbertson — H-6
Cullom — Pg. 148, K-2
Curtis — G-6
Dakota City — D-12
Dalton — E-3
Danbury — H-6
Dannebrog — F-9
Davenport — H-10
David City — F-11
Dawson — J-13
Daykin — H-11
Debolt — Pg. 148, C-3
Decatur — E-12
Denton — G-11
Deshler — H-10
Dewitt — H-11
Dickens — G-6
Diller — H-11
Dix — F-2
Dodge — E-11
Doniphan — G-9
Dorchester — G-11
Douglas — H-12
DuBois — J-12
Dunbar — G-12
Duncan — F-10
Dunning — E-7
Dwight — G-11
Eddyville — G-7
Edgar — H-10
Edison — H-7
Elba — F-9
Elgin — E-9
Eli — C-5
Elk Creek — H-12
Elkhorn — F-12
Ellsworth — D-4
Elm Creek — G-8
Elmwood — G-12
Elsie — G-5
Elsmere — D-7
Elwood — G-7
Elyria — E-8
Emerson — D-11
Emmet — D-9
Enders — H-5
Endicott — J-11
Ericson — E-9
Eustis — G-7
Exeter — G-10
Fairbury — H-11
Fairfield — H-10
Fairmont — H-10
Falls City — J-13
Farnam — G-7
Farwell — F-9
Filley — H-11
Firth — H-11
Fordyce — D-11
Fort Crook — Pg. 148, H-4
Foster — D-10
Franklin — H-8
Fremont — F-12
Friend — G-10
Fullerton — F-10
Funk — H-8
Gandy — F-6
Garrison — F-11
Geneva — H-10
Genoa — F-10
Gering — E-2
Gilmore — Pg. 148, H-4
Giltner — G-9
Glenvil — H-9
Goehner — G-11
Gordon — C-4
Gothenburg — G-7
Grafton — G-10
Grainton — G-5
Grand Island — G-9
Grant — G-5
Greeley — F-9
Greenwood — G-12
Gresham — G-11
Gretna — F-12
Guide Rock — J-9
Gurley — F-3
Hadar — E-11
Haigler — H-4
Hallam — H-11
Halsey — E-7
Hamlet — H-5
Hampton — G-10

Harrisburg — E-2
Harrison — C-2
Hartington — D-11
Harvard — H-9
Hastings — H-9
Hay Springs — C-4
Hayes Center — H-5
Hazard — F-8
Hebron — H-10
Hemingford — D-3
Henderson — G-10
Herman — F-12
Hershey — F-6
Hildreth — H-8
Holdrege — H-7
Holstein — H-9
Hooper — F-11
Hoskins — E-11
Howells — E-11
Humboldt — J-12
Humphrey — E-10
Huntley — H-8
Hyannis — D-5
Vicinity — Pg. 148
Imperial — G-5
Inavale — J-9
Indianola — H-6
Inman — D-9
Ithaca — F-11
Johnson — H-12
Johnstown — D-7
Juniata — G-9
Kearney — G-8
Kenesaw — G-9
Kennard — F-12
Keystone — F-5
Kilgore — C-6
Kimball — F-2
La Vista — Pg. 148, F-3
Lakeside — D-4
Laurel — D-11
Lawrence — H-9
Lebanon — H-7
Leigh — E-11
Lemoyne — F-5
Lewellen — F-4
Lewiston — H-12
Lexington — G-8
Liberty — J-12
Lincoln — G-12
Linwood — F-11
Lisco — E-4
Litchfield — F-8
Lodgepole — F-4
Long Pine — D-7
Loomis — H-7
Louisville — G-12
Loup City — F-8
Lyman — D-2
Lynch — C-9
Lyons — E-12
Madison — E-11
Madrid — G-5
Magnet — D-10
Malmo — F-11
Marquette — G-10
Martell — H-11
Martinsburg — D-11
Mason City — F-8
Max — H-5
Maxwell — F-6
May — Pg. 148, F-3
Maywood — G-6
McCook — H-6
McCool Jct. — H-10
McGrew — E-2
Mead — F-12
Meadow — Pg. 148, K-1
Melbeta — E-2
Memphis — G-12
Merna — F-7
Merriman — C-5
Milford — G-11
Millard — Pg. 148, F-1
Miller — G-8
Milligan — H-10
Mills — C-9
Minden — H-8
Minitare — E-2
Mitchell — D-2
Monowi — C-9
Moorefield — G-6
Morrill — D-2
Mullen — D-6
Murray — G-12

Nenzel — C-6
Newman Grove — E-10
Newport — D-8
Nickerson — F-12
Niobrara — C-10
Norden — C-7
Norfolk — E-10
North Bend — F-11
North Loup — F-9
North Platte — F-6
O'Neill — D-9
Oak — H-10
Oakdale — E-10
Oakland — F-12
Obert — D-11
Oconto — F-7
Octavia — F-11
Odell — J-11
Odessa — G-8
Ogallala — F-5
Ohiowa — H-10
Omaha — F-12
Vicinity — Pg. 148
Ong — H-10
Ord — E-8
Oreapolis — Pg. 148, J-5
Orleans — H-8
Osceola — F-10
Oshkosh — E-4
Osmond — D-10
Overton — G-8
Oxford — H-7
Page — D-9
Palisade — H-5
Palmer — F-9
Palmyra — G-12
Panama — H-12
Papillion — G-12
Vicinity — Pg. 148, G-3
Parks — H-4
Pawnee City — J-12
Paxton — F-5
Pender — E-12
Petersburg — E-10
Phillips — G-9
Pickrell — H-11
Pierce — D-10
Pilger — E-11
Plainview — D-10
Platte Center — F-10
Plattsmouth — G-12
Vicinity — Pg. 148, K-5
Pleasanton — G-8
Plymouth — H-11
Polk — G-10
Poole — G-8
Potter — F-3
Prague — F-11
Primrose — F-9
Prosser — G-9
Purdum — D-7
Raeville — E-10
Ragan — H-8
Ralston — Pg. 148, F-2
Randolph — D-11
Ravenna — G-9
Raymond — G-11
Red Cloud — H-9
Republican City — H-8
Reynolds — J-11
Richfield — Pg. 148, H-2
Richland — F-11
Rising City — F-11
Riverdale — G-8
Riverton — H-9
Roca — G-11
Rockville — F-9
Rogers — F-11
Rosalie — E-12
Rose — D-8
Roseland — H-9
Rushville — C-4
Ruskin — H-10
Saint Edward — F-10
Saint Helena — C-11
Saint Libory — G-9
Saint Mary — H-12
Saint Paul — F-9
Santee — C-10
Sargent — E-8
Saronville — H-9
Schuyler — F-11
Scotia — F-9
Scottsbluff — D-2
Scribner — F-11
Seneca — D-6
Seward — G-11
Shelby — F-10
Shelton — G-8
Shickley — H-10

Sholes — D-11
Shubert — H-12
Sidney — F-3
Silver Creek — F-10
Smithfield — G-7
Snyder — E-11
South Bend — G-12
South Souix City — D-12
Spalding — E-9
Sparks — C-7
Spencer — C-9
Springfield — G-12
Vicinity — Pg. 148, J-1
Springview — C-8
Stamford — H-7
Stanton — E-11
Staplehurst — G-11
Stapleton — F-6
Steele City — J-11
Steinauer — H-12
Stockville — G-6
Strang — H-10
Stratton — H-5
Stromsburg — F-10
Stuart — D-8
Summerfield — J-12
Sumner — G-8
Superior — J-10
Surprise — G-10
Sutherland — F-6
Sutton — H-10
Syracuse — H-12
Table Rock — H-12
Tarnov — F-10
Taylor — E-8
Tecumseh — H-12
Tekamah — E-12
Terrytown — D-2
Thayer — G-10
Thedford — E-6
Thurston — E-12
Tilden — E-10
Tobias — H-11
Trenton — H-6
Trumbull — G-9
Tryon — E-6
Uehling — E-12
Ulysses — G-11
Unadilla — G-12
Upland — H-8
Valentine — C-7
Valley — F-12
Valparaiso — G-11
Venango — G-4
Verdel — C-10
Verdigre — D-10
Verdon — J-13
Waco — G-10
Wahoo — F-12
Wakefield — D-11
Wallace — G-5
Walthill — E-12
Wauneta — H-5
Wausa — D-10
Waverly — F-11
Wayne — D-11
Weeping Water — G-12
Weissert — F-8
Wellfleet — G-6
West Point — E-11
Western — H-11
Westerville — F-8
Whitman — D-5
Whitney — C-3
Wilber — H-11
Wilcox — H-8
Willow Island — G-7
Wilsonville — H-7
Winnebago — D-12
Winnetoon — D-9
Winside — E-11
Winslow — F-12
Wisner — E-11
Wolbach — F-9
Wood Lake — C-7
Wood River — G-9
Wymore — J-12
Wynot — C-11
York — G-10

NEVADA

NEVADA
Page 54
Population: 800,493
Capital: Carson City
Land Area: 109,893 sq. mi.

Adaven — F-5
Alamo — G-5
Ash Springs — G-5

NEVADA

Austin D-4
Babbitt E-2
Baker E-6
Battle Mountain . . . C-4
Beatty H-4
Beowawe C-4
Blue Diamond J-5
Boulder City J-6
Bracken . . . Pg. 126, H-2
Bunkerville H-6
Cactus Springs H-5
Cal Nev Ari J-6
Caliente G-6
Carlin C-5
Carp G-6
Carson City E-1
Carver's E-3
Caselton F-6
Cherry Creek D-6
Coaldale F-3
Cold Spring D-3
Contact A-6
Crescent Valley C-4
Currant E-5
Currie C-6
Deeth B-5
Duckwater E-5
Dyer F-3
Eagle Picher Mine . . C-2
East Ely E-6
East Las Vegas . . . . Pg. 126, J-4
Elko C-5
Ely E-6
Empire C-2
Eureka D-5
Fallon D-2
Fernley D-2
Frenchman E-3
Gabbs E-3
Gerlach C-2
Glendale H-6
Golconda B-3
Gold Point G-3
Goldfield G-3
Goodsprings J-5
Halleck B-5
Hawthorne E-2
Henderson J-6
  Vicinity . . Pg. 126, K-4
Hiko G-5
Imlay C-3
Indian Springs H-5
Ione E-3
Jack Creek B-5
Jackpot A-6
Jarbridge A-5
Jean J-5
Jiggs C-5
Kimberly E-5
Lage's D-6
Lamoille C-5
Las Vegas J-5
  Vicinity . . Pg. 126, G-1
  Detailed City . Pg. 244
Las Vegas Beach . . . . . Pg. 126, H-7
Laughlin K-6
Lee C-5
Lida G-3
Lovelock C-2
Lund E-6
Luning F-3
Major's Place E-6
McDermitt A-3
McGill D-6
Mercury H-5
Mesquite H-6
Midas B-4
Middle Gate E-3
Mill City C-3
Mina F-3
Moapa H-6
Montello B-6
Mountain City A-5
Nelson J-6
Nixon D-2
North Las Vegas . . . J-6
  Vicinity . . Pg. 126, E-2
Nyala F-5
Oasis B-6
Oreana C-3
Orovada B-3
Overton H-6
Owyhee A-5
Panaca G-6
Paradise Valley B-3
Pioche F-6
Preston E-6
Rachel G-5

Reno D-1
Round Mt. E-4
Ruby Valley C-5
Ruth E-5
Sandy J-5
Schurz E-2
Scotty's Jct. G-4
Searchlight K-6
Shantytown C-5
Silver City D-2
Silver Peak F-3
Silver Springs D-2
Sloan J-5
Sparks D-2
Sulphur B-2
Sutcliffe D-1
Thousand Springs . . B-6
Tonopah F-3
Tuscarora B-4
Unionville C-3
Ursine F-6
Valmy C-4
Virginia City D-2
Wadsworth D-2
Wann . . . . . Pg. 126, E-3
Warm Springs F-4
Weed Heights E-2
Wellington E-2
Wells B-6
Winnemucca B-3
Yerington E-2

NEW HAMPSHIRE
Page 55
Population: 920,610
Capital: Concord
Land Area: 8,993 sq. mi.

Albany E-6
Allenstown H-6
Alstead H-3
Alton G-6
Alton Bay G-6
Amherst J-5
Andover G-5
Antrim J-4
Ashland F-5
Ashuelot K-3
Atkinson J-6
Auburn J-6
  Vicinity . . Pg. 133, B-4
Barnstead H-6
Bartlett E-6
Bath E-4
Bayside J-7
Bedford J-5
  Vicinity . . Pg. 133, C-2
Belmont G-5
Bennington J-4
Berlin D-6
Bethlehem D-5
Boscawen H-5
Bow Center H-5
Bradford H-4
Brentwood J-6
Bretton Woods E-5
Bridgewater G-5
Bristol G-5
Brookfield G-6
Brookline K-5
Canaan G-4
Canaan Center F-4
Candia J-6
Carroll D-5
Cascade D-6
Center Conway E-6
Center Ossipee F-6
Charlestown H-3
Cheever J-5
Chester J-6
Chesterfield J-3
Chichester H-5
Chocorua F-6
Cilleyville G-4
Claremont G-4
Coburn G-6
Cold River H-3
Colebrook B-5
Columbia B-5
Concord H-5
Contoocook H-5
Conway E-6
Coos Junction D-5
Cornish City G-3
Cornish Flat G-3
Crystal C-6
Danbury G-5
Davisville H-5

Derry J-6
  Vicinity . . Pg. 133, E-5
Derry Village J-6
  Vicinity . . Pg. 133, D-5
Dixville B-6
Dorchester F-4
Dover H-7
Drewsville H-3
Dublin J-4
Dummer C-6
Durham H-7
East Alton G-6
East Barrington H-6
East Derry . Pg. 133, D-5
East Grafton G-4
East Hebron F-5
East Kingston J-6
East Lempster H-4
East Madison F-6
Easton E-5
Eaton Center F-6
Effingham Falls F-6
Elkins G-4
Epping J-6
Epsom H-6
Epsom Four Corners H-6
Errol C-6
Exeter J-7
Fabyan D-5
Farmington G-7
Fish Market M-5
Francestown J-4
Franconia D-5
Franklin G-5
Freedom F-6
Fremont J-6
Gerrish H-5
Gilford G-6
Gilmans Corner F-4
Gilmanton G-6
Gilsum J-4
Glen E-6
Glen House D-6
Glendale G-5
Goffs Falls J-5
Goffstown J-5
Gorham D-6
Goshen H-4
Gossville H-6
Grafton G-4
Grantham G-4
Grasmere . . Pg. 133, B-1
Greenfield J-4
Greenville K-4
Groton F-4
Groveton C-5
Guild G-4
Guildhall C-5
Hampton J-7
Hampton Beach J-7
Hancock J-4
Hanover F-4
Hanover Center F-4
Harts Location E-6
Haverhill E-4
Hebron F-4
Henniker H-5
Hillsborough H-4
  Vicinity . . Pg. 133, E-5
Hinsdale J-3
Hooksett H-6
Hopkinton H-5
Hoyts Corner H-4
Hudson K-6
  Vicinity . . Pg. 133, G-3
Hudson Center . . . . Pg. 133, G-3
Jackson D-6
Jaffrey J-4
James City H-6
Jefferson D-5
Jefferson Highlands . D-5
Keene J-3
Kensington J-7
Kidderville B-5
Kingston J-6
Laconia G-5
Lancaster D-5
Laskey Corner G-7
Leavitts Hill H-6
Lebanon G-4
Lincoln E-5
Lisbon E-4
Litchfield . Pg. 133, E-2
Little Boars Head . . . J-7
Littleton D-5
Londonderry Pg. 133, E-4
Loudon H-5
Lower Shaker Village G-4
Lower Village J-3
Lyme F-4
Lyme Center F-4

Madbury H-7
Madison F-6
Manchester J-5
  Vicinity . . . . . . Pg. 133
Marlborough J-4
Marlow H-4
Martin J-6
Martins Corner . . . . Pg. 133, B-3
Mason K-5
Meadows D-5
Meredith F-6
Meriden G-3
Merrimack J-5
  Vicinity . . Pg. 133, E-2
Milan C-6
Milford J-5
Milton G-6
Mirror Lake F-6
Monroe D-4
Mont Vernon J-5
Moultonborough . . . F-6
Moultonville F-6
Mount Sunapee H-4
Munsonville J-4
Nashua K-5
  Vicinity . . Pg. 133, G-2
New Durham G-6
New Hampton G-5
New Ipswich K-4
New London G-4
New Rye H-6
Newbury H-4
Newfields J-7
Newington H-7
Newmarket J-7
Newport H-4
Newton J-6
North Chatham D-6
North Conway E-6
North Grantham . . . G-4
North Groton F-5
North Haverhill D-4
North Londonderry . . . . . . Pg. 133, D-3
North Pelham . . . . Pg. 133, G-4
North Rochester H-6
North Sandwich F-6
North Stratford C-5
North Sutton H-4
North Wakefield . . . G-6
North Woodstock . . . E-5
Northfield G-5
Northumberland . . . C-5
Northwood H-6
Orford F-4
Orfordville F-4
Ossipee F-6
Otterville G-4
Pages Corner H-5
Parker J-5
Pearls Corner K-6
Pelham K-6
Pembroke H-6
Penacook H-5
Peppermint Corner . . . . . . Pg. 133, E-5
Peterborough J-4
Pinardville . . . Pg. 133, B-2
Pittsburg B-6
Pittsfield H-6
Plainfield G-3
Plaistow J-6
Plymouth F-5
Portsmouth H-7
Potter Place G-4
Province Lake F-7
Randolph D-6
Raymond J-6
Redstone E-6
Reeds Ferry Pg. 133, E-2
Richmond K-3
Rindge K-4
Riverton D-5
Rochester H-6
Rollinsford H-7
Rowes Corner . . . . Pg. 133, A-4
Rumney F-5
Rye J-7
Rye Beach J-7
Salem J-6
Salisbury H-5
Sanbornton G-5
Sanbornville G-7
Sandwich F-6
Seabrook Beach J-7
Severance . . Pg. 133, B-4

Sharon J-4
Shelburne D-6
Somersworth H-7
South Acworth H-3
South Cornish G-3
South Danbury G-5
South Hooksett . . . . Pg. 133, B-3
South Merrimack . . . . Pg. 91, K-6
South Stoddard J-4
South Weare J-5
Spofford J-3
Springfield G-4
Squantum J-4
Stark C-6
Stewartstown B-6
Stoddard H-4
Stratford C-5
Stratham J-7
Sunapee G-4
Surry J-3
Sutton H-4
Swiftwater E-4
Tamworth F-6
Temple J-4
Thornton F-5
Thorntons Ferry . . . . Pg. 133, E-2
Tilton G-5
Trapshire J-3
Troy J-4
Tuftonboro F-6
Twin Mountain D-5
Union G-7
Wakefield G-7
Wallis Sands J-7
Walpole H-3
Warner H-5
Warren F-4
Washington H-4
Weare J-5
Wendell H-4
Wentworth F-4
Wentworths Location B-6
West Campton F-5
West Lebanon G-3
West Milan C-6
West Ossipee F-6
West Rindge K-4
West Rumney F-5
West Stewartstown . . B-5
West Swanzey J-3
West Windham . . . . Pg. 133, F-4
Westmoreland J-3
Westville J-6
Willey House E-5
Wilson . . . . Pg. 133, D-4
Wilton J-5
Winchester J-3
Windham . . . Pg. 133, F-5
Windsor H-4
Winnisquam G-5
Wolfeboro G-6
Wonalancet F-6
Woodman H-5
Woodsville E-4

NEW JERSEY
Pages 56-57
Population: 7,364,823
Capital: Trenton
Land Area: 7,468 sq. mi.

Absecon M-6
  Vicinity . . . Pg. 91, H-3
Adelphia H-7
Allamuchy D-4
Allendale . Pg. 142, D-4
Allentown H-6
Alloway M-2
Alpha E-3
Alpine B-6
  Vicinity . . Pg. 142, F-7
Andover D-4
Asbury Park G-8
Atlantic City N-7
  Vicinity . . . Pg. 91, H-4
Atlantic Highlands . . F-8
Atsion K-5
Audubon K-4
Audubon Park . . . . Pg. 150, F-7
Avalon P-5
Avenel . . . . Pg. 143, P-1
Baptistown F-4
Barnegat K-8
Barnegat Light K-8

Barrington . . Pg. 150, G-7
Bay Head H-8
Bay Point N-3
Bayonne D-8
  Vicinity . . Pg. 143, M-4
Beach Haven M-7
Beachwood J-7
Bedminster E-5
Beesley Pt. N-5
Belleplain N-4
Belleville D-7
Bellmawr K-3
  Vicinity . . Pg. 150, G-6
Belmar H-8
Belvidere D-3
Bergenfield C-8
Berlin K-4
Bernardsville D-6
Beverly J-4
  Vicinity . . Pg. 150, C-9
Blairstown C-4
Blawenburg F-5
Bloomfield D-7
  Vicinity . . Pg. 142, D-1
Bloomingdale C-7
  Vicinity . . Pg. 142, G-4
Bloomsbury E-3
Bogata . . . . Pg. 142, G-6
Boonton C-7
Bordentown H-5
Bound Brook F-6
Bradley Beach H-8
Branchville B-5
Bridgeboro Pg. 150, D-9
Bridgeport K-2
Bridgeton M-2
Brielle H-8
Brigantine N-6
  Vicinity . . . Pg. 91, F-3
Broadway D-4
Brooklawn Pg. 150, G-6
Browns Mills J-6
Budd Lake C-5
Buena M-4
Burlington H-4
Butler C-7
Buttzville D-4
Caldwell . . Pg. 143, H-1
Califon E-5
Camden J-3
  Vicinity . . Pg. 150, E-6
Cape May Q-4
Cape May Court House Q-4
Cardiff . . . . Pg. 91, J-3
Carls Corner M-3
Carlstadt . Pg. 143, H-5
Carneys Pt. L-1
Carteret E-6
  Vicinity . . Pg. 143, P-2
Cassville H-7
Cedar Bridge K-7
Cedar Grove J-8
  Vicinity . . Pg. 142, G-2
Cedarville N-3
Centerton M-3
Chatham D-6
  Vicinity . . Pg. 142, G-4
Chatsworth K-6
Cherry Hill J-4
  Vicinity . . Pg. 150, F-7
Chesilhurst K-4
Chester D-5
Cinnaminson J-4
  Vicinity . . Pg. 143, N-1
Clarksburg H-6
Clarksville A-6
Clayton L-3
  Vicinity . . Pg. 150, G-6
Clermont P-5
Cliffside Park Pg. 143, J-6
Clifton D-8
  Vicinity . . Pg. 142, H-3
Clinton E-4
  Vicinity . . Pg. 142, E-7
Closter . . . Pg. 142, E-7
Colesville A-5
Collingswood J-3
  Vicinity . . Pg. 150, F-7
Cologne . . . Pg. 91, J-1
Colonia . . . Pg. 143, P-1
Colts Neck G-7
Columbus H-5
Conovertown Pg. 91, G-3
Corbin City N-5
Cranbury G-6
Cranford . . Pg. 143, M-1
Cresskill B-8
  Vicinity . . Pg. 142, F-7
Crestwood Village . . J-7

Croton F-4
Cumberland N-4
Deacons J-5
Deerfield M-3
Delaware C-3
  Vicinity . . Pg. 143, M-4
Demarest . Pg. 142, F-7
Denville C-6
Devonshire . Pg. 91, K-1
Dividing Creek N-3
Dover . . . . Pg. 142, F-6
Dumont . . . Pg. 142, F-6
Dunellen E-6
East Newark Pg. 143, K-4
East Orange D-7
  Vicinity . . Pg. 142, B-1
East Rutherford . . . . Pg. 143, H-4
East Vineland M-4
Eatontown G-8
Edgewater Park J-4
Edinburg G-5
Edison F-6
  Vicinity . . Pg. 150, C-9
Egg Harbor M-6
Egg Harbor City . . . . Pg. 91, K-1
Elizabeth E-7
  Vicinity . . Pg. 143, M-3
Elmer L-3
Elmwood Park . . . . Pg. 142, G-4
Elwood M-5
Emerson . . Pg. 142, E-6
Englewood C-9
  Vicinity . . Pg. 142, G-7
Englewood Cliffs . . . A-6
  Vicinity . . Pg. 142, B-1
English Creek Pg. 91, K-4
Englishtown G-7
Erskine . . . Pg. 142, B-2
Estell Manor N-5
Everittstown E-4
Ewingville G-5
Fair Haven H-8
Fair Lawn C-8
  Vicinity . . Pg. 142, F-4
Fairfield . . Pg. 142, G-1
Fairmount D-5
Fairton N-3
Farmingdale H-7
Flemington F-4
Florham Park D-7
Folsom L-4
  Vicinity . . Pg. 150, E-6
Fords . . . . . Pg. 143, P-1
Forked River K-8
Fort Dix J-6
Fort Lee A-6
  Vicinity . . Pg. 142, H-6
Four Mile F-6
Franklin B-6
  Vicinity . . Pg. 143, N-2
Franklin Lakes . . . . Pg. 142, D-3
Franklinville L-3
Fredon C-5
Freehold G-7
Freewood Acres . . . H-7
Frenchtown F-4
Garfield C-8
  Vicinity . . Pg. 142, G-4
Garwood . . Pg. 143, M-1
Germania . . Pg. 91, J-1
Gibbsboro K-4
Gilford Park J-8
Glassboro L-3
Glen Gardner E-4
Glen Ridge Pg. 143, H-3
Glen Rock . Pg. 142, E-4
Glenwood A-6
Gloucester City K-3
  Vicinity . . Pg. 150, G-6
Gouldtown M-3
Great Meadows D-4
Green Bank K-6
Guttenberg Pg. 143, J-5
Hackensack C-8
  Vicinity . . Pg. 142, G-6
Hackettstown D-5
Haddon Heights . . . . . . Pg. 150, G-7
Haddonfield J-4
  Vicinity . . Pg. 150, F-7
Hainesburg C-4
Haledon . . Pg. 142, F-3
  Vicinity . . . Pg. 91, H-5
Hamburg B-6
Hamilton Sq. G-5
Hammonton L-5
Hampton E-4
Hanover D-6

Harmony D-3
Harrington Park . . . . Pg. 142, E-6
Harrison . . Pg. 143, K-4
Harrisonville L-1
Harvey Cedars L-8
Hasbrouck Hts. . . . . Pg. 142, G-5
Haworth . . Pg. 142, E-6
Hawthorne C-8
  Vicinity . . Pg. 142, F-3
Helmetta G-7
Hewitt A-6
High Bridge E-4
Highland Park F-7
Highlands F-9
Hightstown G-6
Hillsdale B-6
  Vicinity . . Pg. 142, D-5
Ho-Ho-Kus Pg. 142, E-4
Hoboken D-8
  Vicinity . . Pg. 143, K-5
Holmdel G-7
Hopatcong C-5
Hope F-5
Hopewell F-5
Hurdtown C-6
Irvington D-7
  Vicinity . . Pg. 143, L-2
Iselin . . . . . Pg. 143, P-1
Island Heights J-8
Jamesburg G-6
Jersey City D-8
  Vicinity . . Pg. 143, L-5
Johnsonburg C-4
Keansburg F-8
Kearny D-8
  Vicinity . . Pg. 143, K-4
Kenilworth E-7
  Vicinity . . Pg. 143, M-1
Keyport F-8
Kinnelon C-6
Lafayette B-5
Lakehurst J-7
Lakeside B-7
Lakewood H-7
Lambertville G-4
Larisons Cor. F-4
Laurence Harbor . . . F-7
Lavallette J-8
Lawnside . . Pg. 150, G-8
Lawrence E-5
Lebanon E-5
Leeds Point . Pg. 91, F-2
Lenola . . . . (—)
Liberty Cor. E-6
Lincoln Park C-7
  Vicinity . . Pg. 142, F-1
Linden E-7
  Vicinity . . Pg. 143, N-2
Lindenwold K-4
Linwood N-6
Little Egg Harbor . . . M-7
Little Falls . Pg. 142, G-2
Little Ferry Pg. 142, H-5
Livingston . Pg. 143, J-4
Lodi . . . . . Pg. 142, G-4
Long Branch G-9
Long Valley D-5
Longport N-6
  Vicinity . . . Pg. 91, H-5
Lumberton J-5
Lyndhurst . Pg. 143, J-4
Madison D-6
Magnolia F-4
  Vicinity . . Pg. 150, G-8
Mahwah A-6
  Vicinity . . Pg. 142, C-4
Manahawkin L-7
Manalapan G-6
Manasquan H-8
Mantoloking J-8
Manville F-5
Maple Shade J-3
Maplewood Pg. 143, K-2
Marcella C-6
Margate City N-6
  Vicinity . . . Pg. 91, H-5
Marlboro G-7
Marlton . . . Pg. 150, G-9
Marmora P-5
  Vicinity . . . Pg. 91, K-6
Marshallville N-5
Matawan F-7
Maurice River P-4
Mays Landing M-5
Maywood . . Pg. 142, G-5
McAfee B-6
McKee City . Pg. 91, K-3

NEW JERSEY

Medford J-5
Medford Lakes K-5
Mendham D-6
Merchantville
. . . . Pg. 150, E-7
Metuchen E-7
Mickleton K-3
Midland Park Pg. 142, E-4
Milburn . . . Pg. 143, K-1
Milford E-3
Millside Heights
Millstone F-6
Milltown F-6
Millville N-3
Monmouth Jct. G-6
Monroe G-6
Montague A-5
Montclaire . . Pg. 143, H-3
Montvale . . Pg. 142, D-5
Montville C-7
Moorestown J-4
Vicinity . . . Pg. 150, E-8
Morris Plains D-6
Morristown D-6
Morrisville E-3
Mt. Arlington C-6
Mt. Ephraim Pg. 150, G-6
Mt. Holly J-5
Mullica Hill L-3
National Park K-3
Vicinity . . . Pg. 150, G-5
Neptune H-8
Neshanic F-5
Netcong C-5
New Brunswick F-6
New Egypt J-6
New Gretna J-8
New Milford Pg. 142, F-6
New Providence E-6
New Rochelle
. . . . Pg. 142, G-5
Newark D-8
Vicinity . . . Pg. 143, K-3
Detailed City . . Pg. 259
Newfield M-4
Newfoundland B-6
Newton B-5
North Arlington
. . . . Pg. 143, J-4
North Bergen Pg. 143, J-6
North Caldwell
. . . . Pg. 142, G-2
North Cape May Q-4
North Dennis P-4
North Haledon C-7
Vicinity . . Pg. 142, F-3
North Wildwood . . . Q-5
Northfield N-6
Vicinity . . . Pg. 91, J-4
Northvale Pg. 142, D-7
Norwood C-9
Vicinity . . . Pg. 143, E-7
Nutley D-8
Vicinity . . Pg. 143, H-3
Oakland . . Pg. 142, D-2
Oaklyn . . . Pg. 150, F-7
Ocean City N-6
Vicinity . . . Pg. 91, J-6
Ocean Gate J-8
Oceanport G-8
Oceanville . . Pg. 91, G-2
Ogdensburg B-5
Old Bridge F-7
Old Tappan C-8
Vicinity . . Pg. 142, D-6
Oldwick E-5
Oradell . . Pg. 142, F-6
Orange D-7
Vicinity . . . Pg. 143, K-2
Oxford D-4
Palermo . . . Pg. 91, K-7
Palisades Park
. . . . Pg. 142, H-6
Palmyra . . Pg. 150, D-7
Paramus C-8
Vicinity . . Pg. 142, F-5
Park Ridge . . Pg. 142, D-5
Parsippany-Troy Hill D-6
Passaic D-8
Vicinity . . Pg. 142, H-4
Patterson C-7
Vicinity . . Pg. 142, F-3
Paulsboro K-2
Peapack E-5
Pemberton J-6
Pennington G-5
Penns Grove L-2
Pennsauken K-3
Vicinity . . Pg. 150, E-7
Pennsville L-1

Penny Pot M-5
Pequannock Pg. 142, F-1
Perth Amboy F-7
Vicinity . . Pg. 143, Q-2
Phillipsburg E-3
Pine Beach Pg. 142, H-1
Pine Hill K-4
Pitman L-3
Pittstown E-4
Plainfield E-6
Plainsboro G-6
Pleasantville N-6
Vicinity . . . Pg. 91, H-3
Pole Tavern L-3
Pomona M-6
Vicinity . . . Pg. 91, J-2
Pompton Lakes C-7
Vicinity . . Pg. 142, D-1
Pompton Plains B-6
Vicinity . . Pg. 142, E-1
Port Elizabeth N-4
Port Norris P-4
Port Reading Pg. 143, P-2
Port Republic M-6
Vicinity . . . Pg. 91, G-1
Princeton G-5
Princeton Jct. G-5
Prospect Park C-8
Pt. Pleasant H-8
Pt. Pleasant Beach . . H-8
Quinton M-2
Rahway E-7
Vicinity . . . Pg. 143, N-2
Ramsey . . . Pg. 142, C-4
Raritan E-5
Readington E-5
Reaville F-5
Red Bank G-8
Vicinity . . . Pg. 150, G-5
Red Lion K-4
Ridgefield . . Pg. 143, H-6
Ridgefield Park
. . . . Pg. 142, G-6
Ridgewood C-8
Vicinity . . Pg. 142, E-4
Ringwood B-7
Vicinity . . Pg. 142, B-6
Rio Grande Q-4
River Edge Pg. 142, F-5
River Vale B-6
Vicinity . . Pg. 142, E-6
Riverdale C-7
Riverside J-4
Riverton J-4
Vicinity . . . Pg. 150, D-8
Robertsville G-7
Rochelle Park
. . . . Pg. 142, F-5
Rockaway C-6
Rockleigh . . Pg. 142, E-7
Rocky Hill F-5
Roosevelt H-6
Roseland . . Pg. 143, H-1
Roselle E-7
Vicinity . . Pg. 143, M-2
Roselle Park E-7
Vicinity . . Pg. 143, M-2
Ross Corners B-5
Rumson G-8
Runnemede K-3
Vicinity . . . Pg. 150, G-8
Rutherford . . Pg. 143, H-4
Saddle Brook
. . . . Pg. 142, G-5
Saddle River C-8
Vicinity . . Pg. 142, D-4
Salem M-1
Sayreville F-7
Scullville . . . Pg. 91, K-5
Sea Isle City P-5
Seabrook M-3
Seaside Heights . . . J-8
Seaside Park J-8
Seaville P-5
Secaucus . . Pg. 143, J-5
Sewaren . . Pg. 143, P-2
Sharptown L-2
Shiloh M-2
Ship Bottom L-8
Shrewsbury G-8
Silverton J-8
Smithburg H-7
Smithville M-6
Vicinity . . . Pg. 91, G-2
Somerdale F-4
Somers Pt. N-6
Vicinity . . . Pg. 91, J-5
Somerville E-5
South Amboy F-7
South Brunswick . . . G-6
South Dennis P-5

South Hackensack
. . . . Pg. 142, G-5
South Orange
Vicinity . . Pg. 143, K-2
South Plainfield . . . E-6
South River F-7
South Toms River . . . J-7
Sparta C-5
Speedwell K-6
Spotswood F-6
Spring Lakes Heights H-8
Spring Mills E-3
Springdale E-3
Vicinity . . . Pg. 150, G-8
Springfield . . Pg. 143, L-1
Stanhope C-5
Stockholm B-6
Stockton F-4
Stone Harbor Q-5
Stratford K-4
Summit D-7
Surf City L-8
Sussex A-5
Swedesboro K-2
Tabernacle K-5
Tavistock . . Pg. 150, G-8
Teaneck . . Pg. 142, G-6
Tenafly C-9
Vicinity . . Pg. 142, F-7
Teterboro . . Pg. 142, H-5
Tinton Falls G-8
Toms River J-7
Totowa C-7
Vicinity . . Pg. 142, G-3
Trenton G-5
Tuckerton L-7
Tuttles Cor. B-5
Union Beach F-8
Vicinity . . . Pg. 143, L-2
Union City D-8
Vicinity . . . Pg. 143, K-5
Upper Saddle River
. . . . Pg. 142, C-4
Ventnor City N-6
Vicinity . . . Pg. 91, G-5
Vernon B-5
Verona . . . Pg. 143, H-2
Villas Q-4
Vineland M-4
Waldwick C-8
Vicinity . . Pg. 142, D-4
Wallington . . Pg. 142, H-4
Wanaque B-7
Vicinity . . Pg. 142, D-1
Waretown K-8
Warren E-6
Warren Grove K-7
Washington D-4
Washington Crossing G-4
Watchung E-6
Wayne C-7
Vicinity . . Pg. 142, F-2
Weehawken Pg. 143, K-5
Welchville L-2
Wells Mills K-7
Wenonah K-3
West Caldwell
. . . . Pg. 142, H-1
West Cape May . . . Q-4
West Long Branch . . G-8
West Milford B-6
West New York D-8
Vicinity . . . Pg. 143, J-6
West Orange D-7
Vicinity . . . Pg. 143, J-2
West Patterson C-7
Vicinity . . Pg. 142, G-3
West Portal E-4
Westfield E-7
Westville K-3
Vicinity . . . Pg. 150, G-6
Westwood C-8
Vicinity . . Pg. 142, E-6
Weymouth M-6
Wharton C-6
White Horse H-5
Whitehouse E-5
Whitesboro Q-4
Whitesville H-7
Wildwood Q-5
Wildwood Crest . . . Q-5
Williamstown L-4
Winslow L-4
Wood Ridge Pg. 142, H-5
Woodbine P-4
Woodbridge F-6
Vicinity . . . Pg. 143, P-2
Woodbury K-3
Woodbury Heights . . K-3
Woodcliff Lake
. . . . Pg. 142, D-5

Woodlynne . . Pg. 150, F-6
Woods Tavern F-5
Woodstown L-2
Woodsville G-4
Wrightstown J-6
Yardville H-5

NEW MEXICO
Page 62
Population: 1,302,894
Capital: Santa Fe
Land Area: 121,335 sq. mi.

Abbott C-5
Abeytas E-3
Abiquiu C-3
Abo E-4
Alameda D-3
Vicinity . . . Pg. 90, A-9
Alamo E-2
Alamogordo G-4
Albuquerque D-3
Vicinity . . . . . . Pg. 90
Alcalde C-3
Algodones D-3
Alma G-1
Alto G-4
Amalia B-4
Ambrosia Lake D-2
Amistad C-7
Anapra J-3
Ancho F-4
Angus G-4
Animas J-1
Antelope Wells J-1
Apache Creek F-1
Aqua Fria D-4
Arabela E-6
Aragon F-1
Arch E-7
Archuleta B-2
Armijo D-3
Arrey H-2
Arroyo Hondo B-4
Arroyo Seco B-4
Artesia G-6
Atoka H-6
Atriscoe . . . Pg. 90, E-7
Aztec B-2
Bayard H-2
Beklabito B-1
Belen E-3
Bellview D-7
Bent G-4
Berino J-3
Bernal D-5
Bernalillo D-3
Bernardo E-3
Bingham F-4
Black Lake C-5
Black River Village . . H-6
Black Rock D-2
Blanco B-2
Blanco Trading Post . C-2
Bloomfield B-2
Bluewater D-2
Bosque Farms E-3
Brazos B-3
Broadview E-7
Buckhorn G-1
Bueyeros C-6
Caballo G-3
Canjilon B-3
Canon C-3
Canon Plaza B-4
Capitan F-4
Caprock F-6
Capulin B-6
Carlsbad H-6
Carlsbad Caverns . . . H-6
Carrizozo F-4
Causey F-7
Cebolla B-3
Cebolleta D-2
Cebolletita D-2
Cedar Crest D-3
Cedar Hill B-2
Cedarvale E-4
Central H-2
Cerro B-4
Chacon C-5
Chama B-3
Chamberino J-3
Chamisal C-4
Chamizal F-3
Chaparral J-4
Chilili E-4
Chimayo C-4
Cimarron B-5
Clapham C-6

Claunch F-4
Clayton B-7
Cleveland C-4
Cliff G-1
Clines Corners D-4
Cloudcroft G-4
Clovis E-7
Cochiti Lake C-3
Columbus J-2
Conchas D-6
Coolidge D-1
Corona E-4
Costilla B-4
Cotton City J-1
Counselors C-2
Coyote C-3
Coyote Canyon C-1
Crossroads F-7
Crownpoint C-1
Cruzville F-1
Crystal C-1
Cuba C-3
Cuchillo G-3
Cuervo D-6
Cundiyo C-4
Datil F-2
Deming H-2
Derry H-2
Des Moines B-6
Dexter G-6
Dilia D-5
Domingo D-3
Dona Ana H-3
Dora F-7
Dulce B-3
Dunken G-5
Duran E-5
Dwyer H-2
Eagle Nest B-5
Edgewood D-4
El Morro D-2
El Paso Gap J-5
El Porvenir C-4
El Rito C-4
El Vado B-3
Elephant Butte G-3
Elida E-6
Elk G-5
Elk Silver E-6
Elkins E-6
Embudo C-4
Encino E-5
Endee D-7
Engle G-3
Ensenada B-3
Escobosa E-3
Escondida F-3
Espanola C-4
Estancia E-4
Eunice H-7
Fairacres H-3
Farley B-6
Farmington B-1
Fence Lake E-1
Five Points . . . Pg. 90, F-7
Flora Vista B-1
Floyd E-7
Folsom B-6
Forrest E-5
Fort Stanton G-4
Fort Sumner E-6
Fort Wingate D-1
Frijoles C-4
Gage H-2
Galisteo D-4
Gallina C-3
Gallinas C-4
Gallup D-1
Gamerco D-1
Garfield H-3
Gila G-1
Gladstone B-6
Glenrio D-7
Glenwood G-1
Golden D-4
Grady D-7
Gran Quivira E-4
Grants D-2
Greenfield G-6
Grenville B-6
Guadalupita C-5
Hachita J-2
Hagerman G-6
Hanover H-2
Hatch H-3
Hayden C-7
Hernandez C-4
High Rolls G-4
Hilburn City G-7
Hill H-3

Hillsboro G-2
Hobbs G-7
Holman C-4
Hondo G-4
Hope G-5
House E-6
Humble City G-7
Hurley H-2
Jal H-7
Jarales E-3
Jemez Springs C-3
Jicarilla F-4
Kenna E-6
Kingston H-2
Kirtland B-1
Knowles G-7
La Cienega D-4
La Cueva C-5
La Jara C-3
La Joya E-3
La Luz G-4
La Madera C-4
La Mesa J-3
La Mesilla H-3
La Plata B-1
La Puente B-3
La Union J-3
Laborcita F-3
Laguna E-3
Lake Arthur G-6
Lake Valley C-2
Lamy D-4
Las Cruces H-3
Las Nutrias E-3
Las Palomas G-3
Las Vegas C-5
Ledoux C-4
Lemitar F-3
Lincoln G-5
Lindrith C-3
Lingo F-7
Loco Hills G-6
Logan D-7
Lordsburg H-1
Los Alamos C-4
Los Cerrillos D-4
Los Chavez E-3
Los Lunas E-3
Los Ojos B-3
Los Padillas E-3
Los Ranchos de
Albuquerque Pg. 90, B-8
Loving H-6
Lovington G-7
Luis Lopez E-3
Lumberton B-3
Luna F-1
Madrid D-4
Magdalena F-3
Malaga H-6
Maljamar G-6
Manuelito D-1
Manzano E-4
Maxwell B-5
Mayhill G-5
McAlister E-6
McCartys D-2
McDonald G-7
Melrose E-5
Mentmore D-1
Mesa E-6
Mescalero G-4
Mesita D-3
Mesquite H-3
Mexican Springs . . . C-1
Miami C-5
Miera D-4
Milan D-2
Mills C-6
Milnesand F-7
Mimbres H-2
Mineral Hill D-4
Mogollon G-1
Monero B-3
Montezuma C-5
Monticello G-2
Montoya D-6
Monument H-7
Mora C-4
Moriarty D-4
Mosquero C-6
Mountainair E-4
Mt. Dora B-6
Mule Creek G-1
Nadine H-7
Nageezi C-2
Nara Visa D-7
Naschitti C-1
Navajo C-1
Navajo C-1

Newcomb C-1
Newkirk D-6
Ocate C-5
Oil Center H-7
Ojo Caliente C-4
Ojo Feliz C-5
Old Horse Springs . . F-2
Omega E-2
Organ H-3
Orogrande H-4
Oscuro F-4
Paguate D-2
Paradise Hills Pg. 90, A-6
Paraje E-5
Pastura E-5
Pecos D-4
Pena Blanca D-3
Penasco C-4
Pep F-7
Peralta E-3
Pescado D-1
Picacho G-5
Pie Town E-2
Pine Lodge E-6
Pinon H-5
Pinos Altos H-1
Placita G-2
Placitas D-4
Pleasant Hill E-7
Pleasanton G-1
Pojoaque C-4
Portales E-7
Prewitt D-1
Pueblo D-4
Pueblo Bonito C-2
Puerto De Luna E-5
Punta E-4
Quay D-6
Quemado E-1
Questa B-4
Radium Springs H-3
Ragland E-6
Rainsville C-5
Ramah D-1
Ramon E-5
Ranchos De Taos . . . B-4
Ranchvale E-7
Raton B-6
Rayado B-5
Red Hill F-1
Red Rock H-1
Red River B-5
Regina C-3
Reserve F-1
Rincon H-3
Rinconada C-4
Rio Rancho D-3
Riverside G-6
Rociada C-4
Rodeo J-1
Rogers F-7
Romeroville D-5
Roswell E-6
Rowe D-4
Roy C-6
Ruidoso G-4
Ruidoso Downs G-4
Ruther,on B-3
Sabinal E-3
Sacramento H-4
Saint Vrain E-7
Salem H-3
Salt Lake E-1
San Acacia E-3
San Antonio F-3
San Antonio H-3
San Fidel D-2
San Ignacio C-4
San Jon D-7
San Juan H-2
San Lorenzo H-2
San Mateo D-2
San Miguel D-4
San Patricio G-4
San Rafael D-2
Santa Cruz C-4
Santa Fe C-4
Santa Rita H-2
Santa Rosa D-5
Sapello C-5
Sedan C-7
Sena D-5
Seneca B-7
Separ H-2
Seven Rivers H-6
Shadybrook C-5
Sheep Springs C-1
Shiprock B-1
Silver City H-2
Socorro F-3

NEW YORK

Solano C-6
Springer B-5
Standing Rock C-1
Stanley D-4
Sunset G-5
Sunshine J-2
Sunspot H-4
Taiban E-6
Tajique E-3
Talpa C-4
Taos B-4
Tatum G-7
Terrero C-4
Tesuque C-4
Thoreau D-1
Three Rivers G-4
Tierra Amarilla B-3
Tierra Monte C-4
Tijeras D-3
Tinnie G-5
Tohatchi C-1
Tolar E-6
Tome E-3
Torreon C-3
Torreon E-4
Tres Piedras B-4
Tres Ritos C-4
Truchas C-4
Trujillo D-5
Truth or Consequences
. . . . G-3
Tucumcari D-6
Tularosa G-4
Turley B-2
Turn E-3
Tyrone H-1
Ute Park B-5
Vado J-3
Valencia E-3
Vallecitos C-3
Valmora C-5
Variadero D-5
Vaughn E-5
Veguita E-3
Velarde C-4
Villanueva D-5
Virden H-1
Wagon Mound C-5
Watrous C-5
Weed G-5
Wheatland D-7
White Horse C-1
White Oaks F-4
White Rock C-4
White Sands Missile
Range H-4
Whites City H-6
Whitewater D-1
Willard E-4
Williamsburg G-3
Winston G-2
Yeso E-5
Youngsville C-3

NEW YORK
Pages 58-61
Population: 17,558,072
Capital: Albany
Land Area: 47,377 sq. mi.

Adams F-12
Addison N-8
Afton M-13
Airmont . . . Pg. 142, B-4
Akron J-5
Albany K-18
Albion H-6
Alden K-5
Alexander K-5
Alexandria Bay D-12
Alfred M-7
Allegany N-5
Almond M-7
Altamont K-18
Altmar G-12
Amagansett C-9
Amenia O-19
Ames K-16
Amityville . . Pg. 145, N-16
Amsterdam J-18
Andes M-16
Andover N-7
Angelica M-6
Angola L-4
Angola-on-the-Lake . L-3
Antwerp D-13
Apalachin N-12
Arcade L-5
Archville . . . Pg. 142, B-8

NEW YORK

Ardsley . . . . . Pg. 142, D-9
Argyle H-20
Arkport M-7
Arlington O-19
Armonk . . . Pg. 144, C-11
Asharoken Pg. 144, G-17
Astoria . . . Pg. 143, J-8
Athens M-19
Atlantic Beach . . . E-4
Vicinity . Pg. 145, Q-11
Attica K-5
Atwell G-15
Auburn K-10
Aurora K-10
Avoca M-8
Avon K-7
Babylon E-5
Vicinity . Pg. 145, M-14
Bainbridge M-13
Baldwin E-4
Vicinity . Pg. 145, Q-11
Baldwinsville . . . J-11
Ballston Spa J-18
Balmville A-3
Bardonia . . Pg. 142, B-6
Barker H-5
Barneveld H-14
Barnum Island
. . . . . . Pg. 145, Q-13
Batavia J-6
Bath M-8
Bay Park . Pg. 145, P-12
Bay Ridge . Pg. 143, M-6
Bay Shore E-6
Vicinity . Pg. 145, M-19
Bayberry
Vicinity . Pg. 164, A-8
Bayside . Pg. 143, K-10
Bayville D-5
Vicinity . Pg. 145, H-14
Beacon A-3
Bedford B-4
Vicinity . Pg. 144, B-13
Bedford Hills
. . . . . . Pg. 144, A-11
Bellmore . Pg. 145, N-14
Belmont N-6
Bemus Pt. N-2
Benson Hurst
. . . . . . Pg. 143, N-7
Bergen J-6
Bethpage D-5
Vicinity . Pg. 145, L-15
Big Flats N-9
Binghamton . . . N-12
Black River E-13
Blasdell K-4
Blauve . . Pg. 142, C-7
Bloomingburgh . . A-2
Bloomingdale . . C-18
Bloomingdale . . N-18
Bloomington . . N-18
Bolivar N-6
Boonville G-14
Bovsen Bay . . . J-11
Brasher Falls . . . B-16
Brentwood D-6
Vicinity . Pg. 145, L-19
Brewerton J-11
Brewster B-4
Briarcliff Manor . . C-4
Bridgehampton . . C-9
Bridgewater . . . K-14
Brighton . Pg. 156, J-4
Brightwaters
. . . . . . Pg. 145, M-19
Broadalbin J-18
Brockport J-6
Brocton M-2
Bronx . . Pg. 142, G-9
Brooklyn . . Pg. 143, L-7
Brookville . Pg. 145, K-14
Brownsville . . . E-12
Brushton B-16
Buchanan B-3
Buffalo K-4
Vicinity . . . . . Pg. 98
Detailed City . Pg. 212
Burdett M-8
Burke B-17
Bushnell Basin
. . . . . . Pg. 156, K-6
Cairo M-18
Caledonia K-7
Calverton D-7
Cambridge J-20
Camden H-13
Camillus J-11
Canajoharie . . . K-16
Canandaigua . . . K-8
Canarsie . Pg. 143, M-8

Canaseraga M-7
Canastota J-13
Candor M-11
Canisteo M-7
Canton C-14
Cape Vincent . . . E-11
Carthage E-13
Cassadaga M-2
Castile L-6
Castleton Corners
. . . . . . Pg. 143, N-4
Castleton-on-Hudson
. . . . L-18
Castorland F-13
Cato J-10
Catskill M-19
Cattaraugus M-4
Cayuga K-10
Cayuga Heights . . L-11
Cazenovia K-13
Cedarhurst Pg. 145, P-11
Celeron N-2
Center Moriches . . D-7
Center Port Pg. 145, H-17
Centereach D-6
Central Islip Pg. 145, K-20
Central Nyack
. . . . . . Pg. 142, C-7
Central Square . . H-12
Central Valley . . . B-3
Champlain A-19
Chappaqua Pg. 142, A-9
Chateaugay . . . A-17
Chatham M-19
Chaumont E-12
Chelsea . . Pg. 143, N-3
Cherry Creek . . . M-3
Cherry Valley . . . K-16
Chester B-2
Chili Center . Pg. 156, J-2
Chittenango J-13
Churchville J-7
Clarence Center . . J-4
Clarkstown . Pg. 142, B-6
Claverack M-19
Clayton D-12
Clayville J-14
Cleveland H-13
Clifton . . Pg. 156, K-1
Clifton Knolls . . . K-18
Clifton Springs . . K-9
Clinton J-14
Clintondale O-18
Clyde J-9
Cobleskill K-17
Cohocton L-8
Cohoes K-19
Cold Brook H-15
Cold Spring J-11
Vicinity . Pg. 164, A-7
Coldspring Harbor
. . . . . . Pg. 145, J-16
Collamer . Pg. 164, B-10
College Point Pg. 143, J-9
Colonie K-18
Commack . Pg. 145, K-18
Coney Island
. . . . . . Pg. 143, P-7
Constableville . . . G-14
Constantia H-12
Cooperstown . . . K-15
Copenhagen . . . F-13
Copiague . Pg. 145, N-17
Coram D-6
Corfu K-5
Corinth H-18
Corning N-9
Cornwall-on-Hudson . A-3
Cortland L-11
County Knolls . . . J-18
Cove Neck Pg. 145, J-15
Coxsackie M-19
Crittenden . Pg. 156, J-3
Croghan F-13
Croton-on-Hudson . B-3
Cuba N-5
Cutchogue C-8
Dannemora . . . B-18
Dansville L-7
DeRuyter K-13
DeWitt J-11
Deer Park D-5
Vicinity . Pg. 145, L-19
Deferiet E-13
Delanson K-17
Delevan L-5
Delhi M-15
Delmar L-18
Depew J-4
Deposit N-14

Dewitt . . Pg. 164, C-10
Dexter E-12
Dobbs Ferry . . . C-3
Vicinity . Pg. 142, D-8
Dolgeville J-16
Dongan Hills Pg. 143, N-4
Dover Plains O-19
Dresden L-9
Dryden L-11
Dundee L-9
Dunkirk M-2
Earlville K-13
East Aurora K-4
East Bloomfield . . K-8
East Glenville . . . J-18
East Hampton . . C-9
East Hills . Pg. 145, K-13
East Meadow . . . D-4
Vicinity . Pg. 145, M-14
East New York
. . . . . . Pg. 143, M-8
East Northport . . D-5
Vicinity . Pg. 145, J-17
East Penfield Pg. 156, J-7
East Quogue . . . C-9
East Randolph . . N-3
East Rochester . . J-8
Vicinity . Pg. 156, J-6
East Rockaway
. . . . . . Pg. 145, P-12
East Syracuse
. . . . . . Pg. 164, C-10
EastView . Pg. 142, C-9
Eastchester Pg. 142, E-9
Eatons Neck . . . C-5
Vicinity . Pg. 144, H-17
Eden L-4
Edgemere . Pg. 145, Q-11
Edwards C-15
Egypt . . Pg. 156, K-6
Elba J-6
Elbridge J-11
Ellenville O-17
Ellicottville M-4
Ellisburg F-12
Elma K-4
Elmira Hts. N-10
Elmont . . Pg. 145, N-12
Elmsford . Pg. 142, C-9
Elwood . . Pg. 145, J-17
Endicott N-12
Endwell N-12
Esperance K-17
Evans Mills E-12
Fabius K-12
Fair Haven H-10
Fairport J-8
Vicinity . Pg. 156, J-6
Falconer N-3
Farmingdale
. . . . . . Pg. 145, M-16
Farnham L-3
Fayetteville J-12
Fernwood H-19
Fillmore M-6
Firthcliffe A-3
Fishkill A-3
Flatbush . . Pg. 143, M-7
Fleischmanns . . . N-17
Floral Park Pg. 145, M-11
Florida B-2
Flower Hill Pg. 145, K-12
Flushing . Pg. 143, K-9
Fonda J-17
Forest Hills . Pg. 143, L-9
Forest Lawn Pg. 156, F-5
Forestville M-3
Fort Ann G-19
Fort Edward . . . H-19
Fort Johnson . . . J-17
Fort Plain K-16
Fort Salonga
. . . . . . Pg. 144, H-18
Frankfort J-15
Franklin M-15
Franklinville M-5
Freeport E-4
Vicinity . Pg. 145, P-14
Frewsburg N-3
Friendship N-6
Fulton H-11
Fultonville K-17
Gainesville L-6
Galway J-18
Gang Mills N-9
Garden City
. . . . . . Pg. 145, M-12
Gate . . . Pg. 156, H-2
Gateville . Pg. 164, B-8
Geneseo K-7
Geneva K-9

Gilbertsville L-14
Glasco N-18
Glen Cove D-4
Vicinity . Pg. 145, J-12
Glen Head Pg. 145, K-13
Glen Park E-12
Glenham A-3
Glens Falls H-19
Gloversville J-17
Goldens Bridge . . B-4
Goshen B-2
Gouverneur . . . D-14
Gowanda M-3
Grandview-on-Hudson
. . . . . . Pg. 142, C-8
Granville G-20
Great Kills . Pg. 143, P-4
Great Neck D-4
Vicinity . Pg. 145, K-11
Greece J-7
Vicinity . Pg. 156, G-2
Green Island . . . K-19
Green Lawn Pg. 145, J-17
Green Point Pg. 143, K-7
Greenburgh Pg. 142, D-9
Greene M-13
Greenport C-9
Greenwich J-20
Greenwood Lake . B-2
Groton L-11
Hadley H-19
Hagaman J-18
Halesite . Pg. 145, H-16
Hamburg L-4
Hamilton K-14
Hammond C-13
Hammondsport . . M-8
Hampton Bays . . D-8
Hancock O-15
Hannibal H-10
Harriman B-2
Harrison C-4
Vicinity . Pg. 144, F-11
Harrisville E-14
Hastings-On-Hudson
. . . . . . Pg. 142, E-8
Hauppage Pg. 145, K-19
Haverstraw B-3
Haviland O-19
Hawthorne Pg. 142, B-10
Hempstead E-4
Vicinity . Pg. 145, N-13
Henrietta . Pg. 156, K-4
Herkimer J-15
Hermon C-14
Herrings E-13
Heuvelton C-14
Hewlett Bay Park
. . . . . . Pg. 145, P-12
Hewlett Harbor
. . . . . . Pg. 145, P-12
Hicksville D-5
Vicinity . Pg. 145, L-15
Highland O-18
Highland Falls . . . B-3
Highland Mills . . . B-3
Hillburn C-2
Hillcrest . Pg. 142, A-6
Hillside Lake . . . P-19
Hilton H-7
Hobart M-16
Holbrook D-6
Holcomb K-8
Holland L-5
Holland Patent . . H-14
Holley J-6
Holmes M-16
Homer L-11
Honeoye Falls . . K-7
Hoosick Falls . . . J-20
Hornell M-7
Horseheads . . . N-10
Houghton M-6
Hudson M-19
Hudson Falls . . . H-19
Hugenot Park
. . . . . . Pg. 143, Q-3
Huguenot . Pg. 143, Q-3
Hunter M-17
Huntington D-5
Vicinity . Pg. 145, J-16
Huntington Sta. . . D-5
Hurley O-18
Hyde Park A-3
Ilion J-15
Interlaken L-10
Inwood . . Pg. 145, P-11
Irondequoit Pg. 156, G-4
Irvington . Pg. 142, D-8
Island Park Pg. 145, Q-12
Islip D-6

Ithaca M-11
Jamaica . . Pg. 145, N-11
Jamesport C-8
Jamestown N-2
Jefferson Hts. . . . M-18
Jefferson Valley . . B-4
Jeffersonville . . . O-15
Jericho D-5
Johnson City . . . N-12
Johnstown J-17
Jones Island
. . . . . . Pg. 145, Q-14
Jordan J-11
Keeseville C-19
Kenmore K-3
Kensington Pg. 145, L-12
Kerhonkson . . . O-17
Keuka Park L-9
Kinderhook M-19
Kings Park Pg. 145, J-19
Kings Point Pg. 145, K-11
Kingston N-18
Kiryas Joel B-2
Lackawanna . . . K-4
Lacona G-12
Ladentown . Pg. 142, A-5
Lake Carmel . . . A-4
Lake Erie Beach . L-3
Lake George . . . G-18
Lake Luzerne . . . H-18
Lake Placid D-18
Lake Ronkonkoma . D-6
Lakewood N-2
Lancaster K-4
Lansing L-11
Larchmont Pg. 142, F-10
Latham K-18
Lattington . Pg. 145, H-13
Laurel Hollow
. . . . . . Pg. 145, J-15
Laurens L-14
Lawrence Pg. 145, Q-11
LeRoy K-6
Leicester K-6
Levittown E-5
Vicinity . Pg. 145, M-15
Lewiston J-3
Liberty O-16
Lido Beach Pg. 145, Q-13
Lima K-7
Lime Lake M-5
Limestone N-4
Lincoln Park . . . N-18
Lindenhurst E-5
Vicinity . Pg. 145, N-17
Lisle M-12
Little Falls J-16
Little Valley M-4
Liverpool J-11
Vicinity . Pg. 164, B-7
Livingston Manor . O-16
Livonia K-7
Lloyd Harbor . . . D-5
Vicinity . Pg. 145, H-15
Lloyd Neck Pg. 144, H-16
Lockport J-4
Locust Grove
. . . . . . Pg. 145, K-15
Locust Valley
. . . . . . Pg. 145, J-13
Lodi L-10
Long Beach E-4
Vicinity . Pg. 145, Q-12
Long Island City
. . . . . . Pg. 143, K-7
Lorenz Pk. M-19
Lowville F-14
Lynbrook . Pg. 145, P-12
Lyndonville H-5
Lyons J-9
Lyons Falls G-14
Macedon J-8
Machias M-5
Madison K-14
Mahopac B-4
Malone B-17
Malverne . Pg. 145, N-12
Mamaroneck . . . C-4
Vicinity . Pg. 142, E-10
Manchester J-8
Manhasset Pg. 145, K-12
Manhattan . Pg. 143, J-7
Manlius J-12
Mannsville F-12
Manorhaven
. . . . . . Pg. 145, K-11
Marathon M-12
Marcellus J-11
Margaretville . . . N-16

Marlboro P-18
Massapequa E-5
Vicinity . Pg. 145, N-15
Massapequa Park
. . . . . . Pg. 145, N-16
Massena B-15
Mastic D-7
Mastic Beach . . . D-7
Matinecock Pg. 145, J-14
Mattituck C-8
Mattydale J-11
Vicinity . Pg. 164, B-9
Maybrook A-2
Mayfield M-2
Mayville M-2
McGraw L-12
Meadow Island
. . . . . . Pg. 145, Q-14
Mechanicville . . . K-19
Medford D-6
Medina J-5
Melville . Pg. 145, L-16
Menands K-19
Meridian J-10
Merrick . Pg. 145, P-14
Merriewold Lake . . B-2
Mexico H-11
Middle Hope . . . P-18
Middleburgh . . . L-17
Middleport J-5
Middletown A-2
Vicinity . Pg. 156, H-1
Middleville J-15
Milford L-15
Mill Neck Pg. 145, H-14
Millbrook O-19
Millerton N-19
Millport M-10
Milton O-18
Mineola . Pg. 145, K-13
Mineville E-19
Minetto H-11
Minoa J-12
Mohawk J-15
Monroe B-2
Monsey B-3
Vicinity . Pg. 142, B-5
Montauk C-10
Montgomery . . . A-2
Monticello P-16
Montour Falls . . . M-10
Mooers A-19
Moravia L-11
Morris L-15
Morristown C-14
Morrisville K-13
Mount Ivy . Pg. 142, A-6
Mount Kisco B-4
Vicinity . Pg. 144, B-11
Mount Morris . . . L-7
Mount Pleasant
. . . . . . Pg. 142, C-9
MountVernon . . . D-4
Munnsville K-13
Muttontown Pg. 145, K-14
Nanuet C-3
Napanoch O-17
Naples L-8
Nassau L-19
Nelliston K-16
Vicinity . Pg. 145, J-13
New Berlin L-14
New Brighton
. . . . . . Pg. 143, M-5
New Cassel
. . . . . . Pg. 145, M-14
New Dorp . Pg. 143, P-4
New Dorp Beach
. . . . . . Pg. 143, P-4
New Hartford . . . J-14
New Hempstead
. . . . . . Pg. 142, A-5
New Hyde Park
. . . . . . Pg. 145, M-12
New Paltz O-18
New Rochelle . . . D-4
Vicinity . Pg. 142, F-10
New Suffolk C-8
New York City . . . E-3
Vicinity . Pg. 142-145
Detailed City . Pg. 262
New York Mills . . J-14
Newark J-9
Newark Valley . . . M-12
Newburgh . . A-3, P-18
Newfane H-4
Newfield M-11
Newport H-15
Vicinity . Pg. 145, K-11
Niagara Falls . . . J-3
Nichols N-11
Norfolk B-15
North Chili . Pg. 156, J-1

North Collins L-3
North Greece
. . . . . . Pg. 156, F-2
North Haven . . . C-9
North Hills Pg. 145, L-12
North Hornell . . . M-7
North New Hyde Park
. . . . . . Pg. 145, M-12
North Sea C-9
North Syracuse . . C-8
Vicinity . Pg. 164, A-9
North Tarrytown
. . . . . . Pg. 142, B-8
North Tonawanda . J-4
Northville H-17
Norwich (Chenango Cty)
. . . . L-13
Norwich (Nassau Cty)
. . . . . . Pg. 145, K-14
Norwood B-15
Noyack C-9
Nunda L-6
Nyack C-3
Vicinity . Pg. 142, B-7
Oak Beach Pg. 145, P-19
Oakfield J-5
Ocean Beach . . . E-6
Oceanside Pg. 145, P-13
Odessa M-10
Ogden Center
. . . . . . Pg. 156, H-1
Ogdensburg B-13
Oklahoma Beach
. . . . . . Pg. 156, F-5
Olcott H-4
Old Bethpage
. . . . . . Pg. 145, L-16
Old Brookville
. . . . . . Pg. 145, K-13
Old Forge G-14
OldWestbury
. . . . . . Pg. 145, K-13
Olean N-5
Oneida J-13
Oneida Castle . . . J-13
Oneonta M-15
Orange Lake . . . A-3
Orangeburg Pg. 142, D-7
Orangetown Pg. 142, C-6
Orchard Park . . . K-4
Oriskany J-14
Oriskany Falls . . . J-14
Ossining C-4
Oswego H-10
Otego M-14
Otisville A-1
Ovid L-10
Owego N-11
Oxford M-13
Oyster Bay Pg. 145, J-14
Oyster Bay Cove
. . . . . . Pg. 145, J-15
Ozone Park Pg. 143, L-9
Painted Post N-9
Palatine Bridge . . K-16
Palisades . Pg. 142, D-8
Palmyra J-9
Panama N-2
Parish H-12
Parma Center
. . . . . . Pg. 156, F-1
Parma Corners
. . . . . . Pg. 156, G-1
Patchoque D-6
Pawling A-4
Pearl River C-3
Vicinity . Pg. 142, C-6
Peconic C-8
Peekskill B-3
Pelham . Pg. 142, F-9
Pelham Manor
. . . . . . Pg. 142, G-9
Penfield . Pg. 156, J-6
Penfield Center
. . . . . . Pg. 156, H-6
PennYan L-9
Perry K-6
Perrysburg M-3
Peru C-19
Phelps K-9
Philadelphia E-3
Philmont M-19
Phoenix H-11
Piermont . Pg. 142, C-8
Pike L-6
Pine Bush P-18
Pine Hill N-17
Pine Plains N-19
Pitcher Hill . Pg. 164, A-9

Pittsford J-8
Vicinity . Pg. 156, J-5
Plainview D-5
Vicinity . Pg. 145, L-16
Plandome Manor
. . . . . . Pg. 145, K-11
Plattsburgh B-19
Pleasantville . . . C-4
Pocantico Hill
. . . . . . Pg. 142, B-9
Poestenkill K-20
Poland H-15
Pomona B-3
Port Byron J-10
Port Chester
. . . . . . Pg. 144, F-12
Port Dickinson . . N-13
Port Ewen N-18
Port Henry E-19
Port Jefferson . . . C-6
Port Jervis B-1
Port Leyden G-14
Port Richmond
. . . . . . Pg. 143, M-3
Port Washington
. . . . . . Pg. 145, K-12
Port Washington North
. . . . . . Pg. 145, K-12
Portville N-5
Potsdam B-15
Poughkeepsie . . . O-19
Pound Ridge
. . . . . . Pg. 144, B-14
Prospect H-14
Pulaski G-12
Queens . Pg. 143, K-9
Queens Village
. . . . . . Pg. 145, M-11
Quogue D-8
Ramapo . Pg. 142, A-3
Randolph N-3
Ransomville J-4
Ravena L-18
Red Creek H-10
Red Hook N-19
Red Oaks Mill . . . O-19
Remsen H-15
Rensselaer L-19
Rensselaer Falls . . C-14
Rhinebeck N-19
Richburg N-6
Richfield Springs . . K-15
Richmond Hill
. . . . . . Pg. 143, L-9
Richmondville . . . L-17
Richville C-14
Ridge D-7
Riverdale . Pg. 142, F-9
Riverhead D-8
Riverside N-9
Rochester J-7
Vicinity . Pg. 156, H-4
Detailed City . Pg. 278
Rockville Center
. . . . . . Pg. 145, N-13
Rocky Pt. C-7
Roessleville K-18
Rome J-13
Roosevelt Pg. 145, N-14
Roseland . Pg. 156, G-7
Rosedale
Roslyn . Pg. 145, K-12
Roslyn Harbor
. . . . . . Pg. 145, K-13
Roslyn Hts. Pg. 145, L-13
Rossville . Pg. 143, P-3
Round Lake
Rouses Point . . . A-19
Ruby N-18
Rushville K-9
Rye C-4
Vicinity . Pg. 144, F-12
Rye Brook C-4
Vicinity . Pg. 144, F-12
Sackets Harbor . . F-12
Sag Harbor C-9
Saint Johnsville . . J-16
Saint Lawrence Park D-12
Salamanca N-4
Salem H-20
Saltaire . Pg. 145, P-20
San Remo J-19
Sand Ridge J-11
Sands Point Pg. 145, J-11
Sandy Creek . . . G-12
Saranac Lake . . . D-18
Saratoga Springs . J-18
Saugerties N-18
Savona M-9
Sayville D-6

NEW YORK

NORTH CAROLINA

NORTH CAROLINA
Pages 64-65
Population: 5,881,766
Capital: Raleigh
Land Area: 48,843 sq. mi.

NEW YORK

Scarsdale C-4
Vicinity . Pg. 142, E-10
Schaghticoke J-19
Schenectady K-18
Schenevus L-15
Schoharie L-17
Schuylerville J-19
Scotch Town A-2
Scotia K-18
Scottsville J-7
Sea Cliff . Pg. 145, J-12
Seaford . Pg. 145, P-15
Searington Pg. 145, L-12
Selden D-6
Seneca Falls K-10
Severance . Pg. 156, K-2
Sharon Springs . K-16
Shelter Island C-9
Sherburne L-14
Sherman N-1
Sherrill J-13
Shirley D-7
Shortsville K-8
Sidney M-14
Silver Creek L-3
Silver Springs L-6
Sinclairville M-2
Skaneateles K-11
Sloatsburg C-2
Vicinity . Pg. 142, A-3
Smithtown D-6
Smyrna L-13
Sodus H-9
Sodus Point H-9
Solvay J-11
Vicinity . Pg. 164, Q-18
Sound Beach C-6
South Chili . Pg. 156, K-1
South Corning N-9
South Fallsburg O-16
South Farmingdale
. . . . Pg. 145, M-16
South Glens Falls . H-19
South Greece
. . . . Pg. 156, G-2
South Nyack Pg. 142, C-8
Southampton D-8
Southold C-8
Southport N-10
Sparkill . . . . Pg. 142, D-7
Speculator G-17
Spencer N-11
Spencerport J-7
Vicinity . Pg. 156, G-1
Split Rock . . Pg. 164, C-7
Spring Valley C-3
Vicinity . Pg. 142, B-6
Springfield Gdns.
. . . . Pg. 143, M-10
Springs C-9
Springville L-4
Stamford M-16
Stannards N-6
Star Lake D-15
Staten Island
. . . . Pg. 143, N-5
Stillwater J-19
Stony Brook D-6
Stony Pt. B-3
Stottville M-19
Success . Pg. 145, L-12
Suffern C-3
Vicinity . Pg. 142, B-4
Sylvan Beach J-13
Syosset . Pg. 145, K-15
Syracuse K-11
Vicinity . Pg. 164, C-8
Tall Man . Pg. 142, B-4
Tannersville M-18
Tarrytown C-4
Vicinity . Pg. 142, C-8
Theresa D-13
Thornwood Pg. 142, B-10
Ticonderoga F-19
Tillson O-18
Tivoli N-18
Tonawanda J-4
Town Line K-5
Tribes Hill J-17
Troy K-19
Trumansburg L-10
Tuckahoe D-8
Tully K-12
Tupper Lake D-17
Turin F-14
Tuxedo Park B-2
Vicinity . Pg. 142, A-3
Unadilla M-14
Union Hill . Pg. 156, G-7
Union Springs K-10

Uniondale Pg. 145, M-13
Unionville B-15
University Gardens
. . . . Pg. 145, L-11
Upper Brookville
. . . . Pg. 145, J-14
Upper Nyack Pg. 142, B-7
Utica J-15
Valatie L-19
Valhalla . Pg. 144, E-11
Valley Cottage
. . . . Pg. 142, B-7
Valley Falls J-20
Valley Stream E-4
Vicinity . Pg. 145, N-11
Van Etten N-11
Vernon J-14
Verona J-12
Victor K-8
Victory J-10
Village of the Branch
. . . . Pg. 145, J-20
Viola . Pg. 142, A-5
Voorheesville L-18
Waddington B-14
Wading River C-7
Walden A-2
Wallkill A-2
Walton N-15
Walton Park B-2
Wampsville J-13
Wantagh . Pg. 145, N-15
Wappinger Falls . . . A-3
Warrensburg G-19
Warsaw K-6
Warwick B-2
Washingtonville . . . A-2
Waterford K-19
Waterloo K-9
Watertown E-13
Waterville K-14
Watervliet K-19
Watkins Glen M-10
Waverly N-11
Wayland L-7
Wayneport Pg. 156, K-7
Webster J-8
Vicinity . Pg. 156, G-6
Weedsport J-10
Wellsburg N-10
Wellsville N-6
Wesley Hills Pg. 142, A-5
West Carthage F-13
West Chili . Pg. 156, J-1
West End L-15
West Greece Pg. 156, G-2
West Plattsburgh . B-19
West Point B-3
West Sand Lake . L-19
West Walworth
. . . . Pg. 156, H-7
West Webster
. . . . Pg. 156, G-5
West Winfield K-15
Westbury . Pg. 145, M-13
Westfield M-2
Westhampton D-8
Westmere K-17
Westons Mills N-5
Westport D-18
Westvale . Pg. 164, C-8
White Plains C-4
Vicinity . Pg. 142, D-10
Whitehall G-20
Whitesboro J-14
Whitney Point M-12
Willard L-10
Williamsville K-4
Williston Park
. . . . Pg. 145, L-13
Willow Brook Pg. 143, N-4
Wilson H-4
Windsor N-13
Winthrop B-16
Witherbee E-19
Wolcott H-10
Woodbury . Pg. 145, K-15
Woodhull N-8
Woodmere Pg. 145, P-11
Woodridge O-17
Woodsburg Pg. 145, Q-12
Woodstock N-18
Wyadanch Pg. 145, L-17
Wyoming K-6
Yonkers D-3
Vicinity . Pg. 142, E-8
Yorkshire L-5
Yorktown Hts M-12
Yorkville J-13
Youngstown H-3
Zena N-18

NORTH CAROLINA

Abbotsburg E-10
Aberdeen D-8
Acre C-12
Ahoskie A-12
Albemarle D-7
Alexis . Pg. 101, A-1
Allen D-7
Allenton E-9
Andrews D-2
Apex . Pg. 155, J-6
Arapahoe D-12
Arcadia . Pg. 169, F-1
Archdale C-7
Vicinity . Pg. 169, F-7
Arcola B-10
Arlington B-6
Arnold . Pg. 169, G-1
Asbury . Pg. 155, G-4
Asheboro C-8
Asheville C-4
Vicinity . Pg. 91, B-7
Ashland B-12
Askin D-12
Aurora C-12
Avery Creek D-4
Avon C-14
Ayden C-11
Azalea . Pg. 91, B-7
Badin D-7
Bagley C-10
Bald Creek C-4
Baldwin B-5
Bandana C-4
Banner Elk C-4
Barco A-13
Bat Cave D-4
Battleboro B-11
Bayleaf . Pg. 155, D-6
Bear Creek C-9
Beaufort D-13
Belgrade D-11
Belhaven C-12
Belmont D-6
Vicinity . Pg. 101, E-2
Benson C-9
Bertha A-13
Bessemer City D-6
Bethel B-11
Bethel Hill A-9
Bethesda . Pg. 155, D-3
Beulaville D-11
Beverly Hills Pg. 91, C-7
Biltmore . Pg. 91, C-6
Birmingham Heights
. . . . Pg. 91, B-5
Biscoe D-8
Black Mtn. C-4
Bladenboro E-9
Blowing Rock B-5
Bolton E-10
Bonnie Doone
. . . . Pg. 118, C-2
Bonsal . Pg. 155, K-1
Boone B-5
Bottom A-6
Bowdens D-10
Brasstown D-2
Brevard D-4
Bridgeton D-12
Bridgewater C-5
Brookford C-5
Brooks Cross Roads B-6
Brooksdale B-9
Browns Summit . . . B-8
Brunswick F-10
Bryson City D-2
Buena Vista Pg. 91, D-6
Bulade B-4
Bullock A-9
Bunn B-10
Burch B-6
Burgaw E-10
Burlington B-8
Burnsville B-4
Busbee . Pg. 91, D-6
Buxton C-14
Calypso D-10
Camden A-13
Cameron C-9
Candor D-8
Canto C-3
Canton D-3
Caraleigh . Pg. 155, H-6

Carolina Beach F-11
Carpenter . Pg. 155, G-2
Carr B-8
Carrboro B-9
Cary C-9
Vicinity . Pg. 155, G-4
Casville B-8
Cedar Creek D-10
Celo C-4
Centerville B-10
Chadbourn F-10
Chapel Hill C-9
Charlotte D-7
Vicinity . Pg. 101
Detailed City . Pg. 214
Cherokee D-3
Cherryville D-5
China Grove C-7
Chinquapin D-11
Chocowinity C-12
Churchland C-7
Cid . Pg. 155, F-3
Clegg . Pg. 155, F-3
Clemmons B-7
Cliffdale . Pg. 118, D-1
Clinton D-10
Cloverdale . Pg. 155, J-7
Coinjock A-13
Colerain B-12
Colfax . Pg. 169, B-6
College C-11
College View Pg. 155, H-6
Columbia B-13
Columbus D-4
Comfort D-11
Concord D-7
Conover C-6
Conway A-12
Corapeake A-12
Cornelius D-6
Council E-10
Cove Creek C-3
Craggy . Pg. 91, A-5
Cramerton . Pg. 101, E-1
Creedmoor B-9
Creswell B-13
Culberson D-1
Cumberland Pg. 118, E-1
Currie E-10
Dalton B-7
Darden B-12
Davidson C-6
Deep Gap B-5
Deep River . Pg. 169, D-7
Del Mar Beach E-12
Delway E-10
Derita . . . . . Pg. 101, C-7
Dillsboro D-2
Dixie . Pg. 101, F-3
Dobson B-7
Dortches B-10
Dudley D-10
Dunn D-9
Durham D-9
Vicinity . Pg. 155
East Lake B-13
East Laport D-3
Easton View Pg. 169, D-2
Eastwood D-8
Eden A-8
Edenhouse B-12
Edenton B-12
Edneyville D-4
Edward C-12
Ela D-3
Eldorado C-7
Elizabeth City A-13
Elizabethtown E-10
Elk Mountain Pg. 91, A-5
Elk Park B-4
Elkin B-6
Emery C-4
Emma . Pg. 91, B-5
Enfield B-11
Englehard C-13
Enterprise . Pg. 169, F-1
Erwin D-9
Essex B-10
Ether C-8
Evergreen E-9
Fair Bluff F-9
Fairmont E-9
Faison D-10
Falls . Pg. 155, D-7
Farmville C-11
Fayetteville D-9
Vicinity . Pg. 118, D-2
Few . Pg. 155, C-3
Five Points . Pg. 169, D-1
Flat Rock D-4

Fletcher D-4
Folkston E-11
Fontana Village D-2
Forest City D-5
Fountain C-11
Franklin D-2
Freeman E-10
Fremont C-10
Friendship . Pg. 155, J-2
Frisco C-14
Fuquay-Varina C-9
Garner . Pg. 155, J-7
Garysburg A-11
Gastonia D-6
Vicinity . Pg. 101, D-1
Gates A-12
Geenie . Pg. 155, F-2
Gilkey D-5
Gilmer D-3
Glade Valley B-5
Glen Forest Pg. 155, B-3
Glenola . Pg. 169, G-7
Glenview B-10
Glenwood C-5
Gneiss D-3
Godwin D-9
Gold Rock B-11
Goldsboro C-10
Goldston C-8
Gordonton B-9
Gornian . Pg. 155, B-3
Graingers C-11
Grandy A-13
Granite Falls C-5
Granite Quarry C-7
Grantham D-10
Green Level Pg. 155, H-2
Greensboro B-8
Vicinity . Pg. 169
Greenville C-11
Grifton C-11
Grissettown F-10
Grissom . Pg. 155, A-7
Groometown Pg. 169, E-8
Guilford B-8
Vicinity . Pg. 169, C-7
Gumtree . Pg. 169, E-2
Guthrie . Pg. 169, B-3
Halifax A-11
Hamlet D-8
Hampstead E-11
Harbinger B-14
Harmony B-6
Harrells E-10
Harrisburg D-7
Vicinity . Pg. 101, C-9
Hatteras C-14
Hazelwood D-3
Heartsease B-11
Henderson B-10
Hendersonville D-4
Henrietta D-5
Hertford B-12
Hester B-9
Hickory C-5
Hickory Grove
. . . . Pg. 101, E-8
High Hampton D-3
High Point B-7
Vicinity . Pg. 169
Hightowers B-8
Hill Crest B-9
Hillsborough B-9
Hillsdale . Pg. 169, A-8
Hiwassee D-3
Hoffman D-8
Holly Ridge E-11
Holly Springs
. . . . Pg. 155, K-3
Hollyville (Cash Corner)
Hope Mills D-9
House C-11
Hubert D-11
Huckleberry Spring
. . . . Pg. 155, B-1
Hudson C-5
Huntersville Pg. 101, A-6
Ingleside B-9
Jackson A-11
Jacksonville D-11
Jamestown Pg. 169, E-7
Jamesville B-12
Jarvisburg A-13
Johns E-9
Jonas Ridge C-5
Jonesville B-6
Joyland . Pg. 155, C-3
Julian B-8
Justice B-10

Kannapolis C-7
Keene . Pg. 155, D-2
Keener D-10
Kelley E-10
Kenansville D-11
Kenly C-10
Kernersville B-7
Vicinity . Pg. 169, B-4
Kilkenny B-13
King B-7
Kings Mountain . . . D-5
Kinston D-11
Kittrell B-10
Kuhns D-12
Kure Beach F-11
La Grange D-11
Lake Landing C-13
Lakeview D-9
Landis C-7
Lauada D-3
Laurinburg E-9
Lawrence B-11
Leasburg A-9
Leechville C-13
Leesville . Pg. 155, E-5
Lemon Springs C-8
Lenoir C-5
Level Cross B-8
Vicinity . Pg. 169, G-9
Lewis A-9
Lexington C-7
Liberia B-10
Liberty B-8
Lilesville D-8
Lillington C-9
Lincolnton D-5
Linwood C-7
Lizzie C-11
Logan D-5
Long Beach F-10
Longview C-5
Louisburg B-10
Lowell . Pg. 101, D-1
Lowesville . Pg. 101, A-3
Lucama C-11
Lucia . Pg. 101, B-3
Luck C-3
Lumber Bridge D-9
Lumberton E-9
Macedonia . Pg. 155, H-5
Maco E-10
Madison B-7
Magnolia D-10
Maiden C-6
Mamie B-13
Manchester Pg. 118, A-1
Manns Harbor B-13
Manteo B-13
Maple Hill E-11
Marble D-2
Marion C-5
Mars Hill C-4
Marshall C-3
Marshville D-7
Marston D-8
Mathis . Pg. 169, C-4
Matthews D-7
Vicinity . Pg. 101, G-8
Maxton E-9
Mayodan B-8
Maysville D-12
McCullers . Pg. 155, K-6
Mesic C-12
Method . Pg. 155, G-6
Micro C-10
Middleburg A-10
Midway B-12
Vicinity . Pg. 91, E-7
Midway Park E-11
Millbrook . Pg. 155, F-7
Mint Hill D-7
Mocksville C-6
Moncure C-9
Monroe D-7
Monticello B-8
Mooresville C-6
Morehead City D-12
Morgans Corner . . . A-13
Morganton C-5
Morrisville . Pg. 155, G-3
Mount Airy A-7
Mount Gilead D-7
Mount Holly D-6
Vicinity . Pg. 101, D-3
Mount Mourne C-6
Mount Olive D-10
Mountain Home . . . D-4
Mulberry B-6
Murfreesboro A-11

Nags Head B-14
Nakina F-10
Nantahala D-2
Nashville B-11
Nelson . Pg. 155, E-3
Neuse . Pg. 155, E-7
New Bern D-12
New Bridge . Pg. 91, A-6
New Holland C-13
New Salem D-7
Newell . Pg. 101, D-7
Newhill . Pg. 155, K-1
Newport D-12
Newton C-6
Newton Grove D-10
Norlina A-10
Norman D-8
North Wilkesboro . . B-6
Northside B-9
Vicinity . Pg. 155, A-4
Oak Grove B-9
Oak Ridge . Pg. 169, A-6
Oakboro D-7
Ocracoke C-14
Old Dock F-10
Old Ford C-12
Old Fort C-4
Vicinity . Pg. 169, B-1
Oldtown . Pg. 169, B-1
Olivia D-9
Osceola B-8
Oswalt C-6
Oteen C-4
Otto D-3
Oxford B-9
Pantego C-12
Parkwood . Pg. 155, E-2
Patterson B-5
Peachtree D-2
Pembroke E-9
Penderlea E-10
Picks B-9
Pilot Mountain B-7
Pine Ridge A-6
Pinebluff D-8
Pineola B-5
Pinetops B-11
Pineville D-6
Pinnacle B-7
Pireway F-10
Pittsboro C-9
Pleasant Garden
. . . . Pg. 169, E-10
Pleasant Hill A-11
Plymouth B-12
Point Harbor B-13
Polkton D-7
Pollocksville D-11
Portsmouth D-13
Postell D-1
Powells Point B-14
Raeford D-9
Rainbow Springs . . . D-2
Raleigh C-9
Vicinity . Pg. 155
Randleman C-8
Ranger D-1
Ransomville C-12
Rapids A-11
Red Hill B-4
Red Springs E-9
Reidsville B-8
Rheasville A-11
Riceville . Pg. 91, A-7
Rich Square B-11
Roanoke Rapids . . . A-11
Robbinsville D-2
Robersonville B-11
Rockingham D-7
Rodanthe B-14
Roduco A-12
Roper B-12
Rose Hill D-10
Roseboro D-10
Roseneath B-11
Rougemont B-9
Rowan E-10
Rowland E-9
Roxboro A-9
Royal Pines . Pg. 91, E-7
Rudd . Pg. 169, A-10
Ruth D-5
Rutherfordton D-4
Saint Pauls E-9
Salemburg D-10
Salisbury C-7
Salvo B-14
Sand Hill . Pg. 91, C-5

Sanford C-9
Schley B-9
Scotland Neck B-11
Scott's Hill E-11
Scranton C-13
Seabreeze F-11
Seagrove C-8
Sedgefield . Pg. 169, D-8
Selma C-10
Shallotte D-7
Sharpsburg B-11
Shelby D-5
Shopton . Pg. 101, F-3
Siler City C-8
Sioux B-4
Six Forks . Pg. 155, E-6
Skyland C-4
Vicinity . Pg. 91, E-6
Slocomb . Pg. 118, B-3
Smith F-10
Smithfield C-10
Snow Hill C-11
Southern Pines D-9
Southport F-10
Sparta A-6
Spencer C-7
Spivey's Corner . D-10
Spout Springs D-9
Spring Hill B-11
Spring Lake D-9
Vicinity . Pg. 118, B-1
Spruce Pine C-5
Stanhope B-10
Stanley D-6
Vicinity . Pg. 101, B-1
Stanleyville B-7
Vicinity . Pg. 169, A-1
State Road B-6
Statesville C-6
Steeds C-8
Stocksville C-4
Stokes C-12
Stony Point C-6
Stovall A-10
Stratford A-6
Summerfield Pg. 169, A-7
Sunbury A-12
Supply F-10
Surf City E-11
Surl B-9
Swaintown Pg. 169, D-1
Swann C-9
Swannanoa C-4
Swansboro E-12
Swiss C-4
Sylva D-3
Tabor City E-9
Tapoco D-2
Tar Heel E-9
Tarboro B-11
Taylorsville C-6
Teachey D-10
Thomasville C-7
Vicinity . Pg. 169, G-5
Tillery B-11
Tin City E-10
Tobaccoville B-7
Tokay . Pg. 118, C-3
Toluca C-5
Topsail Beach E-11
Topton D-2
Tramway C-9
Trent Woods D-12
Trenton D-11
Trinity . Pg. 169, G-6
Trust C-3
Tryon D-4
Turnersburg C-6
Tuxedo D-4
Twin Oaks A-6
Ulah C-8
Unaka D-2
Union Cross Pg. 169, D-4
Union Ridge Pg. 169, D-1
Upchurch . Pg. 155, G-3
Uwharrie C-7
Valdese C-5
Valley Springs
. . . . Pg. 91, D-6
Vanceboro C-11
Vander D-9
Violet C-7
Wadesboro E-7
Wadeville D-7
Wagram E-9
Wake Forest B-10
Walkertown Pg. 169, A-3
Wallace D-11
Wallburg . Pg. 169, D-3
Walnut C-4
Walnut Creek C-11

NORTH CAROLINA

OHIO

Wanchese B-14
Wards Corner . . . E-10
Warsaw D-10
Waughtown Pg. 169, C-2
Waves B-14
Waynesville D-3
Weaver . . . Pg. 155, B-2
Welcome . . Pg. 169, G-2
Weldon A-11
Wendell C-10
Wesser D-2
West Concord
. . . . . Pg. 101, A-10
West Haven . . Pg. 91, E-5
West Onslow Beach E-12
Westminster D-5
Westover . . Pg. 155, G-5
Whalebone B-14
White Lake E-10
White Oak E-10
Whiteville F-10
Wilbar B-6
Wilders Grove
. . . . . Pg. 155, G-7
Wilkesboro B-6
Willard E-10
Williams Crossroads
. . . . . Pg. 155, K-6
Williamsburg B-8
Williamston B-12
Wilmar C-12
Wilmington F-10
Wilmington Beach . F-11
Wilson C-11
Windsor B-12
Wingate D-7
Winnabow F-10
Winston-Salem . . . B-7
Vicinity . . . . . Pg. 169
Winterville C-11
Winton A-12
Wise A-10
Wise Fork D-11
Woodfin . . . Pg. 91, A-5
Woodland B-11
Woodley B-13
Wrightsville Beach . F-11
Yadkinville B-7
Yancyville A-8
Yeatesville C-12
Youngsville B-10
Zebulon B-10

NORTH DAKOTA
Page 63
Population: 652,717
Capital: Bismarck
Land Area: 69,300 sq. mi.

Abercrombie F-9
Adams B-8
Alamo B-2
Alexander C-2
Alice D-8
Almont E-4
Alsen B-7
Ambrose B-2
Amenia E-9
Amidon E-2
Anamoose C-6
Aneta D-8
Antler A-5
Ardoch C-9
Arena D-6
Argusville E-10
Arnegard C-2
Arthur E-9
Ashley F-6
Ayr E-9
Balfour C-5
Balta C-6
Bantry B-5
Barney F-9
Barton B-6
Bathgate B-9
Battleview B-3
Beach D-1
Belcourt B-6
Belfield D-2
Benedict C-5
Berlin E-7
Berthold B-4
Berwick C-6
Beulah D-4
Binford D-8
Bisbee B-7
Bismarck E-5
Bottineau B-6
Bowbells B-3

Bowden D-6
Bowman E-2
Braddock E-6
Breien E-5
Bremen D-7
Brinsmade C-7
Brocket C-8
Bucyrus F-2
Buffalo E-9
Burlington B-4
Butte C-5
Buxton D-9
Calio B-7
Calvin B-7
Cando B-7
Carbury B-5
Carpio B-4
Carrington D-7
Carson E-4
Casselton E-9
Cathay D-7
Cavalier B-9
Cayuga F-9
Center D-4
Charlson C-3
Churchs Ferry . . . C-7
Cleveland E-7
Clifford D-9
Colehabor D-5
Colfax F-9
Columbus A-3
Conway C-9
Cooperstown D-8
Courtenay D-8
Crary C-8
Crosby A-2
Crystal B-9
Davenport E-9
Dawson F-6
Dazey D-8
Deering B-5
Des Lacs B-4
Devils Lake C-7
Dickey E-7
Dickinson D-3
Dodge D-3
Donnybrook B-4
Douglas C-4
Drake C-6
Drayton B-9
Driscoll E-6
Dunn Center D-3
Dunseith B-6
Dwight F-10
Edgeley F-7
Edinburg B-8
Edmore C-8
Elgin E-4
Ellendale F-8
Elliott F-8
Emerado C-9
Enderlin E-8
Epping B-2
Esmond C-6
Fairdale B-8
Fairfield D-2
Fargo E-10
Farimont F-10
Fessenden D-6
Fingal E-8
Finley D-8
Flasher E-4
Flaxton A-3
Fordville C-9
Forest River C-9
Forman F-8
Fort Ransom E-8
Fort Yates F-5
Fortuna A-2
Freda E-4
Fredonia F-7
Fullerton F-7
Gackle E-7
Galesburg D-9
Gardena B-5
Garrison C-4
Gascoyne F-2
Gilby C-9
Gladstone D-3
Glen Ullin E-4
Glenfield D-8
Golden Valley D-3
Golva D-1
Goodrich D-6
Grafton C-9
Grand Forks C-9
Grandin E-9
Grano B-4
Granville C-5
Grassy Butte C-2

Great Bend F-10
Grenora B-1
Gwinner F-8
Hague F-6
Haley F-2
Halliday D-3
Hamberg C-7
Hampden B-8
Hankison F-9
Hanks B-2
Hannaford D-8
Hannah B-8
Harlow C-6
Harvey C-6
Harwood E-10
Hatton D-9
Havana F-8
Haynes F-3
Hazelton E-5
Hazen D-4
Hebron D-4
Heimdal C-6
Hensel B-9
Hettinger F-2
Hillsboro D-9
Hoopie B-9
Hope D-9
Hunter D-9
Hurdsfield D-6
Inkster C-9
Jamestown E-8
Jud E-7
Karlsruhe C-5
Kathryn E-8
Kenmare B-4
Kensal D-7
Killdeer D-3
Kindred E-9
Kramer B-5
La Moure F-8
Lakota C-8
Landa B-5
Langdon B-8
Larimore C-8
Larson A-3
Lawton C-8
Leal D-8
Leeds C-7
Lehr F-7
Leith E-4
Leonard E-9
Lidgerwood F-9
Lignite A-3
Lincoln E-5
Linton F-6
Lisbon F-9
Litchville E-8
Loma B-8
Ludden F-8
Maddock C-7
Makoti C-4
Mandan E-5
Manfred C-6
Manning D-3
Mantador F-9
Manvel C-9
Marion E-8
Marmarth E-1
Marshall D-3
Martin C-6
Max C-4
Maxbass B-5
Mayville D-9
Maza B-7
McClusky D-5
McHenry D-8
McVille D-8
Medina E-6
Medora D-2
Mercer D-5
Merricourt F-7
Michigan C-8
Milnor F-9
Milton B-8
Minnewaukan . . . C-7
Minot C-4
Minto C-9
Mohall B-4
Monango F-8
Montpelier E-8
Mooreton F-9
Mott E-3
Mountain B-9
Munich B-7
Mylo B-6
Napoleon E-6
Neche B-9
Nekoma B-8
New England E-2

New Leipzig E-3
New Rockford . . . D-7
New Salem E-4
New Town C-3
Newburg B-5
Nome E-8
Noonan A-3
Northwood D-9
Oakes F-8
Oberon C-7
Oriska E-9
Osnabrock B-8
Page D-9
Palermo B-3
Park River C-8
Parshall C-4
Pekin D-8
Pembina B-9
Perth B-7
Petersburg C-8
Pettibone D-7
Pick City D-4
Pillsbury D-8
Pingree D-7
Pisek C-8
Plaza C-4
Portal A-3
Portland D-9
Powers Lake B-3
Prairie Rose E-9
Rawson C-2
Ray B-2
Reeder F-2
Regan D-5
Regent E-3
Rhame E-1
Richardton D-3
Riverdale D-4
Riverside E-9
Robinson D-6
Rock Lake B-7
Rogers E-8
Rolette B-6
Rolla B-6
Ross B-3
Rugby C-6
Ruso C-5
Rutland F-9
Ryder C-4
Saint Thomas B-9
Sanborn E-8
Sarles B-8
Sawyer C-5
Scranton E-2
Selfridge E-5
Sentinel Butte . . . D-1
Sharon D-8
Sheilds E-4
Sheldon E-9
Sherwood A-4
Sheyenne D-7
Sibley D-8
Solen E-5
Souris B-5
South Heart D-2
Spring Brook B-2
Stanley B-3
Stanton D-4
Starkweather B-7
Steele E-6
Strasburg F-6
Streeter E-7
Surrey C-5
Sydney E-7
Sykeston D-7
Tappen E-6
Thompson D-9
Tioga B-2
Tolley B-4
Tolna C-8
Tower City E-8
Towner B-5
Turtle Lake D-5
Tuttle D-6
Underwood D-5
Upham B-5
Valley City E-8
Velva C-5
Venturia F-6
Verendrye C-5
Verona E-8
Voltaire C-5
Wahpeton F-10
Walcott E-9
Wales B-8
Walhalla B-9
Walseth B-5
Warwick C-7
Washburn D-5
Watford City C-2

West Fargo E-9
Westfeild F-5
Westhope B-5
Wheelock B-2
White Earth B-3
Wildrose B-2
Williston B-2
Willow City B-6
Wilton D-5
Wimbledon D-7
Wing D-6
Wishek F-6
Wolford B-6
Woodworth D-7
Wyndmere F-9
York C-6
Ypsilanti E-7
Zap D-4

OHIO
Pages 66-67
Population: 10,797,630
Capital: Columbus
Land Area: 41,004 sq. mi.

Abbeyville . . Pg. 107, J-1
Aberdeen N-3
Ada G-3
Addyston M-1
Adena J-9
Africa . . . Pg. 109, A-5
Akron G-8
Vicinity . . . . . Pg. 89
Albany M-7
Alexandria J-5
Alexis . . Pg. 166, A-5
Alger H-3
Alliance H-9
Alton . . . Pg. 109, F-1
Amanda L-5
Amberley . . Pg. 106, C-5
Amelia M-2
Amesville L-7
Amherst F-6
Amlin . . . Pg. 109, D-1
Amsterdam H-9
Andover E-10
Anna J-2
Ansonia J-1
Antwerp F-4
Apple Creek H-7
Arcadia F-4
Arcanum K-1
Archbold E-2
Arlington G-3
Ashland H-5
Ashley H-5
Ashtabula D-9
Ashville K-5
Athalia O-6
Athens M-7
Attica F-5
Aurora F-8
Austintown . Pg. 170, H-3
Avon Lake E-7
Bainbridge M-4
Baltic H-8
Baltimore K-6
Banker Heights
. . . . . . Pg. 99, D-4
Barberton G-8
Vicinity . . . Pg. 89, E-1
Barnesville K-9
Barnsburg . . Pg. 106, B-2
Batavia M-2
Bath . . . . Pg. 107, K-4
Bath Center Pg. 107, K-4
Bay View E-5
Beach City H-8
Beallsville L-9
Beavercreek K-3
Vicinity . . . Pg. 112, F-4
Beaverdam G-3
Bedford . . . Pg. 107, E-6
Bedford Heights
. . . . . . Pg. 107, E-6
Beechwood . Pg. 107, C-6
Belfort . . . Pg. 99, C-7
Beliot G-9
Bellaire K-10
Belle Center H-3
Belle Valley K-8
Bellefontaine H-3
Bellevue F-5
Bellville H-6
Belmont J-9
Belpre M-8

Belvis . . . Pg. 106, A-2
Bennetts Corner
. . . . . . Pg. 107, H-2
Berea E-7
Vicinity . . . Pg. 107, F-1
Bergholz H-9
Berkey . . . Pg. 166, A-1
Berlin Heights . . . F-6
Bethel N-2
Bethseda J-9
Bettsville F-5
Beverly L-8
Bexley K-5
Vicinity . . . Pg. 109, F-5
Black Lick . Pg. 109, E-7
Blanchester M-3
Bloomdale F-4
Bloomingburg . . . L-4
Bloomville G-5
Blue Ash . Pg. 107, B-6
Bluffton G-3
Boardman . Pg. 170, K-5
Bolivar H-8
Boston Heights
. . . . . . Pg. 107, H-6
Botkins H-2
Botzum . . Pg. 107, K-5
Bowersville L-3
Bowling Green . . . F-3
Bradford J-2
Bradner F-4
Brathenal . Pg. 107, B-5
Brecksville . Pg. 107, F-4
Bremen K-6
Brewster H-8
Vicinity . . . Pg. 99, E-2
Brice . . . Pg. 109, G-7
Bridgetown . Pg. 106, D-1
Briggsdale Pg. 109, G-3
Brilliant J-10
Broadview Heights
. . . . . . Pg. 107, G-4
Brook Park Pg. 107, E-2
Brooklyn . Pg. 107, D-3
Brooklyn Heights
. . . . . . Pg. 107, D-4
Brunswick F-7
Vicinity . . . Pg. 107, J-2
Bryan E-2
Buchtel L-7
Bucyrus G-5
Burton E-9
Butler H-6
Byesville K-8
Cadiz J-9
Cairo G-2
Vicinity . . . Pg. 99, A-6
Caldwell K-8
Caledonia H-5
Cambridge J-8
Camden K-1
Vicinity . . . Pg. 170, J-7
Campbell F-10
Canal Fulton H-8
Vicinity . . . Pg. 99, B-2
Canal Winchester . K-5
Vicinity . . . Pg. 109, J-7
Canfield G-9
Vicinity . . . Pg. 170, K-3
Canton H-8
Vicinity . . . . . Pg. 99
Cardington H-5
Carey G-4
Carroll K-5
Carrollton H-9
Castalia F-5
Cedarville K-3
Celina H-1
Centennial . Pg. 166, A-2
CenterVillage
. . . . . . Pg. 109, B-7
Centerburg J-5
Centerville L-2
Vicinity . . . Pg. 112, H-6
Chardon E-9
Chauncey L-7
Chautaqua . Pg. 112, K-7
Chesapeake O-6
Chesterhill L-7
Cheviot M-1
Vicinity . . . Pg. 106, C-4
Chillicothe L-5
Christianburg J-3
Churchill . . Pg. 170, G-6
Cincinnati M-2
Vicinity . . . . . Pg. 106
Detailed City . Pg. 217
Circleville L-5
Clarington K-9
Clarksville L-3

Cleveland E-7
Vicinity . . . . . Pg. 107
Detailed City . Pg. 218
Cleveland Heights . E-8
Vicinity . . . Pg. 107, C-6
Cleves L-1
Clinton . . Pg. 99, A-1
Clyde F-5
Coal Grove O-6
Coalburg . Pg. 170, G-6
Coalton M-6
Coitsville Center
. . . . . . Pg. 170, J-7
Coldwater H-1
Columbiana G-10
Columbus J-4
Vicinity . . . . . Pg. 109
Detailed City . Pg. 220
Columbus Grove . . G-2
Comet . . . Pg. 99, A-3
Commercial Point
. . . . . . Pg. 109, K-3
Conneaut D-10
Continental F-2
Convoy G-1
Coolville M-7
Corning L-7
Cortland F-10
Coshocton J-7
Covington J-2
Craig Beach G-9
Crestline G-5
Cridersville H-2
Crissey . . Pg. 166, C-2
Crooksville K-7
Crown City O-6
Crystal Lake Pg. 112, F-1
Crystal Spring
. . . . . . Pg. 99, B-3
Cuyahoga Falls . . . F-8
Vicinity . . . Pg. 107, K-7
Cuyahuga Heights
. . . . . . Pg. 107, D-5
Cygnet F-3
Dalton G-8
Danville H-6
Darbydale K-4
Vicinity . . . Pg. 109, J-1
Dayton K-2
Vicinity . . . Pg. 112, J-3
Detailed City . Pg. 225
De Graff J-3
Delaware J-4
Delphos G-2
Delta E-3
Dennison H-9
Derby . . . Pg. 109, K-1
Deshler F-3
Dover H-8
Dresden J-7
Dublin J-4
Vicinity . . . Pg. 109, C-2
Dunkirk G-3
Dunlap . . Pg. 106, A-4
Duvall . . . Pg. 109, K-5
East Canton G-9
Vicinity . . . Pg. 99, D-7
East Cleveland . . . E-7
Vicinity . . . Pg. 107, B-5
East Greenville
. . . . . . Pg. 99, C-1
East Lawn . Pg. 166, D-7
East Liverpool . . . H-10
East Palestine . . . G-10
East Sparta H-8
Eastlake E-8
Eaton K-1
Edgerton E-1
Edison H-5
Eldon E-1
Eldorado K-1
Ellerton . . Pg. 112, K-5
Ellsworth . Pg. 170, K-2
Ellsworth Station
. . . . . . Pg. 170, K-1
Elmore E-4
Elmwood Place
. . . . . . Pg. 106, C-4
Elyria F-7
Emery . . . Pg. 107, D-6
Englewood K-2
Enon K-3
Euclid E-8
Vicinity . . . Pg. 107, A-6
Evandale . . Pg. 106, B-5
Everett . . . Pg. 107, J-5
Fairborn . . Pg. 112, F-3
Fairfax . . . Pg. 106, D-6

Fairfield L-1
Fairhope . . Pg. 99, C-7
Fairlawn F-8
Fairport Harbor . . . D-9
Fairview Park
. . . . . . Pg. 107, D-1
Fayette E-2
Felicity N-2
Ferry . . . Pg. 112, G-7
Findlay G-3
Five Points . Pg. 112, H-7
Flint . . . Pg. 109, C-4
Flushing J-9
Forest G-4
Forest Park M-1
Vicinity . . . Pg. 106, A-3
Fostoria F-4
Frankfort L-4
Franklin L-2
Vicinity . . . Pg. 112, K-7
Frazeysburg J-7
Fredericksburg . . . H-7
Fredericktown . . . H-6
Freeport J-8
Fremont F-5
Frytown . . Pg. 112, K-4
Ft. Jennings G-2
Ft. Loramie J-2
Ft. Recovery H-1
Ft. Shawnee H-2
Gahanna J-5
Galena . . . Pg. 109, A-6
Galion H-5
Gallipolis N-7
Galloway . Pg. 109, G-2
Gambier J-6
Garfield Heights . . F-8
Vicinity . . . Pg. 107, D-5
Garrettsville F-9
Geneva E-9
Geneva-on-the-Lake D-9
Genoa E-4
Georgetown N-3
Georgeville Pg. 109, H-1
Germantown L-1
Gettysburg J-1
Ghent . . . Pg. 107, K-4
Gibsonburg F-4
Girard F-10
Vicinity . . . Pg. 170, G-4
Glandorf G-2
Glendale . . Pg. 106, A-4
Glenwillow Pg. 107, G-6
Golf Manor Pg. 106, C-5
Gould Park Pg. 109, D-6
Grafton F-7
Grand Rapids F-3
Grandview Heights
. . . . . . Pg. 109, F-4
Granger . . Pg. 107, J-3
Granville J-6
Gratis L-1
Green Springs . . . F-5
Greenfield L-4
Greenhills . Pg. 106, A-3
Greensburg Pg. 99, A-3
Greentown . Pg. 99, A-5
Greenville J-1
Greenwich G-6
Grove City K-4
Vicinity . . . Pg. 109, H-3
Groveport K-5
Vicinity . . . Pg. 109, J-6
Hamden M-6
Hamersville N-3
Hamilton L-1
Hamler F-3
Hanover J-6
Hanoverton G-9
HarborView Pg. 166, A-6
Harlem . . . Pg. 109, B-6
Harmon . . . Pg. 99, E-2
Harrisburg Pg. 109, K-1
Harrisburg . Pg. 99, A-1
Harrison M-1
Harrod H-3
Hartville G-9
Hayden . . Pg. 109, D-1
Hayesville G-7
Heath K-6
Hebron K-6
Hicksville F-1
Higginsport N-3
Highland Heights
. . . . . . Pg. 107, B-7
Hilliard J-4
Vicinity . . . Pg. 109, E-1

OHIO

Hills and Dales .... Pg. 99, C-4
Hillsboro M-3
Hinckley . Pg. 107, H-2
Hiram F-9
Holgate F-2
Holland E-3
Vicinity . Pg. 166, C-3
Hopedale J-9
Howenstine . Pg. 99, E-6
Hubbard F-10
Vicinity . Pg. 170, G-6
Huber Heights K-2
Vicinity . Pg. 112, G-1
Huber Ridge Pg. 109, C-6
Hudson .... Pg. 107, H-7
Huron F-6
Hyatts . Pg. 109, A-3
Independence .... Pg. 107, F-4
Ironton O-6
Jackson M-5
Jackson Center H-3
Jacksonville L-7
Jamestown L-3
Jefferson E-9
Jeffersonville L-4
Jerome .... Pg. 109, B-1
Jeromesville G-7
Jewett J-9
Johnston Corners .... Pg. 166, C-4
Johnstown J-6
Junction City K-6
Kalida G-2
Kellys Island E-6
Kent F-8
Kenton H-3
Kettering K-2
Vicinity . Pg. 112, H-5
Kileville . Pg. 109, C-1
Killbuck H-7
Kingston L-5
Kirkersville K-6
Kirtland Hills E-9
Lagrange F-7
Lakemore G-8
Lakeview H-3
Lakewood E-7
Vicinity . Pg. 107, C-1
Lancaster K-6
Landsdowne Pg. 170, H-6
Latchie . Pg. 166, E-7
Laurelville L-5
Lebanon L-2
Leesburg L-3
Leetonia G-10
Leipsic G-3
Lewis Center Pg. 109, A-4
Lewisburg K-1
Lexington H-6
Liberty Center E-2
Lima L-4
Lime City . Pg. 166, E-5
Lincoln Heights .... Pg. 106, B-4
Lindsey F-5
Linworth . Pg. 109, C-3
Lisbon G-10
Lithopolis . Pg. 109, K-7
LittleYork . Pg. 112, J-1
Lockburn . Pg. 109, K-4
Lockland . Pg. 106, B-4
Lodi M-3
Logan L-6
London K-4
Lorain E-6
Lordstown F-9
Vicinity . Pg. 170, G-2
Loudonville H-6
Louisville G-9
Vicinity . Pg. 99, B-7
Loveland M-2
Lowell L-8
Lowellville G-10
Vicinity . Pg. 170, K-7
Luckey F-4
Lynchburg M-3
Lyndhurst . Pg. 107, B-7
Lyons E-2
Lytle . Pg. 112, G-7
Macedonia F-8
Vicinity . Pg. 107, G-6
Madeira M-2
Madison E-9
Magnolia H-8
Malta K-7
Malvern H-9
Manchester N-3

Mansfield H-6
Maple Heights .... Pg. 107, E-5
Mapleton . Pg. 99, E-7
Marble Cliff . Pg. 109, F-3
Marblehead E-5
Marchand . Pg. 99, B-4
Marietta L-8
Marimet . Pg. 106, D-6
Marion H-4
Martins Ferry J-10
Martinsville L-3
Marysville J-4
Mason L-2
Massillon G-8
Vicinity . Pg. 99, C-3
Maumee F-3
Vicinity . Pg. 166, D-3
Mayfield Heights .... Pg. 107, B-7
McArthur M-6
McClure F-3
McConnelsville L-7
McDonald . Pg. 170, G-4
McDonaldsville .... Pg. 99, A-3
McGuffey H-3
Mechanicsburg J-4
Medina F-7
Vicinity . Pg. 107, K-1
Medway . Pg. 112, F-1
Mentor E-8
Mentor-on-the-Lake E-8
Metamora E-3
Miami Villa . Pg. 112, H-2
Miamisburg L-2
Vicinity . Pg. 112, K-6
Middle Point G-2
Middleburg Hts. .... Pg. 107, F-2
Middleport M-7
Middletown L-1
Midvale H-8
Midway K-4
Vicinity . Pg. 166, D-1
Milan F-6
Milford L-2
Milford Center J-4
Millbury . Pg. 166, D-7
Millersburg H-7
Millersport K-6
Millville L-1
Mineral City .... H—8
Minerva G-9
Minerva Park J-5
Vicinity . Pg. 109, D-4
Mingo Junction J-10
Minster H-2
Mitchaw . Pg. 166, A-2
Moline . Pg. 166, D-6
Monclova . Pg. 166, D-3
Monroe L-2
Monroeville F-5
Montpelier E-1
Moraine L-2
Vicinity . Pg. 112, K-5
Moreland Hills .... Pg. 107, D-7
Morrow L-2
Mt. Air . Pg. 109, B-3
Mt. Blanchard G-4
Mt. Gilead H-5
Mt. Healthy . Pg. 106, B-3
Mt. Orab M-3
Mt. Sterling K-4
Mt. Vernon H-6
Mt. Victory H-4
Mudsock . Pg. 109, E-1
Murlin Heights .... Pg. 112, J-1
Murray City L-7
Napoleon F-2
Navarre H-8
Vicinity . Pg. 99, E-3
Nelsonville L-6
Nevada G-5
New Albany Pg. 109, C-7
New Boston N-5
New Bremen H-2
New Carlisle K-3
Vicinity . Pg. 166, J-3
New Concord K-7
New Germany .... Pg. 112, G-3
New Holland L-4
New Knoxville H-2
New Lebanon K-1
New Lexington L-7
New London G-6
New Madison K-1

New Matamoras L-9
New Miami L-1
New Middletown . G-10
New Paris K-1
New Philadelphia . H-8
New Richmond N-2
New Rome . Pg. 109, F-2
New Straitsville L-7
New Vienna L-3
New Washington .. G-5
New Waterford . G-10
Newark J-6
Newburgh Heights .... Pg. 107, D-4
Newcomerstown .. J-8
Newman . Pg. 99, C-2
Newton M-2
Newton Falls F-9
Niles F-10
Vicinity . Pg. 170, K-7
North Baltimore F-3
North Bend M-1
North Canton G-8
North Canton Pg. 99, B-5
North College Hill .... Pg. 106, C-3
North Fairfield F-6
North Jackson .... Pg. 170, H-2
North Kingsville .. D-10
North Lawrence .... Pg. 99, B-1
North Lewisburg .. J-4
North Olmsted F-7
North Randall .... Pg. 107, D-6
North Ridgeville F-7
North Royalton .... Pg. 107, F-3
Northfield . Pg. 107, G-6
Northridge . Pg. 112, H-2
Northwood E-4
Vicinity . Pg. 166, G-8
Norton G-8
Vicinity . Pg. 89, D-1
Norwalk F-6
Norwood . Pg. 106, D-4
Oak Harbor E-5
Oak Hill N-6
Oakwood (Paulding Cty) ... F-2
Vicinity . Pg. 112, H-4
Oakwood (Montgomery Cty) K-2
Vicinity . Pg. 107, F-6
Oberlin F-6
Obetz K-5
Vicinity . Pg. 109, H-5
Ohio City G-1
Ontario H-6
Orange . Pg. 107, D-7
Orangeville F-10
Oregon E-4
Vicinity . Pg. 166, B-7
Orient . Pg. 109, K-2
Orrville G-7
Orwell E-9
Ottawa G-3
Ottawa Hills E-3
Vicinity . Pg. 166, B-4
Ottoville F-2
Otway N-4
Owensville M-2
Oxford L-1
Painesville E-9
Pandora G-3
Parma F-8
Vicinity . Pg. 107, E-3
Parma Heights .... Pg. 107, E-2
Pataskala K-6
Paulding F-2
Payne G-1
Pemberville F-4
Peninsula . Pg. 107, J-5
Pepper Pike Pg. 107, C-6
Perry E-9
Perry Heights Pg. 99, D-4
Perrysburg E-4
Vicinity . Pg. 166, C-5
Perrysville H-6
Philo K-7
Phoneton . Pg. 112, G-1
Pickerington K-5
Pigeon Run . Pg. 99, C-5
Piketon M-5
Pioneer E-1
Piqua J-2
Plain City J-4
Pleasant Corners .... Pg. 109, J-2

Pleasant Hill J-2
Pleasantville K-6
Plymouth G-6
Point Place . Pg. 166, A-7
Poland G-10
Vicinity . Pg. 170, K-6
Pomeroy M-7
Port Clinton E-5
Port Washington .. J-8
Portsmouth N-5
Powell . Pg. 109, B-3
Powhatan Point K-9
Proctorville O-6
Prospect H-4
Put-in-Bay E-5
Quaker City K-8
Quincy J-3
Raab Corners .... Pg. 166, B-1
Racine M-7
Rathbone . Pg. 109, A-2
Ravenna F-9
Reading M-2
Vicinity . Pg. 106, B-5
Reese . Pg. 109, H-5
Remsen Corners .... Pg. 107, K-3
Republic F-5
Reynolds Corner .... Pg. 166, B-3
Reynoldsburg K-5
Vicinity . Pg. 109, F-7
Richfield . Pg. 107, H-5
Richfield Center .... Pg. 166, B-1
Richmond H-9
Richmond Heights .... Pg. 107, A-6
Richville . Pg. 99, D-4
Rio Grande N-6
Ripley N-3
Rising Sun F-4
Rittman G-7
Riverlea . Pg. 109, D-4
Roachton . Pg. 166, E-3
Roaming Shores .. E-10
Rock Creek E-9
Rockford H-1
Rocky River Pg. 107, C-1
Rome N-4
Roseville K-7
Rossford E-4
Vicinity . Pg. 166, C-5
Rushsylvania H-3
Russells Point H-3
Rutland M-7
Sabina L-3
Sagamore Hills .... Pg. 107, G-5
Saint Bernard .... Pg. 106, D-4
Saint Clairsville J-9
Saint Henry H-1
Saint Marys H-2
Saint Paris J-3
Salem G-9
Salineville H-9
San Margherita .... Pg. 109, F-2
Sandusky E-6
Sarahsville K-8
Sardinia N-3
Scio J-8
Seaman N-4
Sebring G-9
Senecaville K-8
Seven Hills Pg. 107, E-4
Seven Mile L-1
Seville G-7
Shadeville . Pg. 109, J-4
Shadyside K-9
Shaker Heights H-7
Vicinity . Pg. 107, C-6
Sharonville . Pg. 106, A-5
Shawnee L-7
Shawnee Hills .... Pg. 109, B-1
Sheffield Lake E-6
Shelby G-6
Sherwood F-1
Shiloh H-7
Shreve H-7
Sidney J-2
Silica . Pg. 166, B-2
Silverton . Pg. 106, C-5
Sinking Spring N-4
Sippo . Pg. 99, C-2
Smithfield J-10
Sodom . Pg. 170, G-5
Solon . Pg. 107, E-7

Somerset K-6
South Bloomfield .. K-5
South Charleston .. K-3
South Euclid .... Pg. 107, B-6
South Hill Park .... Pg. 166, C-5
South Lebanon L-2
South Point O-6
South Russell F-9
South Webster N-5
South Zanesville .. K-7
Spanker . Pg. 112, J-1
Spencer F-7
Spencerville H-2
Spring Valley L-3
Springboro L-2
Vicinity . Pg. 112, J-7
Springdale . Pg. 106, A-4
Springfield K-3
Stanwood . Pg. 99, D-1
Stockport L-8
Stoutsville L-5
Stow F-8
Vicinity . Pg. 107, K-7
Strasburg H-8
Streetsboro F-9
Stringtown . Pg. 112, K-2
Strongsville F-7
Vicinity . Pg. 107, G-1
Struthers F-10
Stryker E-2
Stuebenville H-10
Vicinity . Pg. 166, E-2
Sugar Grove L-6
Sugarcreek H-8
Sulphur Grove .... Pg. 112, G-1
Sunbury J-5
Swanton E-3
Sycamore G-4
Sylvania E-3
Vicinity . Pg. 166, A-3
Syracruse M-7
Tallmadge G-8
Taylorsburg . Pg. 112, K-2
Taylorsville . Pg. 112, H-1
Terrace Park M-2
Thornville K-6
Tiffin G-5
Tiltonsville J-10
Tipp City K-2
Toledo E-4
Toronto H-10
Trenton L-1
Trimble L-7
Trotwood K-1
Vicinity . Pg. 112, J-2
Troy J-2
Tuscarawas H-8
Twinsburg . Pg. 107, G-7
Uhrichsville J-8
Union K-1
Union City J-1
University Heights .... Pg. 107, C-6
Upper Arlington K-4
Vicinity . Pg. 109, E-3
Upper Sandusky .. G-4
Urbana J-3
Urbancrest K-4
Vicinity . Pg. 109, H-3
Utica J-6
Valley View . Pg. 107, E-3
Valleyview . Pg. 109, F-2
Van Wert G-1
Vandalia K-2
Vicinity . Pg. 112, H-1
Vermilion E-6
Versailles J-2
Vinton L-7
Waco . Pg. 99, D-6
Wadsworth G-7
Wakeman F-6
Walbridge E-4
Vicinity . Pg. 166, D-6
Walton Hills Pg. 107, F-6
Wapokoneta H-2
Warren F-10
Vicinity . Pg. 170, F-3
Warrensville Heights .... Pg. 107, D-6
Warsaw J-7
Washington C.H. .. L-4
Washington Mills .... Pg. 112, F-6
Washingtonville .. G-10
Waterloo . Pg. 109, J-7
Waterville E-3

Wauseon E-2
Waverly M-5
Wayne F-4
Waynesburg G-9
Waynesfield H-3
Vicinity . Pg. 166, D-4
Waynesville L-3
Wellington F-6
Wellston M-6
Wellsville H-10
West Alexandria .. K-1
West Austintown .... Pg. 170, J-3
West Carrollton K-2
Vicinity . Pg. 112, K-5
West Farmington .. F-9
West Jefferson J-4
West Lafayette J-8
West Liberty J-3
West Mansfield H-4
West Milton K-2
West Richfield .... Pg. 107, H-4
West Salem G-7
West Union N-2
West Unity E-2
Westerville J-5
Vicinity . Pg. 109, C-5
Westfield Center F-3
Weston F-3
Whitehall K-5
Vicinity . Pg. 109, F-6
Whitehouse E-3
Vicinity . Pg. 166, E-2
Whitfield . Pg. 112, K-5
Wickliffe . Pg. 107, A-7
Wilkesville M-6
Willard G-5
Williamsburg M-2
Williamsport L-4
Willoughby E-8
Willoughby Hills E-8
Willowby Hills .... Pg. 107, A-7
Willowick E-8
Willshire H-1
Wilmington L-3
Winchester N-3
Windham M-2
Wintersville H-10
Woodbourne Pg. 112, H-5
Woodlawn . Pg. 106, B-4
Woodmere Pg. 107, D-7
Woodsfield K-9
Woodville F-4
Woodville Gardens .... Pg. 166, D-7
Wooster G-7
Worthington J-5
Vicinity . Pg. 109, C-4
Wyoming . Pg. 106, B-4
Xenia L-3
Yellow Springs K-3
Yorkville J-10
Youngstown F-9
Vicinity . Pg. 170, H-5
Zanesville K-7

OKLAHOMA

OKLAHOMA
Pages 68-69
Population: 3,025,487
Capital: Oklahoma City
Land Area: 68,655 sq. mi.

Achille J-11
Acme G-8
Ada C-13
Adair C-13
Addington H-9
Afton C-13
Agawam G-9
Agra E-10
Ahloso G-13
Albany H-11
Albert F-8
Albion G-13
Alcorn C-9
Alderson G-12
Aledo E-7
Alex F-9
Alfalfa F-8
Aline C-8
Allen G-11
Alpers G-9
Altus G-6
Alva C-7
Amber F-9
Ames D-8
Amorita B-8

Anadarko F-8
Angora E-6
Antioch G-9
Apache F-8
Apperson C-10
Apple H-12
Aqua Park . Pg. 147, E-13
Arapaho E-7
Arcadia E-9
Vicinity . Pg. 147, A-7
Ardmore H-10
Arnett D-6
Arpelar F-12
Asher F-10
Ashland G-11
Atoka H-11
Atwood F-11
Avant C-11
Avard C-7
Avery E-10
Aydelotte E-10
Babbs F-7
Bache F-12
Bado D-7
Bald Hill E-12
Balko C-5
Barnsdall C-11
Barr D-8
Bartlesville C-11
Battiest G-13
Baum H-11
Bearden F-11
Beggs E-11
Bellvue E-11
Belva C-7
Bengal G-13
Bennington H-11
Bernice C-13
Bessie F-7
Bethany . Pg. 147, D-2
Bethel H-13
Bethel Acres F-10
Big Cabin C-13
Big Cedar G-13
Bigheart C-11
Billings C-9
Binger F-8
Bison D-9
Bixby D-12
Vicinity . Pg. 167, K-5
Blackburn D-11
Blackwell C-10
Blair G-6
Blanchard F-9
Blocker F-12
Blue H-11
Boise City C-2
Boley E-11
Bomar J-10
Boswell H-11
Bowden . Pg. 167, H-1
Bowlegs F-11
Box E-13
Boyd C-4
Boynton E-12
Brace C-7
Braggs E-12
Braman C-9
Bray G-9
Briartown F-13
Bridgeport E-8
Brinkman F-6
Bristow E-11
Broken Arrow D-11
Vicinity . Pg. 167, H-6
Broken Bow H-13
Bromide H-11
Brooksville F-10
Brown H-11
Brushy E-13
Bryan's Corner C-4
Bryant F-11
Buffalo C-6
Bugtussle F-12
Bunch E-13
Burbank C-10
Burlington C-8
Burmah G-13
Burns Flat F-7
Butler E-7
Byars G-10
Byng G-10
Byron C-8
Cabiniss F-11
Cache G-8
Caddo H-11
Calvin F-12
Camargo D-7
Canadian F-12
Canadian Club City . F-9

Caney H-11
Canton D-8
Capron C-8
Carleton D-8
Carmen C-8
Carnegie F-8
Carney E-10
Carrier F-6
Carter F-6
Cartwright J-10
Cashion E-9
Castle E-11
Caston F-13
Catesby C-6
Catoosa D-12
Vicinity . Pg. 167, E-7
Cedar Springs D-8
Cement F-8
Centrahoma G-11
Centralia C-12
Ceres D-10
Cestos D-7
Chandler E-10
Chattanooga G-7
Checotah E-12
Chelsea C-12
Cherokee C-8
Chester D-7
Cheyenne E-6
Chickasha F-8
Childers C-12
Chilocco B-10
Chisney F-10
Chloeta C-13
Chockie G-11
Choctaw . Pg. 147, E-7
Choska E-12
Chouteau D-12
Cimmarron City E-9
Claremore D-12
Clayton G-12
Clemscott H-9
Cleo Springs D-8
Cleveland D-11
Clinton E-7
Cloud Chief F-7
Coalgate G-11
Cogar F-8
Colbert J-11
Cole F-9
Coleman H-11
Collinsville D-12
Vicinity . Pg. 167, A-6
Colony F-8
Comanche H-9
Commerce B-13
Connerville G-11
Cookietown H-8
Cookson E-13
Cooperton G-7
Cora C-7
Cordell F-7
Corinne H-13
Corn F-7
Cornish H-9
Corum H-8
Council Hill E-12
Courtney H-9
Covington D-9
Cowden F-8
Coweta D-12
Cowlington F-13
Coyle D-10
Crawford E-6
Crekola E-12
Crescent D-9
Creta G-6
Criner F-10
Cromwell F-11
Crowder F-12
Curtis C-7
Cushing D-10
Custer City E-7
Cyril G-8
Dacoma C-8
Daisy G-12
Dale F-10
Darwin H-12
Davenport E-10
Davidson H-7
Davis G-10
Deer Creek C-9
Del City . Pg. 147, F-5
Delaware C-12
Dempsey E-6
Denman F-13
Devol H-7
Dewey C-12
Dibble F-9

Dickson H-10
Dill City F-7
Dillworth B-10
Dougherty G-10
Douglas D-9
Dover D-9
Doxey F-6
Drake H-10
Driftwood C-8
Drummond D-8
Drumright D-11
Duke G-6
Dunbar G-12
Duncan G-9
Durant H-11
Durham E-6
Durwood H-10
Dustin F-11
Eagle City D-8
Eakly F-8
Earlsboro F-10
Eason F-10
Eddy C-9
Edith C-7
Edmond . . . Pg. 147, A-5
El Reno E-8
Eldon D-13
Eldorado G-6
Elgin G-8
Elk City E-6
Elmer G-6
Elmore City G-9
Elmwood C-5
Emet H-10
Empire City G-8
Enid D-9
Enterprise F-12
Erick F-6
Eubanks G-12
Eufaula F-12
Eva C-3
Fair Oaks D-12
   Vicinity . . Pg. 167, F-7
Fairfax C-11
Fairland C-13
Fairmont D-9
Fairview D-8
Fallis E-10
Fallon H-12
Fanshawe F-13
Fargo D-6
Farris H-12
Faxon G-8
Fay E-7
Featherston F-12
Felt C-2
Fewell G-13
Fillmore H-11
Finley H-12
Fireworks City
   . . . . Pg. 147, G-2
Fittstown G-10
Fitzhugh G-10
Fleetwood H-9
Fletcher G-8
Floris B-5
Folsom H-11
Foraker C-11
Forest Park . Pg. 147, D-5
Forgan B-5
Fort Arbuckle G-9
Fort Cobb F-8
Fort Gibson E-13
Fort Supply C-6
Fort Towson H-13
Forty One F-7
Foss E-7
Four Corners C-3
Fowler E-10
Fox H-9
Foyil C-12
Francis G-10
Frederick G-7
Freedom C-7
Gage D-6
Gans F-13
Gansel D-9
Garber C-9
Garvin H-13
Gate C-6
Gay H-12
Geary E-8
Gene Autry H-10
Gerty F-11
Gibbon B-8
Gideon D-13
Glencoe D-10
Glenpool D-11
   Vicinity . . Pg. 167, K-3
Glover H-13

Goldsby F-9
Goltry C-8
Goodland H-12
Goodwell C-3
Goodwin D-6
Gore E-13
Gotebo F-7
Gould G-6
Gowen G-12
Gracemont F-8
Grady H-9
Grainola B-11
Grandfield H-7
Granite F-6
Grant H-12
Gray C-4
Grayson E-12
Green D-13
Greenfield E-8
Griggs C-3
Grove C-13
Guthrie E-9
Guymon C-3
Haileyville G-12
Hall Park
   Vicinity . . Pg. 147, K-6
Hammon E-6
Harden City G-10
Hardesty C-4
Hardy B-10
Harmon D-6
Harrah E-10
Hartshorne G-12
Haskell E-12
Hastings H-8
Hayward D-9
Haywood G-11
Hayworth J-13
Headrick G-7
Healdton H-9
Heavener G-13
Hectorville E-12
Helena C-8
Hennepin G-9
Hennessy D-9
Henryetta E-11
Hickory G-10
Higgins G-12
Hillsdale C-8
Hinton E-8
Hitchcock D-8
Hobart F-7
Hodgen G-13
Holdenville F-11
Hollis G-6
Hollister H-7
Hollow C-12
Homestead D-8
Hominy D-11
Honobia G-13
Hooker B-4
Hoot Owl D-13
Hopeton C-7
Hough B-3
Howe F-13
Hucmac D-7
Hugo H-12
Hulah B-11
Hulbert D-13
Hulen G-8
Humphreys G-7
Hunter C-9
Huskey H-12
Hydro E-8
Idabel H-13
Indiahoma G-7
Indianola F-12
Ingersoll C-8
Inola D-12
Isabella D-8
Jay C-13
Jefferson C-9
Jenks D-11
   Vicinity . . Pg. 167, J-3
Jennings D-11
Jesse G-11
Jet C-8
Jones . . . . Pg. 147, C-7
Joy G-9
Kansas D-13
Karma J-11
Karns E-8
Kellyville E-11
Kendrick E-10
Kent H-12
Kenton B-2
Keota F-13
Keyes C-3
Kiamichi G-12
Kiefer D-11

Kildare C-10
Kingfisher E-9
Kingston H-10
Kinta F-13
Kiowa G-11
Knowles C-5
Konawa F-10
Kosoma H-12
Kremlin C-9
Kusa E-12
Lacey D-8
Lahoma D-8
Lake Aluma Pg. 147, C-5
Lake Valley F-7
Lamar F-11
Lambert C-8
Lamont C-9
Lane H-11
Langston E-10
Latta G-10
Laverne C-6
Lawton G-8
Leach D-13
Lebanon H-10
Leedey E-6
Lehigh G-11
Lela D-10
Lenapah B-12
Leon H-9
Leonard E-11
Lequire F-13
Letitia G-8
Lewisville F-12
Lexington F-10
   Vicinity . . Pg. 147, K-5
Lima F-10
Lincoln G-6
Lindsay G-9
Little Axe F-9
Little City H-10
Loco H-9
Locust Grove D-12
Lone Grove H-9
Lone Wolf F-7
Longdale D-8
Lookeba F-8
Lookout B-7
Lovedale C-6
Loveland H-7
Lovell D-9
Loyal D-8
Lucien D-9
Lugert F-7
Lula G-11
Luther E-10
Lyman C-10
Lyons E-13
Macomb F-10
Madill H-10
Manchester B-9
Mangum F-6
Manitou G-7
Mannsville H-10
Maramac D-10
Marietta H-9
Marland C-10
Marlow G-9
Marshall D-9
Martha F-6
Mason E-11
Maud F-10
May C-6
Mayfield F-6
Maysville G-9
Mazie D-12
McAlester F-12
McBride H-11
McCurtain F-13
McLoud E-10
McQueen C-11
McWillie C-8
Mead H-10
Medford C-9
Meeker E-10
Meers G-8
Meno D-8
Meridian E-10
Messer H-12
Miami C-13
Middleberg F-9
Midwest City Pg. 147, E-6
Milburn H-11
Milfay E-11
Mill Creek G-10
Millerton H-13
Milo H-9
Milton F-13
Minco F-9
Mingo . . . Pg. 167, D-5
Mocane B-5
Moore . . . Pg. 147, H-5

Mooreland C-7
Morris E-12
Morrison D-10
Mounds E-11
Mountain View . . . F-7
Moyers H-12
Mulhall D-9
Muldrow E-13
Muskogee E-12
Mustang F-9
   Vicinity . . Pg. 147, F-1
Mutual D-7
Narcissa C-13
Nardin C-9
Nash C-8
Nashoba G-13
Navina E-9
Nebo H-10
New Alluwe C-12
New Eucha D-13
New Prue D-11
New Ringold H-13
New Tulsa D-12
New Woodville . . . H-10
Newcastle F-9
   Vicinity . . Pg. 147, J-2
Newkirk C-10
Nichols Hills Pg. 147, C-4
Nicoma Park Pg. 147, D-7
Nida H-11
Ninnekah F-9
Noble F-9
Norge F-8
Norman F-9
   Vicinity . . Pg. 147, K-5
North Miami B-13
Nowata C-12
Numa C-4
Oakhurst . . Pg. 167, G-1
Oakland H-10
Oaks D-13
Oakwood D-7
Ochelata C-12
Octavia G-13
Oilton D-11
Okeene D-8
Okemah F-11
Okesa C-11
Okfuskee E-11
Oklahoma City . . . F-9
   Vicinity . . . . Pg. 147
   Detailed City . Pg. 266
Okmulgee E-11
Oleta H-12
Olney G-11
Olustee G-6
Omega E-8
Onapa F-12
Oneta E-12
   Vicinity . . Pg. 167, J-7
Oologah D-12
Optima C-4
Ord H-12
Orienta D-8
Orion D-7
Orlando D-9
Osage D-11
Ottawa B-13
Overbrook H-10
Owasso D-12
   Vicinity . . Pg. 167, C-6
Owen B-11
Ozark G-7
Paden E-11
Panama F-13
Panola F-12
Paoli G-10
Patton C-13
Pauls Valley G-10
   Vicinity . . Pg. 167, A-2
Pawhuska C-11
Pawnee D-10
Payne G-9
Pearson F-10
Pearsonia C-11
Peggs D-13
Peoria B-13
Perkins D-10
Perry D-10
Pershing C-11
Petersburg H-9
Pharoah F-11
Phillips G-11
Picher B-13
Pierce F-12
Pink F-9
Pittsburg G-12
Plainview C-7
Platter H-11
Poccasset F-8
Ponca City C-10
Pond Creek C-9

Pontotoc G-11
Pooleville G-9
Porter E-12
Porum F-13
Poteau F-13
Prague E-10
Preston D-11
Proctor D-13
Pryor D-12
Pumpkin Center . . G-8
Purcell F-9
Purdy G-9
Putnam E-7
Pyramid Corners . . C-12
Quapaw B-13
Quay D-11
Quinlan C-7
Quinton F-12
Ralston C-11
Ramona C-11
Randlett H-8
Rankin C-11
Ratliff City G-9
Rattan H-12
Ravia H-10
Reagan H-10
Red Bird E-12
Red Fork . . Pg. 167, G-2
Red Oak F-13
Red Rock D-10
Redden G-12
Reed F-6
Remus F-10
Renfrow C-9
Retrop F-7
Reydon E-6
Rhea D-7
Richards Spur G-8
Ringling H-9
Ringold H-13
Ringwood D-8
Roberta H-11
Rocky F-7
Roff G-10
Roll E-6
Roosevelt G-7
Rose D-13
Rosedale G-10
Rosston B-6
Rubottom H-9
Rush Springs G-9
Ryan H-9
Saddle Mountain . . G-7
Saint Louis F-10
Salem F-12
Salina D-13
Sallisaw E-13
Salt Fork C-9
Sand Springs D-11
   Vicinity . . Pg. 167, G-1
Sapulpa E-11
   Vicinity . . Pg. 167, J-1
Sasakwa F-10
Sayre F-6
Scraper D-13
Scullin G-10
Seiling D-7
Selman C-6
Seminole F-11
Sentinel F-7
Shamrock E-11
Sharon D-6
Shattuck D-6
Shawnee F-10
Shidler C-11
Skedee D-10
Skiatook D-11
   Vicinity . . Pg. 167, A-2
Slapout C-6
Slaughterville F-10
Slick E-11
Smith Village Pg. 147, E-5
Smithville G-13
Snow G-12
Snyder G-7
Soper H-12
South Coffeyville . . C-12
Southard D-8
Sparks E-10
Spear H-12
Spencer . . Pg. 147, D-6
Sperry D-11
   Vicinity . . Pg. 167, C-3
Spiro F-13
Springer H-10
Stanley G-12
Steadman G-11
Stecker F-8
Sterling G-8
Stidham F-12

Stigler F-13
Stillwater D-10
Stilwell E-13
Stonewall G-11
Stratford G-10
Stringtown G-11
Strong City E-6
Stroud E-11
Stuart G-11
Sturgis B-3
Sugden H-9
Sulphur G-10
Summerfield G-13
Summit E-12
Sumner D-10
Sumpter C-10
Surrey Hills B-3
Sweetwater E-6
Sylvian F-11
Tabler F-9
Taft E-12
Tahlequah E-13
Talala C-12
Talihina G-13
Taliaferro C-11
Taloga D-7
Tangier C-6
Tatums G-9
Taylor H-8
Tecumseh F-10
Tegarden C-7
Temple H-8
Terlton D-11
Terral H-9
Texola F-6
The Village . Pg. 147, C-3
Thomas E-7
Three Sands C-10
Tiawah D-12
Tiger . . . . Pg. 167, E-6
Tipton G-7
Tonkawa C-10
Trail D-7
Tribbey F-10
Trousdale F-10
Troy H-10
Tryon E-10
Tullahassee E-12
Tulsa D-11
   Vicinity . . . . Pg. 167
Tupelo G-11
Turley . . . Pg. 167, D-3
Turpin C-4
Tushka H-11
Tuskahoma G-13
Tuttle F-9
   Vicinity . . Pg. 147, H-1
Tyrone B-4
Unger H-12
Union City F-8
Utica H-11
Valley Brook Pg. 147, F-5
Valliant H-13
Vanoss G-9
Velma G-9
Vera C-12
Verdigris D-12
Vernon F-11
Vian E-13
Vici D-7
Vinita C-12
Vinson F-6
Wade H-11
Wadena H-12
Wagoner D-12
Wakita C-9
Wanette F-10
Wapanucka H-11
Warner E-12
Warr Acres . Pg. 147, C-2
Warren G-2
Warwick E-10
Waters H-8
Watonga E-8
Watova C-12
Watson G-13
Waukomis D-8
Waurika H-9
Wayne F-10
Waynoka C-7
Weatherford E-7
Webb City C-10
Webbers Falls E-12
Welch C-13
Weleetka F-11
Wellston E-10
Welty E-11
Westport D-11
Wetumka F-11
Wewoka F-11

Wheeless C-2
White Bead G-9
White Oak C-12
Whitefield F-12
Whitesboro G-13
Wilburton F-12
Willis J-10
Willow F-6
Wilson H-9
Wolco C-11
Woodford H-10
Woodlawn Park
   . . . . Pg. 147, D-2
Woodward D-7
Wyandotte C-13
Wynnewood G-10
Wynona C-11
Yale D-10
Yeager F-11
Yewed C-8
Yost D-10
Yuba J-11
Yukon F-9
   Vicinity . . Pg. 147, C-1
Zeb E-13
Zena C-13

OREGON
Pages 70-71
Population: 2,633,105
Capital: Salem
Land Area: 98,184 sq. mi.

Adair Village D-3
Adams C-9
Adel J-7
Adrian G-11
Agness H-1
Albany D-3
Algoma J-5
Alicel C-10
Allegany F-2
Alpine E-3
Alsea E-3
Amity C-3
Andrews J-9
Antelope D-6
Applegate J-2
Arlington C-7
Arock H-10
Ashland J-3
Ashwood D-6
Astoria A-3
Athena C-9
Aurora C-4
Austin E-9
Azalea H-3
Baker E-10
Bandon G-2
Banks B-3
Barlow C-4
Bay City B-2
Beatty J-5
Beaver C-2
Beaverton . . Pg. 153, F-2
Belknap Springs . . E-4
Bend F-5
Biggs C-7
Birkenfeld B-3
Blalock C-7
Blodgett D-2
Blue River E-4
Bly J-5
Boardman B-8
Bonanza J-5
Bonneville C-5
Boring C-4
Breitenbush Springs . D-5
Bridge G-2
Bridgeport E-10
Brightwood C-5
Broadbent G-2
Brogan F-10
Brookings J-1
Brooks D-4
Brothers F-6
Brownsville E-4
Burns G-8
Burns Jct. H-9
Butte Falls H-4
Buxton B-3
Camas Valley G-2
Camp Sherman . . . E-5
Canby C-4
Cannon Beach B-2
Canyon City E-9
Canyonville H-2
Carlton C-3
Cascade Locks C-5

Cascadia E-4
Cave Junction J-2
Cecil C-7
Central Point J-3
Charleston G-1
Chemult G-5
Cheshire E-3
Chiloquin H-5
Christmas Valley . . G-6
Clatskanie A-3
Cloverdale C-2
Coburg E-3
   Vicinity . . Pg. 116, H-4
Colton C-4
Columbia City B-3
Condon D-7
Coos Bay F-1
Coquille G-2
Corvallis D-2
Cottage Grove F-3
Council Crest
   . . . . Pg. 153, E-3
Cove D-10
Crabtree D-4
Crane G-9
Crawfordsville E-4
Crescent G-5
Crescent Lake G-4
Creswell F-3
Culp Creek F-3
Culver E-5
Curtin F-3
Cushman E-2
Dairy J-5
Dallas D-3
Days Creek H-3
Dayton C-3
Dayville E-8
Dee C-5
Deer Island B-3
Denmark G-1
Depoe Bay D-2
Detroit D-4
Dexter F-3
Diamond H-9
Diamond Lake G-4
Dillard G-2
Disston F-4
Donald C-4
Dorena F-4
Drain F-3
Drew H-3
Drewsey F-9
Dufur C-6
Dunes City F-2
Durham . . . Pg. 153, G-3
Durkee E-10
Eagle Creek C-4
Eagle Point J-3
Eastside G-2
Echo C-8
Eddyville D-3
Elgin C-10
Elk City D-2
Elkton F-2
Elmira E-3
Enterprise C-11
Estacada C-5
Eugene F-3
   Vicinity . . Pg. 116, J-6
Falls City D-3
Falls Creek F-4
Fields J-8
Flora B-11
Florence E-2
Forest Grove C-3
Fort Klamath H-4
Fort Rock G-6
Fossil D-7
Fox E-8
Frenchglen H-8
Friend C-6
Gales Creek B-3
Gardiner F-2
Garibaldi B-2
Gaston C-3
Gates D-4
Gaylord H-2
Gearhart A-2
Gervais C-4
Gibbon C-9
Gilchrist G-5
Glenada E-2
Glendale H-2
Gleneden Beach . . . D-2
Glenwood B-3
Glide G-3
Goble B-4
Gold Beach H-1
Gold Hill H-3

OREGON

Goshen F-3
Vicinity . . Pg. 116, G-7
Government Camp . . C-5
Grand Ronde C-3
Grangeville B-12
Granite D-9
Grants Pass H-2
Grass Valley C-6
Gravelford G-2
Greenhorn E-9
Gresham C-4
Haines D-10
Halfway D-11
Halsey E-3
Hamilton D-8
Hammond A-2
Hampton G-6
Harbor J-1
Hardman D-7
Harlan D-2
Harper F-10
Harrisburg E-3
Hebo C-2
Heceta Beach E-2
Helix B-9
Heppner C-8
Hereford E-10
Hermiston B-8
Hillsboro C-3
Hillsdale . . . Pg. 153, E-3
Hines G-8
Holley E-4
Homestead D-11
Hood River B-5
Horton Blachly E-3
Hoskins D-3
Hubbard C-4
Huntington E-10
Idanha D-5
Ideyld Park G-3
Imbler C-10
Imnaha C-11
Independence D-3
Ione C-8
Ironside E-10
Irrigon B-8
Island City C-10
Jacksonville J-3
Jamieson F-10
Jasper E-3
Jefferson D-4
Jewell B-3
John Day E-9
Jordan Valley H-10
Joseph D-11
Junction City E-3
Juntura G-9
Kamela C-9
Keizer D-3
Kendall . . . . . Pg. 153, E-6
Keno J-4
Kent D-6
Kerby J-2
Kernville D-2
Kimberly D-7
King City . . . Pg. 153, G-2
Kings Valley D-3
Kinzua D-7
Klamatch Agency . . . H-4
Klamath Falls J-4
La Grande D-9
La Pine G-5
Lacomb D-4
Lafayette C-3
Lake Grove . . Pg. 153, G-3
Lake Oswego Pg. 153, F-3
Lakecreek J-3
Lakeside F-1
Lakeview J-7
Langlois G-1
Lawen G-9
Leaburg E-4
Lebanon D-4
Lexington C-7
Lincoln Beach D-2
Lincoln City D-2
Lonerock D-7
Long Creek E-8
Lorane F-3
Lostine C-11
Lowell E-4
Lyons D-4
Mabel E-4
Madras D-6
Malin K-5
Manning C-3
Manzanita B-2
Mapleton E-2
Marcola E-3
Marion D-4

Maupin C-6
Mayville D-7
McCredie Springs . . F-4
McKenzie Bridge . . . E-5
McMinnville C-3
McNary B-8
Meacham C-9
Medford J-3
Medical Springs . . . D-10
Merlin H-2
Merrill K-5
Metolius E-6
Metzger . . . . Pg. 153, F-2
Midland J-5
Mikkalo C-7
Mill City D-4
Millersburg D-3
Millican F-6
Milo H-3
Milton Freewater . . . B-10
Milwaukie . . Pg. 153, F-5
Minam C-10
Mission C-9
Mist B-3
Mitchell E-7
Mohawk E-4
Mohler B-2
Molalla C-4
Monmouth D-3
Monroe E-3
Monument D-8
Moro C-6
Mosier C-6
Mount Hood C-5
Mount Vernon E-8
Mt. Angel C-4
Mulino C-4
Multnomah . Pg. 153, E-3
Murphy J-2
Myrtle Creek G-3
Myrtle Point G-1
Nehalem B-3
Neskowin C-2
Netarts C-2
New Bridge E-11
New Princeton G-9
Newberg C-3
Newport D-2
North Bend F-2
North Plains B-4
North Powder D-10
Norway G-2
Noti E-3
Nyssa F-11
O'Brien J-2
Oak Grove . Pg. 153, G-5
Oakland G-3
Oakridge F-4
Oceanside C-2
Odell C-5
Olene J-5
Ontario F-11
Ophir H-1
Oregon City C-4
Otis C-2
Otter Rock D-2
Owyhee F-11
Pacific City C-2
Paisley H-6
Parkdale C-5
Paulina E-7
Pendleton C-8
Philomath D-3
Phoenix J-3
Pilot Rock C-9
Pinehurst J-4
Pistol River J-1
Pleasant Hill F-4
Pleasant Valley E-10
Plush H-7
Port Orford H-1
Portland C-4
Vicinity . . . . . Pg. 153
Detailed City . . Pg. 275
Post E-7
Powell Butte E-6
Powers H-2
Prairie City E-9
Prescott B-4
Prineville E-6
Prospect H-4
Rainier B-3
Raleigh Hills Pg. 153, E-3
Redmond E-5
Reedsport F-2
Remote G-2
Rhododendron C-5
Richland E-11
Riddle G-2
Riley G-8

Ritter D-8
Riverton G-1
Rockaway B-2
Rogue River H-3
Rome H-10
Roseburg G-3
Rufus C-7
Saginaw F-3
Saint Helens B-4
Saint Paul C-4
Salem D-3
Sandy C-5
Scappoose B-3
Scio D-4
Scottsburg F-2
Seal Rock D-2
Seaside A-2
Selma J-2
Seneca F-8
Shady Cove H-3
Shaniko D-6
Sheaville H-11
Shedd D-3
Sheridan C-3
Sherwood C-3
Siletz D-2
Siltcoos F-2
Silver Lake G-6
Silverton D-4
Sisters E-5
Sitkum G-2
Sixes G-1
Skipanon A-2
Sodaville E-4
South Beach D-2
Sprague River J-5
Spray D-7
Springfield E-3
Vicinity . . . Pg. 116, G-7
Stanfield B-8
Stayton D-4
Sublimity D-4
Summer Lake H-6
Summerville C-10
Sumner G-2
Sumpter E-9
Sunriver F-5
Sutherlin G-3
Sweethome E-4
Swisshome E-3
Talent J-3
Tangent D-3
Telocaset D-10
Tenmile G-2
Terrebonne E-5
The Dalles C-7
Tidewater E-2
Tiernan E-2
Tigard C-4
Vicinity . . . Pg. 153, F-2
Tillamook C-3
Tiller H-3
Timber B-3
Toledo D-2
Trail H-3
Troutdale C-5
Troy B-10
Tualatin C-4
Vicinity . . . Pg. 153, G-2
Turner D-3
Tygh Valley C-7
Ukiah D-8
Umapine B-9
Umatilla B-8
Umpqua G-2
Union D-10
Union Creek H-3
Unity E-10
Vale F-10
Valley Falls J-6
Valsetz D-2
Veneta E-3
Vernonia B-3
Vida E-4
Waldport E-2
Walker F-3
Wallowa C-10
Walterville E-4
Walton E-2
Wamic C-6
Warm Springs D-5
Warren B-3
Warrenton A-2
Wasco C-7
Waterloo D-4
Wedderburn H-1
Wemme C-5
West Fir F-4
West Linn C-4
Vicinity . . . Pg. 153, G-4

West Slope . Pg. 153, D-2
West Stayton D-3
Westfall F-10
Weston B-9
Westport A-3
Wheeler B-2
White City J-3
Whitney E-9
Wilbur G-3
Wilderville J-2
Willamina C-3
Williams J-3
Willow Creek F-10
Wilsonville C-4
Winchester G-2
Winchester Bay F-1
Winston G-3
Wolfcreek H-2
Wonder J-2
Woodburn C-3
Yachats E-2
Yamhill C-3
Yoncalla F-3
Zigzag C-5

PENNSYLVANIA
Pages 72-73
Population: 11,863,895
Capital: Harrisburg
Land Area: 44,888 sq. mi.

Abington . . Pg. 150, B-6
Academy Gardens
. . . . Pg. 150, C-8
Adamstown H-11
Addison K-4
Akron H-11
Alba C-9
Albion C-1
Alburtis G-12
Aldan . . . . . . Pg. 150, F-3
Aliquippa G-2
Allen . . . . Pg. 119, K-1
Allentown G-13
Vicinity . . . Pg. 91, J-2
Altoona G-6
Ambler H-13
Vicinity . . Pg. 150, A-4
Ambridge G-2
Andersontown
. . . . Pg. 119, K-3
Andorra . . . . Pg. 150, C-4
Archbald D-12
Arendtsville J-8
Armagh G-5
Aronimink . Pg. 150, D-3
Ashley E-11
Vicinity . . Pg. 164, G-1
Ashville G-5
Athens C-10
Austin D-7
Avalon . . . . . Pg. 152, B-1
Avis E-8
Avonmore G-3
Baden G-2
Bala-Cynwyd
. . . . Pg. 150, D-4
Baldwin . . . . . Pg. 152, F-5
Ballietsville . . Pg. 91, B-1
Bally H-12
Bangor F-13
Barnesboro G-5
Bartram Village
. . . . Pg. 150, F-4
Bath G-13
Bear Creek Pg. 164, G-4
Beaver G-1
Beaver Falls F-1
Beavertown F-9
Bedford J-6
Beech Creek E-8
Belle Valley Pg. 116, G-2
Belle Vernon J-2
Bellefonte F-7
Bellevue G-2
Vicinity . . Pg. 152, B-2
Bellwood G-6
Ben Avon . . Pg. 152, A-1
Bendersville J-8
Benson H-5
Benton E-10
Berlin J-4
Berrysburg G-9
Berwick F-11
Bessemer F-1
Bethel Park H-2
Vicinity . . Pg. 152, G-2
Bethlehem G-13
Vicinity . . . Pg. 91, B-4

Big Beaver F-1
Big Run F-5
Birdsboro H-12
Black Horse Pg. 150, F-1
Blain H-7
Blairsville G-4
Blakely D-12
Blooming Valley C-2
Bloomsburg F-10
Blossburg C-9
Blue Bell . . Pg. 150, A-3
Bolivar H-4
Boswell H-4
Bowmansdale
. . . . Pg. 119, K-3
Bowmanstown F-12
Boyertown H-12
Brackenridge G-3
Bradford C-5
Brennemans Mill
. . . . Pg. 119, H-3
Brontwood . Pg. 152, F-4
Bressler . . . Pg. 119, J-5
Briar Creek F-11
Bridgeport . Pg. 150, B-2
Bridgeville H-2
Bristol J-14
Broad Axe . Pg. 150, A-4
Broad Top City H-6
Brockway E-5
Brookhaven J-13
Vicinity . . Pg. 150, G-1
Brookville E-4
Broomall . . . Pg. 150, D-2
Brownstown C-5
Vicinity . . Pg. 164, D-4
Brownsville J-2
Bruin F-3
Bryn Athyn Pg. 150, A-7
Bryn Mawr . Pg. 150, D-2
Burgettstown H-1
Burlington C-10
Burnham G-8
Bustleton . . Pg. 150, B-7
Butler F-2
Buttonwood Pg. 164, F-1
Calico Corner
. . . . Pg. 150, B-9
California J-2
Callensburg E-3
Callery F-2
Cambridge Springs . C-2
Camp Hill . . Pg. 119, J-3
Canonsburg H-2
Canton D-9
Carbondale D-12
Carlisle H-9
Carmichaels J-2
Carnegie H-2
Carroll Park Pg. 150, D-4
Carroll Valley K-8
Carrolltown G-5
Cassandra H-5
Castle Shannon
. . . . Pg. 152, F-3
Catasauqua G-12
Vicinity . . . Pg. 91, B-2
Catawissa F-10
Cedarbrook Pg. 150, B-5
Center Moreland
. . . . Pg. 164, B-1
Center Square
. . . . Pg. 150, A-3
Center Valley Pg. 91, E-3
Centerville
(Washington Cty) . . J-2
Centerville
(Crawford Cty) . . . C-3
Central City J-5
Centre Hall F-7
Chalfont H-13
Chambersburg H-7
Charleroi H-2
Cherry Tree G-5
Chester J-13
Vicinity . . Pg. 150, F-1
Chester Heights J-12
Chester Hill F-6
Chestnut Hill Pg. 150, C-4
Chicora F-3
Chinchilla . . Pg. 164, A-5
Clairton H-2
Clarendon C-4
Clarion E-4
Clarks Green
. . . . Pg. 164, A-5
Clarks Summit D-12
Clearfield F-6
Cleona H-10
Clifton Heights
. . . . Pg. 150, F-3

Clintonville E-3
Clymer G-4
Coalport G-5
Coatesville J-12
Cobbs Creek
. . . . Pg. 150, D-4
Cochranton D-2
Cokeburg H-2
Collegeville H-13
Colling Dale Pg. 150, F-3
Colonial Park
. . . . Pg. 119, G-6
Columbia J-10
Vicinity . . Pg. 119, G-3
Colwyn . . . . . Pg. 150, F-4
Conneautville C-1
Connellsville J-3
Connoquenessing . . F-2
Conshohocken J-13
Vicinity . . Pg. 150, B-3
Conway G-2
Conyngham F-11
Coopersburg G-13
Cooperstown D-3
Coraopolis G-2
Cork Lane . Pg. 164, D-3
Cornwall H-10
Corry C-3
Corsica E-4
Coudersport D-7
Courtdale . Pg. 164, E-1
Cove . . . . . . Pg. 119, F-3
Crafton . . . . Pg. 152, D-2
Cranesville C-2
Creekside G-4
Cresson H-5
Cressona G-11
Croydon . . . Pg. 150, B-10
Curwensville F-6
Dallastown J-10
Dalton D-12
Danville F-10
Darby J-13
Vicinity . . Pg. 150, F-3
Dauphin G-9
Vicinity . . Pg. 119, F-4
Dayton F-4
Deepdale . . Pg. 164, C-1
Delaware Water Gap F-13
Delta K-11
Denver H-11
Derry H-4
Dickson City D-12
Dillsburg J-9
Donegal J-4
Donora H-2
Dormont . . . Pg. 150, D-7
Vicinity . . Pg. 152, E-2
Dover J-9
Downingtown J-12
Doylestown H-13
Dresher . . . Pg. 150, A-5
Driftwood E-6
DuBois E-5
Duboistown E-9
Dudley H-6
Dunbar J-3
Duncannon H-9
Duncansville H-6
Dunmore D-12
Vicinity . . Pg. 164, C-6
Dupont . . . . Pg. 164, D-4
Duryea . . . . Pg. 164, D-4
Dushore D-10
Eagles Mere D-10
Eagleville . . Pg. 150, A-1
East Berlin J-9
East Brady F-3
East Butler F-3
East Falls . . Pg. 150, D-5
East Greenville H-12
East Lansdowne
. . . . Pg. 150, D-3
East Mt. Airy Pg. 150, C-5
East Oak Lane
. . . . Pg. 150, C-6
East Stroudsburg . . . F-13
East Texas . Pg. 91, E-1
East Washington H-2
Eastlake . . . Pg. 150, F-4
Eastwick . . . Pg. 150, F-4
Eau Claire F-3
Ebensburg H-5
Economy G-2
Eddington Park
. . . . Pg. 150, B-9
Eddystone . . Pg. 150, G-0
Edinboro C-2
Edwardsville
. . . . Pg. 164, E-1
Eldred C-6

Elizabethtown H-10
Elizabethville G-10
Elkland C-8
Ellport F-2
Ellwood City F-1
Elmwood . . Pg. 150, F-4
Elwyn . . . . . Pg. 150, F-1
Emlenton E-3
Emmaus G-12
Vicinity . . . Pg. 91, E-2
Emporium D-6
Enhaut . . . . Pg. 119, J-5
Enola . . . . . Pg. 119, G-3
Ephrata H-11
Erie B-2
Vicinity . . Pg. 116, G-1
Etna . . . . . . Pg. 152, B-5
Evans City F-2
Everett J-6
Everson J-3
Exeter . . . . . Pg. 164, D-3
Factoryville D-12
Fairchance J-3
Fairfield K-8
Fairview B-2
Fairview Park Pg. 119, K-6
Fairview Village
. . . . Pg. 150, A-5
Falls . . . . . . Pg. 164, B-2
Falls Creek E-5
Farrell E-1
Fawn Grove K-10
Fentonville . Pg. 150, D-6
Fern Brook . Pg. 164, D-1
Fern Rock . . Pg. 150, C-6
Fitzwatertown
. . . . Pg. 150, A-5
Fleetwood G-12
Flemington E-8
Flourtown . . Pg. 150, B-4
Folcroft . . . Pg. 150, F-3
Ford City G-3
Ford Cliff G-3
Forest City D-12
Forest Park Pg. 164, G-3
Forksville D-10
Fort Hunter Pg. 119, F-4
Fort Washington
. . . . Pg. 150, A-4
Forty Fort . . Pg. 164, E-1
Vicinity . . Pg. 164, E-2
Fountain Hill G-13
Vicinity . . . Pg. 91, D-3
Foxcroft . . . Pg. 150, D-3
Frackville F-11
Frankford . . Pg. 150, D-7
Franklin E-3
Franklin Park G-2
Freeburg G-9
Freedom F-2
Freeland F-12
Freemansburg Pg. 91, D-3
Freeport G-3
Friedensville Pg. 91, E-3
Galeton C-8
Gallitzin G-5
Garrett J-4
Geistown H-5
Georgetown Pg. 164, E-2
Germantown Pg. 150, D-5
Gettysburg K-9
Girard B-2
Gladwyne . . Pg. 150, C-3
Glen Campbell F-5
Glen Hope F-6
Glen Rock K-10
Glendale . . . Pg. 164, D-5
Glenolden . Pg. 150, F-3
Glenside . . Pg. 150, B-6
Godard . . . . Pg. 116, G-3
Good Hope . Pg. 119, H-3
Good Hope Mill
. . . . Pg. 119, H-3
Gordon G-11
Grampian F-5
Grantham . . Pg. 119, K-3
Gratz G-10
Great Bend C-12
Greencastle K-7
Greensboro K-2
Greensburg H-3
Greentree . . Pg. 152, E-2
Greenville D-1
Grove City E-2
Halifax G-9
Hallstead C-12
Hamburg G-11
Hammett . . . Pg. 116, H-8
Hanover K-9
Harding . . . . Pg. 164, C-3

Harmonville Pg. 150, B-3
Harmony F-2
Harrisburg H-9
Vicinity . . Pg. 119, G-4
Harrisville F-2
Harveys Lake D-11
Hastings G-5
Hatboro H-13
Havertown . Pg. 150, D-3
Hawley D-13
Hawthorn F-4
Hazelton F-11
Heckton . . . Pg. 119, F-4
Hecktown . . Pg. 91, A-4
Heidelberg . Pg. 152, E-1
Hellertown . Pg. 91, D-4
Herndon G-9
Hershey H-10
Highspire . . Pg. 119, J-6
Hilldale . . . . Pg. 164, E-3
Hogestown . Pg. 119, H-2
Hollidaysburg H-6
Holmesburg Pg. 150, C-7
Homer City G-4
Homestead . Pg. 152, E-6
Honesdale D-13
Honey Brook J-12
Hooversville H-5
Hop Bottom C-12
Hopewell H-6
Houston H-2
Houtzdale F-6
Hudson . . . . Pg. 164, E-2
Hughesville E-10
Hulmeville . Pg. 150, A-9
Hummelstown H-10
Vicinity . . Pg. 119, H-7
Huntingdon G-7
Huntingdon Valley
. . . . Pg. 150, B-7
Hydetown C-3
Hyndman K-5
Indian Lake J-5
Indiana G-4
Industry G-1
Ingram . . . . Pg. 152, D-1
Inkermin . . . Pg. 164, D-4
Irvona F-5
Ithan . . . . . . Pg. 150, C-1
Jackson Center E-2
Jacobus J-10
Jamestown D-1
Jeanette H-3
Jeddo F-12
Jefferson D-12
Jeffersonville Pg. 150, A-2
Jenkintown . Pg. 150, B-6
Jennerstown H-4
Jermyn D-12
Jersey Shore E-9
Jim Thorpe F-12
Johnsonburg D-5
Johnstown H-5
Jonestown H-10
Juniata . . . . Pg. 150, D-6
Kane C-5
Karns City F-3
Kearsarge . . Pg. 116, K-3
Keelersburg Pg. 164, A-1
Kennett Square J-12
Kensington . Pg. 150, E-6
Ketcham . . . Pg. 164, C-1
King of Prussia
. . . . Pg. 150, B-1
Kingston E-12
Kistler H-7
Kittanning F-3
Knox E-3
Knoxville C-7
Kreidersville Pg. 91, A-2
Kulpmont F-10
Kutztown G-12
Laflin . . . . . Pg. 164, D-4
Lake City B-2
Lancaster J-11
Landisburg H-8
Lanesboro C-12
Langhorne H-14
Langhorne Manor
. . . . Pg. 150, A-9
Lansdale H-13
Lansdowne J-13
Vicinity . . Pg. 150, E-3
Lansford F-12
Laporte D-10
Larchmont Meadows
. . . . Pg. 150, E-1
Larksville . . Pg. 164, F-1
Latrobe H-4
Laurel Run . Pg. 164, F-2

PENNSYLVANIA

Laureldale H-12
Lawn Crest C-7
Lawnton .... Pg. 119, H-6
Lawrence Park ...... Pg. 150, D-2
Le Raysville C-11
Lebanon H-10
Leesport G-11
Lehighton F-12
Leithsville .. Pg. 91, E-4
Lemoyne H-9
  Vicinity .. Pg. 119, H-3
Levittown H-14
Lewisburg F-9
Lewistown G-8
Lexington Park ...... Pg. 150, C-7
Liberty D-9
Ligonier H-4
Lilly H-5
Lincoln H-11
Linesville C-1
Linglestown Pg. 119, F-5
Lisburn .... Pg. 119, K-4
Lititz J-11
Little Meadows .. C-11
Littlestown K-9
Liverpool G-8
Lock Haven E-8
Logan .... Pg. 150, D-6
Loganton E-8
Loomis Park Pg. 164, G-1
Loretto G-5
Lower Burrell G-3
Lumar Park . Pg. 150, B-8
Lumber City F-5
Luzerne .. Pg. 164, E-1
Lykens G-10
Macungie G-12
Mahanoy City F-11
Manayunk . Pg. 150, D-4
Manchester J-10
Manheim J-11
Manns Choice J-5
Mansfield C-9
Maplewood Heights ...... Pg. 164, D-1
Marble Hall . Pg. 150, B-4
Marcus Hook K-13
  Vicinity .. Pg. 150, F-3
Marianna J-2
Marietta J-10
Marion Center H-6
Marklesburg H-6
Mars G-2
Marshwood . Pg. 164, B-6
Martinsburg H-6
Marysville H-9
Marysville .. Pg. 119, F-6
Masontown J-2
Matamoras D-14
Mayfair .. Pg. 150, C-7
McKean B-2
McKeesport H-2
McSherrytown K-9
McVeytown G-7
Mckee's Rocks ...... Pg. 152, C-2
Meadville D-2
Mechanicsburg H-9
  Vicinity .. Pg. 119, J-3
Media .. Pg. 150, F-1
Mercer E-2
Mercersburg K-7
Meshoppen D-11
Meyersdale K-4
Middleburg G-9
Middletown H-10
  Vicinity .. Pg. 119, K-7
Midland G-1
Midvale .. Pg. 164, E-2
Mifflinburg F-9
Mifflintown H-8
Milesburg F-7
Milford E-14
Mill City .. Pg. 164, A-2
Mill Creek H-7
Mill Hall E-8
Mill Village C-2
Millbourne . Pg. 150, D-3
Millerbrook . Pg. 150, C-8
Millersburg G-9
Millerstown G-9
Millersville J-10
Millheim F-8
Millridge . Pg. 150, D-2
Milton F-9
Milwaukee . Pg. 164, B-4
Minersville G-11
Mohnton H-11

Monaca G-2
Monessen H-2
Monroe C-10
Monroeville G-3
Mont Alto J-8
Montoursville E-9
Montrose C-12
Moosic D-12
  Vicinity .. Pg. 164, C-5
Morrisville H-14
Morton .. Pg. 150, C-5
Moscow E-12
Mountain Top Pg. 164, G-1
Mountville J-10
Mt. Allen .. Pg. 119, K-2
Mt. Carmel F-10
Mt. Holly Springs .. J-9
Mt. Jewett C-5
Mt. Joy J-10
Mt. Pleasant H-3
Mt. Pocono E-13
Mt. Union H-7
Mt. Wolf J-10
Murrysville G-3
Myerstown H-11
Nanticoke E-11
Nantilly .... Pg. 119, K-3
Nanty-Glo G-5
Narberth J-13
  Vicinity .. Pg. 150, D-3
Nauvo .... Pg. 119, K-4
Nay Aug .. Pg. 164, C-6
Nazareth G-13
Nescopeck F-11
New Albany D-10
New Alexandra H-3
New Beaver F-1
New Berlin F-9
New Bethlehem F-4
New Brighton F-1
New Buffalo G-9
New Castle F-1
New Centerville J-4
New Cumberland H-9
  Vicinity .. Pg. 119, J-4
New Eagle H-2
New Florence H-4
New Freedom K-10
New Holland J-11
New Kensington G-3
New Kingstown ...... Pg. 119, J-1
New Lebanon D-2
New Milford C-12
New Oxford J-9
New Paris J-5
New Philadelphia . G-11
New Salem J-2
New Stanton H-3
New Wilmington E-1
Newburg (Clearfield Cty) .. F-5
Newburg (Bedford Cty) .. J-8
Newport G-9
Newry H-6
Newton .. Pg. 164, B-3
Newtown .. Pg. 164, F-1
Newtown Heights ...... Pg. 150, E-1
Newtown Square ...... Pg. 150, D-1
Newville H-8
Nicetown-Tioga ...... Pg. 150, D-5
Nicholson D-12
Normandy . Pg. 150, B-8
Norristown J-13
  Vicinity .. Pg. 150, A-2
Norritonville . Pg. 150, A-2
North Apollo G-3
North Belle Vernon .. H-3
North East B-3
North Hills . Pg. 150, B-5
North Wales H-13
North York J-10
Northampton G-12
  Vicinity .. Pg. 91, B-1
Northumberland F-9
Norwood .. Pg. 150, G-3
Nuangola E-11
Oakland C-12
Oakleigh .. Pg. 119, H-5
Oakmont G-3
Oberlin .. Pg. 119, J-5
Ohiopyle J-3
Oil City D-3
Old Boston . Pg. 164, E-4
Old Forge D-12
  Vicinity .. Pg. 164, C-4

Oliver Mills . Pg. 164, F-2
Olyphant D-12
  Vicinity .. Pg. 164, A-6
Orange .. Pg. 164, C-1
Orangeville E-10
Orbisonia H-7
Orrstown J-8
Orwigsburg G-11
Osceola Mills F-6
Oswayo C-7
Overbrook . Pg. 150, D-4
Overview . Pg. 119, G-3
Oxford K-11
Palmerton F-12
Palmyra H-10
Parker E-3
Parkesburg J-11
Parkside . Pg. 150, G-2
Patton E-5
Paxtang .. Pg. 119, H-5
Paxton G-9
Paxtonia .. Pg. 119, G-5
Pen Argyl F-13
Penfield .. Pg. 150, D-3
Penn Square Pg. 150, A-2
Pennsburg H-13
Penobscot . Pg. 164, G-2
Perdix .. Pg. 119, F-3
Perkasie H-13
Petersburg G-7
Petrolia F-3
Philadelphia
  Vicinity .... Pg. 150
  Detailed City . Pg. 271
Philipsburg F-6
Phoenixville H-12
Picture Rocks E-10
Pillow G-9
Pine Grove G-10
Pittsburgh G-2
  Vicinity .... Pg. 152
  Detailed City . Pg. 274
Pittston E-11
  Vicinity .. Pg. 164, D-3
Plainfield .. Pg. 119, K-6
Plainsville .. Pg. 164, E-2
Platea B-2
Pleasant View Summit ...... Pg. 164, G-5
Pleasantville (Venango Cty) .. D-3
Pleasantville (Bedford Cty) .. H-5
Plum G-3
Plumville F-4
Plymouth Valley ...... Pg. 150, B-3
Point Marion K-2
Polk D-2
Port Allegany C-6
Port Carbon G-11
Port Matilda F-7
Port Royal G-8
Portage H-5
Portersville F-2
Portland F-13
Pottstown H-12
Pottsville G-11
Progress .. Pg. 119, G-5
Prospect Park ...... Pg. 150, G-3
Punxsutawney F-4
Pymble .. Pg. 150, F-1
Quakertown G-13
Quarryville J-11
Queen City . Pg. 91, D-2
Radnor .. Pg. 150, C-2
Rainsburg J-5
Ramey .. Pg. 164, C-3
Ransom .. Pg. 164, C-3
Reading H-12
Red Hill H-13
Red Lion J-10
Renovo E-7
Reynoldsville E-5
Rices Landing J-2
Richland H-11
Richlandtown G-13
Richmond .. Pg. 150, D-6
Ridgewood . Pg. 164, G-3
Ridgway D-5
Ridley Park . Pg. 150, G-3
Rimersburg E-3
Ringtown F-11
Riverside F-10
Roaring Spring H-6
Robesonia H-11
Rockledge . Pg. 150, B-6
Rockville .. Pg. 119, F-4
Rockwood J-4

Rome C-11
Rose Valley Pg. 150, F-1
Rosemont . Pg. 150, D-2
Roseto F-13
Roseville C-9
Roslyn .. Pg. 150, B-6
Rosslyn Farms ...... Pg. 152, D-1
Rouseville D-3
Roxborough Pg. 150, C-4
Royersford H-12
Rural Valley F-4
Rutherford Heights ...... Pg. 119, H-6
Rutledge .. Pg. 150, G-2
Saegertown C-2
Saint Clair G-11
Saint Marys D-5
Saint Petersburg .. E-3
Salisbury K-4
Salladasburg E-9
Saltillo H-7
Saltsburg G-3
Sandy Lake D-2
Sankertown G-5
Saxonburg F-3
Saxton H-6
Sayre C-10
Scalp Level H-5
Schultzville . Pg. 164, A-3
Schuylkill Haven .. G-11
Scottdale H-3
Scranton D-12
  Vicinity .. Pg. 164, B-5
Seemsville .. Pg. 91, A-2
Selinsgrove F-9
Sellersville H-13
Seward H-4
Shade Gap H-7
Shades Glen ...... Pg. 164, G-5
Shamokin F-10
Shamokin Dam F-9
Sharon E-1
Sharon Hill . Pg. 150, F-3
Sharpsburg . Pg. 152, B-5
Shaverton .. Pg. 164, D-1
Shenandoah F-11
Shepherdstown ...... Pg. 119, K-2
Shickshinny E-11
Shillington H-11
Shinglehouse C-6
Shippensburg J-8
Shippenville E-3
Shiremanstown ...... Pg. 119, J-3
Shirleysburg H-7
Shoemakersville .. G-11
Shoenersville Pg. 91, B-3
Shrewsbury K-10
Siddonsburg Pg. 119, K-3
Slatington F-12
Sligo E-3
Slippery Rock E-2
Smethport C-6
Smithfield K-3
Snow Shoe F-7
Society Hill . Pg. 150, D-5
Solomon Gap ...... Pg. 164, G-2
Somerset J-4
Somerton . Pg. 150, B-8
Souderton H-13
South Bethlehem .. F-4
South Coatesville .. J-12
South Connellsville .. J-3
South Fork H-5
South Philadelphia ...... Pg. 150, F-5
South Renovo E-7
South Waverly B-10
South Williamsport . E-9
Spangler G-5
Spartansburg C-2
Sporting Hill Pg. 119, H-3
Spring City H-12
Spring Grove J-9
Spring Mill Pg. 150, B-3
Springboro C-1
Springfield . Pg. 150, F-2
Stanwood .. Pg. 150, B-9
State College F-7
Steel City .. Pg. 91, C-4
Steelton .. Pg. 119, H-6
Stillwater E-10
Stoneboro D-2
Stoystown J-4
Strasburg J-11
Strattanville E-4

Strausstown G-11
Stroudsburg F-13
Sugar Grove B-4
Sugar Notch Pg. 164, G-1
Sugarcreek G-3
Summerdale Pg. 119, G-3
Summerhill H-5
Summerville E-4
  Vicinity .. Pg. 152, G-5
Summit Hill F-12
Summit Lawn Pg. 91, D-2
Sunbury F-10
Suscon .. Pg. 150, E-4
Susquehanna C-12
Swanville .. Pg. 116, K-3
Swarthmore Pg. 150, F-2
Swoyersville Pg. 164, E-2
Sykesville F-5
Sylvania B-9
Tamaqua F-11
Tatamy G-13
Taylor D-12
  Vicinity .. Pg. 164, C-3
Telford H-13
Temple H-12
Terre Hill H-11
Thompsontown G-9
Thornburg . Pg. 152, D-1
Three Springs H-7
Throop .. Pg. 164, B-6
Tidioute C-4
Timberlake . Pg. 150, E-1
Tioga C-9
Tionesta D-3
Titusville D-3
Tooley Corners ...... Pg. 164, D-6
Topton G-12
Towanda C-10
Tower City G-10
Trainer J-13
Trappe H-12
Treichlers .. Pg. 91, A-1
Tremont G-10
Trooper .. Pg. 150, A-1
Troutville F-5
Troy C-10
Trucksville . Pg. 164, E-1
Tullytown H-14
Tunkhannock D-11
Tyrone G-6
Union City C-3
Union Dale C-11
Union Deposit ...... Pg. 119, G-7
Uniontown J-3
Upland .. Pg. 150, G-1
Upper Exeter Pg. 164, B-2
Upper Fairview ...... Pg. 150, A-1
Upper Roxborough ...... Pg. 150, C-4
Ursina K-4
Vandergrift G-3
Venango C-2
Vernon .. Pg. 164, B-1
Villanova . Pg. 150, D-2
Walnutport G-12
Wampum F-1
Warren C-4
Washington H-2
Waterford C-2
Waterloo Mills ...... Pg. 150, D-1
Watsontown E-9
Wattsburg B-3
Waymart D-13
Wayne .. Pg. 150, C-1
Waynesboro K-8
Waynesburg J-2
Weatherly F-12
Wellersburg K-5
Wellsboro C-8
Wellsville J-9
Wesleyville D-2
  Vicinity .. Pg. 116, G-1
West Brownsville .. J-2
West Catasauqua ...... Pg. 91, B-2
West Chester J-12
West Conshohocken ...... Pg. 150, D-2
West Easton G-13
West Fairview ...... Pg. 119, H-4
West Falls . Pg. 164, A-2
West Gate Hills ...... Pg. 150, D-2
West Grove K-12
West Hazleton F-11

West Homestead ...... Pg. 152, E-5
West Kensington ...... Pg. 150, D-6
West Kittanning F-3
West Liberty F-2
West Middlesex E-1
West Mifflin G-3
  Vicinity .. Pg. 152, G-5
West Newton H-3
West Oak Lane ...... Pg. 150, C-5
West Philadelphia ...... Pg. 150, D-4
West Pittston E-12
West Reading H-11
West View . Pg. 152, A-2
West Wyoming ...... Pg. 164, D-2
West York J-10
Westfield C-8
Westminster Pg. 164, E-4
Westmont H-5
Westover G-5
Wheatland E-1
White Haven E-12
White Marsh Pg. 150, A-6
White Oak H-3
Whitehall G-12
Wilkes-Barre E-12
  Vicinity .. Pg. 164, F-2
Wilkinsburg G-3
Williams Grove ...... Pg. 119, K-2
Williamsburg G-6
Williamsport E-9
Williamstown G-10
Willow Grove Pg. 150, A-6
Wilson G-13
Wind Gap F-13
Windber H-5
Winterstown K-10
Witinski Villa Pg. 164, G-1
Womelsdorf H-11
Woodbury H-6
Wormleysburg ...... Pg. 119, H-4
Worthington F-3
Wrightsville J-10
Wyalusing D-11
Wyola .. Pg. 150, D-1
Wyoming .. Pg. 164, D-2
Wyomissing H-11
Yardley H-14
Yeadon J-13
  Vicinity .. Pg. 154, K-6
York J-10
York Springs J-9
Youngsville C-4
Youngwood H-3
Zelienople F-2

RHODE ISLAND
Page 25
Population: 947,154
Capital: Providence
Land Area: 1055 sq. mi.

SOUTH CAROLINA
Pages 64-65
Population: 3,121,820
Capital: Columbia
Land Area: 30,203 sq. mi.

Albion .... Pg. 154, E-3
Ashton E-8
Ashton .. Pg. 154, F-3
Auburn F-9
  Vicinity .. Pg. 154, J-4
Barrington F-10
  Vicinity .. Pg. 154, K-5
Berkeley E-8
  Vicinity .. Pg. 154, F-4
Bristol G-10
Carolina H-9
Centerdale Pg. 154, D-4
Central Falls Pg. 154, G-4
Charlestown H-9
Chepachet E-9
Clayville F-8
Comstock Gardens ...... Pg. 154, J-2
Conimicut . Pg. 154, K-4
Cranston F-9
  Vicinity .. Pg. 154, J-3
East Greenwich G-9
East Providence F-10
  Vicinity .. Pg. 154, H-5
Esmond F-9
  Vicinity .. Pg. 154, G-3
Exeter G-9

Fiskeville F-9
  Vicinity .. Pg. 154, K-2
Foster Center F-8
Georgiaville Pg. 154, G-2
Glocester E-8
Greenville . Pg. 154, G-2
Harmony F-8
  Vicinity .. Pg. 154, G-1
Harris .. Pg. 154, K-2
Harrisville E-9
Homestead G-10
Hope F-9
  Vicinity .. Pg. 154, K-1
Hope Valley G-8
Hughesdale Pg. 154, H-2
Jamestown G-10
Knightsville Pg. 154, J-2
Lime Rock . Pg. 154, F-3
Lippitt F-9
  Vicinity .. Pg. 154, K-2
Little Compton G-10
Lonsdale . Pg. 154, F-3
Mapleville E-9
Middletown G-10
Millville E-9
Narragansett Pier . H-9
Nasonville E-9
Newport G-10
Nooseneck G-9
North Foster F-8
North Providence ...... Pg. 154, G-3
North Scituate F-9
North Tiverton G-10
Pascoug E-8
Pawtucket F-10
  Vicinity .. Pg. 154, G-4
Portsmouth G-10
Primrose .. Pg. 154, E-2
Providence F-9
  Vicinity .. Pg. 154, H-3
Riverside .. Pg. 154, J-5
Saundersville Pg. 154, H-1
Saylesville Pg. 154, G-3
Slatersville E-9
South Attleboro ...... Pg. 154, F-5
Spragueville Pg. 154, G-1
Tarklin .. Pg. 154, F-5
Thorton .. Pg. 154, J-3
Usquepaug G-9
Valley Falls Pg. 154, F-4
Vernon F-8
Wakefield H-9
Warren F-10
  Vicinity .. Pg. 154, K-6
Warwick G-10
  Vicinity .. Pg. 154, K-4
Washington F-9
Waterman Four Corners
West Barrington ...... Pg. 154, K-5
West Greenwich G-8
Westerly H-8
Wickford G-9
Wood River Jct. H-8
Woodville H-8
Woonsocket E-9

SOUTH CAROLINA

Abbeville F-4
Adams Run J-7
Aiken G-5
  Vicinity .. Pg. 93, A-7
Allendale H-6
Almeda J-6
Anderson F-4
Andrews G-9
Antreville F-4
Appleton H-6
Arcadia Lakes Pg. 108, B-5
Arthur .. Pg. 108, D-2
Ashley Hall . Pg. 100, D-2
Ashley Heights ...... Pg. 100, B-2
Awendaw H-8
Aynor F-9
Ballentine F-6
  Vicinity .. Pg. 108, A-1
Bamberg H-6
Barnwell H-6

Batesburg G-5
Bayboro F-9
Beech Island Pg. 93, D-4
Belton E-4
Belvedere Pg. 93, A-4
Bennettsville E-8
Bethany D-6
Bethune F-7
Bishopville F-7
Blacksburg D-7
Blackville H-6
Blenheim E-8
Bonneau H-7
Bowman H-7
Boykin F-7
Bradley F-4
Branchville H-6
Brownsville E-8
Bruner .. Pg. 108, E-7
Buffalo E-5
Bullock Creek E-6
Cades H-8
Cainhoy
  Vicinity .. Pg. 100, B-6
Calhoun Falls F-4
Camden F-7
Canadys H-7
Carlisle E-6
Cassatt F-7
Cayce F-6
  Vicinity .. Pg. 108, D-4
Centenary F-9
Centerville . Pg. 100, F-3
Central E-3
Chappells F-5
Charleston J-8
  Vicinity .. Pg. 100
Chelsea K-7
Cheraw E-8
Chesnee D-5
Chester E-6
Chesterfield E-8
Clarkshill F-4
Clearwater Pg. 93, B-4
Clemson E-3
Cleveland D-4
Clinton F-5
Clio E-8
Clover D-6
Columbia F-6
  Vicinity .. Pg. 108, C-5
Conagree . Pg. 108, E-2
Conway G-9
Cool Spring F-9
Cresent Beach G-10
Cross H-7
Cross Hill F-5
Cross Keys E-5
Dalzell F-7
Darlington F-8
De Kalb F-7
Debidue Beach H-9
Deer Park . Pg. 100, A-1
Denmark H-6
Denny Terrace ...... Pg. 108, B-4
Dentsville . Pg. 108, B-6
Dillon E-9
Dixiana . Pg. 108, E-4
Dovesville E-8
Drayton .. Pg. 100, D-2
Due West F-4
Edgefield G-5
Edgemoor E-6
Edisto Beach J-8
Edisto Island J-7
Effingham H-6
Ehrhardt H-6
Elgin F-7
Enoree E-5
Estill J-6
Eureka F-4
Evergreen F-8
Fair Bluff F-9
Fairfax J-6
Fenwick Crossroads ...... Pg. 100, G-1
Filbert D-6
Florence E-8
Floydale F-9
Folly Beach J-8
Forest Acres Pg. 108, C-5
Forest Beach K-7
Foreston G-7
Fork F-9
Fork Shoals E-4
Fort Mill D-6
Fountain Inn E-5
Furman J-6
Gaffney D-5

SOUTH CAROLINA

Galivants Ferry F-9
Garden City G-9
Gardens Corner J-7
Garnett J-6
Georgetown G-9
Givhans H-7
Gloverville .. Pg. 93, B-6
Goose Creek H-8
  Vicinity ... Pg. 100, A-2
Gourdin G-8
Gowensville D-4
Graniteville .. Pg. 93, A-6
Grays J-6
Great Falls E-6
Greeleyville G-8
Green Pond J-7
Green Sea F-9
Greenville E-4
Greenwood E-4
Greer E-4
Hampton J-6
Hanahan H-8
  Vicinity ... Pg. 100, B-3
Hannah F-8
Harbison .. Pg. 108, D-3
Hardeeville K-6
Hartsville F-7
Hemingway G-8
Hickory Grove F-9
Hickory Grove D-5
Hilda H-6
Hilton Head Island . K-7
Holly Hill H-7
Honea Path F-4
Horrel Hill .. Pg. 108, D-7
Indiantown G-8
Inman D-4
Irmo ..... Pg. 108, A-1
Islandton H-7
Isle of Palms J-8
  Vicinity ... Pg. 100, E-7
Iva F-4
Jackson H-5
Jacksonboro H-7
Jacksonville .. Pg. 93, B-5
James Island J-8
  Vicinity .. Pg. 100, F-4
Jamestown H-8
Jefferson E-7
Jenkinsville F-6
Joanna F-5
Johns Island Pg. 100, F-1
Johnston G-5
Jonesville E-5
Kershaw E-7
Kingsburg F-8
Kingstree G-8
Kinsler .. Pg. 108, E-3
Kitchings Mill G-5
Kline H-6
Ladson .. Pg. 100, A-1
Lake City G-8
Lamar F-7
Lancaster E-6
Landrum D-4
Lane G-8
Latta F-8
Laurens E-4
Leeds E-5
Lena J-6
Lesslie E-6
Lewis E-6
Lexington F-6
  Vicinity .. Pg. 108, D-1
Liberty E-4
Litchfield Beach .. G-9
Little River F-10
Lockhart E-5
Lodge H-6
Loris F-9
Lykesland .. Pg. 108, E-2
Manning G-8
Manville F-7
Marietta D-4
Marion F-8
Martin H-5
Mauldin E-4
Mayesville F-7
McBee E-7
McColl E-8
McConnells E-5
McCormick G-4
Moncks Corner .. H-8
Montgomery Pg. 108, A-3
Mount Pleasant ... J-8
  Vicinity .. Pg. 100, E-5
Mountville F-5
Mt. Carmel G-4
Mullins F-9
Myrtle Beach G-10

New Ellenton H-5
New Prospect D-5
Newberry F-5
Nichols F-9
Nine Times E-3
Ninety Six F-5
Nixonville F-9
North G-6
North Augusta G-5
  Vicinity ... Pg. 93, B-3
North Charleston .. H-8
  Vicinity .. Pg. 100, C-2
Oatland G-9
Oats F-8
Olanta F-8
Olar H-6
Orangeburg G-6
Outland G-9
Owdoms G-5
Pacolet E-5
Pageland E-7
Pamplico F-8
Parksville G-5
Patrick E-7
Pauline E-5
Pawleys Island ... G-9
Pelion G-6
Pendleton E-3
Pickens E-4
Pierpont .. Pg. 100, E-2
Pineland J-6
Pineville G-8
Pinewood G-7
Plum Branch G-5
Pontiac F-6
  Vicinity .. Pg. 108, A-7
Prosperity F-5
Pumpkintown E-4
Rantowles J-8
Red Bank .. Pg. 108, E-1
Red Top ... Pg. 100, E-1
Rhems G-8
Richburg E-6
Ridgeland J-6
Ridgeway F-6
Riverland .. Pg. 100, G-3
Riverland Terrace
  ... Pg. 100, F-2
Rock Hill E-6
Rockton F-6
Rockville J-8
Rocky Bottom E-3
Ruby E-7
Salters G-8
Saluda F-5
Sampit H-9
Sandy Run G-6
Santee G-7
Sardinia G-8
Sardis F-8
Scranton F-8
Seneca E-3
Sharon E-6
Simpson E-4
Simpsonville E-4
Smallwood F-6
Smoaks H-7
Snowden .. Pg. 100, D-5
Society Hill E-8
Spartanburg E-5
Springdale Pg. 108, D-3
Springfield G-6
St. George H-7
St. Matthews G-7
St. Stephen G-8
Starr F-4
Stateburg F-7
Steedman G-6
Stoney Hill F-5
Stuckey G-9
Sullivans Island ... J-8
  Vicinity .. Pg. 100, F-6
Summerton G-7
Summerville H-7
Sumter G-7
Surfside Beach ... G-9
Sweetwater Pg. 93, A-3
Switzerland K-6
Sycamore E-3
Tamassee E-3
Tatum E-8
Taylor E-4
Ten Mile .. Pg. 100, C-7
Timmonsville F-8
Tradesville E-7
Travelers Rest E-4
Trenton G-5
Ulmer H-6

Union E-5
Varnville J-6
Wagener G-6
Walhalla E-3
Walterboro J-7
Ward G-5
Ware Shoals F-4
Warrenville .. Pg. 93, A-6
Wateree G-7
Weddell .. Pg. 108, A-6
Wells H-7
West Columbia
  ... Pg. 108, C-3
Westminster E-3
Westville E-7
Whitehall J-8
Whitmire E-5
Willington F-4
Williston H-5
Winnsboro F-6
Woodruff E-5
Yauhannah G-9
Yemassee J-7
Yonges Island J-8
York D-6

SOUTH DAKOTA
Page 74
Population: 690,768
Capital: Pierre
Land Area: 75,952 sq. mi.

Aberdeen C-8
Agar C-6
Akaska C-10
Albee F-10
Alcester E-8
Alexandria D-8
Alpena D-10
Altamont C-9
Andover C-9
Arlington D-10
Armour F-8
Artas B-6
Artesian E-8
Ashton C-8
Astoria D-10
Aurora D-10
Badger D-9
Bancroft D-9
Batesland F-4
Belle Fourche C-2
Belvidere E-5
Beresford F-10
Bison B-3
Blunt D-6
Bonesteel F-7
Bowdle C-7
Bradley C-9
Brandon E-10
Brandt D-10
Brentford C-8
Bristol C-9
Britton B-9
Broadland D-8
Brookings D-10
Bruce D-10
Bryant D-9
Buffalo B-2
Buffalo Gap E-2
Burke F-7
Bushnell D-10
Butler C-9
Camp Crook B-2
Canova E-9
Canton F-10
Carthage D-9
Castle Rock C-2
Cavour D-8
Centerville F-9
Central City D-2
Chamberlain E-7
Chelsea C-8
Claire City B-9
Clark C-9
Clear Lake D-10
Colman E-10
Colton E-9
Columbia B-8
Conde C-8
Corona C-10
Corsica E-8
Cottonwood E-4
Cresbard C-7
Crooks E-9
Custer E-2
Dallas F-6
Dante F-8
De Smet D-9

Deadwood D-2
Dell Rapids E-10
Delmont F-8
Dimock E-8
Doland E-8
Dolton E-9
Draper E-5
Dupree C-4
Eagle Butte C-5
Eden B-9
Edgemont E-2
Elk Point G-10
Elm Springs D-3
Emery E-9
Enning D-3
Erwin D-9
Estelline D-9
Ethan E-8
Eureka B-7
Fairburn E-2
Fairfax F-7
Fairpoint C-3
Fairview F-10
Faith C-4
Farmer E-9
Farmingdale D-3
Faulkton C-7
Flandreau E-10
Florence C-9
Fort Pierre D-6
Fort Thompson ... D-7
Frankfort C-8
Frederick B-8
Freeman F-9
Fruitdale C-2
Fulton E-8
Gann Valley E-7
Garden City C-9
Garretson E-10
Gary D-10
Gayville F-9
Geddes F-8
Gettysburg C-6
Glad Valley B-4
Glenham B-6
Goodwin C-10
Gregory F-7
Grenville C-9
Groton C-8
Hammer B-9
Harrisburg F-10
Harrold D-6
Hayti D-9
Hecla B-8
Hermosa E-2
Herreid B-6
Herrick F-7
Highmore D-7
Hill City D-2
Hillsview B-7
Hitchcock D-8
Hosmer B-7
Hot Springs E-2
Houghton B-8
Hoven C-6
Howard E-9
Howes D-4
Huron D-8
Interior E-4
Ipswich C-7
Irene F-9
Iroquois D-9
Isabel B-5
Java B-6
Jefferson G-10
Kadoka E-4
Kennebec E-6
Keystone D-2
Kimball E-7
Kranzburg C-10
Kyle E-4
La Bolt C-10
La Plant C-6
Lake Andes F-8
Lake City B-9
Lake Preston D-9
Lane E-8
Langford B-9
Lead D-2
Lebanon C-6
Lemmon B-4
Lennox F-10
Leola B-7
Letcher E-8
Lily C-9
Little Eagle B-5
Lodgepole B-3
Long Lake B-7
Long Valley E-4

Lowry C-6
Loyalton C-7
Ludlow B-3
Madison E-9
Marion F-9
Martin F-4
Marty F-8
Marvin C-10
Maurine C-3
McIntosh B-5
McLaughlin B-5
Meadow B-4
Mellette C-8
Menno F-9
Midland D-5
Milbank C-10
Miller D-7
Mission E-5
Mitchell E-8
Mobridge B-6
Monroe E-9
Montrose E-9
Morristown B-4
Mound City B-6
Mount Vernon ... E-8
Mud Butte C-3
Murdo E-5
Naples D-9
New Effington ... B-10
Newell C-2
Nisland C-2
North Sioux City .. G-10
Northville C-8
Nunda E-9
Oacoma E-6
Oelrichs E-2
Oglala F-3
Okreek E-5
Oldham D-9
Olivet F-9
Onaka C-7
Onida D-6
Orient C-7
Ortley C-9
Parker F-9
Parkston F-8
Parmelee E-5
Philip D-4
Pierpont C-9
Pierre D-6
Pine Ridge F-3
Plainview D-3
Plankinton E-8
Platte F-7
Pollock B-6
Prairie City B-3
Presho E-6
Pringle E-2
Provo E-1
Pukwana E-7
Quinn D-4
Ramona E-9
Rapid City D-3
Ravinia F-8
Raymond C-8
Redfield C-8
Redig B-2
Ree Heights D-7
Reliance E-7
Revillo C-10
Ridgeview C-5
Rockerville D-2
Rockham C-7
Roscoe C-7
Rosebud F-5
Roslyn C-9
Roswell C-7
Saint Charles F-7
Saint Francis F-5
Saint Lawrence ... D-7
Salem E-9
Scenic E-3
Scotland F-9
Selby B-6
Seneca C-7
Shadehill B-4
Sherman E-10
Sioux Falls E-9
Sisseton B-10
Sorum B-3
South Shore C-10
Spearfish D-2
Springfield F-8
Stephan D-7
Stickney E-8
Stockholm C-10
Stoneville C-3
Stratford C-8
Sturgis D-2
Summit C-10

Tabor F-9
Tea F-10
Timber Lake B-5
Tolstoy C-7
Toronto D-10
Trail City B-5
Trent E-10
Tripp F-8
Tulare D-8
Turton C-8
Tyndall F-9
Union Center D-3
Veblen B-9
Verdon C-8
Vermillion G-9
Viborg F-9
Vienna D-9
Vilas E-9
Vivian E-6
Wagner F-8
Wakonda F-9
Wall D-4
Wallace C-9
Ward E-10
Wasta D-3
Watertown D-9
Waubay C-9
Webster C-9
Wessington D-7
Wessington Springs E-8
Westport B-8
Wetonka B-8
Wewala F-6
White D-10
White Butte B-4
White Lake E-8
White River E-5
Whitewood D-2
Willow Lake D-9
Wilmot C-10
Winner F-6
Wood E-5
Woonsocket E-8
Worthing F-10
Yale D-9
Yankton F-9
Zeona C-3

TENNESSEE
Pages 38-39
Population: 4,591,120
Capital: Nashville
Land Area: 41,155 sq. mi.

Adams F-6
Adamsville J-4
Aetna H-5
Alamo H-3
Alcoa H-11
Alexandria G-8
Algood G-8
Allardt G-9
Allens H-3
Allisona H-7
Allred G-9
Alpine G-9
Altamont J-8
Alto J-7
Amherst .. Pg. 126, C-2
Antioch .. Pg. 139, F-7
Arlington J-2
  Vicinity .. Pg. 134, A-10
Arrington H-7
Arthur F-11
Asbury .. Pg. 126, C-6
Ashland City G-6
Ashport H-2
Athens H-10
Atoka H-2
Atwood G-4
Avondale .. Pg. 139, C-8
Bailey .... Pg. 134, F-9
Banner Hill G-13
Bartlebaugh Pg. 99, F-6
Bartlett J-2
  Vicinity .. Pg. 134, C-7
Beacon .. Pg. 139, G-6
Bean Station G-12
Bearden .. Pg. 126, C-3
  Vicinity .. Pg. 139, D-7
Beersheba Springs . H-8
Belfast J-7
Bell Bridge . Pg. 126, B-2
Bell Buckle H-7
Belle Meade G-6
  Vicinity .. Pg. 139, E-4
Bellevue .. Pg. 139, F-2
Bells H-3
Belvidere J-7

Benjestown Pg. 134, B-3
Benton J-10
Berry Hill . Pg. 139, E-5
Bethel J-6
Bethel Springs ... J-4
Big Sandy G-4
Big Springs J-9
Birchwood J-9
Blaine G-11
Bluff City F-13
Bogota G-3
Bolivar J-3
Bolton .. Pg. 134, A-9
Bon Air H-8
Braden H-2
Bradford G-4
Brentwood G-6
  Vicinity .. Pg. 139, G-5
Briceville G-10
Brighton H-2
Bristol F-13
Brooklin . Pg. 139, G-8
Brownsville H-3
Bruceton G-4
Brunswick . Pg. 134, B-8
Bulls Gap G-12
Bumpus Mills ... F-5
Burlington Pg. 126, B-6
Burlison H-2
Burns J-6
Byington .. Pg. 126, C-1
Byrdstown F-9
Calhoun J-9
Camden G-5
Camelot F-12
Capleville J-2
  Vicinity .. Pg. 134, G-6
Carlisle G-5
Carthage G-7
Caryville G-10
Cash Point J-6
Cedar Bluff Pg. 126, D-1
Cedar Hill F-6
Celina F-8
Center Point J-6
Centerville H-6
Central G-3
Charleston J-9
Charlotte G-5
Chattanooga J-9
  Vicinity ..... Pg. 99
Church Hill F-12
Clarksburg H-4
Clarksville F-5
Claxton .. Pg. 126, A-1
Cleveland J-9
Clifton J-5
Clinton G-10
Coalmont J-8
Collegedale J-9
  Vicinity .. Pg. 99, G-7
Collierville J-2
  Vicinity .. Pg. 134, F-10
Collinwood J-5
Columbia H-6
Cookeville G-8
Copperhill J-10
Cordova .. Pg. 134, D-8
Corinth ... Pg. 126, A-5
Cornersville J-6
Cosby H-11
Covington H-2
Crab Orchard ... H-9
Cross Plains F-6
Crossville H-9
Culleoka H-6
Cumberland City . G-5
Cumberland Furnace G-5
Cumberland Gap . F-11
Dancyville H-3
Dandridge G-11
Darden H-4
Dayton H-9
Decatur H-9
Decaturville H-5
Decherd J-8
Dibrell H-8
Dickson G-5
Dixon Springs ... G-8
Donelson G-7
  Vicinity .. Pg. 139, D-7
Dover F-5
Dowalltown G-8
Doyle H-8
Dresden G-4
Ducktown J-10
Dunlap J-9
Dyer G-3
Dyersburg G-3

Eads .... Pg. 134, C-10
Eagan F-10
East Brainerd Pg. 99, H-6
East Ridge J-9
  Vicinity .. Pg. 99, J-5
Eastview J-4
Egypt .... Pg. 134, B-6
Elizabethton G-13
Elkton J-6
Ellandale .. Pg. 134, B-7
Elmore Park Pg. 134, C-7
Elora J-7
Elza G-10
Englewood J-10
Erin G-5
Erwin G-13
Estill Springs J-7
Ethridge J-6
Etowah J-10
Evensville H-9
Fairview H-6
Farmington H-6
Fayetteville J-7
Finley G-3
Fisherville Pg. 134, D-10
Flat Woods H-5
Flatcreek J-7
Forbus F-9
Forest Hill . Pg. 134, F-8
Forest Hills Pg. 139, F-4
Foster Corners
  ...... Pg. 139, F-8
Fountain City Pg. 126, B-3
Franklin H-6
Friendship G-3
Fruitvale H-3
Gadsden H-3
Gainesboro G-8
Gallatin G-7
Gates H-3
Gatlinburg H-11
Germantown Pg. 139, B-8
Germantown J-2
  Vicinity .. Pg. 134, E-8
Gibson H-4
Gildfield .. Pg. 134, A-8
Gilt Edge H-2
Gleason G-4
Glendale .. Pg. 99, F-3
Goodlettsville ... G-7
Goodspring J-6
Gordonsville G-7
Gower ... Pg. 139, E-3
Grand Junction ... J-3
Grandview H-9
Gray G-13
Graysville H-9
Green Hill . Pg. 139, C-9
Greenback H-10
Greenbrier G-6
Greeneville G-12
Greenfield G-4
Grimsley G-9
Habersham F-10
Haletown J-8
Halls G-3
Halls Crossroads . G-11
  Vicinity .. Pg. 126, A-4
Hampshire H-5
Hampton G-13
Hanging Limb ... G-9
Hanillville .. Pg. 99, F-4
Harriman H-10
Harrison .. Pg. 99, F-6
Harrogate F-11
Hartsville G-7
Henderson H-4
Hendersonville ... G-7
  Vicinity .. Pg. 139, A-8
Henning H-2
Henry G-4
Hermitage Hills
  ...... Pg. 139, C-8
Hickory Valley ... J-3
Highland J-5
Hohenwald H-5
Hopewell . Pg. 139, C-8
Hornsby J-3
Humboldt H-3
Hunter G-13
Huntingdon G-4
Huntland J-7
Huntsville G-10
India J-7
Inglewood
  Vicinity .. Pg. 139, C-6
Iron City J-5
Isham F-10
Ivydell F-10

Jacksboro G-10
Jackson H-3
Jamestown J-8
Jasper J-8
Jefferson City G-11
Jellico F-10
Joelton G-6
  Vicinity . . . Pg. 139, A-4
John Sevier Pg. 126, A-6
Johnson City G-13
Jonesboro G-12
Karns . . . . . Pg. 126, C-1
Keeling H-2
Kelso J-7
Kenton G-3
Kimberlin Heights
  . . . . Pg. 126, D-7
Kimbro . . . Pg. 139, G-8
Kingsport F-13
Kingston H-10
Kirkland H-7
Knoxville H-10
  Vicinity . . . Pg. 126, B-5
Kodak H-11
Kyles Ford F-12
La Vergne G-7
  Vicinity . . Pg. 139, G-9
LaFollette G-10
Laager J-8
Lafayette F-8
Lake City G-10
Lake Mont H-10
Lakesite J-9
Lancing G-9
Lascassas H-7
Latham G-4
Lawrenceburg . . . J-5
Leach G-4
Lebanon H-7
Leipers Fork H-6
Lenoir City H-10
Lenow . . . . Pg. 134, C-9
Lewisburg H-6
Lexington H-4
Liberty H-7
Lickton . Pg. 139, A-5
Linden H-5
Little Creek . Pg. 139, B-5
Livingston H-8
Lobelville H-5
Locke J-2
Lookout Mountain
  . . . . Pg. 99, H-2
Loretto J-5
Loudon H-10
Lucy . . . . . Pg. 134, A-6
Luttrell G-11
Lutts J-5
Lyles H-6
Lynchburg J-7
Lynnville J-6
Madisonville H-10
Malesus H-3
Maloneyville Pg. 126, A-5
Manchester H-7
Marrowbone Pg. 139, C-1
Martin G-4
Maryville H-10
Mascot . . . Pg. 126, A-6
Mason H-2
Maury City H-3
Mayland G-8
Maynardville G-10
McBurg J-6
McEwen G-5
McKenzie G-4
McMinnville H-8
Meadowbrook
  . . . . Pg. 126, C-2
Medina H-4
Medon H-3
Memphis J-1
  Vicinity . . . . . Pg. 134
  Detailed City . Pg. 250
Mercer J-4
Michie J-4
Middleton J-3
Midtown H-10
Milan H-4
Milledgeville J-4
Milligan College . . G-13
Millington J-2
Minor Hill J-6
Miston G-2
Monteagle J-8
Monterey G-9
Morgantown H-9
Morris Chapel . . . J-4
Morrison H-7
Morristown G-11

Moscow J-3
Mosheim G-12
Moss F-8
Mound City . . Pg. 134, C-2
Mount Carmel . . . F-12
Mount Crest H-9
Mount Juliet G-7
  Vicinity . Pg. 139, C-10
Mount Olive H-11
  Vicinity . . . Pg. 126, D-4
Mount Pleasant . . H-6
Mount Vernon . . . J-10
Mount Zion . Pg. 139, A-2
Mountain City . . . F-14
Mule Hollow Pg. 126, C-6
Munford H-2
Murfreesboro H-7
Nashville H-7
  Vicinity . . . . . Pg. 139
  Detailed City . Pg. 257
New Hope K-8
New Johnsonville . G-5
New Market G-11
New River G-10
New Tazewell G-11
Newbern G-3
Newport G-11
Niota H-10
Nixon J-4
Nobles G-4
Norris G-10
North Chattanooga
  . . . . Pg. 99, G-4
Norwood B-3
Nunnelly H-5
Oak Hill . . Pg. 139, F-6
Oak Ridge G-10
Oakdale G-9
Oakland J-2
Oakville . . Pg. 134, F-5
Oakwood F-5
Obion G-3
Ocoee J-9
Oglesby . . Pg. 139, G-6
Old Hickory . Pg. 139, B-8
Olivehill J-4
Oliver Springs . . . G-10
Oneida F-9
Ooltewah . . Pg. 99, G-7
Palmer J-8
Palmyra F-5
Parago Mill . Pg. 139, F-7
Paris G-4
Parrottsville G-12
Parsons H-4
Pasquo . . . Pg. 139, F-3
Peak . . . . . Pg. 126, A-1
Peakland H-9
Pegram G-6
Pelham J-8
Petersburg J-7
Philadelphia H-10
Pigeon Forge H-11
Pikeville H-9
Pinewood H-5
Pinson H-4
Pisgah . . . Pg. 134, D-10
Pleasant Hill G-8
Pleasant View . . . G-6
Portland F-7
Powell . . . Pg. 126, B-2
Providence . Pg. 139, C-9
  Vicinity . . . Pg. 139, F-7
Pulaski J-6
Puncheon Camp . . G-11
Puryear G-4
Quebeck H-8
Raleigh H-7
  Vicinity . . . Pg. 134, B-6
Ramer J-4
Ramsey . . Pg. 126, C-6
Ramsey . . Pg. 134, A-4
Raus J-7
Rayon City . Pg. 139, B-7
Red Bank J-9
  Vicinity . . . Pg. 99, F-3
Red Boiling Springs F-8
Riceville J-10
Richland . . Pg. 139, D-3
Rickman G-8
Ridgely G-3
Ridgetop G-6
Ripley H-3
Ritta . . . . . Pg. 126, A-5
Riverdale . . Pg. 126, C-7
Rives G-3
Roan Mountain . . . G-13
Robbins G-9
Rockwood H-9
Rocky Fork G-12

Rogersville G-12
Rossville J-2
Rural Hill . . Pg. 139, F-8
Russelville G-12
Rutherford G-3
Rutledge G-11
Ryall Springs Pg. 99, H-6
Sadlersville F-6
Saint Bethlehem . . F-5
Saint Joseph J-5
Sale Creek J-9
Saltillo H-4
Sardis H-4
Saundersville
  . . . . Pg. 139, A-9
Savannah J-4
Scotts Hill H-4
Selmer J-4
Sequoyah Hills
  . . . . Pg. 126, C-3
Seven Points Pg. 139, E-9
Sevierville H-11
Sewanee J-8
Shacklett G-6
Shady Valley F-13
Sharon G-3
Shelby Farms
  . . . . Pg. 134, D-7
Shelbyville H-7
Shook . . . . Pg. 126, D-6
Shooks Gap D-11
Shop Springs G-7
Signal Mtn. . Pg. 99, G-4
  Vicinity . . . Pg. 99, F-3
Silver Point G-8
Skiem J-6
Smartt H-8
Smith Springs
  . . . . Pg. 139, F-8
Smithville H-8
Smyrna G-7
Sneedville F-11
Soddy-Daisy J-9
Somerville J-2
South Carthage . . G-8
South Dyersburg . . G-3
South Fulton F-3
South Pittsburg . . J-8
Sparta H-8
Spencer H-8
Spring City H-9
Spring Creek H-4
Spring Hill H-6
Spring Lake Pg. 134, B-7
Springfield F-6
Stanton H-2
Sullivan Gdn. F-12
Summertown J-5
Summit . . . Pg. 99, G-6
Sunbright G-9
Sunrise . . . Pg. 126, A-6
Surgoinsville F-12
Sweetwater H-10
Sycamore . Pg. 139, A-1
Taft J-6
Tarpley H-4
Tazewell F-11
Tekoa . . . . Pg. 126, B-2
Tellico Plains J-10
Tennessee Ridge . . G-5
Three Points Pg. 126, A-7
Timberlake H-4
Tiptonville F-3
Toone J-3
Tracy City J-8
Trenton G-3
Trezevant G-4
Triune H-7
Troy F-3
Tullahoma J-7
Tusculum G-12
  Vicinity . . . Pg. 139, F-6
Una . . . . . Pg. 139, F-7
Unicoi G-13
Union City G-3
Union Grove J-9
Union Hill . Pg. 139, A-5
Vaughlans Gap
  . . . . Pg. 139, F-4
Victoria J-8
Viola H-8
Violet J-10
Vonore H-10
Waco J-6
Walden J-9
Walkertown J-4
Walling H-8
Wartburg G-10
Wartrace H-7
Watertown H-8

Waverly G-5
Waynesboro J-5
Webber City J-5
West Meade Pg. 139, E-4
West Shiloh J-4
Westmoreland . . . F-7
White Bluff F-6
White House F-7
White Pine G-12
Whites Creek
  . . . . Pg. 139, B-4
Whites Village
  . . . . Pg. 126, D-5
Whitesburg G-12
Whiteville J-3
Whitwell J-8
Wilder G-9
Williston J-3
Winchester J-8
Winfield F-10
Woodale . . . Pg. 126, B-7
Woodbury H-8
Woodland Mills . . . F-3
Woodstock . . Pg. 134, B-5
Wrencoe . . Pg. 139, G-7
Wyanoke . . Pg. 134, E-1
Wynnburg G-3

TEXAS

Pages 75-79

Population: 14,229,191
Capital: Austin
Land Area: 262,017 sq. mi.

Abernathy E-7
Abilene G-10
Acala J-2
Ackerly G-7
Acme D-10
Adamsville J-12
Addicks L-15
  Vicinity . . . Pg. 121, D-1
Addison . . . Pg. 111, A-8
Adrian C-7
Agua Dulce P-12
Aiken E-8
Alamo Heights
  . . . . Pg. 159, D-5
Alanreed C-9
Alba F-15
Albany G-10
Aldine L-15
  Vicinity . . . Pg. 121, B-5
Aledo F-12
Alexander H-12
Alfred P-12
Algoa M-16
Alice P-12
Allamoore J-3
Allen F-14
Alleyton L-14
Allison B-10
Allred F-6
Almeda . . . Pg. 121, G-4
Alpine K-5
Altair M-14
Alto H-16
Alvarado G-13
Alvin M-16
Alvord E-12
Amarillo C-7
Ambrose E-14
Ames L-16
Amherst E-7
Anderson K-15
Andice K-12
Andrews G-6
Angleton M-16
Anna E-14
Annona A-16
Anson G-10
Antelope F-12
Anthony H-2
Anton E-7
Apple Springs J-16
Aquilla H-13
Aransas Pass P-13
Archer City E-11
Argyle F-13
Arlington G-13
  Vicinity . . . Pg. 110, E-5
Arp G-16
Artesia Wells P-10
Arthur City E-14
Asherton N-10
Ashtola C-8
Aspermont F-9
Athens G-15
Atlanta F-17

Aubrey E-13
Austin L-13
  Vicinity . . Pg. 93, H-5
Austonio J-15
Austwell N-14
Avery F-16
Avinger F-17
Avoca G-10
Azle G-13
Bacliff M-16
Bagwell E-16
Baird G-10
Bakersfield K-7
Balch Springs G-14
  Vicinity . Pg. 111, E-11
Balcones Heights
  . . . . Pg. 159, D-3
Ballinger H-10
Balmorhea J-5
Bandera L-11
Bangs H-11
Barclay J-13
Bardwell H-14
Barksdale L-10
Barnhart J-8
Barrett L-16
  Vicinity . . . Pg. 121, C-10
Barry H-14
Barstow J-5
Bartlett K-13
Bassett F-17
Bastrop L-13
Batesville N-10
Batson L-16
Bay City M-15
Baytown L-16
  Vicinity . . . Pg. 121, C-7
Beasley M-15
Beaumont L-17
  Vicinity . . Pg. 95, G-1
Beaumont Place
  . . . . Pg. 121, C-7
Beckville G-17
Bedford . Pg. 110, C-5
Bedias K-15
Bee Cave L-12
Beeville N-12
Belfalls J-13
Bellaire . . . Pg. 121, E-3
Bellevue E-12
Bellmead H-13
Bells E-14
Bellville L-14
Belmont M-13
Belton J-13
Ben G-15
Ben Arnold J-14
Ben Bolt P-12
Benavides Q-11
Benbrook G-13
  Vicinity . . . Pg. 110, E-1
Benchley K-14
Benjamin F-10
Bertram K-12
Bettie G-16
Big Lake J-7
Big Sandy G-16
Big Spring H-8
Big Wells N-10
Bigfoot M-11
Birthright F-15
Bishop Q-12
Bivins F-17
Black D-7
Blackwell H-9
Blanco L-11
Blanket H-11
Bleakwood K-18
Bledsoe E-6
Blessing N-15
Blewett M-9
Blooming Grove . . . H-14
Bloomington N-13
Blossom E-15
Blue Mound Pg. 110, C-3
Blue Ridge E-14
Bluegrove E-12
Bluff Dale G-12
Bluffton K-11
Boca Chica S-13
Boerne L-11
Bogata F-15
Boling M-14
Bomarton F-10
Bon Wier K-18
Bonham E-14
Booker A-9
Boonsville F-12
Borger B-8
Boston F-17

Bovina D-6
Bowie E-12
Boxelder F-16
Boyd F-13
Boys Ranch Tacosa B-7
Brackettville M-9
Bradshaw H-10
Brady J-10
Brandon H-14
Brashear F-15
Brazoria M-15
Breckenridge G-11
Bremond J-14
Brenham L-14
Brice D-9
Bridge City L-18
  Vicinity . . . Pg. 95, H-7
Bridgeport F-12
Briggs K-12
Briscoe B-9
Britton Davis Pg. 116, B-5
Broaddus J-17
Bronco F-6
Bronson J-17
Bronte H-9
Brookeland J-17
Brookesmith J-11
Brookshire L-15
Brookside Village
  . . . . Pg. 121, G-6
Brownfield F-7
Brownsboro G-15
Brownsville S-13
Brownwood H-11
Brundage N-10
Bruni Q-11
Bryan K-14
Bryson F-12
Buchanan Dam . . . K-12
Buckholts K-13
Buda L-12
Buena Vista Pg. 159, H-5
Buffalo J-15
Buffalo Gap G-10
Bula E-6
Bulcher E-13
Bullard H-16
Buna K-17
Bunavista B-8
Bunker Hill Pg. 121, D-2
Burke J-16
Burkburnett E-11
Burkett H-10
Burkeville J-18
Burleson G-13
  Vicinity . . . Pg. 110, G-3
Burlington J-14
Burnet K-12
Burton L-14
Bushland C-7
Bustamante R-11
Butler K-13
Byers E-12
Bynum H-14
Cactus A-7
Caddo G-11
Caddo Mills F-15
Caldwell K-14
Calf Creek J-10
Call K-18
Calliham N-12
Calvert K-14
Camden K-16
Cameron K-14
Camilla K-16
Camp Verde L-11
Camp Wood L-10
Campbell F-15
Campbellton N-12
Canadian B-9
Canton G-15
Canutillo H-1
  Vicinity . . . Pg. 116, A-2
Canyon C-7
Caps G-10
Carbon G-11
Carlos K-15
Carlsbad H-9
Carlton H-12
Carmine L-14
Carmona J-16
Carrizo Springs . . . N-10
Carrollton G-13
  Vicinity . . . Pg. 111, A-8
Carta Valley L-9
Carthage H-17
Cash F-15
Cassin . . . . Pg. 159, H-4
Castle Hills M-11
  Vicinity . . . Pg. 159, C-4

Castroville M-11
Cat Spring L-14
Catarina N-10
Cayuga H-15
Cedar Creek L-13
Cedar Hill . . Pg. 111, F-7
Cedar Park K-12
Celeste F-14
Celina F-14
Center H-17
Centerville J-15
Central Gardens
  . . . . Pg. 95, J-4
Chandler G-15
Channelview L-16
  Vicinity . Pg. 121, D-8
Channing B-7
Chapman H-16
Chapman Ranch . . P-13
Chappell Hill L-15
Charco N-13
Charlotte N-11
Cherokee J-11
Cherry Spring K-11
Chester J-17
Chico F-12
Childress D-9
Chillicothe D-10
Chilton J-13
China L-17
China Grove Pg. 159, F-7
Chireno J-17
Chisos Basin M-5
Christine N-11
Christoval J-9
Circle Back E-6
Cisco G-11
Cistern L-13
Clairemont F-9
Clairette H-12
Clarendon C-9
Clarksville E-16
Claude C-8
Clayton H-17
Clear Lake City
  . . . . Pg. 121, G-9
Cleburne G-13
Cleveland K-16
Clifton H-13
Clint H-1
  Vicinity . Pg. 121, F-6
Cloverleaf . Pg. 121, D-8
Clute M-16
Clyde G-10
  Vicinity . . Pg. 93, K-5
Coahoma H-8
Cockrell Hill Pg. 111, D-8
Coffey City H-15
Coldspring K-16
Coleman H-10
College Station . . . K-14
Colleyville . Pg. 110, B-5
Collinsville F-13
Colmesneil K-17
Colorado City G-9
Columbus L-14
Comanche H-11
Combes R-12
Comfort L-11
Commerce F-15
Como F-15
Comstock L-8
Concan M-10
Concepcion Q-12
Concord H-16
Conroe K-16
Converse L-11
Conway C-8
Cooks Point K-14
Cookville F-16
Coolidge H-14
Cooper F-15
Coppell . . . . Pg. 111, A-7
Copperas Cove . . . J-12
Cornudas H-3
Coronado Hills
  . . . . Pg. 116, B-3
Corpus Christi P-13
Corrigan J-16
Corsicana H-14
Coryell City J-13
Cost M-13
Cotton Center E-7
Cottonwood K-15
Cottonwood K-15
Cotulla N-10
Country Campus . . K-16
Coy City N-12
Coyanosa J-5
Crabbs Praire K-15
Crandall G-14

Crane J-6
Cranvills Gap H-13
Crawford J-13
Cresson G-13
Crews H-10
Crockett J-15
Crosby L-16
  Vicinity . . . Pg. 121, B-9
Crosbyton E-8
Cross K-15
Cross Cut H-11
Cross Plains H-11
Cross Roads H-16
Crow G-16
Crowell E-10
Crowley G-13
  Vicinity . . Pg. 110, F-3
Crystal City N-10
Cuero M-13
Cumby F-15
Cushing H-16
Cut & Shoot K-15
Cypress L-15
Cypress Mill K-12
D'Hanis M-10
Dabney M-9
Dacosta N-14
Daingerfield F-16
Daisetta K-16
Dalhart B-7
Dallas G-14
  Vicinity . . . . . . Pg. 111
  Detailed City . Pg. 224
Dalworthington Gardens
  . . . . Pg. 110, E-4
Damon M-15
Danbury M-15
Danevang M-15
Darrouzett A-9
Dawn C-7
Dawson H-14
Dayton L-16
De Berry G-17
De Kalb F-16
De Leon H-11
DeWees M-12
DeSoto . . . Pg. 111, F-8
Deanville K-14
Decatur F-13
Deer Park L-16
  Vicinity . Pg. 121, F-6
Del Rio M-8
Del Valle L-13
  Vicinity . . Pg. 93, K-5
Dell City H-3
Denison E-14
Denton F-13
Denver City F-6
Deport F-15
Derby N-11
Desdemona H-12
Devers L-17
Devine M-11
Dew H-15
Deweyville K-18
Diana G-16
Diboll J-16
Dickens E-9
Dickinson L-15
Dilley N-11
Dime Box K-14
Dimmitt D-7
Dinero P-12
Divot N-11
Dobbin K-15
Dodd City E-15
Donie J-14
Donna S-12
Doole J-10
Doss K-11
Doucette K-17
Dougherty E-8
Douglass H-16
Douglassville F-17
Dozier C-9
Draw F-8
Dripping Springs . . L-12
Driscoll P-12
Dryden L-7
Dublin H-12
Dumas B-7
Dumont E-9
Duncanville Pg. 111, F-7
Dunlay M-11
Dunn G-9
Dyersdale . . Pg. 121, B-6
Eagle Lake M-14
Eagle Pass N-9
Early H-11

TEXAS

Earth D-7
East Columbia . . M-15
East Houston
. . . . . . Pg. 121, C-7
Easterly J-14
Eastland G-11
Easton G-16
Edcouch R-12
Eddy J-13
Eden R-12
Edgecliff . . Pg. 110, E-3
Edinburg R-12
Edmonson D-7
Edna M-14
Edom G-15
Edroy P-13
Egypt M-14
El Campo M-14
El Lago . . Pg. 121, G-10
El Paso H-2
Vicinity . . Pg. 116, D-5
El Sauz R-10
Elbert F-11
Eldorado K-9
Electra E-11
Elgin K-13
Elkhart H-15
Ellinger L-14
Elmendorf M-12
Vicinity . Pg. 159, J-7
Elmo G-15
Elsa R-12
Elysian Fields G-17
Emory F-14
Encinal P-10
Encino Q-12
Energy H-12
Enloe F-15
Ennis G-14
Enochs E-6
Escobas Q-11
Estelline D-9
Etoile J-17
Etter B-7
Euless . . Pg. 110, C-6
Eureka H-14
Eustace F-14
Evadale K-17
Evant J-12
Evergreen K-16
Everman . . Pg. 110, F-3
Fabens H-1
Fairbanks . Pg. 121, C-2
Fairfield H-15
Fairlie F-14
Fairview (Collin Cty) F-14
Fairview (Howard Cty) G-8
Fairy H-12
Falcon R-11
Falfurrias Q-12
Falls City N-12
Fannett L-17
Fannin N-13
Farmers Branch
. . . . . . Pg. 111, B-8
Farmersville F-14
Farrar J-14
Farwell D-6
Fauna . . . . Pg. 121, C-8
Fayetteville L-14
Fedor K-13
Fentress L-13
Ferris G-14
Vicinity . Pg. 111, G-10
Fieldton E-7
Fink E-14
Finney E-9
Flatonia M-13
Flomot D-8
Florence J-12
Floresville M-12
Flower Mound
. . . . . . Pg. 110, A-6
Floydada E-8
Fluvanna F-8
Follett A-10
Forest J-16
Forest Hill . . Pg. 110, F-3
Forestburg F-13
Forney G-14
Fort Clark Springs . M-9
Fort Davis K-5
Fort Gates J-12
Fort Griffin G-10
Fort Hancock J-2
Fort McKavett K-10
Fort Stockton J-6
Fort Worth G-13
Vicinity . . . . . . Pg. 110
Detailed City . Pg. 233

Fostoria K-16
Four Points . Pg. 93, F-2
Fowlerton N-11
Frame Switch . . . K-13
Francitas N-14
Francis J-14
Frankel City G-6
Franklin J-14
Frankston H-15
Fransworth A-9
Fred K-17
Fredericksburg . . . L-11
Fredonia K-11
Freeport N-16
Freer P-11
Friday J-16
Frio Town M-10
Friona D-6
Frisco F-13
Fritch B-8
Frost H-14
Fruitland F-12
Fruitvale G-15
Fulbright F-16
Fullbright F-16
Fulton P-13
Funston G-10
Gail G-8
Gainesville F-13
Galena Park Pg. 121, E-7
Galveston M-16
Ganado M-14
Garden City H-8
Garden Oaks
. . . . . . Pg. 121, D-4
Garden Valley . . . G-15
Garden Villas
. . . . . . Pg. 121, F-6
Gardendale H-8
Vicinity . . Pg. 159, E-7
Garland F-14
Vicinity . . Pg. 111, B-10
Garrison H-17
Garwood M-14
Gary H-17
Gatesville J-12
Gause K-14
Geneva J-17
Genoa . . . Pg. 121, G-8
George West N-12
Georgetown K-13
Geronimo L-12
Giddings L-13
Gilchrist M-17
Gillett M-12
Gilliland E-10
Gilmer G-16
Girard F-9
Girvin J-7
Gladewater G-16
Glazier B-9
Glen Cove H-10
Glen Flora M-15
Glen Rose H-13
Glenn E-9
Glenn Heights
. . . . . . Pg. 111, G-8
Glenrio C-6
Glenwood G-16
Glidden L-14
Gober F-15
Godley G-13
Golden Acres
. . . . . . Pg. 121, F-8
Goldsboro H-10
Goldthwaite J-11
Goliad N-13
Gonzales M-13
Goodland E-6
Goodlett D-10
Goodnight C-8
Goodrich K-16
Gordon G-12
Gordonville E-13
Goree F-10
Gorman H-11
Gouldbusk J-10
Graford F-12
Graham F-11
Granbury G-12
Grand Prairie G-13
Vicinity . . Pg. 111, D-6
Grand Saline G-15
Grandfalls J-6
Grandview G-13
Granger K-13
Grapeland J-15
Grapevine . Pg. 110, B-6
Grassland F-8
Grayback E-11
Greens Bayou
. . . . . . Pg. 121, D-7
Greenville F-15

Grey Forest Pg. 159, A-1
Grit K-10
Groesbeck J-14
Groom C-8
Groves L-17
Vicinity . . . . Pg. 95, K-5
Groveton J-16
Gruver A-8
Gun Barrel City . . G-14
Gustine H-12
Guthrie E-9
Guy M-15
Hagansport F-15
Hale Center E-7
Halletsville M-14
Hallsville G-16
Haltom City Pg. 110, C-3
Hamilton H-12
Hamlin F-9
Hamshire L-17
Happy C-7
Hardin K-16
Hargill R-12
Harker Heights . . J-13
Harleton G-16
Harlingen S-13
Harper L-10
Harrisburg . Pg. 121, E-6
Harrold E-11
Hart D-6
Hartley B-7
Harwood L-13
Haskell F-10
Haslet . . . . Pg. 110, A-3
Hatchel H-10
Hawkins G-16
Hawley G-9
Hearne K-14
Hebbronville Q-11
Hebert . . . . Pg. 95, J-3
Hebron . . . Pg. 111, A-8
Hedley C-9
Hedwig . Pg. 121, D-3
Helena N-13
Helotes . . Pg. 159, B-1
Hemleigh G-9
Hemphill J-18
Hempstead L-14
Henderson G-16
Henrietta E-12
Hereford C-6
Hext K-10
Hico H-12
Hidalgo S-12
Higgins B-10
Highbank J-14
Highland Park
. . . . . . Pg. 111, C-9
Highlands L-16
Vicinity . . Pg. 121, D-9
Hill Country Village
. . . . . . Pg. 159, A-5
Hillebrandt . Pg. 95, K-2
Hillister K-17
Hillsboro H-13
Hillshire Village
. . . . . . Pg. 121, D-3
Hilltop Lakes J-14
Hindes N-11
Hitchcock M-16
Hobson N-12
Hochheim M-13
Hockley L-15
Holland K-13
Holliday E-11
Hollywood Park
. . . . . . Pg. 159, A-5
Hondo M-11
Honey Grove E-15
Horizon City H-1
Houmont Pk. Pg. 121, C-7
Houston L-15
Vicinity . . . . . . Pg. 121
Detailed City . Pg. 237
Houston Gardens
. . . . . . Pg. 121, C-6
Howe F-14
Hubbard H-14
Huckabay G-12
Hudson J-16
Huffman . Pg. 121, A-9
Hughes Springs . G-16
Hull K-16
Humble K-16
Vicinity . . Pg. 121, A-7
Hunt L-10
Hunters Circle
. . . . . . Pg. 121, D-3
Huntington J-17
Huntsville K-15

Hurlwood E-7
Hurst . . . Pg. 110, C-5
Hutchins G-14
Hutto K-13
Vicinity . Pg. 111, E-10
Hye L-11
Idalou E-7
Imperial J-6
Inadal G-9
Independence . . . L-14
Indian Gap J-12
Industry L-14
Inez N-14
Ingleside P-13
Ingram L-11
Iola K-15
Iowa Park E-11
Ira G-8
Iraan K-7
Iredell H-12
Ireland J-12
Irving F-13
Vicinity . . Pg. 111, C-7
Italy G-13
Itasca H-13
Jacinto City Pg. 121, D-7
Jacksboro F-12
Jacksonville H-15
Jamestown J-18
Jarrell K-13
Jasper J-17
Jayton F-9
Jean F-11
Jefferson G-17
Jermyn F-12
Jersey Village
. . . . . . Pg. 121, B-2
Jewett J-14
Joaquin H-17
Johnson City L-11
Johntown F-16
Jolly E-12
Jollyville K-12
Jones Creek M-15
Jonesboro H-12
Jonestown K-12
Joshua G-13
Jourdanton N-11
Joy E-12
Juarez
Vicinity . Pg. 159, C-2
Junction K-10
Juno L-8
Justiceburg F-8
Justin F-13
Kalgary F-8
Kamay E-11
Kanawha E-16
Karnack G-17
Karnes City N-12
Katemcy K-10
Katy L-15
Kaufman G-14
Keene G-13
Keller . . . Pg. 110, B-4
Kellerville C-9
Kemp G-14
Kempner J-12
Kendleton M-15
Kenedy N-12
Kennard J-16
Kennedale . Pg. 110, E-4
Kenney L-14
Kent J-4
Kenwood . Pg. 121, B-6
Kerens H-14
Kermit H-5
Kerrville L-11
Kilgore G-16
Killeen J-13
Kings Mill C-8
Kingsland K-11
Kingsville Q-12
Kirby . . . Pg. 159, D-6
Kirbyville K-17
Kirkland D-9
Kirvin H-14
Kleberg . Pg. 111, E-11
Knickerbocker . . . J-9
Knippa M-10
Knott G-7
Knox City F-10
Kopperl H-13
Kosse J-14
Kountze K-17
Kress D-7
Krum F-13
Kyle L-12
La Gloria R-11
La Grange L-13

La Grulla R-11
La Joya R-11
La Marque M-16
La Paloma S-13
La Porte . Pg. 121, F-7
La Pryor N-10
La Reforma R-12
La Vernia M-12
La Villa R-12
La Ward N-14
Ladonia F-15
Lago Vista K-12
Laguna Park H-13
Lake Hills M-11
Lake Jackson . . . M-15
Lake Worth . Pg. 110, C-2
Lakeport G-16
Lakeside . Pg. 110, C-1
Lakeside Village . . H-13
Lakeview D-9
Lamesa G-7
Lamkin H-12
Lampasas J-12
Lancaster G-14
Vicinity . . Pg. 111, F-9
Lane City M-15
Langtry L-7
Laredo Q-10
Lariat D-6
Lark C-8
Larue H-15
Lasara R-12
Latexo J-15
Lavon F-14
Lawn H-10
LeFors C-9
League City L-15
Leakey L-10
Leander K-12
Leesburg F-16
Leesville M-13
Leggett K-16
Lehman E-6
Leigh G-17
Lela C-9
Lelia Lake C-9
Leming M-12
Lenorah G-7
Leon Springs . . . L-11
Leon Valley L-11
Vicinity . Pg. 159, C-2
Leona J-15
Leonard F-14
Levelland E-7
Lewisville F-13
Vicinity . Pg. 111, A-6
Lexington K-13
Liberty L-16
Liberty Hill K-12
Libscomb A-9
Lincoln L-13
Linden F-17
Lindsay E-13
Lingleville H-12
Lipan G-12
Live Oak . . Pg. 159, B-7
Liverpool M-16
Livingston K-16
Llano K-11
Lobo J-3
Lockett E-10
Lockhart L-13
Lockney E-8
Lodi F-17
Loma Alta L-8
Lomax H-8
Lometa J-11
London K-10
Lone Star F-16
Long Branch H-16
Long Mott N-14
Longview G-16
Longworth G-9
Loop F-7
Lopeno R-11
Loraine G-9
Lorena J-13
Lorenzo E-8
Los Angeles N-11
Los Fresnos S-12
Losoya . . . Pg. 159, J-5
Lott J-14
Louise M-14
Lovelady J-15
Lovell Lake . Pg. 95, K-2
Loving F-11
Loyal Valley K-11
Lubbock F-8
Luckenbach L-11
Lueders G-10

Lufkin J-16
Luling L-13
Lumberton K-17
Lutie C-9
Lydia F-16
Lyford R-13
Lynchburg . Pg. 121, E-9
Lyons K-14
Lytle M-11
Mabank G-15
Macdona . Pg. 159, G-1
Madisonville J-15
Magnolia M-15
Magnolia Park
. . . . . . Pg. 121, E-6
Malakoff H-15
Malta F-16
Manchester Pg. 121, E-7
Mangus Corner
. . . . . . Pg. 159, H-2
Mankins E-11
Manor . . . Pg. 93, G-7
Mansfield G-13
Vicinity . . Pg. 110, F-5
Maple E-6
Marathon K-5
Marble Falls K-12
Marfa K-4
Marietta F-17
Marion M-12
Markham M-15
Marlin J-14
Marquez J-15
Marshall G-16
Marshall Ford Pg. 93, F-1
Mart J-14
Martindale L-13
Martinez M-12
Vicinity . Pg. 159, E-7
Martinsville H-17
Maryneal G-9
Mason K-11
Masterson B-7
Matador E-8
Matagorda N-15
Mathis P-12
Maud F-17
Mauriceville L-17
Maxwell L-12
May H-11
Maydelle H-16
Maypearl G-13
McAdoo E-8
McAllen S-12
McCamey J-7
McCaulley G-9
McDade L-13
McFaddin N-13
McGregor J-13
McKinney F-14
McLean C-9
McLeod F-17
McMahan L-13
McNary J-2
McQueeney L-12
Meadow F-7
Meadowbrook
. . . . . . Pg. 121, F-7
Medicine Mound . D-10
Medina L-11
Megargel F-11
Melissa F-14
Melrose H-17
Melvin J-10
Memphis D-9
Mendoza L-13
Mentone H-5
Mercedes S-12
Meridian H-13
Merkel G-9
Mertzon J-8
Mesquite G-14
Vicinity . Pg. 111, C-11
Mexia H-14
Miami B-9
Mico M-11
Midfield N-14
Midland H-7
Midlothian G-14
Midway K-15
Milam J-18
Milano K-14
Miles H-9
Milford H-13
Millersview J-10
Millett N-11
Millican K-15
Mineola G-15
Mineral N-12
Mineral Wells . . . G-12

Mingus G-12
Mirando City Q-11
Mission S-12
Missouri City Pg. 121, G-3
Mobeetie C-9
Moline J-12
Monahans H-6
Monkstown E-15
Monroe L-17
Mont Belvieu L-16
Montague E-12
Montalba H-15
Monte Alto R-12
Montgomery K-15
Monthalia M-13
Moody J-13
Moonshine Hills
. . . . . . Pg. 121, A-7
Moore M-11
Mooring K-14
Moran G-11
Morgan H-13
Morgan Mill G-12
Morgans Point
. . . . . . Pg. 121, F-10
Morse B-8
Morton E-6
Morton Valley G-11
Moscow J-16
Moss Hill K-16
Moulton M-13
Mount Calm H-13
Mount Enterprise . H-16
Mount Pleasant . F-16
Mount Sylvan G-15
Mount Vernon . . . F-16
Mountain Home . L-10
Muenster E-13
Muldoon L-14
Muleshoe D-6
Mullin J-11
Mumford K-14
Munday F-10
Murchison G-15
Murphy . Pg. 111, A-11
Mykawa . Pg. 121, G-6
Myrtle Springs . . . G-15
N. Richland Hills
. . . . . . Pg. 110, C-4
Nacogdoches H-16
Nada M-14
Naples F-16
Nash F-17
Natalia M-11
Navasota K-15
Nazareth D-7
Neches H-15
Nederland K-17
Vicinity . . Pg. 95, J-4
Needmore E-6
Needville M-15
Nelsonville L-14
New Baden J-14
New Boston F-17
New Braunfels . . . L-12
New Caney L-16
New Deal E-7
New Gulf M-15
New Home F-7
New London G-16
New Summerfield . H-16
New Sweden . Pg. 93, F-7
New Ulm L-14
New Waverly K-15
Newark . . . Pg. 110, A-1
Newcastle F-11
Newlin D-9
Newman H-2
Newsome F-16
Newton K-18
Nixon M-13
Nocona E-12
Nolan G-9
Nolanville J-13
Nome K-16
Noodle G-10
Nordheim N-13
Normandy N-9
Normangee J-15
Normanna N-13
North Houston
. . . . . . Pg. 121, B-3
North Shadydale
. . . . . . Pg. 121, C-6
North Zulch K-14
Northcrest M-13
Northfield D-9
Norton H-9
Notrees H-6
Novice H-10

Nuevo Laredo P-10
Nursery N-13
O'Brien F-10
O'Donnell F-7
Oak Hill L-12
Vicinity . . . . Pg. 93, K-1
Oakalla M-11
Oakland M-14
Oakwood H-15
Odem P-13
Odessa H-7
Oglesby H-13
Oilton Q-11
Oklaunion E-11
Old Boston F-17
Old Center H-17
Old Glory F-9
Old Ocean M-15
Olden G-11
Oldenburg L-14
Olivia N-14
Olmito S-13
Olmos Park Pg. 159, D-4
Olney F-11
Olton E-7
Omaha F-16
Oplin H-10
Orange L-18
Orange Grove P-12
Orangefield Pg. 95, G-6
Ore City F-16
Orla H-5
Osceola H-13
Ottine M-13
Ovalo H-10
Overton G-16
Ovilla . . . . Pg. 111, G-8
Oxville . . . . Pg. 93, F-5
Ozona K-8
Paducah E-9
Paige L-13
Paint Rock J-10
Painview D-7
Palacios N-14
Palestine H-15
Palmer G-14
Palo Pinto G-12
Pampa B-8
Pandora M-13
Panhandle C-8
Panna Maria M-12
Panola G-17
Pantego . Pg. 110, E-5
Paradise F-13
Paris E-15
Park Place . Pg. 121, F-6
Parnell D-9
Pasadena L-16
Vicinity . Pg. 121, E-7
Patricia G-7
Patroon H-17
Pattonville E-16
Pawnee N-12
Paxton H-17
Pearland . Pg. 121, G-6
Pearsall N-11
Pecos J-5
Peggy N-12
Penwell H-6
Perrin F-12
Perry J-13
Perryton A-9
Petersburg E-8
Petrolia E-12
Pettus N-12
Petty E-15
Peveto . . . . Pg. 95, F-7
Pflugerville K-13
Phalba G-15
Pharr S-12
Phillips B-7
Pilot Point F-13
Pine Mills G-16
Pinehurst K-17
Pineland J-17
Pioneer H-11
Pipecreek L-11
Pittsburg F-16
Placedo N-14
Plains F-6
Plano F-14
Vicinity . Pg. 111, A-10
Plantersville K-15
Plata L-4
Pleasanton N-12
Point Comfort N-14
Pollok J-16
Ponder F-13
Ponta H-16
Pontotoc K-11

TEXAS

Poolville F-12
Port Aransas P-13
Port Arthur L-17
  Vicinity . . . Pg. 95, K-4
Port Bolivar L-16
Port Isabel S-13
Port Lavaca N-14
Port Mansfield R-13
Port Neches L-17
  Vicinity . . . Pg. 95, J-5
Port O'Connor . . . N-14
Porter L-16
Portland P-13
Posey F-8
Post F-8
Poteet N-11
Poth M-12
Pottsboro E-14
Pottsville H-12
Powderly E-15
Powell H-14
Poynor H-15
Prairie Dell K-13
Prairie Hill H-14
Prairie Lea L-12
Prairie View L-15
Premont Q-12
Presidio L-4
Priddy H-11
Princeton F-14
Pritchett G-16
Proctor H-12
Prosper F-14
Purmela J-12
Putnam G-11
Pyote H-5
Quail C-9
Quanah D-10
Queen City F-17
Quemado N-9
Quinlan G-14
Quitaque D-8
Quitman G-15
Rachal R-12
Ralls E-8
Ramirez Q-11
Randado Q-11
Randlett Charlie . . E-12
Randolph H-14
Ranger G-11
Rankin J-7
Ratcliff J-16
Ravenna E-14
Rayland E-10
Raymondville R-12
Raywood L-17
Reagan J-14
Realitos Q-11
Red Bluff . . Pg. 121, G-10
Red Oak G-13
  Vicinity . . Pg. 111, G-9
Red Springs E-10
Redford M-4
Reese Vill. E-7
Refugio P-13
Reklaw H-16
Reno E-15
Retta . . . . . Pg. 110, G-4
Rhome F-13
Ricardo Q-12
Rice H-14
Richardson F-13
  Vicinity . . Pg. 111, A-9
Richland G-14
Richland Hills
  . . . . Pg. 110, C-4
Richland Springs . . J-11
Richmond L-15
Richwood M-16
Ridge J-15
Riesel J-13
Ringgold E-12
Rio Grande City . . R-11
Rio Vista H-13
Riomendina M-11
Rios Q-12
Rising Star H-11
River Oaks (Tarrant Cty)
  . . . . Pg. 110, D-2
River Oaks (Harris Cty)
  . . . . Pg. 121, E-4
Riverside H-16
Riviera Q-12
Roanoke . . . Pg. 110, A-4
Roans Prairie K-15
Robbins J-15
Robert Lee H-9
Robinson H-13
Robstown P-13
Roby G-9

Rochelle J-11
Rochester F-10
Rock Island M-14
Rockdale K-14
Rockland J-17
Rockport P-13
Rocksprings L-9
Rockwood J-10
Roganville K-17
Rogers K-13
Rollingwood . . Pg. 93, J-2
Roma R-10
Romayor K-16
Roosevelt K-9
Ropesville F-7
Rosanky L-13
Roscoe G-9
Rose City . . . Pg. 95, G-3
Rosebud J-14
Rosenberg M-15
Rosevine J-17
Rosser G-13
Rotan G-9
Round Mountain . . K-12
Round Rock K-13
Round Top L-14
Rowena H-9
Rowlett . . . Pg. 111, B-11
Roxton E-15
Royalty J-6
Rule F-10
Runge M-12
Rusk H-16
Rye K-16
Sabinal M-10
Sachse . . Pg. 111, A-11
Sacul H-16
Sadler E-14
Sagerton F-10
Saginaw G-13
Saint Hedwig M-12
Saint Jo E-13
Salado J-13
Salt Falt H-3
Samnorwood C-9
San Angelo J-9
San Antonio M-12
  Vicinity . . . . . Pg. 159
  Detailed City . Pg. 285
San Augustine . . . H-17
San Benito S-13
San Diego P-12
San Elizario H-1
San Felipe L-14
San Gabriel K-13
San Isidro R-11
San Juan R-12
San Marcos L-12
San Patricio P-12
San Perlita R-13
San Saba J-11
San Ygnacio Q-10
Sanderson L-6
Sandia P-12
Sanford B-8
Sanger F-13
Sansom Park
  . . . . Pg. 110, C-2
Santa Anna H-11
Santa Elena R-12
Santa Fe L-15
Santa Maria S-12
Santa Rosa S-12
Saragosa J-5
Saratoga K-17
Sarita Q-12
Satsuma . . . Pg. 121, B-1
Savoy E-14
Schertz M-12
Schulenburg L-14
Scotland E-11
Scottsville G-17
Scranton G-11
Seabrook L-16
  Vicinity . . Pg. 121, G-10
Seadrift N-14
Seagraves F-6
Sealy L-14
Sebastian R-13
Sebastopol K-16
Segovia K-10
Seguin M-12
Selma . . . . . Pg. 159, A-7
Seminole G-6
Seven Points G-14
Seymour E-11
Shafter L-4
Shallowater E-7
Shamrock C-9

Shannon F-12
Sharpstown . . Pg. 121, F-3
Shavano Park
  . . . . Pg. 159, A-4
Sheffield K-7
Shelbyville H-17
Sheldon L-16
  Vicinity . . Pg. 121, C-9
Sheridan M-14
Sherman F-14
Sherwood J-9
Shiner M-13
Shiro K-15
Shoreacres Pg. 121, G-10
Sidney H-11
Sierra Blanca J-3
Silsbee K-17
Silver H-9
Silverton D-8
Simms F-16
Singleton K-15
Sinton P-13
Sisterdale L-11
Sivells Bend E-13
Skellytown B-8
Skidmore P-12
Slaton F-8
Slidell F-13
Slocum H-16
Smeltertown Pg. 116, C-3
Smiley M-13
Smyer E-7
Snook K-14
Snyder G-8
Socorro H-1
Somerset M-11
  Vicinity . . Pg. 159, J-1
Somerville K-14
Sonora K-9
Sour Lake L-17
South Bend F-11
South Houston
  . . . . Pg. 121, F-7
South Padre Island . S-13
South Plains D-8
Southlake . . Pg. 110, B-5
Southland E-7
Southton . . . Pg. 159, H-6
Spade E-7
Spanish Fort E-12
Speaks M-14
Spearman B-8
Spicewood K-12
Splendora L-16
Spofford M-9
Spring L-15
Spring Branch L-11
Spring Valley Pg. 121, D-3
Springlake D-7
Springtown F-12
Spur F-9
Spurger K-17
Stafford M-15
  Vicinity . . Pg. 121, G-2
Stamford F-10
Stanton H-7
Star J-12
Stephenville H-12
Sterling City H-8
Stinnett B-8
Stockdale M-12
Stoneburg E-12
Stoneham K-15
Stonewall L-11
Stowell L-16
Stratford A-7
Strawn G-11
Streetman H-14
Study Butte M-5
Sudan E-7
Sugar Land L-15
  Vicinity . . Pg. 121, G-1
Sullivan City S-11
Sulphur Sprs. F-15
Summerfield D-6
Sumner E-15
Sundown F-6
Sunnyvale Pg. 111, C-11
Sunray B-7
Sunrise Acres
  . . . . Pg. 116, B-4
Sunset F-13
Sunset Valley . Pg. 93, K-2
Sutherland Springs M-12
Sweeny M-15
Sweetwater G-9
Swenson F-9
Taft P-13
Tahoka F-7
Talco F-16
Talpa H-10

Tankersley J-9
Tarpley M-10
Tarzan G-7
Tatum G-17
Taylor K-13
Taylor Lake Village
  . . . . Pg. 121, G-9
Teague H-14
Telegraph K-9
Telephone E-15
Telferner N-14
Tell D-9
Temple J-13
Tenaha H-17
Teneseee Colony . H-15
Tennyson H-9
Terlingua M-5
Terrell G-14
Terrell Hills . Pg. 159, D-5
Texarkana F-17
Texas City M-16
Texhoma A-8
Texico D-6
Texline A-6
Thackerville E-13
Thalia E-10
The Grove J-13
The Woodlands . . . L-16
Thelma . . . . Pg. 159, K-5
Thomaston M-13
Thorndale K-13
Thornton J-14
Thorp Spring G-12
Thrall K-13
Three Rivers N-12
Throckmorton F-10
Tilden N-11
Timpson H-17
Tioga F-13
Tira F-15
Tivoli N-14
Toco E-15
Tolar G-12
Tomball K-15
  Vicinity . . Pg. 121, A-4
Tool H-14
Topsey J-12
Tornillo H-1
Toyah J-5
Trent G-10
Trenton F-14
Trickham H-11
Trinidad H-14
Trinity J-15
Troup H-16
Troy J-13
Tucker H-15
Tuleta N-13
Tulia D-7
Turkey D-9
Turnertown H-16
Tuscola G-10
Twin Sisters L-12
Twitty C-9
Tye G-10
Tyler G-16
Tynan P-12
Umbarger C-7
Unity E-15
Universal City M-12
University Park
  . . . . Pg. 111, C-9
Utopia M-10
Uvalde M-10
Valentine K-4
Valera H-10
Valley Mills H-13
Valley Spring K-11
Valley View F-13
Van G-15
Van Alstyne F-14
Van Horn J-3
Van Vleck M-15
Vancourt J-9
Vanderbilt N-14
Vanderpool L-10
Vashti E-12
Vealmoor G-8
Vega C-7
Venus G-13
Vera E-10
Vernon D-11
Victoria N-13
Vidor L-17
  Vicinity . . . Pg. 95, F-4
Village Mills M-15
Vincent G-8
Voca J-11
Von Ormy . . Pg. 159, H-2
Voss H-10
Votaw K-17

W. University Place
  . . . . Pg. 121, E-4
Waco H-13
Wadsworth N-15
Waelder L-13
Waka A-9
Wake Village E-17
Wall J-9
Waller L-15
Wallis L-14
Walnut Sprs. H-13
Warda L-13
Warren K-17
Washington K-15
Waskom G-17
Watauga . . . Pg. 110, C-4
Water Valley H-9
Waters Park . Pg. 93, F-4
Watson K-12
Watsonville . Pg. 110, F-5
Waxahachie G-14
Wayside D-8
Weatherford G-12
Weaver F-15
Webberville . Pg. 93, K-7
Webster M-16
Weches J-16
Weesatche N-13
Weimar L-14
Weinort F-10
Welch F-7
Wellington D-9
Wellman F-7
Wells J-16
Weslaco S-12
West H-13
West Columbia . . . M-15
West Lake Hills
  . . . . Pg. 93, H-2
West Orange K-17
West Point L-13
Westbrook G-8
Westfield L-16
  Vicinity . . Pg. 121, A-4
Westhoff M-13
Westlake . . . Pg. 110, A-4
Westover F-11
Westover Hills
  . . . . Pg. 110, D-2
Westworth Village
  . . . . Pg. 110, D-2
Wharton M-15
Wheeler C-9
Wheeler G-15
Wheelock K-14
White Deer C-8
White Settlement
  . . . . Pg. 110, D-1
Whiteface E-6
Whiteflat E-9
Whitehouse G-15
Whitesboro E-13
Whitewright F-14
Whitharral E-7
Whitney H-13
Whittsett N-12
Wichita Falls E-12
Wickett H-5
Wiergate J-18
Wildorado C-7
Wildwood K-17
Wilkinson F-16
Willow City K-11
Wills Point G-15
Wilmer . . . . Pg. 111, F-10
Wilson F-8
Wimberly L-12
Winchell J-11
Windcrest . . Pg. 159, C-7
Windom F-15
Windthorst E-12
Winfield F-15
Wingate H-9
Wink H-5
Winnie L-17
Winnsboro F-15
Winona G-16
Winters H-9
Wolfe City F-15
Wolfforth F-7
Woodlake J-16
  Vicinity . . Pg. 121, E-2
Woodlawn G-17
Woodsboro P-13
Woodson F-11
Woodville K-17
Woodward J-13
Wortham H-14
Yoakum M-13
Yorktown M-13

Ysleta . . . . . Pg. 116, E-6
Zavalla J-17
Zephyr H-11
Zorn L-12

UTAH
Pages 80-81
Population: 1,461,037
Capital: Salt Lake City
Land Area: 82,073 sq. mi.

UTAH

Abraham H-4
Adamsville K-4
Alpine F-5
Alta F-6
Altamont F-8
Alton L-4
American Fork F-5
Aneth M-9
Angle K-5
Annabella J-5
Antimony K-5
Arcadia F-8
Aurora J-5
Austin J-5
Axtell H-5
Bear River City . . . D-5
Beaver K-4
Benjamin F-5
Beryl K-2
Bicknell K-5
Birdseye G-6
Black Rock J-4
Blanding L-9
Blue Cr. C-4
Bluebell F-8
Bluff L-9
Bluffdale F-5
Bonanza G-9
Boneta F-7
Boulder K-6
Bountiful E-5
  Vicinity . . Pg. 157, F-6
Brian Head L-4
Bridgeland F-8
Brigham City D-5
Bryce Canyon L-4
Burmester E-4
Burrville J-5
Cannonville L-4
Carbonville G-7
Castle Dale H-7
Castle Rock E-6
Cave C-5
Cedar City L-3
Cedar Creek C-3
Cedar Fort F-5
Cedar Springs D-4
Cedarview F-8
Center Creek F-6
Centerfield H-5
Centerville E-5
Central J-5
Central L-2
Charleston F-6
Chester H-5
Circleville K-4
Cisco J-9
Clarkston C-5
Clawson H-6
Clear Creek C-3
Clearcreek G-6
Clearfield E-5
Cleveland H-7
Clinton D-5
Clover E-4
Coalville E-6
Colton G-7
Corinne D-5
Cornish C-5
Cove Fort J-4
Crescent Jct. J-8
Croydon E-6
Delle E-4
Delta H-4
Deseret H-4
Desert Mound L-3
Dividend G-5
Draper F-5
Dugway F-3
East Carbon City . . H-8
Eastland L-9
Echo E-6
Elberta G-5
Elmo H-7
Elsinore J-5
Emery J-6
Enoch L-3

Enterprise L-2
Ephraim H-6
Escalante L-5
Etna D-2
Eureka G-5
Fairfield F-5
Fairview G-6
Farmington E-5
Faust F-4
Fayette H-5
Ferron H-6
Fillmore H-5
Fish Springs G-3
Flowell H-4
Fort Duchesne . . . F-8
Fountain Green . . . G-5
Francis F-6
Freedom G-5
Fremont K-5
Fremont Jct. J-6
Fruit Heights E-5
Fruitland F-7
Fry Canyon L-8
Gandy G-2
Garden City C-6
Garrison H-2
Geneva F-5
Genola G-5
Glendale L-4
Glenwood J-5
Goshen G-5
Grantsville E-4
Green Lake E-9
Green River H-8
Greenville K-4
Greenwich J-5
Greenwood H-4
Grouse Creek C-2
Gunlock L-2
Gunnison H-5
Gusher F-8
Hamilton Fort L-3
Hanksville K-7
Hanna F-7
Harrisville D-5
Hatch L-4
Hatton J-4
Heber City F-6
Helper G-7
Henefer E-6
Henrieville L-5
Herriman F-5
Hiawatha H-6
Hinckley H-4
Holden H-5, H-5
Holladay F-5
Honeyville D-4
Hot Springs D-5
Howell C-4
Hoytsville E-6
Huntington H-7
Huntsville D-6
Hurricane M-3
Hyde Park C-5
Hyrum D-5
Indianola G-6
Ioka F-8
Iron Springs L-3
Ivins M-2
Jensen F-9
Jericho G-5
Joseph J-5
Junction K-4
Kamas F-6
Kanab M-4
Kanarraville L-3
Kanosh J-4
Kaysville E-5
Kearns E-3
Kelton D-4
Kenilworth G-7
Kimball Jct. E-6
Kingston K-5
Knolls E-3
Koosharem J-5
La Sal K-9
La Sal Jct. K-9
La Verkin L-3
Lake Pt. Jct. E-4
Lake Shore F-5
Lake View F-5
Laketown C-6
Lapoint F-8
Leamington H-5
Leeds L-3
Leeton L-4
Lehi F-5
Leota F-9
Levan G-5

Lewiston C-5
Loa J-6
Logan D-5
Long Valley Jct. . . . L-4
Low E-3
Lucin D-2
Lund K-3
Lyman J-6
Lynndyl G-4
Maeser F-9
Magna F-5
  Vicinity . . Pg. 157, J-2
Manderfield J-4
Manila E-8
Manti H-6
Mantua D-5
Mapleton F-6
Marion E-6
Marysvale J-4
Mayfield H-6
Meadow J-4
Meadowville C-6
Mendon D-5
Mexican Hat M-8
Midvale E-5, F-6
Midway F-6
Milburn G-6
Milford J-3
Mills H-5
Minersville K-3
Moab J-9
Modena K-2
Molen H-6
Mona G-5
Monarch F-8
Monroe J-5
Montezuma Creek . M-9
Monticello K-9
Moore H-6
Morgan E-6
Moroni G-6
Mountain Home . . . F-7
Mt. Carmel L-4
Mt. Carmel Jct. . . . L-4
Mt. Emmons F-7
Mt. Pleasant G-6
Murray E-5, E-6
Myton F-8
N. Logan C-6
N. Salt Lake F-5
  Vicinity . . Pg. 157, F-5
Naples F-9
Neola F-8
Nephi G-5
New Harmony L-3
Newcastle L-2
Newton C-5
Oak City H-5
Oakley E-6
Oasis H-4
Ogden D-5
Orangeville H-6
Orderville L-4
Orem F-6
Ouray F-9
Panguitch K-4
Paradise D-5
Paragonah K-4
Park City E-6
Park Valley C-3
Parowan K-4
Payson F-6
Peoa E-6
Perry Willard D-5
Pigeon Hollow Jct. . H-6
Pine Valley L-2
Pintura L-3
Plain City D-5
Pleasant Grove . . . F-6
Pleasant View D-5
Plymouth C-5
Portage C-5
Porterville E-6
Price G-7
Providence D-5
Provo F-6
Randolph D-6
Redmond J-5
Richfield J-5
Richmond C-5
Riverdale D-5
Riverton F-5, H-5
Rockville M-3
Roosevelt F-8
Rosette C-3
Rowley Jct. E-4
Roy D-5
Ruby's Inn L-4
Saint George M-3
Saint John Sta. . . . F-4

UTAH

Salem G-5
Salina H-5
Salt Lake City F-4
  Vicinity . . . . . . Pg. 157
  Detailed City . . Pg. 283
Sandy F-5, G-6
Santa Clara M-2
Santaquin G-5
Scipio H-5
Scofield E-3
Sevier J-4
Shivwits M-2
Sigurd J-5
Silver City G-5
Smithfield C-5
Smyths J-3
Snowville C-4
Soldier Summit G-7
South Jordan . . F-5, G-5
South Ogden D-5
South Salt Lake . . . E-5
  Vicinity . . . Pg. 157, J-5
Spanish Fork F-6
Spring City H-6
Spring Lake G-5
Springdale M-3
Springville F-6
Sterling H-6
Stockton F-4
Summit K-3
Summit Pt. K-3
Sunnyside G-8
Sunset E-5
Sutherland H-4
Syracuse E-5
Tabiona F-7
Talmage F-7
Taylors J-5
Teasdale K-6
Terrace D-6
Thistle G-6
Thompson H-9
Tooele F-4
Toquerville L-3
Torrey K-6
Tremonton D-5
Tropic L-5
Trout Cr. G-2
Tucker G-6, E-5
Upalco F-7
Uvada L-2
Venice J-5
Vernal F-7
Vernon F-4
Veyo L-2
Virgin M-3
W. Valley City E-5
Wahsatch D-6
Wales H-5
Wanship E-5
Washington M-3
Washington Terrace . D-5
Wellington G-7
Wellsville D-5
Wendover E-2
West Jordan . . F-5, F-4
West Point D-4
West Valley City . . . F-5
  Vicinity . . . Pg. 157, J-4
Whiterocks F-8
Widtsoe Jct. K-6
Woodruff D-6
Woods Cross E-5
  Vicinity . . . Pg. 157, J-5
Woodside H-8
Zane K-2

VERMONT
Page 55
Population: 511,456
Capital: Montpelier
Land Area: 9,273 sq. mi.

Addison E-1
Albany C-3
Alburg B-1
Arlington J-1
Ascutney G-3
Averill B-5
Bakersfield B-2
Barnard F-3
Barnet D-4
Barre E-3
Barton C-4
Bellows Falls H-3
Bennington J-1
Bethel F-3
Bloomfield C-5

Bomoseen G-1
Bondville H-2
Bradford E-4
Brandon F-2
Brattleboro J-3
Bridgewater Cors. . . G-3
Bridport E-1
Bristol E-1
Broadford Cen. . . . E-3
Brunswick Sprs. . . . C-5
Burlington D-1
Cambridge J-1
Cambridgeport H-3
Canaan B-5
Castleton G-1
Charlotte D-1
Chelsea F-3
Chester H-3
Chester Depot H-3
Chimney Cor. C-2
Concord D-4
Cornwall E-1
Danby G-2
Dorset H-1
E. Barnet D-4
E. Berkshire B-2
E. Braintree E-3
E. Brookfield E-3
E. Burke C-4
E. Calais D-3
E. Dorset H-2
E. Fairfield C-2
E. Granville E-2
E. Hardwick D-3
E. Haven C-4
Eden C-3
Eden Mills C-3
Enosburg Falls B-2
Essex Jct. D-2
Fair Haven G-1
Fairfax C-2
Ferrisburg E-1
Franklin B-2
Gassetts H-3
Gaysville F-3
Glover C-4
Grafton H-3
Grand Isle C-1
Granville E-2
Groton D-3
Guilford J-3
Hancock F-2
Hardwick D-3
Heartwellville J-2
Hinesburg D-2
Holland B-4
Hubbardton F-1
Hyde Park C-3
Irasburg B-3
Irasville E-3
Island Pond C-4
Jacksonville J-2
Jamaica H-2
Jay B-3
Jeffersonville C-2
Johnson C-3
Lake Elmore C-3
Leicester F-2
Londonderry H-2
Lowell B-3
Ludlow G-2
Lunenberg D-5
Lyndon D-4
Lyndonville C-4
Maidstone C-5
Manchester H-2
Manchester Cen. . . H-2
Marlboro J-2
Marshfield D-3
Middlebury E-1
Middletown Sprs. . . G-1
Mill Village E-3
Montgomery Cen. . . B-3
Montpelier D-3
Morgan Cen. B-4
Morrisville C-3
New Haven E-1
New Haven Jct. . . . E-1
Newbury E-4
Newfane J-2
Newport B-3
North Concord D-4
North Dorset H-2
North Hero C-1
North Hyde Park . . . C-3
North Rupert H-1
Northfield E-2
Norton B-4
Norwich F-3
Orleans B-4

Orwell F-1
Passumpsic D-4
Pawlet H-1
Pittsfield F-2
Pittsford F-2
Pittsford Mills F-2
Plainfield D-3
Plymouth C-2
Plymouth Union . . . G-2
Pompanoosuc F-3
Post Mills F-3
Poultney G-1
Pownal J-1
Pownal Cen. J-1
Putney J-3
Quechee G-3
Randolph F-2
Richford B-2
Richmond D-2
Ripton E-2
Robinson E-2
Rochester F-2
Roxbury E-2
Royalton F-2
Rutland G-2
Saint Albans B-2
Saint George D-2
Saint Johnsbury . . . D-4
Searsburg J-2
Shafsbury J-1
Shafsbury Cen. . . . J-2
Shelburne D-1
Sherburne Cen. . . . G-2
Shoreham F-1
Simonsville H-2
South Burlington . . . D-1
South Dorset G-2
South Hinesburg . . . D-2
South Royalton F-3
South Ryegate E-4
South Shafsbury . . . J-2
South Starksboro . . E-2
South Walden D-3
South Wallingford . . G-2
Springfield H-3
Starksboro E-2
Stockbridge F-2
Sudbury F-1
Sunderland J-2
Swanton B-1
Ticonderoga F-1
Townshend J-2
Troy B-3
Tunbridge F-3
Tyson G-2
Underhill Flats D-2
Union Village F-3
Vergennes E-1
Vershire E-3
Waits River E-3
Waitsfield E-2
Wallingford G-2
Waltham E-1
Wardsboro J-2
Warren E-2
Washington E-3
Waterbury D-2
Waterbury Ctr. D-3
Websterville E-3
Wells G-1
West Addison E-1
West Braintree E-2
West Bridgewater . . G-2
West Burke C-4
West Danville D-3
West Dover J-2
West Fairlee F-3
West Groton E-3
West Hartford F-3
West Rutland G-2
West Topsham E-3
West Wardsboro . . . J-2
Westfield B-3
White River Jct. . . . G-3
Whiting F-1
Wilmington J-2
Windsor G-3
Wolcott C-3
Woodbury D-3
Woodford J-1
Woodstock G-3
Worcester D-3

VIRGINIA
Pages 82-83
Population: 5,346,818
Capital: Richmond
Land Area: 39,703 sq. mi.

Abingdon K-3
Achilles H-12
Alexandria E-12
  Vicinity . . . Pg. 168, F-5
Altavista J-8
Amelia H-10
Amherst H-8
Annandale . . Pg. 168, F-3
Appalachia J-1
Appomattox H-9
Arlington D-12
  Vicinity . . . Pg. 168, E-4
Ashland G-10
Atlee . . . . . Pg. 156, B-1
Bailey's Crossroads
  . . . . Pg. 168, E-4
Ballston . . . Pg. 168, E-5
Bassett J-7
Bastian J-5
Bavon H-13
Bedford H-8
Belle Haven G-13
Bellwood Manor
  . . . . Pg. 156, B-6
Bensley . . . Pg. 156, C-6
Berryville D-10
Big Island H-8
Big Stone Gap J-2
Blacksburg H-6
Blackstone J-11
Bluefield H-4
Bon Air H-7
  Vicinity . . . Pg. 156, E-4
Boones Mill H-7
Bowling Green F-11
Boydton K-9
Bridgewater F-8
Bristol K-3
Broadway E-8
Brodnax J-10
Brookneal J-8
Buchanan H-7
Buckingham G-9
Buena Vista G-8
Burgess G-12
Burke . . . . Pg. 168, G-2
Burkeville H-9
Cape Charles H-13
Carmel Church G-10
Castlewood J-3
Cedarbluff J-4
Central Garage G-11
Centralia . . . Pg. 156, C-7
Charlottesville G-9
Charlottsville F-9
Chase City J-9
Chatham J-8
Cheriton H-13
Chesapeake J-13
  Vicinity . . . Pg. 146, K-4
Chester H-11
  Vicinity . . . Pg. 156, C-7
Chesterfield . . Pg. 156, C-7
Chilhowie K-4
Chincoteague F-14
Christiansburg J-6
Churchville F-8
Clarksville K-9
Claudville K-6
Clifton Forge G-7
Clinchco H-3
Clintwood J-3
Coeburn J-3
Colonial Beach F-11
Colonial Hts. H-11
Courtland J-11
Covington G-6
Craigsville F-8
Craney Island Estates
  . . . . Pg. 156, B-3
Crewe H-10
Crittenton . . Pg. 146, E-1
Crozet G-9
Culpeper E-10
Cumberland H-9
Dale City E-11
Damascus K-4
Dante J-3
Danville K-7
Dayton E-8
Deerfield Estates
  . . . . Pg. 156, D-7
Deltaville G-13

Dillwyn H-9
Drakes Branch J-9
Dublin J-5
Dugspur J-6
Eagle Rock G-7
Eastville H-13
Edinburg E-10
Elkton E-9
Emporia K-11
Ewing K-1
Exmore H-13
Fairfax F-11
  Vicinity . . . Pg. 168, E-1
Falling Creek
  . . . . Pg. 156, E-6
Falls Church Pg. 168, E-3
Falmouth E-11
Farmville H-9
Fieldale K-7
Floyd J-6
Franconia . . Pg. 168, G-4
Franklin K-11
Fredericksburg F-10
Fries K-5
Front Royal D-9
Galax K-5
Gate City K-2
Glade Spring J-4
Gladys J-8
Glasgow G-8
Glen Allen . . Pg. 156, D-1
Gloucester H-12
Gloucester Pt. H-12
Gordonsville F-9
Goshen F-8
Gretna J-8
Grottoes F-8
Groveton . . . Pg. 168, G-5
Grundy H-3
Gum Springs G-10
Gwynn H-13
Halifax J-8
Hampden-Sydney . . H-9
Hampton J-13
  Vicinity . . . Pg. 146, A-2
Hanover G-11
Harrisonburg E-8
Herndon D-10
Highland Springs
  . . . . Pg. 156, A-3
Hillsville J-6
Hollins H-7
Holly Glen Estates
  . . . . Pg. 156, C-1
Honaker J-3
Hopewell H-11
Hunton . . . . Pg. 156, D-1
Hurt J-8
Independence K-4
Iron Gate G-7
Irvington G-12
Jarratt J-11
Jonesville K-1
Keene Mill Heights
  . . . . Pg. 168, G-2
Kenbridge J-10
Keysville J-9
Kilmarnock G-12
King & Queen C.H. . . G-12
Kiptopeke H-13
La Crosse K-10
Lakeside . . . Pg. 156, C-2
Lancaster G-12
Land O' Pines
  . . . . Pg. 156, D-6
Lawrenceville J-10
Lebanon J-3
Leesburg D-10
Lexington G-7
Longwood Acres
  . . . . Pg. 156, D-5
Lottsburg G-12
Lovingston G-8
Luray E-9
Lynchburg H-8
Madison F-9
Madison Hts. H-8
Manassas E-10
Mappsville G-14
Marion J-4
Marshall E-10
Martinsville K-7
Mathews H-13
McKenney J-10
McLean . . . . Pg. 168, D-3
Mechanicsville G-11
  Vicinity . . . Pg. 156, A-3

Middleburg D-10
Middletown D-9
Monterey F-8
Montross F-12
Mt. Jackson E-9
Narrows J-5
Nassawadox H-13
New Castle H-7
New Market E-9
Newport News J-12
  Vicinity . . . Pg. 146, A-1
Norfolk J-13
  Vicinity . . . . . . Pg. 146
  Detailed City . Pg. 263
Norton J-2
Oak Grove F-12
Onancock G-13
Onley G-14
Orange F-10
Palmyra G-9
Pamplin City H-8
Parksley G-13
Patrick Henry Heights
  . . . . Pg. 156, B-1
Patrick Springs K-7
Pearisburg H-6
Pembroke H-6
Pennington Gap . . . J-2
Petersburg H-10
Pimmit Hills Pg. 168, D-3
Pole Green . Pg. 156, A-2
Poquoson H-12
  Vicinity . . . Pg. 146, A-3
Port Royal F-11
Portsmouth J-12
  Vicinity . . . Pg. 146, F-3
Pound J-2
Powhatan H-10
Prospect Hill Pg. 168, C-2
Pulaski J-5
Purcellville D-10
Quantico E-11
Radford J-6
Ravensworth Pg. 168, F-2
Red Ash J-3
Remington E-10
Richlands E-4
Richmond H-10
  Vicinity . . . Pg. 156, C-4
  Detailed City . Pg. 277
Richmond Heights
  . . . . Pg. 156, B-5
Ripplemead H-6
Roanoke H-7
Rocky Mount J-7
Ruckersville F-9
Rural Point . Pg. 156, A-1
Rural Retreat J-5
Rustburg H-8
Salem H-7
Saltville J-4
Sandston H-11
  Vicinity . . . Pg. 156, A-4
Saxis G-13
Seaford H-12
Shady Oak . . Pg. 168, B-1
Shenandoah E-9
Shipman G-8
Smithfield J-12
South Boston K-8
Sperryville E-9
Spring Grove H-11
Springfield . . Pg. 168, G-3
St. Paul J-3
Stafford F-11
Stanley E-9
Stanleytown J-7
Staunton F-8
Stephens City D-9
Strasburg D-9
Stuart K-6
Stuarts Draft F-8
Suffolk J-12
  Vicinity . . . Pg. 146, H-1
Sugar Grove J-4
Surry H-12
Sussex J-11
Sydnorsville J-7
Tangier G-13
Tappahannock G-11
Tazewell J-4
Timberville E-8
Triangle E-11
Tysons Corner
  . . . . Pg. 168, D-2
Urbanna G-12
Vanderpool F-7
Vansant H-3
Varina . . . . . Pg. 156, A-5

Verona F-8
Victoria J-9
Vienna D-11
  Vicinity . . . Pg. 168, E-2
Vinton H-7
Virginia Beach J-13
  Vicinity . . . Pg. 146, H-7
Volens J-8
Wakefield J-12
Warm Springs F-7
Warrenton E-10
Warsaw F-12
Waverly J-11
Waynesboro F-8
Weber City K-3
West Point H-12
Williamsburg H-11
Winchester D-9
Windsor J-12
Wise J-2
Woodbridge E-11
Woodlawn K-5
Woodstock E-9
Wylliesburg J-9
Wytheville J-5
Zion G-9

WASHINGTON
Pages 84-85
Population: 4,132,156
Capital: Olympia
Land Area: 66,511 sq. mi.

Aberdeen F-3
Acme B-6
Addy B-13
Airway Heights D-14
Albion F-14
Alderwood Maner
  . . . . Pg. 163, A-4
Algona E-6
Almira D-11
Altoona H-3
Anacortes B-5
Anatone H-14
Appleyard E-9
Arlington C-6
Asotin G-14
Auburn E-6
Battle Ground J-5
Bellevue D-6
  Vicinity . . . Pg. 163, E-6
Bellingham A-5
Benton City H-10
Bickleton H-9
Bingen J-7
Black Diamond E-6
Blaine A-5
Bonney Lake F-6
Bossburg B-13
Bothell D-6
  Vicinity . . . Pg. 163, B-5
Boundary A-13
Bremerton D-5
Brewster C-10
Bridgeport C-10
Brier D-16
  Vicinity . . . Pg. 163, A-4
Browns Point Pg. 164, D-8
Bryn Mawr . Pg. 163, H-5
Buckley E-6
Bucoda F-5
Burien . . . . . Pg. 163, H-3
Burlington B-6
Camas J-5
Carbonado F-6
Carnation D-6
Cashmere E-9
Castle Rock H-4
Cathlamet G-4
Centralia G-5
Chehalis G-5
Chelan D-9
Cheney E-14
Chewelah C-13
Clarkston G-14
Clayton C-13
Cle Elum E-8
Coalfield . . . Pg. 163, H-6
Coles Corner D-8
Colfax F-14
College Place H-12
Colton G-14
Colville B-13
Conconully B-10
Concrete B-7
Connell G-12
Copalis Beach E-2
Cosmopolis F-3

Coulee City D-11
Coulee Dam C-11
Coupeville C-5
Crescent Bar E-9
Creston D-12
Cusick C-14
Danville A-12
Darrington C-7
Davenport D-13
Dayton H-13
Deer Park C-14
Deming A-6
Des Moines E-6
  Vicinity . . . Pg. 163, K-3
Disautel C-11
Discovery Bay C-5
Dodge G-13
Duluth J-5
Dusty F-13
Duvall D-6
East Wenatchee . . . E-9
Eastgate . . . Pg. 163, F-6
Eatonville F-6
Edgewood . Pg. 164, F-10
Edmonds D-5
  Vicinity . . . Pg. 163, A-2
Edwall E-13
Elbe F-6
Eldon D-4
Electric City D-11
Ellensburg F-9
Elma F-4
Elmer City C-11
Endicott F-13
Entiat D-9
Enumclaw E-6
Ephrata E-10
Eureka H-12
Everett C-6
Everson A-6
Fairfield F-14
Fairholm C-3
Farmington F-15
Ferndale A-5
Fife . . . . Pg. 164, F-9
Fircrest E-5
  Vicinity . . . Pg. 164, F-7
Forks C-2
Friday Harbor B-5
Garfield F-14
George F-10
Gifford C-13
Gig Harbor E-5
Glenoma G-6
Gold Bar D-7
Goldendale J-8
Grand Coulee D-11
Grandview H-9
Granger G-9
Granite Falls C-6
Greenwater F-7
Hamilton B-6
Harrah G-9
Harrington E-12
Hartline D-11
Hatton G-11
Hoodsport E-4
Hoquiam F-3
Humptulips E-3
Husum J-7
Hyak E-7
Ilwaco G-3
Index D-7
Ione B-14
Issaquah E-6
Joyce C-3
Juanita . . . . Pg. 163, C-4
Kahlotus G-12
Kalama H-5
Keller C-12
Kelso H-5
Kenmoore . . Pg. 163, B-4
Kennewick H-11
Kent E-6
  Vicinity . . . Pg. 163, J-4
Kettle Falls B-13
Kingston . . . Pg. 163, A-1
Kirkland D-6
  Vicinity . . . Pg. 163, D-5
Kittitas F-9
Klaus G-5
Klickitat J-7
Krupp E-11
La Center J-5
La Conner B-5
La Crosse F-13
La Push C-2
Lacey F-5
Lake Stevens C-6
Lamont E-13
Langley C-5

WASHINGTON

WASHINGTON
WISCONSIN

Latah . . . E-14
Leavenworth . . . D-9
Lebam . . . G-3
Lind . . . F-12
Littlerock . . . F-4
Long Beach . . . G-3
Longview . . . H-4
Lyman . . . B-6
Lynden . . . A-5
Lynnwood . . . D-6
  Vicinity . . . Pg. 163, A-3
Mabton . . . H-9
Malone . . . G-4
Maltby . . . Pg. 163, A-6
Mansfield . . . D-10
Manson . . . D-9
Maplewood . . . Pg. 163, H-5
Marcus . . . B-13
Marysville . . . C-6
Mattawa . . . G-10
McCleary . . . F-4
Medical Lake . . . E-13
Megler . . . H-3
Menlo . . . G-3
Mercer Island . . . D-5
  Vicinity . . . Pg. 163, F-4
Mesa . . . G-11
Metaline . . . A-14
Metaline Falls . . . A-14
Methow . . . C-9
Midland . . . Pg. 164, G-9
Millwood . . . D-14
Milton . . . Pg. 164, E-10
Monroe . . . D-6
Montesano . . . F-3
Morton . . . G-6
Moses Lake . . . F-11
Mossyrock . . . G-4
Mount Baker . . . A-7
Mount Vernon . . . B-5
Mountlake Terrace . . . D-5
  Vicinity . . . Pg. 163, A-3
Moxee City . . . G-9
Mukilteo . . . C-6
Naches . . . F-8
Napavine . . . G-4
Naselle . . . E-3
Neah Bay . . . B-2
Neilton . . . E-3
Newcastle . . . Pg. 163, G-5
Newport . . . C-14
Normandy Park . . . E-5
  Vicinity . . . Pg. 163, J-2
North Bend . . . E-7
North Bonneville . . . J-6
North Cove . . . F-2
North Puyallup . . . Pg. 164, F-10
Northport . . . A-13
Oak Harbor . . . C-5
Oakesdale . . . E-13
Oakville . . . F-4
Ocean Park . . . G-3
Ocean Shores . . . F-2
Odessa . . . E-12
Okanogan . . . C-10
Olympia . . . F-5
Omak . . . B-10
Orchards . . . J-5
Orient . . . A-13
Oroville . . . A-10
Orting . . . F-6
Othello . . . F-11
Ozette . . . C-2
Pacific . . . E-6
Pacific Beach . . . E-2
Packwood . . . G-7
Palouse . . . F-14
Pasco . . . H-11
Pateros . . . C-10
Pe Ell . . . G-4
Pomeroy . . . G-14
Port Angeles . . . C-4
Port Gamble . . . D-5
Port Orchard . . . E-5
Port Townsend . . . C-5
Poulsbo . . . D-5
Prescott . . . H-12
Prosser . . . H-10
Pullman . . . G-14
Puyallup . . . F-5
  Vicinity . . . Pg. 164, G-10
Queets . . . D-2
Quincy . . . E-10
Rainier . . . F-5
Randle . . . G-6
Raymond . . . F-3
Reardan . . . D-13
Redmond . . . D-6
Renton . . . E-6
  Vicinity . . . Pg. 163, H-4

Republic . . . B-12
Richland . . . H-11
Richland Highlands . . . Pg. 163, B-3
Richmond Beach . . . Pg. 163, B-3
Ridgefield . . . J-5
Rimrock . . . G-7
Ritzville . . . F-12
Riverside . . . B-10
Rochester . . . F-4
Rock Island . . . E-9
Rockford . . . E-14
Rockport . . . B-7
Rollingbay . . . Pg. 163, D-1
Roosevelt . . . J-9
Rosalia . . . E-14
Rosburg . . . G-3
Roslyn . . . E-8
Roy . . . F-5
Royal City . . . F-10
Ryderwood . . . G-4
Salmon La Sac . . . E-8
Sappho . . . C-2
Seattle . . . D-5
  Vicinity . . . Pg. 163
  Detailed City . . . Pg. 291
Sedro Woolley . . . B-6
Selah . . . G-9
Sequim . . . C-4
Shelton . . . E-4
Silver Creek . . . G-5
Skykomish . . . D-7
Snohomish . . . D-6
Snoqualmie . . . E-7
Soap Lake . . . E-10
South Bend . . . G-3
South Cle Elum . . . F-8
South Prairie . . . F-6
Spangle . . . E-14
Spokane . . . D-14
Sprague . . . E-13
Springdale . . . C-13
St. John . . . F-14
Stanwood . . . C-6
Starbuck . . . G-13
Steilacoom . . . E-5
Stella . . . H-4
Steptoe . . . F-14
Stevenson . . . J-6
Sultan . . . D-6
Sumas . . . A-6
Summit . . . Pg. 164, G-9
Sumner . . . E-6
Sunnyside . . . H-10
Tacoma . . . E-5
  Vicinity . . . Pg. 164, F-8
Taholah . . . E-2
Tekoa . . . E-14
Telma . . . D-8
Tenino . . . F-5
Tieton . . . G-8
Toledo . . . G-5
Tonasket . . . B-10
Toppenish . . . H-9
Trout Lake . . . H-7
Tukwila . . . E-6
Tumwater . . . F-4
Twisp . . . C-9
Union . . . E-4
Union Gap . . . G-9
Uniontown . . . G-14
University Place . . . Pg. 164, F-6
Vader . . . G-4
Vancouver . . . J-5
  Vicinity . . . Pg. 153, A-5
Vantage . . . F-9
Vashon Heights . . . Pg. 163, G-1
Vashon Island . . . Pg. 163, K-1
Waitsburg . . . H-13
Walla Walla . . . H-12
Wallula . . . H-11
Wapato . . . G-9
Warden . . . F-11
Washougal . . . J-5
Washtucna . . . G-12
Waterville . . . D-9
Wauconda . . . B-11
Waverly . . . E-14
Wenatchee . . . E-9
Wenatchee Heights
West Richland . . . H-11
Westport . . . F-2
White Salmon . . . J-7
White Swan . . . H-8
Wickersham . . . B-6
Wilbur . . . D-12

Wilkeson . . . F-6
Wilson Creek . . . E-11
Winlock . . . G-4
Winslow . . . D-5
Winthrop . . . B-9
Wishram Heights . . . J-8
Withrow . . . D-9
Wollochet . . . Pg. 164, E-6
Woodinville . . . Pg. 163, B-6
Woodland . . . J-5
Yacolt . . . J-5
Yakima . . . G-9
Yelm . . . F-5
Zillah . . . G-9

WEST VIRGINIA
Pages 82-83
Population: 1,949,644
Capital: Charleston
Land Area: 24,119 sq. mi.

Alderson . . . G-6
Arnoldsburg . . . E-5
Ashton . . . E-4
Athens . . . H-5
Augusta . . . D-8
Baileysville . . . G-4
Baker . . . D-9
Barboursville . . . F-3
Barrackville . . . C-7
Beckley . . . G-5
Belington . . . D-7
Belmont . . . D-5
Bethlehem . . . B-6
Beverly . . . E-7
Big Chimney . . . F-4
  Vicinity . . . Pg. 100, H-5
Big Otter . . . E-5
Birch River . . . E-6
Blacksville . . . C-6
Blount . . . Pg. 100, J-4
Bluefield . . . H-5
Bradley . . . G-5
Bramwell . . . G-5
Bream . . . Pg. 100, H-5
Bridgeport . . . D-7
Buckhannon . . . D-6
Buffalo . . . E-4
Burnsville . . . E-6
Cairo . . . D-5
Camden-on-Gauley . . . F-6
Cameron . . . C-6
Cedar Grove . . . F-5
Center Pt. . . . C-6
Chapmanville . . . G-3
Charles Town . . . D-10
Charleston . . . F-4
  Vicinity . . . Pg. 100
Chesapeake . . . F-4
Chester . . . A-6
Cinco . . . Pg. 100, J-6
Clarksburg . . . D-6
Clay . . . E-5
Clendenin . . . E-5
Coal Fork . . . Pg. 100, K-5
Coco . . . Pg. 100, H-7
Coxs Mills . . . D-6
Craigsville . . . F-6
Creed . . . Pg. 100, H-4
Danville . . . F-4
Davis . . . D-8
Delbarton . . . G-3
Dunbar . . . F-4
  Vicinity . . . Pg. 100, H-1
Dunmore . . . E-7
Durbin . . . E-7
East Bank . . . F-4
Eleanor . . . E-4
Elk . . . Pg. 100, J-3
Elk Garden . . . C-8
Elkins . . . D-7
Ellenboro . . . D-5
Etowan . . . Pg. 100, H-3
Fairmont . . . C-6
Fairview . . . C-6
Farmington . . . C-6
Fayetteville . . . G-5
Fivemile . . . Pg. 100, J-6
Flatwoods . . . E-6
Follansbee . . . A-6
Forest Hill . . . H-5
Franklin . . . E-7
Friendly . . . C-5
Ft. Ashby . . . C-8
Ft. Gay . . . F-3
Gandeeville . . . E-4
Gap Mills . . . H-6
Gary . . . H-4
Gassaway . . . E-5

Gauley Bridge . . . F-5
Gerrardstown . . . C-9
Gilbert . . . G-4
Gilmer . . . E-5
Glen Dale . . . B-6
Glenville . . . D-6
Grantsville . . . E-5
Guthrie . . . Pg. 100, H-3
Hambleton . . . D-7
Hamlin . . . F-3
Harman . . . E-8
Harrisville . . . D-5
Hedgesville . . . C-9
Henderson . . . E-3
Hillsboro . . . F-6
Hinton . . . H-6
Hundred . . . C-6
Huntington . . . F-3
Hurricane . . . F-3
Huttonsville . . . E-7
Iaeger . . . H-4
Ingleside . . . H-5
Institute . . . Pg. 100, H-1
Inwood . . . C-10
Jane Lew . . . D-6
Jolo . . . H-4
Junction . . . C-8
Junior . . . D-7
Kenna . . . E-4
Kenova . . . F-3
Kermit . . . G-3
Keyser . . . C-8
Keystone . . . H-4
Kimball . . . H-4
Kingwood . . . C-7
Leon . . . E-4
Lester . . . G-5
Lewisburg . . . G-6
Liberty . . . E-4
Linn . . . D-6
Logan . . . G-3
Lost City . . . D-8
Lost Cr. . . . D-7
Lumberport . . . C-6
Mabscott . . . G-5
Madison . . . F-4
Malden . . . Pg. 100, K-5
Man . . . G-4
Mannington . . . C-7
Marlinton . . . G-6
Marmet . . . F-4
  Vicinity . . . Pg. 100, J-5
Martinsburg . . . C-9
Mason . . . D-4
Masontown . . . C-7
Matewan . . . G-3
Matoaka . . . H-5
Meadow Bridge . . . G-5
Middlebourne . . . C-6
Midkiff . . . F-3
Mill Creek . . . E-7
Milliken . . . Pg. 100, H-5
Milton . . . F-3
Monongah . . . C-6
Montgomery . . . F-5
Montrose . . . D-8
Moorefield . . . D-9
Morgantown . . . C-7
Mossy . . . F-5
Moundsville . . . B-6
Mt. Hope . . . G-5
Mt. Storm . . . D-8
Muddlety . . . F-5
Mullens . . . H-5
Naoma . . . G-4
Neola . . . G-7
Nettie . . . F-6
New Cumberland . . . A-6
New Haven . . . D-4
New Martinsville . . . C-6
Newton . . . E-5
Nitro . . . F-4
Nutter Fort . . . D-6
Oak Flat . . . E-8
Oak Hill . . . G-5
Oceana . . . G-4
Omar . . . G-3
Paden City . . . C-5
Parkersburg . . . D-5
Parsons . . . D-7
Paw Paw . . . C-9
Pennsboro . . . D-5
Petersburg . . . D-8
Peterstown . . . H-5
Philippi . . . D-7
Piedmont . . . C-8
Pinch . . . Pg. 100, H-6
Pine Grove . . . C-5
Pineville . . . H-4
Poca . . . E-4
Pocatalico . . . E-4

Port . . . Pg. 100, K-5
Prichard . . . F-3
Princeton . . . H-5
Pt. Pleasant . . . E-3
Quick . . . Pg. 100, H-7
Racine . . . F-4
Rainelle . . . G-5
Rand . . . F-4
  Vicinity . . . Pg. 100, K-5
Ranson . . . D-10
Ravenswood . . . D-4
Reedy . . . E-5
Renick . . . G-6
Rensford . . . Pg. 100, J-5
Rhodell . . . H-5
Richwood . . . F-6
Ridgeley . . . C-9
Ripley . . . E-4
Riverview . . . Pg. 100, J-4
Roanoke . . . E-6
Rock Cave . . . E-6
Romney . . . D-9
Ronceverte . . . G-6
Rowlesburg . . . D-7
Rupert . . . G-6
Ruth . . . Pg. 100, K-2
Rutledge . . . Pg. 100, H-5
Salem . . . D-6
Scherr . . . D-8
Seneca Rocks . . . E-8
Shepherdstown . . . C-10
Shinnston . . . C-6
Slatyfork . . . F-6
Smithers . . . F-5
Smithfield . . . C-6
Snow Hill . . . Pg. 100, J-4
Sophia . . . G-5
South Charleston . . . F-4
  Vicinity . . . Pg. 100, J-1
South Malden . . . Pg. 100, K-4
South Park . . . Pg. 100, K-4
Spencer . . . E-5
Spring Fork . . . Pg. 100, K-5
St. Albans . . . F-4
St. Mary's . . . C-5
Star City . . . C-7
Stonewood . . . D-7
Summersville . . . F-5
Sylvester . . . G-4
Tad . . . Pg. 100, J-5
Terra Alta . . . C-8
Thomas . . . D-7
Thornwood . . . E-7
Triadelphia . . . B-6
Tunnelton . . . D-7
Union . . . H-6
Valley Head . . . E-7
Van . . . G-4
Vienna . . . D-4
War . . . H-4
Wardensville . . . D-8
Wayne . . . F-3
Webster Spr. . . . E-6
Weirton . . . A-6
Welch . . . H-4
Wellsburg . . . A-6
West Hamlin . . . F-3
West Logan . . . G-4
West Union . . . D-5
Weston . . . D-6
Westover . . . C-7
Wheeling . . . B-6
White Sulphur Spr. . . . G-6
Whitesville . . . G-4
Williamson . . . G-3
Williamstown . . . D-4
Yawkey . . . F-4

WISCONSIN
Pages 86-87
Population: 4,705,767
Capital: Madison
Land Area: 54,426 sq. mi.

Abbotsford . . . F-5
Adams . . . H-5
Adell . . . J-8
Algoma . . . G-8
Alma . . . G-2
Alma Center . . . G-4
Almena . . . E-2
Altoona . . . G-3
Amery . . . E-2
  Vicinity . . . Pg. 136, F-6
Aniwa . . . F-6
Antigo . . . F-6
Appleton . . . G-7
Arcadia . . . H-3
Argyle . . . K-5

Arlington . . . J-6
Ashland . . . D-4
Ashwaubenon . . . G-7
Athens . . . F-5
Auburndale . . . G-5
Augusta . . . G-4
Avoca . . . K-5
Baldwin . . . F-2
Balsam Lake . . . E-2
Bangor . . . H-4
Baraboo . . . J-5
Barneveld . . . K-5
Barron . . . F-3
Bay City . . . G-2
Bayfield . . . C-4
Bayside . . . K-8
  Vicinity . . . Pg. 136, A-6
Beadstown . . . J-4
Beaver Dam . . . J-7
Belgium . . . J-8
Belleville . . . K-6
Belmont . . . K-5
Beloit . . . L-6
Benton . . . L-5
Berlin . . . H-6
Big Bend . . . Pg. 136, H-1
Birchwood . . . E-3
Birnamwood . . . F-6
Black Creek . . . G-7
Black Earth . . . K-5
Black River Falls . . . G-4
Blair . . . H-3
Blanchardville . . . K-5
Bloomer . . . F-3
Bloomington . . . K-4
Bonduel . . . G-7
Boscobel . . . K-4
Boyceville . . . F-2
Boyd . . . F-4
Brandon . . . J-7
Brillion . . . H-8
Brodhead . . . L-6
Brokaw . . . F-6
Brookfield . . . Pg. 136, D-3
Brown Deer . . . Pg. 136, A-5
Browntown . . . L-6
Bruce . . . F-3
Buena Park . . . Pg. 136, K-1
Buffalo . . . H-2
Burlington . . . K-8
Butler . . . Pg. 136, C-3
Butternut . . . D-5
Cable . . . D-3
Caddy Vista . . . Pg. 136, J-6
Cadott . . . F-4
Caledonia . . . Pg. 136, K-6
Cambria . . . J-6
Cambridge . . . K-7
Cameron . . . F-3
Camp Douglas . . . H-5
Campbellsport . . . J-8
Cascade . . . J-8
Casco . . . G-8
Cashton . . . J-4
Cassville . . . K-4
Catawba . . . E-4
Cazenovia . . . J-5
Cecil . . . G-7
Centuria . . . E-1
Chetek . . . F-3
Chilton . . . H-8
Chippewa Falls . . . F-3
Clayton . . . F-2
Clear Lake . . . F-2
Cleveland . . . H-8
Clinton . . . L-7
Clintonville . . . G-7
Cochrane . . . H-3
Colby . . . G-5
Coleman . . . F-8
Colfax . . . F-3
Colgate . . . Pg. 136, A-1
Coloma . . . H-6
Columbus . . . J-7
Coon Valley . . . J-4
Cornell . . . F-4
Cottage Grove . . . Pg. 133, C-7
Couderay . . . E-3
Crandon . . . E-7
Crivitz . . . F-8
Cross Plains . . . K-6
  Vicinity . . . Pg. 133, C-1
Cuba City . . . L-4
  Vicinity . . . Pg. 136, F-6
Cudahy . . . K-8
Cumberland . . . E-2
Dane . . . J-6
Darien . . . L-7
Darlington . . . K-5

De Pere . . . G-8
De Soto . . . J-4
DeForest . . . J-6
Deerfield . . . K-6
Delavan . . . K-7
Denmark . . . G-8
Dickeyville . . . L-4
Dodgeville . . . K-5
Dorchester . . . F-5
Dousman . . . K-7
Dresser . . . F-1
Duplainville . . . Pg. 136, D-2
Durand . . . G-2
Eagle . . . K-7
Eagle River . . . E-6
East Troy . . . K-7
Eastman . . . K-4
Eau Claire . . . G-3
Eden . . . J-7
Edgar . . . F-5
Edgerton . . . K-6
Egg Harbor . . . F-9
Elano . . . F-6
Eleva . . . G-3
Elk Mound . . . G-3
Elkhart Lake . . . H-8
Elkhorn . . . K-7
Ellsworth . . . G-2
Elm Grove . . . Pg. 136, D-3
Elmwood . . . G-2
Elroy . . . J-5
Embarrass . . . G-7
Ephraim . . . F-9
Ettrick . . . H-3
Evansville . . . K-6
Exeland . . . E-3
Fairchild . . . G-4
Fall Creek . . . G-4
Fall River . . . J-7
Fennimore . . . K-5
Ferryville . . . J-4
Fifield . . . E-5
Fitchburg . . . Pg. 133, C-5
Florence . . . E-7
Fond Du Lac . . . H-7
Fontana . . . L-7
Footville . . . L-6
Fort Atkinson . . . K-7
Fountain City . . . H-3
Fox Lake . . . J-7
Fox Point . . . Pg. 136, B-6
Francis Creek . . . H-8
Franklin . . . K-8
  Vicinity . . . Pg. 136, K-4
Frederic . . . E-2
Fremont . . . H-7
Friendship . . . H-6
Galesville . . . H-3
Gays Mills . . . J-4
Genoa . . . J-3
Genoa City . . . L-8
Germantown . . . J-8
  Vicinity . . . Pg. 136, A-3
Gillett . . . F-7
Gilman . . . F-4
Glen Flora . . . E-4
Glendale . . . Pg. 136, B-6
Glenwood City . . . F-2
Grafton . . . J-8
Granton . . . G-5
Grantsburg . . . E-1
Gratiot . . . L-5
Green Bay . . . G-8
Green Lake . . . H-6
Greendale . . . Pg. 136, G-4
Greenfield . . . Pg. 136, F-5
Greenwood . . . G-4
Gresham . . . G-7
Hales Corners . . . Pg. 136, G-4
Hammond . . . F-2
Hancock . . . H-6
Hartford . . . J-7
Hartland . . . K-8
Haugen . . . E-2
Hawkins . . . E-4
Hawthorne . . . D-3
Hayward . . . E-3
Hazel Green . . . L-5
Heafferd Jct. . . . E-5
Highland . . . K-5
Hilbert . . . H-8
Hillsboro . . . J-5
Holmen . . . H-3
Hope . . . Pg. 133, D-6
Horicon . . . J-7
Hortonville . . . G-7
Howard . . . G-8

Howards Grove . . . H-8
Hudson . . . F-1
Hurley . . . D-5
Husher . . . Pg. 136, J-6
Independence . . . E-4
Ingram . . . E-4
Iola . . . G-6
Iron River . . . C-3
Jackson . . . J-8
Janesville . . . K-7
Jefferson . . . K-7
Johnson Creek . . . K-7
Junction City . . . G-5
Juneau . . . J-7
Kaukauna . . . H-8
Kendall . . . H-5
Kennan . . . E-4
Kenosha . . . L-8
Keshena . . . F-7
Kewaskum . . . J-8
Kewaunee . . . G-9
Kiel . . . H-8
Kimberly . . . H-8
Kingston . . . J-6
La Crosse . . . H-3
La Farge . . . J-4
Lac Du Flambeau . . . D-5
Ladysmith . . . E-3
Lake Delton . . . J-5
Lake Geneva . . . L-7
Lake Nebagamon . . . D-3
Lancaster . . . K-4
Lannon . . . Pg. 136, B-2
Lena . . . F-8
Linden . . . K-5
Little Chute . . . H-8
Livingston . . . K-4
Lodi . . . J-6
Loganville . . . J-5
Lomira . . . J-7
Lone Rock . . . J-5
Loyal . . . G-4
Lublin . . . F-4
Luck . . . E-2
Luxemburg . . . G-8
Madison . . . K-6
  Vicinity . . . Pg. 133
Manawa . . . G-7
Manitowish . . . D-5
Manitowoc . . . H-9
Maple Bluff . . . Pg. 133, B-5
Marathon City . . . F-5
Marinette . . . F-8
Marion . . . G-7
Markesan . . . J-6
Marshall . . . K-6
Marshfield . . . G-5
Mason . . . D-4
Mauston . . . H-5
Mayville . . . J-7
Mazomanie . . . J-6
McFarland . . . Pg. 133, D-6
Medford . . . F-5
Meeker . . . Pg. 136, A-2
Mellen . . . D-4
Melrose . . . H-4
Melvina . . . H-4
Menasha . . . H-7
Menomonee Falls . . . J-7
  Vicinity . . . Pg. 136, A-2
Menomonie . . . F-2
Mequon . . . K-8
  Vicinity . . . Pg. 136, A-5
Merrill . . . F-5
Merrillan . . . G-4
Middleton . . . K-6
  Vicinity . . . Pg. 133, C-2
Milltown . . . E-2
Milton . . . K-7
Milwaukee . . . K-8
  Vicinity . . . Pg. 136
  Detailed City . . . Pg. 253
Mineral Point . . . K-5
Minong . . . D-3
Mishicot . . . H-8
Mondovi . . . G-3
Monico . . . E-6
Monona . . . Pg. 133, D-5
Monroe . . . L-5
Montello . . . H-6
Montfort . . . K-5
Monticello . . . K-6
Montreal . . . D-5
Mosinee . . . G-6
Mount Horeb . . . K-6
Mount Sterling . . . K-4
Mukwonago . . . K-7
Muscoda . . . K-4
Muskego . . . K-8
  Vicinity . . . Pg. 136, G-2

WISCONSIN

Necedah H-5
Neenah H-7
Neillsville G-4
Nekoosa H-5
Nelson G-2
Nelsonville G-6
Neshkoro H-6
New Berlin K-7
  Vicinity . . Pg. 136, E-2
New Glarus K-5
New Holstein H-8
New Lisbon H-5
New London G-7
New Richmond . . . F-2
Niagara E-8
North Cape Pg. 136, K-4
North Fond du Lac . H-7
North Hudson F-1
Norwalk H-4
Oak Creek K-8
  Vicinity . Pg. 136, G-6
Oconomowoc K-7
Oconto F-8
Oconto Falls G-8
Omro H-7
Onalaska H-3
Ontario J-4
Oostburg J-8
Orfordville K-6
Osceola F-1
Oshkosh H-7
Osseo G-3
Owen F-4
Oxford H-6
Paddock Lake L-8
Palmyra K-7
Pardeeville J-6
Park Falls E-4
Park Ridge G-6
Patch Grove K-4
Pembine E-8
Pepin G-2
Peshtigo F-8
Pewaukee . Pg. 136, C-1
Phelps D-6
  . . . . Pg. 133, C-3
Phillips E-5
Pigeon Falls G-3
Pittsville G-5
Plain J-5
Plainfield H-6
Platteville K-4
Plover G-6
Plum City G-2
Plymouth H-8
Poplar C-3
Port Edwards H-5
Port Washington . . . J-8
Portage J-6
Potosi K-4
Pound F-8

Prairie du Chien . . . K-4
Prairie du Sac J-5
Prentice E-5
Prescott G-1
Princeton H-6
Pulaski G-8
Racine K-8
Radisson E-3
Randolph J-7
Raymond . Pg. 136, K-4
Redgranite H-6
Reedsburg J-5
Reedsville H-8
Rhinelander E-6
Rib Lake F-5
Rice Lake E-3
Richland Center . . . J-5
Ridgeland F-2
Ridgeway K-5
Rio J-6
Ripon H-7
River Falls G-1
River Hills . . Pg. 136, A-5
Riverside D-2
Roberts F-2
Rosendale H-7
Rosholt G-6
Rothschild G-5
Saint Croix Falls . . . F-2
Saint Francis K-8
  Vicinity . . Pg. 136, F-7
Sauk City J-5
Saukville J-8
Schofield G-5
Seymour G-7
Sharon L-7
Shawano G-7
Sheboygan H-9
Sheboygan Falls . . . J-8
Sheldon F-3
Shell Lake E-2
Shiocton G-7
Shorewood . Pg. 136, C-7
Shorewood Hills
  . . . . Pg. 133, C-3
Shullsburg L-5
Siren D-2
Sister Bay F-9
Soldiers Grove J-4
Solon Springs D-3
Somerset F-1
South Milwaukee . . K-8
  Vicinity . Pg. 136, G-7
Sparta H-4
Spencer G-5
Spooner E-3
Spring Green J-5
Spring Valley G-2
Springfield Pg. 133, B-2

Springfield Corners
  . . . . Pg. 133, A-2
Stanley F-4
Stevens Point G-5
Stockbridge H-7
Stockholm G-2
Stoddard J-4
Stoughton K-6
Stratford G-5
Strum G-3
Sturgeon Bay F-8
Sturtevant K-8
Sun Prairie K-7
  Vicinity . . Pg. 133, A-7
Superior C-2
Suring F-7
Sussex . . . Pg. 136, B-1
Tabor . . . . Pg. 136, J-7
Taylors Falls E-1
Tennyson K-4
Theresa J-7
Thompsonville
  . . . . Pg. 136, K-5
Thorp F-4
Tichigan . Pg. 136, J-1
Tigerton G-7
Token Creek Pg. 133, A-6
Tomah H-4
Tomahawk E-6
Tony F-4
Trego E-3
Trempealeau H-3
Turtle Lake F-2
Two Rivers H-9
Union Center J-5
Union Church
  . . . . Pg. 136, J-4
Union Grove K-8
Unity G-5
Valders H-8
Vernon . . . Pg. 136, G-1
Verona K-6
  Vicinity . . Pg. 133, E-2
Vesper G-5
Village of Superior . C-2
Viroqua J-4
Walworth L-7
Washburn C-3
Waterford K-7
Waterloo K-6
Watertown K-7
Waukesha K-7
  Vicinity . Pg. 136, E-1
Waunakee K-6
Waupaca H-6
  Vicinity . Pg. 133, A-3
Waupun J-7
Wausau F-6
Wausaukee F-8

Wautoma H-6
Wauwatosa K-8
  Vicinity . . Pg. 136, D-4
Webster E-2
West Allis . Pg. 136, E-4
West Bend J-8
West Milwaukee
  . . . . Pg. 136, E-5
Westby J-4
Westfield H-6
Weyauwega G-6
White Lake F-7
Whitefish Bay K-8
  Vicinity . . Pg. 136, C-6
Whitehall G-3
Whitelaw H-8
Whitewater K-7
Whiting G-6
Wild Rose H-6
Wind Pt. K-8
Winneconne H-7
Winter E-4
Wisconsin Dells . . . J-6
Wisconsin Rapids . . G-5
Withee F-4
Wittenberg G-6
Wonewoc J-5
Woodruff E-6
Wrightstown G-8
Wyeville H-5
Wyocena J-6
Yuba J-4

WYOMING
Pages 88-89
Population: 469,559
Capital: Cheyenne
Land Area: 96,989 sq. mi.

Acme B-8
Afton F-3
Aladdin B-12
Albany J-9
Albin H-12
Alcova F-9
Alpine Jct. E-3
Alva B-11
Arapahoe F-6
Arlington H-9
Arminto E-8
Arvada B-9
Atlantic City G-6
Auburn F-3
Baggs J-7
Bairoil G-7
Banner B-8
Bar Nunn F-9

Barnum D-8
Basin C-7
Beckton B-8
Bedford F-3
Beulah B-12
Big Horn B-8
Big Piney G-4
Big Sandy F-5
Big Trails D-8
Bill E-10
Bitter Creek H-6
Bondurant E-4
Border G-3
Bosler H-10
Boulder F-5
Boxelder F-10
Buffalo C-8
Burgess Jct. B-7
Burlington C-6
Burns J-12
Burntfork J-4
Burris E-5
Byron B-6
Calpet G-4
Canyon Jct. B-4
Carpenter J-12
Carter J-4
Casper F-9
Centennial J-9
Cheyenne J-11
Chugwater H-11
Clareton D-11
Clark B-5
Clearmont B-9
Cody C-5
Cokeville G-3
Colony B-12
Cora F-4
Cowley B-6
Creston Jct. H-7
Crowheart E-5
Daniel F-4
Dayton B-8
Deaver B-6
Devil's Tower Jct. . . B-11
Diamondville H-3
Dixon J-7
Douglas F-10
Dubois E-5
East Thermopolis . . D-7
Eden G-5
Edgerton E-9
Egbert J-12
Elk Basin B-6
Elk Mountain H-9
Elkol H-4
Elmo H-9
Emblem C-6
Encampment J-9

Ethete F-6
Etna E-3
Evanston J-3
Evansville F-9
Fairview F-3
Farson G-5
Federal J-11
Fort Bridger J-4
Fort Laramie G-11
Fort Washakie F-5
Four Corners C-12
Frannie B-6
Freedom F-3
Frontier H-4
Garland B-6
Gillette C-10
Glendo F-11
Glenrock F-10
Granger H-4
Grass Creek D-6
Green River H-5
Greybull C-7
Grover F-3
Guernsey G-11
Hamilton Dome . . . D-6
Hampshire D-11
Hanna H-9
Hartville G-11
Hawk Springs H-12
Hiland E-8
Hillsdale J-12
Hobock Jct. E-3
Horse Creek H-11
Hudson F-6
Hulett B-11
Huntley H-12
Hyattville C-8
Iron Mountain H-11
Jackson E-3
Jay Em G-12
Jeffrey City G-7
Jenny Lake D-3
Kaycee D-9
Keeline F-11
Kelly E-4
Kemmerer H-3
Kinnear E-6
Kirby D-7
La Barge G-4
La Grange H-12
Lake Jct. B-4
Lamont G-8
Lance Creek E-11
Lander F-6
Laramie J-10
Leiter B-9
Lightning Flat B-11
Linch D-9
Lingle G-12

Little America J-4
Lonetree J-4
Lost Cabin E-8
Lost Springs F-11
Lovell B-6
Lucerne D-7
Lusk F-12
Lyman J-4
Lysite E-7
Madison Jct. B-3
Mammoth Springs Jct.
  . . . . B-3
Manderson C-7
Manville F-11
Marbleton F-4
Mayoworth D-8
McFadden H-10
McKinnon K-4
Medicine Bow H-9
Meeteetse C-6
Merna F-4
Midwest E-9
Millburne J-4
Mills F-9
Moneta E-7
Moorcroft C-11
Moose D-3
Moran Jct. D-4
Morrisey D-11
Morton E-6
Mountain Home . . . J-10
Mountain View J-4
Mule Cr. Jct. E-12
Natrona E-9
New Haven B-11
Newcastle D-12
Node F-12
Norris Jct. B-3
Old Faithful C-3
Opal H-4
Orin F-11
Orpha F-10
Osage D-12
Oshoto B-11
Otto C-7
Parkman B-8
Pavillion E-6
Piedmont J-4
Pine Bluffs J-12
Pine Tree Jct. D-10
Pinedale F-5
Pitchfork D-5
Point of Rocks H-6
Powder River F-8
Powell B-6
Quealy J-5
Ralston B-6
Ranchester B-8
Rawlins H-8

Recluse B-10
Red Desert H-7
Redbird E-12
Reliance H-6
Reno Jct. D-10
Riverside J-9
Riverton F-7
Robertson J-4
Rochelle D-11
Rock River H-10
Rock Springs H-5
Rocky Point B-11
Rozet C-10
Sage H-3
Saint Stephens . . . F-6
Saratoga J-9
Savageton D-10
Savery J-8
Shawnee F-11
Shell C-7
Sheridan B-8
Shirley Basin G-9
Shoshoni E-7
Sinclair H-8
Slater H-11
Smoot F-3
South Pass City . . . G-6
Spotted Horse B-10
Story C-8
Sundance C-12
Sunrise G-11
Superior H-6
Sussex D-9
Table Rock H-7
Ten Sleep D-8
Teton Village D-3
Thayne F-3
Thermopolis D-6
Tie Siding J-10
Torrington G-12
Tower Jct. B-4
Turnerville F-3
Ucross C-9
Upton C-11
Urie J-4
Valley C-5
Van Tassell F-12
Veteran G-12
Walcott H-9
Waltman E-8
Wamsutter H-7
West Thumb Jct. . . . C-3
Weston B-10
Wheatland G-11
Wilson E-3
Woods Landing . . . J-10
Worland D-7
Wright D-10
Yoder H-12